Springer Series on Social Work

Albert R. Roberts, PhD., Series Editor

2007 Handbook of Forensic Mental Health With Victims and Offenders: Assessment, Treatment, and Research
David W. Springer, PhD and Albert R. Roberts, PhD

2006 Clinical Practice and Psychopharmacology, Second Edition
Sophia F. Dziegielewski, PhD, LCSW

2006 Cognitive Behavior Therapy in Clinical Social Work Practice
Arthur Freeman, EdD and Tammie Ronen, PhD

2005 Multicultural Perspectives in Working with Families, Second Edition
Elaine P. Congress, ACSW, DSW

2004 Research Methods for Clinical Social Work
John S. Wodarski, PhD

2004 Dilemmas in Human Services Management: Illustrative Case Studies
Pauline Myers, PhD

2004 The Changing Face of Health Care Social Work: Professional Practice in Managed Behavioral Health Care, Second Edition
Sophia F. Dziegielewski, PhD, LCSW

2003 Adolescent Pregnancy: Policy and Prevention Services
Naomi Farber PhD, MSW

2002 Human Behavior and the Social Environment: Integrating Theory and Evidence-Based Practice
John S. Wodarski, PhD, and Sophia F. Dziegielewski, PhD, LCSW, Editors

2002 A Guide for Nursing Home Social Workers
Elise M. Beaulieu, MSW, ACSW, LICSW

2002 New Routes to Human Services: Information and Referral
Risha W. Levinson, DSW

2001 Social Work Practice and Psychopharmacology
Sophia F. Dziegielewski, PhD, LCSW, and Ana Leon, PhD, LCSW

2001 Understanding Narrative Therapy: A Guidebook for the Social Worker
Paul Abels, MSW, PhD, and Sonia L. Abels, MSW

2001 Theoretical Perspectives for Direct Social Work: A Generalist-Eclectic Approach
Peter Lehmann, PhD, and Nick Coady, PhD, Editors

2001 Law and Social Work Practice, Second Edition
Raymond Albert, MSW, JD

2000 Evidence-Based Social Work Practice With Families: A Lifespan Approach
Jacqueline Corcoran, PhD

1999 Homeless Families With Children
Namkee Choi, PhD, and Lydia Snyder, MSW

1998 The Privatization: of Human Services
Volume I: Policy and Practice Issues
Volume II: Cases in the Purchase of Services
Margaret Gibelman, DSW, and Harold W. Demone, PhD, Editors

1998 The Changing Face of Health Care Social Work: Professional Practice in the Era of Managed Care
Sophia F. Dziegielewski, PhD, LCSW

Dr. David Springer is the Associate Dean for Academic Affairs, Graduate Adviser, and a University Distinguished Teaching Professor in the School of Social Work at The University of Texas at Austin, where he also holds a joint appointment with the Department of Psychology. Dr. Springer has conducted research funded by the National Institute of Mental Health, the National Institute on Drug Abuse, and the Hogg Foundation for Mental Health. His areas of interest include: clinical assessment and intervention with adolescents and families; evidence-based substance abuse and mental health treatment with youth; applied psychometric theory and scale development; juvenile delinquency; intervention research with adolescents; and leadership in social work higher education. Dr. Springer currently serves on the editorial board of several professional journals. He is a co-author, with Dr. C. Aaron McNeece and Dr. Elizabeth Mayfield Arnold, of *Substance Abuse Treatment for Criminal Offenders: An Evidence-Based Guide for Practitioners* and has authored or co-authored numerous articles, book chapters, and reports that coalesce around assessment and intervention with troubled adolescents and their families.

Albert R. Roberts, Ph.D., is a Professor of Social Work at the School of Social Work, Rutgers University, New Brunswick, NJ. Dr. Roberts conducts seminars and teaches courses on research methods, crisis intervention and brief treatment, program evaluation, family violence intervention, adolescence, victimology, social policy, and juvenile justice. He previously taught at the Indiana University School of Social Work in Indianapolis. He received his doctorate in social work at the University of Maryland School of Social Work in 1978. Dr. Roberts is a Fellow of the American Orthopsychiatric Association, a lifetime member of the Academy of Criminal Justice Sciences, and an active member of the National Association of Social Workers and the council on Social Work Education. Dr. Roberts is the founding editor of the Springer Series on Family Violence and the Springer Series on Social Work. He has authored or edited over thirty books, including *The Social Worker's Desk Reference* and *Crisis Intervention Handbook: Assessment, Treatment, and Research, Third Edition*. He is the current editor of the journal *Brief Treatment and Crisis Intervention*.

Handbook of Forensic Mental Health With Victims and Offenders: Assessment, Treatment, and Research

Editors
David W. Springer, Ph.D., LCSW
Albert R. Roberts, Ph.D., DABFE

SPRINGER PUBLISHING COMPANY
New York

Springer series on social work

Springer Publishing Company, LLC.
11 West 42nd Street
New York, NY 10036
www.springerpub.com

Acquisitions Editor: Philip Laughlin
Managing Editor: Mary Ann McLaughlin
Production Editor: Matthew Byrd
Cover design by Mimi Flow
Typeset by Techbooks

07 08 09 10/5 4 3 2 1

ISBN-13: 978-0-8261-1514-0

Library of Congress Cataloging-in-Publication Data

Handbook of forensic mental health with victims and offenders : assessment, treatment, and research / co-edited by David W. Springer, Albert R. Roberts.
    p. cm. – (Springer series on social work)
    Includes index.
    ISBN 0-8261-1514-4
  1. Social work with criminals—United States.   2. Criminals—Mental health—United States.   3. People with mental disabilities and crime.   4. Prisoners—Mental health services.
5. Criminals—Mental health services.   I. Springer, David W.   II. Roberts, Albert R.

HV7428.H28   2007
364.4'0453—dc22

2006033865

Printed in the United States of America by Edwards Brothers.

Contents

Contributors   ix

Foreword   xiii

Preface   xv

Acknowledgments   xvi

Section I: Introduction and Overview

1   Forensic Social Work in the 21st Century   3
    David W. Springer and Albert R. Roberts

Section II: Forensic Risk Assessment, Roles, and Specialized Practices

2   Double Jeopardy: Risk Assessment in the Context of Child Maltreatment
    and Domestic Violence   25
    Aron Shlonsky and Colleen Friend

3   Prevention of Prisoner Sudden Deaths: Safety Guidelines and Suicide
    Screening Protocols   53
    Kenneth R. Yeager and Albert R. Roberts

4   Forensic Social Work and Expert Witness Testimony in Child
    Welfare   67
    Carlton E. Munson

5   Expert Testimony on Woman Battering and Its Effects   93
    Evan Stark

6   The Role of the Forensic Social Worker in Developing Mitigation
    Evidence   125
    John P. Niland

7   Emerging Trends in Batterer Intervention Programming: Equipping
    Forensic Workers for Effective Practice   151
    Fred Buttell and Michelle Mohr Carney

Section III: Juvenile Justice Process, Assessment, and Treatment

8   Treatment Effectiveness With Dually Diagnosed Adolescents: Implications
    for Juvenile Offenders   173
    Kimberly Bender, Johnny S. Kim, and David W. Springer

9   Forensic Practices and Serving Dually Diagnosed Youth Involved With the
    Juvenile Justice System   205
    Gerald Landsberg and Jo Rees

10 Psychopathic Traits in Juveniles   225
    Diana Falkenbach

11 Sex, Drugs, and Rock 'n' Rolling With Resistance: Motivational
    Interviewing in Juvenile Justice Settings   247
    Sarah W. Feldstein and Joel I. D. Ginsburg

12 From Augustus to BARJ: The Evolving Role of Social Work
    in Juvenile Justice   273
    Jonathan B. Singer

13 Social Work in Juvenile Courts   299
    Allison Benesch, F. Carole Bryant, and Richard LaVallo

14 Multisystemic Treatment of Serious Clinical Problems in Youths and Their
    Families   315
    Scott W. Henggeler, Ashli J. Sheidow, and Terry Lee

15 Treatment of Mentally Ill Juvenile Offenders   347
    Lisa Rapp-Paglicci

16 Overrepresentation of African Americans Incarcerated for Delinquency
    Offenses in Juvenile Institutions   363
    James Herbert Williams, Peter S. Hovmand, and Charlotte L. Bright

Section IV: Forensic Services and Programs for Adult Offenders

17 Drug Courts   385
    Steven Belenko, David DeMatteo, and Nicholas Patapis

18 Jail Mental Health Services   425
    Diane S. Young

19 Trauma and Posttraumatic Stress Disorder
    in Inmates With Histories of Substance Use   445
    Sheryl Pimlott Kubiak and Isabel M. Rose

20   Best Practices With HIV Infected/Affected Incarcerated Women   467
     Elizabeth C. Pomeroy, Michele A. Rountree, and Danielle E. Parrish

21   Aftercare and Recidivism Prevention   491
     Jose B. Ashford, Bruce D. Sales, and Craig Winston LeCroy

Section V: Restorative Justice and Victim–Offender Mediation

22   Victim-Offender Mediation and Forensic Practice   519
     Marilyn Peterson Armour and Mark S. Umbreit

23   Restorative Justice: Cultural and Gender Considerations   541
     Katherine van Wormer and Morris Jenkins

24   Posttrauma Intervention: Basic Tasks   563
     Gary Behrman and William H. Reid

25   Epilogue: Social Work and Criminal Justice?   573
     Harris Chaiklin

Author Index   587
Subject Index   611

Contributors

Marilyn Peterson Armour, Ph.D.
Assistant Professor
School of Social Work
The University of Texas at Austin
Austin, TX

Jose B. Ashford, Ph.D.
Professor
Arizona State University
School of Social Work
Tempe, AZ

Gary Behrman, Ph.D.
Director of Financial Aid & M. Social Work
    Admissions
Saint Louis University
St. Louis, MO

Steven Belenko, Ph.D.
Professor
Department of
    Criminal Justice
Temple University
Philadelphia, PA

Kimberly Bender, M.S.W.
Doctoral Candidate
The University of Texas at Austin
School of Social Work
Austin, TX

Allison Benesch, M.S.S.W., J.D.
Assistant District Attorney
    Travis County Child Abuse Unit
Austin, TX

Charlotte L. Bright, MSW
Doctoral Student
George Warren Brown School of Social Work
Washington University
St. Louis, MO

F. Carole Bryant, J.D.
Clinical Professor
The University of Texas at Austin
School of Law
Austin, TX

Fred Buttell, Ph.D., LCSW
Associate Professor and Ph.D. Program
    Director
Tulane University
School of Social Work
New Orleans, LA

Michelle Mohr Carney, Ph.D.
Associate Professor
School of Social Work
University of Georgia
Athens, GA

Harris Chaiklin, Ph.D.
Professor Emeritus
School of Social Work
University of Maryland
College Park, MD

David DeMatteo, J.D., Ph.D.
Assistant Professor
Co-Director, J.D./Ph.D.
    Program in Law and Psychology

Department of Psychology
Drexel University
Philadelphia, PA

Diana Falkenbach, Ph.D.
Assistant Professor
The City University of New York
John Jay College of Criminal Justice
New York, NY

Sarah W. Feldstein, M. S.
Doctoral Candidate in Clinical Psychology
University of New Mexico
Albuquerque, NM

Colleen Friend, Ph.D.
California State University at Los Angeles
Department of Social Work
School of Public Policy and Social Research
Los Angeles, CA

Joel I. D. Ginsburg, Ph.D., C. Psych
Psychologist
Correctional Service of Canada
Fenbrook Institution
Gravenhurst, Canada

Scott W. Henggeler, Ph.D.
Director, Family Services Research Center
Professor of Psychiatry and Behavioral
    Sciences
University of South Carolina Medical School
Charleston, SC

Peter S. Hovmand, Ph.D.
Assistant Professor
George Warren Brown School of Social Work
Washington University
St. Louis, MO

Morris Jenkins, J.D., Ph.D.
Assistant Professor
Department of Criminal Justice
University of Toledo
Toledo, OH

Johnny S. Kim, Ph.D.
Assistant Professor
University of Kansas

School of Social Welfare
Lawrence, KS

Sheryl Pimlott Kubiak, Ph.D.
Assistant Professor
Michigan State University
College of Social Sciences
School of Social Work
East Lansing, MI

Gerald Landsberg, Ph.D.
Professor and Director
Initiatives Against Violence
New York University
School of Social Work
New York, NY

Richard LaVallo, M.S.S.W., J.D.
Senior Attorney, Advocacy, Incorporated
    and Adjunct Professor
The University of Texas at Austin
School of Social Work
Austin, TX

Craig Winston LeCroy, Ph.D.
Professor
School of Social Work
Arizona State University
Tempe, AZ

Terry Lee, M.D.
Assistant Professor
Public Behavioral Health and Justice
    Policy
University of Washington
Seattle, WA

Carlton E. Munson, Ph.D.
Professor
School of Social Work
University of Maryland-Baltimore
Baltimore, MD

John P. Niland, J.D.
Director, Capital Trial Project
Texas Defender Service
Austin, TX

Danielle E. Parrish, M.S.W.
Doctoral Student
School of Social Work
The University of Texas at Austin
Austin, TX

Nicholas Patapis, Psy.D.
Treatment Research Institute
University of Pennsylvania
Philadelphia, PA

Elizabeth C. Pomeroy, Ph.D.
Professor
The University of Texas at Austin
School of Social Work
Austin, TX

Lisa Rapp-Paglicci, Ph.D
Associate Professor
University of South Florida, Lakeland
Lakeland, FL

Jo Rees, M.S.W., J.D.
Director of Clinical Services
Friends of Island Academy
New York, NY

William H. Reid, D.S.W., deceased
Distinguished Professor Emeritus
SUNY-Albany
School of Social Work
Albany, NY

Isabel M. Rose, Ph.D.
Assistant Professor
School of Social and Behavioral Sciences
Marist College
Poughkeepsie, NY

Michele A. Rountree, Ph.D
Assistant Professor
The University of Texas at Austin
School of Social Work
Austin, TX

Bruce D. Sales, Ph.D., J.D.
Professor of Psychology, Psychiatry, Sociology,
   & Law

University of Arizona
Tucson, AZ

Ashli J. Sheidow, Ph.D.
Assistant Professor of Psychiatry and
   Behavioral Sciences
Family Services Research Center
Medical University of South Carolina
Charleston, SC

Aron Shlonsky, PhD
Associate Professor
Faculty of Social Work
University of Toronto
Toronto, Ontario

Jonathan B. Singer, LCSW
Doctoral Student
University of Pittsburgh
Pittsburgh, PA

Evan Stark, Ph.D.
Associate Professor and Director
Graduate Department of Public
   Administration
Rutgers University and University of Medicine
   and Dentistry School of Public Health
New Brunswick and Piscataway, NJ

Mark. S. Umbreit, Ph.D.
Professor and Director
Center for Restorative Justice and Peacemaking
University of Minnesota
Minneapolis, MN

Katherine van Wormer, Ph.D.
Professor and Director of BA Program
Department of Social Work
University of Northern Iowa
Cedar Falls, IA

James Herbert Williams, Ph.D.
Foundation Professor for Youth and
   Diversity
School of Social Work
Arizona State University
Phoenix, AZ

Kenneth R. Yeager, Ph.D.
Assistant Professor of Clinical Psychiatry
The Ohio State University
University Medical Center
Columbus, OH

Diane S. Young, Ph.D.
Director, Baccalaureate Social Work
   Program
Syracuse University School of Social Work
Syracuse, NY

Foreword

Social workers have been involved in forensic tasks—matters related to the courts and legal proceedings—ever since the profession's formal inauguration in the late 19th century. Although the term *forensic* was not used by social work's earliest practitioners, without question many of the profession's original functions were forensic in nature. Perhaps the most visible manifestation included social workers' involvement in the creation of the first juvenile court in 1899 as an alternative to handling minors in adult criminal courts. These pioneering social workers were visionary; they recognized that vulnerable people—in this case minors—could best be served by professionals who understand the importance of social services in the context of legal proceedings.

Since those significant, yet modest, beginnings, forensic social work has evolved and matured. Social work's earliest practitioners hardly could have imagined the remarkably diverse functions performed by today's forensic social workers, the settings in which they work, or the clinical, organizational, policy, and ethical challenges they face. Today's forensic social workers provide expert witness testimony, assessments and diagnoses, clinical services, evaluations, mediation, arbitration, supervision, and research expertise. They work in settings as diverse as juvenile and adult courts, psychiatric hospitals, community-based mental health clinics, child welfare agencies and programs, domestic violence programs, and independent practice. Forensic social workers wrestle with complex ethical issues concerning possible conflicts of interest and individuals' civil liberties and rights to informed consent, self-determination, privacy, confidentiality, and privileged communication. They must be adept at interdisciplinary training and willing to identify and implement "best practices" based on the latest empirical research and evidence.

The education required to be a competent forensic social worker has grown exponentially in recent years. Contemporary forensic practitioners must be knowledgeable about and proficient in clinical assessments and interventions, legal rights and procedures, ethical issues, and research, in addition to being competent in their primary field of practice (mental health, addictions, child welfare, domestic violence, juvenile justice, criminal justice, aging, and so on).

Historically, forensic social workers have had to rely on knowledge and information drawn from diverse disciplines and sources. Only recently have forensic social workers been able to rely on literature produced explicitly by and for them. Springer and Roberts'

Handbook of Forensic Mental Health With Victims and Offenders is a vitally important addition to this emerging and essential body of knowledge. This compelling publication places between two covers a broad collection of informative, original essays on core issues in forensic social work. This engaging volume offers readers keen insights into forensic practice related to child abuse and neglect, domestic violence, suicide, psychiatric care and mental illness, juvenile justice, adult corrections, addictions, trauma, and restorative justice.

As the *Handbook of Forensic Mental Health With Victims and Offenders* clearly demonstrates, social workers are uniquely positioned for forensic tasks. Social work's explicit and deliberate endorsement of a generalist perspective, which includes simultaneous focus on individuals' private troubles and the environmental circumstances and public policies that surround them, is particularly well suited to forensic practice. Social workers in court, correctional, child welfare, mental health, addictions treatment, and domestic violence settings must attend to both complex clinical issues and daunting organizational, community, and policy dynamics that affect offenders, clients, and victims. Competent forensic practitioners must understand the ways in which these diverse and wide-ranging phenomena influence mental illness, criminal conduct, child and elder abuse and neglect, addictions, and domestic violence; in addition, they must grasp the ways in which these same phenomena can help people address the troubling issues in their lives and lead to the design, funding, and implementation of meaningful services, programs, and policies. Social work's broad-based perspective, education, training, and practice are ideal for this daunting task.

Further, social work stands alone among human service professions in its firm, unambiguous, clearly stated commitment—as expressed in the preamble of the National Association of Social Workers *Code of Ethics*—to assisting our world's most vulnerable, oppressed, and disadvantaged citizens. The intersection between social work's formal mission statement and the goals and tasks of forensic practice is compelling.

Many years ago I started my formal social work career working in the criminal justice system as a group worker in a federal correctional institution. At the time I was relatively unaware of the broader field of forensic practice. Many years later, my work in the criminal justice field continues, currently in the form of my longtime service as a member of a state parole board. Along the way I have watched the forensic field mature. The context in which I practice today is vastly different from the one that existed when I entered the field. Today we have a much firmer, clearer, and more enlightened understanding of the nature of forensic practice, including the challenging roles, functions, responsibilities, and dilemmas that this field of practice offers. The contents of Springer and Roberts' *Handbook of Forensic Mental Health With Victims and Offenders* provide ample evidence of that fact.

Frederic G. Reamer
Professor
School of Social Work
Rhode Island College
Providence, Rhode Island

I n this completely new text—in collaboration with a distinguished team of 45 justice, forensic, and mental health experts—we have set out to provide an authoritative resource on the delivery of evidence-based forensic mental health services with victims, offenders, and their families.

Consider some sobering statistics. Early in the 21st century, the U.S. Department of Justice and the FBI reported that 26 million rapes, burglaries, robberies, and thefts took place annually. A woman is battered every 9 seconds somewhere in the United States, and 40 to 70% of juvenile and adult offenders have a mental health disorder.

Indeed, forensic social workers have a formidable and critical role in providing risk assessments, expert testimony, mental health care, substance abuse treatment and other timely best practices to both victims and offenders. Accordingly, the common thread that binds together the 25 chapters in this book is a collective response to the overarching question: **What is being done to advocate for, and deliver, critically needed mental health interventions and social services to perpetrators and survivors of serious and violent crimes?** Consider just a few of the topics and issues covered in this handbook: forensic risk assessment, expert testimony, developing mitigation evidence, batterer group treatment, juvenile justice policies, juvenile offender assessment and treatment, substance abuse treatment, mental health treatment, multisystemic treatment of juveniles, motivational interviewing, criminal and drug court practices, adult correctional services and programs, PTSD and substance abuse treatment, services for HIV infected and incarcerated female offenders, community-based aftercare and recidivism prevention programs, restorative justice, and victim-offender mediation.

It is our sincere hope that this handbook will be a useful and timely resource among administrators, professionals, educators, and students in social work, psychology, and criminal justice. Editing a book of such volume is a formidable task. Yet, if it helps improve the life of just one offender or victim, it will have been worth the effort.

Acknowledgments

Most important, we particularly thank our diligent team of distinguished authors for writing their cutting-edge chapters. We are extremely grateful to Theodore C. Nardin, CEO and Philip Laughlin, Senior Editor of Springer Publishing Company, for their responsiveness in quickly offering us a contract based on the completed manuscript that we submitted. Special thanks to the diligent editorial and production leadership of Matthew Byrd, production manager at Techbooks. The systematic support throughout the editing and camera-ready copy preparation process for this book by Hollee Ganner, Diana Villarreal, Kathleen Kelleher, and Maya Mills of The University of Texas at Austin is sincerely appreciated. The cover design by Mimi Flow at Springer Publishing adds a colorful dimension to the Handbook, and we applaud her for her creative contribution. David Springer would like to thank his wife, Sarah, for her lively spirit and sense of humor. Al Roberts would like to thank his wife, Beverly, for wise counsel.

David W. Springer, Ph.D.   Albert R. Roberts, Ph.D.
Austin, TX   Kendall Park, NJ

Introduction and Overview

Forensic Social Work in the 21st Century

Introduction

To forensic practitioners, the study of and intervention with victims as well as offen-ders is certainly a challenging and most worthy endeavor. Forensic practitioners have a formidable role in providing risk assessments, expert testimony, mental health care, substance abuse treatment, and other timely best practices to both victims and offenders. During the past decade, the pendulum has finally swung from neglecting crime victims to providing full federal, state, and local funding for comprehensive social services, police response, court intervention, computerized court case notification, emergency shelter, emergency medical care, mental health services, victim compensation, advocacy, and crisis intervention for crime victims and survivors of domestic violence.

David W. Springer
Albert R. Roberts

Violent crime victimizations are pervasive throughout American society, and the costs are enormous. Early in the 21st century the U.S. Department of Justice and the FBI reported that 26 million rapes, burglaries, robberies, and thefts took place annually (Roberts, 2003). In addition, a women is battered every 9 seconds somewhere in the United States, and approximately 8.7 million women are battered annually (Roberts & Roberts, 2005). With regard to the cost of crime, the Bureau of Justice Statistics (BJS) has indicated that tangible and intangible costs total over $500 billion annually; this includes property and productivity losses, medical expenses, pain and emotional suffering, disability, and risk of death (Roberts, 2003). *What is being done to advocate for, and deliver, critically needed social services and interventions to survivors of violent crimes?* All 25 specially written chapters in this new book examine the current developments and the most promising evidence-based practices in child maltreatment and domestic violence assessment and treatment; assessment and treatment of juvenile offenders; mental health, drug treatment, medical treatment, and aftercare for adult offenders; trauma survivor assistance; victim–offender mediation; batterers intervention programs; restorative

3

justice; expert testimony in child welfare and woman battering cases; and social worker mitigation testimony in death penalty cases. The victim rights and services movement is flourishing, especially with the recent passage of the Violence Against Women Act (VAWA III), which allocates $3.9 billion for the years 2006 to 2010 for programs to aid battered women and sexual assault victims, as well as education and training for victim advocates, social workers and nurses, law enforcement officers, prosecutors, and judges in victim issues, and effective intervention strategies. In contrast, the funding picture for practitioners in correctional settings has a long way to go and varies from state to state.

Unfortunately, all too often juvenile and criminal justice policies have been promulgated based on erroneous and magnified fears that all criminal offenders are violent and dangerous, and as a result need many years of incarceration and punishment.

> The fact is that the overwhelming majority—more than 80 percent—of crime victimizations in the United States are the result of property-related crimes, rather than violent crimes. However, the violent murders committed by a very small number of offenders receive a disproportionate amount of attention from the news media. (Roberts & Brownell, 1999, p. 359)

In addition, a large number of mental health professionals are unaware of the fact that many juvenile and adult offenders were victims of child physical abuse or sexual abuse, child neglect, and/or domestic violence while growing up.

> Many of today's politicians and citizens are unaware that the revenge, punishment, and confinement-oriented policies of the 1800s did not work but led instead to inmate violence and offenders who, on release from incarceration, were far more violent and hateful than they were before confinement. If an inmate is treated like a wild animal, in all likelihood, he will become a violent predator. However, if convicted people are given opportunities for education, vocational training in a marketable skill, social skills training, confrontational group therapy, and substance abuse treatment (that is, therapeutic communities like Synanon and Daytop Village of the 1960s and 1970s), then there is a viable opportunity for them to seek a law-abiding lifestyle, particularly if they are young offenders and have not been corrupted by habitual and chronic convicted felons in maximum-security institutions and sadistic guards. (Roberts & Brownell, 1999, p. 360)

These are challenging times for the practitioners who are employed in or who hope to be employed as correctional treatment specialists or counselors in adult correctional facilities, and as victim advocates in victim assistance and domestic violence intervention programs. Capital spending for prison building projects, custody and security, and law enforcement staff has increased significantly. The increased funding for custody, security, and law enforcement can provide some opportunities for forensic practitioners as long as law enforcement and correctional administrators recognize the important roles and complementary skills of forensic practitioners. According to the BJS (2004), funding for major criminal justice functions—corrections (529% increase), police (281% increase), and judicial (383% increase)—has steadily increased over the last 2 decades (from 1982 to 2001). As a result of "three strikes and you're out" punitive legislation, state and federal governments have built more prisons, and judges have meted out longer prison sentences.

> Starting in the early 1990s, the public furor over the amount of highly publicized, violent crime being committed by former offenders led to a new trend in which some state

legislatures enacted laws to put habitual offenders (upon their third conviction) regardless of whether or not it was a minor offense in prison for the rest of their life, creating
a new philosophy or 'three strikes and you're in prison with a life sentence.' (Roberts,
1997, p. 7)

The critical issues of punishment versus rehabilitation, deterrence, and the determination of whether individual offenders are capable of change—long the topics of public
debate—have never been more relevant than they are today. The type of treatment that
the accused offender receives during and after arrest, adjudication, and conviction will
have a profound effect on the individual and on society. As forensic practitioners, many
of us believe in the offender's potential for change, provided he or she is given opportunities for legal and system advocacy, individual and group therapy, substance abuse
treatment, motivational interviewing and strength-based treatment, social services, and
vocational rehabilitation. Unfortunately, the emphasis on custody and punishment in
many states has led to the elimination of many mental health professional positions in
adult corrections, while other states have hired more forensic practitioners to work with
juvenile offenders and to prepare adult offenders better to transition to their reentry into
the community (Roberts, 1997).

Five of the chapters in this new book focus on forensic risk assessment roles and
measures, expert testimony essentials and guidelines, methods of developing mitigation
evidence related to child maltreatment and domestic violence, and the effectiveness of
batterer group treatment modalities. The next nine of the chapters focus on the most
promising juvenile justice policies, juvenile offender assessment measures, juvenile court
procedures and practices, substance abuse treatment, mental health treatment, multisystemic treatment of juveniles and their families, motivational interviewing, and the continuum of mental health and case-management services needed by mentally ill juvenile
offenders. The final eight chapters in this new book focus on criminal and drug court
practices, adult correctional services and programs, best practices for posttraumatic stress
disorder (PTSD) and substance abuse treatment, medical services for HIV-infected and
incarcerated female offenders, community-based aftercare and recidivism prevention
programs, and restorative justice and victim-offender mediation.

With violent crime and the fear of violence pervading American society, two major growth industries exist. The first is of paramount importance for social workers,
counselors, and criminal justice professionals: expanding victim assistance, domestic violence intervention, rape crisis intervention, and sexual assault prevention programs.
The second growth industry—creating more punitive prisons and incarcerating offenders for longer sentences—is often diametrically opposed to the helping profession's role
of facilitating rehabilitation and the delivery of humane social services. In the epilogue,
social work pioneer Professor Emeritus Harris Chaiklin points out that too many ill-
informed and conservative politicians and legislators blindside the public by repeatedly
dramatizing punishment and long-term incarceration as the only solution to criminality.
With all of the research studies that have been completed in the past 40 years, educated
legislators and correctional administrators should realize that the only thing that does
work in preventing recidivism is a wide range of programs and resources dedicated to
humane treatment and rehabilitative services, and community-based options in the least
restrictive environments for offenders who have gone astray.

Social workers as change agents, legislative advocates, policymakers, and program
administrators can have an important influence on the development of humane and

cost-effective programs for both victims and offenders. Consider the career of one so-cial worker, Dr. Noël Bridget Busch, who has served in each of these roles. Dr. Busch is Assistant Professor and Director of the Institute on Domestic Violence and Sexual Assault at The University of Texas at Austin School of Social Work. When Professor Springer and Professor Roberts approached Dr. Busch about contributing to this book, she was asked to share her story about how her career had evolved. Accordingly, her biographical narrative is exactly that—a narrative written in the first person.

Noël Bridget Busch, PhD, LMSW, MPA, Assistant Professor, The University of Texas at Austin

I am a social worker, and I have worked in the criminal justice system for the past 18 years. As my role as a social worker has evolved in various social institutions, I have come to believe strongly in the role of forensic social workers in prison, parole, and the court systems. I began my professional career in the criminal justice system as a student intern with the North Carolina Department of Correction, Division of Parole Services, in 1987. In 1989, after completing an internship and earning a bachelor's degree in psychology, I served as the assistant director for a prerelease program funded by the North Carolina Department of Correction Parole Services. This community-based program, located in Greensboro, North Carolina, offered incarcerated men alcohol and drug treatment, interviewing and employment skills, group and individual counseling, stress management, and numerous other life skills programs with the goal of reducing recidivism. I regularly visited prisons in North Carolina, where my supervisor and I educated prison personnel on the benefits of the program and recruited potential clients. Clients attended the community-based program for 30 days and graduated with a certificate of completion.

After approximately 2 years in that position, the program was disbanded because of state budget cuts, and I became a parole officer and managed a caseload of paroled men and women in two North Carolina counties. Because of the high caseloads of 80–120 parolees and the structure of parole services, officers had little time to devote to supportive service for their clients. In my capacity as a parole officer, I was responsible for monitoring the whereabouts of my parolees, screening for drug use, ensuring that restitution and child support were paid, and verifying employment and nightly curfews. Ultimately, in my position as a parole officer I was charged with the responsibility of reporting to the court system if any of my clients were in violation of their parole requirements or absconded, and when the court so ordered I served arrest warrants.

In 1991, frustrated with the lack of services for paroled men and women, I de-cided to attend graduate school at the University of South Carolina, earning an MSW degree in 1993. As a student with emergent interests in feminism, I was placed at Sistercare, an organization that serves battered women and their children in Columbia, South Carolina. Because I was a second-year graduate student with a macro concentration, the agency charged me with organizing a statewide effort to ad-vocate for incarcerated battered women who had killed their partners in self-defense. One of my first tasks was to research and document the numbers of incarcerated, battered women who had killed their partners in South Carolina. I analyzed the circumstances of their cases by reading trial transcripts and interviewing the women in prison. A statewide coalition was organized that included a steering committee comprised of incarcerated women and advocates. I met weekly with the coalition and, with their guidance and the supervision of the agency director, developed a strategic plan to advocate for early parole consideration for these women. In order to enhance my therapeutic skills, I also began to co-facilitate support groups for other incarcerated battered women in Columbia, SC. After months of planning and seeking the advice of many leaders of national women's organizations, the coalition decided to use the legislative process to seek early parole consideration for these women. In 1994, the South Carolina Legislature passed a law that provided for early parole consideration of incarcerated individuals who had a history of intimate partner violence that may have contributed to her or his crime. I and the members of the coalition led a legislative effort that included educating members of the state assembly; organizing testimony of experts and incarcerated, battered women before house and senate subcommittees; and mobilizing a grassroots effort. The majority of women who qualified for early parole consideration and were later judged to be no longer a threat to society had also been engaged in therapeutic support groups for battered women, in individual counseling, and with social workers while incarcerated. As a part of the review for early parole, the coalition provided evidence that their histories of intimate partner abuse contributed to the commission of their crimes. The law also required that these offenders serve at least one-third of their sentences before being considered for early parole. Due to the efforts of many advocates, dozens of cases of incarcerated battered women who killed in self-defense have been reviewed by the parole commission, and subsequently many women have been released on parole.

After returning from 2 years as a Peace Corps volunteer in Romania, I earned a master of public administration degree from the University of South Carolina in 1997 and began a doctoral program in social work. At this time, I was reemployed with the same agency servicing battered women in Columbia, SC, and assisted in preparing additional cases for the parole commission. In December 2000, I completed a Ph.D. degree in social work from the University of South Carolina. My dissertation was entitled *Battered Women's Moral Reasoning: Conception and Considerations of 'Right' and 'Wrong,'* and it was later published in condensed form as an article in the *Journal of Social Work Education* in 2004. No statistically significant differences on the Defining Issues Test (DIT), a measure of moral development, between battered and nonbattered women were found. Moreover, in-depth interviews revealed that while battered women defined their violent relationships as "wrong," many reported that they were unable to leave their relationships because of fear of reprisal and threats of retribution by their abusers.

I joined the faculty at the School of Social Work at The University of Texas at Austin as an assistant professor in December 2001. I am now the Director and Principal Investigator of The University of Texas Institute on Domestic Violence and Sexual Assault and have managed over 20 research and direct service projects, totaling over $1.2 million dollars worth of external funding. I served as the principal investigator of the first statewide study of the prevalence of sexual assault in Texas. The information from this study has been used to educate legislators; state, county, and local leaders; and community members about the crime of sexual assault. I testified twice to members of the Texas Legislature about sexual assault crimes and the Uniform Crime Report. Since moving to Texas, I have continued my direct social work practice with women in prison as a volunteer co-facilitator of a support group for survivors of intimate partner violence and sexual assault at the women's prison in Gatesville, Texas.

In addition, I have served as an expert witness in a dozen cases involving victims of domestic violence or sexual assault from across the state of Texas. In my capacity as an expert witness, I have educated judges, attorneys, and juries in immigrant, civil, and criminal courts and parole services on the complex dynamics of interpersonal violence. I have provided written biopsychosocial assessments on clients and given oral testimony. In one federal immigration case, my written report and oral testimony provided critical analysis for understanding the plight of undocumented battered women. Consistent with the federal Violence Against Women Act (VAWA), I explained to the court the circumstances of extreme cruelty and extreme hardship that an undocumented battered woman faces and the power and control strategies that batterers utilize to instill fear and maintain silence in their intimate partners. Many undocumented victims of intimate partner violence report that they do not seek police intervention or assistance from local agencies serving victims because their abusive partners have threatened to report them to immigration services or physically harm or kill them and their children. These women feel trapped. My expert testimony provided the court with critical information that resulted in a favorable ruling for the victim. I recall arguing that "social workers should have a central role in forensic work. We are professionals highly skilled to complete in-depth assessments with clients that provide a broad, ecological framework for understanding complex circumstances and situations. Improvements in the jails and prisons, courts, and in the aftercare systems will only be achieved with the thorough and thoughtful professional consideration that social workers provide. It is a matter of striving toward social and economic justice for some of the most disenfranchised citizens in our society."

[Editor's Note: At the time of this writing, Dr. Noël Bridget Busch was awarded the 2006 Distinguished Recent Contributions Award by the Council on Social Work Education (CSWE).]

The Future

Social workers like Noël Busch embolden the future of forensic practice. What can we expect in the year 2017 and beyond? Will federal and state agencies continue to allocate billions of dollars to more and more jails and prisons? Will the skyrocketing costs and relative ineffectiveness of prisons result in a reallocation of scarce funds toward the more cost-efficient alternatives to incarceration such as pretrial diversion, electronic monitoring, family counseling, restorative justice and restitution, and victim–offender mediation? There seems to be a consensus among justice social work authorities that community-based alternatives to incarceration need to be expanded throughout the nation.

We predict that the future of forensic practice will become increasingly grounded in evidence-based practice as scientific research continues to be conducted. It is important to strike the right balance between corrections and treatment. A key point of contention among practitioners and researchers who work with juvenile and adult offenders has been an operational definition of the term *effective treatment* or *evidence-based practice (EBP)*.

Simply defined, evidence-based practice is the use of treatments for which there is sufficiently persuasive evidence to support their effectiveness in attaining the desired outcomes (Rosen & Proctor, 2002). It is very important to underscore that EBP is also a process in which the practitioner poses a well-structured question, queries a database and the literature to find current evidence, evaluates the evidence found, and applies the evidence to the client taking into consideration the client's values, preferences and clinical context (Sackett, Straus, Richardson, Rosenberg, & Haynes, 2000).

Take substance-abusing criminal offenders as one subset of offenders. The Treatment Outcome Working Group, a panel of treatment and evaluation experts sponsored by the Office of National Drug Control Policy (ONDCP), established the following results and outcomes that define effective treatment with substance-abusing offenders:

1 reduced use of the primary drug;
2 improved functioning of drug users in terms of employment;
3 improved educational status;
4 improved interpersonal relationships;
5 improved medical status and general improvement in health;
6 improved legal status;
7 improved mental status; and
8 improved noncriminal public safety factors such as reduction in diseases (ONDCP, 1996).

It is safe to assert that for most offenders, effective treatment must address the offender's medical, psychological, social, vocational, and legal problems. The contemporary debate over what constitutes effective treatment with offenders is at least 4 decades old. In 1966, Robert Martinson, Douglas Lipton, and Judith Wilkes were charged by the New York State Governor's Special Committee on Criminal Offenders to examine "what works" in rehabilitating criminal offenders. The Committee was formed on the premise that prisons could rehabilitate, that New York State's prisons were not making serious efforts at rehabilitation, and that they should be transformed from serving a custodial function to a rehabilitative one (Martinson, 1974).

In their 6-month search of the literature reviewing all rehabilitation studies published in English from 1945 to 1967, Martinson and colleagues found 231 studies that met the following operationalization of rehabilitation: the extent to which a prisoner adjusted to prison life, experienced vocational and educational achievements, underwent personality and attitudinal changes, made a general adjustment to society, and returned to crime (recidivism). To be included, the study had to have a control or comparison group.

Martinson's (1974) first published account synthesizing the 1,400-page report addresses only "the effects of rehabilitative treatment on recidivism, the phenomenon which reflects most directly how well our present treatment programs are performing the task of rehabilitation" (p. 24). However, Martinson noted that even this one measure brings with it several methodological limitations, such as the challenge of determining whether what works for one offender also works for another given the disparate groups being studied and the wide range of definitions ascribed to the term *recidivism rate* across studies. Nevertheless, in response to seven questions explored in Martinson's (1974) article, he provided the following bold summary of the findings: *"With few and isolated exceptions, the rehabilitative efforts that have been reported so far have had no appreciable effect on recidivism*" (p. 25, italics in original). Ignoring the major methodological limitations noted by Martinson, the politicians and media honed in on this dim summary.

In response to Martinson's (1974) seminal work, others have conducted systematic and sophisticated analyses over the years to determine what treatment strategies are effective with different populations. Throughout this handbook, a review of what treatments work with specific populations will be a recurring theme.

The evidence-based practice movement has gained considerable momentum in the social work profession, both in North America and the United Kingdom. The most recent comprehensive addition to the social work literature is the *Evidence-Based Practice Manual*, by Roberts and Yeager (2004). In this book, Proctor and Rosen (2004) suggest that evidence-based practice is comprised of three assertions: (a) intervention decisions based on empirical, research-based support; (b) critical assessment of empirically supported interventions to determine their fit to and appropriateness for the practice situation at hand; and (c) regular monitoring and revision of the course of treatment based on outcome evaluation. We assert that evidence-based practice in forensic social work should be a recurring theme in social work curriculum.

Curriculum for Social Work in the Justice System

Treger and Allen (1997) asserted that the university will need to play a unique role in preparing social work students to fill the needs of the field in contemporary society. Nearly a decade later, this assertion is even more amplified. Schools of social work must assume leadership positions that will contribute to the inclusion of diversity and forensic content in the curriculum. Social workers entering the field of criminal and juvenile justice must possess knowledge of legal aspects and organizational systems unique to helping profession practice. In particular, it is critical that bachelor and master of social work (BSW and MSW) programs train social workers who are equipped to collaborate with criminal justice personnel such as judges, correctional treatment specialists, and probation officers. Accordingly, the curriculum requires a holistic approach to social work, including knowledge of the subculture of other human service professions and the processes of cooperation and achieving social change. Where possible, forensic social work courses should be cross-listed across social work, psychology, and criminal justice departments so that students from these disciplines have opportunities to learn from one another, integrate a range of perspectives, apply Socratic questioning to challenge their own assumptions, and build a common language from which to work.

In short, the fields of social work, psychology, and criminal justice simply must do a better job of bridging a nexus. Consider the following excerpt from chapter 17 as Belenko, DeMatteo, and Patapis examine the role of the social worker in drug courts: "It is important for social workers in drug courts to understand fully the adjudication process, the legal rights of offenders, criminal procedure, which rights are waived by those agreeing to participate in the drug court, and other aspects of the criminal courts. Cross-training on these issues is important so the social worker understands and appreciates how adjudicatory decisions are made and how such decisions may conflict with the clinical interests of the client. Although drug courts are a treatment-oriented intervention, they are part of the criminal court system, and the first priorities are always adequate resolution of the criminal case and public safety." This is just one example, but it highlights the importance of practitioners understanding their roles within the context of the criminal justice system.

In chapter 4, Carlton E. Munson shares the results of a study conducted by the National Organization of Forensic Social Work (NOFSW), which found that only 4.3% of accredited social work programs offered a course in forensic social work, and only 4.3% offered a forensic specialization. Only 14% of the schools surveyed had plans to develop a forensic specialization. Sixty-four percent of the schools reported offering a course in social work and the law, but there was no indication that the courses focused on forensic social work (Neighbors, Green-Faust, & van Beyer, 2002).

If social work is to become increasingly relevant to the justice system, it must reconceptualize the field of practice and narrow the gap between education and the needs in the field. A mutually useful relationship between educational institutions and the community may provide a cost-effective model for stimulating the kind of interchange and development that provides multiple benefits to a range of systems. When education involves itself with contemporary problems, it may become more effective in improving the conditions of life—both in the states and abroad.

International collaborations must be given higher priority. College students are increasingly looking for study-abroad opportunities as part of their collegiate program of study. For example, UT–Austin is placing an increased emphasis on supporting study-abroad opportunities for students and faculty, as are many universities. The UT–Austin School of Social Work recently collaborated on a symposium entitled *Youth, Education, and Juvenile Justice: Perspectives from the U.S. and Brazil.*

International comparisons place Brazil in fourth place with regard to the number of general population homicides and in fifth place with respect to juveniles (Waiselfisz, 2004). Further review of these data show a homicide rate among the general population as being relatively stable since 1980, yet the rate involving juveniles has almost doubled in the last 20 years (1980: 30 homicides per 100,000; 2000: 54.5 homicides per 100,000; Waiselfisz, 2004). One encounters a similar pattern involving juveniles in the United States. Furthermore, in relationship to other large geographical regions, Latin America and the United States are the only regions where the rates of juvenile homicides are significantly greater than those observed in the general population (Waiselfisz, 2004).

Despite the progress in the legislative arena, recent reports indicate that serious problems continue to be encountered in the transformation of a protective doctrine, expressed by the Child and Adolescent Act, in educational interventions for juvenile offenders. The most obvious findings reported include:

- lack of reliable and complete data relative to juvenile crimes;
- poor communication among responsible service providers working with juvenile offenders (police, district attorneys, judges, program administrators, and nongovernmental agencies offering socioeducational services);
- lack of a stable, socioeducational services system that address the needs of juvenile offenders;
- lack of research studies on interventions for this specific group of adolescents; and
- lack of systematic evaluation models to assess the efficacy of these efforts in spite of a variety of existing, isolated initiatives.

With this in mind, it is evident that a need exists for more in-depth, systematic investigation by those invested in the success of juvenile offenders, such as teachers, social workers, correctional officers, and judges—a multidisciplinary effort involving different disciplines and service providers. Another important aspect is the need for open, informed analysis and discussions of the experiences of others confronting similar challenges.

In response to such concerns, the UT–Austin School of Social Work entered a collaborative model with numerous other entities, namely various other units at UT–Austin (Brazil Center, Teresa Lozano Long Institute of Latin American Studies, School of Law, School of Education), the Texas Youth Commission, the Texas Juvenile Probation Department, the Federal University of Rio Grande do Sul, and the Brazilian Ministry of Education. Such a collaboration has the potential not only to inform the research of professors, but also to enhance the educational opportunities for college students interested in studying (in this case) juvenile justice. Consider the project's four objectives:

1 elaborate an integrated data system to capture essential information relative to the juvenile offenders and incorporate it into the existing Rio Grande do Sul database relating to children and youth;
2 identify and systematize current effective educational and rehabilitative practices with youth offenders;
3 study promising pedagogic practices whose goals are to facilitate the education of youth with diverse behavior profiles in the general education system; and
4 elaborate formative and summative models of evaluation to assess the effectiveness of implemented educational and rehabilitative interventions used with youth offenders.

During the spring of 2005, visitors from Brazil visited Austin, Texas, for the first part of the symposium. At the time of this writing, Professor Springer had just returned from a visit to Porto Alegre, Brazil, with a team of delegates (faculty, community administrators and practitioners, and graduate students) from Austin to learn firsthand about Brazil's juvenile justice system and to lay the groundwork for future faculty and student exchanges (including graduate student research and internships). If social work programs are truly to prepare social workers for culturally competent, holistic, community-based practice, interdisciplinary and international collaborations like the Brazil initiative highlighted previously may be worth exploring as part of the future of the social work curriculum.

Of course, we must also examine different ways of infusing forensic social work content into existing curricula. Possibilities might range from simple course offerings to a more formalized dual course of study leading to both the Master of Social Work (MSW) and a law degree. Professor Noël Busch, in her role as director of the Institute on Domestic Violence and Sexual Assault, has spearheaded an effort to infuse domestic violence and sexual assault content throughout the curriculum, not only in the UT–Austin School of Social Work but also across the UT campus. These are just a few examples of how social work curriculum can be enhanced to prepare students for work in the field of forensic social work.

The course description and objectives from a forensic social work elective syllabus offered at the UT–Austin School of Social Work is provided here. The emphasis in the course description that is placed on delineating and managing the dilemmas between social work and legal ethics, the social worker's authority, and the tension between social control and social support is done so deliberately.

Forensic Social Work Syllabus

Course Description

Forensic social work is the practice specialty that focuses on the intersection between law and health and human services. It requires the ethical knowledge and skill capacity to balance the mutual and conflicting interests of client and community. Multidisciplinary in nature, forensic social workers are found in such settings as child protective services, guardian ad litem programs, juvenile offender treatment programs, mitigation services, victim services, witness assistance programs, and domestic violence shelters. Apart from work in forensic settings, social workers increasingly encounter client problems (e.g., termination of parental rights, vulnerable adults, child abuse and neglect, and foster and permanency placement) that require them to work effectively in cross-disciplinary settings with police, court personnel, attorneys, and corrections officers.

The purpose of this course, therefore, is to gain familiarity with the structure of the American criminal and civil legal system with an emphasis on those areas relevant to forensic social work, including expert testimony, rules of evidence, risk assessment and management, and theories of causation of violence and aggression. The course also focuses on delineating and managing the dilemmas between social work and legal ethics, the social worker's authority, and the tension between social control and social support.

Course Objectives

Upon successful completion of the course, students will be able to:

1 understand forensic social work including purposes, functions, practice roles, and practice settings.
2 demonstrate familiarity with the adversary process including the steps in civil matters and criminal prosecution.
3 identify relevant social work values and ethics, apply them toward resolving ethical dilemmas encountered in forensic social work practice, and critically appraise the relationship between legal and social work ethics.
4 comprehend and articulate relevant theories and models of offender causation including the influence of oppression and socioeconomic injustice.
5 demonstrate an understanding of best practices in developing mental health evidence for forensic purposes.
6 utilize assessment skills relevant to determining competency of an accused to understand rights, waive rights, be tried, and be executed.
7 apply the biopsychosocial assessment process to evaluate (a) degree of criminal responsibility, (b) relevant mental and/or substance disorders, and (c) collateral information including records, testing, and medical reports.
8 apply the knowledge and skills required to present court testimony, including the role and responsibilities associated with being an expert witness.

9 utilize skills in forensic social work as it relates to child welfare including the interviewing of children and adults, giving of testimony, writing reports required by the courts, and assessing foster care and adoption placements.

10 understand the concept of mitigation in criminal cases and demonstrate an understanding of effective methods of developing skills in mitigating evidence in capital and noncapital cases.

11 identify and evaluate methods of risk assessments and risk management for their applicability to the criminal justice process.

Further examples of expanded social work roles addressed in social work curriculum are reflected throughout the remainder of the book. This handbook is broken down into five sections.

Section I of the book, comprised of chapter 1, examines the role and functions of forensic social workers and provides the conceptual foundation for the rest of the book. An emphasis is placed on evidence-based policies and practices to guide forensic social work. In chapter 1, David W. Springer and Albert R. Roberts examine the vast potential for professional social workers to become involved and responsive to both criminal offenders and their innocent victims. We also examine current evidence-based policies and practices, update trends and research findings, and focus on the most effective interventions—best practices for the 21st century.

Section II of this book, comprised of chapters 2 to 7, coalesces around forensic risk assessment issues and measures and forensic social work with special populations. This section covers a range of topics, such as expert witness testimony in child welfare, expert witnessing in criminal and civil cases involving woman battering, correctional social work with criminal offenders and their children, the role of the forensic practitioner in developing mitigation evidence, practice with HIV-infected women offenders, and emerging trends in group treatment approaches with batterers.

In chapter 2, Aron Shlonsky and Colleen Friend address risk assessment in the context of child maltreatment and domestic violence. Their chapter is conceptualized in the context of responding to child maltreatment allegations. That is, it assumes that the entry point for co-occurring child maltreatment and domestic violence cases is a child maltreatment allegation. From this perspective, the literature is reviewed with respect to the prevalence of domestic violence and how it is linked to child maltreatment. The authors examine the challenges in making predictive assessments in both domestic violence and child protection, positing that a nested or layered risk classification system offers the greatest potential to assist caseworkers in making service decisions. Key to this nested approach is the integration of safety and risk assessment information with a detailed assessment of child and family functioning. This should include consideration of the survivor's perception of risk and the potential for long-term harm that could accompany a range of responses from either a child's placement or removal from the home, as well as the child's remaining in the home. Professors Shlonsky and Friend suggest that engaging in the process of evidence-based practice encompasses the use of these two elements (risk and contextual assessment) and extends to the identification and continued evaluation of services for both child maltreatment and domestic violence.

In chapter 3, Kenneth R. Yeager and Albert R. Roberts examine the high rates of preventable deaths in jails and prisons as a result of hanging, hog-tying, Taser shocks, and cutting off the inmates' breathing with four-way restraints within juvenile and adult correctional facilities. The objectives of this chapter are threefold: to examine potential risk factors for inmate death, to highlight statistics associated with inmate suicide, and to examine risks associated with the practice of restraint within the criminal justice system. This chapter combines actual cases and case exemplars designed to highlight contributing factors and to discuss potential interventions to minimize potential foreseeable negative outcomes of inmate abuse, harm, self-harm and injuries, victimization, and death.

In chapter 4, Carlton E. Munson addresses expert witness testimony (EWT) in child welfare. Professor Munson explains that the forensic roles are primarily in three interrelated areas: (a) performing evaluations for courts and attorneys, (b) serving as consultants to attorneys, and (c) providing direct and rebuttal EWT. The author defines and explores the role of expert witness, including expert witness qualification factors, the content of EWT, and the selection of experts. Despite the challenge associated with the lack of a body of scientific studies regarding forensic social work practice, or perhaps because of it, Professor Munson underscores the importance of preparing for forensic social work practice and EWT. The chapter covers forensic child evaluations and diagnoses, depositions, affidavits, and interrogatories. Professor Munson reminds us that the ultimate intervention in forensic social work is the provision of EWT. Accordingly, he provides step-by-step guidelines for how to be professional and act in the best interest of the parties in a case.

In chapter 5, Evan Stark provides an overview of expert witnessing in criminal and civil cases involving woman battering, with an emphasis on how such testimony bears on cases also involving the welfare of children. The first part of the chapter reviews the background and most significant milestones in the evolution of expert testimony on battering; the rationale, scope, and general applicability of domestic violence testimony; and the major conceptual approaches to representing women's experience of abuse. The second part focuses on how to conduct a domestic violence evaluation in preparation for trial. Drawing on his experience as a witness in a pathbreaking class action lawsuit against the child welfare system in New York, *Nicholson v. Williams*, Professor Stark also examines the role of the expert in cases where children have been exposed to domestic violence. In the final sections, the author outlines the factors that can assist in evaluation and risk assessment. Although there is often a need to assess victims, perpetrators, or children in domestic violence cases clinically, this chapter is limited to the most common scenario in which domestic violence experts are called, when an attorney or prosecutor wants to provide the finder of fact or a jury with general information about woman battering and its effects, including its effects on children.

In chapter 6, John P. Niland explores the role of the practitioner in developing mitigation evidence; he defines mitigating evidence as anything that can justify a more lenient sentence. In the context of a death penalty case, effective mitigating evidence can spell the difference between life and death. In the noncapital case, mitigating evidence can be used to support a sentence that the defense feels is appropriate in light of the mitigation offered.

In chapter 7, Fred Buttell and Michelle Carney examine emerging trends in batterer intervention programming. Professors Buttell and Carney begin their chapter by tackling the debate surrounding the prevalence of domestic violence, asserting that the answer to this debate will ultimately drive solutions. Their review of the literature continues to address complex issues. Given that most men in batterer intervention programs are there as convicted offenders, the authors review the sequence of events that leads to the adoption of pro-arrest policies in police calls involving domestic violence. They go on to critically appraise outcome evaluations of treatment programs for domestic violence perpetrators. The intervention program described in more detail is a structured, intensive, 26-week, feminist-informed, and cognitive-behavioral group treatment program that focuses primarily on anger management and skills development. A central issue for those treating this population is determining how to do so within the constraints of both legal mandates regarding arrest and state-legislated programming.

Section III of this book, comprised of chapters 8 to 16, examines the assessment and treatment of juvenile offenders and the emerging role of the social worker and other mental health professionals in juvenile justice. After increasing for a number of years, and contributing to the spread of "get-tough," punitive legislation, juvenile crime peaked in 1994 and then declined almost every year for the past 12 years. However, despite overall declines in juvenile arrests and even in violent arrests, arrests in some categories have increased. The two areas of concern in recent years are simple assaults and drug violations. One plausible explanation is the fact that more than a decade of rapidly spreading get-tough and punitive policies increasingly placed juveniles in largely ineffective and potentially dangerous environments such as boot camps, adult prisons, and large, overcrowded juvenile facilities. On the positive side, we have recently witnessed a slow yet gradual return to the rehabilitation-focused roots of the juvenile justice ideal. To a large extent, this therapeutic and rehabilitative movement is the focus of this section.

In chapter 8, Kimberly Bender, Johnny S. Kim, and David W. Springer systematically review randomized clinical trials of interventions for dually diagnosed adolescents. To accomplish this goal, the authors systematically reviewed empirical intervention studies and, for each intervention examined, asked the following questions: (a) What is the evidence in support of this intervention as an effective treatment for dually diagnosed adolescents? (b) What degree of change is associated with this intervention? (c) Given certain common factors among treatments with demonstrated effectiveness, what are some preliminary guidelines for treating dually diagnosed youth? Results examining both between-group effect sizes indicate the efficacy of several treatment modalities in improving specific aspects of treatment needs but highlight family behavior therapy and individual cognitive problem-solving therapy as showing large effect sizes across externalizing, internalizing, and substance abuse outcomes in dually diagnosed youth. Preliminary guidelines for treating dually diagnosed adolescents are derived from a review of those treatments shown to be most effective, and these findings are then examined in light of their implications for juvenile offenders.

In chapter 9, Gerald Landsberg and Jo Rees assert that for practitioners to be effective in their multiple roles as direct providers and as advocates they need to be cognizant of the pathways of mentally ill or dually diagnosed youth into the juvenile justice system. This chapter provides an overview of the pathways of youth into the juvenile justice system, highlights potential points in the process in which helping professionals can intervene, and gives examples of intervention based on New York City experiences that are also of value in other locations, describes training offered to practitioners, and then discusses the importance of advocacy and recommendations for systems-change activities.

In chapter 10, Diana Falkenbach examines the psychopathic juvenile offender. Professor Falkenbach explores psychopathic traits that constitute the construct of psychopathy, including an in-depth discussion of the downward extension of the construct of psychopathy to youthful populations and the controversy surrounding this shift. There is potential benefit in practitioners exploring psychopathic traits in juveniles, such as developing early prevention strategies. Given the importance of false positives and false negatives, the complexities surrounding the assessment of psychopathic traits in juveniles are a core focus of this chapter.

In chapter 11, Sarah W. Feldstein and Joel I. D. Ginsburg address the use of motivational interviewing with juvenile delinquents. This intervention strategy may be particularly useful for work with adolescents who experience ambivalence about changing their behavior. Rather than interpreting ambivalence as a sign of indecision or pathology, ambivalence is considered crucial to the practice of motivational interviewing. The authors describe and apply motivational interviewing to address a range of problems experienced by juveniles and review the effectiveness of this approach to date.

In chapter 12, Jonathan B. Singer provides an overview of the juvenile justice system, highlighting where social work values and practice can and should be employed. Balancing the scholarly with the practical, he presents both findings from research and insights from professionals in the field. Singer presents the current organization of the juvenile justice system and discusses roles of the practitioner and juvenile probation officer, including adjunctive helping profession services such as crisis intervention and family-based services. He concludes with a discussion of the Balanced and Restorative Justice (BARJ) model of juvenile justice that seeks to make the traditional rehabilitative–punitive framework obsolete. This discussion is very timely because the Office of Juvenile Justice and Delinquency Prevention has supported the adoption of BARJ since 1998 and most states have included the principles in their statement of purpose.

In chapter 13, F. Carole Bryant, Allison Benesch, and Richard LaVallo explore the role of the helping professional in juvenile courts. The role of the helping professional in the juvenile court system has evolved considerably since the inception of social work as a bona fide profession in the late 1800s. At that time, social workers were considered social activists who advocated for change on behalf of people whom they encountered in prisons and social welfare agencies. In recent years, social workers have become an integral part of the criminal justice system as a whole, especially in the juvenile courts. The authors examine a range of issues, including the importance for social workers to become familiar with legal issues that have a direct impact on their role in the courts, social work qualifications, the reliability of expert testimony, the credibility of a witness, hearsay statements, confidentiality, therapist privilege, and immunity. The chapter concludes with reflections and words of wisdom from Allison Benesch, a former associate judge for the Travis County District Courts in Texas, where she has presided over juvenile delinquency, child protective services, and family law cases.

In chapter 14, Scott W. Henggeler, Ashli J. Sheidow, and Terry Lee provide an in-depth presentation of multisystemic therapy (MST), an intensive family- and community-based treatment that has been applied to a wide range of serious clinical problems presented by youths, including chronic and violent criminal behavior, substance abuse, sexual offending, psychiatric emergencies (i.e., homicidal, suicidal, psychotic), and, recently, serious health care problems. Youths with these types of serious clinical problems present significant personal and societal (e.g., crime victimization) costs, and,

due to their high rates of expensive out-of-home placements, consume a grossly disproportionate share of the nation's mental health treatment resources. Across these clinical
populations, the overarching goals of MST programs are to decrease rates of antisocial
behavior and other clinical problems, improve functioning (e.g., family relations, school
performance), and reduce use of out-of-home placements (e.g., incarceration, residential
treatment, hospitalization). The steps of MST, and the effectiveness and transportability
of MST in alleviating these problems in juvenile delinquents, are examined starting with
the statewide programs in Missouri and South Carolina.

In chapter 15, Lisa Rapp–Paglicci draws on research studies in California, Virginia,
Florida, Colorado, New York, North Carolina, and other states that indicate that the
majority of juvenile offenders have one or more mental disorders and explores the complexity of treating this population. Professor Rapp-Paglicci examines the importance of
conducting a thorough biopsychosocial assessment, ascertaining risk factors associated
with offending behavior and mental health problems, and using screening instruments
to aid in assessment with this population. She also reviews cognitive-behavioral therapy,
educational rehabilitation, functional family therapy, MST, and wraparound programs
as promising interventions to treat mentally ill juvenile offenders. Contraindicated approaches are also discussed, including boot camps, incarceration, and nondirective counseling. Recently, President Bush signed into law the Mentally Ill Offender Treatment
and Crime Reduction Act of 2004. This law has set the stage to begin to address mentally
ill offenders in the juvenile justice system in a new manner and to provide the desperately needed treatment that they require, as opposed to punitive-oriented boot camps or
prison.

In chapter 16, James Herbert Williams, Peter S. Hovmand, and Charlotte L. Bright
review the intersections between race and disparities in the juvenile justice system utilizing case examples of two communities at different stages in addressing disproportionate
minority confinement, reviewing the salient literature, and providing an overview of
practical approaches to address this significant issue.

Section IV of this book, comprised of chapters 17 to 21, explores forensic services and
programs for adult offenders in drug courts, jails, state prisons, and aftercare settings in
the community. Approximately 6.6 million people were on probation, in jail or prison, or
on parole in the United States at the beginning of this century. We know that the rates of
mental health and substance use disorders are typically much higher among incarcerated
adults than the corresponding rates among general community populations. Therefore,
this section identifies and discusses a range of important issues in adult corrections,
including the role and effectiveness of drug courts in facilitating addictions treatment
services, special needs of female offenders and their families, jail mental health services,
the treatment of PTSD in inmates, and the restorative justice movement.

According to the BJS (2005), during 2004 the total federal, state, and local adult
correctional population—incarcerated or under community supervision—grew by approximately 59,900 to reach the nearly 7-million mark. About 3.2% of the U.S. adult
population, or 1 in every 31 adults, was incarcerated or on probation or parole at year-end
2004. Four states had an increase of 10% or more in their probation population in 2004:
Kentucky (15%), Mississippi (12%), New Mexico (11%), and New Jersey (10%). The
adult probation population decreased in 21 states. Washington was the only state with
a double-digit decrease (down 27%). We are starting to see an increase in community

treatment of offenders under parole supervision in some states. Specifically, a total of 10 states saw double-digit increases in their parole population in 2004, led by Nebraska (24%). Nine states had a decrease in their parole population. Nevada, down 13%, was the only state with a decrease of more than 10%.

In chapter 17, Steven Belenko, David DeMatteo, and Nicholas Patapis examine drug courts as one means of helping drug-involved offenders. Grounded in a philosophy of therapeutic jurisprudence, drug courts have become an increasingly important model for linking drug-involved offenders to community-based treatment. The authors cover drug courts in depth, addressing key operational components of drug courts, eligibility for drug courts, the role of the drug court judge and other staff, application of sanctions and rewards, clinical assessment, and delivering treatment in drug court settings. A thorough review of the outcome research related to the effectiveness of drug courts is provided, and gaps in the drug court research literature are highlighted. Finally, critical issues, such as "creaming" and "net widening," related to drug courts are discussed, and recommendations for improving the effectiveness of clinical services are made. Regarding the role of the practitioner, the authors conclude that given the case management, clinically oriented approach of drug courts, helping professionals can play a vital role in ensuring that the clinical and other service needs of drug-involved offenders are being met.

In chapter 18, Diane S. Young provides an overview of jail mental health services, beginning with a discussion of the scope of the problem. The legal basis for jail mental health care and the generally accepted standards for jail mental health services are presented. The organization of jail mental health services, including a description of current practices—what services are actually provided and by whom—are explained. Special clinical issues and dilemmas that occur in jail mental health practice are presented. Finally, promising approaches for the provision of jail mental health services are explored.

In chapter 19, Sheryl Pimlott Kubiak and Isabel M. Rose discuss the prevalence of trauma exposure and co-occurring trauma and substance use disorders among men and women involved in the criminal justice system. The authors examine methods for assessing trauma exposure and trauma-related disorders, as well as promising interventions appropriate for institutional settings.

In chapter 20, Elizabeth C. Pomeroy, Michelle A. Rountree, and Danielle E. Parrish examine best practices with HIV-infected/affected incarcerated women. The authors review rates of infection among this population, as well as epidemiological and etiological determinants of risk. They then summarize best practices, including targets for change, preventative and treatment modalities, and the use of culturally grounded treatments. The chapter concludes with a detailed description of a successful psychoeducational treatment that has been developed, implemented, and evaluated by the lead author, Professor Pomeroy.

In chapter 21, Jose B. Ashford, Bruce D. Sales, and Craig Winston LeCroy examine factors relevant to formulating strategies for maintaining changes achieved in the treatment process and in achieving specific rehabilitative objectives for preventing relapse. The authors begin with a description of similarities and differences in the historical development of aftercare in the fields of corrections and mental health. This is followed by an examination of the outcome literature on case management, intensive supervision, psychosocial rehabilitation, and relapse prevention. In reviewing these approaches, Professors Ashford, Sales, and LeCroy identify unexamined areas and issues affecting the integration of correctional and mental health technology in caring for offenders in the community, which, if unattended to, are associated with relapse and recidivism.

Section V consists of four chapters focusing on restorative justice dialogues, victim–offender mediation programs, healing potential and outcome measures of restorative justice practices, and posttrauma group interventions in New York City in the aftermath of the September 11, 2001, mass terrorist murders.

In chapter 22, Marilyn Peterson Armour and Mark S. Umbreit explore victim–offender mediation (VOM), which is the oldest, most widely developed, and most empirically grounded expression of restorative justice. VOM provides interested victims the opportunity to meet with the juvenile or adult offender, in a safe and structured setting, with the goal of holding the offender directly accountable for his or her behavior while providing important assistance and compensation to the victim. Professors Armour and Umbreit discuss the values and traditions in which this approach is grounded and provide a brief history of the restorative justice movement. The authors go on to describe the context and stages of the VOM dialogue and address the role of the mediator based on their in-depth work in Minnesota, Illinois, Indiana, Texas, Utah, and other states as well as Canada, Australia, New Zealand, and England. The effectiveness of VOM is reviewed, as are pitfalls and unintended consequences of VOM. In the end, Professors Armour and Umbreit conclude that the widespread practice of VOM in thousands of cases each year and the empirical evidence generated over the past 25 years across many sites in numerous countries strongly indicate that VOM contributes to increased victim involvement and healing, to offenders taking responsibility for their behaviors and learning from this experience, to community members participating in shaping a just response to law violation, and to more positive public attitudes toward juvenile and criminal courts.

In chapter 23, Katherine van Wormer and Morris Jenkins examine the restorative justice movement, which represents a paradigm shift from conventional forms of resolving wrongdoing to a focus on the harm to victims and communities. The authors begin their chapter by addressing the scope of the problem, viewed as interpersonal violence (violence and other forms of violation by one person or the other) as well as structural violence at the societal level. Four models of restorative justice are explored, and in their review of the literature on the effectiveness of restorative justice, Professors van Wormer and Jenkins examine questions such as these: What does the literature show us about the long-term effectiveness of these restorative justice models? Are lives altered thereby? Does healing of the participants—victims and offenders—take place? The authors also explore gender-based restorative initiatives in situations of battering and rape, as well as cultural issues in restorative justice.

In chapter 24, Gary Behrman and the late William H. Reid present a task-based group treatment approach to posttrauma intervention. When persons are traumatized, much of what they assume about themselves, others, and the purposes of their lives are disrupted, resulting in multiple disconnections from their past. The model is designed to help individuals and their communities recreate these connections in meaningful, creative, and responsible ways, which may result in change on informative, reformative, or transformative levels. The model makes use of nine basic tasks in which the practitioner, individuals, and community are active participants. The tasks comprise welcoming, reflecting, reframing, educating, grieving, amplifying, integrating, empowering, and terminating/revisiting. Use of the model is illustrated in the first author's work with employees of the New York City Adult Protection Services, who were witness to the World Trade Center disaster.

In chapter 25, the epilogue, Harris Chaiklin provides an introduction and overview of key issues in correctional practice, addresses curriculum-related issues for practitioner education, and provides a historical perspective in order to bridge the past to the future of correctional practice and the improved delivery of social services to inmates.

Conclusion

To the extent that articles appearing in the *Social Work* journal published by the National Association of Social Workers (NASW) is a reflection of the field's interest in forensic social work, the interest has seemed to wax and wane over the years. From July 1998 to July 2005, the *Social Work* journal published a total of 13 articles (an average of just one article every 6 months!). By contrast, from November 1998 to November 2005, the *Research on Social Work Practice* journal published 29 articles related to forensic social work (an average of one article nearly every 2 months). It is worth noting that the *Research on Social Work Practice* journal, edited by Dr. Bruce Thyer of Florida State University, is sponsored by the Society for Social Work and Research. It is difficult to speculate why *Research on Social Work Practice* has published many more articles related to forensic social work in the past 7 years than has *Social Work*. Is it because *Research on Social Work Practice* is associated with the Society for Social Work and Research, a professional organization that overtly commits itself to the development and dissemination of evidence-based practice? Is it because Dr. Thyer has been the sole editor of *Research on Social Work Practice* since its inception, while *Social Work* rotates its editors, who may have different editorial priorities and perspectives, on a 4-year cycle? Does it have something to do with the type of manuscripts being submitted to these respective journals? Perhaps it is because the NASW does not recognize forensics as a helping profession practice area. Whatever the reason, the relatively few number of forensic social work publications appearing in *Social Work* is of concern. With approximately 150,000 members of NASW (all of whom receive the journal), practice strategies for improving the criminal justice system have the potential to reach a wide audience. Yet, an alternative view is that we should feel emboldened. The Society for Social Work and Research continues to grow its membership, and all members are given the choice to receive *Research on Social Work Practice*.

RESOURCES AND REFERENCES

Bureau of Justice Statistics. (1991). *Probation and parole, 1990.* Washington, DC: U.S. Department of Justice.

Bureau of Justice Statistics. (2004). *Bureau of Justice statistics bulletin.* Washington, DC: U.S. Department of Justice.

Bureau of Justice Statistics. (2005, November). *Bureau of Justice statistics bulletin.* Washington, DC: U.S. Department of Justice.

Costin, L. B., Harper, B. C., Piliavin, I., & Whaley, B. (1972). Barriers to social justice. In B. Ross & C. Shireman (Eds.), *Social work practice and social justice* (pp. 1–9). Washington, DC: NASW.

Martinson, R. (1974). What works? Questions and answers about prison reform. *The Public Interest, 35,* 22–54.

Neighbors, I. A., Green-Faust, L., & van Beyer, K. (2002). Curriculum development in forensic social work at the MSW and post-MSW levels. In I. Neighbors, A. Chambers, E. Levin, G. Nordman, & C. Tutrone (Eds.), *Social work and the law: Proceedings of the National Organization of Forensic Social Work, 2000* (pp. 1–11). New York: Haworth.

Office of National Drug Control Policy. (1996, March). *Treatment protocol effectiveness study.* Washington, DC: U.S. Government Printing Office.

Proctor, E. K., & Rosen, A. (2004). Concise standards for developing evidence-based practice guidelines. In A. R. Roberts & K. R. Yeager (Eds.), *Evidence-based practice manual: Research and outcome measures in health and human services* (pp. 193–199). New York: Oxford University Press.

Roberts, A. R. (1997). Introduction and overview. In A. R. Roberts (ed.), *Social work in juvenile and criminal justice settings* (2nd ed., pp. 7–18). Springfield, IL: Charles C. Thomas.

Roberts, A. R. (2003). Crime in America: Critical issues, trends, costs, policies, and legal remedies. In A. R. Roberts (Ed.), *Critical issues in crime and justice* (pp. 3–22). Thousand Oaks, CA: Sage.

Roberts, A. R., & Brownell, P. (1999). A century of forensic social work: Bridging the past to the present. *Social Work, 44* (4), 359–370.

Roberts, A. R., & Roberts, B. S. (2005). *Ending intimate abuse: Practice guidelines and survival strategies.* New York: Oxford University Press.

Roberts, A. R., & Yeager, K. R. (Eds.). (2004). *Evidence-based practice manual: Research and outcome measures in health and human services.* New York: Oxford University Press.

Rosen, A., & Proctor, E. (2002). Standards for evidence-based social work practice. In A. R. Roberts and G. J. Greene (Eds.), *Social workers' desk reference* (pp. 743–747). New York: Oxford University Press.

Sackett, D. L., Straus, S. E., Richardson, W. S., Rosenberg, W., & Haynes, R. B. (2000). *Evidence-based medicine: How to practice and teach EBM* (2nd ed.). New York: Churchill Livingstone.

Treger, H., & Allen, G. F. (1997). Social work in the justice system: An overview. In A. R. Roberts (Ed.), *Social work in juvenile and criminal justice settings* (2nd ed., pp. 19–33). Springfield, IL: Charles C. Thomas.

Waiselfisz, J. J. (2004). *Mapa da violência IV. Os jovens do Brasil. Juventude, Violência e Cidadania.* Brasília: UNESCO, Instituto Ayrton Senna, Secretaria Especial dos Direitos Humanos.

Forensic Risk Assessment, Roles, and Specialized Practices

Double Jeopardy: Risk Assessment in the Context of Child Maltreatment and Domestic Violence

Aron Shlonsky
Colleen Friend

Molly is an ongoing caseworker for a Citiville Children's Protective/Protection Services (CPS) agency. One of her ongoing family reunification cases involves the Smith family. The family initially came to the attention of CPS due to concerns of neglect (involving mother's and father's substance abuse of crack cocaine) and domestic violence (DV; father charged with assault). The three children, Tom, age 13, Cara, age 7, and Marie, age 3, were all placed with kin. Now, 1 year later, mother has been in recovery and is seeking the return of the children. Father was briefly jailed, but managed to hold on to his job. After about 6 months of a traditional batterers' intervention treatment program, he claims to have cleaned up and is

The authors gratefully acknowledge the substantial contributions made to this chapter by Raelene Freitag (Children's Research Center), Linda Mills (NYU), and Dennis Wagner (Children's Research Center).

supposedly not living in the home. The children come home on a 30-day trial visit. The CPS worker receives a cross-report called in to the child abuse hotline that describes a "domestic violence" incident involving both parents, where father was allegedly "high" and the now 14-year-old son, Tom, was seen chasing Mr. Smith out of the home with a baseball bat. The CPS worker checks with the police and learns that the father was slightly injured and was arrested.

First: Assess CPS risk.

- What will happen if I do nothing (weighing the risks of any course of action or inaction)?
- Considering safety as the most important goal, how should I proceed?
- How does domestic violence interact with neglect to increase risk?
- Is the risk here low, medium, or high?
- How often do I need to reevaluate the risk?

Second: Assess DV risk.

- What is my role when domestic violence is involved?
- Are all DV cases dangerous to kids?
- How are the kids affected psychologically?
- Are there any physical injuries? Do any injuries require emergency room treatment?
- How dangerous is this situation?
- What are the limitations of predictions about this family?
- Is the risk here low, medium, or high?
- How is the substantiation decision shaped by the DV incident?

Third: Assess context.

- What are the family dynamics? Is there substance abuse involved?
- Are there social supports and strengths to be built upon?
- What is the family's perception of the situation?
- How will I attend to some of the risk factors pressing in order to reduce the likelihood that Mrs. Smith, the children, or Mr. Smith will be harmed or killed?
- How do domestic violence and CPS interact in terms of understanding the family? Must I find a way to treat and/or prevent both?
- What available services would be most effective?

Introduction

Responding to child maltreatment is far more complicated than keeping children safe or protected from their own parents. The twin goals of safety and permanence imply that caseworkers must consider both the safety and ultimate well-being of the child. That is, at each decision point, caseworkers must weigh the potential for harm if nothing is done (i.e., leaving the child in a potentially abusive home) with the risk that intrusive actions aimed at child protection will ultimately prove to be harmful (i.e., unnecessarily separating a child from his or her parent). This is no simple equation, and the stakes are high. Yet the combination of severe consequences, the inherent difficulty of making accurate assessments, and differences in skill levels among CPS workers is a set up for unreliable case decision making (Shlonsky & Wagner, 2005).

CPS has begun to deal with this complicated decision-making context by using various assessment tools (Rycus & Hughes, 2003; Shlonsky & Wagner, 2005). These include one or more of the following:

1 Safety assessments: consensus-based lists of factors thought to be related to the likelihood of immediate harm.
2 Actuarial risk assessments: empirically derived estimations of the likelihood of maltreatment recurrence over time.
3 Structured contextual assessments: detailed appraisals of individual and family functioning.

The combination of such approaches allows caseworkers to more simply and reliably assess whether children might be safe if left in the home (safety assessment), generates a more reliable and valid prediction of the likelihood of future harm (actuarial risk assessment), and compiles detailed information that can be used to develop an individualized case plan (contextual assessment). Nonetheless, children and families who are reported for maltreatment often present with multiple problems spanning several service systems, each carrying its own risk of harm. Among the most serious of these is domestic violence. While domestic violence is often included as an item in safety and risk assessments, the intersection of these two threats to children may necessitate an expanded course of action.

This chapter is conceptualized in the context of responding to child maltreatment allegations. That is, it assumes that the entry point for co-occurring child maltreatment and domestic violence cases is a child maltreatment allegation. From this perspective, the literature is reviewed with respect to the prevalence of domestic violence and its link to child maltreatment. Next, we examine the challenges in making predictive assessments in both domestic violence and child protection, positing that a nested or layered risk classification system offers the greatest potential to assist caseworkers in making service decisions. Key to this nested approach is the integration of safety and risk assessment information with a detailed assessment of child and family functioning. This should include consideration of the survivor's perception of risk and the potential for long-term harm that could accompany a range of responses from either a child's placement or removal from the home, as well as the child's remaining in the home. Finally, we suggest that engaging in the process of evidence-based practice (EBP) encompasses the use of these two elements (risk and contextual assessment) and extends to the identification and continued evaluation of services for both child maltreatment and domestic violence. At the outset, we concede that the science of predicting human behavior, especially when it comes to violence, is complex, risky, and not likely to be mastered. Nevertheless, there is a public expectation that vulnerable children and parents will be protected from repeated assault and that state intervention is both necessary and acceptable to prevent such injury (Finkelhor, 1990). Though imperfect, this integrated approach appears to hold promise for minimizing harm and providing effective services.

Domestic Violence and Children's Protective/Protection Services: Scope and Consequences

The terms *domestic violence* and *intimate partner violence* can be used interchangeably to represent a pattern of battering or abusive acts in the context of an intimate relationship. Domestic violence spans a continuum of severity and includes physical, sexual, and emotional abuse (Roberts, 2001). In the 1985 U.S. National Family Violence Survey, 16% of American couples (married and cohabitating) reported experiencing at least one episode of physical violence over the course of the relationship (Straus & Gelles, 1986).

Each year in the United States, at least 3 to 8 million women of all races and classes are battered by an intimate partner (Roberts, 1998; Straus, Gelles, & Steinmetz, 1980). As disconcerting as these figures are, they likely underestimate the true prevalence of single and multiple acts of domestic violence. Such approximations are based on self-report, and survey respondents may be reluctant to disclose events that cause them to harbor feelings of shame or embarrassment. Indeed, Straus and Gelles (1986) estimated that only 14.8% of victims officially report DV incidents. Experts generally agree that women are more likely than men to be seriously physically injured by domestic violence because of men's greater use of force and severity of tactic (Barnett, Miller-Perrin, & Perrin, 1997). Further compounding these gender differences, women are far more likely to experience an injury as a result of assault than are men (Straus, 1993).

Although there is still controversy as to whether domestic violence is *bidirectional*, involving aggression by both parties, the issue is relevant to a discussion of domestic violence and child maltreatment for two important reasons: Most reports of child abuse and neglect are made against women (American Association for Protecting Children, 1988; Gelles & Cornell, 1990), and battered women sometimes mistreat their own children (Casanueva, 2005; Ross, 1996). Women's involvement in violence (not merely as responders, but as an initiators) has been documented in over 100 studies (Straus, 1999), yet this seemingly intractable finding is at odds with the dominant DV advocacy paradigm, which sees women only as victims (Dutton & Nicholls, 2005). This lack of clarity has caused tension between DV advocates and child protection services, the latter of which operates from the standpoint that the child is always the victim.

Estimates of the number of American children exposed to domestic violence vary greatly and are also calculated from data in national surveys. Based on earlier calculations that 3 million American households experienced at least one incident of interpersonal violence in the past year (Straus et al., 1980), Carlson (1998) estimated that 3.3 million children per year are at risk of exposure to parental violence. In their latest (1985) national survey, Straus and Gelles (1990) found that 30% of parents self-reported that their children witnessed at least one incident of physical violence over the course of that marriage. Although this estimate includes incidents that have a wide range of severity, some of which would not be considered by CPS to qualify as child maltreatment, the magnitude of the problem in the general population is of grave concern.

Children exposed to parental violence are frequently the victims of co-occurring maltreatment. This co-occurrence has been investigated in single-site clinical samples and shelter samples of abused women and their physically abused children, with rates of co-occurrence ranging from 30 to 60% (Appel & Holden, 1998; Edleson, 1999). In Canada, where exposure to domestic violence is treated as a maltreatment category, approximately 34% of substantiated cases in 2003 involved exposure to domestic violence,[1] and 28% of indicated maltreatment reports were substantiated primarily for DV exposure, making domestic violence the second most common form of substantiated maltreatment (Trocmé et al., 2005).

Clearly, children are at risk of abuse from both adults in the household. As already discussed, the risk of child maltreatment from battered mothers is an important consideration when discussing risk assessment. It is equally important to note that in households where the male batterer abuses his partner, batterers may also physically abuse the child. Estimates of such co-occurrence range from 47% to 80% (Hart, 1992; O'Keefe, 1995), making it imperative that DV advocates and child protection workers understand and come to terms with both forms of abuse (Mills et al., 2000). Several studies and scholars have identified child protection workers' tendency to hold the mother to a higher standard of responsibility than her partner in protecting her children (Davidson, 1995; Davis, 1995; Magen, 1999; Mills, 2000). DV advocates propose that this is a gender bias, and the differential perception of the role of the battered woman and the batterer has led to friction between the two service systems (Beeman, Hagemeisten, & Edleson, 1999; Hartley, 2004; Saunders & Anderson, 2000). Edleson (1999) aptly notes that the Children's Protective/Protection Services system may lack the authority to hold a male batterer accountable if he is not the father of the children. As Hartley (2004) correctly points out, not all reported child maltreatment cases in families with domestic violence are inaccurate in their assessment of failure to protect. In some cases, children are also being physically abused or neglected by both parents. Thus, domestic violence and child maltreatment (including neglect) can be two simultaneously occurring events (Hartley, 2004). Having found a surprisingly high level of neglect by mothers in families with severe domestic violence, she argues for a continuing shift from a view of mother's failure to protect to a view that recognizes the need for interventions focusing on the circumstances that endanger both mother and child (Hartley, 2004).

New information about domestic violence in the context of CPS services is also emerging from the National Survey of Children and Adolescent Well-Being. This survey begins with a U.S. national probability sample of children investigated for abuse and neglect between October 1999 and December 2000 and follows them for the next 3 years. Casanueva, Foshee, and Barth (2004) used these data to investigate hospital emergency room (ER) visits by children. Although the survey is limited to the primary caregiver's self-report of domestic violence, and only a few caregivers were willing to acknowledge that their child's injury was due to domestic violence, mothers' reports of current, severe domestic violence were positively associated with children's use of the ER. The authors went on to find that maternal depression (a key factor associated with child neglect) and lack of supervision (an element of child neglect) were also associated with children's injuries. They concluded that the identification of current, severe domestic violence in the home and depression among mothers would help prevent future injuries to children. Taken as a whole, Casanueva's (2005) and Hartley's (2004) work supports an earlier finding made by a Los Angeles juvenile court in *In re Heather A.* (1997). Here the Los Angeles Court of Appeals supported the lower court's finding that children's exposure to domestic violence, even if only secondary, constituted neglect on the part of the battering father.

Best practice for families affected by both DV and child maltreatment calls on advocates and child protection workers to "see double," meaning they need to draw from knowledge and understanding of both perspectives (Fleck-Henderson, 2000). But seeing double comes with its own set of impediments, relative to the way these families enter and behave in the two systems. In the DV track, women may self-report and voluntarily remain for services after the violence becomes intolerable. On the other hand, entrance into the Children's Protective/Protection Services system is typically not self-initiated. Services are generally involuntary, and the child's removal is feared by most families.

Children who witness domestic violence can experience a broad range of harmful responses including behavioral, emotional, or cognitive problems that may follow them into adulthood (Edelson; 1999; Felitti, 1998; Groves, 1999; *Nicholson v. Williams*, 2002). When children both witness and experience abuse, they are more likely to exhibit severe behavior problems than children who only witness domestic violence or children who are not exposed at all (Hughes, 1988), making effective intervention all that more important. Despite the increased risk of poor outcomes, some children display remarkable resiliency in the face of exposure to violence. Such resilience may be moderated by the level of violence, degree of exposure, child's exposure to other stresses, and his/her innate coping skills (Edelson, 1999). On the other hand, Groves (1999) attributes this resiliency to children being able to talk about the problem and the presence of another adult who can both mediate the experience and promote coping, which would coincide with the findings of resiliency studies (Werner, 1995; Werner & Smith, 1992). Canadian researchers found that 26% of the children in their school sample could be classified as resilient, despite their exposure to domestic violence (Wolfe, Jaffe, Wilson, & Zak, 1985). While not immediately obvious, such findings have serious implications for responding to domestic violence in the context of child maltreatment. A U.S. district court judge found these arguments of resiliency to be persuasive when he ordered New York City's Administration for Children's Services to stop removing children solely because they saw their mother being beaten (*Nicholson v. Williams*, 2002). This challenge to a common practice in one of the largest public child welfare agencies in the country put the entire CPS system on notice that decisions about removal had to adequately protect the rights of the nonabusing parent and consider the overall well-being of the child.

The Challenge of Prediction

The challenges posed in making protective services risk determinations have been detailed elsewhere (Gambrill & Shlonsky, 2001; Wald & Woolverton, 1990), as have risk decisions in DV response (Cattaneo & Goodman, 2005; Dutton & Kropp, 2000). However, few studies have integrated the two areas. DV and child maltreatment assessment share many of the same methodological issues in terms of predicting risk and making subsequent service decisions. Specifically, the discovery of child maltreatment and domestic violence begs the following questions: Will it happen again if nothing is done? What are the consequences if it does recur? How might my actions, as a worker, forestall this eventuality? Who is my client—the child, the battered parent(s), the abusing parents, or all three? At the agency and policy level, what can we do to make sure that we are expending scarce resources only on cases where child maltreatment and/or domestic violence are most likely to recur? How can we tell whether services are effective?

Cognitive Biases and Thinking Errors

Clearly in both fields, clinical prediction of risk is marked by cognitive biases and thinking errors, resulting in decisions that tend to have limited predictive validity (Dawes, 1994; Grove & Meehl, 1996). The sheer volume of observed information, the speed in which decisions must be made, and the pressure to get it right can influence a worker's assessment of risk (Shlonsky & Wagner, 2005). Yet there is little evidence that, in the face of such demands, workers can make reliable and valid predictions of future events. In fact, the opposite is likely true, even for those armed with good information and experience (Dawes, 1994; Dawes, Faust, & Meehl, 1989). One of the major reasons for this shortcoming involves the inability of most people to accurately weigh and combine large amounts of disparate and often conflicting information, prompting the worker to select factors for the decision that have no relationship to the behavioral outcome being forecast (Faust, 1984; Shlonsky & Wagner, 2005). For example, in a child maltreatment case, an investigative worker might understandably focus on a parent's combativeness with the caseworker rather than on his or her overall parenting skills. There are situations in which experts can quickly and accurately make judgments (Klein, 1998), but these rarely involve long-term predictions of human behavior.

Fortunately, formal risk assessment measures have been developed in both child protection (Rycus & Hughes, 2003) and DV services (Cattaneo & Goodman, 2005; Dutton & Kropp, 2000) in order to combat the shortfalls of unassisted clinical judgment. Tools such as the California Family Risk Assessment for child protection and the Spousal Assault Risk Assessment (SARA) for domestic violence are designed to guide decision makers to those characteristics and observed behaviors that best predict the event of interest. While there is still some debate about whether tools based on a consensus of experts (consensus-based) or that employ statistics to generate an optimal combination of factors that predict the event (actuarial) are more predictive, actuarial instruments tend to perform at least as well as consensus-based tools and almost always outperform unassisted clinical judgment (Dawes, 1994; Grove & Meehl, 1996). Certainly, this is the case in child protection, where the most rigorous of studies testing actuarial and consensus-based tools favor the actuarial approach (Baird & Wagner, 2000; Baird, Wagner, Healey & Johnson, 1999).[2]

Laying this argument aside, then, what other issues should be considered? Why not merely find an actuarial tool that works for both child maltreatment and domestic violence, implement it, and be done? If only the world were that simple. While decisions informed by evidence (in this case, validated tools) promise to be better than decisions based on other sources, their predictive capacity is quite limited due to the nearly impossible task of predicting human behavior, as well as the difficulty of accurately predicting events with a low base rate of occurrence (e.g., femicide, child death by maltreatment). In other words, tools can go only so far. In addition, there are several methodological and contextual factors that must be addressed when considering both child maltreatment and domestic violence. Finally, actuarial tools are designed for a very specific purpose: making an optimal classification of risk (e.g., low, medium, or high). They are not inclusive of all risk factors, and there is no guarantee that risk factors are causal for recurrence rather than links in a chain originating elsewhere. That is, the factors contained in a risk assessment instrument cannot be used to develop a comprehensive service plan.

The Tools and Their Capacities

Risk assessment tools for domestic violence have been under development and in use for at least the last decade (Fein, Vossekuil, & Holden, 1995), but there has been somewhat limited success in predicting recidivism (Hilton & Harris, 2005). Two commonly used and validated instruments are the Danger Assessment (DA) and its revision (DA2) (Campbell, 1995, 2004), and the SARA (Kropp, Hart, Webster, & Eaves, 1995). The DA and DA2 are measures designed to predict the risk that a woman will be killed (femicide) by her partner. The DA was validated retrospectively on a small sample, calling its properties into question and presenting some interpretive problems (Dutton & Kropp, 2000). Acknowledging these limitations, Campbell (2004) recruited a larger and more diverse multisite sample and revised the instrument based on her findings (2004). All but 1 of the 15 yes/no items were significant predictors of intimate partner femicide, and the nonpredictive item (perpetrator's suicidality) was retained due to its theoretical relationship with femicide. Five items were added, and a few were combined and otherwise modified. The DA2 (see Figure 2.1) contains 20 items and is reported to have acceptable reliability ranging from 0.74 to 0.80. Given that the DA2 is predicting lethality, a fairly rare event, there are concerns about its ability to identify simultaneously women at risk of femicide and women who are not at risk. That is, as sensitivity (ability to detect women who will be killed) is increased, the specificity (ability to predict women who will not be killed) decreases. For example, in Campbell's (2004) study, a cutoff score of 4 produced a sensitivity of 83.4%, meaning that 83% of the women who were killed were correctly identified retrospectively.[3] The trade-off for such a sensitive instrument is a specificity of 39.2%. As a result of this statistical dilemma, the number of false positives (number of women incorrectly predicted to be killed) is very high. This does not mean that the instrument is not valuable or well constructed but, as we will discuss, it does raise philosophical and political questions about where the bar should be set.

While the DA and DA2 are important factors for intimate partner femicide, this represents a small (albeit important) part of all DV assaults. The most common forms of family violence are so-called minor violent acts, and those acts are performed by both genders (Straus & Gelles, 1990). The SARA, on the other hand, is a consensus-based clinical checklist of 20 factors clustered into five areas. The SARA's original purpose was to structure and enhance professional judgments about risk (Dutton & Kropp, 2000). Similarly to actuarial tools in use in child protection (Wagner & Johnson, 2003), the SARA allows for clinical overrides in order to incorporate some level of clinical judgment into risk decisions (Dutton & Kropp, 2000). Although the SARA's interrater reliability is reported to be high and its internal consistency moderate, evidence of predictive validity (the ability of the tool to predict domestic violence) is modest (Heckert & Gondolf, 2004). In addition, it is unclear whether the SARA's psychometric properties have been tested on a CPS sample. The Sara's 20 factors each have a range of response categories consisting of three items: 0 (*absent*), 1 (*subthreshold*), and 2 (*present*). Each of these items is totaled, and risk of domestic violence is said to increase as the score increases, but, unlike an actuarial approach, there appear to be no pre-established cutpoints to establish low, moderate, or high degree of risk. Unlike the DA, the SARA is completed by a

DANGER

Jacquelyn C. Can

Copyright 2004 Johns Hop

Several risk factors have been associated with incr
violent relationships. We cannot predict what will hap
danger of homicide in situations of abuse and for you

Using the calendar, please mark the approximate d
partner or ex partner. Write on that date how bad the

1. Slapping, pushing; no injuries and
2. Punching, kicking; bruises, cuts, a
3. "Beating up"; severe contusions, I
4. Threat to use weapon; head injur
5. Use of weapon; wounds from wea
(If **any** of the descriptions for the higher num

34

The Ontario
oped for use h
context, ap
Cormie
cons

Mark **Yes** or **No** f
("He" refers to your husband, partner, ex-husband, ex-partner, or whoever is currently physically hurting you.)

Yes	No		
		1.	Has the physical violence increased in severity or frequency over the past year?
		2.	Does he own a gun?
		3.	Have you left him after living together during the past year?
			3a. (If have *never* lived with him, check here____)
		4.	Is he unemployed?
		5.	Has he ever used a weapon against you or threatened you with a lethal weapon?
			5a. (If yes, was the weapon a gun?____)
		6.	Does he threaten to kill you?
		7.	Has he avoided being arrested for domestic violence?
		8.	Do you have a child that is not his?
		9.	Has he ever forced you to have sex when you did not wish to do so?
		10.	Does he ever try to choke you?
		11.	Does he use illegal drugs? By drugs, I mean "uppers" or amphetamines, speed, angel dust, cocaine, "crack", street drugs or mixtures.
		12.	Is he an alcoholic or problem drinker?
		13.	Does he control most or all of your daily activities? (For instance: does he tell you who you can be friends with, when you can see your family, how much money you can use, or when you can take the car?
			(If he tries, but you do not let him, check here: ____)
		14.	Is he violently and constantly jealous of you?
			(For instance, does he say "If I can't have you, no one can.")
		15.	Have you ever been beaten by him while you were pregnant?
			(If you have never been pregnant by him, check here: ____)
		16.	Has he ever threatened or tried to commit suicide?
		17.	Does he threaten to harm your children?
		18.	Do you believe he is capable of killing you?
		19.	Does he follow or spy on you, leave threatening notes or messages on answering machine, destroy your property, or call you when you don't want him to?
		20.	Have you ever threatened or tried to commit suicide?

Total "Yes" Answers

Thank you. Please talk to your nurse, advocate or counselor about
what the Danger Assessment means in terms of your situation.

Revised Danger Assessment to assist in prediction of partner femicide.

caseworker and, ultimately, yields an estimation of harm rather than lethality. Although they differ in the severity of what they seek to measure, the good news is that both the SARA and the DA2 share certain comments, indicating that there may be reasonable convergence between the two. The measures also appear to have fairly good reliability and are easily completed. Nonetheless, overall predictive validity of both tools remains modest.

Domestic Assault Risk Assessment (ODARA) is an actuarial tool devel-
by police officers conducting domestic violence investigations and, in this
pears to predict recidivism better than the SARA (Hilton, Harris, Rice, Lang,
& Lines, 2004). Hilton and Harris (2005) describe the tool as a 13-item scale
sting of domestic violence history, general criminal history, threats and confinement
ring the most recent assault, children in the relationship, substance abuse, and victim
barriers to support. Similar to other actuarial tools, each item is binary (0, 1) and the
total score is used to generate a probability of recidivism. This tool holds promise for a
number of reasons. First, its psychometric properties (Hilton et al., 2004) appear to be
similar to other actuarial tools used in different fields. Somewhat related, its simple, easy-
to-use structure will likely increase the reliability of domestic violence risk ratings and,
by extension, the validity of such predictions. Moreover, the tool was designed for police
investigations, and such inquiries have at least some similarity to child maltreatment
investigations in terms of their immediacy and inherently coercive nature. Nevertheless,
like the DA and SARA, the ODARA has not been normed on a CPS sample.

Child protection safety and risk assessment tools have also been in use for some
time (Fluke, Edwards, Bussey, Wells, & Johnson, 2001; Johnson & L'Esperance, 1984;
McDonald & Marks, 1991; Wald & Woolverton, 1990), though the quality of the measures
and the integrity of their application vary. In general, these tools are designed to predict
either (1) risk of immediate harm (safety assessment) or (2) risk of maltreatment recurrence over time (risk assessment). The safety assessment is usually completed shortly
after the initial contact with the family, and the risk assessment is usually completed
toward the end of the investigation period. Unfortunately, most of the early tools lacked
sufficient predictive validity to be of much use in the field (Lyons, Doueck, & Wodarski,
1996). More recently, however, safety and risk assessment tools have been successfully
used in the field to contend more accurately with unsafe situations and high-risk families
(Fluke et al., 2001; Johnson, 2004; Wagner & Johnson, 2003). However, these instruments
also suffer from an inability to predict at high levels of accuracy for the same problems
detailed previously (i.e., high sensitivity and low specificity). There is some evidence,
though, that a well-constructed, easily scored actuarial instrument can be effectively
used in the field. Following up on the retrospective validation of the California Family
Risk Assessment, a similar tool (Baird & Wagner, 2000), Wagner and Johnson (2003) and
Johnson (2004) conducted a prospective validation the California Family Risk Assessment using a sample using over 7,000 Children's Protective/Protection Services cases
from a variety of California counties. Each tool was completed by trained workers in the
field during the course of their investigation. They found that the instrument maintained
its psychometric properties indicating that, with proper training of caseworkers using it,
the instrument transfers well to the field.

The Challenge of Measuring and Defining Outcomes

The prediction of child maltreatment is made difficult in the face of vague definitions
and outcome measures (Gambrill & Shlonsky, 2000; Wald & Woolverton, 1990), and this
likely translates into the DV sphere as well. Arguably, physical and sexual abuse can be
more readily defined and classified in terms of severity than other forms of maltreatment.
However, child neglect, the most pervasive and common form of maltreatment in the
United States (Hines & Malley-Morrison, 2005) is subject to widely ranging definitions

and cutpoints (measurable point beyond which one can say neglect has occurred) across studies (Zuravin, 1999). Defining domestic violence itself might be an easier task, but defining when domestic violence becomes child abuse is another matter. Although there are those who would argue that witnessing domestic violence is a form of child maltreatment, and to some extent they may be right, this is not always a viable reason for mandated services and, ultimately, removing a child from his or her family or home (*Nicholson v. Williams*, 2002). At what point does CPS become involved in the response to domestic violence? If we base this on emotional harm to the child, how is this measured? The subtleties involved may make the creation of valid cutpoints untenable. The presence of children who appear to be resilient to some of the measurable effects of domestic violence (Edelson, 1999) indicates that children may react differently to similar types of exposure to violence. What is not clear is whether these same children would remain resilient if they were removed from the care of their parents. That is, if resilience is a confluence of personal and situational factors, a change in situation might result in a change in resilience. If resilience involves personal coping strategies, insight capacity, and parental relationship, then removal might compromise or overwhelm the individual's capacity to maintain these so-called traits.

Many risk assessment tools use substantiation or indication (social work finding that maltreatment has occurred) as the sole measure of maltreatment recurrence with the acknowledgment that it is limited to known recurrence. For instance, there are an unknown number of children who are maltreated but are not reported to CPS (English, Marshall, & Orme, 1999). Similarly, there may be a surveillance effect (families receiving CPS services are under increased scrutiny), and such children may be reported more often than would otherwise be expected (Fluke et al., 2001; Lindsey, 1994, 2004). Practically speaking, however, substantiation remains the best measure available for reabuse. In addition, valid instruments that measure risk re-report, child injury, and foster care placement have been developed and can be used to inform the decision-making process (Johnson, 2004; Wagner & Johnson, 2003). For example, a high risk rating for a child on the injury scale may inform a service decision differently than a high risk rating for re-report. DV studies have a similar problem in that they largely rely on subsequent police reports to measure recurrence, though there have been studies that use victim self-report as well (Dutton & Kropp, 2000).

Reliability and validity of the tools is also a challenge. DV and child maltreatment risk assessment tools range in quality, and it is exceedingly important to ascertain a tool's psychometric properties. However, even the best tools have limitations. Risk of domestic violence and child maltreatment is not static. That is, risk likely changes over time in child maltreatment cases (DePanfilis & Zuravin, 1998), and about half of DV incidents are single occurrences (Dutton & Kropp, 2000); thus, we may be observing an escalation or de-escalation at any given moment in time. If escalation is always assumed at the point of risk assessment, the false-positive rate might be very high, whereas if escalation is not assumed the number of false negatives might be high (Gambrill & Shlonsky, 2000).

In addition, attempts to make simple (yes/no) predictions of whether a child will be reabused are problematic. For instance, the California Family Risk Assessment instrument, while meeting key standards for reliability, is unable to predict maltreatment recurrence at acceptable levels if it is constrained to simply predict whether maltreatment will recur (more detail presented later in this chapter and in Shlonsky & Wagner, 2005). Again, this is due to the near impossibility of trying to predict complex human behavior.

Thus, even the best risk assessment tools should not be used as the sole decision-making device, but a good actuarial classification system can be used to reasonably inform service decisions.

Goal and Role Confusion

The co-occurrence of domestic violence and child maltreatment raises some serious questions about the very nature of services involving children and families. Much of the emphasis in child protection is focused on keeping children safe and facilitating a permanent home. Yet, a child is less likely to be safe if the parent is not safe. Clearly, the welfare of children depends on the welfare of parents. Likewise, a response to domestic violence that does not consider issues of child maltreatment that go beyond domestic violence (i.e., that the assaulted parent may also be abusive or neglectful) errs in the other direction.

For the purposes of this chapter, we are focusing only on children who are reported for maltreatment. Even with this smaller population, a number of different types of risk are present when factoring in the occurrence of domestic violence. These risks generally fall into two categories, risk of harm to the child and risk of harm to the parent, and include

1 child maltreatment that is not directly DV involved.
2 child maltreatment as a direct result of domestic violence.
3 child emotional harm as a result of observing domestic violence.
4 parent physical harm as a result of domestic violence, potentially limiting the parent's ability to meet the child's needs.
5 parent emotional harm as a result of domestic violence, potentially limiting the parent's ability to meet the child's needs.

These overlapping risks pose considerable challenges to both measurement and service response. Actuarial models of risk assessment are statistically derived sets of factors that estimate the likelihood of an event. The items themselves are not necessarily causal. That is, their presence may predict an event without actually causing it. While it seems logical that domestic violence is both a risk factor and causal for maltreatment recurrence, most tools use overall maltreatment recurrence as a benchmark,[4] rather than recurrence in the context of a DV incident. That is, the presence of the risk factor of domestic violence indicates that some children are probably reabused as a direct result of domestic violence between partners, but this is a subset of the larger group of children who are reabused for other reasons. Thus, predicting maltreatment is not predicting domestic violence, and vice versa.

Additionally, items on child protection risk assessment instruments often ask questions about whether there is currently domestic violence in the home or whether the primary caregiver has a history of domestic violence. What is generally not asked is whether the child was physically or emotionally injured during a DV episode. This is a critical point of inquiry; otherwise, there may not be a child protection issue. The relationships between prior violent acts (presumably including physical abuse of children) as well as battery while pregnant have been established as markers for femicide (Campbell, 1995). Child injury during a DV incident likely indicates a level of severity that should not be ignored. Along these same lines, consideration should be given as to whether a parent was injured as part of the DV issues that brought the family to the attention of CPS.

Integrated Assessment Strategies: A Proposed Solution

Despite the fact that actuarial prediction is likely to produce results that are better than clinical decisions alone, the reality is that we are currently unable to predict either child maltreatment recurrence or DV lethality or injury at sufficient levels to make outright statements about whether either will occur in the future. There are just too many unexplained factors, and the phenomena being predicted occur too infrequently to attain great accuracy. To illustrate this point, Shlonsky and Wagner (2005) combined the four classifications (low, moderate, high, and very high) of the California Family Risk Assessment instrument into two risk classifications forming a simple (yes/no) prediction of whether maltreatment would recur. While this configuration predicted at levels slightly greater than chance, the rate of false positives (predicting that individuals would reabuse when they, in fact, did not) was exceedingly high. For such a low base rate of recurrence, the best prediction would be that it would not happen. Similarly, the DA2, while clearly reliable in the sense that it predicts lethal domestic violence quite a bit better than chance alone, suffers from the same inability to make an outright (yes/no) prediction (Campbell, 2004; see also www.dangerassessment.com). The limited predictive capacity of high-quality tools means that the best we can do is to develop classification systems that categorize people into varying degrees of risk and tailor the intensity of the response according to these groupings. In other words, we make a statistically informed guess about what will happen in the future and respond accordingly. Given the level of accuracy of risk assessment tools in these fields, a forensic conclusion would never say more than whether a family is at higher risk than most other families for one or both of these outcomes.

With this limitation in mind, actuarial approaches categorize individuals and/or families into graded levels of risk. Examples of this approach in child protection are the Michigan Actuarial Model, which was validated retrospectively (Baird, Wagner, Healy, & Johnson, 1999; Baird & Wagner, 2000), and the California Family Risk Assessment, which has now been validated prospectively (Johnson, 2004; Wagner & Johnson, 2003). These models consist of a short set of questions, mostly binary, that have been found to predict abuse and neglect separately. Again, despite its limitations, this actuarial model clearly differentiates level of risk for resubstantiation, subsequent child placement, and child injury (see Figure 2.2). As level of risk increases, the percentage of children experiencing these outcomes increases. Children classified in the highest risk categories have a higher likelihood of experiencing these events, while children classified in the lower risk levels have a lower likelihood. The model does not claim to be right every time, nor is it intended to be the sole source for decision making. The risk assessment tool simply assigns a level of risk relative to other cases (Shlonsky & Wagner, 2005). If an instrument cannot adequately distinguish between risk categories, then it cannot serve as a decision aid. That is, if high-risk cases end up recurring as often as moderate-risk cases, the decision maker would not gain any information from the tool. A comparison of this approach (Baird & Wagner, 2000) to two commonly used consensus-based tools found that the actuarial

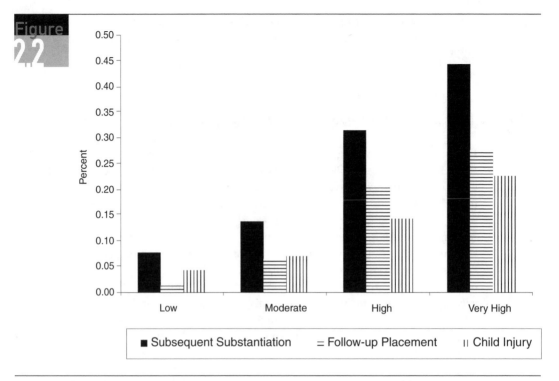

California Final Family Risk Classification by follow-up substantiation, placement, and injury. Originally reported in Baird and Wagner, 2000.

tool differentiated between risk levels while the two expert-driven models struggled to distinguish between risk levels (see Figure 2.3).

Nested Risk Assessment

The presence of related yet separate risk constructs (in this case, maltreatment recurrence and DV recurrence) requires careful consideration with respect to risk instrumentation and application. One of the problems with assessment instruments is their implementation in the field. Instruments that are too long or too difficult to complete are unlikely to be used by practitioners. Clients, too, especially involuntary clients, may not engage with a practitioner who asks them countless questions contained on an endless instrument. Thus, a comprehensive risk assessment instrument that covers all areas of risk would be ill advised. There are statistical as well as practical concerns. How do two instruments interact to alter risk? That is, are all children who are at high risk for DV recurrence also at high risk for child maltreatment? Perhaps so, depending on the definition of maltreatment. But is the converse true? Are all cases at high risk for child maltreatment recurrence also at high risk of DV recurrence? Clearly not. Domestic violence may not have occurred the first time, making an assessment of recurrence somewhat nonsensical. If we are functioning within the Children's Protective/Protection Services realm, it would seem that the primary assessment of risk should be child maltreatment in all its forms.

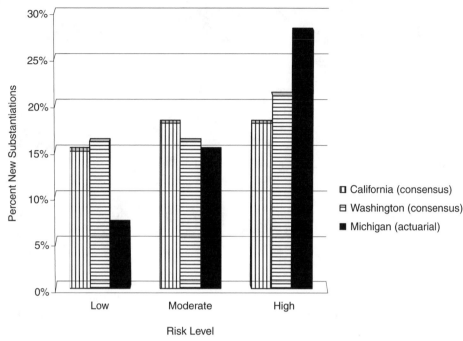

Actuarial versus consensus-based classification of subsequent substantiations. Originally reported in Baird and Wagner, 2000.

A nested approach to risk assessment, with risk of child maltreatment recurrence as the first-order assessment, has the potential to optimally employ more than one type of risk assessment instrument. That is, a hierarchy of instruments, beginning with a maltreatment recurrence measure and moving to other assessment instruments as needed, would provide valuable information for making key service decisions. In child protection, one common approach is to screen cases for investigation, assign a service priority (i.e., immediate or more delayed response), conduct a safety assessment, determine whether the maltreatment occurred (substantiation decision), complete a risk assessment, and decide whether to open a case for services. This is followed by a contextual assessment and the development of a service plan (see, for example, Wagner & Johnson, 2003). This approach can be enhanced by conducting a DV risk assessment at various points along this continuum if there is an indication that domestic violence is a current and ongoing issue for this family (see Figure 2.3). If the original allegation includes issues of domestic violence or domestic violence is discovered during the safety assessment, a joint assessment for risk of domestic violence might also be conducted focusing specifically on the immediate risk of harm or danger from domestic violence (e.g., DA2). At the end of the investigation period, the original allegations are found to be substantiated or indicated (the maltreatment occurred), unsubstantiated (insufficient evidence), or unfounded (the maltreatment did not occur). At this point, a child protection risk assessment is completed prior to the decision about whether or not to open a case for services. The decision is informed by the level of risk as well as caseworker input and agency guidelines. If opened

Table 2.1	Service Decisions Based on Risk of Recurrence for Child Maltreatment and Domestic Violence		
Recurrence Risk	**Child Protection Risk**		
	Low	**Medium**	**High**
Low	Community referral only, no DV referral	Community referral only, no DV referral	High intensity CW services, no DV services
Domestic Violence Risk Medium	Community referral only	Community referral, DV prevention referral	High intensity CW and DV services
High	Community referral only, DV prevention referral	Community CW referral, high intensity DV prevention services	High intensity CW and DV services

for services (ranging from referral to child placement) and domestic violence has been identified in the child protection risk or contextual assessments as a current family issue, a DV screener for general risk of DV recurrence could be administered and the information used for case planning purposes.

Table 2.1 presents an example of a framework for service decisions based on risk level of both child maltreatment recurrence and domestic violence. These responses are suggestions only. Risk assessment should not dictate service response due to the issues touched on in this chapter and in greater detail elsewhere (Gambrill & Shlonsky, 2000; Shlonsky & Wagner, 2005; Wald & Woolverton, 1990). Especially with mandated services, decisions should be made by carefully weighing risk assessment information and clinical judgment. Due to political considerations and population dynamics, individual agencies may decide on a different set of responses. At the outset, it is acknowledged that most DV instruments have not been extensively tested and, to our knowledge, have not been normed on a CPS sample. This framework is merely a suggestion, and any instruments used in this context should meet basic psychometric standards as well as be rigorously evaluated once implemented.

Beginning with the primary assessment for maltreatment recurrence, low-risk cases would result in referrals to services only. The main function of the Children's Protective/ Protection Services system is to keep children safe from maltreatment. Low-risk families, despite the likelihood of having fairly serious problems, should generally not be forced to receive such services. High-risk cases, on the other hand, call for joint evaluations and greater intensity of services. High-intensity services might range from voluntary family preservation services to child placement. If a case is rated as having a high likelihood of maltreatment recurrence but is classified as low risk for domestic violence, then the mix of services would not include DV prevention support. Thus, scarce DV resources would be conserved for families with the highest likelihood of having a subsequent DV incident. As risk for both child maltreatment and domestic violence increases, so too does the intensity of the service mix.

A classification of risk, whether obtained from a consensus or actuarial assessment, estimates the probability that an event will occur among families with similar characteristics. It is not a perfect predictor, nor is it a cookbook for service decisions. Certainly, it is not a substitute for sound professional judgment, and the finding should not be the sole basis for a case decision. Appropriate use in the field requires that workers understand how actuarial risk assessments work, know the limitations of the estimates they make, and receive the training and policy guidance necessary to employ them effectively in the field (Shlonsky & Wagner, 2005). An important component of both the California Actuarial Tool and the SARA is the presence of an agency and clinical override feature. This option allows caseworkers to upgrade the risk level (generally in consultation with their supervisor) in order to respond to information that may not be accounted for in the risk assessment instrument. However, this feature should be used sparingly. The very structure of a good actuarial instrument would suggest that, on average, clinical overrides will result in less accuracy. This is not to say that a clinical override used on an individual family will always be the wrong decision. It simply means that, over time, the instrument will be correct more often than the clinical decision maker.

The Integration of Actuarial and Clinical Approaches

Despite the advantages of using actuarial tools (e.g., more reliable and accurate assessment of risk) there are clear limitations, some of which have been detailed here. Perhaps the greatest limitation of the actuarial approach is that its intended use, assessment of risk, tells us nothing about people except how likely they are to act in a certain way. They are not designed to obtain a detailed understanding of family dynamics and functioning, and they are certainly not designed to be the sole basis of a treatment plan (Shlonsky & Wagner, 2005). Actuarial and clinical judgment must be integrated with the client's perception of the situation to make prudent decisions about the type and scope of services offered to children and families. This combination offers the greatest opportunity for improving casework decisions.

A comprehensive, contextualized family assessment identifies and clarifies relevant strengths and needs at the individual, family, community, and societal level (Gambrill, 1997); it explicates the reasons the family came into contact with the Children's Protective/Protection Services system; and it provides insight into the type and scope of services that might be necessary to prevent maltreatment and DV recurrence. An example of such an integration is the Children's Research Center's Structured Decision-Making approach. As detailed in Shlonsky and Wagner (2005) and in various state reports (see http://www.nccd-crc.org), the actuarial risk assessment tool is used to help agencies establish the intensity of services. However, case planning relies on a structured assessment of "Family Strengths and Needs" that is completed after the risk assessment and is used to organize clinical assessment findings. This consensus-based assessment is sometimes completed as part of a case or family group decision-making conference, allowing families the opportunity to participate more fully in the assessment and case planning process, and includes such elements as substance abuse, mental health, domestic violence, physical health, family relationships, housing, and social support. Standardization makes worker assessments more reliable, furnishes a brief format for documenting case notes, supplies additional criteria for classifying cases based on prioritized service or treatment needs,

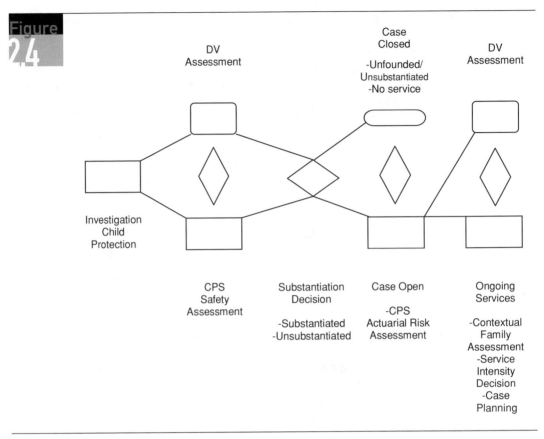

Process of assessing family strengths and needs.

and provides useful information for constructing fundamental progress indicators (see Figure 2.4).

The Link to Evidence-Based Practice as a Process

This integrated approach to risk assessment can be seen as the beginning of the full-scale implementation of the process of EBP (Shlonsky & Gibbs, 2004) in Children's Protective/ Protection Services (Wagner & Shlonsky, 2005). As outlined for evidence-based medicine (EBM) by Sackett, Richardson, Rosenberg, and Haynes (1997) and adapted for the helping professions by Gibbs (2003), EBP is the integration of current best evidence, clinical expertise, and client state/preferences. This integration is achieved through the process of posing an answerable question, querying a database in order to find current best evidence, evaluating evidence found, and applying it to client and clinical context (Sackett, Straus, Richardson, Rosenberg, & Haynes, 2000). Thus, EBP is more than simply the application of an intervention that has some evidence of effectiveness. Rather,

Figure
2.5

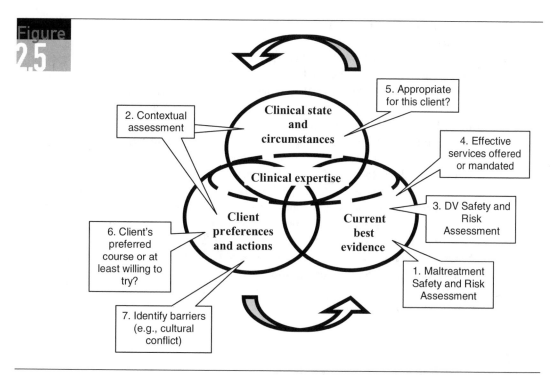

The cycle of EBP. Original Venn diagram appeared in Haynes, Devereaux, and Guyatt, 2002.

it is a *process* that allows agencies and practitioners to truly take account of what is known about both the clients and the challenges they face.

The nested risk assessment approach described in this chapter fits within the EBP conceptual model when the model is conceptualized as a recursive *cycle* rather than a single event. Using a more recent conception of the EBM model by Haynes, Devereaux, and Guyatt (2002), risk assessment can be seen as an entry point, targeting scarce resources to clients at highest risk (see Figure 2.5). Moving counterclockwise around the circle, a search is conducted for current best safety and risk assessment instruments for use in child protection. Relevant data sources on current best evidence include the Cochrane and Campbell Collaborations, Medline, PsycINFO, CINAHL, Social Services Abstracts, Social Work Abstracts, and others. Next, the contextual assessment uses clinical expertise to elicit key strengths and needs as well as client preferences as movement is made toward service provision. If, during the investigation process, current domestic violence or a history of domestic violence is discovered, current best evidence is again sought with respect to DV assessment tools (this process would work equally well if other problems such as depression or child behavior problems were discovered). At this stage, service decisions are made with consideration of risk level on both tools (perhaps using a predefined matrix similar to Table 2.1), family circumstances and preferences, and agency mandates. This stage should include a search of the literature for the current best evidence given the family's specific problems. Again, rather than simply throwing services at unwilling clients, consideration of the family's individual and group functioning, their preferences for providers or service type, and any barriers to service that might exist should be carefully weighed and, to the extent possible, used to modify services provided.

There is some debate as to whether conducting a detailed search with every client is realistic given the time constraints faced by caseworkers in the field (Mullen, Shlonsky, Bledsoe, & Bellamy, 2005). Initial searches by caseworkers will be more time consuming but will amount to updates as problems faced by families are encountered for a second time. There may also be ways for the agency to anticipate the challenges faced by their clients, conduct specific searches for current best evidence with respect to risk assessment tools and effective services, and begin obtaining or developing such resources for use by caseworkers. Web Resources for Child Welfare and Family Violence Information (see Figure 2.6) might serve as a starting point for gathering those resources. Some large CPS agencies have already formed in-house special research units to assist line workers and policy makers (for example, ACS in New York City and DCFS in Los Angeles). These could provide the necessary infrastructure for an EBP approach at the site or broader agency level. This would not preclude the need for continued searches and revisions of the assessment and service constellation due to the quickly changing state of evidence. Nonetheless, the anticipation of assessment and service provides a solid evidence base on which to guide service decisions.

Recommendations for Future Directions

Our examination of risk assessment in the context of child maltreatment and domestic violence has led us to see a number of pressing needs. First, there should be more cross-disciplinary work. To their credit, states such as Massachusetts have pioneered joint CPS and DV case assessments (Aron & Olson, 1997), but far more needs to be done. DV risk assessment instruments must be normed on CPS populations in order to use these instruments with greater confidence or modify them. For instance, although the SARA is not necessarily a predictive instrument (Dutton & Kropp, 2000), it does contain sets of risk factors that can be developed into an actuarial instrument built upon CPS cases.

Good assessment tools and the skills to use them are meaningless if services are not effective at ameliorating the problems that bring families to the attention of Children's Protective/Protection Services. After evaluating multiple batterers' treatment programs, the most recent national analysis called for improved program evaluations and concluded that it was too early to abandon the concept, and too early to believe we have all the answers (Jackson, Feder, Forde, Davis, Maxwell, & Taylor, 2003). Similarly, the literature is clear in recommending group treatment and various components for battered women's counseling, but program evaluations have been scarce to nonexistent (Lipchik, Sirles, & Kubicki, 1997). In other words, we are not sure what works for whom and at what point. Critics of the current service approaches for domestic violence argue that Western feminist ideology has been the driving force behind the menu of services offered battered women, but that this has been done without adequate evaluation that these approaches lead to enhanced safety (Mills, 2003). Regarding children, Cunningham and Baker (2004) have identified only 11 evaluations of children's treatment programs for DV exposure in the published literature, none addressing treatment effectiveness. Thus, we have a small

Family Violence Prevention Fund http://endabuse.org	Focuses on public education and contains information on national awareness campaigns. It also posts legislative updates.
Danger Assessment http://www.dangerassessment.com	Centers on Jacqueline Campbell's instrument. It provides access to the instrument, information on its free use and psychometric data, and links to other domestic violence resources.
Child Welfare League of Canada http://www.cwlc.ca/index_e.htm	Provides information advocacy, statistics on abuse and neglect, publications, and membership. There are links to other sites, including the Canadian Incidence Study (2003), whose reports on child abuse and neglect findings can be accessed from this site.
American Profession Society on the Abuse of Children http://apsac.fmhi.usf.edu/	Focuses on all aspects of services for maltreated children and provides links to other resources, membership, their publications, and guidelines.
Child Welfare League of America http://www.cwla.org	Provides information on child advocacy, statistics on abuse and neglect, foster care, child welfare, and membership. Their *Children's Monitor* is a public policy update that can be read free online.
Child Welfare Information Gateway http://www.childwelfare.gov/ 1-800-394-3366	Provides information on statistics, child welfare, child abuse and neglect prevention, and state statutes. Many publications can be viewed free online. There is a section for professionals that addresses a range of topics from promising practices to workforce and training resources, including e-learning training.
Minnesota Center Against Violence and Abuse http://www.mincava.umn.edu	Offers information and resources on violence and various types of abuses. Provides links to related resources, published articles, and other manuscripts; many articles can be downloaded from this site.
Center for Excellence for Child Welfare http://www.cecw-cepb.ca/home.shtml	Fosters research, develops policy, forges networks, and disseminates information. Family violence research can be conducted with the search functions. The Center is part of the Bell Canada Child Welfare Research Unit, located at the University of Toronto.
Canadian Incidence Study http://www.phac-aspc.gc.ca/cm-vee/csca-ecve/index.html	Reports on child abuse and neglect in Canada.
California Evidence Based Clearinghouse For Child Welfare http://www.cachildwelfareclearinghouse.org	Provides up to date information on evidence based child welfare practices. Facilitates the utilization of evidence based practices as a method of achieving improved outcomes in safety, permanency and child well being.

Web Resources for Child Welfare and Family Violence Information.

set of DV-specific services that consist largely of shelter care, none have been adequately evaluated, and, where viable programs for families who decide to remain intact exist, they need to be better publicized. These shortcomings must be addressed by moving beyond standard DV service provision, perhaps toward a harm reduction approach.

Given that risk assessments tend to be abuser focused, Cavenaugh and Gelles' (2005) review of the literature found that most male offenders in the low-to-moderate category do not escalate over time. They make a case for matching these typologies with treatment interventions, much like the stages of change approach (Prochasha, DiClemente, & Norcross, 1992). Batterers appear to be a heterogeneous population as opposed to the homogeneous, ever-escalating group typified by current approaches to treatment and intervention. Thus, we need to find specific strategies that are effective with particular risk groups. The danger of mismatching a batterer to treatment services, according to Cavenaugh and Gelles (2005), is that it is possible, and perhaps likely, that a batterer may complete a program without having his needs addressed. At its worst, a homogenous approach could undermine the victim's future safety.

Understanding that battered women are (for the most part) keenly and uniquely aware of their own danger, we need to study how their knowledge can enhance the performance of risk assessment instruments. Perhaps alternative treatment approaches such as the work of Penell and Burford (2002) in Family Group Decision Making and the experiment in restorative justice approaches for batterers proposed and underway by Mills (2005) hold promise for improving prediction and reducing recurrence by engaging the extended family and community members to monitor and provide acceptable resources for at-risk families.

Conclusion

Having explored the connection between child maltreatment and domestic violence, as well as the challenges in making predictive assessments, we are advocating a nested risk assessment that considers child maltreatment recurrence first, and then proceeds with a DV risk assessment. Both of these then lead to a comprehensive and contextual family assessment that is the basis of connecting the family with appropriate services. Further, anchoring this within an EBP framework will help workers understand the limits as well as the strengths of risk assessment instruments, the proper use of contextual assessment measures, and the range of effective treatment options available to children and families. Integral to this approach, we recommend the following:

- Child protection workers need more specific focused training in understanding risk assessment. They need to understand the terms discussed in this article (i.e., reliability, validity, sensitivity, specificity), as well as the current state of what Cash (2001) calls the art and science of risk assessment. Similarly, managers and policy makers must understand that there is no way to eliminate risk; there is only the minimization of harm through risk management (Gambrill & Shlonsky, 2001).
- In addition, child protection workers need more training in determining where and when to intervene and how to conduct interviews that are sensitive to the

issues surrounding domestic violence. Beyond prediction, the workers' goal is to prevent recurrence of harm. On the whole, good risk assessment instruments outperform clinical judgment with respect to prediction, but there is a role for the worker in assessing the dynamic context of child maltreatment and domestic violence. In particular, this will aid in the selection of appropriate treatment. Because instruments such as the DA rely so heavily on victim self-report, workers also need training in engendering a battered woman's trust, as she may accurately perceive that honesty may put her at risk of losing her children.

- Reliably placing families into graded levels of risk can be readily accomplished with instruments such as the DA and the California Family Risk Assessment tool. As identified earlier, these gradations may be useful in matching typologies to treatment.

- More research is needed to discover how domestic violence and child maltreatment might interact to alter risk levels. For instance, they may have shared pathways that converge in child neglect. We are just beginning to understand how such markers as children's use of the ER, maternal depression, and severe domestic violence are linked. Because we know that both child maltreatment (Lindsey, 1994) and domestic violence (Edelson, 1999) correlate with poverty, the role of unemployment needs to be excavated fully with respect to both risk assessment and prevention of recurrence.

- Effective services must be identified and made available for locally prevalent problems (Shlonsky & Wagner, 2005). Each agency should identify a core set of commonly needed services for the treatment and prevention of domestic violence, child maltreatment, and their related problems. Where such services do not exist or cannot be found, old services should be evaluated and innovations sought using the EBP methods discussed here. In any case, the current state of knowledge (or lack thereof) should be acknowledged rather than ignored.

Children's Protective/Protection Services workers face the monumental and often impossible task of trying to prevent maltreatment while keeping families together. The presence of another unpredictable and harmful family problem, domestic violence, raises the stakes even higher. Risk assessment tools, despite their ability to predict future harm, are only the beginning of what is needed to prevent harm. Such tools must be integrated with a structured assessment of family functioning and a set of effective, individualized services geared toward addressing both concerns.

NOTES

1. A child has directly or indirectly (e.g., observed physical injuries or overheard the violence) witnessed violence occurring between a caregiver and his/her partner (Trocmé et al., 2005).
2. One recent study testing actuarial versus clinical approaches (Baumann, Law, Sheets, Reid, & Graham, 2005) favored clinical approaches in certain instances. However, serious methodological issues have been raised that call these findings into question (Johnson, 2005).
3. Since Campbell was investigating lethality, her informants were often mothers, sisters, and friends of the decedent.
4. The California Family Risk Assessment tool and other Children's Research Center measures do distinguish between physical abuse and neglect as outcomes.

RESOURCES AND REFERENCES

American Association for Protecting Children. (1988). *Highlights of official child neglect and abuse reporting.* Denver: American Humane Association.

Appel, A. E., & Holden, G. W. (1998). The co-occurrence of spouse and physical child abuse: A review and appraisal. *Journal of Family Psychology, 12*(4), 578–599.

Aron, L., & Olson, K. (1997). Efforts by child welfare agencies to address domestic violence. *Public Welfare, 55*(3), 4–13.

Baird, C., & Wagner, D. (2000). The relative validity of actuarial and consensus-based risk assessment systems. *Children and Youth Services Review, 22*(11/12), 839–871.

Baird, C., Wagner, D., Healy, T., & Johnson, K. (1999). Risk assessment in Children's Protective/Protection Services: Consensus and actuarial model reliability. *Child Welfare, 78*(6), 723–748.

Barnett, O., Miller-Perrin, C., & Perrin, R. (1997). *Family violence across the lifespan: An introduction.* Thousand Oaks, CA: Sage.

Baumann, D. J., Law, J., Sheets, J., Reid, G., & Graham, J. (2005). Evaluating the effectiveness of actuarial risk assessment models. *Children and Youth Services Review, 27*(5), 465–490.

Beeman, S., Hagemeisten, A., & Edelson, J. (1999). Child protection and battered women's services: From conflict to collaboration. *Child Maltreatment, 4*(2), 116–126.

Campbell, J. (Ed.). (1995). *Assessing dangerousness: Violence by sexual offenders, batterers, and child abusers.* Thousand Oaks, CA: Sage.

Campbell, J. (2004, September). *Lethality and risk of re-assault: An overview with new data and practical techniques.* Paper presented at the International Conference on Family Violence, San Diego, CA.

Carlson, B. (1998). Children's observations of interpersonal violence. In A. R. Roberts (Ed.), *Battered women and their families: Intervention strategies and treatment programs* (pp. 147–167). New York: Springer.

Casanueva, C. (2005, December). *Child abuse and neglect and its relevence among intimate partner violence victims involved with child protective services.* Paper presented at the American Public Health Association, Philadelphia, PA.

Casanueva, D., Foshee, V., & Barth, R. P. (2004). Intimate partner violence as a risk factor for children's use of the emergency room and injuries. *Children and Youth Services Review, 27*(11), 1223–1242.

Cash, S. (2001). Risk assessment in child welfare: The art and science. *Children and Youth Services Review, 23*, 811–830.

Cattaneo, L. B., & Goodman, L. A. (2005). Risk factors for reabuse in intimate partner violence: A cross-disciplinary critical review. *Trauma, Violence, & Abuse, 6*(2), 141–175.

Cavenaugh, M., & Gelles, R. (2005). The utility of male domestic violence offender typologies: Directions for research, policy, and practice. *Journal of Interpersonal Violence, 20*(2), 155–166.

Cunningham, A., & Baker, L. (2004). *What about me.* Retrieved Sept. 21, 2005, from www.lfec.on.ca/what_about_me.html

Davidson, H. A. (1995). Child abuse and domestic violence: Legal connections and controversies. *Family Law Quarterly, 29*, 357–373.

Davis, J. (1995). Failure to protect and its impact on battered mothers. *Courts and Communities Confronting Violence in the Family, 1*, 6–7.

Dawes, R. M. (1994). *House of cards: Psychology and psychotherapy built on myth.* New York: Free Press.

Dawes, R. M., Faust, D., & Meehl, P. E. (1989). Clinical versus actuarial judgment. *Science, 243*, 1668–1674.

DePanfilis, D., & Zuravin, S. J. (1998). Rates, patterns, and frequency of child maltreatment recurrences among families known to CPS. *Child Maltreatment, 3*(1), 27–42.

Dutton, D. G., & Kropp, P. R. (2000). A review of domestic violence risk instruments. *Trauma, Violence, & Abuse, 1*(2), 171–181.

Dutton, D. G., & Nicholls, T. L. (2005). The gender paradigm in domestic violence research and theory: Part 1—The conflict of theory and data. *Aggression and Violent Behavior, 10*(6), 680–714.

Edelson, J. L. (1999). The overlap between child maltreatment and woman battering. *Violence Against Women, 5*(2), 134–154.

English, D. J., Marshall, D. B., & Orme, M. (1999). Characteristics of repeated referrals to Children's Protective/Protection Services in Washington state. *Child Maltreatment: Journal of the American Professional Society on the Abuse of Children, 4*(4), 297–307.

Faust, D. (1984). *The limits of scientific reasoning.* Minneapolis: University of Minnesota Press.

Fein, R. A., Vossekuil, B., & Holden, G. W. (1995). *Threat assessment: An approach to prevent targeted violence*. Washington, DC: National Institute of Justice.

Felitti, V. J. (1998). *The relationship of adverse childhood experiences to adult health: Turning gold into lead*. Retrieved from www.acesstudy.org/docs. Last accessed, January 20, 2006.

Finkelhor, D. (1990, Winter). Is child abuse overreported? *Public Welfare, Winter*, 22–29.

Fleck-Henderson, A. (2000). Domestic violence in the child protection system: Seeing double. *Children and Youth Services Review, 22*, 333–354.

Fluke, J., Edwards, M., Bussey, M., Wells, S., & Johnson, W. (2001). Reducing recurrence in Children's Protective/Protection Services: Impact of a targeted safety protocol. *Child Maltreatment: Journal of the American Professional Society on the Abuse of Children, 6*(3), 207–218.

Gambrill, E. (1997). *Social work practice: A critical thinker's guide*. New York: Oxford University Press.

Gambrill, E., & Shlonsky, A. (2000). Risk assessment in context. *Children and Youth Services Review, 22*(5/6), 813–837.

Gambrill, E., & Shlonsky, A. (2001). The need for a comprehensive risk management system in child welfare. *Children and Youth Services Review, 23*(1), 79–107.

Gelles, R. J., & Cornell, C. P. (1990). *Intimate violence in families* (2nd ed.). Newbury Park, CA: Sage.

Gibbs, L. (2003). *Evidence-based practice for the helping professions: A practical guide with integrated multimedia*. Pacific Grove, CA: Brooks/Cole-Thomson Learning.

Groves, B. D. (1999). Mental health services for children who witness domestic violence. *The Future of Children, 9*(3), 122–132.

Grove, W. M., & Meehl, P. E. (1996). Comparative efficiency of informal (subjective, impressionistic) and formal (mechanical, algorithmic) prediction procedures. *Psychology Public Policy and Law, 2*(2), 293–323.

Hart, B. (1992). Battered women and the duty to protect children. In state codes on domestic violence: Analysis, commentary, and recommendations. *Juvenile Family Court Journal, 43*(4), 79–80.

Hartley, C. (2004). Severe DV and child maltreatment: Considering child physical abuse, neglect and failure to protect. *Children and Youth Services Review, 26*, 373–392.

Haynes, R. B., Devereaux, P. J., & Guyatt, G. H. (2002). Clinical expertise in the era of evidence-based medicine and patient choice. *Evidence-Based Medicine, 7*, 36–38.

Heckert, D. A., & Gondolf, E. W. (2004). Battered women's perceptions of risk versus risk factors and instruments in predicting repeat reassault. *Journal of Interpersonal Violence, 19*(7), 778–800.

Hilton, Z. N., & Harris, G. T. (2005). Predicting wife assault: A critical review and implications for policy and practice. *Trauma, Violence, & Abuse, 6*(1), 3–23.

Hilton, Z. N., Harris, G. T., Rice, M. E., Lang, C., Cormier, C. A., & Lines, K. (2004). A brief actuarial assessment for the prediction of wife assault recidivism: The Ontario Domestic Assault Risk Assessment. *Psychological Assessment, 16*(3) 267–275.

Hines, D., & Malley-Morrison, K. (2005). *Family violence in the United States: Defining, understanding and combating abuse*. Thousand Oaks, CA: Sage.

Hughes, H. M. (1988). Psychological and behavior correlates of family violence in child witness and victims. *American Journal of Orthopsychiatry, 58*, 77–90.

Jackson, S., Feder, L., Forde, D., Davis, R., Maxwell, C., & Taylor, B. (2003). *Batterer intervention programs: Where do we go from here?* Washington, DC: National Institute of Justice.

Johnson, W., & L'Esperance, J. (1984). Predicting the recurrence of child abuse. *Social Work Research and Abstracts, 20*(2), 21–26.

Johnson, W. (2004). *Effectiveness of California's child welfare structured decision-making (SDM) model: A prospective study of the validity of the California Family Risk Assessment*. Oakland, CA: Alameda County Social Services Agency.

Johnson, W. (2005). The risk assessment wars: A commentary: Response to "Evaluating the effectiveness of actuarial risk assessment models" by Donald Baumann, J. Randolph Law, Janess Sheets, Grant Reid, and J. Christopher Graham, *Children and Youth Services Review, 27*(5), 465–490. *Children and Youth Services Review, 28*(6), 704–714.

Klein, G. (1998). *Sources of power: How people make decisions*. Cambridge, MA: MIT.

Kropp, P. R., Hart, S. D., Webster, C. W., & Eaves, D. (1995). *Manual for the Spousal Assault Risk Assessment Guide* (2nd ed.). Vancouver, BC: British Columbia Institute Against Family Violence.

Lindsey, D. (1994). *The welfare of children*. New York: Oxford University Press.

Lindsey, D. (2004). *The welfare of children*. (2nd ed.) New York: Oxford University Press.

Lipchik, E., Sirles, E., & Kubicki, A. (1997). Multifaced approaches in spouse abuse treatment. *Journal of Aggression, Maltreatment, and Trauma 1997, 1, 131–148*.

Lyons, P., Doueck, H. J., & Wodarski, J. S. (1996). Risk assessment for Children's Protective/Protection Services: A review of the empirical literature on instrument performance. *Social Work Research, 20*(3), 143–155.

Magen, R. H. (1999). In the best interests of battered women: Reconceptualizing allegations of failure to protect. *Child Maltreatment, 4,* 127–135.

McDonald, T., & Marks, J. (1991). A review of risk factors assessed in Children's Protective/Protection Services. *Social Service Review, 65,* 112–132.

Mills, L. G. (2000). Woman abuse and child protection: A tumultuous marriage. *Children and Youth Services Review, 22,* 199–205.

Mills, L. G. (2003). *Insult to injury: Rethinking our responses to intimate abuse.* Princeton, NJ: Princeton University Press.

Mills, L. G. (2005). *A comparison study of batterer intervention and restorative justice programs for domestic violence offenders.* (National Science Foundation Award #0452933).

Mills, L. G., Friend, C., Fleck-Henderson, A., Krug, S., Magen, R. H., Thomas, R. L., et al. (2000). Child protection and domestic violence: Training, practice, and policy issues. *Children and Youth Services Review, 22,* 315–332.

Mullen, E., Shlonsky, A., Bledsoe, B., & Bellamy, J. (2005). From concept to implementation: Challenges facing evidence-based social work. *Journal of Evidence and Policy, 1*(1), 61–84.

Nicholson v. Williams, 203 F. Supp. 2nd 153 (E.D. N.Y. 2002).

O'Keefe, M. (1995). Predictions of child abuse in maritally violent families. *Journal of Interpersonal Violence, 10*(1), 3–25.

Penell, J., & Burford, G. (2002). Feminist praxis: Making family group conferencing work. In H. Strang & J. Braithwaite (Eds.), *Restorative justice and family violence* (pp. 108–127). Cambridge, UK: Cambridge University Press.

Prochasha, J., DiClemente, C., & Norcross, J. (1992). In search of how people change. *American Psychologist, 47,* 1102–1114.

Roberts, A. R. (1998). *Battered women and their families: Intervention strategies and treatment approaches* (2nd ed.). New York: Springer.

Roberts, A. R. (2001). Myths and realities regarding battered women. In A. R. Roberts (Ed.), *Handbook of intervention strategies with domestic violence: Policies, programs and legal remedies* (pp. 3–21). New York: Oxford University Press.

Ross, S. M. (1996). Risk of physical abuse to children of spouse abusing parents. *Child Abuse and Neglect, 17,* 197–212.

Rycus, J. S., & Hughes, R. C. (2003). *Issues in risk assessment in Children's Protective/Protection Services: A policy white paper.* Columbus, OH: North American Resource Center for Child Welfare Center for Child Welfare Policy.

Sackett, D. L., Richardson, W. S., Rosenberg, W., & Haynes, R. B. (1997). *Evidence-based medicine: How to practice and teach EBM.* New York: Churchill Livingstone.

Sackett, D. L., Straus, S. E., Richardson, W. S., Rosenberg, W., & Haynes, R. B. (2000). *Evidence-based medicine: How to practice and teach EBM* (2nd ed.). New York: Churchill Livingstone.

Saunders, D. G., & Anderson, D. (2000). Evaluation of a domestic violence training for child protection workers and supervisors. Initial results. *Children and Youth Services Review, 22,* 373–395.

Shlonsky, A., & Gibbs, L. (2004). Will the real evidence-based practice please step forward: Teaching the process of EBP to the helping professions. *Journal of Brief Therapy and Crisis Intervention, 4*(2), 137–153.

Shlonsky, A., & Wagner, D. (2005). The next step: Integrating actuarial risk assessment and clinical judgment into an evidence-based practice framework in CPS case management. *Children and Youth Services Review, 27*(3), 409–427.

Straus, M. A., & Gelles, R. J. (1990). *Physical violence in American families.* Brunswick, NJ: Transaction.

Straus, M. A. (1993). Physical assaults by wives: A major social problem. In R. J. Gelles & D. R. Loseke (Eds.), Current controversies on family violence (pp. 67–87). Newbury Park, CA: Sage.

Straus, M. A. (1999). The controversy over domestic violence by women: A methodological, theoretical and sociology of science analysis. In X. Arriaga & S. Oskamp (Eds.), *Violence in intimate relationship* (pp. 17–44). Thousand Oaks, CA: Sage.

Straus, M. A., & Gelles, R. J. (1986). Societal change and family violence from 1975 to 1985 as revealed by two national surveys. *Journal of Marriage and the Family, 48,* 465–479.

Straus, M. A., & Gelles, R. J. (1990). *Physical violence in American families.* New Brunswick, NJ: Transaction Books.

Straus, M. A., Gelles, R. J., & Steinmetz, S. (1980). *Behind closed doors: Violence in American families.* New Brunswick, NJ: Transaction Books.

Trocmé, N., Fallon, B., MacLaurin, B., Daciuk, J., Felstiner, C., Black, T. et al. (2005). *Canadian Incidence Study of reported child abuse and neglect – 2003: Major findings.* Ottawa, Canada: Minister of Public Works and Government Services.

Wagner, D., & Johnson, K. (2003). *The California structured decision making risk revalidation: A prospective study.* Madison, Wisc: Children's Research Center.

Wald, M. S., & Woolverton, M. (1990). Risk assessment: The emperor's new clothes? *Child Welfare, 69*(6), 483–511.

Walker, L. (1984). *The battered woman syndrome.* New York: Springer.

Werner, E. E. (1995). Resilience in development. *Current Directions in Psychological Science, 4*(3), 81–85.

Werner, E. E., & Smith, R. S. (1992). *Overcoming the odds: High risk children from birth to adulthood.* Ithaca, NY: Cornell University Press.

Wolfe, D. A., Jaffe, P., Wilson, S. K., & Zak, L. (1985). Children of battered women: The relation of child behavior to family violence and maternal stress. *Journal of Consulting and Clinical Psychology, 53*, 657–665.

Zuravin, S. (1999). Child neglect: A review of definitions and measurement research. In H. Dubowitz (Ed.), *Neglected children: Research, practice, and policy* (pp. 24–46). Thousand Oaks, CA: Sage.

Prevention of Prisoner Sudden Deaths: Safety Guidelines and Suicide Screening Protocols

Kenneth R. Yeager
Albert R. Roberts

Introduction

It is critically important to address high rates of preventable deaths in jails and prisons as a result of hanging, hog-tying, Taser shocks, and cutting off the inmate's breathing with four-way restraints within juvenile and adult correctional facilities. Suicide is the number one cause of death in jails and correctional institutions. Offenders with a preexisting mental disorder, alcohol or substance abuse problem, depressive disorder, and/or previous suicide attempt history are at especially high risk when incarcerated. The suicide risk for juvenile and adult detainees and offenders increases when they have been held in detention centers or lockups with no way to post bail, or are incarcerated for the first time in state prisons. Efforts to understand the environmental factors that contribute to inmate deaths in jails and state prisons are relatively new. The Death in Custody Reporting Act of 2000 (PL 106-297) has led the way to compiling and analyzing detailed information related to inmate deaths.

The objectives of this chapter are to examine potential risk factors for inmate death, to highlight statistics associated with inmate suicide, and to examine risks associated with the practice of restraint within the criminal justice system. This chapter will combine actual cases and case exemplars designed to highlight contributing factors and to discuss potential interventions to minimize potential foreseeable negative outcomes of inmate abuse, harm, self-harm and injuries, victimization, and death.

In compliance with the Death in Custody Reporting Act, the U.S. Bureau of Justice Statistics began collecting inmate death records from all local jails in 2000. This was expanded to include reporting from all state prisons in 2001. The first report was issued in August 2005 as a Bureau of Justice Statistics Special Report, titled *Suicide and Homicide in State Prisons and Local Jails*. In this report, authored by Bureau of Justice Statistics policy analyst Christopher J. Mumola, characteristics related to high risks of suicide and homicide within the inmate population are highlighted and trends related to suicide and homicide are outlined and discussed in detail (Mumola, 2005).

This report documents that jail suicide rates have declined steadily from 129 per 100,000 inmates in 1983 to 47 per 100,000 in 2002. It is reported that in 1983 suicide accounted for the majority of jail deaths (56%). However, by 2002, the most frequently cited cause of death (52%) was reported to be from natural causes, well ahead of suicides (32%). Suicide rates in state prisons fell from 34 per 100,000 in 1980 to 16 per 100,000 in 1990 and appear to have stabilized since 1990.

In 2002 the suicide rate in the nation's 50 largest jail systems (29 per 100,000 inmates) was half of other jails (57 per 100,000 inmates). More importantly, offenders with a history of violence, incarcerated for violent offenses in both local jails and state prisons, had suicide rates of 92 per 100,000 inmates in local jails and 19 per 100,000 in state prisons. Two major data points emerge from this study. First is the remarkable difference between numbers of suicides in local jails versus state prisons. The average annual suicide rate of state prisoners (14 suicides per 100,000 prisoners) was one third that of local jail inmates (48 suicides per 100,000 prisoners). The second major data point is the over twice as high suicide rate of violent offenders as opposed to nonviolent offenders (31 and 9 per 100,000, respectively; Mumola, 2005). See Figure 3.1.

However, the national data do not portray the true scope of the problem because there are significant differences between states. During a 2-year period, there were no *prison* suicide deaths in three states—New Hampshire, Nebraska, and North Dakota—while six states reported prison suicide rates of 5 or less per 100,000 prisoners. However, 13 states reported prison suicide rates of at least 25 per 100,000 prisoners. States reporting the greatest number of prison suicides were led by South Dakota (71) and Utah (49), followed by Vermont, Alaska, and Arkansas with each reporting 36 suicides per 100,000 prisoners (Mumola, 2005).

A logical question to ask at this juncture is what causes this large variation in prisoner suicide. The U.S. Department of Justice described six key components to the identification of suicide risk and prevention of suicide. Those are

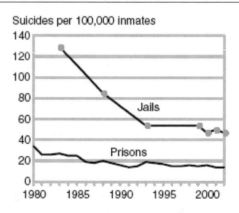

Suicides per 100,000 inmates. Adapted with permission from Mumola (2005).

1 Presence of a suicide prevention policy in place.
2 Staff training.
3 Screening and assessment.
4 Elements of safety within housing units.
5 Suicide watch levels (in minutes).
6 Intervention strategies.

At the time of this writing, the combined U.S. Department of Justice National Institute of Corrections and National Center on Institutions and Alternatives (NCIA) report *Prison Suicide: An Overview and Guide to Prevention* came to the following conclusions:

> Only three departments of correction (California, Delaware, and Louisiana) had suicide prevention policies that addressed all six critical components and that an additional five departments of correction (Connecticut, Hawaii, Nevada, Ohio, and Pennsylvania) had policies that addressed all but one critical component. Thus, only 15 percent of all departments of correction had policies that contained either all or all but one critical component of suicide prevention. In contrast, 14 departments of correction (27%) had either no suicide prevention policies or limited policies—3 with none, and 11 with policies that addressed only one or two critical components. The majority (58%) of DOCs [departments of correction] had policies that contained three or four of the critical components. (Hayes, 1995, p. 18, bold in original)

It is possible that the strongest correlative factor in the prevention of inmate suicide, according to *Prison Suicide* (Hayes, 1995), is staff training and interaction with the inmate population. This report indicates the following:

> The key to any suicide prevention program is properly trained correctional staff, who form the backbone of any prison facility. Very few suicides are actually prevented by mental health, medical, or other professional staff because suicides usually are attempted in inmate housing units and often during late evening and on weekends when inmates are outside the purview of program staff. These incidents must therefore be thwarted by correctional staff who have been trained in suicide prevention and have developed an intuitive sense about the inmates under their care. Correctional officers are often the only staff available 24 hours a day; thus, they form the front line of defense in preventing suicides. (Hayes, 1995, p. 25)

Recent efforts to increase effectiveness in the identification and prevention of inmate suicide have greatly decreased the numbers of completed suicides. Efforts to increase effectiveness in assessment and screening, specifically within the critical first weeks of incarceration, have proven to be effective. Issues addressing observation, close observation, and one-to-one surveillance have also been effective in decreasing suicide among the inmate population. Policies and procedures have been implemented in a growing number of correctional facilities, including inmate suicide assessment and screening protocols, suicide watch programs, crisis intervention programs, and systematic record keeping and data collection.

However, there are still no uniform suicide prevention standards, and there is too much variation in the extent of suicide screening and prevention programs both from state to state and within many states. The following exemplar provides a springboard for the next steps in suicide prevention standards within the jail and prison sectors.

Case Example Rob

Rob, a new inmate, is entering his second week of a 5-year sentence in the state prison system. Rob is expecting to spend approximately 10 to 14 months prior to being released on probation. He is approached by Nick, a seasoned inmate with a history of being the "deal maker." Rob is told by a peer that "this is the guy who can get you anything, I mean anything you need while in the joint." The story appears to be true, as Nick offers Rob what seems to be a reasonable deal. He offers Rob a nearly new iPod, a very hot commodity within the prison system, for the modest price of six packs of cigarettes per week for the next 3 years. While Rob smokes, he is not a heavy smoker and hopes to quit. He is able to have a carton per week provided by his family. Rob naively accepts the deal.

Shortly after the deal is inked, Rob hears through the grapevine that Marco, a notoriously dangerous inmate, is furious because his iPod has been taken, and he vows to find out who has stolen his property . . . and there will be "hell to pay." Confused and frightened, Rob isn't really sure what to make of the situation. Should he give the iPod back? Should he hide it? Should he give it to someone else? He is aware that there will be consequences from Nick should the return of the iPod be tracked back to Nick.

With only hours before time in the community room begins, where both Nick and Marco will be, Rob feels pressured to come up with a method to isolate himself and thus remain safe. He complains of physical illness, but this is met with little response. Desperate, he is able to make himself physically ill, and on the way to the nursing area, Rob decides the next step is to strike out by hitting someone. That way, he will be placed in seclusion where he will be safe until he can speak with a guard he trusts to assist in working out the situation. Rob randomly hits another inmate whom he doesn't know as he is escorted down the corridor. Unfortunately, his plan does not go as intended. He is immediately restrained, physically subdued, and taken back to his cell and placed on 15-minute checks (suicide precaution).

Word of this event travels fast, and the implication is clear to almost everyone. Rob is somehow connected with the missing iPod, and he is trying to find a safe haven. Even worse, there are grumblings that Nick is aware and feels he will have to "take out" Rob to protect himself.

Knowing the word is out, he feels hopeless, confused, and depressed. Rob concludes he will not be able to survive in this system. Feeling unable to withstand the punishment that awaits him, and with overwhelming anxiety and anger, Rob quietly begins his next plan. He removes the sheet from his mattress and ties one end to the back edge of the bed frame. He then wraps the sheet around his neck. Rob is careful to be certain that there is only enough sheet to extend 6 inches beyond the end of the bed frame while he is on the top bed. Rob then ties a loop in the remainder of the sheet, which he slips his hands through and tightens. The rest is simply a matter of rolling off the bunk. Rob's plan is nearly complete. Within 4 minutes he is found by corrections staff, and a code is called. Staff respond, and attempts to resuscitate are implemented, but not before brain death occurs. After 72 hours in a local hospital ICU, life supports are removed, and death is pronounced.

In the case of Rob, as is true with many cases of suicide in prisons and jails, staff questioned exactly what happened to cause such an event. Even other inmates were struck by this desperate action. Many concerned asked why this was not prevented. Many felt that it should or could have been prevented. Others felt this was simply the kind of event that is going to happen from time to time, given the population.

Suicide Prediction and Prevention

Unfortunately, there is no evidence-based formal assessment of specific guidelines that can reliably predict a suicide attempt or those who will commit suicide (American Psychiatric Association [APA], 2003; Glancy & Chaimowitz, 2005; Kanapaux, 2005; Paterson, Claughan, & McComish, 2004; Sherer, 2003). Informal and unstructured assessments of suicide also have limitations. Malone, Szanto, Corbitt, and Mann (1995) identified that clinicians did not document prior suicide attempts of admitted suicide patients nearly 25% of the time. Additionally, clinicians failed to include recent suicidal ideation or planning behavior in discharge summaries in 38% of patients. Bush, Fawcett, and Jacobs (2003) conducted a chart review study of 76 completed inpatient suicides and found inadequate suicide assessments. Results are as follows: 51% lacked documentation of prior suicide attempt; 29% were on no suicide precaution; 28% had current no self-harm contracts; of 50 patients who had suicidal ideation information available in the chart, 78% denied ideation in their last contact with staff (Bush et al., 2003).

While there is no clear evidence that a clinical assessment tool is effective in identification of potential inpatient suicide, such an assessment is helpful in providing a consistent template for staff in questioning suicidal ideation, directing thought process along the lines of risk assessment, and in formalizing communication patterns and assessments of risk within and between staff members. Such an assessment tool facilitates utilization of a common language and a common basis for communication of concerns related to patient safety needs. The APA guideline for the assessment and treatment of patients with suicide behavior provides such a common framework (APA, 2003). Initial and ongoing assessment of suicidality provides the foundation for safe care within the inpatient psychiatric setting. The APA (2003) indicates that a comprehensive suicide assessment should include:

- Identification of psychiatric signs and symptoms.
- Assessment of past suicidal behavior, including intent of self-injurious acts.
- Review of past treatment history and treatment relationships.
- Identification of family relationships, family history of suicide, mental illness, and dysfunction.
- Identification of current psychosocial stressors and nature of current crisis.

- Appreciation of psychological strengths and vulnerabilities of the individual patient.
- Specific inquiry about suicidal thoughts, plans, and behaviors.
- Elicitation of the presence or absence of suicidal ideation.
- Elicitation of the presence or absence of a suicide plan.
- Assessment of the patient's degree of suicidality, including suicidal intent and lethality of plan.
- History of suicide attempts or self-harm.
- Employment status.
- Psychosocial situation.
- Recognition that suicide assessment scales have very low predictive values and do not provide reliable measures of suicide risk.
- Establishment of a multiaxial diagnosis.
- Estimation of suicide risk.

Unit Assessment of Safety

Evaluation of the built environment serves as the framework for prevention of unit-based suicide within correctional facilities. However, there is an overwhelming lack of awareness of the potential for safety risks in the form of suicide and self-harm within the correction facilities.

Most DOC policies reflect the importance of housing as it relates to a suicide prevention program. The NCIA's analysis found that 39 DOCs (75%) addressed the issue of housing in their suicide prevention policy or other administrative directives. But while most procedures addressed the issues of inmate clothing, only a few addressed bedding or the physical environment in consideration of suicidal risk. Some policies identified specifically the use of isolation or seclusion to protect inmates; however, many policies did not address the removal of obvious protrusions in cells, which can be utilized as attachment points for hanging. In addition, few procedures were tailored to the level of an inmate's suicide risk (Hayes, 1995).

Units should be assessed to determine the following risks for suicide, including attachment points at three levels:

- Support of body weight off of the floor.
- Support of body weight in a sitting or kneeling position.
- Attachment point permitting a twisting method of hanging.

Doors, beds, bars, plumbing pipes, and fixtures should all be considered for risk of self-harm. Any exposed pipes, plumbing fixtures, door hinges, or bed frames that can be utilized as fixtures for attachment must be considered and modified to the greatest extent possible. Additionally, items that provide the opportunity for hanging, for example, sheets and electric cords, should be accounted for and removed from general areas. Electrical fixtures should be examined and frequently tested to assure special ground fault circuits are functional. Shower grab bars should be plated to remove potential for hanging. Exposed plumbing fixtures such as p-traps, water supply lines, or toilet flush mechanisms should be enclosed to prevent hanging from a sitting or kneeling position.

Supervision of Inmates

Research indicates that the overwhelming majority of suicide attempts in custody are by hanging. Medical experts warn that brain damage from strangulation can occur within 4 minutes, death often within 5 to 6 minutes. In prisons, the promptness of the response to attempted suicide is often driven by the level of supervision afforded the inmate. Supervision means more than observing in specified intervals or even direct observation. As strangulation can occur within 4 minutes, it is obvious that 15-minute checks for inmates at risk is an ineffective method of observation. The standard within psychiatric facilities are roving staff persons making continuous rounds and observations of the patient population.

As within psychiatric facilities, such observation would provide a greater blanket of protection of the inmate population. Additional tools to enhance observation are the utilization of personal data assistants (PDAs) and/or laptop computers to complete required paperwork. These devices are portable and easy to use, and such tool applications can free up corrections staff to move efficiently throughout the facility and provide greater levels of observation.

Utilization of Facility Safety Rounds

Assessing safety on inpatient units is an ongoing process. Three approaches are recommended: continuous internal observation, monthly internal review, and yearly external review.

First is an approach that includes direct or line staff/officers because they are the persons who are most affected and at risk should a unit turn volatile and unsafe. This process facilitates input into the unit's safety plan from correctional treatment and mental health specialists, who are more likely than others to know current inmate methods of self-harm and to identify potential environmental risks. In this model, line staff/correctional officers are assigned to sweep the unit on an ongoing basis while conducting safety checks.

Jail and correctional officers should examine the unit for slight changes. For example, what is going on in the inmate's cell? Are the items in the same place, and if not, why have they been moved? Are shoelaces in the shoes? Are all of the sheets on all of the beds? Are there any missing blankets? Have there been any alterations to the safety features put into place within the facility? For example, have any of the room fixtures been altered in any way? Finally, operational or correctional line staff will have the best sense of levels of inmate acuity. As a result, it is often the line correctional officer or sergeant who will have the best idea of the need to increase staffing levels to address shifting inmate acuity levels or to identify inmates demonstrating increased levels of anxiety and/or agitation. This is important since anxiety and agitation have been identified as precursors to self-harm.

This frontline process has the greatest potential to minimize risk associated with inmate safety.

The second level of safety assessment is a monthly review of the safety features by administrative staff. It is good to have persons who are not on the floor on a daily basis examining all areas to determine if there are any significant changes that have limited the unit safety features. In some cases, administrative rounds will find breaks in safety features or items that have been reintroduced to the cellblock or unit environment that have previously been identified as risk factors. Finally, administrative rounds are designed to maintain the overall safety structure and examine units for outdated products, decreases or changes in cleanliness of the unit, needed maintenance items such as cleaning equipment, infection control issues, and changes within the physical environment that would lead to decreases in inmate safety.

The third and final level is an external review of inmate safety. It is recommended that one time per year staff from a similar size and type of correctional facility examine the facility in question to assure safety features have not changed over time without identification by staff within the previous year. More importantly, collaborative environmental review provides an opportunity for sharing of ideas to move inmate safety programming forward. In this case, administrators and supervisors for similar facilities can share innovative approaches to patient safety that can be combined or compared to find best practices. A final benefit of collaborative safety reviews is the tendency for them to be based in the current reality of corrections facilities versus the assumptions of safety that are developed from day-to-day practice. Frequently, it is all too easy to slip into the rationalization of the facility being safe because there have not been any recent safety problems such as suicide gestures or attempts.

Finally, utilize the data collected to inform staff of progress made, needed areas for improvement, and benchmarking against like facilities nationally. Investment of time and staff to increase the understanding of inmate risks and to reduce environmental factors that will contribute to the risk of inmate self-harm will, in all likelihood, continue to drive down the number of incidents of self-harm within each facility. Collective review of this data can provide the opportunity to share in collaboration the best practices for establishment of harm reduction strategies.

Lethality Risk Associated With Physical Restraint

On April 12, 1999, a 21-year-old schizophrenic man named Timothy Perry was found dead in an observation cell hours after being placed in four-point restraints. Perry, who suffered from schizoaffective disorder, impulse control disorder, borderline personality disorder, major depressive disorder, and oppositional defiant disorder and was estimated to have an intelligence quotient (IQ) of 76 was placed in restraints and strapped to a bed in a cell of the mental health unit of Connecticut's Hartford Correctional Center.

Timothy Perry was well known to the mental health network because he had been treated in many of Connecticut's state facilities. Perry's anxiety and agitation level had begun to escalate during his hospitalization in Cedarcrest Regional Hospital, and he had taken several violent actions against staff. At this time, Cedarcrest called in police to arrest

Perry. Following his arrest, Perry was sent to the correctional center, a local detention facility under the control of the DOC. While incarcerated, Perry continued to decompensate, with increasing episodes of acting out in increasingly aggressive manners. On the evening of April 12, corrections officers decided to place Perry in physical restraints.

Perry was carried to a holding cell, where he was placed face down on a mattress. With verbal orders from a DOC psychiatrist, Perry was sedated and moved to yet another cell equipped with four-point restraints, where the officers' actions were videotaped. The now-naked Perry was placed in the restraints by officers using "techniques of pain compliance against the heavily sedated Perry." The unresponsive Perry was left in the cell. Approximately 2 hours later, a nurse noticed that Perry's feet had become discolored and that he was completely still. When she had the cell door opened, it was found that Perry had no pulse, his body was cold, and he had been dead for some time.

The case of Timothy Perry received wide publicity. The circumstances of the case were so egregious and the correctional officers' and medical staff's noncompliance with policy led to state settlement of the lawsuit. In the single largest wrongful death settlement ever paid by the state of Connecticut in the death of a single man without children, Perry's estate was awarded $2.9 million.

Forensic physician review of the evidence related to the events leading to the death of Perry indicated that Perry was placed face down in a prone position with his hands restrained behind his back, his legs restrained, and a towel held over his mouth, placing him at significant physical risk. Such a positioning inhibits chest wall motion and compromises breathing. It was determined that the actions taken by the officers were indeed the cause of death in this case.

Despite the wide media response to this case, such incidents continued to recur, and reports of sudden death of individuals who were restrained while prone, with many of the cases being reported as hog-tying, appeared throughout the 1990s. The description of *hog-tying* refers to the restraint of a person in a prone position with his or her wrists and ankles bound together behind the back. Given the adverse effects of this type of restraint, many law enforcement entities have discussed the issue of sudden death during restraint procedures and have attempted to modify or even eliminate the use of this procedure. However, sudden death during restraint in the prone position continues to occur.

This is evidenced in the March 2000 article by O'Holloran and Lewman titled "Asphyxial Death During Prone Restraint: A Report of 21 Cases," published in the *American Journal of Forensic Medicine and Pathology*. In this article, O'Holloran and Lewman examine the concept that sudden death of individuals held prone during police restraint may be due to asphyxia, even though neck holds were not applied. O'Holloran and Lewman (2000) conclude that it is not reasonable to calculate lethality to the extent that an assignment of blame should be placed; however, given the amount of discussion in the forensic pathology, emergency medicine, and law enforcement literature regarding the risk of death during hog-tying, the argument for classification as accidental becomes weaker. O'Holloran and Lewman (2000) report, as is the case with many forms of asphyxial death, that autopsy findings are subtle and nonspecific, which indicates that each case should be evaluated on its own merit. Regardless of the findings, safety concerns remain related to the use of restraint, with best practice indicating complete discontinuation of hog-tying or any form of prone restraint that has the potential to impact respirations, limit chest movement, or result in asphyxial death.

An Emerging Trend in Safety Risk in Corrections

While the risk of asphyxial death is decreasing, there is a new and growing concern related to the use of stun guns or Tasers. Taser guns or electroshock stun weapons are dart-firing weapons designed to cause incapacitation instantly through the delivery of a 50,000-volt shock. Tasers fire two barbed darts, which remain attached to the gun by wires, approximately 20 feet. The hooks are approximately 2 inches in length and are designed to impact and penetrate the target's clothing and/or skin to deliver a high-voltage but low-amperage shock. National statistics on Taser-related deaths vary. The American Civil Liberties Union reports more than 130 deaths in the United States, while Amnesty International reports more than 120 deaths in the United States and Canada—both figures since June 2001. As in the case of restraint asphyxia, coroners have for the most part attributed the cause of death to factors other than the mechanism of the Taser or stun gun. These factors generally are drug intoxication or preexisting heart conditions. However, there is growing concern of the role the stun gun has played. Current evidence suggests that Tasers have become the most prevalent force tool within many law enforcement and correctional agencies. Currently, in 49 U.S. states testing of Tasers in anticipation for adoption is underway. In Canada approximately 60 police departments have been issued and are now employing the use of Tasers. It is important to note that all of this application is occurring in the absence of rigorous, independent, and impartial study into the use of and the effects of Tasers, particularly in persons with identified heart disease or in those under the influence of mood-altering substances, especially amphetamine or stimulant compounds.

It is clear that the use of prone physical restraint is at least connected to unanticipated negative outcomes in the form of contributing factors that have led correctional officers and law enforcement to reconsider application of such procedures on prisoner populations. It may be possible that the same is true of the utilization of Tasers within the criminal justice and correctional arenas. Most disturbing regarding each of the examples provided is the application of procedures without an informed approach to understanding the implications of use of the procedure or technology. In the case of Tasers, it is possible that there will need to be a case similar to the case of Timothy Perry before the approach is eliminated, changed, or at least refined.

What is most evident is the lack of application of evidence in the development of procedures. It is time that corrections facilities assume the responsibility of gathering and utilizing data to refine practices. This has occurred in other industries, such as aviation, pharmaceuticals, and health delivery. Corrections facilities should be held to the same standards. It is also time that data related to prisoner death, whether due to suicide, homicide, health issues, or utilization of excessive force, be considered. Professionals understand that, at times, drastic methods are required with the population being addressed. However, there is increasing data related to the care and management of chronically mentally ill populations that providing care in a manner that is less restrictive can be equally effective in a population that is equally difficult to manage. Thus, correctional staff and safety managers could benefit from building upon established information within psychiatric facilities.

Establishment of a clearly defined approach to enhance methods of prisoner management within correctional facilities should be provided through clear leadership and direction by defining and articulating a mission and philosophy as well as developing and implementing a performance improvement action plan and holding people accountable. This core strategy includes the elevation of oversight of every unusual event by quality care review. The government and organizational leadership should assure the creation of an action plan based on the most current evidence-based approach and best-practice application for prisoner management and the monitorship of this plan by the principles of continuous quality improvement (Huckshorn, 2005).

Utilization of Data

Improvement of prisoner management and reduction of unforeseen bad outcomes can be fostered and developed by using data in a nonpunitive though competitive way. This includes using data to analyze characteristics of facility management by unit, shift, day, and staff member; identify facility baseline; set improvement goals; and monitor use and changes comparatively over time not only to document the effectiveness of best practices but also to inform best practices across the nation.

Training of Safety Approaches

Creation of an environment within correctional facilities where policy, procedures, and practices are based on the knowledge and principles of safety management and the characteristics of trauma-informed systems utilized within mental health settings to create an environment that is less likely to be coercive or conflictual and can be applied, adapted, and measured for levels of effectiveness to inform best practices. This type of intervention includes, but is not limited to, the communication of facility expectations for staff knowledge, skills, and abilities with regard to establishing and maintaining environmental and prisoner safety through job descriptions, performance evaluations, new employee orientations, and other similar activities (Huckshorn, 2005).

Utilization of Case Analysis and Debriefing

Actively seeking to disseminate knowledge gained from contentious and rigorous analysis of safety-related events and the use of this knowledge to inform policy, procedures, and practices should help correctional facilities avoid repeated episodes of sudden death in the future. Recommended debriefing activities include two phases: an immediate postevent acute analysis and the more formal problem analysis with line staff to inform the processes leading to the unanticipated event (Huckshorn, 2005).

Conclusion

Within the United States, correctional facilities are facing numerous remarkable challenges. As populations shift, correctional facilities are dealing with larger numbers of mentally ill and substance-abusing individuals. Challenges present daily in the management of this increasingly difficult population. With the emergence of new challenges, it will be a natural reflex to seek quick, effective methods to manage this difficult population. Some will point to new technology as the best method of intervention. The purpose of this chapter is to provide a sense of the need to move forward with informed caution. While there may be quick, effective, technologically driven solutions available, we suggest that the reader stop and consider the full potential impact of actions being taken. Over the past decade significant progress has been made in the collection and analysis of data related to prisoner death within state and local correctional facilities. It appears that the time is right for transformation of the correction facilities with regard to application of safety and quality improvement to inform the level of safety provided within correction facilities. It is time for the extensive application of quality and operational improvement measures within the corrections settings as well as the establishment of benchmark approaches to uniform safety features within correctional facilities. It also appears the time is right to establish application of processes and protocols to address difficult populations within correctional facilities across the nation based on research and informed practice.

With appropriate analysis of data- and quality-informed approaches to inmate management, adoption of standardized protocols, and implementation of tested safety protocols, the number of deaths by suicide and other unforeseen events can continue to be significantly reduced. It is time to examine thoroughly our approach to safety across the correction facilities of our nation and to improve safety for incarcerated persons and for those working within corrections facilities. This chapter has examined potential issues; however, time and space are limited. It is clear that there is much more to be learned and explored. It is equally clear that there is great opportunity for extensive research and application of the knowledge gained within the nation's correctional facilities. It is our hope that this chapter will serve as a springboard to launch new concepts and approaches to correctional facility safety.

RESOURCES AND REFERENCES

American Psychiatric Association. (2003). American psychiatric association practice guideline for the assessment and treatment of patients with suicidal behaviors. *American Journal of Psychiatry, 160*, 1–50.

Bush, K., Fawcett, J., & Jacobs, D. (2003). Clinical correlates of inpatient suicide. *Journal of Clinical Psychiatry, 64*, 14–19.

Glancy, G. D., & Chaimowitz G. (2005). The clinical use of risk assessment. *Canadian Journal of Psychiatry, 50*(1), 12–16.

Hayes, L. M. (1995). *Prison suicide: An overview and guide to prevention.* Washington, DC: National Center on Institutions and Alternatives and U.S. Department of Justice National Institute of Corrections.

Huckshorn, K. A. (2005). *Creating violence free and coercion free mental health treatment environments for the reduction of seclusion and restraint: A snapshot of six core strategies for the reduction of seclusion and restraint. Training curriculum for the reduction of seclusion and restraint.* Alexandria, VA: National Technical Assistance Center.

Kanapaux, W. (2005). Guideline to aid treatment of suicidal behavior. *Psychiatric Times, 21*(8), 17–23.

Malone, K. M., Szanto, K., Corbitt, E. M., & Mann, J. J. (1995). Clinical assessment versus research methods in the assessment of suicidal behavior. *American Journal of Psychiatry, 152*(11), 1601–1607.

Mumola, C. J. (2005, August). *Suicide and homicide in state prisons and local jails. Bureau of Justice Statistics special report* (Report No. NCJ 210036).

O'Holloran, R. L., & Lewman, L. V. (2000). Asphyxial death during prone restraint: A report of 21 cases. *American Journal of Forensic Medicine and Pathology, 21*(1), 39–52.

Paterson, B., Claughan, P., & McComish, S. (2004). New evidence or changing population? Reviewing the evidence of a link between mental illness and violence. *International Journal of Mental Health Nursing, 13*(1), 39–53.

Sherer, R. A. (2003). Psychiatrists strive to assure patients' safety. *Psychiatric Times, 20*(6), 23–29.

Yeager, K. R., Saveanu, R., Roberts, A. R., Reissland, G., Mertz, D., Cirpili, A. et al. (2005). Measured response to identified suicide risk and violence: What you need to know about psychiatric patient safety. *Brief Treatment and Crisis Intervention, 5*, 121–141.

Carlton E. Munson

Introduction

The content of this chapter is based on the premise that forensic social work activities must be conducted in the context of the evidence-based practice model that is evolving in most helping professions, including social work practice (Roberts & Yeager, 2004). This chapter deals with forensic social work practice related to children, adolescents, and their families, but most of the content can be applied to any form of forensic social work. For the sake of brevity, the terms *child* and *children* will be used to refer to children and adolescents. The abbreviation *EWT* is used in this chapter to refer to expert witness testimony. The conceptual content of this chapter will be illustrated by the following case example as well as brief vignettes. Most of the practical suggestions for forensic work in this chapter are drawn from this case example.

Case Example

Mary S., a 27-year-old single parent, and her 6-year-old son were referred to a clinical social worker for an evaluation associated with a department of social services (DSS) planning for a termination of parental rights (TPR) hearing for Mary. The court, at a permanency planning hearing for the child, ordered the evaluation. The child first came to the attention of the DSS staff after a female adult brought the child to the DSS office and stated that the boy was left at her home by someone, but the woman was not sure who was the mother of the child. DSS sheltered the child in foster care and began a search for the mother. The mother was found, and the child was returned to the mother's care after she complied with the DSS reunification plan. Over the next 4 years, DSS provided services to the mother on six occasions. Two of the service periods were at the mother's request. The mother would bring the child to the DSS office and request voluntary placement of the child because she could not care for him. The service was later discontinued and the case closed because of the mother's noncompliance with the DSS service plan. The mother had a chronic polysubstance abuse disorder and a diagnosis of severe bipolar disorder with rapid cycling. She was suicidal during the depressive phase of the disorder, and her son was removed from her care by the DSS child protective services four times because of neglect and physical abuse. The child was found to have cigarette burns on the forehead and bruises on his arms. Mary had attempted suicide in the presence of her son while in a state of "substance intoxication" (American Psychiatric Association, 2000a). The most recent removal occurred after the mother was convicted of stealing money from her employer to support her substance dependence. The mother was sent to jail for 18 months. DSS filed for termination of Mary's parental rights under the Adoption and Safe Families Act of 1997. The child was in his third foster care placement, and the current placement was a preadoptive home.

As part of the TPR process, the DSS sought a court-ordered evaluation by a clinical social worker to assess the mother's suitability to parent and the degree of attachment the child had with the mother and the preadoptive parents.

The mother was evaluated at the prison. The child was evaluated at the social worker's office and was observed in the preadoptive parents' home. The mother was given a protocol of standardized testing that included assessment of intellectual capacity, academic functional skills, personality, parenting skills, depression, dissociation, and substance/alcohol history. A clinical interview was conducted that included gathering a thorough social history. The mother by self-report described a family history of dysfunction with several out-of-home placements. Mary dropped out of high school and was introduced to substances and alcohol by an older male companion. She lived with several men who committed domestic violence, and her son's father was currently in jail for arson and murder. His parental rights had been terminated. The mother had five past psychiatric hospitalizations for the bipolar disorder. An attachment assessment was conducted. After a lengthy review process, arrangements were made with the prison for the mother to be brought to the DSS office for the attachment assessment. The attachment assessment was a modified set of procedures based on the "strange situation" developed by Ainsworth (Ainsworth, Bell, & Stayton, 1971; Cassidy & Shaver, 1999).

The mother was in a prerelease center at the prison and was scheduled to be released within 6 months, but no planning had been accomplished with respect to living arrangements, employment, therapy, and substance counseling and screening after her release. Mary was alienated from her family, and her parents wanted no contact with her after she was released from prison.

The child's evaluation included IQ testing, behavioral scales, trauma scales, a child depression scale, an ADHD scale administered to the caregivers, and a structured clinical interview of abuse history. The foster parents were seasoned foster parents and had adopted two children in the past. The attachment assessment was done in the clinician's office through use of one-way mirror observation. The clinician reviewed the DSS files, the child's school records, the prison psychiatrist's notes, and the prerelease center records, and interviewed the prison nurse who administered Mary's medications and provided her psychiatric care in the prison.

The evaluation report was submitted to the court 2 weeks before the TPR hearing. The social worker testified at the hearing after testimony of the six DSS social workers who had worked with the mother over the years. The workers laid the foundation for the clinical social worker's testimony about the evaluations. Attorneys had been appointed for the mother and the child. The clinician's testimony focused on the history of the mother's illness and disorders and her failure to protect and failure to make her child safe. The clinician did not testify to the "ultimate issue" (decision to be made by the court) of whether or not the child should be adopted. The clinician focused on the lack of attachment with the mother; the positive, significant, secure attachment with the preadoptive foster parents; and the fact that the mother would not be able to recover sufficiently in a reasonable period after her release. This testimony was based on the expectation of the Adoption and Safe Families Act of 1997 that the parent must be able to be reunified within 14–18 months in order to prevent adoption. The expert used scientific studies to support reasoned testimony that it would be very difficult for the mother to recover sufficiently within a brief time frame for reunification to occur. The clinician's vita was not admitted into evidence at the hearing because the clinician had testified many times in the court. The judge overruled objections by the mother's attorney that the clinician was not qualified to testify and the reports submitted did not meet the legal requirements for expert testimony. The judge ruled the clinician could testify as an expert in clinical social work and child welfare. The mother's attorney subjected the clinician to intense cross-examination. The judge ordered that the mother's parental rights be terminated. The mother's attorney appealed the decision, and two appeals courts upheld the trial court's ruling.

Scope of the Problem and Literature Review

Forensic social work is a social work practice specialty that focuses on legal issues and litigation, both criminal and civil, in the areas of child welfare, custody, divorce, juvenile delinquency, nonsupport, relative's responsibility, welfare rights, mandated treatment, and competency. Forensic social workers can be utilized to prepare other professionals for expert and fact witness testimony. Forensic social workers educate law professionals about social welfare issues and the interface of the law and the practice of social work (Barker, 1999). Social workers are increasingly performing forensic work related to child welfare domestically and internationally (Munson, 2005a). The forensic roles are primarily in three areas: (a) performing evaluations for courts and attorneys, (b) serving as consultants to attorneys, and (c) providing direct and rebuttal EWT (Gutheil & Applebaum, 2000). Many times the three roles are interrelated.

The extensive changes in family structure and functioning in the 1960s ushered in a new era of social scientists' and the helping professions' involvement in the law (Krause, 1986). Brieland and Lemmon (1977), in one of the early modern texts on social work and the law, called attention to the vital role practitioners have always held in providing services and advocacy for children. Today forensic work and EWT are particularly important in legal actions involving very young children who are not able to speak for themselves and are barred from testifying on the grounds that young children cannot understand the concept of truthfulness. Also, children are often prevented from making their wishes known to a court because of the concept of "considered judgment" or "reasoned judgment." These concepts are based on a presumption that children cannot make decisions that are necessarily in their best interest because of cognitive immaturity (Best, 2004). The expert in these cases becomes a voice for the underaged or impaired child along with the attorney representing the child. Providing such protection for the child is an awesome responsibility and should be far removed from the strategizing that lawyers often use, especially in high-conflict divorce and custody disputes. The prevailing legal standard and concept that an expert forensic specialist must adhere to is the best interest of the child. The best interest standard is used in most U.S. jurisdictions (Benjamin & Gollan, 2003).

Social workers do not generally have training in how to perform these forensic social work tasks. Social work education programs at the baccalaureate, master, or doctoral level do not provide academic instruction in forensic social work, and there are limited continuing education offerings in this area. A study reported by the National Organization of Forensic Social Work (NOFSW) found that only 4.3% of accredited social work programs offered a course in forensic social work and only 4.3% offered a forensic specialization. Only 14% of the schools surveyed had plans to develop a forensic specialization. Sixty-four percent of the schools reported offering a "social work and the law" course, but there was no indication that the courses focused on forensic social work (Neighbors, Green-Faust, & van Beyer, 2002). Schools of social work do not test clinical testing methods and practices, which is problematic because EWT standards mandate an empirical basis for testimony. There are very few continuing education workshops devoted specifically to the needs and expectations of forensic social workers. The NOFSW does offer workshops as part of their annual meeting.

The National Association of Social Workers (NASW) does not recognize forensics as a social work practice area. The NASW *Encyclopedia of Social Work* (NASW, 1995b), which is described by its editors as a "comprehensive and exhaustive . . . objective overview of the profession" (p. xvi), does not contain any reference to forensic social work. One NASW study reported that less than 4% of social workers are employed in "courts–justice system" settings (Gibelman & Schervish, 1997). This statistic is not a good indicator of the extent of forensic social work practice because many who work for courts and other criminal justice settings do not do forensic work, and many who do forensic work are not employed by courts or criminal justice settings. The NASW study includes forensic social work under the rubric of "criminal justice," but distinguishes forensic social work as a specialty within criminal justice. There is no mention in the NASW data of forensic social work in connection with child welfare services (Gibelman, 1995). The latest edition of the study does include a section on social work EWT (Gibelman, 2004). The NASW Code of Ethics does not mention forensic social work, and the only reference to legal matters pertains to confidentiality of records with regard to a court request for disclosure of information (NASW, 1995a, section 1.07j). The NASW Code of Ethics differs from the American Psychological Association Code of Ethics that makes four references to forensic work in the areas of roles, assessment, evaluation, and testimony (American Psychological Association, 2002). NASW has not established practice standards for forensic social work. For a fee, NASW does make available law notes on specific areas of practice, and there is a law note for social work EWT.

Social work regulatory boards do not generally recognize or comprehend the nature of forensic social work practice, especially when it involves matters related to children.

It is rare that social work regulatory boards have forensic social work members, and boards have limited numbers of clinical members who are more likely to have a better appreciation of forensic social work. The lack of regulatory board knowledge of forensics is problematic because forensic practitioners are more vulnerable to regulatory complaints than other specialties. This is especially the case in custody disputes where child forensic social workers are often involved (Munson, 2005b).

Statistics regarding the extent of social work EWT is currently the best indicator of the amount of forensic social work practice, but this indicator is limited because all forensic social work does not involve testimony. Also, there is no comprehensive tabulation of the number of federal, state, and local jurisdictions that accept and reject EWT. Forensic social workers write verified reports, affidavits, and evaluations for attorneys as preparation for EWT, but can be denied the opportunity to testify by judges. There is no statistical record of this forensic work. One study of federal civil trials (Krafka, Dunn, Johnson, Cecil, & Miletich, 2002) found that 43% of EWT involved the category of "medical/mental health," and 16% of the cases involved EWT by professionals who were not physicians. Social work was in the "other" category that included 19 disciplines, and approximately 2% of the total medical/mental health EWT in federal courts was provided by social workers. It is unfortunate that no comprehensive statistics about social work EWT are currently compiled and have not been historically gathered.

Clinical and Legal Issues

Expert Witness Defined

An expert witness has been defined by the Society of Expert Witnesses (2000) as "anyone with knowledge or experience of a particular field or discipline beyond what is expected of a layman. An expert witness is an expert who makes his or her knowledge available to a court (or other judicial or quasi-judicial body) to help it understand the issues of a case and reach a sound and just decision" (p. 2). A general definition of EWT is "Opinion evidence of some person who possesses special skill or knowledge in some science, profession or business which is not common . . . and which is possessed by the expert by reason of his special study or expertise" (Black, 2004, p. 298).

There are several types of expert witnesses: (a) "pure consultant" is an expert who acts as a consultant on a case and never testifies in court; (b) "maybe expert" is a person who may or may not be called to testify as an expert witness; (c) "rebuttal expert" is a person who testifies in response to an expert on the other side in a case; and (d) "physical or mental examination expert" is a professional who evaluates a person and testifies about the evaluation (Bishop, 2004). The social worker in the previous case example served as a mental health examination expert after conducting an extensive evaluation of the mother and the child, and eventually provided EWT as part of the parental rights legal action.

To be qualified as an expert, the forensic specialist must have knowledge, skill, experience, training, or education in a particular subject (Bernstein & Hartsell, 2005; Mueller & Kirkpatrick, 2005). The expert can be qualified in one or more of these areas. A child expert witness could be qualified on the basis of 20 years' experience treating maltreated children, or another person may never have treated children but has conducted research with samples of children who have been maltreated. In some complex cases, attorneys will use several experts to cover the range of possible testimony needed. The best expert will qualify in all five areas.

Expert Witness Qualification Factors

Expert testimony is admitted, in the form of an opinion, if the court determines that the testimony will assist the "trier of fact" (judge or jury) in understanding the evidence or to determine a fact that is in question. The *Federal Rules of Evidence* (U.S. House of Representatives Committee on the Judiciary, 2004) codified and adopted by Congress in 1975 defines who can testify as an expert witness (see Hess, 1999; Mueller & Kirkpatrick, 2005). The *Federal Rules of Evidence* has been adopted by most states and applies to most state and local courts. Forensic social workers should become familiar with Rules 701 through 706, which define the regulations regarding expert witnesses. In making the determination of who can testify as an expert, the court must establish (a) whether the witness is qualified as an expert by knowledge, skill, experience, training, or education; (b) the appropriateness of the expert testimony on the particular subject; and (c) whether a sufficient factual basis exists to support the expert testimony. An expert opinion is not inadmissible because it embraces an ultimate issue (issue to be decided by the trier of fact). An expert witness testifying with respect to the mental state or condition of a defendant in a criminal case may not state an opinion or inference as to whether the defendant had a mental state or condition constituting an element of the offense because that issue is for the trier of fact to decide. This exception does not apply to an ultimate issue of criminal responsibility (U.S. House of Representatives, 2004). Expert witnesses can give opinions and inform the trier of fact in order for courts to make the best possible decision in cases. For this reason, judges are granted liberal discretion in allowing expert testimony (Mueller & Kirkpatrick, 2005).

Attorneys will attempt to persuade experts to believe that the outcome of a case depends on the expert, but the reality is that the outcome of a case is determined by many factors. Most experienced expert witnesses can give accounts of highly successful expert testimony that has been undermined by attorneys who mismanaged the case. Experts should perceive their function as to offer findings and opinions in a truthful, fair, and factual manner, which can *assist* the trier of fact in making a decision. The role of providing assistance to the court should be paramount in an expert's perception of the effect of expert testimony. The ultimate outcome of the case is determined by many variables and is the responsibility of the trier of fact.

Fact and Expert Witnesses

Expert witnesses and fact witnesses are different in most jurisdictions. For example, a mental health professional can be called to testify to the treatment that has been provided to a person and would testify only to the facts of the treatment. If the witness is not testifying as an expert, the testimony is in the form of opinions or inferences limited to those that are rationally based on perception and helpful in clarifying factual testimony.

Social workers are often confused about the roles of fact and expert witnesses in the courtroom. A social work fact witness is not usually a forensic social worker. A fact witness is most often a therapist or counselor of a client who is appearing in court. The social worker is called to testify to the facts of the treatment or counseling provided to the person and to advocate for the person. An expert witness is used to render an opinion about the person based on scientific knowledge and is not to advocate for the person but is to present a balanced and unbiased view of what is scientifically important for the court to know in making a decision. A fact witness usually testifies before an expert to lay the foundation for the expert's testimony. For example, in the case of Mary S. presented previously, the DSS social workers who had provided service to Mary S. testified to the facts of her repeated failure to comply with the services offered her by DSS. The workers testified to the arrests for substance abuse and the referrals to the substance counseling programs that did not lead to recovery. The workers testified to the psychiatric hospitalizations they arranged for Mary S. after they had gone into her home and witnessed the neglect and abuse of her son. The expert was then called to testify about the findings of the evaluation that substantiated Mary S.'s substance dependence, psychiatric illness, mental capacity, lack of attachment, lack of support network, inadequate housing, and no employment. The forensic social worker then rendered an opinion, based on the scientific research evidence, regarding the low statistical probability that Mary S. would be able to provide adequate care for the child in the near future. The expert witness rendered an opinion about what would be in the best interest of Mary S.'s son given the mother's history of dysfunction and the child's enduring bond with and attachment to the preadoptive caregivers. The fact witnesses and the expert witness provided the necessary and sufficient evidence for the court to decide the "ultimate issue"—termination of Mary S.'s parental rights. If a foundation for an expert's testimony is not sufficiently established through the testimony of fact witnesses, the court may not permit the expert to testify.

In some cases attorneys will attempt to have fact witnesses testify as experts in the same case, and some judges will allow such testimony in an effort to obtain as much information as possible in making a decision. Practitioners should make every effort to avoid this dual role because it is impossible to be a therapeutic advocate and an unbiased expert at the same time. To perform this combined role could be considered an ethics violation under the NASW Code of Ethics admonition against dual roles that can be harmful to clients (NASW, 1995a, section 1.06c) and does not conform to generally accepted practice of forensic practice (American Psychiatric Association, 1997a, 1997b; American Psychological Association, 1994; Ash & Derdeyn, 1997; Walker, 2002). For example, if the social worker who did the evaluation of Mary S. had previously provided therapy for her son, the social worker would have been required to decline performing the forensic evaluation. Forensic social workers who mistakenly assume such dual roles are significantly deviating from generally accepted forensic practice standards.

Content of Expert Witness Testimony

With respect to expert witnesses, the law is interested in "scientific conservatism," not "speculative interpretation" (Dyer, 1999). This scientific conservatism is grounded in the rules from a series of Supreme Court opinions in which federal appeals courts have interpreted what is admissible scientific expert evidence according to the *Federal Rules of Evidence*. The appeals court opinions define what experts can offer as evidence in their testimony. The first case that dealt with the issue in modern times was *Frye v. United States* in 1923, and the second case was *Daubert v. Merrell-Dow Pharmaceuticals* in 1993. Some states continue to operate under the "Frye rule," and others have adopted the "Daubert test." The Daubert case and the subsequent case law that has refined the Daubert test (*General Electric Co. v. Joiner*, 1997; *Kumho Tire Co. v. Carmichael*, 1999) have become the most widely adopted criteria for EWT. Forensic social workers in the child welfare field need to understand that the *Frye* and *Daubert* standards are the ultimate arbiter of every action of a forensic social work practitioner who testifies as an expert witness. The *Frye* and *Daubert* standards mandate that any child welfare forensic social worker offered to a court as an expert witness must deliver testimony that is scientific and evidence based. The *Frye* decision held that EWT is acceptable if it is based on "... well recognized scientific principle ... sufficiently established to have gained general acceptance in the particular field in which it belongs" (*Frye v. United States*, 1923, p. 1).

The *Daubert* ruling provided much more specificity to the requirements for EWT by holding that the judge's discretion about the admissibility of EWT must be based on a review of whether the proposed testimony can be tested, has been peer reviewed, and is standardized and whether there is maintenance of standards, a known accepted error rate, and widespread acceptance of the evidence. The Daubert ruling made judges the gatekeepers of EWT, which gives them broad discretion regarding what is admitted as expert testimony. In the case of *Kumho Tire Co. v. Carmichael*, the Court extended the Daubert rules to all EWT including "technical and other specialized expert witness testimony." This category of evidence includes forensic social work EWT. Nurcombe and Partlett (1994) have described how psychiatry, psychology, and social work do not perform "pure science" but do have a scientific orientation that is grounded in human sciences and service to clients that qualifies the expert to testify:

> The purpose of clinical social work is to diagnose and treat sick, impaired, or troubled people.... psychiatry, clinical psychology, and clinical social work are not sciences themselves. When legal cross examiners ask clinicians to concede that psychiatry, psychology or social work are not "exact sciences" the truthful answer would be that clinical work is not science, though it may draw on it.
>
> Lawyers and clinicians are alike in identifying with their clients or patients; scientists are (or should be) objective. Lawyers and scientists are akin in their preoccupation with facts; clinicians are absorbed in the personal reality of those they treat. Scientists and clinicians both apply scientific knowledge, but to different ends, the one to advance knowledge, the other to help impaired or troubled people.... The law seeks to monitor professional standards by deferring to professional judgment while at the same time ensuring that accepted measures are not readily dismissed. Lawyers and clinicians are similar in their pragmatism; they borrow information from other fields to judge cases, [and] advance their clients' causes (p. 2)

Forensic social workers should keep this concise description of the relationships among law, science, and clinical practitioners in mind when preparing to offer EWT.

Forensic social workers must conform to the *Daubert* scientific expectation even though judges vary in their use of science in decision making (Munson, 2005b). A study of federal judges found that the Daubert ruling had altered their acceptance or limitation of EWT. Prior to the Daubert decision in 1993, judges excluded or limited expert testimony in 25% of cases, but after Daubert the rate increased to 41% (Krafka et al., 2002). A study of state court trial judges presented a much different picture, with the Daubert standards having negligible impact on EWT in psychological syndrome and profile cases (Dahir et al., 2005; Gatowski et al., 2001). Some forensic social workers testify in federal courts related to international child abduction cases (Munson, 2005a) and some capital criminal cases, but the majority of forensic social work EWT is offered in state and local courts where there is much confusion among attorneys and judges about EWT. In this context, attorneys act as gatekeepers as much as the judge because the attorneys determine what experts to offer for court use. Judges often will admit even questionable expert testimony to get any information possible to aid in difficult decision making. If the testimony is weak or inadequate, the court will decide the weight it will give, if any, to the EWT (English & Sales, 2005).

Selection of Experts

How experts are identified occurs in many ways. Most often the judge or attorneys review scientific literature to identify an expert. Universities and colleges are often contacted in the expert identification process. There are expert referral lists that are maintained by organizations and referral services. Any forensic social worker who joins a referral listing service is at risk of being labeled as a biased "hired gun" by the opposing attorney. It is not recommended that experts become part of such listings because of the bias issue.

Experts are selected by attorneys and judges. Federal Rule 706 governs the appointment of expert witnesses. The court can appoint its own expert, or any party to a case can offer a motion to the court for appointment of an expert as well as make nominations of specific experts to be appointed by the court. A party can request that an expert not be appointed or allowed to testify. An expert witness cannot be compelled to testify. An expert agreed on by the court and the parties is to be notified in writing by the court, and the duties of the expert are defined by the court. The notification is to be filed with the court clerk. The process of written appointment notification does not always occur. The expert witness is to advise the parties of the findings and opinions before testifying.

Expert witnesses should avoid situations in which the court has no prior knowledge of the offering of the expert to a court by an attorney. The rules do not limit the parties in calling expert witnesses of their own selection, but an expert appearing in court the day of a hearing with the expectation that the court will allow the expert to testify is usually an inappropriate use of time because of the high probability that the court will reject hearing from such a casually offered expert. The forensic social worker should make efforts to have attorneys seeking expert testimony to approach the court and request that the court appoint the expert. Court appointed experts have more credibility and legal standing than the casually offered expert. Formal appointment of an expert is critical in high-conflict divorce and custody disputes.

Appointed expert witnesses are entitled to reasonable compensation at a rate set by the court in court-appointed cases. Fees are usually paid from funds provided by law in criminal cases. In civil cases compensation is paid by the parties individually or in proportions ordered by the court.

Ultimate Issue

The ultimate issue is the question the judge or jury must answer in making its decision. The admissibility of forensic social workers' testimony about ultimate issues varies by state. Historically, psychiatrists and psychologists have been statutorily authorized to testify about the ultimate issue. In 2000, the Maryland Court of Appeals ruled (*In re Adoption/Guardianship*, 2000) that a licensed clinical social worker can diagnose, testify as an expert witness, and testify about ultimate issues just as psychiatric and psychological experts can. The court ruling was aided by an amicus curiae (friend of the court) brief that was filed by nine social work organizations, and the Court "ruling had national implications" (Gibelman, 2004, p. 268) for the practice of clinicians in general and forensic social work specifically. Forensic social workers who have their right to testify as experts challenged should provide their attorney with this citation for the Maryland Court of Appeals case and should obtain a copy of the amicus brief that is available from the NASW.

There has been controversy about whether expert witnesses should be allowed to testify to ultimate issues and whether ultimate issue testimony is ethical practice. Ultimate issue testimony has been more restricted in criminal cases than in civil cases, and it has been more restricted in Great Britain than the United States (Ceci & Hembrooke, 1998). Each child forensic social worker must decide whether or not to testify about the ultimate issue in a case. Attorneys will often seek ultimate issue testimony, but the expert is under no obligation to offer such testimony. In the case of Mary S., the expert did not testify to the ultimate issue of the termination of the parental rights, but instead listed the tasks the mother would have to accomplish in order to achieve reunification with her child and the statistical probability that she would or would not successfully complete the tasks within the time frames established by the Adoption and Safe Families Act of 1997 for reunification to occur.

The Science of Social Work Practice

A significant problem for forensic social work practice is the lack of a body of scientific studies regarding social work practice. This limitation is problematic because there is a long-standing standard for EWT that mandates a scientific base for expert witnesses. The clinician in preparing an evaluation report may reach a number of conclusions and make a number of recommendations that are intuitively derived or based on clinical anecdotal experience or practice wisdom, but when the clinician is called on to testify about an evaluation, the standard for acceptance of the testimony will be whether the clinician can affirm that the opinions, conclusions, and recommendations are valid to a reasonable degree of psychological certainty. This requirement introduces a statistical probability that the testimony of the clinician is valid and reliable within the scientific community. Helping professionals have entered the field of EWT late because of its intuitive practice base. Brieland and Lemmon (1977) in their early text on social work and law made little mention of EWT, and Saltzman and Furman (1999) in a recent book on social work and law made few references to EWT. It has been only during the last several years that EWT has become more widespread in practice and more of an issue for the profession. One way to increase the reliability and validity of social work forensic interventions is to use generally accepted practice guidelines, evidence-based practice standards (McDonald, 2001; Munson, 2004a), established protocols (Munson 2001a, 2004b), outcome-based interventions that have been tested, and standardized measurements (Kaplan & Saccuzzo, 2004; Vance, 1998; Wodrich, 1997). In some states the test of knowledge experience and skill can in part be based on the number of hours per week the expert devotes to performing the activity that is the focus of the expert testimony. For example, the Kansas Supreme Court held that a psychiatrist who devoted only 30 to 40% of work hours per week to clinical practice must be disqualified as an expert witness because Kansas law requires that experts devote 50% of their time to clinical practice (*Dawson v. Prager and the Menninger Clinic*, 2003).

Description of Intervention

Forensic Practice Administration

The legal requirement that experts must have knowledge, skill, experience, training, and education to provide testimony—and the criteria that expert testimony must be based on evidence that is tested, peer reviewed, standardized, has known error rates, and is generally accepted—highlights the fact that child forensic social work practice must be evidence based. Entering forensic practice requires acceptance of these standards. If the practitioner is not aware of the standards, negative consequences can result. The following case vignette illustrates the need for preparation for forensic practice.

> John M. was a clinical social worker with 20 years general social work practice experience doing individual and family therapy. On a referral from an attorney, John saw a child who was having difficulty adjusting to the parents' divorce. John was able to help the child and the parents. The attorney asked John to testify in the custody determination hearing as a fact witness regarding the child's improvement. John agreed, but was nervous. The testimony went well, and John was asked his opinion about custody. The judge allowed John to give his opinion after opposition from the opposing attorney. The lawyer told John he did a good job. John found he liked being in the courtroom and decided he would like to do more forensic work.
>
> The attorney contacted John and requested that he see another child for therapy. After 2 months in therapy the lawyer asked John to do a custody evaluation for the child and the parent, and John agreed. When John testified, the opposing attorney accused John of being biased in his opinions because he had interviewed the mother several times when she brought the child to therapy, but he did not interview the father until the custody evaluation was started. The attorney also elicited in John's testimony that the mother was in arrears for her portion of the son's therapy sessions, and the attorney accused him of basing his opinion on the fact that the mother owed him money. The opposing attorney hired a psychologist to give expert testimony that John did not observe generally accepted practice standards and that he was not qualified to testify as a custody evaluator or expert witness. The psychologist wrote an affidavit that contained 17 citations supporting his views. The judge agreed with the opposing attorney's expert witness and commented in his order that he would not give any weight to John's testimony because of bias based on a dual relationship with the mother and lack of qualifications to do a custody evaluation. John was upset by this rejection. The parents never paid him for the custody evaluation.

This case example illustrates a number of points about forensic child practice. John entered forensic work by the route that many helping professionals do, on the basis of a single episode of courtroom work. The initiation of a forensic practice based on such experience is risky. The practitioner needs training and understanding of this area of practice. John did not do research on custody work, he did not consult an experienced custody evaluator, and he did not attend any of the many custody evaluator trainings that are available. John did not understand the concept of bias and how it is applied in legal matters (see Myers, 1998).

Forensic social work practice requires a different orientation from the general practice of social work. The nature and sources of referrals differ, and documentation and record keeping require a different strategy. A thorough and complete record of all activity should be maintained from the time the first contact with a client or an attorney takes place. Practitioners preparing to enter the legal arena in a case should be clear about their role of consultant, evaluator, and/or expert witness. It is generally good practice to work directly with the attorney who represents the client and only indirectly with the client. A letter of agreement should be signed, and it is recommended that the forensic social worker enter a case on a retainer basis to avoid allegations of bias based on fees owed to the practitioner. Any work done on an hourly basis should be billed monthly and submitted to the attorney. If the client falls into significant arrears, work should be discontinued until the payment is updated. Performing forensic activities when the client is substantially in arrears opens the forensic social worker to allegations of bias to obtain back payment. When doing forensic work for public agencies, this approach may need to be altered, but the key guiding principle should be that any act of a forensic social worker should be balanced and unbiased. For example, when working with children the forensic social worker may come into contact with a guardian ad litem (GAL) who represents the child. The forensic social worker should not have a close professional relationship with the GAL within or outside the case. Activities such as working lunches should be avoided. A forensic social worker should not have direct contact with the attorney on the other side without the knowledge of the client's attorney.

Areas of Forensic Practice

Forensic social work with children and adolescents can cover a number of areas including

- short- and long-term effects of
  - neglect
  - physical abuse
  - sexual abuse, and
  - witnessing domestic violence
- mental injury of a child
- custody decisions
- impact of reunification with a parent after a long separation
- TPR
- mental status and functioning of parents in anticipation of reunification with a child
- impact of domestic violence on a child or parent
- assessment of parent alienation activities

Areas of Needed Knowledge and Skill

Forensic child welfare work and EWT require highly specialized training and experience. The primary areas that forensic social workers should have training in should include, but are not limited to, the following (key resources are cited):

- Child and adolescent development (Berk, 1998; Bukatko & Daehler, 1998; Newcombe, 1996).
- Child and adolescent psychopathology (Ollendick & Hersen, 1998).
- Adult psychopathology (Kaplan & Sadock, 1998).
- Attachment theory (Cassidy & Shaver, 1999; Dyer, 1999).
- Traumatic stress theory (Carlson, 1997; Schiraldi, 2000; van der Kolk, McFarlane, & Weisaeth, 1996; Wilson & Keane, 1997; Wolchik & Sandler, 1997).
- Basic developmental neurology (Harris, 1995).
- Basic understanding of psychopharmacology (Fuller & Sajatovic, 2001).
- Basic understanding of genetics (Anderson & Ganetzky, 1997).
- Basic knowledge of substances and alcohol use, abuse, and dependence (American Psychiatric Association, 2000c; Ray & Ksir, 1996).
- Basic child welfare practice (Hobbs, Hanks, & Wynne, 1999; Lutzker, 1998).
- Ability to administer and interpret standardized measures and instruments (American Psychiatric Association, 2000b; Groth-Marnat, 1997).
- Knowledge of local, state, and federal laws relevant to clinical practice, specialization, and expertise (Munson, 2001c).

Forensic Child Evaluations

Forensic evaluations are different from general clinical evaluations that are done at admission for treatment or other purposes (Babitsky & Mangraviti, 2002; Heilbrun, Marczyk, & DeMatteo, 2002; Melton, Petrila, Poythress, & Slobogin, 1997; Righthand, Kerr, & Drach, 2003). General evaluations are usually brief, informally prepared, and for the purpose of planning a course of treatment. General evaluations usually are for the exclusive use of the clinician and are highly confidential. Forensic evaluations are focused on a specific legal question that must be addressed by a court. The evaluation is lengthy, is formally prepared, must be internally and externally accurate, is submitted to a number of parties (lawyers, judges, clients, and agencies), and may become public information if entered as part of a hearing record. In some cases evaluations of children will be kept confidential and can be sealed by the court. The NASW Code of Ethics requires social workers to request that courts protect such records by sealing them (NASW, 1995a, section 1.07j).

A forensic evaluation should consist of a standard protocol that is routinely used with cases based on the clinician's specialty practice area, but there should be flexibility to use alternate methods to accommodate unique aspects of a case. The assessment should include contact with all persons who have relevance to the outcome of the case. Clinical interviews should be conducted with pertinent individuals, and standardized measures should be used when appropriate (e.g., to confirm diagnosis of depression or PTSD, to determine suitability for custody or level of parenting stress). The evaluator should contact collateral sources that may have information relevant to the issues explored in the evaluation (such as child welfare workers, therapists, medical and psychiatric hospitalization reports, police, school counselors, teachers, employers, and probation officers).

Evaluation reports should be clear, concise, and carefully proofread before submission. The summary and conclusions and recommendations sections of a forensic report should use reasoning and logic to arrive at conclusions. The content should be sequenced in a way that aids the trier of fact in understanding how the expert arrived at opinions and recommendations. In sequencing facts, logic, conclusions, and opinions, the forensic expert should adopt strategies that lawyers use in report writing (see Fontham, Vitiello, & Miller, 2002). Various outlines for submission of reports have been devised (Koocher, Norcross, & Hill, 1998; Melton et al., 1997; Nurcombe & Partlett, 1994; Sattler, 1998). The following outline is generally recommended for child and adolescent reports:

- Reason for Evaluation: This should be a brief statement of the purpose of the evaluation and the referral source.
- Procedures: There should be identification of information sources (e.g., prior evaluation reports, school records, court hearing transcripts, deposition transcripts, relevant mental health and medical treatment records, list of persons interviewed, and standardized measures used). A brief statement should be included that describes how suggestive questioning and inducements for participation were avoided (see Ceci & Bruck, 1995).
- Abuse History: Identify the presence or absence of any individual or family history of neglect, physical abuse, sexual abuse, or domestic violence.
- Background: Information relevant to the factors that led to the current presenting problem should be summarized.
- Family History: Detailed family history data including information about parents, siblings, education, employment, social functioning, and religious activity should be described.
- Developmental History: Include a survey of the mother's use of tobacco, alcohol, substances, and prescription medications during pregnancy. Note if there were any complications during pregnancy or at birth. A review for premature birth, low birth weight, eating/feeding problems during infancy, problems with toilet training, or problems entering school should be included.
- Developmental Milestones: Assess and note appropriate developmental milestones of children and adolescents. This can be done with standardized measures or milestone checklists. The most common areas of development are physical, self-help, social, communication, and intellectual (Berk, 1998). Language development can be a crucial indicator of development in combination with maltreatment. Language delays are common (Amster, 1999) and are so prevalent in the child welfare population that they can be used diagnostically for maltreated children (Munson, 2001a).
- History of Out-of-Home Placements: As much information as possible should be included about past and current placements. This applies to children and adults.
- Visitation: If the child is not in the care of the parents, a summary is given of the visitation schedule and whether or not visitation is supervised.
- Criminal Justice History: Supply a history of all arrests, convictions for criminal offenses, and description of civil litigation the child or parent has experienced.

- Substance/Alcohol History: Provide a review of the history of substance/alcohol use, abuse, and dependence by child and parents based on the *Diagnostic and Statistical Manual of Mental Disorders, Fourth Edition, Text Revision* (*DSM–IV–TR*; American Psychiatric Association, 2000a) criteria.
- Medical History: Report major illnesses, injuries, hospitalizations, and family history of illness for the child and parents. Document the date of the last physical examination. If the client has not had a physical examination in the last 30 days, this should be noted and the client referred for medical screening to rule out any general medical conditions that could be a source of dysfunction. Children should also be referred for dental, vision, and hearing screenings if there have been no screenings in the last year.
- Medications: Note past and current medications including dosage information. Review parents and child for use of herbal medications or cultural bound medications. If the client is taking medication, record the most recent administration of medication prior to the evaluation session.
- Mental Health Treatment: Review past and present inpatient and outpatient mental health treatment. Record diagnoses received and names of therapists, quality of relationship with the therapists, and the outcome of the treatment.
- School: For children, report school functioning academically and behaviorally. For adults, report the amount of education.
- Clinical Interview: Record the identified client's mental status, interview behavior and demeanor, speech, language, somatic complaints, perception, cognition, judgment, memory, intellectual functioning, emotions, interpersonal skills, and access to weapons.
- Standardized Measures: Give descriptions and summaries of standardized measures administered. Interpretation of objective measures should be described in clear, concise language. The interpretation should be focused on the purpose of the evaluation and the recommendations.
- Diagnosis: Provide a thorough *DSM–IV–TR* multiaxial diagnosis (see Munson, 2000, 2001a, 2001b).
- Summary and Conclusions: This section should give a concise summary of the case and provide an integrated analysis of the significant aspects of the findings. Conclusions should be supported with citations of empirical research and clinical literature that support findings and conclusions. Include a section of "considerations" for the court to take into account when there are competing solutions to the legal issue before the court.
- Recommendations: Based on the findings of the evaluation and the diagnosis, specific recommendations should be made with justification for each recommendation. Recommendations should be based on facts and should reflect a balanced use of the competing alternatives that may be available to the court in rendering its decision.

In preparing the written report, it is recommended these three guidelines be followed:

1 Indicate sources of statements and use qualifier words when the expert does not have direct knowledge of a fact. Use phrases such as:
  - reported by . . .
  - reportedly . . .

- according to . . .
- the client stated . . .

2 Use professional language, such as:
- "He appeared to be intoxicated," not "He was drunk."
- "Indications are she deliberately made inaccurate statements," not "She lied to me."
- "Limited intellectual capacity," not "mentally retarded," unless diagnosed through standardized tests.
- "This person has a history of and current problem with substance abuse and dependence," not "This person is a long-term drug addict."

3 Use language in reports that is familiar to the courts. This language can be derived from written opinions of appeals courts. Do not attempt to make legal statements, but use brief, legal phrases to express concepts that are being communicated in the report. For example, phrases that can be helpful are:
- best interest of the child
- general well-being of the child
- risk to the child
- safety of the child
- vulnerability of the child
- special-needs child
- influences likely to be exerted on the child
- preference of the child
- fitness of the person seeking custody
- adaptability of the person to the task
- environment and surroundings the child will be reared in
- potential for maintaining natural family relations
- opportunities for the future life of the child
- prior voluntary abandonment or surrender of custody
- parental rights versus performance of parental duties
- chronic and enduring mental illness
- persistent and ongoing problems

Diagnosis and Expert Testimony

There has been controversy about the legal sanction for clinical social workers to do diagnosis. A series of appellate legal opinions have confirmed the admissibility as evidence diagnosis performed by clinical social workers where there is legislative authorization. Diagnosis of mental and emotional disorders is included in most state practice acts and is directly stated in practice acts of 34 states (American Association of State Social Work Boards, 1998). The states that include the word *diagnosis* in their practice acts are Alabama, Alaska, Arizona, Colorado, Connecticut, Delaware, Florida, Hawaii, Illinois, Indiana, Iowa, Kentucky, Louisiana, Maine, Maryland, Massachusetts, Minnesota, Mississippi, Missouri, Nevada, New Hampshire, New Jersey, New Mexico, North Carolina, Ohio, Oklahoma, Oregon, Rhode Island, South Dakota, Texas, Vermont, Wisconsin, Wyoming, and the District of Columbia. All other states, except two, permit diagnosis but use alternate terminology. Forensic social workers should be thoroughly trained in diagnosis. Social work education programs provide uneven coverage of diagnostic criteria, and the forensic social worker should periodically have continuing education in diagnosis because the database for statistical occurrence of disorders and symptoms is constantly evolving.

Attorneys are increasingly learning about diagnosis and will try to discredit an expert's diagnosis by showing that the social work expert does not have thorough training in diagnosis. Parents are more knowledgeable about mental disorders due to the expansion of Internet access. Clinicians need to be able to answer complex questions asked by caregivers as well as to correct distortions lay persons have as a result of learning fragments of information about mental disorders (Munson, 2001b).

Depositions, Affidavits, and Interrogatories

Depositions are sworn statements taken outside the courtroom and are usually conducted in a lawyer's office. Notice of a deposition can be informal or through a subpoena. A subpoena *duces tecum* means to bring to the deposition or hearing documents specified in the subpoena. Some attorneys will command all records pertaining to the case and ask that the entire file be surrendered for review at the deposition. The expert will need legal advice as to whether this is permissible. The expert may have to refuse to surrender an entire record at a deposition. The expert will be asked questions by the attorneys involved. No judge is present. There is a transcriber present, and a transcript of the deposition will be available to the deponent (the expert). The expert should insist on reviewing the transcript of the deposition for accuracy before signing it. The expert should retain a copy of the deposition transcript and review it before testifying. There can be a gap of months between the time of the deposition and actual testimony in court. The attorneys will be looking for discrepancies between the expert's deposition testimony and the courtroom testimony, and the expert will need to explain any discrepancies.

Affidavits are sworn written statements submitted to a court prior to testifying. Affidavits are sought by attorneys and can serve a variety of purposes. An expert who is asked to prepare an affidavit should seek specific information about the necessity for and purpose of the affidavit. The expert may or may not have to testify based on an affidavit. The form for an affidavit can vary by state. The general format is a statement of the expert's qualifications, the facts of the case, the issues addressed, opinions, references, and statement of oath (for a sample affidavit, see Babitsky & Mangraviti, 2002). Affidavits can be very narrow in focus and very brief or broad in scope and lengthy. The expert's affidavit statements should be consistent with subsequent testimony or an explanation should be given for why the expert's opinion has changed.

Interrogatories are lists of questions that an attorney provides to an expert in writing before trial that are to be answered by the expert under oath.

Description of Expert Witness Testimony

The ultimate intervention in forensic social work is the provision of EWT. Providing EWT can have a profound effect on the parties in a legal matter. The expert has a duty to be honest, objective, and unbiased and to perform to the highest professional standards in the courtroom. The following sections provide guidelines for how to be professional and act in the best interest of the parties in a case.

Before the Hearing

An expert witness should request to meet with the attorney who will be offering the expert to the court. Such a meeting can be helpful in preparing how the expert wants to present testimony and what is to be highlighted. It is important to ask the attorney all questions about the nature of the testimony. The attorney should be provided written information about the expert's credentials prior to the hearing. If the expert meets with the attorney, written materials should be organized and key points highlighted. An outline of points separate from any expert reports should be prepared focusing on key points. The points should be committed to memory (Munson, 2002). The expert may be limited during testimony to referring to reports and notes only when asked specific questions about the written materials.

At the Hearing

The classic advice holds regarding attire and demeanor. Dress professionally, act professionally, and arrive at court early. Bring all materials related to the case to court. Avoid talking with anyone in the waiting room, courtroom, or hall while waiting to testify. This includes colleagues, attorneys, police, strangers, or the parent or child the expert is testifying about. Do not smile, laugh, or joke with anyone before, during, or after testifying in the presence of the judge or jury. For confidentiality reasons, do not leave a brief case or hearing materials unattended at any time.

On the Stand

Before testifying, the expert should request the attorney retaining the expert to review the expert's credentials for the court when the expert takes the witness stand. Sometimes attorneys are conscious of the need to proceed rapidly and may do a brief review of the expert's credentials, especially if the expert has testified in the court in the past. If the expert is easily and quickly qualified to testify, it is important to include in the testimony responses that call attention to the expert's qualifications. For example, substantive comments can be prefaced with comments such as "In my 20 years of work with this population, it is my experience that . . ." or "As part of my training, I became familiar with research that supports . . . ." (Munson, 2002). Such comments could be crucial if there is an appeal of the case. Appeal courts review cases only on the basis of the trial court transcripts and the exhibits. If the expert's credentials were not entered in writing, then the appeals court will have only transcript testimony to rely on in assigning weight to the expert's testimony. In the case of Mary S., the expert's credentials were not entered as an exhibit, and the appeals court in the oral arguments raised questions about the expert's credentials.

Procedural qualification of experts focuses on the concepts of knowledge, skill, experience, training, and education identified in Federal Rule 702 because they are basic to qualifying as an expert (Mueller & Kirkpatrick, 2005). The process of expert qualification includes review of professional education (degrees and dates received, internships, specialized training, continuing education, honors, awards, licenses, certifications; Tsushima & Anderson, 1996), employment history, number of clients evaluated or treated, research activity, publications, professional paper presentations, and the amount of prior testimony as an expert witness. The expert should have this information memorized. In some cases the expert may be asked for statistics about the number of times he or she qualified as an expert, in what jurisdictions, and in what areas of specialization. The expert may be asked about the amount of payment for the testimony, and the expert should answer accurately.

The attorney who is challenging the expert's testimony will use the *voir dire* procedure, which is the opposing attorney's opportunity to test and challenge the expert's credentials and competency to testify as well as to challenge expert testimony in general (for example, citing research indicating expert opinions are no more accurate than those of lay persons). There may be attempts to show bias in requesting information about fees received for testimony or the expert's personal history as a victim of abuse or domestic violence to show that the expert is promoting a cause or is engaging in advocacy. *Voir dire* is a standard legal procedure that should not be viewed as a personal attack, although it may seem to be. This can be the most difficult phase of expert testimony because attacks on education, training, and experience can be intense (Tsushima & Anderson, 1996). The key is to be calm and answer questions directly and honestly. Never become defensive or argumentative during this stage of testimony, especially when feeling attacked personally or professionally. For example,

> Attorney question (AQ): It is true that the social work profession is on the lowest tier of therapists, with psychiatrists at the top, psychologists next, and social workers at the bottom, correct?
>
> Expert answer (EA): No, that is not the situation today. It was like that 40 years ago. Clinical practice with children and adolescents today is quite complex and requires multidisciplinary expertise. All recognized mental health professionals are equal members of the treatment team. Social workers have the most historical expertise in child welfare, and we often provide leadership in this area.

A general rule of testimony is to avoid anticipating what the judge or the attorneys are dealing with or attempting to elicit. Simply answer the questions on the basis of what was done, the reason it was done, and the opinions formulated. Ask attorneys to repeat unclear questions. Answer only the questions that are asked, and do not attempt to expand on a previously given answer. Focus on the immediate question being asked. It is recommended the expert look at the judge or jury when giving opinions, look at the attorney when giving facts, and avoid looking at the client when giving difficult testimony. Always look at the judge when giving answers to questions asked by the judge.

If the opposing attorney asks a question directly from the expert's notes or report, ask for the specific page number of the report and answer on the basis of the content of the report. It is also a good policy to make verbal reference to the expert report. Use statements such as "In my report summary section, I indicated ...," "My background information section of the report confirms that ...," and "The results of my testing explained on page 6 of the report indicate that. ... " This is an effective way to call attention to the judge or jury the expert's findings. Do not read from the report. Testify from memory and request the court to allow review of the report or supporting documents if a technical question is asked that requires a precise answer, such as actual test scores or precise dates.

Cross-Examination

Cross-examination is always difficult because it is the opposing attorney's second chance to challenge the expert witness. In the *voir dire* phase of testimony, there is a general challenge to qualifications to testify, and in the cross-examination, there are specific challenges of the validity of the expert's procedures and conclusions in the specific case. It is important to remain calm and factual and not to alter voice level when challenges are made. Do not let the attorney provoke anger. This requires a significant amount of self-control. It is important for the expert to remember that the testimony is to provide facts and opinions related to what was done in conducting assessments and how opinions were reached.

The expert should hesitate when it feels like a question should not be answered. Hesitation will give the attorney an opportunity to object. While on the witness stand, the expert should not attempt to analyze the effect of the testimony. Focus should be on the accuracy and scientific basis of the testimony.

Try to avoid answering hypothetical questions. For example,

AQ: Hypothetically, if my client had a relative who could provide care for this child, could the child adjust to placement under these circumstances?

EA: It depends. It depends on the home study of the relatives, their parenting skills, the child's bond and attachment with the foster parents, and history of contact with the relatives as well as other factors. So it would be difficult for me to answer that question.

During cross-examination an expert can use questions to expand on previous answers or to make additional points. For example,

AQ: My client was evicted from her apartment because she had no job, could not pay her rent, and DSS would not give her assistance, wasn't she?

EA: My notes indicate that she was evicted because she was having loud parties, and the police were called because of substance use. This was consistent with statements she made to me that she had been using cocaine regularly for the last three years. I have no record that she ever asked for assistance with her rent.

AQ: Then all you can testify to is that there were arguments between my client and the companion? There was no real domestic violence in this relationship, was there?

EA: Recurring shouting and belittling are violent acts. In addition, there is increased risk to the child because the caregivers frequently use alcohol. They have been apprehended for violence in the community. There is denial about the domestic violence. The child has special needs and uneasy temperament. All of these facts increase the risk of violence against the child by the parent.

Avoid defensiveness when asked questions that can be viewed as attacks about ethics. It is best to respond with a simple statement of ethical obligations. For example,

AQ: Sir, it is a fact, isn't it, that you wrote these negative descriptions about my client knowing it would harm her in the TPR hearing?

EA: No, my professional ethics code would not allow me to do that. I wrote it because I am required to record all relevant information regarding this case that to the best of my knowledge is true and accurate. I researched every point I wrote about, and I relied on standardized testing to confirm my clinical interview findings.

Conciseness

Testimony should be concise, crisp, and to the point. Answers should be given in a clear, mildly modulated tone of voice. Responses should be quick, but brief delays are acceptable to ponder how thoughts will be formulated. Answer only the question asked. This advice is included in every manual on EWT, but most experts have had the experience of exceeding the expectations of an answer and having the content of the excessive statement used against them. For example, an attachment/bonding expert was asked by an attorney, "Where do you work?" The expert responded, "At the ABC Center for Attachment Intervention." The expert then added, "I don't work there. I am actually one of the owners." By making this statement the expert allowed the attorney to open a new line of questioning about her ownership and the financial status of the center, and the attorney implied that she was biased in accepting clients and in making recommendations because she depended on the clients for income to keep the center open (see Myers, 1998). The second part of the expert's answer was beyond the scope of the question. The judge allowed the line of questioning because the expert had made the statement part of the answer. The expert's assertion about ownership was not asked and did not need to be stated.

An expert should never talk while a judge or an attorney is speaking. If an attorney interrupts, the expert should stop talking and listen to the attorney. The expert should never, ever challenge an attorney. Challenges are the responsibility of the attorney who engaged the expert.

Humor

Experts should avoid attempts at the use of humor. Attorneys are always looking for ways to make points with a jury or judge. Use of humor can make an expert appear flippant and unserious, which decreases credibility. An expert, who was a university professor, was trying to explain a difficult concept during cross-examination and was repeatedly challenged by the attorney. The expert began a point by saying, "If you were one of my students, I would have to explain it this way to you. . . . " The attorney interrupted the expert and stated, "Based on what I have heard you say here today, I would never sign up for one of your classes." The expert gave the attorney a perfect opportunity to plant in jurors' minds doubt about the expert's abilities as a teacher and as a knowledgeable person. It is rare that an expert can make a humorous comment and be successful. The expert should remember that experts are to be serious, factual, scientifically oriented individuals.

Use of Visuals

The use of visuals to support testimony should be reviewed before deciding to use them. Any visuals considered for use should be shared with the attorney who engaged the expert, and the possible effects of the visuals carefully weighed in advance of the testimony. Visuals may be necessary when providing highly technical testimony (Smith & Bace, 2002), but visuals should be used only to explain a complex point that cannot be conveyed effectively orally. In most issues involving children, visuals are not necessary. An expert using visuals that are unnecessary takes the risk of boring the judge or jury. There may be problems with equipment, and judges or jurors may not be able to see the visuals clearly, both of which can decrease the effectiveness of the expert testimony. Most courtrooms are not designed for facilitating visual presentations.

After the Hearing

After a hearing, the best way to prepare for the next court appearance is to review the testimony and think of ways it could have been improved. Do not obsess about the effect of the testimony, but analyze ways future testimony can be improved. Write down key questions from the testimony that may be asked in future cases, and review them before future testimony. Advice given by Brodsky (1999) can be used to formulate a posttestimony self-analysis: "Decide for yourself what it is you dislike in yourself as an expert and what you like. Then, take active steps to diminish the aspects that do not work and enhance the ones that do" (p. 188).

Conclusion

Doing child forensic practice is complex and difficult, but it can be very rewarding when it is related to using our values and ethics to help children have a better chance at a normal and successful life. At the same time, our values of being a helper will not make us immune to attacks by some caregivers and lawyers. The most difficult aspect of EWT is to have an attorney attack an expert's motives, knowledge, and skills when the expert is working to help vulnerable children. The forensic practitioner must remember that attorneys are adhering to their code of ethics when trying to discredit us because their responsibility is to defend their client by any means available. Increasingly, lawyers are refraining from undue attacks because they have recognized that courts show deference to experts in an effort to obtain as much information as possible about the issues in a case. Unjustified attacks may hurt, rather than help, an attorney's case. When the forensic specialist comes under attack, the best defense is to be calm, objective and factual and to rely on empirically derived information and evidence-based practice standards. Forensic social workers should read Susan Daicoff's (2004) *Lawyer, Heal Thyself* for self-comfort when reflecting on lawyers who attack the ethics of other professionals. This book will help expert witnesses better understand the motivations, personalities, and drives of the lawyers who support experts and the lawyers who confront experts in the courtroom. Remember, in the courtroom there will be the supportive attorney who engaged the expert and the attorney or attorneys representing the other side who may or may not strongly challenge the expert. Also, remember that an expert's testimony is only as good as the skills of the attorney who engaged the expert (Munson, in press).

Good forensic work requires much time and effort. Lawyers and courts often dictate the forensic social worker's schedule. Forensic social work is not for the passive and unprepared practitioner. Forensic social work is truly one of the artistic and scientific aspects of practice that requires discipline, skill, and preparation. There are rewards and frustrations. In the case of Mary S., the frustration was that, 2 weeks after the TPR hearing, Mary S. had to be hospitalized because of a psychotic episode associated with her mental illness. The expert's statistical probabilities about Mary S.'s ability to care for her child in the short and long term proved to be accurate. No professional wants to see a parent's rights terminated, and in this case, the expert in one of the considerations offered as part of the expert report and oral testimony advocated for an open adoption, which the preadoptive parents agreed to. In this case the expert played a significant role in providing the best possible outcome for a difficult situation.

NOTE

1. Content of this chapter pertains to legal issues and offers suggestions for helping professionals participating in legal proceedings. No comments in this chapter should be considered as legal advice. The reader should consult an attorney for legal advice regarding cases that are relevant to the content of this chapter. Laws, regulations, and procedures used in forensic work can vary by state and local jurisdiction. Before implementing any strategies discussed in this chapter, the practitioner should confirm that the strategy is compliant with state and local statutes and regulations.

RESOURCES AND REFERENCES

Adoption and Safe Families Act of 1997, Pub. L. No. 105-59 (1997).

Ainsworth, M. S., Bell, S. V. M., & Stayton, D. J. (1971). Individual differences in strange-situation behaviour of one-year-olds. In H. R. Schaffer (Ed.), *The origins of human social relations* (pp. 17–57). New York: Academic Press.

American Association of State Social Work Boards. (1998). *Social work laws and board regulations: A comparison guide*. Culpeper, VA: Author.

American Psychiatric Association. (1997a). Practice parameters for child custody evaluation. *Journal of the American Academy of Child & Adolescent Psychiatry*, 36(10), 57S–68S.

American Psychiatric Association. (1997b). Practice parameters for the forensic evaluation of children and adolescents who may have been physically or sexually abused. *Journal of the American Academy of Child & Adolescent Psychiatry*, 36(10), 37S–56S.

American Psychiatric Association. (2000a). *Diagnostic and statistical manual of mental disorders* (4th ed., text rev.). Washington, DC: Author.

American Psychiatric Association. (2000b). *Handbook of psychiatric measures*. Washington, DC: Author.

American Psychiatric Association. (2000c). *Practice guidelines for the treatment of psychiatric disorders: Compendium 2000*. Washington, DC: Author.

American Psychological Association. (1994). Guidelines for child custody evaluations in divorce proceedings. *American Psychologist*, 49(7), 677–680.

American Psychological Association. (2002). *Ethical principles of psychologists and code of conduct*. Washington, DC: Author.

Amster, B. J. (1999). Speech and language development of young children in the child welfare system. In J. A. Silver, B. J. Amster, & T. Haecher (Eds.), *Young children and foster care* (pp. 117–157). Baltimore: Brookes.

Anderson, P., & Ganetzky, B. (1997). *An electronic companion to genetics workbook*. New York: Cogito.

Ash, P., & Derdeyn, A. (1997). Forensic child and adolescent psychiatry: A review of the past 10 years. *Journal of the American Academy of Child & Adolescent Psychiatry*, 36(11), 1493–1502.

Babitsky, S., & Mangraviti, J. J. (2002). *Writing and defending your expert report: The step-by-step guide with models*. Falmouth, MA: SEAK.

Barker, R. L. (1999). *The social work dictionary* (4th ed.). Washington, DC: NASW Press.

Benjamin, G. A. H., & Gollan, J. K. (2003). *Family evaluation in custody litigation: Reducing risks of ethical infractions and malpractice*. Washington, DC: American Psychological Association.

Berk, L. E. (1998). *Development through the life span*. Boston: Allyn & Bacon.

Bernstein, B. E., & Hartsell, T. H. (2005). *The portable guide to testifying in court for mental health professionals: An A to Z guide to being an effective witness*. Hoboken, NJ: Wiley.

Best, A. (2004). *Evidence: Examples and explanations* (5th ed.). New York: Aspen.

Bishop, E. T. (2004). *Experts: What can be discovered, when, and at whose expense*. Dallas, TX: Strasburger and Price.

Black, H. C. (2004). *Black's law dictionary* (8th ed.). St. Paul, MN: West Publishing.

Brieland, D., & Lemmon, J. (1977). *Social work and the law*. St. Paul, MN: West Publishing.

Brodsky, S. L. (1999). *The expert witness: More maxims and guidelines for testifying in court*. Washington, DC: American Psychological Association.

Bukatko, D., & Daehler, M. W. (1998). *Child development: A thematic approach* (3rd ed.). Boston: Houghton Mifflin.

Carlson, E. B. (1997). *Trauma assessment: A clinician's guide*. New York: Guilford.

Cassidy, J., & Shaver, P. R. (Eds.). (1999). *Handbook of attachment: Theory, research, and clinical applications*. New York: Guilford.

Ceci, S. J., & Bruck, M. (1995). *Jeopardy in the courtroom: A scientific analysis of children's testimony*. Washington, DC: American Psychological Association.

Ceci, S. J., & Hembrooke, H. (1998). *Expert witnesses in child abuse cases: What can and should be said in court*. Washington, DC: American Psychological Association.

Crawford, R. J. (2001). *The expert witness: A manual for experts*. Bloomington, IN: 1st Books.

Dahir, V. B., Richardson, J. T., Ginsburg, G. P., Gatowski, S. I., Dobbin, S. A., & Merlino, M. L. (2005). Judicial application of Daubert to psychological syndrome and profile evidence: A research note. *Psychology, Public Policy, and Law, 11*(1), 62–82.

Daicoff, S. S. (2004). *Lawyer, heal thyself: A psychological analysis of personality strengths and weaknesses*. Washington, DC: American Psychological Association.

Daubert v. Merrell-Dow Pharmaceuticals, Inc., 509 U.S. 579 (1993).

Dawson v. Prager and the Menninger Clinic, Kan. No. 88,077 (2003).

Dyer, F. J. (1999). *Psychological consultation in parental rights cases*. New York: Guilford.

English, P. W., & Sales, B. D. (2005). *More than the law: Behavioral and social facts in legal decision making*. Washington, DC: American Psychological Association.

Fontham, M. R., Vitiello, M., & Miller, D. W. (2002). *Persuasive written and oral advocacy in trial and appellate courts*. New York: Aspen.

Frye v. United States, 54 App. D.C. 46, 293 F. 1013 (1923).

Fuller, M. A., & Sajatovic, M. (2001). *Drug information for mental health*. Cleveland, OH: Lexi-Comp.

Gatowski, S. I., Dobbin, S. A., Richardson, J. T., Ginsburg, G. P., Merlino, M. L., & Dahir, V. B. (2001). Asking the gatekeepers: A national survey of judges on judging expert evidence in a post-Daubert world. *Law and Human Behavior, 25*(5), 433–458.

General Electric Co. v. Joiner, 522 U.S. 136 (1997).

Gibelman, M. (1995). *What social workers do*. Washington, DC: NASW Press.

Gibelman, M. (2004). *What social workers do* (2nd ed.). Washington, DC: NASW Press.

Gibelman, M., & Schervish, P. J. (1997). *Who we are: A second work*. Washington, DC: NASW Press.

Groth-Marnat, G. (1997). *Handbook of psychological assessment* (3rd ed.). New York: Wiley.

Gutheil, T. G., & Applebaum, P. S. (2000). *Clinical handbook of psychiatry and the law* (3rd ed.). Philadelphia: Lippincott Williams & Wilkins.

Harris, J. C. (1995). *Developmental neuropsychiatry: Assessment, diagnosis, and treatment of developmental disorders* (Vol. II). New York: Oxford University Press.

Heilbrun, K., Marczyk, G. R., & DeMatteo, D. (2002). *Forensic mental health assessment: A casebook*. New York: Oxford University Press.

Hess, A. K. (1999). Serving as an expert witness. In A. K. Hess & I. B. Weiner (Eds.), *The handbook of forensic psychology* (2nd ed., pp. 521–555). New York: Wiley.

Hobbs, C. J., Hanks, H. G. I., & Wynne, J. M. (1999). *Child abuse and neglect: A clinician's handbook* (2nd ed.). London: Churchill Livingstone. In re Adoption/Guardianship, No. CCJ14746, 360 Md 634, 759 A.2d 755 (2000).

Kaplan, H. I., & Sadock, B. J. (1998). *Synopsis of psychiatry: Behavior science/clinical psychiatry* (8th ed.). Baltimore: Williams and Wilkins.

Kaplan, R. M., & Saccuzzo, D. P. (2004). *Psychological testing: Principles, applications and issues* (5th ed.). Pacific Grove, CA: Brooks/Cole.

Koocher, G. P., Norcross, J. C., & Hill, S. S. (Eds.). (1998). *Psychologists' desk reference*. New York: Oxford University Press.

Krafka, C., Dunn, M. A., Johnson, M. T., Cecil, J. S., & Miletich, D. (2002). Judge and attorney experiences, practices, and concerns regarding expert testimony in federal civil trials. *Psychology, Public Policy, and Law, 8*(3), 309–332.

Krause, H. D. (1986). *Family law in a nutshell* (2nd ed.). St. Paul, MN: West Publishing.

Kumho Tire Co. v. Carmichael, 97-1709, 131 F.3d 1433, *rev'd*, 526 U.S. 137 (1999).

Lutzker, J. R. (Ed.). (1998). *Handbook of child abuse research and treatment.* New York: Plenum.

McDonald, G. (2001). *Effective intervention in child abuse and neglect: An evidence-based approach to planning and evaluating interventions.* New York: Wiley.

Melton, G. B., Petrila, J., Poythress, N. G., & Slobogin, C. (1997). *Psychological evaluations for the courts: A handbook for mental health professionals and lawyers.* New York: Guilford.

Mueller, C. B., & Kirkpatrick, L. C. (2005). *Federal rules of evidence: With advisory committee notes, legislative history and cases.* Gaithersburg, NY: Aspen Law and Business.

Munson, C. E. (2000). *The mental health diagnostic desk reference: Visual guides and more for learning to use the Diagnostic and Statistical Manual, DSM–IV–TR.* New York: Haworth.

Munson, C. E. (2001a). *Handbook of clinical social work supervision* (3rd ed.). New York: Haworth.

Munson, C. E. (2001b). *The mental health diagnostic desk reference: Visual guides and more for learning to use the Diagnostic and Statistical Manual, DSM–IV–TR* (2nd ed.). New York: Haworth.

Munson, C. E. (2001c). Mental health expert witness testimony (EWT) in family and child welfare practice. *Brief Treatment and Crisis Intervention, 1*(2), 115–130.

Munson, C. E. (2002). Forensic social work and expert witness testimony in child welfare. In A. Roberts & G. Greene (Eds.), *Social workers' desk reference* (pp. 684–690). New York: Oxford University Press.

Munson, C. E. (2004a). Evidence-based treatment for traumatized and abused children. In A. Roberts & K. Yeager (Eds.), *Handbook of practice-focused research and evaluation* (pp. 252–263). New York: Oxford University Press.

Munson, C. E. (2004b). Evolution of protocol-based supervisory practice (PBSP)." In K. Hopkins & M. Austin (Eds.), *Human service supervision in the learning organization* (pp. 85–96). Thousand Oaks, CA: Sage.

Munson, C. E. (2005a). International child abduction and clinical social work intervention. *Proceedings of the 44th Annual Meeting of the International Conference for the Advancement of Private Practice of Clinical Social Work: Changes in law and theory—Impact on best practices* (pp. 95–109). Montreal, Canada.

Munson, C. E. (2005b, April). *Passing the Daubert test: The limits of evidence in social work practice and expert witness testimony.* Paper presented at the 22nd Annual Meeting of the National Organization of Forensic Social Work, New Orleans, LA.

Munson, C. E. (in press). *Clear and convincing evidence: A handbook of expert witness testimony and evidence-based clinical child welfare practice.* New York: Haworth.

Myers, J. E. B. (1998). *Legal issues in child abuse and neglect practice* (2nd ed.). Thousand Oaks, CA: Sage.

National Association of Social Workers. (1995a). *Code of ethics of the National Association of Social Workers.* Washington, DC: NASW Press.

National Association of Social Workers. (1995b). *Encyclopedia of social work* (19th ed.). Washington, DC: NASW Press.

Neighbors, I. A., Green-Faust, L., & van Beyer, K. (2002). Curriculum development in forensic social work at the MSW and post-MSW levels. In I. Neighbors, A. Chambers, E. Levin, G. Nordman, & C. Tutrone (Eds.), *Social work and the law: Proceedings of the National Organization of Forensic Social Work, 2000* (pp. 1–11). New York: Haworth.

Newcombe, N. (1996). *Child development: Change over time* (8th ed.). New York: HarperCollins.

Nurcombe, B., & Partlett, D. F. (1994). *Child mental health and the law.* New York: Free Press.

Ollendick, T. H., & Hersen, M. (Eds.). (1998). *Handbook of child psychopathology* (3rd ed.). New York: Plenum.

Ray, O., & Ksir, C. (1996). *Drugs, society, and human behavior.* St. Louis, MO: Mosby.

Righthand, S., Kerr, B., & Drach, K. (2003). *Child maltreatment risk assessments: An evaluation guide.* New York: Haworth.

Roberts, A. R., & Yeager, K. R. (Eds.). (2004). *Evidence-based practice manual: Research and outcome measures in health and human services.* New York: Oxford University Press.

Saltzman, A., & Furman, D. M. (1999). *Law in social work practice* (2nd ed.). Chicago: Nelson-Hall.

Sattler, J. M. (1998). *Clinical and forensic interviewing of children and families: Guidelines for the mental health, education, pediatric, and child maltreatment fields.* San Diego, CA: Jerome M. Sattler.

Schiraldi, G. R. (2000). *The post-traumatic stress disorder sourcebook: A guide to healing, recovery, and growth*. Los Angeles: Lowell House.

Smith, F. S., & Bace, R. G. (2002). *A guide to forensic testimony: The art and practice of presenting testimony as an expert technical witness*. Boston: Addison-Wesley.

Society of Expert Witnesses. (2000). *What is an expert witness?* Retrieved September 9, 2005, from http://www.sew.org.uk/noidxbar/wel_fs.htm

Tsushima, W. T., & Anderson, R. M. (1996). *Mastering expert testimony: A courtroom handbook for mental health professionals*. Mahwah, NJ: Lawrence Erlbaum Associates.

Uniform Marriage and Divorce Act, § 302 (1971).

U.S. House of Representatives Committee on the Judiciary. (2004). *Federal rules of evidence*. Washington, DC: U.S. Government Printing Office.

Vance, H. B. (1998). *Psychological assessment of children: Best practices for schools and clinical settings* (2nd ed.). New York: Wiley.

van der Kolk, B. A., McFarlane, A. C., & Weisaeth, L. (Eds.). (1996). *Traumatic stress: The effects of overwhelming experience on mind, body, and society*. New York: Guilford.

Vogelsang, J. (2001). *The witness stand: A guide for clinical social workers in the courtroom*. New York: Haworth.

Walker, N. E. (2002). Forensic interviews of children: The components of scientific validity and legal admissibility. *Law and Contemporary Problems, 65*(1), 149–178.

Wilson, J. P., & Keane, T. M. (Eds.). (1997). *Assessing psychological trauma and PTSD*. New York: Guilford.

Wodrich, D. L. (1997). *Children's psychological testing: A guide for nonpsychologists* (3rd ed.). Baltimore: Brookes.

Wolchik, S. A., & Sandler, I. N. (1997). *Handbook of children's coping: Linking theory and intervention*. New York: Plenum.

Resources

The following list of resources is designed to be the most current and most helpful material related to the range of child social work forensic practice.

Benjamin, G. A. H., & Gollan, J. K. (2003). *Family evaluation in custody litigation: Reducing risks of ethical infractions and malpractice*. Washington, DC: American Psychological Association.

Bernstein, B. E., & Hartsell, T. H. (2005). *The portable guide to testifying in court for mental health professionals: An A to Z guide to being an effective witness*. Hoboken, NJ: Wiley.

Ceci, S. J., & Bruck, M. (1995). *Jeopardy in the courtroom: A scientific analysis of children's testimony*. Washington, DC: American Psychological Association.

Ceci, S. J., & Hembrooke, H. (1998). *Expert witnesses in child abuse cases: What can and should be said in court*. Washington, DC: American Psychological Association.

Munson, C. E. (in press). *Clear and convincing evidence: A handbook of expert witness testimony and evidence-based clinical child welfare practice*. New York: Haworth.

Myers, J. E. B. (1998). *Legal issues in child abuse and neglect practice* (2nd ed.). Thousand Oaks, CA: Sage.

Ney, T. (Ed.). (1995). *True and false allegations of child sexual abuse: Assessment and case management*. New York: Brunner/Mazel.

Nurcombe, B., & Partlett, D. F. (1994). *Child mental health and the law*. New York: Free Press.

Righthand, S., Kerr, B., & Drach, K. (2003). *Child maltreatment risk assessments: An evaluation guide*. New York: Haworth.

Expert Testimony on Woman Battering and Its Effects

Introduction

This chapter provides an overview of expert witnessing in criminal and civil cases involving woman battering with an emphasis on how such testimony bears on cases also involving the welfare of children. The first part reviews the background and most significant milestones in the evolution of expert testimony on battering; the rationale, scope, and general applicability of domestic violence testimony; and the major conceptual approaches to representing women's experience of abuse. The second part focuses on how to conduct a domestic violence evaluation in preparation for trial. Drawing on my experience as a witness in a pathbreaking class action lawsuit against the child welfare system in New York, *Nicholson v. Williams*, I also examine the role of the expert in cases where children have been exposed to domestic violence. In the final sections, I outline the factors that can assist in evaluation and risk assessment. Although there is often a need to conduct a clinical assessment with domestic violence victims, perpetrators, or children, this chapter is limited to cases in which domestic violence experts are called on to provide general information about woman battering and its effects, including its effects on children, or to describe the dynamics of abuse in a particular case.

Evan Stark

Part I: The Development of Domestic Violence Testimony

Beyond the "Frye Test"

The admission of expert testimony was traditionally governed by a three-part test: (a) the subject matter had to be "beyond the ken of the average laymen"; (b) the expert had to possess sufficient skill, knowledge, or experience in the field to aid the "trier of fact" in the search for truth; and (c) the state of the scientific knowledge involved had to be sufficiently developed to allow an expert opinion to be rendered (Frye, 1923; Strong, 1999). Meeting the rigorous requirements of what is known as the "Frye test" poses special challenges to relatively new fields of inquiry such as domestic violence. In a criminal case where my testimony was challenged, Connecticut's highest court replaced the stringent test suggested by Frye by requiring only that the expert be qualified by his or her educational background, work experience, and/or research; the testimony focus on a subject not familiar to the average person; and it be helpful to the jury (*State v. Borrelli*, 1993). A similar Supreme Court decision made that same year held that evidence (such as expert testimony) was admissible simply if its relevance outweighed its possible prejudicial effect (*Daubert v. Merrell*, 1993). Relevance can be established by showing that the evidence makes an element of culpability more or less likely or helps a judge or jury understand the evidence in a case or determine a fact that is at issue (Downs, 1996).[1]

Standards for expert testimony similar to those established in Connecticut make it possible for any advocate, social worker, or health or mental health professional with specialized knowledge of or experience with domestic violence to present testimony to help a judge or jury assess evidence or to correct misconceptions about woman battering and its effects.[2] This experience may involve specialized training in domestic violence; clinical or advocacy work that involves a significant proportion of abuse victims, perpetrators, or their children; and/or research in the field. Expert testimony in criminal cases involving domestic violence is by no means uncontroversial. Particularly since the Bobbitt and Menendez trials, a number of critics have claimed that using what Alan Dershowitz (1994) terms the "abuse excuse" in cases involving victims of domestic violence, war-time trauma, rape, child sexual or physical abuse, or compulsive gambling condones vigilantism and frees people who kill from personal responsibility (McCord, 1987; Westervelt, 1999). Critics at the other end of the political spectrum have argued that expert testimony can perpetuate stereotypes that are as demeaning of battered women as the myths it is designed to dispel, particularly when it focuses exclusively on a victim's psychology rather than the "reasonableness" of her actions (Schneider, 2000). Despite these sentiments, courts have generally concluded, as Sue Ostoff (1995), Director of the National Clearinghouse for the Defense of Battered Women, insists, that "the introduction of expert testimony does not promote vigilantism; it promotes fair trials" (p. ii).

Precedents for the Battered Woman's Defense

Expert testimony on woman battering and its effects developed in response to ongoing dilemmas that arose in representing battered women who defended themselves against abuse. In the past, women who committed homicide or other crimes in the context of their battering rarely claimed self-defense or duress. Only three self-defense cases involving women reached the appellate courts in the United States before 1900 (Bochnak, 1981; Gellespi, 1989), and battered women made such claims even less often. Because a history of abuse could provide a motive for the alleged crime, battered women often concealed it. Another important reason for concealment was that a rigid standard of self-defense was applied to women modeled after what "the reasonable man" could be expected to do in a similar situation. This meant that their acts would be excused only if they used a level of force equivalent to the immediate force they confronted. They could kill their assailant only if an armed assault was underway, opportunities to retreat or escape were closed, and the force used was no more than needed to prevent attack (Bochnak, 1981). Anything more and they went to jail, as many thousands of women did. Although the standard allowed for variation in how individuals perceive danger, it typically made no provision for group differences such as those arising from gender inequality or, as significantly, for the fear and entrapment attendant on a history of being battered.

Battered women had few credible alternatives to self-defense. In *Women Who Kill*, Ann Jones (1980) depicted the legal quandary women faced when they retaliated against abusive partners, even in the throes of an assault. Behind the norm of domesticity, the most obvious explanation when an otherwise respectable woman responded violently was that she was insane. It was easier for courts to acquit on the grounds of insanity than to acknowledge that the behavior widely viewed as part of the marriage contract could provoke a rational woman to violence. A variation on this theme was to appeal to the court's paternalism by portraying the abused woman as frail and helpless, promoting the stereotypic belief that women could be acted on but could not act reasonably on their own behalf. A third approach was to argue that the violence a particular victim suffered was far in excess of the norm. In short, the legal system acknowledged abuse only so long as the victim was framed as a passive, helpless, or ladylike victim driven mad by a moral deviate. These terms for protection were acceptable because they supported women's oppression as a class; legitimated the status of women as male property to be used, but not abused; denied women an affirmative capacity for aggression and rationality (which were presumably possessed only by men); sustained the distinction between "respectable" and "rough" women that excluded working class, minority, and unconventional women from protection; and fostered the belief that moderate levels of violence against women were normal, hence, not a topic for public concern.

The domestic violence revolution altered this situation dramatically. As community-based shelters were opened in dozens of communities in the late 1970s (Roberts, 1981), defense attorneys and feminist scholars sought to broaden the range of legal options available to battered women beyond insanity and incapacity. Women's "self-defense work" was designed to remedy the unequal treatment resulting from the application of male norms in the criminal justice system by assisting victimized women to get their voices heard in the courtroom (Schneider, 2000). Expert testimony was one way to do this.

In 1977, shortly after the first battered women's shelters opened in the United States, Michigan housewife Francine Hughes put her children safely in a car, then returned and set fire to the bed in which her husband was sleeping, fatally burning him. Hughes's attorney worried that a traditional self-defense plea would fail, largely because the sleeping husband did not pose the imminent danger required by law. Today, the "burning bed" case is recognized as a transition: Although Francine won by adapting the traditional defense of temporary insanity, thereby reinforcing the view that her act was unreasonable, a precedent was set when the history of abuse was documented for the court as the source of Hughes's distorted perception (McNulty, 1980).

Three months before Hughes set fire to her house, feminist legal scholars Elizabeth Schneider and Nancy Stearns from the Center for Constitutional Law won an appeal from the Washington State Supreme Court that also helped set the stage for a new approach in cases of woman battering. Reversing the murder conviction of Yvonne Wanrow, the Washington court emphasized that a history of sex discrimination predisposed a "reasonable woman" to greater vulnerability than a man, hence, to respond more readily (i.e., with less provocation) and with a higher level of violence than a man would have in an identical situation (Schneider, 2000). Wanrow also challenged the tendency for courts to exclude contextual evidence—such as a prior history of conflict between two parties—from self-defense cases involving battered women, opening the door for experts to argue that the experience of battered women had social validity and commonality, so their retaliatory acts might be reasonable. The decision also implied that women act in self-defense under different circumstances and in different ways than men and that sex-based stereotypes interfere with how jurors interpret these acts.

Temporary insanity caused by abuse and the lower standard for retaliatory violence set by the so-called Wanrow instruction were the two lines of defense available to battered women when psychiatrist Elisa Benedek took the stand in the murder trial of Ruth Childers in Benton, Indiana, in 1978. Childers was charged with murdering her former husband, Clifford, who had battered her for 18 years. Clifford returned to their farm, intoxicated, and began throwing furniture and other things belonging to Ruth and her teenagers out of their rented moving van. After calling the sheriff, Ruth confronted Clifford with a shotgun and told him to leave. He lunged at her, the gun went off, and Clifford was killed. A firearms expert established that the gun had gone off accidentally, reducing the crime to involuntary manslaughter. But full acquittal required an explanation for why she thought the shotgun was necessary in the first place, even though Clifford had neither threatened nor assaulted her that day.

To answer this question for the defense, Dr. Benedek relied on a psychological pattern known as "battered woman's syndrome" (BWS) that had been described by Dr. Lenore Walker (1979, 1984, 1989). Dr. Benedek wove her narrative from two parallel themes that have been emphasized by numerous experts since then: the escalation of violence and the victim's deteriorating psychological state. She depicted Childers's incapacity to perceive alternatives to the shooting as an example of "learned helplessness" induced by violence, a form of depression brought on by abuse according to Walker. Dr. Benedek explained why, based on the sense of futility and dependence imposed by the violence, battered women develop an exaggerated sense of their assailant's power and are convinced they are in greater danger than a third party might perceive. Dr. Benedek's argument failed to persuade the jury. Mrs. Childers was convicted and sentenced to 5 years in prison, the maximum allowed in Indiana for involuntary manslaughter.

Today, expert testimony on battering and its effects has been admitted, at least to some degree, in thousands of cases and in each of the 50 states plus the District of Columbia (Downs, 1996; Schneider, 2000)[3] Of the 19 federal courts that have considered the issue, all but 3 have admitted the testimony in at least some cases (Parrish, 1996).[4] Based largely on the new awareness of battering, governors in Massachusetts, Ohio, Illinois, New York, and 18 other states took the unprecedented step of pardoning battered women imprisoned for killing men who abused them.

The Rationale, Types of Cases, and Scope of Expert Testimony

The importance of expert testimony on abuse reflects the general lack of lay knowledge about the nature of domestic violence, its dynamics and consequences, and its significance in identifying the best interests of children during a custodial dispute. Expert knowledge may also be needed to counteract other psychological assessments that minimize domestic violence, fail to take it into account, mistakenly view a woman's reports of abuse as symptomatic of her psychological problems, depict the violence as an expression of marital discord for which both parties are equally responsible, or believe the woman is responsible for the husband's abuse. In one case, when the court-appointed assessor concluded that a woman's report of abuse was "delusional," she produced a diary in which she had carefully documented assaults extending back 7 years. In response, he changed his diagnosis to "obsessive."

There are two basic ways in which domestic violence expertise is used by courts: to dispel myths about abuse by providing general information about domestic violence and its effects, and to provide a case-specific assessment of abuse, its dynamics, and its consequences. The most common scenario in which expert testimony on battering has been accepted (90% of the states) involves traditional self-defense situations. More than half of the states have found the testimony relevant to assessing the reasonableness of the defendant's belief that she was in danger of imminent harm and/or of her actions in defense of herself or others. A significant number (37%) of the states have found the testimony relevant to the defendant's perception of the temporal proximity of the perceived danger to life or safety. Two states, Ohio and Missouri, limit the admissibility of expert testimony to self-defense cases by statute, and nearly 40% of the states require that the defendant raise a self-defense claim in order to introduce expert testimony (Parrish, 1996). Technically, there is no separate defense based on BWS specifically or battering generally. Thus, expert testimony is properly used to support a woman's claim of self-defense, duress, or necessity, not to replace it. But, particularly as a complement to a woman's testimony, the expert can help to dispel jurors' preconceptions about battered women, illuminate how battering shaped her understanding and response to perceived danger, bolster her credibility, show the existence of mitigating factors (e.g., at sentencing), and explain why her fears were reasonable.[5]

Expert testimony has also been admitted by a substantial number of state courts in nontraditional self-defense situations, such as when a battered woman kills her batterer while he is sleeping (accepted by 29% of the states) or by hiring a third party to kill him (accepted by 20% of the states). I supported the self-defense claim of an Albanian woman, Donna B., who had been assaulted more than 300 times by her husband, though she had never called police and had only one medical visit that could be linked to abuse, when a doctor noted she was seeking an abortion against her will because her husband demanded it. One night, her husband beat her, dragged her across the room by the hair, and kicked her in the side. Then, leaving her on the floor, he went to bed. Donna climbed the stairs, took the gun her husband kept under his pillow, and shot him repeatedly at point-blank range. She then went back downstairs, called the police, and returned to the bedroom to retrieve the weapon, fearful that he would come after her.

In another case, I testified at the sentencing for murder of a woman who put a knife in her sleeve, went into the street, and confronted a former boyfriend who had threatened to come to her apartment that night and "f–k her up really bad," something he had done in the past. Though she had him arrested for previous assaults and had a court order restraining him from contacting her, he repeatedly returned to threaten and assault her. The woman had two daughters in her house with no telephone, the electricity had been turned off, and the boyfriend had broken the lock on her front and back doors. She walked up to the man and told him, "If you're going to do me, do me now," expressing the unbearable anxiety evoked by waiting to be hurt. When he cursed her, repeated his threat, and pushed her away, she stabbed him.

Nonconfrontational situations like these challenge the expert to explain why the victim's sense of imminent danger is as reasonable as if she were confronted by a knife-wielding intruder. Such situations are atypical, though they are often publicized. In fact, in the vast majority (at least 75%) of the cases in which they are charged with murder, battered women kill men in traditional self-defense situations, during an ongoing attack or when the imminent threat can be readily discerned (Maguigan, 1991).

A sizable minority of states have admitted expert testimony in non-self-defense cases, such as where women are charged with crimes they claim to have committed out of duress or necessity caused by battering (16% of the states) or where a battered woman has been charged with a crime against someone other than the batterer (14% of the states). In *U.S. v. Ezeiruaku* (1995), a criminal court permitted the defendant, Mildred Akiagba, to introduce testimony from an expert on BWS and an expert on Nigerian custom. Ms. Akiagba pled guilty to conspiracy to distribute heroin, but she also testified that her estranged husband had coerced her into this and that he had physically abused, controlled, and monitored her as well as threatened her with deportation because he was an American citizen and she was not. While expert testimony in this case was ultimately unsuccessful, the court recognized its general relevance to establishing fear of bodily injury for purposes of mitigating or downgrading a charge or sentencing level on the basis of duress or coercion. I have testified in cases where battering was the context in which a woman signed a fraudulent tax return; allowed narcotics to be stored in her house; sold or carried drugs for her partner; failed to protect or injured her children; embezzled money on behalf of an abusive partner; and fired at a stranger who was pursuing her, killing the woman he used as a shield.

In 29% of the states, the prosecution has offered expert testimony to explain a complainant's recantation or prior inconsistent statements about abuse. In *Commonwealth v. Goetzendanner* (1997), the Appeals Court of Massachusetts upheld the testimony of an expert witness concerning BWS to explain why a woman had a restraining order removed and recanted, though she had earlier presented evidence that the partner punched her in the face and body, beat her with a stick, held a knife to her throat, and raped her. Noting precedents from other state and federal courts, the court also defined the scope of such testimony. "Where relevant," the court held, "evidence of BWS be admitted through a qualified expert to enlighten jurors about behavioral or emotional characteristics common to most victims of battering and to show that an individual victim or victim witness has exhibited similar characteristics." But the court also limited the scope of such testimony "... to a description of the general or expected characteristics shared by typical victims of a particular syndrome or condition." Thus, the testimony "may not relate directly to the symptoms exhibited by an individual victim" (Perry & Lemon, 1998). Twenty percent of the states have explicitly precluded experts from testifying that the defendant is in fact a battered woman or "suffering from 'battered woman syndrome.'"

Given these constraints, the prosecutor or defense attorney may pose hypothetical situations to the expert, hoping that a jury will make connections between the general dynamics associated with battering and the facts in a particular case. In *State vs. Borrelli* (1993), just before trial, a woman recanted her original claim to police that her boyfriend had tied her up, gagged her, and burned her with cigarettes. Although an expert cannot testify about whether or not a given woman is telling the truth, I explained that recantation is common in abuse cases and usually reflects the victim's fear of retaliation if she contributes to his conviction. In other cases, I have been called to discount defense challenges by explaining why it is consistent with battering for a woman to go with the defendant voluntarily during a "kidnapping," deny being abused to friends, lie to medical or mental health personnel, bail the abuser out of jail, or write love letters to him in prison. I have also had to address these issues to support a woman's credibility in custodial disputes, wrongful death suits after police or other authorities failed to respond to pleas for help, or criminal cases. On three occasions, I have been asked to explain why a court should take a woman's claims of abuse seriously even though she married the partner after the abusive incidents she alleged took place. Experts are also called frequently to rebut expert testimony that challenges the credibility of a woman's claim to be abused or discounts its importance. On the other hand, introducing expert testimony can trigger an adverse examination of the victim by an expert for the prosecution or opposing counsel, an issue to be carefully considered (Parrish, 1996).[6]

Expert testimony on battering is also becoming increasingly common in civil cases, particularly those involving tort actions for damages or in custodial disputes where the equity interests of battered women assume particular poignancy. In marked contrast to the past, most states now require courts to at least consider evidence of domestic violence, typically via expert testimony on battering and its effects. In *Burgos v. Burgos* (1997), I testified that Mr. Burgos had battered Mrs. Burgos; prevented her from securing education or employment outside the home; and caused her multiple injuries, chronic stress, and a loss of confidence. Both parties had nearly equitable estates. But the court recognized Mrs. Burgos' noneconomic contributions during the marriage and that her earning capacity had been stunted by Mr. Burgos' conduct. It found that Mrs. Burgos required additional education, which was to be paid for by Mr. Burgos, supplemental income in the form of weekly alimony, and a share in Mr. Burgos' pension benefits.

In a New York City case, the marriage reached its nadir when the husband committed a near fatal assault with a barbell after his wife announced she wanted a divorce. The unemployed husband depended heavily on his wife's considerable income to maintain a luxurious lifestyle and had coerced and controlled her into taking out a new life insurance policy just before he attacked her. Although he admitted the assault, he presented expert psychiatric testimony that a combination of medication and stress caused him to "crack," that his dependency and his idealization of his wife were inconsistent with the profile typical of batterers, and that his previous threats and assaultive acts comprised what the psychiatrist termed "unfortunate, but normal dysfunction" typical of many "bad marriages." Ruling that the man's actions "shocked the conscience of the court," the judge set precedent by awarding her nearly all of the marital assets.

One of the most important roles experts play is to challenge widespread ignorance about battering and its effects on children among mental health professionals. In custodial disputes where physical or sexual abuse is alleged, husbands may claim their wives have fabricated the charges to turn their children against them. Rather than investigate whether the charges can be supported, psychologists often collude in the husband's strategy by diagnosing the child as suffering "parental alienation syndrome" (PAS) and recommending that the father get custody. While behavior designed to turn a child against a parent must be taken seriously, PAS has been adopted less because its causes or dynamics have been supported by research—they have not—than because it gives a family court judge a convenient way to resolve a contentious dispute without becoming embroiled in the tough evidentiary issues raised by abuse.

In a custodial dispute where there was clear evidence the husband had abused his wife, a court-appointed psychologist attributed the refusal of the 9-year-old boy to go to court-ordered visitation with the father to PAS, citing the mother's excessive criticism of her husband. Evidence of the mother's "unreasonableness" was her refusal to drop a restraining order, although the couple had been separated for over a year. The judge ordered the boy taken to a juvenile shelter, where, after 3 days of harassment from the other boys, he agreed to comply.

In *Knock v. Knock* (1993), a 10-year-old girl asked to live with her father, whom the mother charged with abuse. The primary evidence of abuse was contained in a five-volume diary written in Chinese. Translation costs were prohibitive. A psychologist testified that, according to the Minnesota Multiphasic Personality Inventory (MMPI) and several other tests, the father had no propensity for violence. A record from a battered woman's shelter was inadmissible because an advocate had removed a page documenting an outburst when the girl told the mother, "I hope you die."

To rebut the husband's psychiatrist in the New York dispute over marital assets, I summarized research showing that an extremely dangerous subgroup of batterers present with dependent personalities and so idealize their partners that the threat of separation evokes the feeling "If I can't have her, no one will" (Dutton & Kropp, 2000). In the custody case involving the boy, the psychologist naively assumed abuse ended with separation (when, in fact, danger increases after separation) and falsely concluded that the mother's continued fears were exaggerated, so she never asked questions that could have uncovered the dramatic history of postseparation intimidation, including an anonymous note threatening that the mother would be burned with sulphuric acid if she persisted in her custody claims, something the husband had done to a coworker in a dispute. (Mahoney, 1991). Had the mother dropped the restraining order as the psychologist urged, her risk would have increased. In the second custody case, expert testimony was needed to show that standard psychological tests like the MMPI are not diagnostic in identifying abuse. When the mother testified that the husband frequently told her "I hope you die" at the dinner table, the judge could see why the girl repeated this at the shelter and accepted her claim of being abused.

Absence of expert opinion in cases like these may lead courts to hold victims accountable for actions over which they had little control or to approve custodial arrangements that extend the risk to mother and child. The expert can help the family court appreciate the irony involved when mothers are alternately censured for exposing their child to a violent partner (as I discuss in the case of *Nicholson v. Williams* later) and for not cooperating with court orders requiring repeated contact. Of course, the presentation of expert testimony is no guarantee that an abuse victim will be acquitted or successful in a civil or custodial case. Although cases involving domestic violence are reversed on appeal at a far higher rate than other types of cases, often because a court has failed to admit expert

control rather than BWS or when little or no domestic violence occurred (*People v. Daoust*, 1998; see also *Knock v. Knock*, 1993).

A closely linked psychological defense is based on symptoms of posttraumatic stress disorder (PTSD; American Psychiatric Association, 1994, section 309.81), a psychiatric syndrome first described among Vietnam veterans. Like BWS, the premise of the PTSD model is that any normal person would respond in a similar way if confronted by identical circumstances (e.g., external threats and violence) that elicit "intense fear, helplessness, loss of control and threat of annihilation" (Herman, 1992, p. 33). Recognizing that the conventional formulation of PTSD fails to capture "the protean symptomatic manifestations of prolonged, repeated trauma," Herman (1992, p. ll9) identifies three symptom categories of what she terms "complex PTSD": hyperarousal (chronic alertness); intrusion (flashbacks, floods of emotion, hidden reenactments); and constriction, "a state of detached calm . . . when events continue to register in awareness but are disconnected from their ordinary meanings" (p. 44) The fear elicited by the traumatic event also intensifies the need for protective attachments and may lead women to unwittingly move from one abusive relationship to the next. Experts relying on this model assess (or test) the victim for symptoms of PTSD; link the substance of flashbacks to incidents of abuse; and explain how the trauma that overwhelmed the normal coping mechanisms of the self caused the victim to dissociate (e.g., not remember her own violence), become hypervigilant (e.g., to exaggerate the danger posed by a sleeping man), or to use preemptive violence.

Although many of the same criticisms that apply to BWS also apply to PTSD, experts should be sensitive to the existence of these conditions. In addition to helping courts resolve the dilemmas identified previously, testimony based on these models can help courts recognize a new class of psychological harms caused by domestic violence and mitigate a woman's guilt by tracing her action to a psychological state induced by violence. Trauma theories also avoid some of the stigma associated with a traditional insanity defense because they are predicated on the belief that extreme violence would elicit similar cognitive and behavioral changes even in normal persons. At the same time, the images of helplessness and/or psychopathology on which these defenses rest can discredit a woman's credibility by emphasizing her distorted or exaggerated perceptions, impugn her capacity as a parent (e.g., because she is "sick"), and discount the objective parameters or her subjugation (e.g., her responses may be intra- rather than posttraumatic). To compensate for the potentially stigmatizing effects of psychological defenses, psychological experts have included a woman's futile efforts at resistance among the learning experiences that may lead her to conclude that survival requires retaliatory violence (Dutton, 1993), suggested a "psychological self-defense" based on an interactive model of identity (Ewing, 1987), and argued that living in a battering relationship gives victims a special and more astute (rather than distorted) perception of reality than the outsider (Blackman, 1986). Experts are well advised to remain eclectic, adapting a psychological approach that best suits the experiential evidence in a particular case.

Coercive Control

There is increasing evidence that most battered women remain relatively intact psychologically; that the violent infrastructure of assault consists of routine, but noninjurious violence; that they are controlled as well as coerced; and that the deprivation of liberty and autonomy that are due to control tactics more readily explains the durability of abusive relationships—and the victim behaviors that confound the courts—than traumatic violence or psychological dependence. The most common case in which experts are called has been alternatively described as "psychological abuse," "coerced persuasion," "conjugal or intimate terrorism," and "coercive control," the term I prefer. It consists of an ongoing course of malevolent conduct wherein one partner, almost always a male, seeks to dominate the other by deploying violence, intimidation (e.g., through threats and emotional abuse), isolation, and control (exploitation, deprivation, and regulation; Bancroft, 2002; Johnson, 1995, 2001; Jones & Schecter, 1992; Okun, 1986; Stark, 1995).

While psychological and physical harms are included in an assessment of coercive control (see Part II of this chapter), the model depicts a process of entrapment whereby regulation and structural deprivations such as the denial of money, food, transportation, or access to support overlay everyday activities like cooking, cleaning, and socializing and create a condition of objective (rather than merely psychological) dependence that frustrate women's efforts to seek help or to otherwise minimize, stop, resist, prevent, and/or escape from the battering. The expert who assesses for coercive control describes the systematic nature of abuse and outlines the use of violence, intimidation, isolation, and control, as well as the harms to liberty and autonomy that result from the entrapment process. The model highlights the contrast between women's capacities, strengths, and desires and their lived experience of being subordinated; emphasizes what women have been kept from doing for themselves alongside what has been done *to* them; and stresses the same right to a liberatory response that we would give to a person taken hostage, kidnapped, or held as a POW. Reconstructing the battering experience through the prism of coercive control explains how an otherwise intelligent, mentally healthy woman appears to function in dependent, destructive, or self-destructive ways, without resorting to potentially demeaning psychological accounts.

Part II: Preparing the Case

In the initial consultation with a defense attorney, prosecutor, or client, sufficient information is garnered to determine the nature and scope of the testimony required, including whether it involves a case-specific assessment, a report, or merely generic information about battering and its effects. I frankly discuss the strengths and limits of my involvement, including whether a psychiatrist or psychologist might be more appropriate than a forensic social worker. In custodial cases and some other types of litigation, victims are often prompted to make the initial contact because their attorneys have not adequately addressed their experience of abuse. It is important to validate a client's need for support. But, because an expert is only as good as the attorney doing the questioning, effective presentation of domestic violence evidence is possible only if a positive working relationship is established directly with counsel. This often includes educating attorneys about abuse, directing them to relevant reading, exploring alternative models to frame abuse, helping them develop appropriate questions, and suggesting issues they should raise with opposing experts. Consultation is a legitimate role for an expert even if neither a report nor testimony is required.

The Purpose of Evaluation

When a case assessment is required, the purpose of a pretrial evaluation is to answer three questions: (a) Is the client a battered woman? (b) If so, what were the dynamics of abuse? And (c) what are the consequences of abuse for the client and/or any children? If the battered woman is charged with violence or another crime, an assessment may also consider (d) how the history of battering affected her perceptions and behavior related to the event. Documents such as police reports or medical records or interviews with friends, family members, or witnesses may help answer these questions. But the critical information is almost always provided by the client interview.

Approaching Woman Battering as Coercive Control

As I indicated, the coercive control model that I use defines battering as ongoing (therefore, as comprising a pattern rather than a single incident) and as including varying combinations of violent acts, intimidation, isolation, and control. Following this understanding, the assessment explores whether and to what extent the partner employed these tactics, their development and interplay over the course of the relationship, how the woman responded, how she or any children were harmed (injured, exploited, shamed, regulated, etc.), and how these experiences shaped her perceptions and behavior.

The Typology of Abuse

An appropriate forensic framework should be selected based on the facts in a case and the victim's presentation. Three types of cases in which partners use force can be distinguished. The first involves fights or isolated assaults. In one case, when a woman's boyfriend slapped her on a dare, she knocked him down and sat on him, amusing his friends. As she was leaving the after-hours club where this took place, he jumped on her back and she stabbed him fatally. While a court might decide the woman responded in self-defense, after my interview, I decided this was not a case of battering because there was no pattern of abuse or control.

A second type involves a pattern of violence repeated over time, where the force is mainly unidirectional and has the clear malevolent aim of injuring, punishing, or controlling a partner. While emotional or psychological abuse can play a role in these cases, evaluation focuses primarily on the degree, frequency, history, means, dynamics, and effects of violence on a woman's physical integrity, psychological well-being, safety, level of fear, and decision making, as well as any exposure of the children, direct or indirect, to the violence. Such an assessment bears on traditional and nontraditional claims of self-defense, a "duress" defense to a criminal charge (such as embezzlement, drug involvement, or signing a false tax return), assessing damages in a civil suit, or a parent's fitness in custodial disputes. Describing the "typical" incident of physical abuse and its consequences in past encounters is relevant to showing that battered women may be able to predict the seriousness of an impending assault (when a nonabused partner or stranger could not). On the night Donna shot her husband, he failed to "have his way" with her as he usually did after he beat her. This led her to conclude she was disposable in his mind and would kill her if she failed to act first. Other clients have described a changed look in their partner's eyes or a similarly subtle change in routine that signaled heightened danger.

The absence of a traumatic reaction in no way negates the reasonableness of a battered woman's fear. Battered women frequently remain remarkably intact psychologically, even in the face of injurious, life-threatening assaults. This is also true in cases of coercive control, the third context in which partners use force, where physical abuse is complemented by significant deprivations, isolation, and control. These cases are described more fully later in the chapter. Suffice it to say here that, while psychological testing or evaluation may sometimes be useful, the evaluator's focus is on the existential condition of entrapment that compromises a woman's capacity to act independently or to protect herself or her children rather than primarily on mental health dimensions of her predicament.

Documentation

Depending on whether the case is criminal or civil, prior to meeting the client, the evaluator should review available records and evaluations from courts; corrections; criminal justice; medical, mental, and behavioral health agencies; court-ordered evaluations of children; investigative reports of friends, witnesses, and family members; and records of related legal proceedings (depositions, trial transcripts, visitation orders, protection orders, judicial rulings, etc.). It is quite common for official documents to be silent about abuse, even in cases where it is long standing and has involved repeated and injurious violence, or to contain psychiatric and pseudopsychiatric diagnoses frequently misapplied to abused women such as "hysterical" or "hypochondriac." These records may still be useful. A medical record may contain notes about repeated missed visits or "unwanted pregnancies," for instance, or about unexplained "falls," other "accidents," suicide attempts, or complaints of "nervousness" or "pain" that are unsupported by clinical tests.

Unconventional sources can be critical in abuse cases because official documentation of partner violence is rare and of intimidation, isolation, and control virtually nonexistent. I have clients prepare a written chronology of their relationship and ask them to provide any diaries, calendars, letters, and other evidence that may provide contemporaneous evidence of abuse. The chronology helps to facilitate recall and date episodes in relation to key life events. In one case, we used a woman's diary to date abusive episodes extending over their 3-year marriage. After each episode, the husband gave her expensive gifts, presumably evidence of the honeymoon phase described by Walker. The woman had also saved the bills for his gifts in their original envelopes. Importantly, the dates on these envelopes corresponded to another round of beatings for which there were no apologies or gifts. In another custody dispute, the mother provided a credible account of how her sons reacted to her abuse. But the boys denied seeing any violence and described their mother as "out to get" their father, a view accepted by the court-appointed clinician. The boys admitted what they had witnessed only when one son was confronted with a tape of his mother's telephone conversations he had made for his father. The key to the dismissal of murder charges against Donna B. was a log book in which her husband had her record her daily activities (including how each penny was spent, her weekly menus, thoughts of how to improve their family, etc.). He would call her downstairs nightly to defend each entry, then beat her for not doing enough to advance their family. In an embezzlement case, the defendant produced "The List," a multipage set of rules that covered everything from how she should dress, organize her clothes, and alphabetize her CDS to how she should vacuum ("till you see the lines"). The existence of the list helped jurors understand how her boyfriend could get this Vassar graduate to steal to support his gambling habit. While unconventional forms of documentation are not always admissible in court, experts are usually able to introduce them as contributing to how they reached their conclusions.

The Interview

Depending on the framework adapted, the interview is structured to determine the fact of abuse as well as its dynamics, consequences, and significance for a current case.

"Anticipatory empathy," based on what is known about a client's predicament, helps the evaluator prepare appropriate questions. When I meet a client, I introduce the purpose of the interview, describe my role in the trial, say something about my background with "women in a similar situation," and acknowledge how painful or embarrassing it may be to recount an abusive history to a stranger. I also explain that the information they provide may be available to opposing counsel, other experts, or even to their partners via counsel.

Accurate recall is a serious problem in domestic violence evaluations because multiple episodes extending over a long time are often involved and because many battered women adapt to coercion and control by repressing, denying, minimizing, or normalizing the danger they face. Conversely, victims may blame themselves for what happened or exaggerate their culpability, particularly if they feel guilty about their own violence. Donna B.'s husband sent her to Weight Watchers (which she liked because she got out of the house), then put her on a scale and beat her for not losing weight. Overeating is a common adaptation to abuse. But Donna blamed her "stupidity" and "forgetfulness" for the assaults, a self-assessment she pressed on me. Ironically, self-blame can be protective because it helps clients maintain a sense of control in the context of having no control. While evaluation is not counseling, it is appropriate to help clients understand their partners' culpability, normalize their experience, react with feeling (though not overreact) to their maltreatment, and weigh appropriate expressions of their own responsibility against adaptive or defensive postures that could increase their vulnerability at trial. For example, prosecutors often exploit the propensity for battered women to recall abusive episodes they initially denied. In fact, as Herman (1992) suggests, the revision of a woman's story as memories surface is a sign of recovery from trauma and should be so reframed for the court.

To maximize accurate reporting, some practitioners recommend an intensive, all-day interview that follows events in a chronological order, moving gradually from neutral questions about family background, early dating experiences, and the like to more emotion-laden episodes (Thyfault, Browne, & Walker, 1987). This approach has the added benefit of simulating courtroom testimony, where victims may be questioned over hours or even days. Walker and her colleagues also suggest structuring questions about violence—and testimony—around four different battering incidents: the first occurrence of violence in the relationship, the worst episode, the typical episode, and the most recent or fatal incident. They follow each narrative with a matching set of detailed questions about the specific circumstances (e.g., time, place, duration), acts (slap, hit, knife, etc.), and outcomes of the incident (injury, help seeking, retaliation, etc.) before moving to the next episode. Obtaining consistent details about incidents provides a picture of violence that allows comparisons over time that can identify escalation or other changes in behavioral patterns.

In complicated cases, I prefer several shorter interviews spaced over several weeks and proceed from a semistructured narrative in the first meeting to a more structured assessment schedule that probes the occurrence of specific events. Repeated shorter interviews exploit the fact that recall improves dramatically over time, particularly if the abuse has culminated in an event involving extreme violence, and have the added advantage of allowing the interviewer to review notes in the interim and fill gaps and clarify ambiguities. I also find that victims who discharge the anxiety surrounding an extreme episode of violence early in an interview can explore less dramatic facets of the battering more dispassionately and with greater accuracy.

The initial interview (or phase of the interview) captures the woman's story as she understands it, that is, in a rough chronological and narrative form. After reviewing the incident precipitating the evaluation, the interview takes a standard psychosocial history that includes any familial history of violence, sexual abuse, or substance use; a history of earlier relationships, abusive or not; schooling; work history; and a history of major medical, mental health, or behavioral problems. The oft-claimed link between current victimization and violence in childhood is greatly exaggerated. Still, violence in the family of origin or in prior relationships contributes to a woman's understanding of the current relationship. An employment history can counter negative stereotypes of battered women or, conversely, illustrate how the abusive partner disrupted a woman's work life, caused her to lose a job (or workdays), or obstructed her career path. Probing employment also helps clients separate facets of their lives that remained normal and for which they accept respect even when they feel shame about their behavior at home. Information on prior pathology can also illuminate a woman's response pattern. However, the psychosocial history is also mined to provide baseline evidence of independence and resilience against which the effects of subsequent abusive experience can be weighed. Courts frequently want to know whether the victim's current state reflects abuse rather than long-standing personality problems.

The History of Battering

The next phase of the interview focuses on the current relationship and, depending on the framework of harms adapted, seeks to establish the existence and interplay of abusive strategies, the consequences of battering, and how the woman responded. The narrative account is guided by frequent prompts to sharpen recall, direct attention to dimensions of experience not linked with abuse in the popular mind (such as isolation or control), and to keep the focus. This is followed by questions targeting specific dimensions of violence, intimidation (including shaming rituals), isolation, and control not covered in the narrative that research or casework suggest are common and/or are associated with an elevated risk of fatality or entrapment.

Violence: The Adult Trauma History

With respect to the partner's violence, the evaluator seeks information on

- the number, frequency, types, duration, and severity of assaults
- injuries or chronic problems resulting from assault

- the typical assaultive incident
- the presence and/or use of weapons
- sexual assault
- assault during pregnancy
- violence or other criminal conduct outside the relationship
- violence in the presence of others, including children
- violence while under the influence of alcohol or drugs
- physical and/or sexual abuse of children

The narrative begins with the courtship and proceeds from the first episode of abuse ("What is the first abusive episode you remember?" or "When was the first time he laid his hands on you?") to capture as many instances as possible of physical and sexual assault. In addition to asking about specific types of violence (choking, kicking, hitting with objects, etc.), I ask, "What did he do when he really wanted to hurt you?" and/or "What was the worst thing he ever did to you?" and/or "Has your partner ever hurt you so badly you needed a doctor?" and/or "Have you ever thought your partner might kill you?" Sexual coercion should be explored alongside sexual assault. I ask, for instance, "Did your partner ever force you to have sex when you didn't want to" and "Has your partner made you do things sexually that hurt you?" or "made you feel ashamed?" Although the cumulative effects of routine acts of minor violence can be as devastating as injury, these acts can be easily lost in the wake of severe assaults. A client who had stabbed her boyfriend recounted only three incidents of violence, for instance. But when I asked, "Did he ever put his hands on you when you didn't want him to?" she produced a detailed account of daily physical restraint during which this young 118-pound woman felt virtually immobilized by her 269-pound boyfriend.

At the conclusion of the interviews, the expert should be able to summarize the range, frequency, duration, and severity of domestic violence. A typical summary might read:

> Based on the interviews and documents reviewed, I conclude that Dawn S. was battered by Felipe G., starting approximately a year before the stabbing, during the summer of 1992, and extending to head trauma inflicted on the night of the fatality. Including over 50 assaults, the violence included breaking into her apartment, stalking, choking, rape, knocking her down, punching her in the back, kicking her in the head and back, dragging her by the hair, and slapping her repeatedly. In addition, he threatened to shoot her, held a gun to her head, and threatened her with a knife.

Estimates of the number of abusive episodes help neutralize the misconception that only injurious, life-threatening violence constitutes abuse and dramatize the range, frequency, and comumulative effects of partner violence. Donna B.'s husband first slapped her several days after they married, when she laughed on the phone while talking to her husband's uncle. A few nights later, when she said she wasn't feeling well, he tied her hands with a belt and "had his way." She recalled a dozen similar incidents during the first year. Early in the second year, the couple moved into their own apartment, and Mike B. instituted the nightly log ritual. From this point until she shot him 3 years later, Donna described beatings as occurring "nightly," "constantly," and "all the time." Using specific questions about the frequency of assaults during limited time periods bounded by watershed events, I concluded there had been somewhere between 250 and 300 attacks in this relationship, an estimate experience tells me was probably conservative. The expert should be prepared to defend the estimate during cross-examination.

Intimidation

Intimidation, threats, and emotional abuse are used to frighten the victim; induce compliance; and make her feel incompetent, stupid, or weak. An assumption underlying the assessment is that in inhibiting escape, coercion and control are as often the predicates as the sequelae of ongoing assault and play a major role in eliciting stress-related behavioral and psychological problems. With respect to emotional abuse and intimidation, the evaluator should be particularly sensitive to the following factors:

- chronic put-downs of the woman, friends, or family members
- games designed to make the woman feel "crazy" (so-called gaslight games)
- withdrawal from communication (e.g., the silent treatment)
- terrorizing or sadistic behaviors, particularly when the victim is sick or injured
- paranoid, jealous, or homicidal fantasies
- threats against the woman, family, friends, or pets, including threats to kill
- monitoring or stalking
- threats of suicide
- use of children as spies

Compared to an assessment of violent acts, the range, meaning, and dimensions of intimidation tactics are difficult to elicit and specify. Overt emotional abuse can be identified by asking questions like "When your partner wanted to insult you, what names were you called?" "How often did he do this?" or "Has your partner ever made you feel you can't do anything right?" "How does he do this?" I also ask, "What is the worst threat your partner ever made?" But intimidating behaviors are often far less transparent and may be more effective in situations where the threat is perceived only by a partner. In one case, the partner of a star softball pitcher would walk onto the field when he became jealous and offer her a sweatshirt. Although her teammates interpreted this as loving, she understood the implication, that she would need to cover up her bruises that night.

Although fear is an extremely sensitive indicator of actual risk in battering relationships, the ostensible normality of many situations that women describe as "crazy-making" leads them to distrust and even feel guilt about their instincts. One result is that women voluntarily change behaviors—quit school, reject a job offer, or give up a night out with friends—because they sense their partner's disapproval. Worse, inchoate fears may make them do things of which they are ashamed. To get at this situation, it is helpful to ask general questions about fear and about how behaviors have changed because of it. I ask, "Do you ever feel you are walking on eggshells at home?" or even "What are the ways your partner scares you?" and "Are there certain things you don't do or say anymore because you're afraid of how your partner will respond?"

When obsessive jealousy is a factor, intimidating tactics can be uniquely sadistic. In one case, a jealous ex-husband hid in a tree outside the house and jumped down when his former wife attempted to leave, causing the woman to urinate in her pants. Controllers commonly demand their partners wear beepers so they can be located at any moment or that they check in or out or give them a fixed time in which to shop or complete other chores. A former TV anchor woman was so intimidated by her husband's rule that she answer the phone by the third ring ("or else") that a rash formed on her arms and face when someone called during our interview. In other instances, batterers simply "lose it" to frighten their partners, driving at dangerous rates of speed, for example, or putting their fist through car windows. In one case, when a newlywed suggested a plan to redecorate the house, her partner picked up a sledge hammer and started smashing the walls.

Not all verbal attacks, insults, or demands that a partner behave in specific ways are examples of battering. Psychological abuse is effective in frightening or controlling an abused party because the past experience of assaultive violence conveys the implication that either the partner complies "or else. . . . "

Isolation

Isolation from friends, family, helping professionals, and other sources of support removes the moorings from which a positive sense of self derives, increases the victim's dependence on her partner, increases her vulnerability to domestic violence, and keeps abuse secret. Since isolation is a relative state, the evaluator probes changes that have occurred during the target relationship or since the onset of abuse. A key question may be "Do you feel you can come and go as you please and talk to whom you like?" Key issues are

- restricted access to family members, friends, and coworkers
- restricted access to medical care or other sources of help and protection
- restricted access to common social arenas (church, school, work, etc.)
- control over mobility and communication (car, phone, going out alone, etc.)
- invasion of private spaces (e.g., diaries, answering machines, pocketbooks, drawers)

Isolation can be particularly important where a partner restricts a woman's access to an area of activity such as work, the gym, or going to church that she has used as her "safety zone" to feel good about herself or contemplate her options. In the "burning bed" case, Francine Hughes set fire to the house immediately after her partner burned her school books, symbolically closing the one area in her life he did not control. To get at this, I ask, "Were there things that you did or wanted to do that you have given up because your partner doesn't like them?" Often, moving to a new apartment or area is followed by a sharp escalation in violence because the woman is now removed from her support network. In one case, abuse became nearly fatal when the FBI relocated an abusive man who had testified in a federal drug case, forcing the woman to leave her two daughters and go underground. Victims may be so cut off from alternative sources of support and information that they conclude their abusive partner is the only one who can protect them, an example of the "Stockholm syndrome," where victims identify with their oppressors. Some victims increase their own isolation by stopping friendships, work, school, or other activities to placate the batterer. Passive-aggressive tactics can also isolate victims. In one case, a husband outwardly supported his wife's decision to return to work. But she felt compelled to quit after she found children unfed or sleeping on the living room floor when she returned home. The possessiveness or jealousy associated with isolation sometimes feels like love. When her partner said it was unhealthy to take her children to a local diner where her mother and sister worked, the woman concluded that "he wanted to make us his family."

Control

That battering is motivated by power and control is almost a cliché in the domestic violence field. But we now appreciate how often control strategies are also the primary means by which partners exact material benefits from the victim, secure privileges, circumscribe her choices, and deny her access to the means required for safety or autonomy. Three features distinguish the control tactics used in battering: They are personally tailored to a particular woman; they extend across social space as well as over time, like the "beeper game"; and they are gendered, focusing on stereotypic behaviors associated with women's default roles as caretaker and homemaker. Critical dimensions of control include

- control over money and other basic necessities (money, food, etc.)
- control over coming and going
- control over sexuality (when, where, how, with whom, etc.)
- control over access to medical care or other helpers
- control over interactions with friends, family, or children
- violations of personal boundaries (reading diaries, listening to calls)
- control over minute aspects of daily life (dress, domestic chores, etc.)
- control over how the children are disciplined
- control over how time is spent during the day

As with forms of coercion, control strategies extend to a range of microevents (from what she says on the phone to who handles the TV changer) that are too broad to encompass with specific questions. Cases in which men control material necessities (money, food, sex, medications) are common enough and can be usefully explored (and demonstrated in court) with the visual aid of the Power and Control Wheel developed by the Domestic Abuse Intervention Project (DAIP) in Duluth, Minnesota, and readily available from most shelters. Following the wheel, an expert can probe how money was handled in the household, then turn to sexuality, then access to family members, then consider how he exploited "male privilege," and so forth. Or, alternatively, the evaluator can directly ask about major survival-related resources such as "Who controlled the money in your household?" or about the regulation of basic life activities such as driving, socializing, or talking on the phone. Here too, however, what is remarkable is how trivial many regulations are. The very pointlessness of rules like how high the bed cover can be or how a woman walks or manages the TV changer can exacerbate her degradation when she obeys them. The most common focus of microregulation in coercive control is the activities identified as women's work by sex stereotypes, such as how women dress, cook, clean, and care for their children. Control should not be confused with decision making, however. In the New York case involving marital assets discussed previously, the wife was the sole source of income, hired the maids, and decided where the children went to school. The husband was content to design and build his new country estate, garden, and write his memoirs. The critical issue in identifying control is "who decides who decides what."

Evaluating a woman's access to helpers is an important piece of assessing control. Batterers frequently prevent women from seeking help, regulate their interaction with helpers, punish them for help-seeking behavior, or force them to terminate care while they are still at risk. In one case, a physician who was ashamed to have his colleagues see his wife "sick" sprayed her with Raid to cure her cancer. Then, 24 hours after surgery, he insisted she return home, where she contracted an infection and almost died.

Strategies to Prevent Violence

Most victims utilize a range of strategies to limit, minimize, resist, or escape abuse, including separation and seeking help from formal and informal sources. The evaluator catalogues these strategies and their efficacy: Whom did she tell? How, when, and with what consequences did she seek help? What did she do to avoid physical abuse? To minimize its consequences? The relative efficacy of various interventions can also help to frame her choices now. Did violence stop when she called the police in the past? Was the police response helpful or punitive (e.g., was she arrested along with her partner?)? How did her partner respond when she refused sex, left the house, or asked her nephew to sleep over? How did she get around isolation? How did she resist control? Documenting a woman's attempts to establish safety zones and the "search-and-destroy" missions on which her partner tries to enter and close these zones can help convey the degree of entrapment in a relationship. Experts should be aware that if the level of entrapment is high, resistance may go underground and be expressed only in negative ways such as suicide attempts or substance use, a pattern I term *control in the context of no control*. One client took a nearly lethal dose of pills in front of her children when her husband was following her around the house with a video camera to show "how crazy I was." While she could not control whether she was hurt, taking the pills gave her control over when and where. Providing a catalogue of their efforts at resistance can be therapeutic for clients as well as informative in court, particularly if they have internalized the view that they did nothing. By contrast with informal means to minimize or resist the violence, formal intervention is often ineffective in limiting the partner's access, a fact that explains why separation is so risky. The inappropriate, victim-blaming, or ineffective response of helpers is often an important part of a woman's entrapment.

Consequences of Battering

Documenting the consequences of battering bears on the victim's credibility, helps support assessments that battering was serious or life threatening, and supports a range of claims in civil cases, including access to mandated services, alimony, and financial liability. I would reiterate that the benefits of putting evidence of psychological debility on the record should be weighed against the stigma such evidence carries, particularly when custodial issues are concerned. In an Alabama case in which I was consulted, the husband had beaten the wife so badly that she was hospitalized for head trauma. During the custody dispute, the husband's psychiatric witness testified that the woman's IQ had been dramatically lowered by the head trauma. Concluding that the intelligence loss impugned the woman's capacity to parent, the judge ruled that it was in the best interest of the child for the father to have custody.

Apart from injury, problems attributed to abuse should be credibly linked to the research literature and should occur in reasonable proximity to abuse experiences. As in the descriptive narrative, the primary means of identifying health problems will be through the adult trauma history of all known physical consequences of abuse, regardless of whether they prompted a medical visit or produced permanent physical changes (such a loss of teeth or hair), scars, or disability. In addition to the usual bruises, abrasions, and contusions, physical symptoms with a high risk of being linked to abuse include human bites; STDs or HIV disease; chronic pain syndromes; unwanted pregnancies, miscarriage, or multiple abortions; multiple or centrally located injuries, particularly to the face, breast, or abdomen; frequent headaches or nonspecific "pain all over"; and sleep disorders, anxiety, dysphasia, hyperventilation, or other physical problems associated with chronic stress.

There is no single profile of the psychological effects of battering. Battered women's reactions run the gamut and include emotional distress (anxiety, sadness, anger); changes in beliefs and attitudes about the self, others, and the world (self-deprecation, distrust, fear of the world); and symptoms of psychological distress or dysfunction (e.g., flashbacks, sleep problems, rapid weight loss or gain). Whether a particular battered woman meets criteria for a clinical diagnosis depends heavily on her resiliency (based on family history and support systems) as well as on the types, intensity, and duration of violence, coercion, and control; the relative efficacy of adaptive and strategic responses; and the racial, social class, and cultural context. Battering is associated with a dramatically increased risk of alcoholism, drug abuse, attempted suicide, and mental illness, including psychosis, largely because victims self-medicate or attempt to escape from the chronic anxiety of living with coercive control. Even when clients have a previous history of these problems, they often escalate, going from use to abuse or addiction, for instance, in relation to the escalation of coercion and control. Functional assessments can often be key as well, particularly if current behavior is contrasted to behavior prior to the onset of abuse or in arenas where the victim is unaffected by the abuse. There is no population-based or control-study evidence that BWS or PTSD are more common than other psychological diagnoses among battered women. To the contrary, posttraumatic reactions leading to diagnoses other than PTSD (e.g., acute stress disorder, dissociative amnesia, major depressive disorder) as well as those that do not constitute classifiable psychiatric disease (e.g., shame, distrust, transient dissociative reactions) may be far more relevant.

When liability or alimony is an issue, it may also be important to assess the socioeconomic consequences of battering. Psychologically, a victim's capacity to evaluate and respond to new relationships may be compromised by a history of abuse. She may suffer low self-esteem, believe she cannot succeed at her job or in school, and lose confidence in her parenting skills. As in *Burgos v. Burgos* (1997), an abusive partner may be held liable for the costs of treatment, job retraining, or personal support where abuse prevented a woman from advancing to the level normally reached by someone with her education and experience. Even when extraneous causes of debilitation are evident (such as abuse in childhood), the expert may estimate the proportion of the problem (and the associated costs) due to the current abuse, particularly if the partner knowingly exploited the woman's vulnerability.

In many cases, "liberty harms" that involve the loss of the autonomy and freedoms taken for granted by adult citizens are the most significant results of coercive control. The costs of losing personal discretion over how one dresses, cooks, cleans, or spends one's earnings can be calculated as part of pain and suffering. Courts are often more responsive to these constraints than to physical injury or psychological problems. At the same time, the very ordinariness of the behaviors regulated by coercive control can make constraints in these areas invisible, particularly if they involve activities that are already constrained by women's sex role.

The Dynamics of Battering

Once the various elements of battering have been separately elucidated and juxtaposed to their consequences and the victim's strategies, a narrative can be constructed around the relative importance in this relationship of violence, intimidation, isolation, and control; how the interaction of these strategies changed over time; and with what consequences. This narrative bridges the gap between the abstract legal concept of "battered woman" and how coercive control was manifested in a particular relationship. Dynamics may be framed as a staged experience involving watershed events or turning points associated with a change in the pattern, frequency, or severity of abuse. In the case of Donna B., Stage I was characterized by relatively minor and infrequent assaults and ended when the couple moved to their own apartment and was isolated from the Albanian community because the husband had assaulted his mother. Deprived of supportive contacts, including her mother and sisters, Donna B.'s vulnerability increased, leading to a sharp escalation in violence and control in Stage II. In the embezzlement case, the escalation of violence led to the woman's complete isolation from her family and the extended community of support she had built at work. In Stage II, the couple lived apart. But the fear and intimidation already established permitted the boyfriend to impose his rules with only occasional physical "discipline" if she was "bad." Alternatively, dynamics may be described by summarizing each type of abuse in turn. The detailed history of a relationship is normally reserved for a report, but it can also be an extremely useful heuristic device in helping a judge or jury understand a woman's story.

The "Special Reasonableness" of Battered Women

The factors an evaluator considers to explain a woman's response to a particular abusive episode include her experiences of violence (past and present), the immediate signs of impending threat (e.g., risk factors such as the presence of weapons), lessons learned from previous attempts to avoid or limit harm, the objective constraints that constitute her degree of entrapment (e.g., her isolation, access to money, or means of protection), and behavioral problems that might limit her capacity to perceive accurately or take advantage of credible sources of help or support.

The lessons a woman learns from previous attempts to modify abuse can be presented to show the rational basis for her calculated decision to retaliate violently. A client fired at a man when he cut her off on the way to her car and put his hand in his pocket, as if to pull a gun. During the assessment, she explained that previous assaults as well as beatings by two former husbands taught her "when men want to hurt you, they can hurt you bad," helping her to anticipate what the man meant to or could do to her. Elizabeth R. was charged with first-degree assault for stabbing her boyfriend in the downstairs hallway of their apartment house. I described how, to prevent herself from being seriously hurt in the past, she had called the police, screamed for help, called neighbors, taken refuge at a neighbor's house, gone to the emergency room four times, tried to defend herself with a bottle and a golf club, changed apartments, and locked her door. At the time of the stabbing, she was waiting for her brothers to remove Mr. E. from the house. By showing that these efforts had failed to prevent Mr. E.'s escalating attacks—the police had arrested her as well as Mr. E., and he had thrown her down a flight of stairs the previous evening—her own violent act was reframed as the culmination of a rational process of learning rather than as an act of vengeance.

Unraveling the Battered Mother's Dilemma

Special challenges in evaluation are posed when experts are asked to testify in civil or family court on the effects of exposure to domestic violence on children or where a battered mother is charged in the death of her child. Such testimony occurs amid a growing literature on the risks to children who are exposed to domestic violence; mounting political pressure for child protective services (CPS) to intervene in so-called dual-victim families, where both a mother and child are put at risk by an abusive male; and a body of case law that applies the Failure to Protect Doctrine (under state neglect statutes) to nonoffending parents in these families (Stark, 1999/2000, 2002). Following the presumption that witnessing abuse harms children, CPS and the courts in many states, with New York as the leader, have instituted a policy of charging battered mothers with neglect and temporarily removing their children if it is alleged that the children witnessed the violence or were otherwise exposed to it. Because this practice revictimizes battered women, in response to a class action suit brought on behalf of battered mothers and their children in New York City, Federal Judge Jack Weinstein recently found it was unconstitutional, a decision endorsed by New York's highest court. But Judge Weinstein's decision does not remove the acute dilemmas faced when an expert is asked to weigh the disabling effects of coercive control or other abuse on a primary parent against her responsibilities to protect a child from harm.

The allegation that a woman's behavior contributed to a child's death moves the issue of how severely her choices were constrained by coercion and control to center stage. In such cases, I emphasize "the battered mother's dilemma," where an abusive partner repeatedly forces the victim to choose between her own safety and the safety of their children. A particular incident may bring this dilemma into sharp focus, as when a woman realizes that she may be hurt or killed if she attempts to protect her child from an offender's abuse. Typically, however, the battered mother's dilemma describes an ongoing facet of abusive relationships in which the offending partner repeatedly forces a victimized caretaker to choose between taking some action she believes is wrong (such as physically disciplining her child), being hurt herself, or standing by while he hurts the child. Threatening to hurt the primary caretaker if she reports domestic violence or child abuse is a classic instance of the battered mother's dilemma. A parallel dilemma occurs when the abuser shifts his focus to the child, hoping to extend his control of his partner by threatening or hurting her child, a pattern I term *child abuse as tangential spouse abuse*. Confronted with these dilemmas, victims attempt to preserve their rationality and humanity by selecting the least dangerous option, another example of control in the context of no control. Courts often replicate this dilemma by mandating women to both protect their child from domestic violence and to cooperate with their spouse in custodial or visitation arrangements.

How should an expert approach the risks domestic violence poses to children in civil cases and family court cases? To strengthen a mother's case for custody or support the prosecution of a batterer, experts may be expected to testify that domestic violence can have a range of direct and indirect effects on children's well-being. But in a dependency proceeding, they may be confronted by the situation we faced in Nicholson, where the mothers were punished because their children had been exposed to a partner's violence. In Nicholson, no harm had been demonstrated to any of the children. The best approach is probably to review the known risks to children in domestic violence cases; identify the typical dynamics in these cases; and explain the limits of knowledge in this area, which are considerable (Stark, 2002). There is compelling evidence that as many as one child in five may be hurt physically by domestic violence, some seriously, and that many more children can suffer short- or long-term psychological effects because of witnessing. At the same time, the vast majority of battered women retain their capacity to parent, and the vast majority of children exposed remain psychologically normal. Moreover, most of the psychological harms associated with exposure can be resolved with counseling or other supportive services, making removal an inappropriate response. Among the limits of current research is its failure to distinguish the effects of exposure from other environmental hazards, to identify the dosage of exposure required for harm, or to link the types of abuse employed to the types of harms children experience. Thus, although woman battering is possibly the most common context for child abuse and neglect, a case-specific assessment is required to determine whether a particular child has been harmed, or is likely to be harmed, by exposure to abuse. Even in this case, the harms must be weighed against the trauma of removal, a particular problem in abuse cases where children may already blame themselves for a mother's problems.

Assessing Risk

Experts may be asked for a risk assessment at any phase of a criminal or civil process or to help courts select an instrument to predict future violence by offenders against female partners and/or children. Although several promising instruments are currently being tested, there is little published research on the reliability and validity of these tools (Dutton & Kropp, 2000). These tools are designed only to predict subsequent partner violence. So they have little predictive value for coercive control, the most common context in which women seek help. More important, since as many as 80% of perpetrators reassault their original or other partners even after an arrest or the completion of a batterer's intervention program, the most conservative assumption is that all abusive partners will reoffend unless there are compelling checks on their doing so. If anything, because they neglect the range of strategies deployed to oppress women, these instruments overestimate false negatives; that is, they falsely predict abuse will not reoccur in situations where it will, an important limitation. Even when a test is employed, the consensus is that its utility depends on the use of multiple methods and sources, such as those reviewed here.

If risk assessments are relatively unhelpful in predicting whether abuse will reoccur, they can help estimate the level of risk involved. Because the battered mother's dilemma and child abuse as tangential spouse abuse are linked at every point to coercive control, the same factors that predict a mother's level of risk can be applied to the risks faced by children. A promising generic tool is the Spousal Assault Risk Assessment or SARA (Kropp, Hart, Webster, & Eaves, 1998). The SARA is a set of guidelines comprised of 20 items identified by the empirical literature and designed to enhance professional judgment about risk. Since the SARA is not a test (although it includes an analysis of psychological data), it can be used by the nonclinician. The procedure recommended includes interviews with the partner and the victim, standardized measures of physical and emotional abuse, histories of drug and alcohol abuse, and a review of collateral records.

I frequently use risk assessment to help establish the level of danger a defendant faced at the time she used violence against her partner. Psychologist Angela Browne (1987) identified several factors that distinguished women who killed abusive partners from those who did not, including the level and frequency of physical and sexual violence they faced, the batterer's use of drugs and alcohol, the presence of weapons in the household, and the propensity for their partners to threaten or use violence against others, including their children. Another useful instrument is the Danger Assessment (DA) Scale (Campbell, 1995; Campbell et al., 2005) developed to predict spousal homicide around "women's perception of the danger of being killed by their partners." Although the DA has been shown to predict short-term misdemeanor assault with some accuracy (Goodman, Dutton, & Bennett, 2000), its credibility in predicting homicide is still unknown. Based on a multicity study of partner homicide, Glass, Manganello, and Campbell (2004) found that the assailant's access to firearms was the most important risk factor for femicide, particularly if the man had threatened to kill the victim in the past. But two factors unique to relationships also predicted fatality: whether the couple had separated after having lived together, and whether an abuser was highly controlling in addition to being violent. When these factors were combined, the chance that an abused woman would be killed by her partner was nine times higher than when these factors were not present. These same factors are unlikely to predict partner homicides by women.

Based on this evidence, research with abusive men, and my own experience with victims of coercive control, I have distilled the overall factors considered in evaluating the existence and dynamics of coercive control into those that, whether alone or in combination, appear to dramatically increase the chance that battering will culminate in a death. I find it useful to consider the current situation separately from the contribution of past battering. With respect to past violence, the key risk factors considered are

- presence and/or use of a weapon
- sexual abuse
- chronic drug and/or alcohol abuse
- violence against the partner outside the home
- threats to kill (or belief she will be killed)
- control over all aspects of her life
- total or near total isolation from family members, friends, or helping professionals
- denial of food, money, clothes, or other necessities
- paranoid, homicidal, or jealous fantasies
- monitoring or stalking the victim

- violence against children, other family members, or pets
- serial abuse

With respect to the current situation, the factors I assess as high risk include whether the perpetrator is

- depressed or paranoid.
- obsessed with the victim.
- threatening to commit suicide.
- stalking or monitoring the victim.

The victim is

- separated from the perpetrator or considering separation.
- seriously thinking about killing the perpetrator.
- fearful she or the children will be seriously hurt or killed.

Recent changes in the relationship indicating high risk include

- sudden escalation (or change) in the pattern, severity, or frequency of assaults, isolation, intimidation, emotional abuse, or control.
- the introduction of a weapon into the house.
- a recent attack involving the threat of homicide.
- a recent violation of a restraining order.
- the extension of abuse to children.

Tabulating a score based on the number of risk factors presented allows comparison with other cases and a statement of relative risk that supports the client's perceptions or fears.

Assessing Validity

Because the client interview is often the primary source of evidence that battering occurred, the court, as well as opposing counsel, may ask whether and why the expert finds the woman a credible source of information. In lieu of independent corroboration, the expert can establish credibility with a reasonable scientific certainty based only on the external and internal validity of her story. With respect to external validity, the paramount question is whether the pattern of violence and control depicted is consistent with what is known about the dynamics in abusive situations, the personality and behavior of batterers, or the consequences of battering. In testimony, the evaluator may review basic knowledge about battering, and then show why the material provided in the interview was consistent with this knowledge. Consistency between the narrative account and documents reporting specific episodes or witness accounts also helps to validate descriptions of other facets of abuse that are undocumented. But expert assessment never hinges on the occurrence of a single abusive episode. Even setting aside the defense mechanisms that lead victims to minimize or blame themselves for abuse, the complexity and duration of domestic violence often makes it impossible to reconstruct the actual sequence or nature of events. Instead, the major focus of evidence gathering is on the pattern or course of abusive conduct; on routine or typical incidents; and on strategies used to coerce and control victims, as well as to hurt them physically. Clients may mislead even a skilled interviewer about particular episodes. But they are extremely unlikely to simulate credibly a lengthy course of conduct that resembles coercive control. To assess internal validity, I repeat key questions during the interview; look for repetition in word patterns and phrases (which suggest a story is rehearsed); and consider whether victims accept responsibility for their role in events, admit their own acts of aggression or violence, and recall extraneous details of traumatic events. Throughout an evaluation, I make the conservative assumption that the partner would provide an account of events that is diametrically opposed to the account provided by the victim.

Conclusion

Early work on women's self-defense stressed the positive role that expert testimony might play at trial in complementing the defendant's testimony and making her particular experience plausible to a jury. More recently, however, even sympathetic commentators have questioned whether its benefits in specific cases are worth the risk that expert testimony on battering and its effects will replace rather than support women's voices in the courtroom. One way this can happen is by substituting "a statistically derived average experience that women typically share for the detailed, potentially idiosyncratic experiences each of us has" (Scheppele quoted in Schneider, 2000, p. 106). To the extent that the court relies on an expert to provide a window on common experiences, the authority and credibility of women as witnesses to their own experience may be reduced, a possibility reflected in the popular conceit that battering occurs behind closed doors (i.e., without a credible witness). The ambiguous political status of expert testimony is further reinforced by the dominant psychological models of abuse used in defense cases. Indeed, to the extent that the BWS and PTSD models lend the imprimatur of science to images of female dependence, pathology, and incapacity, they replicate the dilemmas that confronted battered women who killed abusers in the past. This approach to woman battering accommodates an obvious social wrong—violence against women—without threatening, indeed by reproducing and even extending, the prevailing sexual hierarchy based on male dominance. Employing the coercive control model resolves some of these dilemmas.

Experts who define their role as a hired gun or, alternatively, as that of a value-neutral forensic scientist may not face ethical dilemmas in cases where a victim's expressed wishes appear to conflict with her best interest. For the rest of us, however, it is often difficult to decide how best to support a woman's voice in the legal setting, particularly when the state requests expert testimony to discount a victim's recantation or refusal to testify. Here, the basic tenet of noninterference with a victim's choices must be weighed against our civic obligation to protect vulnerable others from harm, secure the basic rights and liberties of all citizens, and uphold standards of community justice. After weighing these issues against the limited facts at my disposal, I chose to testify in *State v. Borrelli* but refused the state's request to testify in lieu of an immigrant woman who had been dragged from her workplace by the boyfriend on whom she depended for her residency permit and eventual citizenship.

Another challenge faced by the expert witness is to help the judge and jury walk in the shoes of a woman when the class or cultural underpinnings that frame her decision making are foreign, perhaps even alien, to their own. Moreover, suspicion is warranted of "cultural experts" who suggest that abuse is normal or accepted in certain traditions without exposing the patriarchal origins of these norms. Fortunately, the diversity of the battered women's movement allows us to identify indigenous experts and translators who are also sensitive to nuances in cultural beliefs. Even so, what is decisive is how a particular woman perceives her reality and at what point she draws the line between widely accepted forms of deference and abuse.

Some find the drama that attends a court appearance the hardest part of their role as experts, including having to endure mean-spirited cross-examinations, simulate a level of certainty that is unfamiliar to researchers, or provide an objective appraisal that differs markedly from the stand one would assume as an advocate. If helping a client you believe is legally innocent avoid painful jail time is gratifying, it can be personally devastating when a client you have come to know and care about is convicted, goes to jail, or loses custody of her children to a man you believe will hurt them.

The battered women in whose cases experts become involved have suffered extensive, sometimes shocking harms. In reporting these harms, the expert merely reflects his or her experience. But in asking the court to set aside its judgments, both its harsh assessments of "women like these" or its stereotypic imagery of victimhood and psychological dysfunction, the expert also does something more, asking judge and jury to enter the client's world, suspend their pity, and step inside her life to discover what she is struggling to defend as well as to avoid or escape. The expert should try to portray not merely the suffering this woman endured, but the incredible courage she mustered to survive it, and not merely how she was hurt, but what she could be had she not been subjected to coercion and control. If, despite the seeming totality of their oppression, battered women nonetheless regain a sense of control in the court context, this is because their story has been reconstructed and authenticated through what Herman (1992) terms "the alliance of victim and witness." Whatever the outcome of a case, in simply joining in this alliance, the expert witness puts the survivor of abuse in touch with a larger social context in which, by respecting the reality as she has lived it, her right to safety and independence is affirmed.

NOTES

1. The first case to recognize that the subject matter of woman battering was beyond the ken of the average juror was a 1977 Washington, D.C., case, *Ibn-Tamas v. United States*.
2. Still, according to a review (Parrish, 1995) of state policies, 25% of the states have required some evidence that battered woman syndrome is accepted in the scientific community in order to admit the testimony, while 33% of the states have explicitly required that the proffered expert must be properly qualified as such.
3. On the other hand, 18 states have also excluded expert testimony in some cases; of these, there is still doubt under case law about its admissibility only in Wyoming (Parrish, 1996).

4. A comprehensive search conducted in 1995 by the National Clearinghouse for the Defense of Battered Women for the Women Judges' Fund for Justice located over 350 cases (Parrish, 1996). The database included 238 state court (primarily appellate) decisions, 31 federal court (mostly appellate) decisions, 30 trial court-level cases, 12 appellate decisions on pretrial motions, 13 civil actions, and 31 cases involving prosecution of batterers or male defendants charged with sexual assault where expert testimony on battering or sexual assault was discussed in court. The fact that the research largely excluded local court and civil cases suggests that the actual number of cases where expert testimony has been an issue is probably in the thousands.
5. More than 25% of the states have found an expert can give an opinion on the "ultimate question" for the fact finder of reasonableness or whether the defendant acted in self-defense. But a larger group of states (37%) have held to the contrary.
6. Only Minnesota has found explicitly to the contrary.

RESOURCES AND REFERENCES

American Psychiatric Association. (1994). *Diagnostic and statistical manual of mental disorders* (4th ed.). Washington, DC: Author.

Bancroft, L. (2002). *Why does he do that? Inside the minds of angry and controlling men.* New York: Putnam.

Blackman, J. (1986). Potential uses for expert testimony: Ideas towards the representation of battered women who kill. *Women's Rights Law Reporter, 9,* 227–237.

Bochnak, E. (Ed.). (1981). *Women's self-defense cases: Theory and practice.* Charlottesville, VA: Michie Law Publishers.

Browne, A. (1987). *When battered women kill.* New York: Free Press.

Burgos v. Burgos, WL 120300 (Conn. Super. Ct. 1997).

Campbell, J. C. (1995). Prediction of homicide of and by battered women. In J. C. Campbell (Ed.), *Assessing dangerousness: Violence by sexual offenders, batterers and child abusers* (pp. 96–113). Thousand Oaks, CA: Sage.

Campbell, J., Webster, D., Koziol-McLean, J., Block, C., Campbell, D., Curry, M. A., et al. (2005). *Assessing risk factors for intimate partner homicide.* Washington, DC: National Institute of Justice.

Campbell, J. C., Sharps, P. W., & Glass, N. (2000). Risk assessment for intimate partner violence. In G. Pinard & L. Pagani (Eds.), *Clinical assessment of dangerousness: Empirical contributions* (pp. 136–157). New York: Cambridge University Press.

Commonwealth v. Goetzendanner, 679 N.E.2d 1362 (Mass. Ct. App. 1997).

Daubert v. Merrell Dow Pharmaceuticals, Inc., 61 LW 4807–8 (1993).

Dershowitz, A. M. (1994). *The abuse excuse and other cop-outs, sob stories, and evasions of responsibility.* New York: Little, Brown.

Downs, D. (1996). *More than victims: Battered women, the syndrome society, and the law.* Chicago: University of Chicago Press.

Dutton, D. G., & Kropp, P. R. (2000). A review of domestic violence risk instruments. *Trauma, Violence, & Abuse, 1*(2), 171–181.

Dutton, M. A. (1993). Understanding women's response to domestic violence: A redefinition of battered women's syndrome. *Hofstra Law Review, 21*(4), 1191–1242.

Dutton, M. A. (1996). *The validity and use of evidence concerning battering and its effects in criminal trials: A report to Congress under the Violence Against Women Act.* Washington, DC: U.S. Department of Justice, National Institute of Justice, and U.S. Department of Health and Human Services, National Institute of Mental Health.

Ewing, C. P. (1987). *Battered women who kill: Psychological self-defense as legal justification.* Lexington, MA: DC Heath.

Frye v. United States, 293 F. 1013 (D.C. Cir. 1923).

Gellespi, C. (1989). *Justifiable homicide: Battered women, self-defense and the law.* Columbus: Ohio State University Press.

Glass, N., Manganello, J., & Campbell, J. C. (2004). Risk for intimate partner femicide in violent relationships, *DV Report 9*(2), 1, 2, 30–33.

Goodman, L. A., Dutton, M. A., & Bennett, L. (2000). Predicting repeat abuse among arrested batterers. *Journal of Interpersonal Violence, 15,* 63–74.

Herman, J. L. (1992). *Trauma and recovery.* New York: Basic Books.

Ibn-Tamas v. United States, 407 A.2d 626 (D.C. 1979).

In re Betty J. W. et al., 179 W.Va. 605, 371 S.E.2d 326 (1988).

Johnson, M. (1995). Patriarchal terrorism and common couple violence: Two forms of violence against women. *Journal of Marriage and the Family, 57,* 283–294.

Johnson, M. P. (2001). Conflict and control: Symmetry and asymmetry in domestic violence. In A. Booth, A. Crouter, & M. Clements (Eds.), *Couples in conflict.* Mahwah, NJ: Lawrence Erlbaum Associates.

Jones, A. (1980). *Women who kill.* New York: Fawcett Columbine.

Jones, A. (1994). *Next time, she'll be dead: Battering & how to stop it.* Boston: Beacon Press.

Jones, A., & Schecter, S. (1992). *When love goes wrong.* New York: Harper Collins.

Jones, R. (2000). Guardianship for coercively controlled battered women: Breaking the control of the abuser. *Georgetown Law Journal, 88,* 605–657.

Knock v. Knock, 224 Conn. 776, 621 A.2d 267 (1993).

Kropp, P. R., Hart, S. D., Webster, C. W., & Eaves, D. (1998). *Spousal assault risk assessment: User's guide.* Toronto, Canada: Multi-health Systems.

Lehrman, F. (1996). Elements of interpersonal domestic violence torts: Some non-traditional alternatives. *Domestic Violence Report, 3,* 4.

Maguigan, H. (1991). Battered women and self-defense: Myths and misconceptions in current reform proposals. *University of Pennsylvania Law Review, 140,* 379–384.

Mahoney, M. (1991). Legal images of battered women: Redefining the issue of separation. *Michigan Law Review, 90*(1), 24–30.

McCord, D. (1987). Syndromes, profiles and other mental exotica: A new approach to the admissibility of nontraditional psychological evidence in criminal cases." *Oregon Law Review, 66,* p. 19.

McCord, D. (1990). Evidence of syndromes: No need for a 'better mousetrap. *South Texas Law Review, 37,* 67–69.

McNulty, F. (1980). *The burning bed.* New York: Harcourt, Brace, Jovanovich.

Meier, J. S. (1993). Notes from the underground: Integrating psychological and legal perspectives on domestic violence in theory and practice. *Hofstra Law Review, 21*(4), 1295–1366.

Okun, L. (1986). *Woman abuse: Facts replacing myths.* Albany: State University of New York Press.

Ostoff, S. (1995). Introduction. In J. Parrish (Ed.), *Trend analysis: Expert testimony on battering and its effects in criminal cases.* Philadelphia: National Clearing House for the Defense of Battered Women.

Parrish, J. (1996). Trend analysis: Expert testimony on battering and its effects in criminal cases. *Wisconsin Women's Law Journal, 11*(1), 75, 102–127.

People v. Daoust, 577 N. W.2d 179 (Mich. Ct. App. 1998).

Perry, A. L., & Lemon, N. K. D. (1998). State court decisions regarding the use of battered woman's syndrome testimony. *Domestic Violence Report, 3*(3), 35–42.

Roberts, A. R. (1981). *Sheltering battered women: A national study and service guide.* New York: Springer.

Schechter, S. (1987). *Guidelines for mental health practitioners in domestic violence cases.* Washington, DC: National Coalition Against Domestic Violence.

Schneider, E. (2000). *Battered women & feminist lawmaking.* New Haven: Yale University Press.

Shepard, M., & Campbell, J. (1992). The abusive behavior inventory: A measure of psychological and physical abuse. *Journal of Interpersonal Violence, 7*(3), 291–305.

Stark, E. (1995). Re-presenting woman battering: From battered woman syndrome to coercive control. *Albany Law Review, 58,* 101–156.

Stark, E. (1999/2000). A failure to protect: Unraveling "the battered mother's dilemma." *Western State University Law Review, 27,* 29–110.

Stark, E. (2002). The battered mother in the child protective service caseload: Developing an appropriate response. *Women's Rights Law Reporter 23*(2), 107–131.

State v. Borrelli, 227 Conn. 153, 629 A.2d 1105 (1993).

State v. Kelly, 97 NJ 178, 478 A.2d 364 (1984).

State v. Smith, 198 W.Va. 441, 481 S.E.2d 747 (1996).

Strong, W. (1999). *McCormick's handbook on the law of evidence.* New York: West Publishing.

Thyfault, R., Browne, A., & Walker, L. E. (1987). When battered women kill: Evaluation and expert witness testimony techniques. In D. J. Sonkin (Ed.), *Domestic violence on trial: Psychological and legal dimensions of family violence* (pp. 71–85). New York: Springer.

U.S. v. Ezeiruaku (D. NJ, 1995). WL 263983 (1995).

Walker, L. (1979). *The battered woman.* New York: Harper & Row.

Walker, L. (1984). *The battered woman syndrome.* New York: Springer.

Walker, L. (1989). *Terrifying love: Why battered women kill and how society responds.* New York: HarperCollins.

Walker, L. (1991). Post-traumatic stress disorder in women: Diagnosis and treatment of battered woman syndrome. *Psychotherapy, 28,* 21–29.

Westervelt, S. A. (1999). *Shifting the blame: How victimization became a criminal defense.* Piscataway, NJ: Rutgers University Press.

Wilson, K., Varcella, R., Brems, C., Benning, D. & Renfro, N. (1992). Levels of learned helplessness in abused women. *Women and Therapy, 13,* 53–67.

The Role of the Forensic Social Worker in Developing Mitigation Evidence

6

John P. Niland

I he education and training of the social worker can bring great value to the courtroom in helping to ensure that any punishment that is assessed for both capital and noncapital crimes is suitably individualized to the person charged with the crime. Beginning with the psycho–social history, the forensic social worker can help the defense trial team develop mitigating evidence that will not provide an excuse for the criminal act, but can help the jury understand the behavior of the offender.

While the education and training of the social worker can provide an understanding of the social, cultural and mental health issues involved in humanizing the client and explaining behavior, it is important to note that mitigation work is not social work. The social worker who becomes a mitigation specialist must operate under the norms and ethical guidelines applicable to those who are defending a person charged with a capital crime. To the extent there is a conflict, the norms and guidelines of those defending the criminally accused must control.

The Concept of Mitigating Evidence

Mitigating evidence is anything that can justify a more lenient sentence. In the context of a death penalty case, effective mitigating evidence can spell the difference between life and death. In the noncapital case, mitigating evidence can be used to support a sentence that the defense feels is appropriate in light of the mitigation offered. The mitigation may justify a lower sentence, a deferred sentence, or a probated sentence. While mitigating evidence is most often used during the punishment phase of a trial, or prior to judicial sentencing, the evidence can be extremely useful in determining the client's level of culpability, if any, in the guilt/innocence phase of the trial.

The concept of mitigating evidence finds its roots in the Eighth Amendment to the U.S. Constitution. This portion of the Bill of Rights prohibits the imposition of Cruel and Unusual Punishment. Certainly punishment that is not proportioned to the crime violates the Eighth Amendment (*Atkins v. Virginia*, 2002). It is difficult, if not impossible, for the criminal justice system to make punishment proportional to the crime unless the judge or jury setting the punishment has before it all evidence that is relevant to punishment. This is all evidence that can justify a more lenient sentence or, in the context of a death penalty case, "any circumstance that a juror can use to justify a sentence of life" (*Tennard v. Dretke*, 2004).

Some Eighth Amendment Jurisprudence

The Eighth Amendment cases that have been decided by the U.S. Supreme Court have provided guidance to legislatures, judges, and lawyers as to the appropriate scope of mitigating evidence. In *Lockett v. Ohio* (1978), the Court held that a statute that did not permit a judge or jury to consider all aspects of the defendant's character, record, or circumstances of the offense in a death penalty case violated the Eighth Amendment. The Court later ruled that the refusal of a judge to consider the family history of a 16-year-old murder defendant as a mitigating factor in imposition of the death penalty violated the Eighth Amendment requirement that all relevant factors must be considered (*Eddings v. Oklahoma*, 1982). The exclusion in a capital sentencing hearing of testimony of jailers and others that during his incarceration, before trial, the defendant had adjusted well to prison life violated the accused's right to present all relevant evidence in mitigation (*Skipper v. South Carolina*, 1986).

What can be reasonably inferred from these decisions is that there has been a body of mitigating evidence that is mitigating as a matter of law; that is, each juror must be able to consider this evidence when deciding if a defendant will live or die. The *Tennard* (2004) decision cited previously is important for several reasons. First, the Court strongly disapproved of the "nexus" or relationship requirement that had been put in place by the Texas Court of Criminal Appeals and the Fifth Circuit Court of the United States. These courts held that a defendant must be able to establish a nexus between the mitigating evidence and the facts of the crime. In other words, if the evidence does not tend to show why the defendant committed the crime, it is not admissible. While the ability to show such a nexus can be very persuasive, there should be no requirement that such a relationship must be shown before the evidence is admissible. As seen in *Skipper* (1986), positive adjustment to incarceration has no nexus to the crime, but it is still relevant to sentencing and should be admitted when available.

As can be seen by the Supreme Court opinions cited previously, lower state courts have not been accepting of a broad interpretation of the permissible scope of mitigating evidence. This concept may be best described in *McCoy v. North Carolina* (1988) when the court said:

> Under our decisions, it is not relevant whether the barrier to the sentencer's considera-
> tion of all mitigating evidence is interposed by statute, *Lockett v. Ohio, supra, Hitchcock
> v. Dugger,* 481 U.S. 393 (1987); by the sentencing court, *Eddings v. Oklahoma, supra;*

or by an evidentiary ruling, *Skipper v. South Carolina, supra*. The same must be true with respect to a single juror's holdout vote against finding the presence of a mitigating circumstance. Whatever the cause... the conclusion would necessarily be the same: Because the [sentencer's] failure to consider all of the mitigating evidence risks erroneous imposition of the death sentence, in plain violation of *Lockett*, it is our duty to remand this case for resentencing. *Eddings v. Oklahoma*, 455 U.S., at 117.

The Human Side of Mitigation

Scharlette Holdman, Ph.D., is executive director of the Center for Capital Assistance in San Francisco, California, a nonprofit organization dedicated to providing assistance to defense counsel at all stages in capital litigation. In remarks she gave to the Inter-American Court on November 20, 2001, Dr. Holdman explained the concept of mitigation:

> Mitigating factors stem from the diverse frailties of humankind and are presented to the sentencer to provide insight into the offender's behavior. Mitigation is complex and multifaceted. Theories of mitigation are governed by principles of individualized sentencing and allow for great variation in the information presented to and considered by the sentencer. Mitigation evidence is based on respect for the uniqueness of the individual and requires thoughtful presentation of the character and record of the offender. It covers all relevant facets of the character and record of the individual in order to minimize the risk that the death penalty will be imposed in spite of factors that call for a less severe penalty. It is based on the constellation of factors that were formative in the offender's development, behavior and functioning. Although most mitigation evidence focuses on the offender, it also reflects the nature and circumstances of the offense under the theory that punishment should be proportionate to the offense.
>
> Circumstances of the offense often shed light on an otherwise inexplicable act and call for a penalty less severe than death. Theories of mitigation are governed by principles of individualized sentencing and allow for greater variation in the information presented to and considered by the sentencer. (Holdman, 2001)

Mitigation Themes

The law says that no limitation can be set on the scope of mitigating evidence that can be placed before the jury, so the mitigation themes that may explain the client's behavior are virtually limitless. These themes might involve the dynamics of the family before, during, and after the birth of the client; social and cultural influences in the client's environment; and physical and mental health issues.

While mitigating evidence is not limited to that which explains the client's role in the offense, the most effective evidence will explain the client's behavior before, during, and after the time of the crime. The U.S. Department of Justice has published a meta-analysis of 66 studies that told of research into predictors of violence in the community. The results of the analysis were separated into the categories of individual risk factors, family risk factors, and neighborhood and community risk factors. The study identified the following risk factors in these categories.

Risk Factors for Violence Activity

Individual Risk Factors

These include hyperactivity, concentration problems, restlessness, risk taking, aggressiveness, early initiation of violent behavior, and beliefs and attitudes favorable to deviant or antisocial behavior.

Family Risk Factors

These include parental criminality, child maltreatment, poor family management practices, low levels of parental involvement, poor family bonding, family conflict, residential mobility, parental attitudes favorable to substance abuse and violence, and parent–child separation.

School Risk Factors

These include academic failure, low bonding to school, truancy and dropping out of school, frequent school transitions, and high-delinquency-rate schools.

Peer Risk Factors

These include delinquent siblings, delinquent peers, and gang membership.

Community/Neighborhood Risk Factors

These include poverty, community disorganization (crime, drug selling, poor housing), availability of drugs and firearms, neighborhood adults involved in crime, exposure to violence, and racial prejudice.

It is sobering to review these risk factors and realize that the client has little, if any, control over most of these risk factors. Clients often lead lives that are chosen for them by someone else.

The forensic social worker will likely become involved in the criminal case by working either for the prosecution as a victim liaison or for the defense as a mitigation specialist. This chapter deals with a forensic social worker serving the defense function as a mitigation specialist. So that the reader can see how important the forensic social worker is to the process, the optimum way of developing mental health evidence will be described, with an emphasis on the mitigation specialist's contribution to this important aspect of the litigation.

The mitigation specialist's role as a member of the capital trial team is emphasized. However, it is important to remember that the mitigation specialist can be extremely helpful in the noncapital case as well. Mitigation evidence will be developed for a noncapital case that proceeds to trial, or it can be used as the basis for an alternative sentencing plan when counsel is asking for a deferred sentence or probation. The Fifth Circuit Court of Appeals has held that a lawyer who fails to develop mental health evidence adequately for presentation during the punishment phase of a noncapital trial does not provide the effective assistance of counsel that is guaranteed by the Sixth Amendment to the U.S. Constitution (*Miller v. Dretke*, 2005).

Developing Mental Health Evidence

It is rare that defense counsel will encounter a case of capital murder that does not present issues involving the mental health of the client. For many years it was the practice, of both seasoned and novice attorneys, to develop mental health evidence by delegating the task to a psychologist or a psychiatrist with requests such as "go shrink my client," "run a full battery of tests," or even "go see the client and let me know what my defense is." With this admonition, the mental health professional would often approach the task from a therapeutic standpoint. A number of different standardized tests would be administered just as if the psychologist was beginning the process of diagnosis and treatment. The tests, while often producing valuable information for the trial team, would often generate information that was either useless or damaging. Counsel was then presented with a difficult choice: "Do I use both the valuable and the damaging evidence, or do I go to trial without mental health testimony at all?"

The defense of one charged with a serious crime is generally not an exercise in treatment. While the good defense lawyer will not want his or her client to suffer needlessly from the consequences of mental problems and will make sure that mental health needs are attended to, the goal of the representation is to defend the client within the context of the criminal justice system. Accordingly, a litigation approach, rather than a therapeutic approach, to the evaluation is critical. The mental health evidence must be developed incrementally beginning with a thorough social history, not with a battery of standardized tests.

The case for developing mental health evidence incrementally, beginning with the preparation of a social history, has been advanced by both the U.S. Supreme Court and the American Bar Association. The Court, in the 7–2 decision in *Wiggins v. Smith* (2003), reaffirmed the importance of the social history in the representation of one charged with a serious crime. In this truly important decision, the Court once again recognized the importance of national standards, such as the *American Bar Association Guidelines for the Appointment and Performance of Counsel in Death Penalty Cases* (2003), as "guidelines to determining what is reasonable" (*Wiggins v. Smith*, 2003).

A well-presented mental health case should include evidence from both expert and lay witnesses. Lay witnesses can describe any strange behaviors exhibited by the client, as well as the traumatic abuses suffered by the client before the crime, that were observed by the witness firsthand. It is vital, however, to then explain to the jury how these events or behaviors elucidate the client's conduct and mitigate his or her moral blameworthiness for the offense. This important explanation can often be made only through the presentation of expert testimony. An expert can take powerful lay testimony about physical and sexual abuse, mental illness, or disability and paint the picture for the jury. The expert can help the jurors see why each should not stop with just feeling sorry for the counsel's client; they must be persuaded to spare his or her life.

The terms *mental health evidence* and *mitigation evidence* are sometimes used together or interchangeably in this chapter; that is, they are often one and the same. Both types of evidence help to explain who the client is, why he or she might have done what the state charges, and justify an appropriate sentence other than death in the capital case. Mental health and mitigation evidence help counsel develop a theory of defense at the guilt/innocence phase and a theory for life (or reduced sentence) at the punishment phase of a trial.

The first people hired, in preparation for a capital trial, should be investigators—one to begin the fact investigation and one to compile the client's life history. Thorough fact and mitigation investigations must be done so that counsel can make the necessary informed decisions about what additional experts may be needed as well as what the theories and themes of mitigation should be. Furthermore, making decisions about the direction of a case too early, and without the necessary investigation into the client's background and circumstances of the offense, will often lead to counsel missing important facts that can help in both the guilt/innocence phase as well as the penalty phase.

While more and more lawyers are effectively using mitigation specialists in both capital and noncapital cases, an often dangerous practice is developing. A psychologist may insist on performing the mitigation investigation in addition to serving as a consulting and/or testifying expert. While the psychologist may claim that it is unethical to do his or her job without personally doing the mitigation investigation, the expert in this situation may be wearing too many hats. The problematic consequences of this practice are (a) learning facts during the investigation that compromise the expert's ability to testify and (b) billing at the psychologist's rate for work that can be done at a much lower rate, thus depleting funds that the court will allow for the case. While a denied motion for funding may provide a reasonably good issue on appeal, counsel is generally better off conserving the funding and doing the job right in the first place.

While there may be less risk in the consulting (i.e., nontestifying) psychologist performing the mitigation investigation, this practice is not without its problems. Counsel may still face the funding problem identified previously. However, a greater problem is the lack of familiarity that the psychologist may have with critical social and cultural issues that are relevant to the client's life. Too much emphasis may be placed on mental health issues to the detriment of the social and cultural factors that can be discovered by someone who understands these issues.

It is suggested that a far better practice is to hire a mitigation specialist, often a master of social work (MSW) or licensed clinical social worker (LCSW), and a consulting mental health expert who, along with the other members of the trial team, choose those experts who will ultimately testify before the jury. Needless to say, counsel should also be very careful about using the same expert to both consult and testify. These experts usually serve two different roles, as will be explained later in this chapter.

After counsel has received feedback from the initial investigations of both the fact and mitigation investigators, he or she will need to consider the wide variety of experts who can be used to develop and present the mitigation case—the case for life. For example, if it is discovered that the client was under the influence of drugs or alcohol at the time of the crime, a pharmacologist, toxicologist, or psychopharmacologist can first describe, in laypersons' terms, the quantity of drugs and alcohol in the system. The witness can then explain to the jury the effects this quantity has on the brain and how it influenced the client at the time of the offense. The drugs and/or alcohol likely create a different person. Should the client be addicted to or dependent on drugs or alcohol, the neurobiology of addiction should be explained.

The practitioner may find that the client has been intoxicated for much of his or her life. The practitioner should consider consulting with a neurologist or neuropsychologist to conduct tests (brain imaging by the neurologist and standardized tests by the neuropsychologist) for brain damage resulting from this drug abuse or dependence. The practitioner might also consider consulting with someone to explain what addiction will do to the client's personality, way of life, and thought processes, aside from the changes occurring in the brain as a result of drug dependence. Furthermore, the client's substance abuse or dependence may be a form of self-medication used to block a traumatic event, such as sexual abuse, from his or her memory. Drugs and alcohol may be the client's method of coping with tragic events with which he or she cannot otherwise deal.

Without proper investigation into (and understanding of) the facts of both the offense and the client's life, counsel is likely to make the mistake of treating the client as "just an alcoholic," "just a drug addict," "just plain mean," or "just plain crazy."

Give the Experts the Relevant Materials They Need

Regardless of what kind of experts are retained, counsel must provide them with the relevant information and guidance necessary to develop the evidence that tests and advances the theory of the case. This information will generally be relevant medical records, psychiatric records, records from child protective services, and school records. Unfortunately, some doctors perform these important psychological assessments without reference to these important records. Counsel is likely familiar with the drive-by examination in which the expert talks to the accused for 15 minutes and arrives at a conclusion. This is done without the benefit of (a) an adequate psychosocial history; (b) a thorough physical exam; (c) necessary neurological exams; or (d) information from other sources that will supplement, contradict, or confirm a history given by the client. The quality of the opinion will be determined by the quality of the examiner and the information used to form that examiner's opinion.

The accused in a criminal case is generally not a good historian. The client may not remember important events in his or her medical and psychiatric history. He or she may be in denial about past trauma and its effects and may not think that an abusive situation is important enough to tell the mitigation investigator. The abuse was a normal part of his or her life, so why would anyone be interested in that? Denial or suppression can be a form of coping with trauma. Discussion of the trauma could be embarrassing. Why would anyone want to talk about that kind of thing with a virtual stranger? For a good discussion of these and other mental health issues, see Blume (2002).

Counsel can help the examiner—even one chosen by the prosecution—to reach the right conclusion by making sure that the relevant records are considered by the examiner prior to forming the opinion. The following description is a real-life example of how this process can work: Michael was charged in a felony court with a serious sexual assault on an infant. Michael was a person with mental retardation. He had a very low IQ and suffered from impaired adaptive functioning since childhood. The records all supported this history as well as the legal conclusion that Michael was a person with mental retardation and not competent to stand trial. There was also the issue of whether or not Michael, at the time of the offense, understood that what he did was wrong.

The trial court ordered an evaluation when the motion raising Michael's competency was filed. George R. Sornberger, trial division director of Kentucky's Department of Public Advocacy (DPA) and one of Michael's attorneys, with the help of a consulting psychologist, gathered together Michael's records and forwarded them to the state psychologists performing the evaluation. These evaluators rarely concluded that a defendant was not competent to stand trial. However, faced with the mountain of records that supported that exact conclusion, the psychologists concluded that Michael was indeed a person with mental retardation and that he was not competent to stand trial. After reading the report from the psychiatrists, the prosecution moved to dismiss the indictment against Michael.

Michael lived in squalid conditions prior to being jailed for the described offense. Mental impairments were a part of the fabric of Michael's family. After his case was disposed of, he was removed from his tar-paper shack of a home, which lacked indoor plumbing. He then was placed in a comfortable assisted-living facility, where he lives today.

If the client has been the subject of prior testing by a mental health professional, an evaluating expert, a consultant and/or testifying expert not only should have the test results and the examiner's report, but also receive what is referred to as the *raw data*. Raw data may include all recordings, notes, and test protocols relating to prior tests. This raw data will allow counsel's expert to tell if the tests were administered and scored properly. The procedure for the handling of raw data is covered by the ethical principles governing the practice of psychology (American Psychological Association, 2002b).

The customary procedure is for the raw data to go directly from the test giver to the expert and not directly to the attorney. The test givers are understandably protective of these standardized tests. There is a concern that if the tests enter the public domain not only may the copyright be violated, but also the tests could be studied with the obvious resulting problems (Drogin, 2000).

Informing the Expert About the Law

Counsel should never assume that the expert will know precisely what to do in a given capital case without guidance from the trial team. Some mental health experts and lawyers assume that the experts have a full understanding of the criminal law applicable to the case. Yet some experts may mistakenly assume that the test for insanity is whether or not the client, suffering from severe mental disease or defect, was (a) incapable of appreciating the criminality of his conduct or (b) unable to conform his conduct to the requirements of the law.

This two-pronged test may be used to determine insanity in some jurisdictions, but not in Texas. The Texas definition of insanity is contained in Section 8.01(a) of the Texas Penal Code. The test is whether or not the "Defendant knew his conduct was wrong." Whether or not the client was unable to conform his conduct to the law is likely not relevant (*Freeman v. State*, 1958). A psychotic defendant, one who is suffering from delusions, may be insane in another jurisdiction, but he can be legally sane in Texas (*Morales v. State*, 1970).

Many psychiatrists and psychologists assume that every state has a temporary insanity defense or recognizes what is referred to as "diminished capacity" at the time of the offense. Temporary insanity in Texas is not a separate defense; the issue is the client's mental state at the time of the offense. One can be temporarily insane at the time of the offense but not permanently insane (*Rodriguez v. State*, 1942). Although temporary insanity caused by voluntary intoxication is not a defense to a crime, according to Texas Penal Code Section 8.04, it may be offered in an attempt to mitigate the punishment for the offense. The important thing is that if the practitioner and the mental health expert are going to work together effectively, they have to be reading from the same page. That is, the practitioner and the expert must both understand the law of the case, the theory and themes of the case, and how the mental health findings will apply to the law.

When counsel brings a mental health expert in on a case, he or she must be prepared not only to provide the expert with the relevant records, but also to direct the type of examination that is done. Counsel must not dictate the opinion. However, the examination should serve to test the validity of, and hopefully advance, the theory of the defense. Tests that will produce scores and conclusions irrelevant to the theory of the case will only waste time and money.

Counsel will know what to ask the expert to do only if the attorney understands the client's history, knows the results of the psychosocial history, and has an understanding of the possible mental health theories that will form the basis of the guilt/innocence defense and/or theory of mitigation. Investigating the case, and understanding many of the mental health issues early in the representation, will help to avoid the mistake that many attorneys make. That is, to simply tell the mental health expert, "Go over and evaluate the client and tell me what you think."

Understanding What the Expert Is Talking About

There is no way that a jury will ever understand what the expert is talking about if the trial team does not understand this information. One of the first things that should be done upon retaining someone in a field that the forensic social worker is not completely familiar with is to ask him or her for some article that will educate the clinician on the issues the expert will cover. Then, they should read this material. Defense counsel obviously cannot become an expert in the field. However, counsel must learn enough so that he or she can discuss the issues of the case with the expert, understand the expert's testimony, and make intelligent decisions on how to relate it to the client and the facts of the case. The forensic social worker can be helpful in digesting the current literature and assisting the trial team with the experts.

Expanding the Concept of the Mitigation Presentation

The obvious mitigation specialists are helping professionals. Social workers with MSW degrees have schooling in the preparation of the psychosocial history that is so important in getting the mitigation investigation off to the right start (Andrews, 1991). For an excellent discussion of the importance of the social history in understanding the client's mental health, see Walker (2002). Dr. Walker is with the University of Kentucky Center on Drug and Alcohol Research, Lexington, Kentucky, and wrote the cited article for the Kentucky DPA's *Mental Health & Expert's Manual.*

There is, however, still some resistance by courts in considering social workers as "real experts" (Warren, 1993, p. 11). A larger problem perhaps is that many judges are not accustomed to approving funds for any experts, or all the experts, that are needed for a capital case. It has also been observed that lawyers are unaware that helping professionals are available to aid the trial team, while, at the same time, helping professionals do not know that there is a need for them in capital litigation.

Experts in Specific Areas

The mitigation evidence must be presented in the most powerful manner possible. Mitigation has little impact unless it relates to the client and the facts of the case. By retaining experts who are specifically qualified and interested in the topic the team wishes to present, each important fact can be explained to the jurors so that they can understand the relevance that the testimony has to the offense and the mitigation case as a whole. This will prevent important facts from being neglected or glossed over.

Furthermore, by retaining those with specific expertise, the defense will obtain a wider range of opinions on what mitigating factors may be present in the client's life that a more general expert may miss. It is the same theory on which the public seeks out both family doctors and specialists in different fields of practice. The consultant can act as the gatekeeper or general practitioner and refer the social worker to the specialist that the team needs. Each specialist in turn can make other referrals as necessary.

The Relationship With the Expert

As has been discussed, often the first instinct of many lawyers is to call a psychologist or psychiatrist (many lawyers do not comprehend the difference) and tell him or her to "go evaluate the client and tell me what you think." Here are some problems with the approach discussed earlier in this chapter.

1 Counsel has not given direction to the mental health expert because he or she is unsure about what he or she wants or needs from the expert. Before seeking an evaluation, counsel should work with the forensic social worker to review the records that have been gathered and formulate an initial strategy. The ultimate plan may be to perform no evaluation at all, or to limit the evaluation to specific areas in the hopes of confirming the initial theory of the defense and/or mitigation.
2 Counsel has not obtained the psychosocial history and relevant records on the client that will give the lawyer and the expert some idea about the client's mental health history.
3 Without needed direction, the expert, following a typical therapeutic approach to the case, may very well run a full battery of psychological tests, the results of which may be damaging or not relevant to the defense. For example, the expert may

conclude that the client is suffering from a mental illness that might help explain why he committed the acts with which he has been charged. However, without the forensic social worker's guidance and the benefit of a psychosocial history showing prior diagnoses, the psychologist may perform a Minnesota Multiphasic Personality Inventory (MMPI). This is a standardized test that is used for many purposes. While the MMPI will not likely have any relevance to forensic issues, prosecutors routinely select isolated responses from the MMPI to paint a negative picture of the client. While the reputable scientist knows that MMPI responses should not be used this way, they often are.

The mental health expert needs guidance in utilizing a litigation approach to the evaluation of the client. Understanding the difference between litigation-based and therapeutic-based approaches to mental health issues will make an important difference in obtaining the resources necessary to present a defense (Keefe, 1998). An approach that the trial team might consider is the following:

1 Counsel should interview the client immediately after appointment, thereby hope-fully building the sense of trust that is so important to a successful disposition of the case. The attorneys will learn something about the client, his or her family, and perhaps the facts of the case. The members of the trial team will spend the time necessary to show its interest in the client, dealing with immediate issues that are troubling him or her and stressing the importance of *Skipper* (1986; jail behavior) evidence should the case go to trial.

2 Counsel or the forensic social worker as the mitigation specialist should take authorizations to the jail for the client to sign so that the specialist can start gathering records regarding the client's contact with schools, hospitals, doctors, the military, and so on.

3 The mitigation specialist should review these records as soon as they arrive so that references to other institutions with relevant records can be identified and contacted.

4 Counsel should determine what prior mental health diagnoses have been made. Counsel should be aware that some of the diagnoses that now appear in the *Diagnostic and Statistical Manual of Mental Disorders* (*DSM–IV–TR;* American Psychiatric Association, 2000) may not have been recognized as disorders when a prior evaluation was made, may be called something different now, or may have different diagnostic criteria. Counsel should see that prior diagnoses are updated in light of current understanding. The forensic social worker may have a better understanding of developments in the *DSM–IV–TR*'s diagnostic criteria.

The trial team should look to see if there are less than obvious reasons to explain some conduct that at first glance appears to be harmful. For example, if the client ran away from home, was he or she trying to avoid an abusive, dysfunctional family or family member? If the client was often truant, was it because the parent refused to take him to school? If the client showed aggression to people or animals, was he or she influenced by an older sibling, or was this a coping mechanism to deal with other problems? These issues can be explored by the forensic social worker who is developing the social history.

5 Counsel should review the work of the mitigation specialist, who has compiled a psychosocial history of the client and obtained the relevant records (Andrews, 1991). Based on the mitigation specialist's analysis, he or she may determine that there are signs of mental health problems (and records to support this) that are likely to be a significant factor at trial.

6 Counsel should move for funding to hire a psychologist as a consultant, not as a testifying expert, but as counsel's agent. This is someone who can assist at client interviews, make observations about any disorders, assess the client's credibility, and suggest areas of cross-examination of the state's expert.

The consultant can provide insight on how to deal with the difficult client. He or she can offer advice as well as suggest strategy, tactics, and other experts that are indicated. The Supreme Court in *Ake v. Oklahoma* (1985) suggested that a mental health expert could, among other things, (a) consult on issues relevant to the defense; (b) help determine whether the anticipated defense is viable; (c) assist in the preparation of cross-examination of the state's expert; and (d) aid in the preparation of penalty-phase evidence. This is what a good consultant should be doing.

7 Once the consultant has reviewed the records, interviewed the client, and otherwise familiarized him-or herself with the case, the trial team can consider the next step that should be taken. After a thorough discussion of the case with the consultant, the team has a better idea of what additional experts, if any, are needed, some of whom may testify at trial.

Counsel is now better able to direct what he or she wants the expert(s) to look for and what tests, if any, to perform. The consultant can refer the practitioner to additional experts and provide an affidavit or oral testimony in the ex parte hearing to provide the threshold showing of necessity for other experts. This permits counsel to show the court that the defense is not wildly spending money without thought. The same amount of money will likely be spent, but with the consultant and the testifying expert dividing the work. The attorney can possibly save the cost of an unnecessary or damaging evaluation by heeding the advice of the consultant who has properly reviewed the records on hand.

A good psychologist can be a good consultant or evaluator. However, it is not recommended that the psychologist wear more than one hat. Should he or she serve as a consultant and then as an evaluator, the objectivity of the evaluation may be compromised. It is the evaluator who will likely testify at trial. The expert does not want his or her participation as a consultant to bias later impressions, nor does the team want to give the prosecutor any ammunition on cross-examination. In no event should the psychologist treat the client when he or she has served in either the role of a consultant or an evaluator. The *ABA Criminal Justice Mental Health Standards* has a good discussion of some of these issues in Standard 7-1.1 (American Bar Association, 1986, p. 12).

What Experts Might Want Counsel to Consult

It is important to remember that all experts are not alike. Just because a person has the necessary education and training to become a psychologist or other mental health professional does not mean that the particular background is right for the case in question. Counsel cannot merely go through the yellow pages, look under "Psychology," and pick a name. Careful selection is necessary to make sure that each expert has the qualifications to assist the trial team in the defense of the client.

The team may encounter experts who have exaggerated their experience and degrees. These experts will say anything that the team wants them to say (until they are dismantled on the stand). Some are convinced that they are experts on everything and that there is no such thing as junk science. Others may have personal or professional agendas that cloud their objectivity. They may be thinking more of the money they will be paid than of the work to be done. They may want to play the role of lawyer and consultant. They may be incapable of explaining the concepts to jurors, or they may testify poorly. We all have seen the great expert who does everything right until he or she gets on the stand and then no one can (or wants to) understand a thing that he or she might say.

The team will want to make sure that the expert understands the constraints that attorneys are under and that he or she will abide by them. Investigate the purported expert's reputation. If he or she dropped the ball for other lawyers, it is likely that the ball will be dropped for the team. The team cannot assume that an expert knows how to testify effectively or that he or she has testified before. The expert must thoroughly understand the scope of the direct and potential cross-exam and the importance of maintaining a cool, professional demeanor while on the stand.

Possible Trial Team Members

The team might consider one or more of the following as additional members of the trial team.

Psychologist

These professionals base opinions on discussions with the clients, examination of relevant records, and tests that they administer. There is a whole battery of these tests that counsel should discuss with the psychologist and decide which ones are desired and which ones are not. These tests could be the (a) Beck Depression Inventory; (b) Cognitive Capacity Screening Examination (overview of general cognitive functioning); (c) Trails Test (tests motor functioning and hand-eye coordination); (d) Rey's 15-item test (malingering); (e) Shipley Institute of Living Scale (intellectual functioning); (f) MMPI-2 (psychopathology; be careful here); (g) Millon Clinical Multiaxial Inventory (tests for personality disorders can address anti-social personality and other disorders); (h) Symptom Checklist-90-R (recent acuity of psychiatric symptoms); and (i) 16 Personality Factor Questionnaire (primary personality characteristics). The results of these tests can be augmented by the client's life history and that of his or her family.

These tests can be described as cognitive. This is the operation of the mind by which we become aware of objects of thought or perception. "Cognitive functioning" is a good phrase to use when talking to psychologists. It describes much of what they are looking for, as well as how cognitive functioning, along with other conditions in the clients lives, explain why they do what they do.

When the team is looking at the work of an evaluator, be it for the defense or the prosecution, some of the relevant questions to ask are (a) did the psychologist choose the right tests? (b) were the tests administered properly and under the right conditions? (c) were the tests scored properly? and (d) were the tests interpreted properly? These are issues that counsel will want to ensure that the defense expert can address, both as to the tests he or she administered as well as those that may have been given by others. These tests will probably not be done by an evaluator for the prosecution. However, counsel can be assured that the state will be looking to see how the defense psychologist's work measures up in each of these areas.

The defense consultant can review the raw data generated by state-sponsored experts. Make sure that the raw data is requested immediately after the test results are completed and sent directly to the defense consultant rather than to the lawyers. Also send along an authorization signed by the client releasing any privacy interest in the raw data. If the state has conducted tests, do not wait to subpoena the psychologist to bring the raw data when he or she testifies at trial. Get this ahead of time so that the defense consultant can review the raw data against any conclusion drawn by the state's psychologist.

Psychiatrist

A psychiatrist is a medical doctor. If the client is acting strangely, counsel may not have the expertise to associate the client's behavior with a medical condition. A psychiatrist should be considered if the psychological testing indicates there is a medical reason for the client's behavior at the time of the offense. Psychiatrists can order additional hospital testing as well as understand and prescribe medication. Hopefully the psychiatrist's medical training can alert him or her to abnormalities in the client's physical appearance that would indicate often overlooked mental problems, such as fetal alcohol syndrome or genetic abnormalities.

Should the client be exhibiting psychotic behavior, the team should consider having the behavior recorded by video in the presence of the psychiatrist who can ask probing questions as to the client's ability to understand the difference between right and wrong or to conform his or her conduct to the requirements of the law.

The psychiatrist has the ability to bat clean-up for the mental health team at trial, particularly if the theory of defense is insanity. In forming opinions, psychiatrists reasonably and customarily rely on the results of forensic testing generated by psychologists, information gathered by their own examinations, the results of any hospital tests that were ordered, results of the investigation that was done by the forensic social worker, and any other evidence that supports the theory.

Neurologist

Neurologists are skilled at detecting physical disease and damage to the central nervous system, especially the brain. They can testify about the link between the brain and behavior. They can use brain imaging techniques, blood and spinal fluid analysis, and neurological examination to arrive at conclusions. Neurologists, like psychiatrists, are medical specialists and often have great credibility with the jury (Clark & Monahan, 2002).

Neuropsychologist

Neuropsychology is a specialty branch of psychology devoted to studying the relationship between the brain and behavior. The brain is an organ of behavior, and damage to the organ can result in cognitive, intellectual, behavioral, and emotional changes. Neuropsychologists, with other qualified mental health experts, can testify about competency to stand trial, criminal responsibility, insanity, and mitigating factors. They can determine the presence, location, and severity of brain damage. They can also describe the impaired functions of the brain and both the short- and long-term practical consequences of the impairment. They can also distinguish between psychiatric and neuropsychological problems.

Why use a neuropsychologist and not a neurologist? Neurologists are mostly concerned with lower brain functions, such as reflexes, sensations, and balance, functions that are mediated by the brain stem, midbrain, and cranial nerves. Medical tests are often incomplete and not good for determining the consequences of brain damage and have poor sensitivity and specificity for detecting mild brain damage. Neuropsychologists look at higher brain functions that are mediated by the cerebral cortex. Their tests have better sensitivity for detecting brain function or its impairment.

Getting the Relationship Started

Regardless of the experience and qualifications of the consultant, trial counsel should not assign the job of developing a theory of defense or mitigation to the consultant or other expert. Defense counsel retains the role of the person that is ultimately responsible for the client's life. The consultant wants and needs this direction in the relationship. The expert is not told what conclusions to draw; that is the job of the expert. However, the relationship must be directed by trial counsel. The following is a letter that might be used to get the relationship started.

Dear Dr. Jones:

I have been appointed by the judge of the 41st Judicial District Court to represent Mary Smith. Ms. Smith has been charged by indictment alleging that she committed an intentional murder while in the course of the commission of a robbery. This is a capital offense, and the State is seeking the death penalty. My co-counsel is Carol Johnson.

I am assembling the team that will defend Ms. Smith against this indictment, and I anticipate the need for a consulting psychologist. If you are hired, I will need you to do the following:

1 Meet with the client and client's family and report your observations to designated members of the defense team.
2 Meet in person or by phone as needed with counsel and other members of the defense team.
3 Review and evaluate documents and records that relate to the client's history that have been gathered by the team's mitigation specialist.

4 Consider, evaluate, and review our client's competency to stand trial; to understand and knowingly waive her Miranda rights; and to voluntarily give her statement to investigators.

5 Consider, evaluate, and review our client's criminal responsibility at the time of the alleged offense, including responsibility for any lesser included offense as opposed to the offense charged.

6 Advise the team as to any additional mental health experts that are indicated and what requests should be made of these experts. You will need to provide evidence, by testimony or affidavit, to assist the defense team in establishing the threshold showing of necessity for the funding of these additional experts.

7 Review and evaluate reports of mental health consultants who have examined our client on behalf of the prosecution. I will ask that you determine whether any examination was performed properly and in accordance with accepted scientific standards, referencing the *ABA Criminal Justice Mental Health Standards*.

8 Review any raw data (all recordings, notes, test protocols, and unprocessed responses), test scores, and reports generated by evaluator(s) to determine if the tests were properly chosen, properly administered, properly scored, and properly interpreted.

9 Assist defense counsel in finding weaknesses and errors in the prosecution's analysis of our client's potential for future violent conduct, if any, and prepare counsel for cross-examination of the prosecution's expert witnesses.

10 You will not be asked to evaluate our client for the purpose of testifying at trial nor to testify on any issue or provide treatment.

I am enclosing a copy of the Uniform Offense Report that summarizes the State's investigation of the charges against my client. Should this report, or anything else, alert you to the existence or appearance of a conflict, please let me know.

Should you be hired, you will be considered as one who is employed to assist the defense team in the rendition of professional legal services to Ms. Smith. Any information that comes to you will be by reason of the attorney–client relationship and protected by applicable rules of evidence. We would expect you to observe strictly the confidential nature of this information.

Would you kindly contact me on receipt of this letter? Prior to my moving for funding from the court for your hiring, I will need from you the following:

1 a copy of your curriculum vitae;
2 your hourly fee and an estimate of the total fee that you require;
3 the names and addresses of three lawyers with whom you have consulted in criminal cases in the past; and
4 any reasons why you cannot or should not be associated with this case, including any issues that the prosecution can raise on cross-examination should you be called to testify.

I look forward to hearing from you.

Sincerely,
John Q. Lawyer

Some or all of the previous points may be used in a letter to a proposed consultant. It can be tailored to fit the needs of the situation. The important thing is to establish a clear relationship early.

Consider now that the consultant has reviewed the records, interviewed the client, talked to everyone that he or she feels is relevant, and believes that the team needs a specialist to take the evaluation of the client's mental health to the next level. He recommends that Dr. Adams be contacted as a possible evaluating, and testifying, psychologist. Dr. Adams has agreed. Counsel needs to let Dr. Adams know what is needed. Consider the following letter:

> Dear Dr. Adams:
>
> Thank you for agreeing to conduct an evaluation of our client, Mary Smith. This is a capital offense, and the State is seeking the death penalty. My co-counsel is Carol Johnson. As the team's evaluating psychologist, I will ask you to do the following:
>
> 1 Meet with the client and relevant others as necessary, and orally report your observations to designated members of the trial team.
> 2 You are asked to provide your opinion only on the following issue(s):
>
> [List the issues here on which you want the doctor to provide an opinion.]
>
> 3 Conduct those standardized tests that we mutually agree are appropriate for the purpose of evaluation of the issues identified previously.
>
> [Note: One of the features of the referral letter is to focus the scope of the testifying expert's examination of the client narrowly. Counsel might consider one or more of the following areas of examination, remembering, however, that the State will likely be able to conduct an examination similar in scope to that of the expert. Accordingly, the designated areas from the following list must be carefully chosen and clearly focused. Choose from the tests listed previously, or add those that may be appropriate for the particular case.]
>
> 4 Consider and evaluate our client's competency to stand trial; to understand and knowingly, voluntarily, and intelligently waive her Miranda rights and voluntarily give her statement to investigators.
> 5 Consider and evaluate the client's criminal responsibility at the time of the alleged offense, including responsibility for any lesser offense. Specifically, you will be asked to determine whether (a) at the time of the conduct charged and as a result of a severe mental disease or defect, she did not know her conduct was wrong; and/or (b) whether our client suffers from any condition that would make her more susceptible to anger, rage, resentment, or terror sufficient to render the mind incapable of cool reflection.
>
> Texas Penal Code Section 19.02 appears to call for an objective "person of ordinary temper" standard. However, I would like for you to distinguish those aspects of anger, rage, and resentment that do not relate to temper. I also want you to review the subjective evidence relating to possible anger, rage, and resentment for use as mitigation at the punishment phase of the trial.
>
> 6 Consider and evaluate Ms. Smith's ability to recognize the risks associated with her conduct or to appreciate such risks and to avoid such conduct once the risk

was appreciated. You will also be requested to administer those psychological tests that we agree are indicated and reasonably necessary.

7 Meet in person or by phone as needed with counsel and other members of the defense team.

8 Review and evaluate documents and records that relate to the issue(s) described in #2.

9 You will be asked to advise the team as to any additional mental health experts that are indicated and what requests should be made of these experts. You will need to provide evidence, by testimony or affidavit, to establish the threshold showing of necessity for the funding of these additional experts.

10 Review and evaluate reports of mental health consultants who have examined our client on behalf of the prosecution. I will ask that you determine whether any examination was performed properly and in accordance with accepted scientific standards, referencing the *ABA Criminal Justice Mental Health Standards.*

11 The defense team will ask you to evaluate any claim that the prosecution may make that there is a probability that our client would commit criminal acts of violence that would constitute a continuing threat to society. Naturally, we will not ask you to provide a clinical risk assessment, as these are not scientifically reliable, nor will you examine the client for that purpose. We will, however, expect you to be familiar with the literature in this field and be prepared to testify as to the lack of reliability of clinical predictions of future dangerousness.

12 You will be asked to review any raw data, test scores, interpretations, and reports generated by state-sponsored evaluator(s) to determine if the tests were properly chosen, properly administered, properly scored, and properly interpreted.

13 You should be prepared to testify at trial, if necessary. You may also be asked to testify concerning your findings that support any pretrial suppression motions that are filed.

14 Would you kindly contact me so that we can provide you with those records that are relevant to the focused referral question of your inquiry? We will also need to discuss (a) the nature of the anticipated evaluation of our client and (b) a schedule for completing your evaluation.

I am enclosing a copy of the Uniform Offense Report received from the prosecution. Should you need any more information about the State's investigation please let me know.

We have been given a trial date of __/__/___. Should you conclude that, as a result of one or more severe mental diseases or defects, our client did not know that her conduct was wrong, I will need to give the prosecution at least 20 days notice, prior to trial, of our intent to offer that evidence.

Communications between you, the client, and the defense team shall be deemed privileged unless and to the extent that privilege is waived by your testimony. If at any time you conclude, for any reason, that you cannot or should not be associated with this case, please notify me immediately. I look forward to hearing from you.

Sincerely,
John Q. Lawyer

Many lawyers are naturally concerned about how much information to give the evaluator and how much effort should be devoted, if any, to influence the evaluation.

After all, the team has gone to the trouble of isolating the consultant's role from that of the evaluator so as to avoid contaminating what counsel hopes is an objective evaluation. How should counsel proceed?

First of all, I believe that the evaluator should have all information that is *relevant* to the theory that has been initially selected by the trial team as well as all information that is in the possession of the opposing counsel. This would include all of the information that relates to the present theories and themes that have been worked up by the team. It makes little sense to abandon all of that work and then simply hope that the examining (and likely testifying) expert will arrive at the same conclusion that the trial team has. Send the expert the records that led the trial team to the chosen theory. Anything that is not relevant to that theory, or the issues on which the expert has been asked to testify, will likely waste the expert's time if he or she has to review it.

> The role of the expert witness is very much like that of the judge or jury. Specifically, the expert is going to examine various forms of evidence to reach a decision about the client. There is nothing untoward about employing one's skills as an advocate to reinforce for the expert the aspects of the case that are in the client's favor. Indeed, it is disingenuous at best for lawyers to sit on their hands when virtually every other party interviewed may have a strong, highly opinionated and potentially adverse perspective on their client's behaviors, intentions, and current mental health status. (Drogin, 2000)

Trial lawyers are advocates, and this is no time to stop being an advocate. Allow the expert to understand the tentative theory of the case and what material exists to support it. If the team has chosen a theory that is not supported by the evaluation, the team can reevaluate the theory. It is better to learn that early on, rather than realize in the middle of the expert's testimony that his or her conclusions do not support the trial team's theory. If counsel's initial theory is valid, then all the material that has been accumulated in developing that theory and the supportive themes can be used by the evaluator in making a persuasive presentation to the jury. If the expert, after thoroughly evaluating the client's condition, arrives at a conclusion that does not support the theory, it is not too late to adjust the team's preparation.

Besides, it is not realistic to think that, at this point, counsel does not know enough about the case to have developed a theory for it. Naturally, counsel will want the theory confirmed by the evaluating/testifying expert. However, do not think of the testifying psychologist as the one who will determine the theory. That theory has usually been inferred by examining the psychosocial history gathered from the forensic social worker, client, records, interviews, and discussions with the consulting psychologist and relating all of this to the facts of the case. The expert will be the one who can find the evidence that can support that theory, neutralize what does not appear to support it, and present it cogently to a jury.

Mental Health Language

The experts will use language that the trial team will need to be familiar with. Sometimes a report reviewed by the team provides a five-axis conclusion. All findings within each axis are listed in order of importance, so the first one named under each axis is the most important. What do the axes stand for?

Axis I: Clinical disorders. These are disorders other than personality disorders and mental retardation.

Axis II: Personality disorders and mental retardation.

Axis III: General medical conditions.

Axis IV: Psychosocial and environmental problems (home, school, economic, criminal justice system).

Axis V: Global assessment of functioning (GAF). Assessment is based on a scale of 1–100 at a given time, for example, current, on admission, or at discharge. The average GAF for a well-functioning adult is about 80.

The trial team may often find that the prosecution will attempt to take Axis I clinical disorders and characterize them as Axis II personality disorders that are more frightening to a jury. The trial team, on the other hand, will want to closely examine any perceived Axis II personality disorders to determine those that are actually clinical disorders that can be treated.

Funding for the Mitigation Specialist and Other Experts

Ake v. Oklahoma (1985) stands for the proposition that, when a defendant has made a preliminary showing that his or her sanity at the time of the offense is likely to be a significant factor at trial, the Constitution requires that a state provide access to a psychiatrist's assistance on this issue. *Ake* provides support for more than just an independent evaluation:

> And without a psychiatrist's assistance to conduct a professional examination on issues relevant to the insanity defense, to help determine whether that defense is viable, to present testimony and to assist in preparing the cross-examination of the State's psychiatric witnesses, the risk of an inaccurate resolution of insanity issues is extremely high. (p. 65)

The *Ake* decision allows a defendant the basic tools of an adequate defense. The defendant is entitled access to a competent psychiatrist who will conduct an appropriate examination and assist in evaluation, preparation, and presentation of the defense. The *Ake* holding has been extended to consultants in other areas of expertise.

The *Ake* decision is important because many cases in which the forensic social worker is involved will include indigent clients. However, should the forensic social worker work for a team that has been hired by the client, there is no need to go to the court for funding unless the client becomes indigent at some stage of the representation.

The Ex Parte Motion

This sworn motion must show the judge what is needed, why it is needed, why he or she should grant the relief requested, what counsel will do with the funding, who will provide the assistance, and what it will cost. There is plenty of authority for making the funding request ex parte. *Ake* (1985) says it would be unfair for the defense to be forced to disclose a line of investigation in order to obtain funds to pursue it. What if counsel wants money for someone other than a mental health expert? "Fundamental fairness and due process entitles indigent defendants to an adequate opportunity to present their claims within the adversary system. The requested expert will provide the defendant with one of the basic tools of an adequate defense" (*Ake*, 1985, p. 62). If counsel needs it, counsel should ask for it.

Protecting the Motion

The ex parte nature of the motion means that the prosecutor does not know what assistance the defense counsel is requesting. This serves several purposes, not the least of which is giving the prosecutor sleepless nights trying to figure out what defense counsel is up to. The right to an ex parte hearing helps to level the playing field in the indigent case. If counsel was fortunate enough to have been hired in a capital case, the defense team could go out and hire whomever was needed and would not have to disclose that to the prosecutor. Why should an indigent client be treated any differently?

So as to avoid the appearance of any ethical improprieties, counsel may consider notifying the prosecutor that at some time the defense will be approaching the court, ex parte, for the purpose of obtaining funding. The date and time of the hearing, as well as the assistance sought, should not be divulged. The team can consider the following steps when applying for funding:

1 Make the showing of necessity in an ex parte motion which should include the elements described previously. Attach affidavits from those who can give reasons why the requested expert assistance is warranted.

2 Tender to the judge two orders. One can be entitled "Order Finding Threshold Showing" and merely states that the ex parte contact seeking funds has been made and the judge approved the funding. This will be distributed to parties and will inform the prosecutor of the contact. The second order will designate who is to be hired and how much is authorized for payment. This order will not go to the prosecutor but will note in bold capital letters at the bottom:

THIS ORDER, AND THE DEFENDANT'S EX PARTE MOTION FOR FUNDING, SHALL BE SEALED IN THE RECORD AND SHALL BE SEEN BY AND DISTRIBUTED TO DEFENSE COUNSEL AND THIS COURT ONLY. THE CLERK'S DOCKET ENTRY SHALL NOT NAME THE TITLE OF THIS MOTION NOR THE COURT'S ORDER, BUT SHALL REFER TO THEM AS "EX PARTE MOTION" AND "EX PARTE ORDER."

3 Provide to the clerk a large envelope, and type on the outside of the envelope: THE CONTENTS OF THIS ENVELOPE HAVE BEEN SEALED BY ORDER OF THE COURT DATED __/__/__. FOR THE EYES OF THE COURT AND DEFENSE COUNSEL ONLY. Counsel might consider the need to explain

cordially to the clerk or deputy what is being done and point out the language in the judge's order so that the pleadings are handled properly. Make sure that any docket entry does not include the expert's name.

If these precautions are not taken, it is likely that the motion and order will not be sealed and will wind up in the court's file for all to see and copy.

While it is the attorney who will be drafting the motion and order and litigating the motion, it is important for the forensic social worker to be familiar with the process for payment for services.

Other Areas for Expert Assistance

Adaptability and Positive Prisoner Evidence

The issue of adaptability arises in just about every capital trial. It is often a serious consideration for juries in deliberation. Juries want to know how the defendant will react to the prison environment. They want to be sure that, if they sentence the client to life in prison, he will not continue to commit criminal acts of violence.

Cultural Experts

There may be cultural aspects in the case that relate to a murder, and the jury may not be able to understand or be willing to accept the relationship. If the client is a gang member, for example, it may be useful to have a person knowledgeable about gangs and their role in the client's life. Aggravating factors related to the gang can be lessened if the evidence concerning the gang membership can be explained in the context of the lack of employment or support in the area where the client lives.

Cultural experts can also help to explain how the client's ethnicity, childhood, or developmental experiences are completely different from anything the jurors have experienced. This will prevent the jurors from seeing the client's crime out of context with a life that was chosen for him or her by others. Cultural experts may be sociologists, social workers, or even individuals who are a part of the client's culture and have the required level of knowledge that will be helpful to the jurors in making the appropriate decision.

Substance Addiction or Dependence/Abuse

Substance abuse is a very tricky issue in a capital case because it can both explain the crime and aggravate it in the minds of many. The team should challenge members of the venire who will view evidence of addiction as aggravating rather than mitigating.

It is vital to explain to the jury how the drugs and alcohol that the client consumed affected his or her life and the culpability for the crime he or she committed. Experts on this issue can range from psychologists to those lay witnesses who may work at a rehabilitation center, but usually will be a toxicologist or pharmatoxicologist. The team should have a basic understanding of the neurobiology of addiction. Addiction is very different from substance abuse. Addiction (or dependence in *DSM–IV–TR*) causes physiological changes in the brain. When a client shows indications of addiction, the forensic social worker can involve someone who can help the jury understand why choices made to obtain and take drugs by the addicted person are not often voluntary acts. The chosen expert can work hand in hand with the mitigation specialist and hopefully explain why the client was predisposed to addiction and how that influenced his or her life and the crime.

Geneticist

It is very useful to show that certain aggravating facts about the client were completely beyond the client's control. Most aggravating aspects to a person's conduct can be traced to some origin that he or she did not choose. A geneticist may be able to trace inherited neurological impairment or point out inherited psychological disorders. Furthermore, there may be incest in the client's background, which is often a telling sign of the client's impoverished environment both culturally and materially. A genogram will be used by the geneticist or practitioner to find these links.

Crime Scene

There may be aspects to the crime that in some way lessen the client's culpability. This may be evidence that the client did not intend to kill anyone when he or she began the crime, but was startled or frightened. There may be evidence that suggests a psychosis was involved during the murder. An expert in crime scene analysis or forensic pathology may be able to shed light on evidence from the crime scene that suggests reduced culpability or moral blameworthiness.

Child Development Expert

The client may have suffered from a neglectful and abusive home. These life experiences may mean nothing to a jury unless an expert is able to allow the jurors to understand the consequences of such treatment. Often a client's behavior can be explained by the quality of attachment to the caregiver that was laid down early in life. The expert may help the jurors understand how these life experiences influenced the client's life and the particular crime.

Juror Perceptions of Expert Testimony

The Capital Jury Project has done research on how people who served on capital juries have viewed the process. One article based on this research has noted that many jurors respond negatively to some defense experts (Sundby, 1997). It was noted that jurors often viewed defense experts, such as psychologists and psychiatrists, as hired guns and gave them little credibility. Of course, the testimony of some of these experts is vital, but the main criticism of this testimony is that it is not explained in a way that can be grasped by the juror.

Studies have shown that, in complex cases, jurors may tend to evaluate the credibility of experts in large part on their personal characteristics rather than on the information they presented. Jurors may resolve the issue of conflicting expert testimonies by ignoring both of them (Ivkovvic & Hans, 2003). One of the endless news magazine programs that we are now inundated with recently aired a program dealing with alleged false confessions. The defense hired a nationally known expert on the issue of false confessions. According to jurors who were interviewed after their verdict of guilty, the witness testified brilliantly and explained the many reasons why people feel the need to implicate themselves falsely. He was very informative, but the direct examination never related itself to the facts of the case. The jury heard some interesting testimony, but it was not persuasive, so jurors could not use the information in their decision-making process. While this can be the fault of the witness and his preparation by the trial team, often the testimony is made unpersuasive by limiting orders from the trial judge. The lawyers and witness may want to make the link for the jury, but may be denied this ability by the trial court.

One of the most powerful witnesses discussed by the interviewed capital jurors was what Professor Sundby described as the "lay expert." This is an individual who has personal knowledge and experience with the defendant or the defendant's circumstances outside of the present representation and some basis to give an expert opinion concerning a mitigating factor. One example given in Professor Sundby's article was the use of a director of a rehabilitation center for recovering addicts. The witness was herself once a drug addict and a prostitute, who, in fact, knew the defendant's mother. This witness was qualified to give an opinion on the effects of drug addiction and poverty on children and at the same time could speak from personal experience. Several jurors noted, in giving a life sentence, that this witness was very credible. It is difficult for a prosecutor to cross-examine an expert who has personal knowledge about what they are speaking of and not just academic expertise.

Another example cited was a defendant's commanding officer in the U.S. Marine Corps. This individual testified as to the defendant's ability to conform to a restrictive, structured environment. This testimony was from personal experience, however, and not based on a confusing psychological rating scale. The main focus of these types of witnesses is to be creative. Another excellent type of lay expert is the corrections officer, if the team can obtain his or her cooperation.

Victim Outreach

Most of this chapter has dealt with the role of the forensic social worker in assisting the defense in a criminal case. However, the contribution of the practitioner is not limited to assisting in the defense function. Many criminal acts involve victimization of an innocent person. In the unfortunate case of a homicide, in addition to the tragic death, there are those who survive the victim.

The forensic social worker can assist these victims and survivors as a victim's advocate.

Conclusion

The forensic social worker can bring a wealth of talent to the criminal justice system. The social worker possesses a unique combination of skills that lend themselves to forensic work. These skills are the ability to empathize with those who are in need; an understanding of a broad range of social, cultural, and mental health issues; as well as a sense of compassion and desire for social justice.

Just as the qualified practitioner can benefit the criminal justice system, so too can the system provide the social worker with a rewarding career that can grant a sense of satisfaction found in few areas of work.

RESOURCES AND REFERENCES

Ake v. Oklahoma, 470 U.S. 68 (1985).

American Bar Association. (1986). Mental health. In *ABA criminal justice mental health standards* (Standard 7-1.1). Washington, DC: Author.

American Bar Association. (2003, February). *American Bar Association guidelines for the appointment and performance of counsel in death penalty cases.* Washington, DC: Author.

American Psychiatric Association. (2000). *Diagnostic and statistical manual of mental disorders* (4th ed., text rev.). Washington, DC: Author.

American Psychological Association. (2002a). Standard 2.10 Maintaining test security. In *Ethical principles of psychologists and code of conduct.* Washington, DC: Author.

American Psychological Association. (2002b). Standard 9.04 Release of test data. In *Ethical principles of psychologists and code of conduct.* Washington, DC: Author.

Andrews, A. (1991). Social work expert testimony regarding mitigation in capital sentencing proceedings. *Social Work, 36,* 440–445.

Atkins v. Virginia, 536 U.S. 304 (2002).

Blume, J. H. (2002). Mental health issues in criminal cases: The elements of a competent and reliable mental health examination. In *Mental health & experts manual* (6th ed., chap. 3). Frankfurt: Kentucky Department of Public Advocacy.

Drogin, E. Y. (2000). Evidence and expert mental health witness: A jurisprudent therapy perspective. In *2000 Wiley Expert Witness Update* (pp. 295–313). New York: Aspen Law & Business.

Eddings v. Oklahoma, 455 U.S. 104 (1982).

Freeman v. State, 317 S.W.2d 726 (Texas Crim. App. 1958).

Holdman, S. (2001). Paper presented to the Inter-American Court.

Ivkovvic, S., & Hans, V. (2003). Jurors' evaluations of expert testimony. Judging the messenger and the message. *Law and Social Inquiry, 28,* 441.

Keefe, D. (1998). Mental health issues and the defense of capital cases. Schools of social work will likely offer courses that deal with many of these issues. *The Fight for Life.*

Hess, A., & Weiner, I. (1999) *The handbook of forensic psychology* (2nd ed.). New York: Wiley.

Clark, J., & Monahan, E. (2002). Decision rules for integrating the expert into the case. In *Mental health and expert's manual.* Frankfurt: Kentucky Department of Public Advocacy.

Lockett v. Ohio, 438 U.S. 586 (1978).

McCoy v. North Carolina, 494 U.S. 433 (1988).

Miller v. Dretke, 420 F.3d. 356 (5th Cir. 2005).

Morales v. State, 458 S.W.2d 56 (Tex. Crim. App. 1970).

Rodriguez v. State, 165 S.W.32d 104 (Tex. Crim. App. 1942).

Sundby, S. E. (1997). The jury as critic: An empirical look at how capital juries perceive expert and lay testimony. *Virginia Law Review, 83,* 1109.

Skipper v. South Carolina, 476 U.S. 1 (1986).

Tennard v. Dretke, 124 S.Ct. 2562 (2004).

Texas Penal Code Section 19.02.

Walker, R. (2002). Social histories and forensic mental health evaluations in forensic cases. In *Mental health & experts manual* (6th ed., chap. 9). Frankfurt: Kentucky Department of Public Advocacy.

Warren, J. (1993). The clinical social worker as forensic expert. *Institute of Law, Psychiatry and Public Policy Monograph*, p. 11.

Wiggins v. Smith, 123 S.Ct. 2527 (2003).

Resources for Forensic Social Workers

Texas Defender Service
510 S. Congress, Suite 304
Austin, TX 78704
(512) 320-8300
http://www.texasdefender.org

National Alliance of Sentencing and Mitigation Specialists
National Legal Aid & Defender Association
1140 Connecticut Avenue NW, Suite 900
Washington, DC 20036
(202) 452-0620, ext. 234

National Organization of Forensic Social Work
460 Smith Street
Suite K
Middletown, CT 06457
(860) 613-0254

Emerging Trends in Batterer Intervention Programming: Equipping Forensic Workers for Effective Practice

Fred Buttell
Michelle Mohr Carney

Case Example

What you are doing is crazy. You know good and well that I do not want you to communicate in any way to any member of my family. Yet, you continue to leave messages and even sent an e-mail to my son. If you really love Sally then you would want her marriage to be secure and above all other relationships except for her relationship with God. But, you are ready at any moment to drive into Sally your discontent for her husband. That only brings division between Sally and me. Why can't you people just obey proper authority? Don't you know that I am the one who knows what is best for my family? Who made you the father and husband of this family and marriage? Why have you all exalted yourselves above my legal and spiritual authority for my family?

When I make a statement, I mean it. You are not to communicate with my wife or any of my children until I know that you will obey my authority for my marriage and my family. When I know that you are not a threat to my marriage, my wife, and my children, I will give you permission to communicate with them. I am the only husband to Sally and the only father to our children. You are not either one. You gain access to this family only through me. Do not cowardly write or call Sally or any of our children. If you have a problem with me, then e-mail me. But remember, if I don't see you improve by submitting to my authority as husband for this marriage and father for this family, then you will still be a threat to my family's unity and progress and I will continue this period of silence. Just obey my authority and you will not be estranged forever.

(Excerpt of an e-mail sent from the husband of a battered woman to her sister.)

Scope of the Problem

Among the many controversies in the field of domestic violence, perhaps the oldest is the debate among researchers about the prevalence of the problem. At the heart of the debate lies data drawn from two very different sources. According to the most recent data reported by the U.S. Department of Justice Bureau of Justice Statistics (BJS; Durose et al., 2005), there were 3.5 million victims of family violence in the United States between the years 1998 and 2002. Of the 3.5 million violent crimes committed in the family during those years, approximately 1.7 million were domestic violence crimes involving adults either married or cohabitating. The overwhelming majority of domestic violence victims were women (84%) and, in terms of relationship violence, women accounted for 86% of the victims of abuse suffered at the hands of a boyfriend or girlfriend. Finally, while about 75% of the victims of family violence were female, the data in the report suggests that about 75% of the perpetrators were male. What emerges from the statistical picture portrayed in the BJS report is that domestic violence is a serious social problem that involves males initiating violence against their female intimate partners. From a theoretical perspective, this behavior is consistent with the feminist conceptualization of domestic violence that suggests that the United States is a patriarchy where men use violence to maintain power and control in an intimate relationship. This conceptualization of domestic violence as being almost exclusively perpetrated by males in intimate relationships is important because it has been used to shape public policies to address the problem and has defined cultural awareness of the issue. Interestingly, this idea that men in relationships largely perpetrate domestic violence as part of a strategy to gain power and control in their relationships is not without criticism.

Nationally representative surveys of American families conducted in 1975 and 1985 paint a very different picture of violence occurring in American families than that portrayed by the BJS report. Data from the National Family Violence Surveys (NFVS) in 1975 and 1985, compiled using the Conflict Tactics Scale (Straus, 1979; Straus & Gelles, 1986), suggest gender symmetry in perpetrating couple violence. For *any* use of violence, the 1975 national figures for men and women were 12.1% and 11.6%, respectively. In 1985, the comparable figures were 11.3% and 12.1%. For *serious* violence, or those acts judged to have a high probability of producing serious injury, the 1975 figures were 3.8% for men and 4.6% for women. In 1985, the comparable figures were 3.0% and 4.4%. In all cases, the gender differences are less than 2%. These findings have been used to suggest that the majority of violence in adult intimate relationships in American families is reciprocal and that women and men use violence at roughly equivalent rates. The net result of the contradictory findings of data compiled using police reports and victims of crime surveys (i.e., the BJS data) versus the nationally representative surveys (i.e., the NFVS data) has been to polarize researchers into two camps: (a) those who believe that domestic violence is a power and control tactic used by men to control women in intimate relationships (i.e., feminists) and (b) those who believe domestic violence is a tactic used equally by men and women in intimate relationships to resolve conflict (i.e., sociologists).

It is important to note that this is not an idle debate. Specifically, how one resolves the debate has everything to do with how one conceptualizes solutions. For example, if policymakers believe that there is gender symmetry in domestic violence, then the laws that they craft to address the problem and the intervention programs that they propose to fix the problem will be radically different from those that would be created if they subscribed to the feminist conceptualization of the problem. Unfortunately, the intensity of the debate has tended to polarize the issue to the extent that current solutions tend to be exclusively feminist driven and to completely ignore the view of domestic violence suggested by the sociological camp. According to one prominent family violence researcher, it seems that ideology has trumped empirical research in the field of domestic violence regarding the conceptualization of "domestic violence" (Gelles, 2002). Evidence for his contention can been seen in the federal Violence Against Women Act of 1996, up for renewal in 2005, which allocates federal money to states for shelters and other services and which completely ignores female-initiated violence or male victims of violence. This situation is unfortunate as there is evidence that both camps may be correct in their conceptualizations of domestic violence.

Recently, in an attempt to bridge the acrimonious divide between sociological and feminist scholars, Johnson (1995) developed an argument suggesting that the two groups are both correct in their conceptualizations of violence and that they are really discussing different phenomenon. He contends that there are essentially two distinct forms of family violence, which he refers to as "patriarchal terrorism" and "common couple violence." According to Johnson (1995), common couple violence refers to the phenomenon captured in the NFVS, in which the violence is not coercive or controlling and is gender balanced. In this model, couples may engage in physical violence with one another in the context of a specific argument, but the violence is not meant to control the other person and is likely to be bidirectional or mutual (Johnson & Lebow, 2000). By contrast, patriarchal terrorism refers to the phenomenon described in the case example and seen in shelter populations and criminal courts, in which the violence is male initiated and escalating and represents a man's attempt to dominate and control his partner. In this model, the violence is purposeful and is meant to intimidate and control the female partner. As such, it is not generally confined to physical violence and routinely involves severe emotional abuse and intimidation, and it likely will result in severe injury for the woman (Johnson, 2000). Johnson's conceptualization of domestic violence is helpful because it suggests that both feminist scholars and sociological scholars are correct in their conceptualizations of domestic violence, which has implications for the concept of "mandatory arrest" policies in domestic violence cases that will be discussed later in the chapter.

Literature Review

Placing the controversy aside regarding whether men or women are more violent within intimate relationships, there is no denying the fact that each year there are large numbers of perpetrators of domestic violence entering our criminal justice system in need of intervention. In order to fully understand intervention efforts with batterers, it is necessary to start at the beginning of the sequence of events that most frequently places men in treatment. Specifically, the overwhelming majority of men in batterer intervention programs (BIPs) are there as a part of a criminal sentence. These men are arrested for a domestic violence offense, prosecuted, and sentenced to a community-based BIP as part of a therapeutic intervention that is used instead of incarceration. Consequently, given that most men in BIPs are there as convicted offenders, it is instructive to review the sequence of events that led to the adoption of pro-arrest policies in police calls involving domestic violence.

In the mid-1980s four things happened in close succession that shifted the focus in domestic violence away from victims and onto perpetrators. First, the results of the Minneapolis Domestic Violence Police Experiment, discussed later in the chapter, were published, which concluded that arresting men for committing domestic violence offenses served a protective function for women (Sherman & Berk, 1984). Second, the publication of the U.S. Attorney General's Task Force on Family Violence, also in 1984, suggested that states and local jurisdictions should be doing more to protect women from domestic violence and concluded that there was ample legal precedent to arrest and prosecute domestic violence offenses. Third, in 1985, a large award was granted to a battered woman in a civil suit filed against the police department in Torrington, Connecticut, for failing to protect her from her abusive husband. Finally, continuing pressure was applied to legislators from the women's movement for them to pass laws criminalizing violence against women (for a more extensive discussion of these issues, see Gelles, 1993). As a result of the intersection of these four issues, police and policymakers were searching for a new solution to combat domestic violence at precisely the same time that social science data came to light suggesting that arresting men for domestic violence offenses would protect women from future abuse. Thus, laws criminalizing domestic violence were quickly enacted, and police jurisdictions around the country adopted mandatory or presumptive arrest policies in domestic violence cases.

The original goal of the Minneapolis Domestic Violence Police Experiment was to test the competing hypotheses of specific deterrence and labeling theory (Sherman & Berk, 1984). Specific deterrence indicates that the pains of punishment deter people from repeating the crimes for which they are punished, especially when punishment is certain, swift, and severe. Labeling theory indicates that punishment often makes individuals more likely to commit crimes because they begin to define themselves as criminal. Over an 18-month period, police applied one of three intervention strategies: (a) arrest, (b) ordering the suspect from the premises, or (c) mediation/advice. The study design called for random assignment of arrest, separation, and mediation and a 6-month follow-up period measuring the frequency and seriousness of domestic violence after each police intervention. The design applied to only simple misdemeanor domestic assaults when both the suspect and the victim were present when the police arrived. Excluded from the study were situations where the suspect attempted to assault police officers, a victim demanded arrest, or both parties were injured. The analysis suggested that recidivism was highest for separation and lowest for arrest. Consequently, the researchers concluded that the "arrest intervention certainly did not make things worse and may well have made things better," which "suggests that arrest and initial jail alone may produce a deterrent effect regardless of how the courts treat such cases, and that arrest makes an independent contribution to the deterrence potential of the criminal justice system" (Sherman & Berk, 1984, p. 268). Therefore, they advocated for a *presumption* of arrest in domestic violence cases. These findings had a profound impact on public policy because they were combined with social advocacy and social action in an atmosphere of public support for a new societal response to domestic violence. The net result was that new laws were quickly enacted because legislators perceived it to be both the right thing to do and popular with constituents.

Because the results of the Minneapolis Domestic Violence Police Experiment had such a profound impact on public policy, the National Institute of Justice (NIJ) funded replication studies in six cities. Beginning in 1986 and early 1987, police in Omaha, Miami, Atlanta, Colorado Springs, Milwaukee, and Charlotte began controlled experiments to replicate the Minneapolis findings. In an interesting parallel to the evaluation literature on BIPs (which will be discussed in detail later in the chapter), where the more rigorous studies have discovered negligible positive effects for BIPs, these replication studies corrected the methodological flaws in the original study and discovered that there were no significant differences between the three randomly assigned treatments. Unfortunately, these studies reported that arrest worked unevenly at deterring future domestic violence offenses and, in fact, made some men more violent. In brief, these replication studies discovered both deterrent and unanticipated effects of arrest. Data from each of the six sites suggests that men arrested for domestic violence who lacked a stake in conformity (e.g., employment, marriage versus dating) were significantly more likely to have a repeat offense than their counterparts who were not arrested. Conversely, among those who were married and employed, arrest deterred subsequent violence. In sum, there is general consensus among researchers that arrests for misdemeanor domestic violence offenses do not necessarily prevent recurrences of abuse and, in fact, there is now a feeling that these arrests may even worsen the situation (Berk, Campbell, Klap, & Western, 1992; Binder & Meeker, 1992; Hirschel, Hutchinson, & Dean, 1992; McCord, 1992; Mitchell, 1992; Pate & Hamilton, 1992; Polsby, 1992; Sherman, Smith, Schmidt, & Rogan, 1992).

These findings, when viewed in light of those of Berk et al. (1992), which suggested that there were batterers that were "good risks" or those who seemed to be deterred by arrest, and those who were "bad risks" or likely to be repeat offenders, give further evidence to the idea that batterers are not a homogeneous group. Consequently, when evaluating the deterrent effects of arrest for domestic violence, it would perhaps be helpful to distinguish between "good risks" and "bad risks." In making this distinction, the key risk indicators are employment status and marital status. Unfortunately, it seems that for many men arrested for domestic violence offenses "arrest is more an inconvenience than a traumatic behavior altering deterrent" (Mitchell, 1992, p. 244). From a policy perspective, the most interesting aspect of the data generated by the replication studies is that they have not been used to alter public policy. For example, there has been no change in police policy regarding mandatory arrest in domestic violence cases, whereby police officers are educated about "good risks" and "bad risks" and instructed to arrest only men for whom arrest might serve a deterrent function. Rather, despite the findings from the NIJ replication studies, many victim advocates remain strident in their views that arrest works best. Unfortunately, the confluence of events that led to the adoption of mandatory arrest policies initially no longer exists, which means that this situation is unlikely to change in the near future. However, what does persist are the laws that criminalized domestic violence and led to mandatory arrest policies in domestic violence cases throughout the country and their byproducts, which includes treatment programs for domestic violence offenders.

The remainder of this section provides information on outcome evaluations of treatment programs for domestic violence perpetrators. However, before beginning an analysis of the research evaluating the effectiveness of treatment programs, some methodological issues that impact on their validity warrant comment. First, given the violent, dangerous behavior under study, the random assignment of subjects to different treatment conditions or to a no-treatment control condition is limited by inherent ethical issues. To date, very few evaluation studies have employed random assignment of subjects to different treatment conditions, and most program evaluations have employed quasi-experimental designs, including subjects who either failed to complete treatment or were untreated for various reasons as a control group. Obviously, because these control groups are formed without the benefit of random assignment, the differences that emerge between control subjects and treatment subjects could be the result of confounding variables.

A second issue critical to the evaluation of treatment program effectiveness is the choice of outcome criteria. Despite the potential for biased reporting on a subject as sensitive as domestic violence, empirical studies frequently evaluate treatment effectiveness based solely on subjects' self-reported violence on pre- and posttreatment comparisons of self-report inventory scales. Although some studies have utilized rearrest as an outcome criteria, this is also problematic because there is no way of knowing if those individuals who are not rearrested are also not reoffending. Perhaps the most important issue confounding the evaluation of BIP effectiveness concerns the fact that most empirical studies have reported outcome data only for those subjects who completed treatment and were available at follow-up. As a result, subjects who experienced a beneficial impact from treatment are probably overrepresented in responding samples as less motivated subjects may have withdrawn from treatment prematurely or refused to participate at follow-up.

On the issue of premature dropout, investigations into attrition rates among BIPs have discovered that approximately 40% to 60% of men attending the first session of treatment actually fail to complete treatment (DeMaris, 1989; Edleson & Syers, 1991; Gondolf, 1997; Pirog-Good & Stets, 1986). When evaluated in terms of treatment failure following initial contact with the program, one study discovered that 93% of the men referred to the program never actually completed it (Gondolf & Fisher, 1988). Clearly, the most troubling aspect of these high attrition rates is the fact that the men who drop out of treatment remain at increased risk of abusing their partners (Hamberger & Hastings, 1988). Consequently, there has been an attempt to identify differences between treatment completers and dropouts, with the goal of enhancing retention rates.

Research into the issue of premature termination from BIPs has been organized around exploring differences between dropouts and treatment completers on three issues: (a) demographic and psychological variables, (b) being court-mandated into treatment versus volunteering for treatment, or (c) some combination of the two. Unfortunately, despite a substantial amount of research on this topic, meaningful information on differences between dropouts and completers remains elusive, as many studies report inconsistent and often contradictory findings. For example, there is some literature that suggests that demographic variables (i.e., age, employment status, educational level, alcohol use, income, previous criminal history, and relationship status) can distinguish between treatment completers and dropouts, with dropouts tending to be younger, unemployed, less educated, more likely to abuse alcohol, either single or separated and to have a previous criminal history (Cadsky, Hanson, Crawford, & Lalonde, 1996; Chang & Saunders, 2002; Daly, Power, & Gondolf, 2001; DeMaris, 1989; Grusznski & Carrillo, 1988; Hamberger & Hastings, 1989). Other studies, however, have discovered either inconsistent or nonsignificant differences between treatment completers and dropouts on these variables (Chen, Bersani, Myers, & Denton, 1989; DeHart, Kennerly, Burke, & Follingstad, 1999; DeMaris, 1989; Grusznski & Carrillo, 1988; Hamberger & Hastings, 1989, 1991; Hamberger, Lohr, & Gottlieb, 2000).

Perhaps the best explanation for this confusing situation is that, currently, there has been only one replication study involving a sample drawn from the same location (Hamberger et al., 2000). Consequently, the differences in findings across studies may be attributable to differences in the samples or to systemic variables that could vary by location (e.g., judicial support for the program). If true, individual BIPs would have to develop information on program attrition that is unique to their program and location. In fact, Hamberger et al. (2000) have argued persuasively that the only way to develop meaningful information on program attrition for any specific BIP is to have each program "identify local norms for attrition and their attendant predictors" (p. 550).

Recently, in an attempt to make sense of the confusing situation that emerges from a consideration of the national literature on BIP attrition, one study employed a researcher–practitioner partnership to study variables associated with premature dropout from a court-mandated BIP and create a predictive model that could be used to assist the participating BIP in correctly identifying men at greatest risk for dropping out of the program (Buttell & Carney, 2002). In brief, the collaborative relationship yielded a predictive model that correctly predicted treatment completion for approximately 75% of the sample, which represented a 33% improvement over chance. The benefit of the development of the model for the BIP that participated in the study was their intention to use it to identify the men at risk of not completing the program. Following identification, the program sought to provide these men with additional services aimed at enhancing their likelihood of retention. We believe that the only way for BIPs to improve retention is for them to partner with researchers to develop attrition models specific to the batterers and judicial support in their location, and we believe that the study described previously can serve as a prototype for these types of collaborative relationships.

In terms of the evaluation literature on BIPs, there were several early reviews of the quasi-experimental design evaluation literature conducted, each of which reviewed dozens of single-site program evaluations (Carden, 1994; Eisikovits & Edleson, 1989; Gondolf, 1997; Holtzworth-Munroe, Bates, Smultzer, & Sandin, 1997; Rosenfeld, 1992; Tolman & Bennett, 1990). All of these reviews indicated that BIPs were experiencing some success, with most men (60% to 80%) who complete treatment no longer physically abusive toward their partner at the conclusion of the treatment program. Unfortunately, as mentioned previously, these same reviews also identify serious methodological limitations that detract from the confidence that can be placed in the positive single-site program evaluation data (for an excellent review, see Rosenfeld, 1992).

In direct contrast to the quasi-experimental design studies, more rigorous recent experimental evaluations and meta-analyses of BIPs suggest that these programs are having little or no treatment effect. Three recent experimental evaluations of BIPs, involving random assignment to different treatment conditions and a no-treatment control condition, have indicated that BIPs are having either a small effect or no effect on batterer recidivism (Davis & Taylor, 1999; Davis, Taylor, & Maxwell, 1998; Dunford, 2000; Feder & Dugan, 2002). Although the Dunford (2000) study involved Navy personnel and may not extrapolate well outside of that context and the other experimental evaluations were compromised by several problems, including significant problems with attrition and follow-up issues (Gondolf, 2001), two recent meta-analyses also suggest that BIPs are either ineffective or, if effective, yield a very small effect size (Babcock, Green, & Robie, 2004; Levesque, 1999). Overall, a critical appraisal of this body of literature suggests that treatment effects for BIPs are, at best, modest.

Despite the BIP evaluation research, it would be premature to conclude that BIPs are failing entirely. Specifically, in all of the evaluation studies discussed previously, both experimental and quasi-experimental, data was aggregated across all batterers in a treatment condition. Specifically, none of the studies evaluated the effect of different types of intervention efforts on different subtypes of batterers. Consequently, the findings of null or small effects may be attributable to the fact that batterers are not a homogenous group.

Although the idea that batterers are not a homogenous group is not a new one, it was not until Holtzworth-Munroe and Stuart's (1994) review of 15 previous batterer typology studies that similarities across the individual studies were identified. In brief, Holtzworth-Munroe and Stuart (1994) posited that batterer subtypes could be classified along three descriptive dimensions: (a) severity and frequency of marital violence, (b) generality of violence (i.e., violent only in the family or inside and outside the family), and (c) the batterer's psychopathology or personality disorders (p. 477). Using these three descriptive dimensions, they then identified three different types of batterers: (a) family-only, (b) dysphoric/borderline, and (c) generally violent/antisocial. Family-only batterers represent approximately 50% of batterers, and they are the least violent sub-group. These men engage in the least amount of marital violence, report the lowest levels of psychological and sexual abuse, are the least violent outside the home, and evidence little or no psychopathology. Dysphoric/borderline batterers represent approximately 25% of batterers. These men engage in moderate to severe marital violence, their violence is primarily confined to their wives (although some outside violence may also be present), and they are the most psychologically distressed and the most likely to evidence borderline personality characteristics. Generally violent/antisocial batterers represent approximately 25% of batterers. These men are the most violent subtype, engaging in high levels of marital and extrafamilial violence, and they are the most likely to evidence characteristics of antisocial personality disorder (p. 481–482). Since Holtzworth-Munroe and Stuart's (1994) review of the literature and identification of these three different subtypes of batterers, several other studies have investigated the phenomenon of batterer subtypes (Gondolf, 1999; Gottman et al., 1995; Hamberger, Lohr, Bonge, & Tolin, 1996; Holtzworth-Munroe, Meehan, Herron, Rehman, & Stuart, 2000; Tweed & Dutton, 1998; Waltz, Babcock, Jacobson, & Gottman, 2000). With relatively minor differences (e.g., four subtypes rather than three), these studies have supported the conceptualization of the three subtypes of batterers identified by Holtzworth-Munroe and Stuart (1994).

In summary, the findings of null or small effects in the BIP evaluation literature may be attributable to the fact that batterers are not a homogenous group and different types of batterers may have responded differently to the standardized intervention model being evaluated. If true, then some men may have gotten better in treatment, some men may have stayed largely the same, and some men may have gotten worse. Such a conclusion seems plausible, as the NIJ replication studies discussed previously on the deterrent effect of arrest for domestic violence demonstrated that arrest appeared to deter subsequent violence for some men (e.g., employed men) but may have increased the risk of subsequent violence for other men (Schmidt & Sherman, 1993). Regarding BIPs, as a result of this differential response to the intervention program, the evaluation studies and meta-analyses would suggest that, on average, the intervention program was ineffective, when, in fact, change may be related to subtype. When viewed from this perspective, the recent findings suggesting little or no treatment effect are not disastrous but, instead, appear to provide a compelling argument for identifying batterer subtypes and evaluating client–treatment matching.

Clinical or Legal Issues

At the present time, there appears to be one pressing clinical issue and two legal issues affecting BIPs. First, the effectiveness of mandatory arrest for deterring future domestic violence offenses has been called into question. Specifically, as discussed previously, the NIJ-funded replication studies of the deterrent effects of arrest for domestic violence offenses, rather than confirming the results of the Minneapolis Police Experiment, suggested null findings for the deterrent effect of arrest for domestic violence offenses. In fact, the replication studies discovered that arrest makes some men more violent. The second legal issue involves states legislating standards for BIPs, which serve to legally institutionalize one treatment model at precisely the same time that more rigorous evaluation research is suggesting that the model being instituted through state standards may not be working very well. Finally, the most pressing clinical issue relates to the cultural competency of the intervention model being instituted through state standards, which, unfortunately, intersects with and exacerbates the problems created by the premature creation of state standards for BIPs.

The data on mandatory arrest policies in cases involving domestic violence, when viewed through the lens of BIP attrition and evaluation, suggest some remarkable similarities between the men who fail to be deterred by arrest, the men who drop out of treatment prematurely, and the different subtypes of batterers. As discussed previously, some batterers are deterred from continued use of violence by arrest, but some are not, just as some men remain in BIPs and some do not. Is it possible to identify individual characteristics that would help to categorize those who were likely to drop out of treatment or those who would be deterred by arrest? The answer is yes, but not in a one-size-fits-all way. Differences among batterers' individual characteristics as well as BIPs' geographic location and judicial support are widely varied. Rather than focusing on a list of potentially important characteristics across batterers, what seems more valuable is to identify subtypes of batterers and to engage in client–treatment matching. Unfortunately, however, the current climate in domestic violence suggests that such innovative programming is, at best, unlikely.

Regarding the issue of cultural competency among BIPs, although there is no empirical research investigating the differential effect of the standard cognitive-behavioral treatment program on outcomes for White and African-American batterers, some authors have argued that the lack of cultural competence among treatment programs has a severe negative impact on African-American participants (Bennett & Williams, 2001; Gelles, 2002; Williams, 1992, 1995; Williams & Becker, 1994). In brief, survey research has documented the absence of culturally sensitive intervention approaches among treatment providers nationally (Williams, 1995). This absence of culturally sensitive intervention approaches is disturbing, given both the high rate of violence occurring in African-American relationships (Locke & Richman, 1999; Plass, 1993; Williams, 2000; Wyatt, Axelrod, Chin, Carmona, & Loeb, 2000) and the high attrition rate among African-American men in batterer treatment programs (Gondolf, 1997; Williams, 1995).

One factor operating against the identification of culturally appropriate intervention strategies for minority batterers is the national legislative trend to institutionalize the one-size-fits-all treatment model discussed in the literature (Moore, Greenfield, Wilson, & Kok, 1997; Williams, 1992). In brief, in an effort to create uniformity in BIPs, states have legislated standards for treatment providers. In fact, by 1997, more than half of the United States had instituted standards (Bennett & Williams, 2001). Among the many aspects of batterer intervention addressed by these standards is to formalize program structure and length. As a result, most treatment programs nationally, regardless of theoretical perspective, offer a feminist-informed, cognitive-behavioral, group treatment approach for batterers. The implication of this trend for treatment programs seeking to create culturally sensitive approaches for minority batterers is that they must now seek to create such services within the constraints of the one-size-fits-all model. Specifically, treatment providers are faced with a contradiction in attempting to develop programs that account for diverse client groups. The primary question is how to provide specialized, culturally sensitive intervention services to diverse groups of batterers while, at the same time, adhering to state standards that insist that all batterers, regardless of cultural differences, receive the same intervention program. It is exactly this dilemma that has many prominent domestic violence researchers arguing against the adoption of state program standards (Gelles, 2002).

Despite the problems related to incorporating culturally sensitive programming into BIPs, many authors have created culturally sensitive intervention programs for violent men (for an excellent example see, Almeida, Woods, Messineo, & Font, 1998). For the purposes of this discussion, culturally sensitive interventions are those that acknowledge the intersection of gender and race, adopt a constructivist perspective in learning about the different cultural views of clients, and account for different cultural pathways regarding courtship and marriage. Importantly, culturally sensitive interventions do not sanction violence against women but acknowledge that the cultural backgrounds of the participants may create different pathways to violence. Although culturally sensitive programs for batterers exist, two important issues have yet to be addressed: (a) a lack of any systematic evaluations of these models, comparing their effectiveness with the model that is being institutionalized through state standards; and (b) the adoption of state program standards, without any empirical evidence that the model being adopted works for minority batterers (Gondolf & Williams, 2001).

Description of Intervention

The intervention program is feminist informed and cognitive behavioral in orientation and is consistent in organization and focus to those programs described in the literature (Bennett & Williams, 2001; Gondolf, 1997; Rosenbaum & Leisring, 2002). The intervention program is a structured, intensive, 26-week group treatment program that focuses primarily on anger management and skills development. The intervention program incorporates three phases: (a) orientation and intake interview (two sessions),

(b) psychoeducational classes (22 sessions), and (c) group therapy regarding termination (two sessions). Groups consist of approximately 15 batterers and meet 1 night each week for approximately 2 hours. This batterer treatment program incorporates confrontation, therapy, and educational components. In this setting, the common proximal events of domestic violence are directly addressed with clients and they are given an opportunity to make changes that will positively affect their personal relationships with others.

The 22-week psychoeducational program curriculum can be broken up into three successive series of group experiences. Because most offenders share a common set of defenses (minimization, denial, and blame) that foster aggressive behavior, the first series of group sessions helps participants to recognize and overcome these defense mechanisms. In this series, which lasts 4 weeks, participants are assisted in overcoming their natural resistance to change by helping them achieve insight into their use of defense mechanisms. Thus, the first step toward modifying behavior occurs when clients recognize and accept the fact that the problem is their behavior. In the first session, program rules are reviewed and reasons for using anger are explored. Participants are instructed to examine their use of anger and identify ways to begin to change how they interact with their partners and families. Importantly, the men are required to tell their story and explain to the other group members the reasons for their arrests and referrals to the intervention program. In the second and third sessions, the men are educated about the importance of responsibility and honesty in achieving program goals, and roadblocks to responsibility (i.e., minimization, denial, and blame) are discussed. Following this educational piece, the men are required to retell their story, and group members provide corrective feedback to each other when they hear men utilizing roadblocks in their retelling of the incident that led to the program referral. In the fourth session, the cycle of violence is explained, and the men are asked to consider their relationships from this perspective and share their experiences with the group. At the end of the session, the concept of partnership in relationships is explored and discussed as an alternative to power and control.

The second series of sessions, which last 6 weeks, flows out of the fact that the belief and value systems of most batterers are very similar and foster the notion of traditional sex role stereotypes. This series challenges the batterers' beliefs and values. The sessions are designed to help clients restructure their thinking by modifying the beliefs that promote violent behavior. In the fifth and sixth sessions, a modified form of rational emotive therapy is explained, and participants are encouraged and assisted in applying the model to their own experiences. Also, in the seventh session, the concept of time-out is explained as a method to avoid the escalation that frequently accompanies arguments and results in violence. In the eighth session, irrational beliefs that contribute to violence (e.g., If my partner doesn't do what I want, he or she is deliberately trying to make me angry.) are explored and discussed, and the concept of rational self-talk is proposed as a method of avoiding the kind of irrational thinking that results in anger. In the ninth and tenth sessions, the concept of "thinking traps" (e.g., exaggeration and personalization) are presented to members, and they are required to explore in group how they have used these thinking errors to justify the violence they have inflicted on their partners.

The final series of sessions, which lasts 12 weeks, is designed to help clients increase interpersonal skills by providing them with a repertoire of alternate and appropriate behaviors. In this series, skills such as problem solving, assertiveness, and negotiation are both taught and practiced in the group setting. In the 11th and 12th sessions, the concept of assertiveness is explained, and the men are required to role-play scenarios where an assertive response is required for successful resolution of a problem situation. In the 13th and 14th sessions, roadblocks to communication (e.g., telling others what to do, preaching, and judging) are explained, and participants are encouraged to explore their own uses of these concepts in communicating with their partners. Also, in the 15th session, the concept of assertiveness is continued, and the men are required to role-play problematic communication scenarios with each other in group. In the 16th and 17th sessions, a problem-solving model is presented and applied to the experiences of the men in group. In the 18th and 19th sessions, the generational cycle of violence is presented, and childhood exposure to domestic violence is explored with participants. In the 20th and 21st sessions, negotiation skills are both presented and practiced in the group. In the final session, the concepts of trust, support, tolerance, and acceptance are presented, with an emphasis on how they relate to successful negotiation. Participants are required to discuss and role-play strategies for incorporating negotiation into their interactions with their partners.

Conclusion

While the debate about the prevalence of domestic violence rages on, and the camp of those who either cannot or will not acknowledge female-initiated violence battles those who suggest the possibility that intimate partner violence is bidirectional, mandatory arrest policies remain consolidated and states fight to legislate a one-size-fits-all standardized programming approach to working with batterers.

At issue for those truly interested in identifying and instituting effective practices for intervening with perpetrators of domestic violence is how to do so within the constraints of both legal mandates regarding arrest and state-legislated programming. What seems critical is to wade through the debates to find appropriate methods for intervening with batterers while understanding that they are not a homogenous group any more than persons from different genders or cultures would be assumed to be the same. With this enhanced understanding of batterers, intervention efforts must be tailored to the individual needs of each batterer, and one such way is to identify subtypes of batterers and intervene with each group accordingly.

The convergence of batterer typology studies confirming the tripartite Holtzworth-Munroe and Stuart (1994) conceptualization, and recent evaluations suggesting that BIPs are not working, should provide an impetus for improving intervention efforts by identifying batterer subtypes prospectively and engaging in client–treatment matching. Unfortunately, client–treatment matching becomes particularly problematic in a system where states are legislating one-size-fits-all treatment programs based not on individual needs or batterer subtype, but on uniform standards across the nation. In the absence of agreement regarding effective batterer intervention programming, what is clear is that for those who do remain in treatment—a prospect much more likely when the treatment is appropriately matched to the batterers' needs—the likelihood that they will continue to use violence in intimate relationships is reduced.

Increasing our understanding of battering and BIPs may best be done through enhanced researcher–practitioner relationships. Specifically, stronger collaborative relationships will allow for BIPs better to integrate research documenting the existence of batterer subtypes into programming, which can then be used as a vehicle for engaging in differential client–treatment matching.

RESOURCES AND REFERENCES

Almeida, R., Woods, R., Messineo, T., & Font, R. (1998). Cultural context model. In M. McGoldrick (Ed.), *Re-visioning family therapy: Race, culture and gender in clinical practice* (pp. 404–432). New York: Guilford Press.

Babcock, J., Green, C., & Robie, C. (2004). Does batterers' treatment work? A meta-analytic review of domestic violence treatment. *Clinical Psychology Review, 23*, 1023–1053.

Bennett, L., & Williams, O. (2001). Intervention program for men who batter. In C. Renzetti & J. Edleson (Eds.), *Sourcebook on violence against women* (pp. 261–277). Thousand Oaks, CA: Sage.

Berk, R., Campbell, A., Klap, R., & Western, B. (1992). The deterrent effect of arrest in incidents of domestic violence: A Bayesian analysis of four field experiments. *American Sociological Review, 57*, 698–708.

Binder, A., & Meeker, J. (1992). Implications of the failure to replicate the Minneapolis experimental findings. *American Sociological Review, 57*, 886–889.

Buttell, F., & Carney, M. (2002). Predictors of attrition among batterers court-ordered into treatment. *Social Work Research, 26*, 31–41.

Cadsky, O., Hanson, K., Crawford, M., & Lalonde, C. (1996). Attrition from a male batterer treatment program: Client-treatment congruence and lifestyle instability. *Violence and Victims, 11*, 51–64.

Carden, A. (1994). Wife abuse and the wife abuser: Review and recommendations. *The Counseling Psychologist, 22*, 539–582.

Chang, H., & Saunders, D. (2002). Predictors of attrition in two types of group programs for men who batter. *Journal of Family Violence, 17*, 273–292.

Chen, H., Bersani, C., Myers, S., & Denton, R. (1989). Evaluating the effectiveness of a court-sponsored abuser abatement program. *Journal of Family Violence, 4*, 309–322.

Daly, J., Power, T., & Gondolf, E. (2001). Predictors of batterer program attendance. *Journal of Interpersonal Violence, 16*, 971–991.

Davis, R., & Taylor, B. (1999). Does batterer treatment reduce violence? A synthesis of the literature. *Women and Criminal Justice, 10*, 69–93.

Davis, R., Taylor, B., & Maxwell, C. (1998). *Does batterer treatment reduce violence? A randomized experiment in Brooklyn. National Institute of Justice Final Report* (Grant No. 94-IJ-CX-0047). Washington, DC: National Institute of Justice/NCJRS.

DeHart, D., Kennerly, R., Burke, L., & Follingstad, D. (1999). Predictors of attrition in a treatment program for battering men. *Journal of Family Violence, 14*, 19–35.

DeMaris, A. (1989). Attrition in batterers' counseling: The role of social and demographic factors. *Social Service Review, 63*, 142–154.

Dunford, F. (2000). The San Diego Navy Experiment: An assessment of interventions for men who assault their wives. *Journal of Consulting and Clinical Psychology, 68*, 468–476.

Durose, M., Harlow, C., Langan, P., Motivans, M., Rantala, R., & Smith, E. (2005). *Family violence statistics including statistics on strangers and acquaintances* (NCJ No. 207846). Washington, DC: U.S. Department of Justice.

Edleson, J., & Syers, M. (1991). The effects of group treatment for men who batter: An 18-month follow-up study. *Research on Social Work Practice, 1*, 227–243.

Eisikovits, Z., & Edleson, J. (1989). Intervening with men who batter: A critical review of the literature. *Social Service Review, 37*, 385–414.

Feder, L., & Dugan, L. (2002). A test of the efficacy of court-mandated counseling for domestic violence offenders: The Broward experiment. *Justice Quarterly, 19*(2), 343–375.

Gelles, R. (1993). Constraints against family violence: How well do they work? *American Behavioral Scientist, 36*, 575–586.

Gelles, R. (2002). Standards for programs for men who batter? Not yet. *Journal of Aggression, Maltreatment & Trauma, 5*, 11–20.

Gondolf, E. (1997). Batterer programs: What we know and need to know. *Journal of Interpersonal Violence, 12*, 83–98.

Gondolf, E. (1999). MCMI-III results for batterer program participants in four cities: Less "pathological" than expected. *Journal of Family Violence, 14*, 1–17.

Gondolf, E. (2001). Limitations of experimental evaluations of batterers programs. *Trauma, Violence, and Abuse, 2*, 79–88.

Gondolf, E., & Fisher, E. (1988). *Battered women as survivors: An alternative to treating learned helplessness.* Lexington, MA: Lexington Books.

Gondolf, E., & Williams, O. (2001). Culturally focused batterer counseling for African-American men. *Trauma, Violence, and Abuse, 2*, 283–295.

Gottman, J., Jacobson, N., Rushe, R., Shortt, J., Babcock, J., Talliade, J. et al. (1995). The relationship between heart rate reactivity, emotionally aggressive behavior, and general violence in batterers. *Journal of Family Psychology, 9*, 227–248.

Grusznski, R., & Carrillo, R. (1988). Who completes batterer treatment programs? An empirical investigation. *Journal of Family Violence, 3*, 141–150.

Hamberger, K., & Hastings, J. (1988). Skills training for treatment of spouse abusers: An outcome study. *Journal of Family Violence, 3*, 121–130.

Hamberger, K., & Hastings, J. (1989). Counseling male spouse abusers: Characteristics of treatment completers and drop-outs. *Violence and Victims, 4*, 275–286.

Hamberger, K., & Hastings, J. (1991). Personality correlates of men who batter and nonviolent men: Some continuities and discontinuities. *Journal of Family Violence, 6*, 131–147.

Hamberger, K., Lohr, J., Bonge, D., & Tolin, D. (1996). A large sample empirical typology of male spouse abusers and its relationship to dimensions of abuse. *Violence and Victims, 11*, 277–292.

Hamberger, K., Lohr, J., & Gottlieb, M. (2000). Predictors of treatment dropout from a spouse abuse abatement program. *Behavior Modification, 24*, 528–552.

Hirschel, D., Hutchinson, I., & Dean, C. (1992). The failure of arrest to deter spouse abuse. *Journal of Research in Crime and Delinquency, 29*, 7–33.

Holtzworth-Munroe, A., Bates, L., Smultzer, N., & Sandin, E. (1997). A brief review of the research on husband violence. *Aggression and Violent Behavior, 2*, 65–99.

Holtzworth-Munroe, A., Meehan, J., Herron, K., Rehman, U., & Stuart, G. (2000). Testing the Holtzworth-Munroe & Stuart (1994) batterer typology. *Journal of Consulting and Clinical Psychology, 68*, 1000–1019.

Holtzworth-Munroe, A., & Stuart, G. (1994). Typologies of male batterers: Three subtypes and the differences among them. *Psychological Bulletin, 116*, 476–497.

Johnson, M. (1995). Patriarchal terrorism and common couple violence: Two forms of violence against women. *Journal of Marriage and the Family, 57*, 283–294.

Johnson, M. P. (2000). Conflict and control: Images of symmetry and asymmetry in domestic violence. In A. Booth, A. Crouter, & M. Clements (Eds.), *Couples in Conflict* (pp. 178–204). Hillsdale, NJ: Lawrence Erlbaum Associates.

Johnson, S. M., & Lebow, J. (2000). The "coming of age" of couple therapy: A decade review. *Journal of Marital and Family Therapy, 26*(1), 23–38.

Levesque, D. (1999). *Violence desistance among battering men: Existing interventions and the application of the transtheoretical model of change.* Unpublished doctoral dissertation, University of Rhode Island, Kingston.

Locke, L., & Richman, C. (1999). Attitudes toward domestic violence: Race and gender issues. *Sex Roles: A Journal of Research, 40*, 227–229.

McCord, J. (1992). Deterrence of domestic violence: A critical view of research. *Journal of Research in Crime and Delinquency, 29*, 229–239.

Moore, K., Greenfield, W., Wilson, M., & Kok, A. (1997). Toward a taxonomy of batterers. *Families in Societies, 78*, 352–359.

Mitchell, D. (1992). Contemporary police practices in domestic violence cases: Arresting the abuser: Is it enough? *Journal of Criminal Law & Criminology, 83*, 241–249.

Pate, A., & Hamilton, E. (1992). Formal and informal deterrents to domestic violence: The Dade County spouse assault experiment. *American Sociological Review, 57*, 691–697.

Pirog-Good, M., & Stets, J. (1986). Programs for abusers: Who drops out and what can be done. *Response, 9*, 17–19.

Plass, P. (1993). African-American family homicide: Patterns in partner, parent, and child victimization, 1985–1987. *Journal of Black Studies, 4*, 515–538.

Polsby, D. (1992). Suppressing domestic violence with law reforms. *Journal of Criminal Law & Criminology, 83*, 250–253.

Rosenbaum, A., & Leisring, P. (2002). A group intervention program for batterers. *Journal of Aggression, Maltreatment & Trauma, 5*, 57–71.

Rosenfeld, B. (1992). Court-ordered treatment of spouse abuse. *Clinical Psychology Review, 12*, 205–226.

Schmidt, J., & Sherman, L. (1993). Does arrest deter domestic violence? *American Behavioral Scientist, 36*, 601–609.

Sherman, L., Smith, D., Schmidt, J., & Rogan, D. (1992). Crime, punishment, and stake in conformity: Legal and informal control of domestic violence. *American Sociological Review, 57*, 680–690.

Sherman, W., & Berk, R. (1984). The specific deterrent effects of arrest for domestic assault. *American Sociological Review, 49*, 261–272.

Straus, M. A. (1979). Measuring intra-family conflict and violence: The Conflict Tactics (CT) Scales. *Journal of Marriage and the Family, 41*, 75–88.

Straus, M. A., & Gelles, R. J. (1986). Societal changes and change in family violence from 1975 to 1985 as revealed by two national surveys. *Journal of Marriage and the Family, 48*, 465–479.

Tolman, R., & Bennett, L. (1990). A review of quantitative research on men who batter. *Journal of Interpersonal Violence, 5*, 87–118.

Tweed, R., & Dutton, D. (1998). A comparison of impulsive and instrumental subgroups of batterers. *Violence and Victims, 13*, 217–230.

Waltz, J., Babcock, J., Jacobson, N., & Gottman, J. (2000). Testing a typology of batterers. *Journal of Consulting and Clinical Psychology, 68*, 658–669.

Williams, O. (1992). Ethnically sensitive practice to enhance treatment participation of African-American men who batter. *Families in Society, 73*, 588–595.

Williams, O. (1995). Treatment for African-American men who batter. *CURA Reporter, 25*, 610.

Williams, O. (2000). The public health and social consequences of Black male violence. *Journal of African-American Men, 5*, 71.

Williams, O., & Becker, R. (1994). Domestic partner abuse treatment programs and cultural competence: The results of a national survey. *Violence and Victims, 9*, 287–295.

Wyatt, G., Axelrod, J., Chin, D., Carmona, J., & Loeb, T. (2000). Examining patterns of vulnerability to domestic violence among African-American women. *Violence Against Women, 6*, 495–515.

Relevant Resources for Practitioners

National Coalition Against Domestic Violence
Web site: www.ncadv.org

American Bar Association Commission on Domestic Violence
740 15th Street NW, Washington, DC 20005
Phone: 202-662-1000, Web site: www.abanet.org/domviol

American Institute on Domestic Violence
2116 Rover Drive, Lake Havasu City, AZ 86403
Phone: 928-453-9015, Web site: www.aidv-usa.com

Amnesty International USA, Women's Human Rights Program
322 Eighth Avenue, New York, NY 10001
Phone: 212-633-4292, Web site: www.amnestyusa.org/women

Asian and Pacific Islander Institute on Domestic Violence
450 Sutter Street #600, San Francisco, CA 94108
Phone: 415-954-9988 ext. 315, Web site: www.apiahf.org/apidvinstitute

The Audre Lorde Project
85 S. Oxford Street, Brooklyn, NY 11217
Phone: 718-596-0342, Web site: www.alp.org

The Black Church and Domestic Violence Institute
2740 Greenbriar Parkway #256, Atlanta, GA 30331
Phone: 770-909-0715, Web site: www.bcdvi.org

Bureau of Justice Statistics Clearinghouse
810 Seventh Street NW, Washington, DC 20531
Phone: 800-851-3420, Web site: www.ojp.usdoj.gov/bjs

CAAAV Organizing Asian Communities
2473 Valentine Avenue, Bronx, NY 10458
Web site: www.caaav.org

Childhelp USA
15757 N. 78th Street, Scottsdale, AZ 85260
Phone: 800-422-4453, Web site: www.childhelpusa.org

Child Welfare League of America
440 First Street NW, Third Floor, Washington, DC 20001
Phone: 202-638-2952, Web site: www.cwla.org

Children's Defense Fund
25 "E" Street NW, Washington, DC 20001
Phone: 202-628-8787, Web site: www.childrensdefense.org

Coalition for Justice in the Maquiladoras
4207 Willow Brook, San Antonio, TX 78228
Phone: 210-732-8957, Web site: www.coalitionforjustice.net

Equality Now
P. O. Box 20646, Columbus Circle Station, New York, NY 10023
Web site: www.equalitynow.org

Faith Trust Institute
2400 N. 45th Street #10, Seattle, WA 98103
Phone: 206-634-1903, Web site: www.cpsdv.org

Family Violence Prevention Fund
383 Rhode Island Street #304, San Francisco, CA 94103
Phone: 415-252-8900, TTY: 800-595-4889, Web site: www.endabuse.org

The Feminist Majority and the Feminist Majority Foundation
1600 Wilson Boulevard #801, Arlington, VA 22209
Phone: 703-522-2214
433 S. Beverly Drive, Beverly Hills, CA 90212
Phone: 310-556-2500, Web site: www.feminist.org

Graduate School of Public Affairs, University of Colorado
The Master's Program on Domestic Violence
Phone: 800-990-8227 ext. 4182, Web site: www.cudenver.edu/gspa

Human Rights Watch
350 Fifth Avenue, 34th Floor, New York, NY 10118
Web site: www.hrw.org

The Humane Society of the United States, First Strike Campaign
2100 L Street NW, Washington, DC 20037
Phone: 888-213-0956, Web site: www.hsus.org/firststrike

INCITE! Women of Color Against Violence
Web site: www.incite-national.org

Indigenous Women's Network
13621 FM 78726, Austin, TX 78726
Phone: 512-258-3880, Web site: www.indigenouswomen.org

Institute on Domestic Violence in the African American Community
University of Minnesota School of Social Work, College of Human Ecology
290 Peters Hall, 1404 Gortner Avenue, St. Paul, MN 55108
Phone: 877-643-8222, Web site: www.dvinstitute.org

Jewish Women International
2000 M Street NW #720, Washington, DC 20036
Phone: 800-343-2823, Web site: www.jewishwomen.org

JIST Life / KIDSRIGHTS
8902 Otis Avenue, Indianapolis, IN 46216
Phone: 800-648-5478, Web site: www.jistlife. com

LAMBDA GLBT Community Services
216 S. Ochoa Street, El Paso, TX 79901
Phone: 206-350-4283, Web site: www.lambda.org

Legal Momentum
395 Hudson Street, New York, NY 10014
Phone: 212-925-6635, Web site: www.nowldef.org

Manavi
P. O. Box 3103, New Brunswick, NJ 08903
Phone: 732-435-1414, Web site: www.manavi.org

Mending the Sacred Hoop – Technical Assistance Project
202 E. Superior Street, Duluth, MN 55802
Phone: 888-305-1650, Web site: www.msh-ta.org

The Miles Foundation (violence and the military)
P. O. Box 423, Newton, CT 06470
Phone: 203-270-7861, Web site: members.aol. com/milesfdn/myhomepage

Ms. Foundation for Women
120 Wall Street, 33rd Floor, New York, NY 10005
Phone: 212-742-1653, Web site: www. ms.foundation.org

National Center for Elder Abuse
1201 15th Street NW #350, Washington, DC 20005
Phone: 202-898-2586, Web site: www.elderabusecenter.org

National Center for Victims of Crime
2000 M Street, NW, Suite 480, Washington, DC
Phone: 202-467-8700, Web site: www.ncvc.org

National Center for Youth Law
405 14th Street, 15th Floor, Oakland, CA 94612
Phone: 510-835-8098, Web site: www.youthlaw.org

National Center on Domestic and Sexual Violence
7800 Shoal Creek #120-N, Austin, TX 78757
Phone: 512-407-9020, Web site: www.ntcdsv.org

National Clearinghouse on Abuse in Later Life
Wisconsin Coalition Against Domestic Violence
307 S. Paterson Street #1, Madison, WI 53703
Phone: 608-255-0539, Web site: www.ncall.us

National Clearinghouse on Child Abuse and Neglect Information
330 C Street SW, Washington, DC 20447
Phone: 800-394-3366, Web site: nccanch.acf.hhs.gov

National Coalition for the Homeless
1012 14th Street NW #600, Washington, DC 20005
Phone: 202-737-6444, Web site: www.nationalhomeless.org

National Coalition of Anti-Violence Programs
240 W. 35th Street #200, New York, NY 10001
Phone: 212-714-1184, Web site: www.ncavp.org

National Domestic Violence Hotline
P. O. Box 161810, Austin, TX 78716
Phone: 800-799-7233, TTY: 800-787-3224, Web site: www.ndvh.org

National Gay and Lesbian Task Force
1325 Massachusetts Avenue NW #600, Washington, DC 20005
Phone: 202-393-5177, Web site: www.ngltf.org

National Health Resource Center on Domestic Violence
Family Violence Prevention Fund
383 Rhode Island Street #304, San Francisco, CA 94103
Phone: 888-792-2873, Web site: www.endabuse.org

National Immigration Forum
50 F Street NW #300, Washington, DC 20001
Phone: 202-347-0040, Web site: www.immigrationforum.org

National Latino Alliance for the Elimination of Domestic Violence (ALIANZA)
P. O. Box 672, Triborough Station, New York, NY 10035
Phone: 646-672-1404, Web site: www.dvalianza.org

National Network for Immigrant and Refugee Rights
310 Eighth Street #303, Oakland, CA 94607
Phone: 510-465-1984, Web site: www.nnirr.org

National Network to End Domestic Violence
660 Pennsylvania Avenue SE #303, Washington, DC 20003
Phone: 202-543-5566, Web site: www.nnedv.org

National Organization for Victim Assistance
1730 Park Road NW, Washington, DC 20010
Phone: 800-879-6682, Web site: www.try-nova.org

National Resource Center on Domestic Violence
Pennsylvania Coalition Against Domestic Violence
6400 Flank Drive #1300, Harrisburg, PA 17112
Phone: 800-537-2238, TTY: 800-553-2508, Web site: www.nrcdv.org

National Runaway Switchboard
3080 N. Lincoln Avenue, Chicago, IL 60657
Phone: 773-880-9860 / 800-621-4000, Web site: www.nrscrisisline.org

National Sexual Violence Resource Center
123 N. Enola Drive, Enola, PA 17025
Phone: 877-739-3895, TTY: 717-909-0715, Web site: www.nsvrc.org

National Women's Political Caucus
1634 Eye Street NW #310, Washington, DC 20006
Phone: 202-785-1100, Web site: www.nwpc.org

Planned Parenthood Federation of America
434 W. 33rd Street, New York, NY 10001
Phone: 212-541-7800, Web site: www.plannedparenthood.org

Rape, Abuse & Incest National Network (RAINN)
635-B Pennsylvania Avenue SE, Washington, DC 20003
Phone: 800-656-4673 ext. 3, Web site: www.rainn.org

Resource Center on Domestic Violence: Child Protection & Custody
National Council on Juvenile & Family Court Judges
P. O. Box 8970, Reno, NV 89507
Phone: 800-527-3223, Web site: www.nationalcouncilfvd.org

Sacred Circle
National Resource Center to End Violence Against Native Women
722 Saint Joseph Street, Rapid City, SD 57701
Phone: 877-733-7623

Soroptimist International of the Americas
1709 Spruce Street, Philadelphia, PA 19103
Phone: 215-893-9000, Web site: www.soroptimist.org

STOPDV, Inc.
P. O. Box 1410, Poway, CA 92074
Phone: 858-679-2913, Web site: www.stopdv. com

Violence Against Women Office, U.S. Department of Justice
10th and Constitution Avenue NW #5302, Washington, DC 20530
Phone: 202-616-8994, Web site: www.ojp.usdoj.gov/vawo

Women's Independence Scholarship Program, The Sunshine Lady Foundation
4900 Randall Parkway #H, Wilmington, NC 28403
Phone: 910-397-7742 / 866-255-7742, Web site: www.sunshineladyfdn.org

Juvenile Justice Process, Assessment, and Treatment

Treatment Effectiveness With Dually Diagnosed Adolescents: Implications for Juvenile Offenders

8

Kimberly Bender
Johnny S. Kim
David W. Springer

Introduction

Addressing the unique treatment needs of dually diagnosed adolescents has become increasingly pressing in recent years as a result of high prevalence rates and serious clinical concerns associated with this population. Several issues make comorbid disorders extremely challenging to treat, including complex treatment needs, increased severity of symptoms, high cost of treatment, necessity to integrate several interventions, and low treatment retention among dually diagnosed youth. Despite these complexities, recent studies have demonstrated the effectiveness of interventions aimed at treating dually diagnosed adolescents. The primary aim of this chapter is to systematically review empirically supported interventions for dually diagnosed adolescents.

The juvenile justice system serves a growing number of youth diagnosed with co-occurring mental health and substance use disorders (Teplin, Abram, McClelland, Dulcan, & Mericle, 2002). Approximately 14% of females and 11% of males carry a major mental diagnosis (psychosis, major depression, or manic episode) and a substance use disorder diagnosis, and approximately 30% are dually diagnosed with co-occurring behavioral and substance use disorders (Abram, Teplin, McClelland, & Dulcan, 2003). These rates of dual diagnosis for juvenile offenders are elevated when compared with rates found in nonoffender adolescent samples (Aarons, Brown, Hough, Garland, & Wood, 2001).

The authors wish to acknowledge the researchers who conducted the original research included in this systematic review. This chapter is adapted from Bender, K. Springer, D. W. & Kim, J. S. (2006). Treatment effectiveness with dually diagnosed adolescents. *Brief Treatment and Crisis Intervention, 6*(3), 17–205.

Despite the high prevalence of both mental health and substance use diagnoses in the juvenile justice system, few randomized intervention studies have been conducted in juvenile justice settings. This is most likely due in large part to difficulty in implementing studies within tightly restricted juvenile justice settings, high attrition rates, and feasibility issues regarding randomization (Springer, McNeece, & Mayfield-Arnold, 2003). Due to the lack of outcome studies specifically targeting dually diagnosed juvenile offenders, this chapter reviews the treatment of dually diagnosed adolescents in general. The final discussion then examines findings in light of their implications for juvenile offenders.

Definitions

Dually diagnosed adolescents are identified as simultaneously having substance use disorders (SUDs) and comorbid psychiatric mental health disorders. The term *dually diagnosed* remains rather ambiguous, however, because it encompasses adolescents with a variety of substance use problems and a spectrum of mental health disorders. This lack of uniformity creates challenges for those who seek to study and treat dually diagnosed adolescents (Crome, 2004). For example, adolescents with SUD and comorbid mood disorders may have different needs and responses to treatment than do adolescents with SUD and conduct disorder (CD) or attention-deficit/hyperactivity disorder (ADHD). For the purposes of this review, adolescents with a combination of an SUD and at least one mental health diagnosis are categorized as dually diagnosed. For the purposes of this review, an adolescent is any youth between the ages of 12 to 18 years. Lastly, juvenile delinquency is differentiated from CD such that a youth can be defined as a juvenile delinquent after only one delinquent act while a diagnosis of CD requires a pattern of behavior over an extended period of time that consistently violates the rights of others and societal norms (Springer, 2004).

Prevalence

Despite the difficulty in creating a uniform definition, several studies have reported extremely high prevalence rates of comorbid conditions. Among substance-abusing adolescents, 50% to 90% report comorbid psychiatric problems (Greenbaum, Foster-Johnson, & Amelia, 1996; Greenbaum, Prange, Friedman, & Silver, 1991; Rounds-Bryant, Kristiansen, & Hubbard, 1999). Roberts and Corcoran (2005) assert that dually diagnosed adolescents are in fact not a special subpopulation of adolescents but, instead, the norm. The majority of adolescents seeking services today are thus likely to have substance use problems; mental health diagnoses; as well as myriad social, behavioral, and familial problems.

Characteristics

Dually diagnosed adolescents are characteristically a very challenging population to treat. Although prevalence rates are high, few interventions have been developed or tested to treat this population. There is a dearth of development and testing of treatments for dually diagnosed youth for several reasons. The majority of federally funded mechanisms have been focused on Type I and II clinical trials with homogeneous samples. Dually diagnosed adolescents are likely to have poor attendance in treatment, to be difficult to engage, and to have high rates of noncompliance (Crome, 2004; Donohue et al., 1998; Flanzer, 2005; Wise, Cuffe, & Fischer, 2001). Early termination of treatment is especially problematic for youth with comorbid SUDs and ADHD or CD, while those with comorbid adjustment or mood disorders have better rates of retention (Flanzer, 2005).

Early termination and disengagement is associated with poor treatment outcomes (Williams & Chang, 2000). Consequently, dually diagnosed adolescents are at increased risk for hospitalization, relapse, and poor prognosis (Crome, 2004; Flanzer, 2005). Thus, comorbidity—especially mixed type (internalizing and externalizing disorders in addition to SUD)—is linked to poor treatment outcomes for adolescent substance abusers (Rowe, Liddle, Greenbaum, & Henderson, 2004). Even when initial treatment outcomes are positive, dually diagnosed youth are less likely to sustain treatment gains over time (Dakof, Tejeda, & Liddle, 2001; Shane, Jasiukaitis, & Green, 2003).

Dually diagnosed adolescents also represent a more clinically severe subsample of adolescents seeking treatment. They are likely to have earlier onset of substance use and tend to use substances more frequently and more chronically than adolescents with SUDs alone (Greenbaum et al., 1991; Rowe et al., 2004). Examining severity of SUDs in the population further, Libby, Orton, Stover, & Riggs (2005) found that levels remain similarly high regardless of whether youth developed mental health disorders or SUDs first, suggesting that different pathways to dual diagnosis have consistently high treatment needs.

Not only are substance use risk factors higher among this population, but dually diagnosed adolescents are also more at risk for myriad other social problems, including familial and academic problems, as well as increased criminal behavior (Grella, Hser, Joshi, & Rounds-Bryant, 2001). Many youth who are dually diagnosed have also experienced early significant loss in their lives (Libby et al., 2005). Considering these complex needs, it is not surprising that dually diagnosed youth tend to have more service needs, receive more services during treatment, and are twice as likely to involve family members in treatment (Grella, Vandana, & Hser, 2004).

Treatment

Currently three models of treatment guide interventions for dually diagnosed clients, including serial treatment (treating one disorder before the other), parallel treatment (treating both disorders simultaneously by separate clinicians), and integrated treatment (treating both disorders concurrently).

To date, treatment modalities for dually diagnosed adults have received more empirical attention than have interventions for adolescents. Dumaine (2003) conducted a comprehensive meta-analysis of dually diagnosed adults and reported that intensive case management services followed by standard aftercare services with specialized outpatient psychoeducational groups had the greatest treatment effects, while inpatient treatments had the least effects.

However, studies have found that simply replicating adult-oriented treatments for adolescents is not adequate; adolescents require specialized treatment to meet their unique developmental needs. Lysaught and Wodarski (1996) highlight the importance of integrating treatment formats by addressing the influences of both peers and parents through peer group treatment and parent psychoeducational groups. Many researchers and treatment providers, recognizing the unique clinical needs of dually diagnosed adolescents, have called for better screening and assessment in facilities treating adolescents (Robertson, Dill, Husain, & Undesser, 2004). Others have begun to test treatments with established efficacy for adults for their applicability, with modifications, to dually diagnosed adolescents. For example, Crome (2004) states that the best treatment approaches for dually diagnosed youth are those that combine addiction treatments for adults and treatments for adolescents with behavioral problems.

Intervention researchers may be apprehensive about empirically testing the treatment of dually diagnosed adolescents because it is costly and time intensive and requires interventions that are integrative and complex. For instance, dually diagnosed adolescents often require behavioral treatments unique to their mental health disorders in addition to those treatments required for substance abuse (Flanzer, 2005). Cost of treatment for comorbid adolescents can be twice as high as treatment for adolescents with only one of these disorders (King, Gaines, Lambert, Summerfelt, & Bickman, 2000). Due to these challenges, services for co-occurring youth are often lacking in availability and quality, creating a gap of comprehensive, appropriate treatment for this population (Flanzer, 2005).

Despite this population's challenges and complexities, researchers recognizing the prevalence and severity of needs have begun studying effective treatments for dually diagnosed adolescents. In the following section, we comprehensively describe the recent nonrandomized outcome studies related to treatment of dually diagnosed youth, and then provide a systematic review of six treatment studies that utilized randomized designs.

Nonrandomized Outcome Studies

Pretest–Posttest Designs

We found five studies that utilized a pretest–posttest design to measure improvement in mental health symptoms and substance abuse in dually diagnosed youth (see Table 8.1 for study details). These studies covered a variety of interventions and reported mixed results.

Two studies (Bean, White, Neagle, & Lake, 2005; Clark, Marmol, Cooley, & Gathercoal, 2004) reported positive treatment outcomes. Bean et al. (2005) reported positive outcomes in their study of dually diagnosed youth receiving intensive psychiatric residential services, including reductions in anxiety, depression, CD, and ADHD symptoms. Clark et al. (2004) found similar improvements using wilderness therapy in reducing depressive affect, substance use proneness, delinquency, and impulsivity.

In contrast to these two studies, Whitmore, Mikulich, Ehlers, and Crowley (2000) reported more mixed results. Youth receiving more traditional individual, family, and group outpatient therapy showed improvement in CD, criminality, and ADHD symptoms; however, two major outcomes, depression and substance use, did not improve significantly in this sample (Whitmore et al., 2000).

Table 8.1	Nonrandomized Outcome Studies			
Study	**Sample**	**Design**	**Treatment**	**Findings**
Bean et al. (2005)	Dually diagnosed adolescents ($N = 53$)	Pretest, posttest	Intensive psychiatric residential treatment	Reduction in anxiety symptoms, depression symptoms, conduct disorder, ADHD symptoms. Sig. improvement in family relationships and educational status.
Clark et al. (2004)	Troubled adolescents; 50% dually diagnosed ($N = 109$)	Pretest, posttest	Wilderness therapy	Wilderness therapy improved scores of depressive affect, substance abuse proneness, delinquent predisposition, and impulsive propensity.
Grella et al. (2004)	Adolescents with SUD; 62% dually diagnosed (majority CD) ($N = 810$)	Pretest, posttest	Residential, outpatient, short-term inpatient	Dually diagnosed youth had more service needs, received more services, and were twice as likely to involve family in tx; positive outcomes related to rapport with counselor and participation in 12-step groups.
*Rogers et al. (2004)	Adolescent offenders; 73.2% SUD, 65.9% CD, 26.8% mood disorder ($N = 82$)	Pretest, posttest	Designed especially for youth w/both SUD and behavioral disruptive disorders; psychoeducation, therapeutic groups with behavioral level system	CD did not predict tx outcome; strongest predictor of hospital course and time to discharge was breadth of substance use.
Whitmore et al. (2000)	Dually diagnosed female adolescents ($N = 46$)	Pretest, 1-year post-treatment	Weekly individual, family, and group therapy sessions addressing drug use and criminal behavior	Improvement in CD, criminality, ADHD symptoms, and educational/vocational status; no improvement in substance use or depression; peer problems predicted CD; ADHD symptoms predicted substance outcomes.

(Continued)

Table 8.1	(Continued)			
Study	Sample	Design	Treatment	Findings
*Jenson & Potter (2003)	Dually diagnosed Juvenile detainees (N = 107)	Pretest, 3-month, 6-month follow-up	Cross-system collaborative intervention: psychoeducation, psychiatric, case management, group therapy; substance abuse tx, family therapy	Reduction in MH symptoms, delinquency, and substance use at 6-month postrelease from detention.
Shane et al. (2003)	Three groups: youth with SUD, SUD + either internal or externalizing disorder, SUD + both internal and externalizing disorder (N = 419)	Posttest, 3-month, 6-month, 12-month follow-up	Short-term and long-term residential substance abuse treatment programs	Mixed comorbid youth entered treatment with higher levels of substance use; maintained highest levels through tx and at posttreatment compared to other groups; they initially responded to tx w/decrease in substance use; relapsed at higher rates.
Grella et al. (2001)	Adolescents with SUD; 64% dually diagnosed (majority CD) (N = 992)	Pretest, 12-month follow-up	Drug treatment in residential, outpatient, and short-term inpatient	Dually diagnosed youth had more severe substance use (earlier onset, more substance dependence, greater # of substances); dually diagnosed youth more problems w/ family, school, criminal behavior; at 12-month, showed improvement but still greater use than SUD-only group.
*Randall et al. (1999)	Juvenile offenders with SUD; 72% dually diagnosed (N = 118)	Pretest, posttest, 6-month follow-up	Multisystemic therapy (MST) and community services as usual	Comorbid externalizing disorders associated with worse substance abuse and criminal activity outcomes; the presence of internalizing disorders buffered the effects of externalizing disorders.
*Crowley et al. (1998)	Dually diagnosed male juvenile delinquents (N = 89)	Pretest, 6-month, 12-month, 24-month follow-up	Residential tx; behavior tx, group, family, vocational counseling, 12-step groups, aftercare available	2-year follow-up: improvement in criminality, CD, and depression but no change in substance use; outcomes predicted by intensity of substance involvement, CD severity, and onset of CD as reported at intake.

Note. Studies marked with an asterisk (*) include samples of juvenile offenders.

Two studies (Grella et al., 2004; Rogers, Jackson, Sweell, & Johansen, 2004) identified substance abuse as a particularly persistent and influential factor in treatment. Clarifying the differential effects of drug treatment for dually diagnosed youth versus SUD-only youth, Grella et al. (2004) found that dually diagnosed youth had more severe substance use. While treatment did reduce substance use for this vulnerable group, the dually diagnosed youth still maintained higher levels of use posttreatment. Rogers et al. (2004) further explored the effects of dual diagnosis on treatment, reporting that severity of substance use, not CD, predicted successful completion of treatment in a hospital setting.

Pretest–Posttest and Follow-up Designs

An important aspect of treatment, enduring treatment effects, has been evaluated using follow-up data in a few nonrandomized studies. Again, these five outcome studies report equivocal results.

Among those reporting more positive findings was an evaluation of a cross-system collaborative intervention for dually diagnosed juvenile detainees. The intervention focused on treatment coordination through case management and was associated with a reduction in mental health symptoms, delinquency, and substance use 6 months after being released from detention (Jenson & Potter, 2003). Crowley, Mikulich, MacDonald, Young, and Zerbe (1998) had similar positive findings when they examined the effects of residential treatment on male juvenile delinquents 2 years after leaving treatment. While Crowley et al.'s sample improved in criminality, depression, and CD, they showed no change in substance use.

Three other studies reported more negative results. Shane et al. (2003) found that youth with both externalizing and internalizing mental health disorders in addition to SUD entered treatment with higher levels of substance use when compared to youth with only one type of mental health diagnosis and SUD, or those with SUD only. This mixed group, with more complex diagnoses, maintained elevated rates of substance use throughout treatment and at posttreatment. Furthermore, while mixed comorbid youth initially responded to residential treatment with a decrease in substance use, they relapsed at higher rates (Shane et al., 2003). Grella et al. (2001) similarly found that dually diagnosed youth reduced their substance use after completing treatment in various residential, outpatient, and short-term inpatient substance abuse programs, but 12 months after treatment they were more likely to be using substances and engaging in criminal behavior than adolescents with SUD only (Grella et al., 2001). In a study of multisystemic therapy, Randall, Henggeler, Pickrel, and Brondino (1999) found the presence of externalizing disorders to be especially detrimental; youth with both SUD and externalizing disorders had higher rates of antisocial behavior and worse substance use outcomes at 16-month follow-up. Interestingly, and contrary to Shane et al.'s (2003) finding that youth with mixed disorders had poorer outcomes, Randall et al. (1999) found that the additional presence of internalizing disorders buffered the effects of externalizing disorders and SUD on drug use and criminal behavior.

From the few available studies examining the treatment outcomes of dually diagnosed adolescents, it appears that treatment is a complex task often resulting in mixed outcomes. Substance abuse appears to be a particularly difficult problem to treat, for which maintaining lasting improvements is challenging. The difficulty in treating substance use is further compounded by intertwined mental health conditions, especially comorbid externalizing disorders. Treatments appear to be successful at reducing certain mental health or substance abuse symptoms, but reducing both problem areas to clinically meaningful levels is difficult.

A limitation of the studies discussed previously is lack of randomization, preventing researchers from controlling for various threats to internal validity and drawing causal inferences through isolating the effects of manualized treatments. In other words, the results from these studies cannot be unambiguously interpreted. Thus, the focus of the current study is to systematically review randomized clinical trials of interventions for dually diagnosed adolescents.

Aim

The primary goal of the current study is to systematically review the effectiveness of current empirically supported treatments for dually diagnosed adolescents. To accomplish this goal, the authors systematically reviewed empirical intervention studies and, for each intervention examined, asked the following questions: (a) What is the evidence in support of this intervention as an effective treatment for dually diagnosed adolescents? (b) What degree of change is associated with this intervention? and (c) Examining the common factors among treatments with demonstrated effectiveness, what are some preliminary guidelines for treating dually diagnosed youth?

Method

Review Criteria

To identify intervention studies to be included in this review, the authors conducted several keyword searches of electronic databases, including Education Resources Information Center (ERIC), PsycINFO, MedLine, Social Services Abstracts, and Social Work Abstracts. Terms used in these searches included *adolescent, youth, teen, juvenile, substance abuse, drug abuse, treatment outcome, intervention, efficacy, mental health, co-occurring, dual diagnosis*, and *comorbid*. In addition, the authors reviewed Campbell Collaboration and Cochrane databases to identify studies or other reviews meeting the established selection criteria.

Once studies were identified by topic area, they were reviewed for inclusion according to their ability to best address the research questions of the current study. Studies included in this review were those that met the following selection criteria established by the authors: (a) randomized clinical trials, allowing authors to determine effectiveness; (b) treatment for dually diagnosed disorders, meaning treatment for both substance abuse and mental health disorders concurrently; (c) peer reviewed in the past 10 years, to provide the most current literature available; (d) treatments designed for youth with already existing dual diagnoses, excluding prevention studies; (e) studies published in English; and (f) treatment for youth ages 12–18, narrowing our studies to those of adolescents only.

Data Analysis

To address Aims A and B, studies were examined according to three outcome categories targeted by each study. The three categories included (a) externalizing problems, (b) internalizing problems, and (c) substance abuse problems. The effect-size formulas used in this study are based on Morris and DeShon's (2002) article on effect-size metric. The independent groups design metric is appropriate if the research question examines differences between treatment and control groups while the repeated measures group design metric should be used if the research question examines change within an individual.

For each study, one effect size was calculated for each outcome measure using the independent groups pretest–posttest design sample estimator (Equation 8.1) when pretest and posttest scores for both groups were available:

$$d_{IG} = \frac{M_{post,E} - M_{pre,E}}{SD_{pre,E}} - \frac{M_{post,C} - M_{pre,C}}{SD_{pre,C}}, \tag{8.1}$$

where $M_{pre,E}$ and $M_{pre,C}$ represent the mean pretest scores for the experimental and control groups, $M_{post,E}$ and $M_{post,C}$ represent the mean posttest scores for the experimental and control groups, and SD represents the standard deviation. This allowed us to examine the magnitude of treatment effects between two groups for each of the studies based on the three outcome-measure constructs. It also allowed us to answer the first research question investigating the evidence in support of these interventions as an effective treatment for dually diagnosed adolescents. Effect sizes for pretest–follow-up scores were also calculated using the same formula (Equation 8.1) because we were interested in the long-term sustainability of the treatment effects for the various therapy models.

To address Aim B investigating the degree of change associated with each therapy model, effect sizes were calculated for each treatment modality (excluding services as usual groups), resulting in measures of change for multisystemic therapy (MST), interactional group treatment (IT), family behavior therapy (FBT), individual cognitive problem solving (ICPS), cognitive behavior therapy (CBT), ecologically based family therapy (EBFT), and seeking safety therapy (SS). Calculating effect sizes using Equation 8.2 allows us to examine further whether change occurred within the individual and the magnitude of the treatment effect. A repeated measures design consists of each individual participant in a group being measured before and after treatment with the difference between the individual score representing the estimate of the treatment effect. The formula used to calculate a repeated measures effect size for each of the studies was

$$d_{RM} = \frac{M_{post,E} - M_{pre,E}}{SD_{pre,E}}, \tag{8.2}$$

where $M_{pre,E}$ represents the mean pretest scores, $M_{post,E}$ represents the mean posttest scores, and SD represents the standard deviation. This allowed us to see if there were any treatment effects or changes in individuals based on the different interventions. Again, effect sizes for follow-up scores were also calculated using the same formula (Equation 8.2) because we were interested in the long-term sustainability of the treatment effects for the various therapy models. Effect sizes were interpreted based on classification by

Cohen (1988), with 0.20 or less indicating a small effect size, 0.50 moderate, and 0.80 and above large.

A common issue that arises when calculating effect sizes for a primary study is what to do when there are multiple measures for a single construct. The approach taken for this study is based on Lipsey's (1994) suggestion to calculate individual effect sizes for each of the different measures in a single study and then average them to generate one effect size for that measure. Similarly, a study may have an effect size for all the dependent variables in that primary study. It is recommended that only one effect size value should represent a study in any analysis in order to ensure statistical independence of the data (Bangert-Drowns, 1997; Devine, 1997). In addition, all effect sizes are calculated so that a positive score indicates favorable direction. Effect sizes for measures where a negative score is the desired direction were reserved so that all effect sizes were in the same direction when averaging multiple measures for a single construct.

Results

Our search identified seven interventions for dually diagnosed adolescents reported across six different studies that met our selection criteria. These studies included: MST (Henggeler, Pickrel, & Brondino, 1999), IT (Kaminer & Burleson, 1999; Kaminer, Burleson, Blitz, Sussman, & Rounsaville, 1998), FBT (Azrin, Donohue, Teichner, Crum, Howell, & DeCato, 2001), ICPS (Azrin, Donohue, Teichner et al., 2001); CBT (Kaminer, Burleson, & Goldberger, 2002), EBFT (Slesnick & Prestopnik, 2005), and SS (Najavits, Gallop, & Weiss, in press). Table 8.2 provides a brief overview of each of the selected studies.

Review of Interventions for Dually Diagnosed Adolescents

Multisystemic Therapy

MST (Henggeler & Borduin, 1990; Henggeler, Schoenwald, Borduin, Rowland, & Cunningham, 1998) was developed by Scott Henggeler and his colleagues at the Family Services Research Center, in the Department of Psychiatry and Behavioral Sciences at the Medical University of South Carolina in Charleston. MST is a family- and community-based treatment approach that is theoretically grounded in a social-ecological framework (Bronfenbrenner, 1979) and family systems (Haley, 1976; Minuchin, 1974). The social-ecological model views human development as a reciprocal interchange between the client and "nested concentric structures" that mutually influence each other (Henggeler, 1999). Furthermore, the ecological perspective asserts that one's behavior is determined by multiple forces (e.g., family, school, work, peers) and is supported by causal modeling of delinquency and substance abuse (Henggeler, 1997).

A basic foundation of MST is the belief that a juvenile's acting out or antisocial behavior is best addressed by interfacing with multiple systems, including the adolescent's family, peers, school, teachers, neighbors, and others (Brown, Borduin, & Henggeler, 2001). Thus, the MST practitioner interfaces not just with the adolescent, but also with various individuals and settings that influence the adolescent's life.

Table 8.2	Randomized Clinical Trials of Interventions for Treating Dually Diagnosed Adolescents					
			Intervention Study			
Experimental Group	MST	IT	FBT	CBT	EBFT	SS
Comparison Group	SAU	CBT	ICPS	PET	SAU	SAU
Sample Size	118	32	56	88	124	33
Gender						
Male	79%	61.5%	82%	70%	59%	0%
Female	21%	38.5%	18%	30%	41%	100%
Race/Ethnicity						
Hispanic	1%	0%	16%	0%	42%	
Black	50%	0%	2%	0%	7%	
White	47%	90%	79%	90%	37%	
Other	2%	10%	3%	10%	14%	
Age Range	12–17	13–18	12–17	13–18	12–17	
Mean	15.7	15.9	15.4	15.4	14.9	
Diagnosis (% comorbid)	SUD 72% comorbid	100% comorbid SUD and MH	100% comorbid SUD and MH	Psychoactive SUD; predominantly comorbid	SUD 74.2% comorbid SUD and MH diagnosis	100% comorbid SUD and PTSD
Attrition Rate	2% treatment retention in MST group	50% IT 50% CBT	56/88 completed 8 of 15 sessions	Tx completion rate: 86%, 3-month fu: 80%; 9-month 65%	EBFT: 45% completed all 15 sessions; 77% completed 5 or more sessions	Research attrition: intake: 18 SS/15 SAU post: 14 SS/12 SAU; follow-up: 11 SS/9 SAU
Delivery of Treatment	MST: in home; SAU: outpatient	Outpatient aftercare	Outpatient	Outpatient	SAU = shelter services; EBFT = outpatient	Outpatient
Data Collection	Pre tx, post tx, 6-months	Pre tx, 3-months post tx	Pre tx., post tx, 6-month follow-up	Pre tx, post tx, 3-month, 9-month follow-up	Pre tx, post tx, 6-month, 12-month follow-up	Pre tx, post tx, 3-month follow-up

(Continued)

Table 8.2	(Continued)				

			Intervention Study		
Outcomes: Substance Use	MST sig. reduced alcohol and drug use	CBT better at reducing substance use than IT at 3 months; both showed improvement at 15 months	FBT and ICPS equally effective in reducing alcohol and drug problems; both grps. sig. reduction in illicit drug use pre to post and maintained at follow-up	CBT lower relapse rates than PET at 3 months; similar relapse rates between groups at 9 months	EBFT greater reduction in substance abuse than SAU	SS significantly better improvements in substance use, cognitions related to SUD than SAU, but few gains maintained at follow-up
Outcomes: Related Problems	MST reduced # of days in out-of-home placement and criminal activity	CBT more improvement in family functioning than IT at 3 months; both showed = improvement at 15 months	FBT and ICPS = effective in reducing CD; both groups sig. improved conduct; mood improve sig. in both groups		EBFT and SAU show sig. and = improv. in psychological functioning, family functioning, and HIV knowledge	SS sig. better improvements PTSD cognitions and other psychopathology subscales than SAU

Note. MST = multisystemic therapy (Henggeler et al., 1999); FBT = family behavioral therapy (Azrin et al., 2001); CBT = cognitive behavioral therapy (Kaminer et al., 2002); EBFT = ecologically based family therapy (Slesnick & Prestopnik, 2005); IT = interactional group treatment (Kaminer et al., 1998, Kaminer & Burleson, 1999); PET = psychoeducational therapy; ICPS = individual cognitive therapy; SS = seeking safety (Najavits, Gallop, & Weiss, in press); SAU = service as usual; tx = treatment.

Henggeler (1999) has summarized the MST model of service delivery. The MST practitioner typically carries a low caseload of 5 to 6 families, which allows for the delivery of more intensive services (2 to 15 hours per week) than traditional approaches (normally 1 hour per week). The practitioner is available to the client system 24 hours per day, 7 days per week. Services are delivered in the client's natural environment, such as the client's home or a neighborhood center. Treatment is typically time limited, lasting 4 to 6 months. For a detailed exposition on implementing MST with high-risk youth, the reader is referred to sources that describe MST in detail (cf. Henggeler & Borduin, 1990; Henggeler et al., 1998).

Original Study Findings. Henggeler et al. (1999) examined the use of MST as compared to usual community services in treating a sample of substance-abusing juvenile offenders, most of whom (72%) were dually diagnosed. The sample included 118 adolescents ages 12 to 17, recruited from a juvenile justice system. Participants were predominantly male (79%) and self-identified as Black (50%), White (47%), Hispanic (1%), or other (2%).

The authors report an extremely low treatment attrition rate of 2% in the MST group; the attrition rate for service as usual was not calculated. Frequency of MST sessions was determined by client need; families received services an average of 130 days ($SD = 32$ days), consisting of an average of 40 contact hours ($SD = 28$, range = 12–187). Services as usual (SAU) consisted of a variety of available substance abuse and mental health treatments in the community, including therapeutic groups, school-based, residential, and 12-step programs. However, SAU group members received very little treatment, with over three quarters (78%) not receiving mental health or substance abuse treatment of any kind. Outcome measures included drug use, criminal activity, and days in out-of-home placement. Findings indicate that MST reduced alcohol, marijuana, and drug use, as well as reducing the number of days youth spent in out-of-home placement. However, improvement was not maintained at 6-month follow-up. Criminal activity, while decreased, was not reduced as significantly as found in other MST studies (Henggeler et al., 1999).

Computed Effect Sizes. Effect sizes between the MST experimental group and the SAU control group were calculated using Equation 8.1 with posttest and follow-up scores. Independent group effect sizes for externalizing outcomes were 0.09 at posttest and 0.09 at 6-month follow-up. According to Cohen (1988), both posttest and follow-up effect sizes were considered small. Both effect sizes were near zero, indicating no significant difference between MST and SAU groups. Equation 8.2 for externalizing outcomes resulted in repeated measures effect sizes for the MST group of 0.59 at posttest and 0.81 at 6-month follow-up, demonstrating that MST had a moderate effect size at posttest and a large effect size at follow-up.

For substance use outcome, independent group effect sizes between MST and SAU were 0.38 at posttest and 0.10 at follow-up, indicating a small treatment effect favoring the MST group. Repeated measures effect sizes for the MST group were 0.28 at posttest and 0.26 at follow-up, indicating a small treatment effect at both time measures. Computed effect sizes for this study and others included in this review are reported in Tables 8.3 and 8.4.

Findings from Henggeler et al. (1999) reveal modest results when compared with other studies of MST (Henggeler, 1999), some of which have shown stronger support of MST specifically for treating substance use in juvenile offenders (Henggeler et al., 1991). The authors report that these modest results are likely due to difficulty in transporting MST from its developers into practice. To address limitations in adapting MST, Henggeler and colleagues (1999) mention studies aimed at developing ways to integrate substance use treatment with a focus on other relationship problems (Budney & Higgins, 1998).

Interactional Group Treatment

Interactional therapy focuses on the importance of clients' interpersonal relationships with the goal of developing insights, enhancing self-esteem, and improving self-care. Developed by Yalom and later adapted for group work with adult alcoholics (Brown & Yalom, 1977), IT utilizes group dynamics and immediacy to work on interpersonal relationships, thus improving client affect. Primary goals of IT include exploring how pathology is manifested in interactions within group, enabling self-disclosure and expression of emotions, and ultimately fostering more positive interpersonal relation-ships outside of treatment and decreased symptoms/problem behaviors. To encourage this process, IT therapists aim to help clients develop trust, openness, and cohesiveness within the group through open conversations about the group process and relationship issues in group (Kadden, Litt, Cooney, Kabela, & Getter, 2001).

Original Study Findings. Kaminer et al. (1998) examined IT in comparison to CBT in a clinical trial with a follow-up study at 15-months posttreatment by Kaminer and Burleson (1999). The purpose of the Kaminer et al. (1998) study was to examine whether youth with externalizing versus internalizing comorbid disorders could be matched by treatment. The sample included 32 adolescents between the ages of 13 and 18 who were leaving a partial hospitalization treatment program. Participants were predominantly White (90%) and male (61.5%), and all were dually diagnosed with an SUD and either an internalizing disorder or an externalizing disorder. Treatment attrition was 50% in the IT group and 50% in the CBT group, resulting in 8 youth in each group. Both IT and CBT were provided over a 12-week period in weekly 90-minute sessions. Outcome measures included objective and subjective measures of drug use as well as substance-related problems such as family functioning, academic function, peer social relationships, legal problems, and psychiatric severity.

Findings indicate that CBT was more effective at reducing substance use than IT at 3-months posttreatment; however, both groups showed significant reduction in substance use at the 15-month follow-up. While nonsignificant, other substance-related problems showed a trend in favor of CBT at 3-month follow-up but equal improvements at 15-months posttreatment. There were no significant effects for matching type of psychiatric disorder to treatment type.

Computed Effect Sizes. Effect sizes between the IT experimental group and the CBT control group were calculated using Equation 8.1 with posttest and follow-up scores. Independent group effect sizes for internalizing outcomes were 0.30 at posttest and 0.30 at the 15-month follow-up. Both posttest and follow-up effect sizes were considered small, indicating a small treatment effect favoring the IT group. Equation 8.2 for internalizing outcomes resulted in repeated measures effect sizes for the IT group of 0.84 at posttest and 1.47 at 15-month follow-up, demonstrating that IT had a large effect size at posttest and at follow-up. The repeated measure effect size for the CBT group was 0.52 at posttest and 1.14 at follow-up, indicating CBT had an initial moderate effect but a large effect at follow-up.

For substance use outcome, independent group effect sizes between IT and CBT were –0.35 at posttest and 0.15 at follow-up, indicating a small treatment effect favoring the CBT group at posttest and a small treatment effect favoring IT at follow-up. Repeated measures effect sizes for the IT group were 0.72 at posttest and 0.32 at follow-up, indicating a nearly large effect at posttest but a small effect by follow-up. Repeated measures effect sizes for the CBT group were 1.10 at posttest and 0.48 at follow-up, indicating CBT had a large effect at posttest but a moderate effect at follow-up.

Findings from Kaminer et al. (1998) and Kaminer & Burleson (1999) confirm prior studies that found maintenance of treatment gains independent of therapy type in adult alcoholics (Cooney, Kadden, Litt, & Getter, 1991), and Stephens, Roffman, and Simpson (1994) found similar long-term effects for marijuana use. Limitations of the Kaminer et al.

(1998) and Kaminer & Burleson (1999) studies include lack of a no-treatment control group, high attrition rates, and lack of an objective measure of substance use (such as urinalysis) at follow-up.

Family Behavior Therapy

FBT seeks to decrease drug use and behavioral problems using a behavioral approach. The behavioral perspective guiding FBT views physiological dependence and social peer pressure as reinforcers of continued substance use. Interventions in FBT employ empirically validated strategies to target multiple variables believed to influence substance use and antisocial behaviors, including cognitive, verbal, social, and family factors (Donohue & Azrin, 2001).

FBT therapists follow standard treatment components, while maintaining some flexibility to meet the unique needs of their clients. Standard treatment components include engagement, assessment, drug analysis, sharing of assessment and analysis with youth and family, and selection from a variety of interventions. In order to address all domains of a youth's life, FBT encourages youths' siblings and peers to participate in the youth's treatment process.

Engagement is highly valued in FBT. An empirically validated protocol used to enhance engagement involves calling clients before their first session and after their first session to build rapport and increase the likelihood of retention. Food and drinks are often also a part of creating an engaging atmosphere for youth and their families (Donohue & Azrin, 2001).

Key to this treatment is allowing the youth and his/her family to choose among interventions that will meet the diverse individual, familial, and cultural needs of the client. Clients, with guidance from their therapists, can choose among several FBT interventions that fit their specific needs. For a detailed exposition on the interventions used in the study that we reviewed, including behavioral contracting, stimulus control, urge control, and communication skills training, the reader is referred to Donohue and Azrin (2001). Azrin et al. (2001) conducted a clinical trial comparing FBT to ICPS, which is discussed in the next section.

Individual Cognitive Problem Solving

ICPS employs empirically validated methods geared toward developing self-control and solving problems. Designed to address behavior problems and aggression in adolescents and adults, ICPS is strongly cognitive and is designed to help youth learn a general cognitive strategy that can then be applied to a variety of problems and decision-making situations. Examples of problem-solving steps learned in ICPS include focusing attention by stopping and thinking, defining the problem clearly, acknowledging choices of response, thinking through consequences of each choice, and choosing the best option (Azrin et al., 2001). While this treatment approach often incorporates behavioral components, for the purpose of this study it was provided in a purely cognitive, nondirective manner.

Original Study Findings. Azrin et al. (2001) compared FBT to ICPS in a clinical study that involved 56 youth, between the ages of 12 and 17, referred for treatment by detention staff, judges, probation officers, or school officials. Participants were predominantly White (79%) and male (82%), and all were dually diagnosed with both an SUD and either CD or oppositional defiant disorder. Fifty-six out of the initial 88 adolescents who began treatment completed 8 of 15 sessions and were included in final analysis, resulting in an attrition rate of 36%. Azrin et al. (2001) aimed at providing 15 sessions over a 6-month period, but due to missed appointments, both treatments involved between 8 and 15 1-hour outpatient therapy sessions. Outcome measures included alcohol use, illicit drug use, satisfaction with drug use, overall mood, conduct, and school and work performance. Findings indicate that there was no difference in effectiveness between FBT and ICPS in reducing alcohol and illicit drug use and in improving conduct and mood. Significant improvements in both groups were observed from pretest to posttest and were maintained at follow-up.

Computed Effect Sizes. Effect sizes between the FBT experimental group and the ICPS control group were calculated using Equation 8.1 with posttest and follow-up scores. Independent group effect sizes for externalizing outcomes were −0.02 at posttest and −0.35 at 6-month follow-up, indicating no treatment differences at posttest and a small treatment effect favoring the ICPS group at follow-up. Using Equation 8.2 for externalizing outcomes resulted in repeated measures effect sizes for the FBT group of 0.97 at posttest and 0.89 at 6-month follow-up, demonstrating that FBT had a large effect size at both posttest and follow-up. The repeated measure effect size for the ICPS group was 0.99 at posttest and 1.25 at follow-up, indicating ICPS also had a large effect at posttest and follow-up.

For internalizing outcomes, independent group effect sizes between the FBT and ICPS were 0.16 at posttest and 0.28 at 6-month follow-up, indicating a small treatment effect favoring FBT at both posttest and follow-up. Repeated measures effect sizes for the FBT group internalizing outcomes were 1.00 at posttest and 1.10 at 6-month follow-up, demonstrating that FBT maintained a large effect size at posttest and at follow-up. The repeated measure effect size for the ICPS group was 0.80 at posttest and 0.82 at follow-up, indicating ICPS also maintained a large effect at posttest and follow-up.

For substance use outcome, independent group effect sizes between FBT and ICPS were 0.21 at posttest and 0.15 at follow-up, indicating a small treatment effect favoring the FBT group at posttest and at follow-up. Repeated measures effect sizes for the FBT group were 1.13 at both posttest and at follow-up, indicating a large effect at both time measures. Repeated measures effect sizes for the ICPS group were 0.92 at posttest and 0.97 at follow-up, indicating ICPS had a large effect at posttest and maintained this large effect at follow-up.

Findings from Azrin et al. (2001) confirm prior studies that found FBT to be effective in reducing youths' behavioral problems (Bank, Marlowe, Reid, Patterson, & Weinrott, 1991) and research that finds FBT effective in reducing drug use (Azrin, Donohue, Besalel, Kogan, & Acierno, 1994). The efficacy of ICPS in reducing youth's drug use has not been previously demonstrated in a clinical trial (Azrin et al., 2001); this study extends previous research that supports the efficacy of ICPS in treating young children's (Spivak & Shure, 1974) and preadolescents' (Kazdin, Esveldt-Dawson, French, & Unis, 1987) behavioral problems. Azrin et al.'s (2001) rigorous study had very few limitations, although a larger and more representative sample may have improved power to detect further differences in treatment.

Cognitive Behavior Therapy

CBT views client behavior, including substance abuse and mental health symptoms, as maladaptive ways of coping with problems or of getting needs met. Cognitive therapy is founded on the premise that behavior is adaptive, and there is an interaction between a person's thoughts, feelings, and behaviors. It follows then that clients' behaviors are learned and can be modified by changing thought patterns and using behavior modification techniques. Treatment focuses on identifying antecedents to symptoms, thoughts in response to those triggers, and feelings and behaviors that result from those thoughts. Monitoring this cycle, challenging irrational thoughts, and replacing them with more productive thoughts will result in more healthy behaviors and more positive affect (for more information on the use of CBT with youth, see Reinecke, Dattilio, & Freeman, 2003).

Original Study Findings. Kaminer et al. (2002) examined the efficacy of CBT in comparison to pscychoeducational therapy (PET) for 88 predominantly dually diagnosed youth in outpatient treatment. Participants were largely White (90%) and male (70%) and ranged in age from 13 to 18. Treatment attrition was 14% and did not differ between the two treatment groups. Both CBT and PET participants attended 75- to 90-minute weekly therapy sessions over the course of 8 weeks. Outcome measures included objective (urinalysis) and subjective measures of alcohol and drug use as well as substance-related problems, including academic, family, peer, legal, and psychiatric problems. Findings indicate that CBT was associated with lower substance use relapse rates than PET at 3-months posttreatment. However, this trend toward CBT did not last at 9-month follow-up, at which time differential treatment effects disappeared, and CBT and PET showed similar relapse rates. Thus, this study found CBT had better short-term treatment effects, but long-term effects were equally effective for the two treatment groups.

Computed Effect Sizes. Effect sizes between the CBT experimental group and the PET control group were calculated using Equation 8.1 with posttest and follow-up scores. Independent group effect sizes for internalizing outcomes were 0.03 at posttest and 0.20 at 9-month follow-up, indicating little difference between treatment modalities at posttest and a small treatment effect favoring CBT at follow-up. Using Equation 8.2 for internalizing outcomes resulted in repeated measures effect sizes for the CBT group of 0.30 at posttest and 0.70 at 9-month follow-up, demonstrating that CBT had a small effect size at posttest and a nearly large effect size at follow-up. The repeated measure effect size for the PET group was 0.33 at posttest and 0.55 at follow-up, indicating PET also had a small effect size at posttest and a moderate effect at follow-up.

For substance use outcome, independent group effect sizes between CBT and PET were 0.13 at posttest and −0.02 at follow-up, indicating a small treatment effect favoring the CBT at posttest and little difference in treatment modalities at follow-up. Repeated measures effect sizes for the CBT group were 0.77 at posttest and 0.88 at follow-up, indicating a nearly large effect at posttest and large effect at follow-up. Repeated measures effect sizes for the PET group were 0.64 at posttest and 0.87 at follow-up, indicating PET had a moderate effect at posttest and a large effect at follow-up.

These effect sizes confirm the findings from Kaminer and Burleson's (1999) earlier study comparing CBT and IT, which found the same pattern of early differential effects but similar positive long-term effects regardless of treatment type. This study was limited, like many others, by its largely White sample, raising concerns about generalizability.

Ecologically Based Family Therapy

EBFT is based on the Homebuilders family preservation model but is targeted at runaway adolescents. Homebuilders family preservation models, originating in the early 1970s to prevent out-of-home placements, are based on crisis intervention theory (Kinney, Haapala, Booth, & Leavitt, 1990). This theory posits that people are most open to change during crisis, and family preservation models provide intensive and immediate brief treatment during crises. A single counselor is thus responsible for providing a range of behavioral, cognitive, and environmental interventions catered to the family's needs.

Because the target population for EBFT is runaway adolescents with numerous levels of problems, applying the family preservation model to this population has the same conceptual base as a multisystemic treatment approach. Thus, EBFT attempts to intervene in individual, individual–parent, family, and extrafamilial systems with a family preservation model of response (Slesnick, 2003).

EBFT begins with individual sessions with the adolescent and with the parents separately, preparing the two to come together to discuss factors leading up to the runaway episode. Treatment motivation and engagement are goals of these initial sessions. Next, EBFT utilizes family intervention sessions focused on problem solving, communication, and overt plans to decrease substance use. Following family work, EBFT broadens the system by involving key people in the youth's extrafamilial network in treatment. This overlaps with termination that focuses on extending support networks to agencies and community services that may be of help once treatment has ended (Slesnick, 2003).

Original Study Findings. Slesnick and Prestopnik (2005) examined the efficacy of EBFT as compared to SAU in a runaway shelter. Participants ($N = 124$) were predominantly male (59%) and Hispanic (42%) and ranged in age from 12 to 17 years. Forty-five percent of participants completed all 15 treatment sessions; 77% completed 5 or more sessions. Outcome measures included drug use, psychological functioning (internalizing and externalizing), family functioning, and HIV risk variables. Findings indicate that the EBFT group had greater reduction in overall substance use than SAU, but both groups showed significant and equal improvement in psychological functioning, family functioning, and HIV knowledge. Overall, reductions in high-risk behaviors were maintained through follow-up.

Computed Effect Sizes. Effect sizes between the EBFT experimental group and the SAU control group were calculated using Equation 8.1 with posttest and follow-up scores. Independent group effect sizes for externalizing outcomes were –0.29 at posttest, –0.18 at 9-month follow-up, and –0.12 at 12-month follow-up. This indicates a small treatment effect favoring SAU at posttest and both follow-up periods. Using Equation 8.2 for externalizing outcomes resulted in repeated measures effect sizes for the EBFT group of 0.24 at posttest, 0.56 at 9-month follow-up, and 0.81 at 12-month follow-up, demonstrating that EBFT initially had a small effect size at posttest, but had a moderate effect at the first follow-up and a large effect at the second follow-up.

For internalizing outcomes, the independent group effect sizes between EBFT and SAU were –0.15 at posttest, –0.12 at 9-month follow-up, and –0.15 at 12-month follow-up, indicating that there was a small treatment effect favoring SAU at all time periods. Repeated measures effect sizes for the EBFT group were 0.24 at posttest, 0.43 at 9-month follow-up, and 0.55 at 12-month follow-up, indicating EBFT had a small effect at posttest, but this effect was nearly moderate and moderate at each subsequent follow-up period.

For substance abuse outcome, independent group effect sizes between EBFT and SAU were 0.02 at posttest, –0.02 at 9-month follow-up, and –0.03 at 12-month follow-up, indicating a little difference in treatment modalities at all time periods. Repeated measures effect sizes for the EBFT group were 0.45 at posttest, 0.56 at 9-month follow-up, and –0.03 at 12-month follow-up, indicating a nearly moderate effect at posttest and a moderate effect at first follow-up, but no effect at the second follow-up.

The positive outcomes associated with EBFT confirm prior studies that support family treatment of substance-abusing adolescents (Ozechowski & Liddle, 2000), but the retention rates and engagement in the Slesnick and Prestopnik (2005) study are uncharacteristically high for treatment of runaway youth and their families, who are often described as difficult to engage (Smart & Ogborne, 1994). While this is one of few studies examining the efficacy of EBFT, the findings from this study are similar to other outcome studies finding interaction between treatment group and time for substance use outcomes but no differences by group on psychological or family functioning outcomes (Stanton & Shadish, 1997). The EBFT manual was in early development stages during this study; thus, the study lacks measures of treatment fidelity, a clear limitation.

Seeking Safety Therapy

SS is a manualized psychotherapy designed to treat co-occurring posttraumatic stress disorder (PTSD) and SUD through development of coping skills across cognitive, behavioral, and interpersonal domains. Twenty-five topics spanning these domains each present a "safe coping skill" relevant to both posttraumatic stress and SUDs (Najavits et al., in press). For example, topics include asking for help, coping with triggers, and setting relationship boundaries. Najavits (2002) describes five principles that guide SS, including (a) establishing safety as the first priority; (b) integrating treatment for PTSD and SUD; (c) focusing on ideals; (d) spanning cognitive, behavioral, interpersonal, and case management content; and (e) explicating therapist processes. SS has been modified for treating adolescents by creating optional formats (verbal material presentation vs. written), asking questions more indirectly (what if this happened to your friend?), adding flexibility for discussion topics, and involving parents if the adolescent agrees (www.seekingsafety.org).

Original Study Findings. Najavits et al. (in press), in their study of dually diagnosed adolescent girls, examined the efficacy of SS in comparison to other services clients may attend, including Alcoholics Anonymous, pharmacological intervention, and other individual or group therapies (labeled treatment as usual or TAU). All participants were female ($N = 33$) and met *Diagnostic and Statistical Manual of Mental Disorders* (4th ed.) criteria for both PTSD and SUD. Treatment attrition rates were not reported, but sample size decreased from intake ($n = 18$ for SS and 15 for TAU) to posttreatment

($n = 14$ for SS and 12 for TAU) and further decreased at 3-month follow-up ($n = 11$ for SS and 9 for TAU).

SS participants were offered twenty-five 50-minute sessions over 3 months. The 18 SS participants averaged approximately 12 sessions ($SD = 6.25$). Outcome measures included substance abuse, cognitions about substance use, and psychopathology. Findings indicate that SS participants had significantly better outcomes than participants in the TAU group, including improvements in substance use, cognitions related to SUD/PTSD, and several psychopathology subscales (anorexia, somatization). Only one measure of self-concept was more improved in TAU than SS. The authors report that only some gains were maintained at follow-up, although with attrition, the power to detect significant relationships at follow-up was very low.

Computed Effect Sizes. Effect sizes between the SS experimental group and the TAU control group were calculated using Equation 8.1 with posttest and follow-up scores. Independent group effect sizes for externalizing outcomes were 0.83 at posttest and 0.59 at 3-month follow-up, indicating a large treatment effect favoring SS at posttest and a moderate effect favoring SS at follow-up. Using Equation 8.2 for externalizing outcomes resulted in repeated measures effect sizes for the SS group of 0.66 at posttest and 0.53 at 3-month follow-up, demonstrating that SS had a moderate effect size at posttest and at follow-up.

For the internalizing outcome, independent group effect sizes between SS and TAU were 0.10 at posttest and –0.30 at follow-up, indicating a small effect favoring SS at posttest but a small effect favoring TAU at follow-up. Repeated measures effect sizes for the SS group were 0.46 at posttest and 0.08 at follow-up, indicating that SS had a near moderate treatment effect at posttest with no effect remaining at follow-up.

For the substance use outcome, independent group effect sizes between SS and TAU were 0.94 at posttest and 0.03 at follow-up, indicating a large treatment effect favoring the SS at posttest but little difference in treatment modalities at follow-up. Repeated measures effect sizes for the SS group were 0.72 at posttest and 0.46 at follow-up, indicating a near large effect at posttest and near moderate effect at follow-up.

This is the first study of its kind to utilize SS with a younger population. The positive outcomes associated with SS in this sample of adolescents confirm prior studies with positive results in adult women (Najavits, Weiss, Shaw, & Muenz, 1998). This study was limited by low sample size, especially at follow-up, and by a disproportionately high rate of psychopathology in the TAU group at intake (despite randomization).

Discussion

Analyzing the results discussed previously was a complex and difficult task. The studies examined in this review were not uniform in their research methodology. They differed by type of control group, with some studies that compared the experimental group to SAU while others compared the experimental group to established treatments such as CBT or ICPS. These methodological differences made comparing between-group effect sizes (shown in Table 8.3) across studies challenging. Put simply, those treatments that are

Table 8.3	Independent Groups Effect Sizes Based on Equation 8.1		
Intervention	**Sample total**	**Outcome Measures**	**Effect Size Value – Between Groups**
Study 1 MST vs. SAU Henggeler et al. (1999)	118	Personal Experiences Inventory: alcohol/marijuana and other drugs; Self-reported delinquency	Posttreatment Substance use = 0.38 Externalizing = 0.09 6 months Substance use = 0.10 Externalizing = 0.09
Study 2 IT vs. CBT Kaminer et al. (1998); Kaminer & Burleson (1999)	32	Teen Addiction Severity Index: substance use, psychological	Posttreatment (3 months) Substance use = −0.35 Internalizing = 0.30 15 months Substance use = −0.14 Internalizing = 0.30
Study 3 FBT vs. ICPS Azrin et al. (2001)	56	Days using drugs; Parent and Youth Happiness with Parent and Youth Scales: drug use, illicit behavior, total scale; Life Satisfaction Scale: drug use, total scale score; Child Behavior Checklist: delinquency; Youth Self-Report: delinquency; Eyberg Problem Behavior Inventory: problem, intensity; frequency of arrest; Beck Depression Inventory	Posttreatment Substance use = 0.21 Externalizing = −0.02 Internalizing = 0.16 6 months Substance use = 0.15 Externalizing = −0.35 Internalizing = 0.28
Study 4 CBT vs. PET Kaminer et al. (2002)	88	Teen Addiction Severity Index: alcohol problems, substance abuse problems, psychological	Posttreatment (3 months) Substance use = 0.13 Internalizing = 0.03 9 months Substance use = −0.02 Internalizing = 0.20
Study 5 EBFT vs. SAU Slesnick and Prestopnik (2005)	124	POSIT Days using drugs and alcohol Youth Self-Report: externalizing internalizing	Posttreatment Substance use = 0.02 Externalizing = −0.29 Internalizing = −0.15 6 months Substance use = −0.02 Externalizing = −0.18 Internalizing = −0.12 12 months Substance use = −0.03 Externalizing = −0.12 Internalizing = −0.15
Study 6 SS vs. SAU Najavits et al. (in press)		Personal Experiences Inventory: effects from drug use, social benefits of drug use, polydrug use, psychological benefits of drug use, transitional drug use, preoccupation with drugs, loss of control, deviant behavior; Adolescent Psychopathology Scale: substance use disorder, somatization, major depression, self-concept; Trauma Symptom Checklist for Children, sexual concerns, sexual distress	Posttreatment Substance use = 0.94 Externalizing = 0.83 Internalizing = 0.10 3 months Substance use = 0.03 Externalizing = 0.59 Internalizing = −0.30

Table 8.4

Within-Group Effect Sizes by Treatment Type Based on Equation 8.2							
Externalizing		Internalizing			Substance Abuse		
Pre–Post	D	Pre–Post	D		Pre–Post		D
MST	0.59	IT	0.84		MST		0.28
FBT	0.97	CBT	0.52		IT		0.72
ICPS	0.99	FBT	1.00		CBT		1.10
EBFT	0.24	ICPS	0.80		FBT		1.13
SS	0.66	CBT	0.30		ICPS		0.92
		PET	0.33		CBT		0.77
		EBFT	0.24		PET		0.64
		SS	0.46		EBFT		0.45
					SS		0.72
Pre–Follow-up		Pre–Follow-up			Pre–Follow-up		
MST	0.81	IT	1.47		MST		0.26
FBT	0.89	CBT	1.14		IT		0.32
ICPS	1.25	FBT	1.10		CBT		0.48
EBFT	0.56	ICPS	0.82		FBT		1.13
SS	0.53	CBT	0.70		ICPS		0.97
		PET	0.50		CBT		0.88
		EBFT	0.43		PET		0.87
		SS	0.08		EBFT		0.56
					SS		0.46
Pre–Follow-up 2		Pre–Follow-up 2			Pre–Follow-up 2		
EBFT	0.81	EBFT	0.55		EBFT		−0.03

compared to other established treatments may have very small or negative effect sizes, thereby erroneously tempting us at first glance to assume they are less effective than those treatments that were compared to SAU. Even results for those treatment groups that were compared to SAU may be distorted, as common factors may exist between treatment modalities and services regularly offered, resulting in low effect sizes between the independent groups.

Closer inspection using measures of within-group change (shown in Table 8.4) revealed that several of the treatments were associated with large changes in outcome measures. Thus, the results comparing effectiveness between groups and the results examined from each group individually often revealed different stories. For example, in regard to externalizing outcomes, FBT showed little or no treatment effect when compared to ICPS (effect size = −.02 at posttest, −.35 at follow-up). However, when we looked at the change in externalizing outcomes using repeated measures effect size estimates with the FBT group (effect size = 0.89 at follow-up) and ICPS group (effect size = 1.25 at follow-up) separately, both treatments had large effects in reducing externalizing problems. Therefore, to say that FBT was not effective as a treatment option based on the independent group effect size estimate would be misleading because both FBT and ICPS had large treatment effects for externalizing outcomes when examining pre- and follow-up mean scores for each group.

Table 8.5	Treatments Organized by Effect Size and Outcome Based on Equation 8.2		
		Dual Diagnosis Outcomes	
Effect Size	**Externalizing**	**Internalizing**	**Substance Abuse**
Large	MST**	IT****	FBT**
	FBT**	CBT^a****	ICPS**
	ICPS**	FBT**	CBT^b***
		ICPS**	PET***
		CBT^b***	
Moderate	EBFT**	PET***	EBFT**
	SS*	EBFT**	CBT^1****
			SS*
Small		SS*	MST**
			IT****

Note. Asterisks indicate period of time between pretest and follow-up; *Pretest to 3-month follow-up, **Pretest to 6-month follow-up, ***Pretest to 9-month follow-up, ****Pretest to 15-month follow-up.
^{a}CBT from Study 2 (Kaminer et al., 1998). ^{b}CBT from Study 4 (Kaminer et al., 2002).

This analysis is further complicated by the fact that results vary by outcome measure (externalizing, internalizing, and substance abuse), with some treatments showing more effectiveness for one outcome but not another. Further still, each study varies by follow-up period, making it difficult to compare an effect size at 15-months posttreatment with an effect size at 3-months posttreatment. There is value in knowing how treatment changes for one intervention compared to other treatments. However, for the reasons noted previously, the authors chose to focus the synthesized discussion on repeated measures effect sizes (measures of within-group change for a given treatment approach) across outcome measures at follow-up.

Table 8.5 shows those treatments that had large, moderate, and small effects at follow-up on externalizing, internalizing, and substance abuse outcomes. The table also indicates the follow-up time period, allowing the reader to interpret the effect in the context of the time period in which it was measured.

Externalizing effect sizes were large for the MST, FBT, and ICPS groups. Of interest is that youth receiving MST and ICPS showed moderate to large improvements in externalizing outcomes at posttest, and these effects improved further to large effects at follow-up.

Internalizing effect sizes were large for the IT, CBT, FBT, and ICPS groups. The effects of all four of these interventions improved over time after treatment ended. Especially impressive among these treatments is the sustainability of internalizing outcomes for IT and CBT; youth in these groups demonstrated substantial changes even when evaluated as long as 15 months after treatment ended.

Last, substance abuse effect sizes were large for the FBT, ICPS, PET, and CBT groups. Worth noting is that newer, less established treatments such as EBFT and SS also had moderate effect sizes at posttest and sustained moderate reductions in substance abuse at follow-up.

While analysis identifying effective treatment modalities for individual outcomes is helpful, one challenge of treating dually diagnosed youth is their likely diagnosis with several or all of these conditions. Reviewing these results, FBT and ICPS appeared to be the only interventions to produce large treatment effect sizes across externalizing, internalizing, and substance abuse domains. Furthermore, the large effect sizes for these two treatments were evident at 9-months posttreatment, demonstrating sustainability of effects over time.

The effect sizes computed in this systematic review are impressive when compared with previous community-based outcome studies of adolescents, especially the repeated measures effect sizes for each of the therapy models. For example, Weisz, McCarty, and Valeri (2006) found psychotherapy's mean overall effect sizes on adolescent depression, when including dissertations and using more rigorous effect size calculations than previous meta-analyses on this subject, to be moderate (.34) with a range of –0.66 to 2.02. In addition, they also found that those studies on the effectiveness of psychotherapy on adolescent depression that were conducted in real-world settings had a small overall weighted mean effect size of 0.24. Furthermore, Weisz and Jensen (1999) found average effect sizes for the four broad-based meta-analyses on adolescent psychotherapy conducted in efficacy trials ranged from 0.71 to 0.84, indicating that the treatment effects were large or nearly large. In contrast, effectiveness studies in community settings for child and adolescent disorders found an overall mean effect size of 0.01, indicating no treatment effect, with a range of –0.40 to 0.29. Therefore, the results found in this systematic review appear quite promising, especially given the difficulty inherent in working with dually diagnosed adolescents.

Implications for Juvenile Offenders

Understanding treatment effectiveness with dually diagnosed adolescents is relevant for those working in the juvenile justice system because many juvenile offenders have complex mental health and substance use problems as well as myriad other academic, familial, and social issues. However, juvenile offender treatment also includes unique outcomes of interest, namely, reduction in criminal behavior. For this reason, it is helpful to examine more closely those studies that specifically included juvenile offenders to assess the impact on criminal behavior outcomes. These studies may have implications for working specifically with dually diagnosed juvenile offenders.

Two of the six randomized studies included in this review involved treatment of juvenile offenders (Azrin et al., 2001; Henggeler et al., 1999). Henggeler et al. (1999) reviewed arrest records 11-months posttreatment and found MST youth reduced criminal arrests by 26% and reduced recidivism by 19%, rates lower than youth receiving SAU (although not at a statistically significant level). However, self-reported delinquency rates were not affected by MST. Low rates of criminal activity at follow-up were significantly related to high family collaboration and to caregiver reports of a clear direction in treatment. The authors suggest that treatment adherence by the therapists providing MST is the most plausible explanation for the moderate to low treatment effects because MST has been shown to improve outcomes with juvenile offenders in the past.

Azrin et al. (2001) also studied juveniles referred from juvenile detention center staff, probation officers, judges, and school administrators. As discussed previously, their positive findings included large effect sizes in externalizing, internalizing, and substance use outcomes for juvenile offenders in both the FBT and ICPS treatment groups. Examining their delinquency outcomes more closely, official court records revealed that youths' number of arrests decreased greater than 50% at post- and follow-up assessments. Standardized self-report scales confirmed a significant reduction in conduct behavior. Additionally, self-reports of youth and parent satisfaction with youths' illicit conduct significantly improved, suggesting reduced family conflict around conduct issues. The large effects of both FBT and ICPS provide support for their use with the dually diagnosed juvenile offender population.

In addition to the aforementioned randomized studies, several of the nonrandomized outcome studies shed light on the treatment of dually diagnosed juvenile offenders. Rogers et al. (2004) concluded that breadth of substance use rather than CD symptoms is the strongest predictor of treatment outcomes in dually diagnosed antisocial youth. Furthermore, Crowley et al. (1998) found substance use an especially difficult problem to treat while criminality, CD, and depression improved up to 2-years posttreatment in a group of juvenile delinquents in residential treatment. It appears, however, that the combination of CD and substance use has an especially detrimental influence on criminal activity and antisocial behavior in youth offenders (Randall et al., 1999).

For detained youth and those leaving detention, collaboration between mental health, substance use, and juvenile justice service providers appears especially important in reducing delinquency (Jenson & Potter, 2003). This type of collaboration requires graduate-level clinicians with specialized training in patterns of behavior of dually diagnosed youth. These findings indicate a need for training clinicians on collaborative case management and techniques for integrating treatment for dually diagnosed juvenile offenders. Thus, in addition to integrating the mental health and substance abuse service needs of dually diagnosed adolescents, treatment of the juvenile offender population adds the juvenile justice system into the collaboration mix. Unfortunately, to date, few integrated treatment programs have been developed specifically for dually diagnosed offenders (Kelly, 2001).

Preliminary Guidelines for the Treatment of Dually Diagnosed Adolescents

After thoroughly searching the literature, we found few clear treatment guidelines for effective treatment for dually diagnosed adolescents. Hills (2000) explicates four core principles in treating persons with co-occurring disorders, including (a) treatment engagement, (b) treatment continuity, (c) treatment comprehensiveness, and (d) continued treatment tailoring through reassessment. However, Hills' (2000) work focuses on adults in the justice system and does not address the specific needs of adolescents.

Riggs and Davies (2002) suggest clinical principles for integrated treatment for adolescents dually diagnosed with depression and substance abuse. These principles include (a) motivation, establishing alliance, patient-generated goals, and empirically supported treatments of SUDs; (b) pharmacotherapy for depression; (c) monitoring of substance use, medication compliance, and motivation; (d) if pharmacotherapy is not appropriate, then psychotherapy for depression (CBT or IT suggested), including family therapy and 12-step programs; (e) if depression and SUD do not improve within 2 months, consider more intensive therapy; and (f) relapse prevention. While making a contribution to the field, Riggs and Davies (2002) focus more narrowly on psychiatric

Table 8.6	Ten Preliminary Treatment Guidelines for Dually Diagnosed Adolescents

1. Assessment is multipronged, is ongoing, and includes practitioner, parental, and self-monitoring so that treatment is responsive to the changing needs of the client.
2. Treatment strategically enhances engagement and retention.
3. Treatment plans are flexible and allow for client choice and voice.
4. An integrated treatment approach is used to address both mental health and substance-related disorders concurrently.
5. Treatment is developmentally and culturally sensitive to match the unique needs of the client system.
6. Treatment is ecologically grounded and systems oriented, including important individuals to the client such as family members, friends, and school personnel.
7. Treatment taps several domains of the client's functioning to enhance the client's problem-solving and decision-making skills, affect regulation, impulse control, communication skills, and peer and family relations.
8. Treatment is goal directed, here-and-now focused, and strength based.
9. Treatment requires active participation by all members involved and includes homework assignments.
10. Interventions aim to produce sustainable changes over the course of treatment.

Note. Treatment guidelines developed by Kimberly Bender, David W. Springer, and Johnny S. Kim.

treatment, and their guidelines aim treatment to those adolescents with depression and SUD only.

Due to a lack of existing clear guidelines for treatment, we addressed Aim C of our study by identifying common threads in the effective treatment modalities identified in our review, thereby creating preliminary data-driven guidelines for the effective treatment of dually diagnosed adolescents (see Table 8.6). We reviewed those interventions with large effect sizes (.80 or higher) at follow-up; culled from them commonalities in treatment characteristics; and then, drawing from the data and a narrative review of the randomized studies, developed preliminary guidelines for treatment of dually diagnosed youth. These guidelines should be reviewed as tentative. It is not possible from this review for us to pinpoint active ingredients of these interventions, but merely to attempt to extrapolate commonalities among those interventions that produced large effect sizes. It is our simple hope that these guidelines might serve as a general barometer for the field, perhaps providing a general gauge of how to tailor treatment for dually diagnosed youth.

Implications for Researching Dually Diagnosed Youth

While the findings discussed previously highlight the efficacy of several treatments in improving outcomes for dually diagnosed youth, treatment of this population is by no means straightforward or simple. Rowe et al. (2004) demonstrates the complexity of treating dually diagnosed youth in their study assessing substance abuse outcomes for three categories of adolescents: exclusive substance abusers (SUD only), externalizers (SUD with externalizing psychiatric disorder), and mixed substance abusers (those with SUD and both externalizing and internalizing disorders). Rowe and colleagues (2004) found

SUD-only youth increased use during treatment but showed significant improvement in substance use at 6- and 12-month follow-up. Externalizers followed a similar pattern of increased use and then posttreatment gains, although at a slower rate of improvement. The mixed group initially decreased substance use during treatment but returned to pretreatment levels at follow-up. This study underscores the fact that comorbidity, especially mixed type, is especially difficult to treat. An interaction between mental health and substance abuse problems may render some treatments ineffective for those youth with complex diagnoses, especially over the long term.

In light of our own complex results and studies such as Rowe et al. (2004), it is evident that further research is clearly warranted. There is a paucity of randomized clinical trials of interventions for dually diagnosed youth, and more randomized studies are urgently needed. Future research should examine those interventions with evidence of significant change by comparing such interventions with no-treatment control groups. Furthermore, studies should more clearly identify subgroups of dually diagnosed youth. Youth with specific psychiatric diagnoses and specific SUDs should be grouped and treatments should be evaluated for their effectiveness in treating specific subgroups of dually diagnosed adolescents. Finally, prospective studies that are able to examine putative risk and protective factors for dually diagnosed adolescents are sorely needed, as we need more sophisticated and accurate etiological models of dual diagnoses that can in turn inform prevention and treatment efforts. The state of intervention research targeting dually diagnosed adolescents is in its infancy and has much room for expansion.

Limitations

Certain limitations should be noted about our systematic review. First, only those interventions evaluated through randomized studies that met our search criteria were reviewed in the current study. Potentially effective interventions that have not received rigorous empirical attention may have been excluded. As such, the current review is limited to include only 6 studies, a very small number for which to draw strong conclusions. Many of the original 6 studies themselves had their own limitations, such as predominantly White or male samples, lingering questions about treatment fidelity, small sample sizes, and high attrition rates. Additionally, most measures used in the reviewed studies involved participant self-report. While these standardized measures were reliable and valid, there is a possibility of measurement bias due to social desirability on the part of participants. Furthermore, because measures relied on retrospective recall, these studies assumed accuracy in participant memory of their behaviors, introducing another possible source of measurement error.

Second, given that the participants from the original 6 studies were from community-based samples, it is plausible that these findings do not generalize to more seriously impaired adolescents in clinical inpatient settings. It is possible that adolescents in clinical settings would present with a unique set of psychosocial needs and functional impairment, with treatment needing to be tailored accordingly.

Third, even though we included only randomized clinical trials in our systematic review, it is always possible that some unaccounted extraneous variable(s) account for the proportion of variance explained. For example, in the Najavitis et al. (in press) study, the authors noted a disproportionately high rate of psychopathology in the TAU group (despite randomization). Obviously, while they were minimized through using randomized clinical trials, not all threats to internal validity were controlled for in the original studies. In response to this concern that it is some third variable that explains the observed relationship, Measelle, Stice, and Springer (in press) recently recommended, for example, that future randomized prevention studies manipulate negative affect to test experimentally whether a decrease in negative affect produces a consequent reduction in substance abuse.

A fourth limitation is that, in computing effect sizes for this study, we found some studies used outcome measures that did not clearly fit into our categories of externalizing, internalizing, or substance use outcomes. We chose not to incorporate these more ambiguous outcomes into our calculations, and it is possible that by excluding these measures we deflated our effect sizes from those found in the original studies.

Finally, a fifth limitation is the possibility of overestimation of effect sizes for one-group pretest–posttest designs (Lipsey & Wilson, 2001). Effect sizes calculated for these less rigorous study designs could be misleading because they tend to be higher than the more rigorous experimental designs and therefore should be viewed with caution.

Despite these limitations, the current study provides a preliminary understanding of the effectiveness of existing modalities for treating dually diagnosed youth. Furthermore, this study begins an important dialogue by creating preliminary treatment guidelines for helping this vulnerable population. These guidelines should be explored empirically in order to create clear best practices for those working with dually diagnosed youth. Dually diagnosed adolescents compose a large percentage of adolescents seeking treatment, and they require unique and evidence-based treatment modalities that are designed to meet their complex needs.

RESOURCES AND REFERENCES

References marked with an asterisk (*) indicate studies included in the systematic review.

Aarons, G. A., Brown, S. A., Hough, R. L., Garland, A. F., & Wood, P. A. (2001). Prevalence of adolescent substance use disorders across five sectors of care. *Journal of American Academy of Child and Adolescent Psychiatry, 40*, 419–426.

Abram, K. M., Teplin, L. A., McClelland, G. M., & Dulcan, M. K. (2003). Comorbid psychiatric disorders in youth in juvenile detention. *Archives of General Psychiatry, 60*, 1097–1108.

Azrin, N. H., Donohue, B., Besalel, V. A., Kogan, E., & Acierno, R. (1994). Youth drug abuse treatment: A controlled outcome study. *Journal of Child & Adolescent Drug Abuse, 3*, 1–16.

*Azrin, N. H., Donohue, B., Teichner, G. A., Crum, T., Howell, J., & DeCato, L. A. (2001). A controlled evaluation and description of individual-cognitive problem solving and family-behavior therapies in dually-diagnosed conduct-disordered and substance-dependent youth. *Journal of Child & Adolescent Substance Abuse, 11*(1), 1–43.

Bangert-Drowns, R. L. (1997). Some limiting factors in meta-analysis. In W. J. Bukoski (Ed.), *Meta-analysis of drug abuse prevention programs* (NIDA Report No. 170, pp. 234–252). Rockville, MD: National Institute on Drug Abuse.

Bank, L., Marlowe, J. H., Reid, J. B., Patterson, G. R., & Weinrott, M. R. (1991). A comparative evaluation of parent training interventions for families of chronic delinquents. *Journal of Abnormal Child Psychology, 19*, 15–33.

Bean, P., White, L., Neagle, L., & Lake, P. (2005). Is residential care an effective approach for treating adolescents with co-occurring substance abuse and mental health diagnoses? *Best Practices in Mental Health, 1*(2), 50–60.

Bronfenbrenner, U. (1979). *The ecology of human development: Experiences by nature and design.* Cambridge, MA: Harvard University Press.

Brown, S., & Yalom, I. D. (1977). Interactional group therapy with alcoholics. *Journal of the Study of Alcohol, 38*, 426–456.

Brown, T. L., Borduin, C. M., & Henggeler, S. W. (2001). Treating juvenile offenders in community settings. In J. B. Ashford, B. D. Sales, & W. H. Reid (Eds.), *Treating adult and juvenile offenders with special needs* (pp. 445–464). Washington, DC: American Psychological Association.

Budney, A. J., & Higgins, S. T. (1998). *A community reinforcement plus vouchers approach: Treating cocaine addiction* (NIH Publication No. 98-4309). Rockville, MD: National Institute on Drug Abuse.

Clark, J. P., Marmol, L. M., Cooley, R., & Gathercoal, K. (2004). The effects of wilderness therapy on the clinical concerns (Axes I, II, and IV) of troubled adolescents. *Journal of Experimental Education, 27*(2), 213–232.

Cohen, J. (1988). *Statistical power analysis for the behavioral sciences* (2nd ed.). Hillsdale, NJ: Lawrence Erlbaum Associates.

Cooney, N. L., Kadden, R. M., Litt, M. D., & Getter, H. (1991). Matching alcoholics to coping skills or interactional therapies: Two-year follow-up results. *Journal of Consulting Clinical Psychology, 59*, 589–601.

Crome, I. B. (2004). Comorbidity in youth people: Perspectives and challenges. *Acta Neuropsychiatrica, 16*, 47–53.

Crowley, T. J., Mikulich, S. K., MacDonald, M., Young, S. E., & Zerbe, G. O. (1998). Substance-dependent, conduct-disordered adolescent males: Severity of diagnosis predicts 2-year outcome. *Drug and Alcohol Dependence, 49*, 225–237.

Dakof, G. A., Tejeda, M., & Liddle, H. A. (2001). Predictors of engagement in adolescent drug abuse treatment. *Journal of the American Academy of Child & Adolescent Psychiatry, 40*(3), 274–281.

Devine, E. C. (1997). Issues and challenges in coding interventions for meta-analysis of prevention research. In W. J. Bukoski (Ed.), *Meta-analysis of drug abuse* (NIDA Report No. 170, pp. 130–146). Rockville, MD: National Institute on Drug Abuse.

Donohue, B., & Azrin, N. (2001). Family behavior therapy. In E. F. Wagner & H. B. Waldron (Eds.), *Innovations in adolescent substance abuse interventions* (pp. 205–227). New York: Pergamon.

Donohue, B., Azrin, N. H., Lawson, H., Friedlander, J., Teichner, G., & Rindsberg, J. (1998). Improving initial session attendance of substance abusing and conduct disordered adolescents: A controlled study. *Journal of Child & Adolescent Substance Abuse, 8*(1), 1–13.

Dumaine, M. L. (2003). Meta-analysis of interventions with co-occurring disorders of severe mental illness and substance abuse: Implications for social work practice. *Research on Social Work Practice, 13*(2), 142–165.

Flanzer, J. (2005). The status of health services research on adjudicated drug-abusing juveniles: Selected findings and remaining questions. *Substance Use & Misuse, 40*, 887–911.

Greenbaum, P. E., Foster-Johnson, L., & Amelia, P. (1996). Co-occurring addictive and mental disorders among adolescents: Prevalence research and future directions. *American Journal of Orthopsychiatry, 66*(1), 52–60.

Greenbaum, P. E., Prange, M. E., Friedman, R. M., & Silver, S. E. (1991). Substance abuse prevalence and comorbidity with other psychiatric disorders among adolescents with sever emotional disturbances. *Journal of the American Academy of Child & Adolescent Psychiatry, 30*(4), 575–583.

Grella, C. E., Hser, Y., Joshi, V., & Rounds-Bryant, J. (2001). Drug treatment outcomes for adolescents with comorbid mental and substance use disorders. *Journal of Nervous and Mental Disease, 189*(2), 384–392.

Grella, C. E., Vandana, J., & Hser, Y. (2004). Effects of comorbidity on treatment processes and outcomes among adolescents in drug treatment programs. *Journal of Child & Adolescent Substance Abuse, 13*(4), 13–31.

Haley, J. (1976). *Problem solving therapy.* San Francisco, CA: Jossey-Bass.

Henggeler, S. W. (1997). The development of effective drug-abuse services for youth. In J. A. Egertson, D. M. Fox, & A. I. Leshner (Eds.), *Treating drug abusers effectively* (pp. 253–279). New York: Blackwell.

Henggeler, S. W. (1999). Multisystemic therapy: An overview of clinical procedures, outcomes, and policy implications. *Child Psychology & Psychiatry, 4*(1), 2–10.

Henggeler, S. W., & Borduin, C. M. (1990). *Family therapy and beyond: A multisystemic approach to treating the behavior problems of children and adolescents.* Pacific Grove, CA: Brooks/Cole.

Henggeler, S. W., Bourduin, C. M., Melton, G. B., Mann, B. J., Smith, L., Hall, J. A., et al. (1991). Effects of multisystemic therapy on drug use and abuse in serious juvenile offenders: A progress report from two outcome studies. *Family Dynamics of Addiction Quarterly, 1*, 40–51.

*Henggeler, S. W., Pickrel, S. G., & Brondino, M. J. (1999). Multisystemic treatment of substance-abusing and -dependent delinquents: Outcomes, treatment, fidelity, and transportability. *Mental Health Services Research, 1*(3), 171–184.

Henggeler, S. W., Schoenwald, S. K., Borduin, C. M., Rowland, M. D., & Cunningham, P. B. (1998). *Multisystemic treatment of antisocial behavior in children and adolescents.* New York: Guilford Press.

Hills, H. A. (2000). *Creating effective treatment programs for persons with co-occurring disorders in the justice system.* Delmar, NY: CAIN center.

Jenson, J. M., & Potter, C. C. (2003). The effects of cross-system collaboration on mental health and substance abuse problems of detained youth. *Research on Social Work Practice, 13*(5), 588–607.

*Kaminer, Y., & Burleson, J. A. (1999). Psychotherapies for adolescent substance abusers: 15-month follow-up of a pilot study. *American Journal on Addictions, 8*, 114–119.

*Kaminer, Y., Burleson, J. A., Blitz, C., Sussman, J., & Rounsaville, B. J. (1998). Psychotherapies for adolescent substance abusers: A pilot study. *Journal of Nervous and Mental Disease, 186*(11), 684–690.

*Kaminer, Y., Burleson, J. A., & Goldberger, R. (2002). Cognitive-behavioral coping skills and psychoeducation therapies for adolescent substance abuse. *Journal of Nervous and Mental Disease, 190*(11), 737–745.

Kadden, R. M., Litt, M. D., Cooney, N. L., Kabela, E., & Getter, H. (2001). Prospective matching of alcoholic clients to cognitive behavioral or interactional group therapy. *Journal of the Study of Alcohol, 62*, 359–369.

Kazdin, A. E., Esveldt-Dawson, K., French, N. H., & Unis, A. S. (1987). Problem-solving skills training and relationship therapy in the treatment of antisocial child behavior. *Journal of Consulting and Clinical Psychology, 57*, 522–535.

Kelly, W. R. (2001). *Criminal justice and mental illness: Prevalence and treatment.* Unpublished manuscript, University of Texas at Austin.

King, R. D., Gaines, L. S., Lambert, E. W., Summerfelt, W. T., & Bickman, L. (2000). The co-occurrence of psychiatric substance use diagnoses in adolescents in different service systems: Frequency, recognition, cost, and outcomes. *Journal of Behavioral Health Services & Research, 27*(4), 417–430.

Kinney, J., Haapala, D. A., Booth, C., & Leavitt, S. (1990). The Homebuilders model. In J. K. Whittaker, E. M. Tracy, C. Booth, & J. Kinney (Eds.), *Reaching high-risk families: Intensive family preservation in human services* (pp. 31–36). Hawthorne, NY: Aldine de Gruyter.

Libby, A. M., Orton, H. D., Stover, S. K., & Riggs, P. D. (2005). What came first, major depression or substance use disorder? Clinical characteristics and substance use comparing teens in a treatment cohort. *Addictive Behaviors, 30*, 1649–1662.

Lipsey, M. W. (1994). Identifying potentially interesting variables and analysis opportunities. In C. Harris & H. Larry (Eds.), *The handbook of research synthesis* (pp. 97–109). New York: Russell Sage Foundation.

Lipsey, M. W., & Wilson, D. B. (2001). *Practical meta-analysis* (Vol. 49). Thousand Oaks, CA: Sage.

Lysaught, E., & Wodarski, J. S. (1996). Model: A dual focused intervention for depression and addiction. *Journal of Child & Adolescent Substance Abuse, 5*(1), 55–71.

Measelle, J., Stice, E., & Springer, D. W. (in press). A prospective test of the negative affect model of substance abuse: Moderating effects of social support. *Psychology of Addictive Behaviors.*

Minuchin, S. (1974). *Families and family therapy.* Cambridge, MA: Harvard University Press.

Morris, S. B., & DeShon, R. P. (2002). Combining effect size estimates in meta-analysis with repeated measures and independent-groups designs. *Psychological Methods, 7*(1), 105–125.

Najavits, L. M. (2002). Seeking safety: A new psychotherapy for posttraumatic stress disorder and substance use disorder. In P. Ouimette & P. J. Brown (Eds.), *Trauma and substance abuse: Causes, consequences, and treatment of comorbid disorders* (pp. 147–170). Washington, DC: American Psychological Association.

*Najavits, L. M., Gallop, R. J., & Weiss, R. D. (in press). Seeking safety therapy for adolescent girls with PTSD and substance use disorder: A randomized controlled trial. *Journal of Behavioral Health Services and Research.*

Najavits, L. M., Weiss, R. D., Shaw, S. R., & Muenz, L. R. (1998). "Seeking safety": Outcome of a new cognitive-behavioral psychotherapy for women with posttraumatic stress disorder and substance dependence. *Journal of Traumatic Stress, 11*, 437–456.

Ozechowski, T. J., & Liddle, H. A. (2000). Family based therapy for adolescent drug abuse: Knowns and unknowns. *Clinical Child and Family Psychology Review, 3*, 269–298.

Randall, J., Henggeler, S. W., Pickrel, S. G., & Brondino, M. J. (1999). Psychiatric comorbidity and the 16-month trajectory of substance abusing and substance-dependent juvenile offenders. *Journal of the American Academy of Child and Adolescent Psychiatry, 38*(9), 1118–1125.

Reinecke, M. A., Dattilio, F. M., & Freeman, A. (Eds.). (2003). *Cognitive therapy with children and adolescents: A casebook for clinical practice* (2nd ed.). New York: Guilford.

Riggs, P. D., & Davies, R. D. (2002). A clinical approach to integrating treatment for adolescent depression and substance abuse. *Journal of the American Academy of Child and Adolescent Psychiatry, 41*(10), 1253–1255.

Roberts, A. R., & Corcoran, K. (2005). Adolescents growing up in stressful environments, dual diagnosis, and publisher-names of success. *Brief Treatment and Crisis Intervention, 5*(1), 1–8.

Robertson, A. A., Dill, P. L., Husain, J., & Undesser, C. (2004). Prevalence of mental illness and substance abuse disorders among incarcerated juvenile offenders in Mississippi. *Child Psychiatry and Human Development, 35*(1), 55–74.

Rogers, R., Jackson, R. L., Sweell, K. W., & Johansen, J. (2004). Predictors of treatment outcome in dually-diagnosed antisocial youth: An initial study of forensic inpatients. *Behavioral Sciences and the Law, 22*, 215–222.

Rounds-Bryant, J. L., Kristiansen, P. L., & Hubbard, R. L. (1999). Drug abuse treatment outcome study adolescents: A comparison of client characteristics and pretreatment behaviors in three treatment modalities. *American Journal of Drug and Alcohol Abuse, 25*(4), 573–591.

Rowe, C. L., Liddle, H. A., Greenbaum, P. E., & Henderson, C. E. (2004). Impact of psychiatric comorbidity on treatment of adolescent drug abusers. *Journal of Substance Abuse Treatment, 26*, 129–140.

Shane, P. A., Jasiukaitis, P., & Green, R. S. (2003). Treatment outcomes among adolescents with substance abuse problems: The relationship between comorbidities and post-treatment substance involvement. *Evaluation and Program Planning, 26*, 393–402.

Slesnick, N. (2003). *Treatment manual: Ecologically based family therapy for substance abusing runaway youth*. Unpublished manuscript.

*Slesnick, N., & Prestopnik, J. L. (2005). Ecologically based family therapy outcome with substance abusing runaway adolescents. *Journal of Adolescence, 28*, 277–298.

Smart, R. G., & Ogborne, A. C. (1994). Street youth in substance abuse treatment: Characteristics and treatment compliance. *Adolescence, 29*, 733–745.

Spivak, G., & Shure, M. B. (1974). *Social adjustment of young children: A cognitive approach to solving real life problems*. San Francisco: Jossey-Bass.

Springer, D. W. (2004). Evidence-based treatment of juvenile delinquents with externalizing disorders. In A. Roberts (Ed.), *Juvenile justice sourcebook: Past, present, and future* (pp. 365–380). New York: Oxford University Press.

Springer, D. W., McNeece, C. A., & Mayfield-Arnold, E. (2003). *Substance abuse treatment for criminal offenders: An evidence-based guide for practitioners*. Washington, DC: American Psychological Association.

Stanton, M. D., & Shadish, W. R. (1997). Outcome, attrition, and family—Couples treatment for drug abuse: A meta-analysis and review of the controlled, comparative studies. *Psychological Bulletin, 122*, 170–191.

Stephens, R. S., Roffman, R. A., & Simpson, E. E. (1994). Treating adult marijuana dependence: A test of the relapse prevention model. *Journal of Consulting Clinical Psychology, 62*, 92–99.

Teplin, L. A., Abram, K. M., McClelland, G. M., Dulcan, M. K., & Mericle, A. A. (2002). Psychiatric disorders in youth in juvenile detention. *Archives of General Psychiatry, 59*, 1133–1143.

Weisz, J. R., & Jensen, P. S. (1999). Efficacy and effectiveness of child and adolescent psychotherapy and pharmacotherapy. *Mental Health Services Research, 1*, 125–157.

Weisz, J. R., McCarty, C. A., & Valeri, S. M. (2006). Effects of psychotherapy for depression in children and adolescents: A meta-analysis. *Psychological Bulletin, 132*(1), 132–149.

Whitmore, E. A., Mikulich, S. K., Ehlers, K. M., & Crowley, T. J. (2000). One-year outcome of adolescent females referred for conduct disorder and substance abuse/dependence. *Drug and Alcohol Dependence, 59*, 131–141.

Williams, R. J., & Chang, S. Y. (2000). A comprehensive and comparative review of adolescent substance abuse treatment outcome. *Clinical Psychology: Science and Practice, 7*(2), 138–166.

Wise, B. K., Cuffe, S. P., & Fischer, D. O. (2001). Dual diagnosis and successful participation of adolescents in substance abuse treatment. *Journal of Substance Abuse Treatment, 21*, 161–165.

9

Forensic Practices and Serving Dually Diagnosed Youth Involved With the Juvenile Justice System

Gerald Landsberg

Jo Rees

Introduction

Over the past decade we have witnessed the criminalization of emotionally disturbed juveniles into the juvenile and criminal justice systems. Research indicates that over 100,000 juveniles are held daily in criminal justice–related facilities, and nearly 670,000 youths are processed annually through these systems. The numbers of these youth effected by mental illness is significant. The 2003 report of the National Center for Mental Health and Juvenile Justice (NCMHJJ) suggests that "70 to 80 percent are believed to have a diagnosable mental health disorder" and "at least one out of five has a serious mental disorder" (NCMHJJ 4, 2003). In this population, recent estimates suggest that the percentage experiencing co–occurring alcohol and substance abuse disorders may range from 50 to 70% of these individuals (Landsberg, Sydor, & Rees, 2004). Further, the numbers of juveniles with emotional or dual diagnosis disorders entering justice systems is increasing. The NCMHJJ report cites this increase and provides an example drawn from Texas that reports an increase of 27% in this population from 1995 to 2001 (NCMHJJ, 2003). The Baselon Center for Mental Health and the Law in a July 2004 press release about their testimony to Congress on this issue writes, "children who need a safety net wind up in juvenile detention . . . Thousands of children are locked up because the system isn't offering them the help they need when they need it" (Bazelton Center, 2003).

This criminalization of emotional discords in juveniles provides important challenges as well as opportunities for helping professionals. Why? Social workers are proportionally the largest profession providing mental health service in the community-based system. Further, helping professionals are beginning to play expanded roles in both the institutional- and community-based criminal justice system.

This chapter (a) provides an overview of the pathways of youth into the juvenile justice system, (b) highlights potential points in the process at which helping professionals can intervene and gives examples of intervention based on New York City experiences that are of value in other locations, (c) describes training offered to practitioners, and (d) then discusses the importance of advocacy and recommendations for systems-change activities.

Pathways of Mentally Ill and Dually Diagnosed Youth Into the Juvenile Justice System

For practitioners to be effective in this area in their multiple roles as direct providers and as advocates, they need to be cognizant of the pathways of mentally ill or dually diagnosed youth into the juvenile justice system. The pathways that exist are reflective of the size, scope, and complexity of the juvenile justice, child welfare, and mental health systems in their geographic areas. Smaller cities and suburban or rural communities may have pathways that are not readily difficult to understand. However, large urban centers—for example, New York City—often have highly complex pathways, and in the section that follows, we briefly highlight the New York City system. Even though the complexity in New York City may be substantial, it is our perspective that helping professionals from other localities can gain a better understanding of systems interactions that may occur in their own jurisdictions.

The New York City Example

Adolescents in New York City come into contact with the juvenile justice system in a variety of complex ways. A youth who is living at home with parents or guardians and commits a crime enters the juvenile justice system directly. The same is true for youth in the child welfare system and/or other mental health placement such as a residential treatment facility (RTF). If a young person commits a crime or a delinquent act in school, he or she can become directly involved with juvenile justice as well. Finally, youth with pending delinquency cases in Family Court as well as those presently in the Office of Children and Family Services' (OCFS) aftercare can become known to the juvenile justice system through those channels. These youth all enter juvenile justice with existing access to some systems, such as schools, health clinics, mental health providers, Administration for Children's Services (ACS), and others, and can move throughout different systems during the process. Much of the movement between these systems, not previously recognized, is not recorded in any official database. In the absence of formal data, the Vera Institute conducted information gathering relying on limited sources, including interviews with senior staff at ACS, the voluntary contract agencies, the NYC Department of Probation, the NYC Police Department, family court judges, and professionals in the mental health system.

The juvenile and criminal justice systems frequently overlap with ACS. There is little data documenting the connections between these systems, but studies indicate a substantial flow of ACS teenagers through the criminal and juvenile justice systems. In New York, a teen is considered an adult at age 16, regardless of the offense. Teens as young as 13 years of age can also be prosecuted as adults if they are charged with certain serious offenses. Only youth 16 years old or younger who commit less serious offenses are considered juveniles. Specific information regarding the offenses that determine how a youth is processed can be found in the New York Family Court Act. The juvenile justice system involves a number of government agencies—the police, the Department of Juvenile Justice (DJJ), the Department of Probation, Corporation Counsel (prosecution), the Legal Aid Society's Juvenile Rights Division (JRD), and the courts.

The Vera Institute, in its report *Adolescent Pathways: Exploring the Intersections Between Child Welfare and Juvenile Justice, PINS, and Mental Health,* has developed a five-stage model for youth who come into contact with juvenile justice systems. In Stage 1, after police arrest juveniles, they are supposed to deliver the youth to a subsequent location within 3 hours. That location depends on the seriousness of the offense and on whether parents are available to take juveniles home. Unless the youth is accused of a certain classified serious crime, if a parent comes to the precinct within the 3 hours, the teen is usually released. A teen who commits a serious crime will be brought to Spofford, the secure detention facility operated by the DJJ.

In Stage 2, juveniles who are not immediately released, but rather brought to Spofford, are processed by DJJ. Using its own risk assessment techniques, it determines whether to release the juvenile. In the course of the assessment, DJJ staff is required to try to contact a parent. If the parent is unavailable or detention is deemed appropriate, DJJ retains custody and brings the adolescent to court when it opens. Some experts suggest that the DJJ internal risk assessment protocol is entirely inadequate. It is criticized as not being thorough and/or not completely detailing the individual and family service needs, particularly in terms of substance abuse and/or mental health disorders.

In Stage 3, once the juvenile arrives in court, probation intake is the first step. The officer interviews the adolescent and, if possible, the parent or guardian. From the interviews and records, the officer gathers critical information, such as school attendance, criminal history, and circumstances of the offense. Based on this information, the officer decides whether to divert the case from prosecution. If the offense is minor, the juvenile has no criminal record, and the complainant consents, the probation officer can "adjust" the case. Under this scenario, if the juvenile complies with certain requirements, such as attending school regularly, the officer does not refer the case for prosecution. The problem is that the probation officers are not assessing for mental health and substance abuse needs, but rather, they are simply gathering information. If there is a need for these special services, it is critical to know that at this stage, so the youth can be properly processed. If diversion and probation are recommended, then compliance with special services can be a term of probation, thus reducing the rate of recidivism. Further, deciding on the appropriateness of adjusting a case should be done by determining if existing services needs are presently being adequately met. If the special needs go unnoticed, and subsequently untreated, the youth is at substantial risk for reoffending.

In Stage 4, most cases (89%) are referred to Corporation Counsel, which decides whether to bring charges. When efforts to divert and/or adjust a case fail, or these interventions are not appropriate for the particular youth, the corporation counsel determines if the juvenile will be prosecuted, as well as what will be the specific criminal charges.

In Stage 5, it is the judge, however, who ultimately decides where a juvenile goes while a delinquency case is pending. At the initial court hearing, the teenager appears with an appointed lawyer, usually from the JRD. The judge hears from Probation, Corporation Counsel, and the lawyer. If parents or guardians are present, the judge will consult with them. Judges report that the presence or absence of the parent or guardian is a significant factor in their decisions whether to release adolescents. After a series of initial hearings, the case can move to fact finding—the family court term for a trial. Not all cases go to fact finding; the complainant may not follow up or appear in court, or corporation counsel may move to dismiss.

There is another option, rarely exercised, that allows judges to convert delinquency cases to PINS (person in need of supervision) cases. In recent years there has been such an increase in PINS cases that the court systems are trying to increase efforts at diversion away from PINS. In addition, judges often assume that the juvenile has been assessed through probation for possible diversion or adjustment, and the reason why the case is before the judge is that neither option was deemed appropriate. They are then less likely to recommend PINS. Some mental health and substance abuse experts believe that converting to PINS is a good option over diversion or adjustment because it is less restrictive than probation, but still contains a monitoring component where special needs services are concerned.

If a juvenile is found guilty or makes an admission, the judge sets a sentencing ("disposition") date. When the facts are uncomplicated and adequate information is before the court, the judge may proceed to disposition immediately. If not, the judge orders probation to produce an investigation and recommendation report (the "I and R"), in which it assembles information about the adolescent and recommends a disposition. If substance abuse and mental health screenings were not done before, it is necessary to conduct those now; however, these are not always performed. At disposition, the judge may return juveniles to the community (unsupervised or supervised) or order them placed. The maximum period of placement with OCFS, juvenile justice in New York State, varies with the type of offense: For a misdemeanor, it is 12 months; for a felony, it is 18 months; and for a designated or classified felony, it is 3 to 5 years. Those periods can be extended by petition to the court (Armstrong, 1998).

If special services needs exist, placement does not always mean jail or detention. Placement can be through an OCFS direct or contracted treatment facility. Adolescents with mental health or substance abuse problems have limited residential options. The two types of facilities are hospitals and RTFs, both of which are in short supply. In recent years, hospitals have tightened the criteria for admission to psychiatric beds. Only adolescents who are in the midst of a life-threatening crisis qualify for admission. If admitted, they are usually discharged shortly after they stabilize. RTFs are licensed psychiatric facilities equipped to handle teenagers with complex problems. RTF residents often suffer from problems in addition to mental illness, such as a history of serious delinquency and severe educational deficiencies. Part of the problem is that if a youth in an RTF gets arrested and is absent from the facility for 72 hours or more, regardless of where the child is, the RTF must release and vacate the youth's bed. This is due, in part, to the incredible lack of beds available systemwide. In the entire city, the mental health system provides only 200 residential beds for adolescents.

That being said, alternatives to residential placement in the mental health system must be explored. Creating new beds is extremely expensive and can encourage overplacement. The favored alternative is to bring mental health services directly to clients' homes. Commonly referred to as *wraparound* or *case coordination*, this model uses flexible programming and dollars to create an individualized treatment plan, and the needs of the family dictate the services. For children and adolescents, wraparound relies heavily on the involvement of adults. But ACS adolescents are less likely to have responsible adults to participate in treatment. It is particularly difficult to employ the wraparound model in congregate care facilities, which contain most of the deeply troubled adolescents.

As this report describes, adolescents in crisis are shifted between a host of government agencies—the police, DJJ, probation, mental health, the courts, and ACS. Often, they are passed along as quickly as possible. The lack of cooperation and collaboration between these agencies leads to both over- and underplacement, duplication of services, unnecessary transaction costs, and, most important, poor service for teens and their families (Armstrong, 1998).

A Conceptual Framework for Intervention and Treatment

What steps can practitioners take to intervene and treat youth effectively? Our conceptual framework identifies several key intervention points. These include

1 Screening and assessment.
2 Providing early intervention services through the fostering of collaborative multiagency relationships.
3 Developing discharge planning relations with the juvenile justice and criminal justice systems and providing follow-up and community care.

Screening and Assessment

How do we know if a juvenile who is entering the juvenile justice or criminal justice system has an emotional problem, a substance abuse problem, or both? With the growing knowledge that juveniles with emotional or co-occurring disorders are increasingly found in the justice system, both treatment providers and juvenile justice staff are promoting the development of screening and assessment protocols for juveniles entering the system. The purpose of screening and assessment is to assist mental health, substance abuse, and juvenile justice staffs with disposition and intervention strategies for youth in their system.

What is screening? Screening is a procedure that ideally occurs early in the process of a juvenile's entrance into the justice system. Often this does not occur when a juvenile is adjudicated. Rather, *if* it occurs, it is at the point where a juvenile enters a detention facility. Screening has several useful purposes. First, screening is conducted to identify youth who require special attention and services. Screening is also utilized to determine the current level of mental health and substance abuse functioning. Another important purpose of screening is to identify youth who may have cognitive and/or educational deficits.

How is screening done? The most appropriate method of conducting a screening is by using an existing screening instrument that has shown to have reliability and validity with at-risk youth who are involved with forensic systems. Those instruments for possible use include the Massachusetts Youth Screening Instrument II (MAYSI-2), the Comprehensive Addiction Severity Index for Adolescents (CASI-A), and the Problem-Oriented Screening Instrument for Teenagers (POSIT). In selecting the instrument to be used, there are many key issues that need to be reviewed. Reliability, validity, and sensitivity to age, gender, and culture are necessary. Further, the instrument must have the ability to provide information on mental health status and diagnosis as well as substance abuse involvement. Finally, the ease of which the instrument is administered as well as the amount of human resources needed for the task must be considered.

What is assessment? Assessment is a more in-depth process than screening, is conducted by a mental health professional, and provides more information. Comprehensive and accurate assessment determines the

> level and extent of mental health and substance abuse problems, identifies other psychosocial or psychological problems that may enhance the symptoms of mental health and/or substance abuse problems, [and] determines the extent that youth's family may be useful in treatment, their motivation and ability to maintain family warmth and boundaries. (Underwood, 2004, p.4)

The language that is used to discuss, write about, or collaborate with others in screening and assessment is particularly sensitive for accuracy as well as appropriate service delivery. Some experts at the Urban Institute warn there is no real consistency in the definition and measurement of key terms, such as "emotionally disturbed," "deficit," and others. The government agencies, professional organizations, social service and health agencies, schools, and other entities use different types of information and approaches. Further, there is no universally accepted measurement of mental health or substance abuse problems. Different services providers use one source or a combination of sources of information—biomedical evidence, psychometric evaluations, and clinical judgment (the last of which can be a particularly subjective source of information). The classification approach of the American Psychiatric Association's *Diagnostic and Statistical Manual of Mental Disorders* (4th ed.) focuses on etiology. More often, practitioners and researchers are presently moving toward a functional approach, which generally ignores etiology and focuses on functioning in areas such as cognition, communication, motor and social abilities, and patterns of interaction. There exists considerable variation in ways these problems are being conceptualized in the clinical, research, and academic communities (Mears & Aron, 2003). Currently, striving for open communication about information sources on and intervention approaches to individual cases is the way of addressing this dilemma on a very small scale. Service providers have a responsibility to share comprehensive and accurate information when collaborating in service delivery, and the issues discussed previously are key issues to consider.

Another significant problem in this area is that the utilization of screening and assessment in the juvenile justice system is now done in only a limited number of settings. In other settings, the quality of screening, assessment, and comprehensive conceptualization of each youth remain considerably lacking. As a result, many emotionally disturbed or dually diagnosed juveniles are not identified, and therefore diversion to treatment settings is not an option for them. Expanding screening and assessment programs is an essential goal. Having screening and assessment programs in *all* juvenile justice settings is an ideal goal. Improving existing service delivery by expanded training and education initiatives on new treatment strategies and intervention approaches is a crucial objective to work toward achieving systemwide.

Early Intervention and Collaboration

Early intervention is an especially valuable tool to reduce the potential damages of criminalization, especially the incarceration of youth who may be experiencing emotional distress and those who are dually diagnosed. Project Confirm, piloted by the Vera Institute of Justice and the Administration for Children's Success, is an excellent example of this type of program. It is especially important because it (a) involved collaboration between eight state and local agencies and (b) targeted foster children who are an extremely high-risk group.

The VERA report on Project Confirm describes problems of foster children in the criminal justice system in strict terms:

- Responding to the arrest of a foster child requires the involvement of numerous public and private agencies. Depending on the jurisdiction, an arrest may require action by the police, child welfare, juvenile justice, probation, contract foster care providers, public defenders, family court judges, and juvenile prosecutors. For children not in foster care, parents are responsible for navigating this system. For foster children, the locus of responsibility is often unclear to frontline staff, managers, and foster parents. Confusion about roles, delays in transmitting information, and misunderstandings between frontline workers in the child welfare and juvenile justice agencies may increase the likelihood that arrested foster children are detained in juvenile detention facilities rather than released to foster parents, guardians, or caseworkers.
- Being detained not only deprives foster youth of their liberty but also may disrupt their placement and education, and result in harsher punishments later on in the process. Though foster children comprised less than 2% of the New York City youth population, they accounted for approximately 15% of youth admitted to juvenile justice detention facilities in 1997.
- A review of case records showed no evidence that foster children commit more crimes or crimes of greater severity than nonfoster children—factors that could have explained differential detention rates. Instead, conversations with judges, probation officers, police officers, and juvenile justice workers revealed a strong concern with the impact of the multiple organizational barriers separating the child welfare and juvenile justice agencies. Those interviewed felt that with more information about a youth, and with a caseworker in court to serve as a release resource, many foster children would be released to the caseworker rather than detained in juvenile detention facilities (Ross, Conger, & Armstrong, 2002).

How did Project Confirm actually work? The key element of Project Confirm was the action by VERA workers at the main juvenile detention to inform the Project whenever the police made an arrest. By the end of the project, research compiling telephone calls to the project by police indicated that calls were made nearly 100% of the time. The purpose of the call to Project Confirm staff was to notify ACS care workers to come to represent the foster child in adjudicated proceedings. Over time the project was able to get ACS workers to appear in court 93% of the time.

What was the impact of the project? Project Confirm produced many changes in the juvenile justice and child welfare systems. Communication between agencies increased, and the necessity of working across agency lines became a common understanding among many frontline staff. In some cases, Confirm staff made sure that foster youth received necessary medication while in detention. In general, Confirm became the place where frontline staff could learn more about problems related to the overlap between juvenile justice and child welfare. The program's central goal, however, is to reduce the disparity in detention rates between nonfoster and foster youth.

"Program managers and researchers felt that Confirm could make a difference with some groups more than with others. Specifically, since court officials have few reasons to detain youth facing low-level charges and with minor delinquency records other than the absence of a release-extensive resource, we suspected that Confirm would have a larger impact on these types of cases than it would on more serious cases. The evaluation focused only on Confirm's impact on decisions made by court personnel to detain youth who have already spent 1 night in detention (youth who are referred to as "police admits"), not on decisions to detain youth immediately upon arrest . . . The ultimate findings suggested that Project Confirm did reduce the incidence of unnecessary detention due to the lack of a release resource" (Landsberg, Sydor, & Rees, 2004, p. 18). Officially, the activities of Project Confirm were transferred to the ACS, the NYC agency with primary responsibilities. It should be noted that, although the project did not focus on emotionally disturbed children, it is an excellent example of a model program with significant applications for that population.

Friends of Island Academy: Reaching Out, Reaching In, Rebuilding Young Lives

Friends of Island Academy (Friends) was originally founded in 1990 to work with youth incarcerated at New York City's largest jail, Rikers Island. Reaching in beyond the walls of the institution, Friends offers youth development workshops and individual case management services that are gender and culturally responsive and are informed by an understanding of the individual and societal factors that have contributed to (and increase the likelihood of) youth involvement with the criminal justice system, the complex barriers they face on release, and the challenges they face to remain alive and free. Guided by a youth development perspective, Friends offers a safe passage between youths' lives in jail and the community by beginning a dialogue with young people that aims to steer them toward positive life choices and views them as active participants in the rebuilding of their lives. On release, Friends provides a comprehensive program of daily services that include risk assessment and management, social work services, education, employment assistance and training, mentoring, youth development services, and case management, both on site at the main agency (located in midtown Manhattan) and by reaching out into public schools and the high-risk communities in New York City to which the youth are returning.

Having a holistic view that recognizes and develops strengths and skills in a population of criminal justice–involved youth who have faced (and continue to face) multiple challenges to community inclusion, translates into service provision that targets intervention and support in all areas of their lives. Without such an approach, the chances of their return to custody are significantly high: "When adolescents incarcerated at Rikers Island return home, they face unique challenges, including high rates of substance abuse, homelessness, and unemployment. . . . two-thirds of these youth land back in the criminal justice system within three years" (Vera Institute of Justice, 2004, p. 20).

The following program description will highlight the work of Friends and shows that it combines several key approaches:

- Connection with youth both inside and outside jail and detention.
- Involvement of youth in comprehensive services that provide tools to survive and succeed, in addition to the identification and management of risk.
- Training formerly incarcerated young people as peer leaders to reach out to at-risk youth in public schools and communities, before the cycle of incarceration begins for them.

A comprehensive summary of the services available at Friends of Island Academy is available via its Web site: www.foiany.org.

Reaching In: Working With Incarcerated Youth in Jail and Juvenile Detention

In 2003, figures obtained from the DJJ report that 5,138 youth were sent either to jail (26%) or juvenile detention facilities (74%) in New York City. In order to reach these youth before release, case managers and trained youth leaders from Friends attend the jail twice weekly to provide support (which includes positive youth development activities such as writing workshops) and education on the services that are available in the community, help youth examine the constrictions of jail and gang membership, and provide relevant reasons for pursuing jobs and educations that can lead to salaries and independence. Youth are then encouraged to increase their competencies and transform the skills that led to incarceration to instead excel at work and school.

In addition to providing information and service linkage, Friends also offers formerly incarcerated youth a concrete "safe passage" at the point of release through its Van Program. Prior to September 2005, youth released from detention at Rikers Island were dropped off at the subway station at Queens Plaza at 3:00 a.m. to find their way home. Having served a period of detention, with no money and often no home to return to, youth found themselves waiting in an area with newly released adult ex-offenders where they were vulnerable to drug dealers, prostitution, and gang activity. Although a class action lawsuit brought by mental health advocates in New York City (settled in 2003) compelled the Department of Corrections to start the Rikers Island Discharge Enhancement Program, to facilitate service linkage (and often transport) to community agencies for adult inmates on release, little attention has been paid to the needs of newly released juveniles. Obtaining funding from a private donor to purchase a van, outreach case managers at Rikers Island are now able to offer youth the opportunity to sign up for a safe journey on release—directly to the agency at Friends to begin their lives back in the community.

Rebuilding Young Lives: Membership and Participation at Friends of Island Academy

Due to the complex social and emotional barriers that young returning prisoners face—whether arriving directly at Friends from Rikers Island or referred via probation, social services, community-based organizations, or peer word of mouth—all youth undertake a comprehensive intake and assessment with a case manager at the point of entry.

Portrait of a Youth Coming From Jail

Research has demonstrated that the vast majority of youth in detention come from neighborhoods in New York City having the highest levels of poverty, poor housing, and underperforming schools (Juvenile Justice Project of the Correctional Association of New York [Correctional Association], 2002). Further, the disproportionate representation of youth of color who are arrested, prosecuted, and incarcerated in New York City has been documented. While African American and Hispanic youth make up less than two thirds of the city's youth population, they make up 95% of youth entering incarceration (Correctional Association, 2002). At Friends in 2005, 48% of currently enrolled members are African American and 31.5% are Hispanic, many of whom live in parts of the South Bronx, New York City.

Intake evaluations at Friends show that the average postrelease youth attending the agency reads below the sixth-grade level, is not involved in school, and has no employment history and no income. Of 395 youth enrolled in services at Friends in 2003, 18% of the youth were homeless at point of entry.

In order to begin to address these barriers to rebuilding their lives, all youth entering the agency undertake a comprehensive assessment and are assigned a case manager to help them develop life plans that identify and build on their strengths (e.g., individual, family, and community supports) and address barriers that might negatively impact their transition to the community. To this end, Friends offers on-site teaching, employment services (job readiness, job training, and job placement), and referral to community agencies providing both crisis and long-term housing support.

Example: Tackling Barriers to Education

With many youth returning to the community having achieved an educational level of sixth grade or below, their reentry into public school is further complicated by no prerelease enrollment arrangements and their return to communities with existing high rates of school failure (Correctional Association, 2002). To tackle this barrier to rebuilding lives and to demonstrate that no youth should be left behind, Friends opened an on-site school with four daily classes: Level 1: literacy (Grades 1–3), Level 2: basic education (Grades 4–7), Level 3: pre-GED (Grades 8–10), and Level 4: GED tutoring (Grades 11–12.9). Studies are supplemented by job readiness training, workshops, field trips, and creative writing labs.

It is of note that this model recognizes that formerly incarcerated youth need more than just the rhetoric of a second chance as they return to education. Youth receive intensive support in their attendance and progress at school by case managers and social work staff, who recognize the complexities in the lives of the youth as they make the transition back into the community. In viewing education as part of the overall life plan of the youth, staff support them to achieve, to develop confidence and self-esteem from their progression, and to work through obstacles when they arise. Results are demonstrable as program outcomes: In the 2004/2005 school year, Friends served 103 students, of which 21 were in Level 1 (with 4 students advancing to the next level), 42 in Level 2 (with 7 students advancing), and 41 in Levels 3 and 4 (with 4 earning their GED diplomas). Two students entered college, joining four other Friends' youth who had started the prior year. Recidivism rates for youth enrolled in the agency is consistently below 20% (data collected internally at Friends). However, the statistics on success must always be viewed against the backdrop of the multiple mental health and social stressors faced by formerly incarcerated youth, which require comprehensive risk assessment, management, and treatment in order to facilitate participation in achieving such outcomes.

Mental Health, Trauma, and Substance Abuse

In addition to the comprehensive intake assessment undertaken to identify social, financial, educational, employment, and housing needs at point of entry to Friends, all youth are screened using the MAYSI-2. A self-administered screening tool, which has been shown to have reliability and validity in identifying mental health disorders in criminal justice–involved at-risk youth (ages 12–17 years), the MAYSI-2 has the advantage of being easy to administer (it takes less than 10 minutes to complete), requires a fifth-grade reading level (or it can be read to the youth), and is available in Spanish. It is divided into seven scales designed to detect alcohol and drug use; angry-irritable behavior; depression-anxiety; somatic complaints; suicidal ideation; thought disturbance and traumatic experience. Scored by the intake case manager, the MAYSI-2 provides the information to target youth for immediate attention and further comprehensive assessment by the agency professional clinical staff (there are three staff with master of social welfare degrees [MSWs] and two MSW interns on site).

Immediate clinical risk assessment and risk management services are supported by a formal agency collaboration (funded by a 3-year private grant) with Mount Sinai Adolescent Health Center, which provides access to emergency psychiatric evaluation in addition to full health screening and counseling for trauma and substance abuse. Comprehensive programs of individual (crisis and long-term interventions) and group mental health services (e.g., anger management, gender-specific groups, life-skills, family meetings) are also provided on site by social work staff and case managers, with regular case conferences to monitor and evaluate ongoing risk assessment, management, and treatment planning for members.

In 2003, a random sample of 150 postrelease participants at Friends demonstrated a picture of complex mental health needs and exposure to trauma in the lives of the youth:

- 64% reported a history of substance abuse.
- 56% had undergone traumatic experiences (including histories of physical and sexual abuse and exposure to violence).

- 49% reported symptoms of depression.
- 10% had a history of self-harm and ideation.
- 9% had received psychiatric treatment.

Example: Gender-Specific Programming

Friends has developed gender-specific programming to meet the mental health needs of both the young men (80%) and young women (20%) of youth attending the agency by running weekly support groups. From data collected at assessment, compared to young men at Friends, women report over twice the number of childhood victimizations (including physical and sexual abuse), are over twice as prone to depression, and are five times more likely to have suicidal ideation. An understanding of the differential needs of criminal justice–involved young women is informed by a relational model that identifies the qualities of relationships that foster healthy growth and development in women (Jordan, Kaplan, Miller, Stiver, & Surrey, 1991). To help them build positive connections, Friends offers programs focused on their needs including the Wellness Curriculum for health in six key areas: physical, social, mental, emotional, environmental, and spiritual. Using narrative, art, and writing activities, the young women are encouraged to experience themselves and to develop relationships in ways that are mutual, empathic, creative, and authentic as they begin to rebuild their lives in the community.

Reaching Out Into Public Schools and the High-Risk Communities in New York City: The GIIFT Pack

After a youth is succeeding at education and work, Friends trains him or her to help other at-risk youth bypass lives of crime and incarceration. The training program, called GIIFT Pack (Girls & Guys Insight Into Incarceration for Teens), combines communication and professional skills such as anger management, resume preparation, and interviewing tips. Most importantly, GIIFT Pack empowers youth to become positive leaders in their communities—a far cry from their former gang involvement—leading up to 50 one-hour workshops per year in public schools, which include the following:

- Interactive youth development workshops, which examine factors that lead to life on the streets or in jail and then increase the students' personal competency via six points of youth development: self-esteem, locus of control (taking command of one's actions vs. allowing a gang to dictate), future orientation (identifying and achieving healthy goals), coping skills, conflict resolution skills, and positive peer interaction and responsibility in relationships.
- Group discussions where students can express themselves and process the information and insight gained from the interactive workshops.
- Crisis intervention and mentoring sessions for students referred by school staff.
- Special activities including athletics, field trips, arts, and literacy-related projects.

In summary, Friends works directly at the points of crisis: inside jails, at the point of release from jail, and inside troubled public schools and housing developments in

New York City. A comprehensive holistic approach that both identifies and manages mental health risks and social barriers faced by formerly incarcerated youth is essential to rebuilding young lives and indicates that services—not cells—can create safe, productive communities.

Training Practitioners

In light of the growing criminalization of dually diagnosed or emotionally disturbed youth, there is a growing need to train practitioners and others—such as criminal justice, mental health, substance abuse, child welfare, and other human services professionals—to work with these youth and the systems that serve them. New York University School of Social Work, through its Division of Lifelong Learning and Professional Development, has initiated a Child and Adolescent Forensic Mental Health Certificate Program. This certificate program has been offered several times and has been quite successful.

The Child and Adolescent Forensic Mental Health Certificate Program brings together professionals who serve emotionally disturbed children and adolescents who have contact with the juvenile and adult justice systems. This training consists of six 3-hour courses covering diagnostic and clinical issues, program and administrative matters, and legal and policy-planning material. The faculty consists of experts in legal, judicial, clinical, program-planning, and advocacy matters, and they have extensive experience, knowledge, and skills in working with and on behalf of emotionally disturbed children and adolescents.

Objectives

- Increase understanding of the special needs of children and adolescents who are involved with the judicial and criminal justice systems.
- Introduce students to the methods of assessment and treatment of these children and adolescents.
- Enhance advocacy, program planning, and intersystems skills and knowledge.
- Introduce students to innovative programs that focus on alternatives in the treatment and care of emotionally disturbed children and adolescents who are involved with the judicial and criminal justice systems.

Courses and Course Descriptions

1 *Criminalization of Juveniles With Emotional Disorders: An Overview (3 hours)*. This course focuses on the estimated numbers of juveniles impacted and reviews the factors pushing this trend, the numerous pathways of this population into the criminal justice system, the extremely complex systems that affect this trend, and the lack of effective prevention or intervention strategies to address the problem. The presentation highlights major program and policy issues and suggests needed actions.

2 *"If You Were in My Courtroom, Dr . . .": A Judge's Perspective (3 hours)*. This course presents a view from the bench as to what judges see, expect, need, and

receive in regard to the mental health concerns of the families and children in the criminal justice system. This course helps professionals better prepare mental health material for presentation in court.

3 *Applied Forensics: Why Kids and the Courts Need Good Evaluations (3 hours).* This course examines legal interview techniques to aid in the identification of potential mental health issues of court-involved youth and their families. The course addresses program placement, disposition, and sentence planning. The presentation also discusses effective advocacy for juveniles in the justice system.

4 *Working With Families: Understanding and Managing the System (3 hours).* This course provides case presentations focusing on working with families dealing with three or more systems. Topics include engaging families and youth and getting families comfortable talking about mental health and medication. The presentation examines the importance of advocacy within the systems serving juveniles.

5 *Contemporary Issues Pertaining to Juvenile Offenders (3 hours).* This course reviews issues relevant to juvenile offenders as they come into contact with the criminal justice and forensic mental health systems. Topics covered include assessment of competence, risk assessment and management, amenability to treatment, waivers to adult court, and special treatment needs of juvenile offenders.

6 *Psychiatry in Juvenile Justice: The Tail or the Dog? (3 hours).* This course considers the practical purposes and problems in applying standard psychiatric diagnoses to an antisocial adolescent population. The course includes definitions of the major categories of disorders, the possibilities and limitations of diagnostic assessments in the juvenile justice systems, and the availability of treatment and management resources and alternatives.

Advocacy for Change

Advocacy for change requires that helping professionals join together with others to develop a broad-based advocacy coalition. This coalition needs to involve child advocacy organizations, mental health advocates, child welfare, and other interested parties. This alliance becomes the key to pursue a change agenda to impact on intervention for at-risk youth. A major part of the work of an advocacy coalition is to educate both political leaders and the general public about this issue and the need to create new systems of care.

What should the goals for the advocacy activities be? Based on work in NYC, we have identified the following goals:

1 Establish a high-level government group to foster the coordination and planning of services and interventions for emotionally disturbed and dually diagnosed juveniles. This group needs to have the political clout to bring diverse mental health, criminal justice, substance abuse, child welfare, and other governmental and non-governmental agencies together. This planning and coordinating group must play the key role in promoting systems change and program development. Some of the primary tasks of this group will be:
   A. To develop and implement a 5-year plan with defined goals and to monitor progress that has occurred in meeting those goals.

B. To establish a permanent research and evaluation task force to assess and evaluate program and policy changes.

C. To develop a detailed program and resource inventories.

D. To facilitate regular meetings between key stakeholders to promote coordination of services and programs and cultivate permanent dialogue.

E. To facilitate an ongoing discussion regarding information-sharing strategies, for example, creating a coordinated management information system.

F. To foster the establishment of continuing education programs in an effort to provide effective cross-training to professionals in the fields of mental health, substance abuse, and criminal justice.

2 Establish a specialized, designated, forensic mental health funding source. Given the complexity of agencies and funding arrangements and the underfunding of services for mental health, substance abuse, and criminal justice prevention programs, a key recommendation is to lobby the state to finance a designated funding stream to permit localities to establish creative and innovative programs for the dually diagnosed juveniles at risk of incarceration. Information from states like Texas and California, which have established these funding streams, suggests that they are an invaluable resource for developing and implementing new initiatives.

3 Improve the existing system of community care for the mentally ill and dually diagnosed. Across the country, community care for youth who are mentally ill and dually diagnosed is extremely deficient. Nationwide, and in most localities, there continues to be a shortage of appropriate treatment programs and services; a lack of specialized forensic services and integrated MICA (mentally ill/chemically abusing) services; a lack of coordination between service agencies both in the provision of direct services and follow-up; a shortage of resources to develop and implement needed programs and services for underserved populations such as minorities; deficiencies in training of mental health professionals regarding the needs of the forensic population and interventions tailored for this same group; and a dire shortage of housing resources.

These shortfalls have a major impact on the provision of services to the dually diagnosed juveniles involved in the criminal justice system. Diversion from jail only works if needed community resources, treatment, and housing are available. Effective reintegration on discharge from jails or prison only works if effective community services exist. Advocates have often suggested that the lack of effective community services promotes the use of the criminal justice system as an option to provide treatment and services to the mentally ill and dually diagnosed. The lack of care for youth exacerbates the trend toward criminalization.

4 Understand the pathways of dually diagnosed and emotionally disturbed juveniles into the criminal justice system. For localities to promote change:

> There needs to be an understanding of the "pathways of juveniles with mental illness into the criminal justice system." This understanding should be conceptualized into a roadmap that identifies key intervention points and intervention strategies and agencies. This roadmap serves as a vehicle for effective planning (Landsberg, Sydor, & Rees, 2004, p. 27).

In fact, that roadmap can be seen as the key initial action step because it guides planning and discussions for action.

5 Promote research. Research should be an essential part of the action agenda. This research should focus on two key areas:

A. The size and scope of the problem.

B. Evaluation of intervention strategies to determine their value and efficiency.

6 Enhance training. Training on this issue needs to be developed and offered to a wide range of agency staffs—criminal and juvenile justice, mental health and substance abuse, child welfare, and related areas. The training should be geared toward increasing the awareness of the problem and developing early intervention efforts.

7 Create a court intervention and screening program. Although there are numbers of possible intervention strategies, many of which should be pursued, one essential strategy is to develop family, criminal, or juvenile court screening and interventions. Screening with the purpose of identifying emotionally disturbed and dually diagnosed juveniles offers an early opportunity for possible diversion of those individuals from the criminal justice to the treatment system.

8 Develop a focus on juveniles in foster care. Juveniles in foster care are an especially high-risk population and are incarcerated disproportionately in juvenile or adult detention facilities. Often, they lack effective representation in courts and, therefore, judges frequently choose incarceration as the disposition options. Mental health and substance abuse providers need to link with child welfare agencies to improve care for this population. This is especially needed since mental health and substance abuse services to juveniles in foster care is highly deficient.

These recommendations are general but form an excellent basis for initial work. What is necessary is the political will to pursue change and to improve the lives of the affected population.

Conclusion

The criminalization of mental illness in youth populations has become a stain on the mental health, criminal justice, and child welfare systems. Helping professionals play roles in these systems. It is incumbent on practitioners as providers and advocates to become active and energetic players in this arena.

RESOURCES AND REFERENCES

Armstrong, M. L. (1998, May). *Adolescent pathways: Exploring the intersections between child welfare and juvenile justice, PINS, and mental health.* New York: Vera Institute of Justice.

Bazelton Center for Mental Health and the Law (2003). Suspending Belief—A Report to Congress.

Conger, D., & Ross, T. (2002). *Reducing the foster care bias in juvenile detention decisions: The impact of Project Confirm.* New York: Vera Institute of Justice.

Jordan, J., Kaplan, A., Miller, J. B., Stiver, I., & Surrey, J. (1991). *Women's growth in connection: Writings from the Stone Center.* New York: Guilford.

Juvenile Justice Project of the Correctional Association of New York. (2002, March). *Rethinking juvenile detention in New York City.* Retrieved from http://www.correctionalassociation.org/JJP/publications/rethinking_detention.pdf

Landsberg, G, Sydor, A. & Rees, J. (2004). *Juveniles with a dual diagnosis and the criminal justice system: Directions for improving care.* New York University School of Social Work.

Mears, D. P., & Aron, L. Y. (2003, November). *Addressing the needs of youth with disabilities in the juvenile justice system: The current state of knowledge.* Retrieved October 29, 2004, from the Urban Institute Web site: http://www.urban.org/url.cfm?ID=410885

NCMHJJ 4 (2003). *Screening and Assessing Mental Health and Substance Abuse Disorders Among Youth in the Juvenile Justice Sustem.*

Ross, T., Conger, D., & Armstrong, M. (2002). Bridging child welfare and juvenile justice. *Child Welfare* LXXXI(3), 471–499.

Underwood, L. A. (2004, April). *Screening of emotionally disturbed juveniles in the criminal justice system.* Paper presented at the Strengthening Families Conference, Kansas City, KS.

Vera Institute of Justice. (2004). *Adolescent reentry initiative.* Retrieved June 20, 2004, from http://www.vera.org/project/project1_1.asp?section_id=5&project_id=77

Important Resources and Web Sites

Bazelon Center for Mental Health and Juvenile Justice
1101 Fifteenth Street NW, Suite 1212, Washington, DC 20005
Phone: 202-467-5730
Web site: www.bazelon.org

Center for the Promotion of Mental Health in Juvenile Justice
Colombia University
1051 Riverside Drive, Unit 74, New York, NY 10032
Phone: 212-543-5298
Web site: www.promotementalhealth.org

Children and the U.S. Justice System
Amnesty International USA
322 Eighth Avenue, 10th Floor, New York, NY 10001
Phone: 800-AMNESTY
E-mail: aimember@aiusa.org
Web site: www.amnestyusa.org/rightsforall/juvenile/index.html

Friends of Island Academy
330 West 38th Street, Floor 3, New York, NY 10018
Phone: 212-760-0755
Web site: www.foiany.org

Justice by Gender: The Lack of Appropriate Prevention, Diversion and Treatment Alternatives for Girls in the Juvenile Justice System Web site:
http://www.abanet.org/crimjust/juvjus/girls.html

Juvenile Detention Alternative Initiative
Annie E. Casey Foundation
701 St. Paul Street, Baltimore, MD 21202
Phone: 410-547-6600, Fax: 410-547-6624
E-mail: webmail@aecf.org
Web site: www.kidscount.org/publications/advocasey/winter99/juv/juv1.htm

Juvenile Justice Center
American Bar Association
740 15th Street NW, 10th Floor, Washington, DC 20005
Phone: 202-662-1506
E-mail: juvjus@abanet.org
Web site: www.abanet.org/crimjust/juvjus/home.html

Juvenile Justice Clearinghouse
P. O. Box 6000, Rockville, MD 20849-6000
Phone: 800-638-8736, Fax: 301-519-5212
E-mail: askcjrs@ncjrs.org
Web site: www.nttac.org

Juvenile Justice Information Portfolio
Web site: http://www.unicef-icdc.org/documentation/subject.html#jj
Information portfolio from the United Nations Children's Fund.

Juvenile Justice Policy Network
Child Welfare League of America
440 First Street NW, Third Floor, Washington, DC 20001-2085
Phone: 202-942-0256, Fax: 202-638-4004
E-mail: bricebet@cwla.org
Web site: www.cwla.org/cwla/juvjustc/juvenilejustice.html

Juvenile Mentoring Program: A Progress Review
Web site: http://www.ncjrs.org/html/ojjdp/2000_9_1/contents.html
From the Office of Juvenile Justice and Delinquency Prevention. Juvenile mentoring programs are an
effective means of providing at-risk youth with the adult assistance and positive role models they
require. This bulletin lists the parameters under which the current 164 JUMP projects operate and
describes the scope and methodology of JUMP's ongoing national evaluation.

Legal Information Institute
Cornell University School of Law
E-mail: webmaster@lii.law.cornell.edu
Web site: wwwsecure.law.cornell.edu/topics/juvenile.html
Includes federal and state juvenile justice laws and information.

National Center for Juvenile Justice
710 Fifth Avenue, Pittsburgh, PA 15219
Phone: 412-227-6950

National Center for Mental Health and Juvenile Justice
Policy Research Associates, Inc.
345 Delaware Avenue, Delmar, NY 12054
Phone: 866-962-6455
Email: ncmhjj@prainc.com
Web site: www.ncmhjj.com

National Center on Addiction and Substance Abuse
633 Third Avenue, 19th Floor, New York, NY 10017-6707
Phone: 212-841-5200
Web site: www.casacolumbia.org

National Criminal Justice Reference Service
P. O. Box 6000, Rockville, MD 20849-6000
Phone: 800-851-3420, TTY toll-free: 877-712-9279, TTY local: 301-947-8374
E-mail: askncjrs@ncjrs.org
Web site: www.ncjrs.org, virlib.ncjrs.org/JuvenileJustice.asp

Office of Children and Family Services
New York City Regional Office
80 Maiden Lane, Room 509, New York, NY 10038
Phone: 212-383-1788, Fax: 212-383-1811
Web site: www.ocfs.gov

Office of Juvenile Justice and Delinquency Prevention
810 Seventh Street NW, Washington, DC 20531
Phone: 202-514-9395
Web site: www.ojjdp.gov

Substance Abuse and Mental Health Administration
Center for Mental Health Services
Child and Adolescent Services Branch
5600 Fishers Lane, 11C-16, Rockville, MD 20857
Phone: 301-443-1333
Web site: www.cmhs.gov

Psychopathic Traits in Juveniles

Diana Falkenbach

Review of Psychopathy

Psychopathy is not a diagnostic category; however, theories of psychopathy have been discussed throughout psychological history. While the existence of criminal, immoral, and violent behavior has been documented throughout the centuries, the diagnostic labeling of antisocial behavior has evolved from psychopath, sociopath, and dissocial personality disorder to, finally, antisocial personality disorder (APD; Lykken, 1995; Rogers & Dion, 1991), with the terms often used interchangeably. However, while psychopathy can be defined in terms of personality traits and behavioral features (Cleckley, 1976; Hare, 1980), the *Diagnostic and Statistical Manual of Mental Disorders*, 4th edition (*DSM–IV*; American Psychiatric Association [APA], 1994), criteria for APD include mainly behavioral features (Hare, 1996; Wilson, Frick, & Clements, 1999). This structure of diagnostic criteria has changed through different versions of the *DSM*, and the current criteria, as shown in Table 10.1, were chosen to aid practitioners in reliably diagnosing APD. For example, the features listed include behaviorally specific examples (i.e., Criteria 1 suggests that failure to conform to social norms can be indicated by repeatedly performing acts that are grounds for arrest). However, by marginalizing the personality features, the *DSM* "... fails to recognize that the same fundamental personality structure, with the characteristic pattern of ruthless and vindictive behavior, is often displayed in ways that are not socially disreputable, irresponsible, or illegal" (Millon & Davis, 1996, p. 443). The limitations imposed by marginalizing psychopathic personality features in diagnostic criteria is further evidenced by a strata within the criminal population that display a higher than average risk for negative outcomes such as violence, recidivism, institutional infractions and misconduct, and poor treatment responsiveness. The current research on psychopathy indicates that the construct of psychopathy, with both personality and behavioral features, is a more reliable predictor of these negative outcomes than a diagnosis of APD. The research indicates the importance of looking beyond a behavioral diagnosis of APD to the personality features of psychopathy.

Cleckley (1941) was the first to develop specific criteria to define psychopathy, and the current conceptualization of psychopathy is based on Cleckley's initial 16 "interpersonal, affective, cognitive and behavioral [characteristics] associated with an impulsive, irresponsible, and deceitful lifestyle" (Bodholt, Richards, & Gacano, 2000, p. 56). Cleckley described people with deficits of conscience who acted in ways unacceptable to society and showed no concern for the consequences of their behavior (Lykken, 1995). Psychopaths are often described as selfish and disrespectful of the rights and welfare of others, while simultaneously displaying a lack of guilt or concern for the consequences of their actions. They appear carefree and may act on a whim to satisfy their personal desires. They can be well liked, displaying superficial charm, but they are insincere and incapable of participating in sustained affective relationships with others. They may also be irresponsible and lack concern for their future. Consequently, they may not maintain consistent employment (Hare et al., 1990).

Over the last few decades, studies have demonstrated that psychopathy is associated with a variety of outcomes important to psychology. Psychopathy is associated with more violence convictions (Forth, Hart, & Hare, 1990; Hare, 1980, 1983; Hare & Jutai, 1983), violence and misconduct in prison (Harris, Rice, & Cormier, 1991; Toch, Adams, & Grant, 1989), and both general and violent recidivism (for meta-analytic reviews, see Hemphill, Hare, & Wong, 1998; Salekin, Rogers, & Sewell, 1996) among prisoners (Hart & Hare, 1998), sexual offenders (Quinsey, Rice, & Harris, 1995), civil psychiatric patients (Douglas, Ogloff, Nicholls, & Grant, 1999; Skeem & Mulvey, 2001), and forensic psychiatric patients (Hill, Rogers, & Bickford, 1996). Research has also concluded that psychopaths commit crimes of a greater number, variety, and severity compared to nonpsychopathic criminals.

Psychopaths also have less fear (Lykken, 1995), do not learn well in response to punishment (Schmauk, 1970), do not inhibit aggression (Megargee, 1982), and have less time to reoffense (Serin, 1996; Serin & Amos, 1995). Additionally, some research, though not conclusive, suggests that psychopathy may be associated with poor treatment outcomes and compliance in a variety of adult samples (Hare, Clark, Grann, & Thornton, 2000; Ogloff, Wong, & Greenwood, 1990; Rice, Harris, & Cormier, 1992; but see Salekin, 2002; Skeem, Monahan, & Mulvey, 2002). So there is a specific group of offenders that are a specific problem. While only a small group of inmates causes problems within the prison system, those few consume a large amount of time and resources and commit a disproportionate amount of violent acts toward other inmates and staff (Blackburn & Coid, 1998). These severe ramifications of psychopathic traits within both the criminal justice system and mental health fields have led to more focus being placed on valid and reliable assessment of psychopathy, as well as the early identification and etiology of psychopathy, in order to help aid clinicians and researchers in developing earlier treatment and interventional strategies.

Psychopathy Checklist—Revised

Cleckley's criteria were important in terms of identifying specific characteristics of psychopaths; however, the Psychopathy Checklist–Revised (PCL-R) was the first instrument designed specifically to assess for psychopathy. The PCL-R is currently the gold standard for the measurement of psychopathy in adult male forensic and correctional populations (Hare, 1991). The PCL-R assesses psychopathy in terms of several of Cleckley's original criteria, and most of the clinical and experimental research on the construct of psychopathy has used Hare's PCL-R (Hare, 1991). Additionally, while the original PCL was designed to conduct research with male forensic populations, research is underway using the PCL-R and its derivatives in assessing the psychopathic characteristics in female populations (see Hare, 2003; Vitale, Smith, Brinkley, & Newman, 2002), nonforensic samples, and youth.

As shown in Table 10.1, the PCL-R is a 20-item rating scale. The items reflect 20 core characteristics of psychopathy. Each item is scored on a 3-point Likert-type scale (0–2), with 0 indicating the characteristic *does not apply*, 1 indicating the trait *may or may not apply*, and 2 indicating the trait *definitely applies*. Decisions about scoring are based on a semistructured interview and a file review. The interview is designed to gather historical and interpersonal information directly from the person. The file review is intended to gather collateral information from files, which is necessary given that one of the traits of psychopathy is pathological lying. Based on information gathered, the interviewee is given a score on each of the 20 traits. Scores on items are totaled with a possible range of scores from 0 to 40. Items are omitted if there is insufficient data available to score that item. The total score for that person is then prorated. Psychopathy has traditionally been defined as a PCL-R score greater than 29 (Hart, Hare, & Harpur, 1992). The PCL-R has been shown to be reliable and valid (Hare, 1991, 2003; Hare et al., 1990), and research indicates that it predicts recidivism, violence, and criminal behavior better than APD, criminal history, and personality variables (Harpur, Hare, & Hakstain, 1989; Hart & Hare, 1998; Kosson, Smith, & Newman, 1990).

The developers warn researchers and clinicians that specialized training is necessary when using the PCL-R and its derivatives. There are several reasons that the measures should be used only by those specifically trained in its administration. First, while the items appear self-explanatory (i.e., grandiose sense of self-worth), there are actually specified meanings defined in the manual. Users of the PCL-R should be trained to a specific criterion on the subtleties of decisions about whether a person should be scored a 0, 1, or 2 on each item. Second, scores on the PCL-R are being used in court for decisions on issues such as dangerousness, sexual predator status, sentencing, treatment and institutional placements, and civil commitment. Therefore, there are significant implications for individuals and society if someone is determined to be a psychopath using the PCL-R. Due to these issues, the use of the PCL-R and the training of the administrator are subject to closer scrutiny by attorneys and judges when used in court. The impact of scores on the PCL-R "makes it imperative that the instrument be administered only by qualified clinicians and researchers, and in accordance with accepted professional and ethical standards" (Hare, n.d., para. 2). Hare and Darkstone Research offer official

Table
10.1

Comparison of APD Criteria and PCL-R Items

301.7 Antisocial Personality Disorder[a]	PCL-R Two Factors[b]	PCL-R Four Facets[c]
A. Pervasive pattern of disregard for and violation of the rights of others occurring since age 15, as indicated by three (or more) of the following:	Factor 1 (Interpersonal/Affective)	Factor 1 (Interpersonal/Affective)
1. Failure to conform to social norms with respect to lawful behaviors, as indicated by repeatedly performing acts that are grounds for arrest.	Glibness/superficial charm	_Facet 1 (Interpersonal)_
	Grandiose sense of self-worth	Glibness/superficial charm
2. Deceitfulness, as indicated by repeated lying, use of aliases, or conning others for personal profit or pleasure.	Pathological lying	Grandiose sense of self-worth
	Conning/manipulation	Pathological lying
	Lack of remorse/guilt	Conning/manipulation
3. Impulsivity or failure to plan ahead.	Shallow affect	_Facet 2 (Affective)_
4. Irritability and aggressiveness, as indicated by repeated physical fight or assaults.	Callous/lack of empathy	Lack of remorse
	Failure to accept responsibility for own actions	Shallow affect
5. Reckless disregard for the safety of self or others.		Callous/lack of empathy or guilt
	Factor 2 (Behavioral/Lifestyle)	Failure to accept responsibility
6. Consistent irresponsibility, as indicated by repeated failure to sustain consistent work behavior or honor financial obligations.	Need for stimulation	Factor 2 (Social Deviance)
	Parasitic lifestyle	_Facet 3 (Lifestyle)_
	Poor behavioral controls	Need for stimulation and/or proneness to boredom
7. Lack of remorse, as indicated by being indifferent to or rationalizing having hurt, mistreated, or stolen from another.	Early behavioral problems	Parasitic lifestyle
	Lack of realistic, long-term plans	Lack of realistic, long-term goals
	Irresponsibility	Impulsivity
B. Individual must be a least age 18.	Impulsivity	Irresponsibility
	Juvenile delinquency	
C. There is evidence of conduct disorder with onset before age 15.	Revocation of conditional release	_Facet 4 (Antisocial Behavior)_
		Poor behavioral controls
D. The occurrence of antisocial behavior is not exclusively during the course of schizophrenia or manic episode.	Additional items	Early behavior problems
	Many short-term marital relationships	Juvenile delinquency
	Promiscuous sexual behavior	Revocation of conditional release
	Criminal versatility	Criminal versatility

[a] The data in column 1 are from the _Diagnostic and Statistical Manual of Mental Disorders_ (4th ed., pp. 649–650), by the American Psychiatric Association, 1994, Washington, DC: Author.

[b] The data in column 2 are from Hare (1991)

[c] The data in column 3 are from Hare (2003)

training on the use of the PCL-R along with a comprehensive education on the background and research of its use and psychopathy in general. Details are available online at http://www.hare.org/training.

The PCL-R has generally yielded a two-factor structure. Factor 1 and Factor 2 of the PCL-R correspond to the personality and behavioral features of psychopathy, respectively (see Table 10.1). Factor 1, or the personality-based items (Lilienfeld & Andrews, 1996), describes the affective and interpersonal aspects of psychopathy. Factor 1 includes characteristics such as superficial charm, grandiosity, manipulation, callousness, lack of empathy and guilt, and lack of respect or care for others. These items are thought to more closely resemble Cleckley's (1941, 1976) original criteria, which did not include the requirement of aggressive or violent behavior; therefore, these personality characteristics are currently believed to be the core features of psychopathy. Factor 2 of the PCL-R is composed of behavior-based items and is similar to the criteria for APD (Lilienfeld, 1994; Lilienfeld & Andrews, 1996; Widiger & Corbitt, 1993). Factor 2 reflects chronically antisocial or socially deviant behavior, juvenile delinquency, impulsivity, and criminal versatility. While the two factors are highly correlated ($r = .50$; Harpur, Hakstain, & Hare, 1988), they have different external correlates (Harpur et al., 1989). For example, Factor 1 may be associated with the use of aggression to gain some goal, or instrumental aggression, where Factor 2 may be associated with aggression as a reaction to a provocation or threat, or reactive aggression (Cornell et al., 1996; Falkenbach, 2004). Despite the possible implications for considering factor scores separately, in general, for someone to score high enough to be diagnosed with psychopathy, both the behavioral and personality features must be present (Harpur et al., 1989; Wilson et al., 1999).

More recent research indicates that a three-factor model may better fit the data (Cooke & Michie, 1997; Hare, 2003; Skeem, Mulvey, & Grisso, 2003). This three-factor conceptualization still places emphasis on the affective, interpersonal, and behavioral aspects of the disorder. In this model, Factor 1 is split into two separate factors, labeled Deficient Affective Experience and Deceitful Interpersonal Style. The third factor is Irresponsible Behavioral Style. There are 7 PCL-R items that are not retained in the Cooke and Michie model. These items reflect socially deviant behaviors (e.g., juvenile delinquency, revocation of conditional release, sexual promiscuity, and criminal versatility). Research exploring that model is underway, but Hare maintains that the three factors are incorporated into his original two-factor solution. Additionally, as shown in Table 10.1, in the recently published PCL-R: 2nd Edition, Hare (2003b) suggested a four-facet solution that indicates Factor 1, still labeled Interpersonal/Affective, is comprised of "Facets" 1 (Interpersonal) and 2 (Affective), while the original Factor 2, now labeled Social Deviance, is comprised of Facets 3 (Lifestyle) and 4 (Antisocial Behavior).

Psychopathic Traits in Juveniles

The Downward Extension of the Construct of Psychopathy

Research over the last decade has involved the downward extension of the construct of psychopathy to youthful populations. This area of study is important for both practical and theoretical reasons. Practically speaking, adolescent criminal and violent behavior is an extremely important social issue. Until 1994 there was a continued increase in the overall arrest rates for violent crime among juveniles. In that year alone, 20% of the 645,000 people arrested for violent offenses were youth. Since that time, the violent arrest rate for juveniles has decreased (Butts & Harrell, 1998); however, recent tragic events and severe cases including several school shootings (e.g., Columbine) indicate that juvenile violence continues to be an important social issue.

Longitudinal research suggests that a number of adolescents participate in some degree of relatively minor delinquent behavior. This behavior is so prevalent that it is accepted by many as developmentally normal. For the most part, this offending is "adolescent limited"; that is, the criminal career ends with adolescence and the youth moves on to satisfactory adjustment in adulthood. However, there is a group of "life-course-persistent" offenders, who commit more severe crimes and continue their criminal behavior as adults (Moffitt, 1993). This group of criminal adolescents is the greatest long-term risk to society, and recent research on psychopathic traits in juveniles aims to identify these at-risk youth. Identification of those youth who have the potential to become career criminals may safeguard society from their crimes and potentially save the public more than $1.3 million (Cohen, 1998).

Controversy

There are many potential gains for considering the existence of psychopathic traits in youth. However, while the construct of psychopathy in adults is relatively well defined, with a well-validated measurement procedure, the same cannot be said about the construct as applied to youth. For conceptual, developmental, and theoretical reasons, the very idea of juvenile psychopathy is contentious and controversial (see Edens, Skeem, Cruise, & Cauffman, 2001; Frick, 2002; Lynam, 2002; Seagrave & Grisso, 2002; Steinberg, 2002). For example, some researchers have expressed concern that the label of psychopathy may be misapplied to some adolescents. Adolescence is a turbulent period of development, during which time some degree of delinquent behavior is developmentally normal. Teenagers may exhibit many types of antisocial behaviors such as promiscuity, fighting, theft, lying, and manipulation that might be associated with psychopathy. One problem, as indicated by Moffitt's (1993) adolescent-limited group of offenders, is that these traits and behaviors may, in fact, be transitory in nature. Therefore, while these behaviors may be considered part of the characteristics of psychopathy, for adolescent-limited offenders, exhibiting these behaviors may be unrelated to the construct of psychopathy (Steinberg, 2002).

Additionally, controversy surrounds the idea of labeling a child a psychopath and burdening that child with the negative implications attached to that label. Even when a diagnosis of psychopathy is accurate, applying the term *psychopathy* to a young and developing youth can have longstanding, dramatic, and often detrimental effects on how that child is treated in the future. Psychopathy is a form of an adult personality disorder and potentially can stigmatize those to whom the label might be applied. Given the poor prognosis for psychopathy and the social stigmatization that comes with the label, clinicians, families, and the courts may all assume a poor prognosis for those youth identified with psychopathic traits. Therefore, these youth may be pushed aside and considered untreatable, despite the reality that the research on treatment outcome for psychopathy is inconclusive. The unfortunate consequence may be that youth who may actually have a chance of rehabilitation may lose out on resources and opportunities for treatment because they have been categorized as untreatable psychopaths. Another potential implication is waiver to adult court. The court considers several issues when deciding if an adolescent should be tried as an adult. Poor treatment prognosis and risk for future criminality are key determinants of the decisions made in court and also outcomes associated with psychopathy. Therefore, those youth diagnosed with psychopathic traits will be at greater risk for being waived into adult court (Falkenbach, Poythress, & Heide, 2003).

Finally, there may not be enough evidence that psychopathic traits are demonstrated in youth (Hart, Watt, &, Vincent, 2002). The pathology associated with personality disorders, and psychopathy in particular, is well accepted. However, there is disagreement as to whether these disorders can be identified in youth (Kernberg, Weiner, & Bardenstein, 2000). For example, a diagnosis of a personality disorder requires demonstration of personality characteristics that are stable and consistent over a significant period of life (APA, 1994). However, children, by definition, cannot have demonstrated a long-term stable personality. In youth, certain aspects of personality are still changing. An adolescent's ability to use good judgment, understand the perspectives of others, and have a sense of self are all in flux, which makes it difficult to assess traits such as *lack of empathy* and *grandiose sense of self* (Edens et al., 2001).

Additionally, traits of personality disorders may be manifest differently during different developmental stages (Kagen, 1969). Therefore, psychopathic traits, as defined in adulthood, may be indicative of something different in childhood, or psychopathy may look different in children than it does in adults (Hart et al., 2002). Overall there is a lack of longitudinal research to show if there is an actual continuity between psychopathic traits in youth and psychopathy in adulthood (Edens et al., 2001; Hart et al., 2002).

Evidence of Psychopathic Traits in Youth

While there are serious issues to consider when extending the construct of psychopathy down to youthful populations, studying psychopathic-like features among youth is important. Parallels in the adult and juvenile offending literature, etiological theory, and empirical research suggest there is some connection between psychopathic traits in adulthood and specific characteristics in youth. The research on adult offenders suggests that psychopathic adults begin offending at a younger age than nonpsychopathic offenders. Similarly, the juvenile literature indicates that a younger age of onset is predictive of a greater degree of delinquency (Tolan, 1987). Additionally, while some degree of delinquent behavior is developmentally normal during adolescence (adolescence-limited offenders), there is a small cadre of juveniles who account for a disproportionate amount of delinquent behavior and continue to behave in an antisocial manner into adulthood (life-course-persistent offenders; Moffit, 1993). Likewise, in the adult offender literature, while the majority of offenders meet criteria for APD, there is a small strata within the criminal population, psychopaths, who display a higher than average risk for negative outcomes such as violence, recidivism, institutional infractions, and misconduct. Perhaps those life-course-persistent juvenile offenders may later develop traits associated with adult psychopathy (Lynam, 1996).

These parallels in the literature suggest a connection between certain types of juveniles and psychopathic traits in adulthood. Additionally, some researchers believe that

> the personality structure of the psychopath is first evident from an early age (Frick, O'Brian, Wootton & McBurnett, 1994), and is well defined by early adolescence (Forth, Hart & Hare, 1990). It is stable across time (Harpur & Hare, 1994)...and likely contributes to the maintenance of antisocial behaviors throughout the individual's lifespan. (Hemphill, Hare, & Wong, 1998, p. 140)

Thus, there is also a theoretical basis for exploring that connection.

Lykken (1995) suggests that the behavior problems and aggression of psychopaths are related to difficult temperaments. He proposes that psychopaths are born with a constitutional deficit that includes reduced ability to feel fear or inhibit behavior in response to cues for punishment. Typically, children are punished when they yield to "immoral" impulses or act in an antisocial manner; therefore, they learn to act in appropriate ways. Children who are low in fearfulness are at higher risk for behavior problems because they are not as intimidated by punishments. Those youth who are less concerned with punishment and the opinions of others do not experience guilt, and social conformities are not internalized. Therefore, children who are indifferent to punishment are "unlikely to develop an effective conscience" (Lykken, 1995, p. 62). It is these youth whom Lykken predicts may grow into adult psychopaths.

Numerous studies support the idea that psychopathic traits in adulthood may be observable in childhood. Recent heritability research (Blonigen, Carlson, Krueger, & Patrick, 2003) conducted with adult twins has found some degree of genetic influence. This research indicates that a predisposition to develop psychopathic traits may be heritable. Retrospective studies have also linked adult psychopathy to a number of adolescent behavior problems (Harris, Rice, & Quinsey, 1994) and have shown that children who exhibit psychopathic-like traits also have higher rates of conduct disorder (CD; Forth et al., 1990; Frick, 1998), oppositional defiant disorder (ODD), and a variety of self-reported delinquencies (Salekin, Leistico, Trobst, Schrum, & Lochman, 2005).

The combination of parallel findings in the adult and juvenile criminal literature, theory, and empirical research suggests that psychopathic traits may be detectable and identifiable in youth (Abramowitz, Kossen, & Seidenberg, 2004). Therefore, while caution is necessary, continued research on the existence and assessment of psychopathic traits in juveniles is important. Efforts to understand the etiology of psychopathic traits has prompted the extension of the construct of psychopathy downward into younger populations. In this way, researchers may identify indicators of the disorder in children and adolescents and locate key behavioral and interpersonal traits that may influence later behaviors.

Potential Benefits for Exploring Psychopathic Traits in Youth

Psychopathic features may be potential markers for youth at relatively higher risk for serious and prolonged antisocial behavior. Some research has shown that adult psychopaths are resistant to treatment and do not typically have positive treatment outcomes. There is hope that early identification of the "fledgling psychopath" (Lynam, 1996) may help in terms of identifying potential protective factors against later development of psychopathic traits (Salekin, Neumann, Leistico, DiCicco, & Durios, 2004) or developing early prevention strategies. Identifying those youth at risk may also lead to earlier treatment, at a time when adolescents, whose personalities are not yet fully formed, would theoretically be more amenable to treatment. Second, adolescents account for a proportionately large percentage of violent and nonviolent crime. When more is known about these subgroups of juvenile offenders, researchers can work to develop more effective treatment programs, designed to target particular groups of adolescents—treatments that could ultimately result in a reduction of crime.

Assessing Psychopathic Traits in Youth

Several characteristics have been identified in order to better recognize those youth who may be predisposed to psychopathic-like traits. Additionally, some already existing childhood disorders have been examined, including CD and ODD. These disorders have been associated with behavioral problems that are similar to some traits associated with psychopathy. For example, as shown in Table 10.2, deceitfulness, violation of society rules, and aggression are all traits of CD and are all theoretically related to psychopathy. However, CD does not include the more interpersonal and affective characteristics of psychopathy such as glibness, superficial charm, grandiose sense of self-worth, or shallow affect. Therefore, CD, like APD in adults, explains part of psychopathy but not all of it. The simultaneous presence of CD and attention-deficit/hyperactivity disorder (ADHD), due to its specific characteristic of impulsivity, has also been considered in relationship to psychopathy. There is some contention, however, as to the exact nature of this relationship.

There are three perspectives on the nature of the interaction between ADHD, conduct problems, and psychopathy. First, it is suggested that a combination of both ADHD and conduct problems is predictive of psychopathic traits in juveniles (Lynam, 1996). Second, it is posited that ADHD and conduct problems have independent effects on the development of juvenile psychopathic traits, in that both disorders are separately related to the later development of psychopathic traits (Farrington, Loeber, & Van Kammen, 1990; Taylor, Chadwick, Heptinstall, & Danckaerts, 1996). Finally, it is suggested that no direct relationship exists between ADHD and psychopathic traits in juveniles, but that the relationship between ADHD and psychopathic traits is mediated by CD. Despite these relationships between ADHD, CD, and psychopathic traits, only about half of those youth diagnosed with CD go on to become career criminals. These disorders alone do not indicate psychopathy in youth (Robins, 1978).

Juvenile-Specific Assessment Measures

The determination that psychopathy is conceptually different from any disorders previously identified in youth necessitates the use of assessment measures designed to tap

Table 10.2	Conduct Disorder Diagnostic Criteria

A. A repetitive and persistent pattern of behavior in which the basic rights of others or major age-appropriate societal norms or rules are violated, as manifested by the presence of three or or more of the following criteria in the past 12 months, with at least one criterion present in the past 6 months:

Aggression toward people and animals

1 Often bullies, threatens, or intimidates others
2 Often initiates physical fights
3 Has used a weapon that can cause serious physical harm to others (e.g., a bat, brick, broken bottle, knife, gun)
4 Has been physically cruel to people
5 Has been physically cruel to animals
6 Has stolen while confronting a victim (e.g., mugging, purse snatching, extortion, armed robbery)
7 Has forced someone into sexual activity

Destruction of property

8 Has deliberately engaged in fire setting with the intention of causing serious damage
9 Has deliberately destroyed others' property (other than by fire setting)

Deceitfulness or theft

10 Has broken into someone else's house, building, or car
11 Often lies to obtain goods or favors or to avoid obligations (i.e., cons others)
12 Has stolen items of nontrivial value without confronting a victim (e.g., shoplifting, but without breaking and entering; forgery)

Serious violations of rules

13 Often stays out at night despite parental prohibitions, beginning before age 13
14 Has run away from home overnight at least twice while living in parental or parental surrogate home (or once without returning for a lengthy period)
15 Is often truant from school, beginning before age 13.

B. The disturbance in behavior causes clinically significant impairment in social, academic, or occupational functioning.
C. If the individual is age 18 or older, criteria are not met for antisocial personality disorder.

Note. From the *Diagnostic and Statistical Manual of Mental Disorders* (4th ed., pp. 649–650), by the American Psychiatric Association, 1994, Washington, DC: Author.

specifically into psychopathic traits in youth. Currently used assessment instruments have either been interview and file review ratings using a modified version of the PCL-R like the Psychopathy Checklist: Youth Version (PCL:YV; Forth, Kosson, & Hare, 2003), or parent, teacher, or self-report ratings of psychopathic traits, such as the Antisocial Process Screening Device (APSD; Frick & Hare, 2001), the modified Child Psychopathy Scale (mCPS; Lynam, 1997) or the Youth Psychopathic Traits Inventory (YPI; Andershed, Kerr, Stattin, & Levander, 2002). These inventories have been either created or adapted from adult psychopathy inventories for use in adolescent populations, and they attempt to tap the key interpersonal and behavioral traits associated with the construct of psychopathy. Results from research utilizing these adolescent inventories strongly suggest that traits related to the construct of psychopathy can be observed and measured in juveniles (e.g., Forth, et al., 2003; Lynam, 1997). The use of these measures has not only given researchers and clinicians the ability to understand specific personality correlates associated with psychopathic-like behavior in adolescents, but has also helped to extend theories of adult psychopathy into younger populations.

PCL-R and Derivatives

Modifications of PCL-R

When the exploration of the construct of psychopathy was initiated, no juvenile-specific measures existed. The PCL-R, while it was a well researched and validated measure of psychopathy in adults, had some items that were inappropriate for assessing psychopathic traits in youth. For example, *parasitic lifestyle*, which includes living off or being supported by others, is inappropriate given that youth are expected to be financially supported by their families. Additionally, *many short-term marital relationships* is not an appropriate item given the limited relationship experience of adolescents. Therefore, several initial studies used a modified version of the PCL-R with adolescent samples. For example, Forth et al. (1990) created a modified version of the PCL-R more applicable to youth. First, the items deemed inappropriate for use with youth were omitted (i.e., *parasitic lifestyle* and *many short-term marital relationships*). Second, the scoring criteria were altered for those historical items associated with criminal behavior (i.e., *juvenile delinquency* and *criminal versatility*) because a juvenile by definition would have a truncated history.

Connections are noted between youth high on this adapted PCL-R measure and psychopathic adults, suggesting that a set of symptoms similar to adult psychopathy exists in juveniles (Brandt, Kennedy, Patrick, & Curtin, 1997; Forth et al., 1990; Myers, Burket, & Harris, 1995; Rogers, Johansen, Chang, & Salekin, 1997). However, there are problems interpreting results of research on youth based on a measure designed for adults. For instance, interpretation of the research did not incorporate information regarding the developmental processes and norms for adolescents. The modified PCL-R involved revised scoring for only 2 of 20 items, while many other characteristics may be displayed in a different manner for youth.

Psychopathy Checklist: Youth Version

In order to address some of the issues found in the revised version of the PCL-R for youth, Forth et al. (2003) developed the PCL:YV as an adolescent-specific measure of psychopathy. Similar to the adult PCL-R, the PCL:YV is a rating scale designed to assess the 20 core characteristics of psychopathy in youth ages 12 to 18. As shown in Table 10.3, while the PCL-YV is based on the PCL-R, the PCL:YV eliminated items specific to adults and added in items more appropriately tailored to youth life experiences, such as family life, school, and peer relationships. For example, *unstable personal relationships* replaced *many short-term marital relationships*, and items like *impression management* were added while *glibness/superficial charm* was removed. Additionally, *parasitic lifestyle* was changed to *parasitic orientation*, which does not include depending on one's family for financial support or lack of work history. Also, some changes were made in the scoring criteria for items. For example, the item s*timulation seeking* includes the use of drugs and specifically mentions large amounts of sugar or caffeine used for consciousness altering. When scoring *manipulation for personal gain*, the focus is more on cons and hustles rather than manipulation within the interview (Forth et al., 2003).

Like the PCL-R, each item is scored by a trained rater on a 3-point Likert-type scale where 0 indicates an absence of the trait, 1 indicates the traits are sometimes present, and 2 indicates the traits exist consistently. Scores on items are totaled with a possible

Table 10.3

Psychopathy Checklist: Youth Version Versus Youth Psychopathic Traits Inventory

PCL:YV Items and Factor Structures[a] YPI[b]

PCL:YV	YPI
Factor 1 (Interpersonal/Affective)	**Factor 1 Grandiose/Manipulative (*Interpersonal*)**
Facet 1 (Interpersonal)	Dishonest charm
Impression management	Grandiosity
Grandiose sense of self-worth	Lying
Pathological lying	Manipulation
Manipulation for personal gain	
	Factor 2 Callous/Unemotional (*Affective*)
Facet 2 (Affective)	Unemotionality
Lack of remorse	Remorselessness
Shallow affect	Callousness
Callous/lack of empathy	
Failure to accept responsibility	**Factor 3 Impulsive/Irresponsible (*Behavioral*)**
	Impulsiveness
Facet 3 (Lifestyle)	Thrill seeking
Stimulation seeking	Irresponsibility
Parasitic orientation	
Lack of goals	
Impulsivity	
Irresponsibility	
Facet 4 (Antisocial Behavior)	
Poor anger control	
Early behavior problems	
Serious criminal behavior	
Serious violations of conditional release	
Criminal versatility	
Impersonal sexual behavior	
Unstable interpersonal relationships	

[a] The data in column 1 are from "Assessment of Psychopathy in Male Young Offenders," by A. E. Forth, S. D. Hart, and R. D. Hare, 1990, *Psychological Assessment, 2*, pp. 342–344.
[b] The data in column 2 are from "Psychopathic Traits in Non-referred Youths: A New Assessment Tool," by H. Andershed, M. Kerr, H. Stattin, and S. Levander, 2002, in E. Blauuw and L. Sheridan (Eds.), *Psychopaths: Current International Perspectives* (pp. 131–158), The Hague: Elsevier.

range of scores from 0 to 40. The manual for the PCL:YV reports both the three- and four-factor solutions. The authors also note that, due to the controversy and the limited research available on the measure, only the dimensional scores should be used for clinical purposes, while cutoff scores for categorical assessment should be reserved for research.

Decisions about scoring are based on an integration of information from a semistructured interview and review of collateral information from files. However, the interview questions and procedures were explicitly modified for use with adolescents rather than adults. Research suggests that the PCL:YV demonstrates adequate levels of reliability, good validity, and good relationships to theoretically related constructs (Forth et al., 2003). Specifically, research has found a significant relationship between the PCL:YV and ODD, CD, more violent criminal behavior, earlier age of onset for antisocial behaviors, interpersonal characteristics associated with psychopathy in adults, poor parental attachments, and greater alcohol and substance abuse problems (Forth, 1995; Forth & Burke, 1998; Gretton, McBride, Lewis, O'Shaughnessy, & Hare, 1994; Kossen et al., 1990; Mailloux, Forth, & Kroner, 1997; Spain, Douglas, Poythress, & Eptein, 2004; Toupin, Mercier, Dery, Cote, & Hodgins, 1996). The accumulated research findings indicate that the PCL:YV assesses a construct in adolescents that is theoretically similar to psychopathy in adults (Kossen et al., 1990). However, despite the potential demonstrated by the PCL:YV, there are some inconsistencies in the research. For example, juveniles scoring high on the PCL:YV experience higher levels of anxiety; however, lack of anxiety is one of the core characteristics of adult psychopathy (Brandt et al., 1997). Therefore, additional research is needed to resolve these inconsistencies.

Interview-Based Rating Versus Self-Report

The gold standard for the assessment of psychopathy in adult male forensic populations is the PCL-R (Hare, 1991), and follow-up studies are ongoing regarding its predecessor, the PCL-YV. There are some benefits to an interview-based rating system, and specifically the PCL:YV. First, PCL:YV items are based on decisions made by expert raters who are specifically trained on administration of this measure. Protocol for administration requires that raters are trained until they reach a criterion level of interrater agreement (Hare, 1991). Conversely, parent, teacher, and self-report measures do not always have interrater reliability (Falkenbach et al., 2003; Frick, Lahey et al., 1994). Additionally, the PCL:YV involves a face-to-face, structured interview where raters can conduct behavioral observations. These evaluators also meet the juvenile for the sole purpose of conducting the interview, so they are not involved with the juvenile, allowing for less subjectivity. Similarly, PCL:YV ratings are based on the combination of information from various sources. Data from interviews, behavioral observation, and file reviews are integrated, making the scores less subjective than individual ratings.

However, the PCL-R and its derivatives are not without their shortcomings. They are resource intensive, require specialized training, and take several hours to complete. These measures are limited to use with institutionalized populations for whom there is access to files of past behaviors, and even in a forensic or prison setting the file is not always complete or accessible. There are also questions about the applicability of PCL measures to noninstitutionalized populations for whom there is no history of criminal behavior or institutional files. All of the antisocial behavior features of Factor 2 were not part of Cleckley's original conceptualization of psychopathy and make the PCL-R ill equipped to identify successful psychopaths lacking a criminal history (Lilienfeld & Andrews, 1996). Self or other report questionnaires appear to be a sound solution to these dilemmas.

General Personality Inventories

In the past, clinicians and researchers have looked to self-report measures of personality to assess for psychopathic traits. For instance, in adults, self-report indices from general personality inventories—such as the Psychopathic Deviation scale and Hypomania

scale of the MMPI and the Socialization scale of the California Personality Inventory—
have been utilized as measures of psychopathic traits. These indices, however, have been
shown to be related primarily to Factor 2 of the PCL-R (Harpur et al., 1989). These
scales typically correlate poorly, or not at all, with Factor 1. In other words, they are inadequate measures of the core personality features of psychopathy identified by Cleckley
(1941).

In the juvenile literature, self-report indices from personality measures have not
faired much better. Murrie & Cornell (2000) considered the use of the Millon Adolescent
Clinical Inventory (MCMI; Millon & Davis, 1993) as an indicator of psychopathic traits
in youth. These authors had experts choose items from the complete MCMI that assess
traits associated with psychopathy and used 20 of those items to create the psychopathy
content scales of the MCMI. The psychopathy content scales differentiated between
psychopaths and nonpsychopaths in about 80% of cases. However, the psychopathy
content scores were not as good a predictor of theoretically relevant external correlates
such as aggression as the PCL:YV (Stafford & Cornell, 2003). Additionally, like in adults,
where self-report general personality inventories are more associated with behavioral
aspects of psychopathy, the MCMI psychopathy content scales are more associated with
PCL:YV Factor 2 than Factor 1 (Murrie & Cornell, 2000; Murrie, Cornell, Kaplan,
McConville, & Levy-Elkan, 2004). Ultimately, even the authors suggest that the MCMI
psychopathy content scales are for screening purposes only and is not a substitute for the
thoroughness of the clinical interview and file review required with the PCL:YV (Murrie
& Cornell, 2000; Murrie et al., 2004).

Self-Report Measures Designed to Measure Psychopathy Directly

While several self, parent, and teacher report measures have been developed, three in
particular have been most researched and offer promise in terms of the assessment of
psychopathic traits in juveniles.

The Antisocial Process Screening Device

The APSD (Frick & Hare, 2001) consists of 20 items. It was originally designed in order
for parents and/or teachers to rate youth, ages 6 to 13, on psychopathic traits. A self-
report version was later developed for use with youth ages 13 and older. The items of
the APSD map onto 15 of the 20 dimensions of the PCL-R. Some of the PCL-R items,
such as *grandiose sense of self-worth* and *shallow affect* are represented by more than one
APSD item. Other PLC-R items that do not have comparable age-appropriate traits or
activities, such as *parasitic lifestyle* and *revocation of conditional release*, are not included
on the APSD. Traditionally, independent ratings made by a parent and a teacher on each
of the 20 items are combined for a total score. Early research using the parent/teacher
and self-ratings with clinic-referred youth suggested a factor structure that somewhat
parallels the original PCL-R two-factor structure. The first factor obtained, labeled
Callous/Unemotional (CU) traits, is comprised of six items and is similar to the PCL-
R Factor 1. Included in this factor are items such as *lack of guilt or shame* and *lack of
emotions*. These items primarily reflect the affective and interpersonal characteristics
associated with psychopathy. The second factor, labeled Impulsive/Conduct Problems

(I/CP), includes 10 items associated with the behavioral features captured by PCL-R Factor 2 (Frick et al., 1994). This factor includes items such as *acts without thinking* and *easily bored.*

Later research with justice-involved youth indicated that the self-report APSD was better described as having a three-factor structure. This three-factor solution is analogous to the three-factor structure noted for the PCL-R by Cooke & Michie (1997). The APSD three-factor solution includes an interpersonal factor called Narcissism (NAR, 7 items), an affective factor called Callous/Unemotional (CU, 6 items), and an impulsivity factor called Impulsivity (IMP, 5 items; Vitacco, Rogers, & Neumann, 2003).

Finally, the two- and three-factor models were tested with a community sample. Confirmatory factor analysis revealed that a three-factor model adequately described the structure of the APSD (Frick, Bodin, & Barry, 2000). This three-factor model is the model advocated in the published version of the self, parent, and teacher versions of the APSD (Frick & Hare, 2001).

To date, there is some empirical research published using APSD suggesting its promise as a screening devise for psychopathic traits in juveniles. While most of the research is summarized in the APSD manual (Frick & Hare, 2001), Frick, Bodin, and Barry (2000) suggested that "[s]elf-report becomes more reliable and valid as a child enters adolescence, especially for assessing antisocial tendencies and attitudes that may not be observable to parents and other significant adults" (p. 13). Falkenbach et al. (2003) found adequate psychometric properties for the self-report version, and their results indicated better reliability and validity for the self-report version than the parent-report version. These results are particularly important given that a valid self-report measure of psychopathic features might be useful to justice-involved youth, for whom there is limited access to parents and teachers.

Additionally, Frick et al. (2000) suggested that there is a need for more research to determine whether the APSD can predict a youth's response to interventions. Spain et al. (2004) found that the APSD predicted institutional infractions and treatment progress of juvenile justice youth. These studies are particularly important with juvenile justice youth. These adolescents have the greatest need for prevention and early intervention programs in order to prevent these at-risk youth from career delinquency.

Child Psychopathy Scale

The original Child Psychopathy Scale (CPS; Lynam, 1997) was a 41-item measure that drew items from the Child Behavior Checklist (Achenback, 1991) and a version of the California Child Q-Set (Block & Block, 1980). The original CPS was designed to be rated by parents (Lynam, 1997). However, the authors created the mCPS, which is a rationally derived 55-item self-report measure whose items map onto 14 of the 20 PCL-R dimensions. Each item on the mCPS is rated on a 2-point scale where the youth indicates if a trait is (1 = *yes*) or is not (0 = *no*) like them. There is limited published research using the mCPS at this time; however, Spain et al. (2004) found that the mCPS predicted treatment progress and institutional infractions in juvenile justice youth. Lynam, Raine, and Stouthamer-Loeber (2001) found satisfactory reliability and validity of the 52-item version of the measure.

The factor structure of the mCPS has not been examined. However, because each item maps onto a unique PCL-R dimension, it is possible to construct, on a rational basis, subscales representing the affective, interpersonal, and impulsive psychopathy dimensions. Lynam (1997) suggested creating dimension scores by averaging the scores of items that map onto each dimension. These dimension scores can then be added to create factor scores to which each dimension contributes equally. These rationally derived subscales, which can be labeled AFFECT (affective), INTP (interpersonal), and IMPUL (impulsivity), are roughly comparable to the CU, NAR, and IMP scales from the APSD. Given the limited research on the current version of this measure, the mCPS should be limited to use in research.

Youth Psychopathic Traits Inventory

The YPI (Andershed et al., 2002) is the most recently developed measure for the assessment of psychopathic traits in juveniles. The YPI is a 50-item scale for use with adolescents ages 12 and older. The items on the YPI assess how a youth typically thinks or feels using a 4-point Likert-type scale where 1 indicates the item does not apply at all and 4 indicates the item applies very well. The measure was designed so that higher total scale scores indicate a person is more likely to continue to display antisocial and psychopathic-like behavior into adulthood.

Like the other measures designed to assess psychopathic traits in juveniles, the YPI is based on the Cleckley (1941) model of psychopathy. However, the developers of the YPI included more contemporary theories and were able to correct for some weaknesses in the other assessment inventories. First, the YPI is based on the core personality and interpersonal characteristics. The PCL:YV has been criticized for being heavily weighted with historical items of problem behaviors. By focusing on Cleckley's core traits, the YPI puts less emphasis on the historical and antisocial or violent behaviors that were not part of Cleckley's original conceptualization. As shown in Table 10.3, the YPI consists of 3 main factors that assess *grandiose/manipulative* traits, which represent the interpersonal characteristics; *callous/unemotional* traits, which assess the affective characteristics; and *impulsive/irresponsible* traits, which assess the behavioral characteristics. These factors are made up of 10 subscales including items assessing the core traits in the PCL-R and several items theoretically linked to adult psychopathy. The authors also eliminated those items that are inappropriate for juveniles and those items Cooke and Miche (1997) identified as poor indicators of psychopathic behavior. The intention of the design was to create an assessment instrument consisting of more temporally stable characteristics (Andershed et al., 2002).

Second, while the 10 subscales make the YPI a comprehensive assessment of psychopathic traits, it was also designed to overcome social desirability issues. Given the negative social perception of many traits associated with psychopathy, one weakness of other self-report measures is that people may be unwilling to admit to or endorse the characteristics. Items on the YPI are reframed so they are not perceived as deficits but as neutral characteristics (Andershed et al., 2002).

Finally, one of the criticisms of the PCL:YV is that it is limited to use with those who are institutionalized and have complete files to review for collateral information (see Skeem et al., 2003). The YPI was designed using a community-based sample. Therefore, the measure can be used in both community and forensic settings. Additionally, because scores are based on self-report, it can be used if there is a limit to what file information is available.

The YPI is a new measure with limited research and therefore should be used only for research at this time. However, initial studies do indicate good reliability for both males and females. Validity was also demonstrated, with moderate associations found for relevant variables such as early age of onset (e.g., early contact with criminal justice system and early behavioral problems) and antisocial behavior (Andershed et al., 2002). Similarly, in a delinquent population, scores on the YPI predicted more institutional infractions. Additionally, research shows that the YPI demonstrates the negative relationship with anxiety found in adult psychopaths (Skeem & Cauffman, 2003). The current research on the YPI suggests that it has potential to become a future screening measure for psychopathic traits in youth.

Summary

Studies using the measures of psychopathic traits in juveniles have shown that children with higher psychopathic traits resemble adults with higher psychopathy scores in numerous ways (Frick et al., 1994; Lynam, 1997; O'Brien & Frick, 1996). Edens et al. (2001) reviewed the research on assessment measures of psychopathic traits in juveniles. They concluded that, on average, there was a moderate relationship between these measures and various relevant criminal justice outcome criteria. These results have been found in studies across settings and age groups, using different indices of violence and different measures of psychopathic tendencies. Generally, adolescent psychopathy scores (e.g., APSD, CPS, YPI, and PCL:YV) tend to correlate with other indices of psychopathic behavior including CD symptoms (Forth et al., 1990), impulsive behaviors (Stanford, Ebner, Patton, & Williams, 1994), past violence (Kruh, Frick, & Clements, 2005), future criminal behavior (O'Neil, Lidz, & Heilbrun, 2003), and, postdictively, the number of institutional infractions (Edens, Poythress, & Lilienfeld, 1999).

Conclusion

Despite comparable correlations between the PCL:YV, CPS, APSD, and YPI with indices of aggression and antisocial behavior, the measures have rarely been researched together because they have been applied in different settings. Most studies of the PCL:YV have been conducted in samples of youth involved in juvenile justice, and most research on the APSD and CPS has been with community- and clinic-referred youth (Frick et al., 1994; Lynam, 1997). An exception to this trend was an evaluation of the correspondence between the APSD and the PCL:YV in a juvenile justice sample (Murrie & Cornell, 2002). However, this study was unable to evaluate the relationship between these measures and external correlates.

The development of these measures has allowed for a great deal more research investigating psychopathic traits in juveniles. However, until more research can be conducted with these measures, it is a good idea for researchers to utilize multiple assessments of psychopathic traits (Spain et al., 2004). In terms of clinical utility, evaluations of psychopathic traits in juveniles should be conducted with extreme caution. Specifically, Seagrave and Grisso (2002) suggest that the clinical utility of any measure of psychopathic traits in juveniles is contraindicated. However, if these assessments are to take place, the evaluations should adhere to the most rigorous standards, and evaluators should consider the consequences of decisions, especially when the evaluation will be used for decisions in court or for treatment.

RESOURCES AND REFERENCES

Abramowitz, C. S., Kosson, D. S., & Seidenberg, M. (2004). The relationship between childhood attention deficit hyperactivity disorder and conduct problems and adult psychopathy in male inmates. *Personality and Individual Differences, 36*, 1031–1047.

Achenbach, T. M. (1991). *Child Behavior Checklist/4–18 years* (CBCL/4–18). Burlington: University of Vermont.

American Psychiatric Association. (1994). *Diagnostic and statistical manual of mental disorders* (4th ed.). Washington, DC: Author.

Andershed, H., Kerr, M., Stattin, H., & Levander, S. (2002). Psychopathic traits in non-referred youths: A new assessment tool. In E. Blauuw & L. Sheridan (Eds.), *Psychopaths: Current international perspectives* (pp. 131–158). The Hague: Elsevier.

Blackburn, R., & Coid, L. (1998). Psychopathy and the dimensions of personality disorders in violent offenders. *Personality & Individual Differences, 25*(1), 129–145.

Block, J. H., & Block, J. (1980). *The California Child Q-Set.* Palo Alto, CA: Consulting Psychologists Press.

Blonigen, D. M., Carlson, R. F., Krueger, R. F., & Patrick, C. J. (2003). A twin study of self-reported psychopathic personality traits. *Personality and Individual Differences, 35*, 179–197.

Bodholt, R. H., Richards, H. R., & Gacano, C. B. (2000). Assessing psychopathy in adults: The Psychopathy Checklist–Revised and Screening Version. In C. B. Gacano (Ed.), *The clinical and forensic assessment of psychopathy: A practitioners guide* (pp. 111–136). Mahwah, NJ: Lawrence Erlbaum Associates.

Brandt, J. R., Kennedy, W. A., Patrick, C. J., & Curtin, J. J. (1997). Assessment of psychopathy in a population of incarcerated adolescent offenders. *Psychological Assessment, 9*, 429–435.

Butts, J. A., & Harrell, A. V. (1998). Delinquents or criminals: Policy options for young offenders. Washington, DC: Urban League.

Cleckley, H. (1941). *The mask of sanity: An attempt to reinterpret the so-called psychopathic personality.* St. Louis MO: Mosby.

Cleckley, H. (1976). *The mask of sanity; an attempt to reinterpret the so-called psychopathic personality* (5th edition). St. Louis: Mosby.

Cohen, M. A. (1998). The monetary value of saving a high-risk youth. *Journal of Quantitative Criminology, 14* (1), 5–33.

Cooke, D. J., & Michie, C. (1997). An item response theory analysis of the Hare psychopathy checklist. *Psychological Assessment, 9*, 3–13.

Cornell, D. G., Warren, J., Hawk, G., Stafford, E., Oram, & Pine. (1996). Psychopathy in instrumental and reactive violent offenders. *Journal of Consulting & Clinical Psychology, 64*(4), 783–790.

Douglas, K. S., Ogloff, R. P., Nicholls, T. L., & Grant, I. (1999). Assessing risk for violence among psychiatric patients: The HCR-20 Violence Risk Assessment Scheme and the Psychopathy Checklist: Screening Version. *Journal of Consulting & Clinical Psychology, 67*(6), 917–930.

Edens, J. F., Poythress, N. G., & Lilienfeld, S. O. (1999). Identifying inmates at risk for disciplinary infractions: A comparison of two measures of psychopathy. *Behavioral Sciences & the Law, 17*, 435–443.

Edens, J. F., Skeem, J. L., Cruise, K. R., & Cauffman, E. (2001). Assessment of "juvenile psychopathy" and its association with violence: A critical review. *Behavioral Sciences and the Law, 19*, 53–80.

Falkenbach, D. M. (2004). The subtypes of psychopathy and their relationship to hostile and instrumental aggression. *Dissertation Abstracts International.*

Falkenbach, D. M., Poythress, N. G., & Heide, K. M. (2003). Psychopathic features in a juvenile diversion population: Reliability and predictive validity of two self-report measures. *Behavioral Sciences & the Law, 21*, 787–805.

Farrington, D. P., Loeber, R. & Van Kammen, W. B. (1990). Long-term criminal outcomes of hyperactivity-impulsivity-attention deficit and conduct problems in childhood. In L. N. Robins & M. R. Rutter (Eds.), *Straight and devious pathways from childhood to adulthood* (pp. 62–81). New York: Cambridge University Press.

Forth, A. E. (1995). Psychopathy in adolescent offenders: Assessment, family background, and violence. *Issues in Criminological and Legal Psychology, 24,* 42–44.

Forth, A. E., & Burke, H. C. (1998). Psychopathy in adolescence: Assessment, violence, and developmental precursors. In D. J. Cooke, A. E. Forth, & R. D. Hare (Eds.), *Psychopathy: Theory, research, and implications for society* (pp. 205–230). Dordrecht, the Netherlands: Kluwer Academic.

Forth, A. E., Hart, S. D., & Hare, R. D. (1990). Assessment of psychopathy in male young offenders. *Psychological Assessment, 2,* 342–344.

Forth, A. E., Kosson, D., & Hare, R. D. (2003). *The Psychopathy Checklist: Youth Version.* Toronto, Canada: Multi-Health Systems.

Frick, P. J. (1998). Conduct disorders. In T. H. Ollendick & M. Hersen (Eds.), *Handbook of child psychopathology* (pp. 213–237). New York: Plenum.

Frick, P. J. (2002). Juvenile psychopathy from a developmental perspective: Implications for construct development and use in forensic assessments. *Law and Human Behavior, 26,* 247–253.

Frick, P. J., Bodin, S. D., & Barry, C. T. (2000). Psychopathic traits and conduct problems in community and clinic referred samples of children: Further development of the Psychopathy Screening Device. *Psychological Assessment, 12,* 382–393.

Frick, P. J., & Hare, R. D. (2001). *The Antisocial Process Screening Device.* Toronto, Ontario, Canada: Multi-Health Systems.

Frick, P. J., Lahey, B. B., Applegate, B., Kerdyck, L., Ollendick, T., Hynd, G. W., et al. (1994). DSM-IV field trials for the disruptive behavior disorders: Symptom utility estimates. *Journal of the American Academy of Child and Adolescent Psychiatry, 33,* 529–539.

Frick, P. J., O'Brien, B. S., Wootton, J. M., & McBurnett, K. (1994). Psychopathy and conduct problems in children. *Journal of Abnormal Psychology, 103,* 700–707.

Gretton, H., McBride, M., Lewis, K., O'Shaughnessy, R., & Hare, R. D. (1994, March). Patterns of violence and victimization in adolescent sexual psychopaths. Paper presented at the biennial meeting of the American Psychology-Law Society (Division 41 of the American Psychological Association), Santa Fe, NM.

Hare, R. D. (1980). A research scale for assessment of psychopathy in criminal population. *Personality and Individual Differences, 1,* 111–119.

Hare, R. D. (1983). Diagnosis of antisocial personality disorder in two prison samples. *American Journal of Psychiatry, 149,* 887–890.

Hare, R. D. (1991). *The Hare Psychopathy Checklist–Revised.* Toronto, Canada: Multi-Health Systems.

Hare, R. D. (1996). Psychopathy: A clinical construct whose time has come. *Criminal Justice and Behavior, 32*(1), 25–54.

Hare, R. D. (2003b). *The Hare Psychopathy Checklist – Revised; Second Edition.* Toronto: Multi-Health Systems.

Hare, R. D. (n.d.). *HARE PCL-R TRAINING PROGRAM.* Retrieved September 15, 2005, from http://www.hare.org/training/part1.html

Hare, R. D., Clark, D., Grann, M., & Thornton, D. (2000). Psychopathy and the predictive validity of the PCL-R: An international perspective. *Behavioral Sciences & the Law, 18*(5), 623–645.

Hare, R. D., Harpur, T. J., Hakstain, A. R., Forth, A. E., Hart, S. D., & Newman, J. P. (1990). The revised Psychopathy Checklist: Reliability and factor structure. *Psychological Assessment: A Journal of Consulting and Clinical Psychology, 2*(3), 338–341.

Hare, R. D., & Jutai, J. W. (1983). Criminal history of the male psychopath: Some preliminary data. In K. Van Dusen & S. Mednick (Eds.), *Prospective studies of crime and delinquency* (pp. 23–32). Boston: Kluwer Nijhoff.

Harpur, T. J. Hakstain, A. R., & Hare, R. D. (1988). Factor structure of the Psychopathy Checklist. *Journal of Consulting & Clinical Psychology, 56*(5), 741–747.

Harpur, T. J., Hare, R. D. (1994). Assessment of psychopathy as a function of age. *Journal of Abnormal Psychology, 103*(4), 604–609.

Harpur, T. J., Hare, R. D., & Hakstain, A. R. (1989). Two factor conceptualization of psychopathy construct validity and assessment implications. Psychological Assessment. *A Journal of Consulting and Clinical Psychology, 1*(1), 6–17.

Harris, G. T., Rice, M. E., & Cormier, C. A. (1991). Psychopathy and violent recidivism. *Law and Human Behavior, 15*(6), 625–637.

Harris, G. T., Rice, M. E., & Quinsey, V. L. (1994). Psychopathy as a taxon: Evidence that psychopaths are a discrete class. *Journal of Consulting and Clinical Psychology, 62*, 387–397.

Hart, S. D., & Hare, R. D. (1998). Discrimination validity of the Psychopathy Checklist in a forensic psychiatric population. *Psychological Assessment, 1*(3), 211–218.

Hart, S. D., Hare, R. D., & Harpur, T. J. (1992). The Psychopathy Checklist: Overview for researchers and clinicians. In J. Rosen & P. McReynolds (Eds.), *Advances in Psychological Assessment,* Vol 8 (pp. 103–130). New York: Plenum.

Hart, S. D., Watt, K. A., & Vincent, G. M. (2002). Commentary on Seagrave and Grisso: Impressions of the state of the art. *Law and Human Behavior, 26*, 241–245.

Hemphill, J. F., Hare, R. D., & Wong, S. (1998). Psychopathy and recidivism: A review. *Legal & Criminological Psychology, 3*(1), 139–170.

Hill, C. D., Rogers, R., & Bickford, M. E. (1996). Predicting aggressive and socially disruptive behavior in a maximum security forensic psychiatric hospital. *Journal of Forensic Sciences, 41*(1), 56–59.

Kernberg, P. F., Weiner, A., & Bardenstein, K. (2000). *Personality disorders in children and adults.* New York: Basic.

Kagan, J. (1969). The three faces of continuity in human development. In D. A. Goslin (Ed.), *Handbook of socialization theory and research* (pp. 983–1002). Chicago: Rand McNally.

Kosson, D. S., Smith, S. S., & Newman, J. P. (1990). Evaluating the construct validity of psychopathy in Black and White male inmates: Three preliminary studies. *Journal of Abnormal Psychology, 99*(3), 250–259.

Kruh, I. P., Frick, P. J., & Clements, C. B. (2005). Historical and personality correlates to the violence patterns of juveniles tried as adults. *Criminal Justice and Behavior, 32*, 69–96.

Lilienfeld, S. O. (1994). Conceptual problems in the assessment of psychopathy. *Clinical Psychology Review, 14*(1), 17–38.

Lilienfeld, S. O., & Andrews, B. P. (1996). Development and preliminary validation of a self-report measure of psychopathic personality traits in noncriminal populations. *Journal of Personality Assessment, 66*(3), 488–524.

Lynam, D. R. (1996). The early identification of chronic offenders: Who is the fledgling psychopath? *Psychological Bulletin, 120*, 209–234.

Lynam, D. R. (1997). Pursuing the psychopath: Capturing the fledgling psychopath in a nomological net. *Journal of Abnormal Psychology, 106*, 425–438.

Lynam, D. R. (2002). Psychopathy from the perspective of the five-factor model of personality. In P. T. Costa & T. A. Widiger (Eds.), *Personality disorders and the five-factor model of personality* (pp. 325–348). Washington, DC: American Psychological Association.

Lynam, D., Raine, A., & Stouthamer-Loeber, M. (2001). *Reliability and validity of the Childhood Psychopathy Scale in two samples.* Paper presented at the Annual Meeting of the International Society for Research in Child and Adolescent Psychopathology, Vancouver, BC.

Lykken, D. T. (1995). *The antisocial personalities.* Hillsdale, NJ: Lawrence Erlbaum Associates.

Megargee, E. I. (1982). Psychological determinants and correlates of criminal violence. In M. E. Wolfgang & N. A. Weiner (Eds.), *Criminal violence* (pp. 81–170). London: Cassel.

Mailloux, D. L., Forth, A. E., & Kroner, D. G. (1997). Psychopathy and substance use in adolescent male offenders. *Psychological Reports, 81*, 529–530.

Myers, W. C., Burket, R. C., & Harris, H. E. (1995). Adolescent psychopathy in relation to delinquent behaviors, conduct disorder and personality disorders. *Journal of Forensic Sciences, 40*(3), 435–439.

Millon, T., & Davis, R. (1993). The Millon Adolescent Personality Inventory and the Millon Adolescent Clinical Inventory. *Journal of Counseling and Development, 71*, 570–574.

Millon, T., & Davis, R. D. (1996). *Disorders of personality: DSM–IV and beyond* (2nd ed.). New York: Wiley.

Moffitt, T. E. (1993). Adolescence-limited and life course-persistent antisocial behavior. *Psychological Review, 100*, 674–701.

Murrie, D. C., & Cornell, D. (2002). The Millon Adolescent Clinical Inventory and psychopathy. *Journal of Personality Assessment, 75*, 110–125.

Murrie, D. C., Cornell, D. G., Kaplan, S., McConville, D., & Levy-Elkon, A. (2004). Psychopathy scores and violence among juvenile offenders: A multi-measure study. *Behavioral Sciences and the Law, 22*, 49–67.

O'Brien, B. S., & Frick, P. J. (1996). Reward dominance: Associations with anxiety, conduct problems, and psychopathy in children. *Journal of Abnormal Child Psychology, 24*, 223–240.

Ogloff, J. R., Wong, S., & Greenwood, A. (1990). Treating criminal psychopaths in a therapeutic community program. *Behavioral Sciences & the Law, 8*(2), 181–190.

O'Neill, M. L., Lidz, V., & Heilbrun, K. (2003). Adolescents with psychopathic characteristics in a substance abusing cohort: Treatment and process outcomes. *Law and Human Behavior, 27*, 299–313.

Quinsey, V. L., Rice, M. E., & Harris, G. T. (1995). Actuarial prediction of sexual recidivism. *Journal of Interpersonal Violence, 10*(1), 85–105.

Rice, M. E., Harris, G. T., Cormier, C. A. (1992). An evaluation of a maximum security therapeutic community for psychopaths and other mentally disordered offenders. *Law and Human Behavior, 16*(4), 399–412.

Robins, L. N. (1978). Etiological implications in studies of childhood histories relating to antisocial personalities. In R. D. Hare & D. Shalling (Eds.), *Psychopathic behavior: Approaches to research* (pp. 255–271). Chichester, UK: Wiley.

Rogers, R., & Dion, K. L. (1991). Rethinking the *DSM III–R* diagnosis of antisocial personality disorder. *Bulletin of the American Academy of Psychiatry & the Law, 19*(1), 21–31.

Rogers, R., Johansen, J., Chang, J. J., & Salekin, R. T. (1997). Predictors of adolescent psychopathy: Oppositional and conduct-disordered symptoms. *Journal of the American Academy of Psychiatry and Law, 25*, 261–271.

Salekin, R. T. (2002). Psychopathy and therapeutic pessimism: Clinical lore or clinical reality? *Clinical Psychology Review, 22*(1), 79–112.

Salekin, R. T., Leistico, A. R., Trobst, K. K., Schrum, C. L., & Lochman, J. E. (2005). Adolescent psychopathy and personality theory—the interpersonal circumplex: Expanding evidence of a nomological net. *Journal of Abnormal Child Psychology, 33*, 445–460.

Salekin, R. T., Neumann, C. S., Leistico, A. R., DiCicco, T. M., & Durios, R. L. (2004). Psychopathy and comorbidity in a youth offender sample: Taking a closer look at psychopathy's potential importance over disruptive behavior. *Journal of Abnormal Psychology, 33*(4). 731–742.

Salekin, R. T., Rogers, R., & Sewell, K. W. (1996). A review and meta-analysis of the Psychopathy Checklist and Psychopathy Checklist–Revised: Predictive validity of dangerousness. *Clinical Psychology: Science & Practice, 3*(3), 203–215.

Schmauk, F. J. (1970). Punishment, arousal, and avoidance learning in sociopaths. *Journal of Abnormal Psychology, 76*(3), 325–335.

Seagrave, D., & Grisso, T. (2002). Adolescent development and the measuremsent of juvenile psychopathy. *Law and Human Behavior, 26*, 219–239.

Serin, R. C. (1996). Violent recidivism in criminal psychopaths. *Law & Human Behavior, 20*(2), 207–217.

Serin, R. C., & Amos, N. L. (1995). The role of psychopathy in the assessment of dangerousness. *International Journal of Law & Psychiatry, 18*(2), 231–238.

Skeem, J. L., & Cauffman, E. (2003). Views of the downward extension: Comparing the youth version of the Psychopathy Checklist with the Youth Psychopathic Traits Inventory. *Behavioral Sciences and the Law, 21*, 737–770.

Skeem, J. L., Monahan, J., & Mulvey, E. P. (2002). Psychopathy, treatment involvement, and subsequent violence among civil psychiatric patients. *Law & Human Behavior, 26*(6), 577–603.

Skeem, J. L., & Mulvey, E. P. (2001). Psychopathy and community violence among civil psychiatric patients: Results from the MacArthur Violence Risk Assessment Study. *Journal of Consulting & Clinical Psychology, 69*(3), 358–374.

Skeem, J. L., Mulvey, E.P, & Grisso, T. (2003). Applicability of traditional and revised models of psychopathy to the Psychopathy Checklist: Screening version. *Psychological Assessment, 15*(1), 41–55.

Spain, S. E., Douglas, K. S., Poythress, N. G., & Epstein, M. (2004). The relationship between psychopathic features, violence, and treatment outcome: The comparison of three youth measures of psychopathic features. *Behavioral Sciences and the Law, 22*, 85–102.

Stafford, E., & Cornell, D. (2003). Psychopathy scores predict adolescent impatient aggression. *Assessment, 10*, 102–112.

Stanford, M. S., Ebner, D., Patton, J. H., & Williams, J. (1994). Multi-impulsivity within an adolescent psychiatric population. *Personality and Individual Differences, 16*: 395–402.

Steinberg, L. (2002). The juvenile psychopath: Fads, fictions, and facts. National Institute of Justice Perspectives on Crime and Justice 2001 Lecture Series, 5, 35–64.

Taylor, E., Chadwick, O., Heptinstall, E., & Danckaerts, M. (1996). Hyperactivity and conduct problems as risk factors for adolescent development. *Journal of the American Academy of Child & Adolescent Psychiatry, 35*(9), 1213–1226.

Toch, H., Adams, K., & Grant, J. D. (1989). *Coping: Maladaptation in prisons*. New Brunswick, NJ: Transaction.

Tolan, P. H. (1987). Implications of age of onset for delinquency risk. *Journal of Abnormal Child Psychology, 15*, 47–65.

Toupin, J., Mercier, H., Dery, M., Cote, G., & Hodgins, S. (1996). Validity of the PCL-R for adolescents. *Issues in Criminological & Legal Psychology, 24*, 143–145.

Vitacco, M. J., Rogers, R., & Neumann, C. R. (2003). The antisocial process screening device: An examination of its construct and criterion-related validity. *Assessment, 10*, 143–150.

Vitale, J. E., Smith, S. S., Brinkley, C. A., & Newman, J. P. (2002). The reliability and validity of the Psychopathy Checklist–Revised in a sample of female offenders. *Criminal Justice and Behavior, 29*(2), 202–231.

Wilson, D. L., Frick, P. F., & Clements, C. B. (1999). Gender, somatization, and psychopathic traits in a college sample. *Journal of Psychopathology and Behavioral Assessment, 21*(3), 221–235.

Widiger, T. A., & Corbitt, E. M. (1993). Antisocial personality disorder: Proposals for DSM-IV. *Journal of Personality Disorders, 7*(1), 63–77.

Sex, Drugs, and Rock 'n' Rolling With Resistance: Motivational Interviewing in Juvenile Justice Settings

11

Sarah W. Feldstein
Joel I. D. Ginsburg

Case Examples

Billy

Nothing about Billy's life has been simple. Uncertain about whether she was or wanted to be pregnant, Billy's mom never quit smoking nor sought prenatal care. Billy arrived into this world in a haggard state, premature and of a low birth weight. As he grew up, Billy realized that his mom was not good at looking after him. Billy came to understand that he could rely on only himself.

Despite his inability to sort out the order or sounds of the letters, Billy managed to pass each year of elementary school. However, by junior high, his trouble with letters made the school day frustrating. Therefore, Billy stopped attending his difficult classes. With the principal's threats of expulsion for misbehavior and truancy, Billy realized that it would be simpler to just stop attending school altogether.

Thus, Billy returned home to spend his days goofing around and watching television. One day, Billy's mother asked him to do her a favor. She handed him a small package and told him to run it to the neighbor's house. Billy was a skilled athlete, and he knew he could get it to the neighbor's at lightning speed. In fact, it took him a mere 15 minutes to run to the neighbors, exchange the package for some cash, and return home. Billy's mother was delighted with his speed and said that she loved him. While Billy believed that he did not need to hear those words, it felt good to hear that she loved him. Soon, Billy was running errands for her throughout the day and night.

A few months in, something went wrong during one of the runs. The man he was dealing with had a strange look in his eye. Without paying, the man took the package from Billy and ran. Billy knew that he could not return home without the money; his mother would be furious. Desperate, Billy chased after him. As Billy approached the man, he pulled out the pocketknife that he kept for emergencies. Holding up the knife, Billy demanded that the man give up the money. Neighbors called the police when they saw the flash of a knife. The police arrested Billy for aggravated assault. When Billy arrived at the station, he called his mom, hoping that she would come get him. However, Billy's mother was irate that he had called her with the police nearby. She called him "stupid" and told him not to bother coming home again.

Marie

Marie's mother was a prostitute who had contracted HIV from one of her "Johns." The antiretroviral medication was expensive and beyond their family's means. Two years after discovering that she had AIDS, she died. At her funeral, Marie's Auntie Belle invited Marie to come and live with her. Although she was currently healthy, Auntie Belle had also become HIV positive through her evening work. Similarly, without the money to pay for the medication, Auntie Belle soon became very ill.

When Auntie Belle died a year later, Marie felt lost and alone. Marie spent the first month after her Auntie's death walking about the streets, trying to figure out what to do. One evening, during one of her evening walks, a handsome man approached her. He told her that his name was James. James told Marie that she looked like she was in trouble, but she need not worry because he was going to take care of her. Marie could not believe her luck. She felt like some higher power had acknowledged everything that she had done for her mother and her Auntie and was rewarding her. Without a second thought, Marie climbed into the passenger seat of James' fancy car. A week later, James stationed Marie under the highway bridge, advertising her as his "youngest girl yet." After ignoring two police warnings to stay away from the bridge, Marie was arrested for prostitution.

Scope of the Problem

Mental Health and Risk-Taking Behavior Within the U.S. Juvenile Justice System

Although the overall rates of juvenile crimes have been decreasing, the last decade witnessed a 19% increase in drug abuse violations (Snyder, 2005). The correlates of drug use are also evident in the mental health issues of the juvenile justice population. Abram, Teplin, McClelland, and Dulcan (2003) recently completed a large-scale survey of the rates of mental disorders as classified by the *Diagnostic and Statistic Manual of Mental Disorders* (*DSM–III–R*, *DSM–IV*, *DSM–IV–TR*; American Psychiatric Association [APA], 1987, 1994, 2000), derived from a sample of youth ages 10 to 18 years interviewed within 2 days of their intake into the Cook County (Chicago) Juvenile Temporary Detention Center.

Prevalence of *DSM* Diagnoses

Within this sample, Abram et al. (2003) examined the prevalence of *DSM–III–R* diagnoses (APA, 1987), including major depression, dysthymia, mania, psychotic disorder, panic, separation anxiety, obsessive-compulsive disorder, attention-deficit/hyperactivity disorder (ADHD), conduct disorder (CD), oppositional defiant disorder (ODD), and substance use disorders. They found that the minority of juveniles met diagnostic criteria for only one disorder (females = 17%, males = 20%), while the majority met diagnostic criteria for at least two disorders (females = 57%, males = 46%). In a previous study, these researchers found that the most prevalent disorders among both male and female juveniles were substance use (females = 47%, males = 51%) and disruptive behavior disorders such as ODD and CD (females = 46%, males = 41%; Teplin, Abram, McClelland, Dulcan, & Mericle, 2002). Similarly, in their most recent study, Abram et al. (2003) found that most of their sample met diagnostic criteria for a substance use disorder along with a disruptive behavior disorder or ADHD. Interestingly, when compared with the juveniles who did not meet diagnostic criteria for a major mental disorder (defined by the authors as psychosis, mania, or a major depressive episode), juveniles with a major mental disorder had significantly greater odds (1.8 – 4.1) of having a co-occurring substance use disorder (Abram et al., 2003).

Even after excluding substance use and disruptive behavior disorders, 34% of female and 24% of male juveniles still met diagnostic criteria for two or more disorders (Abram et al., 2003). These disorders included affective disorders (females = 28%, males = 19%), anxiety disorders (females = 31%, males = 21%), ADHD (females = 21%, males = 17%), and psychotic disorders (females = 1%, males = 1%; Teplin et al., 2002).

Independent of the Chicago research group, the Patterns of Youth Mental Health Care in Public Services System study, which includes Garland, Aarons, and colleagues, have been evaluating 1,715 youth (ages 6 – 17 years) in five sectors of San Diego public care. Those sectors include alcohol and drug services, child welfare, juvenile justice, mental health services, and public school services for youth with serious emotional disturbance. Within this sample, Garland et al. (2001) found similar rates of *DSM–IV* diagnoses as found in the Chicago studies. Across their juvenile justice system, 52% of their sample met diagnostic criteria for one or more disorders. Specifically, 30% of their sample met the diagnostic criteria for CD, 15% for ODD, 13% for ADHD, 9% for anxiety disorders (separation anxiety = 4%, posttraumatic stress disorder = 3%), and 7% for mood disorders (major depression = 5%; Garland et al., 2001).

Substance Abuse and Dependence

To understand the prevalence of substance use within this sample, McClelland, Elkington, Teplin, and Abram (2004) further examined the manifestation of related diagnoses. As measured by the Diagnostic Interview Schedule for Children, version 2.3 (DISC version 2.3), youth reported relatively low rates of substance abuse (less than 1% to 6%) and high rates of substance dependence (2% – 38%) during the 6 months prior to intake. In their sample of over 1,700 youth, when the authors combined abuse and dependence into the broader category of substance use disorders (SUDs), 50% of males and 45% of females met criteria for at least one SUD. In addition, 20% of males and females had two or more SUDs. While the prevailing SUDs were marijuana abuse and dependence, alcohol use was not far behind. Specifically, approximately 40% of the sample reported both alcohol and marijuana SUDs.

In collaboration with the San Diego public sector study, Aarons, Brown, Hough, Garland, and Wood (2001) investigated the prevalence of substance use in a juvenile justice sample, finding similar rates of SUDs to those reported in the McClelland et al. (2004) sample. In the Aarons et al. (2001) sample, 62% of the youth met *DSM–IV* diagnostic criteria for any SUD during their lifetimes, while 37% met diagnostic criteria for SUDs during the past year. Also, like the findings of McClelland et al. (2004), Aarons et al. (2001) found that most justice system juveniles were using marijuana (lifetime prevalence = 45%, past-year prevalence = 15%) and alcohol (lifetime prevalence = 49%, past-year prevalence = 28%). Aarons and colleagues found much lower rates for the use of amphetamines (lifetime = 23%, past year = 10%), hallucinogens (lifetime = 9%, past year = 3%), cocaine (lifetime = 2%, past year = < 1%), and opiates (lifetime = <1%, past year = <1%).

Sexual Risk-Taking Behavior

Along with substance use and externalizing behaviors, sexual risk-taking behavior is often seen as another component in the cluster of delinquent behaviors. Although it is not diagnosable within the *DSM*, the health implications of risky sexual behavior are serious. Through the self-report instruments of the AIDS Risk Behavior Assessment and items from the DISC version 2.3, Teplin, Mericle, McClelland, and Abram (2003) examined the sexual behavior of the Chicago youth. Across ages, the majority of the youth were sexually active (females = 87%, males = 91%). Most males (61%) and a quarter of the females (26%) reported having had more than one sexual partner within the past 3 months (Teplin et al., 2003). In addition, over 95% of this sample engaged in at least three, and 65% in at least 10, HIV/AIDS-related risk behaviors (i.e., unprotected vaginal or anal sex, vaginal or anal sex with high-risk partner; Teplin et al., 2003).

Age Considerations

Throughout these studies, clear differences between the younger (ages 13 and under) and older (ages 14 and older) youth emerged. As may be predicted by increasing age and experience, older youth reported symptoms consonant with higher rates of *DSM* diagnoses (Teplin et al., 2002), as well as greater sexual activity and risky sexual behavior, including unprotected sex (Teplin et al., 2003).

Gender Considerations

In addition, when examined together, gender differences appeared. Significantly more females than males met diagnostic criteria for *DSM–III–R* disorders (Teplin et al., 2002), even after excluding substance use and CD (met criteria for two or more disorders: females = 34%, males = 24%; Abram et al., 2003). In addition, Teplin et al. (2003) found that significantly more males engaged in sexual risk-taking behaviors, including having more than three partners within the past 3 months (females = 5%, males = 37%) and having sex when drunk or high (females = 52%, males = 68%). In contrast, males and females reported equal rates of unprotected intercourse, when sober (females = 41%, males = 35%) as well as when drunk or high (females = 33%, males = 33%; Teplin et al., 2003). Together, these data indicate that while females reported greater overall mental health issues, males engaged in more sexual risk-taking behavior.

Racial/Ethnic Considerations

Throughout these studies, there were also multiple racial/ethnic differences. White juveniles reported the highest rates of psychiatric comorbidity, while African American juveniles reported the lowest (Abram et al., 2003). In addition, within this sample, more Caucasian and Hispanic than African American juveniles (particularly females) met diagnostic criteria for one or more SUDs (Abram et al., 2003; McClelland et al., 2004). In contrast with African American youth, White and Hispanic youth reported higher use of illicit drugs other than marijuana (McClelland et al., 2004). Teplin et al. (2002) summarized their paradoxical finding that while most of the juveniles in the justice system were from minority cultures, White juveniles had the highest rates of most *DSM* disorders. Teplin et al. (2002) posit that, on average, White youth in the justice system may have greater psychological difficulties than minority youth.

Literature Review

Background

Abilities, skills, and psychosocial functioning continue to develop throughout adolescence (Schulenberg & Maggs, 2002). While some juveniles demonstrate responsibility and emotional maturity in employment or academics, many operate in ways that are consistent with middle childhood. Specifically, the executive functioning is generally the last to develop, leaving adolescents to function with immature forms of reasoning, impulse control, and planning (Cicchetti & Rogosch, 2002). Unfortunately, not all juveniles will develop mature reasoning, impulse control, and planning capacities. However, there are therapeutic approaches and interventions, such as motivational interviewing (MI) that may be flexible enough to work with the range of adolescent ability and functioning. Specifically, throughout the theoretical literature, MI has been posited as a potentially effective approach with child and adolescent clients in general (Baer & Peterson, 2002; DiGiuseppe, Linscott, & Jilton, 1996; Miller & Sanchez, 1994; Tober, 1991), in pediatric practice (Sindelar, Abrantes, Hart, Lewander, & Spirito, 2004), with respect to decreasing substance use and related risks with children and adolescents (Baer, Peterson, & Wells, 2004; Breslin, Li, Sdao-Jarvie, Tupker & Ittig-Deland, 2002; Colby, Lee, Lewis-Esquerre, Esposito-Smythers, & Monti, 2004; D'Amico & Fromme, 2000; Dishion, Kavanagh, Schneiger, Nelson, & Kaufman, 2002; Hawkins, Cummins, & Marlatt, 2004; Masterman & Kelly, 2003; Myers, Brown, & Kelly, 2000; Myers, Brown, & Vik, 1998; Rivers, Greenbaum, & Goldberg, 2001; Waldron & Kaminer, 2004; Winters, 1999), with late adolescent and college students (Barnett et al., 2004; Larimer & Cronce, 2002; Neal & Carey, 2004; Saunders, Kypri, Walters, Laforge, & Larimer, 2004; Tevyaw & Monti, 2004), with respect to safer sexual behavior (Brown &

The Spirit of Motivational Interviewing
1. Motivation for change is elicited from the client, not imposed upon the client.
2. It is the client's task, not the counselor's, to articulate and resolve his or her ambivalence.
3. Direct persuasion is not an effective method for resolving ambivalence.
4. The counseling style is generally a quiet and eliciting one.
5. The counselor is directive in helping the client to examine and resolve ambivalence.
6. Readiness to change is not a client trait, but a fluid product of interpersonal interaction.
7. The therapeutic relationship is more like a partnership than expert/recipient roles.

Note. Adapted from "*Introduction to Motivational Interviewing*," by T. B. Moyers, 2005, Workshop presented at the Center on Alcoholism, Substance Abuse, and Addictions, Albuquerque, NM.

Lourie, 2001; Cowley, Farley, & Beamis, 2002), in school settings (Lambie, 2004), and in juvenile justice settings (Coll, Juhnke, Thobro, & Haas, 2003).

The Spirit of MI

Ambivalence is the state in which a person feels two ways about something. Ambivalence is believed to play a role in most psychological difficulties (Miller & Rollnick, 2002). Rather that interpreting ambivalence as a sign of indecision or pathology, ambivalence is considered crucial to the practice of MI. Specifically, within the practice of MI, addressing and resolving ambivalence is believed to help move a person toward change (Miller & Rollnick, 2002).

In contrast to communication styles that elicit client resistance, MI operates through client and practitioner collaboration (Miller & Rollnick, 2002). MI's guiding approach draws on clients' inherent desire and ability to move toward change (Miller & Rollnick, 2002). As defined by its developers, MI is a "client-centered, directive method for enhancing intrinsic motivation to change by exploring and resolving ambivalence" (Miller & Rollnick, 2002, p. 25). More than a set of techniques, MI is a way of being with people. This style involves exploring ambivalence around a target behavior through the examination of a person's relevant values, interests, and concerns (Miller & Rollnick, 2002). See Table 11.1 for a list of the major characteristics of MI.

Although developed 2 decades ago, the foundational beliefs of MI are supported by 3 decades of research. Specifically, in the early 1970s, Truax and colleagues found that certain therapist characteristics such as openness, genuineness, and empathy facilitated therapeutic gain with juvenile delinquent clients (Truax, 1971; Truax, Wargo, & Volksdorf, 1970). Moreover, they found that less collaborative efforts, such as persuasion, could not incite change with juvenile delinquents (Truax & Lister, 1970). However, this finding has been found not only in the juvenile justice literature. Across demographic categories, confrontational practitioner behaviors have been found to decrease collaboration and increase resistance (DiCicco, Unterberger, & Mack, 1978; Miller, Benefield, & Tonigan, 1993; Miller & Wilbourne, 2002; Patterson & Forgatch, 1985). The approach of MI emerged from these data; confrontation, education, and authority are believed to elicit client resistance, while collaboration, evocation, and autonomy facilitate therapeutic alliance and foster an environment ready for positive change (Miller & Rollnick, 2002).

Table 11.2	Four Principles of Motivational Interviewing: REDS
	1. Roll with resistance (R) Tools: Reframe resistance, normalize ambivalence, and emphasize personal control 2. Express empathy (E) Tools: Affirm, ask open questions, and use reflective listening 3. Develop discrepancy (D) Tools: Ask evocative questions and employ decisional balance 4. Support self-efficacy (S) Tools: Affirm, characterize successful adolescents, and encourage a success story

Note. Adapted from "*Introduction to Motivational Interviewing,*" by T. B. Moyers, 2005, Workshop presented at the Center on Alcoholism, Substance Abuse, and Addictions, Albuquerque, NM.

Specifically from these data, the foundations of the MI approach have been established as empathy, development of discrepancy, rolling with resistance, and support of self-efficacy (Table 11.2). Consonant with the work of Carl Rogers (1980), empathy within MI (Miller & Sanchez, 1994) is the skillful and deliberate ability to convey a sense of being present, as well as an understanding of the client's words, emotions, and underlying meaning.

In addition to providing a genuine expression of empathy, MI practitioners help their clients develop discrepancy between their current behavior and their treatment goal, by supporting the client's self-efficacy and inherent abilities, and without being distracted by resistance (referred to as *rolling with resistance*; Miller & Rollnick, 2002). Through reflective and empathic listening, the practitioner conveys a sense of collaboration with the client through acceptance, understanding of ambivalence, and ultimate support of the client's autonomy to change or not change (Miller & Rollnick, 2002).

Approaches and Relevant Tools

Operationally, MI relies on the practitioner's use of open questions, reflective listening, affirmation, summary statements unifying and reinforcing client statements, and eliciting change talk (Miller & Rollnick, 2002). In contrast to closed (i.e., yes/no or short answer) questions (i.e., "Were you also using when you were running drugs for your mom?" "How many times did you prostitute yourself last week?"), MI relies on the use of open questions that allow a client to provide thoughtful, and even unanticipated, responses (i.e., "Tell me about how things are going with your mom." "What is going well and not so well at home?" "How does your recent arrest fit in with your hopes and dreams?").

Reflective listening is one of the most frequently used strategies within MI. Specifically, it is a method of checking in with a client to move beyond his or her spoken words to determine meaning and affect. It can range from the simple restatement of the client's words (i.e., Client: "I hate being here." Therapist: "You hate being here.") to the more sophisticated and complex, including the addition of affect or the continuation of a client's thoughts (i.e., Client: "I hate being here." Therapist: "You're angry about how this all worked out.").

In juvenile justice settings, practitioners frequently need to provide clients with information, such as the requirements for release. Consistent with the MI style, the

Table 11.3	Giving Information: Using the Elicit–Provide–Elicit Formula
Elicit:	*Ask the client what he or she already knows about the topic.*
Example:	"Tell me what you know about what is going to happen once you leave the detention center."
Provide:	*Begin by providing a summary of what the client already knows. Next, ask for the client's permission to provide information. If permission is given, then provide information in a neutral and objective fashion. The information, not the counselor, confronts the client.*
Example:	"It sounds like you already know some things that happen once you leave here. As you said, you have to go to school. And, if the school reports you as truant, you can be arrested again. I have some additional information about what happens to kids once they leave the detention center. Could I share it with you?"
If permission is granted . . .	
	"Kids who have been arrested, and who are arrested again, end up having more serious punishments for the same crime. If the judge is afraid that you will continue running into trouble without getting help, then he or she may tell you to go to a treatment center or a lockdown facility."
Elicit:	*Ask for the client's response to the information you have provided.*
Example:	"What do you make of that?" "Any thoughts on that?"

Note. Adopted from *Health Behavior Change: A Guide for Practitioners*, edited by S. Rollnick, P. Mason, and C. Butler, 1999, Edinburgh, UK: Churchill Livingstone.

elicit–provide–elicit (Table 11.3) formula allows a practitioner to use open questions to find out what a client already knows about certain topics (i.e., "What do you know about the court's requirements for school attendance?"). Once a client's knowledge has been elicited, a practitioner may offer to provide additional information to the client (i.e., "I have a little more information about the court's requirements for your case. May I share that with you?"). In the MI style of supporting autonomy, a practitioner may proceed in sharing information only once the client's permission has been granted. After the provision of information, the practitioner can once again elicit the reaction of the client to determine what the client thinks about or how he or she has integrated the additional information (i.e., "What do you think about that?" "How does that fit with your plans for after your release?").

In addition, practitioners can utilize four approaches to resolving ambivalence. First, a practitioner might ask the juvenile to engage in an imagination experiment, in which the juvenile is asked to state where she or he hopes to be in a few years. After eliciting a client's reaction, the practitioner may ask how the juvenile's current behavior fits or does not fit with that goal. For example, "How does your marijuana use fit with your plans to be a professional basketball player?" If clients state that they do not have or do not know their future goals and hopes, reflection of that is an appropriate response (i.e., "You're here in the detention center right now, and you're not sure where you'd like to be in 5 years. Tell me a little bit more about that.").

Table 11.4

Readiness Rulers

Readiness:

On a scale of 0–10, where 0 is *not at all ready* and 10 is *very ready*, how ready are you to change [X behavior] now? What makes you choose a [number chosen] instead of a 0?

Importance:

On a scale of 0–10, where 0 is *not at all important* and 10 is *very important*, how important is it for you to change [X behavior] now? What makes you choose a [number chosen] instead of a 0?

Confidence:

On a scale of 0–10, where 0 is *not at all confident* and 10 is *very confident*, how confident are you that you could change [X behavior] if you wanted to? What makes you choose a [number chosen] instead of a 0?

Note. Adopted from *Health Behavior Change: A Guide for Practitioners,* edited by S. Rollnick, P. Mason, and C. Butler, 1999, Edinburgh, UK: Churchill Livingstone.

Second, a practitioner can use readiness rulers (Table 11.4) to approach ambivalence. Using these rulers can help a juvenile client express the importance of changing the target behavior, the degree of readiness to change the behavior, and the level of confidence in his or her ability to make the change. As rulers are often used, a client might describe the importance of a court mandate (such as increasing school attendance; i.e., "On a scale of 0 to 10, where 0 is not at all important and 10 is the most important thing in your life, how important is it for you to start attending school more?"). Once a number is given, the practitioner may ask the juvenile why he or she expressed that particular degree of importance as opposed to a lesser degree. Even if a juvenile client expresses a low value (such as a "1"), asking why the activity is not at an even lower value (such as "0") maintains the effect of enhancing the individual's sense of self-efficacy. If the client is willing, the practitioner may follow up by asking the client how he or she might move the level of importance assigned to the activity from a "1" to a "3," as well as what potential obstacles may hinder that progress.

Third, a practitioner may elicit the juvenile's beliefs of the pros and cons of the target behavior. Specifically, using an open and supportive approach, this can take the form of brainstorming about the extremes of the consequences of changing and not changing the target behavior. A practitioner might start by asking, "What's good about working for James?" In the spirit of a collaborative approach, a practitioner might use a summary statement and an open question to elicit the negative side of the target behavior. For example, "You've said that working for James has not been as bad as everyone else makes it out to be. For example, he gives you clothes, food, and a place to sleep. However, you have also mentioned that it can sometimes be scary out there by yourself under the bridge. What other things might not be so good about working for James?"

Fourth, to increase a juvenile's sense of self-efficacy, a practitioner might ask a client to relate a success story (i.e., "Tell me a story of when you did something really well."). If a juvenile is expressing difficulty coming up with a success story, or even positive attributes of him- or herself, an adjective checklist (Table 11.5) may help elicit the client's strengths.

Table 11.5	Characteristics of Successful Adolescents				
	Instructions: Please circle the characteristics that best describe you.				
	Accepting	Committed	Flexible	Persevering	Stubborn
	Active	Competent	Focused	Persistent	Thankful
	Adaptable	Concerned	Forgiving	Positive	Thorough
	Adventuresome	Confident	Forward-looking	Powerful	Thoughtful
	Affectionate	Considerate	Free	Prayerful	Tough
	Affirmative	Courageous	Happy	Quick	Trusting
	Alert	Creative	Healthy	Reasonable	Trustworthy
	Alive	Decisive	Hopeful	Receptive	Truthful
	Ambitious	Dedicated	Imaginative	Relaxed	Understanding
	Anchored	Determined	Ingenious	Reliable	Unique
	Assertive	Die-hard	Intelligent	Resourceful	Unstoppable
	Assured	Diligent	Knowledgeable	Responsible	Vigorous
	Attentive	Doer	Loving	Sensible	Visionary
	Bold	Eager	Mature	Skillful	Whole
	Brave	Earnest	Open	Solid	Willing
	Bright	Effective	Optimistic	Spiritual	Winning
	Capable	Energetic	Orderly	Stable	Wise
	Careful	Experienced	Organized	Steady	Worthy
	Cheerful	Faithful	Patient	Straight	Zealous
	Clever	Fearless	Perceptive	Strong	Zestful

Note. Adapted from "*COMBINE Monograph Series, Volume 1. Combined Behavioral Intervention Manual: A Clinical Research Guide for Therapists Treating People With Alcohol Abuse and Dependence*," edited by W. R. Miller, 2004, DHHS Publication No. NIH 04-5288, Bethesda, MD: NIAAA, p. F-18.

For example, a practitioner might present the list and state, "This is a list of adjectives that describes adolescents who were successful after release. Please circle the adjectives that describe you." After the juvenile circles the appropriate adjectives, a practitioner might use open questions to draw out more information about the circled adjectives (i.e., "You circled that you were 'alive.' Tell me more about that."). In addition, to demonstrate affirmation and support of a juvenile's efforts, a practitioner might reflect, "Your life is not easy. Most kids in your situation would run into trouble. You are handling a very tough situation really well. How do you do it?"

Review of Related Research

The vast majority of research regarding MI, as well as other empirically validated approaches, has been conducted with adult samples. Due to the paucity of research on effective treatments with adolescents (DiGiuseppe et al., 1996), many practitioners have had to rely on a combination of nonempirically based approaches, personal knowledge, and professional experience to guide their interactions with juveniles in the justice system. While some of the anecdotal and descriptive literature on therapeutic work with adolescents supports the use of methods that resemble MI, empirical research remains necessary to determine the fit of MI with juvenile justice settings.

On the other hand, significantly more research has been done supporting the use of client-centered approaches in family treatment and parent-training settings. In some settings, particularly those with younger or cognitively challenged children, the development of therapeutic alliance with the child's parents may be more important to treatment compliance than the development of the therapeutic alliance with the child (DiGiuseppe et al., 1996). Even when the child is not very young or disabled, working with parents can yield beneficial results for the entire family system. As Patterson and Forgatch (1985) found in their study working with families referred because of child management problems, therapists' efforts to teach and confront significantly increased parent noncompliance. However, in line with client-centered approaches, compliance increased concomitantly with therapists' demonstrations of support and use of techniques that facilitate change.

With juvenile samples, the areas with the most empirical support include interventions targeting the use of tobacco, alcohol, marijuana, and, polysubstance use. Although the majority of the following studies report extensive training of their practitioners in MI techniques and spirit, no practitioner training measures such as the Motivational Interviewing Skill Code (MISC) or treatment fidelity measures such as the Motivational Interviewing Treatment Integrity Manual (MITI) were reported. As a result, it is difficult to determine whether the practitioners assigned to use MI employed "true" MI or adaptations such as techniques or components of MI but not the full approach (i.e., using reflective listening and open questions, but without being directive; using importance and confidence rulers, but being confrontational; Rollnick & Miller, 1995).

Tobacco Use

Many youth believe that substance use is normative and find it neither necessary nor desirable to cease (Lawendowski, 1998). If an adolescent smoker does not want to change smoking behavior, it is important to attend to the client's position. Rollnick and Miller (1995) posit that intervening in a manner that moves ahead of the client is likely to increase the client's resistance to treatment. Thus, with overt risk behaviors like smoking, it may be tempting for practitioners to highlight the potential risks of the behavior (e.g., "Smoking will kill you."). Yet lecturing about the potential harmfulness of smoking to adolescent smokers who are not yet ready to quit is unlikely to be an effective intervention and may even produce iatrogenic effects (Stein, Colby, & O'Leary, 2002). In contrast, MI requires attending to clients' statements, reinforcing their self-efficacy and autonomy, and collaboratively exploring the pros and cons of behaviors like smoking (Rollnick & Miller, 1995).

As a brief intervention for adolescent smoking administered in inpatient units and emergency departments, MI has shown small effects (Brown et al., 2003; Colby et al., 1998; Colby, Monti, & Tevyaw, 2005) in comparison with brief advice. However, the reduction of tobacco use in the MI condition has rarely yielded statistical significance (Brown et al., 2003; Colby et al., 1998). However, youth who have received MI around smoking have reported greater ambivalence about their smoking and greater self-efficacy in their ability to quit (Brown et al., 2003), as well as higher abstinence rates (Colby et al., 2005). However, some of these differences have not been supported by biochemical assays (Colby et al., 2005).

Alcohol Use

Because most juveniles do not self-refer (Tevyaw & Monti, 2004), they are a distinctly different group than the adult samples who seek alcohol treatment. However, many adolescent alcohol problems are likely to emerge in other settings (Tevyaw & Monti, 2004), such as when adolescents are sent to detention. Commonly referred to as opportunities or teachable moments, justice settings may provide opportune and timely settings to intervene with adolescent alcohol use.

In another teachable setting, the team of researchers at Brown University has researched the effectiveness of MI in reducing alcohol use with adolescents (ages 13–19 years) receiving emergency health services (Barnett, Monti, & Wood, 2001; Monti et al., 1999; Spirito et al., 2004; Tapert et al., 2003). With their late-adolescent sample (ages 18–19 years), their studies have found that both an MI and standard hospital care groups display reductions in alcohol use (Barnett, et al., 2001; Monti et al., 1999). However, at the 6-month follow-up, the recipients of MI have demonstrated significantly greater reductions in alcohol-risk behavior, including decreased episodes of drinking and driving, lower levels of alcohol-related injuries, and fewer alcohol-related problems (i.e., with parents, friends, police, and school). Unfortunately, those same differences were not found within the younger adolescents (Barnett et al., 2001; Spirito et al., 2004). However, the authors posit that the more attentive (and less harried) standard of care in the pediatric versus adult emergency room may have obscured treatment effects (Barnett et al., 2001). In addition, Spirito et al. (2004) suggest that in order to effect change in alcohol-related behaviors with younger adolescents, it may be integral to involve the child's parents. Spirito et al. (2004) hypothesize that increasing parental communication and monitoring may be the best way to achieve alcohol use reduction with younger clients.

Although in many ways college-age samples have drastic demographic differences compared to juvenile justice samples, the majority of the research on MI's efficacy in reducing alcohol use in adolescent samples has been conducted with college youth ages 18 to 21 years. With this mindset, important lessons can be derived about the possible fit of MI in juvenile justice settings.

Studies of MI as an Intervention for Alcohol Use With Late Adolescents

With a sample of undergraduates preselected by baseline alcohol use as measured by drinking at least 13 drinks per week and endorsement of one or more problems on the Rutgers Alcohol Problem Index (RAPI; White & Labouvie, 1989), Murphy et al. (2004) invited 54 late adolescents to participate in an intervention for credit (mean age: 19 years, 69% female, 94% White, 52% membership in the Greek-system housing). After having their alcohol consumption assessed, participants received personalized drinking feedback (PDF) with or without an MI condition. Those who received only the personalized feedback never met with a clinician and, instead, reviewed their feedback sheet for 30 minutes. The feedback sheet included rankings that compared the student's weekly drinking with normative drinking rates, estimates of the student's blood alcohol concentration (BAC), risks associated with the student's frequency of heavy drinking, the list of alcohol-related consequences that the student endorsed on the RAPI, risks related to the student's family history of alcohol use, the amount of time that the student allocated to drinking and recovering, the amount of calories present in the student's alcohol choices, and a sheet of advice regarding harm-reduction strategies (Murphy et al., 2004). The students who also received MI were given the same feedback, but in the format of a 30- to 50-minute motivational interview where the contents of the sheet were discussed (Murphy et al., 2004). At the 6-month follow-up, Murphy et al. (2004) found moderate drinking reductions in terms of reported drinks per week, frequency of drinking per week, and frequency of heavy drinking per week in both groups. However, female students demonstrated slightly greater levels of reductions than males. In addition, students who also received an MI session showed slightly greater effect sizes for drinking reductions than those students who only received the PDF ($d = 0.42$ for PDF; $d = 0.48$ for PDF + MI).

At the University of Washington, with the Marlatt and Larimer team, Baer and colleagues (1992) used a 2-year longitudinal design to investigate the drinking levels and alcohol-related problems for high-risk student drinkers placed in three types of interventions. To qualify for the study, students had to report at least one drinking-related problem, report drinking at least twice a week, and have peak BAC that approached .10. The sample was comprised of 75 students, approximately 50% female and 91% White with a mean age of 21 years. Students were randomized into an information-based classroom intervention, a self-help correspondence group, or a group that received feedback and a MI. Assessments taken four times throughout the 2-year period demonstrated patterns of increases and reductions in drinking. Namely, drinking levels appeared to increase around the participants' 21st birthdays. However, participants in all three intervention groups showed comparable reductions in drinking levels overall.

Baer, Kivlahan, and Blume (2001) also investigated an intervention with high school students matriculating into a 4-year undergraduate program who displayed high-risk drinking, in which 348 students agreed to participate. The authors also gathered a sample of 113 students (28 who also showed high-risk drinking) to provide a no-intervention comparison group. Those individuals in the intervention condition received an individualized feedback session during the first semester of their first year. The intervention was delivered in an MI style and highlighted discrepancies, explored ambivalence, and determined how drinking fit in with the students' goals. With the students, practitioners reviewed their baseline assessment results, their drinking diary cards, age-appropriate drinking norms, myths and perceptions about drinking, facts regarding the metabolism of alcohol, the physiological correlates and consequences of drinking, and harm-reduction strategies (Baer et al., 2001). Those in the prevention condition received information regarding their drinking during the middle of their second year of college. Specifically, they received mailed feedback regarding specific information about their drinking and comparing their patterns with those of their age-matched peers. The students who showed the highest risk drinking behavior also received phone calls from the research team, during which team members expressed their concern and offered additional feedback sessions. Through this intervention, 34 students in this arm of the study received MI sessions, mostly by phone. Baer et al. (2001) found that within the 4 years of this study, students who received MI interventions demonstrated significant reductions in negative consequences associated with drinking, the majority of which emerged within the first of the annual assessments. Quantity and frequency of drinking generated the smallest effects in this program.

Marlatt et al. (1998) also found that, compared with college students in a no-treatment control condition, high-risk drinking college students who received a brief MI-based intervention during their freshman year showed reductions in drinking rates (as measured by the Alcohol Dependence Scale) and associated harmful consequences (on the RAPI) through a 2-year follow-up period. The authors also found main effects for gender on drinking, where women showed significantly greater reductions in drinking problems over time, as well as for those students living in Greek-system housing. Yet, the data indicated that the brief interventions were effective independent of demographic or other risk factors. The data from Marlatt et al. (1998) also indicated that all high-risk students, those in the intervention and those in the no-treatment control groups, displayed significant reductions in drinking rates and related problems through the 2-year follow-up. The authors highlighted the developmental salience of aging with drinking behavior, positing that perhaps binge drinking is generally a time-limited event that is likely to decrease as adolescents move into adulthood and gain more responsibilities (Marlatt et al., 1998).

In a replication of Marlatt et al.'s (1998) study, Larimer et al. (2001) targeted their MI intervention at freshman members of 12 intact fraternities and 6 sororities. The participants were 296 Greek housing members (mean age: 18 years, 82% White), randomized by house to either an MI-based individual and house-based feedback condition or an assessment-only control condition. Larimer et al. (2001) found that in comparison to the assessment-only control-group members who showed an increase in drinking throughout their first year (14.5 to 17 drinks weekly and no change in peak BAC), Greek-system housing members who received the individual and house-based intervention demonstrated significant reductions in overall drinking in terms of total weekly alcohol consumption (15.5 to 12 standard drinks weekly) and typical BAC (BAC: .12 to .08). However, unlike the Marlatt et al. (1998) and Baer et al. (2001) studies, the reductions in drinking observed in the intervention group did not correspond with concomitant reductions in alcohol-related consequences or with reductions in symptoms of alcohol dependence. In addition, Larimer et al. (2001) noted that although there was a significant difference between the intervention and assessment-only group, drinking levels remained high in both conditions. Interestingly, Larimer et al. (2001) found that participants in the intervention condition who received feedback from trained peer undergraduates demonstrated equivalent or greater reductions in alcohol use than those who received feedback from professional providers. A limitation of this study was that Larimer et al. (2001) were not able to parse out which of the effects were due to the individual intervention and which were due to the housewide interventions.

With students recruited from an introductory psychology course, Borsari and Carey (2000) screened for baseline drinking levels. Male students who reported drinking five or more drinks and female students who reported drinking four or more drinks per occasion on at least two occasions during the past month were eligible to participate in their study. Twenty-nine participants were randomized into the brief intervention group, and 31 were placed in the control group. Students were approximately 18 years old, 57% female, and 88% White. The majority of the participants lived in campus dormitories. The students in the intervention group received an hour-long MI. At the 6-week follow-up, participants who received the intervention reported high levels of satisfaction with the intervention and stated that they would recommend an MI-style session to a student who had equal or greater drinking levels and related problems. Borsari & Carey (2000) found small to medium effect sizes for students who received the MI intervention in reductions in weekly drinking (ES = 0.21), monthly drinking frequency (ES = 0.28), and binge drinking (ES = 0.12). Like the Larimer et al. (2001) study, Borsari & Carey (2000) found no relationship between the intervention and control groups with respect to drinking-related problems. One limitation was that there was no experimental control for practitioner effects because the first author performed all of the MI interventions (Borsari & Carey, 2000).

Marijuana and Polysubstance Use

At this time, there are several new areas in which the efficacy and effectiveness of MI are being evaluated. This includes emergent prevention and intervention programs for marijuana use and polysubstance use (Dennis et al., 2002; Diamond et al., 2002; Doyle, Swan, & Roffman, 2003; McCambridge & Strang, 2004a, 2004b, 2004c; Stephens, Roffman, & Fearer, 2004).

With a sample of 16 through 20 year olds engaged in polysubstance use (i.e., alcohol, tobacco, and marijuana), McCambridge & Strang (2004c) found harm-reduction effects with MI. The participants were able to choose which substances they preferred to discuss during their MI: marijuana was the most extensively discussed substance and the one for which the most impressive effect size was obtained (Strang & McCambridge, 2004). Rather than commencing abstinence, adolescent participants who received MI moderated their substance use, still representing a significant decrease in use. As the authors indicate, the true benefit of MI with traditionally unreachable adolescent populations may be its ability to initiate any substance use reduction (McCambridge & Strang, 2003, 2004c).

In their large randomized, controlled trial comparing short-term (90 days or less) outpatient treatments, including the MI-based therapy, motivational enhancement therapy (MET) with cognitive behavioral therapy (CBT), family support network, the adolescent community reinforcement approach (ACRA), and multidimensional family therapy with mid-adolescent, predominantly White male marijuana users, Dennis et al. (2004) found that all five treatments demonstrated effectiveness. Specifically, adolescents receiving all forms of therapy increased days of abstinence during the following 12 months, though effect sizes were small (Dennis et al., 2004). A combination of MET with CBT (MET/CBT5 and MET/CBT12, meaning with 5 or 12 sessions of CBT) and ACRA emerged as the most cost-effective treatments.

Summary of MI Approaches With Adolescent Samples

Compared with the extensive research evaluating MI and brief interventions with adults, there have been fewer studies evaluating brief strategies to reduce alcohol use with adolescents. However, this is becoming an increasingly prolific field. The previous studies (i.e., Brown et al., 2003, Larimer & Cronce, 2002; Tevyaw & Monti, 2004) provide preliminary data that MI may be able to effect change with adolescents, possibly due to MI's good fit with the developmental stage of adolescence. As a supportive, flexible, idiographic, brief, and autonomy-based intervention, MI overlaps well with adolescents' individual needs, competing attentional demands, developing identities, and desire to assert independence (Berg-Smith et al., 1999; Channon, Smith, & Gregory, 2003), possibly catalyzing maturation and development (Tevyaw & Monti, 2004).

MI in Adult Justice Settings

Aside from overlapping well with the needs of adolescents, MI has also been recommended for use with adult criminal justice clients. Like their juvenile counterparts, adult offenders show high rates of substance abuse and dependence and other *DSM* disorders. Moreover, many adult offenders also exhibit deficits in executive functioning, critical reasoning, and impulse control. In fact, Andrews and Bonta (2003) discussed antisocial cognitions and personality (e.g., self-control deficits), parenting practices, substance abuse, and intelligence in their coverage of the "Big Eight" predictors of recidivism, which overlap with the etiological factors of delinquency. Because many parallels exist between the juvenile and adult offender populations, the evidence supporting the use of MI with adult offenders is informative.

Although comprised primarily of nonoffenders, Project MATCH Research Group (1993) offered evidence that indicates the potential good fit of MI with juvenile and adult justice clientele. A multisite comparison of 12-step facilitation, CBT, and MET (MI with the provision of feedback; U.S. Department of Health and Human Services, 1995), Project MATCH explored potential fits between client characteristics and alcohol treatment. Findings indicated that outpatients with high anger ratings had better posttreatment drinking outcomes following MET (Project MATCH Research Group, 1997). Mattson (1998) cited the nonconfrontational nature of MET as a potential source of success with angry individuals. Because adult and juvenile forensic clientele frequently display anger, the efficacy of MET with angry clients is highly relevant.

MI has been used with adult offenders, but its history in this capacity is brief and its use is sparse. Much of the literature in this area consists of recommendations rather than empirical research. For example, McMurran and Hollin (1993) suggest using MI with alcohol-abusing young offenders. In addition, Annis and Chan (1983) question the value of highly intensive and confrontational group treatment for substance abuse with offenders.

Similar recommendations exist for treating sex offenders (e.g., Garland & Dougher, 1991; Kear-Colwell & Pollock, 1997). The field was brought a step closer toward implementing MI-based interventions with the work of the National Organization for the Treatment of Abusers (Mann, 1996). This group developed a practice manual guiding the use of MI with the assessment and treatment of sex offenders. Moreover, Mann and Rollnick (1996), in their case study of a sex offender who believed that he was innocent despite his conviction of sexual assault, also support an MI approach. Focusing on assessment alone, Mann, Ginsburg, and Weekes (2002) discuss the use of MI in collaborative risk assessment. Across assessment and treatment approaches, MI may help convert a potentially adversarial forum into a more active, meaningful, and pleasant experience for the offender.

Moving from sex offending and assessment, Ginsburg, Mann, Rotgers, and Weekes (2002) provide a review of the use of MI with substance-abusing offenders. Overall, they found that research findings have been mixed. While some studies have found modest results favoring the use of MI, others have not yielded significant differences between MI and other approaches. Methodological factors such as insufficient statistical power, questionable practitioner expertise, and treatment fidelity may explain some of the findings. However, more research is clearly needed prior to drawing definitive conclusions.

For practitioners interested in clinical applications of MI, Jamieson, Beals, Lalonde, and Associates (2000) provide a curriculum for delivering an MI-friendly group intervention to substance-abusing offenders. Moreover, Ginsburg, Farbring, and Forsberg (in press) discuss a protocol used in the Swedish criminal justice system. This protocol includes multisession individual intervention, based heavily in the spirit and techniques of MI. In addition, MI and relevant adaptations have been built into existing correctional treatment programs and interventions targeting a wider array of mandated clients (e.g., Lincourt, Kuettel, & Bombardier, 2002).

In recent years, a major thrust has been directed toward delivering large-scale MI training initiatives to program delivery staff and probation and parole personnel in various jurisdictions in Canada, the United States, and Sweden. Organizational change might be an even greater challenge than changing behavior at the client or micro level. However, it is a foundational step toward realizing the potential efficacy of MI with adult and juvenile clients. In the context of managing sex offenders within the criminal justice system, Birgden (2004) addresses this organizational challenge by advocating for the use of motivational techniques (including MI) by legal and correctional practitioners to maximize the therapeutic effects of the law. This therapeutic jurisprudence minimizes antitherapeutic consequences of the law.

Another important note in thinking about adult offending is that any efforts to intervene early, thereby disrupting a possible trajectory toward lifelong recidivism, are important. Despite treatment approaches that may work with adult samples, prevention and early treatment strategies effective with juveniles may yield the most psychosocially valuable results.

Clinical and Legal Issues

There are important legal caveats when considering treatment within the juvenile justice system. In some states, regardless of age, if a juvenile is deemed competent by the treating therapist, then the juvenile can receive mental health services. Yet, even if a therapist deems a juvenile competent, he or she still does not have legal power in any other domain until the client's 18th birthday. Moreover, a juvenile can be adjudicated competent for legal purposes (such as being sentenced as an adult), yet remain unentitled to other adult rights in their lives (Koocher, 2003).

In addition, in some states there are legal entitlements that all juveniles have. For example, in terms of health care, a child or adolescent of any age can consent to receive contraception, be tested for sexually transmitted diseases, and, if under the umbrella of outpatient mental health services, receive drug or alcohol treatment (Boonstra & Nash, 2000). These rights exist because many juveniles would rather go without treatment than notify their parents of potential problems in these areas (Kuther, 2003). Therefore, it was determined that these treatments ought to be accessible without parental consent, rather than reduce the likelihood that juveniles may access them by requiring it (Koocher, 2003).

Thus, how do these considerations relate to treatment? Let us recall Marie, recently arrested for prostitution. At her arraignment, the court system decides to send her to detention and compel her to attend therapy. During her first session, Marie tells her therapist that she does not want to be in therapy, but does want to appease her juvenile parole officer (JPO). The JPO has indicated that if Marie does well in therapy, then her stay in detention will not exceed 2 weeks. However, he has also stipulated that if she fails to attend or take therapy seriously, he will extend her remand for another month.

Thus, Marie arrives at therapy frustrated and angry. Koocher (2003) suggests that therapists consider all of the players involved in a juvenile's psychotherapy, as well as realize that each has incongruent goals for the process. In Marie's case, Marie, the court system, her friends, and the psychotherapist will all have disparate expectations.

Confidentiality is a paramount concern. Marie will likely want all that she shares to remain within the walls of the therapy room. However, as stipulated by her court hearing, the therapist might have to report her attendance and progress to the JPO. As posited by Taylor and Adelman (1989), the therapist's dilemma is to balance privileged communication and cooperating with other child welfare providers. Many who work with children and adolescents suggest outlining this dilemma with clients during the first therapy session (Kearney, 1998; Koocher, 2003). Specifically, Taylor and Adelman (1989) suggest stating, in a developmentally appropriate manner, that there are limits to confidentiality and that those limits exist to protect the child and ensure her safety. Moreover, if an issue arises that needs to be disclosed to parents or outside authorities, the therapist can state that he or she will discuss this with the client prior to disclosure (Taylor & Adelman, 1989).

Thus, relevant to Marie and other juveniles, what issues could constitute limits to confidentiality? This varies greatly between states. Therefore, a practitioner ought to be familiar with his or her state's statutes on these issues. Moreover, it is important to detail these limits to confidentiality with each juvenile client. Belitz (2004) suggests giving enough examples that both the juvenile and his or her parents can understand what may warrant JPO or parental notification. In addition, it might be helpful to mention that the examples given do not constitute the only incidents that may warrant parent notification. Disclosure may be a difficult, but necessary, step in keeping the child client safe (Kearney, 1998; Taylor & Adelman, 1989) and will inevitably affect the therapeutic relationship. However, if discussed early in the therapeutic relationship, the negative impact may be minimal (Kearney, 1998; Koocher, 2003; Taylor & Adelman, 1989).

Different state laws may provide clinicians with freedom in determining how best to serve their juvenile clients; thus, it is important to know the relevant state statutes. In the spirit of MI, a practitioner may find it helpful to be genuine and transparent about confidentiality and the relevant limits. Although the client may not be enthusiastic about the upcoming intervention (Koocher, 2003), through being clear and direct with one's expectations and limitations, a practitioner may be able to safeguard clients and develop an effective therapeutic relationship.

Description of the Intervention

To illustrate how MI might work with a client in the juvenile justice setting, consider the following dialogue:

Counselor: Hi, Billy, I'm glad that you were able to make it in today. I know
             that you've had a lot going on. I'd like to introduce myself. My name
             is Sarah, and I am the counselor who works with arrested boys in this
             facility. (*Introductory statement, genuineness, openness*)
Billy: (*arms folded over chest, does not respond*)

Counselor: Man, you couldn't want to be here less if you tried! I can see that you are feeling pretty pissed about this. (*Complex reflection, based on emotion indicated in nonverbal behavior*)

Billy: (*looks up but still says nothing*)

Counselor: Wow, you can't imagine a world in which it might feel good to talk with someone about what's been going on. (*Complex reflection, continuing to be based on nonverbal behavior*)

Billy: Nope.

Counselor: That's right. Things are going pretty well, and you don't need anyone's help. (*Affirmation and undershoot-style reflection*)

Billy: That's right.

Counselor: I hear you loud and clear. You've been taking care of yourself and you'd like to be left alone. (*Complex reflection*)

Billy: Um hm.

Counselor: Well, we have this half hour to use. What would be the best way to use our time today? (*Open question*)

Billy: I don't know.

Counselor: Okay. Wait, let me back up. I can see I'm getting ahead of myself. Let's start with you telling me a little bit about what's going on with you. (*Counselor staying with the client, open question*)

Billy: I was arrested.

Counselor: Go on. (*Evocative statement asking for elaboration*)

Billy: Haven't you seen my record?

Counselor: Nope. I don't look at those because I prefer hearing my clients' story as they experienced it. Why don't we start there? (*Genuineness, validating the client's perspective, open question*)

Billy: Okay . . . (*Begins to tell story*)

If the dialogue continued, through open-ended questions, affirmations, reflections, and summary statements, the counselor would work with Billy in order to hear Billy's story, as he experienced it. In MI, it is important to be genuine and empathetic, and to stay with your client; MI works when the client and the counselor are walking through the client's thoughts and feelings, with the client ultimately guiding the direction. The role of the therapist is to help walk with the client toward the direction of positive change.

Conclusion

Although an MI session may help catalyze change, the exact nature of the power of MI remains elusive. Moreover, although Miller and Rollnick (2002, 2004) highlighted styles and strategies that may be helpful in effecting change within this therapeutic style (often captured in fun acronyms, such as OARS and DARN-C), the factors necessary and sufficient for positive outcomes with this strategy remain unknown (Baer & Peterson, 2002) and are currently the source of a tremendous amount of process research.

Despite the extant empirical research evaluating the efficacy of MI in juvenile justice settings, for many reasons, it appears to be a good match for this setting. First, approximately half of the juvenile justice system clients sampled met diagnostic criteria for at least one *DSM* diagnosis (Abram et al., 2003; Garland et al., 2001; Teplin et al., 2002), indicating a need for mental health services within this setting. Moreover, the most frequent diagnoses within the juvenile justice system took the form of substance use/dependence and disruptive behavior disorders (Aarons et al., 2001; Abram et al., 2003; McClelland et al., 2004; Teplin et al., 2002). Although the empirical validation of MI has been demonstrated mostly with late adolescents and adults, the empirical evidence supporting the use of MI in reducing alcohol, marijuana, and polysubstance use in adolescents appears to be emergent. In addition, because Garland et al. (2001) found that the majority of the youth within the juvenile justice setting are older rather than younger adolescents, MI seems to be well suited for this setting.

However, despite the importance of intervention efforts within the juvenile justice system, it is essential to continue to evaluate and implement prevention efforts to reduce the involvement of children within the juvenile justice system. The *need* is for the development of a system of care that addresses the mental health, physical health, and drug and alcohol problems that frequently present in these young people but are traditionally managed by different agencies that do not work easily together. The *challenge* is to identify a preferred system of holistic care that allows for a seamless transfer of the young person from the detention center to the community in a supported fashion that encourages ongoing mental health follow-up, reduces substance abuse, strengthens family and community support, and decreases the risk of recidivism (Stathis & Martin, 2004, p. 749).

RESOURCES AND REFERENCES

Aarons, G. A., Brown, S. A., Hough, R. L., Garland, A. F., & Wood, P. A. (2001). Prevalence of adolescent substance use disorders across five sectors of care. *Journal of the American Academy of Child and Adolescent Psychiatry, 40*(4), 419–426.

Abram, K. M., Teplin, L. A., McClelland, G. M., & Dulcan, M. K. (2003). Comorbid psychiatric disorders in youth in juvenile detention. *Archives of General Psychiatry, 60*, 1097–1108.

American Psychiatric Association. (1987). *Diagnostic and statistical manual of mental disorders* (3rd ed., rev.). Washington, DC: Author.

American Psychiatric Association. (1994). *Diagnostic and statistical manual of mental disorders* (4th ed.). Washington, DC: Author.

American Psychiatric Association. (2000). *Diagnostic and statistical manual of mental disorders* (4th ed., text rev.). Washington, DC: Author.

Andrews, D. A., & Bonta, J. (2003). *The psychology of criminal conduct* (3rd ed.). Cincinnati, OH: Anderson.

Annis, H. M., & Chan, D. (1983). The differential treatment model. Empirical evidence from a personality typology of adult offenders. *Criminal Justice and Behavior, 10*(2), 159–173.

Baer, J. S., Kivlahan, D. R., & Blume, A. W. (2001). Brief intervention for heavy-drinking college students: 4-year follow up and natural history. *American Journal of Public Health, 91*(8), 1310–1316.

Baer, J. S., Marlatt, G. A., Kivlahan, D. R., Fromme, K., Larimer, M. E., & Williams, E. (1992). An experimental test of three methods of alcohol risk reduction with young adults. *Journal of Consulting and Clinical Psychology, 60*(6), 974–979.

Baer, J. S., & Peterson, P. L. (2002). Motivational interviewing with adolescents and young adults. In W. R. Miller & S. Rollnick (Eds.), *Motivational interviewing: Preparing people for change* (2nd ed., pp. 320–332). New York: Guilford.

Baer, J. S., Peterson, P. L., & Wells, E. A. (2004). Rationale and design of a brief substance use intervention for homeless adolescents. *Addiction Research and Theory, 12*(4), 317–334.

Barnett, N. P., Monti, P. M., & Wood, M. D. (2001). Motivational interviewing for alcohol-involved adolescents in the emergency room. In E. F. Wagner & H. B. Waldron (Eds.), *Innovations in adolescent substance abuse interventions* (pp. 143–168). Oxford, UK: Elsevier Science.

Barnett, N. P., Tevyaw, T. O., Fromme, K., Borsari, B., Carey, K. B., Corbin, W. R., et al. (2004). Brief alcohol interventions with mandated or adjudicated college students. *Alcoholism: Clinical and Experimental Research, 28*(6), 966–975.

Belitz, J. (2004). Caring for children. In L. W. Roberts & A. R. Dyer (Eds.), *Concise guide to ethics in mental health care* (pp. 119–134). Washington, DC: American Psychiatric Publishing.

Berg-Smith, S. M., Stevens, V. J., Brown, K. M., van Horn, L., Gernhofer, N., Peters, E., et al. (1999). A brief motivational intervention to improve dietary adherence in adolescents. *Health Education Research, 14*(3), 399–410.

Birgden, A. (2004). Therapeutic jurisprudence and sex offenders: A psycho-legal approach to protection. *Sexual Abuse: A Journal of Research and Treatment, 16*(4), 351–364.

Boonstra, H., & Nash, E. (2000). Minors and the right to consent to health care. *The Guttmacher Report on Public Policy, 3*(4), 4–8.

Borsari, B. E., & Carey, K. B. (2000). Effects of a brief motivational intervention with college student drinkers. *Journal of Consulting and Clinical Psychology, 68*, 28–733.

Breslin, C., Li, S., Sdao-Jarvie, K., Tupker, E., & Ittig-Deland, V. (2002). Brief treatment for young substance abusers: A pilot study in an addiction treatment setting. *Psychology of Addictive Behaviors, 16*(1), 10–16.

Brown, L. K., & Lourie, K. J. (2001). Motivational interviewing and the prevention of HIV among adolescents. In P. M. Monti, S. M. Colby, & T. A. O'Leary (Eds.), *Adolescents, alcohol, and substance abuse* (pp. 244–274). New York: Guilford.

Brown, R. A., Ramsey, S. E., Strong, D. R., Myers, M. G., Kahler, C. W., Lejuez, C. W., et al. (2003). Effects of motivational interviewing on smoking cessation in adolescents with psychiatric disorders. *Tobacco Control, 12*(4), 3–11.

Channon, S., Smith, V. J., & Gregory, J. W. (2003). A pilot study of motivational interviewing in adolescents with diabetes. *Archives of Disease in Childhood, 88*, 680–683.

Cicchetti, D., & Rogosch, F. A. (2002). A developmental psychopathology perspective on adolescence. *Journal of Clinical and Consulting Psychology, 70*(1), 6–20.

Colby, S. M., Lee, C. S., Lewis-Esquerre, J., Esposito-Smythers, C., & Monti, P. M. (2004). Adolescent alcohol misuse: Methodological issues for enhancing treatment research. *Addiction, 99*(Suppl. 2), 47–62.

Colby, S. M., Monti, P. M., Barnett, N. P., Rohsenow, D. J., Weissman, K., Spirito, A., et al. (1998). Brief motivational interviewing in a hospital setting for adolescent smoking: A preliminary study. *Journal of Consulting and Clinical Psychology, 66*(3), 574–578.

Colby, S. M., Monti, P. M., & Tevyaw, T. O. (2005). Brief motivational intervention for adolescent smokers in medical settings. *Addictive Behaviors, 30*(5), 865–874.

Coll, K. M., Juhnke, G. A., Thobro, P., & Haas, R. (2003). A preliminary study using the Substance Abuse Subtle Screening Inventory – Adolescent Form as an outcome measure for adolescent offenders. *Journal of Addictions and Offender Counseling, 24*, 11–22.

Cowley, C. B., Farley, T., & Beamis, K. (2002). "Well, maybe I'll try the pill for just a few months..." Brief motivational and narrative-based interventions to encourage contraception use among adolescents at high risk for childbearing. *Families, Systems, & Health, 20*(2), 183–204.

D'Amico, E. J., & Fromme, K. (2000). Implementation of the risk skills training program: A brief intervention targeting adolescent participation in risk behaviors. *Cognitive and Behavioral Practice, 7*, 101–117.

Dennis, M. L., Godley, S. H., Diamond, G., Tims, F. M., Babor, T., Donaldson, J., et al. (2004). The Cannabis Youth Treatment (CYT) study: Main findings from two randomized trials. *Journal of Substance Abuse Treatment, 27*, 197–213.

Dennis, M., Titus, J. C., Diamond, G., Donaldson, J., Godley, S. H., Tims, F. M., et al. (2002). The Cannabis Youth Treatment (CYT) experiment: Rationale, study design, and analysis plans. *Addiction, 97*(Suppl. 1), 16–34.

Diamond, G., Godley, S. H., Liddle, H. A., Sampl, S., Webb, C., Tims, F. M., et al. (2002). Five outpatient treatment models for adolescent marijuana use: A description of the Cannabis Youth Treatment Interventions. *Addiction, 97*(Suppl. 1), 70–83.

DiCicco, L., Unterberger, H., & Mack, J. E. (1978). Confronting denial: An alcoholism intervention strategy. *Psychiatric Annals, 8*(11), 596–606.

DiGiuseppe, R., Linscott, J., & Jilton, R. (1996). Developing the therapeutic alliance in child-adolescent psychotherapy. *Applied and Preventive Psychology, 5*, 85–100.

Dishion, T. J., Kavanagh, K., Schneiger, A., Nelson, S., & Kaufman, N. K. (2002). Preventing early adolescent substance use: A family-centered strategy for the public middle school. *Prevention Science, 3*(3), 191–201.

Doyle, A., Swan, M., & Roffman, R. (2003). The marijuana check-up: A brief intervention tailored for individuals in the contemplation stage. *Journal of Social Work Practice in the Addictions, 3*(4), 53–71.

Garland, A. F., Hough, R. L., McCabe, K. M., Yeh, M., Wood, P. A., & Aarons, G. A. (2001). Prevalence of psychiatric disorders in youths across five sectors of care. *Journal of the American Academy of Child and Adolescent Psychiatry, 40*(4), 409–418.

Garland, R. J., & Dougher, M. J. (1991). Motivational intervention in the treatment of sex offenders. In W. R. Miller & S. Rollnick (Eds.), *Motivational interviewing. Preparing people to change addictive behavior* (pp. 303–313). New York: Guilford.

Ginsburg, J. I. D., Farbring, C. A., & Forsberg, L. (in press). Motivational interviewing and antisocial personality disorder. In F. Rotgers & M. Maniacci (Eds.), *Comparative treatments of antisocial personality*. New York: Springer.

Ginsburg, J. I. D., Mann, R. E., Rotgers, F., & Weekes, J. R. (2002). Using motivational interviewing with criminal justice populations. In W. R. Miller & S. Rollnick (Eds.), *Motivational interviewing: Preparing people for change* (2nd ed., pp. 333–346). New York: Guilford.

Hawkins, E. H., Cummins, L. H., & Marlatt, G. A. (2004). Preventing substance abuse in American Indian and Alaska Native youth: Promising strategies for healthier communities. *Psychological Bulletin, 130*(2), 304–323.

Jamieson, Beals, Lalonde, & Associates, Inc. (2000). *Motivational enhancement treatment (MET) manual. Theoretical foundation and structured curriculum. Individual and group sessions* [Developed for the State of Maine, Department of Mental Health, Mental Retardation, and Substance Abuse Services, Office of Substance Abuse]. Ottawa: Author.

Kear-Colwell, J., & Pollock, P. (1997). Motivation or confrontation. Which approach to the child sex offender? *Criminal Justice and Behavior, 24*(1), 20–33.

Kearney, E. M. (1998). Ethical dilemmas in the treatment of adolescent gang members. *Ethics and Behavior, 8*(1), 49–57.

Koocher, G. P. (2003). Ethical issues in psychotherapy with adolescents. *Journal of Clinical Psychology, 59*(11), 1247–1256.

Kuther, T. (2003). Medical decision-making and minors: Issues of consent and assent. *Adolescence, 38*(150), 343–358.

Lambie, G. W. (2004). Motivational enhancement therapy: A tool for professional school counselors working with adolescents. *Professional School Counseling, 7*(4), 268–276.

Larimer, M. E., & Cronce, J. M. (2002). Identification, prevention and treatment: A review of individual-focused strategies to reduce problematic alcohol consumption by college students. *Journal of Studies on Alcohol, 14*, 148–163.

Larimer, M. E., Turner, A. P., Anderson, B. K., Fader, J. S., Kilmer, J. R., Palmer, R. S., et al. (2001). Evaluating a brief alcohol intervention with fraternities. *Journal of Studies on Alcohol, 62*, 370–380.

Lawendowski, L. A. (1998). A motivational intervention for adolescent smokers. *Preventive Medicine, 27*, A39–A46.

Lincourt, P., Kuettel, T. J., & Bombardier, C. H. (2002). Motivational interviewing in a group setting with mandated clients. A pilot study. *Addictive Behaviors, 27*, 381–391.

Mann, R. E. (Ed.). (1996). *Motivational interviewing with sex offenders: A practice manual*. Hull, UK: National Organization for the Treatment of Abusers.

Mann, R. E., Ginsburg, J. I. D., & Weekes, J. (2002). Motivational interviewing with offenders. In M. McMurran (Ed.), *Motivating offenders to change: A guide to enhancing engagement in therapy* (pp. 87–102). Chichester, UK: Wiley.

Mann, R. E., & Rollnick, S. (1996). Motivational interviewing with a sex offender who believed he was innocent. *Behavioural and Cognitive Psychotherapy, 24*, 127–134.

Marlatt, G. A., Baer, J. S., Kivlahan, D. R., Dimeff, L. A., Larimer, M. E., Quigley, L. A., et al. (1998). Screening and brief intervention for high-risk college student drinkers: Results from a 2-year follow-up assessment. *Journal of Consulting and Clinical Psychology, 66*(4), 604–615.

Masterman, P. W., & Kelly, A. B. (2003). Reaching adolescents who drink harmfully: Fitting intervention to developmental reality. *Journal of Substance Abuse Treatment, 24*, 347–355.

Mattson, M. E. (1998). Finding the right approach. In W. R. Miller, & N. Heather (Eds.), *Treating addictive behaviors* (2nd ed., pp. 163–172). New York: Plenum.

McCambridge, J., & Strang, J. (2003). Development of a structured generic drug intervention model for public health purposes: A brief application of motivational interviewing with young people. *Drug and Alcohol Review, 22*, 391–399.

McCambridge, J., & Strang, J. (2004a). Drug problem—what problems? Concurrent predictors of selected types of drug problems in a London community sample of young people who use drugs. *Addiction Research and Therapy, 12*(1), 55–66.

McCambridge, J., & Strang, J. (2004b). Patterns of drug use in a sample of 200 young drug users in London. *Drugs: Education, Prevention, and Policy, 11*(2), 101–112.

McCambridge, J., & Strang, J. (2004c). The efficacy of single-session motivational interviewing in reducing drug consumption and perceptions of drug-related risk and harm among young people: Results from a multi-site cluster randomized trial. *Addiction, 99*, 39–52.

McClelland, G. M., Elkington, K. S., Teplin, L. A., & Abram, K. M. (2004). Multiple substance use disorders in juvenile detainees. *Journal of the American Academy of Child and Adolescent Psychiatry, 43*(10), 1215–1224.

McMurran, M., & Hollin, C. R. (1993). *Young offenders and alcohol related crime: A practitioner's guidebook.* Chichester, UK: Wiley.

Miller, W. R. (Ed.). (2004). *COMBINE Monograph Series, Volume 1. Combined behavioral intervention manual: A clinical research guide for therapists treating people with alcohol abuse and dependence* (DHHS Publication No. NIH 04-5288). Bethesda, MD: NIAAA.

Miller, W. R., Benefield, G., & Tonigan, J. S. (1993). Enhancing motivation for change in problem drinking: A controlled comparison of two therapist styles. *Journal of Consulting and Clinical Psychology, 61*(3), 455–461.

Miller, W. R., & Rollnick, S. (2002). *Motivational interviewing: Preparing people for change* (2nd ed.). New York: Guilford.

Miller, W. R., & Rollnick, S. (2004). Talking oneself into change: Motivational interviewing, stages of change, and therapeutic process. *Journal of Cognitive Psychotherapy, 18*(4), 299–308.

Miller, W. R., & Sanchez, V. C. (1994). Motivating young adults for treatment and lifestyle change. In G. Howard & P. E. Nathan (Eds.), *Alcohol use and misuse by young adults* (pp. 55–81). Notre Dame, IN: University of Notre Dame Press.

Miller, W. R., & Wilbourne, P. L. (2002). Mesa Grande: A methodological analysis of clinical trials of treatment for alcohol use disorders. *Addiction, 97*(3), 265–277.

Monti, P. M., Colby, S. M., Barnett, N. P., Spirito, A., Rohsenow, D. J., Myers, M., et al. (1999). Brief intervention for harm reduction with alcohol-positive older adolescents in a hospital emergency department. *Journal of Consulting and Clinical Psychology, 67*(6), 989–994.

Moyers, T. B. (2005, July). *Introduction to motivational interviewing.* Workshop presented at the Center on Alcoholism, Substance Abuse, and Addictions, Albuquerque, NM.

Murphy, J. G., Benson, T. A., Vuchinich, R. E., Deskins, M. M., Eakin, D., Flood, A. M., et al. (2004). A comparison of personalized feedback for college student drinkers delivered with and without a motivational interview. *Journal of Studies on Alcohol, 65*, 200–203.

Myers, M. G., Brown, S. A., & Kelly, J. F. (2000). A smoking intervention for substance abusing adolescents: Outcomes, predictors of cessation attempts, and post-treatment substance use. *Journal of Child and Adolescent Substance Abuse, 9*(4), 77–91.

Myers, M. G., Brown, S. A., & Vik, P. W. (1998). Adolescent substance use problems. In E. J. Mash & R. A. Barkley (Eds.), *Treatment of childhood disorders* (2nd ed., pp. 692–729). New York: Guilford.

Neal, D. J., & Carey, K. B. (2004). Developing discrepancy with self-regulation theory: Use of personalized normative feedback and personal strivings with heavy-drinking college students. *Addictive Behaviors, 29*, 281–297.

Patterson, G. R., & Forgatch, M. S. (1985). Therapist behavior as a determinant for client noncompliance: A paradox for the behavior modifier. *Journal of Consulting and Clinical Psychology, 53*(6), 846–851.

Project MATCH Research Group. (1993). Project MATCH: Rationale and methods for a multisite clinical trial matching patients to alcoholism treatment. *Alcoholism: Clinical and Experimental Research, 17*(6), 1130–1145.

Project MATCH Research Group. (1997). Project MATCH secondary a priori hypotheses. *Addiction, 92*(12), 1671–1698.

Rivers, S. M., Greenbaum, R. L., & Goldberg, E. (2001). Hospital-based adolescent substance abuse treatment: Comborbidity, outcomes, and gender. *Journal of Nervous and Mental Disease, 189*(4), 229–237.

Rogers, C. R. (1980). *A way of being.* New York: Houghton Mifflin Company.

Rollnick, S., Mason, P., & Butler, C. (1999). *Health behavior change: A guide for practitioners.* Edinburgh, UK: Churchill Livingstone.

Rollnick, S., & Miller, W. R. (1995). What is motivational interviewing? *Behavioural and Cognitive Psychotherapy, 23,* 325–334.

Saunders, J. B., Kypri, K., Walters, S. T., Laforge, R. G., & Larimer, M. E. (2004). Approaches to brief intervention for hazardous drinking in young people. *Alcoholism: Clinical and Experimental Research, 28*(2), 322–329.

Schulenberg, J. E., & Maggs, J. L. (2002). A developmental perspective on alcohol use and heavy drinking during adolescence and the transition to young adulthood. *Journal of Studies on Alcohol, 14,* 54–70.

Sindelar, H. A., Abrantes, A. M., Hart, C., Lewander, W., & Spirito, A. (2004). Motivational interviewing in pediatric practice. *Current Problems in Pediatric and Adolescent Health Care,34*(9), 322–339.

Snyder, H. N. (2005). *Juvenile Arrests 2003.* Washington, DC: Office of Juvenile Justice and Delinquency Prevention.

Spirito, A., Monti, P. M., Barnett, N. P., Colby, S. M., Sindelar, H., Rohsenow, D. J., et al. (2004). A randomized clinical trial of a brief motivational intervention for alcohol-positive adolescents treated in an emergency department. *The Journal of Pediatrics, 145*(3), 396–402.

Stathis, S., & Martin, G. (2004). A transdisciplinary approach to adolescent forensic mental health. *Australian and New Zealand Journal of Psychiatry, 38,* 746–752.

Stein, L. A. R., Colby, S. M., & O'Leary, T. A. (2002). Response distortion in adolescents who smoke: A pilot study. *Journal of Drug Education, 32*(4), 271–286.

Stephens, R. S., Roffman, R. A., & Fearer, S. A. (2004). The marijuana check-up: Reaching users who are ambivalent about change. *Addiction, 99*(10), 1323–1332.

Strang, J., & McCambridge, J. (2004). Can the practitioner correctly predict outcome in motivational interviewing? *Journal of Substance Abuse Treatment, 27,* 83–88.

Tapert, S. F., Colby, S. M., Barnett, N. P., Spirito, A., Rohsenow, D. J., Myers, M. G., et al. (2003). Depressed mood, gender, and problem drinking in youth. *Journal of Child and Adolescent Substance Abuse, 12*(4), 55–68.

Taylor, L., & Adelman, H. S. (1989). Reframing the confidentiality dilemma to work in children's best interests. *Professional Psychology: Research and Practice, 20*(2), 79–83.

Teplin, L. A., Abram, K. A., McClelland, G. M., Dulcan, M. K., & Mericle, A. A. (2002). Psychiatric disorders in youth in juvenile detention. *Archives of General Psychiatry, 59,* 1133–1143.

Teplin, L. A., Mericle, A. A., McClelland, G. M., & Abram, K. M. (2003). HIV and AIDS risk behaviors in juvenile detainees: Implications for public health policy. *American Journal of Public Health, 93*(6), 906–912.

Tevyaw, T. O., & Monti, P. M. (2004). Motivational enhancement and other brief interventions for adolescent substance abuse: Foundations, applications, and evaluations. *Addiction, 99*(Suppl. 2), 63–75.

Tober, G. (1991). Motivational interviewing with young people. In W. R. Miller & S. Rollnick (Eds.), *Motivational interviewing: Preparing people to change addictive behavior* (pp. 248–249). New York: Guilford.

Truax, C. B. (1971). Degree of negative transference occurring in group psychotherapy and client outcome in juvenile delinquents. *Journal of Clinical Psychology, 27*(1), 132–136.

Truax, C. B., & Lister, J. L. (1970). Effects of therapist persuasive potency in group psychotherapy. *Journal of Clinical Psychology, 26*(3), 396–397.

Truax, C. B., Wargo, D. G., & Volksdorf, N. R. (1970). Antecedents to outcome in group counseling with institutionalized juvenile delinquents: Effects of therapeutic conditions, patient self-exploration, alternate sessions, and vicarious therapy pretraining. *Journal of Abnormal Psychology, 76*(2), 235–242.

U.S. Department of Health and Human Services. (1995). *Motivational enhancement therapy manual. A clinical research guide for therapists treating individuals with alcohol abuse and dependence* (NIH Publication No. 94-3723). Rockville, MD: Author.

Waldron, H. B., & Kaminer, Y. (2004). On the learning curve: The emerging evidence supporting cognitive-behavior therapies for adolescent substance abuse. *Addiction, 99*(Suppl. 2), 93–105.

White, H. R., & Labouvie, E. W. (1989). Towards the assessment of adolescent problem drinking. *Journal of Studies on Alcohol, 50*(1), 30–37.

Winters, K. C. (1999). Treating adolescents with substance use disorders: An overview of practice issues and treatment outcomes. *Substance Abuse, 20*(4), 203–225.

Relevant Resources for Practitioners

Practitioners interested in continuing work in our understanding of MI are referred to the following MI-relevant resources:

Center on Alcoholism, Substance Abuse, and Addictions. *Assessment instruments* [List of public domain instruments that can be used in MI]. Available from http://casaa.unm.edu/inst.html.

Miller, W. R., & Rollnick, S. (2002). *Motivational interviewing: Preparing people for change* (2nd ed.). New York: Guilford.

Wagner, C., & Conners, C. (2006). *The motivational interviewing Web site*. Available from http://www.motivationalinterview.org.

From Augustus to BARJ: The Evolving Role of Social Work in Juvenile Justice

Jonathan B. Singer

Introduction

The juvenile justice system has been described as a perpetual tug-of-war between two conflicting approaches, rehabilitation and punishment (Maloney, Romig, & Armstrong, 1988a). The rehabilitative perspective recognizes juveniles as works in progress, products of their environment, and children learning how to live in the adult world. The goal of rehabilitation is to help juveniles to become productive and law-abiding citizens. Because of the emphasis on development and the multidirectional influence of systems, the rehabilitative approach is congruent with the historical and contemporary goals and values of social work. The punitive approach sees juveniles as a fundamentally flawed product. The goal of the punitive juvenile justice system is to protect the public from these youthful offenders. A clinician practicing with the punitive approach will experience significant role conflict. At times, juvenile probation has appeared more like social work (rehabilitation), and at other times more like police work (punishment; Steiner, Purkiss, Kifer, Roberts, & Hemmens, 2004). Although the back and forth between perspectives has occurred over decades, a juvenile probation officer (JPO) might in a single day act as a social worker in the morning and a police officer in the afternoon. This flux between rehabilitation and punishment has been the defining conflict between social work and juvenile justice.

The rehabilitation–punishment approach has been challenged in the last dozen years by a new paradigm called *balanced and restorative justice* (BARJ; Freivalds, 1996;

The author thanks the research staff at the National Council on Juvenile Justice. He is also grateful to Dr. Jeffery Shook for sharing an in-press version of his article on juvenile transfer.

Maloney, Romig, & Armstrong, 1988b). BARJ takes an approach to juvenile justice that eschews the traditional rehabilitative–punitive dichotomy in favor of an alternative philosophy: restorative justice. Although I will discuss BARJ in more detail later in the chapter, it is useful to understand that BARJ takes a balanced approach that holds offenders accountable for their behavior, enables them to make amends to their victims and the community, and provides them with competencies designed to make them better citizens and people (Bazemore & Umbreit, 1998, 2004). BARJ is an approach that is congruent with social work values and a natural fit for many JPOs. BARJ provides an organizing framework that provides direction and congruence in daily decision making. The Office of Juvenile Justice and Delinquency Prevention (OJJDP) has supported the adoption of BARJ since 1998 (Bazemore & Umbreit, 1998), and most states have included the principles in their statements of purpose (Griffin & Torbet, 2002).

In this chapter I provide an overview of the juvenile justice system, highlighting places where social work values and practice can and should be employed. In order to balance the scholarly with the practical, I present both findings from research and insights from professionals in the field. It is my aim to encourage discussion about the role of helping professionals in today's juvenile justice system. I start with a brief history of the juvenile justice system and define key terms that are a standard part of the juvenile justice parlance. Next, I present the current organization of the juvenile justice system and discuss roles of the practitioner and JPO, including adjunctive social work services such as crisis intervention and family-based services. I conclude with a discussion of the BARJ model of juvenile justice that seeks to make the traditional rehabilitative–punitive framework obsolete.

Key Terms

In the juvenile justice system, youth who are arrested for illegal activities are considered *delinquent*. The system distinguishes between activities that are illegal only for minors, called *status offenses* (e.g., underage drinking, truancy, or curfew violation), and activities that are illegal for anyone, called *index offenses* (e.g., rape, robbery, or murder). There are other activities that, depending on the situation and severity, may be considered either status or index offenses (e.g., joyriding, buying stolen goods, or damaging property; Henggeler, Schoenwald, Borduin, Rowland, & Cunningham, 1998). A first-time status offense, like breaking curfew, might result in *voluntary probation* (also referred to as preadjudication probation, contract probation, or double-secret probation). Voluntary probation allows youth to avoid formal adjudication pending successful completion of the terms of probation. It differs from *mandatory probation* only in that that there is no official record of the probation upon successful completion. If diversion or voluntary probation is not appropriate, offenses are brought before a judge in an *adjudicatory hearing* (the juvenile version of the trial in the criminal court). If the juvenile has been found to have committed the offense, the court will proceed to a *disposition* hearing (the juvenile version of sentencing in adult court). The *court* is the judicial branch and is responsible for making the determination of delinquency and dictating detention or the terms of probation. *Corrections* is the action branch and is responsible for the supervision, treatment, rehabilitation, and, most frequently, the punishment of young offenders (Schwartz, 2001).

A Brief History of the Juvenile Justice System

All 50 states and the District of Columbia have juvenile courts that have jurisdiction over delinquent acts committed by children (Griffin & Torbet, 2002). The role and function of these courts has changed since the first juvenile court was established in Cook County, Illinois, in 1899. Over a century of changes in technologies (electronic monitoring, shared computerized records), interventions (detention, medications, evidence-based therapies), and philosophies (from rehabilitation to coercion to restorative justice) has brought about a corresponding change in the roles of JPOs and social workers associated with the juvenile justice system. These roles are increasingly specialized. For example, JPOs will do intakes, community-based work, or work in detention, but rarely does one JPO perform all three tasks. It is almost certain that these roles will continue to evolve. A historical perspective on the evolution of the role of juvenile justice systems provides a context for understanding these changes.

Three assumptions supported the creation of juvenile courts (Sarri et al., 2001). First, children are works in progress. An important part of becoming an adult is learning how to live within the law. Research suggests that nearly everyone (male and female) commits a delinquent offense while young, although most are never arrested (Snyder, 1996). Second, the adult criminal justice system is inadequate to address the developmental needs of juveniles. In 2002 (the most recent statistics available), there were 33,356,500 youth between the ages of 10 and 17, 7% of whom were arrested (Snyder, Puzzanchera, & Kang, 2005). Of juveniles who are arrested, 43% are never adjudicated (Stahl, 2003). Third, juvenile delinquency results from environmental factors, rather than free will. The majority of arrests are for status offenses, like truancy (Snyder et al., 2005). In contrast to the image portrayed in the media, most youth are law abiding, and most arrests are for nonviolent crimes. Taken together, these assumptions supported a rehabilitative approach to working with juvenile offenders. Although the rehabilitative approach was the official policy through the 1970s, the use of punitive measures (e.g., detention over a period of years, removal from family of origin, etc.) were not unknown, and their use would soon be central to a series of Supreme Court decisions (*In re Gault*, 1967; *In re Winship*, 1970; *Kent v. United States*, 1966) that would shift the focus from rehabilitation to punishment.

The tension between the system's punitive and rehabilitative goals was highlighted in the 1967 Supreme Court case *In re Gault* (1967). "The *Gault* decision recognized that the rehabilitative rhetoric but punitive operation of the court provided the worst of both worlds. Youths received neither the rehabilitative benefits justifying procedural informality nor due process protections of the criminal court" (Sarri et al., 2001, p. 7). As a result of *Gault*, juveniles were granted the rights of due process (National Council of Juvenile and Family Court Judges [NCJFCJ], 2005). Rather than encourage a more successful approach to rehabilitation, however, the lawsuits in the 1960s and 1970s resulted in more punitive responses to juvenile crime (Griffin & Torbet, 2002).

From the 1980s through the mid-1990s, the juvenile justice system took an increasingly punitive approach to juvenile crime. Critics of the rehabilitative approach pointed to an increase in juvenile violent crimes; from 1966 to 1994 the arrest rate for violent crimes increased from 58 to 231 per 100,000 (Stanfield, 1999). The public increasingly saw juvenile crime as a threat, and public opinion shifted in support of more punitive responses to juvenile crime (Stanfield, 1999). This change in public opinion was accompanied by a change in the assumptions about the nature of juvenile crime (Stanfield, 1999). The first assumption was that juvenile delinquents are damaged goods with little hope for change. Second, the juvenile system is inadequate to address the criminal natures of the most violent offenders, and therefore transfer to the adult system is acceptable. And the third assumption is that juvenile delinquency is a result of free will, rather than environmental forces such as socioeconomic status, peers, education, family, and ethnocultural biases. When these forces are acknowledged, they are seen as having failed, and therefore the court system is obligated to protect the juvenile from his or her environment, while at the same time protecting the public from the juvenile. These assumptions resulted in a greater emphasis on punitive measures (e.g., longer probations or more detention time), court oversight of juvenile activities, and transfer of juveniles to the adult criminal justice system[1] (Griffin & Torbet, 2002; Shook, 2005), placing greater emphasis on the best interest of society than on the best interest of the child (Steiner et al., 2004).

Since the mid-1990s, we have seen a shift away from a punitive approach in response to changes in crime rates, legal decisions, and new philosophies. The juvenile crime rate has declined since 1995 (Snyder et al., 2005). In 2005, in *Roper v. Simmons*, the U.S. Supreme Court determined that capital punishment was disproportionate punishment, and therefore unconstitutional for youth under the age of 18 (NCJFCJ, 2005). The publication of a 1988 monograph on balanced and restorative justice (Maloney et al., 1988b) provided a new philosophy from which to approach juvenile justice. The shift away from a punitive approach provides practitioners with an opportunity to become involved again in the lives of these juveniles.

The Role of Social Work in Juvenile Justice

Social work has played a historic role in the development of the juvenile justice system (Mitchell, 2004). Current practice guidelines from the National Association of Social Workers (NASW) support the continued involvement of social workers with youth involved in the juvenile justice system. According to the NASW *Standards for the Practice of Social Work with Adolescents* (2005), social workers are expected to: (a) understand the services provided by the juvenile justice system; (b) provide "essential services in the environments, communities, and social systems that affect the lives of youths" (p. 6); and (c) recognize that the process of adolescent identity development "may include a natural form of rebelliousness and rejection of authority" (p. 8). Even if social work's practice guidelines did not specify the juvenile court population, there is a clear mandate to work with youth with mental illness. Although 93% of youth are not involved in the juvenile justice system, the majority of court-involved juveniles meet criteria for a mental illness (Teplin, Abram, McClelland, Dulcan, & Mericle, 2002). Based on social work's professional guidelines, juveniles involved in the court system fall within social work's policy and practice mandate.

Rather than being key players in juvenile justice, social workers mostly provide adjunctive social services, such as crisis assessments and outpatient treatment for individuals, families, and groups. Graduates from disciplines such as criminal justice and counseling are the primary providers of services to juvenile delinquents. Even the traditional domains of mental health and substance abuse treatment are increasingly provided by non–social workers. For example, most substance abuse treatment is provided by licensed chemical dependency counselors, not social workers. The treatment of juvenile sex offenders is a highly regulated practice with its own code of ethics requiring separate certification and oversight beyond the social work license (Knox, 2002). Since there is virtually no scholarly discussion of the role of the social worker, it is unclear if the abandonment of juveniles in the juvenile justice system by social work is intentional.

Although NASW suggests that social workers ought to be able to provide services to youth regardless of their adjudication status, the practice of social work in juvenile and criminal justice settings (also known as *forensic* social work) requires specialty training that is not provided by most schools of social work. In a survey of 72 masters in social work programs accredited by the Council on Social Work Education, only 4 out of 72 (4.3%) of schools reported offering a course in forensic social work. Only 10 out of 72 (14.3%) reported that the school was expanding its program to include forensic social work (Neighbors, Green-Faust, & van Beyer, 2004). Social workers who are unaware of the different expectations and requirements of forensic and traditional social work are likely to provide substandard services, placing themselves and their clients at risk.

Roberts and Rock (2002) identified seven professional functions and responsibilities of forensic social workers. The four functions most applicable to juveniles include (a) assessing risk for future violence and reoffense by offenders who are mentally ill and substance abusing, (b) assessment and treatment of mentally ill youth in criminal justice settings, (c) developing reports for juvenile court, and (d) assessing and treating involuntary offenders (Roberts & Rock, 2002). Involuntary clients can be categorized as either legally mandated or nonvoluntary clients (Rooney, 2002). *Legally mandated* clients seek services because failure to do so will result in a legal sanction against them. For example, adjudicated youth who attend treatment as required by their terms of probation are legally mandated clients. In contrast, *nonvoluntary* clients seek services due to pressure outside of the legal system. Children who are brought in for counseling by their parents are an example of nonvoluntary clients.

There are four ways in which the treatment of adjudicated youth differs from the treatment of nonadjudicated youth. First, adjudicated youth are usually court ordered to participate in treatment, making them legally mandated clients (Rooney, 2002). While youth rarely volunteer to participate in treatment, the pressure on the youth of legal sanctions for failure to participate adds a dimension not usually present in treatment. Second, adjudicated youth are at increased risk for violating the law (Wright & Thomas, 2003). Therefore, in addition to the clinical treatment, social workers are responsible for predicting future actions that might result in criminal offense. Third, the primary treatment goals are usually dictated by the court and reflect the infraction (e.g., terroristic threat or carjacking), rather than the clinical issue (e.g., substance abuse or serious mental illness). Fourth, social workers are often required to present courtroom testimony, either in person or in a written assessment. Testifying requires a set of skills that are rarely taught in social work programs. Testimony requires the disclosure of information that might normally be considered confidential. The specter of such disclosure can affect the therapeutic relationship from the first day.

Although current social work practice guidelines identify expectations for work with youth involved in the juvenile justice system, the overwhelming majority of schools of social work do not provide the types of training that are most needed to work with that population. Social work's systems perspective, commitment to serving people who are oppressed and vulnerable and increasing emphasis on using evidence-based practice, is an ideal package to offer to juvenile offenders. The biggest challenge for the juvenile justice system, and thus the biggest opportunity for social workers, is how to teach juveniles how not to break the law (Schwartz, 2001). Social work has the opportunity to answer a different question: "How can I help this child to behave well?"

The Role of Probation in Juvenile Justice

John Augustus, a Boston shoemaker, is credited with creating both adult and juvenile probation in the mid-1800s (Griffin & Torbet, 2002). His approach to working with delinquent youth was simple but systematic. If the youth were of "good character," then Augustus would post bail and enroll the youth in school or find them apprenticeships. He would periodically check up on them and make informal reports to the court. Today, JPOs perform the same tasks, although with greater oversight and accountability (Steiner, Roberts, & Hemmens, 2003). Augustus and his contemporaries, like fellow Bostonite and founder of the Mental Hygiene movement Dorothea Dix, believed that social ills could be eliminated (Trattner, 1998). These predecessors of modern social work identified social problems and became personally involved with the people these social problems most affected. Today, many JPOs feel a similar sense of mission in their jobs (Alarcon, 2004). However, the pull between competing purposes of social welfare and social control can ultimately lead to role confusion and burnout.

The tension between the rehabilitative and punitive functions of JPOs is reflected in the experience of newly hired JPOs. Interviews of juvenile court employees that I conducted in September 2005 revealed a common theme: Graduates of criminal justice programs tend to be too demanding of juveniles and their families, whereas graduates from social work or counseling programs tend to be too lenient. Curtis Demps, a social worker with the Juvenile Court Family Preservation Program in Austin, Texas, explained the developmental process of the new JPO:

> JPOs with social work backgrounds start out giving these kids the benefit of the doubt. When [the new JPOs] get manipulated, which they inevitably do, they get angry, become rigid and go to the opposite extreme. The JPOs with criminal justice backgrounds do the same, but in reverse. They think that kids should just obey them because they're probation officers. Then they see how the schools have abandoned these kids, how their parents ignore them, and how their friends are no good for them. It takes time, but they learn that they can't do their job pretending to be a cop. The JPOs that stick around reach a middle ground. They have no other choice if they want to do their jobs. (C. Demps, personal communication, September 23, 2005)

Demps concludes that successful JPOs find a middle ground between rehabilitation and punishment. Although individual education influences JPOs' initial outlook, institutional requirements exert an equally powerful influence on the roles that JPOs play.

JPOs play many roles in the juvenile justice system. Research indicates that JPOs in all 50 states perform three basic tasks: intake screening, presentence investigations, and postadjudication supervision (Griffin & Torbet, 2002; Steiner et al., 2003; Torbet

1996). JPOs were responsible for a greater number of community protection duties than accountability or competency development. These three roles are the three corners of the BARJ triangle. This finding suggests that although states are responding to the recommendations to adopt the BARJ philosophy, the implementation of the sections intended to balance out the punitive function has been, ironically, unbalanced. Interestingly, the least common regulations included explaining juveniles' rights and liaising between court and agencies (Steiner et al., 2003).

Since 1990, there has been an increase in the number of juveniles placed on probation and a corresponding increase in JPOs' caseloads. Juvenile probation can be either court ordered or voluntary. The increase in voluntary probation reflects a philosophical shift toward the role of the courts as the primary agent responsible for the oversight of juveniles who have committed any type of offense. As previously stated, voluntary probation allows youth to avoid formal adjudication pending successful completion of the terms of probation. In 1999, 40% of the 1.7 million juveniles referred to court were placed on probation. JPOs' caseloads increased by 27%. During that time, the overall number of juveniles placed on probation increased by 44% (Puzzanchera, 2003). In 1999, JPOs could, on average, expect that 59% of their caseload would be court ordered and the remaining 41% would be juveniles who "voluntarily" chose probation. Although the demographic profile of probation cases has changed little since 1990, the number of formally processed voluntary probation cases has increased by 12% (Puzzanchera, 2003). Despite the apparent acceptance of voluntary probation as an effective alternative, some JPOs have reported that voluntary probation is less effective than mandatory probation:

> I don't like working with consent decrees [voluntary probation]. There are real confidentiality issues, because nobody is allowed to know they are on probation. They call it "double secret" probation. Unlike my regular probationers, I can't use the leverage of the courts to help them "get it." The parents don't take it seriously. I find that at the end of probation most of my consent decrees still have the attitudes and problems. Voluntary probation is like a game to them. (A. Swaggert, personal communication, September 26, 2005)

In fact, the *Desktop Guide* recommends reserving probation only for adjudicated youth for whom there is no alternative community-based treatment available (Griffin & Torbet, 2002).

The Structure of the Juvenile Justice System

Juvenile justice can be seen as one system within a larger system in which youth development (the processes that advance health and well-being) can occur (Benson & Saito, 2001). The larger system includes schools, social services, health care, recreation, faith community, and community-based youth-serving organizations. The influence of the larger systems varies depending on the setting (families, neighborhoods, communities, and cultures). Placing juvenile justice within the context of other systems and settings reaffirms the youth developmental process. It also reminds us that juvenile justice need not be an insular system, even though most of the funding for youth seems to be funneled directly into corrections. Finally, identifying the juvenile justice system as part of a larger societal system is consistent with social work's systems orientation.

Although the federal OJJDP recommends national guidelines, juvenile justice in the United States is not a single system operating under a unified philosophy (Guarino-Ghezzi & Loughran, 1991). States, rather than the federal government, oversee juvenile justice. In 2000, 39 states administered their juvenile justice system through a state social service agency and 11 states administered juvenile justice through the adult corrections system (Wilson, 2000). Within each state, jurisdictions not only offer widely divergent services, but also may operate under different philosophies. Shook (2005) illustrates how contiguous states can approach the same offense in very different ways:

> For example, a 13-year-old youth charged with murder would be ineligible for transfer [from the juvenile to the adult system] in Ohio, automatically excluded from the juvenile court in Illinois, subject to being tried as an adult in the family court in Michigan based on the discretion of the prosecutor, and subject to being transferred to the criminal court by a judge in Indiana (Sarri et al., 2001, cited in Shook, 2005).

It is not hard to imagine that these four states fall on different points in the rehabilitative–punitive continuum. Amy Swaggert, a community-based JPO in Butler County, Pennsylvania, explains how the expectations of service provision are different for her in Pennsylvania than they were for her in Ohio, where she had previously worked:

> When I worked in Ohio, the JPOs were only required to have high school diplomas.[2] The services were poorly funded; each county was given a lump-sum of money and expected to be creative with the programs it produced. The focus wasn't on helping the kids get better, though. The role of the court was to protect the public. In Butler County [Pennsylvania], however, the services are very progressive. I can't think of a single colleague who doesn't have a master's degree in either criminology, or one of the counseling professions. Another difference is that our supervisors are always pushing us to be creative and rehabilitative, rather than punitive. (A. Swaggert, personal communication, September 26, 2005)

Swaggert describes two systems with completely dissimilar expectations and requirements of their JPOs. The amount of role conflict felt by JPOs will reflect the congruence or lack thereof between the philosophy of the individual and the philosophy of the juvenile justice system. Swaggert's background in counseling and social work are appreciated and encouraged in Butler County, Pennsylvania, which currently works under the BARJ philosophy. As such, she reports very little role conflict. Ohio, however, operates under the more traditional punitive philosophy. JPOs with a corrections focus will find that the job expectations in Ohio produce less role conflict.

Just as philosophies differ from state to state, so do minimum educational requirements for JPOs. According to a comparison of educational requirements on the National Center for Juvenile Justice (NCJJ) Web site, most states require a minimum of a bachelor's degree, some states have no minimum educational requirement, and some states recognize experience in lieu of a degree (NCJJ, 2004). A summary of differences can be found in Table 12.1.

Table
12.1

Minimum Educational Requirements for Juvenile Probation Officers in the United States, 2004

State	Bachelors or Equivalent	Associates	GED or High School	None	Certification
Alabama	*				*
Alaska	*b				
Arizona	*				*
Arkansas				*	*
California			*		
Colorado	*				
Connecticut				*	
Delaware	*				
Dist. of Col.	*b				
Florida	*b				
Georgia				*	
Hawaii	*b				
Idaho			*		*a
Illinois	*				*
Indiana	*				*
Iowa	*				
Kansas	*				
Kentucky	*				
Louisiana	*				*
Maine	*				
Maryland		*			*
Massachusetts	*b				*
Michigan	*b				
Minnesota	*				*
Mississippi^c					
Missouri	*				
Montana	*				
Nebraska	*				
Nevada					*
New Hampshire	*b				*
New Jersey	*				
New Mexico	*b				
New York	*				
North Carolina	*				
North Dakota	*				*
Ohio		*			
Oklahoma	*				
Oregon				*	*a
Pennsylvania	*				
Rhode Island	*				*
South Carolina	*				
South Dakota	*				
Tennessee		*			
Texas	*b				*
Utah	*				*
Vermont				*	
Virginia	*				
Washington	*				
West Virginia	*				
Wisconsin^c					
Wyoming	*				*

Note. The data are from *State Juvenile Justice Profiles,* by the National Center for Juvenile Justice, 2004. Retrieved October 19, 2006, from http://www.ncjj.org/stateprofiles.
[a] Voluntary certification; [b] Requires a bachelor's degree plus one to three years experience. Years of experience can be substituted for a master's degree. [c] Data unavailable.

The differences in educational requirements are represented in the four states with the largest juvenile probation populations: New York, California, Florida, and Texas. In California, educational requirements vary from county to county. Although most counties require a bachelor's degree, some counties require only a high school diploma. New York, Texas, and Florida have statewide minimum requirements. New York requires a minimum of a bachelor's degree. Both Texas and Florida require a minimum of a bachelor's degree plus either 1 year of graduate education (Texas) or 1 year of related experience (Florida). In both Texas and Florida, experience can be substituted with a master's degree in one of the social sciences.

Points of Service

Although each jurisdiction organizes the process differently, there are generally eight decision points in the contemporary juvenile justice system: diversion, referral, intake, detention, transfer, adjudication, disposition, and release (Schwartz, 2001). Social workers can play central roles at each of these decision points. For readers interested in a more legal perspective on improving juvenile court practices, please consult the *Juvenile Delinquency Guidelines* (NCJFCJ, 2005).

Diversion

Diversion prior to referral occurs when a juvenile commits either a status offense or a crime and is absorbed by community programs prior to involvement with the juvenile justice system.[3] It is prior to formal involvement with the juvenile justice system that social workers have the most freedom to provide traditional services. Although individual or family therapy can be provided if services are sought, neighborhood involvement is another time-honored alternative to formal adjudication. However, there is a debate as to the goal of diversion programs.

One argument for diversion is that it can reduce recidivism without using juvenile justice resources. Griffin (2003) argues that in order for diversion programs to be successful, they need to provide services to youth who are most at risk for being locked up, rather than the nonviolent entry-level offenders who pose little or no risk to the community. For example, in Philadelphia, for many years community alternatives had no effect in reducing overcrowding in the city's detention facility. In response, Philadelphia developed the Detention Diversion Advocacy Project to provide intensive case management to monitor and support juveniles with extensive prior records, who were currently accused of aggravated assault or drug dealing, or who had histories of failure in preadjudication supervision programs (Griffin, 2003).

However, some argue that the most successful diversion programs are community-based programs that provide targeted services to a relatively small number of youth. In the early 1970s, the House of Umoja in West Philadelphia provided support and encouragement in a family-like environment for gang-involved youths (Woodson, 1981). The project continues today and has served over 3,000 youth (http://www.houseofumoja.org). More recently, Pennsylvania's State Advisory Group has invested federal juvenile justice funds in community-based programs. These programs are intended to address the disproportionate confinement of minority youth (Welsh, Jenkins, & Harris, 1999). Schwartz (2001) cautioned against transforming "indigenous groups into formal components of the juvenile justice system" (p. 239) but encourages developing support networks between the juvenile justice system and community organizations.

A different type of community-based diversion program is the Neighborhood Conference Committee (NCC) in Austin, Texas. Originally adapted from a program in El Paso, Texas, the NCC organized community members into neighborhood-based committees. The committees worked with nonviolent youthful offenders from the neighborhood as an alternative to involvement with the juvenile justice system. Erik Olson, former coordinator of the NCC, illustrates the strengths and limitations of such a program:

> It didn't matter which neighborhood we were in, we saw the same kinds of crimes being committed. After a while, you ask yourself, "What were they [the juveniles] thinking, smoking pot in school, or shoplifting in the neighborhood?" But everyone cared, was excited, and was looking for an alternative to detention for these kids. The tough part was finding resources. For example, if [kids] came in with drug and alcohol problems, they had to get their drug education and rehab from somewhere. If the neighborhood committee had no resources to utilize, then they couldn't do their job. Because we were a small program among thousands of people in a zip code we didn't make an impact on the overall recidivism rates in Austin. But, we were a small piece of a larger system of services. (E. Olson, personal communication, September 29, 2005)

As these examples illustrate, diversion from involvement in the juvenile justice system can take many forms. Yet each program engages the community and provides services to juveniles in less restrictive environments. Schools of social work can play valuable roles in such projects by organizing community-needs assessments and identifying best practices for at-risk populations. Students can be involved through class projects and internships.

Referral

Referral is the formal entrance into the juvenile justice system (Schwartz, 2001). Referrals can be made by police (in the form of arrests) or private petitioners (e.g., a school or neighbor), or they can result from the transfer from criminal court. Youth under the age of 10 are often referred to another social service agency. Juveniles 18 or older, or those who have been charged with certain offenses (e.g., murder), are referred to the criminal courts. The remaining two thirds of arrests are processed through the juvenile courts (Snyder et al., 2005). Some observers feel that, for fiscal and other reasons, the juvenile justice system has become a dumping ground for emotionally disturbed juveniles who have nowhere else to go (Redding, 2000). Intensive mental health treatments, particularly residential programs, are difficult to access and pay for, for both individuals and community agencies. According to Redding (2005), "One 'solution' is to file a petition or else wait for the inevitable arrest, shifting responsibility for monitoring, controlling, and treating the youth to the juvenile justice system" (p. 4). Communities with few treatment alternatives are more likely to rely on the juvenile justice system for services. However, as noted in the beginning of the chapter, the juvenile justice system is often mired in conflicting goals. A referral for services best provided outside of the juvenile justice system (e.g., mental health) places an unnecessary burden on the intake workers, whose job it is to screen out youth who do not belong in the system.

Intake

The intake assessment is one of the most important responsibilities of a JPO (Griffin & Torbet, 2002). The JPO intake can be distinguished from a mental health intake assessment based on the two questions that intake workers must answer: "Is the complaint legally sufficient? If so, what action should be taken?" (Griffin & Torbet, 2002, p. 43). JPOs' training will influence what information they gather beyond these two questions. The *Desktop Guide* (Griffin & Torbet, 2002) recommends the use of simple screening instruments to screen for substance abuse, mental illness, or other problems.

Screening for mental illness can occur quickly (usually in a matter of minutes) and is often performed by the intake officer (Grisso & Underwood, 2004). Although screening is often done informally, use of standardized screening and assessment measures provides more accurate information to decision makers, increases consistency in identifying mental illness, and reduces the need for extensive training of JPOs in mental health diagnosis (see Hoge, 2002, for an extensive review of screening measures). A majority of adjudicated juveniles meet criteria for a mental health disorder, and 20% meet criteria for a serious mental illness (Grisso & Underwood, 2004). Teplin et al. (2002) found that nearly two thirds of boys and nearly three quarters of girls detained in a Chicago juvenile facility had at least one psychiatric disorder. This compares to a 15% incidence rate of psychiatric illness in the general youth populations (Griffin & Torbet, 2002). A delinquent act (either status or index) can be viewed as a symptom of a larger problem or can be seen as the problem itself. In a study by Murrie, Cornell, and McCoy (2005), the label of mental illness did not significantly influence JPO attitudes, but the symptoms of the mental illness did. That is, a label of "antisocial" did not influence the JPOs' decisions as much as the delinquent acts that resulted in the diagnosis of "antisocial." Adolescents can enter the juvenile justice system with a preexisting mental health diagnosis, or diagnosis can be identified during the adjudication process. The *Desktop Guide* recommends diversion to community-based treatment providers if the intake officer determines that a juvenile has a serious mental illness (Griffin & Torbet, 2002). If the screening procedure uncovers suicidal ideation, crisis workers should be brought in for immediate assessment and recommendations (Griffin & Torbet, 2002). An example of a suicide assessment in a detention facility is discussed in the next section.

Griffin and Torbet (2002) cautioned that if information gathered during the screening process is used punitively at trial, the youth will be unlikely to disclose important information later in the process. In the United States, psychological assessments are usually provided by a mental health service provider who is either employed directly through the juvenile justice system or as an outside consultant (Hoge, 2002). In contrast, the United Kingdom and parts of Canada have implemented a model wherein the provision of mental health services is entirely separate from the decision-making process of the juvenile justice system (Hoge, 2002). This model is rehabilitative and community oriented, and it places a more limited role on the juvenile justice system. Mark Peterson, a senior substance abuse counselor in the juvenile justice system in Austin, Texas, and former supervisor of a number of community mental health programs, notes,

I was able to do much better clinical work when I wasn't housed in the same building as the probation officers. The kids see us together and start to doubt the counseling relationship. They wonder how confidential can things be. I don't blame them. (personal communication, September 17, 2005)

Thus, there are both individual and systemic challenges to screening for mental illness and the subsequent treatment if mental illness is found. The worst-case scenario is an informal mental health screen that results in a referral to an in-house provider that has primary allegiance to the court. The best-case scenario is a standardized mental health screen that results in a referral to a community provider with no formal ties to the juvenile justice system.

Detention

Although some JPOs use detention as a form of punishment, the argument has been made that detention is a treatment similar to tough love (Schwisow, 2005). In contrast, Stanfield (1999) argued that detention is neither treatment nor punishment. She contended that detention serves three purposes: (a) securing a child who poses a flight risk prior to adjudication, (b) protecting the community from a violent offender, and (c) holding a youth for whom the system has no better placement (Stanfield, 1999). Using detention facilities to house youth for whom other placements are more appropriate contributes to overcrowding. Overcrowding creates a stressful situation that promotes violence between detainees, increases suicide rates, and leads to more forceful and restrictive measures by JPOs (Hayes, 2004; Stanfield, 1999). As a result, detention can be a high-risk environment for detainees with existing mental health problems.

There are a number of reasons for social workers to provide treatment to youth in detention. First, youth who were in treatment prior to arrest need continuity of care to maintain gains and reduce the adverse effects of the high-risk detention environment, such as harm toward self and others. Second, for youth who were not in treatment prior to intake, but who were identified as having a mental illness at intake, detention is often the first opportunity to address the mental health issues that precipitated the crime. Additionally, a comprehensive assessment over the course of treatment can provide information that can influence judicial decisions. Finally, the detention environment itself can be a beneficial adjunct to traditional treatment. Rather than seeing a client's detention as a barrier to treatment, or even a sign of treatment failure, social workers can see detention as a great place to do therapy. For example, while in detention, juveniles cannot use the excuses of not having time for or transportation to treatment. One of the challenges in community-based treatment is determining the extent to which problems are due to the environment (e.g., chaotic households or unsupportive schools) or are due to a mental illness. Because detention provides a structured and secure environment, the social worker can isolate influences and focus on thoughts, feelings, and actions that are symptomatic of the illness. Additionally, for some youth, detention itself can be a form of reality therapy. I worked with many youth who routinely disrespected their parents, only to become homesick for some of mom's good cooking and the comfort of clothes that were not orange after spending a few days in detention. For these youth, detention provided a perspective that no amount of miracle questions (Berg, 1994) could generate.

One important concern, as noted previously, is that youth in detention are at higher risk for suicide attempts. Social workers can play an important role in providing suicide assessments for detained youth. In the late 1990s, I worked for a community mental health clinic that was under contract by the juvenile court to provide crisis assessments. JPOs in intake or detention called us whenever a juvenile was suicidal or psychotic.

Our responsibility was to assess the youth's risk of current and future harm to self. A significant challenge was judging the veracity of the youths' comments; that is, are they really suicidal, or do they just want to get out of detention? Whereas youth in the community rarely make suicidal statements in order to go to a psychiatric hospital, youth in detention often see the psych ward as the preferable alternative. Other challenges of providing suicide assessments in detention facilities include (a) developing rapport and trust with the youth, (b) tailoring the assessment to meet the needs of the court, and (c) identifying the most important referral based on competing needs.

Developing rapport and trust is a cornerstone of clinical work. Roberts's seven-stage model of crisis intervention (Roberts, 2005) identifies rapport building as either the first or second stage of crisis intervention, depending on lethality. Developing rapport is particularly important when working with youth because they are often involuntary clients. The juveniles whom I assessed in the facility did not ask to be there, and they rarely requested social work services. Rooney (2002) recommended five steps in maintaining informed consent with involuntary clients:

1 Be proactive in describing the nature of interactions. Tell the truth about why you are there.
2 Describe potential risks, including the fact that not all risks can be anticipated.
3 Describe time lines and potential consequences.
4 Describe limits to confidentiality.
5 Describe divided obligations and responsibilities (p. 710).

Although Rooney had not yet published these steps in the late 1990s, the "rap" I gave to all of my detention clients prior to starting the assessment met all but the second criteria listed previously:

Hi, my name is Jonathan. (*Step 1*) I work with kids who talk about killing themselves, killing other people, or hearing voices or seeing things. I'm here because the intake worker said you made suicidal statements. I'm here to find out what's going on. (*Step 5*) I'm not a probation officer and I'm not employed by juvenile court. The good news is that I have no power to lock you up based on what you tell me. The bad news is that I have no power to get you released. (*Step 4*) At the end of our time together I have to tell the JPO whether or not I think you are at risk for killing yourself now or in the near future. If I do think you are at risk, I will recommend transfer to a psychiatric hospital. If you feel like your side of the story was not accurately recorded by the intake worker, you can tell me and I'll include your words in my report, which becomes part of the court record. (*Step 3*) Since you and I will have only about an hour together, I promise I will be honest with you and I will assume you're being honest with me until you do something to make me think otherwise. So tell me, what did you say or do that made the JPO want to call me? . . .

Once my assessment was complete, my write-up focused on immediate and future risk for harm to self or others. I noted mental health issues that might compromise the youth's ability to be successful in the detention setting. For example, poor impulse control and poor judgment, two symptoms of attention-deficit/hyperactivity disorder (American Psychiatric Association, 1994), can result in fights with other detainees and disrespectful interactions with detention staff. Based on the presence of a mental illness, I had to determine whether or not the youth would be further harmed by remaining in detention, or if there was a community referral that would be more appropriate.

Despite the challenges inherent in detention facility assessments, I commend the probation department in Travis County, Texas, for recognizing the importance of screening for suicidality and generally following through with social workers' recommendations. Mental health assessments often provide important information in the next three decision points in the process: transfer, adjudication, and disposition.

Transfer

Transfer, adjudication, and disposition are points of decision where the social worker and JPO work most closely with the court function of the justice system. Because decisions are made during these processes, JPOs and social workers are key players in determining the future of the juvenile.

Transfer is the process by which juveniles are tried as adults (Griffin & Torbet, 2002). Courts have exercised the option to use transfer since the 1900s. Due process was not required in making decisions regarding transfer until the 1966 Supreme Court decision *Kent v. United States* (1966). Since the mid-1990s, transfers have risen dramatically despite a corresponding decrease in juvenile crime. This trend suggests a further blurring of the lines between juveniles and adults regarding culpability and responsibility for criminal acts. Shook illustrates this double standard:

> Legal regulations prohibit youth from consuming alcohol until the age of 21, smoking until 18, driving until 16 (in most states) and voting until 18, yet do not prohibit a youth from being tried as an adult in the juvenile justice system at ages as low as 10. A juvenile may be tried as an adult and convicted of a felony that takes away his or her right to vote without ever having been able to exercise that right. (Shook, 2005)

Adjudication

After the intake, a juvenile will have the opportunity to declare guilt or innocence at an adjudication hearing. Most juveniles enter pleas of guilt (Wilson, 2000). When they do not, the information gathered by the JPO through his or her investigation helps the judge to make a ruling regarding guilt or innocence. Prior to the 1970s, JPOs were key players in adjudication hearings (Needleman, 1997). However, today prosecutors and defense attorneys provide most of the evidence, with JPOs and to a lesser extent social workers filling in the gaps. For a critique of the shift in power from JPOs to prosecutors, see Shook (2005).

Prior to the disposition hearing, JPOs staff the case in order to determine what options are available for the judge. The experience and training of the JPO are evident in the predisposition staffing. When the JPO presents the findings of his or her investigation, omitting evidence of mental illness, substance abuse, family conflict, academic problems, or other problems will have a direct impact on the recommendations that will be made.

Kathy Smith, Judicial Service Manager for Travis County Juvenile Court in Austin, Texas, illustrates the importance of such an investigation:

> It bothered me when the court record was lacking a mental health assessment. I'd say that the vast majority of the kids that go through here have mental health problems. Substance abuse is not too far behind. Now how are you going to make the right choice when you don't have all the information? POs didn't do mental health assessments because they were not aware of the problems, or they didn't have the skills to do a complete one. But that's their problem, not the kid's. I'm not going to send off this kid because the PO before me didn't know enough to get all the information. (K. Smith, personal communication, September 30, 2005)

Staffing allows the JPO to tailor the treatment options to the juvenile's unique situation. The degree to which such tailoring is possible depends on the quantity and quality of social services. For example, if the juvenile was found guilty of possession of an illegal substance, a variety of substance abuse treatment options would be discussed. If, however, it was obvious that the juvenile was in violation of curfew because of family conflict, the staffing recommendation might be to emphasize counseling services. Because of the sensitive information gathered in a predisposition hearing, the *Juvenile Delinquency Guidelines* (2005) recommends completing an investigation after the adjudication hearing determines that disposition is appropriate.

The predisposition staffing illustrates the difference between the punitive–rehabilitative dichotomy and the BARJ approach. The *Juvenile Delinquency Guidelines* (2005) recommends using the BARJ approach in developing dispositions. Rather than limit the disposition options to either rehabilitation (counseling or drug treatment) or punishment (3-months lockup or placement out of county at a corrections facility), the staffing focuses on what competencies the juvenile needs to develop, how to better protect the community from the juvenile, and how the juvenile and the community can learn to be accountable to each other.

Disposition

Once a juvenile has been found guilty of committing a crime, a disposition hearing determines the consequences and treatments needed by the juvenile and his or her family. The two most common dispositions are formal probation, which accounts for 60% of adjudicated youth, and residential placement, which accounts for 30% of adjudicated youth (Wilson, 2000). The *Juvenile Delinquency Guidelines* (2005) reported that graduated responses, sanctions and incentives that increase in response to the progress of the juvenile, are more effective when they encourage the existing strengths of the youth. When mental health is a primary concern, the *Juvenile Delinquency Guidelines* directs decision makers to follow the recommendations by mental health providers, particularly when their recommendations include evidence-based treatments. This recommendation provides social workers with significant leverage to address issues of racial disparity and overrepresentation of minority youth in the system. Several studies have identified barriers to service for minority youth once they enter the juvenile justice system (Cross, Bazron, Dennis, & Issacs, 1989; Gibbs & Huang, 1998; National Mental Health Association,

2000). Social work recommendations during disposition should reflect evidence-based and culturally competent practice.

The OJJDP has identified a number of best practices for treatment of adjudicated youth. Two best-practices treatments that are congruent with social work values and practice that have been identified as exemplary programs by the OJJDP are multisystemic therapy (MST) and brief strategic family therapy (BSFT). MST has demonstrated efficacy with antisocial youth and juvenile sex offenders. BSFT has demonstrated efficacy with Latino and African American substance-abusing adolescents and their families. One of the ways that social workers can establish a mutually beneficial relationship with the juvenile population is by providing evidence-based services that are recommended by the OJJDP and by other national juvenile justice organizations.

MST is a family- and community-based treatment that takes a systemic approach to the treatment of youth and their families (Henggeler et al., 1998). MST is an appropriate intervention for the juvenile population since the juvenile offenders have been the primary focus of outcome studies (Curtis, Ronan, & Borduin, 2004). It has also been demonstrated to reduce recidivism by juvenile offenders and reoffense by juvenile sex offenders (Center for Sex Offender Management, 1999; Griffin & Torbet, 2002). Finally, MST targets family strengths and resiliencies, antisocial peer groups, school performance, and informal social support systems. Treatment can focus on any combination of the individual, family, and extrafamilial (e.g., peer, school, or neighborhood) factors.

BSFT is a family-systems intervention that treats adolescent drug use and co-occurring problems (National Institute on Drug Abuse, 2003). BSFT is an appropriate intervention for the juvenile population since successful outcome studies have used juvenile offenders as participants. BSFT has been demonstrated to reduce marijuana use, to decrease association with antisocial peers, and to improve acting-out behavioral problems. This treatment targets patterns of interactions (e.g., the way the juvenile speaks to his or her mother) rather than the content of interactions (e.g., what the juvenile says to his or her mother; Robbins & Szapocznik, 2000). The BSFT approach allows the family to create systemic changes that influence multiple problems, rather than targeting the content of a single problem. BSFT can be delivered in either the office or the family's home in 8 to 12 weekly sessions. One of the strengths of this treatment is that it was developed with Spanish-speaking Cuban Americans and has been adapted to English-speaking Latino families as well as African American families.

Both MST and BSFT have found an inverse relationship between successful individual treatment and family dysfunction (Curtis et al., 2004). For example, juveniles who are successfully meeting their individual therapy goals report that their family functioning has gotten worse since the start of therapy. Family systems theory explains this phenomenon by looking at the relationship between the identified patient (in this case the juvenile delinquent) and the rest of the family. If the juvenile has been the scapegoat for most, if not all, of the family's dysfunction, then a reduction in scapegoat behaviors transfers the dysfunction back on to the family. This finding is particularly relevant for social workers and JPOs. When the disposition orders the juvenile to be removed from the home, the family dysfunction will remain. Unless it is addressed, the juvenile will return to a chaotic, dysfunctional household and will be at greater risk for reoffense in the future. Treatment that omits the family sets the juvenile up to fail. Therefore, systemic treatments such as MST and BSFT are recommended to address the dysfunctional patterns.

Release

Release occurs upon completion of the terms of probation. The role of the social worker will differ slightly if the youth is being released from community probation or from a locked facility. Juveniles released from community probation typically have no further contact with the system unless a crime is committed. If the youth has a mental illness, social work involvement can play a significant role in reducing the likelihood of reoffense. Juveniles with a mental illness are at significantly higher risk for reoffense than are juveniles without a mental illness (Schwartz, 2001). Continued involvement postrelease is the key to maintaining the juvenile in the community where treatment of his or her mental illness can be the primary focus.

Release from a locked facility presents additional challenges for the youth and the social workers. Placement in a locked facility disrupts peer-group development, connection with teachers, and participation in family lifecycle events and rituals. Juveniles often feel like a stranger in their own communities upon release. Locked facilities are highly structured environments where the youth's every action is monitored. It is impossible for the home environment to replicate the schedule and the structure of a secure facility. Therefore, juveniles often feel unsafe at home and unclear about expectations upon release. Juveniles released from a locked facility are placed on "after-care probation services" (Schwartz, 2001, p. 255). In theory, these services will encourage the juvenile to reintegrate successfully back into the community. However, due to large caseloads and few resources, JPOs are often unable to provide more than basic monitoring services. As such, release presents an opportunity for social workers to have a significant impact on the lives of juveniles involved with the justice system.

In Austin, Texas, I worked with the Family Preservation Program (FPP), a community-based program similar to MST. FPP provides services to children, including those recently released from locked facilities, who were at risk for being removed from their homes. The goal of FPP is to preserve the family by keeping the youth out of the courts by keeping the family together. This program was designed so that each social worker had no more than eight families on a caseload, allowing 4 to 6 hours of services per week per family. FPP workers travel to the home, school, recreation center, and library—wherever the family and the worker agreed services would be most beneficial. FPP workers provide service coordination, medication maintenance, and individual and family therapy and performed all of the roles discussed in introduction to social work texts (e.g., Hepworth, Rooney, & Larsen, 2002): advocate, mediator, broker, and others.

When working with youth recently released from a locked facility, I would engage the family in two specific activities. First, I worked with the juvenile and the family to institute structure into the family's daily routine. We set up schedules for morning and evening routines, including wake-up and bedtime, meals, homework, and recreation (phone, videos, etc.). Second, I helped the family develop and sign a contract stipulating what each member could contribute to make this schedule a success and what would be the consequences for noncompliance. Although the rules were specific to the family, the juvenile always included his or her terms of probation. In addition, each family member had to include one way he or she would try to sabotage the schedule, which provided a bit of comic relief and gave the family the opportunity to support each other not to fall into old habits. This intervention provided a structured environment that supported the juvenile to be successful in the home. One outcome was that the juvenile felt safer and was less likely to accidentally violate his or her terms of probation. A second outcome was that the family was held accountable for their actions as well as the juvenile's. Because we had developed a structured environment, it was easier to identify where the juvenile was being set up for success or for failure. Finally, the intervention made it easier to testify in front of the judge. Rather than discussing details of the treatment, I was able to report whether or not the family was successfully participating in treatment.

In sum, social workers can influence the future of youthful offenders in at least eight points along the juvenile justice decision-making process. Diversion programs set up by social workers and community members can be used to provide alternatives to juvenile justice involvement. Social workers' training in crisis intervention, assessment, and treatment is invaluable when working with mental health problems during intake, detention, and release. Furthermore, the current emphasis in schools of social work on training students in evidence-based treatments meets the recommendations of national juvenile justice organizations for treatment of juveniles. Two of the evidence-based treatments discussed in this chapter, MST and BSFT, are designed to recognize the interactive influence among offender, victim, and community. As I discuss in the next section, one of the emerging approaches to juvenile justice, BARJ, places the relationship among the offender, victim, and community on center stage.

Social Work and Juvenile Probation in the 21st Century

Throughout this chapter, I have looked at the formulation of juvenile justice as a pendulum swinging between the concepts of rehabilitation and coercion. In the late 1980s a third approach, BARJ, was articulated as an alternative (Maloney et al., 1988a) to the rehabilitation–coercion dichotomy. Today, the stage is set for a new partnership between social workers and JPOs.

The BARJ approach was developed through the OJJDP in the early 1990s as one of a series of restorative justice initiatives dating back to the mid-1970s (Freivalds, 1996). Based on the work of Maloney and colleagues (Maloney et al., 1988a), BARJ provides an alternative to the traditional intervention models discussed in this chapter (rehabilitation and punishment). Freivalds (1996) argues that the goals of rehabilitation and punishment are in constant conflict. Focusing entirely on rehabilitation fails because it results in applying labels (like depressed or hyper) and provides excuses for unhealthy behavior. Focusing entirely on punishment fails because it does not allow the offender to develop empathy and self-control (Harp, 2002). In the old paradigm, both treatment and punishment focused all of the resources on the offender. The BARJ philosophy states that the focus needs to be on the victim, the community, and the offender. The "balance" in BARJ refers to a balancing of community safety, offender accountability, and juvenile competency development (Harp, 2002). In juvenile justice settings, these three concepts are collectively referred to as "the triangle" (see Figure 12.1). Treatment goals reflecting the triangle are often complementary. The "restorative justice" in BARJ refers to a focus on repairing the damage to the relationship between the offender and the victim (individual or community).

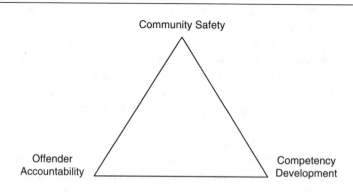

The balanced and restorative justice (BARJ) triangle.

BARJ offers a welcome opportunity for social workers and the juvenile justice system to take their best skills and apply them to a new framework:

> Practitioners have used techniques consistent with this approach for years. . . . However, they have lacked a coherent philosophical framework that supports restorative practice and provides direction to guide all aspects of juvenile justice practice. The BARJ model provides an overarching vision and guidance for daily decisions . . . there is no single "right way" to implement the BARJ Model. Within the general principles and values of restorative justice, implementation may vary based on local resources, tradition and culture. (Bazemore & Umbreit, 1998, p. 1)

The extent to which JPOs can put BARJ principles into practice relies on interagency cooperation and community involvement. For example, a good relationship with the school system can yield more useful information about probationers than does a mere tally of days of school attended, classes skipped, and number of referrals. This type of agency and community partnership facilitates competency development and offender accountability.

Bazemore and Umbreit (2004) argued that the juvenile justice system cannot implement BARJ in a vacuum where the focus on youth excludes the victim and the community. They suggest that partnerships with victim-advocacy groups and community-based organizations will result in a more balanced approach. Bazemore and Umbreit criticize traditional social work treatment as youth focused and thus incompatible with the BARJ approach. This view, however, fails to recognize the breadth of services provided by social work and the congruence of the systems perspective with BARJ. Social work has a historical commitment to community organizing and development of community-based services. Social workers have always been the primary service providers to victims (e.g., sexual assault and domestic violence). And, until the juvenile justice system switched its focus from rehabilitation to punishment, social workers had been the primary providers to youthful offenders. More than any other group, social workers have existing connections with the areas that BARJ emphasizes. The ecosystemic orientation of social work fits naturally with the BARJ approach. A strong partnership between juvenile justice and social work has the potential to make the implementation of BARJ more successful.

The issue of dual-jurisdiction youth highlights the benefits of a partnership between social work and juvenile justice in achieving the goals of the BARJ philosophy. According to Siegel and Lord (2004), cases where youth are involved in both child welfare and juvenile justice are called *dual jurisdiction*. The connection between child maltreatment and later juvenile delinquency has been confirmed in many studies (Siegel & Lord, 2004).

Until recently, however, the two systems that addressed child maltreatment and juvenile delinquency, child welfare and juvenile justice, did not work together. Each system usually has distinct and often conflicting goals regarding the juvenile and his or her family. The child welfare system protects children from those who seek to hurt them, whereas the juvenile justice system seeks to protect those whom juveniles might hurt. The One Judge/One Family program in Allegheny County, Pennsylvania (which includes Pittsburgh), is an example of research influencing practice because in Allegheny County both social workers and JPOs work together to benefit the juvenile (Seigel & Lord, 2004). While it might not be possible or useful to reconcile their differences, the One Judge/One Family program attempts to reduce misunderstanding and streamline case processing. Caseworkers and JPOs receive cross-training to help them understand each others' roles. When a foster child is arrested, court dates are coordinated with representatives from both agencies. In a practical way, the needs of the child are balanced with the needs of the community. Programs like One Judge/One Family are being established around the country (Seigel & Lord, 2004) and represent a needed partnership between social work and juvenile justice.

The BARJ model, however, is not without criticisms. Harp (2002) noted that popular programs in the 1990s focusing on restorative justice gave the impression that the tenets of BARJ were appropriate only for low-level and first-time offenders. BARJ has also been criticized for being community driven, rather than juvenile-justice driven. The danger of community-driven restoration comes from the tentative quality of voluntary participation (Marshall, 1999). In order for community restoration to occur, there first has to be a community; then the community must be willing to participate. Marshall acknowledged that, in practice, communities are likely to participate, but nevertheless he cautioned against the viability of the model if communities continue to fragment. Other critics have argued that the philosophical values of restorative justice cannot be translated into practical application (Morris, 2002). While there are undoubtedly poor applications of BARJ, findings from recent literature as well as interviews with JPOs suggest that there are successful practical applications of BARJ (Bazemore & Umbreit, 1998; DeAngelo, 2005; Morris, 2002). For example, in Pennsylvania, where the language of BARJ is written into the statutes, I interviewed JPOs who believed that the administration encouraged creative interventions as a result of BARJ. One JPO commented that BARJ gives the department "permission" to have her visible in the community, actively developing relationships that will help her meet the goals of accountability and community safety. As a result, she has reduced by half the number of youth she places in detention.

Conclusion

The relationship between social work and juvenile probation extends back to the mid-19th century. Shifts in policy, legal precedent, and public opinion have changed the focus of juvenile justice. This shift has resulted in changing roles and expectations of JPOs and social workers alike. JPOs have become increasingly specialized in their duties. Social workers have become increasingly marginalized in the juvenile justice system. However, professional social work guidelines indicate that adolescents, regardless of setting or system, fall under the purview of social work practice. In this chapter, I identified areas where the duties of the JPOs and social workers coincide and where they diverge. Despite the absence of discussion in the literature about social work and juvenile justice, the analysis of the points of service reveals that social workers can make valuable contributions in almost every facet of the juvenile justice process. Finally, the emergence of the BARJ model suggests a different approach to juvenile justice, one that combines the best qualities of social work and juvenile probation. Although the BARJ model lacks a solid research base and is thus open to criticisms, the newness of the philosophy provides social work with a unique opportunity to become involved in shaping the approach to working with youth involved in the juvenile justice system. As we move into the 21st century, we will see that social work has a historic opportunity to make the circle whole again.

NOTES

1. On June 30, 2000, 1% (7,600) of adult corrections inmates were under the age of 18. The majority of youths in adult prison are 17 years old, males, minorities, and person offenders (Sickmund, 2004).
2. According to the National Center for Juvenile Justice, counties in Ohio generally require either an associates or bachelors degree. However, in some counties experience may be substituted for a degree. Pennsylvania requires a minimum of a bachelor's degree with at least 18 credits in the social sciences (NCJJ, 2004).
3. Although some authors refer to the process of trying juveniles in criminal court as "diversion," I use the term to reflect maintenance in a least restrictive environment rather than placement in a more restrictive environment.

RESOURCES AND REFERENCES

Abrams, L. S., Kim, K., & Anderson-Nathe, B. (2005). Paradoxes of treatment in juvenile corrections. *Child and Youth Care Forum, 34*(1), 7–25.
Alarcon, F. J. (2004). Juvenile corrections: Why would anyone want to work in this business? *Corrections Today, 66*(1), 8–10.
American Psychiatric Association. (1994). *Diagnostic and statistical manual of mental disorders* (4th ed.). Washington, DC: Author.
Baumrind, D. (1991). The influence of parenting style on adolescent competence and substance use. *Journal of Early Adolescence, 11*(1), 56–95.
Bazemore, G., & Umbreit, M. (1998). *Guide for implementing the balanced and restorative justice model—Report of the Office of Juvenile Justice and Delinquency Prevention (OJJDP)*. Washington, DC: U.S. Department of Justice, Office of Juvenile Justice and Delinquency Prevention.
Bazemore, G. & Umbreit, M. (2004). Balanced and restorative justice: Prospects for juvenile justice in the 21st century. In A. R. Roberts (Ed.), *Juvenile justice sourcebook: Past, present, and future.* (Ch. 19). New York: Oxford University Press.
Benson, P. L., & Saito, R. N. (2001). The scientific foundations of youth development. In P. L. Benson & K. J. Pittman (Eds.), *Trends in youth development: Visions, realities and challenges* (pp. 135–154). Boston: Kluwer Academic.
Berg, I. K. (1994). *Family based services: A solution-focused approach.* New York: W. W. Norton.
Bourgon, G., & Armstrong, B. (2005). Transferring the principles of effective treatment into a "real world" prison setting. *Criminal Justice and Behavior, 32*, 3–25.

Breda, C. S. (2003). Offender ethnicity and mental health service referrals from juvenile courts. *Criminal Justice and Behavior, 30*(6), 644–667.

Brookman, M. (2003). Juvenile justice: A role for health professionals. *Journal of Ambulatory Care Management, 26*(1), 91–92.

Brown, R., Killian, E., & Evans, W. P. (2003). Familial functioning as a support system for adolescents' postdetention success. *International Journal of Offender Therapy and Comparative Criminology, 47,* 529–541.

Brown, W. K. (2005). Turning your life around: Tips from an ex-juvenile delinquent. *Reclaiming Children and Youth, 13*(4), 218–224.

Burnett, D. M. R., Noblin, C. D., & Prosser, V. (2004). Adjudicative competency in a juvenile population. *Criminal Justice and Behavior, 31,* 438–462.

Campbell, M. A., & Schmidt, F. (2000). Comparison of mental health and legal factors in the disposition outcome of young offenders. *Criminal Justice and Behavior, 27,* 688–715.

Center for Sex Offender Management. (1999). *Understanding juvenile sexual offending behavior: Emerging research, treatment approaches and management practices.* Silver Spring, MD: Center for Sex Offender Management.

Colley, L., Culbertson, R. G., & Latessa, E. J. (1987). Juvenile probation officers: A job analysis. *Juvenile & Family Court Journal, 38,* 1–12.

Cowles, C. A., & Washburn, J. J. (2005). Psychological consultation on program design of intensive management units in juvenile correctional facilities. *Professional Psychology: Research and Practice, 36*(1), 44–50.

Cross, T. (2004). What works with at-risk youths. *Corrections Today, 66*(2), 64–68.

Cross, T. L., Bazron, B. J., Dennis, K. W., & Issacs, M. R. (1989). *Toward a culturally competent system of care.* Washington, DC: CASSP Technical Assistance Center.

Curtis, N. M., Ronan, K. R., & Borduin, C. M. (2004). Multisystemic treatment: A meta-analysis of outcome studies. *Journal of Family Psychology, 18*(3), 411–419.

DeAngelo, A. J. (2005). The evolution of juvenile justice: Community-based partnerships through balanced and restorative justice. *Corrections Today, 67*(5), 104–107.

Engels, R. C. M. E., Luijpers, E., Landsheer, J., & Meeus, W. (2004). A longitudinal study of relations between attitudes and delinquent behavior in adolescents. *Criminal Justice and Behavior, 31,* 244–260.

Freivalds, P. (1996, July). *Balanced and Restorative Justice Project (BARJ).* Washington, DC: Office of Juvenile Justice and Delinquency Prevention, Office of Justice Programs, U.S. Department of Justice.

Funk, S. J. (1999). Risk assessment for juveniles on probation. *Criminal Justice and Behavior, 26*(1), 44–68.

Gavazzi, S. M., Wasserman, D., Partridge, C., & Sheridan, S. (2000). The growing up fast diversion program: An example of juvenile justice program development for outcome evaluation. *Aggression and Violent Behavior, 5*(2), 159–175.

Gavazzi, S. M., Yarcheck, C. M., Rhine, E. E., & Partridge, C. R. (2003). Building bridges between the parole officer and the families of serious juvenile offenders: A preliminary report on a family-based parole program. *International Journal of Offender Therapy and Comparative Criminology, 47*(3), 291–308.

Gibbs, A. (2001). Partnerships between the probation service and voluntary sector organizations. *British Journal of Social Work, 31*(1), 15–27.

Gibbs, J., & Huang, L. (1998). *Children of color: Psychological interventions with culturally diverse youth.* San Francisco: Jossey-Bass.

Granello, P. F., & Hanna, F. J. (2003). Incarcerated and court-involved adolescents: Counseling an at-risk population. *Journal of Counseling and Development, 81*(1), 11–18.

Gray, P. (in press). The politics of risk and young offenders' experiences of social exclusion and restorative justice. *British Journal of Criminology.* Advance Access published on March 21, 2005, DOI 10.1093/bjc/azi018.

Griffin, P. (2003, July). Juvenile detention: The Philadelphia alternative. *Pennsylvania Progress, 9*(4), 1–12.

Griffin, P., & Torbet, P. (2002). *Desktop guide to good juvenile probation practice.* Pittsburgh, PA: National Center on Juvenile Justice.

Grisso, T. & Underwood, L. (2004). *Screening and assessing mental health and substance use disorders among youth in the juvenile justice system: A resource guide for practitioners.* Washington, D.C.: Office of Juvenile Justice and Delinquency Prevention, document number 204956. Retrieved online September 19, 2005 at http://www.ncjrs.gov/pdffiles1/ojjdp/204956.pdf.

Guarino-Ghezzi, S., & Loughran, E. J. (1991). *Balancing juvenile justice*. New Brunswick, NJ: Transaction.

Harp, C. (2002). *Bringing balance to juvenile justice*. Washington, DC: U.S. Department of Justice, Office of Juvenile Justice and Delinquency Prevention.

Hayes, L. (2004). *Juvenile suicide in confinement: A national survey*. Baltimore: National Center on Institutions and Alternatives.

Henggeler, S. W., Schoenwald, S. K., Borduin, C. M., Rowland, M. D., & Cunningham, P. B. (1998). *Multisystemic treatment of antisocial behavior in children and adolescents*. New York: Guilford.

Hepworth, D. H., Rooney, R., & Larsen, A. J. (2002). *Direct social work practice: Theory and skills* (6th ed.). New York: Brooks/Cole.

Hoge, R. D. (1999). An expanded role for psychological assessments in juvenile justice systems. *Criminal Justice and Behavior, 26*, 251–266.

Hoge, R. D. (2002). Standardized instruments for assessing risk and need in youthful offenders. *Criminal Justice and Behavior, 29*, 380–396.

In re Gault, 387 U.S. 1 (1967).

In re Winship, 397 U.S. 358 (1970).

Kent v. United States, 383 U.S. 541 (1966).

Knox, K. (2002). Juvenile sex offenders risk assessment and treatment. In A. R. Roberts & G. J. Greene (Eds.), *Social workers' desk reference* (pp. 698–701). Oxford, UK: Oxford University Press.

Kvarfordt, C. L., Purcell, P., & Shannon, P. (2005). Youth with learning disabilities in the juvenile justice system: A training needs assessment of detention and court services personnel. *Child and Youth Care Forum, 34*(1), 27–42.

Lambert, E. G., Hogan, N. L., & Barton, S. M. (2002). Satisfied correctional staff: A review of the literature on the correlates of correctional staff job satisfaction. *Criminal Justice and Behavior, 29*, 115–143.

Maccoby, E. E., & Martin, J. A. (1983). Socialization in the context of the family: Parent–child interaction. In P. H. Mussen (Series Ed.) & E. M. Hetherington (Vol. Ed.), *Handbook of child psychology: Vol. 4. Socialization, personality, and social development* (4th ed., pp. 1–101). New York: Wiley.

Maloney, D., Romig, D., & Armstrong, T. (1988a). Juvenile probation: The balanced approach. *Juvenile and Family Court Journal, 39*(3), 1–63.

Maloney, D., Romig, D., & Armstrong, T. (1988b). The balanced approach in daily juvenile probation practice. *Juvenile and Family Court Journal, 39*(3), 39–51.

Marshall, T. F. (1999). *Restorative justice: An overview*. Retrieved September 28, 2005, from the Home Office Research Development and Statistics Directorate Web site: http://www.homeoffice.gov.uk/rds/pdfs/occ-resjus.pdf

Mitchell, J. (2004). Is social work Y2K compliant? Adapting to the mandates of future practice. In I. Neighbors, A. Chambers, E. Levin, G. Nordman, & C. Tutrone (Eds.), *Social work and the law: Proceedings of the National Organization of Forensic Social Work, 2000* (Ch. 6). Binghamton, NY: Haworth Press.

Morgan, R. D., Van Haveren, R. A., & Pearson, C. A. (2002). Correctional officer burnout: Further analyses. *Criminal Justice and Behavior, 29*, 144–160.

Morris, A. (2002). Critiquing the critics: A brief response to critics of restorative justice. *British Journal of Criminology, 42*(3), 596–615.

Murrie, D. C., Cornell, D. G., & McCoy, W. K. (2005). Psychopathy, conduct disorder, and stigma: Does diagnostic labeling influence juvenile probation officer recommendations? *Law and Human Behavior, 29*(3), 323–342.

National Association of Social Workers. (2005). *NASW standards for the practice of social work with adolescents*. Washington, DC: NASW Press.

National Center for Juvenile Justice. (2004). *State juvenile justice profiles: Ohio*. Retrieved October 11, 2005, from http://www.ncjj.org/stateprofiles

National Council of Juvenile and Family Court Judges. (2005). *Juvenile delinquency guidelines: Improving court practice in juvenile delinquency cases*. Reno, NV. Retrieved online August 15, 2005, from http://www.ncjfcj.org/images/stories/dept/ppcd/pdf/JDG/00intro.pdf.

National Institute on Drug Abuse. (2003, August). Brief strategic family therapy for adolescent drug abuse (NIH Publication No. 03-4751). Retrieved August 27, 2005, from http://www.nida.nih.gov/TXManuals/bsft/BSFTIndex.html

National Mental Health Association. (2000). *Mental health and youth of color in the juvenile justice system.* Retrieved September 27, 2005, from http://www.nmha.org/children/justjuv/colorjj.cfm

Needleman, C. (1997). Conflicting philosophies of juvenile justice. In A. R. Roberts (Ed.), *Social work in juvenile and criminal justice settings* (2nd ed., pp. 215–223). Springfield, IL: Charles C. Thomas.

Neighbors, I. A., Green-Faust, L., & van Beyer, K. (2004). Curricula development in forensic social work at the MSW and post-MSW levels. In I. Neighbors, A. Chambers, E. Levin, G. Nordman, & C. Tutrone, (Eds.), *Social work and the law: Proceedings of the National Organization of Forensic Social Work, 2000* (pp. 3–27, Ch. 1). Binghamton, NY: Haworth Press.

Nordness, P. D., Grummert, M., Banks, D., & Schindler, M. L. (2002). Screening the mental health needs of youths in juvenile detention. *Juvenile and Family Court Journal, 53,* 43–51.

Perkins-Dock, R. E. (2001). Family interventions with incarcerated youth: A review of the literature. *International Journal of Offender Therapy and Comparative Criminology, 45,* 606–625.

Puzzanchera, C. M. (2003). *Juvenile delinquency probation caseload, 1990–1999.* Washington, DC: U.S. Department of Justice, Office of Juvenile Justice and Delinquency Prevention.

Redding, R. (2000). Barriers to meeting the mental health needs of offenders in the juvenile justice system. *Juvenile justice fact sheet.* Charlottesville, VA: Institute of Law, Psychiatry & Public Policy, University of Virginia.

Roberts, A. R. (2005). Bridging the past and present to the future of crisis intervention and crisis management. In A. R. E. Roberts (Ed.), *Crisis intervention handbook: Assessment, treatment and research, 3rd ed.* (pp. 3–34). New York: Oxford University Press.

Roberts, A. R., & Rock, M. (2002). An overview of forensic social work and risk assessments with the dually diagnosed. In A. R. Roberts & G. J. Greene (Eds.), *Social workers' desk reference* (pp. 661–667). Oxford, UK: Oxford University Press.

Robbins, M. S., & Szapocznik, J. (2000, April). *Brief strategic family therapy. Juvenile justice bulletin.* (pp. 1–11). Washington, DC: Office of Juvenile Justice and Delinquency Prevention. Retrieved online August 29, 2005 at http://www.ncjrs.gov/html/ojjdp/jjbul2000_04_3/contents.html

Roiblatt, R. E., & Dinis, M. C. (2004). The lost link: Social work in early twentieth-century alcohol policy. *Social Service Review, 78*(4), 652–675.

Rooney, R. (2002). Working with involuntary clients. In A. R. Roberts & G. J. Greene (Eds.), *Social workers' desk reference* (pp. 709–713). Oxford, UK: Oxford University Press.

Sarri, R., Shook, J. J., Ward, G., Creekmore, M., Albertson, C., Goodkind, S., et al. (2001). *Decision making in the juvenile justice system: A comparative study of four States.* Ann Arbor, MI: Institute for Social Research.

Schmidt, F., Hoge, R. D., & Gomes, L. (2005). Reliability and validity analyses of the Youth Level of Service/Case Management Inventory. *Criminal Justice and Behavior, 32,* 329–344.

Schroeder, J., & Trainham, A. (2002). Empowering drug courts through evaluation: Serving as change agents to help others help themselves. In I. Neighbors, A. Chambers, E. Levin, G. Nordman, & C. Tutrone (Eds.), *Social work and the law: Proceedings of the national organization of forensic social work, 2000* (pp. 47–58). Binghamton, NY: Haworth Press.

Schwartz, R. G. (2001). Juvenile justice and positive youth development. In P. L. Benson & K. J. Pittman (Eds.), *Trends in youth development: Visions, realities and challenges* (pp. 231–267). Boston: Kluwer Academic.

Schwisow, A. (2005, March). *It's been seven years of 'tough love' for one of nation's youngest convicted killers.* Retrieved October 1, 2005, from http://www.detnews.com/2005/metro/0503/06/metro-108061.htm

Shook, J. J. (2005). Contesting childhood in the U. S. justice system: The transfer of juveniles to adult criminal court. *Childhood, 12*(4), 461–478.

Siegel, G., & Lord, R. (2004). *When systems collide: Improving court practices and programs in dual jurisdiction cases.* Pittsburgh, PA: National Center for Juvenile Justice.

Silver, E., & Chow-Martin, L. (2002). A multiple models approach to assessing recidivism risk: Implications for judicial decision making. *Criminal Justice and Behavior, 29,* 538–568.

Smith, M., Usinger-Lesquereux, J., & Evans, W. (1999). Rural juvenile first offenders describe what is working and what is not. *International Journal of Offender Therapy and Comparative Criminology, 43,* 322–337.

Snyder, H. (1996). The juvenile court and delinquency cases. *The Juvenile Court, 6*(3), 53–63.

Snyder, H., Puzzanchera, C., & Kang, W. (2005). *Easy access to FBI arrest statistics 1994–2002.* Retrieved September 19, 2005, from the Office of Juvenile Justice and Delinquency Prevention Web site: http://ojjdp.ncjrs.org/ojstatbb/ezaucr

Springer, D. W., McNeece, C. A., & Arnold, E. M. (2003). *Substance abuse treatment for criminal offenders: An evidence-based guide for practitioners* (Forensic Practice Guidebooks Series). Washington, DC: American Psychological Association.

Stahl, A. (2003). *Delinquency cases in juvenile courts, 1999*. Washington, DC: U.S. Department of Justice, Office of Juvenile Justice and Delinquency Prevention.

Stanfield, R. (1999). *The JDAI story: Building a better detention system. Pathways to juvenile detention reform (overview)*. Baltimore, MD: Annie E. Casey Foundation.

Steiner, B., Roberts, E., Hemmens, C. (2003). Where is juvenile probation today? The legally prescribed functions of juvenile probation officers. *Criminal Justice Studies, 16*(4), 267–281.

Steiner, B., Purkiss, M., Kifer, M., Roberts, E., & Hemmens, C. (2004). Legally prescribed functions of adult and juvenile probation officers: Worlds apart? *Journal of Offender Rehabilitation, 39*(4), 47–68.

Stoolmiller, M., & Blechman, E. A. (2005). Substance use is a robust predictor of adolescent recidivism. *Criminal Justice and Behavior, 32*, 302–328.

Takagi, P., & Shank, G. (2004). Critique of restorative justice. *Social Justice, 31*(3), 147–164.

Teplin, L. A., Abram, K. M., McClelland, G. M., Dulcan, M. K., & Mericle, A. A. (2002). Psychiatric disorders in youth in juvenile detention. *Archives of General Psychiatry, 59*, 1133–1143.

Torbet, P. (1996). *Juvenile probation: The workhorse of the juvenile justice system*. Washington, DC: U.S. Department of Justice, Office of Juvenile Justice and Delinquency Prevention.

Torbet, P., & Thomas, D. (1997, October). Balanced and restorative justice: Implementing the philosophy. *Pennsylvania Progress, 4*(3), 1–6. Retrieved online September 28, 2005, at http://www.pccd.state.pa.us/pccd/LIB/pccd/pubs/progress/oct97.pdf

Trattner, W. (1998). *From poor law to welfare state: A history of social welfare in America* (6th ed.). New York: Free Press.

Wasserman, G. A., Ko, S. J., & McReynolds, L. S. (2004). *Assessing the mental health status of youth in juvenile justice settings*. Retrieved September 28, 2005, from the Office of Juvenile Justice and Delinquency Prevention Web site: https://sslvpn.pitt.edu/GPO/LPS53603

Welsh, W. N., Jenkins, P. H., & Harris, P. W. (1999). Reducing minority overrepresentation in juvenile justice: Results of a community-based delinquency prevention in Harrisburg. *Journal of Research in Crime and Delinquency, 36*, 87–110.

Wilson, J. (2000). *Employment and training for court-involved youth*. Washington, DC: U.S. Department of Justice, Office of Juvenile Justice and Delinquency Prevention.

Woodson, R. L. (1981). *A summons to life: Mediating structures and the prevention of youth crime*. Cambridge, MA: Ballinger.

Wright, R., & Thomas, W. (2003). Disproportionate representation: Communities of color in the domestic violence, juvenile justice, and child welfare systems. *Juvenile and Family Court Journal, 54*, 87–97.

Allison Benesch
F. Carole Bryant
Richard LaVallo

Introduction

Making generalizations about helping professionals in the juvenile court system is a daunting, if not impossible, task since both juvenile courts and the role of helping professionals in such courts vary greatly from state to state. In some states, the juvenile courts handle delinquency, child protection, custody, and adoption cases. Whereas in other states, the jurisdiction of juvenile courts is limited to only delinquency cases. Similarly, there are differences in the role of helping professionals in the juvenile court systems around the country. For example, in most states, a social worker may qualify as an expert witness based on his or her education and experience in social work (*Taylor v. Tex. Dept. of Protective & Regulatory Servs.*, 2005). However, there are some jurisdictions where a social worker must possess additional knowledge and expertise to qualify as an expert witness (*In re Interest of D.S.P.*, 1992). In short, it is important that a practitioner be familiar with the juvenile court system in the state where he or she practices social work.

The role of social workers in the juvenile court system has evolved considerably since the inception of social work as a bona fide profession in the late 1800s. At that time, social workers were considered social activists who advocated for change on behalf of people whom they encountered in prisons and social welfare agencies (Barker & Branson, 2000). Some focused their efforts on poverty, the inhumane conditions in prisons (Barker & Branson, 2000) and juvenile delinquency (Brownell & Roberts, 1999), while others led political movements to address larger societal issues such as child labor and women's rights (Barker & Branson, 2000). These early social workers lobbied for laws to diminish what they saw as injustice against the socially disadvantaged and supported better law enforcement (Barker & Branson, 2000).

Many of the lawyers who formed charity organizations began utilizing the first professional social workers to affect change (Barker & Branson, 2000). Because of this relationship between lawyers and social work, many early social workers were involved in courts, prisons, and law firms (Barker & Branson, 2000). After the establishment of the first juvenile court in 1899 (Brownell & Roberts, 1999), many social workers continued their work in those courts. Often, social workers in juvenile courts "stood up for children, families, and the state in the same proceeding" and then served as the probation officer in juvenile delinquency cases (Barker & Branson, 2000, p. 6).

In the 1930s, social work as a profession shifted its focus from the courts to promoting mental health as a means of effectuating social change (Barker & Branson, 2000). Social workers had an increased presence in mental health clinics (Barker & Branson, 2000). During the Great Depression, positions for social workers in police departments and courts were drastically cut (Brownell & Roberts, 1999). The role of social workers in juvenile courts suffered a further setback with the U.S. Supreme Court decision in *In re Gault* (1967), which extended the due process rights afforded to adults in criminal cases to children facing delinquency charges (Barker & Branson, 2000). As a result, juvenile proceedings became more adversarial, and trained lawyers were needed to perform the roles that had once belonged to social workers (Barker & Branson, 2000). While social workers were not entirely eliminated from the juvenile justice system, their involvement was dramatically reduced.

With the gradual movement of the social work profession from the court system to more humanistic concerns, many states lost interest in licensing standards for social workers (Barker & Branson, 2000). Nevertheless, social workers were still called on to testify in court about matters related to their clients. By 1993, every state had regulated its social workers, with most requiring formal licensure (House Health & Human Services Comm., 1993). Such change can be attributed to the increasing litigiousness of society and insurance companies' fears of malpractice claims against social workers testifying in court (Barker & Branson, 2000). Further, many believed that the licensing requirements would promote and advance social work as a profession (House Health & Human Services Comm., 1993). Despite this movement toward regulation, not all practicing "social workers" are actually trained and licensed in social work; many caseworkers, especially in the field of child welfare, hold degrees in other fields.

In recent years, social workers have become an integral part of the criminal justice system as a whole, especially in the juvenile courts. Social workers hold highly specialized positions within police departments, district attorney offices, and child protection agencies. They provide services such as counseling and victim assistance. They deliver rehabilitative services to children and families involved in delinquency and child abuse cases such as substance abuse treatment and family preservation services. Social workers serve as juvenile probation officers in juvenile delinquency cases as well as guardians ad litem in child custody cases. They also conduct social studies and make recommendations to the court regarding the placement of children. Social workers also supervise and assist court appointed special advocates (CASA) or volunteer advocates in child protective services cases (Tex. Fam. Code § 107.031). With the increased privatization of social services, social workers are moving into the private sector to work for adoption agencies, child placing agencies, and residential treatment centers that serve children in juvenile court. Social workers have worked to make the juvenile justice system adopt a more holistic and compassionate approach to helping children and their families.

Issues in Social Worker Involvement With the Courts—A Case View

It is important for social workers in the juvenile court system to become familiar with legal issues that have a direct impact on their role in the courts. This section will focus on the qualifications of a social worker to testify as an expert witness, the type of information that a social worker is permitted to testify about, the confidentiality of the social worker's records, and a social worker's immunity from being sued. Since such legal issues are often determined by case law, selected court opinions will be used to illustrate the effect of these legal issues on social workers.[1]

Social Worker Qualifications

Social workers must meet certain qualifications to testify as a witness in court. As a "fact witness," a social worker may be allowed to testify only about matters within their personal knowledge.[2] As an "expert witness," a social worker may give opinion testimony to assist the judge or jury to understand the evidence or to determine the issue to be decided in the case.[3] In order to testify as an expert witness, the court must examine the social worker's qualifications including knowledge, skill, experience, training, or education to determine whether the social worker can help the judge or jury.[4]

The expert testimony of a social worker falls under the definition of scientific evidence (*Daubert v. Merrell Dow Pharmaceuticals, Inc.*, 1993; *E.I. DuPont DeMemours & Co. v. Robinson*, 1995). Expert testimony must be reliable to constitute scientific evidence and relevant in order to assist the judge or jury. Scientific evidence that is not grounded in the methods and procedures of science is no more than "subjective belief or unsupported speculation" (*E.I. DuPont DeMemours & Co. v. Robinson*, 1995). Unreliable evidence is of no assistance to the judge or jury and therefore inadmissible (*E.I. DuPont DeMemours & Co. v. Robinson*, 1995).

Social work is currently considered a "soft" science because it is based primarily on experience and training as opposed to the scientific method. The requirement of reliability applies to social work but with less rigor than the "hard" sciences (*Nenno v. State*, 1998). For a soft science such as social work, the court must determine (a) whether the field of expertise is a legitimate one, (b) whether the subject matter of the expert's testimony is within the scope of that field, and (c) whether the expert's testimony properly relies on and/or utilizes the principles in the field (*Nenno v. State*, 1998).

Reliability of Expert Testimony

Taylor v. Texas Department of Protective and Regulatory Services (2005) illustrates the application of the reliability test for the expert opinion of a social worker. In this termination of parental rights case, a grandmother challenged the admissibility of a home study conducted by a social worker, which recommended that a child not be placed in her home. The grandmother argued that the admission of the home study was improper because the opinions and testimony of the social worker were scientifically unreliable. The social worker testified at length about her qualifications, training, and experience and described her investigation, interviews, and conclusions in detail. The court noted:

> In fulfillment of her duties, Payne visited and took photographs of Taylor's home. She interviewed Taylor and Taylor's boyfriend Gary Russell, as well as Taylor's employer, and family and church friends. She thoroughly investigated Taylor and Russell's backgrounds and explained her findings and conclusions in the report. As a result of her investigation, Payne determined that Taylor's home was inappropriate for D.A.C. (*Taylor v. Texas Department of Protective and Regulatory Services*, 2005, p. 651)

The court further held:

> Taylor disagrees with Payne's conclusion but makes no specific criticism of Payne or the study. She does not explain how or in what manner Payne's qualifications are inadequate. Although she claims that Payne's testimony is not scientifically reliable, we find that the trial court did not abuse its discretion under the [soft science] standard. Considering Payne's education, training, and experience, and the fact that she explains her findings and conclusions in depth, we do not believe that the district court abused its discretion in holding that Payne was qualified to conduct the study and testify in support of her conclusions. Payne was certified by the Department to conduct these social studies and the governing statute expressly delegates the setting of standards for the studies to the Department. (*Taylor v. Texas Department of Protective and Regulatory Services*, 2005, p. 651–652)

Even though the *Taylor* court applied the reliability standards for the soft sciences, it offered no analysis as to whether the specific requirements of this test were met. The court apparently relied exclusively on the fact that the home study met the criteria for social studies mandated under state law. However, there is a possibility that if no evidence is offered to satisfy the specific requirements for measuring the reliability of an expert's opinion, the testimony of a social worker could be excluded.[5] Finally, in *Taylor*, the social worker's opinion was not founded on evidence-based research. As the field of social work adopts evidence-based practices[6] (Rosen & Proctor, 2002), it is very likely that the courts will require social workers to meet the more stringent reliability standards for hard sciences.

Additional Requirements for Experts

In order to qualify as an expert witness in a particular case or area of the law, a social worker may also be obligated to comply with additional requirements. For example, the Indian Child Welfare Act (ICWA) mandates that the termination of parental rights of a child who is a member of an Indian tribe must be "supported by evidence beyond a reasonable doubt, including testimony of qualified expert witnesses, that the continued custody of the child by the parent or Indian custodian is likely to result in serious emotional or physical damage to the child" (ICWA, 1978).

In *In re the Interest of D.S.P.* (1992), a Wisconsin court addressed the "qualified expert witness" requirement under the ICWA. The court noted that even though Congress did not define what qualifications a person must possess in order to be qualified as an expert witness, it intended the phrase "qualified expert witness" to apply to expertise beyond the normal social worker qualifications. In addition, the Bureau of Indian Affairs promulgated regulations that established the guidelines for qualified expert witnesses under the ICWA.[7] Despite the objections that the two social workers offered by the state in the termination of parental rights case were not qualified expert witnesses, the court concluded that both of these social workers satisfied the requisite training and experience in the field of social work as well as knowledge of the tribe and its customs to qualify as expert witnesses under the federal regulations.

Testimony

Courts impose many restrictions on the nature of testimony that may be offered by social workers as expert witnesses. As stated previously, a social worker who is qualified as an expert may give opinion testimony to assist the court or jury to understand the evidence or to determine a fact in issue (Tex. R. Evid. 702). An expert may give an opinion about the ultimate issue to be decided by the judge or jury (Tex. R. Evid. 704). For example, an expert could give an opinion about whether a child was abused or a defendant was negligent.[8] However, an expert could not give an opinion regarding the credibility of a witness, that is, whether a victim was telling the truth.[9]

When testifying as an expert, a social worker often bases his or her opinion on a combination of personal knowledge, hearsay, and expertise in a given field. An expert is permitted to testify as to his or her opinions or impressions even if the evidence on which the expert's opinion is based is inadmissible evidence, provided that it is of the type relied on by experts in a particular field (Tex. R. Evid. 703). For example, in reaching an opinion on a child's emotional well-being, a social worker ordinarily relies, in part, on a diagnostic interview of the child. The child's out-of-court statements to the social worker are clearly hearsay.[10] But even inadmissible hearsay may form the basis for a social worker's opinion if the child's statement is of a type reasonably relied by experts in the field of social work in forming opinions on the subject. If admitted, the child's hearsay statement may come into evidence only as the basis of the social worker's expert opinion rather than the truth of the statement itself.[11] However, the court could exclude the child's hearsay statement if the danger that it will be used for a purpose other than as explanation or support for the expert's opinion outweighs its value as explanation or is unfairly prejudicial (Tex. R. Evid. 705(d)).

Credibility of a Witness

State v. Catsam (1987), demonstrates the limitation on a social worker's ability to testify about the credibility of a witness. At trial in this criminal sexual assault case of a 10-year-old girl by her mother's boyfriend, a social worker and clinician testified about the truthfulness of child sexual assault victims in general. The Vermont court discussed the fine line between testimony regarding the common psychological and emotional profile observed in children who have been sexually abused and comments on the reliability and truthfulness of those children. The defendant objected to the expert's opinion that children suffering from posttraumatic stress disorder (PTSD) do not make up stories about sexual abuse. He complained that this testimony constituted an expert opinion on the credibility of a complaining witness, which usurps the jury's role in determining the credibility of witnesses, thereby depriving him of a fair trial. Even though the admissibility of profile testimony is useful in assisting the jury to assess the credibility of a complaining child witness, the court found that the challenged expert testimony went beyond the psychological and emotional profile of PTSD sufferers by stating that such children tend to tell the truth about incidents of sexual abuse. It opined:

> When viewed as a whole, the testimony of Ms. Termini was tantamount to a direct comment that the complainant was telling the truth about the alleged sexual assault for which the defendant was charged. By testifying first that sufferers of PTSD generally do not fabricate claims of sexual abuse, and then that the complainant suffers from PTSD, her testimony left one clear and unmistakable inference to be drawn: the complainant would not fabricate this allegation. The fact that the expert does not testify directly to the ultimate conclusion does not ameliorate the difficulty with the opinion on credibility. (*State v. Catsam*, 1987, pp. 187–188)

While the *Catsam* court determined that it was permissible for a social worker to testify about common traits and behaviors associated with children who have been sexually abused, it refused to allow such experts to testify about the truthfulness of sexually abused children. Instead of aiding the jury to assess the credibility of the complaining child abuse witness, this type of expert testimony may unduly influence the jury's judgment about the truthfulness of the sexual abuse victim.

Hearsay Statements

Social workers are sometimes permitted to testify about hearsay statements made by a person outside of a court proceeding. Typically, hearsay is inadmissible (Tex. R. Evid. 802). However, there are limited exceptions to the hearsay rule that allow the introduction of hearsay statements (Tex. R. Evid. 803 & 804). Examples of hearsay exceptions that have been used to allow out-of-court statements made to social workers include a statement made as a result of a startling event;[12] a person's statement about his or her present mental, emotional, or physical condition;[13] and a statement made for purposes of medical diagnosis or treatment.[14]

U.S. v. NB (1995) addressed the issue whether statements made by allegedly abused children to social workers falls under an exception to the hearsay rule. The court examined whether the hearsay statements were admissible under the "catchall" exception to the hearsay rule.[15] N.B. objected to the admission of the testimony because the hearsay testified to by the social workers was not sufficiently trustworthy. In determining the trustworthiness of this type of hearsay testimony, the court considered the training and experience of the social worker, whether the child was interviewed using open-ended questions, the age of the child and whether the child used age-appropriate language in discussing the abuse, length of time between incidents of abuse and making of hearsay statements, and whether the child repeated the same facts consistently to adults. It concluded:

> ...A.B.'s and S.B.'s statements to the three social workers contained sufficient guarantees of trustworthiness. The social workers were well trained and were strangers to the children; the children were very young and used age-appropriate language; the initial two interviewers used open-ended interview techniques; in S.B.'s case, the interview took place close on the heels of the abusive incident; and the children's stories were essentially consistent in the parts relevant to this appeal. (*U.S. v. NB*, 1995, p. 778)

From this case, it is apparent that courts will look to the experience, training, and methods of the social workers who interview children to determine in part whether a hearsay statement is sufficiently reliable to be admissible in court. Often, hearsay statements from adults whom the child has told about the abuse are vital to the state's case. Clearly, then, it is important that social workers who work with abuse victims be well trained and knowledgeable about appropriate interviewing techniques.

Confidentiality

It is common for a social worker to be called to testify about information or communications arising out of his or her professional relationship with a client. A social worker has an ethical and legal obligation to protect the confidentiality of the client during legal proceedings.[16] Unless a client authorizes the disclosure of the confidential information, a social worker must claim the privilege of confidentiality on behalf of the client (Tex. Health & Safety Code § 611.003(b)). In certain judicial or administrative proceedings, a social worker is permitted by statute to disclose confidential information about a client.[17] However, a social worker may be sued for the improper disclosure of confidential information (Tex. Health & Safety Code § 611.005).

Psychotherapist Privilege

In *Jaffee v. Redmond* (1996), the Supreme Court addressed the issue of whether the psychotherapist privilege should extend to clinical social workers. This case involved a clinical social worker who refused to disclose statements made by a police officer during counseling sessions. A federal civil rights action had been brought by the family of a man who had been killed by the police officer. The federal court rejected the social worker's and police officer's argument that the content of their communications was privileged and ordered the disclosure of the counseling notes. This was based on the fact that the federal psychotherapist privilege covered only the confidential communications made to licensed psychiatrists and psychologists.

The Supreme Court, however, ruled that the psychotherapist privilege did extend to social workers. It also found that the significant public and private interests supporting recognition of a psychotherapist privilege outweighed the evidentiary benefit that would result from the denial of the privilege. Effective psychotherapy depended on an atmosphere of confidence and trust, and therefore the mere possibility of disclosure might impede the development of the confidential relationship necessary for successful treatment. The fact that all 50 states and the District of Columbia had enacted into law some form of psychotherapist privilege supported the recognition of the psychotherapist privilege in the federal courts. The Supreme Court concluded:

> All agree that a psychotherapist privilege covers confidential communications made to licensed psychiatrists and psychologists. We have no hesitation in concluding in this case that the federal privilege should also extend to confidential communications made to licensed social workers in the course of psychotherapy. The reasons for recognizing a privilege for treatment by psychiatrists and psychologists apply with equal force to treatment by a clinical social worker such as Karen Beyer. Today, social workers provide a significant amount of mental health treatment.... Their clients often include the

poor and those of modest means who could not afford the assistance of a psychiatrist or psychologist, but whose counseling sessions serve the same public goals. Perhaps in recognition of these circumstances, the vast majority of States explicitly extend a testimonial privilege to licensed social workers. We therefore agree with the Court of Appeals that "drawing a distinction between the counseling provided by costly psychotherapists and the counseling provided by more readily accessible social workers serves no discernible public purpose." (*Jaffee v. Redmond*, 1996, pp. 15–16)

Therefore, by recognizing a psychotherapist privilege, the Supreme Court held that the conversations between the clinical social worker and the police officer and the notes taken during those counseling sessions were protected from compelled disclosure by the court.

Access to Child's Mental Health Records

Abrams v. Jones (2000) dealt with the issue of whether a parent is entitled to the mental health records of his daughter. After extended litigation between her parents over her custody, Karissa, an 11-year-old girl, was seen by a therapist. During her first session, Karrisa was reluctant to talk with the therapist because she was afraid her parents would find out what she had said to him. The therapist promised to give her parents only a general description of what was discussed without any specifics. Karissa's father and his attorney met with the therapist and requested copies of her records. After the therapist refused to provide the father with his notes of his detailed conversations with Karissa, the father filed a lawsuit to compel the release of the records. The father took the position that he had an unconditional right of access to his daughter's records. At a hearing, the therapist testified that Karissa had asked him not to reveal the details of their conversations. The trial court held that the father was entitled to the records. The therapist appealed the order.

Even though the father had the right of access to his daughter's mental health records under the Family Code, the Texas Supreme Court held that the Family Code did not override the provision in the Health and Safety Code that specifically addressed parents' rights to the mental health records of their children. Under this provision, only a parent who is acting on behalf of the child is entitled to access to the child's mental heath records. When a parent is acting on behalf of the child, a therapist could deny access to the records if the therapist determines that the release of the records would be harmful to the child's physical, mental, or emotional health. If a therapist denies a parent access to the child's records, the parent may either select another professional to treat the child who must be given the records by the therapist and may then decide to release the records to the parent or file suit against the therapist for the failure to disclose the records.

Although the father never indicated that he was seeking the records on behalf of Karissa, the Texas Supreme Court found that the father's testimony that he was "partially" motivated to seek the records by what he perceived to be his former wife's custody tactics did not conclusively prove he was not acting on behalf of his daughter. However, it did conclude that the therapist's uncontradicted testimony that it would be harmful to Karissa to release her records justified the therapist's denial of access to his detailed notes.

Hence, under Texas law, a parent does not have unfettered access to a child's mental health records irrespective of the child's circumstances or the parents' motivations. A social worker is not required to provide access to a child's confidential records if a parent who requests them is not acting on behalf of the child. An obvious example is when a parent has sexually abused a child and demands access to the child's treatment records. Such a parent cannot be deemed as acting on the child's behalf.

Immunity

Immunity from lawsuit protects social workers from having to defend themselves in trial and perhaps from paying monetary damages if liable. Immunity is defined as an exemption from liability (Garner, 1999). A social worker who in good faith files a report of abuse or neglect of a child, elderly person, or person with disability is immune from civil or criminal liability based on the report.[18] Immunity is also granted for testimony made during the course of a judicial proceeding (*Bird v. W.C.W.*, 1994). A social worker, who is an employee of a local or state government, may be immune from civil liability under governmental or qualified immunity.[19]

Statutory Immunity for Reporting Abuse

Blum v. Julian (1998) illustrates how the statutory immunity for reporting child abuse applies to social workers. In this case, a father accused of child abuse filed suit for malicious prosecution and intentional infliction of emotional distress against a counselor who had evaluated his daughters for sexual abuse. The counselor concluded that the girls had been abused. Criminal charges were filed against the father, who was acquitted at trial. The counselor claimed that she was immune from liability under the Family Code because she had a duty to report abuse. The immunity provision provides:

> A person acting in good faith who reports or assists in the investigation of a report of alleged child abuse or neglect or who testifies or otherwise participates in a judicial proceeding arising from a report, petition, or investigation of alleged child abuse or neglect is immune from civil or criminal liability that might otherwise be incurred or imposed. (*Blum v. Julian*, 1998, p. 822)

Even though the father asserted causes of action that were related to the counselor's investigation, diagnosis, and report of alleged child abuse concerning his daughters, the court found that this was the type of lawsuit the Family Code immunity provisions were designed to prevent. Hence, the counselor was entitled to immunity unless she acted in bad faith or with malice.

Qualified Immunity

Hernandez v. Texas Department of Protective and Regulatory Services (2004) demonstrates how qualified immunity provides a shield from liability for social workers employed by governmental entities. Parents brought a civil rights action against two child protective services social workers after their infant child died from suffocation in a substandard foster home. The parents alleged that the child's clearly established right to personal security and reasonably safe living conditions had been violated by his placement in a foster home where other children were suspected of having been abused and neglected. The social workers claimed that they were immune from suit based on qualified immunity.

The qualified immunity analysis is a two-stepped inquiry. First, the court must determine whether a plaintiff's allegation establishes a violation of clearly established law. Second, the court must decide whether the governmental official's conduct was objectively reasonable in light of clearly established law at the time of the incident. Even if the official's conduct violates clearly established law, the official is entitled to qualified immunity if the conduct was objectively reasonable.

In *Hernandez*, there was no dispute that the child had a constitutional right to personal security. In order for the social workers to be held liable for the death of the child, the parents had the very high burden of proving that the social workers were deliberately indifferent to the child's right to personal security. That is, "[t]he central inquiry for a determination of deliberate indifference must be whether the state social workers were aware of facts from which the inference could be drawn, that placing children in the Clauds foster home created a substantial risk of danger" (*Hernandez v. Texas Department of Protective and Regulatory Services*, 2004, p. 882). The fact that the actions and decisions of the social workers were merely inept, erroneous, ineffective, or negligent did not amount to deliberate indifference and did not divest them of qualified immunity.

Both social workers were entitled to qualified immunity. Even though the first social worker may have negligently investigated prior complaints about abuse in the foster home, the court did not find "that Lilly merely turned a blind eye to the allegations because ... records show that Lilly conducted unannounced investigations into both complaints" (*Hernandez v. Texas Department of Protective and Regulatory Services*, 2004, p. 883). The second social worker, on the other hand, was aware of two complaints of possible abuse in the foster home prior to the placement of the child. She did nothing with respect to one complaint and only contacted the CPS investigator regarding the second complaint. She visited the home about eight times over the course of 2 years and never felt there was substantial danger of harm to the children placed there. In granting her qualified immunity, the court stated:

> Hence, while the quality of state agency supervision over the care giving offered by the Clauds appears highly questionable, at best the plaintiffs have made out a case of negligence in the part of the state social workers. Based on these facts, we cannot conclude that evidence of a slight bruise on a cheek, without more, is sufficient for the plaintiffs to overcome our circuit's high burden of demonstrating deliberate indifference. (*Hernandez v. Texas Department of Protective and Regulatory Services*, 2004, p. 885)

Social workers are often faced with making difficult decisions to protect children from abuse. They need to make such determinations without fear that their opinions or actions will subject them to being sued. By providing immunity to social workers who report abuse or work for governmental entities charged with the responsibility of protecting children in foster care, the legislature and the courts have lessened the likelihood that they would be sued. However, social workers who report abuse in bad faith or consciously disregard the clearly established rights of foster children are not entitled to immunity.

Concluding Thoughts: A Judge's Perspective[20]

From the juvenile court bench, I had the privilege of hearing social workers testify on numerous occasions. Representatives from child protective services, the community mental health and mental retardation system, and the state psychiatric hospital, as well as other community organizations frequented my courtroom. As a trained social worker myself, there were times I wanted to leap off the bench to give social workers unsolicited pointers, which I shall do now.

I will touch on the obvious pointers first and briefly. First impressions are made on some of the easiest things to do. Witnesses should always be punctual. Having to wait for a witness makes for a bad initial impression. The courtroom is a formal setting and as such is best treated with the respect it deserves. Oftentimes in juvenile court, children, parents, or witnesses would expect us to change their appointment. I was often forced to explain that a court setting is not like having a haircut. Emergencies can certainly call for court settings to be reset, but it is the attorneys who must obtain a new setting from the court.

Witnesses should always be prepared. The witness chair is not the place to review records regarding a client for the first time. That information should be fresh on the mind. Refreshing memory with details is to be expected. However, when a witness cannot recall obvious facts in a case such as the age of a client or why the client was being seen, the rest of what the witness has to testify to lacks credibility.

The first time I felt the urge to jump off the bench and save a fellow social worker from humiliation was to yell at her, "Never wear flip-flops to court." Dress appropriately, as this too goes to first impressions. Social workers, who perhaps purposely dress casually to blend in while out in the field, have come to court wearing capri pants and flip-flop sandals. Needless to say, it is difficult to appear professional and be taken seriously when the attire is so inappropriately casual for the environment, in this case, the courtroom. A witness can be the most brilliant, articulate professional, but if inappropriately attired in a courtroom setting, he or she is asking to be discredited.

Social workers should know the following point more than most. Body language is key. Witnesses have heightened credibility when they can walk that fine line of appearing confident yet not cocky, humble yet not insecure. A witness who appears full of him- or herself is a turnoff to the trier of fact, be that a judge or jury. This is hard to teach as it often goes to the basic level of confidence inherent in the person who comes to the courtroom as witness. I suggest that any professional who faces the possibility of being a witness in a court proceeding should find the time to observe witnesses testifying in court. Potential witnesses should think about response patterns and body language as a vehicle for preparation to testify as much as they should prepare by reviewing the material in their case files.

I have learned that a witness who does poorly in a courtroom setting is not necessarily a professional who performs poorly in the field. I have equally found that the reciprocal is true. I have tried not to be critical of those who perform poorly while under the immense pressure of direct and cross-examination. The courtroom is not everyone's cup of tea. Social workers may likely be in the field they have chosen for reasons that do not blend with comfort in an adversarial environment. The courtroom is like any other place in life.

The more familiar one becomes with the atmosphere, the more relaxed and therefore convincing one is as a witness. Unfortunately, regular Court TV viewers cannot glean from the television that level of comfort that can be obtained only by being in court and participating in its procedures. Observing the process and ultimately testifying are the best lessons available. Like everything in life, with time and experience come a comfort level that turns into confidence and self-assuredness, qualities that make any witness credible.

NOTES

1. This section's reliance on Texas law is due solely to the fact that the authors practice law in Texas. Since comparable case law and statutes exist in other jurisdictions, the Texas cases and statutes cited herein are only for illustrative purposes.

2. In order to testify as a fact witness, evidence must be offered that the social worker has personal knowledge about the matter that he or she is testifying about (TEX. R. EVID. 602). See *Oliver v. State* (2000), in which a psychotherapist was not allowed to testify about a child's past history of sexual abuse in a criminal case because she had no knowledge of the past abuse; *In re J.G.* (2003), in which a probation officer was permitted to testify about the contents of his probation report; and *Salazar v. State* (2004), in which counselors of sexually abused children testified that the children expressed feeling sad, scared, embarrassed, and nervous during counseling sessions.

3. TEX. R. EVID. 702. See *Key v. State* (1989), in which testimony of a rape counselor was permitted in a date rape case in determining whether the rape victim consented to have intercourse with the defendant; and *Scuguza v. State* (1997), in which testimony of a program services director of a battered woman's shelter was allowed in a domestic violence case to explain why some victims of spousal abuse eventually recant their accusations.

4. TEX. R. EVID. 702. See *Rodriguez v. State* (2002), in which a victim services coordinator, who was employed by different rape crisis centers for 4 years, received specialized training in rape trauma and taught classes on rape trauma to law enforcement, was qualified to testify as an expert in a sexual assault case; and *Maldonado v. Maldonado* (2003), in which a private therapist, who had a bachelor of arts degree in sociology, a master's degree in clinical social work, and an advanced practitioner license from the state of Texas with experience as a social worker in child adoption, child protective services, and mental health and as a therapist in both the private and public sectors, was qualified to testify that the husband could provide adequate care for the children in a divorce action.

5. For instance, in *In re K.L.R.* (2005), the court held that testimony of a licensed professional counselor that a mother be given only supervised visitation with her child based on the results of a Minnesota Multiphasic Personal Inventory and interview of the mother and observations of the child at school and home did not meet the soft science reliability test for an expert. This was due to the fact that there was no evidence that counseling was a legitimate field of expertise and that the counselor's testimony properly relied on and/or utilized principles in her field. Despite this, the court refused to reverse the trial court's decision because the recommendations of the counselor were not followed and the testimony of the counselor was similar to the testimony presented by other witnesses.

6. Evidence-based practice is defined as the use of the best scientific evidence available in deciding how to intervene with clients. In other words, "practitioners will select interventions on the basis of their empirically demonstrated links to desired outcomes" (Rosen & Proctor, 2002, p. 743).

7. D.4. Qualified Expert Witnesses

    (a) Removal of an Indian child from his or her family must be based on competent testimony from one or more experts qualified to speak specifically to the issue of whether continued custody by the parents or Indian custodians is likely to result in serious physical or emotional damage to the child.

    (b) Persons with the following characteristics are most likely to meet the requirements for a qualified expert witness for purposes of Indian child custody proceedings:

        (i) A member of the Indian child's tribe who is recognized by the tribal community as knowledgeable in tribal customs as they pertain to family organization and childrearing practices.

(ii) A lay expert witness having substantial experience in the delivery of child and family services to Indians, and extensive knowledge of prevailing social and cultural standards and childrearing practices within the Indian child's tribe.

(iii) A professional person having substantial education and experience in the area of his or her specialty.

8. See *Perez v. State* (2003), in which a psychiatrist was permitted to testify as an expert to the characteristics of sexually abused children.

9. See *Cohn v. State* (1991) and *Burns v. State* (2003), in which a psychologist's testimony that the results of tests suggest that the child was answering questions in an open, nondefensive, and truthful manner did not constitute an impermissible comment on the child's truthfulness.

10. Hearsay is defined as a statement, other than one made by a person while testifying in court, offered in evidence to prove the truth of the matter asserted (TEX. R. EVID. 801(d)).

11. See *Decker v. Hatfield* (1990). In this child custody case, a statement made to a psychologist by a child that he preferred to live with his mother was admitted in evidence because it served as the basis of the psychologist's opinion that the child should be placed with his mother.

12. See *Cortez v. State* (2003), in which a statement made by a victim on the morning of the assault to a rape crisis counselor that she was physically and sexually abused was admissible.

13. See *Salazar v. State* (2004), in which children's statements to a counselor about how they felt about being sexually abused were admissible.

14. See *In re M.G.* (2002), in which statements made to professional counselors by a child that the child told her mother about sexual abuse and that the man who lived with the mother tried to stab someone in her mother's bedroom was admissible in a termination of parental rights case.

15. Federal Rule of Evidence 803(24) states:

> Other exceptions. A statement not specifically covered by any of the foregoing exceptions but having equivalent circumstantial guarantees of trustworthiness, if the court determines that (A) the statement is offered as evidence of a material fact; (B) the statement is more probative on the point for which it is offered than any other evidence which the proponent can procure through reasonable efforts; and (C) the general purposes of these rules and the interests of justice will best be served by admission of the statement into evidence. However, a statement may not be admitted under this exception unless the proponent of it makes known to the adverse party sufficiently in advance of the trial or hearing to provide the adverse party with a fair opportunity to meet it, the proponent's intention to offer the statement and the particulars of it, including the name and address of the declarant.

16. The National Association of Social Worker's Code of Ethics 1.07 (j) provides:

> Social workers should protect the confidentiality of clients during legal proceedings to the extent permitted by law. When a court of law or other legally authorized body orders social workers to disclose confidential or privileged information without a client's consent and such disclosure could cause harm to the client, social workers should request that the court withdraw the order or limit the order as narrowly as possible or maintain the records under seal, unavailable for public inspection.

> Similarly, under the social work licensing regulations, a social worker shall safeguard the client's right to confidentiality within the limits of the law (22 Tex. Admin. Code §781.401(8)) and shall not disclose any confidential information except as provided in the Texas Health and Safety Code, Chapter 611, or other applicable state or federal statutes or rules (22 Tex. Admin. Code §781.402(s)). These confidentiality laws include mental health records (Tex. Health & Safety Code §§611.001 et seq.), substance abuse records (42 C.F.R. §§2.1–2.67), medical records (45 C.F.R. Parts 160-164), education records (34 C.F.R. §§99.1 et seq.), mental retardation records (Tex. Health & Safety Code §§595.001- 595.010), and AIDS/HIV records (Tex. Health & Safety Code §81.046).

17. Such proceedings include a judicial or administrative proceeding brought by the client against the social worker, including malpractice action; a judicial or administrative proceeding where the client waived his right to the privilege of confidentiality in writing; a judicial proceeding affecting the parent–child relationship; a judicial proceeding in which, after having been informed that the

communication would not be privileged, the client made communications to a social worker in the course of a court-ordered examination; any criminal proceeding as otherwise permitted by law; involuntary commitment proceeding for court-ordered treatment; and a legal proceeding where the court or agency has issued an order or subpoena (Tex. Health & Safety Code §611.006).

18. Tex. Fam. Code §261.106 (child abuse or neglect); Tex. Hum. Res. Code §48.054 (elder or disabled abuse).

19. Public employees may claim governmental or official immunity if they are acting within the scope of their authority for the good faith discharge of their duties that involve personal deliberation, decision, and judgment. Public officials are entitled to qualified immunity if they adhere to their duties and do not violate clearly established constitutional or statutory rights. (Garner, 1999).

20. Coauthor Benesch is a former associate judge for the Travis County District Courts in Texas. She has presided over juvenile delinquency, child protective services, and family law cases.

RESOURCES AND REFERENCES

Abrams v. Jones, 35 S.W.3d 620 (Tex. 2000).

Barker, R. L., & Branson, D. M. (2000). *Forensic social work: Legal aspects of professional practice* (2nd ed., pp. 4–5). Binghamton, NY: Haworth Press.

Bird v. W.C.W., 868 S.W.2d 767,770–771 (Tex. 1994).

Blum v. Julian, 977 S.W.2d 819 (Tex. App. Fort Worth 1998, no pet.).

Brownell, P., & Roberts, A. R. (1999). A century of forensic social work: Bridging the past to the present. *Social Work, 44*(4), 359–369.

Burns v. State, 122 S.W.2d 434, 437 (Tex. App. Houston [1st Dist.] 2003, pet. ref'd).

Cohn v. State, 804 S.W.2d 572, 575 (Tex. App. Houston [14th Dist.] 1991, writ denied).

Cortez v. State, 2003 WL 21664888 (Tex. App. Amarillo 2003).

Daubert v. Merrell Dow Pharmaceuticals, Inc., 509 U.S. 579 (1993).

Decker v. Hatfield, 798 S.W.2d 637 (Tex. App. Eastland 1990, writ dism'd).

E.I. DuPont DeMemours & Co. v. Robinson, 923 S.W.2d 549 (Tex. 1995).

Garner, B. A. (Ed.). (1999). *Black's law dictionary* (7th ed., p. 752). St. Paul, MN: West Publishing.

Hernandez v. Tex. Protective & Regulatory Servs., 380 F.3d 872 (5th Cir. 2004).

House Health & Human Services Comm., Bill Analysis, Tex. S.B. 1426, 73rd Leg. R.S. (1993).

Indian Child Welfare Act, 25 U.S.C. § 1912(f) (1978).

In re Gault, 387 U.S. 1 (1967).

In re Interest of D.S.P., 480 N.W.2d 234 (Wis. 1992).

In re J.G., 112 S.W. 3d 256, 261 (Tex. App. Corpus Christi 2003, no pet.).

In re K.L.R., 162 S.W.3d 291, 307 (Tex. App. Tyler 2005, no pet.).

In re M.G., WL 31599020 (2002).

Jaffee v. Redmond, 518 U.S. 1 (1996).

Key v. State, 765 SW2d 848, 850 (Tex. App. Dallas 1989, pet. ref'd).

Maldonado v. Maldonado, 2003 WL 21653876 (Tex. App. San Antonio 2003).

Nenno v. State, 970 S. W. 2d 549 (Tex. Crim. App. 1998).

Oliver v. State, 32 S.W.3d 300, 304 (Tex. App. San Antonio 2000, pet. ref'd).

Perez v. State, 113 S.W.3d 819, 832–835 (Tex. App. Austin 2003, pet. ref'd).

Rodriguez v. State, 2002 WL 2027328 (Tex. App. El Paso 2002).

Rosen, A., & Proctor, E. K. (2002). Standards for evidenced-based social work practice: The role of replicable and appropriate interventions, outcomes, and practice guidelines. In A. R. Roberts & G. J. Greene (Eds.), *Social workers' desk reference* (pp. 743–747). New York: Oxford University Press.

Salazar v. State, 127 S.W.3d 355 (Tex. App. Houston [14th Dist.] 2004, pet. ref'd).

Scuguza v. State, 949 S.W.2d 360, 363 (Tex. App. San Antonio 1997, no pet.).

State v. Catsam, 534 A.2d 184 (Vt. 1987).

Taylor v. Tex. Dept. of Protective & Regulatory Servs., 160 S.W.3d 641 (Tex. App. Austin 2005, pet. denied).

Tex. Fam. Code § 107.031.

Tex. Fam. Code § 261.106.

Tex. Health & Safety Code § 611.003(b).

Tex. Health & Safety Code § 611.005.

Tex. Health & Safety Code § 611.006.
Tex. Hum. Res. Code § 48.054.
TEX. R. EVID. 702.
TEX. R. EVID. 703.
TEX. R. EVID. 704.
TEX. R. EVID. 705 (d).
TEX. R. EVID. 802.
TEX. R. EVID. 803 & 804.
U.S. v. NB, 59 F.3d 771 (8th Cir. 1995).

Multisystemic Treatment of Serious Clinical Problems in Youths and Their Families

14

Scott W. Henggeler
Ashli J. Sheidow
Terry Lee

Overview

Multisystemic therapy (MST) is an intensive family- and community-based treatment that has been applied to a wide range of serious clinical problems presented by youths, including chronic and violent criminal behavior, substance abuse, sexual offending, psychiatric emergencies (i.e., homicidal, suicidal, psychotic), and, recently, serious health care problems. Youths with these types of serious clinical problems present significant personal and societal (e.g., crime victimization) costs and, due to their high rates of expensive out-of-home placements, consume a grossly disproportionate share of the nation's mental health treatment resources. Across these clinical populations, the overarching goals of MST programs are to decrease rates of antisocial behavior and other clinical problems, improve functioning (e.g., family relations, school performance), and reduce use of out-of-home placements (e.g., incarceration, residential treatment, hospitalization).

Portions of this chapter were published previously in *Evidence-Based Psychotherapies for Children and Adolescents*, edited by A. E. Kazdin and J. R. Weisz, 2003, New York: Guilford Press. We greatly appreciate the permission from Guilford Press to reprint this material. In addition, revisions of this chapter were supported by National Institute on Drug Abuse Grants K23DA015658, R01DA08029, R01DA10079, R01DA08029, and R01DA13066; National Institute on Alcoholism and Alcohol Abuse and the Center for Substance Abuse Treatment Grant R01AA122202; National Institute of Mental Health Grant R01MH65414; and the Annie E. Casey Foundation.

315

Theoretical Framework

With roots in social ecological (Bronfenbrenner, 1979) and family systems (Haley, 1976; Minuchin, 1974) theories, MST views youths as embedded within multiple interconnected systems, including the nuclear family, extended family, neighborhood, school, peer culture, and community. The juvenile justice, child welfare, and mental health systems also might be involved. In assessing the major determinants of identified problems, the clinician considers the reciprocal and bidirectional nature of the influences between a youth and his or her family and social network as well as the indirect effects of more distal influences (e.g., parental workplace). For a treatment to be effective, the risk factors across these systems must be identified and addressed. Hence, the "ecological validity" of assessing and treating youth in the natural environment is emphasized under the assumption that favorable outcomes are more likely to be generalized and sustained when skills are practiced and learned where the youth and family actually live.

Conceptual Assumptions

Several assumptions are critical to the design and implementation of MST interventions.

Multidetermined Nature of Serious Clinical Problems

As suggested from the social-ecological theoretical model and supported by decades of correlational and longitudinal research in the area of youth antisocial behavior, such behavior is multidetermined from the reciprocal interplay of individual, family, peer, school, and community factors. As such, MST interventions assess and address these potential risk factors in a comprehensive, yet individualized, fashion.

Caregivers as Key to Long-Term Positive Outcomes

Ideally the caregiver is a parent, but another adult (e.g., grandparent, aunt, uncle, sibling) with an enduring emotional tie to the youth can serve in this role. Often, other caring adults from the youth's ecology are identified to provide social support as well. Professional supports are introduced only after exhausting resources in the family's natural ecology. Paid professionals may genuinely care, but invariably leave the youth's life for reasons such as professional advancement or termination of treatment. Thus, by focusing clinical attention on developing the caregiver's ability to parent effectively and strengthening the family's indigenous support system, treatment gains are more likely to be maintained.

Integration of Evidence-Based Practices

MST incorporates empirically based treatments insofar as they exist. Thus, MST programs include cognitive behavioral approaches, the behavior therapies, behavioral parent training, pragmatic family therapies, and certain pharmacological interventions that have a reasonable evidence base (U.S. Department of Health and Human Services [DHHS], 1999). As suggested by other assumptions noted in this section, however, these treatments are delivered in a considerably different context than usual. For example, consistent with the view that the caregiver is key to achieving long-term outcomes, an MST cognitive behavioral intervention would ideally be delivered by the caregiver under the consultation of the therapist.

Intensive Services That Overcome Barriers to Service Access

In light of the serious clinical problems presented by youths and their families in MST programs (i.e., referral criteria include high-risk of out-of-home placement) and the high dropout rates of such youths and families in traditional treatment programs, clinicians provide intensive services with a commitment to overcome barriers to service access. The home-based model of service delivery employed in MST facilitates the provision of intensive services and overcomes barriers to service access, as described subsequently.

Rigorous Quality Assurance System

Treatment fidelity is needed to achieve desired clinical outcomes. Hence, intensive quality assurance protocols are built into all MST programs, which differentiates MST from most mental health practices. The quality assurance system, which includes training and monitoring components, is detailed subsequently. Together, these quality assurance components aim to enhance clinical outcomes through promoting treatment fidelity. Empirical validation of several key aspects of the MST quality assurance system also is described in more detail subsequently.

Characteristics of MST Treatment

Treatment Principles

The complexity of serious clinical problems presented by adolescents and their families requires considerable flexibility in the design and delivery of interventions. As such, MST is operationalized through adherence to nine core treatment principles that guide treatment planning (see Table 14.1).

Treatment Format

MST works with youth, family members, and all pertinent systems in which the youth is involved including peers, school, extended family, family supports, the neighborhood, community groups, and other involved agencies such as child welfare or juvenile justice. Early in treatment, specific measurable overarching goals and functionally meaningful outcomes are set in collaboration with the family and, as appropriate, other stakeholders. MST overarching goals are broken down into measurable weekly goals. Any person or agency that may influence attainment of these goals is engaged by the therapist and caregiver with specific interventions designed to encourage actions that will facilitate goal achievement.

Table 14.1	MST Treatment Principles

1. **Finding the fit:** The primary purpose of assessment is to understand the fit between identified problems and their broader systemic context and how identified problems make sense in the context of the youth's social ecology.

2. **Positive and strength focused:** Therapeutic contacts emphasize the positive and use systemic strengths as levers for positive change. Focusing on family strengths has numerous advantages, such as decreasing negative affect, building feelings of hope, identifying protective factors, decreasing frustration by emphasizing problem solving, and enhancing caregivers' confidence.

3. **Increasing responsibility:** Interventions are designed to promote responsible behavior and decrease irresponsible behavior among family members. The emphasis on enhancing responsible behavior is contrasted with the usual pathology focus of mental health providers and kindles hope for change.

4. **Present focused, action oriented, and well defined:** Interventions are present focused and action oriented, targeting specific and well-defined problems. Such interventions enable treatment participants to track the progress of treatment and provide clear criteria to measure success. Family members are expected to work actively toward goals by focusing on present-oriented solutions (versus gaining insight or focusing on the past). Clear goals also delineate criteria for treatment termination.

5. **Targeting sequences:** Interventions target sequences of behavior within and between multiple systems that maintain the identified problems. Treatment is aimed at changing family interactions in ways that promote responsible behavior and broaden family links with indigenous prosocial support systems.

6. **Developmentally appropriate:** Interventions are developmentally appropriate and fit the developmental needs of the youth. A developmental emphasis stresses building youth competencies in peer relations and acquiring academic and vocational skills that will promote a successful transition to adulthood.

7. **Continuous effort:** Interventions are designed to require daily or weekly effort by family members, presenting youth and family with frequent opportunities to demonstrate their commitment. Advantages of intensive and multifaceted efforts to change include more rapid problem resolution, earlier identification of treatment nonadherence, continuous evaluation of outcomes, more frequent corrective interventions, more opportunities for family members to experience success, and family empowerment as members orchestrate their own changes.

8. **Evaluation and accountability:** Intervention effectiveness is evaluated continuously from multiple perspectives with MST team members assuming accountability for overcoming barriers to successful outcomes. MST does not label families as "resistant, not ready for change, or unmotivated." This approach avoids blaming the family and places the responsibility for positive treatment outcomes on the MST program.

9. **Generalization:** Interventions are designed to promote treatment generalization and long-term maintenance of therapeutic change by empowering caregivers to address family members' needs across multiple systemic contexts. The caregiver is viewed as the key to long-term success. Family members make most of the changes, with MST therapists acting as consultants, advisors, and advocates.

Strong engagement with the family is essential for successful outcomes, and the MST treatment model incorporates strategies to encourage cooperative partnering. Families are treated with respect and are assumed to be doing the best they can. Other youth-associated systems are viewed as vital partners in the treatment process. The MST team focuses on system strengths (Principle 2) and is responsive to families' needs. Barriers to engagement are evaluated continuously and addressed as needed (Principles 1 and 8).

Model of Service Delivery

MST is provided via a home-based model of service delivery, and the use of such a model has been crucial to the high engagement and low dropout rates obtained in MST outcome studies (e.g., Henggeler, Pickrel, Brondino, & Crouch, 1996). The critical service delivery characteristics utilized in MST include the following:

1 Low caseloads to allow intensive services: An MST team consists of two to four full-time therapists, one half-time supervisor per team, and appropriate organizational support. Each therapist works with four to six families at a time. The therapist is the team's main point of contact for the youth, family, and all involved agencies and systems.
2 Delivery of services in community settings (e.g., home, school, neighborhood center) to overcome barriers to service access, facilitate family engagement in the clinical process, and provide more valid assessment and outcome data.
3 Time-limited duration of treatment (4 to 6 months) to promote efficiency, self-sufficiency, and cost effectiveness.
4 24 hour/day and 7 day/week availability of therapists to provide services when needed and to respond to crises. MST is proactive, and plans are developed to prevent or mitigate crises. Crisis response can be taxing, but most families are appreciative, and a supportive response can enhance engagement. Moreover, the capacity to respond to crises is critical to achieving a primary goal of MST programs—preventing out-of-home placements.

Skills and Achievements Emphasized in Treatment

Interventions are designed to be consistent with the nine core principles of MST, to be empirically based whenever possible, and to emphasize behavior change in the youth's natural environment that empowers caregivers and youth. A more extensive description of the range of problems addressed and clinical procedures used in MST can be found in the MST treatment manuals (Henggeler, Schoenwald, Borduin, Rowland, & Cunningham, 1998; Henggeler, Schoenwald, Rowland, & Cunningham, 2002).

Family Interventions

Engagement and assessment usually begin with meeting the family and youth to explain MST philosophies and principles. In the MST model, the therapist is more closely aligned with the caregivers, relative to the youth. Allying and engaging with caregivers is a critical component of the initial phase of treatment. Youth also are involved in the intake process, but, as might be expected, some are reluctant to engage in a process that usually aims to place them under increased parental control. Each household member's perspective of the presenting problem and goals for treatment are solicited. A genogram is created, and information is obtained about the family, other people living in the home, extended family members, family supports, and the quality of important relationships. Guided by information obtained from the initial family meeting and other referring agencies, the MST therapist meets with these individuals or other organizations (e.g., school personnel, community members) to gain their perspectives. Each system is assessed for strengths and weaknesses, and values of the ecology are incorporated into the treatment plan. Based on these initial data, hypotheses are generated concerning the factors that might facilitate goal achievement, serve as barriers to progress, and maintain negative behaviors. Hypotheses are testable, and hypothesis testing establishes the basis for interventions.

The MST therapist and treatment team must be well informed about research pertaining to family patterns and effective interventions relevant to youth antisocial behavior and related clinical problems. Family risk factors for antisocial behavior, for example, include low caregiver monitoring, low warmth, ineffective discipline, high conflict, caregiver psychopathology, and family criminal behavior, while protective factors include secure attachment to caregivers, supportive family environment, and marital harmony. Thus, the therapist must be capable of assessing the affective bond between caregiver and youth, parental control strategies on a permissive to restrictive continuum, and instrumental aspects of parenting such as structure and consistency. These family processes are assessed with direct questioning, observation, and response to homework assignments. Subsequent interventions aim to optimize strengths that already exist and develop competencies in critical areas that are lacking.

The MST therapist chooses specific parenting interventions with the assistance of the MST supervisor and expert consultant. The assessment of the fit of the particular problem to be addressed and the process of the implementation are pivotal to the selection. In a supportive and nonblaming manner, MST therapists praise positive aspects of parenting (Principle 2), while diplomatically identifying current parenting practices that might be changed for the benefit of all. For example, in a situation in which increased disciplinary structure is needed, interventions likely would occur in three stages. First, the caregivers learn to develop clearly defined rules for observable youth behavior. Second, the caregivers establish rewards and consequences that closely, consistently, and naturally are connected to youth behavior. Third, caregivers learn to monitor their child's compliance with the rules, including when the youth is not being observed directly by the caregiver. In so doing, guidelines specified by Munger (1993, 1998) often are followed. Expected behaviors are clearly defined and specified so the youth and everyone involved with the youth can determine whether the behavior has occurred. The rules should be posted in a public place and reinforced 100% of the time, in an emotionally neutral manner. Praise should accompany the dispensation of rewards. When two caregivers are involved, rules should be mutually agreed on and enforced by both caregivers. Consequences need to be meaningful and appropriate to the specific youth. That is, rewards need to be items or activities that the particular youth is motivated to earn, while negative consequences should be disliked. Basic privileges such as food, clothing, shelter, and love are to be provided unconditionally and are not withheld or varied in their availability to the youth. Activities that promote prosocial development (e.g., sports teams) are considered growth activities and typically should not be withheld. Because of changes in the system or understanding of the fit, components of the behavior plan such as the target behaviors, rewards, and consequences need to be continuously assessed and modified when appropriate.

Importantly, frequent barriers to the success of these family interventions pertain to caregiver difficulties such as substance abuse or untreated mental illness. In such cases, the therapist's primary task is to remove these barriers to caregiver effectiveness by treating them directly. For example, a substance-abusing parent might be treated with a variation of the community reinforcement approach (Budney & Higgins, 1998), which has a strong empirical base in the area of adult substance abuse (Roozen et al., 2004). Similarly, when caregiver effectiveness is compromised due to high levels of stress, the therapist works closely with the caregiver to identify sources of stress that might be modified and to develop strategies for such change. For example, a single working parent might have significant daily demands from employment responsibilities, caring for younger children, and providing support for an elderly relative. This parent might not have the time and energy needed to provide the high level of monitoring and supervision a problem adolescent often requires. Hence, the therapist would collaborate with the parent in developing and implementing strategies to achieve the desired goals (e.g., engaging the adolescent in structured after-school activities, enlisting other supports to help with the elderly relative). When barriers to effectiveness are removed, the caregiver is then in a position to function as the key change agent.

Peer Interventions

Peer relations affect youth functioning in many ways. Socialization with antisocial or substance-using peers is associated with these respective behaviors, while involvement with prosocial peers is a protective factor. Assessment of peer relations involves interviewing caregivers, school personnel, siblings, and the youth, as well as observation. The MST therapist attends to the number and quality of the peer relations, reputations of peers, social and academic functioning of peers, homogeneity versus heterogeneity of the peer group, monitoring of peers by their respective caregivers, and the caregivers' familiarity with youth's peers and their parents.

Limited or poor social skills will contribute to rejection and isolation from peers. The MST therapist should assess the caregiver's social skills and address any caregiver factors that may be contributing to youth socialization difficulties. Some awkwardness may be due to a basic lack of skills or cognitive distortions. Depending on the problem, youth may respond to direct instruction, coaching techniques, and role-playing as described by Forman (1993), for example; the MST therapist will also help the caregiver to assist the youth as indicated.

Conversely, youth who are rejected actively are at risk for externalizing behaviors. Peer groups can contribute directly to the youth's disruptive behavior through diverting youth from more socially acceptable activities, endorsing antisocial behavior as the group norm, providing access to drugs, and encouraging resistance to caregiver monitoring. If the youth is socializing with negative peers, the MST therapist will help the caregiver to have calm discussions about potential negative consequences and avoid criticizing the peers valued by the youth. Interventions to back up these conversations might include systemic monitoring of the youth, caregiver and supportive adults searching places where the deviant peer group tends to socialize if the youth is unaccounted for, asking law enforcement to assist with checking and monitoring, and disallowing telephone contact with antisocial peers. Thus, a relatively stringent plan is put into place to provide significant sanctions for continued association with problem peers. Concomitantly, MST therapists support caregivers to encourage and reinforce youth contact with prosocial peers and participation in socially accepted and monitored activities. Critical to the success of these interventions is the proactive development of plans to ensure implementation of positive and negative consequences contingent on the youth's peer interactions. Such plans often include the therapist and several adults in the family's social network.

School Interventions

School is critical for both academic and social development. Risk factors for disruptive behavior in school include limited intellectual functioning, low achievement, learning disabilities, chaotic family functioning, negative family–school linkage, low commitment to education, and chaotic school environment. Protective factors include high intellectual functioning, commitment to schooling, and good caregiver–school communication. During all school interventions, MST therapists must respect the school's policies and procedures.

A frequent goal of treatment is to develop a collaborative relationship between the youth's caregivers and school personnel, in a context that typically has grown conflictual. The therapist supports the caregiver in interacting with the school but becomes directly involved if necessary. For instance, when there is a family–school conflict impasse, the MST therapist might intervene in a diplomatic manner, emphasizing the best interests of the youth. The MST therapist performs a careful assessment of the nature of the conflict and understands the views of all involved parties to help establish trust with both the family and the school. Unseen efforts of the school can be conveyed to the caregivers, and vice versa, while some misperceptions can be challenged gently. Common ground is highlighted, with a goal of setting up collaborative interactions between the school and caregivers. Ideally, these collaborations emphasize positive, constructive changes that can help the youth and avoid revisiting prior decisions that cannot be changed or assigning blame for any real or perceived negative events. Importantly, arrangements often are made in which the parent is responsible for implementing contingencies at home based on youth behavior in school.

Individually Oriented Interventions

Whether for youth or caregivers, MST individually oriented interventions always occur in the context of a larger systemic treatment plan. Individually oriented interventions can be categorized as those addressing any of the following: continued problematic behaviors after the implementation of systemic interventions; continued problematic behaviors that occur in the face of psychiatric disorders that are being optimally treated from medication and systems perspectives; sequelae of victimization that relate to the presenting problems; and situations where extensive efforts to engage caregivers in changing their behavior are unsuccessful, and the youth will continue to live in the home.

Cognitive-behavioral therapy (CBT) is an individual treatment approach that frequently is used in MST individual interventions. Considering the range of all individual treatments provided to youth, the empirical support for CBT for anxiety, depression, and externalizing conditions is relatively strong (Weisz & Jensen, 1999). CBT is consistent with MST in that it is present focused and action oriented (Principle 4), is individualized to the developmental level of the youth (Principle 6), is evaluated from multiple perspectives (Principle 8), and provides a skill that potentially is generalizable (Principle 9). Briefly, CBT involves first evaluating the youth's cognitions in areas related to the identified problem. This may include examining the youth's planning in achieving an objective, attributions regarding the motivation of others, social problem solving, perspective taking, or assessment of consequences of actions. The relationships between these cognitions and the youth's feelings and behaviors also are evaluated. Cognitive deficiencies and distortions are assessed as they apply to the presenting problem. Cognitive deficiencies are addressed with the acquisition of additional skills. When cognitive distortions are identified, they are tested; underlying maladaptive assumptions are delineated, and the validity of the maladaptive assumptions is tested. More adaptive cognitions and behaviors are then learned. Fortunately, several excellent resources for CBT interventions for various conditions are available (e.g., Forman, 1993; Kendall, 2005), and MST therapists are referred to and supervised in the implementation of these works as appropriate.

Psychiatric Interventions

MST therapists must be familiar with and able to recognize youth and adult conditions that may respond to psychiatric medication. For example, attention-deficit/hyperactivity disorder (ADHD) often is comorbid with disruptive behaviors, and the prognosis of comorbid ADHD and conduct disorder is associated with more negative outcomes than conduct disorder or ADHD alone. Stimulant medications are well studied, and positive effects have been demonstrated for on-task behavior and various externalizing behaviors, while side effects also are characterized well and generally are manageable.

If the MST treatment team feels that symptoms consistent with ADHD are interfering with goal achievement, a stimulant trial may be indicated. If reluctant to follow through on the referral, the feelings of the family should be respected, while determining the fit and appropriate interventions. MST teams should seek child and adolescent psychiatrists who are systems oriented and well versed in empirically based treatments. The MST therapist can promote a positive working relationship by supporting youth and family follow-through with appointments and medication compliance, while helping empower youth and caregivers to collaborate actively and assertively with the psychiatrist. After establishing a diagnosis of ADHD, a double-blind placebo trial may address some family concerns regarding efficacy and short-term side effects. Research suggests that for optimal pharmacological treatment of ADHD, ongoing medication management is needed (Vitiello et al., 2001).

Interventions for Increasing Family Social Supports

A major goal of MST is to develop and maintain social supports for the youth and family in order to promote sustainability of treatment gains. Youth disruptive behavior is associated with increased need for family supports and resources, yet many of the families referred to MST have few resources. Low socioeconomic status, social disorganization, and lack of supportive structures in and of themselves are risk factors for disruptive behavior (Loeber & Farrington, 1998). Conversely, resources can help families manage the challenges of raising children as well as mitigate the negative effects of many hardships (Wolkow & Ferguson, 2001).

Assessment of family social supports occurs during the assessment of other youth-involved systems. Social supports can be characterized by type of support—instrumental, emotional, appraisal, and informational (Unger & Wandersman, 1985)—and also on a continuum ranging from informal proximal relationships to more distal professional and formal systems. The preference is to develop more proximal informal supports, as these are likely to be more responsive, accessible, and maintainable over time. To maintain long-term informal social supports, families who receive support must reciprocate. For example, a neighbor might be enlisted to help monitor the after-school time of a problem adolescent with working parents, and in return, the adolescent might cut the neighbor's lawn each week. Even with strong indigenous support, however, family needs can sometimes overwhelm the informal support system, necessitating the use of more formal supports. Hence, the MST treatment team should have a good understanding of the available formal supports in the community.

Treatment Termination

The average duration of MST treatment is 4 to 6 months. MST typically ends in one of two ways. Either the goals are met, by mutual agreement of the therapist and family and, as appropriate, stakeholders; or the goals are unmet, but it is felt that treatment has reached a point of diminishing returns for time invested. It is important for the MST team to recognize situations where progress is not being made, despite varied attempts to address barriers to effective change. In such cases, the decision to terminate MST services will contribute to the cost effectiveness of MST and provide the family an opportunity to try another type of treatment that might be helpful.

Approximately two thirds of MST cases in community settings end with successful achievement of the goals specified by the family and influential stakeholders. The latter stage of MST is spent preparing the youth, family, and stakeholders for the withdrawal of MST services, and termination is openly discussed. Caregiver competence is highlighted, and mechanisms for maintaining progress are identified. If there is a need for further services, appropriate referrals are made. However, it should not be assumed that families need ongoing services.

Sample Case Summary

Markus, a 15-year-old male, was referred to an MST program by his probation officer for assault and property destruction. He also engaged in verbal and physical aggression toward his primary caregiver (his grandmother, Ms. K). Markus had a 3-year arrest history, with the most recent arrest following an argument with a peer that led to a physical altercation resulting in the peer being hospitalized for injuries. Markus often broke curfew to hang out with his friends and had been arrested with them for throwing rocks through windows of abandoned buildings. At home, Markus and his sister, Amy, rarely followed household rules. The family often argued loudly with one another. Ms. K had attempted to discipline Markus many times by removing privileges or valued items; however, most attempted discipline resulted in Markus being physically aggressive or leaving home. Ms. K had been widowed for 19 years, after her husband died in a work-related accident. Following the death of Ms. K's husband, Ms. K's daughter moved back home and subsequently gave birth to Markus and, 3 years later, to Amy. The children's mother died 6 years ago from pneumonia. Ms. K did not know the father of either child.

As indicated by the MST analytical process, the MST therapist began treatment by conducting an initial assessment with Markus and his family members to identify each person's desired outcomes. The therapist also identified other key participants in the youth's ecology including the probation officer, Ms. Lynch (a neighbor with whom the children spent Wednesday nights when Ms. K worked late), Aunt Sue and Uncle Tim (who "took Markus and Amy some weekends" for respite), and Mr. Alvarez (the school's Spanish teacher, who had taken interest in Markus and with whom Markus enjoyed spending time). The MST therapist worked to engage these indigenous supports and asked about their desired treatment outcomes for Markus. She and the family devised overarching goals for treatment that encompassed both the referral behaviors and the key participants' desired outcomes, and methods for monitoring progress toward these goals. The overarching goals focused on (a) eliminating Markus' criminal behavior and fighting in the community; (b) increasing Markus's and Amy's adherence to household rules, curfew, and chore list; and (c) improving the family's communication and cohesion.

Consistent with the nine MST principles, the therapist identified numerous strengths in Markus' ecology. In addition to being engaged with several supportive adults, the therapist identified Markus's interest in Hispanic culture and his enjoyment in spending time at his aunt and uncle's home as important strengths. Markus also displayed capable interpersonal skills with the therapist and other adults in his ecology such as Mr. Alvarez and Ms. Lynch, and Markus and Amy shared similar interests such as music and cooking. Ms. K worked long hours to provide for her grandchildren and was thankful for her neighbor's and sister's assistance in caring for them.

The next step in the MST analytical process delineated the "drivers" of the target behaviors. The therapist, working with the key participants, identified the factors that appeared to be causing or sustaining the negative behaviors stated in the overarching goals. To determine these drivers, the therapist guided the family through identification of the sequence of events that often led up to problem behaviors, and led the family through enactments of both negative and positive sequences. In addition, she observed Markus at his aunt and uncle's home and at Ms. Lynch's home. Through these steps, the therapist also was able to detect possible drivers promoting Markus's use of appropriate behavior, as Markus consistently displayed praiseworthy behavior in both settings.

Upon identifying and prioritizing drivers, the therapist and MST team generated interventions that would target these drivers, leveraging the strengths of Markus's social ecology. The therapist identified that Markus's involvement in delinquent behavior (the first overarching goal) appeared to be immediately precipitated by boredom. For example, he reported that he and his friends made up a game whereby a player gained points for hitting window panes of abandoned warehouses. The game required both skill and strategy, as it had elaborate rules with bonus points based on where a player stood and what size rock was used, and deducted points for hitting nonselected windows (the recent assault occurred as a result of an argument over the game rules). Thus, boredom and lack of alternative recreational activities were significant drivers for Markus's criminal behavior. In addition, the therapist determined quickly that Markus's involvement in delinquent activity always occurred on nights when he missed curfew and when he was with two specific youths who lived down the street and were distant cousins to Markus.

The therapist began addressing the identified drivers by assisting Ms. K to reconnect with her distant cousin, Emily (i.e., the parent of the two youths arrested with Markus). The two women, who had grown up together but now were estranged, became allies to eliminate their boys' ability to avoid monitoring. To address boredom and lack of alternative recreational opportunities, the therapist leveraged the ecological supports and assisted the family in identifying and generating enjoyable activities for the youth. Ms. Lynch enjoyed having young people at her home and was able to assist Ms. K and Emily in organizing a weekly game night. These evenings included activities such as teaching the youth complex card games that involved skill and strategy. Seeing the success of this endeavor, Emily, Ms. K, and Ms. Lynch jointly expanded this to other evenings. At termination, the women had hosted 5 weeks of biweekly events and had gained the assistance of other caregivers in the neighborhood. They also had made participation in the events contingent on completion of homework and, with assistance from the MST therapist, they obtained small prizes to be won each evening.

To identify drivers of behavior for the second overarching goal, the therapist leveraged the knowledge that Amy and Markus followed the household rules at their Aunt Sue and Uncle Tim's home. It became apparent that Markus's aunt and uncle employed a concrete behavior plan that clearly explicated the rules and responsibilities, as well as associated rewards and consequences. Because Aunt Sue and Uncle Tim did not feel familiar enough with the children's interests, they had held regular meetings with the children to decide on the rewards and consequences for each rule and to be certain that everyone understood each of the rules. Although Ms. K had a similar list of household rules and responsibilities, including rewards and consequences, she had not thought to hold a meeting with the children because she felt she already knew about their interests. On comparison of the plans across households, the need for a revision of Ms. K's rewards and consequences was recognized. The therapist empowered Ms. K to identify effective rewards and consequences by teaching Ms. K the skills to help the children generate a rewards and sanctions menu that could be used in the behavior plan. This included role-playing the family meeting with Ms. K so that she was able to conduct the meeting with only minimal therapist input.

To address the third overarching goal, the MST therapist used family sessions to assess and alter systematically the family's communication patterns. One prioritized driver of poor communication was that the family often tried to speak over one another. This caused the original speaker to raise his or her voice, and the second speaker to respond in kind, until they were yelling at one another. The therapist used simple techniques in family sessions to manage this behavior, such as setting session rules and passing a pen to encourage taking turns (only the holder of the pen could speak, and the therapist controlled the pen). Ms. K and the children enjoyed this strategy so much that they began using it during the weekly family meetings that they started having on their own. Moreover, it became clear that Ms. K and the children had become very inactive in each other's lives and, consequently, had little to talk about when the therapist attempted certain enactments. When given the task to increase their involvement with each other,

Ms. K and the children developed the plan for having weekly family meetings. The MST therapist assisted in planning and attended the first few of these meetings. The children enjoyed teaching Ms. K and the MST therapist about their favorite music, which had a Hispanic origin. It was at this meeting that the children came up with the idea to include a family meal preparation in this weekly event, as well as to invite Mr. Alvarez periodically. Mr. Alvarez had hosted Markus and Amy at his house on a few occasions, where they learned about cooking foods from his native country of Mexico.

MST with Markus and his family was concluded following sustained reduction in the targeted behaviors for 1 month and after an identified plan had been developed for sustaining the key factors driving the improved behaviors. One year from the time of referral, Markus had not been involved in further delinquency and was off probation. Ms. K and her neighbors had sustained the neighborhood activities. Although Markus and his peers tested their limits on occasion, the caregivers were supporting one another with monitoring the youth in the neighborhood. Upon the urging of Markus and Amy, Mr. Alvarez had begun a Spanish club at the school for youth interested in Hispanic culture. Aunt Sue and Uncle Tim continued to have Markus and Amy over, but it was no longer viewed by the grandmother as respite. Ms. K, Amy, and Markus continued to have family meetings regularly, and although they frequently had to make modifications to improve the behavior plan, the family was able to make these changes of their own accord without the consult of a professional.

Quality Assurance System

Considerable resources have been devoted to the development of quality assurance mechanisms aimed at enhancing MST treatment fidelity, and this has taken place for two primary reasons. First, considerable research supports the link between therapist adherence to MST treatment principles and youth outcomes (e.g., Henggeler, Melton, Brondino, Scherer, & Hanley, 1997; Henggeler, Pickrel, & Brondino, 1999; Huey, Henggeler, Brondino, & Pickrel, 2000; Schoenwald, Henggeler, Brondino, & Rowland, 2000). Hence, the development and testing of a strong quality assurance is critical toward the goal of optimizing youth and family outcomes. Second, with the transport of MST programs to community settings, which began in the mid 1990s and has expanded to include programs in more than 30 states and 10 nations treating approximately 12,000 youths annually, procedures to support the effective implementation of MST in distal sites became critical.

Figure 14.1 provides a representation of the MST quality assurance system (Henggeler & Schoenwald, 1999). As described extensively by Henggeler, Schoenwald, Rowland, and Cunningham (2002), the therapist's interactions with the family are viewed as primary because of their critical role in achieving outcomes. Several structures and processes are used to support therapist adherence to MST when interacting with families. These include manualization of key components of the MST program, ongoing training of clinical and supervisory staff, ongoing feedback to the therapist from the supervisor and MST expert consultant, objective feedback from caregivers on a standardized adherence questionnaire, and organizational consultation. By providing multiple layers of clinical and programmatic support and ongoing feedback from several sources, the system aims to optimize favorable clinical outcomes through therapist support and adherence.

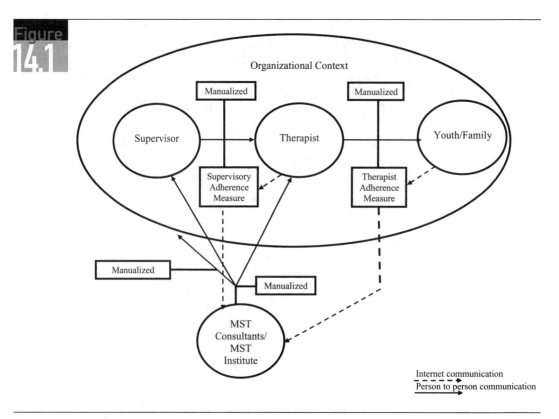

MST continuous quality assurance system.

Manualization of Program Components

All components of the quality assurance system are manualized. The treatment man-
uals for antisocial behavior (Henggeler et al., 1998) and serious emotional distur-
bance (Henggeler, Schoenwald, Rowland, & Cunningham, 2002) are available from
Guilford Press. The other manuals are provided to MST sites through MST Services,
Inc. (www.mstservices.com), which has the exclusive license for the transport of
MST technology and intellectual property through the Medical University of South
Carolina.

Treatment: Specifying MST clinical protocols based on the nine core treatment
principles (Henggeler et al., 1998).
Supervision: Specifying the structure and processes of the weekly on-site supervisory sessions and ongoing development of therapist competencies (Henggeler &
Schoenwald, 1998).
Expert consultation: Specifying the role of the MST consultant in helping teams
achieve youth outcomes and in building the competencies of team therapists and
supervisors (Schoenwald, 1998).
Organizational support: Addressing administrative issues in developing and sustaining an MST program (Strother, Swenson, & Schoenwald, 1998).

Training

Training provided to MST sites by MST Services, Inc., is ongoing and consists of several components:

Site assessment: The development of a new MST program is a process that requires significant community collaboration and often takes up to 12 months to complete.

Initial orientation: A 5-day training program aimed at orienting clinical staff to program philosophy and intervention methods is provided prior to start-up.

Expert consultation: Weekly telephone clinical consultation aimed at promoting treatment fidelity and youth outcomes and building team competencies are ongoing.

Ongoing enhancement of therapist and supervisor competencies: The development and implementation of individualized therapist and supervisor development plans is an important component of all MST programs.

Quarterly booster training: Quarterly boosters are provided by expert consultants to address challenging clinical (e.g., caregiver cocaine abuse) or system (e.g., low referral rate) problems that are impeding the success of the program.

Outcome-Monitoring Components

As discussed subsequently, considerable research efforts are underway to develop and validate an MST quality improvement system. Components that currently are validated include the following:

Therapist Adherence Measure (TAM; Henggeler & Borduin, 1992): This 26-item measure uses caregiver reports to track therapist adherence to MST treatment principles.

Supervisory Adherence Measure (Schoenwald, Henggeler, & Edwards, 1998): Based on therapist reports, this 43-item measure assesses supervisor adherence to the MST supervisory protocol (Henggeler & Schoenwald, 1998).

Youth Outcome Measure: A brief measure of ongoing youth outcomes is in development.

Evidence for Effectiveness of Treatment

Federal entities such as the Surgeon General (U.S. DHHS, 1999; U.S. Public Health Service, 2001), National Institute on Drug Abuse (1999), National Institutes of Health (2004), Center for Substance Abuse Prevention (2000), and the President's New Freedom Commission on Mental Health (2003); leading reviewers (e.g., Burns, Hoagwood, & Mrazek, 1999; Elliott, 1998; Farrington & Welsh, 1999; Kazdin & Weisz, 1998; Stanton & Shadish, 1997); and consumer organizations (e.g., National Alliance for the Mentally Ill, 2003; National Mental Health Association, 2004) have identified MST as either demonstrating or showing considerable promise in the treatment of youth criminal behavior, substance abuse, and emotional disturbance. These conclusions are based on the findings from 15 published outcome studies (14 randomized, 1 quasi-experimental) with youths presenting serious clinical problems and their families. As presented in Table 14.2, these studies included more than 1,300 families. Findings from these studies are summarized next, according to the defining characteristics of the study sample and the types of outcomes targeted.

Juvenile Justice Outcomes

Following favorable psychosocial outcomes (e.g., decreased behavior problems, improved family relations) achieved in the first MST delinquency study (Henggeler et al., 1986), which used a quasi-experimental design, three randomized trials of MST with violent and chronic juvenile offenders were conducted in the 1990s. In the Simpsonville, South Carolina, Project, Henggeler, Melton, and Smith (1992) studied 84 juvenile offenders who were at imminent risk for out-of-home placement because of serious criminal activity. Youth and their families were randomly assigned to receive either MST or the usual services provided by the Department of Juvenile Justice (DJJ). At posttreatment, youth who participated in MST reported less criminal activity than their counterparts in the usual-services group; at a 59-week follow-up, MST had reduced rearrests by 43%. In addition, usual-services youth had an average of almost three times more weeks incarcerated (average = 16.2 weeks) than MST youth (average = 5.8 weeks). Moreover, treatment gains were maintained at long-term follow-up (Henggeler, Melton, Smith, Schoenwald, & Hanley, 1993). At 2.4 years postreferral, twice as many MST youth had not been rearrested (39%) as usual-services youth (20%).

In the Missouri Delinquency Project (Borduin et al., 1995), participants were 176 chronic juvenile offenders and their families who were referred by the local DJJ. Families were randomly assigned to receive either MST or individual therapy (IT). Replicating results from the earlier studies, MST decreased youth behavior problems and improved family relations at posttreatment. Four-year follow-up arrest data showed that youth who received MST were arrested less often and for less serious crimes than counterparts who received IT. Moreover, while youth who completed a full course of MST had the lowest rearrest rate (22.1%), those who received MST but prematurely dropped out of treatment had better rates of rearrest (46.6%) than IT completers (71.4%), IT dropouts (71.4%), or treatment refusers (87.5%). Moreover, an almost 14-year follow-up (Schaeffer & Borduin, 2005) showed that MST participants had 54% fewer arrests and spent 57% fewer days of confinement in adult detention facilities than did their IT counterparts. This differential in recidivism applied across violent, drug, and nonviolent offenses.

In the Multisite South Carolina Study, Henggeler et al. (1997) examined the role of treatment fidelity in the successful dissemination of MST. In contrast with previous clinical trials in which the developers of MST provided ongoing clinical supervision and consultation (i.e., quality assurance was high), MST experts were not significantly involved in treatment implementation and quality assurance was low. Participants were 155 chronic or violent juvenile offenders who were at risk of out-of-home placement because of serious criminal involvement and their families. Youth and their families were randomly assigned to receive MST or the usual services offered by the DJJ. Not surprisingly, MST treatment effect sizes were smaller than in previous studies that had greater quality assurance. Over a 1.7 year follow-up, MST reduced rearrests by 25%,

| Table 14.2 | Published MST Outcome Studies | | | |

Study	Population	Comparison	Follow-up	MST Outcomes
Henggeler et al. (1986) $N = 57^a$	Delinquents	Diversion services	Posttreatment	Improved family relations Decreased behavior problems Decreased association with deviant peers
Brunk, Henggeler, & Whelan (1987) $N = 33$	Maltreating families	Behavioral parent training	Posttreatment	Improved parent–child interactions
Borduin, Henggeler, Blaske, & Stein (1990) $N = 16$	Adolescent sexual offenders	Individual counseling	3 years	Reduced sexual offending Reduced other criminal offending
Henggeler et al. (1991)^b	Serious juvenile offenders	Individual counseling Usual community services	3 years	Reduced alcohol and marijuana use Decreased drug-related arrests
Henggeler, Melton, & Smith (1992) $N = 84$	Violent and chronic juvenile offenders	Usual community services – high rates of incarceration	59 weeks	Improved family relations Improved peer relations Decreased recidivism (43%) Decreased out-of-home placement (64%)
Henggeler et al. (1993)	Same sample		2.4 years	Decreased recidivism (doubled survival rate)
Borduin et al. (1995) $N = 176$	Violent and chronic juvenile offenders	Individual counseling	4 years	Improved family relations Decreased psychiatric symptomatology Decreased recidivism (69%) Decreased rearrests (54%)
Schaeffer & Borduin (2005)	Same sample		13.7 years	Decreased days incarcerated (57%)
Henggeler, Melton, et al. (1997) $N = 155$	Violent and chronic juvenile offenders	Juvenile probation services – high rates of incarceration	1.7 years	Decreased psychiatric symptomatology Decreased days in out-of-home placement (50%) Decreased recidivism (26%, nonsignificant) Treatment adherence linked with long-term outcomes

(Continued)

Table 14.2	(Continued)			

Study	Population	Comparison	Follow-up	MST Outcomes
Henggeler, Rowland, et al. (1999) N = 116 (final sample = 156)	Youths presenting psychiatric emergencies	Psychiatric hospitalization	4-months postrecruitment	Decreased externalizing problems (CBCL) Improved family relations Increased school attendance Higher consumer satisfaction
Schoenwald et al. (2000)	Same sample		4-months postrecruitment	75% reduction in days hospitalized 50% reduction in days in other out-of-home placements
Huey et al. (2004)	Same sample		16-months postrecruitment	Decreased rates of attempted suicide
Henggeler, Rowland, et al. (2003)	Same sample		16-months postrecruitment	Favorable 4-month outcomes, noted above, dissipated
Sheidow et al. (2004)	Same sample		16-months postrecruitment	MST cost benefits at 4 months, but equivalent costs at 16 months
Henggeler, Pickrel, & Brondino (1999) (N = 118)	Substance-abusing and dependent delinquents	Usual community services	1 year	Decreased drug use at posttreatment Decreased days in out-of-home placement (50%) Decreased recidivism (26%, nonsignificant) Treatment adherence linked with decreased drug use
Schoenwald et al. (1996)	Same sample		1 year	Incremental cost of MST nearly offset by between-groups differences in out-of-home placement
Brown et al. (1999)	Same sample		6 months	Increased attendance in regular school settings
Henggeler, Clingempeel, et al. (2002)	Same sample		4 years	Decreased violent crime Increased marijuana abstinence
Borduin & Schaeffer (2001) – preliminary (N = 48)	Juvenile sex offenders	Usual community services	8 years	Decreased behavior problems and symptoms Improved family relations Decreased sex offender recidivism (70%) Decreased recidivism for other crimes (53%) Decreased days incarcerated (62%)

Table 14.2	(Continued)			
Study	**Population**	**Comparison**	**Follow-up**	**MST Outcomes**
Ogden & Halliday-Boykins (2004) ($N = 100$)	Norwegian youths with serious antisocial behavior	Usual Child Welfare Services	6-months postrecruitment	Decreased externalizing and internalizing symptoms Decreased out-of-home placements Increased social competence
Ogden & Hagen (in press)	Same sample		18-month follow-up	Increased consumer satisfaction Decreased externalizing and internalizing symptoms Decreased out-of-home placements
Ellis, Frey, et al. (2005) ($N = 127$)	Inner-city adolescents with chronically poorly controlled type 1 diabetes	Standard diabetes care	7-months postrecruitment	Increased blood glucose testing Decreased inpatient admissions Improved metabolic control
Ellis, Naar-King, et al. (2005)	Same sample			Decreased medical charges and direct-care costs
Ellis et al. (in press)	Same sample			Decreased diabetes stress
Rowland et al. (2005) ($N = 31$)	Youths with serious emotional disturbance	Hawaii's intensive Continuum of Care	6-months postrecruitment	Decreased symptoms Decreased minor crimes Decreased days in out-of-home placement (68%)
Timmons-Mitchell et al. (2006) ($N = 93$)	Juvenile offenders (felons) at imminent risk of placement	Usual community services	18-month follow-up	Improved youth functioning Decreased rearrests (37%)
Henggeler et al. (2006) ($N = 161$)	Substance-abusing and dependent juvenile offenders in drug court	Four treatment conditions, including Family Court with usual services and Drug Court with usual services	12-months postrecruitment	MST enhanced substance use outcomes Drug court was more effective than family court at decreasing self-reported substance use and criminal activity

[a]Quasi-experimental design (groups matched on demographic characteristics); all other studies are randomized.
[b]Based on participants in Henggeler et al. (1992) and Borduin et al. (1995).

which was lower than the 43% and 70% reductions in rearrest in the previous MST studies with serious juvenile offenders. Days incarcerated, however, were reduced by 47%. Importantly, high therapist adherence to the MST treatment protocols, as assessed by caregiver reports on the TAM, predicted fewer rearrests and incarcerations. Thus, the modest treatment effects for rearrest in this study might be attributed to considerable variance in therapists' adherence to MST principles.

The transport of MST programs to community settings began in the mid-1990s and provided an opportunity for independent evaluations of the effectiveness of MST in treating adolescent antisocial behavior, and two of these replications have been published. Ogden directed a four-site randomized trial in which participants were 100 seriously antisocial adolescents in Norway (Norway does not have a juvenile justice system). The youths were randomized to MST versus usual Child Welfare Services conditions. Short-term outcomes at 6 months postrecruitment showed that MST was significantly more effective at reducing youth internalizing and externalizing symptoms and out-of-home placements as well as increasing youth social competence and family satisfaction with treatment (Ogden & Halliday-Boykins, 2004). Importantly, analyses demonstrated differential site effects: The one site with problematic adherence to the MST intervention protocols had the worst outcomes. In addition, a 2-year follow-up has shown that MST effects on out-of-home placements and youth internalizing and externalizing problems were maintained (Ogden & Hagen, in press). This study is important for demonstrating the effective transport of MST to distal community settings.

In the United States, Timmons-Mitchell, Bender, Kishna, and Mitchell (2006) have also provided an independent replication of MST effectiveness with juvenile offenders in community settings. Ninety-three juvenile offenders were randomized to MST versus treatment-as-usual (TAU) services. At 6 months postrecruitment, youths in the MST condition evidenced significantly improved functioning in several areas and had significantly fewer rearrests than TAU counterparts at 18-month follow-up. These results provide further support for the capacity of MST to achieve favorable outcomes when implemented in community practice settings.

In summary, across several trials with violent and chronic juvenile offenders, MST produced 25% to 70% decreases in long-term rates of rearrest, and 47% to 64% decreases in long-term rates of days in out-of-home placements. A recent meta-analysis that included most of these studies (Curtis, Ronan, & Borduin, 2004) indicated that the average MST effect size for both arrests and days incarcerated was 0.55, with efficacy studies having stronger effects than effectiveness studies.

Substance Use Outcomes

Sheidow and Henggeler (in press) provide a comprehensive overview of MST substance-related research, which is a focus of much of the Family Services Research Center's (FRSC)'s current research portfolio. This work was prompted by the many similarities between the treatment needs of juvenile offenders and those of substance-abusing adolescents (see Henggeler, 1993).

Substance-related outcomes were examined in two of the early randomized trials of MST with violent and chronic juvenile offenders (Borduin et al., 1995; Henggeler et al., 1992), and these substance-related findings were published in a single report (Henggeler et al., 1991). Findings in the first study (Henggeler et al., 1992) showed MST treatment effects at posttreatment for self-report alcohol and drug use. In the second study (Borduin et al., 1995), substance-related arrests at 4-year follow-up were 4% in the MST condition versus 16% in the comparison condition, a significant difference. Moreover, an almost 14-year follow-up of participants in this study showed that MST participants continued to have fewer drug-related arrests than did their counterparts who received IT (Schaeffer & Borduin, 2005). In a meta-analysis of family-based treatments of drug abuse (Stanton & Shadish, 1997), the MST effect sizes were among the highest of those reviewed.

Subsequent to the findings from these two trials, the effectiveness and transportability of MST was examined in a study with 118 juvenile offenders meeting *DSM–III–R* criteria for substance abuse (56%) or dependence (44%) and their families (Henggeler, Pickrel, & Brondino, 1999). Participants were randomly assigned to receive MST versus usual community services, which entailed probation services, outpatient substance abuse services (typically, weekly 12-step program meetings) or inpatient/residential treatment, and mental health services (public or private outpatient, school-based, family preservation, residential, and/or inpatient). Compared to the usual-services condition, MST reduced self-reported alcohol and marijuana use at posttreatment, decreased days incarcerated by 46% at the 6-month follow-up, decreased total days in out-of-home placement by 50% at 6-month follow-up (Schoenwald, Ward, Henggeler, Pickrel, & Patel, 1996), and increased youth attendance in regular school settings (Brown et al., 1999). Cost data from this study showed that the incremental cost of MST was offset by the reduced placement (i.e., incarceration, hospitalization, and residential treatment) of youths in the MST condition (Schoenwald et al., 1996). Moreover, a 4-year follow-up (Henggeler, Clingempeel, Brondino, & Pickrel, 2002) demonstrated significantly higher rates of marijuana abstinence, based on drug urine screens, for MST participants (55% abstinent) compared to participants who had received usual services (28% abstinent). The young adults who had participated in MST as youths 4 years earlier also engaged in significantly less criminal activity than did usual-services participants, based on archival and self-report indices. For example, MST participants had an average of 0.15 convictions per year for violent crimes versus 0.57 convictions per year in the usual-services group.

More recently, we have attempted to enhance MST substance-related outcomes by integrating contingency management (CM) interventions into MST treatment protocols. CM techniques (e.g., functional analysis of drug use, tracking, and providing consequences for substance use) are theoretically and clinically compatible with MST, and CM has considerable empirical support (Petry, 2000; Roozen et al., 2004). Specifically, within the context of a randomized trial conducted in collaboration with juvenile drug court (Henggeler et al., 2006), we evaluated (a) the effectiveness of juvenile drug court, per se; (b) the effects of integrating an evidence-based treatment (i.e., MST) as the community intervention component of the drug court process; and (c) whether the integration of CM techniques into the MST treatment protocol would improve substance use outcomes for MST. To conduct these comparisons, 161 juvenile offenders meeting diagnostic criteria for substance abuse or dependence were randomized to one of four treatment conditions.

1 Family court with community services: Youths appeared before a family court judge on average once or twice per year and received outpatient alcohol and drug abuse services from the local center of the state's substance abuse commission.

2 Drug court with community services: Youths appeared before the drug court judge once a week for monitoring of drug use (urine screens) and participated in outpatient alcohol and drug abuse services from the local center of the state's substance abuse commission.

3 Drug court with MST: Youths received an evidence-based treatment (MST) rather than community services in conjunction with drug court.

4 Drug court with MST enhanced with CM: Youths received MST enhanced with key components of CM in conjunction with drug court.

Over a 1-year assessment period, measures of adolescent substance use, criminal behavior, mental health symptomatology, and days in out-of-home placement were assessed. In general, findings supported the view that drug court was more effective than family court services in decreasing rates of adolescent substance use and criminal behavior. Possibly due to the greatly increased surveillance of youths in drug court, however, these relative reductions in antisocial behavior did not translate to corresponding decreases in rearrest or incarceration. In addition, findings supported the view that the use of evidence-based treatments within the drug court context improved youth substance-related outcomes. For example, during the first 4 months of drug court participation, 70% of the urine screens were positive for youths in the drug court with community services condition, in comparison with only 28% and 18% for counterparts in the drug court with MST and drug court with MST enhanced with CM conditions, respectively. These findings support the viability of juvenile drug courts and seem to show that CM can facilitate substance-related treatment gains when integrated into MST protocols. In addition, clinical- and cost-related outcomes are being examined in a 5-year follow-up.

In summary, research findings have provided clear support for the effectiveness of MST in treating adolescent substance use problems. MST provides a comprehensive framework that can efficiently integrate specific interventions into a unified, methodical strategy. Based on this approach and experience from clinical trials, CM is a specific intervention that is consistent with the MST model and can be integrated readily into MST treatment for adolescent substance abuse.

Sex Offending Outcomes

With the exception of higher rates of internalizing symptoms and deficient relations with same-age peers, research suggests that adolescent sexual offenders may have more in common with other delinquents than is generally assumed (Blaske, Borduin, Henggeler, & Mann, 1989; Van Wijk et al., 2005). Such findings suggest that effective treatments for delinquency hold promise in treating juvenile sexual offenders. This proposition was first tested in a small randomized trial ($N = 16$) conducted by Borduin and his colleagues (Borduin, Henggeler, Blaske, & Stein, 1990). Juvenile sex offenders were randomized to MST versus individual counseling treatment conditions. At a 3-year follow-up, MST was significantly more effective at preventing recidivism for sexual offending (i.e., 12.5% for MST vs. 75% for individual counseling) and other criminal offending (25% for MST vs. 50% for individual counseling).

These excellent results led to a larger study by Borduin and colleagues (preliminary findings reported in Borduin & Schaeffer, 2001) in which 48 juvenile sex offenders (50% had arrests for aggressive sexual offenses) and their families were randomized to MST versus usual sex offender treatment conditions. MST was significantly more effective than usual services at decreasing youth behavior problems and symptomatology, improving family relations, decreasing violence toward peers, and improving academic performance. Importantly, at a 9-year follow-up, MST was also significantly more effective at preventing sexual offending (12.5% recidivism for MST vs. 42% for usual services), other criminal offending (29% for MST vs. 63% for usual services), and incarceration (i.e., MST produced a 62% decrease in days incarcerated during adulthood). Finally, highly significant cost benefits were demonstrated for both aggressive and nonaggressive sex offenders treated with MST.

The promising results from these two efficacy trials (i.e., doctoral students as therapists, Borduin as the clinical supervisor) formed the foundation for a larger ($N =$ 131) effectiveness trial (i.e., using community-based practitioners) that is currently in progress, with Henggeler, Letourneau, Borduin, and Schewe as the investigators. In this trial, the MST adaptations for problem sexual behavior (MST-PSB) have been clearly specified and include clear family safety plans for community protection, interventions to address the offender's grooming strategies for victims, and interventions to reduce family denial and minimization of the offense. This larger trial is comparing MST-PSB with a traditional cognitive behavioral group sex offender treatment delivered by juvenile probation. Youths adjudicated for hands-on sex crimes are being recruited for participation, and outcomes are being followed for 24 months postrecruitment. Outcomes analyses are anticipated for 2008. If this effectiveness study proves as successful as the two efficacy studies, MST will be conceptualized as a treatment for youth with delinquent behaviors, including aggressive and nonaggressive sexual offenses.

Mental Health Outcomes

In light of the favorable decreases in psychiatric symptoms in three MST studies with juvenile offenders (Borduin et al., 1995; Henggeler et al., 1997; Henggeler et al., 1986) and the lack of evidence for the effectiveness of inpatient psychiatric hospitalization, a randomized clinical trial was conducted to examine the viability of MST as an alternative to the inpatient treatment of youths presenting psychiatric emergencies (e.g., suicidal, homicidal, psychotic). As described in the corresponding treatment manual (Henggeler, Schoenwald, Rowland, & Cunningham, 2002), several clinical adaptations were made to the basic MST model to address better the needs of youths presenting psychiatric emergencies and their families (MST-Mental Health [MST-MH]). The MST-MH team received increased resources (e.g., decreased caseloads, additional training in evidence-based practices for adult psychopathology and substance abuse, increased clinical supervision, a crisis caseworker, and a continuum of placement options such as shelters and the hospital inpatient unit) to address the mental health and substance use needs of the youths and their caregivers. Child psychiatry (i.e., evidence-based pharmacotherapy) was also fully integrated into the intervention model.

Participants included 156 youths presenting psychiatric crises and approved for emergency hospitalization by an independent physician. These participants were recruited in local emergency rooms and the admissions office of the child psychiatric hospital. Following recruitment, youths and their families were randomized to MST-MH or admission to the inpatient unit. For youths randomized to MST-MH, the treatment team attempted to stabilize the psychiatric emergency outside the hospital if at all possible—with youth safety the overriding priority. Clinical and service outcomes at

4-months poststudy entry strongly favored MST-MH (Henggeler, Rowland et al., 1999). In comparison with psychiatric hospitalization followed by usual community services, MST-MH was significantly more effective at decreasing youth symptomatology, improving family relations, and increasing school attendance. Moreover, MST-MH resulted in a 72% reduction in days hospitalized and a 50% reduction in other out-of-home placements (Schoenwald, Ward, Henggeler, & Rowland, 2000). At an approximately 16-month follow-up, MST-MH was significantly more effective at decreasing rates of attempted suicide (Huey et al., 2004), but the favorable short-term clinical, school, and placement results dissipated (Henggeler et al., 2003). Similarly, economic analyses (Sheidow et al., 2004) showed that MST-MH produced better outcomes at a lower cost during the initial 4-months postrecruitment, but equivalent costs and outcomes during the follow-up period.

The favorable short-term findings in the alternative to hospitalization study have been replicated recently by Rowland et al. (2005). In a study with Hawaii's Felix Class Youths, 31 youths with serious emotional disturbance at imminent risk of out-of-home placement were randomized to MST-MH versus the intensive Hawaii Continuum of Care. At 6 months after intake and in comparison with counterparts receiving the Continuum of Care services, youths in the MST-MH condition reported significantly greater reductions in externalizing symptoms, internalizing symptoms, and minor criminal activity; additionally, archival records showed that MST-MH youths experienced 68% fewer days in out-of-home placements. Together, these studies provide strong support for the capacity of MST-MH to produce favorable short-term clinical and service outcomes for youths presenting serious mental health problems. However, in contrast with the favorable long-term outcomes that MST has achieved for criminal activity (Schaeffer & Borduin, 2005) and drug use (Henggeler, Clingempeel et al., 2002), these favorable short-term outcomes have not been sustained for this challenging mental health population.

Maltreatment Outcomes

Addressing the psychosocial, mental health, and substance abuse needs of maltreating families—child abuse and neglect—has become one of the leading areas of treatment development and research among FSRC investigators. The foundation of this research was based on the first randomized trial of MST that was conducted almost 20 years ago (Brunk, Henggeler, & Whelan, 1987) with 33 maltreating families. Families were randomized to MST versus behavioral parent training conditions, and posttreatment outcomes showed that family interactions for families in the MST condition changed in ways that reflected the use of more favorable parenting strategies. More recently, Swenson (2006) has completed a randomized trial with 86 families in which the adolescent has been physically abused. In this study, MST adapted for maltreatment (MST-Child Abuse and Neglect; MST-CAN) is being compared with an evidence-based behavioral parent training condition, and clinical (e.g., symptoms, parenting, maltreatment) and service (e.g., placement and cost) level outcomes are being examined through 16-months postrecruitment. MST-CAN includes several important clinical adaptations to the basic MST model, including interventions for posttraumatic stress disorder and rigorous guidelines for assuring child safety. This work has led to additional projects that have recently begun that integrate MST-CAN with reinforcement-based therapy

(Jones, Wong, Tuten, & Stitzer, 2005) in the treatment of families in which the caregiver has a significant substance abuse problem that is contributing to the identified maltreatment.

Pediatric Health Care Outcomes

Researchers at Wayne State University have taken the lead in adapting and evaluating the use of MST for improving the health outcomes of youths with challenging and costly health care problems (MST-Health Care [MST-HC]). MST was selected as the platform for this work because of its capacity to overcome barriers to service access and to address the multidetermined nature of difficulties in following complex medical adherence regimens. Encouraged by results from a successful pilot study (Ellis, Naar-King, Frey, Rowland, & Greger, 2003), Ellis, Naar-King, and their colleagues evaluated the capacity of MST-HC to improve the health status of adolescents with type 1 diabetes who had chronically poor metabolic control (Ellis, Frey et al., 2005; Ellis, Frey et al., in press). In a randomized design, 127 inner-city adolescents with chronically poor metabolic control were randomized to receive either MST-HC with standard medical care or standard medical care. At 7-months postreferral, significant findings favoring the MST-HC condition emerged for several key outcomes. Youths in the MST-HC condition, in comparison with counterparts receiving standard care alone, had improved metabolic control, engaged in blood testing more frequently, reported less diabetes-related stress, and had fewer diabetes-related inpatient hospitalizations, which led to significantly lower medical charges and direct care costs (Ellis, Naar-King et al., 2005). Moreover, mediational analyses showed that MST-HC improved metabolic control through increased regimen adherence. The investigators are currently examining the long-term stability of these favorable outcomes.

In light of the promising outcomes for youths with poorly controlled diabetes, this research group is testing adaptations of the MST model for other challenging health problems. For example and again bolstered by successful pilot research (Cunningham, Naar-King, Ellis, Pejuan, & Secord, 2006), Ellis, Naar-King, and colleagues (Ellis, Naar-King, Cunningham, & Secord, 2006) conducted an uncontrolled study to examine the capacity of MST-HC to reduce viral loads in 19 children with perinatally acquired HIV who exhibited high viral loads in the absence of viral resistance. By focusing interventions on addressing identified barriers to medication compliance, the average viral loads for these youths decreased from 37,972 to 1,848 during the 6 months of MST-HC, and these reductions were stable during a 3-month follow-up. The investigators plan to conduct a more rigorous (i.e., randomized) evaluation of MST-HC with HIV+ youths who have high viral loads. In addition, Naar-King, Ellis, and colleagues have recently been funded to adapt and pilot test MST-HC to improve food choices and weight loss in obese African American youth. This research team is clearly forging new ground in the extension and adaptation of MST for challenging and costly health care problems, and their commitment to rigorous research is exemplary.

Testing the MST Quality Assurance System

One of the long-term goals of the MST quality assurance system is to develop strategies that enable continuous tracking of therapist adherence and youth outcomes. Such a system, however, requires the demonstration of empirical linkages between key components of quality assurance. This section describes the empirical status of the linkages shown in Figure 14.1.

Five published studies have demonstrated significant associations between therapist fidelity and youth outcomes. Analyses of data collected in two randomized trials showed that caregiver reports of high adherence on the MST TAM during treatment were associated with low rates of rearrest and incarceration of chronic juvenile offenders at a 1.7-year follow-up (Henggeler et al., 1997) and with decreased criminal activity and out-of-home placement in substance-abusing juvenile offenders approximately 12-months postreferral (Henggeler, Pickrel et al., 1999). Using data from these two randomized trials, findings from Huey et al. (2000) and Schoenwald et al. (2000) supported the view that therapist adherence to MST principles influences those processes (e.g., family relations, association with deviant peers) that sustain adolescent antisocial behavior. In addition, the 45-site MST transportability study (Schoenwald, Sheidow, Letourneau, & Liao, 2003), discussed subsequently, also demonstrated a significant association between therapist adherence and youth outcomes. Thus, the connection between therapist fidelity to MST treatment principles and improved youth outcomes (see Figure 14.1) is relatively well established.

Two large-scale studies have examined additional linkages in the MST quality assurance system depicted in Figure 14.1. A nine-site study with 74 MST therapists, 12 MST supervisors, and 285 families of youths presenting serious clinical problems examined the link between MST supervisory practices and therapist fidelity in community-based MST programs. Findings showed that supervisor expertise in MST and empirically supported treatments was associated positively with therapist fidelity to MST treatment protocols (Henggeler, Schoenwald, Liao, Letourneau, & Edwards, 2002). In contrast with expectations, however, supervisory focus on MST treatment principles and the development of therapist competence were associated with low therapist adherence. To explain these latter findings, therapist adherence difficulties were hypothesized as the driver of these appropriate supervisor behaviors.

In what might be the most extensive study of the functioning of an evidence-based practice in community settings that has been conducted to date, Schoenwald and her colleagues have conducted a 45-site transportability study that included 405 MST therapists and 1,711 families that these therapists treated (Schoenwald, Letourneau, & Halliday-Boykins, 2005; Schoenwald, Sheidow, & Letourneau, 2004; Schoenwald, Sheidow et al., 2003). One set of findings (Schoenwald et al., 2004) from this project showed that the competence of MST consultants (see Figure 14.1) was associated with increased therapist adherence and improved youth outcomes. On the other hand, when consultants focused on maintaining a supportive alliance with therapists, especially in the absence of consultant competence, therapist adherence and youth outcomes were attenuated. These findings demonstrate the important role that "experts" can play in the effective transport of evidence-based practice to community settings, but caution that not all consultative emphases are useful in achieving program goals. Other findings (Schoenwald, Sheidow et al., 2003) have depicted complex relations by which the organizational climate and structure of provider agencies can either enhance or mitigate therapist adherence and corresponding youth outcomes. In addition, consistent with findings from the nine-site transportability study (Schoenwald, Halliday-Boykins, & Henggeler, 2003), therapist–caregiver similarity in ethnicity and gender have emerged as important predictors of therapist adherence and youth outcomes (Halliday-Boykins, Schoenwald, & Letourneau, 2005; Schoenwald et al., 2005).

In sum, research on the MST quality assurance system is finding anticipated and unanticipated associations among the various linkages depicted in Figure 14.1. Importantly, this work will continue to inform efforts to transport MST to community-based providers effectively—in ways that support the work of therapists, supervisors, and other stakeholders to achieve the same types of favorable outcomes that have been obtained in MST randomized trials for youths presenting serious clinical problems.

Conclusion

MST is a family- and community-based treatment for youths presenting serious clinical problems including criminal behavior and violence, substance abuse, serious emotional disturbance, and health care challenges. The evidence base for MST, especially in treating serious antisocial behavior in adolescents, is relatively strong, with several published randomized trials with violent and chronic juvenile offenders showing reductions in recidivism and out-of-home placement. On the strength of this record, MST programs focusing on adolescent antisocial behavior have been adopted by provider organizations in more than 30 states and 10 nations. Importantly, multisite transportability research is examining the capacity of MST programs in community-based settings to achieve outcomes comparable to those attained in clinical trials.

The success of MST has been based largely on research literatures developed across several disciplines during the past 20 to 30 years. For example, decades of correlational and longitudinal research have delineated key risk factors in the development and maintenance of antisocial behavior in adolescents. MST interventions focus on these risk factors. Similarly, a cadre of outstanding efficacy researchers have developed and validated models of intervention for particular well-defined clinical problems. MST intervention protocols make extensive use of this evidence base. On the other hand, the MST model has gone against the traditions of much of the mental health treatment community by, for example, emphasizing the importance of provider accountability for outcomes and quality assurance systems to facilitate program fidelity, viewing caregivers as the key to long-term outcomes, and making programmatic commitments to overcome barriers to service access. Nevertheless, careful review of major federal reports (e.g., Surgeon General's reports on mental health and youth violence) and the conclusions of leading theorists and researchers suggests that such programmatic emphases represent a valuable direction for the field.

RESOURCES AND REFERENCES

Blaske, D. M., Borduin, C. M., Henggeler, S. W., & Mann, B. J. (1989). Individual, family, and peer characteristics of adolescent sex offenders and assaultive adolescents. *Developmental Psychology, 25*, 846–855.

Borduin, C. M., Henggeler, S. W., Blaske, D. M., & Stein, R. (1990). Multisystemic treatment of adolescent sexual offenders. *International Journal of Offender Therapy and Comparative Criminology, 35*, 105–114.

Borduin, C. M., Mann, B. J., Cone, L. T., Henggeler, S. W., Fucci, B. R., Blaske, D. M., et al. (1995). Multisystemic treatment of serious juvenile offenders: Long-term prevention of criminality and violence. *Journal of Consulting and Clinical Psychology, 63,* 569–578.

Borduin, C. M., & Schaeffer, C. M. (2001). Multisystemic treatment of juvenile sexual offenders: A progress report. *Journal of Psychology & Human Sexuality, 13,* 25–42.

Bronfenbrenner, U. (1979). *The ecology of human development: Experiments by design and nature.* Cambridge, MA: Harvard University Press.

Brown, T. L., Henggeler, S. W., Schoenwald, S. K., Brondino, M. J., & Pickrel, S. G. (1999). Multisystemic treatment of substance abusing and dependent juvenile delinquents: Effects on school attendance at posttreatment and 6-month follow-up. *Children's Services: Social Policy, Research, and Practice, 2,* 81–93.

Brunk, M., Henggeler, S. W., & Whelan, J. P. (1987). A comparison of multisystemic therapy and parent training in the brief treatment of child abuse and neglect. *Journal of Consulting and Clinical Psychology, 55,* 311–318.

Budney, A. J., & Higgins, S. T. (1998). *A community reinforcement plus vouchers approach: Treating cocaine addiction* (Publication No. NIH 98-4309). Washington, DC: U.S. Department of Health and Human Services, National Institutes of Health.

Burns, B. J., Hoagwood, K., & Mrazek, P. J. (1999). Effective treatment for mental disorders in children and adolescents. *Clinical Child and Family Psychology Review, 2,* 199–254.

Center for Substance Abuse Prevention. (2000). *Strengthening America's families: Model family programs for substance abuse and delinquency prevention.* Salt Lake City, UT: Department of Health Promotion and Education, University of Utah.

Cunningham, P. B., Naar-King, S., Ellis, D. A., Pejuan, S., & Secord, E. (2006). Achieving adherence to antiretroviral medications for pediatric HIV disease using an empirically supported treatment: A case report. *Journal of Developmental and Behavioral Pediatrics, 27,* 44–50.

Curtis, N. M., Ronan, K. R., & Borduin, C. M. (2004). Multisystemic treatment: A meta-analysis of outcome studies. *Journal of Family Psychology, 18,* 411–419.

Elliott, D. S. (1998). *Blueprints for violence prevention* (Series Ed.). University of Colorado, Center for the Study and Prevention of Violence. Boulder, CO: Blueprints Publications.

Ellis, D. A., Frey, M. A., Naar-King, S., Templin, T., Cunningham, P. B., & Cakan, N. (2005). Use of multisystemic therapy to improve regimen adherence among adolescents with type 1 diabetes in chronic poor metabolic control: A randomized controlled trial. *Diabetes Care, 28,* 1604–1610.

Ellis, D. A., Frey, M. A., Naar-King, S., Templin, T., Cunningham, P. B., & Cakan, N. (in press). The effects of multisystemic therapy on diabetes stress in adolescents with chronically poorly controlled type 1 diabetes: Findings from a randomized controlled trial. *Pediatrics.*

Ellis, D. A., Naar-King, S., Cunningham, P. B., & Secord, E. (2006). Use of multisystemic therapy to improve antiretroviral adherence and health outcomes in HIV-infected pediatric patients: Evaluation of a pilot program. *AIDS, Patient Care, and STDs, 20,* 112–121.

Ellis, D. A., Naar-King, S., Frey, M. A., Rowland, M., & Greger, N. (2003). Case study: Feasibility of multisystemic therapy as a treatment for urban adolescents with poorly controlled type 1 diabetes. *Journal of Pediatric Psychology, 28,* 287–293.

Ellis, D. A., Naar-King, S., Frey, M. A., Templin, T., Rowland, M., & Cakan, N. (2005). Multisystemic treatment of poorly controlled type 1 diabetes: Effects on medical resource utilization. *Journal of Pediatric Psychology, 30,* 656–666.

Farrington, D. P., & Welsh, B. C. (1999). Delinquency prevention using family-based interventions. *Children & Society, 13,* 287–303.

Forman, S. G. (1993). *Coping skills interventions for children and adolescents.* San Francisco: Jossey-Bass.

Haley, J. (1976). *Problem-solving therapy.* San Francisco: Jossey-Bass.

Halliday-Boykins, C. A., Schoenwald, S. K., & Letourneau, E. J. (2005). Caregiver–therapist ethnic similarity predicts youth outcomes from an empirically based treatment. *Journal of Consulting and Clinical Psychology, 73,* 808–818.

Henggeler, S. W. (1993). Multisystemic treatment of serious juvenile offenders: Implications for the treatment of substance abusing youths. In L. S. Onken, J. D. Blaine, & J. J. Boren (Eds.), *Behavioral treatments for drug abuse and dependence: National Institute on Drug Abuse Research Monograph 137* (NIH Publication No. 93-3684). Rockville, MD: National Institutes of Health.

Henggeler, S. W., & Borduin, C. M. (1992). *Multisystemic Therapy Adherence Scales.* Unpublished instrument, Department of Psychiatry and Behavioral Sciences, Medical University of South Carolina.

Henggeler, S. W., Borduin, C. M., Melton, G. B., Mann, B. J., Smith, L., Hall, J. A., et al. (1991). Effects of multisystemic therapy on drug use and abuse in serious juvenile offenders: A progress report from two outcome studies. *Family Dynamics of Addiction Quarterly, 1*, 40–51.

Henggeler, S. W., Clingempeel, W. G., Brondino, M. J., & Pickrel, S. G. (2002). Four-year follow-up of multisystemic therapy with substance abusing and dependent juvenile offenders. *Journal of the American Academy of Child & Adolescent Psychiatry, 41*, 868–874.

Henggeler, S. W., Halliday-Boykins, C. A., Cunningham, P. B., Randall, J., Shapiro, S. B., & Chapman, J. E. (2006). Juvenile drug court: Enhancing outcomes by integrating evidence-based treatments. *Journal of Consulting and Clinical Psychology, 74*, 42–54.

Henggeler, S. W., Melton, G. B., Brondino, M. J., Scherer, D. G., & Hanley, J. H. (1997). Multisystemic therapy with violent and chronic juvenile offenders and their families: The role of treatment fidelity in successful dissemination. *Journal of Consulting and Clinical Psychology, 65*, 821–833.

Henggeler, S. W., Melton, G. B., & Smith, L. A. (1992). Family preservation using multisystemic therapy: An effective alternative to incarcerating serious juvenile offenders. *Journal of Consulting and Clinical Psychology, 60*, 953–961.

Henggeler, S. W., Melton, G. B., Smith, L. A., Schoenwald, S. K., & Hanley, J. H. (1993). Family preservation using multisystemic treatment: Long-term follow-up to a clinical trial with serious juvenile offenders. *Journal of Child and Family Studies, 2*, 283–293.

Henggeler, S. W., Pickrel, S. G., & Brondino, M. J. (1999). Multisystemic treatment of substance abusing and dependent delinquents: Outcomes, treatment fidelity, and transportability. *Mental Health Services Research, 1*, 171–184.

Henggeler, S. W., Pickrel, S. G., Brondino, M. J., & Crouch, J. L. (1996). Eliminating (almost) treatment dropout of substance abusing or dependent delinquents through home-based multisystemic therapy. *American Journal of Psychiatry, 153*, 427–428.

Henggeler, S. W., Rodick, J. D., Borduin, C. M., Hanson, C. L., Watson, S. M., & Urey, J. R. (1986). Multisystemic treatment of juvenile offenders: Effects on adolescent behavior and family interactions. *Developmental Psychology, 22*, 132–141.

Henggeler, S. W., Rowland, M. D., Halliday-Boykins, C., Sheidow, A. J., Ward, D. M., Randall, J., et al. (2003). One-year follow-up of multisystemic therapy as an alternative to the hospitalization of youths in psychiatric crisis. *Journal of the American Academy of Child & Adolescent Psychiatry, 42*, 543–551.

Henggeler, S. W., Rowland, M. R., Randall, J., Ward, D., Pickrel, S. G., Cunningham, P. B., et al. (1999). Home-based multisystemic therapy as an alternative to the hospitalization of youth in psychiatric crisis: Clinical outcomes. *Journal of the American Academy of Child & Adolescent Psychiatry, 38*, 1331–1339.

Henggeler, S. W., & Schoenwald, S. K. (1998). *The MST supervisory manual: Promoting quality assurance at the clinical level.* Charleston, SC: MST Services.

Henggeler, S. W., & Schoenwald, S. K. (1999). The role of quality assurance in achieving outcomes in MST programs. *Journal of Juvenile Justice and Detention Services, 14*, 1–17.

Henggeler, S. W., Schoenwald, S. K., Borduin, C. M., Rowland, M. D., & Cunningham, P. B. (1998). *Multisystemic treatment of antisocial behavior in children and adolescents.* New York: Guilford.

Henggeler, S. W., Schoenwald, S. K., Liao, J. G., Letourneau, E. J., & Edwards, D. L. (2002). Transporting efficacious treatments to field settings: The link between supervisory practices and therapist fidelity in MST programs. *Journal of Clinical Child Psychology, 31*, 155–167.

Henggeler, S. W., Schoenwald, S. K., Rowland, M. D., & Cunningham, P. B. (2002). *Serious emotional disturbance in children and adolescents: Multisystemic therapy.* New York: Guilford.

Huey, S. J., Henggeler, S. W., Brondino, M. J., & Pickrel, S. G. (2000). Mechanisms of change in multisystemic therapy: Reducing delinquent behavior through therapist adherence and improved family and peer functioning. *Journal of Consulting and Clinical Psychology, 68*, 451–467.

Huey, S. J., Jr., Henggeler, S. W., Rowland, M. D., Halliday-Boykins, C. A., Cunningham, P. B., Pickrel, S. G., et al. (2004). Multisystemic therapy effects on attempted suicide by youth presenting psychiatric emergencies. *Journal of the American Academy of Child & Adolescent Psychiatry, 43*, 183–190.

Jones, H. E., Wong, C. J., Tuten, M., Stitzer, M. L. (2005). Reinforcement based therapy: 12-month evaluation of an outpatient drug-free treatment for heroin abusers. *Drug and Alcohol Dependence, 79*, 119–128.

Kazdin, A. E., & Weisz, J. R. (1998). Identifying and developing empirically supported child and adolescent treatments. *Journal of Consulting and Clinical Psychology, 66*, 19–36.

Kendall, P. C. (Ed.). (2005). *Child and adolescent therapy: Cognitive-behavioral procedures.* New York: Guilford.

Loeber, R., & Farrington, D. P. (1998). *Serious & violent juvenile offenders: Risk factors and successful interventions.* Thousand Oaks, CA: Sage.

Minuchin, S. (1974). *Families & family therapy.* Cambridge, MA: Harvard University Press.

Munger, R. L. (1993). *Changing children's behavior quickly.* Lanham, MD: Madison Books.

Munger, R. L. (1998). *The ecology of troubled children: Changing children's behavior by changing the places, activities and people in their lives.* Cambridge, MA: Brookline Books.

National Alliance for the Mentally Ill. (2003, Fall). *NAMI beginnings.* Arlington, VA: Author.

National Institute on Drug Abuse. (1999). *Principles of drug addiction treatment: A research-based guide* (NIH Publication No. 99-4180). Bethesda, MD: National Institutes of Health.

National Institutes of Health. (2004). *Preventing violence and related health-risking social behaviors in adolescents: An NIH State-of-the-Science Conference.* Bethesda, MD: Author.

National Mental Health Association. (2004). *Mental health treatment for youth in the juvenile justice system: A compendium of promising practices.* Alexandria, VA: Author.

Ogden, T., & Hagen, K. A. (in press). Multisystemic therapy of serious behaviour problems in youth: Sustainability of therapy effectiveness two years after intake. *Journal of Child and Adolescent Mental Health.*

Ogden, T., & Halliday-Boykins, C. A. (2004). Multisystemic treatment of antisocial adolescents in Norway: Replication of clinical outcomes outside of the US. *Child & Adolescent Mental Health, 9*(2), 77–83.

Petry, N. M. (2000). A comprehensive guide to the application of contingency management procedures in clinical settings. *Drug & Alcohol Dependence, 58*(1/2), 9–25.

President's New Freedom Commission on Mental Health. (2003). *Achieving the promise: Transforming mental health care in America. Final Report.* Rockville, MD: U.S. DHHS.

Roozen, H. G., Boulogne, J. J., van Tulder, M. W., Van Den Brink, W., De Jong, C. A., & Kerkhof, A. J. (2004). A systematic review of the effectiveness of the community reinforcement approach in alcohol, cocaine and opioid addiction. *Drug & Alcohol Dependence, 74*(1), 1–13.

Rowland, M. R., Halliday-Boykins, C. A., Henggeler, S. W., Cunningham, P. B., Lee, T. G., Kruesi, M. J. P., et al. (2005). A randomized trial of multisystemic therapy with Hawaii's Felix Class youths. *Journal of Emotional and Behavioral Disorders, 13,* 13–23.

Schaeffer, C. M., & Borduin, C. M. (2005). Long-term follow-up to a randomized clinical trial of multisystemic therapy with serious and violent juvenile offenders. *Journal of Consulting and Clinical Psychology, 73*(3), 445–453.

Schoenwald, S. K. (1998). *Multisystemic therapy consultation guidelines.* Charleston, SC: MST Institute.

Schoenwald, S. K., Halliday-Boykins, C. A., & Henggeler, S. W. (2003). Client-level predictors of adherence to MST in community service settings. *Family Process, 42,* 345–359.

Schoenwald, S. K., Henggeler, S. W., Brondino, M. J., & Rowland, M. D. (2000). Multisystemic therapy: Monitoring treatment fidelity. *Family Process, 39,* 83–103.

Schoenwald, S. K., Henggeler, S. W., & Edwards, D. (1998). *MST Supervisor Adherence Measure.* Charleston, SC: MST Institute.

Schoenwald, S. K., Letourneau, E. J., & Halliday-Boykins, C. (2005). Predicting therapist adherence to a transported family-based treatment for youth. *Journal of Clinical Child and Adolescent Psychology, 34,* 658–670.

Schoenwald, S. K., Sheidow, A. J., & Letourneau, E. J. (2004). Toward effective quality assurance in evidence-based practice: Links between expert consultation, therapist fidelity, and child outcomes. *Journal of Clinical Child and Adolescent Psychology, 33,* 94–104.

Schoenwald, S. K., Sheidow, A. J., Letourneau, E. J., & Liao, J. G. (2003). Transportability of multisystemic therapy: Evidence for multilevel influences. *Mental Health Services Research, 5,* 223–239.

Schoenwald, S. K., Ward, D. M., Henggeler, S. W., Pickrel, S. G., & Patel, H. (1996). MST treatment of substance abusing or dependent adolescent offenders: Costs of reducing incarceration, inpatient, and residential placement. *Journal of Child and Family Studies, 5,* 431–444.

Schoenwald, S. K., Ward, D. M., Henggeler, S. W., & Rowland, M. D. (2000). MST vs. hospitalization for crisis stabilization of youth: Placement outcomes 4 months post-referral. *Mental Health Services Research, 2,* 3–12.

Sheidow, A. J., Bradford, W. D., Henggeler, S. W., Rowland, M. D., Halliday-Boykins, C., Schoenwald, S. K., et al. (2004). Treatment costs for youths in psychiatric crisis: Multisystemic therapy versus hospitalization. *Psychiatric Services, 55,* 548–554.

Sheidow, A. J., & Henggeler, S. W. (in press). Multisystemic therapy with substance using adolescents: A synthesis of research. In N. Jainchill (Ed.), *Understanding and treating adolescent substance use disorders*. Kingston, NJ: Civic Research Institute.

Stanton, M. D., & Shadish, W. R. (1997). Outcome, attrition, and family-couples treatment for drug abuse: A meta-analysis and review of the controlled, comparative studies. *Psychological Bulletin, 122*, 170–191.

Strother, K. B., Swenson, M. E., & Schoenwald, S. K. (1998). *Multisystemic therapy organizational manual*. Charleston, SC: MST Institute.

Swenson, C. C. (September, 2006). Moving MST from delinquency to maltreatment: The journey. Presentation at the 17th World Congress of the International Association for Child and Adolescent Psychiatry and Allied Professions. Melbourne, Australia.

Timmons-Mitchell, J., Bender, M. B., Kishna, M. A., Mitchell, C. C. (2006). An independent effectiveness trial of multisystemic therapy with juvenile justice youth. *Journal of Clinical Child and Adolescent Psychology, 35*, 227–236.

Unger, D. G., & Wandersman, A. (1985). The importance of neighbors: The social, cognitive, and affective components of neighboring. *American Journal of Community Psychology, 13*, 139–169.

U.S. Department of Health and Human Services. (1999). *Mental health: A report of the Surgeon General*. Rockville, MD: U.S. Department of Health and Human Services, National Institutes of Health, National Institute of Mental Health.

U.S. Public Health Service. (2001). *Youth violence: A report of the Surgeon General*. Washington, DC: Author.

Van Wijk, A., Loeber, R., Vermeiren, R., Pardini, D., Bullens, R., & Doreleijers, T. (2005). Violent juvenile sex offenders compared with violent juvenile nonsex offenders: Explorative findings from the Pittsburgh Youth Study. *Sexual Abuse, A Journal of Research and Treatment, 17*, 333–352.

Viteillo, B., Sever, J. B., Greenhill, L. L., Arnold, L. E., Abikoff, H. B., Bukstein, O. G., et al. (2001). Methylphenidate dosage for children with ADHD over time under controlled conditions: Lessons from the MTA. *Journal of the American Academy of Child and Adolescent Psychiatry, 40*(2), 188–196.

Weisz, J. R., & Jensen, P. S. (1999). Efficacy and effectiveness of child and adolescent psychotherapy and pharmacotherapy. *Mental Health Services Research, 1*, 125–157.

Wolkow, K. E., & Ferguson, H. B. (2001). Community factors in the development of resiliency: Considerations and future directions. *Community Mental Health Journal, 37*(6), 489–498.

MST Resources

Treatment Manuals

Henggeler, S. W., Schoenwald, S. K., Borduin, C.M., Rowland, M. D., & Cunningham, P. B. (1998). *Multisystemic treatment of antisocial behavior in children and adolescents*. New York: Guilford.

Henggeler, S. W., Schoenwald, S. K., Rowland, M. D., & Cunningham, P. B. (2002). *Serious emotional disturbance in children and adolescents: Multisystemic therapy*. New York: Guilford.

Swenson, C. C., Henggeler, S. W., Taylor, I. S., & Addison, O. W. (2005). *Multisystemic therapy and neighborhood partnerships: Reducing adolescent violence and substance abuse*. New York: Guilford.

Publications

See www.musc.edu/fsrc for a list of MST-related publications and directions for requesting copies.

Program Development

See www.mstservices.com for information on the development of MST programs.

15

Treatment of Mentally Ill Juvenile Offenders

Lisa Rapp-Paglicci

Case Example

Lydia is a 14-year-old female who is very familiar with the juvenile justice system. That is because she has been involved with this system as well as the mental health system for 2 years. She has been shunted back and forth between two systems because neither one is able to help her. Lydia has a history of sexual abuse and has engaged in running behaviors, truancy, and defiance to authority. She presents as angry, irritable, and depressed. She currently is not suicidal but has made two prior attempts. Her social worker worries that her next attempt may be successful.

Mario is a 17-year-old male who has been diagnosed with attention-deficit/hyperactivity disorder (ADHD) and conduct disorder. Mario has struggled with impulsivity, an inability to sustain his attention, problems listening, and problems with organization. In addition, he frequently lies, steals, and destroys others' property, and he refuses to follow directives. He has been expelled from three schools in the past 5 years and has been involved with the juvenile justice system for the past 3 years. He is currently being held in a detention center to await long-term placement for auto theft. He has been waiting for 4 months, and there is no indication about when an opening will be available.

Scope of the Problem

There is a growing recognition that youth being seen in the juvenile justice system have multiple and complex problems beyond delinquent and aggressive behaviors. In fact,

347

research studies indicate that the majority of juvenile offenders have one or more mental disorders, with recent studies estimating that number to be at least two thirds (Teplin, Abram, McClelland, Dulcan, & Mericle, 2002), with as many as 20% having what would be considered a severe mental disorder (MacKinnon-Lewis, Kaufman, & Frabutt, 2002). Specifically, Pliszka, Sherman, Barrow, and Irick (2000) found 15 to 42% of detained youth had major affective disorders such as bipolar and depression, 20 to 46% of juvenile offenders also met the criteria for ADHD, and 50 to 90% met the criteria for conduct disorder. According to a study by McGarvey and Waite (2000), 40% of incarcerated youth met the criteria to receive special education, and nearly 50% of their sample scored 6 years below their chronological age on language achievement scores.

Many females in the juvenile justice system share one unfortunate characteristic: Over 92% have been victims of physical, psychological, and/or sexual abuse (Quinn, Poirier, & Garfinkel, 2005). Cauffman, Feldman, Waterman, and Steiner (1998) found that female juvenile delinquents were nearly six times more likely to suffer from PTSD both currently and at some time in their lives than the general population and 50% more likely to exhibit current symptoms of PTSD than male delinquents. In general, about 82% of females in the juvenile justice system suffer from comorbid mental disorders (Quinn et al., 2005).

Studies of incarcerated youth have also shown high prevalence rates of current suicidal ideation (20%; Rohde, Seeley, & Mace, 1997). Especially at risk are juveniles who suffer from depression and conduct disorder (Rapp & Wodarski, 1997). Other research indicates a strong correlation between violent and homicidal juvenile offenders and psychotic disorders. For example, a study evaluating juvenile murderers indicated that up to 96% of the youth met criteria for at least one diagnosis and 71% had a history of psychotic symptoms (Myers, Burgess, & Burgess, 1995).

The little research that does exist on juveniles who access both the mental health and juvenile justice systems suggests that these youth are more likely to abuse substances, to have been physically abused, to be a minority, and to have a parent with criminal involvement (Rosenblatt, Rosenblatt, & Briggs, 2000). In general, comorbid youth tend to have a worse prognostic picture, more peer rejection, and a higher risk for adult criminality; they also report more dangerous, impulsive, and illegal activities (McConaughty & Skiba, 1993) than juvenile offenders without a mental disorder.

A diagnosis of a mental illness or juvenile offending alone is problematic for practitioners in the mental health and juvenile justice systems. That is because research regarding the etiology, course, and treatment of these problems in children and youth lags significantly behind that of adults. However, comorbid conditions, in which a juvenile has two separate and distinct problems at the same time, pose significant theoretical, conceptual, diagnostic, and treatment planning difficulties. Add to this the fact that comorbid conditions bridge two fragmented delivery systems (juvenile justice and mental health or special education) and that problem becomes a crisis (Rapp-Paglicci & Roberts, 2004).

Comorbid conditions spawn confusion and questions with regard to the course of the disorders. For example, are observed symptoms part of one disorder or both? How does one disorder affect the occurrence or onset of another disorder? Did the disorders begin at the same time, or should one be considered primary? Treatment issues also muddy the waters. For instance, should both disorders be treated simultaneously, or should one disorder be treated first? If so, which one and with which types of interventions? In addition, how can disorders that seem to be polar opposites occur in an individual at the same time (e.g., depression and offending behaviors)?

These statistics and concerns present the reality of the juvenile justice population. It is clear that most youth being seen in this system have multiple problems and do not fit neatly into a single diagnostic category (Rapp-Paglicci & Roberts, 2004). It is also a reality that these youth, even those presenting with suicidal ideation, do not receive adequate screening, assessment, services, or treatment (MacKinnon-Lewis et al., 2002). These youth have frequently been shunted to the juvenile justice system, which is ill equipped to assess, contain, or treat them (Cocozza & Skowyra, 2000). At other times, these youth are dumped into the mental health system, which is also unprepared to handle their complex problems. Some youth are literally transferred back and forth between systems, as neither system is able to address fully the needs of these youth and their families (Scott, Snowden, & Libby, 2002). Instead of integrated services from the mental health and juvenile justice systems, a revolving door may more aptly describe the current situation.

At first look, the populations of the juvenile justice and mental health systems may appear the same; however, closer inspection indicates that youth who eventually end up in the juvenile justice system are more likely to be from minority or economically disadvantaged backgrounds (Murphy, 2002). Managed care organizations have severely limited the services in the mental health system for impoverished youth and their families (Atkins et al., 1999). Therefore, youth with the same symptoms are treated in different systems. Though neither system is well prepared to assist them, those juveniles placed into the juvenile justice system have more stigmas and long-term ramifications, such as difficulty obtaining employment and reintegrating back into society, than those in the mental health system.

Mentally ill juvenile offenders compose a majority of our current juvenile offenders and are inadequately evaluated and treated in both the mental health and juvenile justice systems. Practitioners' confusion about comorbid conditions and their treatment also exists and adds to the difficulty in assisting these youth. However, research has begun to identify screening instruments and effective treatments for mentally ill juvenile offenders, and this chapter provides the latest information regarding empirically based interventions and best practices for work with these youth.

Practical Inserts

The formal assessment before a youth is placed within the juvenile justice system should include a thorough history of the youth's development from birth to the current age; the family background; and psychological, social, and academic histories. Details regarding child abuse, alcohol, drugs, lethality, family violence, traumas, and previous mental health issues are crucial. A formal assessment by the school for learning disabilities that may have previously gone unnoticed is also a must. The offending behavior must be explicitly identified in order to assess the severity and chronicity of the offenses. The following is a model biopsychosocial assessment.

Biopsychosocial Assessment

Presenting problems

Record current problems as reported by the youth, family, referral source, and any pertinent others. Include the history and development of the problem, circumstances surrounding the problem, and previous attempts to solve the problem.

Development (Birth to Current Age)

Describe prenatal care, birth, achievement of developmental milestones, delays, and birth defects.

Family Background

Describe the family constellation, family functioning, and communication. Include socioeconomic, educational, and occupational information. Describe family childrearing and parenting tactics.

Academic History

Describe academic functioning, including learning disabilities, testing information, peer interaction, and school behavior.

Psychological History

Describe previous diagnoses and the history of psychological problems and services. Include medication history and any history of self-injurious behaviors and/or suicide attempts.

Substance Use History

Describe the youth's use and abuse of all substances; include length, method, and location of use and the family history of substance use.

Juvenile Justice or Legal History

Describe previous encounters with the juvenile justice system and the history of illegal behaviors and status offenses. Include timeline, type, and circumstances of offenses, as well as the family history of legal problems.

Violence and Abuse History

Detail psychological, verbal, physical, and sexual abuse of the youth and include a timeline. Identify perpetrators and describe whether the abuse occurred in or outside of the family. Describe any family or dating violence that the youth was exposed to, as well as any violence or abuse that the youth perpetrated. Include any other traumas the youth was exposed to.

Table 15.1	Risk Factors for Juvenile Offending	
Individual	Substance abuse Mental health problems, particularly ADHD and depression Poor social problem-solving skills Learning disabilities Cognitive impairments, especially affecting verbal abilities	
Family	Poor parental supervision Ineffective discipline practices Exposure to domestic violence	
School	Truancy Poor academic achievement Untreated learning disabilities	
Peer	Association with delinquent peers Gang membership	
Community	Exposure to violence Exposure to drug dealing	

Medical History

Describe the history of medical conditions, diseases, and medications of the youth. Include the family medical history.

Cultural History

Identify the ethnicity and race of the youth and family, and include any issues noted regarding bicultural identity, immigration status, language barriers, acculturation, and discrimination.

Lethality

Clearly identify any concerns with lethality of the youth either toward him- or herself or others, and describe the plan for addressing this lethality.

Risk Factors

Professionals should also consider the known risk factors for offending behavior and mental health problems (see Tables 15.1 and 15.2). These risk factors can assist in understanding the severity and potential severity of problems the youth may have. For instance, a youth who has only two risk factors for mental illness will have less of a chance for developing these problems than one who has four. The age of the youth in combination with the known risk factors should be considered. Overall, youth who have more risk factors for mental illness should probably be served in the mental health system because their mental disorders may be exacerbated if placed within the juvenile justice system.

352

Table 15.2	Risk Factors for Mental Illness	
Family	Large family size or overcrowding	
	Paternal criminality	
	Maternal psychiatric disorder	
	Severe marital discord	
Community	Poverty	

Note. From Rutter, M., MacDonald, H., LeCouteur, A., Harrington, R., Bolton, P., & Bailey, A.(1990). Genetic factors in child psychiatric disorders_ II. Empirical findings. *Journal of Child Psychology & Psychiatry & Allied Disciplines, 31,* 39–71.

Screening Instruments

Mental health screening instruments have the potential to assess juveniles readily and easily, and the use of these instruments holds important potential for the juvenile justice system. For instance, the use of these instruments can reduce the risk of harm to the youth and others, prevent and alleviate suffering, provide the necessary information for appropriate referrals, and reduce potential legal liability (Reppucci & Redding, 2000). Previous budget cuts and little interest regarding youth in the juvenile justice system have forced many states into hiring untrained staff. These screening instruments can be utilized by untrained staff to obtain information quickly and accurately. The following are two instruments that show promise as brief screening instruments for screening youth upon entry to the juvenile justice system.

MAYSI-2

The MAYSI-2 (Massachusetts Youth Screening Instrument; Grisso, Barnum, Fletcher, Cauffman, & Peuschold, 2001) was designed specifically for evaluating psychological distress of youth entering the juvenile justice system. It does not focus on psychological diagnoses, but rather on situational and characterological distress in youth who are in the juvenile justice system. The instrument has seven subscales, including alcohol and drug use, angry-irritable, depressed-anxious, somatic complaints, suicidal ideation, thought disturbance, and traumatic experiences. Scores above the cutoff warrant mental health referrals. The instrument has been proven reliable and valid with youth in the juvenile justice system, and with only 52 items it can be completed in 10 minutes. It is also very easy to score.

BSI

The Brief Symptom Inventory (BSI; Derogatis, 1979) was designed to measure current psychological symptoms and render a diagnosis. The instrument can be administered in 10 minutes and is easily scored. It has established reliability and validity and is available in several languages. The inventory does not have a specific suicide subscale, nor does it assess alcohol, drug use, or aggression (Reppucci & Redding, 2000). The BSI is useful for a quick psychological screening; however, other instruments would need to be utilized with it for a comprehensive assessment.

Although screening instruments are helpful tools to screen rapidly for mental health and behavioral problems, they should be used with caution. Youth with mental health problems and certainly offending youth often minimize or deny problems. Therefore, it is crucial that assessments include information from parents/guardians, relatives, teachers, school personnel, counselors, probation officers, religious leaders, and anyone who may have information regarding the youth. In addition, previous juvenile justice, probation, medical, counselor, and academic records should be reviewed to obtain and corroborate all necessary information. The accuracy of the assessment is of great concern since appropriate referrals cannot be completed and treatment will not be effective without the initial step of assessment.

Clinical or Legal Issues

Given the complexity of the issue of mental illness and offending behaviors, it is no wonder that practitioners, juvenile justice personnel, and researchers consider these youth some of their greatest challenges. Social workers have identified many barriers in their attempts to intervene with these youth, including inadequate screening and assessment of youth entering the juvenile justice system, lack of training of juvenile justice personnel regarding mental illness, a lack of staff to deliver services, ineffective or nonexistent services for juvenile offenders suffering from combined mental illness and offending behaviors, confusion and arguments across social service agencies and the juvenile justice system regarding which agency is responsible for assisting these youth, lack of empathy for all juvenile offenders in light of the recent "get tough" policies regarding juveniles, and differing opinions between professionals regarding which problem to treat first and how to treat it. These are serious and complex questions that cannot be answered quickly, yet youth enter the juvenile justice system each day with mental health concerns and these concerns must be addressed.

Social workers can make a difference with these youth by assisting in reforming the juvenile justice system's policies regarding mentally ill juvenile offenders and by intensely advocating for their needs with judges, police officers, probation officers, case managers, and parole officers. Social workers can also be crucial in the juvenile justice process by providing comprehensive assessments to all youth. Many youth suffer from acute psychological and emotional distress, particularly at the preadjudicatory stage, but some are suffering from serious mental illness that has gone undetected or untreated for years (Cocozza & Skowyra, 2000). Youth with undetected mental health problems who are placed in the juvenile justice system can decompensate over time, especially if exposed to a stressful environment like detention, incarceration, or boot camps. They can also be at risk for suicide or violent behavior toward other youth and staff, particularly if they are found to be impulsive and depressed.

The juvenile justice system is in dire need of trained social work professionals to assist with assessment and treatment. Preferably, these professionals should conduct extensive assessments; however, until trained professionals are hired and incorporated into this system, the onus of assessment will continue to lie with juvenile justice personnel. As one means to address these issues, juvenile mental health courts that incorporate assessment as well as treatment are being tried on a small scale. Therapeutic jurisprudence provides a rationale for specialized court approaches that integrate treatment in the legal process.

In May 2005, President Bush signed into law the Mentally Ill Offender Treatment and Crime Reduction Act of 2004. The act provides up to $50 million in grant money to promote treatment programs that are aimed at keeping mentally ill juvenile offenders out of prisons (Rigby, 2005). This is an important policy that social workers can utilize to advance the treatment and programming needs of mentally ill juvenile offenders.

Literature Review and Description of Intervention

Despite the concerns and remaining questions regarding comorbidity, researchers have begun to identify a clear set of comprehensive strategies for effectively reducing delinquency and ameliorating the symptoms of mental illness in youth. Effective interventions usually begin early. In fact, the Office of Juvenile Justice and Delinquency Prevention advocates for prevention programs targeted to at-risk youth (Redding, 2000a). Typically, there is not just one cause of a juvenile's problems. To this end, effective programs need to address multiple risk factors (i.e., individual, family, and community) and intervene at multiple levels (with the youth, family, and larger systems). Interventions that have been shown to be effective are ones that can be tailored to address the particular risk factors present for that youth and his or her situation. Additionally, interventions must be of sufficient duration to produce change. Although brief treatment is currently in vogue and demanded by managed care, seriously mentally ill and delinquent youth require intense and ongoing assistance. Studies have suggested that short-term treatments with no follow-up or booster sessions are usually inadequate (Cocozza & Skowyra, 2000). Finally, community-based programs have generally been found to be more effective than incarceration in reducing recidivism.

The following are some examples and explanation of programs or interventions that have been found to be empirically efficacious.

Cognitive Behavioral Approaches

Cognitive behavioral approaches have become some of the most effective treatment protocols for at-risk behavior, conduct disorder, violent behaviors, depression, and anxiety. Recent studies have specifically found cognitive behavioral skill-based programs highly effective for youths and their families (Kaufman, Rohde, Seeley, Clarke, & Stice, 2005; Kazdin, 2005; Phillips, 2005; Sukhodolsky, Golub, Stone, & Orban, 2005; van Manen, Prins, & Emmelkamp, 2004). The skills-based programs are efficacious in individual, family, and group modalities.

Cognitive behavioral treatment is based on cognitive behavioral theory, which suggests that cognitions are determinants of affect and behavior (Dodge, 1993). This mode of treatment attempts to train participants to identify and then alter their cognitions or distorted thinking. Since depressed, anxious, and offending youth all manifest distortions in attributions, self-evaluations, locus of control, and perceptions of events, this approach is especially conducive for work with offending youth with mental health problems (Kendall, 1993; Rapp & Wodarski, 1997).

Cognitive behavioral approaches usually include specific training modules and manuals. Frequently, they include social skills training, parenting skills training, anger management, problem-solving skills, and behavioral contracting. Teaching multiple skills tailored to the youth's and family's particular needs have been found to be the most efficacious (Bray, Heiserman, & Hosley, 2002). The "skill-streaming" component teaches a progression of very specific prosocial skills through performance feedback, role-playing, and modeling. The anger control element helps youth learn what triggers their anger and how to modify and control it. Problem-solving components teach strategies for identifying problems, alternative actions, and pros and cons of actions. Parenting skills training helps guardians learn to develop behavior modification plans, utilize various reinforcement schedules, and develop creative discipline for youth. Cognitive behavioral programs differ in which skill components they offer. Therefore, professionals and agencies may wish to choose programs carefully to address the specific needs they identify in the youth and families they serve.

Education

Educational rehabilitation is often an essential part of treatment for any offender, but it is especially pertinent for those youth who suffer from developmental or learning disabilities. Many times, children with learning disabilities go undiagnosed or misdiagnosed for years. Children with these disabilities often have a more difficult time following directions, obeying rules, controlling their impulses, and understanding expectations (Block, 2000). Therefore, they frequently violate rules at school. Expulsion or transfer to an alternative school has been the de facto practice of most schools; however, this procedure does not assist the youth. Rather, it sets the youth up for future academic and employment failure. Schools that file charges against learning disabled students are using the juvenile court system to criminalize learning disabilities. On the other hand, schools have been criticized for not addressing dangerous students prior to a crisis (school shootings). Schools have been placed in a damned if they do, damned if they don't position. The bottom line remains the same; special education services are desperately needed by many juvenile offenders and have shown to help decrease offending behaviors when delivered to youth with learning disabilities (Lexcen & Redding, 2000). The best location for the delivery of these services is certainly in the juvenile's own school; however, if a youth's behaviors warrant an alternative placement, these special education needs must be addressed in the least restrictive environment possible, one that implements small class sizes and preferably works in conjunction with other supportive community services (Doll & Hess, 2004).

Functional Family Training

Functional family therapy (FFT) has been found to be an effective practice in the mental health arena with families and youth. It has also been found to reduce recidivism in youth involved in corrections and substance abuse and with very serious juvenile offenders. Additionally, FFT has also been found effective with diverse youth in various geographic areas. Sexton and Alexander (2000) found reductions in offending recidivism rates from 25 to 60%. They also found a reduction in sibling offending behaviors as well as reduced costs when compared to other family interventions (Bray et al., 2002).

Trained therapists utilizing FFT work to modify the family's functioning and, therefore, the youth's symptoms that are thought to be a symptom of problematic family functioning. Improving communication within the family is a crucial element in FFT. The emphasis for change and treatment is on the family as opposed to singling out or blaming the youth for all of the problems of the family. This approach requires frequent family sessions and helps families change their behaviors, parenting tactics, and communication styles to improve functioning.

Multisystemic Therapy

One approach that has repeatedly demonstrated positive outcomes is multisystemic therapy (MST; Henggeler, 1997). MST is an intensive multimodal family-based treatment approach focusing on the juvenile and his or her family, peers, school, and community networks. MST aims to improve parental discipline practices and family relations, decrease the youth's contact with deviant peers, improve the youth's academic performance, and develop support systems to maintain the changes. The approach uses intensive case management and a team of other professionals to target multiple problems (Ellis & Sowers, 2001). The team is available to the family 24 hours per day, 7 days per week, and utilizes various therapies in addition to multiple concrete services to meet the needs of the youth and family. Again, the main goal is to divert the youth from juvenile justice and mental health residential placements and help the youth and family progress toward their life goals. Studies have shown that serious juvenile offenders completing MST had recidivism rates of 22% as compared to 71% for those completing outpatient therapy (Borduin et al., 1995; Tate, Reppucci, & Mulvey, 1995). Even juveniles completing only a portion of the MST program had lower recidivism rates (41%; Redding, 2000a). This intensive intervention is also beneficial to juveniles who were identified early and may have been prevented from entering the juvenile justice system (Hinton, Sheperis, & Sims, 2003). It may also be of use to offenders who have spent a long period of time in the juvenile justice system and who are now being released back into the community. The reader is referred to chapter 14 for a detailed exposition on MST.

Community-Based Alternatives

Due to the serious concerns for mentally ill offenders placed in typical youth facilities with few resources or supports and the serious problem of overcrowding in youth facilities, there are currently attempts to divert mentally ill and seriously disturbed youth from the system and provide efficacious and cost-effective services in the community. Graduated community-based sanctions is one such approach that involves a continuum of sanctions and treatment alternatives tailored to youths' offenses and particular needs. Intensive supervision is utilized with incarceration only as a last resort. Instead of incarceration, group homes, house arrest, detention, restitution programs, day treatment, intensive supervision, and aftercare are utilized alone or in combination based on the offense and the needs of the juvenile, his or her family, and the community. According to Redding (2000b), this approach reduces cost, increases accountability by the juvenile and community, and addresses the individual needs of the juvenile. Another study found this approach the most effective for preventing recidivism, even in violent offenders (Tate et al., 1995).

The community-based treatment needs to be long term, which can be costly; however, this approach is still less expensive than residential programs.

Wraparound Programs

Wraparound services provide an array of formal and informal services to youth and their families while maintaining youth in their community. These programs are effective for low-risk or first-time offenders, since community safety must always be assured. The wraparound programs focus on the youth and family's strengths and build on the natural supports that exist within the family. They expect family involvement in the treatment and utilize individualized service plans. Kamradt (2000) found that recidivism dropped to as low as 17% for youth and families using wraparound programs. In addition, residential treatment decreased by 60%, inpatient hospitalization decreased by 80%, and the average overall cost of care per child decreased by at least $3,300 per month. The level of impairment averaged in the high range at initiation of the program, but after 1 year, the average dropped to the low moderate range for these youths. In addition, recidivism rates dropped from 34% to 17%. These figures suggest strong support for these diversion services.

While the use of community-based services is a promising approach for the effective treatment of mental illness and offending behaviors, it requires intense interagency collaboration and planned integration of services. In other words, various agencies within the community must work together smoothly and comprehensively. Few professionals in any field would reject the notion of collaboration, yet its actual practice is uncommon and difficult (Murphy, 2002). However, with the increasing number of mentally ill juvenile offenders in multiple systems, no one agency can control, house, or rehabilitate them alone. Community agencies have no choice but to collaborate, and these agencies should include schools, adolescent mental health, adult mental health, probation, group homes, substance abuse agencies, Child Protective Services, social services, juvenile justice, and other entities. Agencies need to have good working relationships with each other, clear goals for the juvenile and his or her family, a clear understanding of their scope and the scopes of other agencies, and the programs developed to serve this population effectively. Communities intent on developing community-based programs will also need to address differing philosophies of agencies, funding questions, record and data integration, and citizen support (Redding, 2000b). Without this integration, the community-based approach will fail. Borum and Modzeleski (2000) also emphasize that graduated sanctions in the community include early intervention and have a proactive stance. Agencies should not wait to intervene until a serious offense occurs but rather should identify and respond to beginning, minor offenses or early signs of mental illness with the intent to prevent further and escalating offenses and serious mental illness.

Contraindicated Treatment Approaches

It is vital that ineffective treatments for mentally ill juvenile offenders are understood. In the past, it was thought that any intervention was better than nothing. However, research studies shed light on this inaccurate claim and provide data to prove that some interventions are not just ineffective, but also contraindicated. In other words, some interventions make the youth and his or her family and situation worse than no treatment at all. Obviously, this is not the intent of services and programs; however, these studies should remind us that research is always necessary to identify whether a procedure, treatment, or program is effective and safe.

Adult Facilities

The very first interventions for youth were adult prisons. Unfortunately, many young juveniles are still sent to adult facilities due to the offenses they have committed or because of mandatory sentencing laws. Although juveniles are supposed to be incarcerated separately from adults, some older adolescents are housed with adults and receive very little, if any, treatment or vocational and educational rehabilitation. Clearly, this is not a particularly effective route to changing youth behaviors or reducing mental illness (Ellis & Sowers, 2001). In fact, several large-scale studies have found higher and faster recidivism rates for juveniles transferred to adult facilities than nontransferred juveniles (Myers, 1999; Winner, Lanza-Kaduce, Bishop, & Frazier, 1997).

Juveniles in adult facilities often learn more criminal behaviors and attitudes from adult inmates; are often isolated or sent to lockdown; are abused or neglected by other prisoners and guards; often lose ties with family, peers, and community; and often come out of adult facilities worse than when they entered (Redding, 2000c; Seltzer, 2001). Juveniles also have fewer chances of future employment after adult criminal justice system processing (Freeman, 1992). Clearly, this is not the intended outcome of adult facilities, but if they are contraindicated for mentally healthy juveniles, then their use should definitely be discouraged for mentally ill offenders.

Boot Camps

Boot camps are used as a type of diversion for youth from typical residential facilities. Often they are used for first offenders to attempt to shock or scare them into appropriate behavior. The boot camps are usually from 3 to 6 months long and based on a military schedule and discipline. Rigorous physical training is part of the foundation along with education, but most programs do not provide therapy, vocational training, or life skills training. Most studies have not found support for these types of programs for offenders who are not mentally ill (Ellis & Sowers, 2001). Boot camps are contraindicated for mentally ill offenders because of the intense stress induced and lack of treatment (Seltzer, 2001).

Incarceration Alone

Programs that have relied on punishment alone without any programming or services have overwhelmingly been ineffective and have exacerbated youths' problems. Many youth have been abused and neglected in their homes and communities, and incarceration is often seen as a continuation of this process. Youth often feel distrustful and blatantly oppositional when faced with staff whose focus is harsh punishment and retribution. Ironically, a study conducted by Sherman (1993) found that punishment actually encouraged future lawbreaking, as juveniles focused on "doing their time" as opposed to the harm they had caused to the victim and the community. Deterrence programs administering punishment alone, including isolation or physical restraints, have repeatedly been very ineffective for youth (Ellis & Sowers, 2001). Furthermore, administering abusive conditions to youth who are learning disabled and/or mentally ill will only exacerbate conditions and should in all reality be considered abusive.

Juveniles who are suffering from depression are especially at risk when incarcerated without treatment. According to Ryan (2001), incarceration usually increases feelings of hopelessness and despair, which are precursors to suicide. The death rate from suicide is 4.6 times higher in juvenile detention centers than in the general population (Sheras, 2000). Juvenile facilities also lack the adequate staffing necessary to provide sufficient supervision for suicidal youth. The serious lack of funding prohibits hiring and training more staff and prevents mental health services from being developed within these facilities.

Unspecified and Nondirective Counseling Modalities

Juveniles who engage in offending behaviors and who may have learning disabilities and mental illness have not benefited from nondirective therapy, and in some instances this therapy has been harmful to them (Losel, 1996). Since research studies have repeatedly identified cognitive behavioral approaches as effective, this modality should be utilized. Unspecified modalities, based on weak theoretical foundations and not supported by research, are contraindicated for juvenile justice clients. Psychodynamic interventions are also not supported by the current research literature and should not be used with this population.

It is obvious from this discussion that there has been a substantial body of research that has been conducted on interventions for juvenile offenders. This research should guide social workers as well as juvenile justice programs in beginning to develop effective interventions and programs for juveniles who have comorbid offending and mental illness and/or learning disabilities. It is clear which procedures and programs do not work, and social work professionals working in the juvenile justice system should lead the reforms that are necessary in this system.

Conclusion

Approximately, two thirds of juvenile offenders present with a comorbid mental illness in the juvenile justice system. Unfortunately, these youth tend to have a poorer prognosis than other juvenile offenders unless provided with effective treatment early. They are often herded between the mental health and juvenile justice systems due to each system's lack of resources in meeting their needs and are occasionally even given contraindicated treatment or placements.

Recently, President Bush signed into law the Mentally Ill Offender Treatment and Crime Reduction Act of 2004. This law has set the stage to begin to address mentally ill offenders in the juvenile justice system in a new manner and to provide the desperately needed treatment that they require, as opposed to boot camps or prison. The future is changing for mentally ill juvenile offenders as more effective interventions are utilized and as more social workers become aware of these youths' needs. Yet, social workers will need to continue advocating for this vulnerable group so that these youth receive the critical resources they need and deserve.

RESOURCES AND REFERENCES

Atkins, D., Pumariega, A., Rogers, K., Montgomery, L., Nybro, C., Jerrers, G. et al. (1999). Mental health and incarcerated youth: I. Prevalence and nature of psychopathology. *Journal of Child and Family Studies, 8*, 193–204.

Block, A. (2000). Special education law and delinquent children: An overview. *Juvenile justice fact sheet.* Charlottesville, VA: Institute of Law, Psychiatry, & Public Policy, University of Virginia.

Borduin, C., Mann, B., Cone, L., Henggeler, S., Fucci, B., Blaske, D. et al. (1995). Multisystemic treatment of serious juvenile offenders: Long-term prevention of criminality and violence. *Journal of Consulting and Clinical Psychology, 63*, 569–578.

Borum, R., & Modzeleski, W. (2000). *U.S.S.F. Safe School Initiative: An interim report on the prevention of targeted violence in schools.* Washington, DC: U.S. Secret Service, National Threat Center.

Bray, C., Heiserman, M., & Hosley, C. (2002). Providing community-based interventions to juveniles with mental health disorders: The uniting networks for youth program. *Juvenile Justice Update, 8*(4), 1–15.

Cauffman, E., Feldman, S., Waterman, J., & Steiner, H. (1998). Posttraumatic stress disorder among female juvenile offenders. *Journal of the American Academy of Child and Adolescent Psychiatry, 37*(11), 1209–1216.

Cocozza, J., & Skowyra, K. (2000). Youth with mental health disorders: Issues and emerging responses. *Juvenile Justice, 7*(1), 3–13.

Derogatis, L. (1979). *Brief Symptom Inventory.* Minneapolis, MN: National Computer Systems.

Dodge, K. (1993). Social-cognitive mechanisms in the development of conduct disorder and depression. *Annual Reviews of Psychology, 44*, 559–584.

Doll, B., & Hess, R. (2004). School dropout. In L. Rapp-Paglicci, C. Dulmus, & J. Wodarski (Eds.), *Handbook of preventive interventions for children and adolescents* (pp. 359–380). New York: Wiley.

Ellis, R., & Sowers, K. (2001). *Juvenile justice practice: A cross-disciplinary approach to intervention.* Belmont, CA: Brooks/Cole.

Freeman, R. (1992). Crime and employment of disadvantaged youth. In G. Peterson & W. Vroman (Eds.), *Urban labor markets and job opportunity* (pp. 201–238). Washington, DC: National Academy Press.

Grisso, T., Barnum, R., Fletcher, K., Cauffman, E., & Peuschold, D. (2001). Massachusetts Youth Screening Instrument for mental health needs of juvenile justice youths. *Journal of American Academy of Child and Adolescent Psychiatry, 40*(5), 541–548.

Henggeler, S. (1997). Multisystemic therapy: An overview of clinical procedures, outcomes, and policy implications. *Child Psychology & Psychiatry Review, 4*(1), 2–10.

Hinton, W., Sheperis, C., & Sims, P. (2003). Family-based approaches to juvenile delinquency: A review of the literature. *The Family Journal: Counseling and Therapy for Couples and Families, 11*(2), 167–173.

Kamradt, B. (2000). Wraparound Milwaukee: Aiding youth with mental health needs. *Juvenile Justice, 7*(1), 14–23.

Kaufman, N., Rohde, P., Seeley, J., Clarke, G., & Stice, E. (2005). Potential mediators of cognitive-behavioral therapy for adolescents with comorbid major depression and conduct disorder. *Journal of Consulting and Clinical Psychology, 73*(1), 38–46.

Kazdin, A. (2005). Child, parent, and family-based treatment of aggressive and antisocial child behavior. In E. Hibbs & P. Jensen (Eds.), *Psychosocial treatments for child and adolescent disorders: Empirically based strategies for clinical practice* (2nd ed., pp. 445–476). Washington, DC: American Psychological Association.

Kendall, P. (1993). Cognitive-behavioral therapies with youth: Guiding theory, current status, and emerging developments. *Journal of Consulting and Clinical Psychology, 61*(2), 235–247.

Lexcen, F., & Redding, R. (2000). Mental health needs of juvenile offenders. *Juvenile justice fact sheet.* Charlottesville, VA: Institute of Law, Psychiatry, & Public Policy, University of Virginia.

Losel, F. (1996). Working with young offenders: The impact of meta-analyses. In C. Hollin & K. Howells (Eds.), *Clinical approaches to working with young offenders.* New York: Wiley.

MacKinnon-Lewis, C., Kaufman, M., & Frabutt, J. (2002). Juevenile justice and mental health: Youth and families in the middle. *Aggression and Violent Behavior, 7*(4), 353–363.

McConaughty, S., & Skiba, R. (1993). Comorbidity of externalizing and internalizing problems. *School Psychology Review, 25*, 687–691.

McGarvey, E., & Waite, D. (2000). Profiles of incarcerated adolescents in Virginia: 1993–1998. *The national longitudinal study: A summary of findings*. Washington, DC: Office of Special Education Programs: U.S. Department of Education.

Murphy, R. (2002). Mental health, juvenile justice, and law enforcement responses to youth psychopathology. In D. Marsh (Ed.), *Handbook of serious, emotional disturbance in children and adolescents* (pp. 351–374). New York: Wiley.

Myers, D. (1999). *Excluding violent youths from juvenile court: The effectiveness of legislative waiver*. Unpublished doctoral dissertation, University of Maryland.

Myers, W., Burgess, S., & Burgess, A. (1995). Psychopathology, biopsychosocial factors, crime characteristics, and classification of 25 homicidal youths. *Journal of the American Academy of Child and Adolescent Psychiatry, 34*, 1483–1489.

Phillips, J. (2005). An evaluation of school-based cognitive-behavioral social skills training groups with adolescents at risk for depression (Doctoral dissertation, 2005). *Dissertation Abstracts International Section A: Humanities & Social Sciences, 65*(7), 2768.

Pliszka, S., Sherman, J., Barrow, M., & Irick, S. (2000). Affective disorder in juvenile offenders: A preliminary study. *American Journal of Psychiatry, 157*, 130–132.

Quinn, M., Poirier, J., & Garfinkel, L. (2005). Girls with mental health needs in the juvenile justice system: Challenges and inequities confronting a vulnerable population. *Exceptionality, 13*(2), 125–139.

Rapp, L., & Wodarski, J. (1997). The comorbidity of conduct disorder and depression in adolescents: A comprehensive interpersonal treatment technology. *Family Therapy, 24*(2), 81–100.

Rapp-Paglicci, L., & Roberts, A. (2004). Mental illness and juvenile offending. In A. Roberts (Ed.), *Juvenile justice sourcebook: Past, present, and future* (pp. 290–307). New York: Oxford.

Redding, R. (2000a). Characteristics of effective treatments and interventions for juvenile offenders. *Juvenile justice fact sheet*. Charlottesville, VA: Institute of Law, Psychiatry, & Public Policy, University of Virginia.

Redding, R. (2000b). Graduated and community-based sanctions for juvenile offenders. *Juvenile justice fact sheet*. Charlottesville, VA: Institute of Law, Psychiatry, & Public Policy, University of Virginia.

Redding, R. (2000c). Recidivism rates in juvenile versus criminal court. *Juvenile justice fact sheet*. Charlottesville, VA: Institute of Law, Psychiatry, & Public Policy, University of Virginia.

Reppucci, N., & Redding, R. (2000). Screening instruments for mental illness in juvenile offenders: The MAYSI and BSI. *Juvenile justice fact sheet*. Charlottesville, VA: Institute of Law, Psychiatry, & Public Policy, University of Virginia.

Rigby, M. (2005). President Bush signs Mentally Ill Offender Treatment and Crime Reduction Act of 2004. *Prison Legal News, 16*(5), 41.

Rohde, P., Seeley, J., & Mace, D. (1997). Correlates of suicidal behavior in a juvenile detention population. *Suicide and Life Threatening Behavior, 27*, 164–175.

Rosenblatt, J., Rosenblatt, A., & Briggs, E. (2000). Criminal behavior and emotional disorder: Comparing youth served by the mental health and juvenile justice systems. *Journal of Behavioral Health Services and Research, 27*, 227–237.

Rutter, M., MacDonald, H., LeCouteur, A., Harrington, R., Bolton, P., & Bailey, A. (1990). Genetic factors in child psychiatric disorders. II. Empirical findings. *Journal of Child Psychology & Psychiatry & Allied Disciplines, 31*, 39–71.

Ryan, E. (2001). Mood disorders in juvenile offenders. *Juvenile justice fact sheet*. Charlottesville, VA: Institute of Law, Psychiatry, & Public Policy, University of Virginia.

Scott, M., Snowden, L., & Libby, A. (2002). From mental health to juvenile justice: What factors predict this transition? *Journal of Child and Family Studies, 11*(3), 299–311.

Seltzer, R. (2001). Juveniles with mental disabilities: When incarceration makes youth worse. *Juvenile Justice Update, 7*(2), 9–10.

Sexton, T., & Alexander, J. (2000, December). Functional family therapy. *Juvenile Justice Bulletin*. Washington, DC: Office of Juvenile Justice and Delinquency Prevention.

Sheras, P. (2000). Depression and suicide in juvenile offenders. *Juvenile justice fact sheet*. Charlottesville, VA: Institute of Law, Psychiatry, & Public Policy, University of Virginia.

Sherman, L. (1993). Defiance, deterrence, and irrelevance: A theory of the criminal sanction. *Journal of Research in Crime and Delinquency, 30*, 445–473.

Sukhodolsky, D., Golub, A., Stone, E., & Orban, L. (2005). Dismantling anger control training for children: A randomized pilot study of social problem-solving versus social skills training components. *Behavior Therapy, 36*(1), 15–23.

Tate, D., Reppucci, N., & Mulvey, E. (1995). Violent juvenile delinquents: Treatment efficacy and implications for future action. *American Psychologist, 50,* 777–785.

Teplin, L., Abram, K., McClelland, G., Dulcan, M., & Mericle, A. (2002). Psychiatric disorders in youth in juvenile detention. *Archives of General Psychiatry, 59,* 1133–1143.

van Manen, T., Prins, P., & Emmelkamp, P. (2004). Reducing aggressive behavior in boys with a social cognitive group treatment: Results of a randomized, controlled trial. *Journal of the American Academy of Child & Adolescent Psychiatry, 43*(12), 1478–1487.

Winner, L., Lanza-Kaduce, L., Bishop, D., & Frazier, C. (1997). The transfer of juveniles to criminal court: Reexamining recidivism over the long term. *Crime and Delinquency, 43*(4), 548–563.

Relevant Resources for Practitioners

Newsletters
Juvenile Correctional Mental Health Report
Juvenile Justice Digest
Juvenile Justice Update
OJJDP Fact Sheet
OJJDP Juvenile Justice Bulletin

Periodicals
Behavioral Sciences and the Law
Crime & Delinquency
Criminal Justice and Behavior
Journal of Adolescence
Journal of Interpersonal Violence
Journal of the American Academy of Child and Adolescent Psychiatry
Prison Legal News
Youth Violence and Juvenile Justice

Web sites
Blueprints for Violence, www.colorado.edu/cspv/blueprints/
Campbell Collaboration, www.campbellcollaboration.org/
Cochrane Collaboration, http://www.cochrane.org/index0.htm
Institute of Law, Public Policy, and Practice, www.ilppp.virginia.edu/
National Institute of Mental Health, www.nimh.nih.gov/healthinformation/childmenu.cfm
Office of Justice Programs, www.ojp.usdoj.gov/
U.S. Department of Justice, www.usdoj.gov/

Overrepresentation of African Americans Incarcerated for Delinquency Offenses in Juvenile Institutions

James Herbert Williams
Peter S. Hovmand
Charlotte L. Bright

Introduction

The overrepresentation of African American youth in the juvenile justice system across the United States has been a growing concern over the past 30 years. The rates of overrepresentation of African American youth at various decision points (e.g., arrest, intakes, detention, probation, and incarceration) are many times double or triple that of other racial or ethnic groups (Williams, Ayers, Outlaw, Abbott, & Hawkins, 2001).

The overall increase in the rates of overrepresentation of African Americans in juvenile justice are indicative of policy changes in the previous decade designed to "get tough" with juvenile offenders (Hawkins, Laub, Lauritsen, & Cothern, 2000; Walker, Spohn, & DeLone, 1996). The get-tough policies have influenced all aspects of the decision-making processes in juvenile justice (e.g., police attitudes, patrolling patterns, court referrals, rates of detention, and community attitudes). The literature identifies several theoretical mechanisms of disproportionate minority confinement (DMC) and the overrepresentation of African American youth in the justice system processing (Engen, Steen, & Bridges, 2002). Differential involvement suggests that differences in the severity and history of offending leads to disparities in confinement for African American and White youths (Engen et al., 2002; Wilbanks, 1987). Differential treatment/discrimination posits that African American youth are subjected to more formal and more severe forms of social control than comparable White youth at all stages of juvenile justice processing. Differential levels of social control may be directly related to race or factors often associated with race (e.g., socioeconomic status [SES], family

363

structure, and school status) (Engen et al., 2002). Structural-processual theory contends that biases exist at different decision-making points within the juvenile justice system (e.g., at the point of arrest, referral to juvenile court authorities, or commitment to a state institution). These biases may have a cumulative effect on disparities. Additionally, biases at early stages of the juvenile justice process should have a greater effect on differences in confinement than those detected at later stages. Macrocontextual theory asserts that social-structural or contextual characteristics (e.g., size of African American populations, poverty, and urbanization) are related to differential levels of formal social control and subsequent disparities in confinement (Blalock, 1967; Engen et al., 2002). Numerous studies have provided empirical evidence regarding the inequities in the juvenile justice system in how it processes and treats African American youths as compared to White youths. These studies will be highlighted later in this chapter.

Race is an important determinant in juvenile justice processing. This chapter will review the intersections between race and disparities in the juvenile justice system, utilizing case examples of two communities at different stages in addressing DMC, reviewing the salient literature, and providing an overview of practical approaches to address this significant issue.

Case Examples

Community A

In 1994, juvenile crime was peaking in Community A and the surrounding communities with a detention rate of 25% for African American youth and 12% for White youth (Multnomah County Department of Community Justice [MCDCJ], 1999). The high visibility of juvenile crime promoted increasingly negative perceptions of juveniles by community residents. The electronic and print media were instrumental in perpetuating negative stereotypes of juveniles and other negative community opinions. Community reform was needed but difficult to achieve due to the law-and-order agenda of the local governmental leaders. Individuals wanting an overall reform effort to decrease juvenile crime and detentions were considered to be "soft" on crime (MCDCJ, 1999). According to the 2000 census report, the population of Community A was approximately 670,000, of which more than 77% were classified as White, 6% African American, 6% Asian, and 8% Hispanic/Latino.

Community A's overall population has shown significant increases over the previous 30 years. Twenty-two percent of the population of Community A was younger than age 18 (U.S. Census, 2004a). The median household income was $41,000, with 13% of the population living below the poverty level (U.S. Census, 2004a).

In 1994, Community A developed a detention reform committee. This committee consisted of representatives from the minorities' communities and elected officials. This culturally diverse group consisted of approximately 40 community stakeholders. After a series of planning meetings, committee members concluded the need to develop a juvenile justice system that would distinguish between high-risk youth and high-need youth. High-risk youth are considered those with a high potential to reoffend, and high-need youth are those youth with special emotional and behavioral needs. They concluded that a detention incarceration facility may be more suitable for high-risk youth and not a suitable alternative for high-need youth (MCDCJ, 1999).

One significant challenge for the reform effort was getting community stakeholders to realize that there may be more effective means to meet juveniles' needs than using a secure detention as an alternative for other services. Community A built their reform from existing programs. They also secured seed funding from a local foundation to develop alternative programs and technical assistance. Community A developed a policy and decision-making team to formulate the philosophical goals of the reform initiative and develop new policies to address overrepresentation. The reform initiative was data driven and outcome based. A risk assessment tool was developed to reflect the new philosophy, policies, and community values. After 2 years of planning, the community stakeholders and political decision makers organized to implement an overall detention reform plan (MCDCJ, 1999). The plan focused on case processing, detention admissions criteria, minority disproportionality, alternative program development, confinement conditions, and data collection (MCDCJ, 1999). From 1994 to 2000, Community A decreased detention rates for African American youth by 50% and for White youth by 30% (MCDCJ, 1999). The result was a reduction of 29% in the ratio of African American detention rates to White detention rates, from 2 to 1.5. The sustained success of Community A in decreasing minority overrepresentation in their juvenile justice system established their efforts as a model program for other communities (Middaugh & Mendel, 2003).

Community B

In 2000, Community B became part of a mandated statewide effort to investigate the rates of overrepresentation and DMC. Community B was an urban area with high crime rates and with increasing rates of juvenile offending behavior (St. Cyr & Decker, 2003). African American youth represented 88% of all detained youth while Whites represented 10% from 2000 to 2001, and African American males accounted for 69% of all detained youth during that period (St. Cyr & Decker, 2003). Similar to Community A, juvenile crime in Community B also received high visibility from the electronic media and local politicians. Political pressure was brought to bear by local and state governmental officials on the two major urban areas of the state to investigate and document the level of DMC and develop programmatic efforts to address the overrepresentation of African American youth in the juvenile justice system. Small grants were provided to Community B by the state government to begin the process of addressing the DMC problem.

The demographics of Community B differed from Community A. Whereas Community A increased in total population, Community B decreased by approximately 50% over the course of 30 years from 622,000 in 1970 to 332,000 in 2000. Of the 332,000, 44% were classified as White, 51% African American, 2% Asian, and 2% Hispanic/Latino. Twenty-five percent of the population in Community B was younger than age 18 (U.S. Census, 2004b). The median household income was $27,000, with 26% of the population living below the poverty level (U.S. Census, 2004b). In 2002, judges and juvenile court and detention facilities administrators invited 125 community stakeholders to attend a community presentation by the W. Haywood Burns Institute, a leading national organization working to address the overrepresentation of youth of color in the juvenile justice system (W. Haywood Burns Institute, 2005). This initial meeting served as a catalyst to assemble a DMC advisory board consisting of community stakeholders to assist in the development of a communitywide strategy to address DMC. A previous community advisory group on juvenile court recidivism merged with the newly established DMC Advisory Board for a more focused approach to addressing this significant community problem. Community representatives from the judicial system, schools, law enforcement, city government, state social services, churches, youth development organizations, and local universities were represented on this advisory board. The juvenile courts and detention facilities engaged two researchers from the local university to document the extent of DMC for African American youth. A DMC coordinator was hired to refine existing and implement new programmatic efforts.

Several challenges have delayed the reform efforts for Community B. The lack of adequate funds and community organizational commitment continues to be a challenge. Juvenile justice leaders are motivated to pursue alternatives to confinement, but the lack of funding hinders planning and implementation. Limited funding has been secured for two alternative programs (i.e., electronic monitoring and voice recognition) and limited consulting and technical assistance. Community B has implemented a DMC education and training program for juvenile officers. Similar to Community A, Community B has also developed a risk assessment tool to achieve a more objective decision-making process for confinement focusing on court case decisions, detention admissions criteria, alternative program development, and data collection. However, there has been no significant DMC decrease since the development of the DMC Advisory Board, and African Americans (especially males) continue to be overrepresented in arrests and detentions (Martin & Decker, 2005).

Scope of the Problem

The overrepresentation of minority youth has been well documented in the juvenile justice system. National-level government attention focused on the concept of "disproportionate minority confinement" in 1988, with amendments to the Juvenile Justice and Delinquency Prevention Act of 1974 (JJDP Act) that compelled states to evaluate and address the overrepresentation of youth of color in locked facilities (Devine, Coolbaugh, & Jenkins, 1998). A 2002 amendment to the JJDP Act strengthens this legislation, obliging states to attend to disproportionate minority involvement in all stages of juvenile justice processing (Hsia, Bridges, & McHale, 2004). In assessing overrepresentation, all states found some degree of disparity between the number of minority youth in the population and the number involved in the various phases of processing (Leiber, 2002).

In particular, African American males have long been arrested, detained, and incarcerated disproportionately. Figures 16.1a and 16.1b provide an overview of delinquency referrals and detentions between 1988 and 1997 for African American and White youth. While racial disparity in juvenile justice has decreased somewhat in the past 2 decades, 2003 statistics indicate that African American youths composed 53% of arrests for person offenses and 28% of arrests for property offenses, but only 16% of the youth population. National data do not show overrepresentation in arrests for American Indian and Asian youth (Snyder, 2005), although state-by-state data indicate that these youth are

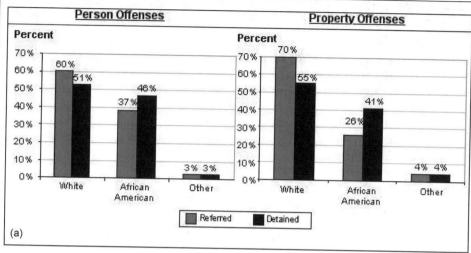

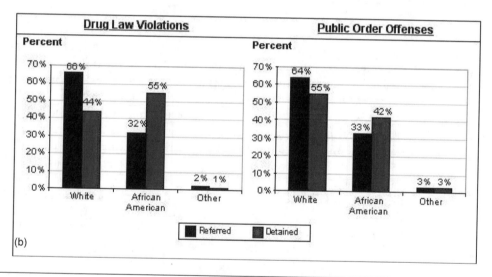

Racial proportions of referred and detained delinquency cases. 1997.
Source: Easy Access to Juvenile Court Statistics: 1988–1997 [data presentation and analysis package].
Office of Juvenile Justice and Delinquency Prevention (1999).

overrepresented in some state juvenile justice systems (Leiber, 2002). It is important to note that official data collection tends to categorize youth arrests by race rather than ethnicity, meaning that most Latinos are designated "White," and thus rates of arrest among Latinos cannot be accurately estimated (Snyder, 2005). Data collection to capture the ethnic diversity of each state is improving, however, as a result of new funding requirements through the Office of Juvenile Justice and Delinquency Prevention (OJJDP) formula grants (Nellis, 2005). In addition, some researchers cited in this section have gathered data about a variety of ethnic groups, not only Whites and African Americans.

The racial composition of the juvenile population in 2003 was 78% White, 16% African American, 4% Asian/Pacific Islander, and 1% American Indian. Most

Table 16.1	Percentage of African American Arrests in 2003	
	Offenses	**Percentages**
	Murder	48
	Forcible rape	33
	Robbery	63
	Aggravated assault	38
	Burglary	26
	Larceny/theft	27
	Motor vehicle theft	40
	Weapons	32
	Drug abuse violations	26
	Runaways	20
	Vandalism	18
	Liquor laws	4

Note. U.S. Department of Justice, Federal Bureau of Investigation. *Crime in the United States – 2003.* Retrieved August 23, 2005, from http://www.fbi.gov/ucr/cius_03/pdf/03sec4.pdf.

Hispanics/Latinos (an ethnic designation, not a race) were classified as White. In contrast to their representation in the population, African American youth were overrepresented in juvenile arrests for violent crimes and, to a lesser extent, property crimes (see Table 16.1). Of all juvenile arrests for violent crimes in 2003, 53% involved White youth, 45% involved African American youth, 1% involved Asian youth, and 1% involved American Indian youth. For property crime arrests, the proportions were 69% White, 28% African American, 2% Asian, and 1% American Indian (Snyder, 2005).

The violent crime arrest rate (i.e., arrests per 100,000 juveniles in the racial group) in 2003 for African American juveniles (752) was more than 4 times the rates for American Indian juveniles (172) and White juveniles (186) and more than 8 times the rate for Asian juveniles (88). For property crime arrests, the rate for African American juveniles (2,352) was about double the rates for American Indian juveniles (1,366) and White juveniles (1,237) and nearly four times the rate for Asian juveniles (614; Snyder, 2005).

During the period from 1980 through 2003, the African American-to-White disparity in juvenile arrest rates for violent crimes declined (see Figure 16.2). In 1980, the African American juvenile arrest rate for violent crime was 6.3 times the White rate; in 2003, the rate disparity had declined to 4.0. This reduction in arrest rate disparities between 1980 and 2003 was primarily the result of the decline in African American-to-White arrest rate disparities for robbery (from 11.5 in 1980 to 8.4 in 2003) because the disparity in the arrest rates for aggravated assault changed little (3.2 vs. 3.1; Snyder, 2005).

Self-report statistics suggest that part of this differential pattern of arrest may be due to real differences in offending behavior. According to some sources, African American youth report more frequent and serious offenses than White youth (American Prosecutors Research Institute, 2001; Elliott, 1994; Griffin, Botvin, Scheier, Doyle, & Williams, 2002). In other studies, African American and White youth do not show significantly different prevalence rates but do show a greater probability of committing an offense than Asian youth (Farrington et al., 2003; Hill, Hawkins, Etchison, & Williams, 2004). A meta-analysis of 65 studies addressed the question of differential offending and found

Murder

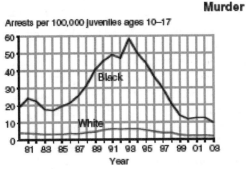

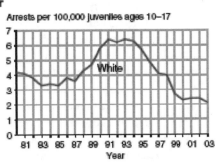

Robbery

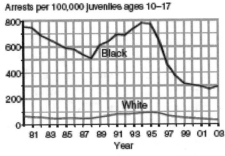

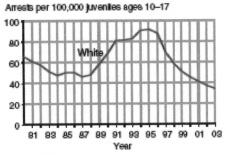

Aggravated Assault

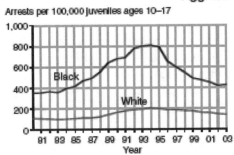

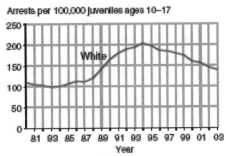

Property Crime Index

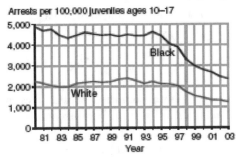

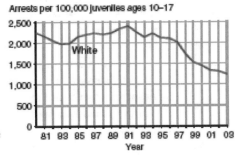

Arrest rates for African American and White youth.

that, while controlling for prior offenses decreased the prevalence of direct race effects, differences in behavior did not explain the racial disparities in juvenile justice processing (Engen et al., 2002). That is, inequities in the system cannot be explained by racial and ethnic behavioral differences.

Assessing specific causes of the disproportionate system involvement of minority youth is a very difficult task. A number of contextual and individual factors have been examined, and research has evaluated correlates of youth offending by race with a number of different and sometimes contradictory results. This problem is compounded by the complex etiology of juvenile crime, as well as by the lack of much information on racial and ethnic groups other than African Americans and Whites. Some of the knowledge that has been accumulated to date, however, is summarized briefly here.

Poverty and Associated Risk Factors

Ever since Shaw and McKay (1969) posited that neighborhood context is criminogenic, juvenile justice researchers have focused on the pivotal role of poverty and its attendant social problems as a precursor to or correlate of delinquent behavior. African American, Latino, and American Indian youth are more likely than White youth to live in poverty (Bruce, 2004; National Center for Children in Poverty, 2004; Snipp, 2005), and Asian Americans have lower average incomes than Whites (Segal, Kilty, & Kim, 2002). This has undeniable implications for the racial and ethnic composition of youth involved in the juvenile justice system.

Comparing self-report data for African American, Latino, and White youth, Kaufman (2005) found that African Americans are more likely to live in impoverished neighborhoods than Hispanic/Latinos, who are in turn more likely to live in impoverished neighborhoods than Whites. In addition, Hispanic/Latino and African American youth are significantly more likely than White youth to have witnessed violence or been victims of violent acts. "Neighborhood and SES measures reduce, but do not eliminate, the association between race and violence. However, this combination of measures explains the association between ethnicity (i.e., being Latino vs. Non-Hispanic White) and violence" (Kaufman, 2005, p. 241). Hawkins and colleagues (2000) also note that poverty and its attendant social problems are associated with violent offending among youth, and African American youth are disproportionately affected by these structural conditions. In addition to poverty itself, neighborhood decay and unemployment (factors associated with low-income families and communities) may also contribute to delinquency (Nellis, 2005).

Much has been made of the perceived connection between family structure and juvenile justice system involvement. In particular, it has been suggested that youth from single-parent homes are more likely than youth from two-parent homes to participate in criminal behavior (Anderson, 2002) or that they are more likely to receive punitive sanctions once in the system due to beliefs that their families cannot provide needed structure and guidance (DeJong & Jackson, 1998). Youth of color are more likely than White children to grow up in single-parent, predominantly female-headed households (McNulty & Bellair, 2003). Single-parent family structure may mediate the connection between delinquent behavior and race or ethnicity. Thus, actual differences, discrimination in the system, or both could be at work to contribute to disproportionate juvenile justice system involvement through family structure.

Racism and Discrimination in Society

Racism and discrimination in the broader societal context have been linked both theoretically and empirically to differential rates of offending. As with self- and official-report statistics, little has been studied regarding the perceived or actual effects of racism on youth of color who are not African American. This is a gap in the literature that clearly should be addressed; however, what is summarized in this chapter is mainly specific to African American youth.

Feld (2003) identifies a political and media tendency to exaggerate the percentage of young offenders who are violent and African American; policies that are "tough on crime" therefore constitute camouflaged racism entrenched in the political and cultural landscape. In elaborating on the experiences of African American youth, one study demonstrated that emotions such as anger and depression tend to mediate the relationship between discrimination and criminal behavior (Simons, Chen, Stewart, & Brody, 2003). Examining school data in Florida, Eitle and Eitle (2003) discovered that episodes of school violence were most likely in schools that were desegregated but existed in a larger community context of racial inequality. This adds support to the theory that racist and discriminatory practices at the macro level contribute to severe delinquent behavior. Caldwell, Kohn-Wood, Schmeelk-Cone, Chavous, and Zimmerman (2004) collected data from African American youth transitioning from high school to young adulthood and found that having faced discrimination was associated with a higher likelihood of having committed violent acts. They concluded that violence may be conceptualized as a maladaptive but understandable response to racism in society.

Racism and Discrimination in the Juvenile Justice System

In addition to broader societal issues of racism and discrimination, discriminatory practices have been identified within the juvenile justice system itself, leading to inequitable outcomes for White and African American youth. As Frazier and Bishop (1995) note, several stages of juvenile justice processing exist, small differences in each of which can eventually yield a large cumulative effect by the time a child is referred for treatment or incarceration.

Police officers, who make arrest decisions, may show some bias. One study, using vignettes to simulate arrest decision making, found that police are more likely to charge African American youth and release White youth (Sutphen, Kurtz, & Giddings, 1993), while another study documented discriminatory arrest patterns in situations where violent crimes were perpetrated by African Americans against White victims (Pope & Snyder, 2003). Police may have more opportunities to come into contact with African American youth than with White youth because much of their time is spent monitoring neighborhoods characterized by high levels of crime, or neighborhoods with larger proportions of African Americans (Hsia et al., 2004).

Probation officers, prosecutors, and judges make the majority of decisions beyond the point of arrest. Poe-Yamagata and Jones (2003) note that African American youth are overrepresented in referrals to juvenile court (intake), placement in locked detention facilities, waiver to adult criminal court, and residential placement as opposed to probation as a disposition. Some evidence also suggests that community-level variables, such as racial inequality and segregation, may condition system responses in that overall status of African American residents is negatively associated with disproportionately harsh treatment of youth in the juvenile court (Leiber & Stairs, 1999). Qualitative research findings indicate that some juvenile justice officials, from probation officers to judges, perceive African American youth in stereotypical terms and that existing diversion alternatives are not always culturally responsive (Pope, 1995).

Approaches to Prevention and Intervention

Approaches to reducing DMC for violent juvenile offenses must focus on strategies that reduce the flow of cases into or out of juvenile confinement. Flows affecting the cases in juvenile confinement can be conceptualized as exchanges or pathways across three major system levels: confinement including detention and incarceration, the juvenile justice system, and the community (see Figure 16.3). Across these three system levels, there are essentially six different types of pathways that can influence DMC: (a) entry into the juvenile justice system, (b) diversion, (c) entry into juvenile confinement, (d) waivers into the adult criminal justice system, (e) release from juvenile confinement into the community, and (f) release from the adult criminal justice system into the community (see Figure 16.4). The causes of the DMC problem will vary by community and across time in terms of these six pathways.

This poses a challenge for practitioners and other community stakeholders with applying evidence-based practices to DMC because the influential pathways change over time and across communities. What may have worked for one community may not work for a community experiencing a different set of dynamics, or even the same community some years after the initially successful intervention. It may even be the case that the current DMC problem for some communities is the result of previously successful past interventions. McCord (2003), for example, has noted the importance of considering the unanticipated and harmful outcomes of crime prevention programs. Thus, it is imperative that helping professionals consider how the juvenile justice system is functioning as a whole with respect to the DMC problem in their community and evaluate the appropriateness of empirically based practices accordingly.

The following sections provide an overview of the state of empirically based practices with respect to the DMC problem for African American youths with aggressive or violent behaviors (see also Figure 16.4). The OJJDP actively maintains a web-based search tool for identifying empirically supported juvenile justice intervention programs according to demographics, continuum along juvenile justice interventions, program type, and a variety of other characteristics. The OJJDP assigns model programs ratings of promising, effective, and exemplary. *Promising programs* have some empirical support and a reasonable framework, but their evidence is limited by a weak research design or inconsistent findings. *Effective programs* have been implemented with fidelity, rely on an established conceptual framework, and have demonstrated effectiveness through quasi-experimental research designs. *Exemplary programs* have also been implemented with fidelity and used sound theoretical frameworks; additionally, they have been found to be effective across settings and populations using high-quality experimental research

Overview of pathways contributing to the disproportionate minority confinement problem.

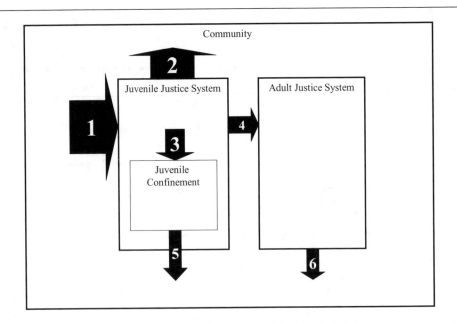

Main classification of pathways contributing to disproportionate minority confinement.

designs. The classification of approaches to interventions to reduce DMC for violent offenses is summarized in Table 16.2.

Approaches that reduce the entry into the juvenile justice system generally consist of prevention efforts that target risk factors at a variety of levels for violent or aggressive behaviors and initial entry into the juvenile justice system. These factors vary from the macro sociocultural level, which include the extralegal factors such as racism and discrimination that influence decision making that contributes to differential handling of African American youth, to the micro levels of the family and individual (see Figure 16.3). The vast majority of empirically based programs currently available for reducing African American youth at risk for confinement from violence or aggression fall into this category, with 58 programs that meet the criteria for being promising, effective, or exemplary with African American youth for preventing violence or aggression. Of these, 17 meet the OJJDP's criteria for effective programs while 15 meet the criteria for exemplary programs. Despite the concern over the influence of extralegal factors such as a race in juvenile arrest decisions by police (Leiber & Stairs, 1999), no systematic attention has been given to discerning effective from ineffective interventions with police, and this remains a much needed area of research for reducing DMC.

Juvenile Justice System → Community

Strategies that increase the utilization of diversion programs generally emphasize offering an alternative for first-time offenders to confinement or waivers into the adult criminal system. Such programs also stress the importance of addressing the underlying causes of delinquent behavior as a way to reduce the likelihood of reentry into the juvenile justice system. Presently, there are only seven programs considered by the OJJDP that

Table
16.2

Approaches to Prevention and Interventions for Disproportionate Minority Confinement by Major Pathways

Pathway	Intervention Goals	Promising	Effective	Exemplary
Community→ Juvenile justice system	Reduce violent offenses, reduce risk factors for committing violent offenses	• All Stars • Broader Urban Involvement and Leadership Development Detention Program (BUILD) • Facing History and Ourselves • Families and Schools Together (FAST) • Get Real About Violence • Girls' Circle • Great Body Shop • Healthy Families America • Nurturing Parenting Program • Oakland Beat Health Program • Open Circle • Operation Ceasefire • Peace Works • Philadelphia Youth Violence Reduction • Primary Mental Health Project • Responsive Classroom • Rural Education Achievement Project (REAP) • Say it Straight • SCARE Program • Second Step: A Violence Prevention Curriculum • Social Decision Making/Problem Solving • Supporting Adolescents with Guidance and Employment • TRIBES • Violence Prevention Curriculum for Adolescents • Woodrock Youth Development Programs • Wraparound Milwaukee	• Aggression Replacement Training • Al's Pals • CASASTART • Child–Parent Center • Consistency Management & Cooperative Discipline • First Step to Success • Gang Resistance Education and Training • I Can Problem Solve • Kansas City Gun Experiment • Multidimensional Family Therapy • Raising a Thinking Child: I Can Problem Solve for Families • Resolving Conflict Creatively Program • School Violence Prevention Demonstration Program • Schools and Families Educating Children (SAFE Children) • Skills, Opportunity, and Recognition (SOAR) • SMART Talk (Students Managing Anger and Resolution Together) • Success in Stages	• Big Brothers/Big Sisters • Coping Power Program • Early Risers "Skills for Success" Program • Fast Track • Functional Family Therapy • Good Behavior Game • Guiding Good Choices • Multidimensional Treatment Foster Care • Multisystemic Therapy • PeaceBuilders • Promoting Alternative Thinking Strategies • Responding in Peaceful and Positive Ways • Strengthening Families Program for Parents and Youths 10–14 • The Incredible Years • Too Good for Violence

(Continued)

Table 16.2 (Continued)

Pathway	Intervention Goals	Promising	Effective	Exemplary
Juvenile justice system → Community	Increase utilization of effective diversion and probation programs for violent juvenile offenders	• Project Back-on-Track • Wraparound Milwaukee • Jefferson County Juvenile Gun Court	• Bethlehem Police Family Group Conferencing Project • Baton Rouge Partnership for the Prevention of Juvenile Gun Violence	• Functional Family Therapy • Multisystemic Therapy
Juvenile justice system → Confinement	Decrease utilization, detention, and incarceration for violent juvenile offenders; shorten duration of sentences	No research demonstrating relationship between prevention/intervention approaches and juvenile confinement		
Juvenile justice system → Adult criminal justice system	Decrease utilization of waivers to adult court	No research demonstrating relationship between prevention/intervention approaches and use of waivers into adult criminal justice system		
Juvenile confinement → Community	Increase utilization of effective aftercare programs for juvenile violent offenders exiting juvenile confinement, shorten duration of sentences, decrease recidivism		• Aggression Replacement Training • Mendota Juvenile Treatment Center	
Adult criminal justice system → Community	Increase utilization of effective aftercare programs for juvenile violent offenders exiting adult system, shorten duration of sentences, decrease recidivism		• Aggression Replacement Training	

Note. Adapted from *The Office of Juvenile Justice and Delinquency Prevention Programs (OJJDP) Model Programs' Guide (MGP)*, by the Office of Juvenile Justice and Delinquency Prevention, 2004, retrieved August 23, 2005, from http://www.dsgonline.com/mpg2.5/mpg_index.htm.

are promising, effective, or exemplary, and only two programs that meet the criteria for exemplary and two programs that meet the criteria for effective. Notably, functional family therapy and multisystemic therapy are considered exemplary approaches to both prevention and early intervention.

Juvenile Justice System → Confinement

Approaches to reducing the entry into juvenile confinement have for the most part focused on changes in juvenile court decision making, including the use of determinant sentencing policies and changes in administrative procedures (Nellis, 2005). Advocates for both toughness on crime and equity and consistency in sentencing have sought changes that make sentencing less subjective (Forst, Fisher, & Coates, 1985). Despite the long history of research on how race affects sentencing decisions, there are still no empirically based interventions for reducing DMC with respect to sentencing.

Juvenile Justice System → Adult Criminal Justice System

Approaches to reducing DMC by transferring serious offenders into the criminal justice system are controversial. While administrative and legislative changes can result in the increased use of waivers and thereby decrease the number of youth likely to face juvenile confinement, the results have been criticized as disproportionately affecting African American youth, harmful, and ultimately mixed in their outcomes (Rodriguez, 2003; Steiner & Hemmens, 2003).

Juvenile Confinement → Community

Interventions that focus on juvenile confinement into the community consist of reentry programs that help juveniles adapt to life in a community and reduce the likelihood of recidivism. Only two programs have been found effective for African American youth with violence or aggression problems: aggression replacement training and the Mendota Juvenile Treatment Center. Thus, this remains another area for future research.

Criminal Justice System → Community

The increasing use of waivers or transfers from the juvenile justice system will by definition create a demand for programs that address reentry. Failing to address this will inevitably feed back to affect the community-level risk factors for another generation of juvenile offenders. Aggression replacement therapy is currently the only empirically supported intervention available for adaptation to an intervention program specific to the reentry of juvenile offenders from the criminal justice system.

Conclusion

Most of the epidemiological information presented in this chapter documents racial disparity in juvenile justice processing, in particular between African American and White youth. In-depth data on other racial and ethnic groups, in particular Latinos, American Indians, and Asians, are sorely lacking in the literature to date. More comprehensive data collection is now mandated through the OJJDP formula grant process, which should improve our understanding of the complex relationships between race, ethnicity, and overrepresentation.

DMC has been extensively reviewed by the National Research Council Panel on Juvenile Crime and other researchers (McCord, Widom, & Crowell, 2001; Pope & Feyerherm, 1995; Stahl, 2001). Studies have concluded that African American youth are overrepresented at all stages of the juvenile justice system, and this disproportionality can be explained by numerous theoretical hypotheses. There is a large body of epidemiological research documenting the extent of overrepresentation of African American youth in the juvenile justice system.

Keeping the limitations of the extant data in mind, we can generalize that African American overrepresentation in juvenile justice is attributable to a variety of social and structural problems and that it needs to be addressed through community action to attend to inequality as well as through justice system intervention and change. There is little research investigating the extent that African American overrepresentation can be explained by differences in risk factors.

When communities are presented with such a significant problem as DMC of juvenile offenders, one of the most acceptable methods of addressing the problem is to engage research and data collection. This satisfies the need to identify the problem and to document legitimately the issue that is to be addressed. The community examples used in this chapter initially engaged in data collection to obtain a better perspective of the level of the overrepresentation of African American youth in their juvenile justice systems.

Overall, most of the empirically based interventions focus on reducing risk factors for initial entry into the juvenile justice system or early interventions. Given that it may be difficult to distinguish first-time offenders from repeat offenders by administrative records alone, a robust strategy would include interventions that are effective as both prevention and early intervention. Functional family therapy and multisystemic therapy both meet this criteria, but additional research should be developed to see to what extent prevention efforts can be extended into early intervention programs.

Specificity of sentencing procedures and transfer decisions to state legislation and local jurisdictional rules will make it difficult to assess the effectiveness of interventions that focus on confinement and transfer decisions. However, more research is urgently needed in order to assess both the short-term and long-term impact of such changes, especially given public support for transfers to adult court for serious or violent juvenile offenders. Likewise, increased attention needs to be paid toward developing effective reentry programs, especially for juveniles transferred to the criminal justice system and sentenced to prison.

The prominent trend in juvenile justice during the 1990s was a tough, hard-nosed approach to juvenile crime. The majority of states including the District of Columbia passed laws to transfer juvenile offenders to adult courts. Overall, the literature revealed that this approach was counterproductive and was not achieving the expected results (McCord et al., 2001). Studies found that many times youth transferred to adult courts had higher rates of reoffending and committed more serious crimes than youth remaining under the custody of the juvenile courts (McCord et al., 2001).

Between 1992 and 1999 the Annie E. Casey Foundation designed and funded a national multisite demonstration project, the Juvenile Detention Alternative Initiative

(JDAI; Mendel, 2003). Recently, the Annie E. Casey Foundation released a series of technical reports as part of their Juvenile Detention Alternatives Initiative (Annie E. Casey Foundation, 2005). One publication from this series, "*Reducing Racial Disparities in the Juvenile Justice System,*" provides the following strategies for addressing DMC at a community level: (a) Formulate a vision and related policy goals, (b) create structure (e.g., task forces and advisory boards) charged with sustaining a focus on DMC, (c) collect data and conduct research on where disparities exist, and (d) build coalitions and alliances with people of color (Annie E. Casey Foundation, 2005). The DMC strategies undertaken by Communities A and B closely follow the strategies outlined in the Annie E. Casey publication.

Effective DMC intervention must be implemented at the policy level for continual development and expansion of effective programs. These programs should promote effective and ongoing system monitoring of various decision-making stages of the juvenile justice process. Strategies for policy changes need to be formulated by the various community stakeholders. This process is evident in Community A. It is important to engage all community stakeholders (e.g., community leaders, community residents, juvenile justice functionaries, and local and state elected leaders) to achieve success with any communitywide programmatic effort to reduce DMC. The complex nature of DMC requires a comprehensive and inclusive approach for determining accomplishable evidence-based solutions. Communities must leverage monetary resources, exercise decision-making power, and utilize influence to position themselves to adequately reduce racial disparities in the juvenile justice system.

RESOURCES AND REFERENCES

American Prosecutors Research Institute. (2001). *Disproportionate minority confinement: Practical solutions for juvenile justice professionals.* Retrieved August 23, 2005, from http://www.ndaa-apri.org/pdf/dmc_2002.pdf

Annie E. Casey Foundation. (2005). *Juvenile Detention Alternatives Initiative. Reducing racial disparities in juvenile detention.* Retrieved December 4, 2005, from http://www.aecf.org/initiatives/jdai/

Anderson, A. L. (2002). Individual and contextual influences on delinquency: The role of the single-parent family. *Journal of Criminal Justice, 30*(6), 575–587.

Blalock, H. M. (1967). *Toward a theory of minority group relations.* New York: Wiley.

Bruce, M. A. (2004). Contextual complexity and violent delinquency among Black and White males. *Journal of Black Studies, 35*(1), 65–98.

Caldwell, C. H., Kohn-Wood, L. P., Schmeelk-Cone, K. H., Chavous, T. M., & Zimmerman, M. A. (2004). Racial discrimination and racial identity as risk or protective factors for violent behaviors in African American young adults. *American Journal of Community Psychology, 33*(1/2), 91–105.

DeJong, C., & Jackson, K. C. (1998). Putting race into context: Race, juvenile justice processing, and urbanization. *Justice Quarterly, 15*(3), 487–504.

Devine, P., Coolbaugh, K., & Jenkins, S. (1998, December). Disproportionate minority confinement: Lessons learned from five states. *Juvenile Justice Bulletin.* Retrieved August 20, 2005, from http://www.ncjrs.gov/pdffiles/170606.pdf

Eitle, D., & Eitle, T. M. (2003). Segregation and school violence. *Social Forces, 82*(2), 589–615.

Elliott, D. S. (1994). Serious violent offenders: Onset, developmental course, and termination—The American Society of Criminology 1993 Presidential Address. *Criminology, 32*(1), 1–21.

Engen, R. L., Steen, S., & Bridges, G. S. (2002). Racial disparities in the punishment of youth: A theoretical and empirical assessment of the literature. *Social Problems, 49*(2), 194–220.

Farrington, D. P., Jolliffe, D., Hawkins, J. D., Catalano, R. F., Hill, K. G., & Kosterman, R. (2003). *Gender and race differences in self-reported offending and court referrals.* Manuscript submitted for publication.

Feld, B. C. (2003). The politics of race and juvenile justice: The "due process" revolution and the conservative reaction. *Justice Quarterly, 20*(4), 765–800.

Forst, M. L., Fisher, B. A., & Coates, R. B. (1985). Indeterminate and determinate sentencing of juvenile delinquents: A national survey of approaches to commitment and release decision-making. *Juvenile and Family Court Journal, 36*, 1–12.

Frazier, C. E., & Bishop, D. M. (1995). Reflections on race effects in juvenile justice. In K. Kempf-Leonard, C. E. Pope, & W. H. Feyerherm (Eds.), *Minorities in juvenile justice* (pp. 16–46). Thousand Oaks, CA: Sage.

Griffin, K. W., Botvin, G. J., Scheier, L. M., Doyle, M. M., & Williams, C. (2002). Common predictors of cigarette smoking, alcohol use, aggression, and delinquency among inner-city minority youth. *Addictive Behaviors, 28*(6), 1141–1148.

Hawkins, D. F., Laub, J. H., Lauritsen, J. L, & Cothern, L. (2000, June). Race, ethnicity, and serious and violent juvenile offending. *Juvenile Justice Bulletin*. Retrieved August 20, 2005, from http://www.ncjrs.org/pdffiles1/ojjdp/181202.pdf

Hill, K. G., Hawkins, J. D., Etchison, K., & Williams, J. H. (2004). *Advancing knowledge on disproportionate minority confinement: Findings from the Seattle Social Development Project.* Unpublished manuscript, Social Development Research Group, University of Washington, Seattle.

Hsia, H. M., Bridges, G. S., & McHale, R. (2004, September). *Disproportionate minority confinement: 2002 update.* Retrieved August 20, 2005, from http://www.ncjrs.gov/pdffiles1/ojjdp/201240.pdf

Kaufman, J. M. (2005). Explaining the race/ethnicity-violence relationship: Neighborhood context and social psychological processes. *Justice Quarterly, 22*(2), 224–251.

Leiber, M. J. (2002). Disproportionate minority confinement (DMC) of youth: An analysis of state and federal efforts to address the issue. *Crime and Delinquency, 48*(1), 3–45.

Leiber, M. J., & Stairs, J. M. (1999). Race, contexts, and the use of intake diversion. *Journal of Research in Crime and Delinquency, 36*(1), 56–86.

Martin, K., & Decker, S. H. (2005). *Disproportionate minority confinement report: First and second degree tampering-specific results.* Report prepared for the DMC Advisory Board of the 22nd Judicial Circuit Family Court-Juvenile Division. St. Louis, MO: Author.

McCord, J. (2003). Cures that harm: Unanticipated outcomes of crime prevention programs. *Annals of the American Academy of Political and Social Science, 587*, 16–30.

McCord, J., Widom, C. S., & Crowell, N. A. (2001). *Juvenile crime, juvenile justice.* Washington, DC: National Academy Press.

McNulty, T. L., & Bellair, P. E. (2003). Explaining racial and ethnic differences in adolescent violence: Structural disadvantage, family well-being, and social capital. *Justice Quarterly, 20*(1), 1–31.

Mendel, D. (2003). And the walls keep tumbling down: A demonstration project has come and gone, but detention reform continues to gather steam. *AdvoCasey: Documenting Programs that Work for Kids & Families, 5*(1), 18–27.

Middaugh, S., & Mendel, D. (2003). On racial balance: A breakthrough. *AdvoCasey: Documenting Programs that Work for Kids & Families, 5*(1), 26.

Multnomah County Department of Community Justice. (1999). *Juvenile detention reform initiative.* Portland, OR: Author.

National Center for Children in Poverty. (2004, May). *Low-income children in the United States.* Retrieved September 13, 2005, from http://www.nccp.org/media/cpf04-text.pdf

Nellis, A. M. (2005, January). *Seven steps to develop and evaluate strategies to reduce disproportionate minority contact (DMC).* Retrieved August 20, 2005, from http://www.jrsa.org/jjec/about/dmc_guidebook.html

Office of Juvenile Justice and Delinquency Prevention. (2004). *The Office of Juvenile Justice and Delinquency Prevention's Model Programs Guide (MPG).* Retrieved August 23, 2005, from http://www.dsgonline.com/mpg2.5/mpg_index.htm

Poe-Yamagata, E., & Jones, M. (2003). *And justice for some.* Retrieved August 23, 2005, from http://www.buildingblocksforyouth.org/justiceforsome/jfs.pdf

Pope, C. E. (1995). Equity within the juvenile justice system: Directions for the future. In K. Kempf-Leonard, C. E. Pope, & W. H. Feyerherm (Eds.), *Minorities in juvenile justice* (pp. 201–216). Thousand Oaks, CA: Sage.

Pope, C. E., & Feyerherm, W. (1995). *Minorities and the juvenile justice system: Research summary* (Report No. NCJ-145849). Second printing. Rockville, MD: Juvenile Justice Clearinghouse. (ERIC Document Reproduction Service No. ED 461 681).

Pope, C. E., & Snyder, H. N. (2003, April). Race as a factor in juvenile arrests. *Juvenile Justice Bulletin*. Retrieved August 20, 2005, from http://www.ncjrs.gov/pdffiles1/ojjdp/189180.pdf

Rodriguez, N. (2003). Youth transfer decisions: Exploring county variations. *Juvenile and Family Court Journal, 54*, 33–46.

Segal, E. A., Kilty, K. M., & Kim, R. Y. (2002). Social and economic inequality and Asian Americans in the United States. *Journal of Poverty, 6*(4), 5–21.

Shaw, C., & McKay, H. (1969). *Juvenile delinquency and urban areas* (Rev. ed.). Chicago: University of Chicago.

Simons, R. L, Chen, Y., Stewart, E. A., & Brody, G. H. (2003). Incidents of discrimination and risk for delinquency: A longitudinal test of strain theory with an African American sample. *Justice Quarterly, 20*(4), 827–854.

Snipp, C. M. (2005, August). *American Indian and Alaska Native children: Results from the 2000 Census.* Retrieved September 13, 2005, from http://www.prb.org/Template.cfm?Section=PRB&template=/ContentManagement/ContentDisplay.cfm&ContentID=12788

Snyder, H. N. (2005, August). Juvenile arrests 2003. *Juvenile Justice Bulletin.* Retrieved August 24, 2005, from http://www.ncjrs.org/pdffiles1/ojjdp/209735.pdf

Stahl, A. L. (2001). *Delinquency cases in juvenile courts, 1998: OJJDP Fact Sheet #31.* Washington, DC: Office of Juvenile Justice and Delinquency Prevention.

St. Cyr, J. L., & Decker, S. H. (2003). *Disproportionate minority confinement report: Year and offense specific results.* Report to the Advisory Board of the 22nd Judicial Circuit Family Court-Juvenile Division. St. Louis, MO: Author.

Steiner, B., & Hemmens, C. (2003). Juvenile waiver 2003: Where are we now? *Juvenile and Family Court Journal, 54*, 1–24.

Sutphen, R., Kurtz, P. D., & Giddings, M. (1993). The influence of juveniles' race on police decision-making: An exploratory study. *Juvenile and Family Court Journal, 44*(2), 69–78.

U.S. Census Bureau. (2004a). *US Census Bureau State & County Quickfacts: Multnomah County, Oregon.* Retrieved November 27, 2005, from http://quickfacts.census.gov/qfd/sates/41/41051.html

U.S. Census Bureau. (2004b). *US Census Bureau State & County Quickfacts: St. Louis City, Missouri.* Retrieved November 27, 2005, from http://quickfacts.census.gov/qfd/sates/29/2965000.html

U.S. Department of Justice, Federal Bureau of Investigation. *Crime in the United States – 2003.* Retrieved August 23, 2005, from http://www.fbi.gov/ucr/cius_03/pdf/03sec4.pdf

Walker, S., Spohn, C., & DeLone, M. (1996). *The color of justice: Race, ethnicity, and crime in America.* New York: Wadsworth.

W. Haywood Burns Institute for Juvenile Justice Fairness and Equity. (2005). *Reducing disproportionality locally.* Retrieved December 4, 2005, from http://www.burnsinstitute.org/reducing.html

Wilbanks, W. (1987). *The myth of a racist criminal justice system.* Belmont, CA: Wadsworth.

Williams, J. H., Ayers, C. D., Outlaw, W. S., Abbott, R. D., & Hawkins, J. D. (2001). The effects of race in juvenile justice: Investigating early stage processes. *Journal for Juvenile Justice and Detention Services, 16*(2), 77–91.

IV

Forensic Services and Programs for Adult Offenders

Drug Courts

Scope of the Problem

Steven Belenko
David DeMatteo
Nicholas Patapis

Changes in U.S. drug policy initiated in the early 1980s led to a rapid increase in the numbers of individuals incarcerated for drug-related offenses (Belenko, 1990, 2000a; Zimring & Hawkins, 1991). As a result, prison and jail admissions more than quadrupled over the past 2 decades to more than 2 million inmates (Harrison & Karberg, 2004), with drug violations accounting for approximately 60% of the increase in the federal inmate population and one third of the increase in the state inmate population (Belenko & Peugh, 1999; Harrison & Beck, 2003). At the end of 2001, drug offenders composed 55% of federal prison inmates and over 20% of state prison inmates in this country (Harrison & Beck, 2003).

Drug Use and Crime

The connections between illegal drug abuse and crime have been well documented (Bradford, Greenberg, & Motayne, 1992; Goldstein, 1985), and substance abusers are disproportionately represented in criminal justice populations. Approximately 80% of state and federal prison and jail inmates (Belenko & Peugh, 2005), 67% of probationers (Bureau of Justice Statistics [BJS], 1998), and 80% of parolees (BJS, 2001; Travis, Solomon, & Waul, 2001) were arrested for a drug- or alcohol-related offense, were intoxicated at the time of their offense, reported committing their offense to get money to buy drugs, or have a demonstrated history of a substance abuse problem. A range of 42 to 86% of adult male arrestees (39 sites) and 52 to 82% of female arrestees (25 sites) tested positive for marijuana, cocaine, opiates, methamphetamine, or PCP (Zhang, 2004). Among male arrestees, a range of 24 to 50% was at risk for drug dependence (31–63% of females). Illicit drug use by the offender has been implicated in 50% of violent crimes (National Institute on Drug Abuse [NIDA], 1993; National Institute of Justice [NIJ], 2000), 50% of domestic violence crimes (Center for Substance Abuse Treatment, 2000), 80% of substantiated child abuse and neglect cases (Child Welfare League of America, 1990), 50 to 75% of theft and property offenses (French et al., 2000; NIJ, 2000), and 75 to 99% of prostitution and drug dealing/manufacturing offenses (Hunt, 1990; NIJ, 2000).

Inmates who regularly use drugs have higher recidivism rates than other inmates (Belenko, 2002). Within 3 years, 95% of released state inmates with drug use histories return to drug use (Marlowe, DeMatteo, & Festinger, 2003; Martin, Butzin, Saum, & Inciardi, 1999), 68% are rearrested, 47% are reconvicted, and 25% are sentenced to prison for a new crime (Langan & Levin, 2002). Without treatment interventions, about 85% of drug-abusing offenders relapse within the first 6 to 12 months (Beck & Shipley, 1989; Hanlon, Nurco, Bateman, & O'Grady, 1998; Marlowe, 2002; Martin et al., 1999; McLellan, 2003; Nurco, Hanlon, & Kinlock, 1991).

Other Offender Health and Social Service Needs

Drug-involved offenders typically present with other problems in addition to drug abuse or dependence (Belenko & Peugh, 1999; Hammett, Gaiter, & Crawford, 1998; Hammett, Roberts, & Kennedy, 2001). For example, given the connections among crime, poverty, and poor health, many offenders need medical services (Anno, 1991; Hammett, Harmon, & Maruschak, 1999; Marquart, Merianos, Hebert, & Carroll, 1997). Health services of particular relevance for drug-involved offenders include treatment and prevention of HIV and other infectious diseases (Hammett et al., 1998). The large numbers of at-risk offenders suggest a need to educate them about reducing their HIV risk behaviors and to give them the tools to lower HIV infection incidence after release (Belenko, Langley, Crimmins, & Chaple, 2004; Braithwaite & Arriola, 2003). Offenders under probation or parole supervision are also at high risk for HIV but receive few effective interventions to reduce risk (Belenko, Langley, et al., 2004; Martin, O'Connell, Inciadi, Beard, & Surratt, 2003). Offenders also have high rates of mental health conditions and comorbid substance abuse/mental health disorders (Belenko, Lang, & O'Connor, 2003; Ditton, 1999; Lamb & Weinberger, 1998); 32% of regular drug users and 28% of alcohol-involved inmates had indications of a mental health problem (Belenko, 2002). In addition, high rates of psychopathy, including antisocial personality disorder, have been linked to reoffending (Festinger et al., 2002; Gendreau, Little, & Goggin, 1996; Marlowe, Festinger, & Lee, 2003) and treatment failure (Peters, Haas, & Murrin, 1999). But treatment for comorbid mental health and substance abuse problems presents substantial complications that are seldom addressed (Belenko et al., 2003; Broner, Borum, & Gawley, 2001; Hoff & Rosenheck, 1999). Offender treatment retention studies have found that mental health disorders are predictive of early termination (Lang & Belenko, 2000), and those with a comorbid psychiatric diagnosis are less likely to enter substance abuse treatment in the first place (Claus & Kendleberger, 2002).

Employment problems can affect long-term recovery and complicate community transition (Belenko & Peugh, 2005; Leukefeld, McDonald, Staton, & Mateyoke-Scrivner, 2004; Travis et al., 2001). Offenders with few marketable skills and job opportunities are more susceptible to relapse and reoffending (Laub & Sampson, 2001; Platt, 1995). Further, for many offenders their physical or mental health problems make it difficult to sustain employment or successfully complete educational programs (Belenko, 2002). Accordingly, an important goal of an effective intervention is to identify employment and training needs; to provide the skills training that enables the offender to be reintegrated into the legitimate labor market; or to provide basic literacy skills, GED certification, and life skills. Offenders who receive vocational training, or have higher employment and earnings rates, have lower reoffending risk (Finn, 1999; Needels, 1996; Seiter & Kadela, 2003). In addition, lack of access to health insurance or other benefits limits offenders' access to housing, health care, and treatment (Hammett et al., 2001; Nelson & Trone, 2000). Offenders also have poor education: 39% of regular drug users in prison have less than 4 years of high school and no GED, and only 38% of all inmates received some academic education within prison since their admission (Belenko, 2002).

Many drug-involved offenders grow up in families with high rates of substance use and dysfunction (Belenko & Logan, 2003; Henggeler, Clingempeel, Brondino, & Pickrel, 2002). Family drug use and criminal activity and low levels of parental involvement are risk factors for juvenile substance abuse and delinquency (Loeber & Farrington, 1998) and entry into the juvenile justice system (Farrington, 1998; Sampson & Laub, 1993). Offenders have limited access to programs that prepare parents to reintegrate with their children, families, or community, or to improve parenting skills (Petersilia, 2000). Taxman, Young, Byrne, Holsinger, and Anspach (2003) point to the importance of strengthening family and community support for released inmates (Beckerman, 1998), as do NIDA's principles of effective treatment (NIDA, 1999).

Substance-involved offenders also have social networks of peers with high rates of drug use and criminal behavior (Belenko & Peugh, 1999; Friedman, Curtis, Neaigus, Jose, & Des Jarlais, 1999), an important risk factor for initiation into and maintenance of substance abuse and criminal behavior (Keenan, Loeber, Zhang, Stouthamer-Loeber, & Van Kammen, 1995; Wills & Cleary, 1999). Conversely, association with prosocial peers may protect substance-involved offenders from relapse and recidivism (Carvajal et al., 1999; Hoge, Andrews, & Leschied, 1996); social networks must be considered in designing effective offender supervision and service plans. Because at-risk offenders are likely to belong to a peer group with lower social status, simply changing peer groups may be difficult (La Greca, Prinstein, & Fetter, 2001). Educating offenders about peer group risk for substance use and criminal behavior may be important, but helping them gain more positive friendships may be equally critical for sustaining treatment effects (McBride, VanderWaal, Terry, & VanBuren, 1999; Prinstein, Boergers, & Spirito, 2001).

Finally, access to affordable, stable drug-free housing is important for offenders (Rossi, 1989; Travis et al., 2001). Many of them face obstacles to finding adequate, stable, and sober housing due to poor family ties, lack of financial resources for a rental deposit, ineligibility for public housing, or discrimination by landlords (Hammett et al., 2001). Public housing may be denied because of their criminal records or history of drug involvement. Offenders also tend to come from low socioeconomic strata and have relatively high rates of prior homelessness (Belenko, 2002).

The Economic Consequences of Drug-Related Crime

Substance abuse and dependence and their consequences are associated with substantial health and social costs in the United States (Belenko, Patapis, & French, 2005). Large numbers of Americans continue to suffer from the effects of substance abuse, and it remains one of the nation's most serious health and social problems (Office of National Drug Control Policy [ONDCP], 2001). As a result, federal, state, and local governments have invested substantial amounts of money over the past 35 years for prevention and treatment programs aimed at reducing the impact of alcohol and illegal drug use. Yet, despite this spending, only a small percentage of the 24 million Americans with alcohol or drug problems are actively engaged in treatment (Office of Applied Studies, 2003).

The health and social costs of illegal drug and alcohol use in this country are substantial, reflecting the effects of substance abuse on crime, productivity, health problems, premature death, underemployment, and family stability. The ONDCP (2001) estimated the total societal costs of illegal drug use in 1998 at $143.4 billion ($168 billion in 2004 dollars). Nearly two thirds of these costs (62%) are related to the enforcement of drug laws and the effects of illegal drug use on criminal behavior, including $31.1 billion in public criminal justice costs (in 1998 dollars), $30.1 billion in lost productivity due to incarceration, $24.6 billion in lost productivity due to crime careers, and $2.9 billion in other costs including property damage and victimization. Other large costs are due to drug-related illness ($23.1 billion), premature mortality ($16.6 billion), drug abuse treatment and prevention ($7.1 billion), HIV/AIDS ($3.4 billion), and other medical consequences or hospitalization ($4.1 billion).

The costs to society of alcohol abuse and its consequences are even greater (Rice, Kelman, Miller, & Dunmeyer, 1990). The most recent estimate of the overall economic cost of alcohol abuse was $185 billion in 1998 (Harwood, 2000). More than 70% of the estimated costs of alcohol abuse for 1998 were attributed to lost productivity ($134.2 billion), including losses from alcohol-related illness ($87.6 billion), premature death ($36.5 billion), and crime ($10.1 billion). The remaining costs include health care expenditures ($26.3 billion, or 14.3% of the total), such as the cost of treating alcohol abuse and dependence ($7.5 billion), the costs of treating the adverse medical consequences of alcohol consumption ($18.9 billion), property and administrative costs of alcohol-related motor vehicle accidents ($15.7 billion), and criminal justice system costs of alcohol-related crime ($6.3 billion).

In general, recent reviews of the economic impacts of substance abuse treatment are consistent in finding that substance abuse treatment interventions yield net economic benefits to society (Belenko et al., 2005; Cartwright, 2000; Harwood et al., 2002; McCollister & French, 2003). Cost–benefit studies of different treatment modalities and client populations continue to report significant cost savings and positive returns on treatment investments; a primary component of the economic benefit is the reduction in crime and victimization following treatment.

Drug Treatment and the Criminal Justice System

Traditional correctional or punitive approaches have had little influence on drug use or criminal recidivism among offenders (for reviews, see Marlowe, 2002, 2003). Between 50% and 70% of probationers fail to comply with applicable conditions for drug testing and attendance in drug treatment (Langan & Cunniff, 1992; Nurco et al., 1991). Moreover, no incremental benefits are obtained from intensive supervision probation programs,[1] and some studies have found *worse* outcomes because infractions were more likely to be detected (Gendreau, Cullen, & Bonta, 1994; Petersilia & Turner, 1993). Finally, results of dozens of evaluations have revealed *no* effects on criminal recidivism or drug use for "intermediate sanctions" such as boot camps, electronic monitoring, house arrest, or shock incarceration (e.g., Gendreau, Goggin, Cullen, & Andrews, 2000; Gendreau, Smith, & Goggin, 2001; Sherman et al., 1997; Taxman, 1999a).

Community-Based Drug Treatment Outcomes

Success rates for drug-involved offenders are also limited in traditional community treatment settings, largely because offenders fail to remain long enough to receive a minimally adequate dosage of services. Results from national treatment studies suggest that 3 months of drug treatment may be a threshold for detecting dose–response effects for the interventions, and 6 to 12 months may be a threshold for observing meaningful reductions in drug use (Simpson, Joe, Fletcher, Hubbard, & Anglin, 1999). Approximately 50% of clients who complete 12 months or more of drug treatment remain abstinent for an additional year following completion of treatment (McLellan, Lewis, O'Brien, & Kleber, 2000). Unfortunately, few drug-abusing offenders reach these thresholds. For example, between 40% and 70% of probationers and parolees drop out of treatment or attend irregularly within 3 to 6 months (Langan & Cunniff, 1992; Nurco et al., 1991; Taxman, 1999a; Young, Usdane, & Torres, 1991), and over 90% drop out within 12 months (e.g., Satel, 1999). Yet reductions in drug use have been found to be associated with significant reductions in future crime and violence among offenders (e.g., Chaiken & Chaiken, 1990; Newcomb, Galaif, & Carmona, 2001; Nurco, Kinlock, & Hanlon, 1990).

Treatment Alternatives in the Criminal Justice System

Given the high rates of substance involvement among offenders, various initiatives have been devised to provide community-based supervision and treatment to drug offenders in lieu of criminal prosecution or incarceration. Prior to the late 1980s, there were few systematic efforts to divert or otherwise link drug-involved offenders to treatment programs, especially felony offenders (Belenko, 2000b). However, over the past decade a number of different treatment alternatives have been developed, implemented, and tested with varying degrees of success. These range in intensity from true diversion programs, to probation-supervised treatment, to judicially supervised programs such as the Treatment Accountability for Safer Communities case management programs (Anglin, Longshore, & Turner, 1999), to drug courts. Treatment alternatives can be implemented at almost any stage of the criminal justice process: prior to adjudication (diversion), during the pretrial period, as a condition of probation, in lieu of incarceration, or as a condition of parole.

True diversion programs permit low-level misdemeanor offenders to have their charges dropped and their arrest record expunged contingent on completion of a prescribed regimen of supervised drug treatment and perhaps community supervision by a probation or pretrial services officer. Record expungement permits the individual to respond truthfully on an employment application or similar document that he or she has not been arrested for a drug-related offense. Although prosecutorial resistance means that most diversion programs serve low-level misdemeanor or first-time offenders, a few exceptions exist. Notably, the Drug Treatment Alternative to Prison program (DTAP), operated by the Kings County (Brooklyn, NY) District Attorney's Office, diverts offenders charged with drug sale who are facing mandatory state prison time because of a prior felony conviction (Hynes & Swern, 2002). DTAP participants enter long-term residential drug treatment in therapeutic communities for 18 to 24 months and upon completion withdraw their guilty plea, have the charges dropped, and avoid incarceration. Research on this program has found that it achieves high retention rates (Lang & Belenko, 2000), reduces recidivism (Belenko, Foltz, Lang, & Sung, 2004), and results in substantial cost savings to the criminal justice system (Zarkin, Dunlap, Belenko, & Dynia, 2005).

A few states, including Arizona, California, the District of Columbia, and Hawaii, have enacted laws expanding eligibility for a probation–without–verdict model of diversion to all nonviolent drug-possession offenders who are not currently charged with another felony or serious misdemeanor offense and who have not previously been convicted of or incarcerated for such an offense within a specified time period. Pursuant to California's Proposition 36 (California Substance Abuse and Crime Prevention Act of 2000), for example, if an offender violates a drug-related condition of probation or commits a new drug-possession offense, the state can revoke probation only if it can prove by a preponderance of the evidence that the offender is a "danger to the safety of others." For a second drug-related violation of probation, the state must prove that the offender is either a danger to the safety of others or is "unamenable to drug treatment" to accomplish a revocation (e.g., *In re Mehdizadeh*, 2003).

The Drug Court Intervention

Over the past 15 years, drug courts have become an increasingly important model for linking drug-involved offenders to community-based treatment. Although drug courts existed as far back as the early 1950s (Belenko, 2000b; Lindesmith, 1965), the current interest in drug courts emerged from various drug case management programs established in the late 1980s (Belenko & Dumanovsky, 1993; Jacoby, 1994) as a result of surging drug caseloads (Goerdt & Martin, 1989) fueled by the law enforcement response to the crack epidemic (Belenko, 1993; Belenko, Fagan, & Chin, 1991; Zimring & Hawkins, 1991). Some of these programs added treatment referral components that eventually evolved into some of the early drug courts (Belenko, 1999a; Cooper & Trotter, 1994). The first program began in Dade County, Florida, in 1989 (Finn & Newlyn, 1993; Goldkamp & Weiland, 1993).

Drug courts have expanded rapidly and in many jurisdictions are now the preferred mechanism for linking drug-involved offenders to treatment. As of December 31, 2004, there were 1,621 operational drug court programs in the United States, a 37% increase from 2003 (Huddleston, Freeman-Wilson, Marlowe, & Roussell, 2005). Drug courts are now operating in all 50 states, 3 U.S. territories (Guam, Puerto Rico, and the Virgin Islands), and 8 countries. Adult drug courts compose the majority of drug court programs in the United States, with 811 programs as of December 31, 2004 (Huddleston et al., 2005). In addition, there were 357 juvenile drug courts, 153 family or dependency drug courts, 54 tribal drug courts, 176 DUI courts, 68 reentry drug courts, and 1 campus drug court. Moreover, drug courts are now serving as a model for several new breeds of "problem-solving courts," including mental health courts for chronically and persistently mentally ill offenders, dependency courts for child abuse and neglect cases, reentry courts for parolees, and domestic violence courts for domestic violence offenders. This chapter will focus on adult drug courts, the predominant model in the United States. Descriptions of the other types of drug courts can be found in Huddleston et al. (2005).

Drug courts are separately identified criminal court dockets that provide long-term, judicially supervised drug abuse treatment and case management services to nonviolent, drug-involved offenders in lieu of criminal prosecution or incarceration. The key operational components of drug courts typically include:

1 Judicial supervision of structured community-based treatment.
2 Timely screening, assessment, and enrollment of eligible defendants and referral to treatment and related services as soon as possible after arrest.
3 Regular status hearings before a judge to monitor treatment progress and program compliance.
4 Progressive sanctions for program infractions and positive rewards for program accomplishments.
5 Mandatory periodic or random drug testing.
6 Establishment of specific treatment program requirements.
7 Dismissal of the charges or reduction in sentence upon successful program completion (Belenko, 1998; National Association of Drug Court Professionals [NADCP], 1997).

There are two basic drug court models: pre-plea and post-plea. In "pre-plea" drug courts, prosecution is deferred and offenders can have their charges dropped upon successful program completion; in many jurisdictions they may have their current arrest record expunged (or erased) if they remain arrest free for an additional waiting period. Graduates of "post-plea" drug courts may avoid a sentence of incarceration, have their probation sentence reduced, be allowed to plead guilty to a misdemeanor rather than a felony, or receive a sentence of time-served in the program. Terminated clients have their original case prosecuted (pre-plea drug courts) or have the sentence imposed (post-plea courts). Figure 17.1 is a flow chart showing how cases are typically processed in plea drug courts.

The structure and underlying philosophy of drug courts represent a dramatic shift in jurisprudence and treatment–criminal justice linkages (Belenko, 2001; Hora, Schma, & Rosenthal, 1999) and are substantial departures from standard practices in criminal courts (Eisenstein & Jacob, 1977; Kamisar, LaFave, & Israel, 1995). The relative popularity of drug courts and the support for the drug court model across the political spectrum may have had other effects on the criminal justice system and antidrug policy. The shifting view toward drug offenders, the acceptance of treatment interventions and treatment efficacy, the adoption (explicit or implicit) of a "therapeutic jurisprudence" model (Hora et al., 1999; Slobogin, 1995), and an increasing discomfort about soaring incarceration rates among drug offenders may in part be attributed to the visibility and popularity of drug courts. Because drug courts emphasize both accountability and treatment, they are attractive both to those favoring "just deserts" and those favoring a "utilitarian" approach to criminal punishment, and this represents a rare consensus of opinion regarding appropriate strategies for addressing drug-related crime. The two case examples that follow illustrate the two main types of drug courts, the processes involved in both successful and unsuccessful treatment outcomes, and their associated jurisprudential results.

Case Example of a Pre-Plea Drug Court Process for an Unsuccessful Client

Nineteen-year-old TY was cited for public intoxication and possession of alcohol by a minor outside of a college sporting event. Before releasing TY at the scene with

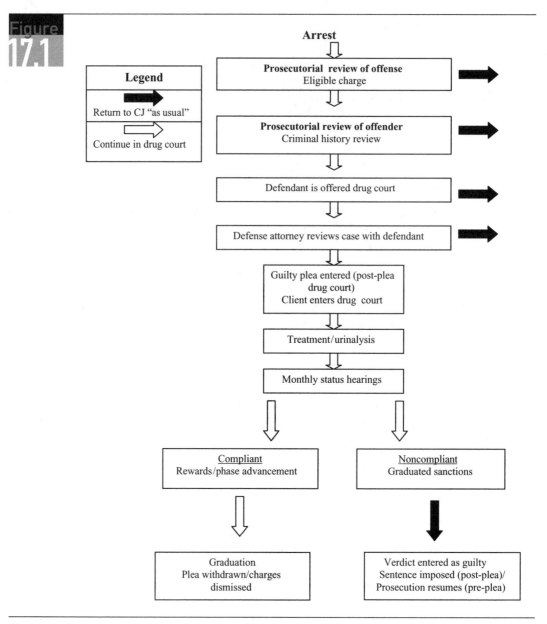

Drug court flow chart

a citation, the officer noted that TY's pupils were fully dilated and his attention span was vigilant to his surroundings, conditions inconsistent with alcohol intoxication. Having probable cause, the officer inspected TY's backpack and found a small (>2 grams) bag of a white powder. A field-reagent test indicated that the substance was cocaine, and TY was arrested for possession of narcotics. In addition, 40 pills (subsequently identified as a Schedule IV prescription sedative) were found on TY's person.

The assistant district attorney (ADA) agreed to modify the charges if TY pled no contest to possession of cocaine and entered the city's drug court program in lieu of prosecution. TY initially refused the ADA's offer, retained private defense counsel, and was strongly against any plea bargain, especially one requiring drug treatment. However, prior to his preliminary hearing TY was unable to produce verification that the pills he possessed at his arrest were prescribed by a physician. The ADA used this fact as additional leverage to encourage TY into treatment by deferring referral of TY's prescription charges to the U.S. Attorney pending entry to drug court. Under advice of counsel TY agreed.

During the drug court admission hearing, TY strongly denied having a drug problem. Despite this denial he was assessed by the caseworker as needing intensive outpatient services (IOP); TY was also required to attend Narcotics Anonymous (NA) meetings at least three times per week. Based on TY's college schedule and part-time employment, the judge modified the caseworker's recommendations and entered an order for outpatient services two times per week, as well as the NA meetings.

Prior to TY's first judicial status hearing, TY attended only half of his scheduled treatment appointments and provided no clean urine samples. He produced an NA attendance slip, but its authenticity was suspect. The judge angrily confronted TY with his performance during the previous 4 weeks and highlighted TY's testimony at his entry hearing when he denied drug use. TY continued to deny use and presented alternative causes for his dirty urine, including incompetent handling of the specimen and possible environmental exposure. The judge reminded TY that he faced a substantial sentence if convicted on cocaine possession. He increased TY's treatment requirement to 3 times per week and sanctioned TY to 1 day in the jury box and a 200-word essay on relapse.

At the next month's status hearing, it was revealed that TY showed no improvement in attendance and did not provide a single clean urine during that period. The treatment team indicated that TY would require inpatient treatment, especially in light of his strong denial. After TY's case manager reviewed his progress in open court, the ADA requested that TY be committed to inpatient treatment for 30 days or terminated from the program. TY's private attorney asked for continued IOP treatment, citing TY's college attendance and employment. After a heated exchange, the judge ordered TY to a weekend in jail and a status hearing the following week. TY was to report to the warden Friday after class and he would be released Sunday evening. TY appeared in court the following week and gave a clean urine, was complimented for his 7 days of sobriety, and was given a 2-week date for his next status hearing.

TY attended two out of six treatment appointments and refused to provide urine both times. At one session, he stated that he was dehydrated and could not produce a sample. At the second session, he left the building without reporting to the nurse as instructed. At TY's next status hearing, the ADA requested that a show-cause hearing be scheduled and that TY be terminated from the program due to his lack of compliance with treatment, open disrespect to staff, and continued denial of drug use. The judge agreed with the ADA but stated that the protocol in this case required that TY be given inpatient treatment prior to being terminated from the program. TY was given 2 days to sort out his personal and educational matters and then was to report to inpatient treatment for a 90-day stay. At the following week's status hearing, TY's case manager noted that TY had not reported to the inpatient treatment center. The judge issued a bench warrant for TY. The following week TY was picked up by the warrant unit at his dormitory.

The ADA reentered her request for a show-cause hearing, which was granted. TY ultimately pled guilty to felony drug possession and was sentenced to 18 months in the county jail, less the 2 weeks time served awaiting his sentencing. He was released 17 months and 2 weeks later. He was subsequently rearrested after attempting to buy sedatives from an undercover narcotics officer.

Case Example of a Post-Plea Drug Court Process for a Successful Client

RJ was arrested for possession of marijuana after a neighbor called the police to report a domestic disturbance in RJ's apartment. When the police arrived, RJ was arguing with his girlfriend and marijuana was visible on the table. He was charged with simple possession, which carried a possible sentence of 12 to 24 months in jail and a permanent felony record if convicted. Because this was a drug court–eligible offense, the case was referred to a narcotics ADA for review and recommendation. The ADA noted that RJ met the inclusion criteria for drug court for the following reasons:

1 RJ was a resident of the court's jurisdiction.
2 The instant charges did not include charges against a person.
3 RJ had no previous felony convictions.
4 The charges did not involve trafficking.
5 RJ reported significant marijuana use and occasional excessive alcohol use.

RJ tendered a plea of no contest to simple possession of marijuana and officially entered the drug court on January 1, 2004. He was subsequently assessed by an in-house caseworker, who recommended that RJ needed outpatient treatment and suggested that two sessions per week were needed. The judge accepted her recommendations and formally entered the case manager's treatment recommendation as a condition of RJ's requirements for compliance. RJ was given a date in mid-February to reappear in court for his first monthly status hearing before the judge, and he was given an appointment time and location for his first outpatient treatment session.

RJ missed his first scheduled treatment appointment but, to his credit, promptly called and rescheduled. He arrived for his rescheduled intake on the following Monday. RJ gave urine specimens that were positive for THC at all of his subsequent treatment sessions. The judge addressed this issue at his first monthly status hearing. The judge did not sanction RJ based on his urine analysis results during the first 2 weeks in the program because cannabinoid metabolites can remain in the body for several weeks after last use. However, the judge treated the subsequent positive urines as infractions and sanctioned RJ to write an essay on relapse. He cautioned RJ that sanctions would escalate if he continued to test positive for drugs, and he verbally reprimanded RJ in open court.

RJ tested negative for drugs at both appointments the next week. However, the following week he tested positive for benzodiazepines (BZDs). RJ disputed the test results, and another urine test was ordered. That test confirmed the presence of BZDs, and RJ was sanctioned to 1 day in the jury box. RJ pled a strong case against the test results, including a lack of a BZD abuse history. The judge reminded RJ that drug court proceeds by stipulation and that no formal challenges to the evidence can be made. The judge admonished RJ, saying, "The drugs got into your system somehow and you are responsible for that. I don't care if you took them or someone put them into your food or drink. If those are the people you associate with then you need to change who your friends are."

Between his second and third status hearings, RJ gave two drug-free urines, but failed to show for any other treatment session. RJ's case was discussed in the pre-status hearing conference, and all agreed RJ was in need of increased treatment, from two to three times per week, and that his sanction should include jail time. That day, RJ was sanctioned to a weekend in the county jail. He was removed from the court immediately by the sheriff and ordered to a "short-listing" schedule, which meant that he was to attend status hearings every 2 weeks until otherwise stated. After RJ's weekend in jail, his compliance with treatment improved significantly over the next 2 months. He had no dirty urines and attended all of his scheduled treatment appointments. He was advanced to Phase II of the drug court program based on his demonstration of 30 days of sobriety. When the announcement was made, RJ received applause from the gallery and was presented with a Phase I certificate.

At the next status hearing, RJ's case manager reported that RJ had been AWOL from treatment and had not contacted her, and the judge issued a bench warrant for RJ. Several months passed and finally RJ, after being picked up on another drug possession charge, was brought before the judge on his outstanding warrant. RJ pled with the judge for a second chance, as did his defense attorney. Although the new charges were dropped, the ADA requested a show-cause hearing as well as RJ's termination from the drug court program. She stated, however, that she would accept a sanction of 7 days detention in lieu of a show-cause hearing to give RJ "time to think about his behavior." RJ returned to court after his detention and reaffirmed his commitment to the drug court program.

Although RJ did not make all of his scheduled appointments, he continued to provide drug-free urines. He received minor sanctions for his poor attendance, 4 hours of community service for each missed session. On August 19, 2005, RJ graduated from the drug court program after demonstrating 90 days of sobriety, finishing his community service requirements, and paying his court costs and fees.

Eligibility for Drug Courts

The initial screening of potential drug court clients is generally conducted by the prosecutor and is first based on the arrest charge, or the charge arrived at via plea bargaining or contained in the prosecutor's accusatory instrument. In general, drug courts are open to nonviolent offenders charged with drug possession, and nearly all drug courts exclude offenders whose charges include trafficking, sale, or possession with intent to distribute. This exclusion can be waived if the prosecutor determines that an offender's selling of one drug is to support his or her addiction to another (e.g., selling marijuana to buy cocaine). Additional exclusions typically include those with a history of a violent offense or another serious felony offense, such as robbery or burglary. As a condition of receiving federal funding, drug courts cannot treat violent offenders, defined as those who have been charged with or convicted of an offense involving the use of a weapon, death or serious injury to a victim, or force against another person (Violent Crime Control and

Law Enforcement Act of 1994). However, even in cases where such offenses are statutorily disqualified, prosecutors have broad discretion in how charges are ultimately filed, despite the charge made at the time of arrest. Thus, some drug courts do accept offenders charged with drug sale or nondrug charges.

The Key Role of the Drug Court Judge

Although embodying a nonadversarial approach, the drug court model incorporates a more central and proactive role for the judge, who, in addition to presiding over the legal and procedural issues of the case, seeks to improve client compliance and success through behavioral management. This includes the administering of sanctions for noncompliant behavior and incentives or other encouragement for positive client behavior or achievement of specific goals (Marlowe & Kirby, 1999; Satel, 1998). In addition to imposing sanctions or rewards, the judge is the only member of the drug court team who can terminate clients from the drug court program. Drug court participants also seem to view the judge's role as a key component of the drug court. In a survey of drug court clients, 75% said that monitoring of treatment progress by a judge was an important difference between the drug court and prior treatment program experience, 82% cited the possibility of sanctions for noncompliance as a very important difference, and 70% thought that the opportunity to talk about their progress and problems with a judge was a "very important" factor in keeping them in the program (Cooper, 1997).

Other Drug Court Staff

Drug Court Coordinator

Drug court coordinators play a key role in the drug court team. Not only do they function as primary assistants to the drug court judge, but also they provide information on clinical resources for defense and prosecuting attorneys. When court is out of session, the drug court coordinator is the primary liaison between clinical case managers and the court staff. The coordinator is also typically responsible for chairing the pre-status hearing case conferences ("staffings") that usually precede each drug court session. In this conference, the coordinator reviews the progress of individual clients based on the reports from case managers and therapists. Through this process, the judge and the rest of the drug court team are made aware of which clients are in compliance with their treatment protocols (i.e., attended sessions, provided clean urine samples) and which clients are noncompliant. The treatment team can then come to an agreement prior to the hearing as to who will be sanctioned and what that sanction will be. Usually, any legal issues that arise between defense counsel and prosecution occur behind closed door in the pre-status hearing conference. In this way, the entire team can present a unified front for presentation to the client and the rest of the court spectators (mostly clients awaiting their own status hearings). Finally, drug court coordinators often represent the drug court team at meetings with other agencies, funders, and conferences.

Case Managers

Case managers, who are often social workers, are responsible for maintaining oversight of the clinical services received by the clients in their caseloads and acting as a liaison between the court and treatment and other service programs. They also attend status hearings and report on the clients' progress in treatment or other services; the level of involvement in this process may depend on whether a liaison from the treatment program attends the hearings, as is the case in some drug courts. As with case managers who work with traditional probation or parole clients, drug court case managers may also conduct assessments, be responsible for administering drug tests, make referrals for other health and social services, and monitor clients' attendance in treatment and other services. Unlike traditional probation case managers, drug court case managers report infractions directly to the judge at status hearings.

Assistant District Attorney/Prosecutor

The district attorney's office, usually represented on the drug court team by an ADA, plays a critical role in the drug court process. First, initial eligibility screening for entry into drug courts is generally performed by the prosecutor (and sometimes by probation staff). However, final determination of an offender's drug court eligibility typically rests with the drug court judge, who may reject the potential client's plea or make a finding of ineligibility during the initial drug court hearing. As the gatekeepers to the initial drug court hearing, however, prosecutors have substantial power to control the types of offenders that can be considered for drug court. Once a client is admitted to drug court, the ADA generally plays an advisory role on the drug court team, participating in staffings, representing the people's interest in the underlying criminal case, and providing input for termination or graduation decisions.

Public Defender

Drug courts are also staffed by a representative from the public defender's office. As with all defense attorneys, their primary role is to protect their clients' legal rights and achieve the best outcome in the resolution of the case. However, the unique nonadversarial nature of the drug court means that both prosecutors and defense attorneys may sometimes play nontraditional roles, presenting unique challenges for attorneys on both sides of the aisle. For example, a drug court prosecutor may advocate for a second chance for a client who has committed an infraction. Similarly, the public defender may occasionally support a more severe sanction for a given client. In the end, both attorneys are fulfilling their respective roles: The prosecutor is executing his or her responsibility to protect the public, and the defense attorney is protecting his or her client from a criminal record and a protracted jail or prison sentence. If a defense attorney legitimately believes that a sanction of jail time may alter a client's behavior enough to keep him or her in the drug court program, in lieu of being terminated and sentenced, then advocating for such a sanction may be appropriate, although there is controversy about such behavior in the legal community (Boldt, 1998; Nolan, 2003).

Application of Sanctions and Rewards

One of the unique aspects of drug courts is their use of behavioral management techniques to reduce noncompliant behavior and encourage positive behavior. Basic principles of behavior theory (as well as theories of punishment in the criminal justice system) indicate that, to be effective, responses to behaviors must incorporate the principles of certainty, celerity, and proportionality (Marlowe & Kirby, 1999; Taxman, 1999b). Thus, if a drug court client is not sanctioned for dirty urines (or is only rarely sanctioned), potential sanctions may be meaningless. Second, if drug use is detected, the response (a sanction, for example) must be rapid. Finally, if severe sanctions are imposed for a relatively minor infraction, drug court clients may feel frustrated or helpless, or feel that the drug court process is unfair. Sanctions and incentives are unlikely to be effective unless they follow these basic principles. Most drug courts use a system of graduated sanctions that increase in severity with each subsequent infraction. This lays the behavioral groundwork for clients to recognize that sanctions will be certain, swift, and fair.

Sanctions used by judges typically range from verbal reprimands in open court to brief periods of incarceration. Incarceration is usually short term (e.g., overnight or for a weekend), which is consistent with the behavioral principle of magnitude or proportionality, and also consistent with other brief sanctions such as contempt of court. However, the imposition of sanctions requires some clinical sensitivity in that what is aversive to one client may not be to another, but at the same time, the judge cannot appear to sanction clients arbitrarily. A recent survey of sanctions and rewards used in a large urban drug court revealed a toolkit of 17 sanctions (Lee & Fox, 2005) including (a) show-cause hearing (opportunity to provide justification to remain in program), (b) 200-word essay, (c) jury box (observe court proceedings all day), (d) direct admission to jail from court hearing for 1–7 days, (e) transfer to residential treatment, (f) recovery house, (g) verbal reprimand, (h) planned weekend incarceration, (i) case management to outpatient treatment, (j) placement in holding cell during hearing, (k) attendance of NA/AA meetings, (l) correctional facility visit for 1–2 days, (m) outpatient to intensive outpatient treatment, (n) termination from treatment court, (o) verbal warning, (p) community service, and (q) house arrest. The most common infractions observed in the same court were (a) missing treatment sessions, (b) missing case management sessions, (c) failing to provide scheduled urines, (d) providing drug-positive urines, (e) missing status hearings, and (f) failing to comply with previous sanctions (i.e., completing essay, attending correctional facility visit).

Typical rewards used in drug court include accelerated advancement to a later treatment phase; verbal acknowledgements; or small tangible items such as candles, store vouchers, key chains, or movie tickets. These rewards may seem to be of much lower magnitude than the sanctions, and some have questioned their effectiveness. The ultimate reward for the drug court client, of course, is of high magnitude and very certain: dismissal of their charges or reduction in sentence upon graduation. In some courts, the clients also have the opportunity for a full expungement of the arrest and written record that accompanied their charges.

Role of Other Agencies

Drug courts incorporate a collaborative process and sometimes function as a coordinating agency for a wide range of ancillary services. Given the health and social services needs of many drug-involved offenders, these services are often necessary to aid clients in maintaining sobriety, receiving medical and other social services, and learning new skills. The aim of incorporating these ancillary services comes out of recognition that a multilevel system of care must be established to maximize the chances that drug court clients will avoid relapse or recidivism.

Aside from their unique relationships with the district attorney and the public defender's office, drug courts interact directly with outside agencies in a manner that is uncommon in the criminal justice system. In typical drug possession cases, an offender is remanded to probation, parole, or the department of corrections and reappears in court only for formal proceedings. Drug courts must coordinate their services not only with the case managers (and sometimes probation or parole officers), but also with community-based treatment providers, public health agencies, employment training and placement, family services, housing assistance services, and other entities. In smaller drug courts, a single outside provider may be responsible for the treatment of all drug court clients. In larger drug courts, a "brokerage" system may be used, with dozens of treatment providers, and each provider may have a different approach to treating addictions, different resources available, and different demands on the clients. Drug courts may have a formal contract with a single dedicated contracted provider in the community, or operate their own treatment program colocated in the drug court.

Delivering Treatment in Drug Courts

Drug courts usually seek to standardize the treatment process by requiring discrete treatment phases, minimum requirements to advance to different program phases, and a minimum length of program involvement. Most drug courts require at least 1 year of participation and incorporate several distinct treatment phases. Phase I usually includes assessment, orientation, and development of a treatment plan and treatment readiness, and generally ranges between 30 and 90 days. During this phase, the client typically has three to four weekly treatment contacts, as well as random urine tests. Phase II is the primary treatment phase, typically lasting 6 months, with treatment contacts and urinalysis similar to Phase I. The final Phase III includes relapse prevention, discharge planning, and vocational and educational training, and lasts between 2 and 4 months. Treatment contacts may be reduced somewhat to one to two times per week, and urine tests are less frequent.

Drug courts can have difficulty accessing effective treatment, and drug court staff are not always adequately trained to identify effective and well-managed treatment providers (Taxman, 1999a; Taxman & Bouffard, 2003). Drug courts may be more likely to respond to poor treatment engagement or compliance with court-based sanctions rather than changes in therapeutic approaches or clinical strategies. In a 1999 survey of 263 drug courts, Peyton and Gossweiler (2001) found a number of service gaps. Many drug courts do not appropriately use screening and assessment instruments for placement decisions; many drug courts have difficulty retaining clients because of lack of treatment motivation or poor "treatment attitude"; and relationships with treatment providers are not well structured. Common reasons for early termination in drug courts include failure to engage in treatment, missing too many treatment appointments, poor attitude, and "lack of motivation" (Peyton & Gossweiler, 2001). Many drug courts initially exclude clients who are deemed to be "not motivated" for treatment, thus further limiting the eligibility pool (Taxman & Bouffard, 2003).

Taxman and Bouffard (2003) found that on average only 22% of observed treatment sessions in drug courts contained any discussion of cognitive-behavioral issues or

strategies, and only 16% of treatment time was spent on cognitive-behavioral components. In addition, information about basic concepts and vocabulary of addiction and
treatment was relatively rarely delivered (32% of sessions), and treatment did not seem
to reflect adequately the drug use habits of the clients. Overall, much of the time in clinical sessions was devoted to administrative tasks and support services. Finally, with their
focus on intervening with clients' substance abuse problems, few drug courts provide
the range of services required to address the important need to restructure their clients'
criminal thinking styles, build or rebuild internal motivating strategies to support prosocial behaviors and constructive decision making, or help clients recognize the impacts of
their previous criminal and drug-taking lifestyles. Drug court case managers therefore
need to increase the motivation of drug court clients to engage in treatment, to link them
to services, and to increase their access to behavioral and cognitive skills training aimed
at reducing substance abuse and criminal behavior.

Because of resource constraints and availability, most drug courts primarily utilize outpatient treatment, which typically emphasizes group counseling. Findings from
national drug treatment outcome studies indicate that outpatient programs averaged
14.8 group sessions per month and only 3.3 individual sessions (Etheridge, Hubbard,
Anderson, Craddock, & Flynn, 1997). Although brief individual sessions are common
supplements in many programs, clients who receive core cognitive behavioral and associated skills training and psycho-education do so in groups of 10 to 15 peers with a
single counselor acting as facilitator. This group modality, however, may pose challenges
for offender treatment: Groups may lose therapeutic focus and effectiveness because of
lack of attention to skills practice, the influence of resistant clients, a classroom style, or
curriculum drift (Morgan, Winterowd, & Ferrell, 1999).

Summary of Findings From Drug Court Research

With their emphasis on judicial supervision and behavioral contingencies, long-term
treatment, clinical assessment, case management, and referral to ancillary services, drug
courts embody many principles of effective treatment (NIDA, 1999). Although methodological problems are common (as they are with substance abuse treatment research in
general), drug court evaluations generally find that these programs maintain offenders
in long-term treatment and reduce drug use and criminal behavior, at least in the short
term (Belenko, 2001). In this section, we summarize what is known about the effects
of drug courts on relapse, recidivism, and other outcomes, as well as the gaps in this
research.

Findings From Research on Drug Court Effectiveness

Belenko (2001) reviewed research findings from 37 evaluations of 36 different drug courts.
The conclusions about drug court impacts drawn from that review were consistent
with those reached from two previous reviews of 59 drug court evaluations (Belenko,
1998, 1999b). Drug courts have achieved considerable local support and provided closely
supervised long-term treatment services (1 year or longer) to offenders with substantial

histories of drug use and criminal justice contacts, previous treatment failures, and high rates of health and social problems.

Drug courts seek to maximize offenders' engagement in long-term treatment services. Treatment research has consistently noted that longer time in treatment is associated with better outcomes (Carroll, 1997; Chou, Hser, & Anglin, 1998; Lang & Belenko, 2000; Simpson, Joe, & Rowan-Szal, 1997). Although there is some variation among drug courts, reviews of drug court research (Belenko, 1998, 1999b, 2001; U.S. Government Accountability Office [GAO], 2005) have noted that overall treatment retention is substantially better than in other community-based treatment programs for offenders. Belenko (1998, 1999b, 2001) concluded that an average of 60% of drug court clients completed at least 1 year of drug treatment, and about 45 to 48% graduated from the program, although there is wide variation across courts (GAO, 2005). This represents a substantial improvement in treatment retention over most probation programs, in which fewer than 10% of clients attend 1 year of treatment (e.g., Goldkamp, 2000; Marlowe, DeMatteo, et al., 2003; Satel, 1999).

Available data suggest that while participants are in the drug court program, drug use prevalence is low. Most evaluations that report data on drug test results during drug court participation find percentages of positive urine screens at less than 10% (Belenko, 1999b, 2001). Several studies with comparative data from samples of probationers have found lower drug-positive rates for drug court clients (Belenko, 1999b). Similarly, drug court evaluations that have examined recidivism during program participation find significantly lower rates for drug court clients compared to similar offender populations under other types of community supervision (Belenko, 1999b, 2001).

Most drug court evaluations that examined post-drug court recidivism, with a suitable comparison group, found reduced recidivism rates for the drug court (Belenko, 1998, 1999b, 2001). Differences were approximately 20 to 30 percentage points during treatment and 10 to 20 percentage points after treatment in drug use and criminal recidivism, compared with offenders receiving standard or intensive probation (Belenko, 2002). In randomized experimental studies, drug court clients exhibited roughly a 15 percentage-point reduction in rearrest rates at 2 and 3 years postadmission compared to probationers (Gottfredson, Najaka, & Kearley, 2003; Turner, Greenwood, Fain, & Deschenes, 1999).

The GAO recently completed a systematic review of 117 evaluations of adult drug court programs published between May 1997 and January 2004 that reported criminal recidivism, substance use relapse, or program completion outcomes. Of the 117 studies, the GAO selected 27 evaluations of 39 drug court programs that met its criteria for methodological soundness. The GAO concluded that drug courts reduce during-treatment recidivism to a greater degree than commonly used criminal justice alternatives, such as probation. Interestingly, there was no conclusive evidence that specific drug court components—such as the behavior of the judge, amount of treatment received, level of supervision provided, and the provision of sanctions for noncompliance with program requirements—affect offenders' during-treatment recidivism rates. The GAO also concluded that drug courts reduce postprogram recidivism (measured up to 1 year after offenders completed the drug court program), particularly for offenders who completed the drug court program. There was mixed evidence supporting the effectiveness of drug courts in terms of reducing substance use relapse.

Gaps in the Drug Court Research Literature

Several important gaps exist in research findings on drug courts. There have been only a few studies that examined the impacts of drug courts on postprogram drug use, employment, or other outcomes (Belenko, 2001; GAO, 2005; Harrell, Cavanagh, & Roman, 1999; Turner et al., 1999). The findings from these studies are inconclusive because of small sample sizes or difficulties with drug court implementation.

Because of limited follow-up periods, little is known about drug courts' long-term postprogram impacts on recidivism (Belenko, 2001; GAO, 2005). In addition, more research is needed about the relative efficacy of different treatment delivery models, the optimum drug court phase structure, and the impacts of different sanction and reward contingency systems. Johnson, Hubbard, and Latessa (2000) suggest that drug court treatment would be improved through closer attention to the type and quality of treatment services, including the application of the principles of effective intervention.

Drug court research also needs to place new emphasis on the treatment process, including client engagement and service delivery (Joe, Simpson, & Broome, 1999; Taxman, 1999a). Very little is known about the effective components of drug courts (Goldkamp, 2000; Longshore et al., 2001), including client, organizational, and system factors (Belenko, 2001). Some studies have examined client factors affecting retention or rearrest (Goldkamp, White, & Robinson, 2001; Peters et al., 1999), but organizational or system factors or alternative treatment delivery models have not been assessed. For example, little is known about the relative efficacy of having a single contracted or court-operated treatment provider compared to referral to multiple community-based programs. The elements of the relationships among drug court staff, treatment and other service providers, and clients that promote or deter successful outcomes are not well studied.

Relatively few evaluations have included data on program services, either because of lack of data or because service delivery was not included in the evaluation design. Yet many researchers and drug court practitioners have noted the importance of looking inside the "black box" of drug court treatment and other services to understand which elements of the drug court process affect client outcomes under which conditions (e.g., Belenko, 2001; Goldkamp et al., 2001; Simpson, Joe, Rowan-Szal, & Greener, 1997; Taxman, 1999a).

The importance of maximizing treatment retention to improve postprogram outcomes suggests that more research is needed on the individual participant, staff, and organizational factors that promote drug court retention. The judge's explicit personal involvement in the offender's treatment outcome, his or her interactions with the offender in court (Satel, 1998), and the embrace of the therapeutic jurisprudence model (Hora et al., 1999; Slobogin, 1995) may be critical. In any event, the unique structure of the drug court model, its interaction with the offender, and the way in which treatment is integrated into the court process all may operate to increase the likelihood of successful program completion. Although a few drug court studies have examined predictors of retention, there is still little extant knowledge to guide the development of new drug court programs or to modify existing programs to reduce dropout and increase graduation rates.

Most important is the need for better-controlled studies of the impacts of various components of drug court interventions, more research on how the components of the drug court model (especially the judicial role) affect program and treatment compliance, studies of the factors affecting in-program relapse and criminal activity as well as postprogram relapse and criminal activity, the importance of using experimental designs for program impact evaluations or the use of more appropriate comparison groups, the collection and analysis of long-term outcome data, and the improvement of automated drug court data systems that can support evaluation. It should be noted that it can be quite difficult to implement experimental designs in criminal justice settings. Defense attorney concerns about due process and equal protection, prosecutorial and judicial resistance to reducing their discretion in case decisions, and the sheer complexity and multiple decision points of the adjudication process are difficult barriers to overcome.

Drug court research has often been hampered by the lack of a well-defined, theoretically grounded drug court intervention. Many drug courts emerged from local grass roots efforts and were experientially rather than theoretically or research based (Goldkamp, 2000; Hora et al., 1999). The recent emergence of suggested frameworks for defining the philosophies, goals, structure, and operations of individual drug courts (Goldkamp et al., 2001; Longshore et al., 2001) will be useful for researchers in defining the measurable components of drug courts and guiding future evaluations. Such frameworks will be helpful to identify the effective and ineffective components of the drug court model. In addition, drug court evaluations have been hampered by a lack of an organizing or theoretical framework for hypothesizing what components of drug courts have what impacts on which types of clients under what conditions. This framework also has to be viewed in the context of the myriad systems involved in drug courts as well as the role of staff and client family members (Belenko, 2001, 2002; Goldkamp et al., 2001; Longshore et al., 2001; Taxman, 1999a).

Legal Issues

"Creaming" and "Net Widening"

Several clinical and operational issues warrant attention if the full potential of drug courts are to be realized. The targeting, eligibility screening, and assessment processes directly drive the number and type of clients that enter drug courts and, by extension, the level and types of clinical services that need to be linked to the drug court. Narrow targeting and strict eligibility screening, as well as program admission procedures that allow higher risk offenders to drop out of the program prior to formal enrollment, may limit the number of participants and produce a "creaming" effect in which the drug court serves mostly low-risk clients. Such courts may show high levels of compliance and good success rates but may not be cost-effective because their clients may have done as well under less intensive adjudication and treatment models (Marlowe et al., 2003). Moreover, the voluntary nature of drug court participation can result in self-selection bias in which highly motivated or lower risk offenders are more likely to choose participation.

Because eligibility criteria for drugs courts are commonly based on an offender's current criminal charge and criminal history, these programs often end up treating the least severely drug-involved individuals and are estimated to serve less than 5% of the drug-addicted offender population (Belenko, 2001). By casting a "wide and shallow net," they capture a large number of individuals who may misuse drugs but who are relatively early in their addiction careers and have not, as yet, progressed to the point of having a diagnosable or clinically significant substance use disorder.

As noted earlier, eligibility for drug courts is typically restricted to drug-possession offenders who do not have a history of a violent offense, drug dealing, or another serious felony offense. As a result, many individuals who are seriously drug-addicted are excluded from drug courts. In fact, it is estimated that roughly 50 to 75% of *all* offenders—including those who commit theft or property offenses, violent offenses, and drug-dealing offenses—have serious drug histories (Belenko & Peugh, 1999; NIJ, 2000). The large majority of these individuals are ineligible for drug court because of their criminal record. This underinclusiveness is another example of "creaming" because the programs are likely to deny entrance to the most severely drug-addicted cases.

Drug courts have also been criticized as being overinclusive because they treat many individuals who do not have a serious substance use problem (DeMatteo, Marlowe, & Festinger, 2006). Recent research suggests that 30 to 40% of drug offenders do not have a diagnosable or clinically significant substance use disorder (Kleiman et al., 2003). In studies conducted by the Treatment Research Institute at the University of Pennsylvania, nearly one half of misdemeanor drug court clients (Marlowe, Festinger, et al., 2003), one third of felony drug court clients (Marlowe, Festinger, & Lee, 2004), and two thirds of pretrial clients in a drug treatment and monitoring programs (Lee et al., 2001) produced "subthreshold" drug composite scores on the Addiction Severity Index (McLellan et al., 1992), similar to a community sample of nonsubstance abusers. Despite having been screened in as requiring drug treatment, more in-depth and confidential assessments revealed that these individuals did *not* have a minimally identifiable disorder. Further, in one study, roughly one third of misdemeanor drug court clients provided a virtually unbroken string of drug-negative urine specimens over nearly a 4-month period following intake (DeMatteo, Festinger, Lee, & Marlowe, 2005). If these individuals could readily abstain from drug use over such an extended interval of time, there may be little clinical justification for labeling their use as compulsive or assuming they need formal treatment.

In a national survey of drug courts, more than 60% of the programs report that defendants initially identified as eligible for the drug court by justice system officials would be disqualified if their substance abuse screening indicates they are not addicted or exhibit only minimal addiction (Peyton & Gossweiler, 2001). In some instances, the defendant may choose not to participate because the incentives for participating in the program are not significant enough to warrant undertaking the intensive program requirements; in other instances, however, the defendant's apparent lack of motivation may, in fact, mask distrust of the justice system generally and/or lack of culturally relevant program services.

Drug Court Clients Must Waive Certain Rights

Once a defendant has been offered drug court by the prosecution and has discussed the offer with his or her defense attorney, there is a series of formal steps that must be taken before the client officially enters the drug court program. In a process known as a colloquy, or a waiver hearing, the defendants must demonstrate to the judge that their decision to enter the drug court is voluntary and that they understand their plea, the rights they are giving up, and the potential outcomes of entering the drug court versus regular court.

The hearing is on the record (there is a court stenographer present) and is due-process based until the entry order is signed by the judge. At the entry hearing, clients stand before the judge and are asked a series of questions. Typical questions include the following: Are you a resident of (jurisdiction)? Are you at least 18 years old? Do you read, write, and understand the English language? Are you currently under the influence of any drugs or medications? Has anybody made any promises or threats to you to bring you here? Are you here on your own free will?

After the defendant satisfactorily answers these questions, the prosecutor addresses the potential client to explain the legal rights he or she is giving up by entering the drug court program. This may simply be a verbal reiteration of the written plea that the client already reviewed with his or her attorney and the ADA (in a post-plea court) and already signed (see Appendix A for an example). In a pre-plea drug court, the discussion of waiver of legal rights focuses on issues such as speedy trial rights, deferral of prosecution, and stipulation to the police report should the case be ultimately prosecuted.

The judge then addresses each client individually: "Mr. Smith, having answered all of my questions satisfactorily and having heard the prosecutor explain the rights you are giving up, do you still want to enter the treatment court program?" If the client declines to enter the drug court, he or she is given a date for a preliminary hearing on the same charge and dismissed from the drug court. If the client agrees to enter, the judge queries the court coordinator and confirms the client's initial level of treatment care. The judge then signs the written colloquy, which has already been signed by the client, ADA, and defense counsel. The client is then given an appointment at a treatment site consistent with the assessed level of care, as well as a date for the first status hearing before the drug court judge.

Why a Plea?

The issue of a plea of either *nolo contendere* (no contest) or guilty is one of great importance to the drug court model. Having a plea on record means that, should a client be consistently noncompliant and nonresponsive to the graduated sanctions and rewards, the judge may enter the plea and sentence the client without a trial. Many drug courts make it clear at the onset that if the client fails the program and is sentenced, they will receive jail time; this is especially true of felony drug courts. The drug court judge must remain consistent to this rule to maintain the element of certainty that is critical to the program as a whole. In other drug courts, however, probation sentences may be the normative sentence for those who are terminated from drug court.

Following unfavorable termination, offenders have limited avenues of appeal available because of the waivers that were agreed to at admission. These appeals are usually limited to issues of voluntariness, lack of jurisdiction, or an illegal or improper sentence. It should be noted that most drug courts are not statutorily commissioned and are usually created through agreements among the DA, defense, and judge. Therefore, the waiver of rights is starting to become an issue for the appeals courts until state legislatures pass laws that officially codify drug courts. This is an obstacle that is arising across the country in drug courts and in other problem-solving courts (see *In re Olivia J.*, 2004).

Clinical Issues

Clinical Assessment

Given the characteristics of their target populations, drug courts can provide an important public health intervention role in the criminal justice system. The drug court screening, assessment, and referral process provides an opportunity to identify participants' health problems and provide linkages to appropriate interventions. The close supervision and case management structure typical of drug courts can help to ensure access to health services and follow-through on treatment and medications (Wenzel, Longshore, Turner, & Ridgely, 2001). Through interagency planning, cross-training, drug treatment access, case management, and close client supervision, drug courts may play an important role in reducing HIV and other infectious disease risks (Belenko, Langley, Crimmins, & Chaple, 2004). The evidence that drug court clients have high rates of mental health problems suggests that programs need to consider inclusion of services for co-occurring disorders (Belenko, 2001; Peters & Hills, 1993). Many drug courts also try to assess and make referrals to address broader clinical issues such as physical and mental health, social service, and employment needs as well as aftercare and support services following treatment completion to ease successful transition into the community (Belenko, 2002).

There are two key dimensions to consider in making appropriate service linkages for substance-involved offenders: drug use severity and other service needs. Evidence that clients with a higher severity of drug use have better outcomes in more intensive or highly structured treatment comes from the Drug Abuse Treatment Outcome Study (Simpson et al., 1999), therapeutic communities (Melnick, De Leon, Thomas, & Kressel, 2001), outpatient settings (Rychtarik et al., 2000; Thornton, Gottheil, Weinstein, & Kerachsky, 1998), and Project MATCH for alcohol patients (Project MATCH Research Group, 1998). In addition, addiction-related problems (i.e., psychiatric, employment, family–social) can have negative impacts on treatment outcomes. Studies in different treatment settings have found that matching services to specific client needs (e.g., psychological services, housing, employment), or the addition of health and/or social services to standard addiction care, improves treatment outcomes (Gastfriend & McLellan, 1997; Hser, Polinsky, Maglione, & Anglin, 1999; Mattson et al., 1994; McLellan, Arndt, Metzger, & O'Brien, 1993; McLellan, Luborsky, Woody, O'Brien, & Druley, 1983).

Because of the other health and social service needs of drug-involved offenders, additional dimensions of drug abuse and its effects need to be assessed for and considered in making clinically appropriate estimates of treatment need (McLellan et al., 1997), in determining intensity of treatment (McLellan & Alterman, 1991), and in crafting appropriate treatment plans (Carise, Gurel, Kendig, & McLellan, 2002). The American Society of Addiction Medicine Patient Placement Criteria indicate that behavioral conditions and consequences of drug use (such as educational and vocational problems, anger management problems, or motor vehicle accidents) should be taken into account in determining level of care (Mee-Lee, Shulman, Fishman, Gastfriend, & Griffith, 2001).

A national survey of drug courts found that 89% conduct clinical assessments prior to admission, although not all use a standardized instrument (Peyton & Gossweiler, 2001). The most frequently used assessment instrument was the Addiction Severity Index (35%

of drug courts). More than one third (35%) use an instrument developed by the drug court staff, and 53% use a variety of other instruments including the Substance Abuse Subtle Screening Inventory, Offender Profile Index, and Level of Service Inventory.

In sum, there are several key challenges for improving assessment and service linkages for drug court clients. First, treatment services are limited in many jurisdictions, and treatment planning may not be individualized or based on adequate assessment using research-based instruments. There is a need to improve treatment planning to identify effective services, facilitate service linkages, and better manage risk in the community. By "effective" referrals, we mean services that are accessible; are relevant and appropriate to the client's risk, need, and cognitive ability levels; and provide data and feedback to the drug court staff and case manager on client progress in meeting service goals. Yet, many drug courts utilize a one-size-fits-all model of treatment delivery. Second, drug court staff, with large caseloads and limited training in health and social services, may not be equipped to provide appropriate service referrals and adequately monitor progress and compliance. The increasing emphasis on offender control and monitoring (even in drug courts) means that high technical violation rates and reincarceration are a consequence of relapse, rather than adjustment of services or re-referral to another provider. Third, many drug courts do not use standardized clinical assessment instruments (Peyton & Gossweiler, 2001). Fourth, the unique profiles and service needs of important drug court subpopulations such as minorities, females, or those with co-occurring disorders are not typically addressed in existing assessment instruments.

Finally, it may be important to assess drug court clients for current conditions, motivational levels, behavioral status, and beliefs or perceptions related to service needs and access. More recent dynamic factors may be more predictive of postadmission success and risk than either static factors or more distal dynamic traits measured prior to arrest (Simourd, 2004). Many assessment instruments include both lifetime and recent (acute) problems and functioning. Lifetime information is designed to help the clinician evaluate problem severity and to develop treatment plans; acute recent problems are also used for these purposes and also used to monitor change. These are very different functions. Although assessment of lifetime functioning is conceptualized as typically applying to treatment intake or baseline, assessment of acute functioning needs to be applicable at intake and subsequent time points. Accordingly, a useful strategy for assessment and developing treatment plans for drug court clients would incorporate assessment tools that: (a) Identify areas of functioning and health that require interventions; (b) assess across multiple dimensions, have sound psychometric properties, are relatively compact and easy to administer and score, and have clinical utility and acceptability in real-world settings; and (c) assess both static and dynamic factors, and distinguish more recent dynamic behaviors and conditions from more distal conditions.

Role of the Social Worker

The role of the social worker or other clinician in the drug court setting poses unique challenges and is different from working with offenders in other contexts. Drug courts are collaborative models that try to strike a balance between rehabilitative public health and public safety goals. This means that public safety considerations, or an accountability framework, may sometimes lead to clinical or adjudicatory decisions that a social worker may feel undermine clinical progress. Social workers must also learn to work within a context of sanctions and rewards that are imposed by the judge. Because the drug court is based in the criminal court, legal, procedural, and public safety issues are paramount. The social worker's perspective may be very different, but he or she has to acknowledge the ultimate authority of the judge and the judicial process, and the role of other members of the drug court team. The judge may even occasionally insert him- or herself into clinical decisions in ways that the social worker may not agree with. Although the judge's ultimate decisions must be accepted and respected, the social worker's role as an advocate for the drug court client and his or her clinical and service needs is an important one. The team approach of drug courts means that social workers or case managers will have opportunities to express their views about how a drug court client is progressing in recovery, what issues are affecting compliance with drug court requirements, and what types of responses are most appropriate for noncompliance. These opportunities usually exist during the staffings or individual client case conferences.

It is also important for social workers in drug courts to understand fully the adjudication process, the legal rights of offenders, criminal procedure, which rights are waived by those agreeing to participate in the drug court, and other aspects of the criminal courts. Cross-training on these issues is important so the social worker understands and appreciates how adjudicatory decisions are made and how such decisions may conflict with the clinical interests of the client. Although drug courts are a treatment-oriented intervention, they are part of the criminal court system, and the first priorities are always adequate resolution of the criminal case and public safety.

Drug Courts as Collaborative Models

The unique structure and philosophy of drug courts provides a potential opportunity to increase access to a broad range of clinical interventions, not just substance abuse treatment. The team approach and relatively nonadversarial nature of the court suggest a higher degree of overt cooperation among the key staff and a lower level of verbal conflict. The drug court approach also assumes that staff have similar training about substance abuse and treatment (and that this training is more extensive than that normally received by court personnel) and share the same overall goal: to assist the participant in succeeding in drug treatment and graduating drug- and crime-free.

Moreover, drug courts typically incorporate formal treatment delivery structures, funding streams, and interagency relationships that are rarely seen in the criminal justice system. Drug courts were designed to address some of the prior integrative problems with criminal justice-based treatment. Yet in many ways drug courts offer a systemic model of treatment different from previous criminal justice-based models, providing a continuity of treatment, monitoring and oversight of services and treatment progress, contingencies to maintain compliance, regular information flow between the provider(s) and the court, and client accountability. In addition, drug courts represent an important and fertile laboratory for studying the organizational, client, and treatment factors that affect the recovery process and desistance from criminal activity.

Improving the Effectiveness of Clinical Services

As in other criminal justice-supervised treatment, drug courts need to improve staff training around substance abuse and treatment, as well as cultural sensitivity and competence. Although some drug courts offer formal training opportunities for judges and staff, others rely more on ad hoc training or the interest and motivation of individual judges. Given the lack of universal training in these areas in standard judicial education, improving and formalizing such training curricula should be a goal of the drug court field. Given the racial, ethnic, and class disparity between the drug client population and criminal justice program staff, improving cultural competence and sensitivity should also be an important part of any training curriculum. Such cultural issues may be closely related to treatment outcomes (Aponte & Barnes, 1995; Fiorentine & Hillhouse, 1999), making it important for treatment and other service providers to be trained in cultural competence, and for drug court services to be structured to address the particular needs and viewpoints of different racial, ethnic, and cultural groups, as well as by gender.

As discussed earlier, little attention has been given to the role of treatment process or the organization of service delivery on drug court offenders' compliance, retention, or outcomes (Taxman, 1999a). Yet a growing body of research notes the importance of treatment process on improving outcomes for criminal justice-based treatment (Simpson, Joe, Rowan-Szal, & Greener, 1997; Joe, Simpson, & Broome, 1998), based on efficient and comprehensive assessment, monitoring, and service delivery (Simpson, Joe, Rowan-Szal, & Greener, 1997). Such systems could be readily implemented within a drug court structure, but few drug courts have implemented either comprehensive and periodic clinical assessments, or regular systematic monitoring of therapeutic interactions. In addition, it may be important for the treatment process to be driven theoretically to engage the client in the treatment process and ameliorate patient risk factors at intake, to motivate the client to change behavior through the use of incentives and sanctions, and to provide a therapeutic environment that actively involves the client in the treatment process (Palmer, 1995). Yet Taxman and Bouffard (2003) suggest that treatment staff often employ theoretically inconsistent approaches to treat clients.

The drug court model incorporates a nonclinical but authoritative figure (the judge) who can make decisions that directly affect the treatment process. Depending on the drug court structure, the knowledge and training of the judge and the drug court staff, and the relationship between the judge and treatment provider(s), judicial behaviors, comments, and decisions can support or undermine the treatment process. The role of the judge thus becomes an important adjunct to the treatment process (Marlowe & Kirby, 1999). In particular, it may be difficult for the judge, other drug court staff, and clinical treatment staff to reach consensus over the appropriate response to relapse. The philosophical or operational tensions surrounding staff's views and attitudes about addiction and recovery can be difficult to resolve, yet may have a profound effect on drug court outcomes (Taxman, 1999a). Careful preprogram implementation planning, timely and appropriate information exchange between the court and clinical staff, and regular stakeholder meetings may mitigate some of these difficulties (NADCP, 1997).

Minimizing tensions between judge and treatment provider or other clinical staff can be difficult, but important to resolve. Not only can judicial attitudes or decisions affect the treatment process, but also clinical decisions can in turn affect the imposition of sanctions, rewards, or phase advancement. The phased treatment structure of drug courts places an inherent time limit on treatment progress. If a client remains too long in one phase (e.g., due to multiple relapses), then the client might be terminated and prosecuted. Although lack of treatment progress may lead to program termination under other models of criminal justice-based treatment supervision (such as probation or parole), retention time under those models is expected to be shorter than under the drug court model, where relapse is expected and more acceptable.

Drug Courts as Coerced Treatment

One criticism often levied against drug courts is that criminal justice clients may be coerced into entering drug court programs. Because these clients must choose between participating in drug court or going to trial and risking jail time, some argue that criminal justice clients do not really have a choice. Moreover, drug courts have also been accused of using coercive techniques to keep participants engaged in treatment.

Part of the difficulty in addressing these concerns is the confusion over the definition of "coercion." In the context of treatment, the term "coercion" is often used interchangeably with "compulsory treatment," "mandated treatment," "involuntary treatment," and "legal pressure into treatment," and it generally refers to any strategies that shape behavior by using external pressure and predictable consequences. Moreover, a client's perception of being coerced into treatment is not always directly related to how the client ended up in a drug treatment program (Wild, Newton-Taylor, & Alletto, 1998). Many clients who are mandated into drug treatment do not report being coerced into treatment (Wild et al., 1998).

Although it is true that drug court clients are required to participate in drug treatment, provide urine samples on request, and fulfill other program requirements—all of which may be perceived as coercive by the clients—it is important to note that available research suggests that coerced-treatment clients often perform better than those entering treatment voluntarily. There is evidence, for example, that substance abusers who participate in treatment as a result of a court order or a requirement of employment benefit as much as, and sometimes more than, individuals who enter treatment voluntarily (Huddleston, 2000; Satel, 1999). In the drug court context, however, more research is needed on the unique coercive elements of drug courts that drive the excellent retention rates (Farabee, Prendergast, & Anglin, 1998; Satel, 1999), and how traditional theoretical deterrence models relate to coerced treatment in the drug court setting (Sung, Belenko, & Feng, 2001; Young & Belenko, 2002).

Conclusion

This chapter has described the underlying philosophy and structure of drug courts, an innovative treatment-oriented intervention that has become quite popular over the past decade. Research on the operations and impacts of drug courts has yielded a number of positive findings, although a number of aspects of drug court effectiveness remain unknown. Nonetheless, drug courts represent one of the most promising programs to date for intervening with offenders with substance abuse problems. Incorporating collaborations among criminal justice and public health systems, structured long-term treatment, a case management approach, accountability, and strong judicial oversight of treatment, drug courts incorporate a number of principles of effective substance abuse treatment as well as behavioral management.

Drug courts offer a unique opportunity for social workers to provide clinical services to a challenging population that generally presents with numerous health and social problems in addition to their drug or alcohol involvement. These clinical and case management services are provided in an environment that incorporates the coercive power of the criminal justice system, the authoritative role of the judge, a system of accountability through sanctions and rewards, and a nonadversarial approach in which clinical decisions are often made by the team. Thus, the drug court can present many challenges for the social worker that differ from typical clinical environments. These challenges include balancing clinical decisions and public health considerations with legal issues, public safety considerations, and the integrity of the drug court process; understanding the complexity of the criminal justice system; recognizing the ultimate authority of the judge; and working with a difficult client population that often requires numerous services.

Despite these difficulties, the drug court has become among the most popular and accepted treatment interventions for offenders, and its principles and problem-solving approach have begun to influence other parts of the criminal justice system, as well as other court systems such as family and juvenile courts. Given the case management and clinically oriented approach of drug courts, social workers can play a vital role in ensuring that the clinical and other service needs of drug-involved offenders are being met.

NOTE

1. Involving specially trained probation officers, reduced client caseloads, and enhanced resources for urinalysis testing and community surveillance.

RESOURCES AND REFERENCES

Anglin, M. D., Longshore, D., & Turner, S. (1999). Treatment alternatives to street crime: An evaluation of five programs. *Criminal Justice and Behavior, 26,* 168–195.

Anno, J. (1991). *Prison health care: Guidelines for the management of an adequate delivery system.* Washington, DC: U.S. Department of Justice, National Institute of Corrections, National Commission on Correctional Health Care.

Aponte, J. F., & Barnes, J. M. (1995). Impact of acculturation and moderator variables on the intervention and treatment of ethnic groups. In J. F. Aponte, R. Y. Rivers, & J. Wohl (Eds.), *Psychological interventions and cultural diversity* (pp. 13–39). Needam Heights, MA: Allyn & Bacon.

Beck, A. J., & Shipley, B. E. (1989). *Recidivism of prisoners released in 1983.* Washington, DC: Bureau of Justice Statistics, U.S. Department of Justice.

Beckerman, A. (1998). Charting a course: Meeting the challenge of permanency planning for children with incarcerated mothers. *Child Welfare, 77,* 513–529.

Belenko, S. (1990). The impact of drug offenders on the criminal justice system. In R. Weisheit (Ed.), *Drugs, crime, and the criminal justice system* (pp. 27–78). Cincinnati, OH: Anderson.

Belenko, S. (1993). *Crack and the evolution of anti-drug policy.* Westport, CT: Greenwood Press.

Belenko, S. (1998). Research on drug courts: A critical review. *National Drug Court Institute Review, 1,* 1–42.

Belenko, S. (1999a). Diverting drug offenders to treatment courts: The Portland experience. In C. Terry (Ed.), *The early drug courts: Case studies in judicial innovation* (pp. 108–138). Newbury Park, CA: Sage.

Belenko, S. (1999b). Research on drug courts: A critical review: 1999 update. *National Drug Court Institute Review, 2*(2), 1–58.

Belenko, S. (2000a). *Drugs and drug policy in America: A documentary history.* Westport, CT: Greenwood Press.

Belenko, S. (2000b). The challenges of integrating drug treatment into the criminal justice process. *Albany Law Review*, *63*(3), 833–876.

Belenko, S. (2001). *Research on drug courts: A critical review: 2001 update*. New York: National Center on Addiction and Substance Abuse at Columbia University.

Belenko, S. (2002). Drug courts. In C. G. Leukefeld, F. Tims, & D. Farabee (Eds.), *Treatment of drug offenders: Policies and issues* (pp. 301–318). New York: Springer.

Belenko, S., & Dumanovsky, T. (1993). *Special drug courts: Program brief*. Washington, DC: U.S. Department of Justice, Bureau of Justice Assistance.

Belenko, S., Fagan, J., & Chin, K. L. (1991). Criminal justice responses to crack. *Journal of Research in Crime and Delinquency*, *28*(1), 55–74.

Belenko, S., Foltz, C., Lang, M. A., & Sung, H.-E. (2004). The impact on recidivism of residential treatment for high risk drug felons: A longitudinal analysis. *Journal of Offender Rehabilitation*, *40*, 105–132.

Belenko, S., Lang, M., & O'Connor, L. (2003). Self-reported psychiatric treatment needs among felony drug offenders. *Journal of Contemporary Criminal Justice*, *19*(1), 9–29.

Belenko, S., Langley, S., Crimmins, S., & Chaple, M. (2004). HIV risk behaviors, knowledge, and prevention among offenders under community supervision: A hidden risk group. *AIDS Education and Prevention*, *16*, 367–385.

Belenko, S., & Logan, T. K. (2003). Delivering effective treatment to adolescents: Improving the juvenile drug court model. *Journal of Substance Abuse Treatment*, *25*, 189–211.

Belenko, S., Patapis, N., & French, M. T. (2005). *Economic benefits of drug treatment: A critical review of the evidence for policy makers*. Philadelphia: Treatment Research Institute.

Belenko, S., & Peugh, J. (1999). *Behind bars: Substance abuse and America's prison population*. New York: National Center on Addiction and Substance Abuse at Columbia University.

Belenko, S., & Peugh, J. (2005). Estimating drug treatment needs among state prison inmates. *Drug and Alcohol Dependence*, *77*, 269–281.

Boldt, R. C. (1998). Rehabilitative punishment and the drug treatment court movement. *Washington University Law Quarterly*, *76*, 1205–1306.

Bradford, J., Greenberg, D. M., & Motayne, G. G. (1992). Substance abuse and criminal behavior. *Clinical Psychiatry*, *15*(3), 605–622.

Braithwaite, R. L., & Arriola, K. R. (2003). Male prisoners and HIV prevention: A call for action ignored. *American Journal of Public Health*, *93*, 759–763.

Broner, N., Borum, R., & Gawley, K. (2001). Criminal justice diversion of individuals with co-occurring mental illness and substance use. In G. Landsberg, M. Rock, & L. Berg (Eds.), *Serving mentally ill offenders and their victims: Challenges and opportunities for social workers and other mental health professionals*. New York: Springer.

Bureau of Justice Statistics. (1998). *Substance abuse and treatment of adults on probation, 1995*. Washington, DC: U.S. Department of Justice.

Bureau of Justice Statistics. (2001). *Trends in state parole, 1990–2000*. Washington, DC: U.S. Department of Justice.

California Substance Abuse and Crime Prevention Act of 2000, Cal. Penal Code §§ 1210 *et seq*. (Deering, 2003).

Carise, D., Gurel, O., Kendig, C., & McLellan, A. T. (2002). *Giving clinical meaning to patient assessment: Technology transfer to improve treatment care planning and service delivery*. Philadelphia: Treatment Research Institute.

Carroll, K. M. (1997). Enhancing retention in clinical trials of psychosocial treatments: Practical strategies. In L. Onken, J. Blaine, & J. Boren, (Eds.), *Beyond the therapeutic alliance: Keeping the drug-dependent individual in treatment* (NIDA Research Monograph Series #165, 4–24). Washington DC: U.S. Government Printing Office.

Cartwright, W. S. (2000). Cost-benefit analysis of drug treatment services: Review of the literature. *Journal of Mental Health Policy and Economics*, *3*, 11–26.

Carvajal, S., Parcel, G., Banspach, S., Basen-Engquist, K., Coyle, K., Kirby, D., et al. (1999). Psychosocial predictors of delay of first sexual intercourse by adolescents. *Health Psychology*, *18*(5), 1–10.

Center for Substance Abuse Treatment. (2000). *Linking substance abuse treatment and domestic violence services: A guide for treatment providers* (TIP No. 25). Rockville, MD: U.S. Department Health and Human Services.

Chaiken, J. M., & Chaiken, M. R. (1990). Drugs and predatory crime. In M. Tonry & J. Q. Wilson (Eds.), *Drugs and crime* (pp. 203–239). Chicago: University of Chicago Press.

Child Welfare League of America. (1990). *Crack and other addictions: Old realities and new challenges.* Washington, DC: Author.

Chou C. P., Hser Y. I., & Anglin M. D. (1998). Interaction effects of client and treatment program characteristics on retention: An exploratory analysis using hierarchical linear models. *Substance Use and Misuse, 33*(11), 2281–2301.

Claus, R. E., & Kendleberger, L. R. (2002). Engaging substance abusers after centralized assessment: Predictors of treatment entry and dropout. *Journal of Psychoactive Drugs, 34*, 25–31.

Cooper, C. (1997). *1997 drug court survey report: Executive summary.* Washington, DC: Drug Court Clearinghouse and Technical Assistance Project, American University.

Cooper, C. S., & Trotter, J. (1994). Recent developments in drug case management: Re-engineering the judicial process. *Justice System Journal, 17*(1), 83–98.

DeMatteo, D. S., Festinger, D. S., Lee, P. A., & Marlowe, D. B. (2005, June). *Substance use patterns in drug court: No problem?* Paper presented at the 67th Annual Scientific Meeting of the College on Problems of Drug Dependence, Orlando, FL.

DeMatteo, D. S., Marlowe, D. B., & Festinger, D. S. (2006). Secondary prevention services for clients who are low risk in drug court: A conceptual model. *Crime & Delinquency,* 52, 114–134.

Ditton, P. M. (1999). *Mental health and treatment of inmates and probationers: Special report* (NCJ 174463). Washington, DC: U.S. Department of Justice, Bureau of Justice Statistics.

Eisenstein, J., & Jacob, H. (1977). *Felony justice: An organizational analysis of criminal courts.* Boston: Little, Brown.

Etheridge, R. M., Hubbard, R. L., Anderson, J., Craddock, S. G., & Flynn, P. (1997). Treatment structure and program services in the drug abuse treatment outcome study (DATOS). *Psychology of Addictive Behavior, 11*, 244–260.

Farabee, D., Prendergast, M., & Anglin, M. (1998). The effectiveness of coerced treatment for drug-abusing offenders. *Federal Probation, 62*, 3–10.

Farrington, D. (1998). Predictors, causes, and correlates of male youth violence. In M. Tonry & M. Moore (Eds.), *Youth violence* (pp. 421–475). Chicago: University of Chicago Press.

Festinger, D. S., Marlowe, D. B., Lee, P. A., Kirby, K. C., Bovasso, G., & McLellan, A. T. (2002). Status hearings in drug court: When more is less and less is more. *Drug and Alcohol Dependence, 68*, 151–157.

Finn, P. (1999). *Washington state's corrections clearinghouse: A comprehensive approach to offender employment* (NCJ 174441). Washington, DC: National Institute of Justice.

Finn, P., & Newlyn, A. K. (1993). *Miami's "drug court": A different approach.* Washington, DC: U.S. Department of Justice, National Institute of Justice.

Fiorentine, R., & Hillhouse, M. P. (1999). Drug treatment effectiveness and client-counselor empathy: Exploring the effects of gender and ethnic congruency. *Journal of Drug Issues, 29*(1), 59–74.

French, M. T., McGeary, K. A., Chitwood, D. D., McCoy, C. B., Inciardi, J. A., & McBride, D. (2000). Chronic drug use and crime. *Substance Abuse, 21*, 95–109.

Friedman, S. R., Curtis, R., Neaigus, A., Jose, B., & Des Jarlais, D. C. (1999). *Social networks, drug injectors' lives, and HIV/AIDS.* New York: Kluwer Academic.

Gastfriend, D. R., & McLellan, A. T. (1997). Treatment matching: Theoretical basis and practical implications. *Medical Clinics of North America, 81*, 945–966.

Gendreau, P., Cullen, F. T., & Bonta, J. (1994). Intensive rehabilitation supervision: The next generation in community corrections? *Federal Probation, 58*, 72–78.

Gendreau, P., Goggin, C., Cullen, F. T., & Andrews, D. A. (2000). The effects of community sanctions and incarceration on recidivism. *Forum on Corrections Research, 12*, 10–13.

Gendreau, P., Little, T., & Goggin, C. (1996). A meta-analysis of the predictors of adult offender recidivism: What works! *Criminology, 34*, 575–596.

Gendreau, P., Smith, P., & Goggin, C. (2001). Treatment programs in corrections. In J. Winterdyk (Ed.), *Corrections in Canada: Social reactions to crime* (pp. 238–263). Toronto, Ontario, Canada: Prentice-Hall.

Goerdt, J. S., & Martin, J. A. (1989, Fall). The impact of drug cases on case processing in urban trial courts. *State Court Journal, 13*, 4–12.

Goldkamp, J. (2000). The drug court response: Issues and implications for justice change. *Albany Law Review, 63*, 923–961.

Goldkamp, J. S., & Weiland, D. (1993). *Assessing the impact of Dade County's felony drug court: Final report to the National Institute of Justice.* Philadelphia: Criminal Justice Research Institute.

Goldkamp, J. S., White, M. D., & Robinson, J. B. (2001). Do drug courts work? Getting inside the drug court black box. *Journal of Drug Issues, 31*(1), 27–72.

Goldstein, P. J. (1985). The drugs/violence nexus: A tripartite conceptual framework. *Journal of Drug Issues, 15*(4), 493–506.

Gottfredson, D. C., Najaka, S. S., & Kearley, B. (2003). Effectiveness of drug courts: Evidence from a randomized trial. *Criminology and Public Policy, 2,* 171–196.

Hammett, T. M., Gaiter, J. L., & Crawford, C. (1998). Reaching seriously at-risk populations: Health interventions in criminal justice settings. *Health Education and Behavior, 25,* 99–120.

Hammett, T., Harmon, P., & Maruschak, L. (1999). *1996–1997 Update: HIV, AIDS, STDs, and TB in correctional facilities.* Washington, DC: U.S. Department of Justice, National Institute of Justice, and Centers for Disease Control and Prevention.

Hammett, T. M., Roberts, C., & Kennedy, S. (2001). Health-related issues in prisoner reentry. *Crime and Delinquency, 47,* 390–409.

Hanlon, T. E., Nurco, D. N., Bateman, R. W., & O'Grady, K. E. (1998). The response of drug abuser parolees to a combination of treatment and intensive supervision. *Prison Journal, 78,* 31–44.

Harrell, A., Cavanagh, S., & Roman, J. (1999). *Final report: Findings from the evaluation of the District of Columbia Superior Court Drug Intervention Program.* Washington, DC: Urban Institute.

Harrison, P. M., & Beck, A. J. (2003). *Prisoners in 2002* (NCJ 200248). Washington, DC: U.S. Department of Justice, Bureau of Justice Statistics.

Harrison, P. M., & Karberg, J. C. (2004). *Prison and jail inmates at midyear 2003* (NCJ 203947). Washington DC: U.S. Department of Justice, Bureau of Justice Statistics.

Harwood, H. (2000). *Updating estimates of the economic costs of alcohol abuse in the United States: Estimates, update methods and data.* Falls Church, VA: Lewin Group.

Harwood, H. J., Malhotra, D., Villarivera, C., Liu, C., Chong, U., & Gilani, J. (2002). *Cost effectiveness and cost benefit analysis of substance abuse treatment: A literature review.* Rockville, MD: Substance Abuse and Mental Health Services Administration. Center for Substance Abuse Treatment.

Henggeler, S. W., Clingempeel, W. G., Brondino, M. J., & Pickrel, S. G. (2002). Four-year follow-up of multisystemic therapy with substance abusing and dependent juvenile offenders. *Journal of the American Academy of Child and Adolescent Psychiatry, 41,* 868–874.

Hoff, R. A., & Rosenheck, R.A. (1999). The cost of treating substance abuse patients with and without comorbid psychiatric disorders. *Psychiatric Services, 50,* 1309–1315.

Hoge, R., Andrews, D., & Leschied, A. (1996). An investigation of risk and protective factors in a sample of youthful offenders. *Journal of Child Psychology and Psychiatry, 37*(4), 419–424.

Hora, P. F., Schma, W. G., & Rosenthal, J. (1999). Therapeutic jurisprudence and the drug treatment court movement: Revolutionizing the criminal justice system's response to drug abuse and crime in America. *Notre Dame Law Review, 74*(2), 439–537.

Hser, Y.-I., Polinsky, M. L., Maglione, M., & Anglin, M. D. (1999). Matching clients' needs with drug treatment services. *Journal of Substance Abuse Treatment, 16,* 299–305.

Huddleston, C. W. (2000). *The promise of drug courts: The philosophy and history.* Alexandria, VA: National Drug Court Institute Training Presentation.

Huddleston, C. W., Freeman-Wilson, K., Marlowe, D. B., & Roussell, A. (2005, May). *Painting the current picture: A national report card on drug courts and other problem solving court programs in the United States* (Vol. 1, No. 2). Alexandria, VA: National Drug Court Institute.

Hunt, D. E. (1990). Drugs and consensual crimes: Drug dealing and prostitution. In M. Tonry & J. Q. Wilson (Eds.), *Drugs and crime* (pp. 159–202). Chicago: University of Chicago Press.

Hynes, C. J., & Swern, A. (2002). *Drug treatment alternative-to-prison, twelfth annual report.* Brooklyn, NY: Office of the Kings County District Attorney.

In re Mehdizadeh, 105 Cal. App. 4th 995 (2003).

In re Olivia J., 124 Cal. App. 4th 698 (2004).

Jacoby, J. (1994). Expedited drug case management program: Some lessons in case management reform. *Justice System Journal, 17*(1), 19–40.

Joe G. W., Simpson D. D., & Broome K. M. (1998). Effects of readiness for drug abuse treatment on client retention and assessment of process. *Addiction, 93*(8), 1177–1190.

Joe, G. W., Simpson, D. D., & Broome, K. M. (1999). Retention and patient engagement models for different treatment modalities in DATOS. *Drug and Alcohol Dependence, 57,* 113–125.

Johnson, S., Hubbard, D. J., & Latessa, E. J. (2000). Drug courts and treatment: Lessons to be learned from the "what works" literature. *Corrections Management Quarterly, 4,* 70–77.

Kamisar, Y., LaFave, W., & Israel, J. (1995). *Modern criminal procedure.* St. Paul, MN: West.

Keenan, K., Loeber, R., Zhang, Q., Stouthamer-Loeber, M., & Van Kammen, W. (1995). The influence of deviant peers on the development of boys' disruptive and delinquent behavior: A temporal analysis. *Development and Psychopathology, 7,* 715–726.

Kleiman, M. A. R., Tran, T. H., Fishbein, P., Magula, M. T., Allen, W., & Lacy, G. (2003). *Opportunities and barriers in probation reform: A case study of drug testing and sanctions.* Berkeley: University of California, California Policy Research Center.

La Greca, A., Prinstein, M., & Fetter, M. (2001). Adolescent peer crowd affiliation: Linkages with health-risk behaviors and close friendships. *Journal of Pediatric Psychology, 26*(3), 131–143.

Lamb, H. R., & Weinberger L. E. (1998). Persons with severe mental illness in jails and prisons: A review. *Psychiatric Services, 49,* 483–492.

Lang, M., & Belenko, S. (2000). Predicting retention in a residential drug treatment alternative to prison program. *Journal of Substance Abuse Treatment, 19,* 145–160.

Langan, P., & Cunniff, M. A. (1992). *Recidivism of felons on probation, 1986–1989.* Washington, DC: U.S. Department of Justice, Bureau of Justice Statistics.

Langan, P. A., & Levin, D. J. (2002). *Recidivism of prisoners released in 1994.* Washington, DC: U.S. Department of Justice, Bureau of Justice Statistics.

Laub, J. H., & Sampson, R. J. (2001). Understanding desistance from crime. In M. Tonry (Ed.), *Crime and justice* (pp. 1–69). Chicago: University of Chicago Press.

Lee, P. A., & Fox, G. (2005). *Sanction practices in felony drug court.* Paper presented at the College on Problems of Drug Dependence annual meeting, University of Pennsylvania, Philadelphia.

Lee, P. A., Marlowe, D. B., Festinger, D. S., Cacciola, J. S., McNellis, J., Schepise, N. M., et al. (2001). Did "Breaking the Cycle" (BTC) clients receive appropriate services? [abstract]. *Drug and Alcohol Dependence, 63*(Supp. 1), S89. Presentation at the 63rd Annual Scientific Meeting of the College on Problems of Drug Dependence, Scottsdale, AZ.

Leukefeld, C., McDonald, H. S., Staton, M., & Mateyoke-Scrivner, A. (2004). Employment, employment-related problems, and drug use at drug court entry. *Substance Use and Misuse, 39,* 2559–2579.

Lindesmith, A. R. (1965). *The addict and the law.* Bloomington, IN: Indiana University Press.

Loeber, R., & Farrington, D. (1998). *Serious and violent juvenile offenders: Risk factors and successful interventions.* Thousand Oaks, CA: Sage.

Longshore, D., Turner, S., Wenzel, S., Morral, A., Harrell, A., McBride, D., et al. (2001). Drug courts: A conceptual framework. *Journal of Drug Issues, 31*(1), 7–26.

Marlowe, D. B. (2002). Effective strategies for intervening with drug abusing offenders. *Villanova Law Review, 47,* 989–1025.

Marlowe, D. B. (2003). Integrating substance abuse treatment and criminal justice supervision. *NIDA Science and Practice Perspectives, 2*(1), 4–14.

Marlowe, D. B., DeMatteo, D. S., & Festinger, D. S. (2003). A sober assessment of drug courts. *Federal Sentencing Reporter, 16,* 153–157.

Marlowe, D. B., Festinger, D. S., & Lee, P. A. (2003). The role of judicial status hearings in drug court. *Offender Substance Abuse Report, 3,* 33–46.

Marlowe, D. B., Festinger, D. S., & Lee, P. A. (2004). The judge is a key component of drug court. *Drug Court Review, 4*(2), 1–34.

Marlowe, D. B., & Kirby, K. C. (1999). Effective use of sanctions in drug courts: Lessons from behavioral research. *National Drug Court Institute Review, 2*(1), 1–32.

Marquart, J., Merianos, D., Hebert, J., & Carroll, L. (1997). Health conditions and prisoners: A review of research and emerging areas of inquiry. *Prison Journal, 77*(2), 184–208.

Martin, S. S., Butzin, C. A., Saum, S. A., & Inciardi, J. A. (1999). Three-year outcomes of therapeutic community treatment for drug-involved offenders in Delaware. *Prison Journal, 79,* 294–320.

Martin, S. S., O'Connell, D. J., Inciadi, J. A., Beard, R. A., & Surratt, H. L. (2003). HIV/AIDS among probationers: An assessment of risk and results from a brief intervention. *Journal of Psychoactive Drugs, 35,* 435–443.

Mattson, M. E., Allen, J. P., Longabaugh, R., Nickless, C. J., Connors, G. J., & Kadden, R. M. (1994). A chronological review of empirical studies matching alcoholic clients to treatment. *Journal of Studies on Alcohol, 12*(Suppl.), 16–29.

McBride, D., VanderWaal, C., Terry, Y., & VanBuren, H. (1999). *Breaking the cycle of drug use among juvenile offenders: Final technical report* (NCJ 179273). Washington, DC: National Institute of Justice. Retrieved September 15, 2005, from http://www.ncjrs.gov/pdffiles1/nij/179273.pdf

McCollister, K. E., & French M. T. (2003). The relative contribution of outcome domains in the total economic benefit of addiction interventions: A review of first findings. *Addiction, 89*, 1647–1659.

McLellan, A. T. (2003). *Investing in drug abuse treatment: A discussion paper for policy makers.* New York: United Nations, Office on Drugs and Crime.

McLellan, A. T., & Alterman, A. I. (1991). Patient treatment matching: A conceptual and methodological review with suggestions for future research. *NIDA Research Monograph 106* (pp. 114–135). Rockville, MD: U.S. Department of Health and Human Services, National Institute on Drug Abuse.

McLellan, A. T., Arndt, I. O., Metzger, D. S., & O'Brien, C. P. (1993). The effects of psychosocial services in substance abuse treatment. *JAMA, 269*, 1953–1959.

McLellan, A. T., Cacciola, J., Kushner, H., Peters, R., Smith, I., & Pettinati, H. (1992). The fifth edition of the Addiction Severity Index: Cautions, additions and normative data. *Journal of Substance Abuse Treatment, 9*, 461–480.

McLellan, A. T., Grissom, G. R., Zanis, D., Randall, M., Brill, P., & O'Brien, C. P. (1997). Problem service "matching" in addition treatment. *Archives of General Psychiatry, 54*, 730–735.

McLellan, A. T., Lewis, D. C., O'Brien, C. P., & Kleber, H. D. (2000). Drug dependence, a chronic medical illness: Implications for treatment, insurance, and outcomes evaluation. *JAMA, 284*, 1689–1695.

McLellan, A. T., Luborsky, L., Woody, G. E., O'Brien, C. P., & Druley, K. A. (1983). Predicting response to alcohol and drug abuse treatment. *Archives of General Psychiatry, 40*, 620–625.

Mee-Lee, D., Shulman, G., Fishman, M., Gastfriend, D. R., & Griffith, J. H. (Eds.). (2001). *ASAM patient placement criteria for the treatment of substance-related disorders: Second Edition–Revised (ASAM PPC–2R).* Chevy Chase, MD: American Society of Addiction Medicine.

Melnick, G., De Leon, G., Thomas, G., & Kressel, D. (2001). A client-treatment matching protocol for therapeutic communities: First report. *Journal of Substance Abuse Treatment, 21*, 119–128.

Morgan, R. D., Winterowd, C. L., & Ferrell, S. W. (1999). A national survey of group psychotherapy services in correctional facilities. *Professional Psychology: Research and Practice, 30*, 600–606.

National Association of Drug Court Professionals. (1997). *Defining drug courts: The key components.* Washington, DC: Office of Justice Programs, U.S. Department of Justice.

National Institute of Justice. (2000). *1999 annual report on drug use among adult and juvenile arrestees.* Washington, DC: U.S. Department of Justice.

National Institute on Drug Abuse. (1993). Numerous factors implicated in drug-related violence. *NIDA Notes, 8*(5), 1–4.

National Institute on Drug Abuse. (1999). *Principles of drug addiction treatment.* Rockville, MD: National Institutes of Health.

Needels, K. E. (1996). Go directly to jail and do not collect? A long-term study of recidivism, employment, and earnings patterns among prison releasees. *Journal of Research in Crime and Delinquency, 33*, 471–496.

Nelson, M., & Trone, J. (2000). *Why planning for release matters.* New York: Vera Institute of Justice.

Newcomb, M. D., Galaif, E. R., & Carmona, J. V. (2001). The drug-crime nexus in a community sample of adults. *Psychology of Addictive Behaviors, 15*, 185–193.

Nolan, J. L. (2003). *Reinventing justice: The American drug court movement.* Princeton, NJ: Princeton University Press.

Nurco, D. N., Hanlon, T. E., & Kinlock, T. W. (1991). Recent research on the relationship between illicit drug use and crime. *Behavioral Sciences and the Law, 9*, 221–249.

Nurco, D. N., Kinlock, T. W., & Hanlon, T. E. (1990). The drugs–crime connection. In J. A. Inciardi (Ed.), *Handbook of drug control in the United States* (pp. 71–90). New York: Greenwood Press.

Office of Applied Studies. (2003). *Results from the 2002 National Survey on Drug Use and Health: National findings* (DHHS Publication No. SMA 03–3836, NHSDA Series H–22). Rockville, MD: Substance Abuse and Mental Health Services Administration.

Office of National Drug Control Policy. (2001). *The economic costs of drug abuse in the United States, 1992–1998.* Washington, DC: Executive Office of the President.

Palmer, T. (1995). Programmatic and nonprogrammatic aspects of successful intervention: New directions for research. *Crime and Delinquency, 41*(1), 100–131.

Peters, R. H., Haas, A. L., & Murrin, M. R. (1999). Predictors of retention and arrest in drug court. *National Drug Court Institute Review, 2*(1), 33–60.

Peters, R. H., & Hills, H. A. (1993). Inmates with co-occurring substance abuse and mental health disorders. In H. J. Steadman & J. J. Cocozza (Eds.), *Mental illness in America's prisons* (pp. 159–212). Seattle, WA: National Coalition for the Mentally Ill in the Criminal Justice System.

Petersilia, J. (2000). *When prisoners return to the community: Political, economic, and social consequences.* Washington, DC: Urban Institute.

Petersilia, J., & Turner, S. (1993). Intensive probation and parole. In M. Tonry (Ed.), *Crime and justice: An annual review of research* (pp. 281–335). Chicago: University of Chicago Press.

Peyton, E. A., & Gossweiler, R. (2001). *Treatment services in adult drug courts: Report on the 1999 National Drug Court Treatment Survey.* Washington, DC: Center for Substance Abuse Treatment and Drug Courts Program Office.

Platt, J. L. (1995). Vocational rehabilitation of drug abusers. *Psychological Review, 117*, 416–433.

Prinstein, M., Boergers, J., & Spirito, A. (2001). Adolescents' and their friends' health-risk behavior: Factors that alter or add to peer influence. *Journal of Pediatric Psychology, 26*(5), 287–298.

Project MATCH Research Group. (1998). Matching alcoholism treatment to client heterogeneity: Project MATCH three-year drinking outcomes. *Alcoholism: Clinical and Experimental Research, 22*, 1300–1311.

Rice, D. P., Kelman, S., Miller, L. S., & Dunmeyer, S. (1990). *The economic costs of alcohol and drug abuse and mental illness: 1985.* Rockville, MD: National Institute on Drug Abuse.

Rossi, P. H. (1989). *Down and out in America: Origins of homelessness.* Chicago: University of Chicago Press.

Rychtarik, R., Connors, G. J., Whitney, R. B., McGillicuddy, N. B., Fitterling, J. M., & Wirtz, P. W. (2000). Treatment settings for persons with alcoholism: Evidence for matching clients to inpatient versus outpatient care. *Journal of Consulting and Clinical Psychology, 68*, 277–289.

Sampson, R., & Laub, J. (1993). *Crime in the making: Pathways and turning points through life.* Cambridge, MA: Harvard University Press.

Satel, S. (1998). Observational study of courtroom dynamics in selected drug courts. *National Drug Court Institute Review, 1*(1), 43–72.

Satel, S. L. (1999). *Drug treatment: The case for coercion.* Washington, DC: American Enterprise Institute.

Seiter, R. P., & Kadela, K. R. (2003). Prisoner reentry: What works, what does not, and what is promising. *Crime and Delinquency, 49*, 360–388.

Sherman, L. W., Gottfredson, D., MacKenzie, D., Eck, J., Reuter, P., & Bushway, S. (1997). *Preventing crime: What works, what doesn't, what's promising* (prepared for the National Institute of Justice). College Park, MD: University of Maryland, Department of Criminology and Criminal Justice.

Simourd, D. J. (2004). Use of dynamic risk/need assessment instruments among long-term incarcerated offenders. *Criminal Justice and Behavior, 31*, 306–323.

Simpson, D. D., Joe, G. W., Fletcher, B. W., Hubbard, R. L., & Anglin, M. D. (1999). A national evaluation of treatment outcomes for cocaine dependence. *Archives of General Psychiatry, 56*, 510–514.

Simpson, D. D., Joe, G. W., & Rowan-Szal, G. A. (1997). Drug abuse treatment retention and process effects on follow-up outcomes. *Drug and Alcohol Dependence, 47*, 227–235.

Simpson, D. D., Joe, G. W., Rowan-Szal, G. A., & Greener, J. M. (1997). Drug abuse treatment process components that improve retention. *Journal of Substance Abuse Treatment, 14*, 565–572.

Slobogin, C. (1995). Therapeutic jurisprudence: Five dilemmas to ponder. *Psychology, Public Policy, and Law, 1*(1), 193–219.

Sung, H., Belenko, S., & Feng, L. (2001). Treatment compliance in the trajectory of treatment progress among offenders. *Journal of Substance Abuse Treatment, 20*, 153–162.

Taxman, F. S. (1999a). Unraveling "what works" for offenders in substance abuse treatment services. *National Drug Court Institute Review, 2*, 93–134.

Taxman, F. S. (1999b). Graduated sanctions: Stepping into accountable systems and offenders. *Prison Journal, 79*, 182–204.

Taxman, F. S., & Bouffard, J. A. (2003). Substance abuse counselors' treatment philosophy and the content of treatment services provided to offenders in drug court programs. *Journal of Substance Abuse Treatment, 25*, 75–84.

Taxman, F. S., Young, D., Byrne, J. M., Holsinger, A., & Anspach, D. (2003). *From prison safety to public safety: Innovations in offender reentry.* Washington, DC: National Institute of Justice.

Thornton, C. C., Gottheil, E., Weinstein, S. P., & Kerachsky, R. S. (1998). Patient-treatment matching in substance abuse: Drug addiction severity. *Journal of Substance Abuse Treatment, 15*, 505–511.

Travis, J., Solomon, A. L., & Waul, M. (2001). *From prison to home: The dimensions and consequences of prisoner reentry.* Washington, DC: The Urban Institute.

Turner, S., Greenwood, P., Fain, T., & Deschenes, E. (1999). Perceptions of drug court: How offenders view ease of program completion, strengths and weaknesses, and the impact on their lives. *National Drug Court Institute Review, 2*, 61–85.

U.S. Government Accountability Office. (2005). *Adult drug courts: Evidence indicates recidivism reductions and mixed results for other outcomes.* Washington, DC: Author.

Violent Crime Control and Law Enforcement Act of 1994, Pub. L. No. 103-322, 108 Stat. 1796, 42 USC §§ 13701 *et seq.* (2003).

Wenzel, S. L., Longshore, D., Turner, S., & Ridgely, M. S. (2001). Drug courts, a bridge between criminal justice and health services. *Journal of Criminal Justice, 29*, 241–253.

Wild, T. C., Newton-Taylor, B., & Alletto, R. (1998). Perceived coercion among clients entering substance abuse treatment: Structural and psychological determinants. *Addictive Behavior, 23*, 81–95.

Wills, T., & Cleary, S. (1999). Peer and adolescent substance use among 6th–9th graders: Latent growth analyses of influence versus selection mechanisms. *Health Psychology, 18*, 453–463.

Young, D., & Belenko, S. (2002). Program retention and perceived coercion in three models of mandatory drug treatment. *Journal of Drug Issues, 32*(1), 297–328.

Young, D., Usdane, M., & Torres, L. (1991). *Alcohol, drugs, and crime: Vera's final report on New York's interagency initiative.* New York: Vera Institute of Justice.

Zarkin, G. A., Dunlap, L. J., Belenko, S., & Dynia, P. A. (2005). A benefit-cost analysis of the Kings County District Attorney's Office Drug Treatment Alternative to Prison (DTAP) Program. *Justice Research and Policy, 7*, 1–25.

Zhang, Z. (2004). *Drug and alcohol use and related matters among arrestees, 2003.* Washington, DC: U.S. Department of Justice, National Institute of Justice.

Zimring, F., & Hawkins, G. (1991). What kind of drug war? *Social Justice, 18*, 104–121.

List of Resources

The following organizations provide information and resources about drug courts and other problem-solving courts, as well as substance abuse and the criminal justice system.

American Bar Association–Judicial Division
DWI courts and other specialized courts
Web site: www.abanet.org

American University Drug Court Clearinghouse and Technical Assistance Program
Information and resources for drug court practitioners and researchers
Web site: spa.american.edu/justice/drugcourts.php

Bureau of Justice Assistance Drug Courts Program Office
Information on federal funding and resources for drug courts
Web site: www.ojp.usdoj.gov/BJA/grant/drugcourts.html

Center for Court Innovation
Community courts, domestic violence courts, drug courts, and other problem solving courts
Web site: www.courtinnovation.org

Council of State Governments
Mental health courts
Web site: www.consensusproject.org

Family Justice
Family Drug courts
Web site: www.familyjustice.org

Justice Management Institute
Community courts, drug courts
Web site: www.jmijustice.org

National Alliance for the Mentally Ill
Mental Health Courts
Web site: www.nami.org

National Association of Drug Court Professionals and the National Drug Court Institute
Adult drug courts, campus drug courts, DWI courts, family dependency treatment courts, reentry drug courts, training resources
Web site: www.nadpc.org or www.ndci.org

National Center for State Courts
Drug courts, DWI courts, and other problem-solving courts
Web site: www.ncsconline.org

National Council of Juvenile and Family Court Judges
Juvenile drug courts
Web site: www.ncjfcj.org

National Criminal Justice Reference Service
Clearinghouse for publications in criminal justice
Web site: www.ncjrs.org

National Institute on Drug Abuse
General information on drug abuse and drug treatment research
Web site: www.drugabuse.gov

National Judicial College
Campus drug courts (Back on TRAC), DWI courts, mental health courts and other problem-solving courts
Web site: www.judges.org

National Mental Health Association
Mental health courts
Web site: www.nmha.org

National Treatment Accountability for Safer Communities
Drug courts and treatment diversion programs, case management of offenders
Web site: www.nationaltasc.org

National Truancy Prevention Association
Truancy courts
Web site: www.truancypreventionassociation.com

National Youth Court Center
Teen courts
Web site: www.youthcourt.net

Native American Alliance Foundation
Native American healing to wellness courts
Web site: www.native-alliance.org

Treatment Research Institute at the University of Pennsylvania
Research on substance abuse treatment and drug courts, Addiction Severity Index and other assessment instruments
Web site: www.tresearch.org

Appendix A: Sample Client Waiver Forms

COURT OF COMMON PLEAS ADULT DRUG COURT PARTICIPANT CONTRACT

1) I, _____, with a birth date of _____/_____/_____, and an address of _____, have entered a guilty plea in Case Docket Number _____, to wit; an admission of the offense(s) of _____ _____, hereby enter into this Drug Court Contract binding myself to its terms. _____

2) I understand that the validity of this contract is conditioned upon my eligibility for the Drug Court Program. If at any time after the execution of this agreement and in any phase of the Drug Court Program, it is discovered that I am, in fact, ineligible to participate in the program, I may be immediately terminated from the program and the sentence I received pursuant to my guilty plea will be executed. I will not be allowed to withdraw my previously entered plea of guilty unless my ineligibility is based on facts or information that should have been known to the prosecutor prior to Drug Court admission, or on Constitutional grounds.

3) I understand that if I enter this program and fail to complete it, I may be barred from future participation.

4) I understand that participation in Drug Court involves a minimum time commitment of 12 months, and may include an aftercare component consisting of up to an additional 6 months.

5) I understand that during the entire course of the Drug Court Program, I will be required to attend court sessions and treatment sessions; submit to random drug testing; and remain clean, sober, and law-abiding. I agree to abide by the rules and regulations imposed by the Drug Court Team. I understand that if I do not abide by these rules and regulations, I may be sanctioned or terminated from the program.

6) I understand that sanctions may include time in custody, increased treatment sessions, increased drug testing, remaining in a particular treatment phase, reduction to a previously completed treatment phase, and/or such other sanctions as may be deemed necessary by the Drug Court Team.

7) I agree to cooperate in an assessment/evaluation for planning an individualized drug treatment program adequate to my needs. I understand that my treatment plan may be modified by the treatment provider or the Drug Court Team as circumstances arise, and I agree to comply with the requirements of any such modifications.

8) I understand that I will be required to pay for some or all of the cost of my treatment, and I will complete a financial declaration if necessary.

9) I understand that I will be tested for the presence of drugs in my system on a random basis according to procedures established by the Drug Court Team and/or treatment provider. I understand that I will be given a location and time to report for my drug test. I understand that it is my responsibility to report to the assigned location at the time given for the test. I understand that if I am late for a test, or miss a test, it will be considered "dirty" and I may be sanctioned.

10) I understand that substituting, altering, or trying in any way to change my body fluids for purposes of testing, including attempts to dilute the sample, will be grounds for sanctions, including termination, imposed at the discretion of the Drug Court Team.

11) I understand that participating in Drug Court requires me to be drug free at all times. I will not possess drugs or drug paraphernalia. I will not associate with people who use or possess drugs, nor will I be present while drugs are being used by others.

12) I agree to be drug tested at any time by a police officer, probation officer, treatment provider, or at the request of the Court or any agency designated by the Court.

13) I agree to inform any law enforcement officer who contacts me that I am in Drug Court. I also agree to inform the _____ County Domestic Relations Office of my participation in Drug Court as long as I have open cases with Domestic Relations.

14) I may not participate in Drug Court if I am currently an affiliated gang member.

15) I will inform all treating physicians that I am a recovering addict and may not take narcotic or addictive medications or drugs. If a treating physician wishes to treat me with narcotic or addictive medications or drugs, I must disclose this to my treatment provider and get specific permission from the Drug Court Team to take such medication.

16) I agree that I will not leave any treatment program without prior approval of my treatment provider and the Drug Court Team.

17) I understand that I may dispute positive test results, but that retesting will be at my expense, and that I may face more severe sanctions if the retest results are still positive.

18) For the purposes of regular Drug Court review hearings, I agree to waive my right to have my attorney of record present. I understand that my case may be discussed without my attorney or the prosecutor present.

19) I understand that my individual course of treatment may include residential treatment, education, and/or self-improvement courses such as anger management, parenting, or relationship counseling.

20) I understand that during the early phases of treatment and recovery, I may be precluded from working or from gaining employment. I further understand that within the time directed by the Drug Court Team, I will seek employment, job training, and/or further education as approved by the Drug Court Team, and that failure to do so may result in sanctions or termination.

21) I agree to keep the Drug Court Team, treatment provider, and law enforcement liaison, if any, advised of my current address and phone number at all times and whenever changed. My place of residence is subject to Drug Court approval, and I will not leave _____ County without prior permission from the Drug Court Team.

22) As a condition of participation in the program, I agree to the search of my person, property, place of residence, vehicle, or personal effects at any time with or without a warrant, and with or without reasonable cause, when required by a probation officer or Drug Court Team member or representative.

23) I agree to execute the Consent for Disclosure of Confidential Substance Abuse Information. I understand that any information obtained from this release will be kept apart from the Court file.

24) I understand that my failure to successfully complete and graduate from the _____ County Court of Common Pleas Adult Drug Court program will result in the imposition of the previously deferred sentence against me. I understand that my failure to complete Drug Court cannot be a basis for the withdrawal of my previously entered guilty plea.

25) Upon my successful completion of the Drug Court program, the criminal charges filed against me will be dismissed. After an appropriate period of time free of criminal activity (one (1) year for misdemeanors and three (3) for felonies), the District Attorney's office, upon motion, will agree to expunge the offense, or the pertinent charges as previously agreed, unless there is an objection from the Court.

I have read the above contract and I understand what I have read. I am willing to enter into this agreement to participate in the _____ County Court of Common Pleas Adult Drug Court program._____

Participant's Signature   Date

_____

Participant's Attorney   Date

_____

Prosecuting Attorney   Date

_____

Drug Court Judge   Date

Appendix B: Drug Court Guilty Plea Colloquy

STATE OF *****:   VS. :   CRIMINAL NO._____
                                INSTRUCTIONS

1. This form is to be used only in the _____ County Court of Common Pleas Drug Court.
2. The Court will explain the elements of the crime(s) to which you are pleading guilty and the possible range of sentences and fines.
3. Complete the answer to every question.
4. Be sure to sign and date the form on the back of page.

_____

You are present before this Court because you and your lawyer have stated that you wish to plead guilty to some or all of the criminal offenses with which you have been charged.

1. Can you read, write, speak, and understand the English language?

2. Are you in any way under the influence of alcohol or drugs, including prescription medications?

3. Do you understand that you are here today to enter a plea of guilty to all of the criminal charges against you?

4. Do you understand that pleading guilty is a condition of participation in Drug Court?

5. Do you understand that if you are terminated from the Drug Court program, you will NOT be permitted to withdraw your guilty plea, unless that termination is based on facts which should have been known to the prosecutor prior to admission, or on Constitutional grounds?

6. Do you understand that if it becomes necessary to sentence you pursuant to your guilty plea, then the sentencing may NOT occur within the ninety (90) days as proscribed by [STATE] Rule of Criminal Procedure 704? I understand and agree to waive the ninety (90) day limitation?

7. Do you understand that should it become necessary to sentence you, it is the Drug Court who will determine the sentence (in other words, this is an open plea)?

8. Do you know that, for a misdemeanor or felony, the Drug Court may impose a sentence in accordance with the sentencing guidelines which place a suggested length of sentence for the type of crime and increase the length of that sentence if you had been previously convicted of other crimes, either as a juvenile or an adult, and that the maximum sentence or sentences of confinement and/or fines applicable to the crimes covered by this guilty plea are as follows:

Charge   Term of Confinement Max.   Fine
_____   _____   _____
_____   _____   _____

9. Do you understand that if you are being sentenced on more than one count, the sentences could be consecutive to each other?

10. Do you understand that you have a right to a trial by jury and that by pleading guilty you are giving up that right?

11. Do you understand that a jury would consist of twelve (12) citizens from _____ County, that you and your attorney would participate in the selection of the jury, and that in order to convict you all 12 members of the jury must agree that you are guilty?

12. Do you understand that you are presumed innocent until proven guilty by the [STATE] beyond a reasonable doubt?

13. Do you understand that the [STATE] must prove each element of each crime beyond a reasonable doubt?

14. Do you understand that if the judge declines to accept your guilty plea, you will be permitted to withdraw it and you will be in the same position as if this plea had not taken place?

15. Do you understand the terms and conditions of Drug Court?

16. Is it your decision to plead guilty?

17. Have you been threatened or forced to plead guilty?

18. Have any promises been made to you to enter a plea of guilty, other than the terms of the Drug Court program as agreed to by me in the Participant Contract?

19. Do you understand that a guilty plea has the same effect as a conviction by a jury or a judge hearing the case without a jury?

I am voluntarily pleading guilty and signing the Drug Court Guilty Plea Colloquy.

_____   _____

Defendant   Date

I have reviewed this Drug Court Guilty Plea Colloquy with my client.

_____

Attorney for Defendant

Jail Mental Health Services

18

Diane S. Young

Case Examples

Molly is 27, White, with a history of legal problems beginning 7 years ago for misdemeanor charges such as petite larceny, prostitution, and various traffic violations. The increasing severity of her legal problems within the recent past results in less frequent but longer incarcerations as a sentenced or an unsentenced inmate. These legal charges include felonies such as aggravated harassment, child abuse, assaults, and drug possession. Molly is diagnosed with bipolar disorder and polysubstance dependence, and she has an extensive history of physical and sexual abuse by family members. Her social history reveals that she has three children, ages 6, 3, and 18 months, all placed in foster care. She does not maintain consistent contacts with her children or with family members. She is unemployed and lives with a male friend who also has a lengthy criminal record. Because of her frequent incarcerations, refusal to comply with outpatient psychiatric treatment, and relapses into substance abuse, she does not receive social welfare benefits on a consistent basis. Efforts to maintain Molly in the community have included intensive case management services, inpatient/outpatient psychiatric and substance abuse treatment, and emergency housing and women's shelter programs. While incarcerated, Molly is usually maintained in the Mental Health Unit. She is referred to a psychiatrist for medications and achieves an appropriate level of medication compliance resulting in psychiatric stability for brief periods of time. (Liette Dennis)

Richard is 39, African American, and single, with an extensive history of legal problems beginning 15 years ago. Initially, his legal problems included misdemeanors such as criminal mischief, disorderly conduct, and petite larceny. Recent charges include felonies, such as

The author wishes to acknowledge Liette Dennis for her contributions to this chapter by writing the case examples.

criminal possession of a weapon, assault, and burglary. Dispositions of charges have ranged from dismissal of charges to brief sentences at the county jail or probation. Richard has been arrested 30 times since age 24. He is diagnosed with bipolar disorder and polysubstance abuse. He has refused to comply with outpatient psychiatric treatment following numerous involuntary hospitalizations in the community and during his incarcerations. He receives Social Security disability benefits and is assigned a payee to assure his housing, food, and clothing needs are met. Because of his extensive legal problems and psychiatric treatment history, he was referred to a forensic intensive case manager, who met with Richard at the jail to begin a discharge plan before he was released into the community. Practitioners in the jail and forensic intensive case managers met with him frequently to encourage his cooperation with a discharge plan. The goal was to stabilize his psychiatric condition while he was incarcerated, find adequate housing, refer him to outpatient psychiatric and medical services, and reinstate Social Security benefits. Regular contacts with social workers and case managers positively influenced his decision to work with a case manager in the community. The benefit of providing case management services is that Richard has been able to maintain himself in the community without an arrest for almost 1 year when previously he would be arrested once or twice each month. (Liette Dennis)

These case illustrations are designed to portray challenging, but not unusual, examples of the complexity of circumstances and service needs that mentally ill offenders bring with them to incarceration. Details have been altered to protect confidentiality, while also maintaining the essence of the cases. The first example indicates problems with family relationships, including with Molly's children; unemployment and insufficient legal income; maintaining treatment and/or medication compliance; aggression toward others; and abuse. The second case describes release-planning efforts with Richard, a seriously mentally ill offender who at first rejected community treatment but now is successfully maintained in the community. Both cases demonstrate the challenges that mentally ill offenders present to jail staff.

Introduction

Jail mental health services are an essential component of the broader network of mental health services established to provide care for persons with mental illnesses. Social workers play key roles in the delivery of these services. Practice within mental health care settings, while rewarding, is also challenging, and provision of services within jails encompasses additional considerations. Jail populations are very diverse and hold pre-trial detainees; individuals serving sentences of less than 1 year; persons convicted of felonies and waiting for sentencing or transportation to prison; probation and parole violators awaiting hearings; and in some jurisdictions, juveniles and individuals with mental illnesses until they can be transported elsewhere. Some local jails also hold state or federal prisoners because of overcrowding in state and federal facilities. In addition, jail populations are very transient, with the majority of individuals staying only a short time.

Jails are the correctional facilities that arrested adults cycle in and out of as mental decompensation occurs. These individuals are often difficult to engage and maintain in treatment in the community, and they continue to present a challenge for successful public health intervention. This is readily seen in both case illustrations. It has been suggested that the central issue confronting mental health activists today is the same one that confronted activists in the 1840s—removing individuals with mental illnesses from jails (Harrington, 1999). In the mid-1800s, it was routine practice to put the insane poor in jails and poorhouses. Dorothea Dix vigorously advocated for the creation of psychiatric hospitals to care for the indigent mentally ill. She argued that it made no sense to jail those who were simply struggling with disease. Within the following 40 years or so, state legislatures opened 30 psychiatric hospitals for the poor, and by 1880, less than one half of 1% of the approximately 92,000 individuals with mental illnesses were kept in jails (Harrington, 1999).

By the late 1940s, however, psychiatric hospitals had deplorable reputations and were in need of serious reform. Within the next few decades, antipsychotic drugs became widely available, and federal programs such as Social Security Disability, Medicaid, and subsidized housing became available. Deinstitutionalization was underway. States tightened up the laws that regulated involuntary hospitalization, requiring the presence of danger to self or others, thus ensuring that the need for hospital beds because of mental illnesses was vastly reduced for the future (Harrington, 1999). Those who had been previously kept in psychiatric hospitals were to live in the community and receive mental health care from community mental health clinics and centers. Unfortunately, this transition was not as successful as intended, and many individuals with mental illnesses were not actively engaged in treatment in their communities.

Indeed, the demand on correctional systems to house and manage severely mentally ill individuals seems to be in direct relationship to the availability of community-care options. Penrose (1939), in a large study of European countries, found a relationship between the number of individuals confined to mental hospitals and the number confined within jails and prisons; as one form of confinement was reduced, the other increased. Scholars who have examined this issue in the United States, through extensive reviews of prior research, have come to a similar conclusion (Lamb & Weinberger, 1998; Torrey, 1997). When community resources for mental health care are minimal or absent, pressure is placed upon the criminal justice system to deal with and manage individuals who, because of their illnesses, create difficulties for others. This places a heavy burden on facilities seldom equipped to understand and address the magnitude of need.

This chapter provides an overview of jail mental health services, beginning first with a discussion of the scope of the problem. The legal basis for jail mental health care and the generally accepted standards for jail mental health services are presented. The organization of jail mental health services, including a description of current practices— what services are actually provided and by whom—are explained. Special clinical issues and dilemmas that occur in jail mental health practice are presented. Finally, promising approaches for the provision of jail mental health services are explored.

Scope of the Problem

Psychiatric disorders and the need for mental health services among jail inmates are fairly extensive (Abram, Teplin, & McClelland, 2003; Ditton, 1999; Lamb & Weinberger,

1998). Based on a 1996 survey of jail inmates (Ditton, 1999), 15.6% of male inmates and 22.7% of female inmates were identified as mentally ill. Ditton identified offenders as mentally ill if they reported a current mental or emotional condition or an overnight stay in a mental hospital or treatment program. Lamb and Weinberger (1998) conducted an extensive review of the literature from 1970 on and found that studies suggest that 6 to 15% of individuals in jails have severe mental illnesses. Another significant proportion could benefit from a level of care equivalent to outpatient mental health treatment while incarcerated. While the definition of mental illness varied across studies, the studies Lamb and Weinberger discussed in their article focused on major mental disorders such as mania, psychotic disorders, and major depression. Abram and colleagues (2003) found that 8% of the jailed women in their sample ($N = 1,272$) had both a severe psychiatric disorder, such as schizophrenia or a major affective disorder, and a substance use disorder.

At midyear 2004, almost 714,000 individuals were held in the nation's approximately 3,400 jails (Harrison & Beck, 2005; Mays & Winfree, 2005). More importantly, many more than this number are booked into jails nationwide on an annual basis, given the rapid turnover within jails. Based on even conservative estimates then, the number of individuals with mental illnesses who are temporarily held in jail in any given year is significant.

Typically, the rates of mental disorders are much higher among incarcerated populations than the corresponding rates among general community populations (Bland, Newman, Thompson, & Dyck, 1998; Regier et al., 1990; Teplin, 1990). Bland and colleagues (1998) found that both 6-month and lifetime prevalence rates were higher among their sample of male inmates than among their sample of community residents for every disorder they examined, including schizophrenia, substance-related, affective, and anxiety disorders.

Findings from Teplin's studies (as reported by the Center for Mental Health Services [CMHS], 1995) have been used to provide a comparison between the prevalence rates of some disorders for jailed inmates and the general U.S. population. In the general population, 1.1% reported major depression currently, 0.9% schizophrenia, and 0.1% mania. On the other hand, among male jail inmates, 3.4% had major depression, 3.0% schizophrenia, and 1.2% mania. Among female jail inmates, 13.7% had major depression, 1.8% schizophrenia, and 2.2% mania.

A more recently reported study (Ford & Trestman, 2005) examined prevalence rates for Axis I and Axis II disorders in 508 randomly selected individuals who did not already have an institutionally defined serious mental health problem in five Connecticut jails. Just over 15% of the males and 23% of the females were diagnosed with depression. One percent of each gender subgroup had mania. Among anxiety disorders, 12.1% of the males and 16.5% of the females were assessed to have posttraumatic stress disorder. The two most commonly occurring personality disorders were antisocial personality disorder, diagnosed in 39.5% of the males and 27.0% of the females, and borderline personality disorder, in 12.9% of the males and 23.2% of the females.

A substantial proportion of mentally ill, incarcerated individuals has alcohol or drug problems (Abram & Teplin, 1991; Ditton, 1999; Regier et al., 1990; Teplin, Abram, & McClelland, 1996; Young, 2003). In the combined community and (prison) institutionalized sample of the five-site Epidemiologic Catchment Area (ECA) Study, Regier and colleagues (1990) found that the lifetime prevalence rate for any alcohol, other drug, and mental disorder was 32.7%. However, among prisoners the lifetime prevalence rate for any of these disorders was 82%. This exceptionally high rate was primarily attributable to the lifetime prevalence rate of a substance-related disorder (72%), although other mental disorders were found in close to 56% of the prisoners as well. About 90% of the prisoners with diagnoses of schizophrenia, bipolar disorder, or antisocial personality disorder also had an addictive disorder (Regier et al., 1990). Ditton (1999) found that almost 65% of mentally ill jail inmates reported being under the influence of drugs or alcohol at the time of the offense. Drug-related offenses were the most serious current offenses for 15.2% of mentally ill jail inmates (compared to 23.3% for all jail inmates; Ditton, 1999).

In a study of 330 jailed adults housed on the mental health units of a county jail, subgroups based on age, gender, and race (White or persons of color) were compared on the prevalence of five major mental health disorder categories (schizophrenia/psychosis, mood, anxiety, adjustment, and substance-related; Young, 2003). Regardless of age, gender, or race, substance-related disorders were the most prevalent type of disorder and present in over 63% of each group. Demographic groups also did not differ significantly in the extent of co-occurring disorders, with at least 41% of each group having both a substance-related disorder and another major mental illness.

Individuals with mental illnesses in jail often have serious problems in addition to substance abuse that make their service needs and successful reentry to the community more complex. For example, 30% reported a period of homelessness within the year prior to arrest, and 47% were not employed during the month prior to arrest (Ditton, 1999). Their family backgrounds are often troubled. Just over 51% of the jailed mentally ill have a family member who was incarcerated at some point, 24% lived in a foster home, agency, or institution while growing up, and 31% had a parent or guardian who abused alcohol or drugs (Ditton, 1999). The rates of prior physical and sexual abuse are also high, with almost 31% of males with mental illnesses and 73% of females with mental illnesses reporting abuse prior to incarceration (Ditton, 1999). In every example given here, the prevalence rates for jailed individuals with mental illnesses are higher than those for jail inmates without mental illnesses.

Severely mentally ill jail inmates are also often harder to manage while incarcerated. Because of their illnesses and the corresponding confusion, suspicion, or fear, they may have trouble understanding jail rules or following orders. Ditton (1999) found that mentally ill inmates were more likely to have been charged with breaking jail rules than other inmates (24.5% and 16%, respectively). In addition, they are vulnerable to abuse by other inmates who are not tolerant of their unusual behavior or who seek to take advantage of them. They are at increased risk for suicide (American Psychiatric Association [APA], 2000), and if they are also physically ill, they may have trouble explaining their medical symptoms and concerns to jail officials in order to get appropriate treatment (Torrey, 1997). Nevertheless, despite the complexities and difficulties in providing care to the mentally ill in jails, there are mandates to do so.

Legal Issues

Jails are not designed or intended to be treatment facilities, yet mental health treatment for severe needs is a legally mandated right of inmates (Alexander, 2000; CMHS, 1995). For pretrial detainees, this right stems from the due process clause of the 14th Amendment to the U.S. Constitution, and for other prisoners, from the protection from cruel and unusual punishment guaranteed by the Eighth Amendment. The intentional failure to provide a minimal level of mental health care to prisoners with severe needs has been found to constitute deliberate indifference to serious medical needs, a violation of the Eighth Amendment (Alexander, 2000). *Estelle v. Gamble* (1976) established prisoners' rights to medical care, and *Bowring v. Godwin* (1977) extended this right to psychiatric treatment (Alexander, 2000). It is important to note, however, that the psychiatric illness must be serious, with great potential for harm if left untreated, before a violation of the right to freedom from cruel and unusual punishment is considered. Correctional facilities are vulnerable to legal action regarding inadequate care if they do not comply with minimally accepted standards of care for individuals with serious mental illnesses.

Ruiz v. Estelle (1980), a class action suit brought against the Texas Department of Corrections over inadequate prison health care, among other concerns, resulted in the setting forth of six basic components for a "minimally adequate mental health treatment program" (Jemelka, Trupin, & Chiles, 1989, p. 484). They are:

- Systematic screening and evaluation to identify those who need mental health treatment.
- Treatment that is more than segregation and close supervision.
- The use of trained mental health providers in adequate numbers to provide individualized treatment for those with serious disorders.
- Record keeping that is accurate, confidential, and complete.
- Careful administration of behavior altering drugs, including adequate review of prescriptions.
- Identification and treatment of inmates with suicidal tendencies.

Beginning in the mid-1970s, standards of adequate mental health care in correctional facilities have been published by the American Public Health Association, the American Correctional Association, the National Commission on Correctional Health Care, and the American Medical Association (CMHS, 1995; Elliott, 1997). Then in 1989, the APA published its Task Force Report on Psychiatric Services in Jails and Prisons, with a revised edition published in 2000 (APA, 1989, 2000). Among the recommendations were that essential mental health services in jails include the following: mental health screening at intake; mental health evaluations by mental health professionals for referred inmates; treatment including crisis intervention, the appropriate use of psychotropic medications, brief therapies, patient education, and a written treatment plan for inmates receiving ongoing services; and discharge or transfer planning (APA, 2000). Although the implementation of published standards by jails is voluntary, such standards can be, and have been, used as a benchmark by the courts when making legal decisions regarding the provision of care (APA, 2000; Lindenauer & Harness, 1981).

Current Practices

According to the APA (2000), the goal of mental health treatment in correctional facilities is to "alleviate symptoms of mental disorders that significantly interfere with an inmate's ability to function" in his or her environment (p. 15). Furthermore, the APA recommends that the same level of mental health care that should be available in the community be available to jailed individuals. Mental health treatment within jails has at least four purposes, including:

- helping patients utilize their rights of due process,
- enhancing the safety of everyone who lives or works in jails,
- relieving unnecessary and severe suffering, and
- assisting inmates to participate in available programs (APA, 2000).

Understanding the goal and purposes of mental health care in jails can serve as a standard against which to compare current practices.

Common Jail Mental Health Services

Some level of mental health care is provided in many jails. Ninety-one percent of the U.S. jails responding to a 1993 survey ($N = 3,076$) reported that they provide at least one of seven mental health services, with larger facilities providing more services (Goldstrom, Henderson, Male, & Manderscheid, 1998). The seven services include crisis intervention, mental health screening during intake, follow-up mental health evaluation, 24-hour mental health (hospital) care, formal therapy, psychotropic medication prescription and monitoring, and case management services. Among jails with average daily populations of 500 or more, two thirds provided all seven services.

The most common mental health services in jails are intake screening and evaluation, crisis intervention and suicide prevention, and the prescription of psychotropic medications. In a study of mentally ill detainees from seven jails, 72.5% of the detainees received medication as the primary treatment, with less than half (43.8%) receiving case management services or individual or group therapy (Veysey, Steadman, Morrissey, & Johnsen, 1997). Goldstrom and colleagues (1998) found the most frequently offered mental health services in 2,797 jails nationwide were crisis intervention (88% of jails), psychotropic medication prescription and monitoring (85%), and mental health screening at intake (84%). Discharge or release planning, so important to maintaining a continuity of care, is utilized less frequently. Veysey and colleagues (1997) report formal discharge plans for about 25% of the mentally ill detainees in their study. Goldstrom and colleagues (1998) found that, of the jails providing at least one mental health service, 64% provided case management services, which may include discharge planning.

Jail Mental Health Service Providers

Practitioners providing mental health services within jails might be on the jail's staff, available through private contract, or from the staff of a publicly funded mental health agency. Based on a large survey of jails, psychiatrists are the most likely of the core mental health practitioners to provide jail mental health services (Goldstrom et al.,1998). Indeed, when psychotropic medications must be prescribed and monitored, access to a psychiatrist is essential. In addition, about one third of jails nationwide use psychologists and one third use social workers to provide mental health services to inmates (Goldstrom et al.,1998). In jails with an average daily population of 250 or more, master's-level social workers were second only to psychiatrists in providing services.

Screening and Evaluation

The APA (2000) recommends that various levels of screening and assessment take place for individuals in jails. Receiving mental health screening should occur immediately upon arrival at the jail and consists of a quick and standardized inquiry into mental health history and symptoms, including previous suicide attempts and ideation and medication use. Appropriately trained custody personnel can do this screening. The Brief Jail Mental Health Screen (BJMHS) is one example of this kind of screening instrument. It is a revision of the Referral Decision Scale (see Teplin & Swartz, 1989) and contains only eight yes or no questions. Its purpose is to identify quickly which incoming inmates need further mental health assessment, and it focuses specifically on recent or acute symptoms of schizophrenia, bipolar disorder, and major depression. The instrument was validated in four jails by comparing data from the BJMHS to data from the Structured Clinical Interview for *DSM–IV* (SCID; Steadman, Scott, Osher, Agnese, & Robbins, 2005). The BJMHS correctly classified 73.5% of males, but only 61.6% of females. Steadman and colleagues recommend that the BJMHS be modified for women and that questions be added that address anxiety symptoms. In the meantime, the BJMHS may be a useful and cost-effective tool for screening incoming male inmates. A copy of the instrument is available at the National GAINS Center (2005) Web site.

Intake mental health screening is a more comprehensive review of all admitted inmates, recommended within 14 days of booking, and conducted by a health care professional. At the time of either receiving or intake mental health screening, if an individual is in need of mental health treatment, he or she should be referred for appropriate services. A brief mental health assessment is recommended within 72 hours of a positive screening or referral when a serious mental illness is suspected, and it is focused on the immediate concern. Mental health personnel should conduct these brief assessments. Finally, comprehensive mental health evaluations consist of an interview with the patient and review of any available health records, and these result in a mental health diagnosis and initial treatment plan, as appropriate (APA, 2000).

Jail mental health personnel use various screening and assessment instruments when conducting evaluations. Alexander (2000, p. 113) describes the ABC model for psychiatric screening with its appearance, alertness, affect, and anxiety (A), behavior (B), and cognition (C) components. A comprehensive evaluation should include exploration of an array of additional factors, such as mental health history and prior psychiatric treatment, medication history and current use, medical concerns, family and social relationships and support, current stressors, history of physical and sexual abuse, drug and alcohol use, employment and educational needs, and criminal history. Peters and Bartoi (1997, pp. 50–52) provide a useful list of areas for exploration when assessing for co-occurring psychiatric and substance use disorders. Because co-occurring disorders are so prevalent in jail populations, treatment plans that ignore substance-related disorders are not likely to be effective.

Mental Health Housing Units

Some jails have special housing units for mentally ill inmates. Both Molly and Richard (see case illustrations) were maintained while in jail in these types of units. Inmates placed in these units have trouble functioning in general housing because of the symptoms related to their mental disorders, but mental health professionals have determined that they do not require acute or emergency psychiatric care. If an inmate is determined to be an immediate danger to self or others, the inmate should be transferred to an acute-care psychiatric facility for inpatient hospitalization, either within the larger corrections system or an outside hospital, until stabilized (Metzner, Cohen, Grossman, & Wettstein, 1998).

Housing units designed for the mentally ill typically house 30 to 50 inmates (Metzner et al.,1998). Metzner and colleagues describe a typical "special needs unit" and suggest minimum physical plant standards. Ideally, corrections officers who work on these units receive training in mental illnesses and ways to manage mentally ill offenders that support therapeutic goals. Although published research on outcomes related to these units is scant (Metzner et al.,1998), one study found that inmates housed in a prison mental health unit had reductions in suicide attempts, the need for emergency medication, and days kept under mental health observation (Condelli, Bradigan, & Holanchock, 1997). One of the recommendations stemming from the Criminal Justice/Mental Health Consensus Project is that inmates placed on these units be evaluated regularly to determine whether their needs have changed (Council of State Governments, 2002). If personnel resources are available, these behavioral health housing units provide a place for psychoeducational groups and individual counseling sessions to occur. More typically, these units are utilized in order to ensure the safety and security of inmates and staff rather than for the provision of treatment per se.

Perhaps because the focus of legal mandates for mental health care is on inmates with serious mental illnesses and correctional health resources are limited, much of the mental health service activity that occurs in jails occurs on special housing units. Table 18.1 lists each type of service activity subsequent to initial screening and assessment, along with a brief description that defines the characteristic elements of each type of service, carried out by social workers employed by a county mental health department to provide mental health services to offenders on special housing units (one unit for males and one for females) in a jail with an average daily population of about 570 (Young, 2002). The table provides a good example of the scope of activities for this jail's mental health staff, excluding psychiatrists, and is probably fairly typical of nonpsychiatric, mental health services provided in similarly sized and staffed jails with behavioral health units. The types of activities and the percentage of the sample ($N = 359$) receiving each type of service were gleaned through an extensive review of progress notes in inmates' mental health records. Each of the services, with the exception of evaluations for housing change and follow-ups, were provided to less than one third of the 359 individuals in the sample (a maximum of 3 weeks' service activity was reviewed for each individual). Despite the relatively brief stay of the majority of the inmates in the sample and the low percentage of inmates receiving many of the services, the sum total of 2,259 services provided by the dozen or so social workers in this jail is not a small number, and it reflects the predominant focuses on brief interventions and maintaining safety and stability and much less emphasis on long-term therapeutic interventions and postrelease planning.

Adequacy of Jail Mental Health Care

As indicated, a majority of jails provide some level of mental health care and many attempt to be responsive to the needs of seriously mentally ill individuals. It is important

Table 18.1	**Types of Jail Mental Health Services Provided by Social Workers and Percentage of Sample Receiving Each Service**
Evaluation for housing change (74.7%)	Fairly quick assessment (usually looking at inmate mood, affect, mental state, and/or suicidal ideation) for the purpose of determining whether an inmate's housing status should change or remain the same. For example, includes decisions about whether the inmate should be moved to general population, whether the inmate should be under closer supervision, or whether razor and sheets should be removed or returned.
Follow-up (58.5%)	A relatively quick touching base or checking in with an inmate. No counseling, but perhaps reassurance or brief information exchanged.
Release planning (31.5%)	Conversation with an inmate related to what the inmate will do upon release with an eye toward the services and supports needed to be successful, or any activity directed toward the inmate's release.
Individual counseling (28.7%)	One-on-one interaction that moves well beyond checking in with an inmate. Issues may include skill development, life changes, relationship or family of origin issues, previous abuse, and/or other personal exploration.
Group work (26.7%)	A psychoeducational group. Group topics might include anger management, substance abuse, personal care, domestic violence, self-esteem, child care, and recreation (games).
Referral to psychiatrist (22.3%)	Referral to an in-house consulting psychiatrist.
Assessment (17.5%)	Further investigation of an inmate's mental status. Conducted with the inmate. Not tied solely to an evaluation for a housing change. Does not include the mental health screening received by all inmates in booking or the more complete mental health evaluation each inmate receives when admitted to the MHU.
Response to self-referral (15.0%)	Meeting with an inmate based upon the inmate's request to be seen. Requests are diverse in nature ranging from simple requests, such as for a book or phone call, to more serious concerns including hearing voices, harassment by other inmates, or a desire to discuss medical, legal, or family concerns.
Consultation (11.7%)	Discussion with another staff member or provider about how to proceed on an issue related to an inmate. For example, consultations might be with the psychiatrist, a security officer, mental health supervisor, or medical provider.

Table 18.1	(Continued)	
	Contact with legal system (8.1%)	Contacting or being contacted by someone within the legal system on behalf of an inmate or assist the inmate in making this contact. For example, a call is made to an attorney or a probation officer to check on the status of a case, or the inmate is assisted with writing a letter to an attorney.
	Contact with outside psychiatric provider (7.0%)	Contacting a provider of psychiatric or mental health services outside of the jail. Typically done to obtain treatment history or verify medications. Providers range from individual therapists to state hospitals, and include doctors and pharmacies for medication verification.
	Contact with inmate's support system (5.0%)	Contacting or being contacted by someone within the inmate's social support system or assist the inmate in making this contact. Often a family member, but also includes other agencies or individuals involved with the inmate or the inmate's family. For example, a call is made to a landlord or to the children's caseworker.
	Crisis intervention (4.5%)	Response to a crisis, where an issue needs immediate attention or is very urgent. Examples include a very distraught inmate, a suicide attempt, or active hallucinations.
	Court-ordered evaluation (3.1%)	Response to the court's request to provide information on an inmate's mental status. Does not include court-ordered evaluations conducted solely by the psychiatrist.
	Referral to other provider (2.5%)	Referral to an in-house provider other than a psychiatrist, such as to a nurse, another social worker, or the personnel of other programs provided in-house.
	Other (5.0%)	Any social work or other nonpsychiatric mental health activity recorded in the progress notes that does not fit in a preceding category.

Note. Adapted from Young, 2002.

to note, however, that the reported presence of a service should not be confused with the quality of the service or whether the level of service provision is adequate to the level of need. Clearly, not all inmates who need services receive them. Teplin, Abram, and McClelland (1997) found that of the 116 female jail inmates needing mental health services in their sample, only 23.5% received them during their jail stay. These findings are similar to Teplin's earlier study of male jail inmates, where 35.5% of the inmates needing services received them. Many jails, particularly smaller ones, do not provide a comprehensive range of services. Where resources for mental health services are scarce, only the most severely disturbed inmates receive much clinical attention. In addition, there has been documentation of severe neglect or substantially inferior treatment for mentally ill inmates in some jails and prisons (Alexander, 1989; Elliott, 1997; Torrey, 1997).

Clinical Issues

Treatment Within a Coercive Setting

Historically, the profession of social work was considerably more involved in adult corrections than it is presently. Several reasons have been offered for the profession's move away from this field. Predominant among these is the coercive nature of corrections, which is contrary to the social work profession's emphasis on client self-determination (Fox, 1983; Miller, 1995). Similarly, within direct social work practice the emphasis is on providing care and treatment to clients from a nonjudgmental stance. Within jails, the emphasis in one's approach to offenders is mostly on control from an authoritarian stance. The primary focuses within jails are public safety and facility security; this is in contrast to the social worker's primary concern with client well-being. These basic philosophical differences between social work and corrections have discouraged active involvement in correctional settings, jails included. In addition, jail settings are decidedly nontherapeutic environments. They have many environmental factors that contribute to poor physical and mental health. These factors include overcrowding, lack of privacy, poor hygienic conditions, poor diet, limited exercise, violence, sexual abuse, loss of control, restriction of meaningful relationships and roles, and, too often, delayed or inadequate health care. These conditions often work against mental health practitioners' efforts to help clients develop and work toward meaningful and realistic goals.

The APA (2000) has concluded, "there is no fundamental incompatibility between good security and good treatment. It should be universally recognized that good treatment can contribute to good security and good security can contribute to good treatment" (p. 25). For this to be attainable, at minimum, adequate resources, trained mental health professionals who work well with other clinicians and security personnel, established and written procedures and policies, and an administrator with clinical expertise and sufficient authority are required (APA, 2000). The implementation of both good security and good treatment in jails has been problematic, and helping professionals have an important role to play in working toward greater balance between these priorities. Where aspects of jail policy need changing, helping professionals should advocate for conditions that would enhance individual well-being and promote therapeutic goals.

Right to Refuse Services and Limits to Confidentiality

Closely related to the issue of providing treatment in a coercive environment are the real limitations that exist on the patient's right to confidentiality while engaged in jail mental health services and the right to refuse services. Mental health professionals will want to become familiar with the institutional and legal policies that determine the limitations to these rights in their particular settings. The National Association of Social Workers (NASW, 1999) Code of Ethics acknowledges that social workers will have mandated clients, and that under these circumstances it is essential to inform clients about "the nature and extent of services and about the extent of clients' right to refuse service" (1.03d). In addition, practitioners should clearly discuss with clients "circumstances where confidential information may be requested and where disclosure of confidential information may be legally required" (NASW, 1999, 1.07e) and the potential consequences of such disclosure (NASW, 1999, 1.07d). Helping professionals have dual responsibility to their clients and to society, and this is particularly true in criminal justice settings where safety and security are essential goals. At the same time, social workers are not given license to disregard those they work with because of their status; rather, they should seek to engage clients "as partners in the helping process" (NASW, 1999), with careful attention to ethical practice. Perhaps it is partially because Richard's cooperation was actively cultivated by the jail social workers and case managers that he continues to live successfully in the community (see case illustration).

Promising Approaches

Release Planning

The importance of making connections quickly and providing short-term interventions for mentally ill offenders in jails cannot be overestimated. To the extent that these individuals are hard to reach in the community, jails provide places of opportunity for intervention to begin. The window of opportunity is very small, however, because many jail detainees are held for only brief periods of time. Young (2002) found that the median length of stay on the mental health units was only 5 days. In this facility, mental health professionals attempted to complete full mental health evaluations within 24 hours of placement on the special housing units. This is commendable, but it is troublesome that so much time goes into assessment if little is done to follow-up on the good information gained through the assessment. When individuals are released soon after their evaluations, there is no opportunity inside the jail to follow through on individualized treatment plans.

Keeping individuals in jail for longer periods of time does not seem like a good solution. Rather, placing more emphasis on release planning and case management services that link inmates to community services is appropriate. When considering jail mental health services, this is the one core component of essential services recommended by the APA's (2000) Task Force that receives the least attention. There is some evidence that case management services provided to mentally ill offenders both in jail and after release from jail is related to reduced recidivism. In a study of 261 inmates who were diagnosed with a *DSM–III–R* Axis I or Axis II disorder and followed for 3 years after release from jail, recipients of community case management services were significantly less likely to have been rearrested within the same county than participants who had not received case management services (60% and 77%, respectively; Ventura, Cassel, Jacoby, & Huang, 1998). In addition, recipients of community case management were significantly more likely to remain in the community longer prior to rearrest (mean of 21 months compared to mean of 14 months, respectively). Interestingly, there were no significant differences in recidivism between inmates who received jail case management services and those who did not. Rather, Ventura and colleagues found the relationship between receiving jail case management services and recidivism to be indirect. Only those inmates who received jail case management later received community case management, and it was the participation in community case management that was linked to reduced rates of rearrest. Richard's participation in case management services, with the connections to services made while he was still incarcerated and continuing after his release, seem to be making a powerful positive impact on his personal recidivism rate (see case illustration).

For release planning to be successful, ongoing partnerships will have to be formed between correctional facilities and community agencies so that continuity of service is available to inmates released from custody. Partnerships must include mental health services, drug and alcohol inpatient and outpatient treatment, and other social services. At present, these types of linkages are not in place in most correctional facilities. Jails operate outside of the social service sector, and social service agencies are often reluctant to work with offenders.

In addition to building community ties, enhancing release-planning services within jails will require new program development in this area, including the allocation of resources to support these efforts. Release-planning activities in many jails, when available at all, too often consist of a brief conversation with an individual about his or her plans upon release from jail. Release dates and times are often not known in advance in jails that serve as holding facilities, detaining inmates pending court appearances. Given the uncertainty about release date and the short amount of time most inmates stay, concerted efforts to engage mentally ill inmates in release planning immediately upon entrance to the jail will be needed, unless it is determined that release is very unlikely. Administrators must demonstrate their approval for these types of efforts by leading the way in forging community ties and by allocating personnel to release-planning tasks. Structuring short-term interventions around stabilization and the development of community-based care plans for inmates likely to be released quickly is one useful way to utilize the assessment information gathered soon after jail entry. Even the inmates who stay longer could certainly benefit from coordinated care plans upon their release.

Exemplary Programs

There are some notable programs that show promise (Conly, 1999; Project Link, 1999). These stand out because they include jail-to-street transitional case management services, housing for the homeless mentally ill upon release, and attention to treating dual diagnoses. The following two programs are highlighted to illustrate some innovative approaches to these gaps in service. They emphasize the possibilities when active community connections are sought on behalf of jailed mentally ill offenders, and plans for this are set in motion during incarceration.

Project Link (1999) received a Gold Achievement Award, an annual award given by the APA, in 1999 in recognition of Project Link's work in addressing the needs of a difficult-to-treat segment of the chronically mentally ill population. This project seeks to prevent repeated incarceration and hospitalization of individuals with severe mental illnesses and to promote their reintegration into the community (Project Link, 1999). Project Link is a consortium of five community agencies and the university department of psychiatry that leads it. A director from each of the participating agencies is a member of the collaborative management team that oversees the project. Case advocates use assertive community treatment principles and intensive case management to engage and maintain persons with severe and persistent mental illness and a criminal justice history. The treatment team is racially and ethnically diverse to help bridge cultural barriers to services. When housing could not be obtained for some of the most impaired clients, especially those with active drug use, Project Link applied for and received a grant and matching local funds to develop a mobile treatment team and treatment residence for dually diagnosed clients.

A 1993 survey of the county jail in the Project Link area first identified the need for improved mental health services for this hard-to-reach segment of the population. Currently, clients are enrolled from the local jail, state correctional facilities, police departments, the public defender's office, hospitals, and emergency rooms (Project Link, 1999). The program is now used as an alternative to incarceration, a condition of release, and in collaboration with probation and parole. Linkages between the criminal justice system, health and social services, and Project Link are actively nurtured. Project Link staff members work with clients in jail and talk with judges, jail staff, and attorneys. Liaison persons are designated within local departments of social services offices to serve as points of contact for Project Link clients. Preliminary cost savings look encouraging. For 46 clients (38 of these had histories of comorbid substance abuse), average monthly jail costs for the group dropped from about $31,000 to $7,000. In addition, average monthly hospital and outpatient costs, including costs for services provided by Project Link, dropped from almost $198,000 to $42,000 for the group (Project Link, 1999).

Another innovative and promising program was featured by the National Institute of Justice in a program focus publication (Conly, 1999). Maryland's Community Criminal Justice Treatment Program (MCCJTP), begun in 1993, has created linkages between jails and communities to provide a continuum of care for mentally ill offenders. The program's distinguishing features include strong collaboration between state and local providers, transitional case management services that connect jailed inmates with community-based services, long-term housing support for homeless mentally ill offenders, and a focus on co-occurring disorders (Conly, 1999). MCCJTP's strategies are based on recommendations of researchers in the past decade. These recommendations include interagency communication, delineation of responsibilities, integrated services, early identification of the mentally ill in correctional settings, distinctive case management services, and specialized services for those with co-occurring substance use disorders (Conly, 1999). Each jurisdiction has at least one case manager who works with individuals while they are in jail. At the time of Conly's (1999) report, evaluation and outcome studies were underway. Preliminary qualitative responses to the program appear to be very positive.

Continuity of Financial Assistance

An important component for successful community reentry is the financial means to sustain oneself. Many individuals with mental illnesses receive federal entitlements: income support through Supplemental Security Income (SSI) or Social Security Disability Income (SSDI) programs, and health coverage through Medicaid or Medicare. The health coverage is often essential to cover the costs of medications necessary for continued psychiatric stability. In many cases, federal entitlement benefits are suspended or terminated upon incarceration (see Bernstein, 2001, for details related to this). Jail mental health staff can perform a significant service by advocating for or assisting inmates in retaining or reestablishing their benefits close to the time of release. For example, a county jail mental health administrator in Oregon advocated for changes in the Medicaid policy that required recipients to be discontinued from eligibility upon arrest (Sherman, Irvin, Yovanoff, & Sowards, 2004). This requirement meant that individuals had to start the lengthy application process over again upon release. The Oregon Office of Medical Assistance Programs has now issued a policy that persons already covered are not disenrolled until they have been in custody at least 2 weeks (Sherman et al., 2004). In addition, jails can develop prerelease agreements between themselves and local Social Security offices (see Bernstein, 2001, for details about these agreements). When these agreements are in place, the jail assists inmates with gathering the information needed for their applications, the Social Security Administration processes claims more quickly, and benefits are often available immediately upon release (Bernstein, 2001). Jail mental health programs that provide these kinds of practical assistance to mentally ill offenders contribute to a continuity of care from jail to community.

Extended Treatment in Jail

Not all individuals with mental illnesses are released quickly, so adequate, ongoing mental health services must be provided within jails. The Criminal Justice/Mental Health Consensus Project was conducted to develop recommendations that will improve the response to persons with mental illnesses who are at risk of involvement or in contact with the criminal justice system (Council of State Governments, 2002). The Project's recommendations are derived from meetings with criminal justice and mental health stakeholders, surveys, document reviews, and the work of four advisory boards. Among its many recommendations, and especially pertinent to jail mental health services, is to utilize the most appropriate psychotherapeutic medications, including the newer generation of medications. In addition, integrated treatment for co-occurring mental illness and substance abuse disorders is recommended. Integrated treatment involves the same clinicians, in the same setting, providing both mental health and substance abuse interventions in combinations that are consistent with the best practices from both fields (Council of State Governments, 2002). Given the large number of dually diagnosed individuals in jail, an integrated response is critical.

For individuals who will spend extended time in jail, mental health providers should develop individualized treatment plans based on comprehensive assessments. The following interventions have evidence of effectiveness in correctional settings: cognitive-behavioral therapy, skill-focused individual and group therapy, training in independent living skills, medication self-management, relapse prevention, and physical exercise programs (Council of State Governments, 2002).

Finally, programs for mentally ill offenders should be both culturally competent and gender specific. In 2004, only about 44% of jail inmates were White; African American and Hispanic inmates composed about 54% (Harrison & Beck, 2005). Cultural influences do have an effect on individuals' willingness to seek out and accept mental health services, and services that are provided in culturally insensitive ways will act as a deterrent. The Council of State Governments (2002) provides recommendations for ensuring that racial and ethnic minorities receive appropriate mental health services. These suggestions can be applied to jail mental health services as well. They include actively recruiting racial and ethnic minority mental health practitioners for clinical and administrative positions, providing a "culturally informed training curriculum" for all mental health practitioners, and forming partnerships between jail mental health services and community organizations that traditionally serve specific racial and ethnic minority groups.

Women compose about 12% of jailed individuals (Harrison & Beck, 2005), and perhaps because of their relatively small representation, their needs are often overlooked when programs are developed to address offenders' mental health. Bloom, Owen, and Covington (2003) prepared a lengthy report on gender-responsive strategies for women offenders based on extensive research literature reviews, national focus groups, and interviews. The guiding principles they set forth are very relevant to the needs of jailed mentally ill women. For example, women require therapeutic environments that are nurturing and mutually respectful. The development of positive and supportive relational connections is essential to women's well-being and good mental health. So many female offenders have experienced trauma, often in the form of physical or sexual abuse, and these personal histories are essential to consider when implementing jail mental health services. Molly's extensive history of physical and sexual abuse by family members is far too typical (see case illustration). Jail environments are not mutually respectful, supportive, or even very positive, and jail mental health administrators and practitioners face considerable challenges when trying to find ways to provide health-promoting environments.

Conclusion

Jail mental health care should not be utilized as a ready replacement for community-based mental health services. Rather, it is essential to improve the response to individuals with mental illnesses prior to incarceration. Programs that divert individuals from jail to treatment and accessible, integrated community treatment for individuals with both psychiatric disorders and substance abuse disorders are two examples of areas where services could be improved and expanded to enhance community care options. In the meantime, jail mental health services must be adequate and accessible to those who need them during incarceration. Jail mental health professionals play critical roles in the identification of those who need services, psychiatric stabilization, connection with appropriate community resources, and provision of ongoing treatment for those with extended jail stays. Helpful standards are in place to assist mental health providers and administrators in these tasks. Too often, severely constrained resources and the lack of appropriately trained mental health personnel impede the provision of quality mental health care behind bars. These issues must be addressed, not only by jail administrators and correctional authorities, but also by the public and government officials who define societal attitudes toward offenders and influence the allotment of resources for correctional treatment.

Evaluation research of contemporary mental health care practices must continue in order to guide the development of effective responses. Release-planning services and making community care connections for jailed individuals with mental illnesses show promise. In addition, expanding the array of treatment modalities for individuals who need ongoing jail mental health services, including the incorporation of integrated mental health and substance abuse treatment, seems necessary if care is to be adequate and effective. Helping professionals can be involved in both advocating for positive changes and implementing quality jail mental health services.

RESOURCES AND REFERENCES

Abram, K. M., & Teplin, L. A. (1991). Co-occurring disorders among mentally ill jail detainees: Implications for public policy. *American Psychologist, 46*(10), 1036–1045.

Abram, K. M., Teplin, L. A., & McClelland, G. M. (2003). Comorbidity of severe psychiatric disorders and substance use disorders among women in jail. *The American Journal of Psychiatry, 160*(5), 1007–1010.

Alexander, R., Jr. (1989). The right to treatment in mental and correctional institutions. *Social Work, 34*(2), 109–112.

Alexander, R., Jr. (2000). *Counseling, treatment, and intervention methods with juvenile and adult offenders.* Belmont, CA: Wadsworth.

American Psychiatric Association. (1989). *Report of the task force on psychiatric services in jails and prisons.* Washington, DC: Author.

American Psychiatric Association. (2000). *Psychiatric services in jails and prisons* (2nd ed.). Washington, DC: Author.

Bernstein, R. (2001). *Finding the key to successful transition from jail to the community.* Retrieved September 7, 2005, from http://www.bazelon.org/issues/criminalization/findingthekey.html

Bland, R. C., Newman, S. C., Thompson, A. H., & Dyck, R. J. (1998). Psychiatric disorders in the population and in prisoners. *International Journal of Law and Psychiatry, 21*(3), 273–279.

Bloom, B., Owen, B., & Covington, S. (2003). *Gender-responsive strategies: Research, practice, and guiding principles for women offenders* (Report No. 018017). Longmont, CO: National Institute of Corrections.

Bowring v. Godwin, 551 F.2d 44 (4th Cir. 1977).

Center for Mental Health Services, Substance Abuse and Mental Health Services Administration, Public Health Service, & U.S. Department of Health and Human Services. (1995, February 24). *Double jeopardy: Persons with mental illnesses in the criminal justice system.* Rockville, MD: Authors.

Condelli, W. S., Bradigan, B., & Holanchock, H. (1997). Intermediate care programs to reduce risk and better manage inmates with psychiatric disorders. *Behavioral Sciences and the Law, 15*, 459–467.

Conly, C. (1999). *Coordinating community services for mentally ill offenders: Maryland's community criminal justice treatment program* (U.S. Department of Justice Publication No. NCJ 175046). Washington, DC: U.S. Government Printing Office.

Council of State Governments. (2002). *Criminal justice/mental health consensus project.* New York: Author.

Ditton, P. M. (1999). *Mental health and treatment of inmates and probationers* (U.S. Department of Justice Publication No. NCJ 174463). Washington, DC: U.S. Government Printing Office.

Elliott, R. L. (1997). Evaluating the quality of correctional mental health services: An approach to surveying a correctional mental health system. *Behavioral Sciences and the Law, 15*, 427–438.

Estelle v. Gamble, 429 U.S. 97 (1976).

Ford, J., & Trestman, R. L. (2005). *Final report: Evidence-based enhancement of the detection, prevention, and treatment of mental illness in the correction systems* (Document No. 210829). Farmington, CT: Authors.

Fox, V. (1983). Forward. In A. R. Roberts (Ed.), *Social work in juvenile and criminal justice settings* (pp. ix–xv). Springfield, IL: Charles C. Thomas.

Goldstrom, I., Henderson, M., Male, A., & Manderscheid, R. W. (1998). Jail mental health services: A national survey. In Center for Mental Health Services, *Mental health, United States, 1998* (pp. 176–187). Washington, DC: U.S. Department of Health and Human Services.

Harrington, S. P. M. (1999). New bedlam: Jails—not psychiatric hospitals—now care for the indigent mentally ill. *The Humanist, 59*(3), 9.

Harrison, P. M., & Beck, A. J. (2005). *Prison and jail inmates at midyear 2004* (U.S. Department of Justice Publication No. NCJ 208801). Washington, DC: U.S. Government Printing Office.

Jemelka, R., Trupin, E., & Chiles, J. A. (1989). The mentally ill in prisons: A review. *Hospital and Community Psychiatry, 40*(5), 481–491.

Lamb, H. R., & Weinberger, L. E. (1998). Persons with severe mental illness in jails and prisons: A review. *Psychiatric Services, 49*(4), 483–492.

Lindenauer, M. R., & Harness, J. K. (1981). Care as part of the cure: A historical overview of correctional health care. *Journal of Prison Health, 1*(1), 56–66.

Mays, G. L., & Winfree, L. T. (Eds.). (2005). *Essentials of corrections* (3rd ed.). Belmont, CA: Wadsworth.

Metzner, J. L., Cohen, F., Grossman, L. S., & Wettstein, R. M. (1998). Treatment in jails and prisons. In R. M. Wettstein (Ed.), *Treatment of offenders with mental disorders* (pp. 211–264). New York: Guilford.

Miller, J. G. (1995). Criminal justice: Social work roles. In *The encyclopedia of social work* (19th ed., pp. 653–659). Washington, DC: National Association of Social Workers.

National Association of Social Workers. (1999). *Code of ethics.* Retrieved September 12, 2005, from http://www.socialworkers.org/pubs/code

National GAINS Center. (2005). Brief jail mental health screen. Retrieved September 14, 2005, from http://www.gainsctr.com/html/resources/MHscreen.asp

Penrose, L. S. (1939). Mental disease and crime: Outline of a comparative study of European statistics. *British Journal of Medical Psychology, 18*, 1–15.

Peters, R. H., & Bartoi, M. G. (1997, April). *Screening and assessment of co-occurring disorders in the justice system.* Delmar, NY: National GAINS Center.

Project Link. (1999). Prevention of jail and hospital recidivism among persons with severe mental illness. *Psychiatric Services, 50*(11), 1477–1480.

Regier, D. A., Farmer, M. E., Rae, D. S., Locke, B. Z., Keith, S. J., Judd, L. L., et al. (1990). Comorbidity of mental disorders with alcohol and other drug abuse: Results from the Epidemiologic Catchment Area (ECA) study. *Journal of the American Medical Association, 264*(19), 2511–2518.

Ruiz v. Estelle, 503 F Supp 1265, 1323 (1980).

Sherman, R. K., Irvin, L. K., Yovanoff, P., & Sowards, S. (2004). Federal demonstration funds at the interface of mental health and criminal justice. *Administration and Policy in Mental Health, 32*(1), 17–29.

Steadman, H. J., Scott, J. E., Osher, F., Agnese, T. K., & Robbins, P. C. (2005). Validation of the brief jail mental health screen. *Psychiatric Services, 56*(7), 816–822.

Teplin, L. A. (1990). The prevalence of severe mental disorder among male urban jail detainees: Comparison with the Epidemiologic Catchment Area Program. *American Journal of Public Health, 80*(6), 663–669.

Teplin, L. A., Abram, K. M., & McClelland, G. M. (1996). Prevalence of psychiatric disorders among incarcerated women. I. Pretrial jail detainees. *Archives of General Psychiatry, 53*(6), 505–512.

Teplin, L. A., Abram, K. M., & McClelland, G. M. (1997). Mentally disordered women in jail: Who receives services? *American Journal of Public Health, 87*(4), 604–609.

Teplin, L. A., & Swartz, J. A. (1989). Screening for severe mental disorder in jails. *Law and Human Behavior, 13*, 1–18.

Torrey, E. F. (1997). *Out of the shadows: Confronting America's mental illness crisis.* New York: Wiley.

Ventura, L. A., Cassel, C. A., Jacoby, J. E., & Huang, B. (1998). Case management and recidivism of mentally ill persons released from jail. *Psychiatric Services, 49*(10), 1330–1337.

Veysey, B. M., Steadman, H. J., Morrissey, J. P., & Johnsen, M. (1997). In search of the missing linkages: Continuity of care in U.S. jails. *Behavioral Sciences and the Law, 15*(4), 383–397.

Young, D. S. (2002). Non-psychiatric services provided in a mental health unit in a county jail. *Journal of Offender Rehabilitation, 35*(2), 63–82.

Young, D. S. (2003). Co-occurring disorders among jail inmates: Bridging the treatment gap. *Journal of Social Work Practice in the Addictions, 3*(3), 63–85.

Resources

American Psychiatric Association. (2000). *Psychiatric services in jails and prisons* (2nd ed.). Washington, DC: Author. Includes guidelines for psychiatric services in jails.

Bazelon Center for Mental Health Law (http://www.bazelon.org). National legal advocacy organization for people with mental illnesses and developmental disabilities.

Civic Research Institute (http://www.civicresearchinstitute.com). Provides reference and practice materials for professionals in the area of behavioral health.

National Alliance for the Mentally Ill (http://www.nami.org). Support and advocacy organization of consumers and friends of people with severe mental illnesses.

National Criminal Justice Reference Service (http:/www.ncjrs.org). Provides information and statistics on criminal justice topics, including health and mental health.

National GAINS Center for People with Co-Occurring Disorders in the Justice System (800-311-GAIN; http://gainscenter.samhsa.gov/html). Operated by Policy Research Associates. Collects and disseminates information about mental health and substance abuse services for people with co-occurring disorders in the justice system.

Policy Research Associates, Inc. (http://www.prainc.com). Conducts research and technical assistance with a focus on mental health services issues.

Trauma and Posttraumatic Stress Disorder in Inmates With Histories of Substance Use

Sheryl Pimlott Kubiak

Isabel M. Rose

Introduction

Rarely is trauma discussed in relation to incarceration—not in terms of the effect of incarceration on those with trauma histories, the prison as a site of new trauma, or the context of the effect of trauma-related disorders on recidivism. This is particularly troublesome given the relationship between post-traumatic stress disorder (PTSD) and substance use disorders (SUD) and the high prevalence of SUD among those involved in the criminal justice system. Men and women entering prisons and jails have considerable histories of psychological trauma prior to incarceration (Gibson et al., 1999; Jordan, Schlenger, Fairbank, & Cadell, 1996; Kupers, 1996; Teplin, Abram, & McClelland, 1996), and certainly the incidence of violence within penal institutions has been well documented (Beck & Hughes, 2005; Kupers, 1996; Toch, 1998; Websdale & Chesney-Lind, 1998). While there is a dearth of information on the prevalence of offenders with both disorders, as many as 50% of those entering community-based substance abuse treatment are thought to have a co-occurring PTSD and generally demonstrate poorer long-term outcomes compared to those without (Ouimette, Finney, & Moos, 1999). Although prison-based substance abuse treatment has generally been successful in reducing recidivism and relapse (Inciardi, Martin, Butzin, Hooper, & Harrison, 1997; Pelissier, Wallace, & O'Neil, 2001; Wexler, De Leon, Thomas, Kressel, & Peters, 1999), only 10% of inmates who need substance abuse treatment actually receive it (Lo & Stephens, 2000). Treatment approaches within prison that recognize and/or address co-occurring substance abuse and trauma-related disorders are rarer yet.

As noted, substance abuse treatment outcomes for those with PTSD have generally been less favorable when compared to those without. In a study comparing outcomes for women with and without PTSD at 3-months posttreatment, those with PTSD were more likely to relapse sooner than those without (Brown, Stout, & Mueller, 1996). In a sample of 1,630 male veterans attending substance abuse treatment, 1-year outcomes for those with co-occurring PTSD were less favorable; those with the dual disorder were more likely to be readmitted for treatment and less likely to be employed than those in the SUD only group (Ouimette, Ahrens, & Moos, 1997). At 2-years posttreatment, the co-occurring SUD and PTSD clients were more likely to report problems related to substance use and more likely to consume alcohol than either the SUD only group or the group with SUD and other psychiatric disorders (Ouimette et al., 1999). Similarly, a recent study found poorer outcomes among male and female prisoners with co-occurring SUD and PTSD when compared to those with SUD only. Those with co-occurring SUD and PTSD were more likely to relapse when released into the community compared to those with only SUD (Kubiak, 2004).

These findings support previous findings and the theory that inattention to PTSD may negate the success of substance abuse treatment (Brown et al., 1996; Najavits, Gastfriend, & Barber, 1998; Najavits, Weiss, & Shaw, 1997; Ouimette, Brown, & Najavits, 1998). Positive outcomes have been found when integrated treatment approaches (broadly defined as a coordination of substance abuse and mental health intervention) for individuals with co-occurring substance use and mental disorders have been used (Drake, Mueser, Clark, & Wallach, 1996; Minkoff, 2001). Initial assessments of integrated approaches to the treatment of trauma and substance-related disorders have been promising (Najavits, Weiss, & Shaw, 1998), but controlled studies are needed. In addition to community-based intervention studies, one cognitive behavioral treatment approach was conducted in a correctional setting with a sample of 17 women (Zlotnick, Najavits, Rohsenow, & Johnson, 2003). At the end of the 3-month treatment period, 53% no longer met criteria for PTSD, and at 6-weeks postrelease 70% did not meet criteria for an SUD (Najavits, 2002; Zlotnick et al., 2003). Treatment for women seems especially salient since women have higher epidemiological rates of PTSD, usually enter prison with more severe SUD, and represent a small proportion of the criminal justice population. However, in general, prison programs have not explicitly attended to this co-occurrence and have only recently been involved in the systematic screening and assessment of substance abuse disorders (see Kubiak, Boyd, Slayden, & Young, 2005).

Attention to trauma-related disorders among incarcerated men and women may be pivotal in preventing relapse and, as a consequence, a return to the institution for failure to comply with parole orders or other types of recidivism. Moreover, unlike many other co-occurring disorders, a substance abuser who abstains (e.g., inability to self-medicate in a forensic setting) may initially experience a marked increase in PTSD symptoms, which, in addition to the severe discomfort the inmate may feel, could place the inmate at risk for noncompliant and/or disruptive behavior in the forensic setting. Thus, the purpose of this chapter is to discuss the prevalence of trauma exposure and co-occurring trauma and SUDs among men and women involved in the criminal justice system. In addition, we will discuss methods for assessing trauma exposure and trauma-related disorders and promising interventions appropriate for institutional settings.

Case Study 1: Rhonda

Rhonda was abandoned as an infant by her biological mother and described her father as loving, but absent. Her father remarried a woman Rhonda described as a "mean drunk" who inflicted severe physical abuse on her. Her half brother sexually abused her when she was between the ages of 6 and 13. She moved out of state after high school and entered a vocational training program. Although she completed training in computer processing, she returned home and worked as a cocktail waitress and topless dancer. She began drug use (cocaine) at the age of 24 after a "friend" sexually assaulted her, and this escalated to heavy use of crack cocaine ("a few hundred dollars per day") the following year. While she indicated multiple arrests (e.g., disorderly conduct, flagging, and accosting and soliciting), most did not result in formal charges. Her first felony conviction brought about a probation sentence, but a probation violation resulted in incarceration in the state prison. Since that time, she has been in and out of prison due to drugs and the inability to successfully complete probation or parole requirements.

Rhonda was sexually molested by two different officers during various points in her incarceration. Rhonda states that she kept the allegations to herself because she could not trust the system: "You don't file complaints if you want to go home." Rhonda reports that the assault experiences during her confinement left her feeling embarrassed, degraded, and humiliated. She had flashbacks of the incidents and, on one occasion, reported a flashback as a result of watching a movie in which someone was sexually assaulted. Rhonda claimed that she had nightmares about the incidents and woke up screaming. She lost weight, often slept 18 hours per day, and sobbed hysterically for no apparent reason. She saw the prison physician for severe headaches, which were diagnosed as stress related. When asked why she did not report these symptoms to the prison psychologist, she said that she did not want to be put on medication: "If you're on medication it doesn't look good to the parole board."

Case Study 2: Joe

Joe was raised by his mother and grandmother. He reports that he was harshly disciplined by both his mother and her boyfriends, and he realized when he was still "just a kid" that he didn't have much control over whether he was beaten—it didn't really seem to matter whether he "behaved or not." He reports that by the time he was 12 he was drinking alcohol and smoking marijuana. In his early teens he committed various offenses such as shoplifting and dealing small amounts of marijuana. His first encounter with the juvenile justice system was at age 14 when he broke into a neighbor's car. He has since been in and out of juvenile detention and jail. Since the age of 18, Joe has been episodically homeless and unemployed. Joe reports that he has encountered a lot of violence on the streets, including violence that he initiates. Joe also reports being a victim of multiple violent encounters. At age 21 he and a few other transients had set up sleeping space under a bridge. During the night a group of intoxicated teens found the men sleeping and started kicking and throwing rocks at them. As the men woke up and tried to get up to defend themselves, the teens "went ballistic" and beat them all bloody. He watched as his friend was dragged from under the bridge, tied to the teens' car door by his shirt, and dragged more than three blocks. The teens stopped the car, untied his friend, and left him dead in the street.

Joe was hospitalized with a broken jaw, broken ribs, and severe bruising. He was released after 2 days of hospitalization to a homeless shelter in spite of experiencing severe alcohol withdrawal symptoms, the inability to eat normally, and limited mobility.

Joe is currently serving time in a state prison after having been convicted of multiple offenses including stalking, harassment, and assault against an ex-girlfriend. Joe was referred to the mental health unit at the prison after complaints from other inmates that Joe was waking them up at night with sporadic screaming. Initially, Joe reports experiencing night sweats and sporadic but severe sensations of being chased or pursued; he reports seeing "... my brother [his friend] being dragged by those White boys ... " Corrections officers have noted that Joe seems to avoid associating with any of the inmates whenever it is possible.

Background and Review of the Literature

The incidence of co-occurring mental health and substance abuse disorders (COD) has been estimated to affect almost half of those with serious and chronic mental health disorders (Kessler et al., 1997; Rogier et al., 1990). As prisons and jails become our de facto mental health institutions, COD should be assessed because individuals with COD may be particularly vulnerable to arrest and incarceration. However, there has been little attention to the issue of COD among incarcerated men and women. The U.S. Department of Justice estimates that in 1999 approximately 16% of inmates in state prisons and locals jails were mentally ill (Ditton, 1999). Furthermore, approximately 13% received mental health therapy or counseling from a trained professional while incarcerated, and 10% received psychotropic medications (Beck & Maruschak, 2001). In addition, estimates of drug or alcohol dependence among incarcerated men and women are considerably higher than epidemiological estimates (Kessler et al., 1997; Warner, Kessler, Hughes, Anthony, & Nelson, 1995), ranging from 51% (Lo & Stephens, 2000) to 70% (Kubiak, Boyd, Slayden, & Young, 2005). In fact, 80% of federal and state inmates were either convicted of a drug-related crime, were using at the time of the offense, or committed their crime to support their drug use (Center for Substance Abuse Treatment, 1998).

Of late, there has been an increased awareness of PTSD co-occurring with SUD. PTSD is one type of anxiety disorder (American Psychiatric Association [APA], 2000) that can occur after direct exposure to an extreme traumatic stressor that involves actual or threatened death or serious injury. Similarly, witnessing such an event or learning of the unexpected or violent death of a loved one can also be a catalyst (APA, 2000). The response to the exposure must involve feelings of "intense fear, helplessness, or horror" (APA, 2000, p. 219). PTSD symptoms involve psychologically reexperiencing the event (intrusion), persistent evidence of increased arousal such as hypervigilance and insomnia (arousal), and efforts to avoid people and places that might trigger memories of the trauma (avoidance). PTSD is usually characterized in one of three ways: acute (symptom duration is less than 3 months), chronic (symptoms persist for 3 months or longer), and delayed onset (a minimum of 6 months has passed between the traumatic event and symptom commencement).

Although research studies have been mixed in support of the "self-medication hypothesis" of drug use, studies of co-occurring SUD and PTSD indicate that trauma exposure usually precedes the development of an SUD (Chilcoat & Breslau, 1998; Stewart, Pihl, Conrod, & Dongier, 1998). In other words, drugs and alcohol are initially used to alleviate the painful symptoms associated with PTSD but then become problems in their own right, which exacerbate PTSD symptoms and increase the risk of subsequent trauma.

Exposure to a traumatic event is not uncommon; however, most people recover psychologically in a relatively brief period of time. For example, the National Comorbidity Study found that 61% of men and 51% of women in the United States experience a trauma over the course of their lifetime, but of those who experience an event, only 8% of men and 20% of women manifest symptoms of PTSD (Kessler, Sonnega, Bromet, Hughes, & Nelson, 1995). However, among those with PTSD, nearly 52% of men and 28% of women experienced an alcohol dependency, and 35% of men and 28% of women reported a co-occurring drug dependency (Kessler et al., 1997). These results suggest that 2.9% of women and 2.5% of men experience co-occurring PTSD and an alcohol abuse disorder. Similarly, 2.9% of women and 1.7% of men would be expected to experience PTSD and a co-occurring drug abuse disorder. Of individuals seeking treatment for substance use, lifetime prevalence rates of PTSD have been estimated as high as 50%, with approximately one quarter to one third meeting criteria for current PTSD (Brown, Recupero, & Stout, 1995; Jacobsen, Southwick, & Kosten, 2001; Najavits et al., 1998).

Although there is little data on the intersection of SUD and PTSD among offenders, we can assume that the high prevalence of SUD in inmate populations translates into an enhanced prevalence of this particular COD. As with SUD, PTSD prevalence rates are higher among the incarcerated than those in the general population (Ehlers, Maercker, & Boos, 2000; Gibson et al., 1999; Jordan et al., 1996; O'Keefe, 1998). One study documented a lifetime prevalence rate for PTSD among incarcerated men at 33% (Ehlers et al., 2000), more than four times higher than the rate for men in the general population. Similarly, Jordan and colleagues (1996) compared the rates of several mental health disorders among women in prison and women from the surrounding geographic area, finding that incarcerated women had twice the rate of depression and had been exposed to a far greater number of traumatic incidents.

Estimates of PTSD may be higher among those incarcerated for several reasons. First, as our case studies illustrate (see discussion later in the chapter), exposure to childhood events such as physical and sexual abuse, as well as parental neglect, is common among those in the criminal justice system (Horowitz, Widom, McLaughlin, & White, 2001; Widom, 1998). Second, involvement in illegal behavior such as drug seeking (Forney, Inciardi, & Lockwood, 1992) and residing in areas of extreme poverty (Kubiak, 2004) may increase exposure. Third, in addition to stress, prison may be a production site of new traumatic experiences, as well as triggering traumatic memories. The threat of violence within male prisons for both physical and sexual assault, as well as the codes of silence maintained by both inmates and guards, has been well documented (Kupers,

1996, 2005; Hochstetler, Murphy, & Simons, 2004; Toch, 1998). Women's prisons have come under greater scrutiny because of the incidence of sexual assault by male corrections staff (General Accounting Office, 1999; Kubiak, Hanna, & Balton, 2005; Websdale & Chesney-Lind, 1998). And recently the Bureau of Justice Statistics released a monograph on reported sexual violence within correctional facilities (Beck & Hughes, 2005).

General Practice Considerations for Trauma Work Within Forensic Settings

It is often challenging to work with men and women in the criminal justice system, and working with those who have these CODs is especially challenging. Along with clinical challenges, there may be structural barriers to clinical practice. These clinical and structural impediments are especially important to consider when discussing intervention around trauma disorders. Therefore, before discussing intervention, we attempt to raise clinical awareness of the effect of the environment on screening, assessment, and intervention.

Working within institutional settings may be difficult for social workers. Treatment professionals enter and exit through locked gates, and treatment concerns are always second to security. Even with picture identification, treatment staff may be subjected to metal detectors, pat downs (body searches over clothing), and carrying emergency notification devices on their person.

Restrictions regarding what can and cannot be taken in to, or out of, the facility (e.g., no keys or cash) are constant reminders of the setting in which the clinician is practicing. In fact, program materials such as books, training videos, and paper generally require advanced clearances and extensive paperwork. Even routine clinical practices common in substance abuse treatment facilities, such as linking clients to other services or contacting family members, may be prohibited by corrections policies.

Once inside, clinical delivery of treatment services can also be affected by institutional rules. Inmates usually require passes, issued by officers, to be able to attend groups or sessions. Required "count" times have to be considered in scheduling groups since inmates/participants have to return to their cells during the multiple counts per day. Rewards and sanctions, often used as treatment incentives in substance abuse programs, also must be dictated by what is feasible from a security and regulation standpoint. A rule infraction that may be handled with a loss of privileges or a clinical intervention in a substance abuse treatment program may be cause for a misconduct ticket inside the prison—potentially effecting the release date from prison.

Similarly, the treatment professional's ethics may be challenged. For example, an inmate might disclose information about an abusive situation within the prison and may not want the social worker to report it. After all, "snitching" is against the code of silence that prevails within the institutional setting. The clinician may then enter into an ethical bind about whether to report it and to whom. As a clinician who is an employee, the social worker may have to report it—making a decision to protect either the client's request or his or her own job. As employees, the formal and informal rules of the institution are paramount. Therefore, it is important to know the reporting requirements of the facility and to understand in advance how these requirements fit with the National Association of Social Workers' (NASW) Code of Ethics and the clinician's personal values. From the outset, social workers need to be prepared to discuss with inmates what they will be required to report and what can be kept confidential. Social workers should also be prepared to explain how clinical records are kept, who has access to them, and under what conditions.

Illustrating this point, we refer to Rhonda's experience of abuse by prison staff. The clinician's initial reaction might be to respect Rhonda's request to keep this information confidential out of his or her ethical responsibility to the standards of confidentiality, but the practitioner also has an obligation to prevent foreseeable harm to the client or others (e.g., the likelihood for prison staff to continue the sexual abuse and potential retaliation). In exploring Rhonda's request, the clinician may find that she has witnessed the retaliatory events by staff toward other women who came forward. Rhonda's main goal is to get her parole and get out of prison, and she fears retaliation could result in bogus tickets that would delay parole. Each practitioner will have to weigh the situation and the unique conditions within his or her particular environment to determine ethical and meaningful solutions. However, the social worker is ethically obligated to educate all potential clients about client–worker confidentiality and its limitations. Informing Rhonda in advance of the kinds of information that the clinician would be required to report is not only ethically required but would also help to prevent potentially damaging the client–worker relationship. Having a working understanding of all legal obligations and employee obligations for reporting is vital.

Another possible scenario is that the clinician is not an employee of the department but is contracted to provide services within the institution. This may provide the clinician some distance from the administrative rules of reporting or documenting within prison files. It may also afford the client more latitude in discussing certain issues. However, reporting requirements need to be established within the contractual agreement and should subscribe to the same ethical standards discussed previously.

One important point—whether you are an employee or contractual staff—is that the American Corrections Association has addressed sexual misconduct of staff with specific standards that all clinicians should be aware of (see Coolman, 2003, for further information). In several states any form of sexual encounter between an inmate and prison staff is illegal. Another important point is that, although some refer to sexual encounters as consensual (whether discussing staff–inmate or inmate–inmate encounters), coercion and power dynamics of the relationship need to be considered. Environmental factors in the prison, including the prison context itself, influence both staff behavior and the perceptions of inmates. Prisons are places designed to confine and control and are generally not conducive to therapeutic intervention (Hearn & Parkin, 2001; Kupers, 1999; Toch, 1998). As "closed organizations," penal institutions involve the total or attempted total control of residents, as people eat, sleep, work, and play under a unified organizational structure (Hearn & Parkin, 2001). Entering this relatively isolated environment as outsiders, treatment professionals have a daunting task in maintaining cohesion with their own personal practice styles and beliefs about treatment.

For helping professionals, maintaining their personal practice styles often involves a desire to differentiate themselves from corrections staff. Similarly, corrections staff may want to differentiate themselves from treatment staff. Correctional officers are primarily responsible for the safety and security of the prison staff and other inmates (Farabee et al., 1999). Their fears of becoming entangled in a treatment system that alters their authority or ability to maintain control, and thus of becoming "soft," parallel treatment staff's fears of being seen as enforcers rather than helpers. Therefore, working collaboratively with prison staff requires mutual respect of roles and the identification of common goals.

In prison settings the ability to collaborate effectively with other health professionals (psychiatrists, psychologists, nurses), paraprofessionals, and corrections staff is imperative. Inmates are often moved around in the facility according to health factors, security needs, cell availability, staffing needs, and so forth. Moreover, inmates are often moved from one prison facility to another throughout the life of their sentences. Practitioners must be flexible and able to work within a dynamic system and one that is designed first and foremost to safely secure inmates.

Practitioners should also consider working with other mental health staff in educating the corrections staff. When possible, it would be to the inmates' advantage to have corrections officers who have a working understanding of the symptoms of PTSD and how those symptoms are manifested in inmate behavior. Corrections officers are in close daily contact with inmates and yet have often been left out of the health education loop. With education, the officers may feel more confident in their ability to manage behaviors and to make referrals when needed. In the case of inmate victimization, educated officers may be less likely to blame the victims for their victimization.

Finally, it is important to note the segregated nature of our criminal justice system and, more specifically, the prison inmate population. Although significantly more Whites are arrested annually than African Americans (e.g., Whites accounted for 76% of all arrests in 2003, and African Americans accounted for 27%; Federal Bureau of Investigation, 2003), racial and ethnic minorities account for 65% of the prison population (Harrison & Beck, 2004). Racial and ethnic differences must be considered in the screening and assessment protocol, as well as in program planning and implementation. Cultural competence is required for this environment, and a working understanding of the NASW standards for cultural competence is recommended (for more information, visit the NASW Web site: www.socialworkers.org).

Intervention

When men and women enter prison, there is usually a period of assessment and testing. As either Rhonda or Joe enters a jail or prison, an initial screening and/or assessment for trauma exposure would be helpful in understanding behavior as well as rehabilitation needs. However, we recognize that in forensic settings screening and assessment may be limited and vary across sites. For example, some state prison systems use standardized mental health and substance use screening for all incoming inmates, yet other states do not. Some jail settings employ mental health clinicians and provide screening, assessment, intervention, and referral services, yet many jail settings do not have this capacity. Mental health treatment priority varies across systems as well. What we describe here follows standards for best practices, although we know that practitioners may need to adjust screening, assessment, and intervention methods accordingly.

Screening

It is important in any case to approach PTSD screening and assessment with caution. Initial screening for trauma exposure should be limited to brief and generalized trauma-related questions such as "As a child were you ever physically hurt by a parent or guardian?" or "Have you ever been hurt sexually by anyone?" Using a brief and generalized screening tool assists the clinician in determining whether a more intrusive assessment is needed. More important, it is imperative not to induce the revisitation of traumatic events. The revisitation of an event may trigger unpleasant memories and lead to a psychologically painful state in a physical space (institution) where the person may not be well equipped to cope. This process requires that the clinician is able to read the verbal and physical cues of the inmates/clients and respect the boundaries and possibly the desire not to discuss the questions further.

Often, generalized trauma screening may be more appropriate in primary care or infirmary settings within the prison where individuals may be presenting with symptoms they are not associating with trauma but may very well be trauma-related. Generalized trauma screening would also be helpful as a part of the intake process in jails and prisons, particularly in settings where trauma counseling is available.

Two brief screening instruments, appropriate in forensic settings and used for determining if an individual meets PTSD Criterion A (exposure to traumatic event) from the *DSM* (see Figure 19.1), are the Traumatic Stress Schedule (TSS; Norris, 1990) and the Trauma History Questionnaire (THQ; Green, 1996). The TSS is a brief screening instrument of 10 items that provides information on event prevalence and was developed with general and multicultural populations. It has been criticized because it does not assess childhood physical and/or sexual abuse and it has only one item related to unwanted sexual activity that may not fully capture other types of sexual assault (see Norris & Riad, 1997). The THQ has 24 questions that provide a comprehensive assessment of Criterion A events as well as other serious stressful events (e.g., simple assault, serious accident).

Many institutions use the Minnesota Multiphasic Personality Inventory-2 (MMPI-2; Butcher, Dahlstrom, Graham, Tellegen, & Kaemmer, 1989) as a routine screening and assessment tool. The MMPI-2 has two scales that suggest the presence of PTSD, the PK (Keane, Malloy, & Fairbank, 1984) and the PS scales (Schlenger & Kulka, 1987, as cited in Greene, 2000). However, both of these scales were developed to assess PTSD among combat veterans and may not be reliable when used in a civilian population (Greene, 2000).

In addition, many institutions provide screening for SUD. For example, Michigan uses the Substance Abuse Subtle Screening Inventory (SASSI) to screen all prisoners who enter the state's prison system (Kubiak, Boyd, Slayden, & Young, 2005). Other brief screening instruments for substance abuse include CAGE-AID (Cut Down, Annoyed, Guilty, Eye-opener-Adapted to Include Drugs) and the Michigan Alcohol Screening Test (MAST). Recently the Substance Abuse and Mental Health Services Administration (SAMHSA) developed a substance abuse screening instrument (the Simple Screening Instrument for Substance Abuse: SSI-SA) that draws items from several validated instruments. The SSI-SA is also recommended as a screening instrument for those with COD (Center for Substance Abuse Treatment, 1998). An excellent resource for substance use screening tools, as well as comprehensive information about substance abuse treatment for individuals with CODs, is the Center for Substance Abuse Treatment's

Part A: Prior to symptoms, a person must have been exposed to a trauma event.
- The trauma exposure must be either experienced directly or witnessed and it must involve actual death or threat of death or serious injury to self or others. The individual may have also encountered this exposure by hearing about the actual death, threat of death, or serious injury to a family member or someone close.
- The person's response needed to be one of intense fear, helplessness, or horror.

Part B: Symptoms after exposure fall into the following clusters:
Cluster I: Reexperiencing the event: reexperiencing must be persistent and manifested in at least one of the following ways:
- recurrent, intrusive, and distressing recollections of the event.
- recurrent event-related dreams that are distressing or trauma-related nightmares.
- acting as if or feeling as if the event is happening again—for example, flashbacks, illusions and hallucinations.
- intense psychological distress when reminded of the event by internal external triggers that are symbolic or resemble the event such as anniversary dates, sounds, or places.
- physiological reactivity such as sweating, shaking, or upset stomach when reminded of the event by internal or external triggers that are symbolic or resemble the event such as anniversary dates, sounds, or places.
Cluster II: Persistent avoidance of trauma-related stimuli and numbing responsiveness (not present prior to event) indicated by three or more of the following:
- effort to avoid trauma-related thoughts, feelings, or conversations.
- effort to avoid activities, places, or people that illicit memories of trauma.
- inability to recall an important aspect of the trauma.
- distinct loss of interest or participation in previously enjoyed activities.
- feelings of estrangement or detachment from others (not feeling connected with others).
- restricted range of affect or inability to feel emotions particularly those associated with love and intimacy.
- lack of a future orientation. The individual may not expect future life experiences such as marriage, children, a career, or long life.
Cluster III: Persistent symptoms of arousal (not present prior to the trauma), as indicated by two or more of the following:
- difficulty falling or staying asleep.
- irritability or outbursts of anger.
- difficulty concentrating.
- hypervigilance (being on guard, heightened sensitivity to surroundings).
- exaggerated startle response.

Diagnostic criteria for posttraumatic stress disorder. Adapted from the *DSM–IV–TR* (APA, 2000, pp. 647–648).

Substance Abuse Treatment for Persons With Co-Occurring Disorders: Treatment Improvement Protocol (TIP) Series 42, which is available from http://www.ncbi.nlm.nih.gov.

Assessment

As in other settings, assessment should entail a comprehensive review of several aspects of the person's social, psychological, and biological functioning. This should be an ongoing process that captures changes in the person's functioning and well-being over time. Our main focus here is assessment of PTSD in the forensic setting. However, we provide suggestions for questions that could be inserted into general psychosocial assessments that may provide evidence that a more comprehensive diagnostic interview is needed.

As explained previously, experiencing a traumatic event does not necessarily mean a person is experiencing symptoms of PTSD. Usually any trauma-related symptoms experienced immediately after an event subside over time. However, in some instances those symptoms do not subside or may reoccur or intensify. For example, symptoms may reoccur when there is a subsequent traumatic event or when the individual is exposed to triggering events such as anniversaries of a traumatic event. Although screening does not require a clinically trained mental health professional, assessment and diagnosis of PTSD do. This is particularly the case with PTSD because distinguishing PTSD from other anxiety disorders can be a complex process. If a practitioner has not been clinically trained and does not have experience in the diagnostic assessment of mental health disorders, then it is important to refer the inmate to professionals with this training.

There are three specific symptom clusters that are used to assess PTSD and affix a diagnosis. Individuals must meet a certain number of symptoms within each cluster to meet criteria for PTSD. These symptom clusters include (a) intrusion, such as psychologically reexperiencing the event; (b) arousal, such as persistent hypervigilance and insomnia; and (c) avoidance, such as efforts to avoid people and places that might trigger memories of the trauma (see Figure 19.1 on *DSM* criteria). PTSD is usually characterized in one of three ways: Acute (symptom duration is less than 3 months), chronic (symptoms persist for 3 months or longer), and delayed onset (a minimum of 6 months has passed between the traumatic event and symptom commencement).

Perhaps the most characteristic symptoms of PTSD are those associated with re-experiencing the event in dreams or flashbacks. General questions could be inserted in the psychosocial assessment that might provide additional information regarding current PTSD symptoms (e.g., Do you have any reoccurring dreams? Do you find yourself thinking about events when you really don't want to?), particularly with individuals who may not have shared their trauma histories during preliminary screening. Similarly, response to routine questions in the psychosocial assessment might also provide clues of symptoms related to trauma exposure. For example, a question such as "Can you tell me about your sleep patterns?" might produce information about nightmares or sleep disturbances that may be related to the trauma. In addition, queries surrounding the use of drugs or alcohol may cue the clinician to trauma symptoms. For example, Rhonda may disclose that she has to be high in order to engage in sexual activity. This would be evidence of avoidant behavior around a potentially triggering event. If this is the case, the general assessment should lead to a more directed diagnostic assessment.

There are a number of diagnostic tools that assist in ascertaining diagnostic status. "Most structured PTSD interviews are based on the DSM-III-R (now the DSM – IV) conceptualization of PTSD and follow the diagnostic criteria closely" (Weathers, Keane, King, & King, 1997, p. 106). One example of this is a commonly used tool known as the Structured Clinical Interview for *DSM–IV* (SCID; Spitzer, Williams, Gibbon, & First, 1990). Among the established psychometric tools that assess PTSD symptoms is the Clinician Administered PTSD Scale (CAPS; Blake et al., 1995), a widely used structured clinical interview. There have been several versions of CAPS, with the most recent version designed to assess PTSD symptoms as they are outlined in the *DSM–V* (National Center for PTSD, 2005).

Some clinicians argue that the symptoms captured in these instruments do not fully capture the full range of posttrauma problems and encourage the recognition of a spectrum of stress-related disorders including acute stress disorder and complex PTSD

(Weathers et al., 1997). They suggest using an instrument like the Trauma Symptom Inventory (TSI; Briere, 1995) to assess the spectrum of posttrauma disorders more fully. However, the 100-item TSI may be too lengthy for prison-based work.

These tools, in conjunction with a clinical interview, in which, among other things, the role the inmate's symptoms play in his or her current functioning and the meaning the inmate attaches to the symptoms are discussed, assist the clinician in the preparation of an intervention plan. McLean (2001) reinforces the need to assess fully the contextual factors that can influence the course of treatment—many of these factors are found in the general psychosocial assessment. He suggests that at minimum the clinician should assess for social supports, cognitive distortions, avoidant coping styles, multiple trauma history, occupational adjustment, physical injury, pain, and litigation. Even in the prison setting, all of these contextual factors are important for inclusion in the psychosocial history assessment.

There are many ways to approach the assessment process and institutional processes, and the experience of professional staff will dictate some aspects. Our main point is to emphasize the need to approach PTSD screening and assessment with sensitivity, clinical and cultural competence, and use of established tools that assess the complexities of the inmate's index trauma and trauma history, the inmate's responses to the trauma, and the impact of the response to the inmate's health and well-being.

Intervention Approaches

The most studied psychosocial treatments for both substance abuse and PTSD are cognitive behavioral interventions (Foa & Meadows, 1997; Najavits, 2001). Particularly for PTSD, these encompass a wide variety of approaches (e.g., systematic desensitization, imaginal and in vivo exposure, eye movement desensitization and reprocessing (EMDR), and cognitive restructuring), with some being more suitable than others for use in forensic settings. When using intensive therapy (an approach that encourages reliving the trauma or intensive exploration of traumatic events) in forensic settings, the clinician must be acutely aware of the importance of providing a safe environment. Providing a safe environment is the first step in intervention with trauma-exposed clients (Herman, 1992). It is difficult in forensic settings to provide this safe environment because one does not have the freedom to leave the stressful event or atmosphere. However, although prison in general may be "unsafe," there is some evidence that prison-based treatment programs, such as therapeutic communities, do in fact provide a safe therapeutic space (Kubiak, manuscript submitted for publication). Therefore, it seems plausible that practitioners could work toward the creation of an organizational climate within prison, or a prison unit, and especially within the therapeutic relationship, in which the inmate/client feels safe.

As in any therapeutic relationship, client engagement is primary. Although building a trusting relationship is most important, this environmental context demands its own strategies for building rapport. In his discussion on barriers to mental health treatment within prisons, Kupers (2005) recommends several steps for overcoming resistance to treatment in prison. Although Kupers specifically refers to men (see section on gender considerations later in the chapter), we believe that similar strategies can be used to engage incarcerated women. The four recommendations are illustrated (in Figure 19.2).

Figure 19.2

1. Honor resistance. The prisoner knows more about the realities of prison life and the risk of revealing personal information and relaxing one's guard. Respect the reasons for resistance.

2. Discuss confidentiality frankly. The clinician must validate the prisoner's fear that what he/she says may become known to custody staff. Prisoners must be told in advance what the therapist is required to disclose so that she/he can make an informed decision about what to disclose.

3. Negotiate what can be realistically accomplished in the context of treatment. The clinician may be limited in how much he/she can help, and being realistic may be another way to establish authenticity and maximize potential gains.

4. Serve as an advocate. Within the ethical requirements of their profession, clinicians may need to advocate on behalf of clients for their rights or treatments. Collaboration between security and clinical staff is necessary, but tensions need to be resolved so that clinical staff do not become security.

General recommendations for overcoming resistance to treatment in prison. Adapted from Kupers (2005, pp. 721–722).

Once engagement is established, there are specific treatment models available to social workers that have been safely implemented in whole or in part in the forensic setting. These models are present-focused and are designed to teach inmates about the intersection of PTSD and SUD. More specifically, these models assist individuals in recognizing the relationship between their trauma exposure, PTSD symptoms, and drug use and how they can learn new strategies for recognizing and coping with symptoms.

Two promising treatment models that use cognitive behavioral techniques and are present-focused are Seeking Safety (Najavits, 2001) and Trauma Recovery and Empowerment Model (TREM; Fallot & Harris, 2002; Harris, 1998). Both have demonstrated evidence of being flexible enough for forensic settings, and both have promising outcomes in the treatment of PTSD and co-occurring SUD.

Seeking Safety is a manualized approach that consists of 24 ninety-minute sessions. The sessions can be held either weekly or biweekly. Seeking Safety is an integrated approach combining four basic therapy skills—cognitive, behavioral, interpersonal, and case management—to promote the development of a feeling of safety, the first step in trauma recovery. The model also teaches clients how to "ground" themselves in the present when a flashback occurs. Seeking Safety has been used with both male and female groups with some success.

TREM is a manualized group approach designed to treat women trauma survivors experiencing severe mental health disorders and substance use problems. The approach does not restrict itself to the reduction of PTSD symptoms and instead embraces an expanded view of trauma-related symptoms (Fallot & Harris, 2002). This model is usually delivered over a 9-month period using weekly meetings. There is an abbreviated model that is 6 months in duration. This model has been used primarily with women who have experienced interpersonal aggression.

When treating inmates with PTSD and those with symptoms of PTSD along with co-occurring substance abuse, the prison context must be an important factor (as discussed previously). The clinician must be cognizant of the environment and what is and is not possible within the context. For example, both of the models discussed previously use group interventions. However, group members here are not anonymous strangers, but people who reside together within the confines of the institution. Here, too, clinicians must be respectful of the resistance, as the inmates' primary job is to protect themselves in the long hours between and after group sessions. In addition to these contextual factors, there are two other considerations. First, we discuss gender and the effect of gender on trauma work and then continuity of care into community settings.

Gender Considerations

Men and women enter incarceration with distinctly different needs. For example, female inmates are more likely to present with more mental (Ditton, 1999) and physical (Acoca, 1998) health care needs than their male counterparts. This holds true for female substance abusers as compared to male substance abusers (Henderson, 1998). Also, women are significantly more likely to report histories of physical and sexual abuse than their male counterparts (Harlow, 1999). Adding to existing health problems and trauma histories is the fact that more than 70% of female inmates have children left behind with relatives and in foster care (Greenfeld & Snell, 1999). Female inmates with children are more likely to have drug histories than inmate fathers and are more likely to need alcohol and drug intervention than their male counterparts (Morash, Bynum, & Koons, 1998), yet prison treatment programming is less abundant for women than it is for men. Practitioners should be prepared to help female inmates manage the added stress, guilt, shame, and increased lack of self-control brought on as a result of leaving their children behind. Not doing so can counteract mental health and substance abuse treatment benefits. Finally, because many women enter institutional settings with histories of physical and sexual abuse—and several states use cross-gender supervision strategies—sexual encounters with custodial staff may amount to a reenactment and reinforcement of trauma (Coolman, 2003; Kupers, 1999). For all of these reasons, gender-responsive strategies and therapeutic activities should be provided throughout the criminal justice continuum of care (Bloom & Covington, 1999; Holtfreter & Morash, 2003; Kassebaum, 1999).

Male inmates generally experience fewer health and mental health problems both in and out of prison compared to female inmates, and they are significantly less likely to report histories of physical and sexual abuse. Moreover, males may be less likely identified as needing mental health services and are less likely than their female counterparts to seek mental health care. However, male prisoners tend to underreport their emotional problems and often do not request help until conditions have deteriorated to the point of psychotic decompensation (Kupers, 2005).

One reason that men may be more resistant to mental health and/or substance abuse treatment services is that "prisoners are often forced to dwell in often-brutal correctional facilities where toughness is the key to survival" (Kupers, 2005, p. 717). Kupers postulates:

> The prison code that reigns in men's prisons is an exaggeration of the unspoken male code on the outside. According to the code, a real man does not display weakness of any kind, does not display emotion other than anger, does not depend on anyone, is never vulnerable, does not snitch, does not cooperate with the authorities, and suffers pain in silence. (p. 718)

However, similar to women, preincarceration trauma may have detrimental effects for men. Hochstetler et al. (2004) found that exposure to violence, previous trauma, and pre-prison events predicted victimization in prison. Victimization in male prisons is common. One study found that half the men in one state prison system had been the victim of a crime, and 10% had been assaulted in the previous 6 months (Wooldredge, 1994). Trauma prior to incarceration may result in "difficulty befriending other prisoners, refraining from participation in the prison economy, and failure to take precautionary measures" (Hochstetler et al., 2004, p. 452). Moreover, supportive relationships in the free world did little to mitigate the distress inmates experienced since these relationships were considered irrelevant in prison and could not protect the prisoner from institutional harm. This demonstrates that screening upon prison admission and providing safe units are important preventative measures in reducing the sequelae associated with institutional violence for men (Hochstetler et al., 2004; Kupers, 1996) as well as women.

Case Study Intervention 1: Rhonda

Treatment of Rhonda during her incarceration begins during screening and assessment with the identification of multiple episodes of sexual abuse. This assessment is particularly important given Rhonda's history of childhood sexual assault (CSA). CSA interferes with psychological as well as physiological development, usually leaving survivors less likely to assess potentially dangerous situations, less likely to trust their own feelings, and more likely to have inappropriate boundaries with others (Banyard, Williams, & Siegel, 2001). Information regarding this CSA may be obtained at early screening, but if not, the Presentencing Investigation (PSI) may be useful. The PSI may or may not verify such history, but it may provide clues as to early childhood victimization, such as a child being removed from the home into protective custody.

In addition to screening for early trauma, Rhonda's chronic history of drug use (in spite of the legal and personal costs) is cause for thorough assessment. Her suspension of use due to incarceration may leave her more vulnerable to experiencing PTSD symptoms. Because of Rhonda's drug abuse history, entrance into a substance abuse treatment program within the prison—or an integrated program as described previously—would assist her in recognizing the association between her trauma and drug use and teach her skills to minimize both the symptoms of PTSD and to manage potential relapse triggers.

More difficult is assessment and treatment of the abuse Rhonda suffered during the incarceration. Her nightmares and stress headaches are symptoms that can be related to her trauma reaction, as well as her inability to advocate for herself in this setting. Although Rhonda may not want to share this information with prison staff, trained professionals may be able to assess her current symptoms as a trauma-related manifestation using the previously noted screening and assessment suggestions. What is important here is not to overlook potential victimization in Rhonda's case as a source of current mental and physical distress.

Treatment strategies may include a group to manage symptoms or a support group for trauma survivors. Although medication may be one way to alleviate some of the symptoms of anxiety, it is not the only way—especially if the client is resistant to pharmacotherapy. Assisting the client in managing the symptoms is very important. For example, grounding techniques that help focus the client on the present (e.g., being aware of immediate surroundings, soothingly orientating the person to the present when she is reliving an experience) may be invaluable in decreasing any disruptive behaviors that could result in segregation or other negative sanctions.

Case Study Intervention 2: Joe

In the case of Joe, his PTSD symptoms were not screened for in the jail setting nor in the state prison system until correctional officers and other inmates began complaining about his behavior. Joe had been living with his symptoms for quite some time prior to entering prison. He assumed that there was no reason to ask for help as he did not view the prison staff as being there to help him. He also felt uneasy talking about his past experiences to the largely White health professionals. He believed that he would be grilled and probably segregated from the general population, and he wanted to avoid anything that would make his time more difficult. Also, Joe was in prison for assaulting his girlfriend, and he did not want to bring much attention to that fact. He claims he did not sexually assault his girlfriend, but he feared that other inmates might assume that he did, which would create an even more threatening environment for him. Joe's hypervigilance was in full force in the prison setting and he was on guard virtually everywhere in the setting. His PTSD symptoms manifested in behaviors assumed to be those of an uncooperative inmate with a hatred for Whites, anger at the system, and an explosive temper. Thus, the initial response was to penalize Joe rather than to refer Joe for a mental health evaluation. The response to Joe's symptoms served only to exacerbate them. For example, Joe increased his refusal to participate in any programming offered in the prison other than what was mandated. Because of the nature of his conviction, Joe was mandated to attend a group for batterers held in the prison. However, because of the confrontational approach used in the prison group, Joe's success in the group was limited. As a result of the prison environment and the batterers group, Joe's sense of feeling threatened was heightened, and intrusive thoughts of both his past abuse as a child and of the event under the bridge increased to the point that his sleep was significantly disrupted and thus disruptive to the other inmates.

For Joe it would be important initially to see him individually if possible. Joe would benefit from having time to address mistrust of staff issues and racial mistrust, and he would likely fare better in a group treatment setting if he had been prepared by having some understanding of his symptoms, some initial coping practice, and education about the group process. This individual time would also assist the clinician in understanding the nuances of Joe's case and would allow time to determine if Joe could benefit from group psychoeducational programming or group therapy if available. Because of Joe's increased problems with sleeping and other daily functioning issues, he may benefit from medication; a number of medications are currently used in the treatment of PTSD as well as the often accompanying disorders such as other anxiety disorders and mood disorders. In cases where the client with PTSD has recently become abstinent, the need for medication to address increased symptom severity is particularly important to consider. Practitioners must work collaboratively with physicians and advocate for evaluations to determine appropriate medication.

Continuity of Care

Many women, in contrast to men, may experience returning to their community—postincarceration—as reentering a traumatic environment. Women not only experience more episodes of trauma, but also are more likely to experience them in the community. This may result in women feeling vulnerable and perhaps reexperiencing their trauma when returning to that environment; thus, lapses or relapses may be attributed to their desire to minimize symptoms that trigger memories of the original event. While we are not suggesting that women feel safe in prison, especially in light of recent investigations and settlements on behalf of women victimized during incarceration (see Greer, 2000), women generally enter prison with significantly more trauma than men (Kubiak, 2004). Therefore, in addition to routine needs upon community reentry such as housing and employment, meeting the needs of traumatized women may require more planning and thoughtfulness. First and foremost, women need to think of maintaining or gaining a safe environment in the community. Deciding what that is and how each woman can achieve this will take some planning. Similar to safety plans devised in domestic violence counseling, women leaving prison may also need to develop a safety plan. These safety plans should include the discovery of places and people who will keep them from harm, in addition to numbers and addresses of local shelters. A related aspect to this is teaching and modeling skills during incarceration that enhance relationships by demonstrating mutual respect and support.

Men may experience greater victimization within the facility as a result of the incarceration than they did prior to incarceration (Kubiak, 2004). Therefore, men leaving the facility may take some comfort in departing from their source of trauma, although they take with them the psychological pain of their prison experience. Prison exit could also explain why men experiencing PTSD symptoms, and perhaps abuse during incarceration, may seek aftercare treatment more than men without PTSD (Kubiak, 2004). This difference between groups may be a desire to confront the trauma and alleviate symptoms by acknowledging their need for ongoing services that address their experiences of trauma during incarceration. However, it is questionable if men receive such services addressing the trauma-related sequelae during reintegration or at any other time. Although male victimization during incarceration, especially sexual assault, is commonly referred to in popular media, it is rarely attended to by clinical professionals during incarceration, in planning reintegration services, or as part of community reentry services. Part of this inattention may be the reluctance of male offenders, as well as service providers, to acknowledge such victimization. Certainly masculine social norms may obstruct such candor. However, practitioners and educators must understand the rules of masculine help seeking (Addis & Mahalik, 2003), as well as prison norms (Toch, 1998), creatively seeking solutions that confront such obstructions to meet men's treatment needs.

Conclusion

The U.S. Surgeon General estimates that between 41% and 65% of individuals with an SUD also have a history of another mental health disorder. Despite the high prevalence of co-occurring mental health and SUD, there are many barriers to the effective assessment and treatment of individuals experiencing these dual disorders (SAMHSA, 2002). Perhaps nowhere are these barriers more acutely felt than in the nation's prisons and jails.

While the lack of appropriate treatment within the criminal justice system may mirror the lack of treatment in the community, in many respects the justice system has become the default provider for many with co-occurring mental health and SUD. The myriad of issues surrounding victimization, trauma, and substance abuse are of particular salience to men and women who are, or have been, incarcerated—as well as their families and the communities they return to. Trauma exposure prior to incarceration may leave an individual more vulnerable to trauma exposure inside the prison, or symptoms of trauma disorders may be exacerbated as a result of incarceration. Recognition of the salience of trauma exposure and symptoms of PTSD on behavior, such as inappropriate use of drugs and alcohol or extreme reactions to stressors within the institution, warrant the screening, assessment, and treatment of PTSD and co-occurring SUD.

This not only is important to the prisoner, but also should be important to correctional staff and administrators. Understanding the effect of trauma exposure and PTSD, and how it influences institutional as well as reentry behaviors, may be an important step in community reintegration. Reduction of exposure as well as symptomatology may decrease community drug use, thereby reducing recidivism and subsequent illegal behavior. However, the presence of helping professionals employed by corrections, or working inside prisons, is extremely low, generating some speculation that social work has abandoned the field of corrections (Gibelman, 1995). Since funding for such opportunities is increasing (Kubiak, manuscript submitted for publication), it is crucial that helping professionals have greater visibility within the prison system, as well as in encouraging and advocating for reform.

Finally, as the United States continues to lead the world in incarceration rates, greater numbers of men and women—especially minority men and women—are experiencing incarceration. Social workers and other mental health professionals should assess incarceration as a possible site trauma. We must not only assess the trauma with which they enter the prison, but also that with which they leave.

RESOURCES AND REFERENCES

Acoca, L. (1998). Defusing the time bomb: Understanding and meeting the growing health care needs of incarcerated women in America. *Crime & Delinquency, 44*, 49–69.

Addis, M. E., & Mahalik, J. R. (2003). Men, masculinity, and the context of help seeking. *American Psychologist, 58*, 5–14.

American Psychiatric Association. (2000). *Diagnostic and Statistical Manual of Mental Disorders* (4th ed., Text rev.). Washington, DC: Author.

Banyard, V. L., Williams, L. M., & Siegel, J. A. (2001). The long-term mental health consequences of childhood sexual abuse: An exploratory study of the impact of multiple traumas in a sample of women. *Journal of Traumatic Stress, 13*, 697–715.

Beck, A. J., & Hughes, T. A. (2005). *Sexual violence reported by correctional authorities, 2004* (NCJ 210333). Washington, DC: U.S. Department of Justice, Bureau of Justice Statistics.

Beck, A. J., & Maruschak, L. M. (2001). *Mental health treatment in state prisons* (NCJ 188215). Washington, DC: Department of Justice, Bureau of Justice Statistics.

Blake, D., Weathers, F., Nagy, L., Kaloupek, D., Gusman, F., Charney, D., et al. (1995). The development of a clinician-administered PTSD scale. *Journal of Traumatic Stress, 8*, 75–90.

Bloom, B., & Covington, S. (1999). *Gender responsivity: An essential element in women's programming. National symposium on women offenders.* Washington, DC: Office of Justice Programs.

Briere, J. (1995). Trauma Symptom Inventory professional manual. Odessa, FL: Psychological Assessment Resources.

Brown, P. J., Recupero, P. R., & Stout, R. (1995). Substance abuse comorbidity and treatment utilization. *Addictive Behavior, 20*, 251–254.

Brown, P. J., Stout, R. L., & Mueller, T. (1996). Post-traumatic stress disorder and substance abuse relapse among women. *Psychology of Addictive Behavior, 10*, 124–128.

Butcher, J. N., Dahlstrom, W. G., Graham, J. R., Tellegen, A., & Kaemmer, B. (1989). *MMPI-2: Manual for administration and scoring.* Minneapolis: University of Minneapolis Press.

Center for Substance Abuse Treatment. (1998). *Planning for alcohol and other drug abuse treatment for adults in the criminal justice system* (CSAT TIP #17). Washington, DC: Substance Abuse and Mental Health Services Administration, Department of Health and Human Services.

Chilcoat, H. D., & Breslau, N. (1998). Investigations of causal pathways between PTSD and drug use disorders. *Addictive Behavior, 23*, 827–840.

Coolman, A. (2003). Sexual misconduct in women's facilities: The current climate. *Corrections Today, 65*(6), 118–121.

Ditton, P. M. (1999). *Mental health and treatment of inmates and probationers* (Bureau of Justice Special Report No. 174463). Washington, DC: U.S. Department of Justice.

Drake, R., Mueser, K., Clark, R., & Wallach, M. (1996). The course, treatment, and outcome of substance disorder in persons with severe mental illness. *American Journal of Orthopsychiatry, 66*, 42–51.

Ehlers, A., Maercker, A., & Boos, A. (2000). Posttraumatic stress disorder following political imprisonment: The role of mental defeat, alienation, and perceived permanent change. *Journal of Abnormal Psychology, 109*, 45–55.

Fallot, R., & Harris, M. (2002). The trauma and recovery empowerment model (TREM): Conceptual and practical issues in group intervention for women. *Community Mental Health Journal, 38*, 475–485.

Farabee, D., Prendergast, M., Cartier, J., Wexler, H., Knight, K., & Anglin, M. (1999). Barriers to implementing effective correctional drug treatment programs. *The Prison Journal, 79*, 150–162.

Federal Bureau of Investigation. (2003). *Uniform crime reports: November 2003.* Retrieved September 5, 2005, from http://www.fbi.gov/ucr/03cius.htm

Foa, E., & Meadows, E. (1997). Psychosocial treatments for posttraumatic stress disorder: A critical review. *Annual Review of Psychology, 48*, 449–480.

Forney, M., Inciardi, J., & Lockwood, D. (1992). Exchanging sex for crack-cocaine: A comparison of women from rural and urban communities. *Journal of Community Health, 17*, 73–85.

General Accounting Office. (1999). *Women in prison: Sexual misconduct by correctional staff. Report to the Honorable Eleanor Holmes Norton House of Representatives.* Washington, DC: Author.

Gibelman, M. (1995). *What social workers do.* Washington, DC: NASW Press.

Gibson, L. E., Holt, J. C., Fondacaro, K. M., Tang, T. S., Powell, T. A., & Turbitt, E. L. (1999). An examination of antecedent trauma and psychiatric comorbidity among male inmates with PTSD. *Journal of Traumatic Stress, 12*, 473–484.

Green, B. L. (1996). Trauma history questionnaire. In B. H. Stamm (Ed.), *Measurement of stress, trauma and adaptation* (pp. 366–369). Lutherville, MD: Sidran.

Greene, R. L. (2000). *The MMPI-2: An interpretive manual* (2nd ed.). Needham Heights, MA: Allyn & Bacon.

Greenfeld, L., & Snell, T. (1999). *Women offenders.* Retrieved September 5, 2005, from http://www.ojp.usdoj.gov/bjs/pub/pdf/wo.pdf

Greer, M. (2000). Human rights and wrongs in our own backyard. Incorporating international human rights protections under domestic civil rights law—A case study of women in U.S. prisons. *Harvard Human Rights Journal, 13*, 71–140.

Harlow, C. (1999). *Prior abuse reported by inmates and probationers.* Retrieved September 5, 2005, from http://www.ojp.usdoj.gov/bjs/pub/ascii/parip.txt

Harris, M. (1998). *Trauma recovery and empowerment.* New York: Free Press.

Harrison, P., & Beck, A. (2004). Prisoners in 2003. (NCJ 19887). Washington, D.C.: Department of Justice, Bureau of Justice Statistics.

Hearn, J., & Parkin, W. (2001). *Gender, sexuality and violence in organizations: The unspoken forces of organizational violence.* London: Sage.

Henderson, D. (1998). Drug abuse and incarcerated women: A research review. *Journal of Substance Treatment, 15,* 579–587.

Herman, J. (1992). *Trauma and recovery.* New York: Basic Books.

Hochstetler, A., Murphy, D. S., & Simons, R. L. (2004). Damaged goods: Exploring predictors of distress in prison inmates. *Crime & Delinquency, 50,* 436–457.

Holtfreter, K., & Morash, M. (2003). The needs of women offenders: Implications for correctional programming. *Women and Criminal Justice, 14,* 137–158.

Horowitz, A. V., Widom, C. S., McLaughlin, J., & White, H. R. (2001). The impact of childhood abuse and neglect on adult mental health: A prospective study. *Journal of Health and Social Behavior, 42,* 184–201.

Inciardi, J., Martin, S., Butzin, C., Hooper, R., & Harrison, L. (1997). An effective model of prison-based treatment for drug-involved offenders. *Journal of Drug Issues, 27,* 261–278.

Jacobsen, L. K., Southwick, S. M., & Kosten, T. R. (2001). Substance use disorders in patients with posttraumatic stress disorder: A review of the literature. *American Journal of Psychiatry, 158,* 1184–1190.

Jordan, K., Schlenger, W., Fairbank, J., & Cadell, J. (1996). Prevalence of psychiatric disorders among incarcerated women. *Archives of General Psychiatry, 53,* 513–519.

Kassebaum, P. A. (1999). *Substance abuse treatment for women offenders: Guide to promising practices* (DHHS Publication No. SMA 99-3303). Rockville, MD: U.S. Department of Health and Human Services, Substance Abuse and Mental Health Services Administration, Center for Substance Abuse Treatment.

Keane, T. M., Malloy, P. F., & Fairbank, J. A. (1984). Empirical development of an MMPI subscale for the assessment of combat related posttraumatic stress disorder. *Journal of Consulting and Clinical Psychology, 52,* 888–891.

Kessler, R., Crum, R., Warner, L., Nelson, C., Schulenberg, K., & Anthony, J. (1997). Lifetime co-occurrence of DSM-III-R alcohol abuse and dependence with other psychiatric disorders in the national comorbidity survey. *Archives of General Psychiatry, 54,* 313–321.

Kessler, R., Sonnega, A., Bromet, E., Hughes, M., & Nelson, C. (1995). Posttraumatic stress disorder in the national comorbidity survey. *Archives of General Psychiatry, 52,* 1048–1060.

Kubiak, S. P. (2004). The effects of PTSD on treatment adherence, drug relapse, and criminal recidivism in a sample of incarcerated men and women. *Research on Social Work Practice, 14*(6), 424–433.

Kubiak, S. P. (manuscript submitted for publication). *Is prison-based treatment an oxymoron? A comparison of prisoner's perceptions of treatment and non-treatment units.*

Kubiak, S. P., Boyd, C. J., Slayden, J., & Young, A. (2005). The substance abuse treatment needs of prisoners. Implementation of an integrated statewide approach. *Journal of Offender Rehabilitation, 41,* 1–19.

Kubiak, S. P., Hanna, J., & Balton, M. A. (2005). "I came to prison to do my time, not to be raped": Coping with sexual assault during incarceration. *Stress, Trauma, and Crisis: An International Journal, 8,* 157–178.

Kupers, T. (1996). Trauma and its sequelae in male prisoners: Effects of confinement, overcrowding, and diminished services. *American Journal of Orthopsychiatry, 66,* 190–196.

Kupers, T. (1999). *Prison madness: The mental health crisis behind bars and what we must do about it.* New York: Jossey-Bass.

Kupers, T. (2005). Toxic masculinity as a barrier to mental health treatment in prison. *Journal of Clinical Psychology, 61,* 713–714.

Lo, C., & Stephens, R. (2000). Drugs and prisoners: Treatment needs on entering prison. *American Journal of Drug and Alcohol Abuse, 28,* 229–245.

McLean, P. (2001). *Anxiety disorders in adults: An evidence-based approach to psychological treatment.* Cary, NC: Oxford University Press.

Minkoff, K. (2001). Best practices: Developing standards of care of individuals with co-occurring psychiatric and substance use disorders. *Psychiatric Services, 52,* 597–599.

Morash, M., Bynum, T., & Koons, B. (1998). *Women offenders: Programming needs and promising approaches.* Washington, DC: National Institute of Justice, U.S. Department of Justice.

Najavits, L. M. (2001). *Seeking Safety: A treatment model for PTSD and substance abuse.* New York: Guilford.

Najavits, L. M. (2002). Seeking Safety: Therapy for trauma and substance abuse. *Corrections Today, 64*, 136–139.

Najavits, L., Gastfriend, D., & Barber, J. (1998). Cocaine dependence with and without PTSD among subjects in the National Institute on Drug Abuse Collaborative Cocaine Treatment Study. *American Journal of Psychiatry, 155*, 214–219.

Najavits, L., Weiss, R., & Shaw, S. (1997). The link between substance abuse and posttraumatic stress disorder in women. *The American Journal on Addictions, 6*, 273–283.

Najavits, L., Weiss, R., & Shaw, S. (1998). "Seeking safety": Outcome of a new cognitive-behavioral psychotherapy for women with posttraumatic stress disorder and substance dependence. *Journal of Traumatic Stress, 11*, 437–456.

National Center for PTSD. (2005). *PTSD assessment instruments.* Retrieved September 24, 2005, from http://www.ncptsd.va.gov/publications/caps.html

Norris, F. H. & Riad, J. K. (1997). Standardized self-report measures of civilian trauma and posttraumatic stress disorder. In J. P. Wilson & T. M. Keane (Eds.), *Assessing psychological trauma and PTSD.* New York: Guilford.

Norris, F. H. (1990). Screening for traumatic stress: A scale for use in the general population. *Journal of Applied Social Psychology, 20*, 1704–1718.

O'Keefe, M. (1998). Posttraumatic stress disorder among incarcerated battered women: A comparison of battered women who killed their abusers and those incarcerated for other offenses. *Journal of Traumatic Stress, 11*, 71–85.

Ouimette, P., Ahrens, C., & Moos, R. (1997). Posttraumatic stress disorder in substance abuse patients: Relationship to 1-year posttreatment outcomes. *Psychology of Addictive Behaviors, 11*, 34–47.

Ouimette, P. C., Brown, P. J., & Najavits, L. M. (1998). Course and treatment of patients with both substance use and posttraumatic stress disorders. *Addictive Behaviors, 23*, 785–796.

Ouimette, P. C., Finney, J. W., & Moos, R. H. (1999). Two-year posttreatment functioning and coping of substance abuse patients with posttraumatic stress disorder. *Psychology of Addictive Behaviors, 13*, 105–114.

Pelissier, B., Wallace, S., & O'Neil, J. (2001). Federal prison residential drug treatment reduces substance use and arrests after release. *American Journal of Drug & Alcohol Abuse, 27*, 315–337.

Rogier, D., Farmer, M., Rae, D., Locke, B., Keith, S., Judd, L., et al. (1990). Comordidity of mental disorders with alcohol and other drug abuse: Results from the Epidemiologic Catchment Area (ECA) study. *Journal of the American Medical Association, 264*, 2511–2518.

Spitzer, R. L., Williams, R. B., Gibbon, M., & First, M. B. (1990). *Structural clinical interview for DSM-IIIR, nonpatient edition.* Washington, DC: American Psychiatric Press.

Substance Abuse and Mental Health Services Administration. (2002). *Report to Congress on the prevention and treatment of co-occurring substance abuse disorders and mental disorders.* Washington, DC: U.S. Department of Health and Human Services.

Stewart, S. H., Pihl, R. O., Conrod, P. J., & Dongier, M. (1998). Functional associations among trauma, PTSD, and substance-related disorders. *Addictive Behaviors, 23*, 797–812.

Teplin, L., Abram, K., & McClelland, G. (1996). Prevalence of psychiatric disorders among incarcerated women. *Archives of General Psychiatry, 53*, 505–512.

Toch, H. (1998). Hypermasculinity and prison violence. In L. H. Bowker (Ed.), *Masculinities and Violence* (pp. 168–178). Thousand Oaks, CA: Sage.

Warner, L., Kessler, R., Hughes, M., Anthony, J., & Nelson, C. (1995). Prevalence and correlates of drug use and dependence in the United States: Results from the national comorbidity survey. *Archives of General Psychiatry, 52*, 219–229.

Weathers, F. W., Keane, T. M., King, L. A., & King, D. W. (1997). Psychometric theory in the development of posttraumatic stress disorder assessment tools. In J. P. Wilson & T. M. Keane (Eds.), *Assessing psychological trauma and PTSD.* New York: Guilford.

Websdale, N., & Chesney-Lind, M. (1998). Doing violence to women: Research synthesis on the victimization of women. In L. H. Bowker (Ed.), *Masculinities and violence* (pp. 55–81). Thousand Oaks, CA: Sage.

Wexler, H., De Leon, G., Thomas, G., Kressel, D., & Peters, J. (1999). The Amity prison TC evaluation: Reincarceration outcomes. *Criminal Justice and Behavior, 26*, 147–167.

Widom, C. S. (1998). Childhood victimization: Early adversity and subsequent psychopathology. In
    B. P. Dohrenwend (Ed.), *Adversity, stress, and psychopathology* (pp. 81–95). New York: Oxford
    University Press.
Wooldredge, J. D. (1994). Inmate crime and victimization in a southwest correctional facility. *Journal
    of Criminal Justice, 22*, 367–381.
Zlotnick, C., Najavits, L. M., Rohsenow, D. J., & Johnson. D. M. (2003). A cognitive-behavioral
    treatment for incarcerated women with substance abuse disorder and posttraumatic stress disorder:
    Findings from a pilot study. *Journal of Substance Abuse Treatment, 25*, 99–105.

Resources

Reports and standards

American Psychiatric Association. (2000). *Psychiatric services in jails and prisons: A task force report of
    the American Psychiatric Association.* Washington, DC: Author.
National Commission on Correctional Health Care. (2003). *Standards for health services in prisons/
    jails.* Chicago, IL: Author.

Organizations and Web sites

National Center for PTSD
Web site: http://www.ncptsd.va.gov

SASSI (Substance Abuse Subtle Screening Instrument) Institute
Web site: http://www.sassi.com

Seeking Safety
Web site: http://seekingsafety.org

Stop Prisoner Rape
Web site: http://www.spr.org/

Best Practices With HIV Infected/Affected Incarcerated Women

Case Examples

Aida, 26-Year-Old Female, Convicted of Felony and Incarcerated for a Term of 6 Years

Elizabeth C. Pomeroy

Michele A. Rountree

Danielle E. Parrish

Aida was interviewed by a social worker who worked for a community-based organization with a 15-year history of providing social services for the criminal justice population recently released from prison. Aida was a 26-year-old Latina, married but separated from her husband, with three children. Aida felt it was important in the first meeting to tell the social worker that she was Dominican and that her people are originally from the Dominican Republic. Aida came to the United States with her family when she was 6 years old, not speaking a word of English.

I remember all of the members of my family being both excited and scared when we came to the States. We came here not speaking English but came to Dorchester, Dorchester, Massachusetts, and found plenty of families from Puerto Rico, the Dominican Republic, Cuba, who spoke Spanish. I was proud of how quickly I picked up English in school. My parents had the toughest time getting use being in the United States. They seemed to be lost among all the cars, people.... the constant pace. My father worked as a car mechanic and my mother worked at the local grocery store in the neighborhood. They wanted the best for both my two sisters and brother.

Aida described how difficult it was to balance the influence of her parent's focus on education, church, and family with the lure of being accepted by her new American friends. "It started out with doing pot at other people's houses when their parents were not home, and then it became more exciting to hang out with what was seen as the cool crowd. For us that meant some of the gang members. That is when I met Jorge and we fell in love." Aida went on to share that along with Jorge's lure also came parties with experimentation from pot to crack cocaine. "Jorge was in and out of jail but I was determined to keep loving him and wait for him with our kids. I did not realize how quickly I had been hooked by the drugs. I started finding more creative ways to support my habit." Aida shared how she found a way to support her habit by selling drugs out of her home. It was not too long before she was arrested and convicted on drug charges. "I was so strung out most of the time. I knew eventually either social services or the cops would get me. I did not care. I was worried about disappointing my kids and parents but I got so lost."

After being out of the fog of active drug using, when Aida entered the substance abuse felony punishment treatment facilities in Massachusetts she expressed being terrified. "At one of the initial orientations at the prison they also mentioned that they offered general HIV education and how those of us with drug histories might be at risk for HIV. I thought, 'Oh my God,' how many times had I shared needles? Even though Jorge told me there was never anyone else, I wanted to believe him." Aida participated in the orientation and decided to get tested. "I felt like I had to for my children's sake. I had 6 years that I would be in here. I did not want my kids to lose me forever if I could do something about [it]." Aida was not surprised but still terrified to have tested positive for HIV. "I was shocked, feeling as though I had been given a death sentence. I know I did a lot of stuff that could have made me positive, but I still thought I wouldn't be." One of the peer educators in the prison also was HIV positive and helped Aida through her grief and fear. The peer educator told Aida about her regime of azidothymidine (AZT) and kept Aida thinking about the day she would be with her children. The social worker interviewed Aida 3 years ago and hired her as a peer educator. She is now living with her children and involved with HIV-related services with the prison.

Carol, 29 Years Old

Carol is a 29-year-old divorced female originally from the West Indies in St. Croix. Carol began the postrelease session with the social worker by saying she thought she would get "AIDS somehow no matter what she did." "HIV and AIDS is nothing new to me. People in my neighborhood had it ... we knew it and they knew it, but no one talked about it. You just do not get into other people's business that way." Carol remembers struggling with substance abuse and drugs since she was a teenager, saying,

> I started out drinking, there was always alcohol in the house, graduated to cocaine and on to the needle. We would share even though we knew we shouldn't, but you also did not want to insult anyone by refusing to share your needles before shooting up, because they may not share with you later on. I did some mad crazy stuff like having sex with men in order to get my fix. Sometimes they would beat me but, hell, who was not getting beat up? So I figured, what made me so special? Condoms? Sometimes, I guess, I was so messed up I could not remember. I did not originally think I was hooking as much as I was trading. I can see how much my thinking was messed up.

Carol felt the worst about her children. When she was convicted on drug felony charges and sent to a prison far away from the city in which she grew up, her children were placed in foster care. Carol took an anonymous HIV test while incarcerated and tested positive. She converted the test result to confidential and was referred to the medication unit and support groups within the prison. Six months prior to her release from prison, Carol has been working with the social worker as her assigned transitional planner to help craft her transition into the community.

Scope of the Problem

Jails, federal prisons, substance abuse felony punishment treatment facilities, and juvenile detention centers in the United States are overwhelmed with the steadily rising number of incarcerated inmates. At the end of 2000, there were a reported 1,313,354 individuals incarcerated in federal and state prisons; 621,149 in local jails; and 8,894 in U.S. Immigration and Naturalization Services facilities. Imprisoned for a variety of offenses, offenders enter the system having engaged in risky practices that place them at heightened risk for HIV/AIDS infection. As a consequence of the engagement in high-risk behaviors, recent estimates suggest that the prevalence of clinical AIDS is 5 times higher and HIV seroprevalence is between 8 and 10 times higher in prison inmates than among the general population (Hammett, Rhodes, & Harmon, 1999). Although the number of known HIV-infected inmates has been steadily decreasing since 1999, only two thirds of local jail inmates report prior testing for HIV (Maruschak, 2004b). Since 1995, the proportion of incarcerated females with HIV has surpassed that of incarcerated males (Maruschak, 2002, 2004a, 2004b).

Disparate testing and reporting policies among correctional facilities make it difficult to present an accurate portrayal of the number of individuals living with HIV in correctional facilities, but it is estimated that incarcerated populations have prevalence rates that are substantially higher for latent tuberculosis (TB), HIV/AIDS, and hepatitis C virus (HCV) than those reported for the general population (Baillargeon et al., 2004). Since AIDS was first identified among prison inmates in 1983, both the rate of HIV infection in incarcerated populations and the spread of HIV infection in prisons have been well documented (Dean, Lansky, & Fleming, 2002; Hammett & Moini, 1990; Hanrahan et al., 1984; Inciardi, 1996; Mutter, Grimes, & Labarthe, 1994; Polonsky et al., 1994). According to Bauserman and colleagues (2003), higher HIV and AIDS rates among the incarcerated are likely the result of two factors. First, due to a number of social, cultural, and political reasons, AIDS cases in the United States are highly concentrated in the African American population, who are also disproportionately incarcerated. Second, incarcerated populations report higher rates of risk behaviors prior to incarceration.

Incarcerated juveniles are at an elevated risk for HIV because of heightened sexual activity, a greater number of partners, greater drug use, and less precautionary behaviors than nonincarcerated youth (Anderson & Farrow, 1998; Lanier, DiClemente, & Horan, 1991). Nader, Wexler, and Patterson (1989) found that when comparing incarcerated adolescents with other youth populations, the incarcerated youth were significantly less knowledgeable about HIV. One in four HIV infections in the United States each year occurs among young people under 21 years of age (National Institute of Justice, 1994). The known high rates of substance abuse, unprotected sexual contact, significant rates of STDs, and unplanned pregnancy among confined youth are indicators of the potential for confirmed cases of HIV/AIDS in late adolescence and early adulthood (Shelton, 2000).

Since populations at greater risk of HIV and AIDS are disproportionately found in correctional settings, it is essential for both those incarcerated and the general population to make HIV/AIDS prevention in these settings a public health priority. Risky behaviors among incarcerated populations are likely to continue upon release. Prison settings offer valuable and essential opportunities to reach this at-risk population in an effort to reduce these risk behaviors. Although prison environments are conducive to the spread of HIV disease, they also provide propitious opportunities for HIV prevention and control of HIV epidemic (St. Lawrence et al., 1997; Yakowitz, Blount, & Gani, 1996).

Criminal Justice Population Rates of HIV/AIDS Infection

Prison inmates present with substantially higher rates of HIV/AIDS than the general population (Dean-Gaitor & Fleming, 1999; Hammett, Widom & Kerr, 1996; Inciardi, 1996; Maruschak, 1999, 2001, 2002, 2004a, 2004b; U.S. Department of Justice, 1997). At the end of 2002, the confirmed rate of AIDS in state in federal prisons was 3.5 times higher than in the U.S. general population (Maruschak, 2004b). The rates of infectious diseases such as HCV, HIV/AIDS, and TB are also elevated in prison populations (Hammett, Harmon, & Rhodes, 2002; Hammett, Harrold, & Gross, 1994; Raba, 1983; Weisfuse et al., 1991; Wu, Baillargeon, Grady, Black, & Dunn, 2001), especially for female inmates (Bauserman et al., 2003). Underestimation of the actual prevalence rate of HIV/AIDS is likely to occur, as certain correctional facilities do not have inmates undergo routine screening or testing for infectious disease.

Female inmates have seropositive HIV rates that exceed those of the general population. Between 1991 and 1995, the number of HIV-infected female prisoners increased at a rate of 88% (Bureau of Justice Statistics, 1997). Van Wormer states, "In New York, 20% of women prison entrants are HIV positive, compared to a 9.2% rate for men. In Texas, Maryland, and North Carolina, as well roughly double the women inmates are seropositive compared to men" (Van Wormer, 2001, p. 246). Higher rates of infection in incarcerated women are attributable, in part, to the greater proportion of women who have drug offenses. McClelland, Teplin, Abram, and Jacobs (2002) have provided empirical evidence that incarcerated women at greatest risk for HIV/AIDS are more frequently arrested for misdemeanors and nonviolent crimes, such as drug crimes, prostitution, and theft. They also note that women with substance abuse disorders and women with severe mental illness have the most extreme sexual risk behaviors (McClelland et al., 2002). Finally, they conclude that since women with these types of charges are being jailed more often and that they return to their communities within a few days, jail provides an especially important point of intervention with these women.

In addition, rates of HIV infection have been higher among African American and Hispanic inmates relative to the unimprisoned population of HIV-positive cases in those racial groups (Beck & Harrison, 2001). Almost 1 in 10 African American men ages 25 to 29 were incarcerated in 2000, compared with 1.1% of White males (Beck & Harrison, 2001). Among females, 1.7% of African American females were detained in a prison setting, compared with 0.7% Hispanic females and 0.3% White females (Bureau of Justice Statistics [BJS], 2005). Likewise, in New York State prisons, 82% of the incarcerated population is African American or Latino (Engle, 1999). The high rates of incarceration and the AIDS epidemic, separately and in combination, have disproportionately affected African American and Latino communities.

Epidemiological and Etiological Determinants of Risk

Pre-Incarceration Risk Behaviors

The high rates of HIV infection among prison populations have been linked to several risk behaviors in which inmates are likely to engage before incarceration, including injection drug use, high-risk sexual activity, and prostitution (Griffin, Ryan, & Briscoe, 1996). Female inmates have consistently reported in high proportions their propensity to engage in injection drug use and/or sexual risk behaviors, such as never or rarely using condoms (Bond & Semaan, 1996; Cotton-Oldenburg, Jordan, Martin, & Kupper, 1999; Hutton et al., 2001; McClelland et al., 2002). Additional HIV/AIDS risk factors that are operative before incarceration include low socioeconomic status, poor access to health care, unhealthy living conditions, high-risk sexual behaviors, history of STDs, and injection drug use (Anno, 1993; Braithwaite, Hammet, & Mayberry, 1996; Hogben & St. Lawrence, 2000; Weisfuse et al., 1991). High levels of risk behavior are consistent with the disproportionate number of HIV and AIDS cases identified among incarcerated persons.

Incarceration Risk Behaviors

The predominant means of HIV exposure reported by inmates with HIV infection and AIDS are unprotected sexual intercourse and needle sharing for injection drug use (Hammett, Harrold, Gross, & Epstein, 1994). These behaviors are especially prevalent among imprisoned drug users, who can spend up to 70% of their drug-use careers incarcerated (Wodak & Deslarlais, 1993). Incarceration rates among injecting drug users (IDUs) have been estimated as exceeding 50% (Muller et al., 1995). In 1997, nearly one fourth of the AIDS cases in men and nearly half of the AIDS cases in women consisted of IDUs (Centers for Disease Control and Prevention [CDCP], 1999). Research suggests that prison inmates who inject drugs while incarcerated are likely to share injection equipment and are unlikely to use bleach or other cleaning agents for sterilizing equipment (Krebs & Simmons, 2002). Tougher sentencing laws without commensurate funding to meet the needs of burgeoning prison populations have resulted in overcrowded conditions and underserved inmates. Both of these factors exacerbate HIV risk in prisons (Hammett et al., 1994).

Post-Incarceration Risk Behaviors

Transmission of HIV/AIDS among the criminal justice population to their home communities without intervention is inevitable. Moreover, because millions of people are released from short-term sentences in correctional facilities each year (Kantor, 1998) and often continue to engage in HIV risk behaviors after their release, these individuals place the larger community at higher risk of HIV infection. Following incarceration, additional risk factors, including psychological stress, crowded living conditions, sexual assault, poor ventilation systems, and increased concentration of immunosuppressed cohabitants, may all contribute to a further increase of infectious disease risk (Anno, 1993; Braithwaite et al., 1996; Griffin et al., 1996; Thorburn, 1995). Providing men and women who exit correctional facilities with HIV education and the necessary health resources is essential for reducing the risk of spreading the disease.

Psychiatric Disorders

The U.S. prison population has high proportions of incarcerated individuals living with psychiatric disorders. These individuals have an increased risk for HIV infection (Kelly et al., 1992; Susser, Valencia, & Conover, 1993). Psychiatric disorders, such as bipolar disorder, schizophrenia, posttraumatic stress disorder, and depression, have been associated with both HIV risk behaviors and HIV infection (Cournos, McKinnon, Meyer-Bahlburg, Guido, & Meyer, 1993; Hutton et al., 2001; Kalichman, Kelly, Johnson, & Bulto, 1994; Kalichman, Sikkema, Kelly, & Bulto, 1995; Kelly et al., 1992; Volavka et al., 1992). Bail-largeon et al. (2003) found bipolar disorder to be most common among HIV-infected inmates.

While many inmates have serious mental health concerns, the literature indicates that women inmates have a much higher incidence of mental health problems than male inmates or the general population (Abram, Teplin, & McClelland, 2003). As many as two thirds of women inmates require mental health services during, or soon after, their initial incarceration (James, Gregory, Jones, & Rundell, 1985). Prior to incarceration, one in five women inmates had received some form of mental health treatment (Gabel & Johnston, 1995).

Many jailed females are dealing with the trauma of child abuse (Shank, 1991). More than half of women in jail report a history of either sexual or physical abuse, compared with only 10% of men (BJS, 2005). Of all persons in jail, 31% grew up in a family with a parent or guardian who abused alcohol or drugs; 12% lived in a foster home or institution; and 46% had a family member who had previously been incarcerated (BJS, 2005). In a study of incarcerated women in North Carolina, 55.9% of those surveyed reported medical issues and 29% were taking medication to address these medical problems (Hogben & St. Lawrence, 2000). Furthermore, almost one fourth of the women reported mental health symptoms such as depression, anxiety, and anger within the past month (Hogben & St. Lawrence, 2000). Over half of the women reported a history of drug use; however, only 4.4% reported self-injecting heroin (Hogben & St. Lawrence, 2000). Singer et al. (1995), using standardized scales, found that 64% of their sample of incarcerated women fell within the clinical range for mental health problems. The same study found that 83% of the women were in the substance abuse range, and 81% had been victimized at some point in their lives.

HIV/AIDS risk behaviors associated with psychiatric disorders include (a) having multiple sex partners (Kelly et al., 1992; Volavka et al., 1992); (b) having sex in exchange for money or drugs (Hutton et al., 2001; Kalichman et al., 1994); (c) having sexual intercourse, including anal sex, with partners with whom they are unfamiliar (Hutton et al., 2001; Kalichman et al., 1994); (d) having sex while under the influence of drugs and alcohol (Kalichman et al., 1994; Kelly et al., 1992); (e) and injecting drugs (Cournos et al., 1993; Kalichman et al., 1995). The elevated risk of these behaviors among patients with psychiatric disorders is attributable to a number of factors, including limited impulse control, difficulties in establishing stable social and sexual relationships, limited knowledge about HIV-related risk factors, increased susceptibility to coercion, and co-morbid alcohol and drug use (Aruffo, Coverdale, Chacko, & Dworkin, 1990; Steiner, Lussier, & Rosenblatt, 1992).

Women With HIV/AIDS

In the decade from 1992 to 2003, the proportion of women in the U.S. with prevalence of AIDS among has steeply increased from 14% to 22% (Centers for Disease Control [CDC], 2005). In addition, African American women are 25 times more likely to be diagnosed with AIDS than White women (CDC, 2005). They are also 4 times more likely to be diagnosed with AIDS than Hispanic women (CDC, 2005). While African American and Hispanic women compose only 25% of all women in the United States, they represent a staggering 83% of AIDS diagnoses reported in 2003 (CDC, 2005).

According to Hoffman (1993), 90% of women with AIDS have dependent children, are single parents, may have lost a partner to AIDS, and are often grappling with issues of poverty. Frequently, HIV/AIDS families are at a pronounced risk of becoming home-less. This situation may be due to a multitude of factors such as discrimination due to infection; declining health and loss of employment; or dwindling finances resulting from intravenous drug use, treatment expenses for infected members, or poverty.

The majority of women infected or affected by HIV/AIDS live in impoverished urban areas. At the beginning of the epidemic, disadvantaged women and intravenous drug users who became infected found little help available in their own communities due to the belief that AIDS was a gay man's disease (Walker, 1991). Today, specific funding is allocated to state and local agencies to provide medical and psychosocial services to women and minority groups. Therefore, women who are released from jail or prison can now more easily access these necessary supportive services in urban areas. However, there is still a lack of HIV services in more rural communities.

Incarcerated Women

The U.S. correction/detention system currently houses over 2 million individuals. Be-tween 1980 and 2000, the population of incarcerated females increased by more than 700% (Poehlmann, White, & Bjerke, 2004). In 1998, an estimated 84,000 women were incarcerated, while 950,000 were under supervision or control of the correctional sys-tem, including parole agencies (van Wormer, 2001). Women in prison or on parole are mothers to over 1.3 million minor children (Mumola, 2000). Women inmates accounted for 6.6% of the state prison population in 2001, and 12% of the local jail population in 2002, up from 10% in 1996 (BJS, 2005). Most recent BJS statistics indicate that 46% of female state prison inmates are African American, while 36.2% are White, and 14.2% Hispanic (Snell & Morton, 1994). In addition, 54% of incarcerated women had used drugs in the month before the current offense, compared to 50% of men (Snell & Mor-ton, 1994). One third of incarcerated women reported having used a needle to inject illegal drugs, compared to one quarter of men (Snell & Morton, 1994). In 2002, over 10% of all female inmates in New York (13.6%) and Maryland (12.1%) were known to be HIV positive (Maruschak, 2004b). The 1996 AIDS rate for incarcerated women was 23 times the national rate for all women (Dean-Gaitor & Fleming, 1999). The majority of women are arrested for nonviolent crimes. Typical offenses include fraud, drugs, and/or prostitution (Van Wormer, 2001).

Jail–Based Psychoeducational Intervention Programs

In an effort to respond to the mental health needs of incarcerated populations, jail-based rehabilitation programs have been established. Most programs implemented within a corrections setting have been educational and preventative in nature (Coulson & Nut-brown, 1992; El-Bassel et al., 1995, 1997) and have focused on providing information to inmates. Psychoeducational groups have been used to address a variety of problem situations. For example, Abel, McIntire, and Dixon (1994) employed a psychoeducational group approach in their work with male inmates who had been incarcerated for offenses related to domestic violence. In addition, a skill building and social support enhancement group was established to prevent HIV/AIDS in drug-abusing incarcerated women (El-Bassel et al., 1995). This pilot study evaluated the effectiveness of this group intervention for reducing the spread of AIDS among 145 female inmates. The study "confirmed the feasibility of implementing a skill-building intervention for drug-using women in jail" (El-Bassel et al., 1995, p. 131). Later in this chapter, we discuss in detail another example of a jail-based psychoeducational program.

Despite the enormous need for interventions targeting women prisoners, there has been only a limited amount of research conducted in this area (Van Wormer, 2001). However, the evidence base for preventing and treating incarcerated men and women with regard to HIV/AIDS is growing. The following section highlights some best practices that have been identified in this literature.

Highlights of Best Practices With Incarcerated Women

A myriad of efforts have been made across the continuum of institutional and community care to reduce HIV/AIDS risk among inmates and provide treatment to those who are infected—from preventative literature to curriculum designed to change attitudes and behavior, and from psychoeducational group interventions to intensive case management following release. As a result, some best practices have emerged. This section summarizes these best practices, including targets for change, preventative and treatment modalities, and the use of culturally grounded treatments. This section will conclude with a detailed description of a successful psychoeducational treatment that has been developed, implemented, and evaluated by one of the authors.

Targets for Change

Effective risk reduction and treatment programs have emphasized disparate targets of change. Maryland's Prevention Case Management Program (PCM) provides individual or group counseling to inmates nearing release to decrease HIV risk behavior (Bauserman et al., 2003). Proponents of this program assert that its success lies in its effort to tailor their program to each individual's personal level of HIV risk. PCM assesses each inmate's overall level of risk, the specific risk behaviors (including heavy drug use), and the psychological factors that are preventing change in these risk behaviors. For each individual, regardless of level of risk, the curriculum emphasizes changes in perceived risk, condom attitudes, condom use self-efficacy, self-efficacy to reduce injection drug risk, and other substance risk and behavioral intentions.

Similarly, Kelly, St. Lawrence, Hood, and Brasfield (1989) suggest that an essential component of an effective HIV risk prevention program is an emphasis on supporting the development of both self-management and interpersonal management skills. Self-management skills include personal awareness, problem solving, and coping that will aid clients in accurately perceiving risks so that they will be motivated to reduce risk behaviors and be better able to identify and navigate successfully through high-risk situations. Interpersonal skills enhance the clients' self-management skills by improving their ability to assert themselves to practice safer sex and to deal with a partner's opposing reactions.

El-Bassel et al. (1997) designed an intervention that used both cognitive–behavioral and skills-building components to reduce HIV risk among incarcerated women. A social support enhancement model was used that involved assisting women in the development of protective behaviors that many of these women had not had prior to the intervention. The intervention also helped women develop the skills to generate social support in their environments to maintain health-promoting outcomes and protective behaviors.

Fisher, Fisher, and Rye (1995), in contrast, use a model based on the theory of reasoned action. The framework is built around the assumption that cognitions lead to attitudes, which then lead to behavioral intentions. Behavioral intentions represent the closest approximation of actual behaviors. In a study by the researchers, this model was supported in its ability to predict AIDS protective behaviors.

St. Lawrence et al. (1997) conducted and evaluated two HIV risk reduction interventions with incarcerated women. They compared an intervention based on social cognitive theory to one that was based on gender and power. The intervention based on social cognitive theory emphasized skills building and resulted in better skills in condom application at 6-month posttest. In contrast, the intervention based on the theory of gender and power resulted in a greater commitment to reduce HIV risk-related behaviors. While the generalizability of the results outside of a prison setting is unknown, these results suggest that these intervention components may be effective in reducing HIV risk among incarcerated women.

Poehlmann and colleagues (2004) review literature on women in prison that details efforts that have attended separately to family relationships and HIV-related issues. In this review, they argue that HIV prevention programs are more likely to be effective if they integrate a family relationship perspective, although they do not report finding any prior interventions that have done this. They draw on *relational developmental theory*, which posits that a woman's identity is grounded in her ability and motivation to interact with others, especially those within her immediate family. They suggest that evidence for this theory has emerged among women offenders, as these women are highly motivated most by their desire to maintain effective ties to their families. In addition, they cite evidence showing a link between HIV-infected women and their heightened motivation to utilize their family relationships as a primary source of support. Since large numbers of women in prison have children and are often driven by the motivation to reunite with their children, they suggest that this provides a valuable opportunity to integrate family programs and HIV interventions for women offenders. Although they have not yet tested this model, they note that the level and type of intervention should be tailored to each individual woman.

From an administrative and planning perspective, prior efforts to reduce HIV risk among the corrections population have proved futile when undertaken by one organization. The research literature suggests that healthy, effective interorganizational collaboration is essential to provide the necessary services to this population (Klein, O'Connell, Devore, Wright, & Birkhead, 2002; Rapposelli et al., 2002). The CDC and Health Resources and Services Administration have also emphasized the importance of federal coordination of prevention and intervention plans to prevent gaps and duplication in service delivery to this high-risk population (Rapposelli et al., 2002). Community-based organizations (CBOs) involvement is especially important given that, when released from prison, inmates return to the community in need of service. Klein et al. (2002) recently reported that collaboration between public health, corrections, and CBOs proved successful in meeting the needs of inmates. Furthermore, several CBOs have a history in serving the criminal justice population, with many of the staff including former inmates. Emphasis on nontraditional qualifications and relevant life experiences of staff members employed by the CBOs is essential. The unique ability and willingness of CBOs to work with in-facility parole officers to develop transitional plans and community parole officers after release have contributed greatly to the successful release of these high-risk inmates.

Prevention and Treatment

Prison and jail facilities provide a critical opportunity to offer behavioral interventions for risk reduction and to identify seropositive individuals, who can then begin appropriate treatment prior to release back into the community. Correctional settings can provide an important and essential setting for HIV risk reduction interventions. Despite the need, relatively few behavioral interventions have been reported that target incarcerated populations (El-Bassel et al., 1995; Grinstead, Zack, & Faigeles, 2001; Grinstead, Zack, Faigeles, Grossman, & Blea, 1999; Magurea, Kang, & Shapiro, 1994; St. Lawrence et al., 1997). The CDC (1999) estimates that for every five HIV-positive persons newly identified by counseling and testing programs, one infection is averted through adoption of safer sex behaviors. In the absence of a cure for or vaccine against HIV, prevention programs in prisons are crucial to combating the HIV epidemic (Fauci, 1988; Fineberg, 1988). It is important to focus efforts on changing the behaviors of offenders who are disproportionately at risk for HIV because of injection drug use and unprotected sex (Baxter, 1991; Griffin, Lurigioi, & Johnson, 1991; Lanier & McCarthy, 1989; Morrison, Baker, & Gillmore, 1994). When compared with a control group of non-HIV-educated offenders, probationers who participated in an HIV education session had more knowledge of HIV-prevention measures and reported that they were more willing to undergo HIV testing, to use condoms, and to refrain from sharing needles (Lurigio, Petraitis, & Johnson, 1992).

A continuum of services for HIV/AIDS prevention and treatment has been used in correctional settings, including HIV counseling and testing, behaviorally based prevention interventions, HIV primary care, supportive services, interventions to prevent HIV-related stigma and discrimination, transitional planning, and community-based case management services at release (Braithwaite et al., 1996; Dean-Gaitor & Fleming, 1999; Gaiter & Doll, 1996; Hammett, 1998; Hammett, Gaiter, & Crawford, 1998). Postrelease efforts have focused on referring out for HIV primary care, support groups for HIV-infected inmates, and coordination with the parole officer on postrelease plan development and referrals. Examples of effective use of available resources for incarcerated individuals have been observed in the efforts of the NYS Department of Health AIDS Institute, the NYS Department of Correctional Services, the NYS Division of Parole, and a statewide network of community-based organizations. These organizations have collaborated to meet HIV prevention and support services needs of inmates and parolees through a continuum of interventions and services.

Effective HIV prevention programs that target risk reduction for incarcerated individuals, both while they are in prison and after they are released, are urgently needed. Incarceration is a time when individuals who engage in extremely high-risk activities, and who are difficult to reach otherwise, are a captive audience for HIV prevention intervention and education (Braithwaite et al., 1996).

Culturally Grounded Practice

The salience of culture in understanding HIV risk behaviors and subsequent attention to these issues in practice has been well documented in HIV prevention literature (Parker, 2001; Amaro, Raj, & Reed, 2001; Wilson & Miller, 2003). Two culturally bound factors identified within the HIV literature have been societal stigmas attached to homosexual relationships and beliefs about gender roles that favor men over women (Wilson & Miller, 2003). Wilson and Miller (2003) define culture as ". . . 'the way of life' among members of a group, including the values, beliefs, attitudes, norms, and standards that might influence some people to put themselves at risk for HIV transmission" (p. 185). Overall, the HIV prevention field has recognized that it is harmful to use prevention programs designed for European Americans with ethnic minority populations, and that the programs that are culturally grounded within the target group's population tend to work better (Wilson & Miller, 2003). In a review of 17 articles that detailed interventions that paid special attention to cultural issues, Wilson and Miller (2003) found two primary strategies that HIV prevention programs have used to integrate culture into their practice: presentation strategies and content strategies.

Attending to Presentation Strategies

The importance of attending to how and what is presented is based on the belief that there are ". . . culturally bound ways of communicating that can only be expressed by members of that group" (Wilson & Miller, 2003, p. 188). Techniques employed to address this cultural concern were use of facilitators or videos that reflected the same race or ethnic background of the target population, use of a familiar physical setting for actors, and the use of scripts or terminology that reflect the target group's cultural use of language.

Attending to Content Strategies

Ten of the 17 interventions relayed a belief in the importance of grounding the intervention in the experiences, norms, and values of the target population. A third of these authors indicated that they had conducted formative research for their intervention with regard to culture, including the use of focus groups and pilot studies to obtain the unique input with regard to culture from the target population.

HIV prevention efforts being implemented in correctional settings must be mindful of the social and contextual factors that contribute to HIV risk behaviors. A solid understanding of these factors should be the basis on which prevention interventions are tailored for disparate prison populations and should be used to help inmates develop prevention skills and personalized strategies that are specific to their needs, circumstances, and capabilities (Bryan, Ruiz, & O'Neill, 2003). Attention to the content and presentation of HIV information and treatment among incarcerated women must take into account the many cultural contexts in which these women live. Salient issues of attention include gender and power, ethnicity, past experiences of abuse and trauma, type of risk behaviors, type and amount of substance abuse, the presence of psychological problems, and the role of family relationships. It is also important to remain cognizant that incarcerated female populations vary in culture by site and region and to make specific efforts to create an HIV/AIDS risk reduction intervention that is culturally grounded for the specific target population.

Example of Best Practice Intervention With Incarcerated Women Infected and Affected by HIV/AIDS

The following sections detail a psychoeducational program for incarcerated women in a large southern metropolitan jail. The project was conducted over a 2-year period and included 87 women inmates in the treatment group and 54 women on a waiting-list comparison group. The group intervention consisted of 10 sessions during a 5-week period. Nine different groups were conducted with eight to nine women in each group. The group was evaluated for the effectiveness of reducing depression, anxiety, and trauma and increasing HIV information among women inmates. An outline of the 10 sessions and results of the intervention are discussed.

Conceptual Framework

The intervention approach utilized in the current study is based on previous research by the authors of a psychoeducational group intervention for family members of people living with AIDS (PLWAs; Pomeroy, Rubin, & Walker, 1996). The psychoeducational approach proved to be very effective in alleviating the emotional turmoil associated with caring for a PLWA. The authors also examined the effectiveness of a psychoeducational group for heterosexuals with HIV/AIDS and found similar positive results (Pomeroy, Rubin, Van Laningham, & Walker, 1997). A psychoeducational approach was also utilized to study the effectiveness of an education and support group for incarcerated non-HIV-positive women in the jail system (Pomeroy, Abel, & Kiam, 1998). Preliminary results of this study indicate the group intervention is effective in alleviating depression, anxiety, and trauma symptoms among these female inmates. Because of the prior success of this intervention with other populations, it was deemed appropriate to modify this approach in order to meet the specific informational needs and emotional concerns of incarcerated women who are infected or affected by HIV/AIDS and then test its effectiveness with this female target population.

The psychoeducational component of the intervention is based on the assumption that persons coping with HIV/AIDS, a difficult illness to define and understand, need accurate information about the disease. Due to the wide variety of rare opportunistic infections that may develop as a result of the illness, people affected by HIV/AIDS often develop inaccurate or false assumptions about the disease. Information about medication is also an important issue that often becomes tied to myths about the disease. People coping with HIV/AIDS are often seeking information that is comprehensible and accurate.

The need for support is also an issue that has been well documented in the literature on coping with a chronic illness (Biegel, Sayles, & Schulz, 1991). Bringing people together in a group can ameliorate the loneliness, isolation, and emotional distress experienced by persons affected by a chronic/terminal illness. Persons infected with HIV/AIDS particularly need this group support due to the high degree of stigma associated with this illness (Pomeroy et al., 1996; Powell-Cope & Brown, 1992).

The intervention also employs elements of the task-centered approach (Reid & Epstein, 1972). The tasks are seen as a way to help clients work on the emotional impact of HIV/AIDS in their lives between group sessions. While information can be readily assimilated if presented in a coherent manner, making emotional changes can be far more time consuming and difficult. Therefore, it is important for clients to spend time working daily on the emotional issues with which they are confronted, especially given the time-limited nature of the intervention. The intervention approach also emphasizes stigma as an important focal point due to the homophobic reactions of society, the fears of contagion, the lack of knowledge about the disease or cure, and the relationship of HIV/AIDS to sexuality.

Theoretical Components of Group Intervention

The educational component of the psychoeducational intervention is based on the assumption that people who are at risk of developing HIV/AIDS need accurate information about the disease. Female inmates in the jail system are a particularly vulnerable population due to the environmental conditions in which they reside. They also need to be informed about their ability to increase their chances of preventing the transfer of this illness to significant others in their lives. From a clinical standpoint, however, it was evident that the inmates had other emotional concerns and stressors that needed to be addressed. Because of these pressing emotional issues, providing HIV education alone would not sufficiently change attitudes and beliefs that lead to risk-taking behaviors. Therefore, a supportive component, which focused on relevant emotional issues that could prevent the use of new information, was included in the framework of the group intervention.

Whereas the psychoeducational approach provides the structure for the group intervention, the conceptual framework also consists of elements of cognitive–behavioral theory and the task-centered approach (Reid & Epstein, 1972). Cognitive–behavioral techniques have proven to be effective in the reduction of anxiety and depression as well as trauma symptoms. Numerous studies have indicated the efficacy of cognitive–behavioral techniques in individual or group therapy settings (Rehm, 1995). The basic assumption underlying cognitive–behavioral theory is that dysfunctional cognitions make people vulnerable to anxiety, depression, and lower self-esteem (Hammen, 1995).

The task component or homework assignments were seen as a way to help clients work on the emotional aspects of their lives between group sessions. While information can be readily assimilated if presented in a coherent manner, making emotional changes can be far more time consuming and difficult. Therefore, it is important for group participants to spend time working daily on the emotional issues with which they are confronted, especially given the time-limited nature of the intervention.

Psychoeducational Group Sessions

Each of the psychoeducational group sessions lasted for 90 minutes. The first part of each session lasted approximately 45 minutes and consisted of a presentation or discussion concerning an educational topic related to HIV/AIDS as well as a discussion of the homework assignment from the previous session. The second part of each session, also 45 minutes, focused on supportive group processes using cognitive–behavioral and task-centered techniques. Some of the topics in the supportive component of the sessions included how to cope with depression and anxiety; how to reduce stress; and the importance of social support, self-esteem, anger management, and coping skills (see Table 20.1). Although individual inmates discussed their own unique feelings and situations, each of the treatment groups received the same structured intervention.

Session 1. The first group session began by having inmates introduce themselves and explain why they decided to join the group. Because most of the inmates had never been in a group led by social workers, the group facilitators outlined the structure of the group for the inmates, explained the importance of being on time for the group, and discussed issues of confidentiality among group participants. One of the goals of this session was to provide the group participants with a general overview of HIV/AIDS. Each group member received a handout about HIV/AIDS that contained information about the virus and how it is transmitted. Although the inmates had a basic knowledge about HIV/AIDS, many participants stated that they knew about HIV/AIDS only because of public service announcements on television. Several inmates asked questions concerning myths about the disease. For example, one inmate asked if you could get HIV/AIDS from toilet seats. Other inmates wanted information about other forms of transmission, such as dirty needles.

A second goal of this initial session was to establish some rapport among the inmates as well as to begin the development of group cohesion. The group facilitator had each inmate talk about four strengths she saw within herself. If an inmate could not think of four assets, the other inmates were allowed to provide her with their insights. This exercise provided group participants with a positive initial group experience as well as common ground on which to build supportive relationships during the group process. After this exercise, the group facilitator had each inmate discuss one feeling that she would like to change by participating in the group process. Several inmates stated they felt very angry, whereas others felt depressed or hopeless most of the time. At the conclusion of the first session, the group facilitators asked each inmate to take a notebook and a pencil provided by the leaders and to make a list that filled one page of notebook paper. Each sentence had to start with the words "I am." The exercise was designed to give the participants a sense of their own identity and self-esteem. The participants were asked to bring the lists back to the next session for discussion.

Table 20.1	Psychoeducational Content of Group Intervention		
Group Session	Educational Component	Support Component	Homework Assignment
1	Overview of HIV/AIDS	Trust and self-esteem; establishing group trust	"I am" exercise
2	Opportunistic infections	Coping with depression; challenging irrational thoughts	Automatic thoughts exercise
3	Preventing transmission of HIV	Depression (continued)	Changing negative thoughts
4	Safer sex practices; healthy versus unhealthy relationships	Dealing with anxiety	Stress reduction exercise
5	Safer sex (continued)	Anxiety (continued)	Stress reduction exercise
6	Drug use and HIV	Coping with anger; communication skills	Anger management
7	Staying healthy	Anger (continued)	Anger management
8	Financial issues; building confidence	Problem solving and goal setting	Goal setting exercise
9	Planning for the future; recognizing personal resources	Empowerment	Strengths exercise
10	Termination	Accomplishments in the group	Moving out and moving on

In summary, the primary goal of the first session was to introduce the inmates to the group process with the attendant rules for group procedures, to initiate a discussion of HIV/AIDS, and to provide the inmates with a positive emotional experience in which they were viewed as important individuals with strengths that could be identified. In this manner, the stage was set for the development of group cohesion and commitment to the process.

Sessions 2 and 3. Beginning with the second session, all remaining sessions began with group members discussing their degree of success with the homework assignment from the previous session. For example, at the beginning of the second session, one inmate stated proudly that she was able to fill an entire notebook page with "I am" sentences and that she had never thought about herself in all those different ways.

The educational component of Session 2 involved a presentation and discussion of various opportunistic infections and their accompanying symptoms that are associated with HIV/AIDS. Session 3 dealt with how HIV/AIDS is transmitted, including myths surrounding this issue. For example, one inmate asked if it were possible to get HIV/AIDS by drinking out of the same glass as someone who is infected. Experts on these topics from a local AIDS organization led the presentations.

The supportive component of Sessions 2 and 3 addressed the emotional issue of depression. Symptoms of depression were discussed as well as the interrelationship between thoughts, feelings, and actions. The notion of automatic thoughts (that is, the repertoire of thoughts that we have about ourselves that we frequently repeat) that lead to depressed feelings also was discussed. The homework assignment for Session 2 involved the inmates writing down their automatic thoughts that they experienced when they felt depressed or under pressure. At the conclusion of Session 3, group participants were asked to keep a log of negative thoughts that they had and the feelings that accompanied those thoughts. Finally, they were asked to reframe the negative thoughts to more positive ones and to write down the attendant feelings.

Sessions 4 and 5. The educational component for Sessions 4 and 5 focused on healthy versus dysfunctional relationships and safer sex practices. This discussion included information on how HIV can be spread through multiple sex partners, prostitution, and lack of precautionary measures. The group facilitators led these discussions with the participants.

Coping with anxiety was the topic for the supportive component for Sessions 4 and 5. Group participants discussed their fears and anxieties about the criminal justice system and about the stressful living conditions in the jail environment. They also discussed their fears about being released from jail and their abilities to get jobs, maintain custody of their children, and support their families. The group facilitators then led the participants through a 30-minute progressive relaxation exercise to alleviate anxieties. To be effective, progressive relaxation must be practiced two or three times per day. During Session 5, group participants were given a relaxation exercise that they could accomplish in a shorter amount of time when they were feeling tense throughout the day. Homework assignments for Sessions 4 and 5 involved having the participants practice progressive relaxation exercises that they had learned during the session from the group facilitator.

Sessions 6 and 7. The use and abuse of drugs and their relationship to HIV/AIDS were presented as the educational topics for Session 6. The transmission of HIV/AIDS through the use of dirty needles was discussed, and the use of bleaching kits to prevent the spread of HIV/AIDS was presented. Participants were given information about where they could obtain bleaching kits in the community. Because many of the participants were being held on drug charges, this topic was particularly relevant and brought about a great deal of discussion among the participants.

In a supportive component of Sessions 6 and 7, the detrimental effects of anger were discussed. Anger management skills such as prelearned responses when confronted with an anger-provoking situation were discussed in detail. Group participants were guided by facilitators through adaptive choices they could make if they were engaged in angry situations. For example, if a group participant was provoked by another inmate, negotiating with the inmate could lead to a more satisfying outcome rather than simply venting their anger. On the other hand, if another inmate was angry at the participant, withdrawing from the situation could be a more successful response than engaging in the confrontation. Homework assignments for Sessions 6 and 7 involved practicing anger management skills that were discussed during those sessions. Specifically, participants were asked to use anger management techniques such as "negotiate," "withdraw," or "avoid" if involved in an angry confrontation and then to write down what the situation was and how they handled their anger in the situation.

Sessions 8 and 9. Sessions 8 and 9 were designed to assist group participants in problem-solving skills and goal setting. Group participants were asked to identify a particular problem that they felt they could resolve. They were then guided through a brainstorming exercise to examine possible solutions to the problem. When a realistic solution was found from the list, they were then asked to list the steps they would take to reach the solution. In addition, each inmate was asked to develop a "discharge plan" that delineated goals before and after being released from jail. The homework assignment for Session 8 included making a list of realistic, attainable goals, both short term while in jail and longer term after being released from jail. These goals were discussed in the following session. The homework assignment for Session 9 involved making a list of strengths and comparing it to the initial list in the first session.

Session 10. The final session focused on termination of the group, the accomplishments of the participants, and moving toward the future. Group participants expressed satisfaction with the group experience and appreciated the fact that the group facilitators cared about their well-being. At the end of Session 10, group participants were given a certificate indicting they had completed the 5-week psychoeducational group intervention.

On two occasions the group facilitators were not allowed to enter the jail facility because the entire jail population had been placed on lockdown. All inmates had to be in their locked cells, and all privileges had been suspended. Therefore, in reality, the 10 sessions took 6 weeks to complete.

Results of the Intervention

The intervention was evaluated using a quasi-experimental research design in which 87 women divided into nine groups received the intervention and 52 women were placed on a waiting list and served as a comparison group. The psychoeducational group was effective in reducing depression, anxiety, and trauma among female inmates infected or affected by HIV/AIDS. It was also effective in increasing the women's knowledge about HIV/AIDS. These findings suggest that therapeutic groups in the correctional system could have a significant and meaningful impact on female inmates. Although women in the study were primarily charged with nonviolent crimes, they had histories of child abuse, substance abuse, prostitution, and domestic violence. Their support systems were generally minimal, unreliable, and dysfunctional. The group leaders' support and the mutual assistance of group members may have been the first time many of these women experienced any real, consistent, and therapeutic help in their lives. The opportunity to discuss crucial issues in their lives in a confidential environment with others who had similar experiences may have played a part in the effectiveness of the intervention.

Group members also appeared to benefit from the information they gained during the group sessions. Most of the female inmates were not knowledgeable about the connection between thoughts, feelings, and behaviors. They also had limited repertoires in terms of coping skills. In addition, group members appeared to benefit from information concerning HIV and AIDS. Many women could not distinguish myth from fact regarding the illness. The group intervention gave these women the opportunity to understand and gain insight about their attitudes and high-risk behaviors (Pomeroy, Kiam, & Abel, 1999). In addition, due to the effectiveness of this group intervention with female inmates, it was modified and implemented with male inmates in the jail system. The group was also found to be effective with this population (Pomeroy, Kiam, & Green, 2000).

Clinical and Ethical Issues

Perhaps the most difficult component of working in a jail facility involved the ethical issues with which the social workers were confronted. Once a sense of trust and connection was established in the group sessions, group members would often come to sessions angry, frustrated, and emotionally distraught due to difficulties they daily confronted with correctional staff such as undue harassment, abuse (physical, sexual, and emotional), or oppression by controlling correctional officers. While the group facilitators could offer the inmates assistance in dealing with these difficult issues, they were unable to change the environmental conditions or attitudes of these officers. When particularly unethical situations arose, the facilitators informed the jail administration; however, the overall conditions remained the same. The facilitators requested continuous supervision pertaining to these ethical dilemmas in order to know how to best navigate their course through the correctional system.

In addition, the issue of confidentiality among group members who participated in the intervention was of paramount importance. The group facilitator thoroughly explained during the initial interview with the potential group member that confidentiality had to be maintained in order to participate in the group intervention. If a group member violated confidentiality, she was immediately removed from the group sessions. The importance of confidentiality in a corrections environment has serious ramifications. Group members must feel safe to disclose personal information. On the other hand, if group members disclosed information that placed inmates or staff in jeopardy, the group facilitator had to report that information to the administration for security reasons. Therefore, limited confidentiality must be addressed before conducting a group intervention.

Table 20.2 contains suggestions for dealing with clinical and ethical obstacles that helping professionals may face in the prison environment. It is recommended that social workers working within the correctional system or social workers who are contracted by the jail or prison system seek outside supervision due to the many ethical issues that arise within this environment.

Conclusion

In this chapter, the problems of HIV/AIDS among incarcerated women are highlighted. The proportion of women in prisons and jails in comparison to males has substantially increased over the past decade. Women are more frequently being arrested for drug offenses, prostitution, and other nonviolent crimes. Many of these women are at a heightened risk for contracting HIV/AIDS. There are a disproportionate number of African American and Latina women affected by this illness, and these women also are more highly represented in the corrections system.

Suggestions to Overcome Obstacles to Service Delivery

Administrative	Service-Related	Sensitivity to Inmates
• Communicate well and coordinate services between organizations. • Make long-term commitments. • Hold frequent meetings among and between service providers. • Circulate Memorandum of Understanding between agencies.	• Inform and engage prisoners in HIV prevention through multiple opportunities and providers. • Implement HIV reporting and partner notification; all agencies involved (public and private) need to assess, revise, and implement roles, policies, and procedures. • Meet the needs of diversity of inmates; provide greater access to HIV education and interventions in Spanish and other languages (Klein et al., 2002). • Make greater use of peer educators, harm reduction information, and access to transitional strategies to encourage more inmates to know their HIV status. • Require all inmates to have medical and mental health examinations at the time of intake, including detailed medical and mental health history, a comprehensive physical examination, and diagnostic procedures. • Ensure that inmates who receive an HIV test and then transfer receive test results, even if paroled. • Use culturally competent services–trained peers (Klein, et al., 2002). • Use peer-led education and discharge planning services with HIV-prevention components; provide a context for operating such programs within correctional facilities (Ehrmann, 2002).	• Do not post medical call-out lists in public areas, indicate reasons for call out, indicate with whom the inmate has an appointment, or reveal length of time of appointments (Klein et al., 2003). • Ensure that inmates who report inmates as partners are not dealt with as security risks. • Require procedures and training of all staff in confidentiality. • Use a variety of testing technologies, providers, and modalities to maximize acceptance by inmates. • Protect inmates from HIV-related stigma and discrimination.

Until recently, there have been few interventions designed specifically for incarcerated women. In the last decade, more attention has been focused on the mental health needs of women in jails and prisons. Interventions related to substance abuse, domestic violence, family relationships, and parenting classes have evolved within the correctional institutions in the United States. Due to the escalating rates of HIV/AIDS among women in the legal system, interventions designed to prevent and treat the disease have begun to emerge. These interventions have included social skills building, cognitive–behavioral approaches, assertiveness training, and social support enhancement to reduce high-risk behaviors and to enhance women's abilities to negotiate safe sex practices in their intimate relationships. Culturally grounded practices are essential in working with this population of women.

An example of empirically supported intervention designed by one of the authors is presented in detail. This psychoeducational group intervention was found to be effective in reducing depression, anxiety, and trauma and in increasing knowledge about HIV/AIDS among women inmates. The intervention is a 5-week, 10-session group design that was delivered in a jail setting. This model can be utilized by social workers working in the jail or prison system due to the efficiency and cost effectiveness of the design. While practitioners in the corrections system are often operating from a crisis case model, this intervention allows practitioners to provide mental health and psychosocial support to groups of inmates infected and affected by HIV/AIDS who might not otherwise receive care.

RESOURCES AND REFERENCES

Abel, E. M., MacIntire, S., & Dixon, R. (1994). *Evaluating the effectiveness of a jail-based intervention program for spouse abusers.* Unpublished manuscript.

Abram, K. M., Teplin, L. A., & McClelland, G. M. (2003). Comorbidity of severe psychiatric disorders and substance use disorders among women in jail. *American Journal of Psychiatry, 160,* 1007–1010.

Amaro, H., Raj, A., & Reed, E. (2001). Women's sexual health: The need for feminist analyses in public health in the decade of behavior. *Psychology of Women Quarterly, 25,* 324–334.

Anderson, B., & Farrow, J. A. (1998). Incarcerated adolescents in Washington State. *Journal of Adolescent Health, 22,* 363–367.

Anno, B. (1993). Health care for prisoners: How soon is soon enough. *JAMA, 269,* 633–634.

Aruffo, J., Coverdale, J., Chacko, R., & Dworkin, R. (1990). Knowledge about AIDS among women psychiatric outpatients. *Hospital and Community Psychiatry, 41,* 326–328.

Bacha, T., Pomeroy, E. C., & Gilbert, D. (1999). The effectiveness of a psychoeducational group for children living with HIV/AIDS: A pilot study. *Health and Social Work, 24,* 303–306.

Baillargeon, J., Black, S., Leach, C. T., Jenson, H., Pulvino, J., Bradshaw, P., et al. (2004). The infectious disease profile of Texas prison inmates. *Preventive Medicine, 38,* 607–612.

Baillargeon, J., Ducate, S., Pulvino, J., Bradshaw, P., Murray, O., & Olvera, R. (2003). The association of psychiatric disorders and HIV infection in the correctional setting. *Annals of Epidemiology, 13,* 606–612.

Bauserman, R. L., Richardson, D., Ward, M., Shea, M., Bowlin, C., Tomoyasu, N., et al. (2003). HIV prevention with jail and prison inmates: Maryland's prevention case management program. *AIDS Education and Prevention, 15*(5), 465–489.

Baxter, S. (1991). AIDS education in the jail setting. *Crime & Delinquency, 37,* 48–63.

Beck, A.J., & Harrison, P.M. (2001). Prisoners in 2000 (NCJ Publication No. 188207). Washington, DC: U.S. Department of Justice.

Biegel, D. E., Sales, E., & Schulz, R. (1991). *Family caregiving in chronic illness: Alzheimer's disease, cancer, heart disease, mental illness and stroke.* Newbury Park, CA: Sage.

Bond, L., & Semaan, S. (1996). At risk for HIV infection: Incarcerated women in county jail in Philadelphia. *Women and Health, 24,* 27–45.

Braithwaite, R., Hammet, T., & Mayberry, R. (1996). *Prison and AIDS: A public health challenge.* San Francisco: Jossey-Bass.

Bryan, A., Ruiz, M. S., & O'Neill, D. (2003). HIV-related behaviors among prison inmates: A theory of planned behavior analysis. *Journal of Applied Social Psychology, 33*(12), 2565–2586.

Bureau of Justice Statistics. (1997, August). *HIV in prisons and jails, 1995* (U.S. DOJ Publication No. NCJ 164260). Washington, DC: U.S. Government Printing Office.

Bureau of Justice Statistics (2005, June). *Criminal offender statistics.* Retrieved August 15, 2005, from http://www.ojp.usdoj.gov/bjs/crimoff.htm

Centers for Disease Control and Prevention. (1999). *CDC update: CDC's role in HIV and AIDS prevention.* Retrieved August, 15, 2005, from http:www.cdc.gov/nchstp

Centers for Disease Control and Prevention. (2005). *HIV/AIDS surveillance report 2004*. Vol. 16 Atlanta: U.S. Department of Health and Human Services, Centers for Disease Control and Prevention.

Cotton-Oldenburg, N., Jordan, B., Martin, S., & Kupper, I. (1999). Women inmates' risky sex and drug behaviors: Are they related? *American Journal of Drug and Alcohol Abuse, 25*, 129–149.

Coulson, G. E., & Nutbrown, V. (1992). Properties of an ideal rehabilitative program for high-need offenders. *International Journal of Offender Therapy and Comparative Criminology, 36*(3), 203–208.

Cournos, F., McKinnon, K., Meyer-Bahlburg, H., Guido, J., & Meyer, R. (1993). HIV risk activity among persons with severe mental illness: Preliminary findings. *Hospital and Community Psychiatry, 44*, 1104–1106.

Dean, H. D., Lansky, A., & Fleming, P. L. (2002). HIV surveillance methods for the incarcerated population. *AIDS Education and Prevention, 14*(Suppl. B), 65–70.

Dean-Gaitor, H. D., & Fleming, P. L. (1999). Epidemiology of AIDS in incarcerated persons in the United States, 1994–1996. *AIDS, 13*, 2429–2435.

Ehrmann, T. (2002). Community-based organizations and HIV prevention for incarcerated populations: Three HIV prevention models. *AIDS Education and Prevention, 14*(Suppl. B), 75–84.

El-Bassel, N., Ivanoff, A., Schilling, R., Gilbert, L., Borne, D., & Chen, D. (1995). Preventing HIV/AIDS in drug-abusing incarcerated women through skill building a social support enhancement: Preliminary outcomes. *Social Work Research, 19*, 131–141.

El-Bassel, N., Ivanoff, A., Schilling, R., Gilbert, L., Borne, D., & Chen, D. (1997). Skill building and social support enhancement to reduce HIV risk among women in jail. *Criminal Justice Behavior, 24*, 205–223.

Engle, L. (1999). It's a crime! HIV behind bars. *Body Positive, 12* (1).

Fauci, A. (1988). The human immunodeficiency virus: Infectivity and mechanisms of pathogenesis. *Science, 239*, 617–622.

Fineberg, H. V. (1988). Education to prevent AIDS: Prospects and obstacles. *Science, 239*, 592–596.

Fisher, W. A., Fisher, J. D., & Rye, B. J. (1995). Understanding and promoting AIDS-preventative behavior: Insights from the theory of reasoned action. *Health Psychology, 14*, 255–264.

Gabel, K., & Johnston, D. (1995). Children of Incarcerated Parents. New York: Lexington Books.

Gaiter, J., & Doll, L. S. (1996). Editorial: Improving HIV/AIDS prevention in prisons is good public health policy. *American Journal of Public Health, 86*(9), 1201–1203.

Griffin, E., Lurigio, A. J., & Johnson, B. R. (1991). HIV policy for probation officers: An implementation and evaluation program. *Crime & Delinquency, 37*, 36–47.

Griffin, M., Ryan, J., & Briscoe, V. (1996) Effects of incarceration on HIV-infected individuals. *National Medical Association, 88*, 639–644.

Grinstead, O., Zack, B., & Faigeles, B. (2001). Reducing post release risk behavior among HIV seropositive prison inmates: The Health Promotion Program. *AIDS Education and Prevention, 13*, 109–119.

Grinstead, O., Zack, B., Faigeles, B., Grossman, N., & Blea, L. (1999). Reducing post release risk behavior among male prison inmates. *Criminal Justice Behavior, 26*, 453–465.

Hammen, C. (1995). The social context of risk for depression. In K. Craig & K. S. Dobson (Eds.), *Anxiety and depression in adults and children* (pp. 82–99). Thousand Oaks, CA: Sage.

Hammett, T., Harmon, P., & Rhodes, W. (2002). *The burden of infectious disease among inmates and releases from correctional facilities. The health status of soon-to-be released inmates.* Chicago: National Commission on Correctional Health Care.

Hammett, T., Harrold, L., & Gross, M. (1994). *Update: HIV/AIDS and STDs in correctional facilities.* Washington, DC: National Institute of Justice and Department of Health and Human Services, Centers for Disease Control and Prevention.

Hammett, T. M. (1998). *Public health/corrections collaborations: Prevention and treatment of HIV/AIDS, STDs and TB. National Institute of Justice and Centers for Disease Control and Prevention Research in Brief,* July 1998. Washington, DC: U.S. Department of Justice, Office of Justice Programs, National Institute of Justice.

Hammett, T. M., Gaiter, J. L., & Crawford, C. (1998). Reaching seriously at-risk populations: Health interventions in criminal justice settings. *Health Education and Behavior, 25*(1), 99–120.

Hammett, T. M., Harrold, L., Gross, M., & Epstein, J. (1994). *1992 Update: HIV/AIDS in correctional facilities: Issues and options.* Washington, DC: National Institute of Justice.

Hammett, T. M., & Moini, S. (1990). *Update on AIDS in prisons and jails.* Washington, DC: National Institute of Justice.

Hammett, T. M., Rhodes, W., & Harmon, P. (1999, August 31). *HIV/AIDS and other infectious diseases among correctional inmates and releasees: A public health problem and opportunity.* Abstract presented at the National HIV Prevention Conference, Atlanta, GA.

Hammett, T. M., Widom, R., & Kerr, S. (1996, July 10). *HIV prevention in prisons and juvenile facilities: A missed "public health opportunity."* Paper presented at the XI International Conference on AIDS, Vancouver, British Columbia. Available from http://hivinsite.ucsf.edu/guide

Hanrahan, J. P., Wormser, G. P., Reilly, A. A., Maguire, B. H., Gavis, G., & Morse, D. L. (1984). Prolonged incubation period of AIDS in intravenous drug abusers: Epidemiological evidence in prison inmates. *Journal of Infectious Diseases, 150,* 262–266.

Hoffman, M. A. (1993). Multiculturalism as a force in counseling clients with HIV-related concerns. *The Counseling Psychologist, 21*(4), 712–731.

Hogben, M., & St. Lawrence, J. S. (2000). HIV/STD risk reduction interventions in prison settings. *Journal of Women's Health & Gender-Based Medicine, 9*(6), 587–592.

Hutton, H., Treisman, G., Hunt, W., Fishman, M., Kendig, N., Swetz, A., et al. (2001). HIV risk behaviors and their relationship to posttraumatic stress disorder among women prisoners. *Psychiatric Services, 52,* 508–513.

Inciardi, J. A. (1996). HIV risk reduction and service delivery strategies in criminal justice settings. *Journal of Substance Abuse Treatment, 13,* 421–428.

James, J. F., Gregory, D., Joesn, R., & Rundell, O. (1985). Mental health status of prisoners in an urban jail. *Criminal Justice and Behavior, 12,* 29–53.

Kalichman, S., Kelly, J., Johnson, J., & Bulto, M. (1994). Factors associated with risk for HIV infection among chronic mentally ill adults. *American Journal of Psychiatry, 151,* 221–227.

Kalichman, S., Sikkema, K., Kelly J., & Bulto, M. (1995). Use of a brief behavioral skills intervention to prevent HIV infection among chronic mentally ill adults. *Psychiatric Services, 46,* 275–280.

Kantor, E. (1998). *HIV transmission and prevention in prisons.* Retrieved August 20, 2001, from the AIDS Knowledge Base: http://hivinside.ucsf.edu/InSite.jsp?page=kb-07-04-13#S5X

Kelly, J., Murphy, D., Bahr, R., Brasfield, T., Davis, T., Hauth, A., et al. (1992). AIDS/HIV risk behavior among the chronically mentally ill. *Am J Psychiatry, 149,* 886–889.

Kelly, J. A., St. Lawrence, J. S., Hood, H. V., & Brasfield, T. L. (1989). Behavioral intervention to reduce AIDS risk activities. *Journal of Consulting and Clinical Psychology, 57,* 60–67.

Klein, S. J., O'Connell, D. A., Devore, B. S., Wright, L. N., & Birkhead, G. S. (2002). Building an HIV continuum for inmates: New York State's Criminal Justice Initiative. *AIDS Education and Prevention, 14*(Suppl. B), 114–123.

Krebs, C. P., & Simmons, M. (2002). Intra-prison HIV transmission: An assessment of whether it occurs, how it occurs, and who is at risk. *AIDS Education and Prevention, 14*(Suppl. B), 53–64.

Lanier, M. M., & McCarthy, B. R. (1989). AIDS awareness and the impact of AIDS education in juvenile corrections. *Criminal Justice and Behavior, 16,* 395–411.

Lanier, M. M., DiClemente, R. J., & Horan, P. (1991). HIV knowledge and behaviors of incarcerated youth: A comparison of high and low risk locales. *Journal of Criminal Justice, 19,* 257–262.

Lurigio, A. J., Petraitis, J. M., & Johnson, B. R. (1992). HIV education for probationers. *AIDS and Education and Prevention, 4,* 205–218.

Magura, S., Kang, S., & Shapiro, S. (1994). Outcomes of intensive AIDS education for male adolescent drug users in jail. *Journal of Adolescent Health, 15,* 457–463.

Maruschak, L. M. (1999). *HIV in prisons, 1997. Bureau of Justice Statistics Bulletin* (Publication No. NCJ 178284). Washington, DC: U.S. Department of Justice.

Maruschak, L. M. (2001). *HIV in prisons, 1999. Bureau of Justice Statistics Bulletin* (Publication No. NCJ 187456). Washington, DC: U.S. Department of Justice.

Maruschak, L. M. (2002). *HIV in prisons, 2000. Bureau of Justice Statistics Bulletin* (Publication No. NCJ 196023). Washington, DC: U.S. Department of Justice.

Maruschak, L. M. (2004a). *HIV in prisons, 2001. Bureau of Justice Statistics Bulletin* (Publication No. NCJ 202293). Washington, DC: U.S. Department of Justice.

Maruschak, L. M. (2004b). *HIV in prisons, 2002. Bureau of Justice Statistics Bulletin* (Publication No. NCJ 205333). Washington, DC: U.S. Department of Justice.

McClelland, G. M., Teplin, L. A., Abram, K. A., & Jacobs, N. (2002). HIV and AIDS risk behaviors among female jail detainees: Implications for public health policy. *American Journal of Public Health, 92*(5), 818–825.

Morrison, D. M., Baker, S. A., & Gillmore, M. R. (1994). Sexual risk behavior, knowledge and condom use among adolescents in juvenile detention. *Journal of Youth and Adolescence, 23,* 271–288.

Muller, R., Stark, K., Guggenmoos-Holzmann, I., Wirth, D., & Bienzle, U. (1995). Imprisonment: A risk for HIV infection counteracting education and prevention programs for intravenous drug users. *AIDS, 9*, 183–190.

Mumola, C. J. (2000). *Special report: Incarcerated parents and their children.* Washington DC: U.S. Department of Justice, Bureau of Justice Statistics.

Mutter, R. C., Grimes, R. M., & Labarthe, D. (1994). Evidence of intra-prison spread of HIV infection. *Archives of Internal Medicine, 154*, 793–795.

Nader, P., Wexler, D. B., & Patterson, T. L. (1989). Comparison of beliefs about AIDS among urban, suburban, incarcerated, and gay adolescents. *Journal of Adolescent Health Care, 10*, 413–418.

National Institute of Justice. (1994). *CDC HIV/AIDS surveillance report: U.S. HIV and AIDS cases reported through December 1994.* Washington, DC: U.S. Department of Justice, National Institute of Justice.

Parker, R. (2001). Sexuality, culture, and power in HIV/AIDS research. *Annual review of Anthropology, 30*, 163–179.

Poehlmann, J., White, T., & Bjerke, K. (2004). Integrating HIV risk reduction into family programs for women offenders: A family relationship perspective. *Family Relations, 53*, 26–37.

Polonsky, S., Kerr, S., Harris, B., Gaiter, J., Fichtner, R. R., & Kennedy, M. G. (1994). HIV prevention in prisons and jails: Obstacles and opportunities. *Public Health Reports, 109*(5), 615–625.

Pomeroy, E. C., Abel, E. M., & Kiam, R. (1998). Meeting the mental health needs of incarcerated women: A pilot study. *Health and Social Work, 23*, 71–75.

Pomeroy, E. C., & Kiam, R., & Abel, E. M. (1999). The effectiveness of a psychoeducational group for HIV-infected/affected incarcerated women. *Research on Social Work Practice, 9*, 171–187.

Pomeroy, E. C., Kiam, R., & Green, D. L. (2000). Reducing depression, anxiety and trauma of male inmates: An HIV/AIDS psychoeducational group intervention. *Social Work Research, 24*, 156–167.

Pomeroy, E. C., Rubin, A., Van Laningham, L., & Walker, R. J. (1997). Straight talk: A psychoeducational group intervention for heterosexuals with HIV/AIDS. *Research on Social Work Practice, 7*(2), 149–164.

Pomeroy, E. C., Rubin, A., & Walker, R. J. (1996). A psychoeducational task-centered group intervention for family members of persons with HIV/AIDS: Strategies for intervention. *Family Process, 35*, 299–312.

Powell-Cope, G. M., & Brown, M. A. (1992). Going public as an AIDS family caregiver. *Social Science and Medicine, 34*(5), 571–580.

Raba, J. (1983). The health status of incarcerated urban males: Results of admission screening. *Journal of Prison Jail Health, 3*(6), 6–24.

Rapposelli, K. K., Kennedy, M. G., Miles, J. R., Tinesly, M. J., Rauch, K. J., Austin, L., et al. (2002). HIV/AIDS in correctional settings: A salient priority for the CDC and HRSA. *AIDS Education and Prevention, 14*, 103–113.

Rehm, L. P. (1995). Psychotherapies for depression. In K. Craig & K. S. Dobson (Eds.), *Anxiety and depression in adults and children* (pp. 183–209). Thousand Oaks, CA: Sage.

Reid, W. J., & Epstein, L. (1972). *Task-centered casework.* New York: Columbia University Press.

Ross, P. H., & Lawrence, J. E. (1998, December). Health care for women offenders. *Corrections Today,* 124–129.

Shank, S. A. (1991). Report of the legal and civil rights subcommittee of the governor's task force on female offenders. *Governor's Office of Criminal Justice Services.*

Shelton, D. (2000). Health status of youthful offenders and their families. *Journal of Nursing Scholarship, 32*(2), 173–178.

Singer, M. Bussey, J., Song, L., & Lunghofer, L. (1995). The psychosocial issues of women serving time in jail. *Social Work, 40*, 103–113.

Snell, T. L., & Morton, D. C. (1994). *Bureau of Justice Statistics Special Report: Women in prison* (NCJ 145321). Washington, DC: U.S. Department of Justice.

Steiner, J., Lussier, R., & Rosenblatt, W. (1992). Knowledge about and risk factors in a day hospital population. *Hospital and Community Psychiatry, 43*, 734–735.

St. Lawrence, J., Elridge, G., Shelby, M., Little, C., Brasfield, T., & O'Bannon, R. (1997). HIV risk reduction for incarcerated women: A comparison of brief interventions based on two theoretical models. *Journal of Consulting and Clinical Psychology, 65*, 504–509.

Susser, E., Valencia, E., & Conover, S. (1993). Prevalence of HIV infection among psychiatric patients in a New York City men's shelter. *American Journal of Public Health, 83*, 568–570.

Thorburn, K. M. (1995). Healthcare in correctional facilities. *Western Journal of Medicine, 163*, 560–564.

U.S. Department of Justice. (1997). *Prison and jail inmates at midyear 1996* (Publication No. NCJ 162843). Washington, DC: Bureau of Justice Statistics, Office of Justice Programs.

Van Wormer, K. S. (2001). Counseling female offenders and victims: A strengths-restorative approach. New York: Springer.

Volavka, J., Convit, A., O'Donell, J., Douyon, R., Evangelista, C., & Czobor, P. (1992). Assessment of risk behaviors for HIV infection among psychiatric inpatients. *Hospital and Community Psychiatry, 43*, 482–485.

Walker, G. (1991). *In the midst of winter: Systematic therapy with families, couples, and individuals with AIDS infection.* New York: W. W. Norton.

Weisfuse, I., Greenberg, B., Back, S., Makkin, H., Tomas, P., & Rooney, W. (1991). HIV-1 infection among New York City inmates. *AIDS, 5*, 1133–1139.

Wilson, B. D. M., & Miller, R. L. (2003). Examining strategies for culturally grounded HIV prevention: A review. *AIDS Education and Prevention, 15*, 184–202.

Wodak, A., & Deslarlais, D. C. (1993). Strategies for the prevention of HIV infection among and from injecting drug users. *Bulletin on Narcotics, 45*, 47–60.

Wu, H., Baillargeon, J., Grady, J., Black, S. A., & Dunn, K. (2001). HIV seroprevalence among newly incarcerated inmates in the Texas correctional system. *Annals of Epidemiology, 11*(5), 342–346.

Yakowitz, S., Blount, M. & Gani, J. (1996). Computing marginal expectations for large compartmentalized models with application to AIDS evolution in a prison system. *IMA Journal of Mathematical Control and Information, 13*, 223-244.

Resources

National Institute of Justice
Web site: http://www.ojp.usdoj.gov/nij

Real Justice
Web site: http://www.realjustice.org

Restorative Justice in the U.S.
Web site: http://www.restorativejustice.org

Substance Abuse Treatment
Web site: http://www.harmreduction.org

Victim Offender Mediation Association
Web site: http://www.voma.org

Women and Prison in the U.S.
Web site: http://www.prisonactivist.org/women

Aftercare and Recidivism Prevention

21

Jose B. Ashford
Bruce D. Sales
Craig Winston LeCroy

P arole supervision can trace its roots to a number of correctional practices: Indenture associated with the houses of refuge and youth reformatories of the early 19th century (Ashford, 1997; Clement, 1993; Pisciotta, 1993), tickets-of-leave from Australian and Irish prison systems (Abadinsky, 1997; Cohn, 1994), indeterminate sentences (Dressler, 1959), and the supervisory release activities of prison societies such as the Philadelphia Society for Alleviating the Miseries of Public Prisons (Giardini, 1959; Hussey & Duffee, 1980; Macht & Ashford, 1991). Aftercare in mental health, on the other hand, is rooted in traditional hospital practices (French, 1940). It was a common practice in the 19th-century hospital for staff to monitor the progress of patients on trial visits with families in the community (Haines, 1920) and not release them from hospital custody until they demonstrated proper functioning in the community (Smith, 1912).

Such mental health aftercare is exemplified by the famous colony for the mentally ill in Gheel, Belgium, where patients were boarded out to families in the community who lived in cottages adjacent to the hospital (Smith, 1912). Under this system, hospitals were responsible for providing services to persons in need of restraint and other acute-oriented services, whereas nondisruptive patients were boarded out to the families (Haines, 1920). Although the nondisruptive patients were in the private care of families, they still were under the public control of hospital authorities. As Adolph Meyer (1992) pointed out, most hospitals offered some form of aftercare before the formal establishment of social casework as a special service for assisting patients in returning to the community.

What emerges from the early descriptions is a portrait of similarities and differences in the development of aftercare in corrections and mental health. As for similarities, both are concerned with the released individual not relapsing (e.g., in corrections, the released offender not recidivating; in mental health, the released patient not having an episode that would require rehospitalization). As for differences, correctional aftercare focused more on monitoring behavior than on being available to provide some community-based services to facilitate successful reintegration into the community.

The lines of development for parole for inmates and aftercare for mentally ill patients began to converge with the introduction of rehabilitation as an alternative correctional goal to punishment (Haines, 1920). By 1930, clinical models of rehabilitation were instituted that changed traditional approaches to parole supervision (Carney, 1980; Hippchen, 1978). Clinical needs and terminology began to usurp the early 19th-century correctional terminology that focused on issues of forced labor, education, and religion. Yet despite this philosophical shift, as we discuss later, implementing this philosophy never achieved that which was envisioned in its rhetoric (Duffee & Clark, 1985; Studt, 1972; Waller, 1974).

As a result, the term *aftercare* to this day means different things to different people within the correctional field. For example, some define aftercare simply in terms of whatever follows a given form of treatment. Others consider aftercare a key component of the posttreatment recovery process (National Institute of Drug Abuse [NIDA], 1993). This chapter focuses on the latter meaning and its significance for the recovery and prevention of recidivism of special-need juvenile and adult offenders.

We begin by clarifying terminology and concepts that integrate and sometimes confound social control and rehabilitation goals for services when offenders are released from juvenile and adult correctional facilities. As part of this discussion, we consider the ways in which needs are defined in the aftercare process and the ambiguity encountered in specifying appropriate goals (outcomes sought) for aftercare services to special-need offenders released from adult and juvenile correctional facilities. We next review the outcome literature on current aftercare services: (a) case management and intensive supervision, (b) psychosocial rehabilitation (e.g., supported housing and supported employment), and (c) relapse prevention. The chapter concludes with a brief discussion of the critical directions for future programmatic research on aftercare services that are needed to improve correctional outcomes and correctional–mental health interactions.

Terminology and Constructs

In juvenile justice, postrelease care from correctional settings is termed *juvenile aftercare*, which includes traditional surveillance services in combination with services designed to assist the juvenile in making a proper adjustment to the community (Ashford, 1997; Ashford & LeCroy, 1993). Although the meaning of adjustment varies within and across states, the juvenile justice system adopted the concept of aftercare to fit with its fundamental commitment to principles of treatment and rehabilitation.

The adult system adopted a concept of parole as its version of aftercare. Parole reflects the correctional system's desire to reinforce its fundamental commitment to notions of accountability, responsibility, and societal protection. Indeed, the word *parole* is derived from the French word that means taking a person on his or her word—in this case, his or her word no longer to engage in criminal activity. Over time, parole as a service emerged to monitor the offender's compliance with the conditions of parole and to assist the offender in readjusting to the community to the extent that such services purportedly would make the offender less likely to recidivate.

Despite this seeming clarity in goals for aftercare in the juvenile and adult systems, aftercare research and services are plagued by a lack of clear terminology and constructs guiding the planning and implementing of these services. This confusion has resulted because states, and jurisdictions within states, have applied different goals over time as the executive, legislative, and judicial branches of government have changed leadership and membership, goals, and views of legal and societal obligations to offenders. For example, should aftercare promote social control in the juvenile justice system or remain true to its historical rehabilitative focus? With the advent of increasing juvenile crime, there is increasing public pressure on states to focus on public safety rather than on rehabilitation when responding to juveniles who come within the purview of the justice system. Even when clinical services are provided to offenders, jurisdictions often show confusion about why the services are provided. Mental health professionals may be focusing on amelioration of pathology, whereas correctional administrators are concerned with reducing recidivism.

The Role of Needs and Goals in the Aftercare Process for Offenders With Special Needs

Questions arise about how we should determine appropriate offender needs, correctional goals (i.e., desired outcomes), and aftercare services to achieve those goals. The answers to these questions depend on whether rehabilitation is still considered an appropriate goal for the criminal justice process. When the adult and juvenile justice systems adopted the rehabilitation ideal, aftercare (parole) services were designed to meet the psychological, physical, and social needs of offenders that placed them at risk for engaging in future criminal behavior (Allen, 1977). This approach to the rehabilitation of offenders dominated correctional practices until the mid-1970s, when a number of studies (Hudson, 1973; Romig, 1978; Wheeler, 1978) indicated that persons placed on aftercare fared no better than persons without aftercare services following release from correctional institutions. The results of these studies and other shifts in criminal justice ideology (American Friends Services Committee, 1971; Martinson, 1974; Pitch, 1995) led to the eventual repudiation of rehabilitation as an appropriate goal for aftercare services.

Today aftercare is not intended to rehabilitate the ordinary offender. Most jurisdictions have shifted the focus of aftercare services from a focus on rehabilitation to a focus on control and surveillance functions (e.g., monitoring offender levels of compliance with the conditions of release), with varying degrees of emphasis on providing services to help offenders make appropriate readjustments to the community (Duffee & Clark, 1985). However, there are certain classes of offenders that are presumably in need of specialized rehabilitation services on release from correctional facilities: substance abusers, sexual offenders, mentally impaired offenders (severely and persistently mentally ill and mentally retarded offenders), and violent offenders (Blackburn, 1996; Clear, Byrne, & Dvoskin, 1993; Henderson & Bell, 1995; Home Office, 1987). These categories of offenders require specialized aftercare services because it is assumed that they have distinct need configurations that influence their relapse potential and likelihood of making a positive adjustment to the community. The first chapter in this book explores different conceptions of offender needs in the criminal justice process; for this reason, it is not necessary to review the controversies plaguing the establishment of clear boundaries between the special and the ordinary needs of offenders. It is enough to say that part of the problem in creating specialized aftercare services for offenders with special needs is the lack of a universally agreed-on definition of offender needs (Andrews & Bonta, 1998; Clements, 1996; Duffee & Clark, 1985; Duffee & Duffee, 1981).

In addition to defining offender needs and special needs to develop appropriate programming for special-need offenders released from correctional facilities, these definitions need to match appropriate clinical and correctional goals and outcomes. To this end, Heilbrun et al. (1988) argued that mental health professionals must treat separately both clinical and criminal targets in designing effective interventions for mentally disordered offenders. Even though their views are consistent with traditional models of rehabilitation, newer developments in mental health services research stress the interaction of services over the use of disease-specific or problem-specific models of intervention. That is, newer models of rehabilitation (Anderson, 1997; Liberman, 1988; Minkoff, 1991; Ragins, 1997) assert that the cure of a clinical pathology and recovery of a noncriminal lifestyle must be pursued concurrently.

This philosophical approach differs substantially from the older models of rehabilitation that stress (a) pursuing a cure of the clinical conditions beforehand and (b) developing recovery strategies (Ragins, 1997). It operates on the assumption that relapse often has less to do with the illness process than with factors relating to the patient's quality of life. In other words, current technology in the field of aftercare is adhering to conceptions of recovery that have expanded the targets for intervention to include other factors besides monitoring symptom and side-effect profiles. Outcomes relevant to recidivism and other psychosocial variables are now assigned a more prominent role in relapse prevention than was previously true of earlier approaches to psychiatric rehabilitation.

In the following sections, we examine aftercare services with some demonstrated effectiveness in preventing relapse and recidivism in populations of offenders with special needs. These services target the clinical and psychosocial needs of offenders with known significance for preventing relapse in clinical populations and recidivism in offenders with special needs. Aftercare technology in corrections has not always responded to the diverse needs of offenders in the justice system. Persons with ordinary and special needs often receive similar aftercare regimens. We begin our examination of aftercare services by analyzing alternative models of supervision for offenders with serious and persistent mental disorders. Persons diagnosed with serious mental disorders have additional outcomes that cannot be ignored in selecting appropriate kinds of supervision in the community.

Supervising Offenders With Serious and Persistent Mental Impairments

Relapse of released persons with mental disorders has been the bane of mental health professionals (Bachrach, 1978; Solomon, Gordon, & Davis, 1984) since the initial recommendations of the Joint Commission on Mental Illness and Health (1961) on aftercare and rehabilitation of mental patients. Most mental health professionals see behavioral and mental state relapse requiring a hospital or correctional facility readmission as an aftercare failure. To avoid such relapse for seriously mentally ill offenders, community-based treatment must be part of aftercare. Yet part of the difficulty in implementing such treatment is the limits placed by managed care on public sector mental health care (Stroup & Dorwart, 1997) in general. This dilemma is exacerbated in correctional aftercare because existing systems of public sector care are obligated to address the complex needs of persons with serious and persistent mental illness (SPMI) who also present with criminogenic needs.

The seriousness of the relapse problem in noncorrectional mental health care has been documented. Numerous studies have shown that one third of hospital admissions of psychiatric patients are in fact readmissions (Glasscote, Cumming, Rutman, Sussex, & Glassman, 1971; Solomon, Gordon, & Davis, 1984). Many patients cycle in and out of hospitals because of problems with aftercare resources in the community (Klinkenberg & Calsyn, 1996). This information is relevant to our discussion because many of these patients also have criminal and substance abuse histories that contribute to their adjustment difficulties.

To cope with the needs of person with SPMI, and in an attempt to address the relapse problem, case management strategies have been instituted to assist patients released from hospitals (Bachrach, 1986; Hawthorne & Hough, 1997; Stein & Santos, 1998; Stein & Test, 1980). Moreover, case management and psychosocial rehabilitation are viewed as key foundations for the development of an effective community support system for persons with serious mental health impairments (Anthony & Blanch, 1989; Hawthorne & Hough, 1997; Stroul, 1989).

Review of Current Aftercare Services

Case Management Services

Case management is designed to assist persons with SPMI in gaining access to existing community services, rather than relying on emergency services and psychiatric hospitals as most mentally ill persons discharged from hospitals in large cities tend to do (Bond, McDonel, Miller, & Pensec, 1991; Stein & Santos, 1998). Therefore, the primary goal of case management is to increase the probability that patients receive the appropriate services when they need them (Reinhardt & Shepherd, 1994). "In particular, the case manager assumes the responsibility for identifying and recommending for the patient those services that he or she believes will most effectively and efficiently return the patient to the expected level of functioning" (Reinhardt & Shepherd, 1994, p. 79).

Case management is not a new concept. It has been viewed as a useful process for the coordination of services for more than a century (Moxley, 1997; Weil, Karls, & Associates, 1985; Zander, 1995). Since the 1960s, case management witnessed increased popularity in human services because of (a) financial pressures to increase the use of particular services for specific populations with specific needs, for limited periods of time, which contributed to the formation of large networks of complex, fragmented, and uncoordinated services for highly specialized groups; and (b) the deinstitutionalization movement (Intagliata, 1982). Within this rapidly changing services environment, networks of services lacked the kinds of coordination needed to ensure quality of care. Fragmented systems of care were particularly burdensome for persons with serious mental impairments who had been previously treated in institutional settings (Intagliata, 1982; President's Panel on Mental Retardation, 1962).

In response to this situation, case management emerged as a fundamental strategy for improving the continuity of care for persons discharged from mental health and mental retardation facilities, even though case management "can simultaneously be described as a system, a role, a technology, a process and a service" (Bower, 1992, p. 2). The continuity of care objective is achieved by a process that involves five basic functions: (a) assessment of client need; (b) development of a services or treatment plan; (c) arrangement and linkage of the person to existing, available services; (d) monitoring of service delivery; and (e) evaluation and follow-up to determine whether the services are achieving the intended goals (Intagliata, 1982; Moxley, 1997; Rose & Moore, 1995). Some case management models include other functions, such as advocacy for client needs (Henderson & Bell, 1995). Advocacy can be implemented in different ways depending on the model of case management under consideration. For example, consumer-oriented approaches to case management handle advocacy differently than systems-oriented approaches (Rose & Moore, 1995). That is, "these functions may be implemented in different ways, depending on the mission of the case management program, so that, for example, programs with administrative missions implement assessment in a gatekeeping fashion while consumer-driven programs engage in assessment through the identification of client wants and strengths" (Moxley, 1997, p. 55).

It is not surprising therefore that the case management process contains a number of inherent tensions and ambiguities surrounding the responsibilities of case managers. "Is the primary responsibility of the case manager to the client, or to the system? Should the case manager be primarily concerned with the efficient use of resources or with the creation of a high quality, individually tailored service?" (Shepherd, 1990, p. 168). These dilemmas increase when case managers are also dealing with issues of public safety and criminal recidivism.

In corrections, there have been a number of approaches to case management, including the formation of community resource management teams. In this, as well as in other approaches to correctional case management, the case manager or team is considered a broker of services and not a provider of direct services (Henderson & Bell, 1995; Spica, 1993). In fact, this is often necessitated because some states do not require field officers, who constitute these teams, to be mental health professionals. Thus, very few correctional agencies see field officers as having the necessary expertise for actually treating offenders with special needs. Even where field officers have social work training, in many jurisdictions today they are no longer expected to use one-to-one principles of casework in responding to offender needs (Henderson & Bell, 1995). This points out an important tension in the case management literature surrounding the roles of case managers. "Are they simply there to link clients to services in a rather bureaucratic, administrative way, as a kind of therapeutic support?" (Shepherd, 1990, p. 169).

Although the debate can be decided politically or by financial exigencies, the choice of which aftercare model to use should be informed by the research literature in aftercare services. For example, broker–of–service approaches to case management has also played a significant role in treating patients with serious mental illness and has been studied in those contexts. The results have been high rates of recidivism among discharged mental patients, which in turn have stimulated a number of experiments in offering alternatives to traditional broker-of-service models. The most widely researched of these approaches is the assertive community treatment (ACT) or the assertive case management model (Stein & Santos, 1998).

ACT differs from traditional broker-of-services models in that it actively tries to help the client (a) obtain material resources to survive in the community; (b) develop coping skills for dealing with the day-to-day requirements of community life; (c) develop a system of support to motivate him or her to remain involved in community life; (d) free him- or herself from relationships that promoted pathological forms of dependency; and (e) learn to relate appropriately to relevant community individuals including family, landlords, and police (Stein & Test, 1980). Thus, ACT provides intensive case support services and is not considered just a human link between the client and a system of services; case management functions are implemented by a team of professionals who share caseloads and who are on call 24 hours per day (Bond et al., 1991; Stein & Santos, 1998). Members of the team have a comprehensive level of responsibility for the individualized treatment of clients in their homes, neighborhoods, and work settings (Intagliata, 1982; Morse et al., 1997). This obligation even entails members of the team assisting clients in daily living activities "such as laundry upkeep, shopping, cooking, restaurant use, grooming, budgeting, and use of transportation" (Stein & Test, 1980, p. 393).

Thus, an important aim of ACT is to improve the quality of a client's life by teaching practical living skills in the natural environment (Duffy & Wong, 1996). When clients do not show up for work or encounter other problems in their daily lives, staff are expected to be assertive in responding to these situations. As Stein and Test (1980) pointed out,

> the program must be assertive, involve patients in their treatment, and be prepared to go to the [client] . . . to prevent drop out. It must also actively insure continuity of care among treatment agencies rather than assume that a [client] . . . will successfully negotiate the often difficult pathways from one agency to another on his own. (p. 293)

ACT also includes the careful monitoring of client symptoms and medical status and relies heavily on the use of low staff–client ratios. This allows team members to help the client find a job or a sheltered work environment and to intervene in a client's job-related problems (Stein & Test, 1980). The case management team also aids the client in learning to use leisure time appropriately and to develop social skills. Because the team is assertive in each of a client's life domains, ACT clients are exposed to a more intensive system of support and treatment than is presumed likely in traditional broker-of-services models of case management.

There are similar movements in the field of community corrections involving increases in the intensity of supervision of persons on conditional release from correctional facilities (e.g., intensive parole supervision and intensive aftercare programs [IAPs]). Both of these movements in intensive case management are confronting, however, important empirical questions. Are intensive case management models effective in achieving complex clinical and behavioral treatment objectives, and how do their outcomes compare with those achieved with traditional models of case management?

One source of information to answer these questions comes from the sizeable body of research that has demonstrated the utility of intensive case management in "facilitating continuity, reducing fragmentation, making appropriate services available, and providing a trusting, consistent relationship for the client with SPMI" (Hawthorne & Hough, 1997, p. 207). This includes several experimental studies that demonstrated that ACT, compared to traditional aftercare, significantly reduces psychiatric inpatient usage (Bond, Miller, Krumwied, & Ward, 1988; Borland, McRae, & Lycan, 1989; Lipton, Nutt, & Sabitini, 1988; Stein & Test, 1980). When ACT clients were compared to a sample of clients receiving services at drop-in centers, ACT clients had fewer state hospital admissions (Bond et al., 1990). When ACT patients were admitted to a hospital, they also required fewer days per admission than participants who received only drop-in center services. Bond and colleagues (1990) also uncovered other benefits. ACT clients reported fewer contacts with police, increased overall program participation, and greater satisfaction with their program than participants receiving the services provided by the drop-in center. Bond et al. (1990) also found that ACT saved more than $1,500 per client. In spite of the fact that findings are mixed regarding cost savings (Curtis, Millman, Streuning, & D'Ercole, 1992; Franklin, Solovitz, Mason, Clemons, & Miller, 1987; Rosenheck, Neale, Leaf, Milstein, & Frishman, 1995; Rossler, Loffler, Fatkenheuer, & Reicher-Rossler, 1992), most research has consistently documented that ACT programs do reduce use of inpatient psychiatric facilities (Olfson, 1990; Rosenheck et al., 1995).

The use of ACT with homeless subpopulations of persons also reveals some promising results. Morse and colleagues (1997) examined three types of case management to determine their relative effectiveness in treating persons with serious mental illness who were homeless or at risk of homelessness. Their study randomly assigned individuals recruited from a psychiatric emergency room to three treatment conditions:

> Broker case management, in which the client's needs were assessed, services were purchased from multiple providers, and the client was monitored; assertive community treatment only, in which comprehensive services were provided for an unlimited period; and assertive community treatment augmented by support from community workers, who assisted in activities of daily living and were available for leisure activities. (Morse et al., 1997, p. 497)

The results of this study indicated that ACT is more effective than brokered case management in providing patients with better program outcomes.

Morse and his colleagues (1997) also found that, compared to brokered case management, patients in ACT achieved more days in stable housing and demonstrated superior outcomes in the area of psychiatric symptoms. However, Morse and his colleagues (1997) did not find that ACT influenced clients' income and abuse of substances. Overall, ACT was more successful than brokered case management in ensuring that clients received intensive levels of services but not necessarily in increasing clients' functioning in all relevant domains of life functioning.

Case management researchers have also examined the relative effectiveness of team and individual caseload approaches to reducing hospital use. Bond and his colleagues (1991) studied the relative efficacy of the individual and team approaches to intensive case management in reducing use of hospitals by patients with a history of frequent use.

The results indicated that team approaches proved more effective over time in reducing hospital use than individual approaches.

ACT has also been evaluated in treating young adults suffering from serious mental illness and substance abuse problems. Bond et al. (1991) examined outcomes for mentally ill substance abusers who were assigned to two different experimental groups (ACT or reference groups [RGs]) and a control group. The RGs were comprised of clients who received four substance abuse group sessions per week led by an RG worker for a specified period of time. The control group received traditional community mental health services. The results indicated that treatment engagement was greater for RG clients and ACT clients than control clients. However, RG clients were significantly lower in the number of hospitalizations than either ACT or control individuals, although ACT patients had significantly lower numbers of hospital days than RG and controls. Finally, unlike other studies, this study found that ACT and RG clients had higher ratings on measures of quality of life than controls, although no significant differences among groups was evident on measures of employment, time in jail, residential status, and residential moves.

Although results of research on ACT with various subgroups in the SPMI population are demonstrating significant promise (e.g., in reducing hospital use), "long-term outcome data documenting improved quality-of-life and functioning are scarce" (Hawthorne & Hough, 1997, p. 207). "Doubts have also been voiced about generalizability of previous studies in support of ACT programs because they were well-funded research/demonstration projects executed by ideologically committed leaders in the field" (Rosenheck et al., 1995, p. 129).

Intensive case management (like ACT) with offenders with serious mental impairments has been subjected, however, to less empirical scrutiny. One noteworthy exception is the randomized trial of case management approaches applied to SPMI clients leaving jails (Solomon & Draine, 1995). Persons leaving jails present a number of special problems for community mental health systems. Their living situations are often more tenuous than other groups of SPMI patients, and they typically are at increased risk for homelessness and reincarceration (Solomon & Draine, 1995). Solomon and Draine randomly assigned 200 inmates from a large urban city jail to one of three conditions: an ACT team, forensic specialist case managers located in community mental health agencies, and the usual referral to a community mental health center. The researchers predicted that offenders receiving case management services would have better psychosocial and clinical outcomes than offenders receiving traditional mental health services. However, they did not find any significant differences among these three conditions. Solomon and Draine (1995) pointed out that we should be cautious in interpreting these results, however, because of the serious lack of fidelity to all aspects of the ACT model noted in how the team implemented the ACT case management supervision returned to jail during the follow-up period. If case management increases the use of jails to control treatment noncompliance, is this a positive outcome in the treatment of persons with chronic disturbances and long histories of treatment resistance?

Part of the problem may lie with the behaviors of the mentally disordered offenders (MDOs) other than treatment noncompliance. Feder (1991b) found in a study of the postrelease and adjustment of MDOs that non-MDOs were more likely than MDOs to have had their parole revoked; however, mentally disordered offenders were more likely than non-MDOs to have committed technical violations. This and other findings (Heilbrun & Griffin, 1993) suggest that MDOs encounter significant difficulties in complying with many of the conditions of parole and other forms of postrelease supervision (Jacoby & Kozie-Peak, 1997). Yet some studies do indicate that appropriate supports can reduce the jail time of mentally ill offenders following release from correctional settings (Wilson, Tien, & Eaves, 1995). However, there are no studies in the literature that have used appropriate comparison groups or adequate sample sizes that would allow for reasonable conclusions about the effectiveness of using specialized support services with MDOs on measures involving positive social adjustment, improvements in quality of life, and recidivism.

Supervising the Other Categories of Special-Need Offenders

Intensive supervision programs (ISPs) have increased in the fields of probation and parole "to manage some special needs of offenders, particularly sex offenders, violent offenders and substance abusers" (Henderson & Bell, 1995, p. 69). A few of these programs incorporate principles of case management derived from the ACT model of care for the SPMI (Martin & Inciardi, 1997). These programs are founded on the assumption that there is a strong correlation between participation in various forms of treatment and levels of recidivism (Fulton & Stone, 1993; Palmer, 1996). That is, if treatment and services are increased for offenders with special needs, then it will reduce recidivism while increasing rehabilitation (Turner, Petersilia, & Deschenes, 1992). Other models of ISPs attempt to increase the monitoring of substance abusers, violent offenders, and sex offenders in all areas of their environment by increasing levels of offender surveillance (Cullen, Wright, & Applegate, 1996; Greer, 1991). "The close monitoring that is part of ISPs provides the control needed for offenders prone to violence" (Henderson & Bell, 1995, p. 72). In other words, ISPs also assume that many offenders with special needs require increased monitoring because of the relationship between their mental impairments or disabilities and lowered inhibitions.

Offenders with substance abuse problems are overwhelming the criminal justice system. Langan and Cunniff (1992) estimated that more than 3 million persons on probation and parole have some form of drug abuse problem. In response to this situation, there is a growing body of literature (Anglin & Hser, 1990; Falkin, Lipton, & Wexler, 1992) that indicates that treatment of drug-abusing offenders can reduce recidivism whether treatment is voluntary or under some form of coercion. Because the problems of substance-abusing offenders are never completely cured, they require various levels of support and supervision in the community for extended periods of time. Although the importance of this form of aftercare is well recognized in the substance abuse treatment literature, aftercare services continue to be inadequate in many service systems (Prendergast, Anglin, & Wellisch, 1995).

Aftercare is also considered an important component of any ISP for monitoring serious juvenile offenders (Goodstein & Sontheimer, 1997). The field of juvenile aftercare or parole has witnessed a marked increase in experiments in intensive aftercare supervision (IAS; Ashford, 1997). A number of these experiments were funded by the Violent Juvenile Offender Research and Development Program (VJO) of the Office of Juvenile Justice and Delinquency Prevention. Unlike many of the early experiments with adult ISPs, the juvenile programs had a much stronger emphasis on treatment and rehabilitation because of the juvenile justice system's primary orientation to principles of rehabilitation (Goodstein & Sontheimer, 1997).

The VJO's approach to aftercare for juveniles has stressed the following themes: social networking, social learning, provision of opportunities, and goal-oriented interventions (Armstrong, 1991; Palmer, 1991). The program has relied on notions of continuous case management, diagnostic assessment, job training skills, placement in work settings, and individual and family counseling to transform the program's pivotal conceptual themes into practice (Ashford, 1997). Palmer (1991) has provided a succinct summary of this project:

> In each of the four test sites that met the minimum participation standards—Boston, Memphis, Newark, and Detroit—program clients...were first placed for an average of six months in "small secure facilities." After that, they were "reintegrated to the community through transitional facilities via a community based residence." This stage was followed by intensive supervision, e.g., frequent contacts in small caseloads, "upon return to neighborhoods." (p. 103)

Each field officer or aftercare worker maintains a case load of between six to eight youths in the identified VJO programs.

The Paint Creek Youth program in Ohio is another experiment for serious delinquent offenders implemented by a private facility. Youths are placed in their parental homes, an independent living setting, or a group home after they are released from the facility. Regardless of their housing arrangement, the youths are placed on house arrest "for the first two weeks but are allowed free movement to attend school, participate in treatment, or go to work" (Ashford, 1997, p. 41). Before youths can be discharged, they must have attended either school or work on a regular basis. The field officers maintain two face-to-face contacts with youths on aftercare status. Other programs with similar caseload and surveillance features are being implemented in other jurisdictions across the United States (Armstrong, 1991). Many of them have structures, however, that focus primarily on achieving community protection and not rehabilitation.

The trend toward ISPs in adult and juvenile community corrections grew dramatically during the 1980s (Cullen et al., 1996). Much of this work was stimulated by early reports of success with experiments with intensive supervision for adults in Georgia and in New Jersey. These programs placed significant emphasis on the use of punitive approaches to the design of offender supervision (Pearson, 1988). The ISPs in Georgia and in New Jersey were also prison-diversion or prison-reduction programs. The aim was to use the ISP as a community alternative for persons eligible for incarceration in prison. The initial evaluation of the Georgia program reported that ISP participants had a reincarceration rate of 16% (Erwin, 1986). However, this initial evaluation of the Georgia program was challenged on a number of methodological grounds by Byrne, Lurigo, and Baird (1989). In particular, they noted stark differences in the levels of comparability between the ISP and control groups.

Initial evaluations of the New Jersey program also pointed to the effectiveness of ISP programs in reducing recidivism (Pearson, 1988). However, the New Jersey study also was criticized for lacking comparable groups in its evaluation design. For this reason, the National Institute of Justice funded the RAND Corporation in Santa Monica, California, to use an improved experimental design to study 14 ISPs in nine different states (Cullen et al., 1996). In this study, offenders were randomly assigned to ISP, probation, parole, or prison. The results indicated that most ISPs were effective in increasing their surveillance and control functions. That is, ISPs have delivered on their promise of increased officer contact with offenders. However, the RAND results about the potential of ISPs to reduce recidivism were not as promising. Offenders assigned to ISP programs had higher arrests (37%) than controls (33%). But recidivism outcomes were improved when increased attention was devoted to providing "higher quality and quantity of treatment, as opposed to emphasizing surveillance and control" (Palmer, 1996, p. 145). That is, "the RAND researchers did detect significant reductions in rearrest for those who participated in treatment programs" (Cullen et al., 1996, p. 87). In fact, ISP participants in treatment in California and Texas had 10% to 20% decreases in recidivism (Petersilia & Turner, 1993). These findings suggest that by giving attention to other aspects of rehabilitation technology, besides recent developments in areas of control and surveillance, we can significantly reduce the levels of recidivism of offenders in need of other forms of treatment. Moreover, although Byrne and Pattavian (1992) concluded from a review of the literature that most evaluations of ISP programs do not "support the notion that intensive supervision significantly reduces the risk of offender recidivism" (p. 296), this may be true only of programs that place minimal attention on providing services that are responsive to significant offender needs.

Altschuler and Armstrong (1990) reviewed IAPs for serious juvenile offenders. They found that the literature lacked a significant body of studies that would allow for reliable conclusions about the effectiveness of IAS programs. Findings from studies by Barton and Butts (1990) and Fagen, Forst, and Vivoam (1988), which adhered to appropriate methodological requirements, support the conclusion that IAS programs are at least as effective as standard approaches (Palmer, 1996). However, "recent experiments in juvenile intensive aftercare and probation have directed equal attention to the close monitoring of severely delinquent juvenile offenders and the provision of specialized services to them" (Altschuler & Armstrong, 1990, p. 3). Such IAPs are demonstrating increased success when social control is combined with increased attention to service and rehabilitation (Altschuler & Armstrong, 1990).

Unfortunately, however, the research is not consistent in its findings. Greenwood, Deschenes, and Adams (1993) evaluated a program of IAPs for high-risk delinquents in Detroit and Pittsburgh. "Youths assigned to the experimental programs were supposed to be released from their residential placement two months early and to receive the intensive aftercare supervision for the next six months" (Greenwood et al., 1993, p. ix). Participation in this program did not significantly affect key behavioral outcomes. That is, researchers did not find significant differences between experimental and control groups in the proportion of youths arrested, in the proportion of self-reported offenses, or in the proportion of drug use. In addition, participation in the experimental group was not found to have any effect on the involvement of youths in work or school. It is hard to be convinced by this study because it did not provide a key causal factor for success in such programs—a clearly conceptualized model for psychosocial rehabilitation.

Psychosocial Rehabilitation Services

Persons with SPMI in the criminal justice system experience serious functional incapacities and role performance difficulties that require a broad range of rehabilitation services. The term *rehabilitation*, initially borrowed from the field of physical medicine, originally incorporated the use of a two-stage process: "(1) treating the symptoms of someone who has become physically disabled, such as by drugs and physiotherapy; and (2) then helping the person to make a relatively permanent adaptation to their environment, such as by providing ramps or a wheelchair" (Ekdawi & Conning, 1994, p. 16). In psychiatric rehabilitation, the interaction of the person with his or her environment is also important, but the primary focus is on the social rather than the physical environment (Watts & Bennett, 1983). According to Wing (1990), professionals are more likely to be on common ground in the field of rehabilitation if their aims are geared to preventing "social disablement by dealing with its major components—disease, disability, disadvantage and demoralization or distress" (Wing, 1990, p. 93). Wing's (1990) view is consistent with newer models of psychiatric and psychosocial rehabilitation (Ekdawi & Conning, 1994; Liberman, 1988; Sperry, Brill, Howard, & Grissom, 1996).

The new generation of models for psychosocial rehabilitation for persons with SPMI adopted the principles of the World Health Organization (Anthony, 1993, p. 12). These models provide an orientation to rehabilitation that assumes that mental disorders cause other negative consequences besides mental impairments or symptoms (e.g., dysfunctions, disabilities, and handicaps) and that these consequences can benefit from rehabilitation services (Anthony, 1993; Liberman, 1988).

When a person has a disorder that impairs the ability to perform a specific task, it is referred to as a *dysfunction* in the rehabilitation literature (Anthony, 1993). A dysfunction includes any restrictions or deficits in a person's ability to perform any activity or task. Examples of dysfunctions commonly seen in persons with SPMI include deficits in self-care skills such as cooking, cleaning, grooming, and other significant daily life activities (Liberman, 1988). Disability refers to all barriers to a person's ability to perform various social roles. According to Gruenberg (1967), who initially formulated the concept of the social breakdown syndrome, disability was only partly influenced by intrinsic impairments. The extrinsic environment includes many factors that contribute to the formation of barriers that place individuals at a relative position of disadvantage to others in society in performing social roles (Bennett, 1983). Today this is referred to in the rehabilitation literature as a *handicap*. Handicaps are the last in a series of consequences of mental disorders that the current rehabilitation model is designed to change (Liberman, 1988).

Most psychosocial rehabilitation approaches to ameliorating dysfunctions, disabilities, and handicaps include a modified conceptualization of recovery, which defines recovery differently from traditional medical models that stress cure as the targeted outcome (Ekdawi & Conning, 1994). The newer psychosocial rehabilitation approaches "conceptualize recovery more in terms of function than pathology" (Ragins, 1997, p. 2). That is, it is not accurate to assume that persons with mental disorders will be restored to their premorbid state. Although disabilities might remain, it is presumed that the dysfunctions and handicaps can be changed. Recovery involves, therefore, "a deeply personal, unique process of changing one's attitudes, values, feelings, goals, skills and/or roles" (Anthony, 1993, p. 15). In other words, it includes many other forms of change beyond recovery from the illness:

> People with mental illness may have to recover from stigma they have incorporated into their very being; from the iatrogenic effects of treatment settings; from lack of recent opportunities for self-determination; from the negative side effects of unemployment; and from crushed dreams. Recovery is often a complex, time-consuming process. (Anthony, 1993, p. 15)

The need for these forms of change also confronts offenders who must adjust to the negative consequences of their incarceration regardless of whether they have additional special needs (Waller, 1974).

Helping people gain or regain skills and resources needed to live an effective life in the community, which is the focus of current rehabilitation technology, is a complex goal because mental disorders affect many domains of life relevant to a person's functioning in the community. These include "activities of daily living, social skills, ability to manage money, social supports, work skills, life satisfaction, family relationships, burden to family members, use of leisure time, physical health care and personal safety" (Dickerson, 1997, p. 898). Skills training is used to remedy dysfunctions in the social, family, and vocational domains. When skills training is limited by the effects of a disorder, the goals of rehabilitation shift to assisting released patients in compensating for their deficits by locating supportive living and work environments (Liberman, 1988). Supportive living and work environments need to be integrated with other rehabilitation technology to prevent relapse of persons with SPMI, substance abuse, violence, sexual deviations, and other special needs.

Supported Housing

There is scarce information in the research literature on the community adjustment of offenders who had required psychiatric hospitalization while in prison (Feder, 1991a), although there is some information on other categories of MDOs (Bogenberger, Pasewark, Gudeman, & Bierber, 1987; Pacht & Cowden, 1974; Rogers & Wettsetin, 1984; Sturgeon & Taylor, 1980). Yet in general it is known that good housing is an essential component for community rehabilitation because it is highly correlated with a number of measures of successful community adjustment (Ogilvie, 1997). Unfortunately, offenders with mental disorders often lack viable housing alternatives that can promote their adjustment in the community following release from correctional facilities. Regardless which category of MDO is studied, available research indicates that they are provided minimal support from family or friends when they are released back to the community (Feder, 1991a, 1991b; Jacoby & Kozie-Peak, 1997). Because they also typically have had extensive histories of marginal social existence before their contacts with the criminal justice system, these offenders generally require some form of assistance with housing on release from correctional settings.

A position statement of the National Association of State Mental Health Program Directors (NASMHPD) asserts that people with serious psychiatric disabilities should have "the option of living in decent stable, affordable, safe housing, fully integrated in the community that maximizes their independence, where they have made the choice and that is coordinated by all key stakeholders" (Ogilvie, 1997, p. 20). Typically, this requires supported housing, which is any form of coordinated housing that complies with these key characteristics identified in the NASMHPD position statement.

Supported housing is considered an important alternative to the traditional forms of residential aftercare described by Budson (1988): transitional halfway houses, long-term group residences, cooperative apartments, lodge programs, work camps, foster care (family care), and board and care homes. These traditional residential services provide consumers a place to live that is not per se "a home in the context of a supportive community" (Telles, 1992, p. 53). That is, in addition to housing and mental health services, supportive housing offers consumers options for sharing a house or an apartment in a supportive social network (consisting primarily of consumers and staff) that will eventually become their permanent system of social support. This social network is also flexible in that the level of social interaction among community participants is determined by the consumers and not by the residential program (Telles, 1992).

Another distinctive characteristic of supported housing is that tenants have the right "to refuse a reasonable number of prospective roommates before financial and other considerations take precedence over their wishes" (Telles, 1992, p. 61). The emphasis is to be placed in the philosophy of supported housing on increasing the choices available to consumers in selecting roommates and other levels of social support in the community, which is what distinguishes this form of housing from other traditional residential aftercare programming (Carling, 1990; Telles, 1992).

The research on supported housing consistently documents that persons living in the worst residential environments are the least likely to have their services met and typically experience increased rates of hospitalization (Ogilvie, 1997). In fact, many studies indicate lower rates of hospitalization for persons receiving supported housing (McCarthy & Nelson, 1991; Rimmerman, Finn, Schnee, & Klein, 1991). Other studies (e.g., Srebnik, Livingston, Gordon, & King, 1995) have documented that consumer choice in housing is positively associated with measures of client satisfaction and personal happiness. In addition, supported housing appears to be associated with having a positive effect on the social networks of patients (Giering et al., 1992) and tends to increase patient levels of independent functioning (Nelson, Hall, & Walsh-Bower, 1998). As might be expected, the influence of the housing program diminishes as support and supervision are reduced, which opens the door for community influences to take over.

Supported Employment

Work has been recognized as an essential prescription for happiness and recovery from mental illness throughout human history (Western Interstate Commission for Higher Education, 1997). It was a key component of the moral treatment developed by Philippe Pinel in the early 1800s. In addition, "Noted authorities such as Rush, Freud and Kraepelin provided support for the role of work in treatment and rehabilitation" (Jacobs, 1988, p. 247). There also has been a long-standing connection between crime and the lack of a regular means for earning a living. Currie (1985) observed a consistent trend that documents this point in the criminological literature from the 1800s to the present. Most of the studies that he reviewed indicated that large percentages of individuals incarcerated in prisons and jails were either without an established occupation or were not working full time in the months before their arrests. In his view, because work is one of the most important ways for individuals to achieve integration in the wider society, "It isn't surprising that those excluded from the world of work will be held less tightly by the bonds that keep a society together" (Currie, 1985, p. 105). Exclusion from work is also highly correlated with "an increase in the incidence of physical and mental illness, asocial behavior, marital problems, and other distress following job loss" (Jacobs, 1988, p. 246).

Although work is included at some level in most measures of quality of life, individuals with serious mental impairments have significant difficulties with obtaining and maintaining employment (Jacobs, 1988; Watts, 1983). In the 1970s, when interest in work rehabilitation regained the attention of the professional community, less than 30% of discharged patients were able to obtain a job (Anthony, Buell, Sharrat, & Althoff, 1972; Watts, 1983). This triggered a number of studies that investigated factors that can predict posthospitalization employment. Many of these studies found that the best predictor was prehospital work history (Jacobs, 1988; Watts, 1983). These and other findings called into question the effectiveness of hospital-based vocational rehabilitation, which was the dominant approach to work restoration at the time.

On the other hand, vocational programs in well-known community rehabilitation centers such as Fountain House of New York (Beard, Malmud, & Rossman, 1978) showed high success rates. The Fountain House program used employment as a central approach to help discharged mental patients adjust to the community (Jacobs, 1988). The results of research in these rehabilitation centers renewed interest in supported employment as a rehabilitation tool. Supported employment clients work for pay in competitive contexts.[1] "Clients work for pay, preferably the prevailing wage rate, as regular employees in integrated settings, and in regular contact with nonhandicapped workers and receive ongoing support" (Bond, Drake, Museser, & Becker, 1997, p. 336). Before the supported employment movement in psychiatric and vocational rehabilitation, most individuals with SPMI worked in nonintegrated or noncompetitive work settings because of myths about schizophrenia (Harding & Zahniser, 1995). For instance, it was widely believed in psychiatric rehabilitation that persons with schizophrenia could only work in low-level positions for short intervals of time. Moreover, it was believed that only about 15% or fewer were able to work in competitive employment. But work prospects for the SPMI changed dramatically in the 1980s.

In the 1980s, supported employment was formally defined in the Rehabilitation Act of 1986 (revised in 1992). This act attempted to provide increased flexibility in developing alternatives to traditional vocational rehabilitation (Bond et al., 1997). It was initially pilot tested with persons with development disabilities as an alternative to the use of sheltered workshops. These pilot tests adhered to a novel approach to vocational rehabilitation that stressed placement before training (Wehman, 1981). Persons were successfully placed in positions with job coaches at the work site. The coaches provided intensive training for the clients to accomplish their job roles. Today, the job coach model is a dominant component of most supported employment programs. Other common components include "a goal of competitive employment, minimal screening for employability, avoidance of prevocational training, individualized placement instead of placement in enclaves or mobile work crews, time unlimited support, and consideration for client preferences" (Bond et al., 1997, p. 336).

As to supported employment, Bond and his colleagues (1997) identified six experimental studies, six descriptive studies, three surveys, and one study that used a quasi-experimental design. All of these identified significant gains in obtaining employment by patients who were participants in supported employment programs. That is, these programs are capable of helping former patients obtain employment in a competitive marketplace. For the available experimental studies, 58% of the supported employment clients were able to achieve competitive employment compared with 21% of the control clients. The results of these experiments also support the conclusion that clients in supported employment spend a longer time in employment and experience increased earnings compared to control individuals. These results suggest that supportive employment programs are a promising approach to the rehabilitation of psychiatric patients.[2]

However, the results of these studies provided minimal support for the conclusion that supported employment can achieve the secondary effect of reducing patient symptoms (Bond et al., 1997). Other interventions, however, such as relapse prevention, are demonstrating significant promise in managing patient symptoms.

Relapse Prevention

Treatment in correctional institutions and hospitals brings about many qualitative and quantitative changes in the behavior of offenders with special needs, but maintaining these changes requires other forms of intervention in the aftercare process. Relapse prevention is an approach to treatment that was developed in the addictions literature and has shown significant promise in preventing relapse in psychiatric (Moller & Murphy, 1997) and in offender populations (Pithers, 1991). It relies heavily on self-help and psychoeducational principles in helping offenders address problems associated with maintaining desired behavioral outcomes achieved from completing the formal phase of a treatment program in a prison, hospital, or community setting (Gendreau, 1996; McMurran, 1996). Before developing relapse prevention, interventions focused primarily on treatment. Accordingly, we knew far more about inducting the cessation of symptoms and problem behaviors than about preventing relapse (George & Marlatt, 1989).

The relapse prevention model is guided by two conceptual principles:

> The first focuses on explaining the processes that operate in situations to promote the occurrence of a lapse and to facilitate escalation from a lapse to a relapse. The second component focuses on explaining the operation of the more subtle processes that can gradually move the recovered addict toward a set of circumstances capable of inciting a lapse. (George & Marlatt, 1989, p. 7)

That is, offenders are taught in the relapse prevention model to identify psychological and situational variables that place them at risk of relapse or reoffending. Lapses are anticipated and offenders are assisted in developing strategies to cope with these "slight slips" (George & Marlatt, 1989). The aim is to prevent the lapse or the behavioral slip from turning into a complete relapse. Treatment personnel are also expected to help offenders understand the connections between "seemingly unimportant decisions" that lead them closer to experiencing a relapse (Laws, 1989) and to help significant others monitor for signs of relapse and provide reinforcement for prosocial behavior (Gendreau, 1996). "In some cases exposure to a particular situation [e.g., social pressure] may trigger the sequence of events leading to an offense; in others, it may be a negative emotional state or specific life event [e.g., interpersonal conflict] such as being reprimanded at work for poor performance" (Epps, 1996, p. 171; see also Cummings, Gordon, & Marlatt, 1980).

However, the sequence of factors that influences a relapse differs from offender to offender (Epps, 1996). The psychological and situational factors are always a concern to treatment professionals but will have different implications for different kinds of behavioral outcomes. That is, a person experiencing a psychiatric relapse needs to focus on different kinds of high-risk situations from that of a person with addiction problems. For instance, Moller and Murphy (1997) have developed a program to aid persons with SPMI in distinguishing between three states of wellness: unstable, stable, and actualized.

In these authors' opinion, relapse occurs when psychiatric symptoms reoccur for more than 24 hours and management strategies are not successful. Their goal is to sensitize patients to take appropriate steps to prevent relapse when they are in a state of stable wellness. In stable wellness, the psychiatric symptoms are present, but the individual is able to maintain daily activities. In sum, although the high-risk situation might differ among treatment groups, it is assumed that the process of relapse prevention for addicts, sexual offenders, and MDOs should follow similar pathways to recovery (NIDA, 1993).

Relapse prevention is a movement in rehabilitation that has triggered interesting research into how best to promote transitions to new crime-free and disorder-free lifestyles. Addiction and crime involve life choices and lifestyles within distinct subcultures that are incompatible with relapse prevention. A cross-cultural project funded by NIDA (1993) for developing effective aftercare for recovering addicts likened the experiences of this recovery process to that of an immigrant. The authors of this project wrote:

> Recovery is not just the cessation and deactivation of drug use: usually, it also demands adjustments to a new way of life within the culture of the larger community.... But—proceeding with the analogy—to make a truly new way of life and not just relocate the old one, people need much more than grit. People must have guidance, acquire new skills, and make new contacts so they can cease being immigrants. (NIDA 1993, p. 9)

This NIDA-sponsored project developed a model of relapse prevention and lifestyle change that included a randomized experimental design of the efficacy of this approach with opiate addicts that was evaluated in both America and Hong Kong. The results showed that during the study's follow-up period, aftercare group members, who received relapse prevention training and other aftercare services, abstained significantly more from the use of illicit opiates when compared to the controls (32% to 18%, respectively). The experimental intervention was also very effective in helping unemployed participants find jobs compared to controls. The substance abuse literature is replete with other outcome studies (Allsop & Saunders, 1989; Marlatt & Gordon, 1980) demonstrating the effectiveness of relapse prevention as an effective aftercare strategy, including dealing with criminal offenders with substance abuse problems (Gorski, Kelley, Havens, & Peters, 1993).

This technology has also been studied with sex offenders. In the early 1980s, California repealed its legislation that allowed mentally disordered sex offenders to be committed to state hospitals. However, a state hospital program was to be established for the voluntary transfer of selected sex offenders to the state hospital during the last 2 years of their prison terms. The Department of Mental Health in California established an evaluation design that compared the postrelease activities of three matched groups of research participants: a treatment group consisting of 77 sex offenders who volunteered for treatment and were randomly selected into the study, a volunteer control group consisting of sex offenders who volunteered for treatment but were not randomly selected for treatment, and a nonvolunteer control group consisting of prisoners who qualified for treatment but did not volunteer to participate. In other words, the design controlled for voluntarism as a factor that might bias the interpretations of the study's results.

Although 77 prisoners were selected into the treatment program, the follow-up study was conducted on 36 offenders who completed the treatment program, had a mean length of stay in the treatment program of 20.8 months, and a mean time at risk in the community of 6.5 months when the final data was collected. This group was compared to a matched sample of volunteer controls ($n = 32$) with a mean time at risk of 4.5 months and a matched sample of nonvolunteer controls ($n = 18$) with a mean time at risk of 6.9 months. The treatment group and volunteer control group both received extensive relapse prevention training in the treatment program and underwent a specialized aftercare phase of the program. Comparisons of the treatment group versus volunteer control group did not differ in terms of criminal history variables, but the volunteer control group had higher rates of offenders with homosexual and bisexual child molester tendencies. The outcome results of this study indicated that one of the participants in the treatment group was returned to prison for a violation of parole. However, none of the participants in the treatment group were arrested for sex crimes. Aftercare providers also did not suspect any reoffenses for the treatment group. There were also no arrests for sex crimes in the other two comparison groups. Each of the other groups had persons returned to prison for parole violations: two in the volunteer control group and three in the control group. The results of this study are inconclusive primarily because individuals were in the community only for approximately 6.5 months (Marques, Day, Nelson, & Miner, 1989).

Another study of relapse prevention with sex offenders was conducted by Pithers and Cumming (1989) using the Vermont Treatment Program for Sexual Aggressors. It demonstrated that relapse prevention holds significant promise for prevention of relapse with this population. The Vermont program involves the collaborative efforts of mental health, probation, and parole professionals. Participants in the program experience special conditions of probation and parole that prohibit the offender from engaging in specific high-risk situations. Of the 167 offenders who received the treatment services in the Vermont project, six relapsed and a seventh was awaiting trail at the time of the evaluation. After 6 years, 4% of the 167 offenders relapsed, which was significantly less than data previously reported for the sex offender population (Pithers & Cumming, 1989). The Pithers (1990) approach to the prevention of relapse is widely regarded in the literature as an effective approach to treating sex offenders (Andrews & Bonta, 1998 Blackburn, 1993; Epps, 1996).

Although relapse prevention is a useful approach in treating persons with SPMI (Birchwood, 1992; Moller & Murphy, 1997), there are no available outcome studies that document its utility in working with MDOs. Among other factors, such research will have to incorporate support-system variables (e.g., monitoring of SPMI) that are likely to affect potential for relapse. For example, as noted previously, monitoring of these persons is essential to identify personal and situational factors associated with relapse. Outcome studies that ignore the critical elements of the *system's* approach to improving relapse prevention are doomed to yield meaningless information.

Where Do We Go From Here

The research on aftercare services suggests that a variety of integrated approaches for handling various categories of offenders with special needs are likely to be effective. Despite this, the data are still relatively silent on integrating specific correctional strategies with proven mental health and psychosocial interventions. In other words, the field lacks data supporting specific models of how to structure the integration of clinical services in mental health with control-oriented services from the field of correctional supervision to achieve desired outcomes. This point is clinically important because control strategies widely used in ISPs can have negative or unforeseen consequences for persons with serious mental impairments.

The picture painted in this chapter of aftercare also illustrates that intensive interventions with teams of professionals providing supportive services is more effective than brokered case management with SPMI persons. However, we still know very little about how to select and how to prescribe the points at which these services should be provided, and we know very little of the relative effectiveness of programs that attempt to improve system linkages between programs in the criminal justice and the mental health systems.

Finally, current literature on aftercare services does not include a clearly defined theory of need that can provide clear goals for actions for the dually diagnosed and the multiple problem offender (Wing, 1990). Our conceptions of need still appear to be highly discretionary (Wing, 1990). Moreover, we have not empirically mapped all the relevant configurations of needs that are associated with proven service responses and differential clinical and criminal justice outcomes. For instance, what is the connection between quality of life needs of persons with SPMI and offender recidivism? Quality of life needs are factors that are highly correlated with forms of symptom and illness relapse. We know very little, however, about their connection with recidivism outcomes in various categories of MDOs. In sum, aftercare is a critical topic in offender rehabilitation that still requires substantial programmatic research to clarify how to connect assessments of criminogenic, psychosocial, and clinical needs with prescriptive actions that have known effects on desired outcomes.

NOTES

1. Supported employment differs from sheltered employment. The latter involves an individual working in a setting that affords them an opportunity to earn a living in a noncompetitive context. That is, sheltered employment provides disabled persons with opportunities for work who are not ready for the competitive marketplace. Although sheltered employment is recognized as a component in the traditional continuum of vocational rehabilitation services, we do not discuss it in this chapter because it is not typically related to offenders on aftercare status.
2. Some experts contend that the transitional employment program implemented at Fountain House differs minimally from current notions of supported employment in the psychosocial rehabilitation literature (Bond et al., 1997). Fountain House pioneered the use of a clubhouse model to make work activities available for all members of the club, regardless of their previous work experience. This model included assignments in transitional employment settings that were identified by staff through negotiations with community employers. Two early outcome studies of this program indicated "that exhospitalized patients who participate in the Fountain House program do better in terms of staying out of the hospital and working than nonparticipants" (Glasscote et al., 1971, p. 61).

RESOURCES AND REFERENCES

Abadinsky, H. (1997). *Probation and parole: Theory and practice* (6th ed.). Upper Saddle River, NJ: Prentice-Hall.

Allen, F. A. (1977). Legal values and the rehabilitative ideal. In S. L. Radzinowicz & M. E. Wolfgang (Eds.), *Crime and justice: Vol. II. The criminal in the arms of the law* (pp. 10–19). New York: Basic Books.

Allsop, B., & Saunders S. (1989). Relapse and alcohol problems. In M. Gossop (Ed.), *Relapse and addictive behaviour* (pp. 11–40). London: Tavistock/Routledge.

Altschuler, D. M., & Armstrong, T. L. (1990). *Intensive aftercare for high-risk juveniles: A community care model.* Washington, DC: U.S. Department of Justice, Office of Juvenile Justice and Delinquency Prevention, Office of Justice Programs.

American Friends Services Committee. (1971). *Struggle for justice.* New York: Hill & Wang.

Anderson, A. J. (1997). Comparative impact evaluation of two therapeutic programs for mentally ill chemical abusers [Electronic version]. *International Journal of Psychosocial Rehabilitation, 1*(4). Retrieved from http://www.psychosocial.com/compare/htm

Andrews, D. A., & Bonta, J. (1998). *The psychology of criminal conduct.* Cincinnati, OH: Anderson.

Anglin, M. D., & Hser, I. (1990). Legal coercion and drug abuse treatment: Research findings and social policy implications. In J. A. Inciardi (Ed.), *Handbook of drug control in the United States* (pp. 151–176). Westport, CT: Greenwood.

Anthony, W. A. (1993). Recovery from mental illness: The guiding vision of the mental health service system in the 1990s. *Psychosocial Rehabilitation Journal, 16*, 11–23.

Anthony, W. A., & Blanch, A. (1989). Research on community support services: What have we learned. *Psychosocial Rehabilitation Journal, 12*, 55–73.

Anthony, W. W., Buell, G. J., Sharrat, S., & Althoff, M. (1972). Efficacy of psychiatry rehabilitation. *Psychological Bulletin, 78*, 447–456.

Armstrong, T. L. (1991). Introduction. In T. L. Armstrong (Ed.), *Intensive interventions with high-risk youths: Promising approaches in juvenile probation and parole* (pp. 1–26). Monsey, NY: Criminal Justice Press.

Ashford, J. B. (1997). Aftercare: The neglected phase of the juvenile justice process. In C. A. McNeece & A. R. Roberts (Eds.), *Policy & practice in the justice system* (pp. 29–47). Chicago: Nelson Hall.

Ashford, J. B., & LeCroy, C. W. (1993). Juvenile parole policy in the United States: Determinate versus indeterminate models. *Justice Quarterly, 10*, 179–195.

Bachrach, L. (1978). A conceptual approach to deinstitutionalization. *Hospital and Community Psychiatry, 29*, 573–578.

Bachrach, L. (1986). Dimensions of disability in the chronic mentally ill. *Hospital and Community Psychiatry, 37*, 981–982.

Barton, W. H., & Butts, J. A. (1990). Viable options: Intensive supervision program for juvenile delinquents. *Crime & Delinquency, 36*, 238–256.

Beard, J. H., Malmud, T. J., & Rossman, E. (1978). Psychiatric rehabilitation and long-term rehospitalization rates: The findings of two research studies. *Schizophrenia Bulletin, 4*, 622–635.

Bennet, D. (1983). The historical development of rehabilitation services. In F. N. Watts & D. H. Bennet (Eds.), *Theory of practice of psychiatric rehabilitation* (pp. 15–420). Chichester, UK: Wiley.

Birchwood, M. (1992). Early intervention in schizophrenia: Theoretical background and clinical strategies. *British Journal of Clinical Psychology, 31*, 257–278.

Blackburn, R. (1993). *The psychology of criminal conduct: Theory, research and practice.* Chichester, UK: Wiley.

Blackburn, R. (1996). Mentally disordered offenders. In C. Hollin (Ed.), *Working with offenders: Psychological practice in offender rehabilitation* (pp. 119–149). Chichester, UK: Wiley.

Bogenberger, R. P., Pasewark, R. A., Gudeman, H., & Bierber, S. L. (1987). Follow-up of insanity acquittees in Hawaii. *International Journal of Law and Psychiatry, 10*, 283–295.

Bond, G. R., Drake, R. E., Museser, K. T., & Becker, D. R. (1997). An update on supported employment for people with severe mental illness. *Psychiatric Services, 48*, 335–346.

Bond, G. R., McDonel, E. C., Miller, L. D., & Pensec, M. (1991). Assertive community treatment and reference groups: An evaluation of their effectiveness for young adults with serious mental illness and substance abuse problems. *Psychosocial Rehabilitation Journal, 15*, 31–43.

Bond, G. R., Miller, L., Krumwied, R., & Ward, R. (1988). Assertive case management in three CMHCs: A controlled study. *Hospital and Community Psychiatry, 39*, 411–418.

Bond, G. R., Witheridge, T. F., Dincin, J., Wasmer, D., Webb, J., & De Graaf-Kaser, R. (1990). Assertive community treatment for frequent users of a psychiatric hospital in a large city: A controlled study. *American Journal of Community Psychology, 18*, 865–891.

Borland, A., McRae, J., & Lycan, C. (1989). Outcomes of five years of continuous intensive case management. *Hospital and Community Psychiatry, 40*, 369–376.

Bower, K. (1992). *Case management by nurses.* Washington, DC: American Nurses Association.

Budson, R. D. (1988). Following hospitalization: Residential aftercare. In J. R. Lion, W. N. Adler, & W. L. Webb, Jr. (Eds.), *Modern hospital psychiatry* (pp. 384–402). New York: W. W. Norton.

Byrne, J., Lurigo, A. J., & Baird, C. (1989). The effectiveness of the new intensive supervision program. *Research in Corrections, 2,* 1–48.

Byrne, J., & Pattavian, A. (1992). The effectiveness issues: Assessing what works in the adult community corrections system. In J. Byrne, A. Lurigio, & J. Petersilia (Eds.), *Smart sentencing: The emergence of intermediate sanctions* (pp. 281–303). Newbury Park, CA: Sage.

Carling, P. J. (1990). Major mental illness, housing supports. The promise of community integration. *American Psychologist, 45,* 969–975.

Carney, L. P. (1980). *Corrections: Treatment and philosophy.* Englewood Cliffs, NJ: Prentice-Hall.

Clear, T. R., Byrne, J. M., & Dvoskin, J. (1993). The transition from being an inmate: Discharge planning, parole and community-based services for mentally ill offenders. In H. J. Steadman & J. J. Cocozza (Eds.), *Mental illness in America's prisons* (pp. 131–157). Seattle, WA: National Coalition for the Mentally Ill in the Criminal Justice System.

Clement, P. F. (1993). The incorrigible child: Juvenile delinquency in the United States from the 17th through the 19th centuries. In A. G. Hess & P. F. Clement (Eds.), *History of juvenile delinquency* (pp. 453–490). Aalen, Germany: Scientia Verlag.

Clements, C. R. (1996). Offender classification: Two decades of progress. *Criminal Justice and Behavior, 23,* 121–143.

Cohn, A. (1994). History of probation and parole. In American Correctional Association (Eds.), *Field officer resource guide* (pp. 1–11). Baltimore: United Book.

Cullen, F. T., Wright, J. P., & Applegate B. K. (1996). Control in the community: The limits of reform. In A. T. Harland (Ed.), *Choosing correctional options that work: Defining the demand and evaluating the supply* (pp. 69–116). Thousand Oaks, CA: Sage.

Cummings, C., Gordon, J. R., & Marlatt, G. A. (1980). Relapse: Strategies of prevention and prediction. In W. R. Miller (Ed.), *The addictive behaviors* (pp. 291–321). Oxford, UK: Pergamon Press.

Currie, E. (1985). *Confronting crime: An American challenge.* New York: Pantheon Books.

Curtis, J. L., Millman, E. J., Struening, E., & D'Ercole, A. (1992). Effect of care management on rehospitalization and utilization of ambulatory care services. *Hospital and Community Psychiatry, 43,* 895–899.

Dickerson, F. B. (1997). Assessing clinical outcomes: The community functioning of persons with serious mental illness. *Psychiatric Services, 48,* 897–902.

Dressler, D. (1959). *Practice and theory of probation and parole.* New York: Columbia University Press.

Duffee, D. E., & Clark, D. (1985). The frequency and classification of the needs of offenders in community settings. *Journal of Criminal Justice, 13,* 243–268.

Duffee, D. E., & Duffee, B. W. (1981). Studying the needs of offenders in prerelease centers. *Journal of Research in Crime and Delinquency, 18,* 251–253.

Duffy, K. G., & Wong, F. Y. (1996). *Community psychology.* Boston: Allyn & Bacon.

Ekdawi, M. Y., & Conning, A. M. (1994). *Psychiatric rehabilitation.* London: Chapman & Hall.

Epps, K. (1996). Sex offenders. In C. R. Hollins (Ed.), *Working with offenders: Psychological practice in offender rehabilitation* (pp. 150–187). Chichester, UK: Wiley.

Erwin, B. S. (1986). Turning up the heat on probationers in Georgia. *Federal Probation, 50,* 17–24.

Fagan, J., Forst, M., & Vivoam, T. (1988). *Treatment and reintegration of violent juvenile offenders.* San Francisco: URSA Institute.

Falkin, G. P., Lipton, D. S., & Wexler, H. K. (1992). Drug treatment in state prisons. In D. R. Gerstein & H. J. Harwood. (Eds.), *Treating drug problems* (Vol. 2, pp. 89–131). Washington, DC: National Academy Press.

Feder, L. (1991a). A profile of mentally ill offenders and their adjustment in the community. *Journal of Psychiatry and Law, 19,* 79–98.

Feder, L. (1991b). A comparison of the community adjustment of mentally ill offenders with those from the general prison population: An 18-month follow-up. *Law and Human Behavior, 15,* 477–493.

Franklin, J., Solovitz, B., Mason, M., Clemons, J. R., & Miller, G. E. (1987). An evaluation of case management. *American Journal of Public Health, 77,* 674–678.

French, L. M. (1940). *Psychiatric social work.* London: Oxford University Press.

Fulton, B., & Stone, S. (1993, Winter). The promise of new ISP. *Perspectives,* 43–45.

Gendreau, P. (1996). The principals of effective interventions with offenders. In A. T. Harland (Ed.), *Choosing correctional options that work: Defining the demand and evaluating the supply* (pp. 117–130). Thousand Oaks, CA: Sage.

George, W. H., & Marlatt, G. A. (1989). Introduction. In D. R. Laws (Ed.), *Relapse prevention with sex offenders* (pp. 1–31). New York: Guilford.

Giardini, G. I. (1959). *The parole process.* Springfield, IL: Charles C. Thomas.

Giering, P., Durbin, J., Foster, R., Boyles, S., Babiak, T., & Lancee, B. (1992). Social networks of residents in supportive housing. *Community Mental Health Journal, 28,* 199–214.

Glasscote, R. M., Cumming, E., Rutman, I. D., Sussex, J. N., & Glassman, S. M. (1971). *Rehabilitating the mentally ill in the community: A study of psychological rehabilitation centers.* Washington, DC: American Psychiatric Association.

Goodstein, L., & Sontheimer, H. (1997). The implementation of an intensive aftercare program for serious juvenile offenders: A case study. *Criminal Justice and Behavior, 24,* 332–359.

Gorski, T. T., Kelley, J. M., Havens, L., & Peters, R. H. (1993). *Relapse prevention and the substance abusing criminal offender.* Rockville, MD: Center for Substance Abuse Treatment.

Greenwood, P. W., Deschenes, E. P., & Adams, J. (1993). *Chronic juvenile offenders: Final results form the Skillman aftercare experiment.* Santa Monica, CA: RAND.

Greer, W. C. (1991). Aftercare: Community integration following institutional treatment. In G. D. Ryan & S. L. Lane (Eds.), *Juvenile sexual offending* (pp. 377–390). Lexington, MA: DC Heath.

Gruenberg, E. M. (1967). Social breakdown syndrome—Some origins. *American Journal of Psychiatry, 123,* 1481–1489.

Haines, T. H. (1920). Lessons from the principals governing the parole procedures in hospitals for the insane. In *Conference on Social Work* (pp. 159–166). Chicago: University of Chicago.

Harding, C. M., & Zahniser, J. (1995). Empirical correction of seven myths about schizophrenia. *Acta Psychiatrica Scandinavica, 90,* 140–146.

Hawthorne, W., & Hough, R. (1997). Integrated services for long-term care. In L. Minkoff & D. Pollack (Eds.), *Managed mental healthcare in the public sector: A survival manual* (pp. 205–216). Amsterdam: Harwood Academic.

Heilbrun, K., Bennett, W. S., Evans, J. H., Offutt, R. A., Reiff, H. J., & White, A. J. (1988). Assessing the treatability in mentally disordered offenders: A conceptual and methodological note. *Behavioral Sciences and the Law, 6,* 479–486.

Heilbrun, K., & Griffin, P. A. (1993). Community-based forensic treatment of insanity acquittees. *International Journal of Law and Psychiatry, 16,* 133–150.

Henderson, A. Z., & Bell, D. K. (1995). Special needs offenders on probation and parole. In American Correctional Association (Ed.), *Field officer resource guide* (pp. 68–81). Baltimore: United Book.

Hippchen, L. J. (1978). Trends in classification philosophy and practice. In Committee on Classification and Treatment, American Correctional Association (Ed.), *Handbook of correctional classification: Programming for treatment and reintegration* (pp. 1–11). Cincinnat, OH: Anderson.

Home Office. (1987). *Mental Health Act 1983: Supervision and after-care of conditionally discharged restricted patients. Notes for the guidance of social supervisors.* London: Home Office Department of Health and Social Security.

Hudson, C. H. (1973). *Summary report: An experimental study of the different effects of parole supervision on a group of adolescent boys and girls.* Minneapolis: Minnesota Department of Corrections.

Hussey, F. A., & Duffee, D. E. (1980). *Probation, parole, and community field services.* New York: Harper & Row.

Intagliata, J. (1982). Improving the quality of community care for the chronically mentally disabled: The role of case management. *Schizophrenia Bulletin, 8,* 655–674.

Jacobs, H. E. (1988). Vocational rehabilitation. In R. P. Liverman (Ed.), *Psychiatric rehabilitation of chronic mental patients* (pp. 245–284). Washington, DC: American Psychiatric Press.

Jacoby, J. E., & Kozie-Peak, B. (1997). The benefits of social support for mentally ill offenders: Prison-to-community transitions. *Behavioral Sciences and the Law, 15,* 483–501.

Joint Commissions on Mental Illness and Health. (1961). *Action for mental health.* New York: Basic Books.

Klinkenberg, W. D., & Clasyn, R. J. (1996). Predictors of receipt of aftercare and recidivism among persons with severe mental illness: A review. *Psychiatric Services, 47,* 487–496.

Langan, P. A., & Cunniff, M. A. (1992). *Recidivism of felons on probation: 1986–89.* Washington, DC: National Institute of Justice.

Laws, D. R. (Ed.). (1989). *Relapse prevention with sex offenders.* New York: Guilford.

Liberman, R. P. (Ed.). (1988). *Psychiatric rehabilitation of chronic patients.* Washington, DC: American Psychiatric Press.

Lipton, F., Nutt, S., & Sabitini, A. (1988). Housing the homeless mentally ill: A longitudinal study of a treatment approach. *Hospital and Community Psychiatry, 39*, 40–45.

Macht, M. W., & Ashford, J. B. (1991). *Introduction to social work and social welfare* (2nd ed.). New York: Macmillan.

Marlatt, G. A., & Gordon, J. R. (1980). Determinants of relapse: Implications for the maintenance of behavior change. In P. O. Davidson & S. M. Davidson (Eds.), *Behavioral medicine: Changing health lifestyles* (pp. 410–452). New York: Brunner/Mazel.

Marques, J. K., Day, D. M., Nelson, C., & Miner, M. H. (1989). *The sex offender treatment and evaluation project: California's relapse prevention with sex offenders* (pp. 247–267). New York: Guilford.

Martin, S. S., & Incardi, J. A. (1997). Case management outcomes for drug-involved offenders. *Prison Journal, 77*, 168–183.

Martinson, R. (1974). What works? Questions and answers about prison reform. *The Public Interest, 35*, 22–54.

McCarthy, J., & Nelson, G. (1991). An evaluation of supportive housing for current and former psychiatric patients. *Hospital and Community Psychiatry, 42*, 1254–1256.

McMurran, M. (1996). Alcohol, drugs, and criminal behavior. In C. R. Hollin (Ed.), *Working with offenders* (pp. 211–242). Chichester, UK: Wiley.

Meyer, A. (1992). Historical sketch and outlook of psychiatric social work. *Hospital Social Service, 5*, 22.

Minkoff, K. (1991). Program components of a comprehensive integrated care system for seriously mentally ill patients with substance disorders. In K. Minkoff & R. E. Drake (Eds.), *Dual diagnosis of major mental illness and substance disorder* (pp. 13–27). San Francisco: Jossey-Bass.

Moller, M. D., & Murphy, M. F. (1997). The three r's rehabilitation program: A prevention approach for the management of relapse symptoms associated with psychiatric diagnosis. *Psychiatric Rehabilitation, 20*, 42–48.

Monahan, J., & Steadman, H. J. (1983). Crime and mental disorder: An epidemiological approach. In N. Morris & M. Tonry (Eds.), *Crime and justice: An annual review of research* (Vol. 3, pp. 145–189). Chicago: University of Chicago.

Morse, G. A., Calsyn, R. J., Klinkenberg, W. D., Gerber, F., Smith, R., Tempelhoff, B., et al. (1997). An experimental comparison of three types of case management for homeless mentally ill persons. *Psychiatric Services, 48*, 497–503.

Moxley, D. P. (1997). *Case management by design: Reflections on principles and practices.* Chicago: Nelson-Hall.

National Institute of Drug Abuse. (1993). *Recovery training and self-help: Relapse prevention and aftercare for drug addicts.* Rockville, MD: National Institute of Drug Abuse.

Nelson, G., Hall, G. B., & Walsh-Bower, R. (1998). The relationship between housing characteristics, emotional well-being and the personal empowerment of psychiatric consumers/survivors. *Community Mental Health Journal, 34*, 57–69.

Ogilvie, R. J. (1997). The state of supported housing for mental health consumers: A literature review. *Psychiatric Rehabilitation Journal, 21*, 122–131.

Olfson, M. (1990). Assertive community treatment: An evaluation of the experimental evidence. *Hospital and Community Psychiatry, 41*, 634–641.

Pacht, A., & Cowden, J. (1974). An exploratory study of five hundred sex offenders. *Criminal Justice and Behavior, 1*, 13–20.

Palmer, T. (1996). Programmatic and nonprogrammatic aspects of successful intervention. In A. T. Harland (Ed.), *Choosing correctional options that work: Defining the demand and evaluating the supply* (pp. 131–182). Thousand Oaks, CA: Sage.

Palmer, T. B. (1991). Interventions with juvenile offenders: Recent and long term changes. In T. L. Armstrong (Ed.), *Intensive interventions with high risk youths: Promising approaches in juvenile probation and parole* (pp. 85–120). Monsey, NY: Criminal Justice Press.

Pearson, F. S. (1988). Evaluation of New Jersey's intensive supervision program. *Crime & Delinquency, 34*, 437–448.

Petersilia, J., & Turner, S. (1993). Evaluating intensive supervision probation/parole: Results of a nationwide experiment. In *Research in brief.* Washington, DC: National Institute of Justice.

Pisciotta, A. W. (1993). Child saving or child brokerage? The theory and practice of indenture and parole at the New York House of Refuge, 1825–1935. In A. G. Hess & P. F. Clement (Eds.), *History of juvenile delinquency* (pp. 533–555). Aalen, Germany: Scientia Verlag.

Pitch, T. (1995). *Limited responsibilities: Social movements and criminal justice.* London: Routledge.

Pithers, W. D. (1990). Relapse prevention with sexual aggressors: A method for maintaining therapeutic gain and enhancing external supervision. In W. W. Marshall, D. R. Laws, & H. E. Barbara (Eds.), *Handbook of sexual assault: Issues, theories, and treatment of offenders* (pp. 343–361). New York: Plenum Press.

Pithers, W. D. (1991). Relapse with sexual aggressors. *Forum on Corrections Research, 3,* 20–24.

Pithers, W. D., & Cumming, G. F. (1989). Can relapses be prevented? Initial outcome data from the Vermont Treatment program for sexual aggressors. In. D. R. Laws (Ed.), *Relapse prevention with sex offenders* (pp. 313–325). New York: Guilford.

Prendergast, M. L., Anglin, M. D., & Wellisch, J. (1995). Treatment for drug-abusing offenders under community supervision. *Federal Probation, 59,* 66–75.

President's Panel on Mental Retardation. (1962). *A proposed program for national action to combat mental retardation.* Washington, DC: U.S. Government Printing Office.

Ragins, M. (1997). Recovery: Changing from a medical model to a psychosocial rehabilitation mode. *The Journal, 5*(3), 1–7.

Reinhardt, B., & Shepherd, G. L. (1994). Behavioral health case review: Utilization review or case management? One company's view. In S. Shueman, W. G. Troy, & S. L. Mayhugh (Eds.), *Managed behavioral health care* (pp. 76–91). Springfield, IL: Charles C. Thomas.

Rimmerman, A., Finn, H., Schnee, J., & Klein, I. (1991). Token reinforcement in the psychosocial rehabilitation of individuals with chronic mental illness: Is it effective over time? *International Journal of Rehabilitation Research, 14,* 123–130.

Rogers, R., & Wettstein, R. (1984). Relapse of NGRI outpatients: An empirical study. *International Journal of Offender Therapy and Comparative Criminology, 28,* 227–235.

Romig, D. A. (1978). *Justice for children: An examination of juvenile delinquent rehabilitation programs.* New York: Human Sciences Press.

Rose, S. M., & Moore, V. L. (1995). Case management. In R. I. Edwards & J. G. Hopps (Eds.), *Encyclopedia of social work* (19th ed., pp. 335–340). Washington, DC: National Association of Social Workers Press.

Rosenheck, R., Neale, M., Leaf, P., Milstein, R., & Frishman, L. (1995). Multisite experimental cost study of intensive psychiatric community care. *Schizophrenia Bulletin, 21,* 129–140.

Rossler, W., Loffler, W., Fatkenheuer, B., & Reicher-Rossler, A. (1992). Does case management reduce the rehospitalization rate? *Acta Psychiatrica Scandinavica, 86,* 445–449.

Sechrest, L., White, S. O., & Brown, E. (Ed.). (1979). *The rehabilitation of criminal offenders: Problem and prospects.* Washington, DC: National Academy of Sciences.

Shepherd, G. (1990). Case management. In W. Watson & A. Grounds (Eds.), *The mentally disordered offender in an era of community care: New directions in provision* (pp. 166–176). Cambridge, UK: Cambridge University Press.

Smith, S. G. (1912). *Social pathology.* New York: Macmillan.

Solomon, P.L., Gordon, B.H., & Davis, J.M. (1984). *Community services to discharged psychiatric patients.* Springfield, IL: Charles C Thomas.

Solomon, P., & Draine, J. (1995). One-year outcomes of a randomized trial of case management with seriously mentally ill clients leaving jail. *Evaluation Review, 19,* 256–273.

Sperry, L., Brill, P. L., Howard, K. I., & Grissom, G. R. (1996). *Treatment outcomes in psychotherapy and psychiatric interventions.* New York: Brunner/Mazel.

Spica, R. (1993, Winter). What is between human services and offender adjustment? *Perspectives,* 24–26.

Srebnik, D., Livingston, J., Gordon, J., & King, D. (1995). Housing choice and community success for individuals with serious and persistent mental illness. *Community Mental Health Journal, 31,* 139–152.

Stein, L. I., & Santos, A. B. (1998). *Assertive community treatment of persons with severe mental illness.* New York: W. W. Norton.

Stein, L. I., & Test, M. A. (1980). An alternative to hospital treatment: Conceptual model, treatment program and clinical evaluation. *Archives of General Psychiatry, 37,* 302–397.

Stroul, B. (1989). Community support systems for persons with long-term mental illness: A conceptual framework. *Psychosocial Rehabilitation Journal, 12,* 9–26.

Stroup, T. S., & Dorwart, R. (1997). Overview of public sector managed mental health care. In K. Minkoff & D. Pollack (Eds.), *Managed mental health care in the public sector: A survival manual* (pp. 1–12). Amsterdam: Harwood Academic Press.

Studt, E. (1972). *Surveillance and service in parole: Report of the parole action study MR-166.* Los Angeles: Institute of Government and Public Affairs, University of California.

Sturgeon, V., & Taylor, J. (1980). Report of a five-year follow up study of mentally disordered sex offenders released from Atascadero State Hospital in 1973. *Criminal Justice Journal, 4,* 31–63.

Telles, L. (1992). The clustered apartment project: A conceptually coherent supported housing model. In L. I. Stein (Ed.), *Innovative community mental health programs* (pp. 53–64). San Francisco: Jossey-Bass.

Turner, S., Petersilia, J., Deschenes, E. P. (1992). Evaluating intensive supervision probation/parole (ISP) for drug offenders. *Crime & Delinquency, 38,* 539–556.

Waller, I. (1974). *Men released from prison.* Toronto Ontario, Canada University of Toronto Press.

Watts, F. (1983). Employment. In F. N. Watts & D. H. Bennett (Eds.), *Theory and practice of psychiatric rehabilitation* (pp. 215–240). New York: Wiley.

Watts, R., & Bennett, D. (1983). Introduction: The concept of rehabilitation. In F. N. Watts & D. H. Bennett (Eds.), *Theory and practice of psychiatric rehabilitation* (pp. 3–14). New York: Wiley.

Wehman, P. (1981). *Competitive employment: New horizons for severely disabled individuals.* Baltimore: Brooks.

Weil, M., Karls, J. M., & Associates. (1985). *Case management in human service practice.* San Francisco: Jossey-Bass.

Western Interstate Commission for Higher Education. (1997). The role of work in recovery from mental illness [Electronic Version]. *West Link, 18*(2). Retrieved from http://www.wiche.edu/mentalhealth/June97

Wheeler, G. R. (1978). *Counter-deterrence.* Chicago: Nelson Hall.

Wilson, D., Tien, G., & Eaves, D. (1995). Increasing the community tenure of mentally disordered offenders: An assertive case management program. *International Journal of Law and Psychiatry, 18,* 61–69.

Wing, J. K. (1990). Defining need and evaluating services. In W. Watson & A. Grounds. (Eds.), *The mentally disordered offenders in an era of community care: New directions in provision* (pp. 90–101). Cambridge, UK: Cambridge University Press.

Zander, K. (1995). Collaborative care: Two effective strategies for positive outcomes. In K. Zander (Ed.), *Managing outcomes through collaborative care: The application of care mapping and case management* (pp. 1–37). Chicago: American Hospital Association.

Restorative Justice and Victim-Offender Mediation

Victim–Offender Mediation and Forensic Practice

22

Marilyn Peterson Armour
Mark S. Umbreit

Shane stole a car and wrecked someone else's car. At the meeting with the victim of the wrecked car, Shane quickly accepted responsibility for the offense and apologized. But at this meeting, the victim refused to let him off so lightly. She interceded: "No, you're going to hear how this affected me," and went on to explain how she couldn't take her asthmatic daughter to emergency, how she couldn't take her son to soccer training, and she couldn't do her shopping. Shane at that stage became a blubbering mess . . . He started to own the offense in its entirety. An action plan was agreed to by both Shane and the victim. It involved Shane giving his car to the victim. Shane would have preferred to go to prison. Giving up his car was deeply embarrassing, because he had to explain to his friends, who saw his car being driven by the victim, what had happened. This humiliating experience had a much more constructive effect on his behavior than a prison sentence would have had.

(Cayley, 1998, cited in Johnstone, 2002)

A youth got drunk, broke into a school along with his friends, and accidentally set fire to the school causing enormous damage. At a meeting with some of the teachers and parents, a young girl showed the youth the scrapbook that she had kept in her classroom. About one-half was just burned to a crisp, and the other half was charred. She said, "This is all I've got as a remembrance of my brother, because this scrapbook is photos of my family and a photo of my brother, and he died not so long ago, about a year ago, and that's all I've got now." And then you saw the tears trickling down the face of the youth. This was the start of a process in which the youth eventually took "ownership" of the offense, apologized to all affected by it, and gave up his weekends to help build a new playground. He did not come to the attention of the police again.

(Cayley, 1998, cited in Johnstone, 2002)

Introduction

Most contemporary criminal justice systems focus on law violation, the need to hold offenders accountable and punish them, and other state interests. Crime is viewed as having been committed against the state. The state, therefore, essentially owns the conflict and determines how to respond to it. Actual crime victims are quite subsidiary to the process and generally have no legal standing in the proceedings.

Restorative justice offers a very different way of understanding and responding to crime. Instead of viewing the state as the primary one offended by criminal acts and placing the actual victims and the community, as well as offenders, in passive roles, restorative justice turns this arrangement around and recognizes crime as fundamentally directed against individual people. It is grounded in the belief that those most affected by crime should be the ones to be actively involved in resolving the conflict. Repairing harm and restoring losses, allowing offenders to take direct responsibility for their actions, and assisting victims to move beyond vulnerability toward some degree of closure stand in sharp contrast to the values and practices of the conventional criminal justice system with its focus on past criminal behavior through ever-increasing levels of punishment (Umbreit, Vos, & Coates, 2005).

Values and Traditions

Restorative justice values, principles, and practices are deeply rooted in the ancient principles of Judeo-Christian culture that set forth the responsibility of offenders to repair directly the harm they caused to individuals, harm that has created a breach in the "Shalom community," the peace of the community. Similar values are also embedded in numerous indigenous cultures throughout the world, including many Native American tribes within the United States and the Aboriginal/First Nation people of Canada, the Maori in New Zealand, Native Hawaiians, African tribal councils, the Afghani practice of jirga, the Arab/Palestinian practice of Sulha, and many ancient Celtic practices found in the Brehon laws (Umbreit et al., 2005).

Restorative Justice Defined

The most succinct definition of restorative justice is offered by Howard Zehr (2002), whom many consider to be the leading visionary and architect of the restorative justice movement. According to Zehr,

> Restorative justice is a process to involve, to the extent possible, those who have a stake in a specific offense and to collectively identify and address harms, needs, and obligations, in order to heal and put things as right as possible. (2002, p. 37)

As such, restorative justice is grounded in the following principles: (a) crime is a violation of a person by another person; (b) the harm suffered by victims must be paramount, and victims must be helped to move beyond their sense of vulnerability; (c) offenders must be encouraged to understand the harm they have caused and be given an opportunity to make amends; and (d) the community must be involved in holding the offender accountable, promoting a healing response to the needs of victims and offenders, and assuming responsibility for the social conditions that contribute to offender behavior (Johnstone, 2002).

History of the Restorative Justice Movement

The mid-1970s marked the beginning of the restorative justice movement. The first restorative justice dialogue program, the Victim Offender Reconciliation Program (VORP), was initially developed in Kitchener, Ontario, in 1974 (Peachey, 1989). From the late 1970s to the early 1980s a number of experimental programs based on restorative justice principles and modeled after the Kitchener program were initiated in several jurisdictions in North America and Europe, with the first VORP in the United States located in Elkhart, Indiana, in 1978 (Umbreit, Vos, & Coates, 2006).

Through the mid-1980s, restorative justice initiatives remained small in size and number and had little impact on the larger system. From the mid-1980s to the mid-1990s the movement slowly began to be recognized in more communities as a viable option for interested crime victims and offenders, though still impacting a very small number of participants. The movement, however, began to enter the mainstream in the mid-1990s with greater recognition by and active collaboration with the formal justice system. Recently, two important international bodies have endorsed restorative justice policies and practices. The United Nations has adopted a set of principles that encourage use of restorative justice programming by member states (United Nations, 2000), and the Council of Europe supports its use in criminal matters (Commission of the European Committees, 2001). Although most victim advocacy groups were quite skeptical in the early years of the restorative justice movement, the growing support for it is evidenced in the National Organization for Victim Assistance's endorsement of "restorative community justice" (Young, 1995).

Victim–Offender Mediation

Victim–offender mediation (VOM) is the oldest, most widely developed, and most empirically grounded expression of restorative justice dialogue (Bazemore & Umbreit, 1995; Umbreit, 2001; Van Ness & Heetderks, 2002; Zehr, 1990, 2002). Many thousands of cases are dealt with annually through more than 300 programs throughout the United States and more than 1,200 programs in primarily Europe, Canada, Israel, Japan, Russia, South Korea, South Africa, South America, and the South Pacific (Umbreit et al., 2006). A total of 29 states in the United States have legislation, in one form or another, that addresses VOM (Lightfoot & Umbreit, 2002). Indeed, the American Bar Association has endorsed VOM and recommends its use in courts throughout the country and has further provided guidelines for its use and development (American Bar Association, 1994).

Approximately two thirds of the cases referred to VOM are misdemeanors; the remaining are felony cases (Umbreit, 2004). The four most common offenses referred to VOM, in order of frequency, are vandalism, minor assaults, theft, and burglary (Umbreit & Greenwood, 1999). The primary referral sources are probation officers, judges, and prosecutors. Juvenile offenders are more likely to be the primary focus of

VOM programs in the United States, with 45% of programs offering services solely to juveniles, and an additional 46% serving both juveniles and adults. The largest number of VOM programs across the United States are offered by private, not-for-profit agencies (43%). Various elements of the justice system are responsible for another 33%, including probation (16%), correctional facilities (8%), prosecuting attorney offices (4%), victim services (3%), and police departments (2%). The remaining 23% are offered by churches or church-related agencies.

These participating programs report a wide range of points in the justice system process at which VOM occurs (Umbreit & Greenwood, 1999). Slightly over a third (34%) are true diversion, occurring after an offender has been apprehended but prior to any formal finding of guilt. Some occur postadjudication but before predisposition (28%). Others occur postadjudication and postdisposition (28%). A small number of programs (7%) report that their mediations could occur at any point in the process, and the remaining 3% report working with cases prior to any court involvement.

VOM usually involves a victim and an offender in direct mediation facilitation by one or sometimes two mediators. Occasionally the dialogue takes place through a third party who carries information back and forth, a process known as "shuttle" mediation. Family group conferencing (FGC) is a closely related cousin to VOM and includes support persons and outside community representatives in addition to the victim and offender. Increasingly over time, distinctions between VOM and FGC have begun to blur. A 1999 survey of VOM programs in the United States found that support persons, including parents in juvenile cases, were present in nearly 9 out of 10 cases (Umbreit & Greenwood, 1999).

With more than 20 years of mediating thousands of cases throughout North America and Europe, VOM has established credibility in the eyes of both citizens and major social institutions. A statewide public opinion poll in Minnesota found that 82% of a random sample of citizens would consider participating in a victim–offender program if they were the victim of a property crime (Pranis & Umbreit, 1992).

Description of the Victim–Offender Mediation Dialogue

VOM is a process that provides interested victims of primarily property crimes and minor assaults the opportunity to meet the juvenile or adult offender, in a safe and structured setting, with the goal of holding the offenders directly accountable for their behavior while providing importance assistance and compensation to the victim (Umbreit, 2001). With the assistance of a trained mediator, victims are able to let offenders know how the crime affected them, to receive answers to questions they may have, and to be directly involved in developing a restitution plan for offenders to be accountable for the losses they incurred. Offenders are able to take direct responsibility for their behavior, learn of the full impact of what they did, and develop a plan for making amends to the person(s) they violated.

Creating the Context for VOM Dialogue

Three conditions form the context within which a restorative dialogue takes place. These conditions are safety of the environment, respectful interaction, and positive energy.

Safe Environment

Safety has been a point of some anxiety for potential dialogue participants for decades (Coates & Gehm, 1989). It is cited by some as giving them reason to hesitate about agreeing to participate in the first place (Coates & Gehm, 1989; Coates, Umbreit, & Burns, 2004). Intimidation, for example, can be quite subtle. Even the clothes a male offender wears may be a reminder to a female victim of violence. Symbols, pictures, topics open for discussion, seating arrangements, and who speaks first can trigger a sense of not being safe. Safety, therefore, is a matter for close mediator scrutiny, whether the case involves vandalism, burglary, or murder (Umbreit, Vos, Coates, & Brown, 2003).

Indeed, concerns for personal safety affect whether or not a victim or an offender agrees to participate in a VOM dialogue. Mediators must assess how likely it is that a face-to-face encounter would cause harm to any of the participants. Mediators will continue to meet with potential participants until they are satisfied and the participants are satisfied that such an encounter can happen without causing harm. This assessment continues during the face-to-face dialogue. Although exceptionally rare in practice, mediators need to be prepared to intervene if the dialogue environment sours or if it becomes unsafe for any participant. Such intervention may be mild, such as reminding participants what they have agreed to not talk about or how they agreed to behave toward one another. In rare instances, the mediator must be prepared to halt the dialogue. This willingness and ability to act sets a tone that serves to establish and maintain a safe environment in which dialogue can occur.

Respectful Interaction

While many values underpin restorative justice, respect is often singled out as the cornerstone value (Zehr, 2002). Respectful interaction refers both to respect for the participants and respect for the process. In their premeetings and at the dialogue session, mediators remind participants to be respectful listeners. They convey the idea that without the bedrock of respect, participants are not yet ready to meet, the likelihood of positive outcomes is slim, and safety will be an issue throughout the process. Mediators must remain mindful of the fact that even though they may evaluate the level of respect shown in a particular dialogue, the final disposition rests with the participants. Did they feel respected by others in the process? By some or all? What actions made them feel respected or disrespected?

Positive Energy

The desirable tone of the VOM dialogue is the least definable and therefore least observable of the necessary conditions. Participants often express feeling powerfully connected with other participants, with the process, and even with a power beyond the process itself. Some describe these feelings in spiritual terms. Some talk about an energetic field. Some find that words fail to capture the profound nature of their experience. Not all participants have or need to have these experiences. However, mediators need to remain open to what participants have to say about the energy of their encounters with the mediator and other participants.

Taken together, safety, respectful interaction, and positive energy create the context for the VOM dialogue. These factors both influence the dialogue and are influenced, in turn, by the dialogue itself.

Stages of the VOM Dialogue Process

The primary goal of VOM is to provide a safe place for dialogue among the involved parties that fosters both offender accountability and growth as well as victim empowerment and assistance. The VOM process has four distinct phases: (a) referral/intake, (b) preparation for mediation, (c) mediation, and (d) follow-up.

Referral/Intake Phase

The VOM process begins when offenders (most often those convicted of such crimes as theft and burglary) are referred by the court. Most programs accept referrals after a formal admission of guilt has been entered with the court. Some programs accept cases that are referred prior to formal admission of guilt, as part of a deferred prosecution effort. Each case is assigned to either a staff or volunteer mediator.

The referral/intake phase begins when the referral of a case (usually from probation) is formally received and ends with assignment of the case to a staff or volunteer case manager who will serve as the mediator. In some programs, cases are referred directly by defense attorneys at either a pre or postconviction level. Most programs use the following criteria to make referrals:

- Type of crime (i.e., property offense such as residential burglary, commercial burglary, theft or vandalism; property offense that involves individuals or small businesses; and simple assault).
- Admission of guilt by the offender.
- Identifiable loss and need for restitution.
- No more than two prior convictions.
- No major mental health problems.
- No major active substance abuse problem.

After the referral is made, there are three tasks that need to be accomplished. These include (a) accurately recording information about the victim and offender on intake forms, (b) mailing letters of introduction to the victim and offender, and (c) assigning the case to a staff or volunteer case manager (mediator).

Preparation Phase

Preparation begins with the assignment of the case to a case manager (mediator) and ends with the beginning of the first joint mediation session. There are three primary tasks to be completed during the preparation for mediation phase. They include (a) explaining the mediation and preparing the offender to participate in the process, (b) securing the victim's consent to participate and preparing the victim for the mediation process, and (c) arranging and scheduling the mediation session. The quality of work done during this phase will have a great impact on the actual mediation session. In fact, unless rapport and trust are effectively established with both the victim and offender, there will be no mediation session. Problems that may occur later in the mediation session often originate during this phase of the process and are likely the result of incomplete preparation.

To prepare the offender, the mediator first asks for and listens to the offender's story about the crime. Then the mediator explains the program and potential benefits, thus encouraging the offender's participation. The mediator also assesses the offender's ability to pay restitution, do work for the victim, or do community service. In some instances, the offender's family members or other support persons may attend and participate in the preparation meeting with the offender as well.

The rhetoric of much of the literature in the field would imply that offender participation in the mediation process is "voluntary." Actual practice in the field would suggest something quite different. When offenders are ordered to mediation by the court, via probation, or are diverted from prosecution if they complete the program, a significant amount of state coercion is being exercised. Research has also indicated that offenders certainly do not perceive the process as "voluntary." Some programs attempt to temper this by trying to get referrals in the least coercive manner possible and to allow those offenders who are strongly opposed to participating or who the program staff has determined are inappropriate for mediation to "choose out" of the program.

To prepare the victim, the mediator first calls and invites the victim to a meeting to learn about mediation and its possible benefits. Every effort is made to avoid having to "sell" the program to the victim over the phone during this initial call. Rather, the mediator attempts to obtain a commitment from the victim to meet at a mutually convenient place in order, first, to listen to the victim's version of the offense and the concerns he or she may have, and, second, to invite the victim's participation in the VOM process. Although the mediator encourages the victim's participation, the mediator also makes clear that participation in the program is absolutely voluntary. Many programs have the first meeting with the offender so that his or her perspective and attitude about the offense can be determined. It can often be helpful for a mediator to share some of what was learned about the offender when the initial meeting with the victim occurs.

It is not uncommon for victims to need time to consider participating, rather than to make a quick decision on the spot. Few victims are immediately enthusiastic about such a confrontation with the offender. While the mediator will attempt to persuade the victim to participate by pointing out a number of potential benefits, the victim, during this preliminary meeting and throughout the VOM process, has complete choice to stay or leave the process. For example, the victim can initially agree to participate and later withdraw. A great deal of sensitivity must be exercised in communicating with victims during the entire process. Because of this, flexibility is required in selecting locations and scheduling meetings, as well as in the overall time frame in which the process will occur. The process is meant to be empowering for victims and to present them with choices.

The importance of the delicate communication process involved in these preliminary meetings cannot be overstated. Victim participation can easily be lost at the first phone call. The initial process of building rapport and trust with both the victim and offender will be essential during the later joint meeting with both individuals. The strongest ethical principle of the VOM process is that the actual mediation program must not again victimize victims, however unintentionally.

Mediation Phase

The mediation phase begins with the first face-to-face conference between the victim and offender and ends with the referring agency's approval of the agreement, either as part of a deferred prosecution program or as a condition of probation. There are four primary tasks to complete during the mediation phase. These include (a) conducting the mediation session; (b) securing signatures on the restitution agreement; (c) securing a follow-up conference, if appropriate; and (d) transmitting the agreement to the referral source.

It is only after the separate preparation sessions with the victim and offender are finished and there is an expression of willingness by both the victim and offender to proceed that the mediator schedules a face-to-face meeting. The meeting begins with the mediator explaining his or her role, identifying the agenda, and stating any communication ground rules that may be necessary. The first part of the meeting focuses on a discussion of the facts and feelings related to the crime. The victim tells the story of discovering the crime. The offender tells the story of having committed the crime. Victims are given the rare opportunity to express their feelings directly to the person who violated them, as well as to receive answers to lingering questions such as "Why me?" or "How did you get into our house?" or "Were you stalking us and planning on coming back?" Victims are often relieved to actually see the offender finally, who usually bears little resemblance to the frightening character they may have conjured up in their minds. Contrary to what many might think, the expression of feelings by the victim typically does not take the form of highly emotional, verbal violence. Some of the initial anger is dissipated through the preliminary meeting with the mediator. Yet, it is often important that some of the initial intensity of feelings be recalled and expressed directly to the offender during the joint meeting.

During the meeting, offenders are put in the very uncomfortable position of having to face the person they violated. They are given the equally rare opportunity to display a more human dimension to their character and even to express remorse in a very personal fashion. Through open discussion of their feelings, both victim and offender have the opportunity to deal with each other as people, often from the same neighborhood, rather than as stereotypes and objects.

Following this important sharing of facts and feelings, the second part of the meeting focuses on a discussion of losses and negotiation of a mutually acceptable restitution agreement, which serves as a tangible symbol of conflict resolution and a focal point for accountability. Actions taken by offenders to repair the harm can take as many forms as creative minds can devise and agree on. And what one victim will accept as adequate reparation another victim may scoff at. Some victims will be pleased only if they receive monetary recompense. Others will want the offenders to take steps to change their behavior to reduce the likelihood that new crimes will be committed. Perhaps these victims will encourage the offender to participate in alcohol or drug counseling. Some victims will want the offenders to repair personal damage caused by careless vandalism. Others will want the offenders to perform some sort of service to the community—whether it is carried out through a formally recognized community service program or not. Some victims want only to hear a genuine apology. And there will be some victims who will feel that simply having the opportunity to tell the story of the pain caused them to the offenders and to see the impact that has on the offenders is enough to repair the harm.

"Repairing the harm" and "making things right" do not mean that situations are restored to where they were before the crime. Some stolen items are irreplaceable. The feeling of having one's life and space invaded and violated may be lessened, but that experience remains part of one's life journey. Yet victims frequently point out that the attitude of the offenders is as important as any other tangible action. Do they believe they see genuine remorse? Do they believe the offenders are really accepting responsibility for what they did? Do they regard the offenders as cocky, or is there a kind of humility expressed as the offenders attempt to repair the harm caused? Is there an apology? Is a plan for repairing harm agreed on? Do participants believe that they had a role in developing the agreement? These questions and their answers suggest that although restitution is an important additional goal, it is, for many programs, secondary to the importance of allowing the parties to talk with each other about the real emotional and practical impact the crime has had on their lives.

Follow-up Phase

The follow-up phase begins with the approval of the restitution agreement by the referring agency and ends with the final closure of the case. There are four primary tasks to complete during this phase: (a) maintaining monthly phone contact with the victim to monitor fulfillment of the restitution agreement; (b) if the offender is out of compliance, working with the offender and probation officer to secure compliance; (c) conducting the prescheduled follow-up joint conference with the victim and offender; and (d) completing the final paperwork related to closing the case.

In order to strengthen the process of personal accountability of the offender to the victim, one or more follow-up meetings between the victim and offender can play a significant role. Although these follow-up meetings are briefer and less structured than the initial VOM session, they provide an informal opportunity to review the implementation of the restitution agreement, to discuss any problems that may have arisen related to the payment schedule, and simply to share small talk if the victim and offender feel so moved.

The need for and willingness to have follow-up meetings is certainly tempered by the actual amount of restitution to be paid. If only a very small amount of restitution is owed, a follow-up meeting might not be appropriate. On the other hand, if a larger amount is due, brief follow-up sessions, including mid-contract and "close-out" meetings, can be quite helpful. As with the initial VOM session, victims must not be coerced into follow-up meetings. To date, only a relatively small proportion of VOM cases include follow-up victim–offender meetings.

The Mediator's Role

While many other types of mediation are largely settlement driven, VOM is primarily dialogue driven, with the emphasis on victim healing, offender accountability, and restoration of losses. VOM mediators, therefore, use a humanistic model of mediation that emphasizes facilitating dialogue and mutual aid; connecting with the parties through building rapport and trust, while not taking sides; identifying the strengths of each party; using a nondirective style of communication; and recognizing and using the power of silence (Umbreit, 1995, 1997, 2001).

Indeed, much of the work of skilled mediators will go unnoticed. When asked, victims and offenders often have difficulty identifying specifically what the mediators did during the face-to-face dialogue. Although mediators may play a very active role in preparation, there is the belief by many, if not most, that their role in a dialogue session is to assure the safety of the environment while staying out of the way as much as possible. Consistent with the desire to empower participants and to encourage them to work out their own entanglements, we expect that a nondirective approach is more restorative that one that is directive.

This does not mean, however, that the mediator is passive. The mediator is acutely aware of what is happening among the participants. Close attention is paid both to nonverbal behavior as well as to what is being said. The mediator must always be ready to act if called on by participants or if the dialogue becomes unsafe. There may be rare moments when participants are stuck and need assistance. These are usually moments when the mediator respects the place of silence, yet there are situations when the mediator will step into the breach. Mediators must, then, be excellent listeners. We do not mean "active" listening, which can interrupt the natural healing that comes from one's story being told without interruption, or "reflective" listening. Rather, the kind of listening required in restorative dialogue is described by mediators as "deep" listening and "listening from the heart." As one mediator stated, "It is like having all your sensors in overdrive while trusting the process."

Effectiveness of VOM

Considerable empirical work has been done over the past 25 years to document the impact of VOM programs. A total of 56 studies were examined for this chapter, including 53 mediation studies and 3 meta-analyses. The following review summarizes the results on participation rates and reasons, participant satisfaction, participant perception of fairness, restitution and repair of harm, diversion, recidivism, and cost.

Participation Rates and Reasons

Approximately 40 to 60% of crime victims eligible to participate in VOM programs choose to become involved, though rates as high as 90% have been reported. A multistate study found that, of 280 victim participants, 91% felt that their participation was voluntary (Umbreit, 1994). Coates, Umbreit, and Burns (2004) found that victims' reasons for choosing to participate were rank ordered as follows: to possibly help the offender, to hear why the offender did the crime, to communicate to the offender the impact of the crime, and to be sure the offender would not return to commit a repeat offense. The most frequent reason for not participating was that it was not worth the time and trouble. Two studies examined offender race/ethnicity as a potential factor in the likelihood of a case coming to mediation. Gehm (1990) found that victims were more likely to mediate if the offender was White. Wyrick and Costanzo (1999), however, found in California that White and Hispanic offenders were equally likely to reach mediation and were significantly more likely to do so than offenders of other minority groups. Victims are also more likely to participate if the offense was a misdemeanor rather than a felony (Gehm, 1990). However, longer time lapses for property cases resulted in fewer mediations, while longer time lapses in personal offenses resulted in more mediations (Wyrick & Costanzo, 1999).

Offenders choosing to participate often want to pay back the victim, to get the whole experience behind them, to impress the court, or to apologize to the victim (Abrams & Umbreit, 2002; Coates & Gehm, 1989). Offenders do not participate because their lawyers told them not to (Schneider, 1986) or they simply did not want "to be bothered" (Coates & Gehm, 1989). Offenders are more likely than victims to report that they do not see their participation as voluntary. In studying juvenile VOM programs in six Oregon counties, nearly half of the juvenile offenders felt they had no choice (Umbreit, Coates, & Vos, 2001).

Participant Satisfaction

Expression of satisfaction with VOM is consistently high for both victims and offenders across sites, cultures, and seriousness of offenses. Eight out of 10 participants report being satisfied with the process and the resulting agreement. Moreover, when comparison groups are studied, VOM participants indicate being more satisfied with the criminal justice system than those victims and offenders who go through traditional court prosecution.

It is hypothesized that personalizing the consequences of crime enhances satisfaction levels with the entire justice process. Indeed, victims report being satisfied with being able to share their stories and the pain resulting from the crime event. Interestingly, victims frequently report that although restitution was the primary motivator for them to participate in VOM what they appreciated most about the program was the opportunity to talk with the offender (Coates & Gehm, 1989; Umbreit & Coates, 1992). A victim stated she had wanted to "let the kid know he hurt me personally, not just the money . . . I felt raped" (Umbreit, 1989, p. 56). Another female victim indicated, "I felt a little better that I've [had a] stake in [the] punishment" (Coates & Gehm, 1989, p. 255). Offenders report surprises about having positive experiences. One youth said, "He understood the mistake I made, and I really did appreciate him for it" (Umbreit, 1991, p. 195). Some reported changes: "After meeting the victim I now realize that I hurt them a lot . . . to understand how the victim feels makes me different" (Umbreit & Coates, 1992, p. 18).

A secondary analysis of satisfaction data from a U.S. and Canadian study yielded remarkably similar results (Bradshaw & Umbreit, 1998; Umbreit & Bradshaw, 2003). Three variables emerged to explain over 40% of the variance. (a) The victim felt good about the mediator; (b) the victim perceived the resulting restitution agreement as fair; and (c) the victim, for whatever reason, had a strong initial desire to meet the offender. Satisfaction with VOM also impacts greater satisfaction with the criminal justice system than for those going through traditional court prosecution (Umbreit, 1995).

Fairness

Studies have found that over 80% of VOM participants across settings, cultures, and types of offenses report believing that the process was fair to both sides and that the resulting agreement was fair (Evje & Cushman, 2000; Umbreit & Roberts, 1996). Again, these experiences led to feelings that the overall criminal justice system was fair. Where comparison groups were employed, those individuals exposed to mediation came away more likely feeling that they had been treated fairly than those going through the traditional court proceedings. In a study of burglary victims in Minneapolis, Umbreit (1989) found that 80% who went through VOM indicated that they experienced the criminal justice system as fair compared with only 37% of burglary victims who did not participate in VOM.

Restitution and Repair of Damage

About half the studies under review addressed the issue of restitution or repair of harm (Umbreit & Coates, 1992; Umbreit et al., 2001). The form of restitution is quite varied and can include direct compensation to the victim, community service, work for the victim, and sometimes unusual paybacks devised between victim and offender. Apologies are also often included in program reports as a component of repairing the harm. Of those cases that reached a meeting, typically 90% or more generated agreements. Approximately 80 to 90% of the contracts are reported as completed.

Results from comparative studies have been somewhat mixed, with some studies reporting higher amounts of restitution and/or greater completion rates for VOM participants than comparison groups (Evje & Cushman, 2000; Umbreit & Coates, 1992) while another reported no difference (Roy, 1993). The meta-analysis covering both mediation and group conferencing found that offenders participating in these programs had substantially higher completion rates than offenders processed in other ways (Latimer, Dowden, & Muise, 2001).

Diversion

Among other reasons, many restorative programs are nominally established to divert offenders from the traditional justice system processes. While such diversion was a goal lauded by many, others expressed concern about the unintended consequence of widening the net—that is, sanctioning offenders who otherwise would not have received sanctions through traditional procedures. Only a handful of the studies reviewed here address this question.

Two mediation studies, both in the UK, have reported a net-widening impact for the intervention. One concluded that at least 60% of the offenders participating in mediation were true diversion from court prosecution, and that overall there was a 13% net-widening effect, much less than expected (Dignan, 1990). In the other, fully 43% of the comparison group cases were not prosecuted and received no sanction, a fairly broad net-widening result (Warner, 1992). Two studies done in the United States found that the mediation programs successfully diverted offenders from court. A North Carolina program apparently reduced court trials by as much as two thirds (Latimer et al., 2001). An Indiana–Ohio study compared consequences for 73 youth and adults going through VOM programs with those for a matched sample of individuals who were processed in the traditional manner (Coates & Gehm, 1989). VOM offenders spent less time incarcerated than did their counterparts, and when incarcerated, they did county jail time rather than state time.

Recidivism

Preventing recidivism is often used as a long-term measure of the effectiveness of VOM programs; clearly, such prevention benefits offenders directly and, more broadly, benefits communities. The following studies used some type of comparison group. Studies simply reporting overall reoffending rates with no comparison are not included.

Results from studies examining the impact of mediation on recidivism have been mixed overall. Several studies found lower rates for mediation participants than for offenders processed through traditional means (Katz, 2000; Schneider, 1986). In addition, five of the six programs examined by Evje and Cushman (2000) also found reduced recidivism. Two studies also found that youths who did reoffend tended to incur less serious charges than their counterparts (Nugent & Paddock, 1995; Umbreit & Coates, 1992). Others reported little or no difference (Roy, 1993; Stone, Helms, & Edgeworth, 1998), as did one of the six programs studied by Evje and Cushman (2000). A study of a countywide restorative program that included VOM as one component found virtually equal recidivism rates between the sample and the control group (Bradbury, 2002).

Three meta-analyses have addressed recidivism issues. Nugent, Umbreit, Wiinamaki, and Paddock (2001) conducted a rigorous reanalysis of recidivism data reported in four previous studies involving a total sample of 1,298 juvenile offenders, 619 who participated in VOM and 679 who did not. Using ordinal logistical regression procedures, the authors determined that VOM youth recidivated at a statistically significant 32%-lower rate than non-VOM youth, and when they did reoffend, they committed less serious offenses than the non-VOM youth.

In a subsequent report, Nugent, Williams, and Umbreit (2003) expanded their data base to include 14 studies. This analysis relied on a combined sample of 9,037 juveniles and similarly found that the mediated adolescents committed fewer and less serious offenses than their counterparts.

The third meta-analysis included both mediation and FGC and found that the two types of programs together yielded reductions in recidivism compared to other, nonrestorative approaches and that offenders in the two program types were significantly more successful during the follow-up periods (Latimer et al., 2001).

Cost

Cost per unit case is obviously influenced by the number of cases handled and the amount of time devoted to each case. Evaluation of a large-scale VOM program in California led the authors to conclude that the cost per case was reduced dramatically as the program went from being a fledgling to being a viable option (Niemeyer & Shichor, 1996). Cost per case was $250. A Missouri program reported total cost per case that ranged from $232 to $338, but did not provide comparison data (Katz, 2000).

As noted earlier, some programs have impacted total incarceration time (Coates & Gehm, 1989), place/cost of incarceration, or reduction of trials (Clarke, Valente, & Mace, 1992). Additionally, time spent to process a case has implications for overall cost. Stone et al. (1998) found that the total time required to process mediated cases was only a third of that needed for nonmediated cases.

In an evaluation of a large-scale restorative program (of which VOM was one component) for youths who would have been referred to state custody, Bradbury (2002) found that the yearly cost per case was less than for the state custody program ($48,396 versus $65,866). Since recidivism was virtually the same between the two groups, the restorative program was less costly on the surface. However, the author concluded that because the restorative youths spent more days in the community, they posed more risk to community residents, so neither program could be designated as clearly superior.

Summary

Just as interest in VOM is growing within the justice arena, so is the body of empirical knowledge collected to evaluate, shape, and refine it. Involving victims, offenders, and community members in sorting out possible solutions to conflicts is yielding, for the most part, positive responses from participants. The vast majority of participants find the experience satisfactory, fair, and helpful. In a number of jurisdictions, rates of restitution completion have climbed. And offenders going through mediation approaches often have lower levels of offending than they did before or than compared with a similar group of offenders who did not meet with their victims.

These differences could be attributed to the effect of self-selection bias; that is, victims and offenders choose to participate in these programs (McCold & Wachtel, 1998). Notwithstanding this issue, the results of the meta-analyses suggest that those individuals who choose to participate in VOM find the process satisfying, tend to display lower recidivism rates, and are more likely to follow through on restitution agreements.

Pitfalls and Unintended Consequences

The restorative justice movement is grounded in values that promote both accountability and healing for all affected by crime. It emphasizes positive human development, mutuality, empathy, responsibility, respect, and fairness. Yet the principles and practices of the restorative justice movement are not inherently benign, incapable of doing harm. Besides receiving adequate training, the ongoing self-care of the mediator helps ensure that full attention can be given to meeting the participants' needs.

Pitfalls

In large part, the pitfalls derive from the inherent difficulty of attempting to balance so many valid needs: needs of victims, needs of offenders, needs of their community, and ultimately the needs of the state that has come to represent them. Sometimes the problem arises from inattention to some of the basic principles and guidelines. For example, well-intentioned judges in two different states took the opportunity during the civil portion of trials involving negligent homicide from drunk driving to refer the offender and the family survivor of the victim to a mediation process—on the surface, a positive restorative option for both. However, in each instance there was no separate preparation of the involved parties, and the persons responsible for facilitating the meetings had no specific training in victim–offender dialogue.

It is not just well-intentioned individuals who make such errors. A nationally recognized exemplary offender reentry project that receives large federal grants to support restorative group conferencing invites victims at the last moment with no preparation, no support, and little involvement. The net result is a feeling of revictimization by those crime victims who participated.

In many jurisdictions there are well-intended juvenile justice officials and judges who mandate young offenders to meet with their victims if the victim is willing to do so, even if the defendant does not own up to the offense or would prefer not to do this type of intervention. Two documented cases occurred in a Midwestern state in both a VOM program and an FGC program. In both cases the victims and their support people felt revictimized by the process because of the attitude projected by the offender who was mandated to attend against his will.

A frequent shortfall is excessive focus on offender rehabilitation, to the exclusion of the needs of the victims and the community. Within the United States, at least one state has adopted legislation to support restorative justice principles because of the restorative justice impact on reducing recidivism and prison overcrowding. A national legal reform organization deeply committed to restorative justice similarly articulates its rationale for such support based on the impact of restorative justice on rehabilitating offenders. Again the significance of the victim's voice gets lost when VOM programs concentrate primarily on the offender's needs.

In the face of these potential pitfalls, mediators and members of the criminal justice system must remain committed to the basic principles and guidelines of VOM, which have by now become well established and well known. These include mediator training, preparation of VOM participants, voluntary participation by all parties, inherent potential for revictimization, and the need for equal concern and commitment to victims and offenders.

Mediator Self-Care

Helping people deal with conflict and pain can take an enormous toll. Self-care is not only carried out for the well-being of the mediator; it is also part of developing the capacity for being fully present with victims and offenders in premeetings, in face-to-face encounters, in follow-up, and in finally letting go of a particular case. Self-care practices vary greatly. Such practices include meditation, yoga, working out at the gym, running, listening to music, resting, cleaning the house, praying, talking with other volunteers, or knowing when to pass on a case because it is too emotionally charged. These same self-care practices also can be used by mediators to center themselves in order to be as available as possible to the dialogue participants. Moreover, self-care after a particularly emotionally grueling experience is vital to self-restoration. Some program managers build in a debriefing to help the mediator integrate the experience, let it go, and move on. Identification of self-care as a continuing critical issue reminds all of us that restorative justice dialogue can impact mediators profoundly as well as victims and offenders. It is a human process. Moreover, mediator self-care can help prevent some of the unintended consequences because self-care can reduce the stress that otherwise contributes to hasty or poor decision making.

Questions for the Future

Although VOM is a widely supported restorative justice dialogue program, there are numerous unresolved and often troubling issues. Many of these speak to the core integrity of the movement, while others pose questions about fair and effective implementation. Some of the most salient issues include the following list:

1 How can VOM reconcile the fact that there is a deep distrust of programs operated by the formal justice system but the public sector is involved in administering these types of programs? Indeed, a study of VOM programs in six Oregon counties found no significant differences in terms of outcomes when programs under public and private nonprofit auspices were compared (Umbreit et al., 2001).
2 How can there be a system-wide commitment to providing local citizens who are victimized by all but the most serious violent crime the opportunity to choose VOM?
3 How can extensive and unfair disparity in sanctions and outcomes be avoided as individual victims and communities are given a wide range of options for holding the offender accountable?
4 Can restorative justice really be a victim-centered approach when the overwhelming emphasis and resources in the system are so heavily focused on identifying, apprehending, processing, and punishing or even treating the offender?
5 Within the United States, the criminal justice system has a vastly disproportionate number of persons of color caught in its policies and practices. How can VOM avoid mirroring this same reality?

Conclusion

Application of alternative dispute resolution techniques in the context of delinquent and criminal behavior is somewhat similar to other types of mediation, but there does exist a number of very clear distinguishing characteristics. The process of VOM is certainly not meant for all victims and offenders. Nor is it meant to diminish the fine work being done by the many other important programs serving the needs of victims or offenders. Rather, the growing practice of VOM, whenever appropriate, represents a much needed presence within the broader fields of alternative dispute resolution and criminal justice.

The wide-spread practice of VOM in thousands of cases each year, and the empirical evidence generated over the past 25 years across many sites in numerous countries, strongly indicates that VOM contributes to increased victim involvement and healing, to offenders taking responsibility for their behaviors and learning from this experience, to community members participating in shaping a just response to law violation, and to more positive public attitudes toward juvenile and criminal courts.

RESOURCES AND REFERENCES

Abrams, L., & Umbreit, M. S. (2002). *Youthful offenders response to victim offender conferencing in Washington County*. St. Paul, MN: Center for Restorative Justice & Peacemaking.
American Bar Association. (1994, August). Policy on legislative and national issues. In American Bar Association, *Policies and procedures handbook* (p. 73). Chicago, IL: Author.
Bazemore, G., & Umbreit, M. S. (1995). Rethinking the sanctioning function in juvenile court: Retributive or restorative responses to youth crime. *Crime and Delinquency, 41*(3), 296–316.

Bradbury, B. (2002). *Deschutes County delinquent youth demonstration project* (Secretary of State Audit Report No. 2002-29). Salem, OR: Office of the Secretary of State.

Bradshaw, W., & Umbreit, M. (1998). Crime victims meet juvenile offenders: Contributing factors to victim satisfaction with mediated dialogue. *Juvenile and Family Court Journal, 49*(3), 17–25.

Cayley, D. (1998). *The expanding prison: The crisis in crime and punishment and search for alternatives.* Cleveland, OH: Pilgrim Press.

Clarke, S., Valente, E., & Mace, R. (1992). *Mediation of interpersonal disputes: An evaluation of North Carolina's programs.* Chapel Hill: Institute of Government, University of North Carolina.

Coates, R. B. and Gehm, J. (1989). An empirical assessment. In M. Wright and B. Galaway (Eds.) *Mediation and criminal justice* (pp. 251-263). London: Sage.

Coates, R. B., Umbreit, M. S., & Burns, H. (2004). Why victims choose to meet with offenders. *Offender Programs Report, 8*(4), 55–57.

Commission of the European Communities (2001). Report from the Commission on the basis of article 18 of the Council Framework Decision of 15 March 2001 on the standing of victims in criminal proceedings, COM (2004) 54 final/2, 16.02.04 Retrieved October 11, 2006 from http://europa.eu/bulletin/en/200012/p104015.htm.

Dignan, J. (1990). *Repairing the damage: An evaluation of an experimental adult reparation scheme in Kettering, Northamptonshire.* Sheffield, UK: Centre for Criminological Legal Research, Faculty of Law, University of Sheffield.

Evje, A., & Cushman, R. (2000). *A summary of the evaluations of six California victim offender rehabilitation programs.* San Francisco: Administrative Office of the Courts.

Gehm, J. (1990). Mediated victim-offender restitution agreements: An exploratory analysis of factors related to victim participation. In B. Galaway & J. Hudson (Eds.), *Criminal justice, restitution, and reconciliation* (pp. 177–182). London: Sage.

Johnstone, G. (2002). *Restorative justice: Ideas, values, debates.* Devon, UK: Willan.

Katz, J. (2000). *Victim–offender mediation in Missouri's juvenile courts: Accountability, restitution, and transformation.* Jefferson City: Missouri Department of Public Safety.

Latimer, J., Dowden, C., & Muise, D. (2001). *The effectiveness of restorative practices: A meta-analysis.* Ottawa, Canada: Department of Justice, Research and Statistics Division Methodological Series.

Lightfoot, E., & Umbreit, M. (2002). *Legislative statutes on victim–offender mediation: A national review.* St. Paul: Center for Restorative Justice & Peacemaking, University of Minnesota.

McCold, P., & Wachtel, B. (1998). *Restorative policing experiment: The Bethlehem Pennsylvania Police Family Group Conferencing Project.* Pipersville, PA: Community Service Foundation.

Niemeyer, M., & Shichor, D. (1996). A preliminary study of a large victim/offender reconciliation program. *Federal Probation, 60*(3), 30–34.

Nugent, W., Umbreit, M., Wiinamaki, L., & Paddock, J. (2001). Participation in victim–offender mediation and severity of subsequent delinquent behavior: Successful replications? *Journal of Research in Social Work Practice, 11*(1), 5–23.

Nugent, W., Williams, R. M., & Umbreit, M. S. (2003). Participation in victim–offender mediation and the prevalence and severity of subsequent delinquent behavior: A meta-analysis. *Utah Law Review, 2003*(1), 137–165.

Nugent, W. M., & Paddock, M. (1995). The effect of victim – offender mediation on severity of reoffense. *Mediation Quarterly, 12*, 353–367.

Peachey, D. E. (1989). The Kitchener experiment. In M. Wright & B. Galaway (Eds.), *Mediation and criminal justice.* London: Sage.

Pranis, K., & Umbreit, M. S. (1992). *Public opinion research challenges perception of widespread public demand for harsher punishment.* Minneapolis, MN: Citizen's Council.

Roy, S. (1993). Two types of juvenile restitution programs in two Midwestern counties: A comparative study. *Federal Probation, 57*(4), 48–53.

Schneider, A. (1986). Restitution and recidivism rates of juvenile offenders: Results from four experimental studies. *Criminology, 24*, 533–552.

Stone, S., Helms, W., & Edgeworth, P. (1998). *Cobb County juvenile court mediation program evaluation.* Carrolton: State University of West Georgia.

Umbreit, M. S. (1989). Crime victims seeking fairness, not revenge: Toward restorative justice. *Federal Probation, 53*(3), 52–57.

Umbreit, M. S. (1991). Minnesota Mediation Center produces positive results. *Corrections Today 53*(5), 194–197.

Umbreit, M. S.. (1994). *Victim meets offender*. Monsey, NY: Criminal Justice Press.

Umbreit, M. S. (1995). *Mediation of criminal conflict: An assessment of programs in four Canadian provinces*. St. Paul, MN: Center for Restorative Justice and Mediation.

Umbreit, M. S. (1997). Humanistic mediation: A transformative journey of peacemaking. *Mediation Quarterly, 14*, 201–213.

Umbreit, M. S. (2001). *The handbook of victim–offender mediation: An essential guide to practice and research*. San Francisco: Jossey-Bass.

Umbreit, M. S. (2004). Victim offender mediation in juvenile or criminal courts. In D. Stienstra & S. Yates (Eds.), *Alternative dispute resolution handbook for judges* (pp. 225-236).Washington, D.C.:American Bar Association.

Umbreit, M. S., & Bradshaw, W. (2003). Factors that contribute to victim satisfaction with mediated offender dialogue in Winnipeg: An emerging area of social work practice. *Journal of Law and Social Work, 9*(2), 35–51.

Umbreit, M. S., & Coates, R. B. (1992). *Victim–offender mediation: An analysis of programs in four states of the US*. Minneapolis: Minnesota Citizens Council on Crime and Justice.

Umbreit, M. S., Coates, R. B., & Vos, B. (2001). *Juvenile victim–offender mediation in six Oregon counties*. Salem: Oregon Dispute Resolution Commission.

Umbreit, M. S., & Greenwood, J. (1999). National survey of victim–offender mediation programs in the US. *Mediation Quarterly, 16*, 235–251.

Umbreit, M. S., & Roberts, A. W. (1996). *Mediation of criminal conflict in England: An assessment of services in Coventry and Leeds*. St. Paul, MN: Center for Restorative Justice and Mediation.

Umbreit, M. S., Vos, B., & Coates, R. B. (2005). *Restorative justice in the 21st century: A social movement full of opportunities and pitfalls*. St. Paul: University of Minnesota, School of Social Work, Center for Restorative Justice & Peacemaking.

Umbreit, M. S., Vos, B., & Coates, R. B. (2006). Restorative justice in the 21st century: A social movement full of opportunities and pitfalls. *Marquette University Law Review, 89*(2), 257–304.

Umbreit, M. S., Vos, B., Coates, R. B., & Brown, K. (2003). *Facing violence: The path of restorative justice & dialogue*. Monsey, NY: Criminal Justice Press.

United Nations. (2000, July 27). *Basic principles on the use of restorative justice programmes in criminal matters* (ECOSOC Res. 2000/14). New York: Author.

Van Ness, D., & Heetderks, K. (2002). *Restoring justice* (2nd ed.). Cincinnati, OH: Anderson.

Warner, S. (1992). *Making amends: Justice for victims and offenders*. Aldershot, UK: Avebury.

Wyrick, P., & Costanzo, M. (1999). Predictors of client participation in victim-offender mediation. *Mediation Quarterly, 16*, 253–267.

Young, M. (1995). *Restorative community justice: A call to action*. Washington, DC: National Organization for Victim Assistance.

Zehr, H. (1990). *Changing lenses: A new focus for crime and justice*. Scottsdale, PA: Herald Press.

Zehr, H. (2002). *The little book of restorative justice*. Intercourse, PA: Good Books.

Relevant Resources

Video Tapes

($20 each, all six for $100)
Produced by the
Center for Restorative Justice & Peacemaking, University of Minnesota

Video 1: Restorative Justice: For Victims, Communities, and Offenders, 25 minutes
This 25-minute video is an excellent resource for broad-based public education about the growing international restorative justice movement. Adapted from the Presbyterian Church USA's *Restoring Justice* video, this version includes research material and resources available in the field. The development of restorative justice in numerous and diverse communities throughout the United States is highlighted. Comments are offered by internationally recognized experts in the field, including Kay Pranis, Mark Umbreit, and Howard Zehr, and many visual examples of restorative justice interventions are presented.

Video 2: Restorative Justice: Victim Empowerment Through Mediation and Dialogue, 25 minutes

This video emphasizes the importance of voluntary participation and victim-sensitive practices through-out the restorative justice and mediation process with a focus on property crimes and minor assaults. An excellent resource for current programs, or for any organization considering the development of such a program, it is particularly helpful to victim assistance agencies and even individual victims who may be considering either supporting or directly participating in the mediation/dialogue process.

Video 3: An Overview of Victim–Offender Mediation and Conferencing, 10 minutes
An overview of the core principles of restorative justice and the victim–offender mediation/conferencing process is provided. Practices that make the mediation/dialogue process more victim sensitive, and ulti-mately more offender sensitive, are identified. The importance of preparation is emphasized throughout the entire video. Intended as a brief overview to inform and guide the viewer through two restorative justice dialogue approaches, this video does not demonstrate in detail the steps required for skilled application of each approach. It is, however, a particularly helpful informational resource to use during brief presentations or workshops.

Video 4: Victim–Offender Mediation and Conferencing: A Multi-Method Approach, 22 minutes
An overview of the core principles of restorative justice and the victim–offender mediation/conferencing process is provided. The importance of adapting restorative justice practices to the expressed needs and cultural context of the people involved is emphasized. Three specific examples are illustrated. First, the use of small group sessions is shown with a one-on-one meeting between victim and offender; next, a conference with support persons present; and third, a brief portrayal of a larger group conference involving neighbors and family members. The importance of preparation is emphasized throughout the entire video. Intended as an overview to inform and guide the viewer through a range of restorative justice dialogue approaches, this video does not demonstrate in detail the steps required for skilled application of each approach. Yet it is a helpful informational resource to use during general presentations about restorative justice conferencing and in training seminars.

Video 5: Complete Victim–Offender Mediation and Conferencing Training: Modeling 2 Cases From Preparation to Mediation, 117 minutes
Following a brief presentation of several key points central to the victim–offender media-tion/conferencing process, two case examples are presented in detail, modeling both the preparation process and the actual face-to-face meeting. The first case involves a home burglary by a young adult in which, after being encouraged to bring a support person, both the victim and offender choose to meet one-on-one. A single mediator is used. The second example is a case of juvenile vandalism perceived as a hate crime against an African American woman. The offender's mother participates in the dialogue; the victim has both her brother and a neighbor present at the meeting. Co-mediators are used in this second case. Each case concludes with a signed agreement for repair of the harm caused by the crime. This 2-hour video is a valuable resource for training mediators/facilitators in the details of the entire victim–offender mediation/conferencing process.

Video 6: Victim Sensitive Offender Dialogue in Crimes of Severe Violence, 70 minutes
In this video, an overview of the victim-sensitive dialogue process in crimes of severe violence is provided by Dr. Mark Umbreit of the Center for Restorative Justice & Peacemaking at the University of Minnesota. The importance of victim-sensitive procedures and humanistic dialogue-driven mediation are highlighted. Segments of separate preparation meetings with the victim and the offender/inmate are shown, followed by a face-to-face meeting of the victim and offender in the presence of a highly trained mediator and co-mediator. The case portrayed is a simulation of an actual murder case. Comments from victim advocates and the Director of the Ohio Department of Corrections and Rehabilitation are offered at the end of the tape. This video is an informational presentation for those unfamiliar with this intervention and can be used in actual advanced training.

Recent Books

Umbreit, M. S. (2001). *The handbook of victim offender mediation: An essential guide to practice and research*. San Francisco: Jossey-Bass. 448 pages, ISBN 0-7879-5491-8.

This is the first resource to provide a conceptual and research-based framework and a practical process for mediating a wide variety of criminal conflicts between victims of crime and their offenders. Step by step, this comprehensive handbook clearly defines how the process works, shows how to identify appropriate victim and offender participants, and reveals what it takes to prepare both sides for the upcoming meeting, which is facilitated through a humanistic dialogue-driven form of mediation.

Umbreit, M. S., Vos, B., Coates, R. B., & Brown, K. B. (2003). *Facing violence: The path of restorative justice and dialogue*. Monsey, NY: Criminal Justice Press. 395 pages, ISBN 1-881798-45-3.

This book presents findings of a 5-year study of victim–officer mediation and dialogue in crimes of severe violence pioneered in the first two states to initiate such a statewide service, in Texas and Ohio. The vast majority of cases involved homicide. The programs are identified, along with case and client characteristics. The experience of participants related to the impact that the dialogue session had on their lives is described, including how helpful the process was, the degree to which it contributed to their healing and growth, how satisfied they were with the process, and other related issues. Specific implications for policy and practice are presented, along with numerous cases studies and review of related research and practice.

Monographs*

1 Armour, M. (2002). Meaning making in the aftermath of homicide.
2 Burns, H. (2002). Citizens, Victims and Offenders Restoring Justice Project: Minnesota Correctional Facility for Women at Lino Lakes.
3 Burns, H. (2001). Citizens, Victims and Offenders Restoring Justice Project: Minnesota Correctional Facility for Women at Shakopee.
4 Coates, R. B., Umbreit, M. S., & Vos, B. (2000). Restorative justice circles in South St. Paul, Minnesota.
5 Fercello, C., Greenwood, J., Schug, R., Umbreit, J., & Umbreit, M. S. (2003). Directory of victim offender mediation programs in the U.S.
6 Roberts, A. W., & Masters, G. (1999). Group conferencing: Restorative justice in practice, Part 1, Part 2, Part 3, Part 4.
7 Umbreit, M. S. (1995). Mediation of criminal conflict: An assessment of programs in four Canadian provinces.
8 Umbreit, M. S. (1995). Victim–offender mediation: An analysis of programs in four US States, 1992.
9 Umbreit, M. S. (2001). Peacemaking and spirituality: A journey towards healing and strength.
10 Umbreit, M. S. (2001). Restorative justice conferencing: Guidelines for victim restorative justice conferencing: Guidelines for victim reparative boards to people, communities, and cultures.
11 Umbreit, M. S. (2002). Forgiveness: An annotated bibliography.
12 Umbreit, M. S., Bradshaw, W., Coates, R. B. (2001). Victim sensitive offender dialogue in crimes of severe violence: Differing needs, approaches, and implications.
13 Umbreit, M. S., & Burns, H. (2002). Humanistic mediation: Peacemaking grounded in core social work values.
14 Umbreit, M. S., Coates, R. B., & Vos, B. (2001). Juvenile victim–offender mediation in six Oregon counties: Final report.
15 Umbreit, M. S., Coates, R. B., & Vos, B. (2001). The victim impact of restorative justice conferencing with juvenile offenders.
16 Umbreit, M. S., Coates, R., & Vos, B. (2002). Systemic change toward restorative justice: Washington County.
17 Umbreit, M. S., Coates, R. B., & Vos, B. (2002). The impact of restorative justice conferencing: A review of 63 empirical studies in 5 countries.
18 Umbreit, M. S., Coates, R. B., & Vos, B. (2003, September). An annotated bibliography of victim–offender mediation.
19 Umbreit, M. S., Lightfoot, E., & Fier, J. (2001). Legislative statutes on victim–offender mediation: A national review.
20 Umbreit, M. S., & Roberts, A. W. (1996). Mediation of criminal conflict in England: An assessment of services in Coventry and Leeds.

*Available free from the Center for Restorative Justice & Peacemaking, University of Minnesota, St. Paul.

Web Sites of Restorative Justice Organizations

- Balanced and Restorative Justice Project Web site: http://www.barjproject.org
- Center for Peacemaking and Conflict Studies, Fresno Pacific University Web site: http://peace.fresno.edu/rjp
- Center for Restorative Justice & Peacemaking, University of Minnesota Web site: http://2ssw.che.umn.edu/rjp/Seminars/Seminars-2005.html
- Centre for Restorative Justice, Simon Frazer University Web site: http://www.sfu.ca/cfrj
- International Victim Offender Mediation Association Web site: http://www.voma.org

For additional assistance, to order materials, and for information related to training opportunities, conferences, technical assistance, and other programs, contact:

Center for Restorative Justice & Peacemaking
University of Minnesota, School of Social Work
105 Peters Hall
1404 Gortner Avenue
St. Paul, MN 55108
PH: (612) 624-4923
FX: (612) 625-8224
EMAIL: rjp@che.umn.edu

Katherine van Wormer
Morris Jenkins

R estorative justice is a movement within (and sometimes outside of) the criminal justice system with special relevance to marginalized populations. Representing a paradigm shift from conventional forms of resolving wrongdoing, restorative justice focuses more attention on the harm to victims and communities, as Zehr (1990) explains, and less on the fact of law breaking. Within modern society, restorative justice represents a paradigm shift, a new vision that has brought people together from various sides of the law and from various backgrounds and lifestyles. Above all, restorative justice is about concern at the macro level and at the micro level about relationships. From the point of view of the offender, restorative justice is about change and redemption; from the view of the victim, it is about healing.

Case Examples

1 When first contacted by the Iowa Administrator of Victim and Restorative Justice Programs to participate in a meeting with the murderer of her daughter, who was now in prison serving out her sentence, Cindy refused. Her daughter had been killed by another woman, Tara, after a dispute over a man. The crime had been horribly brutal; Tara had run over the victim with her car, which had dragged the body, caught underneath the car, for several blocks. The reason Cindy refused this meeting was because, from the way the representative told her about it, she felt that Tara was using the fact that she had been drinking as an excuse. However, when she read Tara's letter requesting the meeting, she was impressed that the

inmate was taking responsibility for the crime. Both women received counseling to prepare them for the encounter. At the prison, the women met for 3.5 hours, each expressing her feelings about the crime. In the end, Cindy told Tara that she wished the best for her, that her daughter would have wanted that for her, that she should try to live a good life, and that she avoid the bad company she had been in before. Since Tara was soon to be paroled, the meeting took on a special significance for both of the participants and resolved a number of difficult issues.

2   A group of priests and ex-priests in treatment for sexual offenders are required to attend a panel in which men and women who were molested as children tell how the molestation affected their lives. Father Brown, who had confessed to molesting a series of young women over the years and had always told himself that his gentle introduction to sex for these innocent adolescents was a blessing to both of them, was suddenly brought face to face with the selfishness of what he had done. He heard of their despair, their betrayal by the father figure in their lives, their sense of guilt, the pain of secrecy, and ultimately their loss of religious faith. And his long-standing defenses were shattered. For the first time, he experienced empathy for those persons who had once been objects of his desire.

3   In the Gullah Islands of South Carolina, many of the long-time inhabitants use a form of culturally specific restorative justice to resolve minor complaints and conflicts (Jenkins, 2006). Many the inhabitants attend semiregular meetings sponsored by the local church to deal with problems that may occur. Prior to one of the meetings, one of the inhabitants was killed by the negligent actions of one of the economically disadvantaged inhabitants of the community. The community, through one of the elders, admonished and chastised the individual for his negligent actions. The elders used the Bible as the foundation for the admonishment, and the individual was told how the community in the past would banish the person from the "church community" until there was a full repentance from the wrong doer. The individual who was negligent did feel shame, but because of his economic position, he could not give the family any financial restitution for his actions. However, over a period of a few months, biweekly baskets of food (basically okra and fish) would mysteriously appear on the doorsteps of the victim's family. In addition, community members would visit and pray with the wrongdoer.

The Restorative Justice Movement

Throughout history, local communities and traditional cultures developed ways of managing conflict and of bringing the offender to accountability to the community. These means of righting the wrong were ritualized but based on communication among members of the community and families of both parties. These forms of justice were found in all cultures. In the Navajo tradition, for example, peacemaking is a form of communal response to help people who have been harmed by another (Sullivan & Tifft, 2001). Community justice operated in early modern Europe, but the emphasis on vengeance became formalized in the Middle Ages as feudal lords and kings consolidated the response to crime through the power of the state (Bazemore & Schiff, 2001). This development was an advance in the sense of preventing family feuds, yet the role of the victim was now relegated to that of witness (Pollard, 2000). Anything that violated the king's peace was interpreted as an offence against the king. Thus, was retributive justice born.

Another development that dominates Anglo–Saxon justice today is the adversarial process. This process harks back to the Middle Ages in England when hired combatants fought duels on behalf of accused individuals (van Wormer, 2006). It is a decidedly masculine system in every respect. Today's trial, in fact, is the counterpart to yesterday's dueling, which was literally trial by combat. Then, as now, it was a case of "may the strong man win." Crime eventually became defined as an offense against the state. The role of judge emerged as a sort of referee between the disputing parties.

Today, deliberation takes place according to a standardized, one-size-fits-all trial or, more often, a plea-bargaining arrangement in which the victim's input tends to be minimal (Van Ness & Strong, 2002). Families and friends of the accused are torn apart from families and friends on the other side of the law. Such court processes and plea bargaining behind closed doors does little to enhance communication and healing among members of the community.

Resolution of conflict through conferencing is the most highly developed in New Zealand, where it is institutionalized throughout the whole system. The similarities between restorative and aboriginal forms of justice coupled with the failure of the existing criminal justice system to deal with the problems of indigenous populations has enhanced its enthusiastic acceptance in New Zealand, as well as in northwest Canada (Roach, 2000).

With the passage of the Sentencing Act of 2002, New Zealand enacted new legislation to make restorative justice processes that had formerly been used with juveniles and families in the child welfare system also available for adult offenders (Parker, 2002), even for situations of domestic violence and rape, which had been excluded from conferencing previously.

Scope of the Problem

The primary problem is violence and other forms of violation by one person or the other, but a larger problem than interpersonal violence is the structural violence at the societal level. Both forms of violence—interpersonal and structural—are often caused by a lack of empathy in society for the victims of crime combined with an extreme degree of punitiveness (zero tolerance) toward convicted offenders. The crimes committed against criminals by society are often as cruel as the original offenses themselves; for example, women sentenced for drug offenses are deprived of visitation with their children and African American men are shut away for years and years in overcrowded and otherwise inhumane conditions. The "get-tough" policies have been inflicted on youth, especially minority youth, sometimes with a vengeance that has been counterproductive and contrary to the ideals of rehabilitation and community building.

The failure of the criminal justice system to meet the needs of victims of crime and to provide an atmosphere in which the offender is rewarded for expressing remorse are common themes in the literature (see Rozee & Koss, 2001; van Wormer, 2006; Zehr, 1990). With regard to intimate partner violence, for example, as Frisch (2003) indicates, the law, which was framed to protect citizens from violence by strangers who are unlikely ever to see each other again, does not easily lend itself to the demands of interpersonal situations. Victims of crime are often revictimized as they seek justice through the criminal justice system. Forced public testimony of the victim at a trial, if it comes to that, may compromise her safety. Moreover, child protective services may start investigating her for her failure to protect the children.

In a similar vein, Rozee and Koss (2001) criticize the handling and outcomes of acquaintance rape at every level of the criminal justice system from the police officer's treatment of the victim to the prosecutor's reluctance to take the case to court to courtroom antics geared to demolish the credibility of the victim as chief witness for the prosecution. Racial-ethnic differences between state officials and the victim compound the lack of consideration and respect. Additionally, as Rozee and Koss further suggest, adversarial justice is experienced as "White imposed" (2001, p. 306); women of color must contend with tension between their needs for justice and felt obligations to buffer racism in the criminal justice system. African American and Latina women may avoid seeking help from the criminal justice system or women's shelters to protect the image held of the minority group in a racist society (Presser & Gaarder, 2004). Women of color are well aware of the brutal and prejudicial treatment inflicted on men of color by the criminal justice system, and they might not want to turn to that system for justice.

In summary, the patriarchal, Anglo–American adversary/plea bargaining system fails to meet the needs of victims in many instances, and of offenders in many others. Even in cases where justice is instituted successfully, for example, where a murderer is given an appropriately lengthy sentence, there is often much business left unfinished. The criminal justice system, in short, is criticized as being ineffective in dealing with crime, the needs of the victim, and the rehabilitation of the offender.

Persons of color have additional criticisms about the criminal justice system and often feel victimized both by offenders (many of whom are African American) as well as by the perceived and real discrimination that occurs throughout the criminal justice system (Johnson, 1993; McCoy, 1993; Miller, 1996; Weitzer, 1996). Even though community members feel victimized by criminals, many in the African American community feel that submitting a fellow brother or sister to the criminal justice system may be an inappropriate response (Austin, 1992). Current responses to crime and delinquency within the African American community, grounded in the substantive criminal law and driven by recent expansion in police powers, have led to a disproportionate number of African Americans in prisons and jails in the United States (Leiber, 2002). Restorative justice has been proposed as a possible solution to this problem.

What Is Restorative Justice?

Restorative justice is a process that is a paradigmatic shift in the approach to crime that could possibly deal with this issue. It seeks to humanize the participants in their quest for justice and requires that the community become an active participant, empowering its members to deal with crime and delinquency (Bazemore, 1994; Umbreit, 1995; Zehr, 1990). This community participation may also offset some of the problems associated with institutional sexism and racism.

More often described in terms of what it is not, rather than what it is, restorative justice is deceptively simple. In fact, this is just one of its many paradoxes. Among the paradoxes, restorative justice is:

- An indigenous approach that can be applied universally and that works well in modern, industrialized societies.
- Seemingly in opposition to the dictates of criminal justice, yet often operating through criminal justice auspices.
- Visionary, yet highly practical.
- A new approach that goes back to ancient customs and traditions.
- A person-centered and kind way of dealing with crime in a "lock-'em-up" era.
- Victim-focused, yet beneficial to the offender as well.
- Secular, yet with spiritual overtones.
- A beacon of light to shine in the darkness.

Models of Restorative Justice

Restorative justice philosophy has generated a wide variety of activities across North America toward a vision of wholeness for all those persons who are harmed by crime. This chapter examines the idea of restorative justice in terms of the scope of the problem—the failure of the present criminal justice system to meet the needs of community and victim in terms of repairing the harm that was done. We briefly describe four various representative forms of restorative initiatives chosen due to their relevance to work with marginalized individuals and populations: victim–offender conferencing, family group conferencing, healing circles, and community reparations. A literature review follows, summarizing evidence-based findings from victim assessments and offender recidivism measures. The heart of the chapter is devoted to a description of victim–offender and community-based initiatives as they pertain to gender and minority needs. Finally, controversies concerning the use of restorative techniques in rape and domestic violence situations are discussed.

Victim–Offender Conferencing

Victim–offender conferencing, sometimes incorrectly referred to as victim–offender mediation, brings together parties for the sake of resolution when one person has injured another and, if possible, to right the wrong. Unlike the mediation model, restorative justice recognizes its participants as victim and offender, rather than as disputants (Presser & Gaarder, 2004). There may be more than one victim and more than one offender. Often an adolescent has acted recklessly or committed a deliberate act such as vandalism. The ritual of the conference brings him or her face to face with community members harmed by the act. The largest programs to date have been offered through victim assistance services of state departments of corrections (Umbreit, Vos, Coates, & Brown, 2003). A trained professional opens the conference and describes the situation in a general sense.

Consider a situation in which an adolescent has endangered the lives of his or her neighbors in some way. The victims, who are the center of the conference, begin by describing their reactions to the act that was perpetrated against them and the aftereffects of having been violated in this way. Supporters of the offender provide background information about the offender and his or her cultural background if relevant, for example, if the person is an immigrant who has newly arrived to the country and has had some difficulties adjusting to the new land or experienced trauma before arriving here. Informal discussion takes place; typically, the offender offers restitution of some sort and expresses remorse for the harm that was done.

In recent years, practitioners have found themselves being asked to bring together victims or survivors of severe forms of violence such as murder of a family member. Such cases, as Umbreit et al. (2003) suggest, require longer case preparation of all participants with special attention paid to their expectations and feelings about the encounter, greater professional skills of facilitators, negotiation with correctional officials, and clarification of boundary issues.

Family Group Conferencing

We can thank the Maori people and social services authorities of New Zealand for the introduction of an innovative program known as family group conferencing (FGC). This model of restoring justice is an outgrowth of both aboriginal and feminist practice concerns stemming from the international women's and children's rights movements of the late 1980s and beyond. Evoking the family group decision-making model in order to try to stop family violence, FGC made its mainstream criminal justice debut in New Zealand in 1989. It also made an appearance about the same time in England and Oregon. This model is currently being tested in Newfoundland and Labrador, as well as in communities in New Zealand, Austria, England, Wales, and North America (see Burford & Hudson, 2000). Despite differences among jurisdictions, one common theme is overriding: FGCs are more likely than traditional forms of dispute resolution to give effective voice to those who are traditionally disadvantaged.

We have filtered out from the literature a number of characteristics of FGC relevant to child welfare practice. Compared to traditional practices in family work, the philosophy of FGC entails:

- Sharing decision-making responsibilities with families.
- A role for the social worker as partner/collaborator rather than expert.
- Decision making by general consensus.
- A process and decision making more likely to reflect the culture, traditions, and needs of the participants.
- Stress on the *quality* of relationships, not family structures.
- Beginning with a broad definition of what constitutes a family.
- Acknowledging the value of kinship care over stranger care for children in need of care.
- A solutions-focused rather than problem-focused framework.
- A proactive rather than investigative model for addressing child mistreatment.
- A focus on building up social networks while not being blind to the risks to children in an unhealthy social environment.

Unlike victim–offender conferencing, the focus here is not on the harm done so much as on the welfare of an abused or neglected child and of the family as a whole. Another difference is the active inclusion of family members, close friends, and other support groups of the main parties to the conference. This approach is appropriate to the needs of women in that the focus is often on parenting and helping the mother with problems in caregiving so that she can take better care of the child, often through support from other relatives and direct help in child care responsibilities. This model works well in close-knit minority communities with extended family ties.

Social work educators Kemp, Whittaker, and Tracy (2000) have adapted a strengths-based *social network model* of FGC for child protection practice. Central to their model is network facilitation to tap into the real power of natural helping. Network meetings are conducted to prepare participants for extended family decision making. The connection between the individual families and community resources is given special attention. For example, advocacy for kinship caregivers to become eligible for the same resources as are available to non-kin foster parents may be undertaken. Interlocking demands of previous poverty, social exclusion, weak community linkages, and troubled extended family relationships are typical challenges facing families seen in child welfare practice. Network facilitation is individually tailored, as Kemp and her colleagues indicate, based on an identification of existing and potential network members. Ideally, FGCs will make creative use of network meetings for reconnecting estranged network members to the family circle.

Healing Circles

Healing circles offer a format borrowed from Native rituals that is especially relevant for work with victims and survivors in providing family and/or community support. Such support is often needed following the trauma caused by a crime of violence such as rape. This innovative approach is ideal for recovering alcoholics and addicts who wish to be reconciled to loved ones as well. The Toronto District School Board has adopted this approach for situations in which students have victimized others at school ("Healing Circle," 2001).

In the healing circle, all the people touched by the offense gather together, review the incident or incidents, try to make sense of it or them, and hopefully reach a peaceful resolution. In order for consensus to be achieved, all participants have a voice in the decision that is reached. In addition to the use of consensus for decision making, several aspects of the circle process reinforce the democratic ideal of equal voice and equal responsibility (Pranis, 2001). A talking piece, which may be a giant bird feather, has an equalizing effect in structuring dialogue as it is passed from speaker to speaker to provide an opportunity for everyone present to speak.

Sometimes on American reservations and Canadian reserves, circles are used for sentencing; this is in lieu of the usual criminal justice process. This is the form of justice increasingly provided by Canada's First Nations Peoples. Circle sentencing as practiced in Canada invites members from across the community to participate in determining appropriate sanctions for offenders. This process typically takes place after a case is concluded and the offender is found guilty in court. The community's role is to engage in discussion, to identify the factors that led to the offending behavior, and to seek ways to eliminate those problems (Doerner & Lab, 2005).

Community Reparation

Restorative initiatives are not limited to work with individuals and families but also can be successfully applied to the unjust treatment of whole populations. At the macro level, *reparation* is the form of restorative justice that occurs outside of the criminal justice and child welfare context. The violator here is the state. Wartime persecutions, rape of the land of the people, slave labor, and mass murder are forms of crimes against humanity that demand some form of compensation for survivors and their families, even generations later, as long as the wounds are palpable. The Truth Commission held in South Africa to address the wounds inflicted by apartheid is one of the most powerful examples of restoration. Compensation came in the form of public testimony and apology (Green, 1998).

Healing for the woundedness of whole populations of people is the ultimate goal of reparative justice. Community reparation generally involves public acknowledgment of responsibility for the crimes against humanity and sometimes monetary compensation. Demands for compensation by African Americans for the cruelty inflicted on their an-cestors through the slave trade and subsequent slavery have received much attention in recent years, but the wrongs have not been redressed. Similarly, the Australian govern-ment continues to deny reparations to the aboriginal people for their "stolen childhoods," a reference to the earlier policy of removing the children of mixed blood and placing them with White families. Reparations have also been denied to the Korean relatives of innocent civilians slaughtered during the American–Korean war.

Successful examples of reparations are U.S. compensation to families of Japanese Americans held in concentration camps during World War II, and German compensation to survivors of slave labor camps. Although social workers have not been involved in any official way in the rewarding of reparations, the values represented in this peacemaking process are highly consistent with social work values, most particularly in regard to social justice, human rights, and empowerment of marginalized populations.

Where there has been victimization and possible trauma, rituals are needed to "heal the damaged souls of the people, to help them find ways to transform hatred into sorrow or forgiveness, to be able to move forward with hope rather than wallow in the evil of the past" (Braithwaite, 2002, p. 207). When the state is the culprit, restorative justice means reparations for the human rights violations that occurred. Reparations may take the form of governmental acceptance of responsibility for the wrongs done, often following a national inquiry.

On a global scale, the most astonishing example of public truth telling and catharsis for crime has taken place in South Africa with the Truth and Reconciliation Commis-sion. Victims of the old regime under apartheid testified, and former officials who had committed unspeakable crimes in the name of apartheid were forced to own up to these crimes. Following the South African example for nationwide ceremonies of healing and in accordance with the inclusion of sexual violence as a war crime by International Criminal Tribunals for former Yugoslavia and Rwanda where large numbers of women had been raped as an act of war, the Truth and Reconciliation Commission in Peru investigated sexual violence against women as a human rights violation (Falcón, 2005). These women had been denied justice and encouraged to keep silent for years about the violence com-mitted against them as the country of Peru was torn by civil war. Sisters and daughters of detained men had been systematically raped and subjected to other forms of sexual abuse to encourage the men to talk. The Commission's final report provided appropriate recognition of the women's victimization and recognition of sexual violence in such cases as crimes against humanity.

Review of the Research Literature

What does the literature show us about the long-term effectiveness of these restorative justice models? Are lives altered thereby? Does healing of the participants—victims and offenders—take place? Of special significance to gendered violence is research on victim–offender conferencing and dialogue in cases of severe violence, crimes for which it was originally believed that restorative processes would be contraindicated, primarily because of safety concerns in cases of family violence (Grauwiler & Mills, 2004). Research in cases of severe violence, according to Umbreit et al. (2003), consistently shows that the process was well received by both victims and offenders. Parents of murdered children have expressed their sense of relief after meeting the inmate, sharing their pain, and developing a better understanding about what happened. Some participants report they are able to let go of their hatred after coming to see the offender as a human being (Umbreit et al., 2003). Grauwiler and Mills (2004) make a strong case, based on their review of the literature and awareness of the inadequacies of conventional criminal justice procedures, for the efficacy of restorative approaches in reducing and preventing family violence.

To provide an aggregate measure of empirical findings on the effectiveness of restorative practices, Latimer, Dowden, and Muise (2001) used the statistical technique of meta-analysis to prepare a comprehensive report for the Department of Justice Canada. Studies selected for inclusion used a control of comparison groups and reported results on victim and offender satisfaction and/or recidivism rates. Curiously, few of the 22 studies that met the criteria were published in peer-reviewed journals. Most of the studies involved young males. Restorative programs were found to be significantly more effective on the basis of all criteria studied. Offenders are more likely to adhere to restitution agreements and not to reoffend when they have gone through the conferencing ritual than are offenders processed through the standard format. Victim–offender conferencing models had especially high victim and offender satisfaction results compared to FGC. Recommendations are for more carefully randomly assigned pilot studies, long-term follow-up studies on victims, and effectiveness studies with female offenders.

An interview with Thomas Quinn (1998) of the National Institute of Justice provides the results of a survey developed by the University of Delaware and sent to a large sample including legislators, judges, and corrections officials. Findings revealed the respondents stressed several positive effects of the interactions: Offenders were more likely to understand the impact of their crimes and to be forced to face the consequences of their acts, and the system worked more efficiently in diverting cases from the formal process and meeting the needs of victims. Concerns expressed about the program were vagueness of the term "restorative justice," due process issues (ensuring that participation was voluntary), the time-consuming nature of the preparatory work, and sentence disparities.

Research on FGC has not been forthcoming until recently. Researchers Morris and Maxwell (2001) found that over a 6-year period two fifths of young offenders who were involved in the FGC process did not reoffend or reoffended only once. Interviews with the parents of offenders who were now doing well revealed the following factors were helpful in their children's favorable outcome: remorse for the crime, active participation by parents in the conference, and acceptance by the parents that the process had been fair. Interviews with the young people themselves revealed that a sense of remorse but not of shame was crucial, as was active involvement in the conference. Morris and Maxwell conclude that helping people take responsibility while reducing elements of public shame is apt to bring out the best in the young people in the study. We can relate this observation to the key importance of having a positive self-concept in promoting law abiding behavior.

A recently released report by the Crime and Justice Research Centre in New Zealand evaluated the results of over 200 restorative conferences for adult offenders. Ten matched groups of conventionally tried offenders were included for comparison. Interviews with key stakeholders showed a high level of victim satisfaction and a lower rate of reoffending by violent offenders who engaged in the conferencing than for the comparison group, although the reconviction rate of the conferenced individuals was not reduced overall (Kingi, Robertson, Poppelwell, & Morris, 2005).

The way it is presently practiced in the United States, FGC is criticized for its occasional failures to prepare adequately the victim and victim's family as well as the offender and his or her family. Based on his extensive survey research of restorative justice participants, Umbreit (2000) cautions FGC organizers against its offender-driven aspects, for example, letting the offender's group choose their seats first. Another idea that requires close monitoring, according to Umbreit, is the tendency to select probation officers and school officials as coordinators. Given the retributive climate of the American criminal justice system, conference coordinators may produce an atmosphere of shaming and blaming of the offender. The recommendation is for social workers or volunteers trained in conflict resolution skills to attend to the emotional needs of the diverse participants.

On the international stage, the thrust for a restorative vision has been embraced through the role of the United Nations. Following consultation with nongovernmental organizations, the UN, through its Commission on Crime Prevention and Criminal Justice, approved a Canadian resolution that encourages countries to use the basic principles of restorative justice and to incorporate restorative justice programming in their criminal justice processes. These principles or guidelines were formulated by representatives of the 38 countries who attended a special UN conference for this purpose (see "UN Crime Commission Acts on Basic Principles," 2002). Sadly, the United States did not participate in the drawing up of these guidelines.

Evaluation of restorative justice programs, as Braithwaite (2002) proposes, could be in accordance with the aims of respect for human rights as spelled out in the Universal Declaration of Human Rights. Relevant articles of the Declaration include the right to protection; to ownership of property; to life, liberty, and security; even to health and medical care and the right not to be subjected to torture or cruel, inhuman treatment. The UN Declaration could provide guidance and a consensual foundation to cover many of the things we look to restore and protect in restorative processes. Above all else, restoration of human dignity to both victim and offender should be primary.

Gender-Based Restorative Initiatives

Like many discussions in the field of restorative and criminal justice, however, such thinking assumes a generic rather than gendered quality, and the special needs of girls and women are not taken into account. When we treat female offenders generically, we often confuse equality with sameness. Gender-blind treatment of girls and women in the criminal justice system subjects them to discipline designed for antisocial men, without making allowance either for the role of motherhood or for a history of personal victimization. Addiction and dependency on drug use and often violent men is another female-specific theme. To help meet the special needs of female offenders, van Wormer (2001) introduced a strengths-restorative approach, which joins a strength-based feminist perspective with a restorative framework.

The finding of distinct gender differences in pathways to lawbreaking is a focus of contemporary studies on female offenders (Belknap & Holsinger, 1997; Chesney-Lind, 1997). Drawing on the empirical finding that there is a disproportionately high rate of multiple victimization for female compared to male offenders, Chesney-Lind describes the pathway that often leads a girl, desperate to escape sexual and physical abuse at home, to run away, seek solace in drugs and "bad company," and survive on the streets through prostitution. Some end up in prison, mostly as a result of incarceration secondary to drug involvement. In their paths, they have victimized others as well—their children, family members, and sometimes strangers—through theft and robbery.

One aspect of victim–offender conferencing that closely relates to women's issues is the use of victim panels in which the individual participants share their personal stories of victimization with offenders who have committed similar crimes. Often the speakers are survivors of crimes like rape, robbery, and attempted murder. Members of the panel are not the victims of the particular offenders in the audience. Victim–offender panels are used as a means of getting male abusers to feel the victims' pain and to feel remorse for the harm they have done.

Minnesota has infused gender-specific programming within its juvenile and adult institutions that is built on restorative justice principles. The Minnesota Department of Corrections furthermore employs restorative justice planners to train people at the county level for diversionary conferencing, emphasizing above all a spirit of dialogue and healing. Burns (2001), a researcher at the Center for Restorative Justice and Peacemaking, describes a process that is a combination of victim–offender conferencing, panels, and healing circles. Meetings held in a circle format at the women's prison at Shakopee were conducted with five crime victims (members of the Parents of Murdered Children support group), six inmates, two facilitators, a neutral advocate, and an observer. Participants who did not know each other before the meetings signed up for certain nights when they would tell their personal stories. Before the conferencing, the victims had favored harsh penalties for such female offenders, but afterward they saw them as people and victims, too, in their own way. Much empathy and remorse was expressed in these exchanges.

In Battering Situations

Restorative practices in the realm of domestic violence have always started at the grass roots level; it is time, argue Grauwiler and Mills (2004), to expand our efforts to include the needs of women who avoid the criminal justice system. Community-based interventions are required that do not rely on criminal prosecution. A postmodern view of justice has developed that, according to Presser and Gaarder (2004), has called into question the ideology of absolute justice, including policies such as forcing the victim to testify in open court against her partner or spouse who assaulted her. Research in the 1990s, as these writers further inform us, found that battering victims who have a say in legal or less formal proceedings may feel more empowered to get help, if not to terminate the abusive relationship. Women of color often see both the courts and social services as adversaries rather than allies, so an emphasis on judicial intervention may turn them away.

One approach to the prevention of domestic violence is the requirement that battering men receive treatment. The aim is to teach offenders new ways of viewing relationships and manhood, and new ways of handling stress and feelings of insecurity. Restorative justice here often takes the form of teaching empathy by having a group of survivors of domestic violence tell their stories, relating what it feels like to be violently victimized by one's spouse or partner. In hearing the stories of pain and suffering that the crimes of violence engendered, those offenders who can be reached will not only feel for the victims as people who were hurt by the careless or cruel behavior of others, but also often will get in touch with their own past victimization. Getting in touch with their own feelings may prepare them for the humanization and rehabilitation process. And just as offenders, in these encounters, see the human face of victims, so the survivors come to see the human face of offenders. In short, two themes—offender accountability and the empowerment of crime victims—ideally come together in the victim–offender initiatives.

An important research question that has not been adequately explored is this: For which type of batterers would a restorative justice approach be effective? More precise knowledge of batterer typologies may ultimately be used to discriminate between offenders who might reasonably be expected to benefit from such an approach and those who are unlikely to benefit or who pose too great a safety threat. While batterer typology systems currently have limited clinical utility (Langhinrichsen-Rohling, Huss, & Ramsey, 2000), we are able through psychological testing to screen out those who show antisocial tendencies, severe depression, or a history of violence directed toward others outside the family, men for whom restorative processes would be unsuitable.

The process of community conferencing as a way of effecting justice for victims of rape and battering is practiced in New Zealand with favorable results (Braithwaite & Daly, 1998). Sentencing in such a system is handled by community groups that include the victim and her family, as well as the offender and individuals from his support system. Power imbalances are addressed in various ways, such as limiting the right of the offender to speak on his own behalf and including community members in a sort of surveillance team to monitor the offender's compliance. Braithwaite and Daly see the potential to use such methods safely by including them in a "regulatory pyramid," utilizing interventions of escalating intensity in refractory cases. While more conventional interventions such as imprisonment may still be used for offenders who do not respond, they see community involvement in decision making, as well as in rituals of shaming and community reintegration, as potentially more beneficial. The victim and other members of the community are given voice and are able to bring social pressures to bear on the offender while both protecting the victim and offering the option of rehabilitation to the offender.

Other reports involving successful community conferencing in cases of severe family violence have come from Canada from traditional native community ceremonies. These are unlike traditional mediation methods used with divorcing couples in that community involvement changes the balance of power. Griffiths (1999), for example, presents the case of a Canadian aboriginal sentencing circle that took up the case of a man who, when drunk, beat his wife. Seated in a circle, the victim and her family told of their distress, and a young man spoke of the contributions the offender had made to the community. The judge suspended sentencing until the offender entered alcoholism treatment and fulfilled the expectations of the victim and of her support group. The ceremony concluded with a prayer and a shared meal. After a period of time, the woman who had been victimized voiced her satisfaction with the process. This case, as Griffiths explains, was clearly linked to the criminal justice system. Others may be handled more quietly, by tribal members. Griffiths concludes on a note of caution: Victims must play a key role throughout the process to ensure that their needs are met and that they are not revictimized. This is a process we can expect to be hearing much more about in the future. The emphasis on restoration rather than retribution can be empowering to all parties involved.

Feminist researcher Mary Koss (2000) advocates what she terms *communitarian justice*, a victim-sensitive model derived from the community-based approaches of New Zealand's Maori people. Such methods are apt to be effective, notes Koss, because they draw on sanctions abusive men fear most: family stigma and broad social disapproval. Such conferencing, as Koss further indicates, is recommended for young offenders without extensive histories of violence.

The goal of such an approach is to help violence-prone men to take responsibility for their actions while at the same time to develop empathy for their victims. Like restorative justice, the aim is to build on positives so as to facilitate the offenders' restoration to the community rather than their further estrangement from it.

In ongoing relationships, an end to the violence is of course crucial. Treatment coupled with close supervision of men who have engaged in battering is an important element in curbing further family violence. Sometimes restorative justice initiatives at the community level take the form of community conferencing, as discussed in the previous section. Participation by all parties is strictly voluntary, and intensive preparation precedes all such conferencing. Issues of power and control for the victim must be addressed (Umbreit, 2000). Hearing directly from the offender of his guilt and remorse while receiving support from family members can help the victim heal while reducing feelings of self-blame. In contrast, few traditional programs address the psychological needs of victims in any meaningful way. Even in situations of violent crime, community conferencing can help victims by bringing the gravity of the violence that they have experienced out into the open. The message to all concerned is that any form of family violence is unacceptable. Such conferencing can attend to the psychological as well as physical abuse a survivor has experienced and counter her sense of helplessness by involving her as an active participant in the process (Koss, 2000). Measures can be taken, moreover, to reduce the survivor's vulnerability such as providing access to an individual bank account or transportation, for example.

Rashmi Goel (2005) believes that restorative justice options are ill suited to application among immigrant South Asian communities for domestic violence cases. Her reasoning is that women from South Asian cultures might be placated by the familiar values of community, cooperation, and forgiveness into seeking restorative justice solutions and ultimately into staying in an abusive situation. Restorative justice is based on the premise that participants are equal and can speak freely in a consensus-based proceeding. But in the South Asian (Indian) cultural tradition, such an assumption cannot be made. Tradition portrays the husband as the sole source of status and support, and Indian women are apt to feel responsible for pain inflicted by the husband. The exact opposite argument is made by Grauwiler and Mills (2004). Their recommendation is for what they call "intimate abuse circles" as a culturally sensitive alternative to the criminal justice system's response to domestic violence. Such circles are especially helpful, they suggest, to immigrant, minority, and religious families where it is more likely that the family will remain intact. This model acknowledges that many people seek to end the violence but not the relationship. Such restorative processes also help partners who would like to separate in a more amicable fashion than through standard avenues.

In Situations of Rape

If criminal justice treatment of victims of crime in general leaves much to be desired, treatment of rape victims is unconscionable. Three main failings of the conventional system are discussed by Braithwaite and Daly (1998). The first of these is the low rate of accountability in the system due to lack of reporting by victim/survivors, the low prosecution rate even when a charge is filed, the perceived lack of credibility of victims of any crime involving sex, and the awareness by authorities of the low conviction rate even if the case does come to trial. Second, rapists who are sentenced to prison are often guilty of repeated offenses that they got away with and are therefore likely to reoffend upon release. Third, women are revictimized under cross-examination by defense attorneys in the courtroom, especially if they were drinking at the time of the offense, they were in an unsafe place late at night, or anything could be uncovered from their past that would seem to shed light on their veracity.

Within this context, Rozee and Koss (2001) describe an American project based on community conferencing principles designed to redress the harm to the victim/survivor in rape cases. A second focus is on restoring justice to the community. Only then do offender-focused goals of rehabilitation and reintegration come into play. The project was introduced experimentally at the University of Arizona to handle several categories of rape and sexual assault for which the standard system of justice was the least able or willing to deal with—sexual intercourse between a young woman 16 to 18 years old and a young man slightly older, alcohol-related rape, date and acquaintance rape, and sexual offenses not involving penetration. Law enforcement is involved initially in the reporting of the crime; the County Attorney in cases appropriate for conferencing meets separately with accuser and accused to inform each party of the benefits and risks of the community justice model and to gain consent to refer the case. Next, if desired, the facilitator meets with the parties and family members to arrange for a conference and for the participation of support systems from each side. A trained male advocate may attend on behalf of either the victim or offender.

The conference is led by a facilitator, generally a mental health professional, who is trained in restorative justice strategies. The offender begins by describing what he did; the victim/survivor speaks next about her experiences; and then family and friends on both sides express the impact of the offense on them. The perpetrator admits to the violation and responds to what he has heard, often with an apology. Options include a formal apology, payment of expenses including counseling for the victim, substance abuse and/or sex offender treatment for the offender, and community service. A written record of the proceedings is provided that includes plans for follow-up accountability. The matter is confidential as long as there is no reoffense, in which case the results of the conference can be used as evidence in any future adjudication.

Advantages of this format as indicated by Rozee and Koss (2001) are the strengthening of community trust, the instituting of trust, release of legal authorities from pressure to take action under difficult circumstances, a forum for volunteer advocates from which to offer antirape messages, and a chance for a student to avoid a stigma that could follow him for life. Community conferencing provides a platform for describing a background of racial and economic oppression without framing such issues as excuses for the bad behavior. Above all, the woman has been listened to, has been given community support, and has received justice. As with all forms of restorative justice, truth telling rather than denial of the truth is encouraged in the process. Although this innovative university program is too new for the long-term results to be clear, the prospects are good in light of the proven effectiveness of similar programming in New Zealand. Presumably, also the university has leverage here inasmuch as the perpetrator is a student enrolled in studies and wishing a clean record whether to remain at this institution or to transfer. For all parties involved, this process should be empowering.

Canadian attorney Ross Green (1998) in his book *Justice in Aboriginal Communities* conducted research on sentencing practices in cases that are sometimes considered too serious for handling outside the normal judicial route. And yet, we could equally argue that such situations are of too great a magnitude for ordinary adversarial methods, especially when members of Indian tribes are involved. The clash between the Anglo-Saxon way of handling criminal matters and aboriginal values is palpable. Photographs provided in the book show large numbers of people seated in a circle at one gathering concerning parents who pleaded guilty to incest. Part I of the book focuses on the conventional Canadian justice system and the clash between this formal adversarial system and aboriginal values. In contrast to modern Euro-American forms of justice, aboriginal justice is about restoring balance to the community. Native peoples have difficulty in standard proceedings because they are apt to feel intimidated and to lack remorse if found guilty. The victim plays a limited role in the formal process as well.

One of the most effective and striking uses of circle conferencing occurred in the Hollow Water (Manitoba) community. In this community, a cycle of sexual abuse had been perpetuated for generations. Because the problem was community-wide, if the victims had gone through normal channels, virtually all the male members of the community would have been removed. The process of circle sentencing was thus chosen as the pragmatic and culturally sensitive approach to an almost overwhelming situation. In the circle, offenders acknowledged the truth of their behavior. "Healing contracts" and a concluding "cleansing ceremony" provided a spiritual dimension to the proceedings. Strong community pressures followed the sessions to keep the offenders in treatment. The process was empowering for all the parties involved and, instead of being divisive, pulled the community together for concerted action toward social change.

Sometimes there is not satisfaction, however, following the handling of serious cases through circles, as Ross (2000) suggests. Complaints have come from women that aboriginal justice had been too lenient in a number of cases and that the victims' interests had not been represented in the decisions that were reached. Rubin (2003), in her examination of women's experiences in restorative processes in Nova Scotia, cautions critics against being overly positive in assessing these alternative forms of justice and ignoring family and community roles in the reinforcement of male control of women. Her recommendations include close attention to women's safety concerns and guarantees for their safety in domestic violence situations.

Cultural Issues and Restorative Justice

Cultural competence is a long-running theme for programs that deal with the oppressed and disenfranchised. Criminal justice and social work practitioners and scholars recognize that culturally competent approaches are needed in both the education and training of professionals in the field (Van Voorhis, 1998; Walker, 2002). Culturally sensitive, specific, or competent approaches are used with disenfranchised ethnic groups (Eisenbruch, de Jong, & van de Put, 2004; Goicoechea-Balbona, 1997; Zellerer, 2003), sexually active gay men (Braun-Harvey, 2003), female ex-offenders (Richie, 2001), and African Americans involved with the juvenile and/or criminal justice systems (Gavazzi, Alford, & McKenry, 1996; Wooldredge, Hartman, Latessa, & Holmes, 1994). This recognition of cultural issues should be and is occurring within the restorative justice movement.

The shift toward restorative justice occurs with difficulty within a society where institutional racism is the foundation for the power imbalance between Whites and non-Whites. Restorative justice scholars and practitioners have recognized that there are multicultural concerns in the movement and believe that institutional racism is a deterrent to an effective restorative justice process (Umbreit & Coates, 1999). However, within the African American community there is a distrust, and at best apprehension, of approaches to crime that appear to come from the Eurocentric framework. Even though much of the literature states that the restorative justice process has its roots in non-European cultures (Benham & Barton, 1996; Melton, 1995; Vyas, 1995; Yazzie, 1997), there are very few academic and popular articles on restorative justice within the African diaspora (Elechi, 1996, 1999; Stern, 2001). These works illustrate key differences and in some cases similarities to the principles of restorative justice. An example of this approach is illustrated by the Kpelle tribe in Liberia.

> [An] informal form of dispute resolution is the moot or house palaver found among the Kpelle of Liberia.... [D]isputes are settled formally in official and unofficial courts of town chiefs or quarter elders, or informally in associational groupings such as church councils or in *moots*. Because the formal court hearings are coercive in nature, they do not provide the best forum for cases involving ongoing relationships. The moot, on the other hand, is an informal airing of grievances that takes place in the home of the complainant before an ad hoc group of kinsmen and neighbors. (Benham & Barton, 1996, p. 632)

These practices were and are being used by people of African descent throughout the Caribbean and South America (Adeleke, 1998; Chung & Chang, 1998). In addition, especially during the times of de jure segregation, many of the problems within the African American community were handled by an informal moot (Brown, 1994).

Jenkins (2006) and Pattison (1998) argue that the use of culturally specific principles within the justice framework could benefit people of color and others. In addition, because of the disproportionate numbers of African Americans who are either offenders or victims of crime or delinquency, Jenkins proposed the use of Afrocentric theory as the foundation within the restorative justice process as a means to dealing with African American offenders, victims, and communities.

Afrocentric and Eurocentric theory differ in four fundamental principles; these fall in the areas of cosmology (worldview), axiology (values), ontology (nature of people), and epistemology (source of knowledge). From the Eurocentric perspective, the dominant worldview focuses on control. Key values include materialism and individualism. People are fundamentally competitive, operating in a dog-eat-dog world. Knowledge is derived through the scientific method. From the Afrocentric perspective, however, worldview focuses on oneness with others. Relationship with the community is valued. There is a belief in the goodness of people and that individuals work together. Spirituality provides a primary source of knowledge (Warfield-Coppock, 1995). Generally, recent crime prevention/intervention efforts, restorative justice processes, and offender rehabilitative programming fall under either the Eurocentric, enculturated, or Afrocentric models. The traditional criminal justice response to crime (or any other social problem) usually is Eurocentric. Many of the programs that are considered culturally sensitive fall under the enculturated model of justice. Programs that are culturally specific may adhere to the Afrocentric principles (see Table 23.1).

Many programs incorporate one or more of each of these principles in their approach to "justice." In addition, other ethnic-centered models incorporate Afrocentric principles. This chapter uses Afrocentric theory as the foundation because of the disproportionate number of African Americans in the system. Last, the authors do not intend to imply that one approach is better than the other, but rather that Afrocentric theory could be an alternative approach within the restorative justice process in the African American community (Jenkins, in press).

Umbreit and Coates (1999) as well as Arrigo and Schehr (1998) argue that there are serious multicultural implications and concerns that must be addressed under the restorative justice model. One's understanding and application of Afrocentric principles does not depend on one's skin color. In fact, two of the Afrocentric principles, worldview and values, are deeply embedded in the restorative justice approach to crime, delinquency, and other social harms. Both restorative justice and Afrocentric theory focus on the community.

An example of a culturally specific restorative justice approach occurred in a medium-sized Midwestern city's approach to offender reentry. This city used the concept of the citizens' circle to help ex-offenders with their reentry into society. Citizens' circles are comprised of concerned citizens from all walks of life, and the primary approach is strength based and uses the citizens' network of friends and associates to assist the ex-offender. In addition, the ex-offender has to be a responsible and socially and politically active member of the community. Most of the ex-offenders in this city are African American, and the circle is comprised mostly of Whites. The approach that the circle uses during its meetings mirrors the rituals that are used in many African American places of worship. Even though the rituals do not use the concept of God or a higher

Table 23.1	Cultural Justice Model Overview		
Group Dimension	Eurocentric Model of Justice (the current legal system)	Enculturated Model of Justice (usually culturally sensitive but not culturally specific)	Afrocentric Model of Justice (culturally specific
Cosmology (worldview)	Control of others. Decisions should be made by a third party (i.e., judges and legal system).	Individual involved in the process makes decisions. Victim needs and offender responsibility dominate.	All parties make decisions equally. Community has the same voice as offender and victim.
Axiology (values)	Individualistic/materialistic. What benefits the individual is important.	Quasi-individualistic. Relationship between victim and offender is primary.	Communal orientation. Relationship with the community is primary.
Ontology (nature of people)	Humans can be good or bad. Humans who are bad need to be punished.	Humans are good, but there are some bad "seeds" that need to be treated or rehabilitated.	Humans are naturally good. Community should support everyone.
Epistemology (source of knowing)	Self-validation through the scientific method. Strictly secular.	Self and spirit are secondary.	Spiritual source is primary.

power as their foundation, the use of food to start the meeting, the readings of the mission and the goals of the circle, and "call and response" praise given to the ex-offender during sessions are very similar to many meetings and fellowships that occur in the African American church. The ex-offenders are always reminded that they must take care not only of their material needs, but also of their spirits and souls. In addition, all members of the circle remind the offender that he or she has a primary responsibility to the family and community.

Relevance to Social Work

Regrettably, the social work profession has largely abandoned the criminal justice field. So states Frederic Reamer (2004). Reamer refers not to employment within criminal justice, a field in which social workers are well represented, but to social work education, research, and scholarship. Yet several decades back, social workers held leading positions in corrections and juvenile justice. A large part of the reason for the declining influence undoubtedly was the state's abandonment of the ideal of rehabilitation and the adoption of a zero-tolerance, punitive response to lawbreaking. It is time, argues Reamer, for social work to reclaim the territory.

Restorative justice is the aspect of criminal justice most compatible with social work values. Recently and for the first time, the social work profession, through the National Association of Social Workers (NASW), gave recognition through its professional newsletter to the principles of restorative justice. Entitled "Restorative Justice: A Model of Healing," the article had as its subtitle "Philosophy Consistent With Social Work Values" (Fred, 2005, p. 4). Indeed, social workers who are schooled in cultural sensitivity and a strengths-empowerment approach will find their values make for a natural fit between their profession and the restorative justice initiatives now being practiced in the criminal justice field. Social workers in New Zealand, Canada, the United Kingdom, and Australia made this discovery years ago. Consider the core values of social work—service, social justice, dignity and worth of the person, importance of human relationships, integrity, and competence (NASW, 1996). Each of these values, as van Wormer (2004) indicates, is congruent with the principles of restorative justice. Restorative justice perhaps will be the door through which the profession of social work will reenter to return to a more central role in criminal justice. This is the challenge for social workers in the United States, to exert leadership where leadership is sorely needed.

Conclusion

This chapter has considered alternative strategies from home and abroad that address crimes ranging from minor offenses to murder. These strategies are included under the rubric of restorative justice. Restorative justice takes wrongdoing and its resolution beyond victims and offenders into the community. This form of justice, like social work, is solution-based rather than problem-based; it is about healing and reconciliation, not inflicting wounds in the interests of retribution.

The restorative justice model, as we have argued in this chapter, is especially relevant to work with women and racial and ethnic minorities in cases of interpersonal wrongdoing as well as in societal violations of human rights. We have described four of the basic restorative models: victim–offender conferencing, FGC, healing circles, and community reparations, and variations thereof. Common to all these models is an emphasis on the needs of the victim, truth telling in one's own voice, direct communication, and accountability of the offender to the victim. Although social work in the United States has been slow to take notice of what may well portend a paradigm shift in criminal justice circles, the profession has now taken notice with public recognition of the viability and possibilities of this model.

RESOURCES AND REFERENCES

Adeleke, T. (1998). Black Americans and Africa: A critique of the Pan-African and identity paradigms. *International Journal of African Historical Studies, 31*, 505–536.

Arrigo, B. A., & Schehr, R. C. (1998). Restoring justice for juveniles: A critical analysis of victim-offender mediation. *Justice Quarterly, 15*, 629–666.

Asante, M. K. (1983). The ideological significance of Afrocentricity in intercultural communication. *Journal of Black Studies, 14*, 3–19.

Austin, R. (1992). The Black community, its lawbreakers, and a politics of identification. *Southern California Law Review, 65*, 1769–1817.

Bazemore, G. (1994). Rehabilitating community service: Toward restorative service sanctions in a balanced system. *Federal Probation, 58,* 24–35.

Bazemore, G., & Schiff, M. (2001). Understanding restorative community justice: What and why now? In G. Bazemore & M. Schiff (Eds.), *Restoring community justice: Repairing harm and transforming communities* (pp. 21–46). Cincinnati, OH: Anderson.

Belknap, J., & Holsinger, K. (1997). Understanding incarcerated girls: The results of a focus. *Prison Journal, 77,* 381–405.

Benham, A., & Barton, A. B. (1996). Alternative dispute resolution: Ancient models provide modern inspiration. *Georgia State University Law Review, 12,* 623–651.

Braithwaite, J. (2002). *Restorative justice and responsive regulation.* Oxford, UK: Oxford University Press.

Braithwaite, J., & Daly, K. (1998). Masculinity, violence and communitarian control. In S. Miller (Ed.), *Crime control and women* (pp. 151–180). Thousand Oaks, CA: Sage.

Braun-Harvey, D. (2003). Culturally relevant assessment and treatment for gay men's online sexual activity. *Sexual and Relationship Therapy, 18,* 371–384.

Brown, E. B. (1994). Negotiating and transforming the public sphere: African American political life in the transition from slavery to freedom. *Public Culture, 7,* 107–146.

Burford, G., & Hudson, J. (Eds.). (2000). *Family group conferencing: New directions in community-centered child and family practice.* New York: Aldine de Gruyter.

Burns, H. (2001, January 23). *Citizens, victims, and offenders restoring justice project.* St. Paul, MN: Center for Restorative Justice and Peacemaking.

Chesney-Lind, M. (1997). *The female offender: Girls, women and crime.* Thousand Oaks, CA: Sage.

Chung, A. Y., & Chang, E. T. (1998). From third world liberation to multiple oppression politics: A contemporary approach to interethnic coalitions. *Social Justice, 25,* 80–100.

Doerner, W., & Lab, S. (2005). *Victimology* (4th ed.). Dayton, OH: Anderson.

Eisenbruch, M., de Jong, J. T., & van de Put, W. (2004). Bringing order out of chaos: A culturally competent approach to managing the problems of refugees and victims of organized violence. *Journal of Traumatic Stress, 17,* 123–131.

Elechi, O. O. (1996). Doing justice without the state: The Afikpo (Ehugbo) Nigeria model of conflict resolution. *International Journal of Comparative and Applied Criminal Justice, 20,* 337–355.

Elechi, O. O. (1999). Victims under the restorative justice systems: The Afikpo (Ehugbo) Nigeria model. *International Review of Victimology, 6,* 359–375.

Falcón, J. M. (2005). The Peruvian truth and reconciliation commission's treatment of sexual violence against women. *Human Rights Brief, 12*(2), 1–4.

Fred, S. (2005, February). Restorative justice: A model of healing. *NASW News,* 4.

Frisch, L. (2003). The justice response to woman battering. In A. Roberts (Ed.), *Critical issues in crime and justice* (2nd ed., pp. 161–175). Thousand Oaks, CA: Sage.

Gavazzi, S. M., Alford, K. A., & McKenry, P. C. (1996). Culturally specific programs for foster care youth: The sample case of an African American rites of passage program. *Family Relations, 45,* 166–174.

Goel, R. (2005, May). Sita's trousseau: Restorative justice, domestic violence, and South Asian Culture. *Violence Against Women, 11*(5), 639–665.

Goicoechea-Balbona, A. (1997). Culturally specific health care model for ensuring health care use by rural, ethnically diverse families affected by HIV/AIDS. *Health & Social Work, 22,* 172–180.

Grauwiler, P., & Mills, L. (2004). Moving beyond the criminal justice paradigm: A radical restorative justice approach to intimate abuse. *Journal of Sociology and Social Welfare, 31*(1), 49–62.

Green, R. G. (1998). *Justice in aboriginal communities: Sentencing alternatives.* Saskatoon, Canada: Purich Publishing.

Griffiths, C. T. (1999). The victims of crime and restorative justice: The Canadian experience. *International Review of Victimology, 6,* 279–294.

Healing circle shows offenders their human toll. (2001, May 26). *Toronto Star,* N1.

Jenkins, M. (2006). Gullah Island dispute resolution: An example of Afrocentric restorative justice. *Journal of Black Studies, 37,* 299–319.

Johnson, S. L. (1993). Racial imagery in criminal cases. *Tulane Law Review, 67,* 1739–1764.

Kemp, S., Whittaker, J. K., & Tracy, E. M. (2000). Family group conferencing as a person-environment practice. In G. Burford & J. Hudson (Eds.), *Family group conferencing: New directions in community-centered child and family practice* (pp. 72–85). New York: Aldine de Gruyter.

Kingi, V., Robertson, J., Poppelwell, E., & Morris, A. (2005). *Court referred restorative justice pilot evaluation.* Retrieved December 4, 2005, from the Crime and Justice Research Centre, Victoria University of Wellington and the Ministry of Justice, Wellington, NZ, Web site: http://www.realjustice.org/library/nzreport05.html

Koss, M. (2000). Blame, shame, and community: Justice responses to violence against women. *American Psychologist, 55*(11), 1332–1343.

Langhinrichsen-Rohling, J., Huss, M. T., & Ramsey, S. (2000). The clinical utility of batterer typologies. *Journal of Family Violence, 15*(1), 37–53.

Latimer, J., Dowden, C., & Muise, D. (2001). *The effectiveness of restorative justice practices: A meta-analysis.* Ottawa, Canada: Research and Statistics Division, Department of Justice Canada.

Leiber, M. (2002). Disproportionate minority confinement (DMC) of youth: An analysis of state and federal efforts to address the issue. *Crime and Delinquency, 48*, 3–46.

McCoy, C. (1993). From sociological trends of 1992 to the criminal courts of 2020. *Southern California Law Review, 66*, 1967–1991.

Melton, A. P. (1995). Indigenous justice systems and tribal society. *Judicature, 79*, 126–133.

Miller, J. G. (1996). *Search and destroy: African American males in the criminal justice system.* Cambridge, UK: Cambridge University Press.

Morris, A., & Maxwell, G. (2001). Restorative conferencing. In G. Bazemore & M. Schiff (Eds.), *Restorative community justice: Repairing harm and transforming communities* (pp. 173–197). Cincinnati, OH: Anderson.

National Association of Social Workers. (1996). *Code of ethics.* Washington, DC: Author.

Parker, L. (2002). *New Zealand expands official recognition of restorative justice.* Retrieved September 21, 2006, from the Restorative Justice Online Web site: http://www.restorativejustice.org/editors/2002A

Pattison, B. (1998). Minority youth in juvenile correctional facilities: Cultural differences and the right to treatment. *Law and Equality Journal, 16*, 573–599.

Pollard, C. (2000). Victims and the criminal justice system: A new vision. *Criminal Law Review, 5*, 13–17.

Pranis, K. (2001). Restorative justice, social justice, and the empowerment of marginalized populations. In G. Bazemore & M. Schiff (Eds.), *Restorative community justice: Repairing harm and transforming communities* (pp. 287–306). Cincinnati, OH: Anderson.

Pranis, K. (2004). The practice and efficacy of restorative justice. In E. Juday & M. Bryant (Eds.), *Criminal justice: Retribution vs. restoration* (pp. 133–157). Binghampton, NY: Haworth.

Presser, L., & Gaarder, E. (2004). Can restorative justice reduce battering? In B. Price & N. Sokoloff (Eds.), *The criminal justice system and women: Offenders, prisoners, victims, and workers* (3rd ed., pp. 403–418). New York: McGraw Hill.

Quinn, T. (1998, March). An interview with former visiting fellow of NIJ, Thomas Quinn. The National Institute of Justice Journal. Office of Justice Programs. Retrieved September 21, 2006, from www.ojp.usdoj.gov/nij/publications.

Reamer, R. (2004). Social work and criminal justice: The uneasy alliance. In E. Judah & M. Bryant (Eds.), *Criminal justice: Retribution vs. restoration* (pp. 213–231). Binghamton, NY: Haworth Press.

Richie, B. E. (2001). Challenges incarcerated women face as they return to their communities: Findings from life history interviews. *Crime & Delinquency, 47*, 368–389.

Roach, K. (2000). Changing punishment at the turn of the century: Restorative justice on the rise. *Canadian Journal of Criminology, 42*(3), 249–282.

Ross, R. (2000). Searching for the roots of conferencing. In G. Burford & J. Hudson (Eds.), *Family group conferencing: New directions in community-centered child and family practice* (pp. 5–14). New York: Aldine de Gruyter.

Rozee, P., & Koss, M. (2001). Rape: A century of resistance. *Psychology of Women Quarterly, 25*, 295–311.

Rubin, P. (2003). *Restorative justice in Nova Scotia: Women's experience and recommendations for positive policy development and implementation. Report and Recommendations.* Retrieved September 21, 2006, from the Ottawa, Canada, National Association of Women and the Law Web site: http://www.restorativejustice.org

Stern, V. (2001). An alternative vision: Criminal justice developments in non-Western countries. *Social Justice, 28*, 88–104.

Sullivan, D., & Tifft, L. (2001). *Restorative justice: Healing the foundations of our everyday lives.* Monsey, NY: Willow Tree Press.

Umbreit, M. S. (1995, Spring). Holding juvenile offenders accountable: A restorative justice perspective. *Juvenile and Family Court Journal, 46*, 31–42.

Umbreit, M. (2000). *Family group conferencing: Implications for crime victims.* Washington, DC: U.S. Department of Justice.

Umbreit, M. S., & Coates, R. B. (1999). Multicultural implications of restorative juvenile justice. *Federal Probation, 63,* 44–51.

Umbreit, M., Vos, B., Coates, R., & Brown, K. (2003). *Facing violence: The path of restorative justice and dialogue.* Monsey, NY: Criminal Justice Press.

United Nations Crime Commission Acts on Basic Principles (2002). Restorative Justice Online. Retrieved September 21, 2006, from www.restorativejustice.org

Van Ness, D., & Strong, K. H. (2002). *Restoring justice* (2nd ed.). Cincinnati, OH: Anderson.

Van Voorhis, R. M. (1998). Culturally relevant practice: A framework for teaching the psychosocial dynamics of oppression. *Journal of Social Work Education, 34,* 121–134.

van Wormer, K. (2001). *Counseling female offenders and victims: A strengths-restorative approach.* New York: Springer.

van Wormer, K. (2004). *Confronting oppression, restoring justice: From policy analysis to social action.* Alexandria, VA: Council on Social Work Education.

van Wormer, K. (2006). Introduction to social welfare and social work: The U.S. in global perspective. Belmont, CA: Wadsworth.

Vyas, Y. (1995). Alternatives to imprisonment in Kenya. *Criminal Law Forum, 6,* 73–102.

Walker, S. (2002). Culturally competent protection of children's mental health. *Child Abuse Review, 2,* 380–393.

Warfield-Coppock, N. (1995). Toward a theory of Afrocentric organizations. *Journal of Black Psychology, 21,* 30–48.

Weitzer, R. (1996). Racial discrimination in the criminal justice system: Findings and problems in the literature. *Journal of Criminal Justice, 24,* 309–322.

Wooldredge, J., Hartman, J., Latessa, E., & Holmes, S. (1994). Effectiveness of culturally specific community treatment for African American juvenile felons. *Crime & Delinquency, 40,* 589–598.

Yazzie, R. (1997). *Aboriginal systems of restoration for victims: Implications for conventional systems of justice.* Paper presented at the International Conference of Justice Without Violence: Views from Peacemaking Criminology and Restorative Justice, Albany, NY.

Zehr, H. (1990). *Changing lenses: A new focus for crime and justice.* Scottsdale, PA: Herald Press.

Zellerer, E. (2003). Culturally competent programs: The first family violence program for aboriginal men in prison. *The Prison Journal, 82,* 171–190.

Resources

Balanced and Restorative Justice Project Web site: http://www.barjproject.org

Center for Peacemaking and Conflict Studies, Fresno Pacific University Web site: http://peace.fresno.edu/rjp

Center for Restorative Justice & Peacemaking, University of Minnesota Web site: http://2ssw.che.umn.edu/rjp/Seminars/Seminars-2005.html

Centre for Restorative Justice, Simon Frazer University Web site: http://www.sfu.ca/cfrj

Posttrauma Intervention: Basic Tasks

Gary Behrman
William H. Reid

I rauma occurs when an experience is perceived as highly unexpected, life threatening, and overwhelming to normal coping skills (Kaplan, 1999). As we know, trauma on a large scale was one of the aftermaths of the horrific events that occurred on September 11, 2001, and during and after Hurricane Katrina. In this chapter we present an approach to posttrauma intervention used in Behrman's work with employees of the New York City Adult Protection Services (APS), who were witness to the World Trade Center disaster at various levels of exposure. The model draws on prior work on posttrauma interventions (Everly & Mitchell, 1997) and the task-centered practice model developed by the second author (Reid, 1992, 1997, 2000; Reid & Epstein, 1972). It is also informed by Behrman's experience and reflections as a licensed clinical social worker trained in critical incident stress debriefings. Although the approach is cast as a social work model, it can also be used by practitioners from other helping professions.

Basic Assumptions

When persons are traumatized, much of what they assume about themselves, others, and the purposes of their lives are disrupted and lose connectedness. The concept of *connections* is integral to this posttrauma intervention model. "Connections are the many different kinds of communicative, productive, and organizational relationships among people

Reprinted from "Posttrauma Intervention: Basic Tasks," by G. Behrman and W. H. Reid, 2002, *Brief Treatment and Crisis Intervention, 2*(1), pp. 39–48.

in socially, historically, and discursively constituted media of language, work, and power, all of which must be understood dynamically and relationally" (Kemmis & McTaggart, 2000, p. 579). In order to maintain and reconstruct those meaningful connections between one's self and community, one needs both the presence of inspirational persons in the community and effective tasks designed by the self. There is a "reaching out and a reaching in" (Kemmis & McTaggart, 2000, p. 579). Together, the individual and the community help recreate these connections in meaningful, creative, and responsible ways, which may result in change on an informative, reformative, or transformative level.

On the informational level, this model "allows the formation of some new meaning and the recapturing of old meanings about the experience and encourages people to begin to create a vision about what might be and take some steps to achieve it" (Saleeby, 1994, p. 357). Providing valuable information and resource development about managing trauma in its aftermath are important components of informative change. Also, creating new meanings that help us understand this experience in new ways leads to informative change. This level of change does not necessarily involve a change in behavior or identity, but challenges us to look beyond what is easily accounted for and examine what does not fit into our conceptions of the world (Sermabeikian, 1994). Applying this new knowledge through tasks will subsequently lead to reformed ways of behaving. This change is then reformative. We have new behaviors that enable us to achieve our desired goals. Transformative change incorporates informative and reformative change but also goes beyond them. Our identity as a person/community is changed, and subsequently how we think, feel, and behave is transformed. We bring a new self into every situation, and this transformed self creates possibilities and relationships that previously were inconceivable.

The Model and an Illustrative Application

The illustration involves Behrman's work with employees of the New York City APS, as referred to previously. As individuals, they can be seen as clients; as a collective, they may be thought of as the APS community. In other applications a community might be a juvenile's school or neighborhood. In its present form this model is designed for diverse populations, including juveniles in the criminal justice system. Research indicates that many youths who are referred to our criminal justice system often suffer from previous traumatic events (Wood, Foy, Goguen, Pynoos, & James, 2002; Wood, Foy, Layne, Pynoos, & James, 2002). Thus, applying this model with this population may be beneficial.

This model is organized around nine basic tasks aimed to further recovery from trauma. The social worker, individual, and community all share in these tasks. The social worker may act as initiator and facilitator, but for the tasks to be effective the client and community must be active participants. The task concept serves to underscore the importance of the actions of the client and community both during and following the intervention. Individual and community rebuilding after a traumatic event is reciprocal. As individuals recover, they help to restore a sense of community. A regenerating community enables individuals to regain their sense of belonging. Critical to this process are tasks undertaken by the individuals, the community, and the social worker.

All tasks are initiated and worked on in group sessions. With the exception of the first and last (Welcoming and Terminating/Revisiting) all tasks can and should be pursued by the client and community between sessions. For this purpose, use can be made of well-developed, empirically tested methods employed in the task-centered practice model (Reid, 1992, 2000; Reid & Fortune, in press). In this chapter, we focus on tasks within the session.

Welcoming

This task involves building rapport, developing trust, and creating a psychologically safe environment in which to accomplish all the other tasks. The social worker communicates to others that he or she is emotionally and socially available and will perform his or her responsibilities with sensitivity, respect for diversity, and professional competence. The client and community must in turn be willing to trust the social worker and be receptive to his or her engagement efforts. Unless these tasks are successfully accomplished, remaining tasks are in jeopardy.

Welcoming can be accomplished through introductions, story telling, icebreakers, or expressions of care and concern for the client and community. At APS, this task began with story telling, informing the group a little bit about myself (Behrman), inquiring about them and their roles at APS, explaining why I was qualified to lead this group, honoring their work, and explaining how privileged I felt to be with them. I was very clear about why I was there and that there were no hidden agendas. We were there to create a healthy community in which all APS workers can maintain and enhance their knowledge, coping skills, and meaningful connections. I also spent some time before the debriefing, walking among them and getting to know their names, where they were born, and what their work responsibilities were.

It was important to me that this debriefing be framed as a community experience, while acknowledging the cultural, religious, and racial differences among the individual participants. Also, the groups were large—60 or more. Thus, striving for healthy outcomes not just for individuals but also for the community seemed appropriate. Another element of the welcoming task is to discuss the ground rules for the upcoming process: What is said will held in confidence; it is not necessary to speak; one should speak only for oneself; all comments should be directed toward the group; everyone should stay for the entire session; the purpose of this intervention is not to evaluate who did what or how well.

At the APS debriefing, it was important to speak first with state officials and the local supervisors about the locations of the offices in relationship to the World Trade Center, how many people work in the offices, where we would be meeting, and how much time would be given to each session. Working with juveniles in the criminal justice system would involve contacting their schools and/or court-appointed officers and social workers. In this instance, I discovered that we would be meeting in a work area and that there would be distractions and disruptions. I was also informed that 50% of the workers were recent immigrants from all over the world, which posed a challenge given our lack of knowledge of the role of race and ethnicity in traumatic experience (Borden, 2000). Finally, I learned that only a few of the caseworkers at APS were social workers.

Reflecting

The purpose of this task, shared by the social worker and the client and community, is to reflect on the core principles that will shape the rebuilding process. What values guide the client's and community's conception of health following the trauma? What do these juveniles value in their lives and what familial, religious, and cultural beliefs are important to them? How have these beliefs shaped behaviors and relationships prior to this traumatic event? These questions will set the stage for the formulation of goals and tasks. Ideally, they will build community identification and a genuine connection between the social worker and the client and community.

Being a reflective practitioner (Schon, 1983) is useful in implementing this task. When the social worker and clients identify together what their underlying principles are, a level of trust and safety should result that will enable them to work together as a team in creating their tasks for healing. Thus, practitioners are called to develop what Berman (1981) termed "participating consciousness" and what Polanyi (1962) described as a "passionate participation of the knower in the act of knowing" (p. viii). Waite (1939) spoke of this task when he remarked, "What the client is responding to is not merely the spoken word but the total impression the worker's personality makes. If we want clients to give us their confidence, we have to become people who inspire confidence" (p. 186).

At the APS offices, there was immense cultural, age, religious, and racial diversity, as noted. The most obvious bonding core principle was their work and their clients. So we talked about the agency's mission and how their own personal and religious beliefs support that mission. There followed a discourse about why they chose to work with vulnerable, neglected, and abused adults and why this was meaningful. During the task, we continued the process of meaning making and naming the principles that unite them as a practice community. Among the principles expressed were commitment to service, respect for each other and their clients, and the dignity and value of everyone in the room. When a helping professional works with juveniles, it is critical that the youth articulate and name what principles they hold in common and respect in one another.

Framing

This task entails framing the traumatic event in meaningful language that makes sense to individuals and the community. This is critical when working with juveniles. The goal is to understand what happened and is happening in their lives so that distorted information about the traumatic event can be reduced and the facts surrounding the event can be clearly communicated. This lowers the risk for rumors disconnecting people from each other.

The task is framed around telling the story of what happened and can be facilitated with these questions: How did the traumatic event happen? Who was involved? Where and when did it occur? The practitioner should refrain during this task from asking questions about why the event happened. Often this will result in blaming someone or something for the trauma, and the process may be thrown off track. With the APS workers, this task was accomplished both in the large group and in small breakouts. If the latter is chosen, it is important to have competent facilitators who can keep the discourse focused on the task.

Educating

In the context of the present model, to educate is to create knowledge that will help restore the health of the individuals and their community. "The process of education and self-education among participants makes critical enlightenment possible" (Kemmis & McTaggart, 2000, p. 598). Educating by the practitioner facilitates the client's and community's complementary task of self-education or learning, the task that must be achieved if the social worker's efforts are to be of any value.

Basic information is provided by the social worker that enables the participants to distinguish between stress and trauma. That is, stress is a reaction to environmental stimuli within the ordinary range of human experience, whereas trauma is perceived as an unexpected life-threatening event, one that overwhelms usual coping strategies (Kanel, 1999). The effects of trauma—such as numbness, fatigue, irritability, and fear— may be persistent. This serves as a "heads-up" type of knowing that can help prepare one for unexpected emotions, behaviors, and cognitions. Loss of focus (increasing risk for accidents), bursts of anger and irritability, headaches and backaches, upset stomachs, and nightmares are all common features of posttrauma experiences. Normalizing these experiences and listening for what may be unique is critical. Also, educating clients regarding some of the potential emotional reactions that may accompany a posttraumatic event—such as denial (numbing), sadness, anger, and blaming—is important. By sharing reactions to the traumatic event, individuals begin to see that there are both similarities and unique responses and that they can learn from one another, a process that helps restore a sense of community.

During this task, the key question for the social worker to ask is "What is different for you physically, emotionally, socially, and spiritually?" Creating a discourse while educating enhances the group's responsibility for describing their symptoms and for developing knowledge about them. Here we are not informing them about what they have just experienced, nor are we telling them what they will be experiencing following a trauma; rather, we are asking them to reveal what their experience has been thus far. Responses by the social worker to this task should be in terms that participants use in their everyday lives, rather than medical, academic, or professional language. The social worker explains that reactions to a traumatic event may vary, many different types of responses are to be expected, and these responses differ from stress reactions. Explanations are given as to why trauma affects us the way it does (Caplan, 1961). Also, we inform participants about sensory experiences or environments that will trigger a sense of reliving the trauma and alert them to these phenomena. Some basic steps in lowering the intensity of the triggers are provided, which include normalizing the experience and identifying what sensory experience might trigger a reexperiencing of the trauma. Is it a smell, sight, sound, taste, or touch? Once this is identified, we acknowledge where the trigger came from and take several deep breaths until the sensory experience dissipates.

The APS workers were very forthcoming about what was different for them physically, emotionally, socially, and spiritually. We compiled an extensive list of symptoms, which served the purpose of instilling within the group a sense of communal suffering as survivors of the trauma. We then discussed ways of coping with the symptoms, which laid the groundwork for tasks that clients could undertake outside the session (see Empowering later in this section).

Grieving

The fifth task is to name what meaningful connections with oneself and others have been threatened or permanently lost. Trauma creates an immense sense of loss, so beginning the grieving process with the client and community is a very valuable task. Discussing different ways of grieving that are culturally, religiously, and gender and age sensitive is incorporated into this task.

Sometimes, when working with a community, it is helpful for the practitioner to meet with community and school representatives to begin this task. Whether working with individuals or communities, this task will help the professional identify what has been individually or communally lost. For example, individual identities were threatened or lost following the bombing of the World Trade Center. APS employees articulated this during the opening debriefing when they described their experience of self since the bombing. A woman with two children, who lost her husband in the bombing, no longer saw herself as a wife and mother in an intact family and struggled with her new identity as a widow with children, all dependent on her extended family. Another said, "Who am I following this trauma? I thought I was a pacifist, but now I am not sure."

This task of the client or community is to assess what is changed or lost in their sense of self. For juveniles entering the criminal justice system, much of their identity is radically changed, both internally and externally, by how they are now identified by the local community. The social worker facilitates this task of assessment with sensitivity and patience, respecting what the client or community has identified as a disconnection from the self and not minimizing what has been named. This task is a process that is never completed, but will change and perhaps enlarge as the client's and community's losses emerge after the trauma. The social worker and the group name what has been lost. A recording device, such as a flip chart, may be useful. Participants begin to see new connections, common experiences, and shared identities, which not only normalizes their posttraumatic reactions but also engages them in community building.

The second part of this task is asking what has been lost with respect to others. Where have unexpected disconnections appeared with families, coworkers, classmates, or communities? When I asked about disconnections from others during the debriefing with the APS workers, a recent citizen of the United States, who emigrated here from the Middle East, said that people on the street questioned his citizenship and his right to be in New York City. He no longer felt connected to his community, and his alienation was mixed with fear and anxiety for his and his family's safety. This experience of alienation may be present among juveniles in the criminal justice system.

The third part of this task is exploring what meaning in their lives has been threatened or lost. These disconnections might appear initially as depression, with such comments as "I don't enjoy my work or school any more, my hobbies and sports have fallen to the sidelines, and I don't want to attend family functions." These are symptoms of a loss of meaning and need to be identified as such. Helping people to maintain and recreate meaning in their lives is a critical task in crisis work (Frankl, 1971). With the APS workers, the social worker facilitated this task by asking the group what loss of meaning frightened them most. Responses varied from not finding it meaningful to live in such a large city to doubting their previously held religious beliefs. This communal discourse around the loss of meaning can begin the process of rebuilding a more supportive community. One way that people recreate their connections with others is through such discourse, which enables them to identify what they can expect from themselves, others, and their environment (Bruner, 1990). This is critical when rebuilding trust after a traumatic event. The social worker assists clients in revisiting those "taken-for-granted meanings and reformulating them into constructions that are improved, matured, expanded and elaborated, and that enhance their conscious experiencing of the world" (Guba & Lincoln, 1986, p. 546). The goal is to create tasks that will enhance behaviors that lead to health.

Amplifying

Amplifying a person's or group's emotional and cognitive experience of the trauma refers to recreating elements of the traumatic experience in a safe environment to facilitate expressions of thoughts and feelings about it. Amplifying requires a competency of the practitioner that lowers the risk that this task will retraumatize the participants. Without competent training in crisis intervention theory and skills, this task can potentially be more harmful than helpful (Everly & Mitchell, 1997). For many persons who have been traumatized, the numbing stage, which prevents the person from fully experiencing the trauma on emotional and cognitive levels, is initially a healthy mechanism. Without this automatic response, many of those experiencing trauma would not be able to carry out activities of daily living. This coping strategy becomes unhealthy when the numbing stage persists. Much later, when the person begins "thawing" and starts to relive the intensity of the trauma, he or she may resort to self-medication techniques that keep the traumatic experience from surfacing. This can be manifested in legal and illegal substance abuse, excessive use of video games and television, harmful sexual behaviors, and other strategies that either distract or numb the person enough so that the trauma never surfaces. It may be critical at some time during the recovery phase for the person or group to create a safe place where amplification can be experienced and related tasks completed. Sometimes people and groups do not have the baseline health, resources, and support to do these tasks.

Amplifying is not recommended during the early weeks following the trauma, and hence it was not used in work with the APS employees reported here. The task can be used only after a full assessment is done by a competent practitioner trained in trauma work, who is able to provide the safety and resources for a person or group to revisit the emotional and cognitive arena of trauma.

The goal is to help participants understand and move through the experience in a purposeful and therapeutic manner. Amplifying is not a task that can be completed in one setting. The amount of time spent on it will depend on the intensity of the traumatic event, its perceived threat to life and safety, and the prior health of the persons traumatized.

If it had been done with the APS employees, amplifying might have made use of videotapes of the destruction of the World Trade Center as a way of recreating the traumatic event. This might have been accompanied by asking participants to recall the sights, sounds, smells, and tastes they might have experienced during the event. For example, at a debriefing session one participant spontaneously recalled that her most vivid sensation was the taste of soot in her mouth. Memories of this kind can be used to help recreate the event in a safe environment. Successfully navigating through these sensory experiences with the help of the practitioner can rob triggers of their ability to create disruptions. Between sessions the client may, under the practitioner's guidance, continue the process through self-exposure to stimuli associated with the traumatic event.

Integrating

The existential questions that eventually arise following a traumatic event is "How does this trauma connect to my overall life? Is it possible to be transformed by this experience, or is the only consequence tragedy and destruction?" The natural strategy is for persons to compartmentalize the traumatic event with the belief that the trauma will not disrupt their health. We often hear, "Don't think about it, forget that it ever happened, and get on with your life!" These sincere suggestions are attempts to compartmentalize the experience rather than to integrate it. If this were the healthiest option, we would never have such organizations as Mothers Against Drunk Drivers. Following the trauma of her daughter's death at the hands of a drunk driver, a woman integrated her traumatic experience to forge a new identity as a national leader and advocate for stricter laws regarding drinking and driving. Who will be transformed following the World Trade Center trauma?

The goal is to create new possibilities for transformative ways of living following the trauma. Through narratives that depict how trauma transformed the lives of ordinary people, the practitioner and clients begin the work of transformation. In telling these stories it is critical that they are told with sensitivity and without setting up unrealistic expectations that everyone should take on a new identity following trauma. Creative ways of inspiring hope and courage are employed. Just raising the question "Is it possible for this tragedy to transform us individually and as a community?" creates a whole discourse with much potential.

Empowering

Thus far, activities within the group sessions have raised various possibilities for the participants' continued taskwork outside the session. Empowering involves identifying, from these possibilities, the most effective and efficient tasks that will facilitate the maintenance and enhancement of healthy outcomes following trauma. It also involves planning ways to obtain the resources necessary to complete these tasks successfully, deciding on methods of task accomplishment, and considering obstacles that may interfere with task attainment.

One approach to facilitating empowerment is Kormanik's (1999) four-S model: self, situation, strategy, support. What resources exist within the self? What is his or her current situation? Are there important resource deficits, such as lack of an adequate income? What past strategies worked or were inadequate when the person or community previously experienced trauma or highly stressful situations? What new strategies did they learn from others? What supports are currently operative in their lives, or what new supports are available that they may not be aware of?

With the APS workers, it was important to ask, "What do you now need? What are your priorities? What is most important for you in regaining or maintaining health?" It is critical that the pressing needs of the individual and community are addressed and that tasks will be responsive to these needs.

Community tasks can be identified and planned with all participants together. The APS employees identified tasks that could be undertaken in groups, such as ongoing team-building meetings, potlucks, and volunteering for service in the city. Also, they agreed to post large sheets of paper in public areas where employees could list tasks they found helpful. Obstacles to tasks were considered. For example, some task possibilities involved obtaining mental health services, but it was not clear how APS employees might obtain these services. Suggestions for securing services were developed by approaching Human Resources for this information.

For more individualized tasks, small breakout groups can be used. At APS, six New York City Department of Mental Health professionals lead small groups. The focus was on the following question: "Now that we have educated each other about how trauma impacts us physically, emotionally, socially, and spiritually, and we have named what is lost in our lives, it is important that we identify what tasks can be developed to address these losses and how these tasks can be carried out." If small group leaders are not available, then the facilitator can circulate among groups or consulting pairs can be utilized. Individual tasks that were identified and developed by APS workers included carrying out volunteer, religious, leisure, and physical activities; eating nutritious meals; and doing relaxation and spiritual exercises.

Terminating and Revisiting

The purpose of terminating is to summarize what has been covered and what has been learned. Attention is given to what has just been created together and how this experience has been helpful. The primary goal is to mark the transition from this structured experience to a fluid one. Care of self and others is emphasized, and the sharing that occurred in the group can be carried on outside this experience.

The facilitator takes the emotional temperature of the group by checking on how the participants are feeling now. Any follow-up sessions are announced, and the group is reminded of long-term resources that were identified. How their participation has helped one another is discussed. The session is closed with some type of ritual that reflects the group's cohesiveness in a genuine and appropriate manner. The practitioner remains available to individuals after the session. Refreshments were served at the APS session, which provided an opportunity for conversation and relaxation.

Many things can change within days and weeks for persons who have been traumatized. It is important to revisit the individuals and community within several weeks, or earlier if warranted. At the follow-up session, the following questions may be considered: What is different since we last met? What new needs have surfaced? What tasks have been effective in maintaining and recreating health? Do any tasks need to be altered or discarded and replaced with new ones? Are there problems with isolation and lack of connectedness? Finally, long-term tasks for maintaining health can be reinforced and further developed at this time.

Conclusion

The model just presented can be applied to any group that has undergone a traumatic experience. Through tasks, participants recreate lost connections affecting the self and community, which enable them to achieve changes at whatever levels are possible. The model is still evolving, and outcomes research is warranted. Directions for future work include developing ways to translate these group tasks, which take place in group sessions, into healing actions that can be carried out in the participant's life and to achieve better articulation between tasks at individual and community levels.

RESOURCES AND REFERENCES

Berman, M. (1981). *The reenchantment of the world.* Ithaca, NY: Cornell University Press.

Borden, W. (2000). The relational paradigm in contemporary psychoanalysis: Toward a psychodynamically informed social work perspective. *Social Service Review, 74*, 352–379.

Bruner, J. (1990). *Acts of meaning.* Cambridge, MA: Harvard University Press.

Caplan, G. (1961). *An approach to community mental health.* New York: Grune & Stratton.

Everly, G. S., & Mitchell, J. T. (1997). *Critical incident stress management. An operations manual for the prevention of traumatic stress among emergency services and disaster workers* (2nd ed.). Ellicott City, MD: Chevron.

Frankl, V. (1971). *Man's search for meaning.* New York: Washington Square Press.

Guba, E., & Lincoln, Y. (1986). Research, evaluation, and policy analysis: Heuristics for disciplined inquiry. *Policy Studies Review, 5*(3), 546–551.

Kanel, K. (1999). *A guide to crisis intervention.* Pacific Grove, CA: Brooks/Cole.

Kaplan, H. (1999). Toward an understanding of resilience: A critical review of definitions and models. In M. Glantz & J. Johnson (Eds.), *Resilience and development: Positive life adaptations.* New York: Plenum.

Kemmis, S., & McTaggart, R. (2000). Participatory action research. In N. Denzin & Y. Lincoln (Eds.), *Handbook of qualitative research* (2nd ed., pp. 567–605). Thousand Oaks, CA: Sage.

Kormanik, M. B. (1999). The cycle of awareness development: A cognitive and psychosocial theory of adult development. In K. P. Kuchinke (Ed.), *Proceedings of the 1999 Academy of Human Resources Management Conference* (Vol. 2, pp. 634–640). Baton Rouge, LA: Academy of Human Resource Management.

Polanyi, M. (1962). *Personal knowledge.* Chicago: University of Chicago Press.

Reid, W. J. (1992). *Task strategies: An empirical approach to social work practice.* New York: Columbia University Press.

Reid, W. J. (1997). Research on task-centered practice. *Social Work Research, 21*(3), 132–137.

Reid, W. (2000). *The task planner.* New York: Columbia University Press.

Reid, W. J., & Epstein, L. (1972). *Task-centered casework.* New York: Columbia University Press.

Reid, W. J., & Fortune, A. E. (2002). The task-centered model. In A. R. Roberts & G. Greene (Eds.), *Social worker's desk reference* (pp. 101–104). New York: Oxford University Press.

Saleeby, D. (1994). Culture, theory, and narrative: The intersection of meaning in practice. *Social Work, 39*(4), 351–359.

Schon, D. (1983). *The reflective practitioner: How professionals think in action.* New York: Basic Books.

Sermabeikian, P. (1994). Our clients, ourselves: The spiritual perspective and social work practice. *Social Work, 39*(2), 178–182.

Waite, F. T. (1939). A little matter of self-respect. In F. Lowry (Ed.), *Readings in social case work, 1920–1938: Selected reprints for the case work practitioner* (pp. 184–186). New York: Columbia University Press.

Wood, J., Foy, D., Goguen, C., Pynoos, R., James, C. B. (2002). Violence exposure and PTSD among delinquent girls. *Journal of Aggression, Maltreatment and Trauma, 6, 1*(11), 109–126.

Wood, J., Foy, D., Layne, C., Pynoos, R., James, C. B. (2002). An examination of the relationships between violence exposure, post traumatic stress symptomatology and delinquent activity: An ecopathological model of delinquent behavior among incarcerated adolescents. *Journal of Aggression, Maltreatment and Trauma, 6, 1*(11), 127–147.

Epilogue: Social Work and Criminal Justice?

Harris Chaiklin

Introduction

Social work has been involved with criminal justice theory and practice since before the profession was formally organized. In contrast, social work education for criminal justice practice has ebbed and flowed. Lately, it has been at a low point. Some years ago I presented an analysis of why education neglects preparation for criminal justice practice (Chaiklin, 2000).[1]

This chapter updates the prior examination. While social work claims that social justice is a key element in the professional ethos, this value apparently does not extend to social lepers. What is odd about this situation is that there are many helping professionals in criminal justice positions, even though their education provided little preparation for this. It is ironic that they have to, in effect, learn on the job (Corcoran & Shireman, 1997). The chapters in this volume and in other sources demonstrate that there is a social work literature that could be used to educate students for positions in the field. See, for example, Brownell and Roberts (2002), Clapp (1998), Menken (1933), Polsky (1962), Pray (1945), Roberts and Brownell (1999), Young (1952), and Young and LoMonaco (2001).

A Broad Definition

The phrase "criminal justice" is used to encompass all the settings and fields of practice where social workers serve. While there are many subspecialties such as forensic, adult, or juvenile, the knowledge and skill needed to work in these areas is essentially the same. Social work education is marked by a tendency to develop specializations to respond to current needs and political demands made on it. If criminal justice education is to have a chance to move into the social work curriculum, it will have to develop a generic base course to support specialized practice courses. Such a course should be given in the first semester of the second year concurrent with a specialized course that relates to the student's field placement.

The lack of criminal justice education in social work has not gone unnoticed. Over the years the issue has been identified and calls for improvement have been made (Goodman, Getzel, & Ford, 1996; Isenstadt, 1995; Sarri, 1995; Witte, 1964; Young, & LoMonaco, 2001). They have had little effect. Social work education seems to content itself with pleas to include content in the curriculum (Young & LoMonaco, 2001). If anything, the organized profession has pulled back even further from involvement. The introductory chapter in this volume notes that the National Association of Social Worker's (NASW's) journal *Social Work* averages only about two articles per year in this area while the much smaller *Research on Social Work Practice* averages six per year. Despite a great deal of prior activity, the Council on Social Work Education (CSWE) has not had a corrections specialist on the staff since 1965. Although the 1962 NASW delegate assembly approved a Corrections Council, it was never implemented because of budgetary restrictions so the Council disbanded (Corcoran & Shireman, 1997).

There is some emphasis in undergraduate social work programs. CSWE does not accredit specific programs in this area, so the schools are left free to develop their own approaches (Reed & Carawan, 1999). While the lack of restrictions permits flexibility, the lack of accreditation makes it difficult to institutionalize this education.

The dominance of sociology and criminal justice departments in educating the personnel needed to staff the criminal justice system began about 50 years ago (Ohlin, 1956). Today there are more than a thousand criminal justice programs which range from junior colleges to doctoral programs. Information about these programs can be accessed on the Web at such sites as www.acjs.org, www.faculty.ncwc.edu/toconnor/jus.grad.htm, and www.criminal justice programs.us. In such departments the largest programs are directed at undergraduate education. Many of these are either joint programs in sociology, criminal justice, and social work or there is a great deal of overlap in course content. Textbooks in this field tend to be directed at all three content areas. Thus, Ellis and Sowers' (2001) text *Juvenile Justice Practice* has as the subtitle *A Cross-Disciplinary Approach to Intervention*. Having so much of the education for criminal justice work concentrated at the bachelor's level is a mixed blessing. It does keep the field alive and provides numerous workers to staff the system. The presence of so many people without advanced professional training tends to hold the field back because it is difficult to raise standards.

At the master's level there is little happening. In the 1990s there were six concentrations in offender rehabilitation, and about 10% of the schools offered an elective course in something related to criminal justice. It is not known how much of this content relates directly to work in prisons. Nor is there any indication of how much content is directed toward reality-oriented social treatment as compared to psychotherapy. For example, in response to the Welfare Reform Act of 1996, many schools revised their curriculums. The University of Michigan, a leading school, created new concentrations in community and social systems, mental health, and the elderly. It dropped courses in ego psychology and deviant behavior (Mulrine, 1997). Such curriculum changes will make it harder for social work students interested in corrections to get the knowledge they need. All of this leads to the conclusion that, even though the need is great and there are opportunities for employment, social work education is not moving to meet this need (Ivanoff & Smyth, 1997).

History

One thing that would help put a spotlight on the need for social work education in criminal justice would be for the organized profession to pay more attention to its history (Chaiklin, 2006). A brief review of this history helps in understanding the continuing need for social work in this area and provides a basis for making some suggestions about how to integrate criminal justice in practice and education.

In the 1860s, 70s, and 80s several organizations formed that either contributed to or became part of what was the beginning of professionally organized social welfare. They show the extent to which social work and criminal justice work had a joint beginning. Franklin B. Sanborn was at the center of many of these groups (Chaiklin, 2005). In 1867 he helped organize the National Prison Association. In 1874, under the auspices of the American Social Science Association's (ASSA) Section on Social Economy and the Massachusetts State Board of Charities, a meeting was held that resulted in creating the Conference of the Boards of Public Charities. Sanborn was the first secretary and remained active in the national conference as it evolved through various name changes. From 1875 to 1879 it was called the Conference of Charities, from 1880 to 1881 it was called the Conference of Charities and Correction, and from 1882 to 1916 it was called the National Conference of Charities and Correction.

Many of the members of the original planning group for the National Conference of Charities and Correction were also leaders in the National Prison Association. For example, Frederick H. Wines was active in attempts to change prisons. Wines's father, Enoch C. Wines, was a noted criminal justice reformer. While secretary of the New York Prison Association he backed Richard L. Dugdale's classic study of the Jukes family. He was a strong supporter of Zebulon Reed Brockway's attempts to reform Elmira prison. He was an early proponent of the indeterminate sentence, which at that time was seen as progress since the prisoner would be released once he had reformed. Enoch Wines wrote two of the earliest books on social services, *Report on Prisons and Reformatories of the United States and Canada* (1867) and *State of Prisons and of Child Saving Institutions in the Civilized World* (1880; Bruno, 1948). This would make him one of the earliest known people to be identified as a social worker.

The diverging interests of charities and corrections manifested themselves fairly early in the development of both professions. In 1917, the name was changed to reflect the split. It became the National Conference of Social Work. It kept that name until 1956 when it became the National Conference of Social Welfare. It kept that name until 1983 when it went out of business. The name changes are indicative of the conference getting farther and farther removed from the basic problems it started out to deal with and the ending of the partnership between lay people and professionals. They also reflect that corrections and social work were going separate ways even though in practice there was and is a large overlap. If schools of social work were to begin requiring a course in the history of the profession, they might provide a springboard for renewed interest in criminal justice education and revive the partnerships that were so successful in bringing social reform.

The Need

Large numbers of people are enmeshed in the criminal justice system. Their service needs fit what social workers are skilled in providing, and their human needs are exemplars of things that social work values address. Chief among these is social justice. Right now the leadership for this is coming from places other than social work. For example, the Innocence Project, which started at Yeshiva University and was founded by Barry C. Scheck and Peter J. Neufeld, has used DNA evidence to show that numerous people were wrongly convicted. Our criminal justice system is in need of constant monitoring. Social workers should be among the leaders in pushing for a fair justice system that treats offenders humanely.

Almost all prisons are overcrowded, and probation and parole caseloads are too large. At the end of 2004 there were 2,135,901 prisoners in federal or state prisons or in local jails. The estimate is that 486 per 100,000 U.S. residents were incarcerated (U.S. Department of Justice, 2006). Despite differences in computing rates by various sources, there is general agreement that right now the United States has the highest rate of imprisonment in the world. The only encouraging note is that the rate of increase is slowing down. There are also selective increases in important categories. Since 1990 the number of women in prison has doubled to 90,688 (Aglilias, 2004). This is a rate that is higher than the male increase (Beck, 2000).

Corrections are expensive, and the system has a large workforce. In 1999 the total cost was $147 billion. Local governments paid more than half of these costs. In March of 1999 the justice system employed 2.2 million people with a payroll of more than $7.2 billion. In terms of personnel distribution 46% were engaged in police work, 21% in judicial, and 33% in corrections. The payrolls follow the personnel distribution with 49% going to police, 22% to judicial, and 29% to corrections (Gifford, 2002).

The unmet needs of offenders are great. Those who are incarcerated have more physical and mental problems than the general population. In 1997, 31% of state and 23.4% of federal inmates had a physical or mental condition. At midyear in 1998 it was estimated that 283,000 mentally ill offenders were imprisoned (Ditton, 1999). The need for services is greatest at the time of release when offenders require help with jobs, housing, and other aspects of dealing with public bureaucracies (Chaiklin, 1972; Petersilia, 2005). Job training and help with placement after release is essential. Only about 6% of prisoners have any meaningful job experience while they are incarcerated. The pressure is so great that correctional systems are beginning to provide some after-release services, something they have traditionally avoided (Travis, 1999). Reentry is clearly an area that would employ social workers if they were educated for this work.

Unfortunately, we are in a period when, despite the need, criminal justice services are being retrenched. In prisons the push is to reduce overcrowding and not to fit services to the offenders' needs. In a somber assessment of this situation, Richard Friedman, former director of the Governors Juvenile Advisory Council in Maryland, says that conditions in both professions contribute to a lack of interest on the part of social work schools for moving into this educational area (R. Friedman, personal communication, 1996). Many social work positions have either been eliminated or downgraded to generic counselor spots with a consequent reduction in pay. Case management is replacing treatment, and prisons are becoming more and more foreboding and punitive. "Frills" are being eliminated, and education and social work are considered superfluous. Criminal justice has become an environment where there is more emphasis on punishment than rehabilitation. My friend Richard Korn once told me that there is a conspiracy of silence created by social workers in the field because they have compromised with a punitive system and those outside the corrections field are so guilty about what their colleagues are doing that they do not say anything. He had good basis for this judgment because he was once director of treatment at the New Jersey State Prison in Trenton and participated in the same thing himself. He spent most of the rest of his career trying to atone for the sins he thought he committed. Social justice is not achieved by talking in abstractions. To attain it takes concrete actions.

Avoiding the Need and Stigmatizing the Offender

Among the common reasons advanced for the movement away from criminal justice education are the deprofessionalization of many social work positions, the emergence of new specializations such as in aging, the increasing importance of private practice using psychotherapy, and the change in correctional emphasis from rehabilitation to punishment (Corcoran & Shireman, 1997; Gumz, 2004). While all of these are factors that affect the profession and its education, there is nothing about them that necessarily says that social work must pull away from criminal justice education. Social workers can play a large role in meeting the needs of offenders (Chaiklin, 1971, 1972).

Offenders are probably the most stigmatized of the populations who need services (Korn & McCorkle, 1961). Miller comments on the high proportion of the prison population that comes from parole or probation revocation: "[F]or the most part these individuals had not engaged in illegal behavior sufficient to warrant an arrest . . ." (1995, p. 656). A situation such as this should be ripe for social work intervention because it calls forth the founding values of the profession that look to help the distressed.

Unfortunately, social work's ambivalence about working with mandated clients has contributed to the lack of a sustained effort at developing practitioners to work in criminal justice. This has been so for a long time. In 1880 Russell called it a "callous corrugated and petrified indifference" (F. Russell, 1880, p. 83). The very first report in the first meeting of the National Conference, then called the Conference of Boards of Public Charities, was about the state of the insane poor. It stated, "It should not be discretionary with a public officer, before whom a case is presented for action, to send an insane person to an asylum, or to an almshouse and jail" (*Official Proceedings*, 1874, p. 61). This issue has never been resolved, for today jails and prisons contain large numbers of prisoners who need treatment for mental problems. One cannot be imprisoned for mental illness, so charges such as disorderly conduct, resisting arrest, or worse are used to swell crime statistics needlessly (Chaiklin, 1985). The jail and prison become storage spaces for the mentally ill. This further impedes the ability of these institutions to do appropriate correctional programming. In 2002 the U.S. Supreme Court (*Atkins vs. Virginia*) ruled that it is illegal to execute a criminal who is retarded. The ruling was based on the Eighth Amendment, which, with elegant simplicity, states, "Excessive bail shall not be required, nor cruel and unusual punishments inflicted." Social work knowledge and skills could contribute a great deal to help clarify a humane approach to offenders that also respects the need for public security. But practitioner and research communities do not communicate. Petersilia says, "when one looks closely at the two enterprises, there is little evidence that research is driving policy, or that policy is driving research" (Petersilia, 2004).

Social workers and other correctional treatment personnel tend to distrust one another. This contributes to social work's avoidance of education for criminal justice in that it is not easy to maintain field placements in correctional settings. The differences in orientation between social workers and other correctional personnel are exacerbated by educational and status differences between them. While neither social work nor criminal justice can claim to be high-status professions, social work does have the edge because of its greater educational requirements and consequent greater income. Criminal justice did not begin moving into university education in a significant way until the 1960s (Kratcoski, 1989). Much of this was spurred by the availability of federal money. The bachelor's degree is still the effective terminal degree for most criminal justice practice.

In contrast, social work education had moved into the university by the early 1930s, and a master's degree in social work quickly became the terminal required degree for practice. Many of those in supervisory and administrative positions in criminal justice had a social work degree because the advanced education was a job requirement. As graduate education became more available in criminal justice, the number of those in administrative positions who had social work degrees diminished. This added to the split between the fields. During the 1960s there was a rapid spread of both masters and bachelor's social work programs. This occurred for the same reason that correctional programs spread—the availability of federal money. While there were high hopes that this expansion would put social work in a leadership role, this has not proved to be the case (Gardner, 1966).

Casework With Authority: Social Work's Unique Contribution to Treatment

It does not go too far to say that social work's lack of response in the face of the great need and the fact that money is available for services reflect a departure from the high ethical standards the field professes. I would suggest that one element in change will be a renewed emphasis on teaching and understanding casework with authority. Most people in the criminal justice system are in situations where their contact with a social worker is mandated.

Casework with authority is social work's one unique contribution to treatment (Fantl, 1958; Hardman, 1959; Hartman, 1963, 1979; Smith & Berlin, 1974; Studt, 1959). The early workers in the juvenile court understood that when the clients were mandated to come to a worker the usual ways of working did not hold. Practitioners had to be comfortable with not personalizing the relationship and with letting the law provide the structure. They also understood that most of the people they worked with did not need psychotherapy but, rather, help in living within the rules of society (Chaiklin, 1971, 1972, 1974). Those who were most skilled as therapists understood that when they were working with offenders who had basic social and material needs and deficits they were doing therapy, but it was not traditional psychotherapy (Studt, 1968). Therapists usually require a relationship in order to proceed. Many mandated clients have never had a decent relationship in their lives. For these people a relationship is not an instrument of help necessary before anything can be done. It is a treatment goal.

Practitioners who understood how to work with authority did not experience any conflict between the needs of custody and the needs of treatment. They knew that unless a situation was secure it was not possible to do work of any kind. Current discussions in social work on involuntary clients continue past patterns without breaking new ground. Some scarcely mention criminal justice (Rooney, 1992). Others stress the complexity of correctional systems and the difficulty of working with involuntary correctional clients (Ivanoff, Blythe, & Tripodi, 1994). And still others continue the hoary debate about whether it is ethical for the social worker to act as an agent of the community (Clark, 1997; O'Hare, 1996; Rothman, Smith, Nakashima, Paterson, & Mustin, 1996). The prospects for increased educational attention to corrections do not seem great despite pleas for this by some social workers (Dwyer, 1997). Since there are jobs in corrections, social workers will fill them whether they are prepared to or not. A survey of the year 2000 master's graduates found that 4% had taken jobs in corrections and criminal justice and 4% in substance abuse (O'Neill, 2002). Those in the field find it is a struggle. A coalition of correctional workers in the Washington, DC, Metro Chapter of NASW abandoned, in 1997, a 5-year effort to get recognized as a section (Hirsch, 1997). What has happened is that an on-the-job training literature has developed. Roberts, for example, has edited a book that offers ideas for workers to use in various settings (Corcoran & Shireman, 1997). There are other examples in the literature (c.f. Draine, & Solomon, 2001; Peoples, 1975; Severson, 1994; Solomon & Draine, 1995; Sternbach, 2000).

Many years ago a great juvenile court judge, Justine Wise Polier, raised the question of whether the social work profession was doing enough to change perceptions about what children need (Polier, 1960). Her observations could stand just as well for adults in the justice system. With her usual sharpness she asked whether the professionals were perpetuating the conditions that they claimed to be correcting. The lack of understanding about working with authority is supported by the ambivalence social workers have when they must work with authority.

Ideologically many social work practitioners, students, and their professors still have trouble accepting that they are agents of the community. They do not accept that a few simple rules fairly enforced contribute to everyone's security. Add to that social work's current ideological commitment to postmodernism, which sees truth as relative, and you have an intellectual style that is not suited to the direct attention to facts and behavior that work in criminal justice agencies requires. To make things worse, they adopt a language style that makes a lot of what is written in this vein almost incomprehensible. It is also a paradoxical stance because postmodernists within social work are apt to characterize the profession as an agent of oppression. They end up as critics rather than supporters of criminal justice (Graves, 1972). This situation was best summed up by Senator Moynihan when he said that "Ideological certainty easily degenerates into an insistence upon ignorance" (Moynihan, 1995, p. 4).

Education as a Key

If there is to be change, one of the first things to be done is to deal with curriculum matters. There are not enough placements, not enough financial support, and not enough correctional content in the curriculum. Social work education is under great pressure to include a large amount of varying material. It responds by tending to jam too much into the curriculum (Vinton & White, 1995; Young & LoMonaco, 2001). The number of specializations and content areas that must be covered grows exponentially. This results in a strong tendency not to teach the basic practice principles and techniques that are applicable in any specialization and setting. All social workers need to know how to listen to the client and to respect the right of self-determination, even where services are mandated.

Another response to the demand is to focus on a few specializations. There are courses or specializations in such things as aging, problem youth, addictions, and AIDS. In these specializations little attention is given to the criminal justice system. Yet, one of the major reasons for the large increase in the correctional population is because of policies concerning imprisoning addicts (Gaiter & Doll, 1996). The AIDS rate in the correctional population is seven times that in the general population, and the addiction rate is even higher (Mahon, 1996).

In addition to the usual resistance to large caseloads and misunderstanding the nature of work with authority, there has also been the belief in social work that no special knowledge is needed to work in corrections (Fox, 1997). In the 1959 Council on Social Work Education Curriculum Study, the conclusion was that no specialized curriculum was needed for corrections. The assumption was that the generic core plus selective course enrichment would provide sufficient preparation for work in corrections (Studt, 1959). Despite this some states began to require the master's in social work for probation officers (Fox, 1997). Even those who say that there should be specialized courses in deviance and social control put more emphasis on the commonality in the core social work curriculum (Austin & Foster, 1972). While the criminal justice system is expensive, it is also chronically short of funds. This contributes to the continuing shortage of personnel (Russell, 1960). This does not prevent those who are working from trying to improve their skills. One 1982 survey of 48 workers in legal services programs showed that more than 70% of them had attended continuing education workshops (Craige, Saur, & Arcuri, 1982). This was at a time when social work continuing education was not widespread or mandatory.

Forensic social work is a well-defined specialty concerned with legal issues and practiced mainly in the courts (Whitmer, 1983). Some have proposed that this might serve as a bridge between the mental health and the criminal justice systems (Barker & Branson, 1993; Brennan, Gedrich, Jacoby, Tardy, & Tyson, 1986). There are other avenues for making more connections between the systems. For example, the pioneering work that Treger has done with the police (Treger, 1980, 1981). The proponents of these ideas also report that there has not been much interest by schools. If it is so difficult to establish specialized education for well-defined subspecialties, it will be even more difficult to make progress on educating for the broadly defined field of corrections.

In not educating for criminal justice, social work does more than just neglect to prepare students for positions where they are needed and where there are employment opportunities. It abandons part of its birthright. Some earlier formulations placed corrections work in the punishment end of the criminal justice system (Studt, 1959). But social work's history in corrections has been one of trying to mitigate the effects of harsh punishment. Social workers played a major role in establishing the juvenile court. Over the years social workers have been effective in working within the criminal justice system (Roberts, 1997).

Conclusion

Social work's style in dealing with education and practice in corrections is disorganized and erratic. In this chapter social work in corrections was defined broadly to include any contact social work and its education has with the justice system. Several factors have combined to draw increased attention to the role social work plays in this area. There is the continued growth of the correctional population along with less tolerance by the public for treatment and other programs directed at offenders (Carlson, 1996, p. 5). At the same time the old prison maxim that "One way or another everyone gets out eventually" holds true. Given the large number of people moving through the justice system all human services will be put under pressure from offenders released into the community without preparation for reintegrating into society.

There are many helping professionals working in the justice system. Their education often does not prepare them for these jobs. In response to this some schools have begun offering courses and field placements in criminal justice, especially in forensic social work. They do this on their own, and there is little evidence that they have communicated with each other about this.

The big impediment in the growing involvement of social workers in criminal justice is that the major professional organizations, the NASW and the CSWE, have shown no interest in organizing the structures and standards that would provide the necessary leadership for recognizing and developing educational standards for social work in criminal justice. What is missing is that there is no systematic effort to find out what is going on. This is because of the abdication of leadership by both the CSWE and the NASW. For example, the *NASW News* reported on a meeting between the head of the American Correctional Association and the director of the NASW (Stoesen, 2004). The story says that both associations had much in common, that social workers were needed in the field, and that there was a need to work to overcome shortages in the field. Despite all the positive testimonials, nothing in the way of action at the organizational level seems to have occurred. So, as with many positive things that have happened in social work, there is activity on the front line, stirring within education, and evidence that progress will be impeded because of the slow response of educational and professional leadership.

The one sign of hope is that the federal government has recently begun to pay attention to the problem of release from prison and has made funds available. As in the past this gets a response from professional organizations. In 2006 the National Association of Social Workers hired a correction specialist to devise ways to tap into these funds.

9

The state of social work education for criminal justice "is hopeless but not serious." This phrase is the part of the title of Watzlawick's (1983) classic book on how people search for unhappiness. A critical analysis does not require that one be in a position where one has no options. There are signs of hope. They come from unexpected places. In Austin, Texas, Julia Cuba is a Girl Scout program executive who is a social work student at The University of Texas (Pace, 2006). She has been part of a Girl Scout program that has social work leadership and uses scouting as a way of breaking family cycles of deviance. The school has gotten involved to the extent that a member of the school's faculty, Dr. Darlene Grant, has been working to guide and evaluate the program for some years.

There is more educational activity than the literature and the formal reports of CSWE and NASW indicate. For example, the University of Illinois gives a course in this area, and in 2005 Fordham University had 20 to 25 corrections placements. Given this undercurrent of action, the absence of a criminal justice emphasis by NASW and CSWE is conspicuous. It would help greatly if NASW and CSWE collaborated in developing a good data base on the extent of social work education and practice in criminal justice.

If both social work and the criminal justice establishment collaborated in educational efforts, it is probable that there would be mutual benefits in terms of being able to cope with current conditions. Enough social workers are working in justice settings to justify setting up an educational specialization in this area. It should not be fractionated into numerous subspecialties like forensics, probation, penal institutions, and so on. This would only perpetuate the problem that it would be designed to correct. Pray said that casework paves the way in preparing prisoners for release (Pray, 1945). It is time to act on this insight.

NOTE

1. It took a long time to get this work published. It was originally submitted in 1993. This update covers more than the last 10 years.

RESOURCES AND REFERENCES

Aglilias, K. (2004). Women in corrections: A call to social work. *Australian Social Work 57*(4), 331–342.
Atkins vs. Virginia, 536 U.S. 304 (2002).
Austin, M. J., & Foster, J. P. (1972). Criminal justice and social welfare: Two emerging systems in search of linkages in the area of service delivery, manpower utilization, and educational planning. In M. J. Austin, E. Kelleher, & P. L. Smith (Eds.), *The Field Consortium: Manpower development and training in social welfare and corrections* (pp. 1–121). Tallahassee: State University System of Florida.
Barker, R. L., & Branson, D. M. (1993). *Forensic social work: Legal aspects of professional practice*. New York: Haworth Press.
Beck, A. J. (2000). *Prisoners in 1999* (pp. 1–16). Washington, DC: U.S. Department of Justice, Bureau of Justice Statistics.
Brennan, T. P., Gedrich, A. E., Jacoby, S. E., Tardy, M. J., & Tyson, K. B. (1986). Forensic social work: Practice and vision. *Social Casework, 67*(6), 340–350.
Brownell, P., & Roberts, A. R. (2002). A century of social work in criminal justice and correctional settings. *Journal of Offender Rehabilitation, 35*(2), 1–17.
Bruno, F. J. (1948). *Trends in social work*. New York: Columbia University Press.
Carlson, P. (1996). Corrections trends for the 21st century: Our future behind the walls and wire. *The Keepers' Voice*, 1–5.

Chaiklin, H. (1971). Social work with the family on release from prison. In *Social work practice, 1971* (pp. 51–61). New York: Columbia University Press.

Chaiklin, H. (1972). Integrating correctional and family systems. *American Journal of Orthopsychiatry, 42*, 784–789.

Chaiklin, H. (1974). Developing correctional social services. In A. R. Roberts (Ed.), *Correctional treatment of the offender* (pp. 294–308). Springfield, IL: Charles C. Thomas.

Chaiklin, H. (1985). *Jail experience and prior mental hospital hospitalization.* Baltimore: University of Maryland School of Social Work and Community Planning.

Chaiklin, H. (2000). Needed: More education for social work practice in criminal justice. *Journal of Law and Social Work, 10*(1/2), 165–174.

Chaiklin, H. (2005). Franklin Benjamin Sanborn: Human services innovator. *Research on Social Work Practice, 15*(2), 127–134.

Chaiklin, H. (2006). A history of social welfare history. *The Maryland Sentinel, January/February* 6.

Clapp, E. J. (1998). *Mothers of all children: Women reformers and the rise of juvenile courts in progressive era America.* University Park: Pennsylvania State University Press.

Clark, M. D. (1997). Withstanding "friendly fire": A frontline reply to O'Hare. *Social Work, 42*(2), 201–202.

Corcoran, K., & Shireman, C. (1997). M.S.W. education for the justice system: From the rehabilitative ideal to generalist practice. In C. A. McNeece & A. R. Roberts (Eds.), *Policy and practice in the justice system* (pp. 251–261). Chicago: Nelson Hall.

Craige, H. B., Saur, W. G., & Arcuri, J. B. (1982). The practice of social work in legal services programs. *Journal of Sociology and Social Welfare, 9*(2), 307–317.

Ditton, P. M. (1999). *Mental health and treatment of inmates and probationers* (pp. 1–12). Washington, DC: U.S. Department of Justice.

Draine, J., & Solomon, P. (2001). Threats of incarceration in a psychiatric probation and parole service. *American Journal of Orthopsychiatry, 71*(2), 262–267.

Dwyer, D. C. (1997). Juvenile corrections: Its implications for social work practice. In A. McNeece & A. R. Roberts (Eds.), *Policy and practice in the justice system* (pp. 19–28). Chicago: Nelson Hall.

Ellis, R. A., & Sowers, K. M. (2001). *Juvenile justice practice: A cross-disciplinary approach to intervention.* Belmont, CA: Brooks/Cole, Thomson Learning.

Fantl, B. (1958). Integrating psychological, social, and cultural factors in assertive casework. *Social Work, 3*(4), 30–37.

Fox, V. (1997). Foreword to the first edition. In A. R. Roberts (Ed.), *Social work in juvenile and criminal justice settings* (pp. xiii–xviii). Springfield, IL: Charles C. Thomas.

Gaiter, J., & Doll, L. S. (1996). Editorial: Improving HIV/AIDS prevention in prisons is good public health policy. *American Journal of Public Health, 86*(9), 1201–1203.

Gardner, J. W. (1966). Remarks. *Journal of Education for Social Work, 2*(1), 5–9.

Gifford, S. L. (2002). *Justice expenditure and employment in the United States, 1999* (pp. 1–12). Washington, DC: U.S. Department of Justice, Bureau of Justice Statistics.

Goodman, H., Getzel, G. S., & Ford, W. l. (1996). Group work with high-risk urban youths on probation. *Social Work, 41*(4), 375–381.

Graves, R. H. (1972). Specialized manpower needs in corrections with emphasis on social work. In M. J. Austin, E. Kelleher, & P. L. Smith (Eds.), *The Field Consortium: Manpower development and training in social welfare and corrections* (pp. 42–51). Tallahassee: State University System of Florida.

Gumz, E. J. (2004). American social work, corrections and restorative justice: An appraisal. *International Journal of Offender Therapy and Comparative Criminology, 48*(4), 449–460.

Hardman, D. G. (1959). Authority in casework: A bread and butter issue. *National Parole and Probation Journal, XXIII* 249–255.

Hartman, H. L. (1963, September). Interviewing techniques in probation and parole. *Federal Probation, 27*, 8–14.

Hartman, H. L. (1979, June). Interviewing techniques in probation and parole. *Federal Probation, 33*, 17–22.

Hirsch, K. (1997). Social workers in the criminal justice system. *The Maryland Sentinel September/October,* 5.

Isenstadt, P. M. (1995). Adult courts. In R. L. Edwards (Ed.), *Encyclopedia of social work* (19th ed., pp. 68–74). Washington, DC: NASW Press.

Ivanoff, A., Blythe, B. J., & Tripodi, T. (1994). *Involuntary clients in social work practice.* New York: Aldine De Gruyter.

Ivanoff, A., & Smyth, N. J. (1997). Preparing social workers for practice in correctional institutions. In A. R. Roberts (Ed.), *Social work in juvenile and criminal justice settings* (pp. 309–324). Springfield, IL: Charles C. Thomas.

Korn, R. R., & McCorkle, L. W. (1961). *Criminology and penology.* New York: Holt, Rinehart, & Winston.

Kratcoski, P. C. (1989). *Correctional counseling and treatment.* Prospect Heights, IL: Waveland Press.

Mahon, N. (1996). New York inmates' HIV risk behaviors: The implications for prevention policy programs. *American Journal of Public Health, 86*(9), 1211–1215.

Menken, A. D. (1933). *On the side of mercy: Problems in social readjustment.* New York: Covici, Friede.

Miller, J. G. (1995). Criminal justice: Social work roles. In R. L. Edwards (Ed.), *Encyclopedia of social work* (pp. 653–659). Washington, DC: NASW Press.

Moynihan, D. P. (1995). Rearranging flowers on the coffin. *Congressional Record: Proceedings and Debates of the 104th Congress, First Session.* Washington, DC: U.S. Government Printing Office.

Mulrine, A. (1997). Career outlook for social work. Retrieved May 3, 1999, from http://www.usnews.com/usnews/edu/beyond/bespc.htm

Official Proceedings of the Annual Meeting: 1874. (1874). New York: Conference of Boards of Public Charities.

O'Hare, T. (1996). Court-ordered versus voluntary clients: Problem differences and readiness for change. *Social Work, 41*(4), 417–422.

Ohlin, L. E. (1956). *Sociology and the field of corrections.* New York: Russell Sage Foundation.

O'Neill, J. V. (2002). Survey eyes job market for grads. *NASW News, June,* 12.

Pace, P. R. (2006). Breaking the mom/daughter prison cycle: Social workers key to lowering incarcerations. *NASW News March,* 6.

Peoples, E. E. (Ed.). (1975). *Readings in correctional casework and counseling.* Pacific Palisades, CA: Goodyear.

Petersilia, J. (2004). What works in prisoner reentry? Reviewing and questioning the evidence. *Federal Probation, 68*(2), 4–8.

Petersilia, J. (2005). Hard time ex-offenders returning home after prison. *Corrections Today, 67*(2), 66–72, 155.

Polier, J. W. (1960). Attitudes and contradictions in our culture. *Child Welfare, 39,* 1–7.

Polsky, H. W. (1962). *Cottage Six: The social system of delinquent boys in residential treatment.* New York: Russell Sage Foundation.

Pray, K. L. (1945). Case work paves the way in preparation for freedom. *Prison Journal, 26,* 166–171.

Reed, J. G., & Carawan, L. W. (1999). Beyond sibling rivalry. *Journal of Criminal Justice Education, 10,* 153–170.

Roberts, A. R. (1997). Introduction and overview. In A. R. Roberts (Ed.), *Social work in juvenile and criminal justice settings* (pp. 7–18). Springfield, IL: Charles C. Thomas.

Roberts, A. R., & Brownell, P. (1999). A century of forensic social work: Bridging the past to the present. *Social Work, 44*(4), 359–369.

Rooney, R. H. (1992). *Strategies for work with involuntary clients.* New York: Columbia University Press.

Rothman, J., Smith, W., Nakashima, J., Paterson, M.A., & Mustin, J. (1996). Client self-determination and professional intervention; striking a balance. *Social Work, 41*(4), 396–405.

Russell, B. (1960). *Current training needs in the field of juvenile delinquency.* Washington, DC: U.S. Department of Health, Education, and Welfare.

Russell, F. (1880). The families of prisoners. In *Seventh Annual Conference of Charities and Correction* (pp. 76–88). Cleveland, OH: A. Williams & Company.

Sarri, R. C. (1995). Criminal behavior overview. In R. L. Edwards (Ed.), *19th Encyclopedia of Social Work* (pp. 637–646). Washington, DC: NASW Press.

Severson, M. M. (1994). Adapting social work values to the corrections environment. *Social Work, 39*(4), 451–456.

Smith, A. B., & Berlin, L. (1974). Self-determination in welfare and corrections. *Federal Probation, 38,* 18–28.

Solomon, P., & Draine, J. (1995). Jail recidivism in a forensic case management program. *Health and Social Work, 20*(3), 167–173.

Sternbach, J. (2000). Lessons learned about working with men: A prison memoir. *Social Work, 45*(5), 413–423.

Stoesen, L. (2004). Corrections: Public safety, public health. *NASW News,* 49.

Studt, E. (1959). Worker-client authority relationships in social work. *Social Work, 4*(1), 18–28.

Studt, E. (1968). Social work theory and implications for the practice of methods. *Social Work Education Reporter, 16*(2), 42–46.

Travis, J. (1999). Prisons, work and re-entry. *Corrections Today, 61*(6), 102–106, 133.

Treger, H. (1980). Guideposts for community work in police-social work diversion. *Federal Probation, 44*(3), 3–8.

Treger, H. (1981). Police-social work cooperation: Problems and issues. *Social Casework, 62*(7), 426–433.

U.S. Department of Justice. (2006). Prison statistics. *United States Bureau of Justice Statistics*. Retrieved February 25, 2006, from http://www.ojp.usdoj.gov/bjs/prisons.htm.

Vinton, L., & White, B. (1995). The 'boutique effect' in graduate social work education. *Journal of Teaching in Social Work, 11*(1/2), 3–13.

Watzlawick, P. (1983). *The situation is hopeless, but not serious: The pursuit of unhappiness*. New York: Norton.

Whitmer, G. E. (1983). The development of forensic social work. *Social Work, 28*(3), 217–223.

Witte, E. F. (1964). Expanding educational facilities for social work manpower. In C. S. Prigmore (Ed.), *Manpower and training for corrections* (pp. 97–115). New York: Council on Social Work Education.

Young, D. S., & LoMonaco, S. W. (2001). Incorporating content on offenders and corrections into social work curricula. *Journal of Social Work Education, 37*(3), 475–489.

Young, P. V. (1952). *Social treatment in probation and delinquency*. New York: McGraw-Hill.

Author Index

A

Aarons, G. A., 173, 200, 249, 250, 266, 268
Abadinsky, H., 491, 510
Abbott, R. D., 249, 363, 381
Abel, E. M., 474, 478, 484, 486, 489
Abikoff, H. B., 323, 345
Abram, K., 173, 200, 203, 248, 249, 250, 251, 266, 269, 270, 276, 284, 298, 348, 362, 427, 428, 435, 442, 443, 445, 465, 470, 471, 472, 486, 488
Abramowitz, C. S., 232, 242
Abrams, L., 294, 529, 534
Abrantes, A. M., 251, 270
Achenbach, T. M., 239, 242
Acierno, R., 188, 200
Acoca, L., 458, 462
Adams, J., 502, 512
Adams, K., 226, 246
Addis, M. E., 461, 462
Addison, O. W., 323, 345
Adeleke, T., 556, 559
Adelman, H. S., 264, 270
Aglilias, K., 576, 582
Agnese, T. K., 432, 443
Ahrens, C., 445, 465
Ainsworth, M. S., 68, 89
Alarcon, F. J., 278, 294
Albertson, C., 275, 280, 297
Alexander, J., 36, 349
Alexander, R., 429, 430, 432, 435, 442
Alford, K. A., 556, 560
Allen, F. A., 493, 510
Allen, G. F., 10, 22
Allen, J. P., 406, 415
Allen, W., 404, 415
Alletto, R., 410, 418
Allsop, B., 508, 510
Almeida, R., 160, 163
Alterman, A. I., 406, 416
Althoff, M., 506, 511
Altschuler, D. M., 502, 510
Amaro, H., 477, 486
Amos, N. L., 226, 245

Amster, B. J., 80, 89
Andershed, H., 234, 236, 240, 241, 242
Anderson, A. J., 494, 510
Anderson, A. L., 370, 379
Anderson, B., 260, 261, 268, 469, 486
Anderson, D., 29, 50
Anderson, J., 400, 413
Anderson-Nathe, B., 294
Anderson, P., 79, 89
Anderson, R. M., 84, 85, 92
Andrews, A., 133, 136, 149
Andrews, B. P., 229, 237, 244
Andrews, D. A., 262, 266, 387, 388, 413, 414, 494, 509, 510
Anglin, M. D., 389, 401, 406, 410, 411, 413, 414, 417, 452, 463, 500, 510, 514
Annis, H. M., 262, 266
Anno, B., 471, 472, 486
Anno, J., 386, 411
Anspach, D., 406, 417
Anthony, J., 448, 449, 464, 465
Anthony, W., 503, 506, 510, 511
Aponte, J. F., 409, 411
Appel, A. E., 29, 48
Applebaum, P. S., 69, 90
Applegate, B. K., 239, 241, 243, 500, 501, 502, 512
Arcuri, J. B., 580, 583
Armour, M. P., 20, 237
Armstrong, M. L., 208, 209, 211, 220
Armstrong, T. L., 273, 274, 276, 291, 296, 501, 502, 510, 511
Arndt, I. O., 406, 416
Arnold, E. M., 298
Arnold, L. E., 323, 345
Aron, L. Y., 44, 48, 210, 220
Arrigo, B. A., 557, 559
Arriola, K. R., 386, 412
Aruffo, J., 473, 486
Asante, M. K., 544, 559
Ash, P., 73, 89
Ashford, J. B., 19, 491, 492, 500, 511, 513
Atkins, D., 349, 360

Austin, L., 476, 489
Austin, M. J., 580, 582
Austin, R., 554, 559
Axelrod, J., 160, 165
Ayers, C. D., 363, 381
Azrin, N. H., 175, 182, 184, 187, 188, 193, 196, 200, 201

B

Babcock, J., 158, 163, 164, 165
Babiak, T., 495, 512
Babitsky, S., 79, 83, 89
Babor, T., 261, 267
Bace, R. G., 88, 92
Bacha, T., 469, 486
Bachrach, L., 494, 495, 511
Back, S., 470, 471, 490
Baer, J. S., 251, 259, 260, 266, 268
Bahr, R., 472, 488
Bailey, A., 352, 361
Baillargeon, J., 469, 470, 472, 486, 490
Baird, C., 31, 34, 37, 38, 39, 48, 501, 511
Baker, S. A., 471, 488
Balton, M. A., 446, 448, 450, 464
Bancroft, L., 104, 122
Banesch, A., 299–313, 307, 312
Bangert-Drowns, R. L., 182, 200
Bank, L., 188, 200
Banspach, S., 387, 412
Banyard, V. L., 461, 462
Barber, J., 446, 464
Bardenstein, K., 231, 244
Barker, R. L., 69, 89, 299, 300, 312, 580, 582
Barnes, J. M., 409, 411
Barnett, N. P., 251, 257, 258, 266, 267, 269, 270
Barnett, O., 28, 48
Barnum, R., 352, 360
Barrow, M., 348, 361
Barry, C. T., 239, 243
Barth, R. P., 28, 48
Bartoi, M. G., 432, 443
Barton, A. B., 556, 560
Barton, S. M., 296
Barton, W. H., 502, 511
Basen-Engquist, K., 387, 412
Bateman, R. W., 386, 414
Bates, L., 158, 164
Baumann, D. J., 47, 48
Baumrind, D., 294
Bauserman, R. L., 469, 470, 486
Baxter, S., 476, 486
Bazemore, G., 274, 292, 293, 294, 521, 534, 542, 544, 560
Bazron, B. J., 288, 295
Beamis, K., 252, 267

Bean, P., 176, 177, 200
Beard, J. H., 506, 511
Beard, R. A., 386, 415
Beck, A. J., 385, 386, 411, 414, 428, 440, 441, 442, 445, 448, 450, 452, 463, 470, 486, 576, 582
Becker, D., 506, 507, 511
Becker, R., 159, 165
Beckerman, A., 387, 411
Beeman, S., 29, 48
Behrman, G., 20
Belenko, S., 10, 19, 385, 386, 387, 388, 389, 390, 391, 400, 401, 402, 403, 404, 406, 410, 411, 412, 415, 417, 418
Belitz, J., 264, 267
Belknap, J., 551, 560
Bell, D. K., 493, 496, 500, 513
Bell, S. V., 68, 89
Bellair, P. E., 370, 380
Bellamy, J., 44, 50
Bender, K., 16, 173–203
Bender, M. B., 333, 334, 345
Benefield, G., 252, 269
Benesch, A., 17
Benham, A., 556, 560
Benjamin, G. A., 70, 89, 92
Bennett, D., 503, 505, 511, 515
Bennett, L., 118, 123, 157, 159, 160, 163, 165
Bennett, W. S., 494, 513
Benning, D., 101, 124
Benson, P. L., 279, 294
Benson, T. A., 258, 259, 269
Berg, I. K., 285, 294
Berg-Smith, S. M., 261, 267
Berk, L. E., 79, 80, 90
Berk, R., 154, 155, 163, 165
Berlin, L., 578, 584
Berman, M., 566, 572
Bernstein, B. E., 71, 90, 92
Bernstein, R., 439, 440
Bersani, C., 157, 163
Besalel, V. A., 188, 200
Best, A., 70, 90
Bickford, M. E., 226, 244
Bickman, L., 176, 202
Biegel, D. E., 479, 486
Bienzle, U., 471, 488
Bierber, S. L., 511, 564
Binder, A., 155, 163
Birchwood, M., 509, 511
Birgden, A., 263, 267
Birkhead, G. S., 476, 485, 488
Bishop, D. M., 358, 362, 371, 380
Bishop, E. T., 71, 90
Bjerke, K., 473, 475, 489
Black, H. C., 71, 90

Black, S., 469, 470, 486, 490
Black, T., 29, 47, 50
Blackburn, R., 236, 242, 493, 509, 511
Blackman, J., 103, 122
Blake, D., 455, 463
Blalock, H. M., 364, 379
Blanch, A., 503, 510
Bland, R. C., 428, 442
Blaske, D. M., 330, 331, 333, 334, 335, 336, 337, 341,
    342, 356, 360
Blea, L., 476, 487
Blechman, E. A., 298
Bledsoe, B., 44, 50
Blitz, C., 182, 186, 193, 195, 202
Block, A., 355, 360
Block, C., 118, 122
Block, J., 239, 242
Block, J. H., 239, 242
Blonigen, D., 232, 242
Bloom, B., 441, 442, 458, 463
Blount, M., 470, 490
Blume, A. W., 259, 260, 266
Blume, J. H., 131, 149
Blythe, B. J., 575, 579, 583
Bochnak, E., 95, 122
Bodholt, R. H., 226, 242
Bodin, S. D., 239, 243
Boergers, J., 387, 417
Bogenberger, R. P., 511, 564
Boldt, R. C., 397, 412
Bolton, P., 352, 361
Bombardier, C. H., 263, 268
Bond, G. R., 495, 497, 498, 506, 507, 511
Bond, L., 471, 486
Bonge, D., 158, 164
Bonta, J., 262, 266, 388, 413, 494, 509, 510
Boonstra, H., 263, 267
Boos, A., 449, 463
Booth, C., 190, 202
Borden, W., 565, 572
Borduin, C. M., 182, 201, 274, 289, 295, 296, 323, 329,
    330, 331, 332, 333, 334, 335, 336, 337, 338, 341, 342,
    343, 344, 345, 356, 360
Borland, A., 498, 511
Borne, D., 474, 475, 476, 487
Borsari, B. E., 251, 260, 261, 267
Borum, R., 357, 360, 386, 412
Botvin, G. J., 368, 380
Bouffard, J. A., 399, 417
Boulogne, J. J., 321, 335, 344
Bourduin, C. M., 182, 185, 201
Bourgon, G., 295
Bovasso, G., 386, 413
Bower, K., 496, 511
Bowlin, C., 469, 470, 486

Boyd, C. J., 446, 448, 453, 464
Boyles, S., 495, 512
Bradbury, B., 531, 535
Bradford, J., 385, 412
Bradford, W., 332, 338, 344
Bradigan, B., 433, 442
Bradshaw, P., 469, 472, 486
Bradshaw, W., 529, 535
Braithwaite, J., 548, 550, 552, 554, 560
Braithwaite, R., 386, 412, 471, 476, 477, 486
Brandt, J. R., 235, 237, 242
Branson, D. M., 299, 300, 312, 580, 582
Brasfield, T., 470, 472, 475, 476, 488, 489
Braun-Harvey, D., 556, 560
Bray, C., 355, 360
Breda, C. S., 295
Brems, C., 101, 124
Brennan, T. P., 580, 582
Breslau, N., 449, 463
Breslin, C., 251, 267
Bridges, G. S., 363, 364, 366, 370, 379, 380
Brieland, D., 69, 76, 90
Briere, J., 456, 463
Briggs, E., 348, 361
Bright, C. L., 18
Brill, P. L., 406, 416, 503, 515
Brinkley, C. A., 227, 246
Briscoe, V., 471, 476, 487
Brodsky, S. L., 88, 90
Brody, G. H., 371, 381
Bromet, E., 449, 464
Brondino, M. J., 178, 179, 182, 184, 185, 193, 196, 197,
    201, 202, 312, 319, 327, 331, 332, 335, 338, 340, 342,
    343, 344, 387, 414
Broner, N., 386, 412
Bronfenbrenner, U., 182, 200, 316, 342
Brookman, M., 295
Broome, K. M., 402, 409, 414
Brown, E. B., 495, 515, 557, 560
Brown, K., 261, 267, 520, 521, 523, 536, 545, 546, 549,
    562
Brown, L., 251–252, 267
Brown, M., 479, 489
Brown, P., 446, 449, 463, 465
Brown, R., 257, 261, 267, 295
Brown, S., 173, 182, 200, 250, 251, 266, 269
Brown, T., 182, 201, 331, 338, 342
Brown, W., 295
Browne, A., 107, 118, 122, 123
Brownell, P., 4, 22, 299, 300, 312, 573, 582, 584
Bruce, M. A., 370, 379
Bruck, M., 80, 90, 92
Bruner, J., 568, 572
Brunk, M., 331, 338, 342
Bruno, F. J., 575, 582

Bryan, A., 478, 486
Bryant, F. C., 17, 299–313
Budney, A. J., 185, 201, 321, 342
Budson, R. D., 504, 511
Buell, G. J., 506, 511
Bukatko, D., 79, 90
Bukstein, O. G., 323, 345
Bullens, R., 336, 345
Bulto, M., 472, 488
Burford, G., 46, 50, 546, 560
Burgess, A., 348, 361
Burgess, S., 348, 361
Burke, H. C., 237, 243
Burke, L., 157, 163
Burket, R. C., 235, 244
Burleson, J. A., 182, 184, 186, 187, 189, 193, 195, 202
Burnett, D. M., 295
Burns, B. J., 329, 342
Burns, H., 523, 529, 530, 531, 535, 551, 560
Busch, N. B., 6–8, 12
Bush, K., 57, 64
Bushway, S., 388, 417
Bussey, J., 472, 489
Bussey, M., 49
Butler, C., 254, 255, 270
Buttell, F., 15, 151–169, 157, 163
Butts, J. A., 230, 242, 502, 511
Butzin, C., 386, 415, 445, 464
Bynum, T., 458, 464
Byrne, J. M., 406, 417, 493, 501, 502, 511

C

Cacciola, J. S., 404, 415, 416
Cadell, J., 445, 449, 464
Cadsky, O., 156, 163
Cakan, N., 333, 339, 342
Caldwell, C. H., 371, 379
Calsyn, R. J., 498, 514
Campbell, A., 155, 163
Campbell, D., 118, 122
Campbell, J., 32, 35, 37, 47, 48, 118, 122, 123
Campbell, M. A., 295
Caplan, G., 567, 572
Carawan, L. W., 574, 584
Carey, K. B., 251, 260, 261, 267, 269
Carise, D., 406, 412
Carling, P. J., 505, 511
Carlson, E. B., 28, 48, 79, 90
Carlson, P., 581, 582
Carlson, R. F., 232, 242
Carmona, J. V., 160, 165, 225, 389, 416
Carney, L. P., 492, 511
Carney, M., 15, 151–169, 157, 163
Carrillo, R., 156, 157, 164
Carroll, K. M., 401, 412

Carroll, L., 386, 415
Cartier, J., 452, 463
Cartwright, W. S., 388, 412
Carvajal, S., 387, 412
Casanueva, C., 28, 29, 48
Cash, S., 46, 48
Cassel, C. A., 437, 443
Cassidy, J., 68, 79, 90
Catalano, R. F., 368, 379
Cattaneo, L. B., 30, 31
Cauffman, E., 226, 230, 231, 241, 242, 245, 348, 352, 360
Cavanagh, S., 402, 414
Cavenaugh, M., 46, 48
Cayley, D., 519, 535
Ceci, S. J., 76, 80, 90, 92
Cecil, J. S., 71, 74, 91
Chacko, R., 473, 486
Chadwick, O., 233, 246
Chaiken, J. M., 389, 412
Chaiken, M. R., 389, 412
Chaiklin, H., 5, 574, 577, 579, 582
Chaimowitz, G., 57, 64
Chan, D., 262, 266
Chang, E. T., 556, 560
Chang, H., 156, 163
Chang, J. J., 235, 245
Chang, S. Y., 175, 203
Channon, S., 261, 267
Chaple, M., 386, 406, 412
Chapman, J. E., 333, 335, 343
Charney, D., 455, 463
Chavous, T. M., 371, 379
Chen, D., 474, 475, 476, 487
Chen, H., 157, 163
Chen, Y., 371, 381
Chesney-Lind, M., 445, 450, 465, 551, 560
Chilcoat, H. D., 449, 463
Chiles, J. A., 430, 442
Chin, D., 160, 165
Chin, K. L., 390, 412
Chitwood, D. D., 386, 413
Chong, U., 388, 414
Chou, C. P., 401, 413
Chow-Martin, L., 297
Chung, A. Y., 556, 560
Cicchetti, D., 251, 267
Clapp, E. J., 573, 583
Clark, D., 226, 243, 497, 512
Clark, J. P., 138, 149, 176, 177, 201
Clark, M. D., 579, 583
Clark, R., 446, 463
Clarke, G., 354, 360
Clasyn, R. J., 495, 513
Claughan, P., 57, 65

Claus, R. E., 386, 413
Clear, T. R., 493, 511
Cleary, S., 387, 418
Cleckley, H., 225, 226, 229, 238, 240, 242
Clement, P. F., 491, 511
Clements, C., 229, 241, 244, 246, 491, 494, 512
Clemons, J. R., 498, 512
Clingempeel, W. G., 332, 335, 338, 343, 387, 414
Coates, R. B., 377, 380, 520, 521, 522, 523, 529, 530, 535, 536, 556, 562
Cocozza, J., 349, 353, 354, 360
Cohen, F., 433, 443
Cohen, J., 182, 185, 201
Cohen, M. A., 230, 242
Cohn, A., 491, 511
Coid, L., 236, 242
Colby, S. M., 251, 257, 258, 267, 269, 270
Coll, K. M., 252, 267
Condelli, W. S., 433, 442
Cone, L. T., 330, 331, 333, 334, 335, 337, 342, 356, 360
Conger, D., 211, 216, 220
Conly, C., 438, 439, 442
Conning, A. M., 503, 512
Connors, G. J., 406, 415, 417
Conover, S., 472, 489
Conrod, P. J., 449, 465
Convit, A., 472, 490
Cooke, D. J., 229, 239, 240, 242
Coolbaugh, K., 366, 379
Cooley, R., 176, 177, 201
Coolman, A., 450, 458, 463
Cooney, N. L., 186, 201, 202
Cooper, C. S., 390, 396, 413
Corbin, W. R., 251, 267
Corbitt, E. M., 57, 65, 229, 246
Corcoran, K., 174, 203, 574, 577, 583
Cormier, C. A., 34, 49, 226, 243, 245
Cornell, C. P., 28, 49
Cornell, D. G., 229, 238, 241, 242, 244, 245, 284, 296
Costanzo, M., 528, 536
Cote, G., 237, 246
Cothern, L., 363, 380
Coulson, G. E., 474, 487
Cournos, F., 472, 487
Coverdale, J., 473, 486
Covington, S., 441, 442, 458, 463
Cowden, J., 504, 514
Cowles, C. A., 295
Cowley, C. B., 252, 267
Coyle, K., 387, 412
Craddock, S. G., 400, 413
Craige, H. B., 580, 583
Crawford, C., 386, 414, 476, 487
Crawford, M., 156, 163
Creekmore, M., 275, 280, 297

Crimmins, S., 386, 406, 412
Crome, I. B., 174, 175, 176, 201
Cronce, J. M., 251, 261, 268
Cross, T. L., 288, 295
Crouch, J. L., 312, 319, 343
Crowell, N. A., 378, 380
Crowley, T. J., 176, 177, 178, 179, 197, 201, 203
Cruise, K. R., 230, 231, 241, 242
Crum, R., 448, 449, 464
Crum, T., 182, 184, 187, 188, 193, 196, 200
Cuffe, S. P., 175, 203
Culbertson, R. G., 295
Cullen, F. T., 388, 413, 500, 501, 502, 512
Cumming, E., 495, 512
Cumming, G. F., 509, 514
Cummings, C., 507, 512
Cummins, L. H., 251, 268
Cunniff, M. A., 388, 389, 415, 500, 513
Cunningham, A., 44, 48
Cunningham, P. B., 274, 289, 296, 319, 323, 327, 328, 332, 333, 335, 337, 338, 339, 342, 343, 344, 345
Currie, E., 505, 512
Curry, M. A., 118, 122
Curtin, J. J., 235, 237, 242
Curtis, J. L., 498, 512
Curtis, N. M., 289, 295, 334, 342
Curtis, R., 387, 413
Cushman, R., 530, 531
Czobor, P., 472, 490

D

Daciuk, J., 29, 47, 50
Daehler, M. W., 79, 90
Dahir, V. B., 75, 90
Dahlstrom, W. G., 134, 137
Daicoff, S. S, 88, 90
Dakof, G. A., 175, 201
Daly, K., 552, 554
D'Amico, E. J., 251, 267
Danckaerts, M., 233, 246
Dattilio, F. M., 189, 203
Davidson, H. A., 29, 48
Davies, R. D., 197, 203
Davis, J., 29, 48
Davis, R., 44, 49, 157, 163, 225, 238, 244
Davis, T., 472, 488
Dawes, R. M., 31, 48
Day, D. M., 509, 513
De Jong, C. A., 321, 335, 344
de Jong, J. T., 556, 560
De Leon, G., 406, 416, 445, 465
Dean-Gaitor, H. D., 470, 473, 476, 487
Dean, H. D., 469, 487
DeAngelo, A. J., 293, 295
DeCato, L. A., 182, 184, 187, 188, 193, 196, 200

Decker, S. H., 365, 366, 380, 381
DeGraaf-Kaser, R., 498, 511
DeHart, D., 157, 163
DeJong, C., 370, 379
DeLone, M., 363, 381
DeMaris, A., 156, 157, 163
DeMatteo, D. S., 10, 19, 79, 90, 386, 401, 403, 404, 413, 415
Dennis, K. W., 288, 295
Dennis, M. L., 261, 267
Denton, R., 157, 163
DePanfilis, D., 35, 48
D'Ercole, A., 498, 512
Derdeyn, A., 73, 89
Derogatis, L., 352, 360
Dershowitz, A. M., 94, 122
Dery, M., 237, 246
Des Jarlais, D. C., 387, 413
Deschenes, E. P., 401, 402, 418, 500, 502, 512, 515
DeShon, R. P., 181, 202
Deskins, M. M., 258, 259, 269
Deslarlais, D. C., 471, 490
Devereaux, P. J., 43, 49
Devine, E. C., 182, 201
Devine, P., 366, 379
Devore, B. S., 476, 485, 488
Diamond, G., 261, 267
DiCicco, L., 261, 267
DiCicco, T. M., 232, 245
Dickerson, F. B., 504, 512
DiClemente, C., 46, 50
DiClemente, R. J., 469, 488
DiGiuseppe, R., 251, 256, 257, 267
Dignan, J., 530, 535
Dimeff, L. A., 259, 260, 268
Dincin, J., 498, 511
Dinis, M. C., 297
Dion, K. L., 233, 245
Dishion, T. J., 251, 268
Ditton, P. M., 386, 413, 427, 428, 429, 442, 448, 458, 463, 576, 583
Dixon, R., 474, 486
Dobbin, S. A., 75, 90
Dodge, K., 354, 360
Doerner, W., 547, 560
Doll, B., 355, 360
Doll, L. S., 476, 487, 580, 583
Donaldson, J., 261, 267
Dongier, M., 449, 465
Donohue, B., 182, 184, 187, 188, 193, 196, 200, 201
Doreleijers, T., 336, 345
Dorwart, R., 495, 515
Doueck, H. J., 34, 49
Dougher, M. J., 262, 268
Douglas, K. S., 226, 237, 239, 241, 242, 245

Douyon, R., 472, 490
Dowden, C., 530, 531, 549, 561
Downs, D., 94, 96, 102, 122
Doyle, A., 261, 268
Doyle, M. M., 368, 380
Drach, K., 79, 91, 92
Draine, J., 494, 495, 499, 515, 579, 583, 584
Drake, R. E., 446, 463, 506, 507, 511
Dressler, D., 491, 512
Druley, K. A., 406, 416
Ducate, S., 472, 486
Duffee, D. E., 491, 497, 512, 513
Duffy, K. G., 497, 512
Dugan, L., 157, 163
Dulcan, M. K., 173, 200, 203, 248, 249, 250, 251, 266, 270, 276, 284, 298, 348, 362
Dumaine, M. L., 175, 201
Dumanovsky, T., 390, 406, 412
Dunford, F., 157, 163
Dunlap, L. J., 390, 418
Dunmeyer, S., 388, 417
Dunn, K., 470, 490
Dunn, M. A., 71, 74, 91
Durbin, J., 495, 512
Durios, R. L., 232, 245
Durose, M., 152, 163
Dutton, D. G., 28, 30, 31, 32, 44, 48, 100, 117, 122, 158, 165
Dutton, M. A., 102, 103, 118, 122, 123
Dvoskin, J., 493, 511
Dworkin, R., 473, 486
Dwyer, D. C., 579, 583
Dyck, R. J., 428, 442
Dyer, F. J., 73, 79, 90
Dynia, P. A., 390, 418

E

Eakin, D., 258, 259, 269
Eaves, D., 32, 49, 118, 123, 500, 516
Ebner, D., 241, 245
Eck, J., 388, 417
Edelson, J. L., 29, 30, 35, 47, 48
Edens, J. F., 230, 231, 241, 242
Edgeworth, P., 531, 535
Edleson, J., 29, 48, 156, 157, 163
Edwards, D., 329, 340, 343, 344
Edwards, M., 49
Ehlers, A., 449, 463
Ehlers, K. M., 176, 177, 203
Ehrmann, T., 485, 487
Eisenbruch, M., 556, 560
Eisenstein, J., 391, 413
Eisikovits, Z., 157, 163
Eitle, D., 371, 379
Eitle, T. M., 371, 379

Ekdawi, M. Y., 503, 512
El-Bassel, N., 474, 475, 476, 487
Elechi, O., 556, 560
Elkington, K. S., 249, 250, 251, 266, 269
Elliott, D. S., 329, 342, 368, 379
Elliott, R. L., 430, 435, 442
Ellis, D. A., 333, 339, 342
Ellis, R., 356, 358, 360, 574, 583
Elridge, G., 470, 475, 476, 489
Emmelkamp, P., 354, 362
Engels, R., 273, 291, 295
Engen, R. L., 363, 364, 370, 379
Engle, L., 470, 487
English, D. J., 35, 48
English, P. W., 75, 90
Epps, K., 507, 509, 512
Epstein, J., 471, 487
Epstein, L., 479, 489, 563, 572
Epstein, M., 237, 239, 241, 245
Erwin, B. S., 501, 512
Esposito-Smythers, C., 251, 267
Esveldt-Dawson, K., 188, 202
Etchison, K., 368, 380
Etheridge, R. M., 400, 413
Evangelista, C., 472, 490
Evans, J. H., 494, 513
Evans, W., 295, 297
Everly, G. S., 563, 569, 572
Evje, A., 530, 531
Ewing, C. P., 103, 122

F

Fader, J. S., 260, 261, 268
Fagan, J., 390, 412, 502, 512
Faigeles, B., 476, 487
Fain, T., 401, 402, 418
Fairbank, J., 445, 449, 453, 464
Falcon, J. M., 548, 560
Falkenbach, D., 17, 225–246, 229, 231, 237, 239, 242
Falkin, G. P., 500, 512
Fallon, B., 29, 47, 50
Fallot, R., 457, 458, 463
Fantl, B., 578, 583
Farabee, D., 410, 413
Farbring, C. A., 247–271, 263, 268
Farley, T., 252, 267
Farmer, M., 428, 429, 443, 448, 465
Farrington, D. P., 233, 242, 324, 329, 342, 343, 368, 379, 387, 413
Farrow, J. A., 469, 486
Fatkenheuer, B., 498, 515
Fauci, A., 476, 487
Faust, D., 31, 48
Fawcett, J., 64
Fearer, S. A., 261, 270

Feder, L., 44, 49, 157, 163, 499, 500, 512
Fein, R. A., 32, 48
Feld, B. C., 371, 379
Feldman, S., 348, 360
Feldstein, S. W., 17, 247–271
Felitti, V. J., 30, 49
Felstiner, C., 29, 47, 50
Feng, L., 410, 417
Ferguson, H. B., 324, 345
Ferrell, S. W., 400, 416
Festinger, D. S., 386, 401, 403, 404, 413, 415
Fetter, M., 387, 415
Feyerherm, W., 378, 380
Fichtner, R. R., 469, 489
Fineberg, H. V., 476, 487
Finkelhor, D., 27, 49
Finn, H., 505, 515
Finn, P., 387, 390, 413
Finney, J. W., 445, 465
Fiorentine, R., 409, 413
First, M. B., 455, 465
Fischer, D. O., 175, 203
Fishbein, P., 404, 415
Fisher, B. A., 377, 380
Fisher, E., 156, 164
Fisher, J. D., 475, 487
Fisher, W. A., 475, 487
Fishman, M., 406, 416, 471, 488
Fitterling, J. M., 406, 417
Flanzer, J., 175, 176, 201
Fleck-Henderson, A., 29, 30, 49, 50
Fleming, P. L., 469, 470, 473, 476, 487
Fletcher, B. W., 406, 417
Fletcher, K., 352, 360
Flood, A. M., 258, 259, 269
Fluke, J., 49
Flynn, P., 400, 413
Foa, E., 456, 463
Follingstad, D., 157, 163
Foltz, C., 389, 412
Font, R., 160, 163
Fontham, M. R., 80, 90
Ford, J., 428, 442
Ford, W. L., 574, 583
Forde, D., 44, 49
Forgatch, M. S., 252, 257, 269
Forman, S. G., 321, 323
Forney, M., 449, 463
Forsberg, L., 247–271, 263, 268
Forst, M. l., 49, 377, 380, 502, 512
Forth, A. E., 226, 227, 232, 234, 235, 236, 237, 241, 243, 244
Fortune, A. E., 565, 572
Foshee, V., 28, 48
Foster, J. P., 580, 582

Foster, R., 495, 512
Fox, G., 398, 415
Fox, V., 436, 442, 583
Foy, D., 564, 572
Frabutt, J., 348, 349, 360
Frankl, V., 568, 572
Franklin, J., 498, 512
Frazier, C., 358, 362, 377, 380
Fred, S., 559, 560
Freeman, A., 189, 203
Freeman, R., 358, 360
Freeman-Wilson, K., 390, 414
Freitag, R., 25
Freivalds, P., 273, 291, 295
French, L. M., 491, 512
French, M. T., 386, 387, 388, 412, 413, 416
French, N. H., 188, 202
Frey, M. A., 333, 339, 342
Frick, P., 225, 229, 230, 232, 234, 237, 238, 239, 241,
  243, 244, 246
Friedlander, J. J., 175, 201
Friedman, R. M., 174, 175, 201
Friedman, S. R., 387, 413
Friend, C., 14, 25–50, 29, 50
Frisch, L., 543, 560
Frishman, L., 498, 499, 515
Fromme, K., 251, 259, 266, 267
Fucci, B. R., 330, 331, 333, 334, 335, 337, 342,
  356, 360
Fuller, M. A., 79, 90
Fulton, B., 500, 512
Funk, S. J., 295
Furman, D. M., 76, 91

G

Gaarder, E., 544, 545, 552
Gabel, K., 472, 487
Gacano, C. B., 226, 242
Gaines, L. S., 176, 202
Gaiter, J., 386, 414, 469, 476, 487, 489, 580, 583
Galaif, E. R., 389, 416
Gallop, R. J., 182, 184, 191, 193, 202
Gambrill, E., 30, 34, 35, 40, 41, 46, 49
Ganetzky, B., 79, 89
Gani, J., 470, 490
Gardner, J. W., 578, 583
Garfinkel, L., 348, 361
Garland, A. F., 173, 200, 249, 250, 266, 268
Garland, R. J., 262, 268
Garner, B. A., 299–313, 307, 312
Gastfriend, D., 406, 413, 416, 446, 464
Gathercoal, K., 176, 177, 201
Gatowski, S. I., 75, 90
Gavazzi, S. M., 295, 556, 560
Gavis, G., 469, 488
Gawley, K., 386, 412

Gedrich, A. E., 580, 582
Gehm, J., 528, 535
Gelles, R. J., 28, 32, 46, 48, 50, 152, 153, 154, 159, 160,
  163, 165
Gellespi, C., 95, 122
Gendreau, P., 386, 388, 413, 507, 512
George, W. H., 507, 512
Gerber, F., 498, 514
Gernhofer, N., 261, 267
Getter, H., 186, 201, 202
Getzel, G. S., 574, 583
Giardini, G. I., 491, 512
Gibbon, M., 455, 465
Gibbs, A., 295
Gibbs, J., 288, 295
Gibbs, L., 42, 50
Gibelman, M., 70, 76, 90, 462, 463
Giddings, M., 371, 381
Giering, P., 495, 512
Gifford, S. L., 576, 583
Gilani, J., 388, 414
Gilbert, D., 469, 486
Gilbert, L., 474, 475, 476, 487
Gillmore, M. R., 471, 488
Ginsburg, G. P., 75, 90
Ginsburg, J. I., 17, 247–271, 262, 263, 268
Glancy, G. D., 57, 64
Glass, N., 118, 122
Glasscote, R. M., 495, 512
Glassman, S. M., 495, 512
Godley, S. H., 261, 267
Goel, R., 553, 560
Goerdt, J. S., 390, 413
Goggin, C., 386, 388, 413
Goguen, C., 564, 572
Goicoechea-Balbona, A., 556, 560
Goldberg, E., 251, 269
Goldberger, R., 182, 184, 189, 193, 202
Goldkamp, J., 390, 401, 402, 403, 413
Goldstein, P. J., 385, 414
Goldstrom, I., 431, 442
Gollan, J. K., 70, 89, 92
Golub, A., 354, 361
Gondolf, E., 32, 49, 156, 157, 158, 160, 163,
  164
Goodkind, S., 275, 280, 297
Goodman, H., 574, 583
Goodman, L., 30, 31, 118, 123
Goodstein, L., 500, 512
Gordon, J., 505, 507, 508, 512, 513, 515
Gorski, T. T., 508, 512
Gossweiler, R., 399, 404, 406, 407, 417
Gottfredson, D., 388, 401, 414, 417
Gottheil, E., 406, 418
Gottman, J., 158, 165, 1643

Grady, J., 470, 490
Graham, J., 47, 48, 453, 463
Granello, P., 295
Grann, M., 226, 243
Grant, I., 226, 242
Grant, J. D., 226, 246
Grauwiler, P., 549, 551, 554, 560
Graves, R. H., 579, 583
Green, C., 158, 163
Green, D. L., 484, 489
Green-Faust, L., 11, 22, 70, 91, 277, 297
Green, R. S., 175, 178, 179, 203
Greenbaum, P. E., 174, 175, 198, 199, 201, 203
Greenbaum, R. L., 251, 269
Greenberg, B., 470, 471, 490
Greenberg, D. M., 385, 412
Greene, R. L., 453, 463
Greener, J. M., 389, 402, 417
Greenfeld, L., 458, 463
Greenfield, W., 160, 164
Greenhill, L. L., 323, 345
Greenwood, A., 226, 245
Greenwood, J., 521, 522, 536
Greenwood, P., 401, 402, 418, 502, 512
Greer, M., 461, 463
Greer, W. C., 500, 512
Greger, N., 339, 342
Gregory, D., 472, 488
Gregory, J. W., 261, 267
Grella, C. E., 175, 177, 178, 179, 201
Gretton, H., 237, 243
Griffin, K. W., 368, 380
Griffin, E., 476, 487
Griffin, M., 471, 472, 487
Griffin, P., 274, 275, 276, 278, 279, 282, 284, 287, 289, 295, 499, 513
Griffith, J. H., 406, 416
Griffiths, C. T., 553, 560
Grimes, R. M., 469, 489
Grinstead, O., 476, 487
Grisso, T., 229, 230, 241–242, 245, 284, 296, 352, 360
Grissom, G. R., 406, 416, 503, 515
Gross, M., 470, 471, 487
Grossman, L. S., 433, 443
Grossman, N., 476, 487
Groth-Marnat, G., 79, 90
Grove, W. M., 31, 49
Groves, B. D., 30, 49
Gruenberg, E. M., 503, 512
Grummert, M., 297
Grusznski, R., 156, 157, 164
Guarino-Ghezzi, S., 280, 296
Guba, E., 569, 572

Gudeman, H., 511, 564
Guggenmoos-Holzmann, I., 471, 488
Guido, J., 472, 487
Gumz, E. J., 577, 583
Gurel, O., 406, 412
Gusman, F., 455, 463
Gutheil, T. G., 69, 90
Guyatt, G. H., 43, 49

H

Haapala, D. A., 190, 202
Haas, A. L., 386, 402, 416
Haas, R., 252, 267
Hagemeisten, A., 29, 48
Hagen, K. A., 333, 334, 344
Haines, T. H., 491, 492, 513
Hakstain, A. R., 226, 227, 229, 238, 243
Haley, J., 182, 201, 316, 342
Hall, G. B., 505, 514
Hall, J. A., 182, 185, 201, 334, 343
Halliday-Boykins, C., 332, 333, 334, 335, 338, 340, 341, 342, 343, 344
Hamberger, K., 156, 157, 158, 164
Hamilton, E., 155, 164
Hammen, C., 479, 487
Hammett, T., 386, 387, 414, 469, 470, 471, 476, 477, 486, 487
Hanks, H. G., 79, 90
Hanley, J. H., 327, 330, 337, 340, 343
Hanlon, T. E., 386, 388, 389, 414, 416
Hanna, J., 295, 446, 448, 450, 464
Hanrahan, J. P., 469, 488
Hans, V., 148, 149
Hanson, C. L., 330, 331, 337, 343
Hanson, K., 156, 163
Harding, C. M., 506, 513
Hardman, D. G., 578, 583
Hare, R. D., 226, 227, 229, 232, 234, 235, 236, 237, 238, 239, 241, 243, 244
Harlow, C., 152, 163, 458, 463
Harmon, P., 386, 414, 469, 470, 471, 487
Harness, J. K., 430, 442
Harp, C., 291, 293, 296
Harpur, T. J., 226, 227, 229, 232, 238, 243, 244
Harrell, A., 230, 242, 402, 403, 414, 415
Harrington, R., 352, 361
Harrington, S., 427, 442
Harris, B., 469, 489
Harris, G. T., 32, 34, 49, 226, 232, 243, 244, 245
Harris, H. E., 235, 244
Harris, J. C., 79, 90
Harris, M., 457, 458, 463
Harris, P. W., 282, 298
Harrison, L., 445, 464

Harrison, P. M., 385, 414, 428, 440, 441, 442, 452, 463, 470, 486

Harrold, L., 470, 471, 487

Hart, B., 29, 49

Hart, C., 251, 270

Hart, S. D., 32, 49, 118, 123, 226, 227, 231, 232, 235, 241, 243, 244

Hartley, C., 29, 49

Hartman, H. L., 578, 583

Hartman, J., 556, 562

Hartsell, T. H., 71, 90, 92

Harwood, H. J., 388, 414

Hastings, J., 156, 157, 164

Hauth, A., 472, 488

Havens, L., 508, 512

Hawk, G., 229, 242

Hawkins, D. F., 363, 380

Hawkins, E. H., 251, 268

Hawkins, G., 385, 390, 418

Hawkins, J. D., 363, 368, 379, 380, 381

Hawthorne, W., 498, 499, 513

Hayes, L. M., 55, 58, 64, 285, 296

Haynes, R. B., 22, 42, 43, 49, 50

Healy, T., 31, 37, 48

Hearn, J., 451, 463

Heather, A., 29

Hebert, J., 386, 415

Heckert, D. A., 32, 49

Heetderks, K., 521, 536

Heide, K. M., 231, 237, 239, 242

Heilbrun, K., 79, 90, 241, 245, 494, 499, 513

Heiserman, M., 355, 360

Helms, W., 531, 535

Hembrooke, H., 76, 90, 92

Hemmens, C., 273, 276, 298, 377, 381

Hemphill, J. F., 226, 232, 244

Henderson, A. Z., 493, 496, 500, 513

Henderson, C. E., 175, 198, 199, 203

Henderson, D., 458, 464

Henderson, M., 431, 442

Henggeler, S. W., 17, 178, 179, 182, 184, 185, 193, 196, 197, 201, 202, 274, 289, 296, 312, 315–345, 319, 323, 327, 328, 329, 330, 331, 332, 333, 334, 335, 336, 337, 338, 340, 341, 342, 343, 344, 345, 356, 360, 387, 414

Heptinstall, E., 233, 246

Hepworth, D. H., 290, 296

Herman, J. L., 101, 103, 107, 121, 123, 456, 464

Herron, K., 158, 164

Hersen, M., 79, 91

Hess, A. K., 72, 90, 149

Hess, R., 354, 360

Higgins, S. T., 185, 201, 321, 342

Hill, C. D., 226, 244

Hill, K. G., 363, 368, 379, 380

Hill, S. S., 80, 90

Hillhouse, M. P., 409, 413

Hills, H. A., 197, 202, 406, 417

Hilton, Z. N., 32, 34, 49

Hines, D., 34, 49

Hinton, W., 356, 360

Hippchen, L. J., 492, 513

Hirsch, K., 579, 583

Hoagwood, K., 329, 342

Hobbs, C. J., 79, 90

Hochstetler, A., 450, 459, 464

Hodgins, S., 237, 246

Hoff, R. A., 386, 414

Hoffman, M. A., 473, 488

Hogan, N. L., 296

Hogben, M., 471, 472, 488

Hoge, R., 284, 296, 297, 387, 414

Holanchock, H., 433, 442

Holdent, G. W., 29, 32, 48

Holdman, S., 127, 149

Hollin, C. R., 262, 269

Holmes, S., 556, 562

Holsinger, A., 406, 417

Holsinger, K., 551, 560

Holtfreter, K., 458, 464

Holtzworth-Munroe, A., 158, 162, 164

Hood, H. V., 475, 488

Hooper, R., 445, 464

Hora, P. F., 391, 402, 403, 414

Horan, P., 469, 488

Horowitz, A. V., 449, 464

Hosley, C., 355, 360

Hough, R. L., 173, 200, 249, 250, 266, 268, 498, 499, 513

Hovmand, P. S., 18

Howard, K. I., 503, 515

Howell, J., 182, 184, 187, 188, 193, 196, 200

Hser, Y. I., 175, 177, 178, 179, 201, 401, 406, 413, 414, 500, 510

Hsia, H. M., 366, 380

Huang, B., 437, 443

Huang, L., 288, 295

Hubbard, R. L., 174, 203, 400, 406, 413, 417

Huckshorn, K. A., 63, 64

Huddleston, C. W., 390, 410, 414

Hudson, C. H., 493, 513

Hudson, J., 546, 560

Huey, S. J., Jr., 327, 332, 338, 340, 343

Hughes, M., 30, 49, 448, 449, 464, 465

Hughes, R. C., 27, 31, 50

Hughes, T. A., 445, 450, 463

Hunt, D. E., 386, 414

Hunt, W., 471, 488

Huss, M. T., 552, 561

Hutton, H., 471, 488
Hynd, G. W., 237, 239, 241, 243

I

Inciardi, J. A., 386, 413, 415, 445, 449, 463, 464, 469, 470, 488, 500, 513
Intagliata, J., 496, 497, 513
Irick, S., 348, 361
Irvin, L. K., 440, 443
Isenstadt, P. M., 574, 583
Israel, J., 391, 414
Issacs, M. R., 288, 295
Ittig-Deland, V., 251, 267
Ivanoff, A., 474, 475, 476, 487, 575, 579, 583, 584
Ivkovvic, S., 148, 149

J

Jackson, K. C., 370, 379
Jackson, R. L., 177, 179, 197, 203
Jackson, S., 44, 49
Jacob, H., 391, 413
Jacobs, D., 57, 64
Jacobs, H. E., 505, 506, 513
Jacobs, N., 470, 471, 488
Jacobsen, L. K., 449, 464
Jacobson, N., 158, 165, 1643
Jacoby, J., 390, 414, 437, 443
Jacoby, S. E., 580, 582
Jaffe, P., 30, 51
James, C. B., 564, 572
James, J. F., 472, 488
Jasiukaitis, P., 175, 178, 179, 203
Jemelka, R., 430, 442
Jenkins, M., 20, 542, 557, 560
Jenkins, P. H., 282, 298
Jenkins, S., 366, 379
Jensen, P. S., 196, 203, 323, 345
Jenson, H., 469, 486
Jenson, J. M., 178, 179, 197, 202
Jerrers, G., 349, 360
Jilton, R., 251, 256, 257, 267
Joe, G. W., 389, 401, 402, 406, 409, 414, 417
Joesn, R., 472, 488
Johansen, J., 177, 179, 197, 203, 235, 245
Johnsen, M., 431, 443
Johnson, B. R., 476, 487, 488
Johnson, D. M., 446, 465
Johnson, J., 472, 488
Johnson, K., 29, 31, 32, 34, 35, 37, 42, 48, 50
Johnson, M. P., 104, 123, 153, 164
Johnson, M. T., 71, 74, 91
Johnson, S. L., 544, 560
Johnson, S. M., 153, 164
Johnson, W., 34, 35, 47, 49

Johnston, D., 472, 487
Johnstone, G., 521, 535
Jolliffe, D., 368, 379
Jones, A., 95, 104, 123
Jones, H., 339, 343
Jones, M., 371, 380
Jones, R., 104, 123
Jordan, B., 471, 487
Jordan, J., 216, 220
Jordan, K., 445, 449, 464
Jose, B., 387, 413
Joshi, V., 175, 178, 179, 201
Judd, L., 428, 429, 443, 448, 465
Juhnke, G., 252, 267
Jutai, J., 226, 243

K

Kabela, E., 186, 202
Kadden, R. M., 186, 201, 202, 406, 415
Kadela, K. R., 387, 417
Kaemmer, B., 453, 463
Kagan, J., 231, 244
Kahler, C. W., 257, 261, 267
Kalichman, S., 472, 488
Kaloupek, D., 455, 463
Kaminer, Y., 182, 184, 186, 187, 189, 193, 202, 251, 270
Kamisar, Y., 391, 414
Kamradt, B., 357, 360
Kanapaux, W., 57, 65
Kanel, K., 567, 572
Kang, S., 476, 488
Kang, W., 275, 276, 283, 298
Kantor, E., 471, 488
Kaplan, A., 216, 220
Kaplan, H., 79, 90, 563, 572
Kaplan, R., 76, 90
Kaplan, S., 238, 241, 244
Karberg, J. C., 385, 414
Karls, J. M., 495, 515
Kassebaum, P. A., 458, 464
Katz, J., 531, 535
Kaufman, J., 370, 380
Kaufman, M., 348, 349, 360
Kaufman, N., 251, 268, 354, 360
Kavanagh, K., 251, 268
Kazdin, A., 188, 202, 315, 329, 343, 354, 360
Keane, T. M., 79, 92, 453, 455, 456, 464, 465
Kear-Colwell, J., 262, 268
Kearley, B., 401, 414
Kearney, E. M., 264, 268
Keefe, D., 135, 149
Keenan, K., 387, 415
Keith, S., 428, 429, 443, 448, 465
Kelley, J. M., 508, 512
Kelly, A. B., 251, 268

Kelly, J., 251, 269, 472, 475, 488
Kelly, W., 197, 202
Kelman, S., 388, 417
Kemmis, S., 564, 567, 572
Kemp, S., 547, 560
Kendall, P., 323, 344, 354, 360
Kendig, C., 406, 412
Kendig, N., 471, 488
Kendleberger, L., 386, 413
Kennedy, M. G., 469, 476, 489
Kennedy, S., 386, 387, 414
Kennedy, W., 235, 237, 242
Kennerly, R., 157, 163
Kerachsky, R., 406, 418
Kerdyck, L., 237, 239, 241, 243
Kerkhof, A. J., 321, 335, 344
Kernberg, P. F., 231, 244
Kerr, B., 79, 91, 92
Kerr, M., 234, 236, 240, 241, 242
Kerr, S., 469, 470, 487, 489
Kessler, R., 448, 449, 464, 465
Kiam, R., 478, 484, 489
Kifer, M., 273, 276, 298
Killian, E., 295
Kilmer, J. R., 260, 261, 268
Kilty, K. M., 370, 381
Kim, J. S., 16, 173–203
Kim, K., 294
Kim, R. Y., 370, 381
King, D., 455, 456, 465, 505, 515
King, L., 455, 456, 465
King, R., 176, 202
Kingi, V., 550, 561
Kinlock, T. W., 386, 388, 389, 416
Kinney, J., 190, 202
Kirby, D., 387, 412
Kirby, K. C., 386, 396, 398, 409, 413, 415
Kirkpatrick, L. C., 71, 72, 84, 91
Kishna, M. A., 333, 334, 345
Kivlahan, D. R., 259, 260, 266, 268
Klap, R., 155, 163
Kleber, H., 404, 416
Kleiman, M., 404, 415
Klein, G., 31, 49
Klein, I., 505, 515
Klein, S. J., 476, 485, 488
Klinkenberg, W. D., 498, 514
Knight, K., 452, 463
Knox, K., 277, 296
Ko, S. J., 298
Kogan, E., 188, 200
Kohn-Wood, L. P., 371, 379
Kok, A., 160, 164
Koocher, G. P., 80, 90, 263, 264, 268
Koons, B., 458, 464

Kormanik, M. B., 570, 572
Korn, R. R., 577, 584
Koss, M., 543, 544, 553, 554, 555, 561
Kosson, D., 227, 232, 234, 236, 237, 242, 243, 244
Kosten, T. R., 449, 464
Kosterman, R., 368, 379
Kozie-Peak, B., 500, 504, 513
Koziol-McLean, J., 118, 122
Krafka, C., 71, 74, 91
Kratcoski, P. C., 578, 584
Krause, H. D., 69, 91
Krebs, C. P., 471, 488
Kressel, D., 406, 416, 445, 465
Kristiansen, P. L., 174, 203
Kroner, D. G., 237, 244
Kropp, P. R., 30, 31, 32, 44, 48, 49, 100, 117, 118, 122, 123
Krueger, R. F., 232, 242
Kruesi, M. J., 333, 338, 344
Krug, S., 29, 50
Kruh, I. P., 241, 244
Krumwied, R., 498, 511
Ksir, C., 79, 91
Kubiak, S. P., 19, 446, 448, 450, 453, 464
Kubicki, A., 44, 49
Kuettel, T. J., 263, 268
Kupers, T., 445, 451, 456, 464
Kupper, I., 471, 487
Kurtz, P. D., 371, 381
Kushner, H., 404, 416
Kuther, T., 263, 268
Kvarfordt, C. L., 296
Kypri, K., 251, 270

L

La Greca, A., 387, 415
Lab, S., 547, 560
Labarthe, D., 469, 489
Labouvie, E. W., 258, 270
Lacy, G., 404, 415
LaFave, W., 391, 414
Laforge, R. G., 251, 270
Lahey, B. B., 237, 239, 241, 243
Lake, P., 176, 177, 200
Lalonde, C., 156, 163
Lamb, H. R., 387, 415, 427, 428, 442
Lambert, E., 176, 202, 296
Lambie, G. W., 252, 268
Lancee, B, 495, 512
Landsberg, G., 16
Landsheer, J., 273, 291, 295
Lang, C., 34, 49
Lang, M., 386, 389, 401, 412, 415
Langan, P., 152, 163, 386, 388, 389, 415

Langhinrichsen-Rohling, J., 552, 561
Langley, S., 386, 406, 412
Lanier, M. M., 469, 476, 488
Lansky, A., 469, 487
Lanza-Kaduce, L., 358, 362
Larimer, M. E., 251, 259, 260, 261, 266, 268, 270
Larsen, A. J., 290, 296
Latessa, E., 295, 556, 562
Latimer, J., 530, 531, 549, 561
Laub, J. H., 363, 380, 386, 415
Lauritsen, J. L, 363, 380
LaVallo, R., 17, 299–313
Law, J., 47, 48
Lawrence, J. E.
Laws, D. R., 507, 513
Lawson, H. J., 175, 201
Layne, C., 564, 572
Leach, C. T., 469, 486
Leaf, P., 498, 499, 515
Lebow, J., 153, 164
LeCouteur, A., 352, 361
LeCroy, C. W., 19, 500, 511
Lee, C. S., 251, 267
Lee, P. A., 386, 398, 403, 404, 413, 415
Lee, T., 17, 315–345, 333, 338, 344
Lehrman, F., 123
Leiber, M., 367, 372, 374, 380, 544, 561
Leisring, P., 160, 164
Leistico, A. R., 232, 233, 245
Lejuez, C. W., 257, 261, 267
Lemmon, J., 69, 76, 90
Lemon, N. K., 98, 123
Leschied, A., 387, 414
L'Esperance, J., 34, 49
Letourneau, E. J., 337, 340, 341, 342, 343, 344
Leukefeld, C., 404, 415
Levander, S., 234, 236, 240, 241, 242
Levesque, D., 158, 164
Levin, D. J., 386, 415
Levy-Elkon, A., 238, 241, 244
Lewander, W., 251, 270
Lewis, D. C., 404, 416
Lewis-Esquerre, J., 251, 267
Lewis, W., 237, 243
Lewman, L. V., 61, 65
Lexcen, F., 355, 360
Li, S., 251, 267
Liao, J. G., 340, 343, 344
Libby, A., 349, 361
Liberman, R. P., 494, 503, 504, 513
Liddle, H. A., 175, 191, 198, 199, 201, 202, 203, 261, 267
Lidz, V., 24, 241
Lightfoot, E., 521, 535
Lilienfeld, S. O., 229, 237, 241, 242, 244

Lincoln, Y., 569, 572
Lincourt, P., 263, 268
Lindenauer, M. R., 430, 442
Lindesmith, A. R., 390, 415
Lindsey, D., 35, 47, 49
Lines, K., 34, 49
Linscott, J., 251, 256, 257, 267
Lipchik, E., 44, 49
Lipsey, M. W., 200, 202
Lipton, D., 9, 500, 512
Lipton, F., 498, 513
Lister, J. L., 252, 270
Litt, M. D., 186, 201, 202
Little, C., 470, 475, 476, 489
Little, T., 386, 413
Liu, C., 388, 414
Livingston, J., 505, 515
Livingstone, C., 254, 255, 271
Lo, C., 445, 448, 464
Lochman, J. E., 233, 245
Locke, B., 428, 429, 443, 448, 465
Locke, L., 160, 164
Lockwood, D., 449, 463
Loeb, T., 160, 165
Loeber, R., 233, 242, 324, 336, 343, 345, 387, 415
Loffler, W., 498, 515
Logan, T. K., 386, 412
Lohr, J., 157, 158, 164
LoMonaco, S. W., 573, 574, 580, 585
Longabaugh, R., 406, 415
Longshore, D., 389, 402, 403, 406, 411, 415, 418
Lord, R., 293, 297
Losel, F., 359, 360
Loughran, E. J., 280, 296
Lourie, K. J., 251–252, 267
Luborsky, L., 406, 416
Luijpers, E., 273, 291, 295
Lunghofer, L., 472, 489
Lurigio, A. J., 476, 487, 488, 501, 511
Lussier, R., 473, 489
Lutzker, J. R., 79, 91
Lycan, C., 498, 511
Lykken, D. T., 225, 226, 232, 244
Lynam, D. R., 230, 232, 233, 234, 239, 240, 241, 244
Lyons, P., 34, 49
Lysaught, E., 175, 202

M

Maccoby, E. E., 296
MacDonald, H., 352, 361
MacDonald, M., 178, 179, 197, 201
Mace, D., 348, 361
Macht, M. W., 491, 513
MacIntire, S., 474, 486
Mack, J. E., 252, 267

MacKenzie, D., 388, 417
MacKinnon-Lewis, C., 348, 349, 360
MacLaurin, B., 29, 47, 50
Maercker, A., 449, 463
Magen, R. H., 29, 49, 50
Maggs, J. L., 251, 270
Maglione, M., 406, 414
Maguigan, H., 98, 123
Maguire, B. H., 469, 488
Magula, M. T., 404, 415
Magura, S., 476, 488
Mahalik, J. R., 461, 462
Mahon, N., 580, 584
Mahoney, M., 100, 123
Mailloux, D. L., 237, 244
Makkin, H., 470, 471, 490
Male, A., 431, 442
Malhotra, D., 388, 414
Malley-Morrison, K., 34, 49
Malloy, P. F., 453, 464
Malmud, T. J., 506, 511
Malone, K. M., 57, 65
Maloney, D., 273, 274, 276, 291, 296
Manderscheid, R. W., 431, 442
Manganello, J., 118, 122
Mangraviti, J. J., 79, 83, 89
Mann, B. J., 182, 185, 201, 330, 331, 333, 334, 335,
    336, 337, 341, 342, 343, 356, 360
Mann, J. J., 57, 65
Mann, R. E., 262, 268
Marczyk, G. R., 79, 90
Marks, J., 34, 49
Marlatt, G. A., 251, 259, 260, 266, 268, 507, 508, 512,
    513
Marlowe, D. B., 386, 388, 390, 396, 398, 401, 403, 404,
    409, 413, 414, 415
Marlowe, J. H., 188, 200
Marmol, L. M., 176, 177, 201
Marques, J. K., 386, 415, 509, 513
Marshall, D. B., 35, 48
Marshall, T. F., 293, 296
Martin, G., 266, 270
Martin, J. A., 296, 390, 413
Martin, K., 366, 380
Martin, S. S., 386, 415, 445, 464, 471, 487, 500, 513
Martinson, R., 9, 10, 21, 493, 513
Maruschak, L. M., 386, 414, 448, 463, 469, 470, 473,
    488
Mason, M., 498, 512
Mason, P., 254, 255, 270
Masterman, P. W., 251, 268
Mateyoke-Scrivner, A., 386, 415
Mattson, M. E., 262, 268, 406, 415
Maxwell, C., 44, 49, 157, 163
Maxwell, G., 550, 561

Mayberry, R., 471, 476, 477, 486
Mayfield-Arnold, E., 174, 203
Mays, G. L., 428, 442
McBride, D., 386, 387, 402, 403, 413, 415
McBride, M., 237, 243
McBurnett, K., 232, 243
McCabe, K. M., 249, 266, 268
McCambridge, J., 261, 269, 270
McCarthy, B. R., 476, 488
McCarthy, J., 505, 513
McCarty, C. A., 196, 203
McClelland, G. M., 173, 200, 203, 248, 249, 250, 251,
    266, 269, 270, 276, 284, 298, 348, 362, 427, 428, 435,
    442, 443, 445, 465, 470, 471, 472, 486, 488
McCold, P., 532, 535
McCollister, K. E., 388, 416
McComish, S., 57, 65
McConaughty, S., 348, 360
McConville, D., 238, 241, 244
McCord, D., 94, 123
McCord, J., 155, 164, 366, 372, 380
McCorkle, L. W., 577, 584
McCoy, C. B., 386, 413, 544, 561
McCoy, W. K., 284, 296
McDonald, G., 76, 91
McDonald, H. S., 404, 415
McDonald, T., 34
McDonel, E. C., 495, 497, 511
McFarlane, A. C., 79, 92
McGarvey, E., 348, 361
McGeary, K. A., 386, 413
McGee, R. A., 49
McGillicuddy, N. B., 406, 417
McHale, R., 366, 371, 380
McKay, H., 370, 381
McKenry, P. C., 556, 560
McKinnon, K., 472, 487
McLaughlin, J., 449, 464
McLean, P., 456, 464
McLellan, A. T., 386, 404
McLellan, A. T., 404, 406, 412, 413, 416
McMurran, M., 262, 269, 507, 513
McNeece, C. A., 174, 203, 298
McNellis, J., 404, 415
McNulty, F., 96, 123
McNulty, T. L., 370, 380
McRae, J., 498, 511
McReynolds, L. S., 298
McTaggart, R., 564, 567, 572
Meadows, E., 456, 463
Mears, D. P., 210, 220
Measelle, J., 200, 202
Mee-Lee, D., 406, 416
Meehan, J., 158, 164
Meehl, P. E., 31, 48, 49

Meeker, J., 155, 163
Meeus, W., 295
Megargee, E. I., 226, 244
Meier, J. S., 123
Melnick, G., 406, 416
Melton, A. P., 556, 561
Melton, G. B., 79, 80, 91, 182, 185, 201, 327, 330, 331, 333, 334, 337, 340, 343
Mendel, D., 365, 379, 380
Menken, A. D., 573, 584
Mercier, H., 237, 246
Merianos, D., 386, 415
Mericle, A. A., 173, 203, 249, 250, 251, 266, 270, 276, 284, 298, 348, 362
Merlino, M. L., 75, 90
Messineo, T., 160, 163
Metzger, D. S., 406, 416
Metzner, J. L., 433, 443
Meyer, A., 491, 514
Meyer-Bahlburg, H., 472, 487
Meyer, R., 472, 487
Michie, C., 229, 239, 240, 242
Middaugh, S., 365, 380
Mikulich, S. K., 176, 177, 178, 179, 197, 201, 203
Miles, J. R., 476, 489
Miletich, D., 71, 74, 91
Miller, D. W., 80, 90
Miller, G. E., 498, 512
Miller, J. B., 216, 220
Miller, J. G., 436, 443, 544, 561
Miller, L. D., 495, 497, 498, 511, 584
Miller, L. S., 388, 417
Miller-Perrin, C., 28, 48
Miller, R. L., 477, 490
Miller, W. R., 251, 252, 253, 256, 257, 265, 269, 270, 271
Millman, E. J., 498, 512
Millon, T., 225, 244
Mills, L. G., 25, 29, 44, 46, 49, 50, 549, 551, 554, 560
Milstein, R., 498, 499, 515
Miner, M. H., 509, 513
Minkoff, K., 446, 464, 494, 514
Minuchin, S., 182, 202, 316, 343
Mitchell, C. C., 333, 334, 345
Mitchell, D., 155, 164
Mitchell, J. T., 276, 296, 563, 569, 572
Modzeleski, W., 357, 360
Moffitt, T. E., 230, 231, 244
Moini, S., 469, 487
Moller, M. D., 507, 509, 514
Monahan, E., 138, 149
Monahan, J., 229, 245, 498, 514
Montgomery, L., 349, 360
Monti, P. M., 251, 257, 258, 261, 266, 267, 269, 270
Moore, K., 160, 164

Moore, V. L., 496, 515
Moos, R. H., 445, 465
Morash, M., 458, 464
Morgan, R. D., 296, 400, 416
Morral, A., 402, 403, 415
Morris, A., 293, 296, 550, 561
Morris, S. B., 181, 202
Morrison, D. M., 471, 488
Morrissey, J. P., 431, 443
Morse, D. L., 469, 488
Morse, G. A., 498, 514
Morton, D. C., 473, 489
Motayne, G. G., 385, 412
Motivans, M., 152, 163
Moxley, D. P., 495, 496, 514
Moyers, T. B., 253, 269
Moynihan, D. P., 579, 584
Mrazek, P. J., 329, 342
Mueller, C. B., 71, 72, 84, 91
Mueller, T., 446, 463
Muenz, L. R., 192, 202
Mueser, K., 446, 463
Muise, D., 530, 531, 549, 561
Mullen, E., 44, 50
Muller, R., 471, 488
Mulrine, A., 574, 584
Mulvey, E. P., 229, 245, 356, 362
Mumola, C. J., 54, 65, 473, 488
Munger, R. L., 320, 343
Munson, C. E., 11, 15, 67–92, 69, 71, 74, 75, 76, 79, 80, 81, 83, 84, 88, 91, 92
Murphy, D. S., 450, 459, 464, 472, 488
Murphy, J. G., 258, 259, 269
Murphy, M. F., 507, 509, 514
Murphy, R., 349, 357, 361
Murray, O., 472, 486
Murrie, D. C., 238, 241, 244, 284, 296
Murrin, M. R., 386, 402, 416
Museser, K. T., 506, 507, 511
Mustin, J., 579, 584
Mutter, R. C., 469, 489
Myers, D., 358, 361
Myers, J. E., 78, 91, 92
Myers, M. G., 251, 257, 258, 261, 267, 269, 270
Myers, S., 157, 163
Myers, W. C., 235, 244, 348, 361

N

Naar-King, S., 333, 339, 342
Nader, P., 469, 489
Nagy, L., 455, 463
Najaka, S. S., 401, 414
Najavits, L. M., 182, 184, 191, 192, 193, 202, 446, 456, 457, 464, 465
Nakashima, J., 579, 584

Nash, E., 263, 267
Neagle, L., 176, 177, 200
Neaigus, A., 387, 413
Neal, D. J., 251, 269
Neale, M., 498, 499, 515
Needels, K., 387, 416
Needleman, C., 287, 297
Neighbors, I. A., 11, 22, 70, 91, 277, 297
Nellis, A. M., 367, 370, 377, 380
Nelson, C., 448, 449, 464, 465, 509, 513
Nelson, G., 505, 513, 514
Nelson, M., 387, 416
Nelson, S., 251, 268
Neumann, C., 232, 239, 245, 246
Newcomb, M. D., 389, 416
Newcombe, N., 79, 91
Newlyn, A. K., 390, 413
Newman, J. P., 226, 227, 237, 243, 244, 246
Newman, S. C., 428, 442
Newton-Taylor, B., 410, 418
Nicholls, T. L., 28, 48, 226, 242
Nickless, C. J., 406, 415
Niemeyer, M., 531, 535
Niland, J. P., 15
Noblin, C. D., 295
Nolan, J., 397, 416
Norcross, J. C., 46, 50, 80, 90
Nordness, P. D., 297
Norris, F. H, 453, 465
Nugent,W. M., 531, 535
Nurco, D. N., 386, 388, 389, 414, 416
Nurcombe, B., 74, 80, 91, 92
Nutbrown, V., 474, 487
Nutt, S., 498, 513
Nybro, C., 349, 360

O

O'Bannon, R., 470, 475, 476, 489
O'Brien, B. S., 232, 241, 243, 244
O'Brien, C. P., 404, 406, 416
O'Connell, D. A., 476, 485, 488
O'Connell, D. J., 386, 415
O'Connor, L., 386, 412
O'Donell, J., 472, 490
Offutt, R. A., 494, 513
Ogborne, A. C., 191, 203
Ogden, T., 333, 334, 344
Ogilvie, R. J., 504, 505, 514
Ogloff, J. R., 226, 245
Ogloff, R. P., 226, 242
O'Grady, K. E., 386, 414
O'Hare, T., 579, 584
Ohlin, L. E., 574, 584
O'Holloran, R. L., 61, 65
O'Keefe, M., 29, 50, 449, 465

Okun, L., 104, 123
O'Leary, T. A., 257, 270
Olfson, M., 498, 514
Ollendick, T., 79, 91, 237, 239, 241, 243
Olson, E., 283
Olson, K., 44, 48
Olvera, R., 472, 486
O'Neil, D., 478, 486
O'Neil, J., 445, 465, 579, 584
O'Neill, M. L., 241, 245
Oram, A., 229, 242
Orban, L., 354, 361
Orme, M., 35, 48
O'Shaughnessy, R., 237, 243
Osher, F., 432, 443
Ostoff, S., 94, 123
Ouimette, P. C., 445, 446, 465
Outlaw, W. S., 363, 381
Owen, B., 441, 442
Ozechowski, T. J., 191, 202

P

Pace, P. R., 582
Pacht, A., 504, 514
Paddock, J., 531, 535
Paddock, M., 531, 535
Palmer, R. S., 260, 261, 268
Palmer, T., 409, 416, 500, 501, 502, 514
Parcel, G., 387, 412
Pardini, D., 336, 345
Parker, L., 543, 561
Parker, R., 477, 489
Parkin, W., 451, 463
Parrish, D. E., 19
Parrish, J., 96, 97, 98, 101, 122, 123
Partlett, D. F., 74, 80, 91, 92
Partridge, C., 295
Pasewark, R. A., 511, 564
Patapis, N., 10, 19, 387, 388, 412
Pate, A., 155, 164
Patel, H., 332, 335, 344
Paterson, B., 57, 65
Paterson, M. A., 579, 584
Patrick, C. J., 232, 235, 237, 242
Pattavian, A., 502, 511
Patterson, G. R., 188, 200, 252, 257, 269
Patterson, T. L., 469, 489
Pattison, B., 557, 561
Patton, J. H., 241, 245
Peachey, D. E., 521, 535
Pearson, C. A., 296
Pearson, F. S., 501 , 514
Pejuan, S., 339, 342
Pelissier, B., 445, 465
Penell, J., 46, 50

Penrose, L. S., 427, 443
Pensec, M., 495, 497, 511
Peoples, E. E., 579, 584
Perkins-Dock, R. E., 297
Perrin, R., 28, 48
Perry, A. L., 98, 123
Peters, E., 261, 267
Peters, J., 445, 465
Peters, R. H., 386, 402, 404, 406, 416, 417, 427, 443,
   508, 512
Petersilia, J., 387, 388, 417, 500, 515, 576, 578,
   584
Peterson, P. L., 251, 259, 266
Petraitis, J. M., 476, 488
Petrila, J., 79, 80, 91
Petry, N. M., 335, 344
Pettinati, H., 404, 416
Peugh, J., 385, 388, 412
Peuschold, D., 352, 360
Peyton, E. A., 399, 404, 406, 407, 417
Phillips, J., 354, 361
Pickrel, S. G., 178, 179, 182, 184, 185, 193, 196, 197,
   201, 202, 312, 319, 327, 331, 332, 335, 338, 340, 342,
   343, 344, 387, 414
Pihl, R. O., 449, 465
Pine, I., 229, 242
Pirog-Good, M., 156, 164
Pisciotta, A. W., 491, 514
Pitch, T., 493, 514
Pithers, W. D., 507, 514
Plass, P., 160, 164
Platt, J. L., 386, 417
Pliszka, S., 348, 361
Poe-Yamagata, E., 371, 380
Poehlmann, J., 473, 475, 489
Poirier, J., 348, 361
Polanyi, M., 566, 572
Polier, J. W., 579, 584
Polinsky, M. L., 406, 414
Pollard, C., 543, 561
Pollock, P., 262, 268
Polonsky, S., 469, 489
Polsby, D., 155, 164
Polsky, H. W., 573, 584
Pomeroy, C., 469, 486
Pomeroy, E. C., 19, 469, 478, 479, 484, 486, 489
Pope, C. E., 371, 372, 378, 380
Poppelwell, E., 550, 561
Potter, C. C., 178, 179, 197, 202
Powell-Cope, G. M.
Power, T., 156
Poythress, N. G., 79, 80, 91, 231, 237, 239, 241, 242,
   245
Prange, M. E., 174, 175, 201
Pranis, K., 522, 535, 547, 561

Pray, K. L., 573, 582, 584
Prendergast, M., 410, 413, 500
Presser, L., 544, 545, 552
Prestopnik, J. L., 182, 184, 190, 191, 193, 203
Prins, P., 354, 362
Prinstein, M., 387, 415, 417
Prochasha, J., 46, 50
Proctor, E. K., 9, 10, 22, 302, 310, 312
Prosser, V., 295
Pulvino, J., 469, 472, 486
Pumariega, A., 349, 360
Purcell, P., 296
Purkiss, M., 273, 276, 298
Puzzanchera, C. M., 275, 276, 279, 283, 297, 298
Pynoos, R., 564, 572

Q

Quigley, L. A., 259, 260, 268
Quinn, M., 348, 361
Quinn, T., 549
Quinsey, V. L., 226, 232, 244, 245

R

Raba, J., 470, 489
Rae, D. S., 428, 429, 443, 448, 465
Ragins, M., 494, 503, 514
Raine, A., 239, 244
Raj, A., 477, 486
Ramsey, S. E., 257, 261, 267, 552, 561
Randall, J., 178, 179, 197, 202, 332, 333, 335, 338, 343
Randall, M., 406, 416
Rantala, R., 152, 163
Rapp, L., 348, 349, 361
Rapp-Paglicci, L., 18, 348, 349, 361
Rapposelli, K. K., 476, 489
Rauch, K. J., 476, 489
Ray, O., 79, 91
Reamer, R., 558, 561
Recupero, P. R., 449, 463
Redding, R., 352, 354, 355, 356, 357, 358, 360, 361
Reed, E., 477, 486
Reed, J. G., 574, 584
Regier, D. A., 428, 429, 443
Rehm, L. P., 479, 489
Rehman, U., 158, 164
Reicher-Rossler, A., 498, 515
Reid, G., 47, 48
Reid, J. B., 188, 200
Reid, W. H., 20
Reid, W. J., 479, 489, 563, 572
Reiff, H. J., 494, 513
Reilly, A. A., 469, 488
Reinecke, M. A., 189, 203
Reinhardt, B., 495, 514
Reissland, G., 65

Renfro, N., 101, 124
Reppucci, N., 352, 356, 361, 362
Reuter, P., 388, 417
Rhine, E. E., 295
Rhodes, W., 469, 470, 471, 487
Riad, J. K., 453, 465
Rice, D. P., 388, 417
Rice, M. E., 34, 49, 226, 232, 243, 244, 245
Richards, H. R., 226, 242
Richardson, D., 469, 470, 486
Richardson, J. T., 75, 90
Richardson, W. S., 22, 42, 50
Richie, B. E., 556, 561
Richman, C., 160, 164
Ridgely, M. S., 406, 418
Rigby, M., 354, 361
Riggs, P. D., 197, 203
Righthand, S., 79, 91, 92
Rimmerman, A.
Rindsberg, J., 175, 201
Rivers, S. M., 251, 269
Roach, K., 543, 561
Robbins, M. S., 289, 297
Robbins, P. C., 432, 443
Roberts, A. R., 3, 3–22, 4, 5, 10, 14, 15, 22, 28, 50,
  53–65, 65, 67, 91, 95, 123, 174, 203, 277, 286, 297,
  299, 300, 312, 348, 349, 361, 529, 536, 573, 581, 582,
  584
Roberts, B. S., 3, 22
Roberts, C., 386, 387, 414
Roberts, E., 273, 276, 298
Robertson, J., 550, 561
Robie, C., 158, 163
Robins, L. N., 233, 245
Robinson, J. B., 402, 403, 413
Rock, M., 277, 297
Rodick, J. D., 330, 331, 337, 343
Rodriguez, N., 377, 380
Roffman, R. A., 186, 203, 261, 268, 270
Rogan, D., 155, 165
Rogers, C. R., 253, 269
Rogers, K., 349, 360
Rogers, R., 177, 179, 197, 203, 226, 233, 235, 239, 244,
  245, 246, 504, 515
Rogosch, F. A., 251, 267
Rohde, P., 348, 354, 360, 361
Rohsenow, D. J., 257, 258, 267, 269, 270, 446, 465
Roiblatt, R. E., 273, 297
Rollnick, S., 252, 253, 254, 255, 257, 262, 265, 268,
  269, 270, 271
Roman, J., 402, 414
Romig, D. A., 273, 274, 276, 291, 296, 493, 515
Ronan, K. R., 289, 295, 334, 342
Rooney, R., 277, 286, 290, 296, 579, 584
Rooney, W., 470, 471, 490

Roozen, H. G., 321, 335, 344
Rose, S. M., 496, 515
Rosen, A., 9, 10, 22, 302, 310, 312
Rosenbaum, A., 160, 164
Rosenberg, W., 22, 42, 50
Rosenblatt, A., 348, 361
Rosenblatt, J., 348, 361
Rosenblatt, W., 473, 489
Rosenfeld, B., 157, 165
Rosenheck, R., 386, 414, 498, 499, 515
Rosenthal, J., 391, 402, 403, 414
Ross, R., 555, 561
Ross, S. M., 28, 50
Ross, T., 211, 216, 220
Rossi, P. H., 387, 417
Rossler, W., 498, 515
Rossman, E., 506, 511
Rotgers, F., 262, 268
Rothman, J., 579, 584
Rounds-Bryant, J., 174, 175, 178, 179, 201, 203
Rounsaville, B. J., 182, 186, 193, 195, 202
Roussell, A., 390, 414
Rowan-Szal, G. A., 389, 401, 402, 409, 417
Rowe, C. L., 175, 198, 199, 203
Rowland, M. D., 274, 289, 296, 319, 323, 327, 328, 332,
  333, 337, 338, 339, 342, 343, 344, 345
Roy, S., 530, 535
Rozee, P., 543, 544, 554, 555
Rubin, A., 478, 479, 489
Rubin, P., 556, 561
Ruiz, M. S., 478, 486
Rundell, O., 472, 488
Rushe, R., 158, 1643
Russell, B., 580, 584
Russell, F., 577, 584
Rutman, I. D., 495, 512
Rutter, M., 352, 361
Ryan, E., 359, 361
Ryan, J., 471, 476, 487
Rychtarik, R., 406, 417
Rycus, J. S., 27, 31, 50
Rye, B. J., 475, 487

S

Sabitini, A., 498, 513
Saccuzzo, D. P., 76, 90
Sackett, D. L., 9, 22, 42, 50
Sadock, B. J., 79, 90
Saito, R. N., 279, 294
Sajatovic, M., 79, 90
Saleeby, D., 564, 572
Salekin, R. T., 226, 232, 233, 235, 245
Sales, B. D., 19, 75, 90
Sales, E., 479, 486
Saltzman, A., 76, 91

Sampl, S., 261, 267
Sampson, R. J., 386, 415
Sanchez, V. C., 251, 253, 269
Sandin, E., 158, 164
Sandler, I. N., 79, 92
Santos, A. B., 495, 497, 515
Sarri, R. C., 275, 280, 297, 574, 584
Satel, S. L., 389, 396, 401, 402, 410, 417
Sattler, J. M., 80, 91
Saum, S. A., 386, 415
Saunders, D. G., 29, 50, 156, 163
Saunders, J. B., 251, 270
Saunders, S., 508, 510
Saur, W. G., 580, 583
Schaeffer, C. M., 330, 331, 332, 335, 336, 338, 342, 344
Schecter, S., 104, 123
Schehr, R. C., 557, 559
Scheier, L. M., 368, 380
Schepise, N. M., 404, 415
Schervish, P. J., 70, 90
Schiff, M., 542, 560
Schilling, R., 474, 475, 476, 487
Schindler, M. L., 297
Schiraldi, G. R., 79, 92
Schlenger, W., 445, 449, 464
Schma, W. G., 391, 402, 403, 414
Schmauk, F. J., 226, 245
Schmeelk-Cone, K. H., 371, 379
Schmidt, F., 295, 297
Schmidt, J., 155, 165
Schnee, J., 505, 515
Schneider, A., 529, 531, 535
Schneider, E., 94, 95, 96, 102, 103, 123
Schneiger, A., 251, 268
Schoenwald, S. K., 274, 289, 296, 319, 323, 327, 328, 329, 330, 331, 332, 335, 337, 338, 340, 341, 342, 343, 344, 345
Schon, D., 566, 572
Schroeder, J., 297
Schrum, C. L., 233, 245
Schulenberg, J. E., 251, 270
Schulenberg, K., 448, 449, 464
Schulz, R., 479, 486
Schwartz, R. G., 262, 274, 278, 283, 290, 297
Schwe, A. L., 337
Schwisow, A., 285, 297
Scott, J. E., 432, 443
Scott, M., 36, 349
Sdao-Jarvie, K., 251, 267
Seagrave, D., 230, 241–242, 245
Sechrest, L., 495, 515
Secord, E., 339, 342
Seeley, J., 348, 354, 360
Segal, E. A., 370, 381
Seidenberg, M., 232, 242

Seiter, R. P., 387, 417
Seltzer, R., 358, 361
Semaan, S., 471, 486
Serin, R. C., 226, 245
Sermabeikian, P., 564, 572
Sever, J. B., 323, 345
Severson, M. M., 579, 584
Sewell, K. W., 226, 245
Sexton, T., 36, 349
Shadish, W. R., 191, 203, 329, 335, 345
Shane, P. A., 175, 178, 179, 203
Shank, S. A., 472, 489
Shapiro, S. B., 333, 335, 343, 476, 488
Sharps, P. W., 118, 122
Sharrat, S., 506, 511
Shaver, P. R., 68, 79, 90
Shaw, C., 370, 381
Shaw, S., 192, 202, 446, 465
Shea, M., 469, 470, 486
Sheets, J., 47, 48
Sheidow, A. J., 17, 315–345, 332, 338, 340, 343, 344
Shelby, M., 470, 475, 476, 489
Shelton, D., 470, 489
Shepard, M., 123
Sheperis, C., 356, 360
Shepherd, G., 495, 496, 514, 515
Sheras, P., 359, 361
Sherer, R. A., 57, 65
Sheridan, S., 295
Sherman, J., 348, 361
Sherman, L. W., 154, 155, 165, 358, 361, 388, 417
Sherman, R. K., 440, 443
Shichor, D., 531, 535
Shipley, B. E., 386, 411
Shireman, C., 574, 577, 583
Shlonsky, A., 14, 25–50, 27, 30, 31, 34, 35, 37, 40, 41, 42, 44, 46, 47, 49, 50
Shook, J. J., 273, 275, 276, 280, 287, 297
Shortt, J., 158, 164
Shulman, G., 406, 416
Shure, M. B., 188, 203
Siegel, G., 293, 297
Siegel, J. A., 461, 462
Sikkema, 472, 488
Silver, S., 174, 175, 201
Simmons, M., 471, 488
Simons, R. L., 371, 381, 450, 459, 464
Simourd, D. J., 407, 417
Simpson, D., 389, 401, 402, 406, 409, 414, 417
Simpson, E., 186, 203
Sims, P., 356, 360
Sindelar, H., 251, 258, 270
Singer, J. B., 17, 273–298, 298
Singer, M., 472, 489
Sirles, E., 44, 49

Skeem, J. L., 24, 226, 229, 230, 231, 241, 242, 245
Skiba, R., 348, 360
Skowyra, K., 349, 353, 354, 360
Slesnick, N., 182, 184, 190, 191, 193, 203
Slayden, J., 446, 448, 453, 464
Slobogin, C., 79, 80, 91, 391, 402, 417
Smart, R. G., 191, 203
Smith, A. B., 578, 584
Smith, D., 155, 165
Smith, E., 152, 163
Smith, F. S., 88, 92
Smith, I., 404, 416
Smith, L. A., 182, 185, 201, 327, 330, 331, 333, 334,
    337, 340, 343
Smith, M., 297
Smith, P., 388, 413
Smith, R. S., 30, 51, 498, 514
Smith, S. G., 491, 515
Smith, S. S., 227, 237, 244, 246
Smith, V. J., 261, 267
Smith, W., 579, 584
Smultzer, N., 158, 164
Smyth, N. J., 575, 584
Snell, T., 458, 463, 473, 489
Snipp, C. M., 370, 381
Snowden, L., 36, 349
Snyder, H. N., 275, 276, 283, 298, 366, 367, 368, 371,
    380, 381
Solomon, P., 494, 495, 499, 515, 579, 583, 584
Solovitz, B., 498, 512
Song, L., 472, 489
Sonnega, A., 449, 464
Sontheimer, H., 500, 512
Southwick, S. M., 449, 464
Sowards, S., 440, 443
Sowers, K. M., 356, 358, 360, 574, 583
Spain, S. E., 237, 239, 241, 245
Sperry, L., 503, 515
Spica, R., 496, 515
Spirito, A., 251, 257, 258, 267, 269, 270, 387, 417
Spitzer, R. L., 455, 465
Spivak, G., 188, 203
Spohn, C., 363, 381
Springer, D. W., 3–22, 14, 16, 173, 173–203, 174, 200,
    202, 203, 298
Srebnik, D., 505, 515
St. Cyr, J. L., 365, 381
St. Lawrence, J., 470, 471, 475, 476, 488, 489
Stafford, E., 229, 238, 242, 245
Stahl, A. L., 298, 376, 381
Stairs, J. M., 372, 374, 380
Stanfield, R., 275, 276, 285, 298
Stanford, M. S., 241, 245
Stanton, M. D., 191, 203, 332, 338, 344
Stark, E., 15, 101, 102, 104, 116, 117, 123

Stark, K., 471, 488
Stathis, S., 266, 270
Staton, M., 404, 415
Stattin, H., 234, 236, 240, 241, 242
Stayton, D. J., 68, 89
Steadman, H. J., 431, 432, 443, 498, 514
Steen, S., 363, 364, 370, 379
Stein, L. A., 257, 270
Stein, L. I., 495, 497, 498, 515
Stein, R., 331, 336, 341
Steinberg, L., 230, 245
Steiner, B., 273, 276, 298, 377, 381
Steiner, H., 348, 360
Steiner, J., 473, 489
Steinmetz, S., 28, 50
Stephens, R. S., 186, 203, 261, 270, 445, 448, 464
Stern, V., 556, 561
Sternbach, J., 579, 584
Stets, J., 156, 164
Stevens, V. J., 261, 267
Stewart, E. A., 371, 381
Stewart, S. H., 449, 465
Stice, E., 200, 202, 354, 360
Stitzer, M. L., 339, 343
Stiver, I., 216, 220
Stoesen, L., 581, 584
Stone, E., 354, 361
Stone, S., 500, 512, 531, 535
Stoolmiller, M., 273, 276, 298
Stout, R. L., 446, 449, 463
Stouthamer-Loeber, M., 239, 244, 387, 415
Strang, J., 261, 269, 270
Straus, M. A., 28, 32, 50, 152, 165
Straus, S. E., 22, 42, 50
Strong, D. R., 257, 261, 267
Strong, K. H., 543, 562
Strong, W., 94, 123
Strother, K. B., 328, 345
Stroul, B., 495, 515
Stroup, T. S., 495, 515
Struening, E., 498, 512
Stuart, G., 158, 162, 164
Studt, E., 492, 515, 579, 580, 581, 584, 585
Sturgeon, V., 504, 515
Sukhodolsky, D., 354, 361
Sullivan, D., 542, 561
Summerfelt, W. T., 176, 202
Sundby, S. E., 147, 149
Sung, H., 389, 410, 412, 417
Surratt, H. L., 386, 415
Surrey, J., 216, 220
Susser, E., 472, 489
Sussex, J. N., 495, 512
Sussman, J., 182, 186, 193, 195, 202
Sutphen, R., 371, 381

Swaggert, A., 279, 280
Swan, M., 261, 268
Swartz, J. A., 432, 443
Sweell, K. W., 177, 179, 197, 203
Swenson, C. C., 323, 338, 345
Swenson, M. E., 328, 345
Swetz, A., 471, 488
Syers, M., 156, 163
Szanto, K., 57, 65
Szapocznik, J., 289, 297

T

Takagi, P., 298
Talliade, J., 158, 1643
Tapert, S. F., 258, 270
Tardy, M. J., 580, 582
Tate, D., 356, 362
Taxman, F. S., 386, 389, 398, 399, 402, 403, 406, 409, 417
Taylor, B., 44, 49, 157, 163
Taylor, E., 233, 246
Taylor, I. S., 323, 345
Taylor, J., 504, 515
Taylor, L., 264, 270
Teichner, G. A., 175, 182, 184, 187, 188, 193, 196, 200, 201
Tejeda, M., 175, 201
Tellegen, A., 453, 463
Telles, L., 504, 505, 515
Tempelhoff, B., 498, 514
Templin, T., 333, 339, 342
Teplin, L. A., 173, 200, 203, 248, 249, 250, 251, 266, 269, 270, 276, 284, 298, 348, 362, 427, 428, 432, 435, 442, 443, 445, 465, 470, 471, 472, 486, 488
Terry, Y., 387, 415
Test, M. A., 495, 497, 498, 515
Tevyaw, T. O., 251, 257, 258, 261, 267, 270
Thobro, P., 252, 267
Thomas, D., 298
Thomas, G., 406, 416, 445, 465
Thomas, R. L., 29, 50
Thomas, W., 277, 298
Thompson, A. H., 428, 442
Thorburn, K. M., 472, 489
Thornton, C. C., 406, 418
Thornton, D., 226, 243
Thyfault, R., 107, 123
Tien, G., 500, 516
Tifft, L., 542, 561
Timmons-Mitchell, J., 333, 334, 345
Tims, F. M., 261, 267
Tinsely, M. J., 476, 489
Titus, J. C., 261, 267
Tober, G., 251, 270
Toch, H., 226, 246, 445, 449, 451, 461, 465

Tolan, P. H., 231, 246
Tolin, D., 158, 164
Tolman, R., 157, 165
Tomas, P., 470, 471, 490
Tomoyasu, N., 469, 470, 486
Tonigan, J. S., 252, 269
Torbet, P., 274, 275, 276, 278, 279, 284, 287, 289, 295, 298
Torres, L., 389, 418
Torrey, E. F., 427, 435, 443
Toupin, J., 237, 246
Tracy, E. M., 547, 560
Trainham, A., 297
Tran, T. H., 404, 415
Trattner, W., 278, 298
Travis, J., 576, 585
Treger, H., 10, 22, 580, 585
Treisman, G., 471, 488
Trestman, R. L., 428, 442
Tripodi, T., 575, 579, 583
Trobst, K. K., 233, 245
Trocmye, N., 29, 47, 50
Trone, J., 387, 416
Trotter, J., 390, 413
Truax, C. B., 252, 270
Trupin, E., 430, 442
Tsushima, W. T., 84, 85, 92
Tupker, E., 251, 267
Turner, A. P., 260, 261, 268
Turner, S., 388, 389, 401, 402, 403, 406, 411, 415, 417, 418, 500, 502, 514, 515
Tuten, M., 339, 343
Tweed, R., 158, 1654
Tyson, K. B., 580, 582

U

Umbreit, M. S., 274, 292, 293, 294, 520, 521, 522, 523, 527, 529, 530, 531, 534, 535, 536, 544, 550, 553, 556, 562
Underwood, L. A., 210, 220, 284, 296
Unger, D. G., 324, 345
Unis, A. S., 188, 202
Unterberger, H., 261, 267
Urey, J. R., 330, 331, 337, 343
Usdane, M., 389, 418
Usinger-Lesquereux, J., 297

V

Valencia, E., 472, 489
Valeri, S. M., 196, 203
van Beyer, K., 11, 22, 70, 91, 277, 297
van de Put, W., 556, 560
Van Den Brink, W., 321, 335, 344
van der Kolk, B. A., 79, 92
Van Haveren, R. A., 296

van Horn, L., 261, 267
Van Kammen, W., 233, 242
Van Laningham, L., 478, 489
van Manen, T., 354, 362
Van Ness, D., 521, 536, 543, 562
van Tulder, M. W., 321, 335, 344
Van Voorhis, R. M., 556, 562
Van Wijk, A., 336, 345
van Wormer, K., 20, 543, 562
VanBuren, H., 387, 415
Vance, H. B., 76, 92
Vandana, J., 175, 177, 179, 201
VanderWaal, C., 387, 415
VanKammen, W., 387, 415
VanWormer, K. S., 470, 473, 474, 489
Varcella, R., 101, 124
Ventura, L. A., 437, 443
Vermeiren, R., 336, 345
Veysey, B. M., 431, 443
Vik, P. W., 251, 269
Villarivera, C., 388, 414
Vincent, G. M., 231, 244
Vinton, L., 580, 585
Vitacco, M. J., 239, 246
Vitale, J. E., 227, 246
Viteillo, B., 323, 345
Vitiello, M., 80, 90
Vivoam, T., 502, 512
Vmbreit, M. P., 20
Vogelsang, J., 92
Volavka, J., 472, 490
Volksdorf, N., 252, 270
Vos, B., 520, 521, 523, 529, 530, 531, 536
Vossekuil, B., 32, 48
Vuchinich, R., 258, 259, 269
Vyas, Y., 556, 562

W

Wachtel, B., 532, 535
Wagner, D., 25, 27, 29, 31, 32, 34, 35, 37, 38, 39, 40, 41, 42, 47, 48, 50, 271
Waiselfisz, J. J., 11, 22
Waite, D., 348, 361
Waite, F. T., 566, 572
Wald, M. S., 30, 34, 40, 50
Waldron, H., 251, 270
Walker, G., 473, 490
Walker, L., 50, 96, 101, 102, 107, 123, 124
Walker, N. E., 73, 92
Walker, R. J., 133, 150, 478, 479, 489
Walker, S., 363, 381, 556, 562
Wallace, S., 445, 465
Wallach, M., 446, 463
Waller, I., 492, 503, 515
Walsh-Bower, R., 505, 514

Walters, S. T., 251, 270
Waltz, J., 158, 165
Wandersman, A., 324, 345
Ward, D. M., 332, 335, 338, 343, 344
Ward, G., 275, 280, 297
Ward, M., 469, 470, 486
Ward, R., 498, 511
Warfield-Coppock, N., 557, 562
Wargo, D. G., 252, 270
Warner, L., 448, 449, 464, 465
Warner, S., 530, 536
Warren, J., 134, 150, 229, 242
Washburn, J. J., 295
Wasmer, D., 498, 511
Wasserman, D., 295
Wasserman, G. A., 298
Waterman, J., 348, 360
Watson, S. M., 330, 331, 337, 343
Watt, K. A., 231, 244
Watts, F., 506, 515
Watts, R., 503, 505, 515
Watzlawick, P., 582, 585
Weathers, F. W., 455, 456, 463, 465
Webb, C., 261, 267
Webb, J., 498, 511
Websdale, N., 445, 450, 465
Webster, C. W., 32, 49, 118, 123
Webster, D., 118, 122
Weekes, J. R., 262, 268
Wehman, P., 506, 515
Weil, M., 495, 515
Weiland, D., 390, 413
Weinberger, L. E., 387, 415, 427, 428, 442
Weiner, A., 231, 244
Weiner, I., 149
Weinrott, M. R., 188, 200
Weinstein, S. P., 406, 418
Weisaeth, L., 79, 92
Weisfuse, I., 470, 471, 490
Weiss, R. D., 182, 184, 191, 192, 193, 202, 446, 465
Weissman, K., 257, 267
Weisz, J. R., 196, 203, 315, 323, 329, 343, 345
Weitzer, R., 544, 562
Wellisch, J., 500, 514
Wells, E. A., 251, 266
Welsh, B. C., 329, 342
Welsh, W. N., 282, 298
Wenzel, S. L., 402, 403, 406, 415, 418
Werner, E. E., 30, 51
Western, B., 155, 163
Westervelt, S. A., 94, 124
Wettstein, R. M., 433, 443, 504, 515
Wexler, D. B., 469, 489
Wexler, H., 445, 452, 463, 465, 500, 512
Whelan, J. P., 331, 338, 342

White, A. J., 494, 513
White, B., 580, 585
White, H. R., 258, 270, 449, 464
White, L., 176, 177, 200
White, M. D., 402, 403, 413
White, S. O., 495, 515
White, T., 473, 475, 489
Whitmer, G. E., 580, 585
Whitmore, E. A., 176, 177, 203
Whitney, R. B., 406, 417
Whittaker, J. K., 547, 560
Widiger, T. A., 229, 246
Widom, C. S., 366, 380, 449, 464, 465
Widom, R., 470, 487
Wiinamaki, L., 531, 535
Wilbanks, W., 363, 381
Wilbourne, P. L., 252, 269
Wild, T. C., 410, 418
Williams, C., 368, 380
Williams, E., 259, 266
Williams, J. H., 18, 241, 245, 363, 368, 380, 381
Williams, L. M., 461, 462
Williams, O., 159, 160, 163, 164, 165
Williams, R. B., 455, 465
Williams, R. J., 175, 203
Williams, R. M., 531, 535
Wills, T., 387, 418
Wilson, D. B., 200, 202, 477, 490, 500, 516
Wilson, D. L., 225, 229, 246
Wilson, J. P., 79, 92, 280, 287, 288, 298
Wilson, K., 101, 124
Wilson, M., 160, 164
Wilson, S. K., 30, 49, 51
Winfree, L. T., 428, 442
Wing, J. K., 503, 510, 516
Winner, L., 358, 362
Winterowd, C. L., 400, 416
Winters, K. C., 251, 270
Wirth, D., 471, 488
Wirtz, P. W., 406, 417
Wise, B. K., 175, 203
Witheridge,T. F., 498, 511
Witte, E. F., 574, 585
Wodak, A., 471, 490
Wodarski, J. S., 34, 49, 175, 202, 348, 349, 361
Wodrich, D. L., 76, 92
Wolchik, S. A., 79, 92
Wolfe, D. A., 30, 49, 51
Wolkow, K. E., 323, 345
Wong, C. J., 339, 343
Wong, F. Y., 497, 512

Wong, S., 226, 232, 244, 245
Wood, J., 564, 572
Wood, M. D., 258, 266
Wood, P. A., 173, 200, 249, 250, 266, 268
Woods, R., 160, 163
Woodson, R. L., 282, 298
Woody, G. E., 406, 416
Wooldredge, J. D., 459, 465, 556, 562
Woolverton, M., 30, 34, 40, 50
Wootton, J. M., 232, 243
Wormser, G. P., 469, 488
Wright, J. P., 500, 501, 502, 512
Wright, L. N., 476, 485, 488
Wright, R., 277, 298
Wu, H., 470, 490
Wyatt, G., 160, 165
Wynne, J. M., 79, 90
Wyrick, P., 528, 536

Y

Yakowitz, S., 470, 490
Yalom, I. D., 182, 200
Yarcheck, C. M., 295
Yazzie, R., 556, 562
Yeager, K. R., 10, 15, 22, 53–65, 65, 67, 91
Yeh, M., 249, 266, 268
Young, A., 446, 448, 453, 464
Young, D. S., 19, 389, 406, 410, 417, 418, 428, 429, 433, 435, 443, 573, 574, 580, 585
Young, M., 519, 534
Young, P. V., 585
Young, S. E., 178, 179, 197, 201
Yovanoff, P., 440, 443
Yuen, S. A., 49

Z

Zack, B., 476, 487
Zahniser, J., 506, 513
Zak, L., 30, 51
Zander, K., 495, 516
Zanis, D., 406, 416
Zarkin, G. A., 390, 418
Zehr, H., 520, 521, 523, 536, 541, 562
Zellerer, E., 556, 562
Zerbe, G. O., 178, 179, 197, 201
Zhang, Q., 387, 415
Zhang, Z., 385, 418
Zimmerman, M. A., 371, 379
Zimring, F., 385, 390, 418
Zlotnick, C., 446, 465
Zuravin, S., 35, 51

Subject Index

A

ABA. *See Criminal Justice Mental Health Standards*
ACA. *See* American Corrections Association
ACLU. *See* American Civil Liberties Union
ACRA. *See* adolescent community reinforcement
    approach
ACS. *See* Administration for Children's Services
ACT. *See* assertive community treatment
actuarial models, 27, 36, 39f, 41–42. *See also* risk
    assessment
ADHD. *See* attention-deficit/hyperactivity disorder
Administration for Children's Services (ACS), 206, 211
adolescent community reinforcement approach
    (ACRA), 261
Adoption and Safe Families Act of 1997, 69
advocacy, goals for, 218
affidavits, 83
African-Americans, 214
    Afrocentric theory, 557
    community and, 544–548
    DMC and, 363–381
    domestic violence, 156–160
    HIV/AIDS and, 470
    inmates, 363–381, 470
    juveniles, 251, 363–381
    restorative justice and, 548
    women, 484
    See also specific topics
aftercare programs, 500
    ACT model, 497–499
    current services, 495–500
    defined, 492
    employment and, 505–507
    mental health and, 491–516
    recidivism and, 492
    special needs and, 493–494
    See also specific groups, programs
AIDS. *See* HIV/AIDS
Ake v. Oklahoma, 144
alcohol abuse
    adolescents and, 258, 258–261
    BIPs and, 156
    costs to society, 388

    gender differences, 250
    MI and, 258–261
    RAPI and, 258
    substance abuse levels and, 249–250
    treatment effects, 192–195
ambivalence, in therapy, 252, 254
American Civil Liberties Union (ACLU), 62
American Corrections Association (ACA), 451, 581
anger management, 160
antisocial behavior, 182
antisocial personality disorder (APD), 225, 228t
Antisocial Process Screening Device (APSD), 234,
    238–239
anxiety, 448, 479
APD. *See* antisocial personality disorder
APSD. *See* Antisocial Process Screening Device
arrest policies, 155, 159
assertive community treatment (ACT), 497–499
assertiveness, 161
assessment tools, 27. *See specific instruments; types*
Atkins vs. Virginia, 578
attention-deficit/hyperactivity disorder (ADHD), 128,
    233, 249, 323, 347

B

balanced and restorative justice (BARJ) model
    balance in, 291, 292f
    development of, 291
    ecosystemic models and, 292
    juvenile justice and, 17
    rehabilitation-punishment, 273, 288
BARJ. *See* balanced and restorative justice model
Baselon Center for Mental Health and the Law, 205
battered woman syndrome (BWS), 96, 98, 102–103
batterer intervention programs (BIPs), 15, 117,
    151–163
    attrition rates, 156
    effects of, 155, 157–158
    meta-analyses of, 157
    racial groups and, 159
battering
    absence of reaction, 106
    abuse excuse, 116–117

battering (*Contd.*)
  arrest policies, 155
  alimony and, 114
  batterer killed, 96–97, 118
  behavior and, 101
  BIPs. *See* batterer intervention program
  BWS. *See* battered woman syndrome
  coercive control and, 103, 105, 112
  conferencing and, 552
  consequences of, 113–115
  custody and, 101
  documentation of, 106–107
  dynamics of, 115
  employment and, 155
  episodic, 109
  expert testimony on, 93–126
  history of, 108
  intervention programs, 151–163
  interviews with victims, 107–108
  intimidation and, 110
  isolation and, 111
  jealousy and, 110
  legal defense, 94–96
  psychological effects of, 114
  restorative practices, 551–553
  risk assessment, 117
  self-defense, 95–98
  shelters, 95
  spousal homicide, 97, 118
  typology for, 158
  See also domestic violence
Beck Depression Inventory, 137
behavioral approach, 187
biopsychosocial assessment, 350–352
BIPs. *See* batterer intervention programs
BJMHS. *See* Brief Jail Mental Health Screen
BJS. *See* Bureau of Justice Statistics
Blum v. Julian, 307
Borrelli decision, 94, 99, 120
Bowring v. Godwin, 430
Brief Jail Mental Health Screen (BJMHS), 432
brief strategic family therapy (BSFT), 289
Brief Symptom Inventory (BSI), 352
broker-of-service models, 497
BSFT. *See* brief strategic family therapy
BSI. *See* Brief Symptom Inventory
Bureau of Justice Statistics (BJS), 3, 152
Burgos v. Burgos, 99, 114
BWS. *See* battered woman syndrome

C

CAGE-AID. *See* Cut-down, Annoyed, Guilty,
    Eye-opener-Adapted to Include Drugs
California Actuarial Tool, 41
California Family Risk Assessment, 31, 35, 37
Campbell Collaboration, 180

Capital Jury Project, 147
CAPS. *See* Clinician Administered PTSD Scale
CASA. *See* court appointed special advocates
case management services, 495–500
CASI-A. *See* Comprehensive Addiction Severity Index
    for Adolescents
Catsam decision, 304
Caucasians, 159, 251, 369f
CBOs. *See* community-based organizations
CBT. *See* cognitive behavior therapy
CD. *See* conduct disorder
Center for Mental Health Services (CMHS) study, 428
Center for Restorative Justice and Peacemaking, 551
charities, 575
Chicago models, 249
child abuse, 4, 14, 26
  allegations of, 27
  case studies, 447
  CPS. *See* Children's Protective Services
  domestic violence and, 40t, 47
  ER visits, 29
  jailed females and, 472
  MST and, 338
  poverty and, 47
  prediction of, 34
  prevention. *See specific legislation, organizations*
  responding to, 27
  risk assessment, 35–36, 40, 40t, 46
  service decisions, 40
  training of social workers, 46
Child and Adolescent Act, 11
Child and Adolescent Forensic Mental Health
    Certificate Program, 217
child development expert, 147
Child Psychopathy Scale (CPS), 234, 239–240
Child Welfare Information Gateway, 45f
Child Welfare League of America, 45f
child welfare system, 15, 239–240, 293
Children's Protection Services (CPS), 27–30, 40, 41
Children's Research Center (CRC), 41
circle sentencing, 547
client engagement, 456
Clinician Administered PTSD Scale (CAPS), 455
CM. *See* contingency management interventions
CMHS. *See* Center for Mental Health Services study
Cochrane-Campbell studies, 43, 180
coercive control model, 105, 410
cognitive-behavioral therapy (CBT), 18
  depression, 479
  dual diagnosis and, 189
  effect sizes and, 181
  HIV risk and, 475
  intervention and, 160, 321–322, 354–355, 456
  MI-based therapy and, 261
  MST and, 322
  PET and, 189

PTSD and, 456
skill-streaming in, 355, 475
substance abuse and, 456
techniques, 479
cognitive bias, 31
Cognitive Capacity Screening Examination, 137
cognitive function, 137. *See also specific instruments*
collaborative intervention, 178, 179t, 252
college education, 11
common couple violence, 153
communitarian justice, 553
community
CBOs. *See* community-based programs
conferencing model, 543
disorganization of, 128
drug abuse programs and, 19
juvenile justice system and, 374–376
postincarceration and, 461
rehabilitation programs, 506
release-planning, 438
risk factors for, 128
safety plans and, 461
service programs, 178t
traumatic environment and, 461
treatment and, 19, 390
community-based organizations (CBOs), 357, 476
community conferencing, 390, 543, 547, 552–555
comorbid disorders, 173–203, 348
ADHD symptoms, 177t
adolescents, 173–203
CBT and, 189
CD and, 177t, 179
collaborative intervention, 178t, 179
definition of, 174
delinquency and, 197
interventions for, 182–192
NYC studies, 206–220
outcome studies, 176
research on, 198
substance use and, 179
SUDs and, 179
therapy models, 175–176, 177t, 181
treatment guidelines, 197–198, 198t
See also specific disorders
Comprehensive Addiction Severity Index for
Adolescents (CASI-A), 210
computer resources, 221–223. *See also* Internet; *specific organizations*
concentration problems, 128
conduct disorder (CD), 232, 234t, 249, 347
conferencing, 390, 543, 547, 552–555
confidentiality, 305–306, 436, 484
Confirm Project, 211
conflict resolution, 216. *See also* mediation
Conflict Tactics Scale, 152
connectivity, professional, 563–564

consensus-based classification, 39f
contextual assessment, 27
contingency management (CM) interventions, 335
coping skills, 191, 216
corrections facilities, 21, 62–63, 285. *See also* jails;
prisons; justice system
Council on Social Work Education (CSWE), 574, 581,
582
court appointed special advocates (CASA), 300
CPS. *See* Child Psychopathy Scale
CPS. *See* Children's Protection Services
CRC. *See* Children's Research Center, 86–87
Crime and Research Centre (New Zealand), 550
Criminal Justice Mental Health Standards (ABA), 136
crisis intervention, 190, 216, 286
cross-examination, 83, 86–87
cross-system interventions, 179
cruel and unusual punishment, 126
CSWE. *See* Council on Social Work Education
cultural factors, 146, 541–562
custody cases, 78, 101
Cut Down, Annoyed, Guilty, Eye-opener-Adapted to
Include Drugs (CAGE-AID), 453

D

DAIP. *See* Domestic Abuse Intervention Project
Danger Assessment Scale, 32, 118
databases, 44
Daubert decision, 73–74, 94
Death in Custody Reporting Act of 2000, 53
Decker v. Hatfield, 311n11
Defining Issues Test (DIT), 7
delinquency, 230, 274, 367f, 544. *See* juvenile justice
system; *specific types*
depositions, 83
depression, 29, 176, 178t, 249, 479
detention, 285
Detention Diversion Advocacy Project, 282
development disabilities, 506
diagnosis, 82–83, 83
Diagnostic and Statistical Manual of Mental Disorders
(APA), 135, 210, 248
Diagnostic Interview Schedule for Children (DISC),
249
DISC. *See* Diagnostic Interview Schedule for Children
discrimination, in justice system, 371–372
disposition hearing, 288–289
disproportionate minority confinement (DMC), 363,
366, 372, 375t, 376t
DIT. *See* Defining Issues Test
diversion prior to referral, 282
DMC. *See* disproportionate minority confinement
Domestic Abuse Intervention Project (DAIP), 112
domestic violence, 4, 8, 14, 35, 109
African-Americans and, 159
arrest policies, 155

domestic violence (*Contd.*)
  battering. *See* battering
  bidirectional, 28
  child abuse and, 25–51
  children's services, 28–30
  common couple violence, 153
  conceptualization of, 153
  court testimony and, 94–104
  family violence, 153
  feminist theory and, 153
  frequency of, 28
  intimate partner violence, 28
  labeling theory, 154
  Minneapolis Police Experiment, 154, 155
  minor violent acts, 32
  offender accountability, 552
  polysubstance use, 261
  poverty and, 47
  predicting, 36
  prevention of, 552
  recidivism, 32
  regulatory pyramid, 552
  rehabilitation process, 552
  research on, 152
  restorative justice and, 552
  risk assessment, 25–51, 552
  safety plans, 461
  service decisions, 40
  sociological approach, 153
  South Asian communities, 553
  specific deterrence, 154
drug abuse, 193t
  addiction and, 146–148
  community-based treatment, 390
  crime and, 385–388
  drug court programs, 390
  dual diagnosis and, 179
  family and, 387
  gender and, 458–459
  HIV risk, 386
  MST and, 334–335
  peers and, 387
  prisons and, 386
  recidivism and, 386
  risk for, 175
  self-medication and, 131
  substance-abusing offenders, 9
  SUDs. *See* substance use disorders
Drug Abuse Treatment Outcome Study, 406
drug courts
  assistant district attorney and, 397
  case managers, 396–397
  clinical assessment and, 406
  coerced treatment and, 410
  coordinators in, 396
  creaming effect, 19, 403–404

  effectiveness of, 400–401
  eligibility for, 395–396
  flow chart for, 392f
  importance of plea in, 405
  judge's role, 396, 408
  justice system and, 385–423
  legal issues, 403
  net widening, 19
  post-plea process, 394–395
  recidivism and, 401
  research on, 400–403
  rewards, 397–398
  sample client waiver forms, 420–423
  sanctions, 397–398
  treatment and, 19, 388–390
  U.S. and, 390
  worker in, 10, 407–408
drug-involved offenders treatment, 19, 388–390
Drug Treatment Alternative to Prison (DTAP) program, 389
DSM. *See* Diagnostic and Statistical Manual of Mental Disorders
DTAP. *See* Drug Treatment Alternative to Prison program
dual jurisdiction, 293
dually diagnosed youth. *See* comorbid disorders
DuPont DeMemours v. Robinson, 301
dysfunction, defined, 503

E

EBFT. *See* ecologically based family therapy
EBM. *See* evidence-based medicine
EBP. *See* evidence-based practice
ecological validity, 316
ecologically based family therapy (EBFT), 181, 190
Eddings v. Oklahoma, 126, 127
Education Resources Information Center (ERIC), 180
educational institutions, 11, 214–215
educational rehabilitation, 355, 386
effect sizes, 181, 182, 185, 195, 196
effective treatment, 9
Eighth Amendment cases, 126
elicit-provide-elicit formula, 254, 254t
emotionally disturbed youth, 205
empathy, 231, 252–253
employment problems, 386, 505
empowerment, of victims, 552
Encyclopedia of Social Work (NASW), 70
environmental problems, 144
ERIC. *See* Education Resources Information Center
Estelle v. Gamble, 430
ethical issues, 86
ethnic groups, 557. *See also specific groups*
evidence-based practice (EBP), 10, 14, 310n6, 316
  cycle of, 43f
  definition of, 42–44, 310n6

EBM and, 42
elements of, 27
EWT. *See* expert witness testimony
expert witness testimony, 67–92
integration of, 316
manual for, 10
Venn diagram for, 43f
Evidence-Based Practice Manual (Roberts and Yeager),
  10
EWT. *See* expert witness testimony
ex parte motion, 145
expert witness testimony (EWT), 71–72
  battering and, 93–126
  child welfare and, 15
  contact letter, 139–141
  content of, 73–75
  credibility of, 303
  cross-examination and, 83, 86–87
  defined, 71
  description of, 83–88
  evidence-based practice and, 67–92
  fact witnesses and, 72
  Federal Rules of Evidence, 72
  forensic social work and, 67–92
  funding for, 144–146
  hearsay statements and, 303
  jury and, 147–148
  lay experts, 148
  nature of testimony, 303
  practice time, 77
  qualification process, 72, 84, 301–302
  rationale for, 97–101
  reliability test, 301
  scope of, 97–101
  selection of, 75
  social workers and, 76, 82–83
  specialized training and, 79
  types of cases, 97–101
externalizing problems, 181, 195

F

family, 18, 355
  assessment of, 42f, 323
  child abuse. *See* child abuse
  FBT. *See* family behavior therapy
  FGC. *See* family group conferencing
  FPP. *See* Family Preservation Program
  protective services and, 41
  punishment and, 232
  social supports for, 323
  substance use and, 387
  violence and, 45, 45f, 154. *See also* domestic
    violence
  See also specific organizations, topics
family behavior therapy (FBT), 181, 187, 197
Family Code, 307

Family Court, 206
family group conferencing (FGC), 550, 582
  mediation and FGC, 531–534
  restorative justice, 546
  social network model, 547
  victim-offender conferencing, 547
family preservation model, 190
Family Preservation Program (FPP), 290
Family Violence Prevention Fund, 45f
Family Violence, Task Force on, 154
FBT. *See* family behavior therapy
Federal Rules of Evidence, 72
feminist theory, 44, 160
FFT. *See* functional family therapy
FGC. *See* family group conferencing
firearms, 118
follow-up designs, 179
forensic child welfare work, 79–83
forensic practice administration, 77–78
forensic social work, 125
  in 21st century, 3–22
  administration of, 77–78
  areas of, 78
  criminal cases and, 128. *See also* justice system
  definition of, 580
  EWT. *See* expert witness testimony
  fact witness and, 72
  focus of, 69
  function of, 3–22
  social work and, 580
  syllabus for, 13–14
  training programs, 217
foster children, 211
Fountain House program, 506
four-S model, 570
FPP. *See* Family Preservation Program
framing, trauma and, 566
Freeman decision, 132
Friends of Island Academy, 212
Frye test, 73, 94
functional family therapy (FFT), 355
funding streams, 219

G

GAF. *See* global assessment of functioning
GAL. *See* guardian ad litem
GAO. *See* U.S. Government Accountability
  Office
Gault decision, 275, 300
gender differences
  alcohol use and, 250
  HIV/AIDS and, 473, 475
  juveniles and, 216
  restorative justice and, 541–562
  risk-taking behaviors, 250
  See also women; *specific topics*

General Electric Co. v. Joiner, 74
geneticist, as witness, 147
GIIFT. *See* Girls&Guys Insight Into Incarceration for
    Teens
Girls&Guys Insight Into Incarceration for Teens
    (GIIFT), 216
global assessment of functioning (GAF), 144
group dynamics, 185
group therapy, 479
guardian ad litem (GAL), 78

H

handicap, defined, 503
heritability research, 232
Hernandez v. Texas Protective Services, 307, 308
Hispanics, 214, 251, 470, 484
HIV/AIDS
    HIV-infected/affected incarcerated women, 19
    infection risk, 19
    jail inmates, 469, 474
    post-incarceration, 471
    prisons and, 467–490
    psychiatric disorders and, 472
    risk behaviors, 471–472, 472, 475
    task-centered approach, 479
    women and, 473, 475
homebuilders family preservation models, 190
homicides, 11
hospital admissions, 495
housing, 387, 498, 504
human development, 182
human rights violations, 548
hyperactivity, 128

I

IAPs. *See* intensive aftercare programs
ICPS. *See* individual cognitive problem solving
ICWA. *See* Indian Child Welfare Act
identity, 568
immunity, 307
index offenses, 274
Indian Child Welfare Act (ICWA), 302
indigenous peoples, 547
individual cognitive problem solving (ICPS), 181,
    187–188, 197
informed consent, 286
insanity plea, 102
integrated approaches, 41–42, 446
intensive aftercare programs (IAPs), 497, 500
intensive supervision programs (ISPs), 500
interactional group treatment (IT), 181, 185–187
internalizing problems, 181, 195
Internet, 180, 221–223
interpersonal relationships, 185
interpersonal skills, 161
interrogatories, 83

intervention, 17, 77–83, 160. *See specific types*
ISPs. *See* intensive supervision programs
IT. *See* interactional group treatment

J

jails
    assessment in, 452
    environment in, 426–427
    evaluation in, 432
    HIV and, 467–490
    legal issues, 429–430
    medical care, 429
    mental disorders and, 428, 472
    Mental Health Screen, 432
    mental health services, 19, 425–444
    overcrowding in, 285
    physical restraint in, 60–62
    preincarceration trauma, 459
    preventable deaths in, 15
    prisons. *See* prisons
    Project Link, 438
    release planning, 437–438
    safety in, 62–63
    safety rounds, 59–60
    screening in, 432
    suicide rates, 54, 54f, 57
    supervision of, 59
    trauma-related disorders and, 446
    victimization within, 461
    women in, 473–474
Japanese Americans, 548
job coach model, 506
Joint Commission on Mental Illness and Health, 495
JPOs. *See* juvenile probation officers
Justice in Aboriginal Communities (Green), 555
justice system, 388–390
    adult system, 262–263, 377
    adversarial process, 543–544
    African-Americans and, 544, 557
    CASA system, 300
    casework with authority, 578
    circle sentencing, 547
    considered judgment and, 70
    creaming in, 19
    crime scene analysis, 147
    cross-examination, 83, 86–87
    cultural issues and, 556
    definition of, 573–575
    delinquency. *See* juvenile justice system
    drugs and. *See* drug courts
    ethnic groups and, 556
    EWT and, 67–92
    fundamental principles of, 557, 573–585
    identity and, 568
    juveniles and. *See* juvenile justice system
    mental health systems and, 580

MI and, 262–263
mitigating evidence and, 127
model for, 557
offender reentry, 557
people in, 576
plea-bargaining system, 544
postmodern theory of, 552
punishment and, 126
rehabilitation and, 574
social work and, 10–21, 558, 573–585
treatment decisions and, 389–390
See also specific topics
juvenile competency development, 291
Juvenile Delinquency Guidelines (2005), 282, 288
juvenile justice system, 247–271
    adjudication hearing, 274, 287
    adult system and, 358, 377
    aftercare. *See* aftercare
    arrests and, 283
    assessment in, 209–212, 233–241, 353
    BARJ. *See* balanced and restorative justice
    children's needs and, 293, 579
    clinical issues, 263–264
    community and, 374–376
    confinement and, 377
    criminal behavior outcomes, 196
    decreasing crime rates, 248
    delinquency, 17, 235, 282, 288
    discrimination in, 371–372
    disposition hearing, 288
    diversion prior to referral, 282
    early prevention strategies, 17
    family structure and, 370
    females in, 348
    five-stage model of, 207
    gender-specific programming, 216
    hearsay evidence, 304
    helping professionals in, 17
    history of, 275
    IAPs for, 502
    identity and, 568
    immunity and, 307
    JPOs. *See* juvenile probation officers
    justice system and, 173–203
    key terms, 274
    mental health records, 306–307, 352
    mentally ill offenders, 18, 347–362
    MI and, 17. *See* motivational interviewing
    overview of, 17
    pathways into, 206–209
    probation and, 278–293
    psychopathic offenders, 17, 229–233
    race and, 18, 363–381. *See specific groups*
    racism and, 371–372
    referral, 283
    rehabilitation and, 500

release, 290, 438
screening in, 209–212, 284, 352
self-report, 238
sexual abuse, 348
social workers in, 17, 276–278, 299–314
statutory immunity, 307
transfer process, 287
triangle of concepts, 291
VOM and, 521
juvenile probation officers (JPOs), 278
    adjudication hearing and, 287
    juvenile probation and, 278
    responsibilities of, 284
    social workers and, 291, 293

K

Kent decision, 275, 287
Knock v. Knock, 100
Kumbo Tire Co. v. Carmichael, 74

L

labeling theory, 154
law enforcement, 299
lawyers, social work and, 300
letter of agreement, 78
Link Project, 438
living skills, 497, 504
Lockett decision, 126, 127

M

MADD. *See* Mothers Against Drunk Drivers
Maldonado case, 310n4
mandatory probation, 274
Maryland Community Criminal Justice Treatment
    Program (MCCJTP), 439
Massachusetts Youth Screening Instrument (MAYSI),
    210, 215, 352
MAST. *See* Michigan Alcohol Screening Test
MATCH project, 262
MAYSI. *See* Massachusetts Youth Screening
    Instrument
MCCJTP. *See* Maryland Community Criminal Justice
    Treatment Program
McCoy v. North Carolina, 126
MCMI. *See* Millon Adolescent Clinical Inventory
MCMI. *See* Millon Clinical Multiaxial Inventory
MDOs. *See* mentally disordered offenders
MDP. *See* Missouri Delinquency Project
mediation
    FGC and, 531, 534
    recidivism and, 531
    restorative justice and, 545–546
    VOM and. *See* victim-offender mediation
Medline, 43, 180
mental health records, 129, 306–307
mental health screening instruments, 352–353

mental health terminology, 143–144
mental ill/chemically abusing (MICA) services, 219
mental retardation, 144
mentally disordered offenders (MDOs), 499
Mentally Ill Offender Treatment and Crime Reduction
    Act of 2004, 18, 354
mentoring sessions, 216
MET. *See* motivational enhancement therapy
meta-analysis, 549
MI. *See* motivational interviewing
MICA. *See* mental ill/chemically abusing services
Michigan Actuarial Model, 37
Michigan Alcohol Screening Test (MAST), 453
Miller v. Dretke, 129
Millon Adolescent Clinical Inventory (MCMI), 238
Millon Clinical Multiaxial Inventory (MCMI), 137
Minneapolis Domestic Violence Police Experiment,
    154, 155
Minnesota Center Against Violence and Abuse, 45f
Minnesota Multiphasic Personality Inventory
    (MMPI), 100, 135, 137
Missouri Delinquency Project (MDP), 330
mitigation
    concept of, 125–130
    evidence and, 15, 125
    mental health records and, 129
    social workers and, 125
    specialists and, 130, 140–146
MMPI. *See* Minnesota Multiphasic Personality
    Inventory
Morales decision, 132
Mothers Against Drunk Drivers (MADD), 570
motivational enhancement therapy (MET), 261
motivational interviewing (MI), 17, 247–271, 252t,
    253t
    alcohol use, 258–261
    collaboration in, 252
    justice system, 262–263
    sex offenders, 262
MST. *See* multisystemic therapy
multidimensional family therapy, 261
Multisite South Carolina Study, 330
multisystemic therapy (MST)
    ADHD and, 323
    BSFT and, 289
    child abuse and, 338
    comorbidity and, 176–177, 178t, 182–185
    conceptual assumptions, 316–317
    delinquency study, 330–339
    description of, 356
    EBFT and, 190
    family interventions, 319–320
    family social supports and, 323
    health care problems, 339
    individually oriented interventions, 322
    interventions and, 321–323

juvenile justice outcomes, 330–339
mental health outcomes, 337–338
outcome studies, 329, 331t, 332t
principles of, 317, 318t
psychiatric symptoms in, 337–338
quality assurance system, 327–340
recidivism and, 196
risk factors, 316
role-playing in, 321
sample case summary, 324–327
school interventions, 322
service delivery, 184, 319
sexual offenders, 336
substance use, 334–335
training in, 329
treatment termination, 324

N

NASMHPD. *See* National Association of State Mental
    Health Program Directors
NASW. *See* National Association of Social Workers
National Association of Social Workers (NASW)
    Code of Ethics, 311n16, 436, 451
    Corrections Council, 574
    Council on Education, 582
    forensics and, 70
    guidelines, 276–277
    journal of, 21, 572
    leadership and, 581
    restorative justice and, 557–558
National Association of State Mental Health Program
    Directors (NASMHPD), 504
National Center for Juvenile Justice (NCJJ), 280
National Center for Mental Health and Juvenile Justice
    (NCMHJJ), 205
National Conference of Social Welfare (NCSW), 575
National Council of Juvenile and Family Court Judges
    (NCJFCJ), 275
National Family Violence Survey (NFVS), 28, 152
National Institute of Justice (NIJ), 155, 549
National Organization of Forensic Social Work
    (NOFSW), 11, 70
National Survey of Children and Adolescent
    Well-Being, 29
NCC. *See* Neighborhood Conference Committees,
    Austin, Texas
NCJFCJ. *See* National Council of Juvenile and Family
    Court Judges
NCJJ. *See* National Center for Juvenile Justice
NCMHJJ. *See* National Center for Mental Health and
    Juvenile Justice
NCSW. *See* National Conference of Social Welfare
negotiation, 161
Neighborhood Conference Committees (NCC),
    Austin, Texas, 283
Nenno decision, 301

nested assessment, 38–41
neuropsychologists, as witnesses, 138–139
NFVS. *See* National Family Violence Survey
Nicholson v. Williams, 15, 30, 35, 93, 100
NIJ. *See* National Institute of Justice
NOFSW. *See* National Organization of Forensic Social
    Work

O

obsessive-compulsive disorder (OCD), 249
OCD. *See* obsessive-compulsive disorder
OCFS. *See* Office of Children and Family Services
ODARA. *See* Ontario Domestic Assault Risk
    Assessment
ODD. *See* oppositional defiant disorder
offender accountability, 291
Office of Children and Family Services (OCFS), 206
Office of Juvenile Justice and Delinquency Prevention
    (OJJDP), 274
Office of National Drug Control Policy (ONDCP), 9,
    387
OJJDP. *See* Office of Juvenile Justice and Delinquency
    Prevention
ONDCP. *See* Office of National Drug Control Policy
One Judge/One Family program, 293
Ontario Domestic Assault Risk Assessment (ODARA),
    34
oppositional defiant disorder (ODD), 232, 249
organizational resources, 165–169

P

Paint Creek Youth program, 501
parasitic lifestyle, 235
parental alienation syndrome (PAS), 100
parole system, 491–516
    aftercare and. *See* aftercare
    caseloads and, 576
    MDOs and, 499
    recidivism and. *See* recidivism
    relapse prevention, 507–510
    See also specific programs
PAS. *See* parental alienation syndrome
Patterns of Youth Mental Health Care in Public
    Services System study, 249
PCL-R. *See* Psychopathy Checklist-Revised
PCL. See Psychopathy Checklist
PCM. *See* Prevention Case Management program
pediatric health care, 339
peers
    interactions among, 216
    risk factors and, 128
    substance use and, 387
personality disorders, 144, 225, 231
Personality Factor Questionnaire (PFQ), 137
Peru, 548
PET. *See* psychoeducational therapy

PFQ. *See* Personality Factor Questionnaire
POSIT. *See* Problem-Oriented Screening Instrument
    for Teenagers
posttraumatic stress disorder (PTSD), 5, 20, 191, 303
    anxiety disorder, 448
    assessment and, 454–455
    BWS and, 103
    cognitive behavioral interventions, 456
    community circle and, 568
    diagnostic criteria, 454f, 455
    gender and, 458–459
    grieving and, 568
    incarceration and, 459
    intervention and, 563–572
    model application for, 564–571
    screening and assessment, 453
    SUD and, 191, 445–466, 448
poverty, 47, 128, 148, 299, 370
Power and Control Wheel (DAIP), 112
Prevention Case Management (PCM) program, 474
prison system, 299
    abuse by staff, 451
    aftercare. *See* aftercare
    assessment and testing, 452
    capital spending for, 4
    drugs and, 386
    HIV and, 467–490
    medical care, 430
    minority confinement, 18
    overcrowding in, 285, 576
    parole. *See* parole system
    physical restraint, 60–62
    preincarceration trauma, 459
    pretest-posttest designs, 176, 179
    preventable deaths in, 15
    prisoner sudden deaths, 53–65
    psychiatric disorders within, 472
    recidivism. *See* recidivism
    safety rounds, 59–60
    staff misconduct, 451
    substance use and, 445–466
    suicides, 53–65, 433
    supervision in, 59
    victimization within, 461
    women in, 7–8, 8, 473–475, 576
    See also justice system
probation
    caseloads and, 576
    ISPs and, 500
    juvenile justice system and, 278–293
    role of, 278–291
    voluntary, 274
    without verdict, 390
Problem-Oriented Screening Instrument for
    Teenagers (POSIT), 210
problem solving, 161

property-related crimes, 4
psychiatrists, as witnesses, 138
psychoeducational therapy (PET), 161, 189, 480–483
psychological abuse, 101–104, 111
psychopathy, 17, 225, 237
    children and, 17, 231–232. *See* Child Psychopathy
        Scale
    Cleckley model, 237
    criteria for, 226
    diagnosis of, 230–232
    PCL. *See* Psychopathy Checklist
    personality and, 225–226, 231
    self-report measures, 238–241
    violence convictions, 226
    youthful populations, 229
Psychopathy Checklist (PCL), 227, 229, 234, 235, 237
PsycINFO, 43, 180
PTSD. *See* posttraumatic stress disorder

Q

quality of life, 505
quasi-experimental design, 157

R

race, 18, 251, 363–381, 367f
racism, 371–372, 556
RAND Corporation, 501
rape, 552, 554
RAPI. *See* Rutgers Alcohol Problem Index
rapport building, 286
raw data, 132
readiness rulers, 255, 255t
recidivism, 9, 10
    aftercare and, 492
    domestic violence and, 32
    drug courts, 386, 401
    ISPs and, 502
    mediation and, 531
    prediction of, 32
    prevention of, 491–516
    prisons and, 386
    rehabilitation and, 20
    substance use and, 387
recovery, 503–505
referral process, 283
rehabilitation
    aftercare and. *See* aftercare
    coercion and, 291
    definition of, 502–503
    juvenile justice system and, 500
    models of, 494
    operationalization of, 9
    recidivism and, 20. *See* recidivism
    relapse and, 495, 507–509
    two-stage process, 502–503
relapse prevention, 495, 507–509

release-planning, 438
reparations, World War II and, 548
Research on Social Work Practice (journal), 21
residential treatment facility (RTF), 206, 504
resources, lists of, 165–169, 221–223. *See specific
        programs, topics*
restorative justice, 20, 550
    African American community and, 548
    BARJ. *See* balanced and restorative justice model
    children and, 550
    cultural factors, 541–562
    definition of, 520, 544–545
    domestic violence and, 552
    ethnic issues and, 557
    FGC and. *See* family group conferencing
    gender and, 541–562
    healing circles, 547
    mediation, 545–546
    meta-analysis, 549
    models of, 20, 545
    movement for, 542
    NASW and, 557–558
    practice in, 20
    racism and, 556
    reparation and, 548
    research literature, 549
    retributive justice and, 543
    United Nations and, 521, 550
    victim assistance programs, 521
    video tapes, 536
    VOM and, 545–546
    VORP and, 521
Rey's test, 137
right refuse services, 436
Rikers Island program, 213
risk assessment, 351–352, 370
    actuarial methods, 27, 36, 41–42
    battering and, 117. *See also* SARA
    children and, 25–51
    classification of risk, 41
    clinical approach, 41–42
    consensus approach, 41
    domestic violence and, 25–51, 32
    integrated strategies, 37–38, 41
    juvenile arrest and, 207
    nested model, 14, 27, 43
    prediction and, 30–31
    service decisions, 40, 40t
    substance use and, 175
    substantiation and, 35
    See also specific instruments, topics
risk-taking behaviors, 128, 250
Rodriguez decision, 133
RTF. *See* residential treatment facility
Ruiz v. Estelle, 430
Rutgers Alcohol Problem Index (RAPI), 258

S

safety assessments, 27
SAMHSA. *See* Substance Abuse and Mental Health
    Services Administration
SARA. *See* spousal assault risk assessment
SASSI. *See* Substance Abuse Subtle Screening
    Inventory
schizophrenia, 506
school failure, 214
school risk factors, 128
SCID. *See* Structured Clinical Interview for *DSM-IV*
scientific evidence, 301
screening instruments, 352–353
Scuguza decision, 310n3
search procedures, 44
seeking safety therapy (SS), 181, 191, 457
self-report measures, 238–241
self, sense of, 216, 231, 255, 568, 570
separation anxiety, 249
September 11 attacks, 20, 564–571
serious and persistent mental illness (SPMI), 495,
    502–503
sex role stereotypes, 161
sexual abuse, 8, 109, 250, 336, 469, 552–555. *See*
    specific topics
Shipley Institute of Living Scale, 137
Simple Screening Instrument for Substance Abuse
    (SSI-SA), 453
skills development, 160, 475, 504
Skipper v. South Carolina, 126, 127
Smith decision, 102
smoking, 257–258
social-ecological model, 182. *See also* multisystemic
    therapy
social network model, 547
Social Security Disability Income (SSDI), 439
Social Work, 21, 574
Social Work Abstracts, 43, 180
social workers
    casework with authority, 578
    code of ethics, 311n16
    confidentiality and, 305–306
    criminal justice theory and, 573–585
    cross-training, 10
    curriculum for, 10–21
    diagnosis and, 82–83
    education and, 580
    EWT. *See* expert witness testimony, 16
    history of profession, 575
    immunity from lawsuit, 307
    influence of, 558
    involuntary clients, 579
    JPOs and, 291
    justice system and, 10–21. *See* juvenile justice
        system

lawyers and, 300
    licensing standards, 300
    mental health services and, 434t
    mitigation specialists, 125
    needs of offenders and, 577–579
    qualifications of, 301
    roles of, 6, 10
    See specific types, topics
Society for Social Work and Research, 21
South Africa, 548
special needs, 493–494
specific deterrence, 154
SPMI. *See* serious and persistent mental illness
spousal assault risk assessment (SARA), 31, 32, 41, 118
SS. *See* seeking safety therapy
SSDI. *See* Social Security Disability Income
SSI-SA. *See* Simple Screening Instrument for
    Substance Abuse
SSI. *See* Supplemental Security Income
status offenses, 274
Stockholm syndrome, 111
Structured Clinical Interview for *DSM-IV* (SCID),
    432, 455
Structured Decision-Making (CRC), 41
substance abuse, 5, 19, 203, 249
    cognitive behavioral treatment, 456
    collaborative intervention, 178t, 179
    crime and, 146, 445–466
    data analysis, 181
    dual diagnosis and, 173–174, 179–181
    educational programs, 386
    employment problems and, 386
    families and, 387
    gender and, 458–459
    HIV risk and, 386
    MST and, 334–335
    offenders and, 500
    peers and, 387
    PTSD and, 191, 445–466
    recidivism and, 387
    risk, 175
    screening for, 453
    stress disorder and, 445–466
    substance use and, 179
    teen addiction index, 193
Substance Abuse and Mental Health Services
    Administration (SAMHSA), 453
Substance Abuse Subtle Screening Inventory (SASSI),
    453
suicide
    APA guideline for, 57
    attachment points, 58
    cause of, 57
    clinical assessment tools, 57
    facilities and, 58
    jails and, 54, 54f, 57

suicide (*Contd.*)
NCIA report, 55
prediction of, 57–58
prevention of, 57–58
prisons and, 53–65, 57
risk factors, 55–58
screening for, 53–65
Supplemental Security Income (SSI), 439
Supreme Court decisions, 275. *See specific cases*
surveillance effect, 35
Symptom Checklist-90-R, 137

T

Taser guns, 62
task-based group treatment, 20
task-centered approach, 479
Taylor decision, 302
temporary insanity, 102
Tennard decision, 126
terminology, mental health, 143–144
therapeutic jurisprudence model, 391
therapist, characteristics of, 252
three strikes legislation, 5
time constraints, on caseworkers, 44
tough love, method, 285
Trails Test, 137
transfer process, 287
trauma, 19
amplifying, 569–570
framing, 566
intervention and, 20, 563–572
PTSD and. *See* posttraumatic stress disorder
self-medication and, 131
substance use and, 445–466
Trauma Recovery and Empowerment Model (TREM), 457
trauma-related disorders, 19, 446
Trauma Symptom Inventory (TSI), 456
TREM. *See* Trauma Recovery and Empowerment Model
Truth and Reconciliation Commissions, 548
Truth Commission, South Africa, 548
TSI. *See* Trauma Symptom Inventory
tuberculosis, 469

U

Uniform Offense Report, 140
Universal Declaration of Human Rights, 550
U.S. Government Accountability Office (GAO), 401
U.S. Supreme Court, 126

V

Van Program, 213
VAWA. *See* Violence Against Women Act
Vera Institute models, 207, 211

victim-advocacy groups, 292
victim-offender mediation (VOM), 20
cost of, 531
description of, 522
diversion through, 530
effectiveness of, 528–532
fairness in, 529
FGC and, 522, 547
follow-up in, 527
mediation phase, 525–527
mediator's role, 527
recidivism and, 530
referral/intake phase, 521, 524, 528
restitution and, 530
shuttle mediation, 522
tapes on, 537
unintended consequences, 532–534
violence
battering. *See* battering
conferencing and, 553. *See* conferencing
cost of, 3
domestic. *See* domestic violence
forms of, 543
initiation of, 128
interpersonal, 543
psychopathy and, 226
risk factors for, 128, 154
strategies to prevent, 113
structural, 543
See also specific groups, types
Violence Against Women Act (VAWA), 4, 8
Violent Crime Control and Law Enforcement Act of 1994, 395–396
Violent Juvenile Offender Research and Development Program (VJO), 500
VJO. *See* Violent Juvenile Offender Research and Development Program
vocational programs, 506
voir dire procedure, 85
voluntary probation, 274
VOM. *See* victim-offender mediation

W

Walker model, 102
Wanrow instruction, 95
Web Resources for Child Welfare and Family Violence Information, 44, 45f
web sites, resources, 221–223
Welfare Reform Act of 1996, 574
Wiggins v. Smith, 129
wilderness therapy, 176
Winship decision, 275
women
African American, 484
battered. *See* battering

domestic violence, 28. *See* domestic violence
HIV/AIDS and, 473, 475
incarceration of, 7, 473–474
involvement in violence, 28
maternal depression, 29
prisons and, 475, 576
rape and, 552, 554

World Trade Center attack, 21, 564–571
wraparound services, 357

Y

youth development workshops, 215
Youth Psychopathic Traits Inventory (YPI), 240–241
YPI. *See* Youth Psychopathic Traits Inventory

Battered Women and Their Families, Third Edition
Intervention Strategies and Treatment Programs

Albert R. Roberts, PhD, DABFE, Editor

"[M]any challenges, problems, intervention strategies, assessment and treatment methods, and empowerment approaches are documented in this book by one of the most brilliant clinical researchers in North America today, Dr. Albert Roberts, together with the highly experienced chapter authors. This is the most practical, evidence-based, inspirational, and well-written book on family violence that I have read in the past 10 years. Every social worker, counselor, nurse, and domestic violence advocate should read this book."

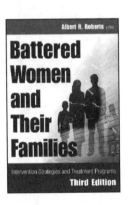

—From the Foreword by **Barbara W. White,**
Dean and Centennial Professor in Leadership,
School of Social Work, University of Texas at Austin.
Former President, Council on Social Work Education (CSWE),
and Former President, National Association of Social Workers (NASW).

The definitive work on battered women is now in a timely third edition. Considered the complete, in-depth guide to effective interventions for this pervasive social disease, *Battered Women and Their Families* has been updated to include new case studies, cultural perspectives, and assessment protocols. In an area of counseling that cannot receive enough attention, Dr. Roberts' work stands out as an essential treatment tool for all clinical social workers, nurses, physicians, and graduate students who work with battered women on a daily basis.

New chapters on same-sex violence, working with children in shelters, immigrant women affected by domestic violence, and elder mistreatment round out this unbiased, multicultural look at treatment programs for battered women.

January 2007 · 656pp · hardcover · 0-8261-4592-2

11 West 42nd Street, New York, NY 10036-8002 • Fax: 212-941-7842
Order Toll-Free: 877-687-7476 • Order On-line: www.springerpub.com